Afr

on a shoestring

Africa on a Shoestring

Published by
Lonely Planet Publications
P O Box 88, South Yarra, Vic 3141, Australia
PO Box 2001A, Berkely CA 94702, USA

Printed by
Colorcraft, Hong Kong

Design by
Graham Imeson

First Published
November 1977 (Africa on the Cheap)

This Edition
July 1986

National Library of Australia
Cataloguing in Publication Data

Crowther, Geoff, 1944-,
Africa on a Shoestring

4th edition
Previous ed: South Yarra, Vic: Lonely Planet 1985
Includes index.
ISBN 0 908086 89 X.

1. Africa – Description and travel – 1977 –.– Guide books.
I. Title.

916'.04328

Geoff Crowther

Born on the Ides of March in Yorkshire, England. Geoff took to his heels early on in the search for the miraculous. The lure of the unknown took him to Kabul, Kathmandu and Lamu in the days before the overland tour bus companies began digging up the dirt along the tracks of Africa. His experiences there led him to join the now legendary but sadly defunct alternative information centre BIT in London in the early '70s. Here he put together their guides, *Overland to India and Australia* and *Overland through Africa*.

Three years and several dingy basement flats later he developed the classic symptoms of a 'burned-out BIT worker' and fled north for a period of healthy living on the bleak, wind-swept mountainsides of rural Cumbria. In 1977 he wrote his first guide for Lonely Planet – *Africa on the Cheap* – followed by *South America on a Shoestring* and *Korea & Taiwan – a travel survival kit*. He has also co-authored *India – a travel survival kit* and *Malaysia,*

Singapore & Brunei – a travel survival kit. When not crashing through the bush in search of gorillas in the Ruwenzoris, tramping over Inca trails in the high Andes or pitting his wits against Indian bureaucracy he lives in a banana shed with 최홍분 in the rain forests of New South Wales and spends his time pursuing noxious weeds, trying to get a house built and brewing mango wine.

ACKNOWLEDGEMENTS

The feedback on the last edition of this book was nothing short of miraculous and I'm extremely grateful to everyone who took the time and trouble to write in with comments, update material, facts about areas and countries not previously covered, street maps and timetables. There were times when I felt I'd be snowed under by the sheer volume of new material but the feedback was too encouraging to allow anything of that nature to happen. It's taken several months of full-time work, often into the wee hours, to collate it all into what is hopefully a coherent form. Obviously with a continent like Africa where nothing stays the same for very long, it's impossible to produce a flawless guidebook. Nevertheless, I'm confident that you'll find this edition even better than the last, and most of the credit for that goes to those who have responded to the request for new material. Please keep writing! There's no substitute for your letters.

I'd like to especially thank Rowland Burley (president, Mountain Club of Kenya) for the information, maps and MCK publications which he sent me on several occasions; Diane Forsland, a former Peace Corps volunteer in Niamey, Niger, for the heaps of information which she sent me on Niger and surrounding countries drawn both from her own experience and from other PC volunteers in the area; Martha Fulford, a Canadian volunteer in Lesotho, who sent me the 'Guide to Lesotho' and heaps of other material about that country; Tom Harriman and Jan King, inveterate travellers from the USA, for their painstaking research and many detailed letters and map collections, and to Katie Seward of the UK for her many long and light-hearted letters prompted by her lone hitch-hiking odyssey from one end of the continent to the other. I'd also once again like to thank Douglas A Cairns of the USA for his contribution to the Egyptian chapter of the last edition. Re-writing that chapter for this edition was so much easier on the basis of what he provided for the last. And many, many thanks to all the people listed on pages 743-4 for their equally valuable contributions.

Last, but by no means least, I'm very grateful to Margaret Moult, Elaine Cushman and Pru Smith who braved tenosynovitis without 'compo' to help type it all out onto discs and to the Lonely Planet team in the USA and Australia who did the editing, proof-reading, typesetting and paste-up.

Contents

A WARNING, A REQUEST & A FEW COMMENTS

Things change and nowhere as fast as they do in Africa. Prices go up, good places go bad, bad places go bankrupt, new places start up and nothing stays the same. If you find things better, worse, cheaper, more expensive, recently opened or long since derelict, then please write to us with details. It doesn't matter if you think we get a lot of mail about certain places and so will probably know already. Confirmation and cross-reference is just as important as being told something we didn't already know. Street maps of cities with whatever you think should be marked on them and transport timetables are particularly appreciated. As in the past, all of those who write in with information will be sent a free copy of any Lonely Planet guide which they request.

Even if you find some of the prices in this book 'of archaeological interest only' or find yourself being 'murdered, ravished or sold into the white slave trade whilst clarifying your abominable directions in the back room of some foul-smelling den of iniquity' or feel that we ought 'to put a caveat in the next edition telling un-suspecting travellers that your directions are an unbridled act of creativity, a spontaneous outpouring of the mango-wine-fuelled imagination,' we'd still like to hear from you. That way we'll get it right in the next edition or even in the mid-term update supplement.

Hope to hear from you!

For the technically-minded, this is the first edition of *Africa on a Shoestring* to be written on a solar-powered computer using a Kaypro 4 microprocessor, four Solarex X100GT solar panels, a Santech inverter and six ex-Telecom 2v 500AH lead-acid batteries.

Introduction

PAPERWORK

The essential documents are a passport and an International Vaccination Card. If you already have a passport, make sure it's valid for a reasonably long period of time and has plenty of blank pages on which stamp-happy immigration officials can do their stuff. If it's only a quarter full and you're thinking of spending a long time in Africa then it might be best to get a new one before you set off. A week spent in either Mali or Niger will result in up to eight pages being filled with immigration and police stamps! If you're British then get one of the 94-page 'jumbo' passports. USA nationals can have extension pages stapled to otherwise full passports at any of their embassies. This facility is also available to UK and other Commonwealth country passport holders at British embassies in various countries such as the Central African Republic. Such extensions cost about US$2.50.

As far as the Vaccination Card goes, whoever supplies you with your vaccinations will provide you with the card and the necessary stamps. If you're taking your own transport or you're thinking of hiring a vehicle to tour certain national parks, get hold of an International Driving Permit before you set off. Any national motoring organisation will fix you up with this provided you have a valid driving licence for your own country. The cost of these permits is generally about US$5.

An International Student Identity Card or the graduate equivalent is also very useful in many places and can save you a small fortune in some countries. Some of the concessions available include airline tickets, train and riverboat fares and free or reduced entry charges to museums and archaeological sites. The card will also exempt you from changing US$260 or the equivalent when entering Algeria. If you're not strictly entitled to a student card, it's often possible to get one if you book a flight with one of the 'bucket shop' ticket agencies that have proliferated in certain European and North American cities. (The deal usually is that you buy an airline ticket from one of them and they'll provide you with a student card.) Another possibility is to buy a fake card (average price around US$10). There always seems to be someone selling these wherever travellers collect in numbers, but examine them carefully before buying, as they vary a great deal in quality. Cairo is an exception, so don't go there expecting to be able to buy a student card.

Another useful thing to have is a Youth Hostels membership card, particularly if you're going to Egypt, Kenya, Morocco, Namibia, South Africa, Tunisia or Zimbabwe, all of which have a network of Youth Hostels.

All the concessions which are possible with an International Student Card or a Youth Hostel membership card are mentioned in the appropriate chapters.

VISAS

Visas are a stamp in your passport permitting you to enter a country and stay there for a specified period of time. They are obtained from the embassy or consulate of the appropriate country either before you set off or along the way. It's best to get them along the way, especially if your travel plans are not fixed, but keep your ear to the ground regarding the best places to get them. Two different consulates of the same country may have completely different requirements before they will issue a visa: The fee may be different; one consulate might want to see how much money you have whereas another won't ask; one might demand an onward ticket while another won't even mention it; one might issue visas while you wait and another insist on referring the application back to the capital (which can take weeks). Whatever you do, don't turn up at a border without a visa if you know one is required unless you're absolutely sure you can get one at the border. If you do this you'll find yourself tramping back to the nearest consulate and, in some countries, this can be a long way.

You'll occasionally come across some tedious, petty power freak at an embassy or consulate whose sole pleasure in life appears to be making as big a nuisance of himself as possible and causing you the maximum amount of delay. If you bite the carrot and display your anger or frustration, the visa will take twice as long to issue. There's one of these creeps born every minute, but if you want that visa don't display any emotion. Pretend you have all day to waste.

Consular officials sometimes refuse pointblank to stamp a visa on anything other than a completely blank page, so make sure your passport has plenty of them. I once persuaded the Sudanese consul in Asmara to stamp a visa on the printed back cover of the passport but it took all day and my back ached after the endless genuflections. Some countries – Zaire is the main one – demand that you produce a letter of recommendation from your own embassy before they will issue a visa. This is generally no problem as your embassy will be aware of this, but you may sometimes have to pay for it. Likewise, if you plan on going to Libya you must have the first few pages of your passport translated into Arabic before you apply for a visa. You can have this done at your embassy either in Tunis or before you leave at the passport office in your own country.

Another important fact to bear in mind about visas is the sheer cost of them. Very few of them are free and some are outrageously expensive. Regardless of what passport you carry, you're going to need quite a lot of visas, and if you're on a tight budget they can eat into your funds in an alarming way. It's a good idea to make a rough calculation of what the visa fees are going to amount to before you set off, and allow for it. Make sure you have plenty of passport-size photographs for visa applications – 24 should be sufficient.

Some countries, it seems, are so suspicious about your motives for wanting to go there that they demand you have a ticket out of the country before they will let you in. So long as you intend to leave from the same place you arrived at, there is no problem, but if you want to enter at one point and leave from another, this can sometimes be a headache. Fortunately, few African countries demand that you have an onward ticket – ex-Portuguese and Spanish colonies, Niger, South Africa and Zimbabwe are the main exceptions – but you can generally get around it by buying an MCO (Miscellaneous Charges Order) from an international airline for, say, US$100. An MCO is similar to having a deposit account with an airline and the beauty of it is that it looks like an airline ticket, but it isn't for any specific flight. It can be refunded in full or exchanged for a specific flight either with the airline you bought it from or with any other airline which is a member of IATA. Most consular and immigration officials accept an MCO as an onward ticket. The other way to get around having an onward ticket is to buy the cheapest ticket available out of the country and then refund it later on. If you do this, make sure you can get a refund without having to wait months for it. Don't forget to ask specifically where you can get the refund (some airlines will only refund tickets at the office where you bought them; some only at their head office).

Most African countries take a strong line against South Africa to the point of refusing entry to nationals of that country. They are also not keen on people whose passports show that they have visited South Africa. If that's the case they may refuse entry. As a rule, the only place you'll encounter this antipathy is in southern Africa – Zambia and Tanzania are the most prominent examples. Likewise the Arab countries of North Africa (except Egypt) refuse entry to Israeli nationals and to anyone with Israeli stamps in their passport. Some countries, like Sudan, have got this down to a fine art and will refuse you a visa even if your passport has no Israeli stamps in it but has Egyptian stamps issued at the Egyptian side of the Egyptian/Israeli border. So if you do visit Israel from Egypt and then want to go through Africa, you may as well throw your passport away and buy a new one. Another intriguing aspect of this sort concerns Australians. Just how they manage to get hold of this kind of information is anyone's guess, but the Nigerians have computer printouts of all Australians who have visited South Africa. Every Nigerian border post has access to this information, so if you're Australian and you've been to South Africa (regardless of whether you have stamps in your passport or not), you can expect a hassle.

One last point to bear in mind about visas is that certain countries take a long time to issue them or impose conditions which make it hardly worth the while. Many ex-Portuguese colonies fall into this category but the main ones which will concern you are Sudan and Nigeria. Sudan takes six weeks to issue visas. Most Nigerian embassies and consulates not only demand that you have sufficient funds and an onward ticket, but that you have a letter of recommendation from a Nigerian citizen together with his/her passport!

In order to balance what has been said above, it should be mentioned that most visas are easily obtained without fuss. It's just that with a total of 52 countries, visas assume an importance in Africa which they don't elsewhere in the world.

MONEY

It's very difficult to make predictions about what a trip to Africa is going to cost since so many factors are involved – how fast you want to travel; what degree of comfort you consider to be acceptable where there's a choice; how much sightseeing you want to do; whether you intend to hire a vehicle to explore a game park or rely on other tourists to give you a lift; whether you're travelling alone or in a group; whether you will be changing money on the street or in banks; and a host of other things. There's only one thing which remains the same in Africa and that's the pace of change. It's fast and things like inflation and devaluations can wreak havoc with your travel plans if you're on a very tight budget. You should budget for at least US$10 per day in the cheaper countries and US$20 in the more expensive ones. This should cover the cost of very basic accommodation, food in local cafés and the cheapest possible transport. It won't include the cost of getting to Africa, safaris in game parks or major purchases in markets. In some countries such as Nigeria and the Ivory Coast you may well find yourself spending considerably more than US$20 per day. On the other hand, if you stay in one place for a long time and cook your own food you can reduce costs considerably since you won't be paying for transport and you'll get a better deal on the cost of accommodation.

However much money you decide on, take a mixture of £ sterling, French francs and US dollars. Francs are the preferred currency in the ex-French colonies and £ sterling/US dollars in ex-British colonies and western-oriented countries such as those on the west coast, southern Africa, Kenya and Zaire. If you take other currencies you'll find it difficult, if not impossible, to find out the exact exchange rate on any particular day.

For the maximum flexibility take the bulk of your money as traveller's cheques and the rest in cash – say up to US$300. American Express, Thomas Cook and First National City Bank cheques are the most widely used and they offer – at least in most cases – instant replacement in the event of loss or theft. Keep a record of the cheque numbers and the original bill of sale for the cheques in a safe place in case you lose them. Replacement is a whole lot quicker if you can produce this information. Even so, if you don't look clean and tidy, or they don't believe your story for some reason or another, replacement can take time because quite a few travellers have been getting up to selling their cheques on the street market (black market) or simply pretending to lose them and then demanding a replacement set. This is particularly so with American Express cheques. You should avoid buying cheques from small banks which only have a few overseas branches, as you'll find them very difficult to change in many places.

Make sure you buy a good range of denominations when you get the cheques – US$10, $20 and $50s (or the equivalent in £ or francs). The reason for this is that if you have too many large bills you may find yourself having to change, say, $50 in a country that you're only going to stay in for a day or two, and end up with a wad of excess local currency which you can only re-convert at a relatively poor rate of exchange. The only exception to this concerns the ex-French colonies. Most of these belong to the Communité Financielle Africaine and use the same unit of currency – the CFA franc. (You may sometimes see this written as the AFR franc but it's the same thing.) In theory, the CFA francs of one country have the same value as those of another and they're freely interchangeable, but the Communité seems to have split into two blocks these days with the Niger/Chad border being the dividing line. That being so, you may well find that the CFA francs of those countries west of this line are not freely interchangeable with those east of this line. It's also well to remember that the CFA is, in effect, a 'hard' currency and freely interchangeable with the French franc on the basis of French franc 1 = 50 CFA.

Having a credit card and a personal chequebook is another way of having secure funds to hand. With these you can generally withdraw up to US$50 in cash and US$500 (sometimes US$1000) in traveller's cheques per week from any branch of the credit card company. This way you can avoid having to carry large wads of traveller's cheques. If you don't have a personal chequebook but you do have a credit card there's usually no problem. Simply present your card and ask for a counter-cheque.

American Express, Diner's Club, Visa and MasterCharge are all widely recognised credit cards. Another which has been brought to our attention is the National Westminster card. This is particularly useful in Africa since National Westminster has many branches in ex-British colonies. They also have a small booklet containing the addresses of all their African branches. With a personal chequebook this is useful because you can get an exact amount of money rather than have to change a large traveller's cheque.

Credit cards also have their uses where 'sufficient funds' are demanded by immigration officials before they will allow you to enter a country. It's generally accepted that you have 'sufficient funds' if you have a credit card.

You cannot always change traveller's cheques in small places or, of course, when the banks are closed; this is one reason why you should bring some cash with you. The major reason for bringing cash is that it allows you to take advantage of any difference between the street rate of exchange (black market) and that offered by the banks. Sometimes you can change traveller's cheques on the black market but this isn't always the case. There are many countries in Africa where you can get considerably more for your hard currency on the streets than you can in the banks. In some cases the difference is little short of spectacular (Ghana, Mozambique, Tanzania and Uganda fall into this category). If you don't take advantage of this then you are going to find many countries very expensive. Conversely, if you do, they'll be relatively cheap. Some people regard the black market as morally reprehensible. It's certainly predatory but, on the other hand, some countries overvalue their currency to such a degree that it's totally unrealistic. The decision is yours but you'll be lucky to come across anyone who isn't using the black market.

If you're setting off from Europe, note that the Credit Suisse bank at Kloten Airport in Zurich, Switzerland, will change all paper money from any country in the world at very reasonable rates and they will also issue paper money in all currencies. Their rate for the Algerian dinar, for example, is about the same as the black market rate inside Algeria.

A few words of warning about changing on the black market. Have available the exact amount you want to change – avoid pulling out large wads of notes. Be very wary about sleight of hand and envelope tricks. Insist on counting out personally the notes that are handed to you. Don't let anyone do this for you and don't hand over your money until you're satisfied you have the exact amount agreed to. If at any point you hand the notes back to the dealer (because of some discrepancy, for example) count them out again when they're handed back to you, because if you don't you'll probably find that all but the smallest notes have been removed. Some operators are so sharp they'd have the shoes off your feet while you were tying up the laces. Don't allow yourself to be distracted by supposed alarms like 'police' and 'danger.' In many countries you won't have to take part in this sort of mini-drama, as money is generally changed in certain shops or with merchants at a market so it's a much more leisurely process. Indeed, in many places it's very unwise to change on the street as you may be set up by a police undercover agent.

Some countries (Egypt and Uganda, for example) have two official exchange rates:

a lower one for international transactions and a higher one for tourists. As a tourist you're entitled to the higher rate which is generally a lot nearer to, if not equal to, the currency's real value vis-a-vis the 'hard' currencies. The idea is to encourage tourism and attempt to stamp out the black market. It doesn't always work. With this book you must treat the official and the black market rates as a guide only. They are correct at the time this book goes to press, but coups, countries defaulting on their external debt repayments, devaluations and IMF strictures can alter the picture dramatically overnight. You must check out all prices and exchange rates with your fellow travellers along the way. They are your best source of current information.

Many African countries issue currency declaration forms on arrival. You must write down how much cash and traveller's cheques you are bringing into the country. Some countries check these very thoroughly when you leave and if there are any discrepancies you're in the soup. Others couldn't care less. Whatever the case, if you intend using the black market inside the country, you must declare less than you are bringing in and hide the excess. More details about the forms can be found in the appropriate country chapters.

There is no 'safe' way to keep your money whilst you're travelling, but the best place is in contact with your skin where hopefully you'll be aware of an alien hand before it disappears. One method is to wear a leather pouch hung around your neck and kept under cover of a shirt or dress. If you do this, incorporate a length of old guitar string into the thong which goes around your neck (the D string should be thick enough). Many thieves carry scissors but few carry wire cutters. Another method is to sew an invisible pocket onto the inside of your trousers. Others prefer a money-belt. Ideally your passport should be in the same place but this isn't always possible as some are either too thick or too stiff. Wherever you decide to put your money, it's a good idea to enclose it in a plastic bag. Under a hot sun that pouch or pocket will get soaked with sweat – repeatedly – and your cash or cheques will end up looking like they've been through the launderette.

If you run out of money whilst you're abroad and need more, ask your bank back home to send a draft to you (assuming you have money in an account there). Make sure you specify the city and the bank branch. Transferred by cable, money should reach you within a few days. If you correspond by mail the process will take at least two weeks, often longer. Remember that some countries will only give you your money in local currency: others will let you have it in US dollars or £ sterling. Find out what is possible before you request a transfer; otherwise you could lose a fair amount of money if there's an appreciable difference between the official and unofficial exchange rates.

If you have taken your entire worldly assets with you and can't lay your hands on another penny, then you have very few options. It's possible to get a job in some places but don't count on it. The one thing you can do is go to your embassy and get repatriated. If you have to do this, many embassies take your passport away from you and you won't get it back until you repay the debt – and they'll fly you back at full-fare economy rates.

BAGGAGE

Take the minimum possible. An overweight bag will become a nightmare. A rucksack is preferable to an overnight bag since it will stand up to rougher treatment and doesn't screw up your posture by putting unequal weight on one side of your body. Choose a pack which will take some rough handling – overland travel destroys packs rapidly. Make sure the straps and buckles are well sewn on and strengthened if necessary before you set off. Whether you take a pack with or without a frame is up to you but there are some excellent

packs on the market with internal frames (eg Berghaus). Probably the best stockists in Britain are the YHA Adventure Centre, 14 Southampton St, London WC2 (tel 01 836 8541). Take a strong plastic bag with you that will completely enclose the pack. Use it on dusty journeys whether your pack is in the luggage compartment of a bus or strapped onto the roof. If you don't, you'll be shaking dust out of your pack for the next week.

A sleeping bag is more or less essential. It gets very cold in the desert at night and, if you'll be visiting mountainous areas, you'll need one there as well. You'll also be glad of it on long bus or train journeys as a supplement to the wooden seats or sacks of potatoes. A sheet sleeping bag – similar to the ones used in Youth Hostels – is also good when it is too hot to use a normal bag. It's cool and keeps the mosquitoes off your body.

Take clothes for both hot and cold climates, including at least one good sweater for use at night in the mountains and the desert. You needn't go overboard, however, and take everything in your wardrobe. Things like T-shirts, cotton shirts and sandals are very cheap in most places and it's usually more interesting and economical to buy these things along the way. It's prohibited to wear clothes that reveal large areas of your body in some places like Tanzania. This includes shorts, short skirts and see-through garments; even flared trousers are frowned on. Much the same applies in Malawi. These sorts of clothes apparently offend the local sense of propriety. It's inadvisable for women to wear anything short in Moslem countries, otherwise they will be hassled endlessly by local men or youths. Most women in these countries are veiled from head to toe so if you go around with little on they will assume you are sexually available. Long skirts and a resilient nature can allay this kind of attention but doesn't guarantee success. On the other hand, being sexually hassled is by no means an exclusively female complaint.

Some people take a small tent and a portable stove. These can be very useful and save you a small fortune but they do add considerably to the weight of your pack. Many local people carry portable stoves around with them. If you take a stove make sure it's leakproof! Don't forget the small essentials: a combination pocket knife or Swiss Army knife; needle and cotton and a small pair of scissors; pair of sunglasses; towel and tooth brushes; oral contraceptives (if used); tampons; a supply of anti-malarial pills; and one or two good novels. Most toiletries – toilet paper, toothpaste, shaving cream, shampoo, etc – are available in all the capital cities and large towns. A water bottle (fabric covered) is very useful when it's hot or for walking in the mountains. It also enables you to give those dubious water holes a miss and so cut down your chances of getting hepatitis.

TAKING YOUR OWN VEHICLE/CARNETS

A carnet (*carnet de passage*) is required for the majority of countries in Africa with the exception of Morocco, Algeria and Tunisia.

The purpose of a carnet is to allow an individual to take a vehicle into a country where duties would normally be payable without the necessity of having to pay those duties. It's a document which guarantees that if a vehicle is taken into a country but not exported, then the organisation which issued it will accept responsibility for payment of import duties. Carnets can only be issued by one of the national motoring organisations (in the UK, this is the AA or RAC; in Australia, the AAA), and before they will issue such a document they have to be absolutely sure that if the need to pay duties ever arises they would be reimbursed by the individual to whom the document is issued.

The amount of import duty can vary considerably but it's usually between one to 1½ times the new value of the vehicle. There are exceptions to this where duty can be three times the new value.

The motoring organisation will calculate the highest duty payable of all the countries that you intend to visit and arrive at what is known as an 'indemnity figure.' This amount must be guaranteed to the motoring organisation by the individual before carnet documents are issued. The indemnity or guarantee can be of two types:

(i) Banks can provide the indemnity but they require an equal amount of cash or other collateral to be deposited with them.

(ii) An insurance company will put up the necessary bond in return for a non-refundable premium. In the UK, for AA carnets, the premium required is calculated at 3% of the indemnity figure subject to a minimum premium of £25. Indemnity figures in excess of £5000 qualify for a slightly lower premium. For RAC carnets, the premium is calculated at 10% of the indemnity figure though half of this is refunded when the carnet is eventually discharged.

If duties ever become payable – for example if you take the vehicle into a country but don't export it again – then the authorities of that country will demand payment of duties from the motoring organisation. It in turn would surrender the indemnity it was holding; if this were a bank indemnity then the bankers would hand over the deposit they were holding. In the case of an insurance company, they would have to settle the claim. If the latter, then the company has the right of recovery from an individual of the amount it has had to pay out, though it's possible to take out a double indemnity with some insurance companies whereby they'll not only make funds available for the issue of the carnet but will also waive the right of recovery from an individual. If you want this kind of cover, the premium you pay will be exactly double that normally required.

To get a carnet you first need to make an application to one of the motoring organisations. They will issue you an indemnity form for completion either by a bank or an insurance company. Once this is completed and a bond deposited with a bank or a premium paid to an insurance company, the motoring organisation issues a carnet. The carnets themselves cost approximately £20. The whole process takes about a week to complete.

Important Points about Carnets

(a) Insurance companies designate certain countries as 'war zones' and no insurance company will insure against the risks of war. This means that for such countries the only options are to get a carnet with a bank deposit or go without a carnet and make transit arrangements at the border. At present, Egypt is regarded as a 'war zone.'

(b) If you intend to sell the vehicle at some point, arrangements have to made with the customs people for the carnet entry to be cancelled. This means surrendering the vehicle into a customs compound from which it will not be released until duties have been paid by the prospective buyer. In some places (eg Niamey, Niger) the buyer has to bribe a minister before a vehicle can change hands. It's fairly easy to sell a car in Ouagadougou (Bourkinafasso) but you must sell it within three days of arrival, otherwise you run into complications. It's legal to sell cars in Togo, Benin and the Ivory Coast without going through customs but the price you get for it is lower because of this. Generally, the older a car, the less duty is payable and therefore the easier it is to sell. In Bamako (Mali) cars under five years old carry prohibitive duty.

(c) Indemnity insurance is issued for a minimum period of one year. You cannot get a reduction in premium or a refund for shorter trips.

The addresses of various motoring organisations are:

UK
Automobile Association, Overseas Operations Dept, Leicester Square, London WC1
Royal Automobile Club, PO Box 92, Croydon CR9 6HN (tel 01-686 2314)

West Germany
ADAC, 11 Konigstrasse, Munchen
ADAC, Bundersalle 9-30, Berlin 31

France
Automobile Club de France, 6 Place de la Concorde, Paris 8e (tel 265 3470)

The above organisations can be very fussy if you're a foreign national or have a vehicle with foreign registration plates. Some of them insist that you must first be a member of one of your own national motoring organisations before they'll issue a carnet. In Germany you also need to have good references.

Legislation about compulsory third-party insurance varies considerably from one country to another. In some places it isn't even compulsory. Where it is, you generally have to buy the insurance on the border but the liability limits on these policies is often absurdly low by western standards and if you have any bad accidents you could be in deep water. Also, you can only guess whether or not the premium is simply pocketed by the person collecting it or is actually passed on to the company. Perhaps this doesn't concern you, but if you want more realistic cover then you will have to arrange this before you leave.

If you're starting from the UK, the company that everyone recommends for insurance policies and for detailed information on carnets is: Campbell Irvine Ltd, 48 Earls Court Rd, London, W8 6EJ (tel 01 937 9407). The people who work here are not only very friendly and will give you personal attention, but they've been handling these kinds of enquiries for years and they know the business inside out. Most of the overland tour companies use them too. Write to them for a copy of their *Overland Insurance* leaflet or call round there and discuss it with them.

Taking a vehicle around Africa requires thorough preparation and is really outside the scope of this book. An excellent guide which discusses all aspects of this is *Sahara Handbook* by Simon and Jan Glen (Lascelles, London, 1980). Another which has been recently updated and doesn't confine itself to the Sahara is *Overland & Beyond* by Jon and Theresa Hewatt (Lascelles, London). In the German language a very good book is *Durch Africa* by K and E Darr (Touring Club Suisse, Zurich, 1977).

Selling Second-Hand Cars in West Africa

For years now large numbers of French, German and Swiss travellers and small entrepreneurs have been buying second-hand cars in northern Europe, driving them across the Sahara Desert and selling them in West Africa. For most travellers this is a one-off affair, the object of which is to reduce the costs of an Africa trip, but there are quite a few people who do it full-time for a living by taking several cars at once on the back of a truck. Several years ago it used to be possible to make a decent profit just on one car but those days are gone. You'll certainly still cover your costs (including the purchase price of the car) and, if you're lucky, you might make a small profit. Even if your car only makes it to Arlit, you shouldn't lose out.

Carnets are not required for Morocco, Algeria or Tunisia. You needn't arrange them in advance for Niger, Togo or Benin because you can buy one on the border of Niger for 5500 CFA per month and this will cover you for all CFA states. This means you can drive all the way down to the West African coast without having to think about carnets ('Carnet de Transit Routier') before you set off.

The same applies to insurance, though it's prohibitively expensive in Arlit (Niger) where it costs US$50 for five days. You can avoid this by going straight south to In Gall and then Agadez, and buying your insurance there.

There's a ready market for certain cars (Peugeot, Renault, Mercedes Benz) in Niger, Bourkinafasso, Benin, Togo and the Ivory Coast, but selling a car in Niger involves a lot of paperwork. In Benin and Togo, on the other hand, all you have to do is register your name and that of the buyer in a book kept for the purpose at a local police station. Make sure it is decided before you sell the car, however, who is going to pay the appropriate fees to the police, the local authorities, customs and the commissioner. Generally, the seller only pays the last. The most sought-after cars are the Peugeot 504 (the 404 is somewhat dated) and Mercedes 280S (not the SE), but avoid injection engines. The vehicle should be at least three years old, though up to seven is acceptable. Left-hand drive and a speedometer calibrated in km per hour are necessary.

To give you an approximate idea of the price you will have to pay for second-hand cars in West Germany, use this as a guide:

Peugeot 504L	US$400 (sell for around US$1200)
Peugeot 504GL	US$600 (sell for around US$1600)
Peugeot 504 Familiale	US$1000 (sell for around US$2000)
Mercedes 280S	US$2000 (sell for around US$4000)

It's easy for non-German residents to get customs plates for the car (though if you buy a car in France and are a foreign national you may have insurance problems), and all the above cars can be driven easily through the Sahara via the Route du Hoggar. Take spare tyres, jerry cans, tools, a couple of radiators, etc. Like the cars, all these accessories are easily sold either with the car or separately. You certainly won't be alone if you decide to do this.

If you're going to be driving in Morocco, make sure you have a Green Card. If you can't produce a Green Card, the police can fine you 35 dirhams which is more than US$6.

HEALTH

Two useful books to read before you set off are: *The Traveller's Health Guide* by Dr A C Turner (Lascelles, London) and *Preservation of Personal Health in Warm Climates* put out by the Ross Institute of Tropical Hygiene, Keppel St, London WC1. Another helpful book on health is David Werner's *Where There is No Doctor: a village health care handbook* published by Macmillan Press Ltd, London.

Vaccinations Before you're allowed to enter most African countries you must have a valid International Vaccination Card as proof that you're not the carrier of some new and exotic plague. The essential vaccinations are cholera (valid for six months) and yellow fever (valid for 10 years). In addition, you're strongly advised to be vaccinated against typhoid (valid one year), tetanus (valid for five to 10 years), tuberculosis (valid for life) and polio (valid for life). Gamma globulin shots are also available for protection against infectious hepatitis (type A) but they are ineffective against serum hepatitis (type B). Depending on how much gamma globulin you receive, protection lasts three to six months. There is a vaccine available for Type B but it's only recommended for individuals at high risk (medical personnel and people expecting to have sexual contact with local people). It's expensive, and the series of three injections takes six months to complete.

You need to plan ahead for these vaccinations, as they cannot all be given at once and typhoid requires a second injection about two or three weeks after the first. Cholera and typhoid jabs usually leave you with a stiff and sore arm for two days afterwards if you've never had them before. The others generally don't have any effect. Tetanus requires a course of three injections.

If your vaccination card expires whilst you're away, there are a number of medical centres in African cities where you can be re-vaccinated, often free of charge. Such centres that we know of are listed in the chapters on the respective countries.

Avoid turning up at borders with expired vaccination cards, as officials may insist on you having the relevant injection before they will let you in. The same needle is often used on a whole host of travellers without any sterilisation between jabs, so you stand a fair chance of contracting serum hepatitis.

Your local physician will arrange a course of injections for you if you live outside a city. Most large cities have vaccination centres which you can find in the telephone book. Fees for injections vary from US$4-9 depending on the vaccine.

You can get vaccinations from the following places:

Belgium
Ministere de la Santé Publique et de la Famille, Cité Administrative de l'Etat, Quartier de l'Esplanade, 1000 Brussels. *Centre Médical du Ministere des Affaires Etrangeres*, 9 Rue Brederode, 1000 Brussel.

France
Direction Départmentale d'Action Sanitaire et Sociale, 57 Boulevard de Sevastopol, 75001 Paris (tel 508 9690).
Institut Pasteur, 25 Rue du Docteur Roux, 75015 Paris (tel 566 5800).
L'Institut d'Hygiene, 2 Quai du Cheval Blanc, 1200 Geneva (tel 022-43 8075).

Holland
Any GGD office or the *Academical Medical Centre*, Amsterdam.

UK
Hospital for Tropical Diseases, 4 St Pancras Way, London, NW1 (tel 01-387 4411). Injections here are free but they're often booked up about a month ahead.
West London Designated Vaccination Centre, 53 Great Cumberland Place, London W1 (tel 01-262 6456). No appoint-

ment is necessary – just turn up. The fees vary depending on the vaccine.

British Airways Immunisation Centre, Victoria Terminal, Buckingham Palace Rd, London, SW1 (tel 01-834 2323). Try to book a few days in advance; otherwise you might have to wait around for a few hours before they can fit you in.

British Airways Medical Centre, Speedbird House, Heathrow Airport, Hounslow, Middlesex (tel 01-759 5511).

Medical Insurance Get some! You may never need it, but if you do you'll be very glad you got it. Only very rarely will you find a country where medical treatment is free. There are many different travel insurance policies available and any travel agent will be able to recommend one. The best thing to do before you choose one is to collect half a dozen different policies and read through them for an hour or two, as the cost of a policy and the sort of cover required can vary quite considerably. Many pitch themselves at the family package tour market and are not really appropriate for a long spell in Africa under your own steam. Usually medical insurance comes in a package which includes baggage insurance and life insurance, etc. You need to read through the baggage section carefully, as many policies put a ceiling on how much they are prepared to pay for individual items which are lost or stolen.

General Health Get your teeth checked and treated if necessary before you set off. Dentists are few and far between in Africa, and treatment is expensive.

The main things which are likely to affect your general health whilst abroad are diet and climate. Cheap food bought in cafés and street stands tends to be overcooked, very starchy (mainly maize and millet) and lacking in protein, vitamins and calcium. Over a period of time the latter two, when combined with lack of exercise for your gums, can seriously affect the health of your teeth, so make sure you supplement your diet with milk or yogurt (where available and pasteurised) and fresh fruit or vitamin/mineral tablets. Avoid untreated milk and milk products – in many countries herds are not screened for brucellosis or tuberculosis. Peel all fruit. Read up on dietary requirements before you set off. And watch out for grit in rice and bread: a hard bite on the wrong thing can lead to a cracked tooth.

In hot climates you sweat a great deal and so lose a lot of water and salt. Make sure you drink sufficient liquid and have enough salt in your food to make good the losses (a teaspoon of salt per day is generally sufficient). If you don't make good the losses, you run the risk of suffering from heat exhaustion and cramps. Heat can also make you impatient and irritable. Try to take things at a slower pace. Hot, dry air will make your hair brittle, so oil it often with, say, refined coconut oil. Take great care of cuts, grazes and skin infections; otherwise they tend to persist and get worse. If they're weeping, bandage them up. Open sores attract flies and there are plenty of those. Change bandages daily and use an antiseptic cream if necessary.

A temporary but troublesome skin condition from which many people from temperate climates suffer initially is prickly heat. Many tiny blisters form on one or more parts of your body – usually where the skin is thickest, such as your hands. They are sweat droplets which are trapped under your skin because your pores aren't large enough or haven't opened up sufficiently to cope with the greater volume of sweat. Anything which promotes sweating – exercise, tea, coffee, alcohol – makes it worse. Keep your skin aired and dry, reduce clothing to a loose-fitting minimum and keep out of direct sunlight. Calamine lotion or zinc oxide-based talcum powder help soothe the skin. Apart from that, there isn't much else you can do. The problem is one of acclimatisation and will go away in time.

Adjustment to the outlook, habits,

social customs, etc, of different people can take a lot out of you too. Many travellers suffer from some degree of culture shock. This is particularly true if you fly direct from your own country to an African city. Under these conditions, heat can aggravate petty irritations which would pass unnoticed in a more temperate climate. Exhausting all-night, all-day bus journeys over bad roads don't help if you're feeling this way. Make sure you get enough sleep.

Drinking Water Avoid drinking unboiled water anywhere that it's not chlorinated unless you're taking it from a mountain spring. Unboiled water is a major source of diarrhoea and hepatitis, as are salads that have been washed in contaminated water and unpeeled fruit that has been handled by someone with one of these infections. This is easier said than done, especially in the desert and in parts of Zaire, and it may be that you'll have to drink water no matter what source it comes from. This is part of travelling and there is no way you can eliminate all risks. Carrying a water bottle and a supply of water-purifying tablets is one way around this. *Halazone, Potable Aqua* and *Sterotabs* are all good for purifying water but they have little or no effect against amoebas or hepatitis virus. For this you need a 2% tincture of iodine – five drops per litre in clear water and 10 drops per litre in cloudy water. Wait 30 minutes and it's safe to drink though it will taste foul.

Malaria This is caused by a blood parasite which is spread by certain species of night-flying mosquito (*anopheles*). Only the female insects spread the disease; you can contract it through a single bite from an insect carrying the parasite. Start on a course of anti-malarial drugs before you set off and keep it up as you travel. The drugs are fairly cheap and any pharmacy will advise you about which kind to buy. There are basically two types: (i) *proguanil* (or *paludrine*) which you take once daily;

or (ii) *chloroquine*, which you take once or twice per week (depending on strength). Both are marketed under various trade names. In some areas of Africa the parasite is beginning to acquire immunity against some of the drugs. This is particularly true in East and Central Africa. In these areas take *Fansidar* (manufactured by Roche in Germany and Switzerland) once weekly, *plus* the normal dose of chloroquine. In Australia and New Zealand *Maloprim* is often substituted for *Fansidar*.

Even if you keep to the above drug regime it's still possible to catch malaria (high fever, severe headaches, shivering) though this is fortunately rare. If you do catch the disease and are not within reach of medical advise the treatment is: One single dose of four tablets (600 mg) of *Chloroquine* followed by two tablets (300 mg) six hours later and two tablets on each following day. As an alternative (or in *Chloroquine*-resistant areas) take a single dose of three tablets of *Fansidar*.

Other than the malaria hazard, mosquito bites can be troublesome and although it's probably useless to say this, *don't scratch the bites*. If you do, and they don't heal quickly, there's a chance of them being infected with something else. You'll come across people in Africa pock-marked with angry sores which started out as insignificant mosquito bites whose owners couldn't resist the urge to scratch them. Don't join them. Will-power works wonders, as does antihistamine cream. If you want to keep the mosquitoes off at night, use an insect repellent on your skin or sleep under a fan at night. Mosquitoes don't like swift-moving currents of air and will stay on the walls of the room in these circumstances.

No vaccination is possible against malaria. Take those pills. (However, at the time of writing there was a news report that a malaria vaccine had been discovered.)

Bilharzia This is caused by blood flukes (minute worms) which live in the veins of

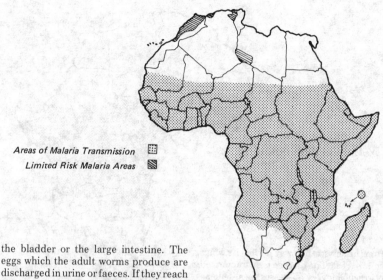

Areas of Malaria Transmission
Limited Risk Malaria Areas

the bladder or the large intestine. The eggs which the adult worms produce are discharged in urine or faeces. If they reach water, they hatch out and enter the bodies of a certain species of fresh-water snail where they multiply for four or more weeks and are then discharged into the surrounding water. If they are to live, they must find and invade the body of a human being where they develop, mate and then make their way to the veins of their choice. Here they start to lay eggs and the cycle repeats itself. The snail favors shallow water near the shores of lakes and streams and they are more abundant in water which is polluted by human excrement. Generally speaking, moving water contains less risk than stagnant water but you can never tell.

Bilharzia is quite a common disease in Africa. If you don't want to catch it, stay out of rivers and lakes. If you drink water from any of these places, boil it or sterilise it with chlorine tablets. The disease is painful and causes persistent and cumulative damage by repeated deposits of eggs. If you suspect you have it, seek medical advice as soon as possible – look for blood in your urine or faeces that isn't

associated with diarrhoea. The only body of water in Africa which is largely free of bilharzia is Lake Malawi. Keep out of lakes Victoria, Tanganyika and Kivu and the rivers Congo, Nile and Zambesi. As the intermediate hosts (snails) live only in fresh water, there's no risk of catching bilharzia in the sea.

Trypanosomiasis (Sleeping Sickness) This is another disease transmitted by biting insects, in this case by the tsetse fly. Like malaria, it's caused by minute parasites which live in the blood. The risk of infection is very small and confined to areas which are only a fraction of the total area inhabited by the tsetse fly. The flies are found only south of the Sahara but the disease is responsible for the absence of horses and cattle from large tracts of central Africa. The fly is about twice the size of a common housefly and recognisable

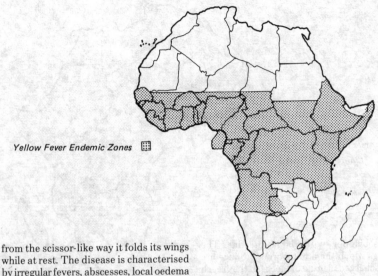

Yellow Fever Endemic Zones ⊞

from the scissor-like way it folds its wings while at rest. The disease is characterised by irregular fevers, abscesses, local oedema (puffy swellings caused by excess water retained in body tissues), inflammation of the glands and physical and mental lethargy. It responds well to treatment.

Yellow Fever As you can see from this map, yellow fever is endemic in much of Africa. Get that vaccination before you set off; then you won't have to worry about it.

Hepatitis This is a liver disease caused by a virus. There are basically two types – infectious hepatitis (known as Type A) and serum hepatitis (known as Type B). The one you're most likely to contract is Type A. It's very contagious and you pick it up by drinking water, eating food or using cutlery or crockery that's been contaminated by an infected person. Foods to avoid are salads (unless you know they have been washed thoroughly in purified water) and unpeeled fruit that may have been handled by someone with dirty hands. It's also possible to pick it up by sharing a towel or toothbrush with an infected person. At the same time, you should remember than an estimated 10% of the population of the Third World are healthy carriers of Type B but the only ways you can contract this form are by having sex with an infected person or by being injected with a needle which has previously been used on an infected person.

Symptoms appear 15 to 50 days after infection (generally around 25 days) and consist of fever, loss of appetite, nausea, depression, complete lack of energy and pains around the base of your rib cage. Your skin will turn progressively yellow and the whites of your eyes yellow to orange. The easiest way to keep an eye on the situation is to watch the colour of your eyes and urine. If you have hepatitis, the colour of your piss will be deep orange no matter how much liquid you've drunk. If you haven't drunk much liquid and/or you're sweating a lot, don't jump to conclusions. Check it out by drinking a lot of liquid all at once. If the urine is still orange then you'd better start making plans to go somewhere you won't mind convalescing for a few weeks. Sometimes the disease lasts only a few weeks and you only get a few really bad days, but it can last for months. If it does get really bad, cash in that medical insurance you took out and fly back home.

There is no cure as such for hepatitis except rest and good food. Diets high in B vitamins are said to help. Fat-free diets have gone out of medical fashion, but you may find that grease and oil make you feel nauseous for a long time. If that's the case, cut them out of your diet until you can handle them again. Seeking medical attention is probably a waste of time and money. There's nothing doctors can do for you that you can't do for yourself other than run tests that will tell you how bad it is. Most people don't need telling; they can feel it! Cut alcohol and cigarettes right off the slate. They'll not only make you feel much worse, they could do permanent damage to a sick liver.

Think seriously about getting that gamma globulin vaccination.

Diarrhoea Sooner or later – unless you're a very exceptional person – you'll get diarrhoea, so you may as well accept the inevitable. You can't really expect to travel halfway around the world without succumbing to diarrhoea at least once or twice, but it doesn't always mean that you've caught a bug. Depending on how much travelling you've done and what your guts are used to, it can be merely the result of a change of food. If you've spent all your life living out of sterilised, cellophane-wrapped packets and tins from the local supermarket, you're going to have a hard time of it at first until you adjust.

There are lots of flies in Africa – flies which live on the various wastes produced by humans and other animals. In most places local people shit fairly indiscriminately wherever the urge takes them. Public toilet facilities are rare or non-existent and that goes for sewage-treatment systems too. Some places are notorious for their open sewers and in very few of them is the connection ever made between food, flies and shit. This is the source of most gut infections which afflict both travellers and local people alike. The situation is changing – but slowly – and travellers are helping to spread the concept of hygiene in many places.

If and when you get a gut infection, avoid rushing off to the chemist and filling yourself with antibiotics. It's a harsh way to treat your system and you can build up a tolerance to them with overuse. Try to starve the bugs out first. Eat nothing and rest. Avoid travelling. Drink plenty of fluids. Have your tea without milk or sugar and add a small amount of dissolved salt to it. Dissolve salt in your fruit juices as well. Diarrhoea will dehydrate you and may result in painful muscular cramps in your guts. The cramps are due to a bad salt balance in your blood, hence the idea of taking a small amount of salt with your tea or fruit juice. Chewing a small pellet of opium or taking a tincture of opium (known as 'paregoric' and often mixed with kaolin – a stronger version of *Milk of Magnesia*) will also relieve the pain of cramps. Something else you may come across, called *RD Sol*, also helps to maintain a correct salt balance and so prevent cramps. It's a mixture of common salt, sodium bicarbonate, potassium chloride and dextrose, and although somewhat unpalatable itself, is OK when mixed with a fruit juice. Two days of this regime should clear you out.

If you simply can't hack starving, keep to a *small* diet of curd, yogurt, lime/lemon juice, boiled vegetables and tea. Stay away from butter, milk, sugar, cakes and non-citrus fruits.

If starving doesn't work or you really have to move on and can't rest for a couple of days, try *Pesulin* (or *Pesulin-O* which is the same but with the addition of a tincture of opium). Dosage is two teaspoons four times daily for five days. Or try *Lomotil* – the dosage is two tabs three times daily for two days.

If you have no luck with either of these, change to antibiotics or see a doctor. There are many different varieties of antibiotics and you almost need to be a biochemist to know what the differences between them are. They include *tetracyclin, chlorostep, typhstrep, sulphatriad, streptomagma* and *thiazole*.

If possible, have a word with the chemist about their differences. Avoid *Enterovioform*, which used to be sold widely in Europe and is next to useless for treating gut ailments in Africa. Anyway, it is now suspected of causing optic nerve damage. With antibiotics, keep to the correct dosage. Overuse will do you more harm than good.

If you are interested in preventing diarrhoea (rather than treating it when you get it) use *Pepto-Bismol* liquid, 60 ml four times a day. It's effective, relatively safe and non-antibiotic but inconvenient to carry. *Vibramycin (doxycycline)*, 200 mg on the first day of travel and 100 mg once per day for three weeks, is also effective but this antibiotic has several potential side effects. *Bactrim DS* or *Septra DS (trimethoprimsulphamethoxazole)*, one tablet per day for two weeks, is also effective but again, it's an antibiotic.

Dysentery This is, unfortunately, quite prevalent in some places. It's characterised by diarrhoea containing blood and lots of mucus and painful gut cramps. (Ah, travellers' toilet tales!) There are two types: (i) bacillary dysentery which is short, sharp and nasty but rarely persistent – the most common variety; (ii) amoebic dysentery which, as its name suggests, is caused by amoebic parasites. This variety is much more difficult to treat and often persistent.

Bacillic dysentery comes on suddenly and lays you out with fever, nausea, painful cramps and diarrhoea but, because it's caused by bacteria, responds well to antibiotics. Amoebic dysentery builds up more slowly but is more dangerous. You cannot starve it out and if it's untreated it will get worse and permanently damage your intestines. If you see blood in your faeces persistently over two or three days, seek medical attention as soon as possible. *Flagyl (metronidazole)* is the most commonly prescribed drug for amoebic dysentery. The dosage is six tablets per day for five to seven days. Flagyl is both an antibiotic and an anti-parasitic as well. It is also used for the treatment of giardiasis and trichomoniasis. Flagyl should not be taken by pregnant women. If you get bacillic dysentery, the best thing for slowing down intestinal movements is codeine phosphate (30-mg tablets – take two once every four hours). It's much more effective than *Lomotil* or *Imodium* and cheaper. Treatment for bacillic dysentery consists of a course of *tetracyclin* or *bactrim* (antibiotics).

If you get heavy 'rice-water' diarrhoea without pains (or almost without pains) then you could have caught a type of cholera – the vaccination you get is not totally effective. If this happens, the most important thing is to drink as much liquid as you can and take salt. Your urine should remain clear, not yellow or concentrated.

Giardia This is prevalent in tropical climates and is characterised by swelling of the stomach, pale-coloured faeces, diarrhoea and, after a while, depression and sometimes nausea. Many doctors recommend *Flagyl* (a dosage of 7 x 250 mg over a three-day period should clear up the symptoms, repeated a week later if not). Flagyl, however, has many side effects and some doctors prefer to treat giardiasis with *Tinaba (tinadozole)* (two grams taken all at once – this normally knocks it right out but if not you can repeat the dosage for up to three days).

Tropical Ulcers These are sores which

often start from some insignificant scratch or burst blister but they never seem to get better and they often get worse and spread to other areas of the body. They're also quite painful. If you keep clean and look after any sores which you get on your arms and legs (eg from ill-fitting shoes or accidents to your feet or from excessive scratching of insect bites) then it's unlikely you will be troubled by them. However, if you do develop sores which won't clear up then you need to hit the anti-biotics quickly. Don't let them spread.

Fellow Travellers – of the insect variety The main ones you're likely to come across are fleas, lice and bed bugs. There isn't a lot you can do about the first. They vary considerably in numbers from one season to another; some places have a lot, others none at all. The less money you pay for a bed or a meal, the more likely you are to encounter them. You can generally avoid lice by washing yourself and your clothes frequently. You're most likely to pick them up in crowded places like buses and trains, but you might also get them by staying in very cheap hotels. You'll occasionally meet tribespeople whose hair is so matted and which hasn't seen water for so long that it's literally crawling with lice. However, it takes a while for lice to get stuck into you so you should get a companion to have a look through your hair about once a week to see if you've acquired any eggs. They are always laid near the base of the hairs. If you find any you can either pick them out one by one (very laborious) or blitz them with insecticide shampoo like *Lorexanne* or *Suleo*. We've had letters from people who have doused their hair in petrol or DDT. You're certainly guaranteed total wipe-out this way but it does seem mildly hysterical and I dread to think what condition it leaves your hair and scalp in!

With luck you won't come across bed bugs too often. These evil little bastards live in the crevices of walls and the framework of beds where they hide during the day. They look like lice but move like greased lightning once you become aware of their presence and switch on the light to see what's happening. Look for tell-tale bloodstains on the walls near beds in budget hotels. If you see them, find another hotel.

On the Road

TRANSPORT

Most African countries offer a choice of railways, buses, taxis (whether shared or private) and trucks. Trains are generally slow – sometimes very slow – but in 3rd class and sometimes 2nd class are often cheaper than other forms of transport. Buses are usually quicker than going by rail or truck but are more expensive. Where there is a good network of sealed roads, you have the choice of going by 'luxury' air-conditioned bus or by ordinary bus. The former naturally cost more but are not always quicker than the ordinary buses. When there are very few or no sealed roads, the ordinary buses tend to be very crowded and stop frequently to pick up or put down passengers. Book in advance if possible.

Most countries also have shared taxis (which take up to five passengers and leave when full) and private taxis. You can forget about the latter if you're on a budget, but shared taxis should definitely be considered. They can cost up to twice the price of the corresponding bus fare, but in some places they're only slightly more expensive and they're certainly quicker and more comfortable.

You should expect to pay a fee for your baggage in addition to the fare on most buses and taxis in West Africa. Also, in countries where the roads quickly turn into mud baths during the rainy season, the fares on buses and taxis can double and even triple.

For many travellers, trucks are the favoured means of transport. They're not only the cheapest way of getting from A to B as a rule, but you can get an excellent view from the top of the load. A few years ago it used to be possible to hitch free on trucks all the way through Africa, assuming you were prepared to wait until the free lifts came along. It's now very difficult to do this and you should expect to pay for

lifts. Hitching is a recognised form of public transport in much of Africa. Most of the time you will be on top of the load, though you can sometimes travel in the cab for about twice what it costs on top. For most regular runs there will be a 'fare' which is more or less fixed, and you'll be paying what the locals pay – but check this out before you agree to a price. Sometimes it's possible to get the truckie to lower the price if there's a group of you (form an impromptu group where possible). Trucks are generally cheaper than buses over the same distance.

There are trucks to most places on main routes every day, but in the more remote areas they may only run once or twice a week. Many lifts are arranged the night before departure at the 'truck park' – a compound/dust patch that you'll find in almost every African town of any size. Just go there and ask around for a truck which is going the way you want to go. If the journey is going to take more than one night or one day, ask whether the price includes food and/or water. Remember that the roads are in many places atrocious and break-downs/getting stuck are a regular feature of the journey. Don't look too closely at the tyres or the springs. When you see the state of many of the roads you'll know why nothing lasts very long. In some places like Zaire, Sudan, Rwanda, Burundi, Tanzania, Zambia and Mozambique the 'roads' just have to be seen to be believed – pot holes as high as a person, bridges washed away, etc. Desert roads in places like Sudan, Chad, Mali, Niger and Mauritania are just a set of tyre tracks left in the sand or the dust by previous trucks. Don't pay any attention to red lines drawn on maps in places like this. Many roads are impassable in the wet season.

In the more developed countries where there are plenty of private cars on the road, it's not only possible to hitch free but, in some cases, very easy indeed, and you may well be offered somewhere to stay the night. Countries where this applies are Algeria, Ghana, Kenya, Libya, Morocco, South Africa, Tunisia, Uganda and Zimbabwe. On the other hand, don't expect much in the way of lifts from expatriate workers. They have a tendency to regard travellers as a lesser form of humanity. Much the same seems to be happening to the attitudes of Peace Corps volunteers and VSOs. Perhaps this is because the hospitality which has been offered in the past has been abused, so if you are offered help by one of these people, please make sure you don't overstay your welcome and that you pay your way. Many of the volunteers have to get by on next to nothing and they haven't gone there in order to be a convenience for travellers. They're committed people who have gone there to help local people improve their lot.

Remember that sticking out your thumb in many African countries is the equivalent of an obscene gesture, although allowances are generally made for foreigners. Wave your hand vertically up and down instead.

Just a word of warning about lifts in private cars. Smuggling across borders does go on, and if whatever is being smuggled is found, you may be arrested even though you knew nothing about it. Most travellers manage to convince police that they were merely hitching a ride and otherwise had nothing to do with the smuggler (passport stamps are a good indication of this), but the convincing can take days. It's unlikely they'll let you ring your embassy during this time, and even if you do you shouldn't count on their ability to help you. If you're worried about this, get out before the border and walk through. A Canadian woman recently spent several days in jail in Francistown, Botswana, after she'd hitched a ride with a 'Malawian businessman' in Livingstone who was heading for Gaborone. The Botswana customs discovered he was smuggling Mandrax which, in Botswana, is lumped in the same bracket as heroin and carries a mandatory seven-year sentence.

ACCOMMODATION

There are many different types of places where you can stay cheaply in Africa. They range from youth hostels in such countries as Egypt, Kenya, Morocco, South Africa, Tunisia and Zimbabwe, through religious missions in the ex-French and ex-Belgian colonies, to government rest houses in such places as Malawi and Namibia and bath-houses (*hammans*) in Algeria. *Hammams* are for men only. The religious missions in the more visited places, however, are becoming less and less willing to take travellers unless they have purpose-built accommodation, but in the more remote areas you should still be able to find a welcome there. Where there are no youth hostels there are often youth centres which can offer floor space or a bed in a dormitory. Most of the above places shouldn't cost you more than a few dollars a night.

The next option is a cheap hotel. Naturally, what you get depends largely on what you pay for. If you're paying less than US$5 a single then, as likely as not, the hotel will double as a brothel. Even US$10 a single won't guarantee that the hotel isn't used for the same purposes in some places. Things like a fan, a private bathroom or a mosquito net, for example, will all bump up the price of a room. In cities and towns where there are distinct 'African' and so-called 'European' quarters (the latter are generally the parts of a city constructed initially by the colonial authorities), the cheapest hotels will be in the 'African' quarter. Hotels which you find in the 'European' quarter will generally be similar in quality to those you find in most western countries.

More and more African countries are setting up purpose-built campsites, but where there are no such places you can always find a place to pitch a tent. In some countries you will be obliged (and it's common courtesy to do so) to first seek permission from the village elder or chief. A tent is also extremely useful if you're thinking of doing a lot of walking, climbing mountains or staying in the bush (especially in Zaire). Never assume, however, that your gear is safe even at a campsite which is supposedly guarded 24 hours a day.

LANGUAGE

The main languages are English, French, Portuguese, Arabic and Swahili, though there are many areas where other languages are widely spoken. Of the latter, Hausa (parts of Nigeria, Niger, Bourkinafasso and Mali), Shona (Zimbabwe), Afrikaans (South Africa and Namibia) and Amharic (Ethiopia) are some of the more important. It is more or less essential to have a working knowledge of English and French, and a smattering of Arabic and Swahili would repay the time spent learning it over and over again. Local people will always warm to any attempt you make to speak their language no matter how botched the effort.

Even if you don't have the time or inclination to learn Arabic, you need to be familiar with the common numerals. They are:

0	*sifr*
1	*wahid*
2	*zouje*
3	*talata*
4	*arba'a*
5	*hamsa*
6	*setta*
7	*seb'a*
8	*thimanya*
9	*tesa'a*
10	*ashara*
11	*hadashara*
12	*etnatashara*
13	*talathashara*
14	*arba'ashara*
15	*hamsahara*
16	*settashara*
17	*sabashara*
18	*thamania ashara*
19	*tisashara*
20	*ishrun*
30	*talat'in*
40	*arba'in*
50	*hamsin*
60	*set'in*
70	*sab'in*
80	*thaman'in*
90	*tis'in*
100	*mia*
200	*miat'in*
1000	*alef*
2000	*alfain*

Some Arabic words which you may find useful are:

yes	*nam*
no	*ley*
thank you	*shokrah*
sir (polite form)	*mansour*
sir (very polite form)	*sidi*
madam (polite form)	*lalla*
greetings	*salaam al laikoum*
hello (Algerian form)	*labass*
river bed	*oued*
sand	*ramia*
mountain	*djebel*
camel	*djemal*
small shops	*souk*
tea	*atai*
coffee	*kahoua*
bread	*khobz*
water	*mey/ma*
how much?	*kem?*
knife	*mouse*
fork	*mtaka*
spoon	*tobsi*

Further south a knowledge of Hausa numbers would be useful. They are:

1	*daya*
2	*biu*
3	*oku*
4	*hudu*
5	*biart*
6	*shida*
7	*bokwai*

8	takwas
9	tara
10	goma
11	gomashadaya
12	gomashabiu
20	ashirin
21	ashirindadaya
22	ashirindabiu
23	ashirindaoku
24	ashirindahudu
30	talatin
1000	CFA Jaka

Some useful Hausa words include:

yes/OK	toh
no	babu
no/don't want it	uhuh
thank you	nagode
thanks very much	nagode quere
good	de kyao
how much?	nowa
expression of surprise	haba/wallahi!
expression of surprise or disgust	khai!
don't want it	shikenah
greetings (very polite)	rankadidi
response to above	sanu (pl sanunku)
welcome (polite)	barka d'azua
welcome (colloquial)	lai'hya loh
reply to the above	nagadjia
water	rua
hot	zafi
cold	sanyi
food	abinchi
rice	shinkafa
okra	guro
onions	albasa
meat	nama
eggs	kwai
fish	kifi
milk	madara
chicken	dantsako
camel	rakumi
salt	gishiri
man	mutum
woman	mache
house	gida
market	kazua
sick	yi shiwo
slowly	sannu sannu
quickly	muza muza
carefully	hunkli hunkli
tomorrow	gobe
this/that	wanun

POST

Have letters sent to you c/o Poste Restante, GPO, in whatever city/town you will be passing through. Alternatively, use the mail-holding service operated by American Express offices and their agents if you're a client (ie if you have their cheques or one of their credit cards). Most embassies no longer hold mail and will forward it to the nearest Poste Restante. Plan ahead. It can take up to two weeks for a letter to arrive even in capital cities, and it sometimes takes much longer in smaller places.

The majority of Poste Restantes are pretty reliable though there are one or two exceptions, Cairo being one of the most notorious. Mail is generally held for four weeks – sometimes more, sometimes less – after which it is returned to the sender. The service is free in most places but in others, particularly ex-French colonies, there is a small charge for each letter collected. As a rule you need your passport as proof of identity. In large places where there's a lot of traffic the letters are generally sorted into alphabetical order, but in smaller places they may all be lumped together in the one box. Sometimes you're allowed to sort through them yourself; sometimes a post office employee will do the sorting for you.

If you're not receiving expected letters, ask them to check under every conceivable combination of your Christian name, surname, any other initials and even under 'M' (for Mr, Ms, Miss, Mrs). This sort of confusion isn't as widespread as many people believe, though most travellers have an improbable story to tell about it. If there is confusion, it's generally because of bad handwriting on the envelope or because the sorter's first language is not English, French or another European language. If you want to make absolutely sure that the fault won't be yours, have your friends address letters as follows:

BLOGGS J
Poste Restante,
GPO,
Nairobi,
Kenya

Avoid sending currency notes through the post. They'll often be stolen by post office employees no matter how cleverly you disguise the contents. There are all sorts of ways of finding out whether a letter is worth opening up. Still, some people do get cash through the mail in this way.

When sending letters yourself, try to use aerogrammes (air letters) rather than ordinary letters, but if you do send the latter make sure that the stamps are franked in front of you. Otherwise there's a fair chance they will be steamed off, re-sold and the letter thrown away.

There's little point in having any letter sent by Express Delivery (called Special Delivery in the UK), as they won't get there any quicker on average than an air letter.

BARGAINING

Most purchases involve some degree of bargaining. This includes hotels, transport, food, cigarettes, etc, but the prices of basic commodities are settled within minutes. It's a way of life in many parts of the world where commodities are looked on as being worth what their owners can get for them. The concept of a fixed price would invoke laughter. If you cop out and pay the first price asked, you'll not only be considered a half-wit but you'll be doing you're fellow travellers a disservice since this will create the impression that all travellers are willing to pay outrageous prices (and all are equally as stupid). You are expected to bargain. It's part of the fun of going to Africa. All the same, no matter

how good you are at it, you'll never get things as cheaply as local people do. To traders, hotel and café owners you represent wealth – whatever your appearance – and it's of little consequence that you consider yourself to be a 'traveller' rather than a 'tourist.' In the eyes of a trader, you're the latter.

Bargaining is conducted in a friendly, sometimes exaggeratedly extrovert manner in most cases, though there are occasions when it degenerates into a bleak exchange of numbers and leaden head-shakes. Decide what you want to pay or what others have told you they've paid, and start off at a price about 50% lower than this. The seller will inevitably start off at a price about 50% higher than what he or she is prepared to accept. This way you can both end up having appeared to be generous. For larger purchases in souks, bazaars and markets, especially in Moslem countries, you may well be served tea as part of the bargaining ritual. Accepting it places you under no obligation to buy, but helps you get to know each other better; anyway your throat gets dry with all that talking. There will be times when you simply cannot get a shopkeeper to lower the prices to anywhere near what you know the product should be selling for. This probably means that a lot of tourists are passing through and if you don't pay those outrageous prices, some mug on an overland tour bus or package tour will. Don't lose your temper bargaining. If you get fed up, go home and come back the next day.

LOOKING FOR SOMEONE TO TRAVEL WITH

Travelling overland is rarely a solo activity unless you want it that way. Even if you set off travelling alone, you'll quickly meet other travellers who are heading in the some direction, as well as others who are returning. This is especially true of the two main north-south routes from the Mediterranean to Central Africa – Algeria to Zaire via Niger, Nigeria, Cameroun and

CAR; and Egypt to Kenya via Sudan and Uganda. Crossroads where travellers congregate are also good places to meet other travellers and team up wth someone. The best are Athens, Bangui, Cairo, Dar es Salaam, Harare, Kampala, Lome, Nairobi, Niamey, Lamu, and any of the Moroccan cities.

If you'd prefer to find someone before you set off, check out the classified advertisements in national newspapers or the noticeboards at colleges and universities before the summer holidays come up. If you're in London, UK, very good places to look are *Time Out, LAM* (London Alternative Magazine), *Australasian Express* and the noticeboard at *Trailfinders*, 48 Earls Court Rd, London, W8. In New York, USA, try the New York Student Centre, Hotel Empire, Broadway and 63rd St (tel 212 695 0291), or get hold of something like the *Village Voice*.

PUBLICATIONS

Maps The best maps of Africa are undoubtedly those published by Michelin. They are much more accurate and far more detailed than those put out by Bartholomew's. The Michelin African series consists of the following:

No 153 North West Africa
No 154 North East Africa
No 155 Southern Africa
No 169 Morocco
No 172 Algeria & Tunisia
No 175 Cote d'Ivoire

The last edition of No 153 was published in 1975 and is in need of revision, but political difficulties have so far prevented research being done and it's not known when a new edition will be published. No 155 is also in need of revision.

If you can't get hold of Michelin maps, then Bartholomew's are adequate for most purposes but they do contain serious errors. Some of the worst errors are the marking of an 'A' class road where none exists or a thin red line where a fully sealed

major highway exists. Tracks which they mark through the desert are largely a figment of the imagination. For small countries (especially Burundi, Rwanda, Lesotho and Swaziland) you needn't even bother opening them since the detail is non-existent. Just don't use them as though they were a road map.

Good suppliers of maps are:

France
Institute Géographie National, 136 bis, Rue de Grenelle, 75700 Paris.

UK
Edward Stanford, 12-14 Long Acre, London WC2 (tel 01-836 1321).
The French Map & Guide Centre, 122 Kings Cross Rd, London WC1 (tel 01-278 0896/7). This latter specialises in Institute Géographie National maps of former French and Belgium colonies.

Other guides Two books which you will find well worth getting hold of as far as the top end of the continent is concerned are:

Sahara Handbook Simon and Jan Glen (Lascelles, London 1980). This is the most comprehensive guide you can get hold of for this part of Africa. It's certainly pitched at those taking their own vehicles, but almost half the book is taken up by very detailed descriptions of all the possible current routes through the Sahara. There are plenty of maps, illustrations and sketches. An excellent book which I recommend to anyone but, because it assumes you'll be sleeping and eating in your own metal box most of the time, it has little to suggest about where to stay and eat and the cost of transport of trucks and buses. You'll be pleased to know they didn't think much of *Africa on the Cheap* (the predecessor of *Africa on a Shoestring*) – 'too underground' . . . 'many errors.' Perhaps they were referring to the red-backed 1977 edition?

Durch Africa Klaus and Erika Darr (Darr Publications). Written in German, this book covers many routes through Africa, though it does concentrate on those taking their own vehicles.

Guide du Sahara B Vaes et al (Hatchette, Guide Bleus, Paris 1977). This is a very detailed guide written in French (as all the Hatchette guides are) which also contains a lot of archaeological and anthropological background information. It does not include Libya or Nigeria and it's pricey.

Backpackers' Africa Hilary and George Bradt (Bradt Enterprises 1977). The descriptions of some 17 walks off the Cape-to-Cairo route described in this book can be entertaining and it does contain some useful addresses but it's very short of maps.

Marokko Erika Darr (Darr Expeditions Service, Kirchheim, 1981). Another of the Darr publications written in German and, like all of them, very detailed and comprehensive with heaps of maps and black-and-white photographs, and a vast Moroccan-German language section. Even if you don't read German, this book is intelligible because of the way it has been put together. It would be very hard to find a book which rivals this. Highly recommended.

Guide to Egypt Michael von Haag (Travelaid, London, 1981). One of the best books ever published on Egypt, especially if you have a yen for ancient Egyptian archaeological sites and Islamic monuments, which it covers in graphic detail together with diagrams and maps. It also has practical sections about where to stay and where to eat. However, in common with travellers who once criticised previous editions of this book for the poor quality of the maps of Cairo and Alexandria, I was very disappointed by the author's attempts at the same and others. After all the effort which obviously went into producing maps for the archaeological sites, he could have done a better job on the cities. A new '85 edition has just been released.

Guide to Mount Kenya & Kilimanjaro ed Iain Allan (Mountain Club of Kenya, Nairobi, 1981). This guide was first published in 1959 and has gone through four editions and is heading for its fifth. As you might expect, being published by the MCK, it has been written and added to continuously over the years by dedicated enthusiasts who spend a large part of their free time doing nothing but exploring these two mountains. What isn't in this book isn't worth knowing. With minute descriptions of each trail (as well as sheer rock faces); good maps and photographs; descriptions of the fauna and flora, climate and geology; and even mountain medicine, it's a must for anyone thinking of spending some time in Kenya or Tanzania. It's also a very convenient size with a plastic cover. Pick up your copy from their HQ at Wilson Airport, Nairobi, or from PO Box 45741, Nairobi.

Guide to East Africa – Kenya, Tanzania, the Seychelles Nina Casimati (Travelaid & Hippocrene Books, London & New York, 1984). This book seems to have started out with good intentions but hit problems. It has very good descriptions of the game parks in East Africa, but beyond that it has left the rails. When it gets down to practical information, especially regarding the lower end of the market, it simply lifts information from earlier editions of *Africa on a Shoestring*.

The Guide to Lesotho David Ambrose (Winchester Press, Johannesburg and Maseru, 1976). David Ambrose is a mountain climber and trekker who has lived and worked in Lesotho since 1965. If the contents of the book are anything to go by, he knows this country like the back of his hand. Although written in the style of an 'official handbook' (and therefore containing a lot of detail of little use to travellers), his descriptions of various treks, climbing possibilities, sights worth seeing, the handicrafts, culture and history of the Basotho are excellent. There are also some stunning colour photographs which, if you haven't already thought about visiting Lesotho, are certainly going to draw you to this beautiful country. Get hold of a copy as soon as you get to Maseru!

Periodicals The best periodical for a very detailed political and economic analysis of every African country except Morocco, Algeria, Tunisia, Libya and Egypt is:

New African Yearbook Alan Rake Ed, (IC Magazines Ltd, 63 Long Acre, London, WC2, tel 01-836 8731). The last edition was published in 1981. It's pricey at US$25 or the equivalent, but there are nearly 400 large format pages. It consists of a collection of essays by many different writers, the majority of whom adopt a dispassionate Marxist point of view. As its name suggests, it concerns itself with largely current issues, so if you're looking for history or cultural developments then you'll need to go to other sources.

Globe (Globetrotters Club, BCM/Roving, London WCIN 3XX, UK). Published six times a year on the first Saturday of February, April, June, August, October, December. Annual membership rate is UK£5 or US$14 worldwide. Chatty, informal newsletter from many diverse contributors, with up-to-date information on exchange rates, visas, accommodation costs, ways of getting there and getting around, etc.

Getting There

If you're setting out from Europe you have the choice of either flying to Africa or going overland to one of the Mediterranean ports from which you can get a ferry to North Africa. If you are departing from any other continent, you'll have to either fly first to Europe or fly direct to Africa. In most cases it's often cheaper to fly first to Europe and then make your way to Africa than it is to fly direct.

As with all travelling which involves flying, some forethought is necessary if you're going to do it as cheaply as possible. There are a bewildering number of possibilities and airline tickets and, unfortunately, there's no magic key which will instantly reveal all about this market. A great deal will depend on such factors as which country you live in; what travel agencies you have access to; whether you can buy your ticket in advance; how flexible you can be about your travelling arrangements; how old you are (it's to your advantage if you're 26 years old or under); and whether you have an international student card. While there are certain ways to go about getting the best deal, you should nevertheless remember the old adage that no matter how little you paid for your ticket, you will inevitably meet someone somewhere who paid less.

The first thing to do is equip yourself with as much information as you can get hold of and be familiar with ticketing jargon. One of the best sources of information about cheap fares all over the world is the monthly magazine, *Business Traveller*, available from newsstands in most developed countries or direct from 60/61 Fleet St, London EC4 & ILA, UK, and from 13th Floor, 200 Lockhart Rd, Hong Kong. Others are *Trailfinder* from Trailfinders Travel Centre, 48 Earls Court Rd, London W8 6EJ, UK; the weekly London entertainment guide, *Time Out*, available from newsstands in London or from Tower House, Southampton St, London WC2E 8QW, UK; and the other free weekly newspaper, *Australasian Express*, also available at the same outlets as *LAM* – London Alternative Magazine. The last three contain what must be one of the world's best collection of advertisements by 'bucket shops' (discount airline ticket shops). Similar publications exist in other parts of the world and, if you're not already familiar with them, a little research will soon unearth them.

The main terms you need to know are:

APEX (and Super-APEX) This means Advance Purchase Excursion and must be bought from 14 days to two months in advance. These tickets are usually only available on a return basis. There are minimum and maximum stay requirements, no stop-overs are allowed and there are cancellation charges.

Excursion Fares These are priced midway between APEX and full economy class. There are no advance booking requirements but a minimum stay abroad is often mandatory. Their advantage over APEX is that you can change your bookings and/or stop-over without surcharge.

Point-to-Point This is a discount ticket which can be bought on some routes in return for the passenger waiving his or her rights to stop-over.

ITX This means Independent Inclusive Tour Excursion and is often available on tickets to popular holiday destinations. It's officially only available as a holiday package deal which includes hotel accommodation, but many agents will sell you one of these for the flight only and issue you phoney hotel vouchers in case you're challenged at the airport (very rare).

Economy Class Symbolised by 'Y' on the airline ticket, this is the full economy fare. Tickets are valid for 12 months.

Budget Fare These can be booked at least

three weeks in advance but the actual travel date is not confirmed until seven days prior to travel. There are cancellation charges.

MCO This means Miscellaneous Charge Order. It is a voucher which looks just like an airline ticket but without a destination or date on it and is exchangeable with any IATA airline for specific flights. Its principal use for travellers is as an alternative to an onward ticket (it's much more flexible than a ticket for a specific flight in those countries which demand an onward ticket).

IATA International Air Transport Association, which to all intents and purposes is a price-fixing cartel to which most airlines belong. Its success at suppressing so-called 'illegal' discounting of tickets has been severely knocked back recently because of falling business. Most American airlines have resigned from the association.

Standby This is one of the cheapest ways of flying – though APEX is often cheaper. You simply turn up at the airport – or, in some cases, an airline's city terminal – without a ticket, and if there are spare seats available on the flight you want, then you get on at a considerable discount. It's become such a common thing since the late 1970s that most airline counters now have a special standby section. To give yourself the best chance of getting on the day you want to fly, get there as early as possible and put your name down on the waiting list – it's first come, first served.

You'll come across many other terms which airlines pull out of the hat in attempts to ginger up business, but they're all variations on the above, with discounts being offered in return for acceptance of certain conditions.

All the above discounted tickets are those which the airlines officially sanction. There are, however, unofficially discounted tickets available through certain travel agents – known in the trade as 'bucket shops.' Despite all the airlines' self-righteous protestations to the contrary, the tickets which these bucket shops sell are released by the airlines through selected travel agents for sale at a considerable discount. The rationale behind this is that it's better for the airlines to fill as many seats as possible rather than to see their planes leave half empty even if some of the passengers are travelling on tickets which cost them less than the airlines are officially prepared to offer. Generally, bucket shops sell tickets at prices lower than an APEX ticket would cost but without the advance purchase or cancellation penalty requirement (though some agents do have their own penalty for cancellation).

Most of the bucket shops are well established and scrupulous but there are a few which are not, so you need to use a little caution when buying a ticket through one of these agents. It's not been unknown for fly-by-night operators to set up an office, take your money and then disappear before they've given you the tickets. Always make sure you have the tickets in hand before you hand over the money or, at the very least, never pay more than a deposit before you see the tickets. Tickets bought from a bucket shop are indistinguishable from those bought from an airline, despite what some people will tell you. The only thing you need to bear in mind is that if you're travelling on a ticket which has been discounted because you're a student, make sure you have the student card with you or you may be required to pay the difference on arrival at the airport.

Three of the best places in the world for bucket shops are London (UK), Amsterdam (Netherlands) and Hong Kong. The shops can also be found in other European cities, in the USA and in all these places where no-one with any sense buys a ticket direct from the airline companies. Australians and New Zealanders are unlucky in this respect, as bucket shops do not exist there – or rather, a few of them do but because unofficial discounting is illegal, it's very difficult to find an agent willing to do so. The Australian government even attempted to prosecute Singapore Airlines some time ago for selling discounted tickets through certain agents.

Having located the best places to buy a ticket, the next thing you need to decide is whether you're going to fix up all your tickets from there or simply buy a one-way ticket to some destination in Europe or Africa and take it from there. A return ticket is always cheaper than two single tickets unless the only flying you are going to do is between America and Europe on standby. Also, with a few exceptions, it's always cheaper to add on places to a long-haul ticket rather than buy a straight A-to-B ticket and then start all over again at the other end.

There is, however, one major constraint you need to bear in mind if you're thinking of flying into Africa on a one-way ticket. Certain countries demand that you have an onward ticket before they'll let you in. If you don't have one, you'll either have to buy one on arrival (naturally at full price and with a limited choice of destinations) or leave a refundable bond which can be as high as US$500. An MCO for, say, US$100, is one way of getting round this. *Don't* buy it from South African Airways, as no other African airline will accept it in exchange for full or part payment on one of their own flights except perhaps Malawi, Zaire, Gabon or Ivory Coast. The main African countries which demand an onward ticket are South Africa, Zimbabwe and sometimes Kenya.

FROM EUROPE

There are numerous ways of getting from Europe to Africa, but if you want to fly there, one outstanding bargain is presently offered by *Point Air-Mulhouse* (popularly known by travellers as 'Le Point'). This company offers weekly 'no frills' flights from Lyon, France, to various West African cities. Fares to Ougadougou, Bourkinafasso, are Fr fr 2550 return. To Bangui, Central African Republic, they are Fr fr 1800 single and Fr fr 2750 return. There is a Fr fr 300 supplement to pay if you fly in July, August or September. Point Air-Mulhouse is a travel club so you have to add on US$12 (Fr fr 80) membership fee to the above fares. They only have one plane, which is an old DC 10. When you book your ticket, you specify whether you are travelling from Paris or Lyon. The price is the same and the bus ride between Paris and Lyon is free, but if you're starting from Britain, Belgium or possibly the Netherlands, it's cheaper to get to Paris than to Lyon. The meeting place in Paris is the Porte d'Orleans (metro station nearby) at 1 am on the day of departure. You arrive at Lyon around 8 am, wait a few hours and then set off. For further details and their flying schedule, write (in French) for a brochure to Point Air-Mulhouse, 4 Rue des Orphelins, 68200 Mulhouse, France (tel 89-42 44 61), or to 54 Rue des Ecoles, 75006 Paris. Book as far in advance as possible, as the Lyon-bangui route is used by many Central African Republic citizens visiting and working in France.

Point Air-Mulhouse is deservedly popular with travellers but it isn't the only cheap deal going. The Travel Club 20/21, Economic Travel, 200 Earls Court Rd, London, W8, also offer a one-way London-Accra via Lagos ticket for just £175. A standard economy fare on Aeroflot from London to Accra via Moscow costs £220.

If you're heading further south, Aeroflot offer London-Lusaka via Moscow for £425 return, and the ticket is valid for one year. KLM offer London-Harare for £555 return and the ticket is valid for three months. Other current air fares from London to various African cities will cost about the following:

Cairo – £144/US$233 one way and £288/US$446 return under 26 years old; or £187/US$289 one way and £231/US$358 over 26.

Dar es Salaam – £224/US$347 one way and £448/US$694 return under 26 years old; or £253/US$392 one way and £374/US$580 over 26.

Johannesburg – £255/US$395 one way and £510/US$790 under 26 years old; or £374/US$579 one way and £432/US$670 return over 26.

Kano – £234/US$363 one way under 26 years old; or £286/US$443 one way over 26.

Nairobi – £192/US$298 one way and £384/US$595 return under 26 years old; or £209/US$324 one way and £314/US$487 return over 26.

These prices should be taken as a guide only; depending on where you buy your ticket, it's possible to get one for up to US$50 less. On the other hand, you may find yourself paying up to US$50 more for one. Another important point to bear in mind as far as costs go is that if you only want to fly as far as Cairo, it's much cheaper (though more time consuming) to take a bus-plane combination. You go by bus as far as Athens and then take a plane to Cairo. The fare from Athens to Cairo on Olympic Airways is 8750 drachmas (about US$82.50) going standby and with a 50% under-26-years-old discount.

If your ultimate destination is Australia starting from London, then the cost of a London-Sydney/Melbourne one-way ticket with stop-overs in Paris, Rome, Athens, Cairo, Khartoum, Nairobi, Johannesburg, Mauritius and Perth will be around £955/US$1480.

Making Your Own Way Across Europe

Whether you're hitching, taking a bus or going by train across Europe, you should decide which of the two routes south through Africa you want to take – through the Sahara from Algeria to West Africa, or down the Nile from Egypt to Uganda/Kenya. The reason for this is that the Egyptian/Libyan border is closed so you cannot swap routes once you get to North Africa, unless you fly between Morocco/Algeria/Tunisia and Egypt.

You can of course, hitch-hike free all the way through Europe to the Mediterranean (other than the cost of a ferry across the English Channel) but this isn't necessarily the cheapest way of going because by the time you've finished paying for overnight accommodation you might as well have bought a ticket on an express bus. There's a wide choice of buses available from such places as London and Amsterdam as well as from other northern European cities, and the fares on the buses from London include the cost of the ferry. Athens is undoubtedly the cheapest place to get to, with fares ranging from £25 to £30. After that it would be Naples (about £43) and Algeciras (about £60). If all you want to do is hop across the channel and hitch from there, it's well worth taking the bus to either Brussels (about £12) or Paris (about £14.50). Most of the agents who sell tickets for these buses also offer a coach-plane deal from London to Cairo (you fly from Athens) for £87. This is a particularly good deal when you consider that the minimum fare on the Piraeus-Alexandria ferry is £47 with *Egyptian Navigation Company* boats and £75 (less with a student card etc) on *Adriatica Line* boats. The addresses of the agents which handle the express buses can be found in any copy of *LAM*, *Time Out* or *Australasian Express* in London.

If you want to make your own way through Europe or don't want to take an express bus and you're starting from London, you must first decide which of the cross-Channel ferries you are going to take. The most popular are Dover-Zeebrugge/Ostend/Dunkirk/Calais/Boulogne, Folkestone-Ostend/Calais/Boulogne and Ramsgate-Dunkirk. If you're hitching to Athens, then Zeebrugge or Ostend would be the best places to go. If you're heading for southern Spain, one of the French ports would be the best place to start from. There are several companies which operate the ferries (*P&O, Townsend Thoresen, Sealink, Hoverspeed* and *Sally The Viking Line*), and all but the last have many departures daily in either direction so there's no chance of you not being able to get on the day you want to go. The cheapest are:

Sally The Viking Line Ramsgate-Dunkirk, drive-on drive-off car ferry. £5-8 for foot passengers and £7 for car passengers. Journey time is 2½ hours.

P&O Dover-Boulogne, drive-on, drive-off car ferry. £7 for foot passengers with a student card. Journey time is 1¾ hours.

Apart from these, Dover-Zeebrugge cost £11 for foot passengers and £9 for car passengers and takes four hours; Dover-Ostend costs £12.50 for foot passengers and £9.50 for car passengers and takes 3½ hours; Dover/Folkestone-Calais costs £11-12.50 for foot passengers and £9-9.50 for car passengers depending on the company you sail with. The journey time is 1-1/4 hours to one hour 50 minutes depending on which port you sail from. There's also a jetfoil available between Dover and Ostend operated by *Sealink*. This costs £17.50 and takes one hour 40 minutes. On all these ferries, it makes a lot of sense to get a lift in a car before it gets to the ferry terminal so you only have to pay the car passenger fare. *Sally The Viking Line* only has two departures daily in either direction at 10.30 am and 10 pm from Ramsgate and 7.30 am and 7 pm from Dunkirk.

There are any number of different ways you can travel overland through Europe to end up in southern Spain, France, Italy or Greece. The choice is yours. Hitching is good in Belgium, Germany, Holland and northern Italy. In the other countries it tends to be slower, particularly in Spain. London to Athens should take four or five days; London to Marseilles two to three days (one if you're lucky); and London to Algeciras up to a week and sometimes more. The cheapest places to stay en route are the Youth Hostels but you need a Youth Hostels membership card to use them.

If you decide to hitch through Italy and then take a ferry across to Greece, there are a number of possibilities. The cheapest are:

R Line Otranto-Corfu/Igoumenitsa, drive-on drive-off car ferry. Daily departures in either direction between 13 June and 18 September and three times per week in either direction between 3 June and 12 June and between 19 September and 3 October (on Monday, Wednesday and Saturday from Otranto and Tuesday, Friday and Sunday from Igoumenitsa/Corfu). There are no ferries on this line during the rest of the year. The minimum fare is £17 and the journey takes 8½ hours.

Ionian Lines Brindisi-Corfu-Patras, drive-on drive-off car ferry. There are departures on alternate days in either direction. The minimum fares are £17 (Brindisi-Corfu) and £19 (Brindisi-Patras). The journey takes 8½ hours and 19½ respectively. A bus meets the ferry on arrival at Patras and costs £5(US$8) for the three-hour journey to Athens.

Other ferries between Italy and Greece are as follows:

Strintzis Lines SA Brindisi-Corfu/Igoumenitsa-Patras, drive-on drive-off car ferry. There are departures on alternate days in either direction. The minimum fares are £20.50 (Brindisi-Corfu) and £22 (Brindisi-Patras).

Libra Maritime Brindisi-Corfu/Igoumenitsa-Patras, drive-on drive-off car ferries. There are daily departures in either direction daily except on Tuesdays from Brindisi and Mondays from Patras. The minimum fare is £21 (Brindisi-Patras) and the journey takes 20 hours. A Patras-Athens bus is available for £5 (US$8) and takes three hours.

Fragoudakis Line Brindisi-Corfu/Igoumenitsa-Patras, drive-on drive-off car ferry. There are departures most days in either direction. The minimum fares are £21 (Brindisi-Corfu) and £22.50 (Brindisi-Patras).

Adriatica Line/Hellenic Mediterranean Lines Brindisi-Corfu/Igoumenitsa-Patras, drive-on drive-off car ferry. There are daily departures in either direction throughout the summer months (less in winter). The minimum fares are £24 (Brindisi-Corfu) and £28 (Brindisi-Patras).

There is also a ferry from Brindisi to Piraeus operated by *Sol Maritime Services Ltd*. It departs once a week in either direction on Wednesdays from Brindisi and Tuesdays from Piraeus. The minimum fare is £31 and the journey takes 22 hours. This ferry does not call at Patras.

If you're hitching down through Italy to Sicily to catch the ferry from Tripani or Palermo to Tunis, there are ferries every 20 minutes in either direction across the Straits of Messina between Italy and Sicily. The ferries run day and night between Messina and Reggio di Calabria and Villa San Giovanni, and cost less than US$1.

The last step to Africa is to take a ferry (or fly) across the Mediterranean. The ferry you take will depend on which way you want to travel through Africa, but in order of cheapness they are: Spain-Morocco; Italy-Tunisia; Greece-Egypt and France-Algeria. A list of these ferries can be found in the next section.

If you're taking a car to either Algeria or Tunisia, the cheapest is the Tunisian Compagnie Tunisie du Navigation boat *Habib Bourguiba*, which goes Tunis-Genova-Tunis-Marseilles-Tunis. Genova to Tunis will cost around US$80 for the car plus US$90 per adult. It's cheaper on the Palermo/Trapani-Tunis car ferry but the cost of driving down through Italy and the freeway fees will just about cancel out the advantages.

MEDITERRANEAN FERRIES

The following list starts from Spain and moves east to finish with Greece. It's not an exhaustive list but includes all the ferries you are likely to use. Many of the ferries from Greece actually start from Venice but would, of course, be much more expensive from there.

Spain-Morocco

1. Algeciras-Tangier There are three different companies which operate ferries along this route.

Compania Transmediterranea has a drive-on drive-off car ferry which departs two to three times daily in either direction. The journey takes 2½ hours and the minimum fare is 990 pesetas.

Transtours operates a hydrofoil service which departs once daily in either direction at 9 am from Algeciras and 4.30 pm from Tangier. The journey takes one hour and the fare is 1350 pesetas or 75 dirham.

ISNASA also operates a drive-on drive-off car ferry which departs once daily in either direction at 11 am from Algeciras and 3 pm from Tangier. The journey takes two hours and the minimum fare is £11.

2. Algeciras-Ceuta (Spanish Morocco) *Compania Transmediterranea* operates a drive-on drive-off car ferry which departs eight times daily in either direction except on Sundays, when there are three departures in either direction. The journey takes 1½ hours and the minimum fare is 740 pesetas.

ISNASA also has a drive-on drive-off car ferry which sails eight times daily in either direction except on Sunday, when there are four departures in either direction. The journey takes 45 minutes and the minimum fare is £5.50.

Note The first of these two ferries is the cheapest way of getting across the Mediterranean.

3. Malaga-Melilla (Spanish Morocco) *Compania Transmediterranea* operates a drive-on drive-off car ferry which departs once daily in either direction except on Saturdays from Malaga and Fridays from Melilla. The journey takes eight to nine hours and the minimum fare is 1390 pesetas.

4. Almería-Melilla (Spanish Morocco) *Compania Transmediterranea* operates a drive-on drive-off car ferry which departs Almería on Monday, Wednesday and Friday at 11.30 pm and Melilla at 11 pm on Tuesday, Thursday and Saturday. The journey takes seven to 8½ hours and the minimum fare is 1390 pesetas.

Gibraltar-Morocco

1. *Transtours* offers a hydrofoil which

departs Gibraltar daily at 5 pm and Tangier daily at 8.30 am. The journey takes one hour and the fare is 2300 pesetas, 130 dirham or £12.

2. The *Bland Line* operates a drive-on drive-off car ferry which departs once daily in either direction except on Mondays and Saturdays. Exact departure times are variable according to the season, so you need to make enquiries with the company. The journey takes 2¼ hours and the fare is £14.

France-Algeria

All the ferries in this section are operated by *Compagnie Nationale Algerienne de Navigation* (CNAN).

1. Marseilles-Oran This service operates in one direction only – from Oran to Marseilles – so it's only of use if you're returning to Europe. There are five departures per month and the journey takes 32 hours.

2. Marseilles-Algiers There is a service almost every day in either direction (you'll never have to wait more than a day for a ferry). The journey takes 20 to 24 hours or 37 to 45 hours if you take a ferry which goes via Palma (Mallorca). It's a car ferry.

3. Marseilles-Annaba There are three or four departures every month in either direction but the schedule is variable according to the month. The journey takes 24 hours.

Note The ferries between France and Algeria are among the most expensive in the Mediterranean.

Italy-Tunisia

The following ferries are all operated by *Tirrenia Line*.

1. Naples-Palermo-Tunis The drive-on drive-off ferry operates once per week in either direction. It departs Naples at 10 am on Fridays, Palermo at 9.30 pm the same day, and arrives at Tunis the following day at 7.30 am. On the return journey, the ferry departs Tunis at 8 pm on Wednesday and arrives at Palermo the following day at 6 am. It departs Palermo the same day at 10 am and arrives at Naples at 7.15 pm. The journey takes 21½ hours from Naples to Tunis and 10 hours from Palermo to Tunis. The minimum fare from Naples to Tunis is £41.20 (October/November/December) and £46.70 (rest of the year). The minimum fare from Palermo to Tunis is £29.10 (October/November/December) and £34.50 (rest of the year).

2. Cagliari-Trapani-Tunis The drive-on drive-off car ferry operates once per week in either direction. It departs Cagliari at 7 pm on Tuesdays, Trapani at 8 am on Wednesdays and arrives in Tunis the same day at 4 pm. In the opposite direction, the ferry departs Tunis at 11.30 am on Saturdays and arrives at Trapani 7 pm the same day. It departs Trapani the same day at 10 pm and arrives in Caliari on Sunday at 8 am. The journey takes 20½ hours from Cagliari to Tunis and 7½ hours from Trapani to Tunis. The minimum fare from Cagliari to Tunis is £21.70 (October/November/December) and £25.80 (rest of the year). The minimum fare from Trapani to Tunis is £18.60 (October/November/December) and £22.10 (rest of the year).

Greece-Egypt

1. Piraeus-Alexandria *Adriatica Line* operates a drive-on drive-off car ferry in either direction two to five times per month depending on the season. The journey takes about 31 hours and the minimum fare is £83 (from 24 June to 27 October) and £75 (rest of the year). The company usually offers reductions on the above fares for holders of International Student Cards, Youth Hostel Cards, Eurail and Eurail Youthpass tickets, so make sure you enquire about these.

The *Egyptian Navigation Company* also operates a ferry along this route but we have no details other than that the minimum fare is £47.

2. Piraeus-Heraklion-Alexandria The *Maritime Company of Lesvos SA* operates a ferry three to four times per month depending on the season in either direction. The journey takes about 42 hours and the minimum fare is US$180 (from 5 July to 22 September) and US$155 (rest of the year). It's a drive-on drive-off car ferry and you have the option of a stop-over on Crete.

3. Piraeus-Larnaca-Latakia-Alexandria The *Black Sea Shipping Company* operates a ferry in either direction along this route twice per month. The trip takes about four days but few travellers appear to use it.

Addresses

Compania Transmediterranea SA
Plaza Manuel Gomez Moreno s/n, Esquina a Orense 4, Madrid 20, Spain
Voyages Melia, 31 Avenue de l'Opéra, 75001, Paris
INTERCONA, 31 Rue Quevado, Tangier, Morocco
Melia, Rokin 32, Amsterdam, Netherlands
Townsend Thoresen, 1 Camden Crescent, Dover, Kent, UK
Melia Reiseburo GmbH, 54 Grosse Bockenheimer, 6 Frankfurt Main 1, West Germany

Transtours
Tourafrica, Estación Maritima, Algeciras, Spain
Smith Imossi & Co Ltd, 47 Irish Town, Gibraltar
4 Rue Jabha al Quatania, Tangier, Morocco

Bland Line
Cloister Building, Gibraltar
Gibmar Travel SA, 22 Avenue Mohammed V, Tangier, Morocco
Cadogan Travel Ltd, Cadogan House, 9/10 Portland St, Southampton, UK

Compagnie Nationale Algerienne de Navigation
2 Quai No 9, Nouvelle Gare Maritime, Algiers, Algeria
SNCM, 61 Boulevard des Dames, 13222 Marseilles, France
CNAN, 29 Boulevard des Dames, 13002 Marseilles, France
SNCM, 12 Rue Godot de Mauroy, Paris 75009, France
CNAN, 25 Rue St Augustin, Opéra, Paris, France

Tirrenia Line
Rione Sirignano 2, PO Box 438, 80121 Naples, Italy
Stazione Marittima, Molo Angiono, Naples, Italy
Via Roma 385, Palermo, Italy
Societé Nationale Maritime Corse Mediterranée, 12 Rue Godot de Mauroy, Paris, France
Serena Holidays, 40/42 Kenway Rd, London SW5, UK
Karl Geuther & Co, Heinrichstrasse 9, 6000 Frankfurt, West Germany

Adriatica Line
Zattere 1411, Palazzo Sociale, 30123 Venice, Italy
De Castro Shipping, 33 Sharia Salah Salem, Alexandria, Egypt
CIT (France), 3 Boulevard des Capucines, 75002 Paris, France
Gilnavi Ltd, 97 Akti Miaouli & Favierou, Piraeus, Greece
Reis-en Passagebureau Hoyman & Schuurman, De Ruyterkade 124, 1011 AB Amsterdam, Netherlands
Sealink UK Ltd, Victoria Station, PO Box 29, London SW1, UK
See Tours International, Weissfrauenstrasse 3, 6000 Frankfurt, West Germany

Egyptian Navigation Company
2 El Nasr St, Alexandria, Egypt
20 Talaat Harb St, Cairo, Egypt
Worms Co, Services Maritime, 30 Avenue Robert Schumann, Marseilles, France
George A Callitsis SA, Callitsis Building, 54 Filonos St, Piraeus, Greece
Alexandria Navigation Company, 35 Picadilly, London W1, UK
Peter W Lampke, Deichstrasse 23, D-2000 Hamburg 11, West Germany

Maritime Company of Lesvos SA
4 Astingos St, Karaiskaki Square, Piraeus, Greece
Louis Tourist Agency (Cyprus) Ltd, 429 Green Lanes, Haringey, London N4, UK

Black Sea Shipping Company
Among Shipping Agency, 71 El Horreya St, PO Box 60764, Alexandria, Egypt
Transtours, 49 Avenue de l'Opéra, 75002 Paris, France
Transmed Shipping SA, 85 Akti Miaouli & 2

Flessa St, Piraeus, Greece
CTC Lines, 1-3 Lower Regent St, London
SW1, UK

FROM THE USA

For a time during the late 1970s and early
1980s, it was possible to get from Los
Angeles/San Francisco to London for as
little as US$199, or from Houston to
London for as little as US$135 – thanks to
Freddie Laker and the effect that his
'Skytrain' had on the standby fares of the
major airlines. Laker collapsed in 1982
and the major airlines which covered
these routes gleefully doubled their
standby prices. However, *People Express*
soon filled the gap and offers a 'no frills'
flight from Newark, New Jersey, to
London for just US$168. Virgin Atlantic
fares are simiilar. At present that is as
cheap as you'll get it.

Standby fares on the other airlines from
the various North American cities to
London are, very approximately: Boston
(US$150), Chicago (US$240), Dallas
(US$260), Houston (US$310), Los Angeles/
San Francisco (US$300), Miami (US$230),
New Orleans (US$275), New York (US$195),
Philadelphia/Washington (US$210), Tor-
onto (C$360), Montreal (C$350), Van-
couver (C$236), Edmonton/Calgary
(C$560) and Winnipeg (C$480).

If your travel plans are not flexible
enough to take a chance on standby or you
would prefer a confirmed booking, you
can usually do this by paying a little more
than you would on standby. But you need
to plan ahead, as the only way you can do
this is through some form of advance
purchase. If you want to fly direct to
Africa, or you think you can get a ticket in
America which is going to be cheaper than
first flying to Europe and then either
flying to Africa or making your way
overland, then it's worth doing some
legwork around the agents to see what
they can offer.

FROM INDIA

A new cargo/passenger service has started
up between Dar es Salaam and India via
various ports on the Arabian Peninsula.
For further details contact *Tanzania
Coastal Shipping Line Ltd*, PO Box 9461,
Dar es Salaam, Tanzania (tel 26192/3;
telex 41124). The ship is called the
Tacoshili.

Algeria

A French colony since 1830, Algeria became independent in 1962 after eight years of guerrilla warfare in which one million Algerians died. A brief struggle for power followed between 'moderates' and 'militants' before Colonel Boumedienne led the Armee de Libération to victory with the 'Front de Libération National.' Ben Bella was elected prime minister, pledged to a 'revolutionary Arab-Islamic state based on the principles of socialism and collective leadership at home and anti-imperialism abroad.'

Landless peasants quickly put these ideals into practice and moved in on the land vacated by the French, setting up cooperative farms to be run by peasant councils. However, with the French common enemy gone, there was rapid polarisation between the advocates of real socialism and those for whom the expulsion of the French meant their chance to become rich. Nationalisation of major industries was carried out but the re-distribution of land was limited to that previously owned by the French, leaving large estates privately owned by rich Algerians. These conservative landowners were frightened by the call for liberation of women in particular. Army revolts, based on the slogan 'Islam is not compatible with socialism' broke out in 1963 and 1964, but with the people tiring of civil disorder and economic stagnation and impatient for the prosperity and progress for which they'd sacrificed a whole generation, most were relieved when Colonel Boumedienne staged a bloodless coup in 1965.

Boumedienne was a competent, if authoritarian, pragmatist who made economic reconstruction his first priority. Economic growth was boosted by the exploitation of vast deposits of natural gas in the Sahara, but unemployment remained high and large numbers of Algerians were forced to go to France to look for work despite a vicious climate of racism there. In Algeria itself, 70% of the working population is employed on the land, but concentration on the industrial sector has meant that productivity is no greater, and in some cases much less, than what was achieved under the French. Since 1971, nearly one million hectares have been distributed on the condition that the land is farmed collectively. Agricultural machinery and expertise have been made available for this, and efforts are being made to improve literacy and improve understanding of agricultural technology.

Algeria is very conscious of its role as a model for less well-endowed Third World countries. It earns a great deal of respect for the intelligence and integrity of its regime and supports a number of liberation struggles around the world. For several years now, Algeria has been deeply committed to supporting the POLISARIO guerrilla army of the Western Sahara in its struggle against Morocco, which occupied the whole of what was formerly the Spanish Sahara following the withdrawal of Mauritania. This support has brought Algeria and Morocco to the brink of war on several occasions and tension between the two remains high. This is the reason why there are only two crossing points between Algeria and Morocco at present.

In its drive to bring about equality between the sexes, the socialist government encouraged the education of women and attempted to change male attitudes in

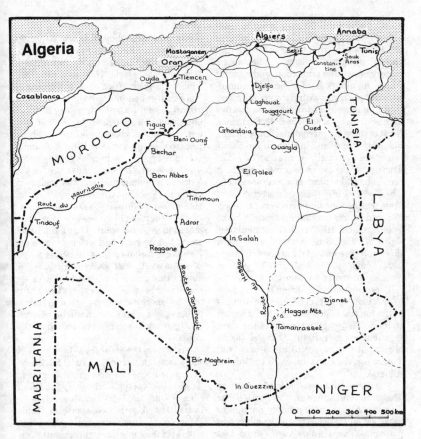

what was essentially an exclusively male-dominated society. It has been relatively successful in the north, especially in the urban areas, but in the south women remain chattels, locked away at the age of 12 and never appearing in public unless veiled and suitably chaperoned. As a result, there's a popular myth that any woman more than 12 years old who isn't locked up or veiled is obviously a whore or at least sexually available. Algeria, of course, holds no exclusive rights on this attitude, which is quite common throughout the Arab world. On the other hand, Algerians in general are a very generous and

hospitable people. Hitching anywhere in the north and even further south is a dream come true and the people who pick you up will often invite you to stay with them for the night.

FACTS

The population is estimated at over 12 million, most of whom live in the north. One-third is concentrated in the cities, with the capital of Algiers having about one million. The least densely populated area is, of course, the Sahara, with less than one person per square km. Of the ethnic groups, the largest is the Berbers, most of whom are farmers living in small towns and villages. Other groups include the Kabyles, a tribe living in the central coastal mountain range which has a long history of popular education, and many of whose members hold important administrative positions within the government. The Chaouias and Mozabites tend to live in the Saharan oases, especially Ghardaia. Most of them are merchants, many owning businesses and land in France. Politically they are strongly conservative. The Tuaregs are nomads who travel throughout the Sahara herding goats and camels. Their way of life, their cohesiveness and their culture have been very severely affected by the continuing drought in the Sahel region (the region immediately south of the true desert), and many thousands are now destitute, scratching a bare living on the outskirts of various Saharan towns and villages.

There are many important Roman ruins in excellent condition (due to the dryness of the desert) which can be visited in this country. The most important of them are at Djemila (near Setif), Timgad (again near Setif but nearer to the desert) and Tipasa (on the coast about 70 km west of Algiers).

Algeria is Africa's second largest country. The mountain range to the north – the Saharan Atlas – runs roughly parallel to the coast and is dissected with valleys and plateaux. The altitude varies from less than 1000 metres in the southern Sahara to over 3000 metres in the Hoggar Mountains near Tamanrasset. There is an important string of oases along the foot of the Atlas Mountains. The temperature and rainfall vary considerably with altitude and position relative to the coast and mountains. Average coastal temperature is between 10 and 12°C in winter and between 24 and 25°C in summer. Inland the temperatures are much higher, varying from 12°C in winter to over 33°C in the summer. Rainfall varies from 70 to 100 cm to zero. Heavy rains in April make make some roads impassable or very difficult.

VISAS

Visas are required by all except nationals of Denmark, Finland, France, Iceland, Italy, Norway, Spain, Sweden, Switzerland, UK and Yugoslavia. Nationals of Israel, Malawi, South Africa, South Korea and Taiwan are not admitted; and if you have a stamp in your passport from any of these countries you will probably be refused entry or your visa application will be rejected. If you are from West Germany, you may experience hassles getting a visa – most West Germans must produce a letter of recommendation from their own embassy. You can avoid this by getting the visa in West Germany before you leave. It's also better not to have a Moroccan stamp in your passport. That's the usual story, but we have had letters from West German travellers saying that visas are no problem at all. Just what distinctions the authorities make isn't clear. If you do encounter hassles, then expect to wait up to one month for your visa to come through, as the application will be referred to Algiers. Visas cannot be issued at the border.

Visas from the embassy in London (UK nationals don't need visas) cost £2.50 and are issued without fuss in 48 hours. In Tunis visas cost 4.50 dinar, require four photos and take around three days to issue. The Algerian consulate in Oujda (Morocco) is friendly and it's possible to get a visa the same day but they're usually very busy. Visas cost 34 dirhams and the consulate is open daily from 9 am to 12 noon.

Visa extensions can be obtained from the Service des Etrangers, Boulevard Zeroud Yousef 19A, Algiers. They take 24 hours to issue.

There are only two possible crossings between Algeria and Morocco at present. They are Oujda-Tlemcen and Figuig-Beni Ounif. You must have a car to get through from Oujda to Tlemcen, but not the other way round. If you don't have a car and you're going from Morocco to Algeria, then you have to cross via Figuig and Beni

Ounif. There are heavy searches at both these border crossings – they're looking mainly for drugs and Algerian dinar. Expect border formalities at Figuig/Beni Ounif to take many hours (six hours isn't unusual).

The biggest shocker about going to Algeria is that you must buy 1000 dinar (about US$210 or the equivalent in another hard currency) at the official rate of exchange regardless of how long you intend to stay. The only people who are exempt from this are those having an international student card and those under 19 years old. Letters on headed paper from a university or college are not acceptable.

If you don't have a student card, there are various scams which are worth considering. The main one applies at border crossings where there are no facilities to change money. Figuig/Beni Ounif and on the train from Constantine to Ghardimaou are two such places. What will happen there is that you'll be issued with a currency form and told to change the required amount of money at the first bank inside the country. Since the only difference between a normal currency form and one issued to a person with a student card is the word 'Edutiante' written across the form, you might as well do this yourself as soon as you're away from the customs officials, and then don't bother to change any money officially. Be careful if you do this, however, because at some borders (eg on the train between Constantine and Ghardimaou) the forms are very thoroughly checked when you leave the country, and that includes traveller's cheques.

Cameroun visas The embassy in Algiers is telling people that visas take one month to come through, so get it somewhere else.

Burkina Faso & CAR visas These are obtainable from the French Embassy. For the Central African Republic the embassy will only issue you a 48-hour transit visa at 37 dinar, so it's hardly worth getting one here.

Mali visas The embassy is at Villa No 14, Cite DNC/ANP, Chemin du Kaddous, Hydra, Algiers. Visas cost 60 dinar (one traveller who was on a British passport said 150 dinar!), require two photos and are issued within 24 hours (sometimes while you wait). There is also a consulate in Tamanrasset where visas cost 100 dinar and are issued while you wait.

Niger visas The embassy is at 54 Rue Vercors, Air de France, Bouzarea, Algiers, and can be difficult to find. It's a long way from the centre, so take a taxi (about 30 dinar). The embassy is open daily except Friday and Saturday from 9 am to 2 pm. Visas cost 1 dinar per day of stay requested (or 20 dinar per month). You must also have a vaccination certificate which includes yellow fever, and the Algerian currency form. The visa takes 24 hours to issue (some travellers say three days). Your application will be refused unless you have all of these. However, although you can usually get a visa without an onward ticket, you will not get into Niger without an onward ticket, especially at the Assamaka border south of Tamanrasset. Don't set off for Niger without reading the details about this in the Niger chapter. Vaccination certificates can be obtained from the Institut Pasteur just below the Monument des Arcades if you don't already have one.

Nigerian visas Visas are priced according to your nationality and range between 15.75 dinar (UK nationals) and 58.50 dinar. They can take a week to come through. However, the staff at this embassy have been variously (but consistently) described as 'a miserable set of bastards' and 'a pack of cretins.'

Zaire visas The embassy is about to move premises, so enquire at the Tourist Office or look it up in the telephone directory.

MONEY

US$1 = 5 dinar
£1   = 7 dinar
Fr 1.8 = 1 dinar

The unit of currency is the Algerian dinar = 100 centimes. Import/export of local currency is allowed up to 50 dinar. There is a thriving black market both inside and outside the country. French francs are the preferred currency (Fr fr 1 = 2-3 dinar) but US dollars (US$1 = 18-20 dinar) and £ sterling (£1 = 20-25 dinar) are acceptable. Avoid changing the latter (£ sterling) if possible. Similar, though usually slightly lower, rates are available in Melilla (Spanish Morocco) and in banks in Germany or Switzerland. The rates in Melilla are better than those in Oujda (Morocco). The Algerian authorities are well aware of these rates, so they're very keen on preventing you from using the black market and, as a result, there are heavy baggage and body searches (shoes off, a quick look in your underpants, etc) at most border posts, though they don't appear to be that keen on checking you and your currency form on exit. If you're taking in black market money, you'll need to hide it very well. If they find the money it will be confiscated.

Currency declaration forms are issued on arrival and you're advised to keep these in order because the customs officials are very strict about them when you leave the country. If you're bringing in valuables such as cameras, jewellery, etc and intend to take them out of the country, then declare them on the currency form if you want to avoid hassles when leaving. If you intend to sell them and don't declare them, you run the risk of having them confiscated. We have had letters from travellers whose cameras and Walkmans were confiscated because they didn't declare them on the currency form. Be careful!

Most travellers bring in a bottle of whisky to sell in order to keep their costs down. A litre bottle (bought semi-duty-free in Melilla, for example) sells for up to 450 dinar, though 200-300 dinar would be more usual. Whisky is easy to sell (they'll find you) – but best prices are in the south. One traveller reported selling 2½ litres of whisky in the Hoggar Mountains for £100. If you have your own vehicle, jerrycans are worth up to £60 each (£6 in the UK). There's also a good market for second-hand clothes, and another traveller even suggested taking coffee to Tunisia.

Petrol costs about £2 per gallon (4.55 litres) in Algeria but only about £1.20 in Melilla, so fill up before you get here. Motor insurance costs 102 dinar per month at the border.

You can buy internal air tickets without producing your currency form, so if you're using black market money they're very cheap. Otherwise, you must pay for boat tickets and international air tickets with hard currency, so don't change money in dinar beforehand for these.

LANGUAGE

The main languages are Arabic, French and Berber. Very little English is spoken. Many Algerians mix French with Arabic or French with Berber without a second thought, so be prepared for this.

GETTING THERE & AROUND
Air

Internal flight tickets can be bought with local currency and you do not have to produce a currency form, so it's a cheap way of getting around if your time is limited. *Air Algerie* also offers a substantial discount for anyone under 22 years old. The price of most flights is only about 20% more than the equivalent fare on an SNTV bus. Tamanrasset to Djanet, for instance, is 110 dinar (though, of course, there's no bus along this route).

Road

Hitching in Algeria is a dream come true. Most Algerians are very hospitable and will go out of their way to help you. They think nothing of packing their cars to the roof, so when an apparently full car screeches to a halt don't give it another thought – just get in. You'd be very unlucky to have to pay for any lifts in the north, but south of the Atlas Mountains you should be prepared to pay. Even so, quite a few travellers are still getting free lifts as far south as Tamanrasset. Whatever you do, get out of the towns before you put your bag down and start hitching. You'll be ignored inside towns and cities. If you're asked to pay for a lift, then it's good to have some idea of what the locals are paying.

Most lifts south of the Atlas Mountains will be on the top of trucks and the 'fare' will be about half the cost of the bus over the same stretch. The drivers of trucks belonging to nationally owned companies are officially forbidden to take on passengers and most of them observe this rule. If you're travelling on top of trucks there are a few essentials you need to take along with you. The first is something to cover your head with. If you don't do this you could come down with sunstroke. The second essential is water. A 10-litre collapsible water container is ideal for this. Otherwise, take several of the two-litre plastic soft-drink bottles that are common in Europe. You also need a sleeping bag as the desert gets very cold at night. A sweater is useful once the sun goes down.

Most of the roads in the north are surfaced so it's easy to get from one place to another quickly. Further south it's a different story. Even on main roads you should expect long stretches of *piste* (corrugated dirt roads) and badly pot-holed roads which were previously surfaced. There are stretches of good, surfaced road (for example, 40 km both north and south of Tamanrasset), and the Algerian army is busy re-surfacing parts of the In Salah-Tamanrasset road, but they're few and far between. Anywhere off the main road and it's *piste* or simply tracks in the dust or sand. The road is sealed as far south as In Salah.

Other than truck transport, there is a good network of long-distance buses operated by the national bus company – SNTV. These are generally comfortable, reliable, fast (where the roads allow) and expensive. It's unlikely you will use them in the north since hitching is so easy, but they may be useful for getting south.

If possible, avoid travelling north from Bechar or Figuig during June, July and August. It's not only unbearably hot (40-50°C but it's holiday time for the soldiers along the Moroccan border and the buses will all be full. At these times you can often find up to 300 people waiting at the bus station, many of whom have been there for days.

Routes to/from Algeria
To/From Morocco

There are only two border crossing points between Algeria and Morocco: Oujda-Tlemcen and Figuig-Beni Ounif. You can cross *from* Algeria to Morocco at either place without complications unless you're driving your own vehicle (in which case you'll have to telephone/telex your own embassy in Rabat to confirm that you intend to re-export the vehicle – you must wait in Oujda until this clearance comes through). If you're going in the opposite direction *from* Morocco to Algeria, however, and you don't have your own vehicle, then you can only cross at Figuig/Beni Ounif. You can cross at either place if you have your own vehicle. There are no buses or trains between the two countries on the Oujda-Tlemcen route but there are trains from Tlemcen to the border. The first one leaves Tlemcen at 9.30 am and costs 9 dinar. From the end of the line you get a bus to the actual border for 2 dinar. There are also three daily buses from Tlemcen to the border. The first leaves at 7 am. From the Moroccan side of the border to Oujda there are taxis for 5 dirhams. Don't be fooled by the Moroccan border officials at Oujda. They'll certainly allow you to walk to the Algerian border without saying a word, but you'll simply be turned back when you get there. It's their idea of a joke.

Between Figuig and Beni Ounif there is no regular transport. It's a three-km walk from Figuig to the border and then another 1½ km from there to Beni Ounif. There are three buses daily in either direction between Bechar and Tlemcen (Bechar is south-west of Beni Ounif).

Expect heavy searches at both border crossings on the Algerian side – they're looking for drugs and Algerian currency.

To/From Tunisia

There are two main routes between Tunisia and Algeria but the southern route is the more interesting one. In the north the Souk Aras-Ghardimaou crossing is the usual route. You can either hitch between the two places or take the daily train in either direction between Souk Aras and Jendouba. If you're hitching and you get stuck, it's a 20-km walk between the two border posts. A new road is under construction between the two border towns and is due for completion at the end of 1985. If you're passing through this border and have excess dinar, they'll be taken off you in return for a receipt (there is no bank at the border). If you return within 12 months then your money will be refunded. At least that's what they tell you, but we've yet to hear the practicalities confirmed. Get rid of your dinar before you arrive at the border. Expect a heavy time from the Tunisian customs. Even if you have no Moroccan stamps in your passport they'll assume you have been to Morocco and that you must have hashish with you.

The more interesting southern route passes through the oasis towns of Touggourt, El Oued, Tozeur and Gafsa. It's very picturesque between El Oued and Tozeur – drifting sand dunes – and there's a good sealed road between Nefta and Gafsa. Tunisian customs are quick and there's no fuss, but be prepared for very thorough searches on the Algerian side.

There are daily buses from the Algerian/Tunisian border to Tozeur which stop at Nefta. You can also get a *louage* from the border to Nefta for 550 millimes. If you have to walk, it's four km between the two border posts.

There is another route along the Mediterranean coast from El Khala (Le Calle) to Tabarka. Although there is regular transport along this route during the day, many travellers have commented on the hostility of the local people.

If possible, avoid taking the train direct from Algiers to Tunis. You will not be allowed to buy your ticket unless you can produce bank receipts. The fare is 149 dinar (2nd class).

Trans-Saharan Routes

There are basically three routes through the Sahara. The most popular and the most reliable (as far as transport and facilities are concerned) is the Route du Hoggar, which runs from El Golea to Agadez (Niger) via In Salah and Tamanrasset. It's an interesting trip which will take you through many of the oasis towns south of the Atlas Mountains and, if you go this way, it's worth making to time to see the Hoggar Mountains east of Tamanrasset. The other main route goes south from Adrar to Gao (Mali) via Reggane and Tessalit and is known as the Route du Tanezrouft. It's more rugged than the Route du Hoggar, takes considerably longer, and there's far less transport along the way. The most westerly route, the Route du Mauritanie – from Bechar to Nouakchott (Mauritania) via Tindouf, Bir Moghreim, F'Derik and Atar – is out of the question at present (and has been for many years) because of the war which is going on between the guerrillas of the POLISARIO front and the Moroccans as a result of the latter's occupation of the former Spanish colony.

There's a much more rugged but far more interesting route if you have plenty of time or your own vehicle. The route goes from Touggourt via In Amenas and

Djanet to Tamanrasset through the Tessili Mountains. There are occasional trucks along this route which connect all three places as well as In Salah and Ouargla, but don't expect free lifts. There's also a bus once a week from In Amenas to Illizi (420 km north of Djanet). Travellers who have gone this way have got stuck here and there. If this happens, there are planes from Illizi, In Amenas and Djanet (Illizi to Djanet for 70 dinar and from Djanet to Tamanrasset for 110 dinar – several times per week). It's possible to pick up free lifts with tourists from Djanet going to Niger.

If you're taking your own vehicle with you across the Sahara or simply planning to take your time across the desert, then get hold of the *Sahara Handbook* by Simon and Jan Glen (Lascelles, London 1980). This excellent book is packed with information about everything you could possibly want to know about crossing the Sahara desert and the places you'll encounter along the way. It's oriented toward people with their own vehicles, but there are plenty of detailed descriptions and maps of places you wouldn't even hear about unless you were part of the archaeology *cognoscenti*. Highly recommended.

Route du Hoggar This is the most easterly of the three routes and runs though the Sahara from Ghardaia to Agadez and Zinder (Niger) via El Golea, In Salah and Tamanrasset. Other than the River Nile, it's the most travelled route between the Mediterranean and Africa south of the desert. Unfortunately, because it is the most travelled route, the road gets worn out very quickly. You'll get used to this further south but what used to be a very good surfaced road between In Salah and Tamanrasset is now so badly pot-holed that it can take three days to do the journey. Here's the latest report from a traveller who kept copious notes:

The road from Ghardaia to In Salah is really lousy but fabulous compared to In Salah-Tamanrasset. Brace yourself 10 km out of In Salah where the *piste* begins. When you get to Arak (gas available) you have to take an 80-km detour – all *piste* – until you hit the ruts again for a while and then after that you must follow a *piste* that runs alongside the main road because the Algerian army is re-surfacing it. 40 km from Tam you hit the completed road and it's like heaven on earth.

The road out of Tam is paved for about 30 km; then it's what you've been waiting for and it's really worth the endless bumps, bruises, etc – the honest-to-god Sahara. The *piste* is marked every five km or so though lots of them are missing. The trucks follow a different route roughly parallel to the *piste.* The truck route is marked (more or less) with piles of stones every 100 metres. There are lots of car bodies, totally stripped, lying around, but don't let that dismay you. In about two days the town of In Guezzam should appear – mud houses, the now typical goat and the border post. There's supposedly a store in town – ask customs. You can get rid of your remaining dinar at the Niger outpost unofficially. Patience is required at the Algerian border post! Be pleasant to the officials – offer them some drinks, munchies, cigarettes or whatever. Shoot the shit with them. I'd heard some horror stories about these guys but they were courteous and never asked me questions about how much I'd spent or about my 'student' card.

Assamaka is about 35 km from In Guezzam. You can't miss it, as it has probably the only trees with shade in that part of the Sahara. Don't get there after 4 pm; otherwise you'll have to spend the night there and put up with unruly soldiers whose only hobby is drinking beer – not much else to do out there. You'll need to show money, but a thick-looking wad of traveller's cheques (even if they only total US$100 in value) should suffice. It's no real hassle but you need patience. There are natural water springs here with sulphur in them; the water is palatable if you add a water-purifying tablet. It's sometimes possible to change dinar here – ask around. Photography is forbidden but you can get away with it if you're discreet.

That's a general outline of the trip, but don't take it as definitive. Other travellers have had considerably different experiences, particularly at the Algerian and Niger customs posts. We've had quite a few reports from women who have been subjected to obnoxious displays of drunken chauvinism and threatening behaviour by the officials at the Algerian border. We've never heard of anyone actually being raped, but it's got pretty close to that on occasion. And don't assume that the officials will be as easygoing about your currency form as they were with the traveller above. They can be very strict about those forms, so keep them in order. People have been sent back to Tamanrasset either because the forms were not in order or the amount declared on the forms didn't tally with the money they were carrying.

The officials and soldiers at the Niger post can be just as unpleasant, but the major hassle here concerns the new requirements about sufficient money and onward tickets. See the chapter on Niger for further details of this.

There are now regular buses all the way from Algiers to Tamanrasset but they're not cheap and many travellers prefer to hitch. It's still possible to hitch free all the way to Tamanrasset, but that would be the exception rather than the rule. Most of the time you'll have to pay for lifts. The most usual form of transport, other than buses, is a truck. Tourists driving their own cars and those who are driving Peugeot 504s to sell in West Africa are usually very conscious of weight and reluctant to give lifts. Coming south from Algiers, there are railways which go as far south as Djelfa and Touggourt. The train from Algiers to Djelfa costs 7 dinar (cheap!). Some examples of transport costs and journey times follow:

Algiers-Laghouat Daily buses in either direction cost 89 dinar.

Algiers-Ghardaia Daily buses in either direction in the morning and evening cost 118 dinar and take about eight hours.

Ghardaia-El Golea A taxi between these two places costs 70 dinar.

Ghardaia-In Salah Daily buses in either direction cost 119 dinar.

Ghardaia-Tamanrasset During the summer there is a daily SNTV bus in either direction, but during the winter it only goes three times per month each way. The fare is 200 dinar.

El Golea-In Salah The bus costs 76 dinar and it's a comfortable ride.

In Salah-Tamanrasset Daily bus in either direction, at 4 am from In Salah and at 8 am from Tamanrasset. The trip costs 120 dinar (not much less than the flight) and can take up to three days because of the state of the road, but it's usually two days with an overnight stop in Arak. Trucks between these two places ask for 300 dinar but are very reluctant to take passengers.

Tamanrasset-In Guezzam There is a bus once a week in either direction which leaves Tamanrasset at 5 am on Wednesdays. The fare is 75 dinar. However, this bus isn't particularly useful, as you have to wait around in In Guezzam for a lift further south. It's much better to arrange a lift all the way to Arlit or Agadez in Tamanrasset.

Tamanrasset-Agadez Trucks between these two places cost 25,000 CFA (about £50) and take two days on average, but can take five if there are problems – soft sand, punctures, etc. The drivers will accept CFA or French francs but not Algerian dinar. It's a rugged journey. Petrol and food are available at In Guezzam and Arlit.

One of the best places to find a lift going south from Tamanrasset is at the customs post where all the trucks have to stop. The gas station is another good bet and you can sometimes pick up a ride at the Restaurant de la Paix on the main street in town. You shouldn't have to wait too long for a ride, as there is a lot of traffic between Algeria and Niger these days.

It's also possible to find lifts from Tamanrasset to Gao (Mali). Quite a few trucks do this route but they're nowhere near as common as the ones going south to Agadez. Expect to pay around 500 dinar or French francs 200.

Route du Tanezrouft

This is the central route which runs from Adrar to Gao (Mali). You can get onto it from Ghardaia via El Golea and Timimoun or from Bechar via Beni Abbes. There are nowhere near as many trucks along this route as there are along the Route du Hoggar. In Adrar you need to stock up on essentials – food, water and (if you're driving) petrol – as it's virtually impossible to get supplies further south until you get to Gao. Even the supplies in Adrar are limited. Adrar is also the last place you will find a hotel for a long time. Don't forget to report to customs in Adrar before you set off.

Finding a lift from Adrar to Gao could take you a week – even longer. Only five or six trucks do the run every week. The road is surfaced as far as Reggane but after that it's *piste* or bush tracks all the way to Gao. It's marked by beacons at regular intervals but the tracks can stretch for several km on either side of the 'road' so you won't always see them. The journey from Adrar to Gao will take about a week, averaging around 200 km per day. Take plenty of water with you. Poste Weygand is derelict and there's no water available, but Poste Maurice Cortier (Bidon Cinq) has been brought back into use and is likely to remain so. The Algerian border post is at Borj Moktar, a small oasis. Formalities will take about four or five hours. The Malian customs are at Tessalit and it takes about three hours to get through formalities. There is one 'hotel' here which serves food and has bucket showers. The next place with any facilities is Bourem. Expect a lot of punctures between Bourem and Gao – the track runs through scrub and dunes and is littered with camel thorns. From Gao you can either go to Mopti and Bamako or to Niamey (Niger). Lifts from Gao to Timbuktu are very hard to find.

This route is sometimes closed between May and September. Make enquiries before you set off. There is no Malian consulate in Adrar, so be sure you get your visa (say, in Algiers) before you set off across the desert. There are regular buses in either direction between Ghardaia and Adrar.

PLACES TO STAY

Algerian hotels are generally expensive, especially if you are paying in dinar bought at the official rate. It's not always easy to find a relatively cheap room as these places fill up very quickly. Many travellers stay in the bath houses (*hammam* in Arabic and *bain maure* in French), as they are the cheapest places you will find. However, they are available for *men only*. There's usually at least one even in the smallest places. For 10 to 15 dinar you will be provided with a mattress on the floor. As you might expect, they're warm but often damp and you usually have to be out early in the morning between 6.30 and 7 am.

Algeria also has an extensive network of Youth Hostels which at 10 dinar per night are a godsend to budget travellers. You can find them in Algiers, Annaba, Bejaia, Biskra, Blida, Bou Saada, Constantine, Djelfa, El Kantaka, El Oued, Ghardaia, Guelma, Khenchela, Laghouat, Mostaganem, M'Sila, Oran, Sisi-bel-Abbes, Tlemcen and Touggourt as well as a number of other less prominent places.

ALGIERS

Information

The Tourist Office is at 2 Rue Hassiba ben Bonali, but don't expect too much.

The Thomas Cook agency is *Sonatour*, 5 Boulevard ben Boulaid.

If you need good maps then have a look at what the civilian mapping agency (Direction des Mines et la Geologie) has to offer.

Useful Addresses

Burkina Faso (Upper Volta) embassy
    Rue Larbi Alik, Hydra
British Embassy
    Batiment B, 7 Chemin de Glycines (tel 605601)

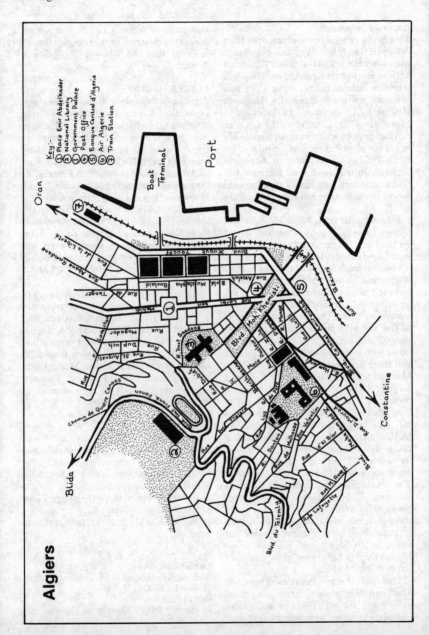

Algiers

Key:-
1. Place Emir Abdelkader
2. National Library
3. Government Palace
4. Post Office
5. Banque Central d'Algérie
6. Air Algerie
7. Train Station

Port

Boat Terminal

Oran

Blida

Constantine

Mali Embassy
  Villa No 14, Cite NNC/ANP, Chemin du
  Kaddous, Hydra
Niger Embassy
  54 Rue Vercors, Air de France, Route de
  Bouzareah
    There is no Niger consulate south of
Algiers but there is now a Mali consulate in
Tamanrasset.

Places to Stay

You should expect to pay at least 50 dinar
for even a cheap hotel in Algiers, and you
may well have to do a lot of walking to find
one which has a spare room. There are a
lot of 'cheap' hotels in the streets around
the railway station. Places signposted
'hotel' (in French) are generally more
expensive than those signposted in Arabic.
Some hotels worth trying:
Hotel des Etrangers, 1 Rue Ali Boumenjel,
Place Port Said, costs 50 dinar for a large
room with two beds, sink and toilet.
Breakfast is included. *Hotel Bearn*, 13
Rue Ahmed Chaib below the Rue Ben
M'Hidi Larbi, costs 25 dinar without
shower (there is an hammam just down the
street). It's a bit of dump but all right for a
short stay. There are other cheap hotels
along the same street if this one is full –
close to the railway and bus stations.
Hotel Rose, 3 Rue Debbih Cherif, costs 65
dinar a double.
Hotel Regina, near the GPO, is clean and
comfortable and costs 55 dinar a double
with shower and toilet. The price includes
breakfast.
Central Tourist Hotel, 9 Rue Abane
Ramdane, is fairly clean and costs 35
dinar a double without shower or
breakfast.
Hotel des Bains de Chatres is off the road
up the hill diagonally from the south-west
corner of Place Port Said. It costs 50 dinar
a double and 25 dinar a single including
breakfast.
Hotel d'Isly is another hotel used quite a
bit by travellers. It's near the university
and costs 30 dinar a single, including
breakfast.

There's a *hammam* close to the centre
of town, between the Place Port Said and
Place des Martyrs. It costs 15 dinar.

Trips from Algiers

The Roman ruins of Tipasa some 65 km
west of Algiers on the coast are well worth
a visit if you have the time. There are
buses from Algiers which cost 10 dinar
and take about two hours. You can camp
on the beach near the village free.

AIN OUSSERA

This is a small town about halfway
between Algiers and Djelfa on the road
going south. Men can stay in the *hammam*
here on the main road near the SNTV bus
stop. It costs 10 dinar downstairs and 40
dinar for a double upstairs. The upstairs
rooms have been described as 'really
crappy.'

ARAK

A small Tuareg settlement, Arak is on the
road between In Salah and Tamanrasset.
There is a small campsite here where you
can rent mats for the night for 10 dinar.
There's also water for washing available
and a small restaurant with a Malian chef
who turns out delicious *couscous*.

BENI-OUNIF

Beni-Ounif is the first Algerian town you
will come to if you're crossing the Moroccan/
Algerian border on foot. There's only one
hotel here and it's expensive at 80 dinar a
double. It has no running water or
electricity and is often full.

CONSTANTINE

The best area to look for accommodation
in Constantine is to the left of the bridge
from the railway station. There are many
cheap hotels here, especially towards the
top of the hill. Don't take *'Complet'* signs
too literally – hotels can generally put you
up even if they're 'full'. Places which have
been recommended here are the *Hotel El
Hana* and the *Hotel Dardamel*. The latter
is at 37 Rue Hamlacui.

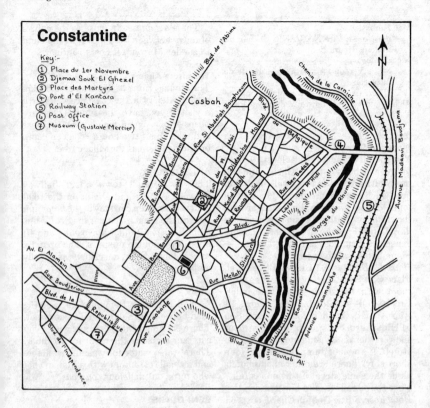

Constantine

Key:-
1. Place du 1er Novembre
2. Djemaa Souk El Ghezel
3. Place des Martyrs
4. Pont d'El Kantara
5. Railway Station
6. Post Office
7. Museum (Gustave Mercier)

DJANET

Stay at the *Hotel Zeribas*, which costs 15 dinar. You are not allowed to camp in the palmerie.

EL GOLEA

El Golea is a beautiful oasis town surrounded by thousands of palm and fruit trees. There are all the usual facilities plus an old fort to visit.

The government-run campsite south of town on the road to In Salah isn't very popular as it's inconvenient for backpackers; it's usually empty. Most people prefer the one north of town, opposite the SNTL truck park, which costs 7 dinar per person, 6 dinar for a small tent, 7 dinar for a large tent, 6 dinar for a small car and 7

dinar for a large car. The water is drinkable and there are showers and washing facilities.

There is also a large market opposite the camp and bread is sold in front of the coffee shop at the entrance. It's a good place for enquiring about lifts if you're hitching.

There are plenty of good restaurants in El Golea. We've had quite a few letters which comment that many of them sell genuine Coca-Cola! Absence makes the heart grow fonder.

In addition to the above, there is the moderately priced *Hotel du Tademait* as well as the expensive *Hotel Boustan* and the *Hotel Grand Erg*.

EL OUED

The *Hotel Oasis* here costs 40 dinar. If you arrive after the banks close, it's possible to change money at the *douai* (customs) near the market.

GHARDAIA

Ghardaia is one of the most fascinating of the oasis towns and well worth exploring. It's actually a cluster of five towns: Ghardaia, Melika, Beni Isguen, Ben Noura and El Atteuf. It's inhabited by a devout Moslem sect known as the Mozabites which broke away from the mainstream of Islam some 900 years ago. Beautiful rugs are woven in the area but they're very expensive. In Beni Isguen there's an interesting **market** every evening except Friday, but you're only allowed in this part of the oasis with a guide and you are not allowed to smoke or take photographs.

It's fairly easy to find someone who will put you up in the palmerie. Just ask around. There used to be an old herbalist called Hadj Said Salah who welcomed travellers for many years but no-one seems to have heard of him recently. A pity. Other than this, men can stay at the *hammam* near the bus station or (for one night only) at the *Maison de Jeunesse* for 10 dinar. The latter is on the main street below the expensive hotel up on the hill by the old Muslim cemetery. There is a campsite two km from the centre on the road beside the riverbed, not far from the major roundabout intersection for the five villages. It costs 55 dinar per night for two people and extra for a vehicle. There are hot showers. The *Youth Hostel* (Auberge de la Jeunesse) costs 15 dinar per night.

Two of the cheapest hotels are the *Hotel Le Napht* and the *Hotel 1001 Nights*. The former is clean and friendly and has a small, pleasant restaurant downstairs. Both cost 50 dinar a double. Others of a similar price you could try include *Le Carrefour*, *La Paix* and *Le Archer*. Avoid the *Hotel l'Atlantide* if possible, as it's dirty and unfriendly.

If meals are not available at the place where you are staying, try *L'Etoile* opposite the Hotel 1001 Nights. You can get a meal here for around 20 dinar.

IN SALAH

In Salah is the most major town between El Golea and Tamanrasset and like the others is an oasis town, but it's populated mainly by Arabs and a few Tuareg.

There are two campsites here, one in the centre of town near the market (10 dinar per person), the other (called *Zribat*) three km south of town. The latter is still under construction but open and should resemble an oasis by the time it is finished. Zribat is run by Hadji of *Restaurant Carrefour* fame and costs 10 dinar per night. As for the Restaurant Carrefour itself, you can get very good meals here – half a chicken, spaghetti, salad, French cheese, orange and coffee – for 30 dinar upstairs and 20 dinar downstairs. Hadji is quite a character and you should find time to talk with him. He'll help you out with any problems you have if it's possible. In addition to the restaurant, he has a pastry shop in the planning stages which will offer yogurt, milk, etc. If you don't want to stay at either campsite, you can camp free in the palmerie west of town near the road to Reggane. Avoid the *hammam* here. There is a bank in In Salah.

ORAN

Oran isn't a particularly interesting place to stay, although if you're passing through it's perhaps worth visiting the **fort of Santa Cruz** outside the city. *Hotel Riad* has been highly recommended as being good value and the staff are friendly. Two other places you might like to try are *Hotel Marhaba* and *Hotel de la Gare* right next to the train station.

OUARGLA

There is an excellent campsite here opposite the *Hotel Trans-Atlantide*.

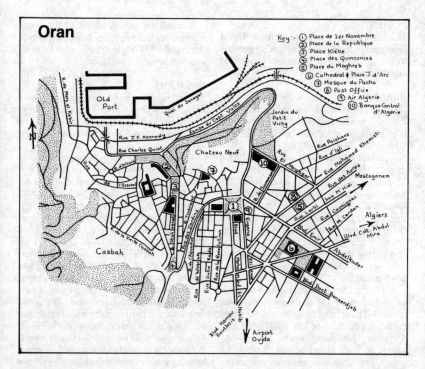

Oran

Key:-
1. Place de 1er Novembre
2. Place de la Republique
3. Place Klébe
4. Place des Quinconces
5. Place du Maghreb
6. Cathedral & Place J. d'Arc
7. Mosque du Pacha
8. Post Office
9. Air Algerie
10. Banque Central d'Algerie

TAMANRASSET

Tamanrasset sits at the foot of the Hoggar Mountains – among the highest mountains in the Sahara – and is the last major town on the route south to Niger. At one time supplies and facilities at Tamanrasset were limited but the place is changing rapidly and supplies are now plentiful. There are also two banks here.

The campsite nearest town – *Zerib* – costs 15 dinar per person and 10 dinar per car. It has washing and showering facilities as well as a restaurant. Breakfast here costs 15 dinar and dinner 35 dinar. It's a good place to get a lift to Niger and to collect information. The site is about two km past the *Hotel Tahat*. The campsite known as *Le Source*, about 15 km from town, isn't quite so good as it used to be but there's an *oued* about three km north of there where you can camp free. Water is

available. If you do stay at Le Source, it costs 10 dinar per night with food available at 12 dinar. There are cold showers only. Zerib is a good place to ask around for lifts, though Peugeot and Mercedes drivers are very conscious of weight and reluctant to take extra passengers. Also, when enquiring about lifts, remember that most of the trucks going to Agadez take the direct western route after Assamaka but tourists are obliged to go via Arlit, so it's best to wait in Tamanrasset until you get a ride going that way.

Other than the campsites, there is the *Hotel Tahat*, which has rooms for 180 dinar a double including breakfast. Single rooms are also available. You should try to get there before 4 pm, otherwise it will be full. You can buy meals here for about 50 dinar each.

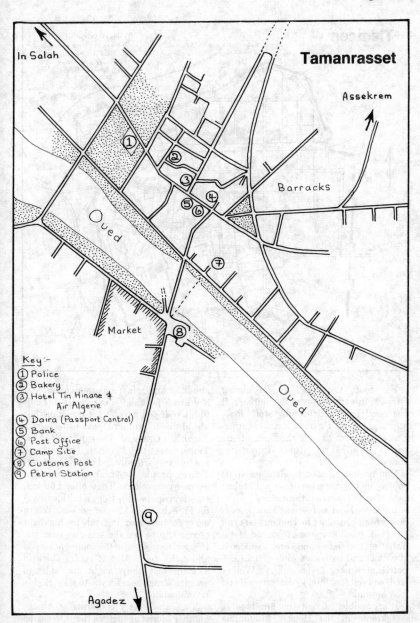

Tamanrasset

In Salah

Assekrem

Barracks

Oued

Oued

Market

Key:-
① Police
② Bakery
③ Hotel Tin Hinane &
    Air Algerie
④ Daira (Passport Control)
⑤ Bank
⑥ Post Office
⑦ Camp Site
⑧ Customs Post
⑨ Petrol Station

Agadez

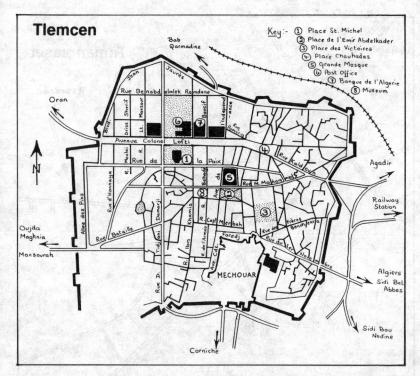

For food, try the *Café Restaurant l'Assiak*, directly opposite the markets. It has good food and friendly staff. *Restaurant de la Paix* gets a variable rating. Some travellers say it's the best; others say it's a flea pit. Check it out for yourself.

You no longer need to clear passport control in Tamanrasset. This is all taken care of at In Guezzam these days.

If you are heading towards Mali there is now a Mali consulate in Tamanrasset (tel 734115). It's 300 metres from the Hotel Tahat on the right-hand side. Visas cost 100 dinar and are issued while you wait. A bottle of whisky (even Johnny Walker Red) will sell for 300-450 dinar here if you look around.

It's possible to visit the **Ermitage** at Assekreme in the Hoggar Mountains

about 85 km from Tamanrasset, but you need transport as it's extremely difficult to hitch. If you haven't got transport but would like to go there, get in touch with *Tarahist*, Gsar El Fougani, BP 144, Tamanrasset (tel 734402). This agency, run by a very friendly and helpful bunch of Tuareg people, has been recommended by many travellers. They offer 200-km, two-day trips into the Hoggar (all inclusive) for French francs 150 per person. 'Worth every centime' and 'Possibly the highlight of our trip to see the sun rise over the Hoggar' were some of the comments made about this tour. Also, if you're stuck in Tamanrasset they might be able to arrange somewhere for you to stay. Highly recommended.

You can also try enquiring at *Altour*, another tourist agency, as they offer trips to a **climbers' refuge** at Assekreme for around 200 dinar. You can stay at the refuge and eat well for 50 dinar per day. It's a magic place and superb walking country, but bring plenty of warm clothes with you as the temperature drops below freezing point at night (it's above 2700 metres). Apart from the climbers' refuge there is also the *Ermitage Hotel* campsite for 7.50 dinar per night.

TLEMCEN

Tlemcen is a beautiful old walled city well worth visiting, but unfortunately not easy to get to these days if you are coming from Morocco (you must have a vehicle to go *from* Oujda to Tlemcen but you can go on foot *from* Tlemcen to Oujda. You can camp for 5 dinar at the Roman ruins just outside town at Mansourah. Cold showers are available. Otherwise, stay at a *hammam* if you're male, or at the *Hotel Majestic* which costs 40 dinar a single without breakfast. There are no showers or hot water.

If you're feeling hot and bothered here then forget about swimming pools. The one at the large hotel costs 50 dinar per hour for non-residents!

OTHER

One traveller who spent time in the Grand Erg Occidental region had this to say about it:

To me this is the true Sahara, with its miles and miles of sand dunes, palm trees and earth houses. It's stunningly beautiful and I would recommend it to all travellers. Beni Abbes was truly fantastic and Taghit is equally beautiful. There are very few tourists here and the bus system is excellent, though expensive. There are only one or two hotels in each oasis town, which cost a minimum of 50 dinar a single going up to 100 dinar, but the people are very hospitable. I didn't stay in a hotel for the entire eight days I was there. You can camp free anywhere. I hitched from Beni Ounif to Bechar (no trouble), bus from Bechar to Beni Abbes (50 dinar), bus from Beni Abbes to Timimoun (70 dinar) and hitched from Timimoun to Adrar (no trouble).

Don't forget to bring a bottle of whisky for sale inside the country if you want to keep your costs down. A litre sells for at least 200 dinar and we've heard of people getting up to 450 dinar for selected brands. Generally, the further south you go the higher the price, but this isn't always so. Some travellers say that everyone keeps their bottle of whisky until they get to Tamanrasset (that's a long way to carry a bottle of whisky!), so you don't get as good a price as you might a little further north. Others say this is nonsense and have got between 300 and 450 dinar for a bottle of quite ordinary whisky in Tamanrasset.

You may come across children in the north-east selling live desert foxes. These animals are fast approaching extinction mainly because of the market that tourists have created for them. Don't buy them even if you plan to free them later, as this just increases the demand for them.

Angola

Angola is still preoccupied with reconstruction after the devastating civil war which engulfed the country when independence was abruptly granted by the Portuguese in 1975. This war, together with continual political and military interference by other countries ever since, resulted in social dislocation on a vast scale, the neglect or abandonment of agriculture and the ruin of the country's road and rail network.

The newly independent country quickly became a classic case of super-power rivalry and has had to face not only full-scale military invasions by the regular troops of South Africa and Zaire but also the activities of European mercenaries and the rebel forces of Jonas Savimbi's South African-supported UNITA. There is also a less serious threat from rebel forces in the oil-rich Cabinda enclave.

Despite all this, much headway has been made in putting the country and its economy back on its feet, with a lot of help from Cuban and Portuguese advisers and voluntary workers. It is the presence of an estimated 19,000 Cuban troops and their real or imagined support of SWAPO guerrillas, however, which the South Africans have used as a pretext for invading the southern half of the country on more than one occasion. These troops have also become a bone of contention in the continuing saga over independence for Namibia.

With security and stability being such elusive commodities in Angola, it's hardly surprising that the government discourages tourism.

Angola suffered one of the most backward forms of colonialism. Portugal itself was – in European terms – a relatively undeveloped country, lacking a substantial industrial base, and simply had neither the inclination nor the resources to develop its African colonies. A settlement was constructed at Luanda on the coast as early as 1575, but there was no attempt to settle the interior until the end of the 19th century, and even then it was done with convict labour from the prisons of the mother country. Before this time the Portuguese were content to milk the area for slaves for their far more lucrative colony of Brazil and to capitalise on the occasional discovery of precious metals and gemstones.

By 1900 there were fewer than 10,000 whites in the colony. This number had grown to around 80,000 by 1950 largely because of the coffee boom which occurred after WW II, but it wasn't until the last 25 years of the colonial era that immigration from Portugal began to take off on a large scale. Even then, about half the new immigrants were illiterate peasants from the more impoverished parts of Portugal. Not only were the vast majority of them destined to spend only a very short time in the colony, but it seems that they weren't cut out for life in the Angolan bush either since only 1% of the European population were established in the rural settlements prior to independence.

Popular resistance had its roots in the system of forced labour, and after WW II spontaneous clashes between the various African communities and the colonial administration became more and more frequent. The first really serious confrontations took place in February and March 1961 and were directed at European and *mestico* plantation owners as well as the jails in Luanda where political

prisoners were held. The protests were organised by supporters of the MPLA (Popular Movement for the Liberation of Angola) and by UPNA (Union of the Populations of Northern Angola – soon to become part of the FNLA (National Front for the Liberation of Angola). Some three years after the formation of the FNLA a group of southerners broke away to form UNITA (National Union for the Total Independence of Angola) in protest at what was perceived to be northern tribalism.

All three groups took to guerilla warfare shortly after the 1961 uprisings as a consequence of the vicious military and political campaign launched by the colonial authorities. There were few major differences between the three groups as far as objectives were concerned, but there were large differences in the sources from which they drew their support. The FNLA appealed to tribal allegiances in the north of the country and was supported by Zaire and a number of western countries opposed to a Communist takeover of the country. For this group the destruction of the MPLA assumed much the same importance as throwing out the Portuguese. The MPLA emphasised the importance of transcending tribalism and appealed to a broad sense of nationalism. It was linked to the liberation movements in the other Portuguese colonies and was supported by the USSR and its allies. Its popular base of support was concentrated in the south and centre of the country. UNITA also drew the bulk of its support from the south and there was fierce rivalry between the two parties. UNITA certainly had the confidence of the Ovimbundu in the early stages but its leaders soon revealed themselves as opportunists. They were not only prepared to come to an accommodation with the right-wing Portuguese forces and to exploit Sino-Soviet rivalry prior to independence, but once it was granted they even formed an open alliance with South Africa!

Following the armed forces movement in Portugal which toppled the fascist regime in 1974, negotiations were immediately begun on a programme for Angolan independence. A transitional government was set up consisting of the three nationalist groups and Portugal, but it broke down and the country was plunged into civil war. A massive airlift was organised during which the bulk of the white population fled to Portugal and other countries. Meanwhile the MPLA, backed by combat troops from Cuba, Guinea and Guinea-Bissau and equipment from Mozambique, Nigeria and Algeria, was able to seize control of the bulk of the country by early 1976. Many years were to pass, however, before the FNLA and FLEC (Front for the Cabinda Enclave) were crushed. UNITA still continues to wreak havoc in the south and south-east though its fortunes wax and wane according to the extent of South African involvement in southern Angola at any particular time. In recent years it has become a valuable bargaining counter for the South Africans in the protracted negotiations for independence in Namibia. While Cuban troops remain in Angola, South Africa will continue to support UNITA and prevaricate over Namibia. Nothing short of an inter-nationally guaranteed settlement is going to bring an end to the civil war in Angola, and even then it's doubtful whether South Africa will negotiate in good faith. All the same, Angola has been pressing ahead at mending fences with the USA and other western countries in the last few years, and American oil companies have been drilling for oil in the Cabinda enclave for many years more or less unaffected by the turmoil in the rest of the country.

VISAS

Visas are required by all. In Europe there are embassies in Lisbon, Paris and Rome. All visa applications have to be referred to DEFA (Direcao de Emigracao e Fronteras de Angola) in Luanda regardless of where they are received, and it can take up to three months for a reply to come through. That being so, you might as well apply direct to DEFA, Luanda, Angola, either by registered mail or by telex (Telex 3127 MIREX AN). You must supply the following details: Your full name; the full names of both your parents; your occupation; your date and place of birth; the purpose of your visit and the proposed length of stay; the number, place and date of issue of your passport; four passport photos; and a photostat of the first six pages of your passport (the latter two only if you are applying by mail – if you apply by telex then you must have the last two on arrival). You'll be given a visa authorisation number and on arrival you'll have to pay US$20 for the visa. It's unlikely your application will be approved unless you have a very good reason for wanting to go there ('tourism' is not regarded as a good reason). One of the best ruses for getting a visa is the need to spend a few days in Angola between flights from one place to another. There is no way you will get a visa if there is any evidence that you have visited South Africa. You must also have an International Vaccination Card for cholera and yellow fever. It also helps if you can prove you have had shots for typhoid and hepatitis.

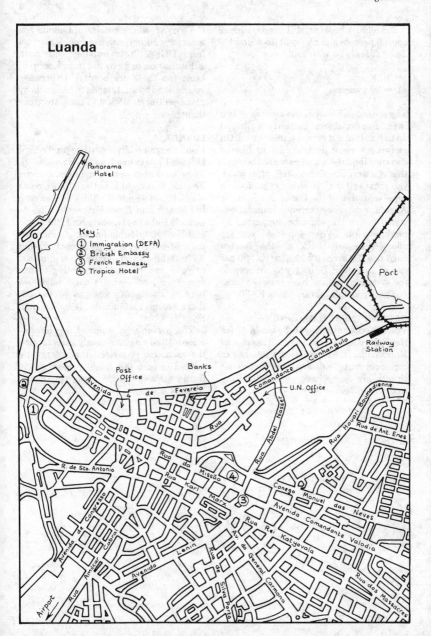

Luanda

Key:
1. Immigration (DEFA)
2. British Embassy
3. French Embassy
4. Tropico Hotel

Panorama Hotel

Port

Railway Station

Post Office

Banks

U.N. Office

Avenida 4 de Fevereia

Rua Comandante Canhangulo

Rua Abdel Nasser

Rua de Ant. Enes

Rua Hovari Boumédienne

R. de Sto. Antonio

Rua da Missão

Rua Karl Marx

Conego Manuel das Neves

Avenida Comandante Valodia

Avenida de Congresso

Rua Amilcar Cabral

Avenida Lenin

Av. de General Carmano

Rua Rei Katyavala

Rua de Silva Porto

Rua dos Mastacres

Airport

Travel anywhere outside Luanda requires special permits and plenty of photographs. Take at least 20 with you!

MONEY
£1 = 50 kwanza

The unit of currency is the kwanza = 100 lweis. Import of local currency is allowed up to Kz 1000 but export is prohibited. On arrival you must declare all your foreign currency (and the searches are so thorough that you won't be able not to!), after which you must sell it all to either customs or a representative of the Banco Nacional de Angola. Any other currency transactions which you make must be supported by bank receipts. When you leave you are allowed to buy back all the foreign currency you arrived with, less Kz 500 per day of your stay. Don't try to circumvent the system or you will have major hassles.

The airport departure tax is Kz 30.

GETTING THERE & AROUND
You can only enter Angola by air. In Africa this is possible from Lusaka, Kinshasa or Brazzaville. There are also a number of connections to Europe. Discounted air tickets are sometimes obtainable from *Aeroflot* or *Balkan Air*.

To go anywhere outside of Luanda you must have authorisation (a *guia de marche*) from DEFA. It is possible with such authorisation to go by rail from Lobito to Luau (on the Zaire border). Otherwise, you must go by air. Luanda to Benguela by plane will cost US$50. There are daily flights.

LUANDA
Hotel accommodation must be pre-booked at least 15 days in advance with *Anghotel*. They have two hotels in Luanda: *Hotel Tropico*, Rua da Missao (tel 31593), costs Kz 2310 single and Kz 3500 double with full board; and *Hotel Panorama*, Ilha de Luanda (tel 37841), costs Kz 1200 single and Kz 1500 double for accommodation only. Meals cost Kz 140 (breakfast) and Kz 360 (lunch and dinner). You must eat in your own hotel as (according to our correspondent – who is not a business-person but doesn't want to be named) there are no restaurants. It is illegal to tip.

The person who supplied this information visited Angola recently and supplied the map. He requested that he not be named in case this might prejudice any future visits he might make to Angola. Thanks anyway.

Benin

For 12 years following independence from France in 1960, Benin (which was known as Dahomey until 1975) lurched from one coup to the next until power was seized by a group of young army officers led by Major Kerekou. Since then the country has taken a sharp turn to the left politically and was for many years known as 'the Cuba of West Africa.' Certainly its policies were based on Marxism-Leninism, but in other ways the comparison was inappropriate since Benin was hardly trying to export its revolution to other countries. Benin made a major effort to break the ties with the colonial era, and the country distanced itself from the more 'moderate' states of West Africa. This was by no means all plain sailing. Tense relations with neighbouring states led to frequent border closures and the disruption of trade. Togo in particular was badly affected by these disruptions and frequently closed its borders in retaliation.

There was also an attempted coup in 1977 led by the French mercenary Bob Denard, who landed at Cotonou in the early hours of the morning along with 50 other European mercenaries and 30 Africans. They were forced to withdraw but they left behind compromising documents which revealed that both Morocco and Gabon had payrolled the operation and that France was also implicated. Subsequently, diplomatic relations with Gabon were broken off, which led to the violent expulsion of some 9000 Beninois living in Libreville and a serious curtail-ment French aid. Nevertheless, Kerekou's regime survived and major reforms have been carried out, particularly in the fields of education and agriculture. Benin is now considered to be one of the most stable states in Africa and there has been a thawing of its frosty relations with neighbouring states of late.

Like many African countries' borders, particularly in West Africa, those of Benin are a legacy of 19th-century colonialism and they could not have been more inappropriate. They completely disregard the fact that from the 16th century onwards a number of independent kingdoms coexisted in the coastal area of this part of Africa. These were the Fon kingdoms of Abomey, Allada and Porto Novo, noted for their sacred societies, witchcraft and elaborate rituals. What is more, these kingdoms were powerful enough to withstand a number of invasions by the Yoruba from neighbouring Nigeria. The wealth of these kingdoms was based on the slave trade which began with the Portuguese in the 16th century but was progressively monopolised by the British and the French during the 17th and 18th centuries. All three European nations established forts on the coast at Ouidah but in 1727 the outpost was recaptured by the local kingdoms.

After the abolition of the slave trade, the European nations began to seek concessions for palm oil plantations from the local rulers. The French were the most successful at this and their involvement gradually led to the declaration of 'protect-orates' over certain areas of the coast. The process was accelerated by the bombard-ment of Porto Novo by the British in 1863 and, some 30 years later, French retal-iation for the attack on their garrisons at Cotonou and Porto Novo by the king of Abomey. Following the defeat of the king, the French declared a 'protectorate' over the whole region.

Pacification of the rest of the colony was not completed until 1914, but this did not quell opposition to French rule. As early as 1923, anti-colonial newspapers were in circulation, set up by French-educated Dahomians and former slaves who had returned from Brazil. Education and trade unionism were major formative influences in the making of the nation between WW II and independence. In addition, large numbers of Dahomians were employed by the French colonial authorities in the administrations of other West African colonies. When independence came to most French colonies in 1960, however, the majority of these workers were forced to return to Benin, where they formed a distinct group of unemployed and grumbling intellectuals. Their interests, along with the factionalism associated with the various kingdoms which had existed before the French conquest, were largely responsible for the endless power struggles which were the order of the day until the coup by Kerekou.

FACTS

Benin is a small but polyglot nation and a lot of thought has gone into guaranteeing the rights of different nationalities, their cultures, languages and traditions. The population of about 3½ million still largely follows traditional religions. Only some 17% are Christian and about 15% Moslem. The major ethnic groups are the Fon, Yoruba (as in western Nigeria), Bariba and Somba.

The southern part of the country has an equatorial climate; most of the year it is very humid. The dry seasons are from January to April and during August. The north is less humid but very hot during March and April. In this area the dry season stretches from November to June.

VISAS

Visas are required by all except nationals of Denmark, France, Germany (West) and

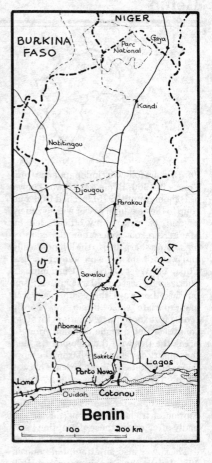

Italy. Nationals of South Africa are not admitted. Suspicion of foreigners and the bureaucracy associated with keeping tabs on them following Bob Denard's failed attempt has diminished considerably over the last few years, and it's now much easier to get a visa. Most people are now issued with a seven-day visa.

There are no Benin embassies in either Lomé (Togo) or Ougadougou (Burkina Faso), so you need to get your visa beforehand in, for instance, Freetown

(Sierra Leone), Abidjan (Ivory Coast), Accra (Ghana), Niamey (Niger) or Lagos (Nigeria). You cannot get visas at the border or from French embassies in countries where there is no Benin consular representative. The only exception to this is if you are entering from Togo via Ouidah, in which case you can get your visa at the border (it seems Benin has finally woken up to the fact that the lack of a Benin embassy in Lome makes it difficult for travellers from Togo). If you buy a visa at this border the cost is 1000 CFA for a one-month visa which will be issued while you wait. A seven-day visa in Niamey costs 1000 CFA and takes 48 hours.

There is also no longer a Benin embassy in Cameroun, so if you're coming up from the Central African Republic that leaves Lagos as the only possible place to get a visa.

Visa extensions are available in Cotonou from Immigration (almost opposite the French embassy) for up to one month and cost 2500 CFA. Two photos are required. The visas are issued in 24 hours – no problems.

Officially you are supposed to have a 'Permit de Circulation' obtained from the police or the Chef du District in each town or city that you stay in overnight, but if you overlook this then make sure that the hotel staff report your presence to the police. You can more or less forget about this in large towns but it's a good idea to register in small towns to avoid arousing suspicions.

It's useful to have a *carte* issued by the tourist office in Cotonou saying you are a bona fide tourist. This is in case you're questioned by the police, especially if you have a camera. Most people, however, have no trouble with police. The cards cost 100 CFA.

It's only necessary to get an exit visa (from Immigration) if you are flying out. In this case they'll issue it while you wait if you make a fuss, but these requirements change from time to time so make

enquiries beforehand. Exit visas can be obtained from Immigration in Cotonou.

Nigerian visas Cotonou is a good place to get these visas. They're issued within 24 hours with little fuss.

MONEY
US$1 = 454 CFA

The unit of currency is the CFA franc. There are no restrictions on the import or export of local currency. There is no black market for local currency, but Cotonou is a good place to buy Nigerian naira if you have excess CFA. Naira 1 is worth approximately 145 CFA.

A good place to change money is the Hotel Sheraton, 15 minutes' walk from the airport. It's open from 8.30 am to 2.30 pm and from 4.30 to 6.30 pm. There are no hassles, no commission on traveller's cheques and no waiting. The bank at the airport is usually closed.

LANGUAGE
French is the official language. The main African languages are Fon, Yoruba, Bariba and Dendi.

POST
The poste restante in Cotonou is good but you must pay for each letter or telex which you receive.

GETTING THERE & AROUND
Air
Quite a few travellers have commented about the possibility of getting cheap air tickets in Cotonou – eg Cotonou-Lagos-London for CFA 80,000, which is about as good as *Le Point* (see the Introductory chapter under 'Getting There'). To get these tickets you must contact a white Frenchman named Maurice either at the Hotel de la Plage or at Cobenham's Travel Agency. Don't deal with anyone else at the Hotel de la Plage who claim they work for him. You fly with *Aeroflot* and the deal involves payment in naira bought on the

black market. You can buy naira by asking around discreetly in the big market next to the bridge (the rate is about CFA 500 = 4 naira).

Many airline companies are only selling return tickets these days regardless of whether you want to use another means of transport at the other end. They're doing this so that they don't end up with the responsibility of returning tourists who are refused entry for whatever reason.

If you're flying out of Cotonou to Lagos, a reservation means nothing. It's all a question of fighting your way onto the plane before anyone else. Maybe it's better to go by road after all?

Road

There are two main routes into Benin, one being the coast road which connects Lagos with Porto Novo, Cotonou, Lome and Accra; and the other through the centre of the country which connects Cotonou with Niamey (Niger) via Parakou and Malanville/Gaya (border). Both roads are in excellent shape. There are buses and shared taxis along both routes or you can hitch. A taxi-brousse from Cotonou to Lome costs 1000 CFA plus 1000 CFA for a pack. The border with Nigeria is closed at present, but should it open up again and you're heading that way, make an early start – it's no joke arriving in Lagos during rush hour or after dark.

As far as the road through the centre of the country goes, there's a daily bus from Niamey to Gaya which leaves at 9 am and costs 1500 CFA. From Gaya to Parakou a shared taxi costs 2500 CFA. There's also a daily bus from Parakou to Malanville which connects with the train from Cotonou. It costs 1800 CFA plus 500 CFA for a pack. If you prefer a Peugeot taxi between the two places, it will cost 2500 CFA plus 200 CFA for a pack, and the ride will take four to six hours.

Rail

Benin has two main railway lines: one follows the coast and links Cotonou, Porto Novo and Lome (Togo); and the other goes north and links Cotonou with Save and Parakou. There is one train daily in either direction between Cotonou and Parakou (between 7 and 8 am from Parakou, but this isn't always the case; sometimes it doesn't depart until 10 am). The fare is 3075 (2nd class) and the journey takes about 10 to 14 hours. Food is available en route. The seats in 2nd class are hard but the train isn't usually crowded.

Boat

It is almost impossible to find a cheap or working passage on a cargo boat to somewhere else in Africa. There are, however, occasional cargo boats which have a number of cabins available to fare-paying passengers. This isn't going to be cheap, but if you're heading to Gabon, for instance, it may well work out slightly less than the one-way air fare.

ABOMEY

Abomey was once the capital of a Fon kingdom and is one of the most interesting places to visit in Benin. There's an excellent **museum** here which covers the history of the kingdoms, as well as the **Fon Palace** and the **Fetish Temple**. The throne of the Abomey kings is made of human skulls! Next to the museum is the **Centre des Artisans**, where there is a good collection of crafts for sale at prices as low as you're likely to find anywhere.

One of the cheapest places to stay is *Le Campement* (now known as the *Foyer des Militants*), which costs 2500 CFA for a single or a double. It's quiet and good value. If it's full then try *Chez Monique*, 300 metres from the Foyer up the small track. Accommodation costs 1000 CFA, though it's not always possible to stay here.

COTONOU

Although Porto Novo is the official capital, most government and diplomatic functions take place in Cotonou. The one

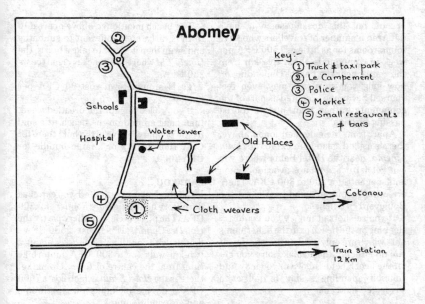

Abomey

Key:-
1. Truck & taxi park
2. Le Campement
3. Police
4. Market
5. Small restaurants & bars

Schools

Hospital

Water tower

Old Palaces

Cloth weavers

Cotonou

Train station 12 Km

thing you must see here, if at all possible, is the **Dan Topka market**, which is held every four days. There is also a good black market for other West African currencies. The poste restante at the main post office in Cotonou is good and will even forward mail if you leave an address.

A very popular place to stay is the *Hotel Babo*, which is well known in the African quarter. The person in reception can be a little off-hand but don't let this put you off, and do have a look at the rooms before taking one. Avoid room No 33 – it's got smelly showers, lumpy beds and crud all over the floor. Rooms cost 3100 CFA a single and 3500 CFA a double with fan. The restaurant next door serves good meals for 300 to 400 CFA, though the price varies every time you go there. A better deal is the *Hotel Pacific* on the other side of the bridge, which leads into the town centre. A room with attached shower and toilet costs 3500 CFA. There are no fans but since the hotel is right next to the ocean you don't really need one; it costs 500 CFA extra. The Pacific is much

quieter than the other hotels and provides more services (three meals a day, baggage storage facilities, etc). There is a breakfast stall right round the corner where you can get a continental breakfast for 100 CFA. You can also catch a taxi to Porto Novo right outside the front door.

Two other places which have been recommended are the *Benin Palace*, which costs 3000 CFA a double; and the *Hotel Le Reve*, which costs 4000 CFA a double.

If you have to stay in Cotonou for a long time (as some travellers have been forced to do because of the closure of the Nigerian border), then the best thing to do is get a group of, say, four people together and rent a house. The cost should be around £200 a month for a well-furnished European-standard house with fans and fridge and at least four bedrooms. This works out much cheaper than the hotels. Ask around in the *Hotel de la Plage* on the seafront not far from the post office.

It's apparently illegal for local people to have you as guests whether you are paying or not, but this doesn't seem to have deterred a number of travellers who have found rooms for as little as 1500 CFA per week in compounds about five km from the centre near the beach. Depending on how long you stay, you may even feel yourself becoming accepted as part of the community rather than just a tourist passing through.

Apart from the café mentioned above, there's a good salad bar next to the *Benin Cinema*, near the Hotel Babo, where you can get lettuce, tomato, avocado, onion and spaghetti for 200 to 300 CFA. There are other restaurants and bars along the Boulevard St Michel.

If you're short of money you could try sleeping on the beach or in the fishermen's huts which are only used during the day. If you do either of these, make sure you get off the beach before dawn or you may find yourself spending a day in jail as a suspected mercenary.

The beach mentioned above nearest to town is dirty, so if you want to sunbathe and swim then it's best to take a taxi to the *Hotel PLM* where the beach is clean (costs 250 CFA).

Taxis around town cost 90 CFA per person.

If you're looking for the dreaded weed, then hang around on the beach. It's sold by the people who live in the huts there for CFA 7000 per kg or a large bundle for CFA 2000.

PARAKOU

If your budget is very limited, you can get a dormitory bed at the *Gare Routiere* for 500 CFA. The place is clean. Otherwise try the *Hotel les Canaris*, which costs 2500 CFA a double with fan. The Canaris is about a two-km walk (or a 300 CFA motorbike ride) from the centre of town. Upmarket there is the *Hotel Benin*, which costs 7000 CFA a double including own bathroom and air-conditioning.

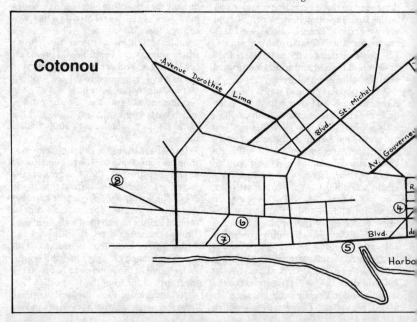

PORTO NOVO

Porto Novo is the official capital of Benin and is only a half-hour journey by minibus from Cotonou (250 CFA).

Try the *Catholic Mission* here for somewhere to stay. It has good facilities.

There is an excellent **museum** here with a fine collection of masks, weapons and musical instruments. It's also possible to get a free ride with the fishermen on the lagoon if you ask around.

OTHER

If you have time while you're in Cotonou, pay a visit to the village of Ganvie, which is built on stilts out in the lagoon. To get there, go first to Calavi by taxi (400 CFA) and there hire a canoe to visit the village. These can cost between 3000-4000 CFA, though it is possible to find cheaper rides in pirogues.

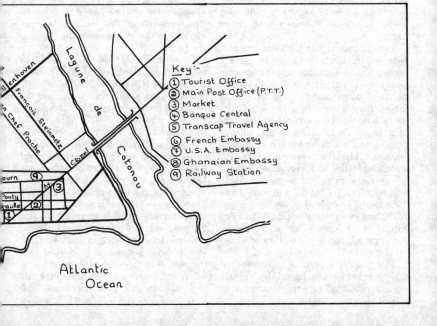

Key:-
1. Tourist Office
2. Main Post Office (P.T.T.)
3. Market
4. Banque Central
5. Transcap Travel Agency
6. French Embassy
7. U.S.A. Embassy
8. Ghanaian Embassy
9. Railway Station

Botswana

Although Tswana peoples had been moving into the watershed of the Limpopo and Shashe since the 18th century, gradually pushing the indigenous Bushmen further north and west, it wasn't until the 1820s that the various clans began to consolidate into a string of nations along what is now the border area between Botswana and South Africa. The change was prompted by the clans' need to defend themselves against the fleeing tide of humanity displaced from the Transvaal and Natal between 1820 and 1840 as a result of Zulu militancy and Boer expansion.

Tswana society was highly structured, each nation being ruled by an hereditary monarch and aristocracy whose economic power was based on the ownership of large herds of cattle and the use of tribute labour. In each one of the eight nations the kings' subjects were compelled to live in centralised towns and satellite villages divided into wards under the control of headmen. The latter were responsible for allocating land and recruiting tribute labour for work on the monarch's fields and pastures. By the second half of the 19th century some of these centralised towns had grown to considerable size. The capital of the Ngwato clan at Shoshong, for example, had a population of about 30,000 by 1860.

The country's borders were secured from further encroachment by various colonisers in 1885 with the declaration of a British protectorate, then known as Bechuanaland. The protectorate was able to retain some degree of economic independence by selling cattle, draught oxen and grain to Europeans streaming north in search of farming land and minerals, but it didn't last long. The construction of a railway through Bechuanaland to Rhodesia and a serious outbreak of rinderpest in the 1890s destroyed the transit trade, and by 1920 the commercial maize farmers in South Africa and Rhodesia were producing grain in such quantities that Botswana no longer had a market.

After that, the country became a labour reservoir for the South African mines and farms with up to a quarter of the entire adult male population away at any one time. The drift south in search of work led to the breakdown of traditional land usage patterns which the aristocrats and a few rich cattle owners were able to turn to their advantage by increasing their areas of cultivation and the size of their herds. The expense of this change was an increase in the gap between the rich and the poor.

Foremost among those who were able to exploit the situation was Tshekedi Khama, the ruler of Ngwato, and it was his son, Seretse Khama, who was to become the country's first president when independence was granted in 1966. Seretse Khama was exiled for six years in the early 1950s by the British authorities for having had the temerity to marry a white woman, but he was later groomed for the presidency by the very same people, being the most moderate of those who aspired to power in the run-up to independence.

Khama was certainly no revolutionary. He guaranteed continued freehold over land held by white ranchers and adopted a strictly neutral stand (at least until near the end of his presidency) over South Africa and Rhodesia. The reason for this was plain to see. Like Swaziland and Lesotho, Botswana was (and still is to a

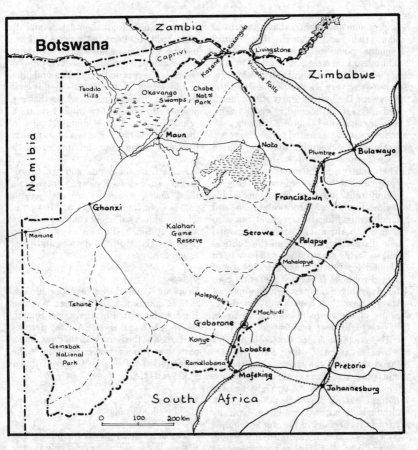

large extent) an economic hostage of South Africa. The wages of Botswana mine workers in South Africa form an important part of the country's income and it is largely dependent on the South African railway system for the transport of its exports to the outside world.

Nevertheless, Khama consistently refused to exchange ambassadors with South Africa and opposed apartheid at various international conferences such as the OAU, UN and Commonwealth. He also had the courage to commit his country to the so-called 'Front Line'

states of Zambia, Tanzania and Mozambique in opposing the Smith regime in Rhodesia. Though he refused to allow the Zimbabwean liberation fighters to set up training camps in Botswana, his vocal support resulted in Rhodesian armed forces 'hot pursuit' raids into the country and the bombing of the Kazangula ferry across the Zambesi River – Botswana's only link with Zambia. (The ferry is again operating). All this took place at a time when Botswana had no army or air force and when a devastating drought had killed off about a third of the national herd.

Economically, things have improved since then and, though the country remains poor, reserves are gradually building up. Seretse Khama died in mid-1980 but his successor, Dr Quett Masire, is pursuing very similar policies and the Botswana Democratic Party still holds 29 of the 32 seats in the country's parliament. As unemployment grows among the country's young educated people, however, strains are developing and there have been serious student demonstrations. The country's problems have also been compounded by the influx of refugees mainly from Zimbabwe (first from Smith's regime, then from Muzorewa's regime and finally from Mugabe's regime) but also from South Africa. The latter are regarded as a disruptive influence on the political and social life of the nation and have been blamed for the increasing incidence of armed robbery. They are presently confined to refugee camps which they may not leave unless they have a job elsewhere. Some of the more disruptive elements have actually been repatriated.

Despite these facets, Botswana remains a peaceful country, which contrasts very favourably with the violence, repression and paranoia so prevalent in its neighbours. The vast majority of travellers have nothing but praise for this country and, although its outback roads are typically African (especially in the wet season), it generates some of the most interesting stories you're likely to come across anywhere on the continent.

FACTS

The bulk of Botswana is semi-desert and scrub inhabited by nomadic groups of Bushmen. Only in the east along the borders with South Africa and Zimbabwe, and in the Okavango Delta north of Maun, is there fertile land with sufficient rainfall for raising crops. It's in these areas that the bulk of the population lives. The climate is hot and dry during the day but cool at night. Most of the rain falls between December and April.

Copper, nickel, cobalt and, less importantly, gold, are mined at Selebe-Phikwe, but the most important source of income is the mining of diamonds. The pipe at Orapa is the second largest diamond pipe in the world; production from this and from the nearby mine at Lethakane amounts to around five million carats a year. The third largest diamond pipe in the world, also in Botswana at Jwaneng, produces some four million carats a year.

Aside from diamonds and the cupronickel at Selebe-Phikwe, Botswana's third major source of mineral wealth comes from the coal mine at Morupule. This produces sufficient coal to power the mines at Selebe-Phikwe as well as to provide electricity for Gaborone and other urban centres.

VISAS

Visas are required by all except nationals of the Commonwealth countries, Western Europe (except Portugal and Spain), South Africa and the USA. Stay permits are issued at the border for 90 days. If you wish to stay longer you must apply to the Immigration & Passport Control Officer, PO Box 942, Gaborone.

MONEY
US$1 = 0.903 pula

The unit of currency is the pula = 100 thebe. There are no restrictions on the import of local currency, but export is limited to 50 pula. There is no black market as such, but you may come across the occasional person who is willing to offer you up to US$1 = 1.25 pula.

HEALTH
Tsetse flies are common in the Okavango Swamps, so take insect repellent and a fly whisk with you. Avoid wearing dark-coloured clothing, as it seems to attract the flies. You can get a checkup for sleeping sickness (which is spread by the tsetse fly) at the hospital in Maun. The

water in the swamps is free of bilharzia and generally safe to drink.

LANGUAGE

English is the official language of the country and the medium of instruction in secondary schools. The most common language, however, which is understood by over 90% of the population and which is the medium of instruction in the primary schools, is Setswana. This is the language of the dominant group – the Tswana – and it's interesting to note that the majority of Tswana speakers live in South Africa, especially in the so-called homeland of Bophuthatswana. Sekalaka is the language of the Kalanga, who are the largest minority group in the country. They live in the north-east in the vicinity of Francistown and are related to the Ndebele people of Zimbabwe.

GETTING THERE & AROUND

You can get into Botswana from Zambia, Zimbabwe and South Africa. Entry from Namibia along the Gobabis-Ghanzi track is considerably more difficult because of the infrequency of transport, but if you do want to go direct between these two countries, then you should seriously consider going via the Caprivi Strip. Much of the road along the Strip is paved, and contrary to what you might hear, this is not a prohibited military area. Refer to the Namibian chapter for details.

Entry from Zambia is via the Kazangula ferry across the Zambesi River. This operates on weekdays only and the customs posts are open from 6 am to 6 pm. The border is closed at weekends so it's pointless to hitch at that time either from Francistown or Maun, as there's no traffic. The ferry is quite an experience. Heavy trucks have to speed on board and come to a sudden halt to provide the ferry with the momentum to break away from the shore. Occasionally a truck will stop a little short or a little long and the whole ferry will flip. Whenever this happens there's quite a mess and a lengthy delay in crossing.

Luckily, it doesn't happen too often. If you're heading north into Zambia, it's possible to pick up South African trucks at Kasane that are going through to Lusaka, Kabwe and Ndola. You cannot change pula into kwacha at the bank in Kasane.

Road

There is a surfaced road all the way from Nata via Francistown, Gaborone and Lobatse to Mafeking, as well as sealed roads from Gaborone to Molepolole and Gaborone to Kanye. Work was also completed recently on surfacing the roads from Nata to Kasane and Nata to Plumtree. The road from Nata to Maun is still a gravel track, but there are plans to surface it within two years. Hitching anywhere along the road between Bulawayo and Mafeking is easy. If you have to pay for lifts, the average price is around 1 pula per 50 km. Gaborone to Francistown should take a day with an early start. There are frequent, privately run minibuses that cover stretches of the main road between Lobatse and Francistown. Lifts with white settlers are usually free, but you should expect to pay black drivers.

Elsewhere in the country there are occasional buses here and there, but generally you'll have to rely on a mixture of cattle trucks, Land-Rovers, supply trucks, mail vans and even planes. Hitching requires a degree of patience and initiative, especially if you're trying to get a ride on a plane. There are quite a few UN agencies, banks and private individuals that operate planes in the more remote areas and you might be offered a ride if they have room. Go out to the airstrip and ask around. Officially, government road vehicles (which have red BX plates) are not supposed to pick up hitch-hikers though many still do, so it's worth checking at the District Council office, the post office or the Central Transport office to see if there's anything going your way. Most Botswana government officials are very helpful about finding lifts for you, especially in the more remote parts of the country. The best way to locate a lift in non-government vehicles is to ask around at trading stores, hotels and among volunteer workers.

Lobatse-Ghanzi-Maun There are beef runs, usually twice a week, from both Maun and Ghanzi to Lobatse. To find a lift in Lobatse, check out the registration numbers of the trucks or ask at the Botswana Meat Corporation. In Ghanzi, the best person to ask is the storekeeper near the Kalahari Arms. Trucks leave Ghanzi on Sundays and Mondays. There's also the faint possibility of getting a lift with the Standard Bank plane which flies up to Ghanzi from Lobatse on Thursday mornings (bank day in Ghanzi).

Between Ghanzi and Maun the most reliable possibility is the mail truck which leaves Maun on Tuesdays and Ghanzi on Thursdays, but there's stiff competition for the five places available. The journey takes about 6½ hours. There are also water trucks on which you might get a lift. Ask at the Central Transport office in either place. Some people have been waiting up to 2½ days for a lift to Ghanzi. For lifts on planes contact Albert Smith at Winnella Airways in Maun.

Lifts west into Namibia from Ghanzi are not that easy to find. There are a few trucks which do the run every week in the dry season, stopping at Kuke overnight and continuing on to Gobabis the next day, but the best place to find them is the Oasis store, as they have a petrol truck which goes to Gobabis every two or three days for supplies. The owner of the Oasis also knows who else is going that way, as he has a two-way radio and everybody stops there for petrol. Afrikaaner farmers go to Gobabis to shop and will usually give you a lift if you ask. The border officials here are very easygoing as virtually no-one uses the crossing. They don't ask for onward tickets or to see how much money you have. Expect delays due to soft sand. There's only one entry/exit point along the whole 1600-km border; it's marked by a high barbed-wire fence.

Francistown-Nata-Maun There are three buses a week in either direction along this stretch, and sometimes more. They generally set off around 11 am. The fare is 16.50 pula and the journey takes about 12 to 16 hours. From Nata they depart at around 3 pm and take about eight hours to Maun. The fare is 11.10 pula. For a lift, ask for Mr Blighaut at the Botswana Game Industries in Francistown or take your chance on the road. Truckies usually ask 10 pula but are sometimes willing to take you for as little as 2 pula. If you're going to be travelling at night on top of a truck, have warm clothes handy. It shouldn't be hard to get a lift as there are about 50 vehicles per day doing this run.

In Maun, the best place to hear about lifts and spare seats on planes to Ghanzi and the Delta is at the Duck Inn restaurant out at the airport.

Maun-Kasane There are usually two to three trucks daily in either direction on weekdays. To find out about them, you need to do the rounds of the council offices in either place at about 8 am and ask if they have anything going. The ride is slow in either direction but even slower from Kasane to Maun, as most tour operators take tours out one way and then fly back. Don't hitch at the weekend, as there will be no traffic (the Kazangula ferry doesn't run at weekends). It's also very difficult to find anything during the wet season and you may well have to go back to Nata or Francistown and then head north up the BOTZAM road to Kasane from there. Again, don't bother hitching along the BOTZAM road at weekends.

Rail

There are both road and rail connections between Botswana and Zimbabwe (Bulawayo-Plumtree-Francistown) and South Africa (Mafeking-Ramatlabama-Gaborone), but the vast majority of travellers take the train. There are two express trains (1st and 2nd classes only) per week in either direction between Bulawayo and Mafeking and one ordinary train (four classes) in either direction daily. 1st class is a reserved sleeping compartment shared with others; 3rd class consists of unreserved sleeping compartments; and 4th class is just rows of wooden benches. There's not a great deal of difference between 3rd and 4th classes. If possible, avoid travelling by train at the end of the month, as miners from Botswana who work in Johannesburg return home on leave at those times and the train will be chock-a-block. During the rest of the month there is usually plenty of room. You need not be at all apprehensive about travelling in 4th class in Botswana.

As in Zimbabwe, fares are based on zones (for more details about this refer to the Zimbabwe chapter), but tickets bought in Botswana are more expensive than those bought in Zimbabwe.

PLACES TO STAY

Most hotels are expensive and you should expect to pay at least 15 pula per night. Some places simply have nowhere cheap to stay, in which case a tent comes in useful. There are hotels in Francistown, Gaborone, Lobatse, Maun, Mahalapye, Mogoditsane, Molepolole, Palapye, Selebe-Phikwe, Serowe, Sherwood Ranch and Tlokweng. Campsites are few and far between and facilities are usually primitive. However, you can camp virtually anywhere – though you should make a point of going to see the village headman before you erect your tent. There is a good possibility that by doing this you will be offered accommodation under a roof somewhere. You may also like to ask around among volunteer workers (Peace Corps, VSO, etc); if you're willing to help out and pay for your keep, they might offer you accommodation. We have had a few irate letters, however, from volunteer workers saying they're getting a bit tired of the constant stream of travellers turning up on their doorsteps and taking it for granted that they'll be offered a place to stay and even a meal. It seems that some travellers have been making too many assumptions, so if you are offered accommodation then please put back as much as you take out, if not more.

FRANCISTOWN

One of the cheapest places to stay here is the campsite at the *Marang Hotel* about six km out of town. It costs 5 pula per site and the charge includes hot showers and the use of the swimming pool. The hotel itself is very pricey. In the centre of town is the *Tati Hotel*, opposite the train station, which charges 35 pula a double (though you can sometimes bargain this down to 25 pula, or 5 pula per person to camp in the back garden). Also in the centre is the *Grand Hotel*, which has similar prices (though here again you can sometimes get a 12-pula single in which two of you can sleep with one on the floor). The Grand is an expatriate hang-out in the evenings. If you're very short of funds you could sleep at the railway station or the police station – no problems.

' If you're looking for lifts south, ask at Guys & Gals clothing store. The truckie who makes the deliveries here does a weekly Francistown-Gaborone-Johannesburg-Maseru run and will usually take passengers free. If you're hitching to Maun you must walk out to the airport turnoff. There is a tree there where the locals wait for the buses and trucks. Most potential lifts won't stop before they get there. Very few lifts will be free, and you'll have to argue about the price.

GABORONE

The **museum** in Gaborone is interesting and worth a visit, as is the excellent **basket store** (the only one) on the square. The work is nice and the pieces are sold according to size.

Most of the hotels here cost 30 to 40 pula per night, though you can get a room at the *Gaborone Hotel*, opposite the railway station, for 19.50 pula a single and 30 pula a double with shared toilets. The

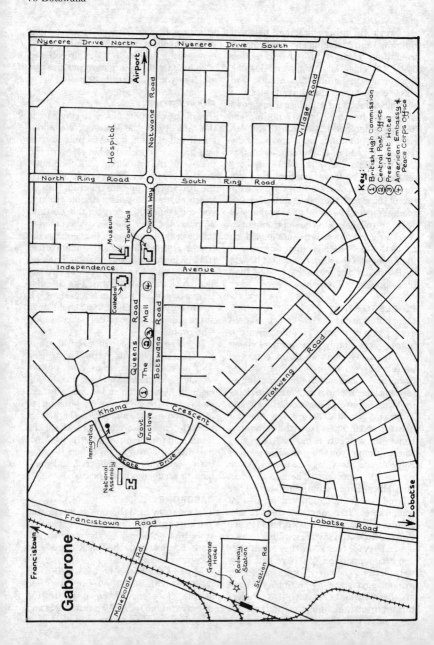

Mago Hotel is even cheaper but it has the disadvantage of being 10 km out of town (a taxi there costs 2-3 pula but there's also a bus for 25 thebe). It's also worth checking out the *Botswana Nurses Association Hostel* opposite the Holiday Inn. You can get a double room here for 10 pula. Some travellers have managed to find a place to sleep with the International Voluntary Sevice, for 2 pula per night. There are also hostels for the Dutch and Canadian volunteers where you might be offered somewhere to stay. One of the best places to meet volunteers here is the bar of the *Holiday Inn* in the evenings. You can also try the balcony of the *President Hotel* overlooking The Mall. If you are short of cash and won't be staying, you can sleep at the railway station without any problems.

For a good meal go to the *Georgina in the Village* restaurant which has been recommended.

GHANZI

The only place to stay in Ghanzi is the *Kalahari Arms Hotel*. A room is very expensive here, but they will let you camp on the grass at the back for 1 pula a night including the use of hot showers. The people are very friendly. They also have relatively cheap rondavel accommodation at the back of the hotel.

KASANE

The best place to stay here is the *Chobe Safari Lodge*, which has a beautiful setting and a campsite costing 5 pula per person per night, but the facilities are nothing special.

MAUN

Riley's Hotel costs 28 pula per night including a 'miserable' breakfast. It is also a popular expatriate hang-out. Camping at *Le Bistrot* just past Riley's used to be possible, but the site is now closed. However, Le Bistrot is a popular hang-out for expatriates, serves good food, and the proprietors, Bernard and Carolynne, are very friendly. Another good place to eat in Maun is the *Paradise Café* behind the GPO. A meat meal here will cost 1 pula.

Many people prefer to head out to one of the three lodges in the Okavango Swamps (about 13 km from Maun), where you can also camp for 1.50 pula per night. If you're looking for a lift out there, ask the woman at *Xaxaba Safaris* for help. It is possible to get out to camps deep inside the delta very cheaply in supply planes, but it's all a question of luck. Try contacting June Leversedge of *Travel Wild* opposite the airport. The *Duck Inn* restaurant at the airport is also an expatriate hang-out and a good place to hear about lifts.

SEROWE

Stay at the *Coop Hotel* here (run by the Brigades – a local cooperative organisation). It's basic and clean and also offers meals. The food is plain but the helpings are large.

GAME RESERVES & NATIONAL PARKS
Okavango Swamps

This area north-west of Maun is really beautiful and abounds with birdlife and other game including elephant, zebra, buffalo, wildebeeste, giraffe, hippo and kudu. You haven't seen Botswana until you've been here. The Swamps are actually the inland delta of the Okavango River, which originates in the mountains of western Angola and eventually spills out over the northern plateau of Botswana. The cone-shaped delta covers an area of over 15,000 square km and is the largest inland delta in the world. The river annually brings more than two million tonnes of sand and silt into the delta, yet less than 3% of the water emerges at the other end to either flood Lake Ngami or cross another 500 km of the Kalahari to enter Lake Xau and the Makgadikgadi Pans.

There are few mosquitoes and tsetse flies around the camps near Maun, but further into the delta they can become unbearable (except in the dry season), so take insect repellent with you and a fly swat to keep them at bay. The bite of the tsetse fly is painful but it doesn't usually itch afterwards like a mosquito bite.

The best time to visit the Swamps is between October and February for big game and between May and August for birdlife, but the camps close down during December and throughout most of January. The area is a national park and entry costs 5 pula per day.

The three lodges closest to Maun are *Island Safaris, Okavango River Lodge* and *Crocodile Camp.* They're all close to each other, about 13 km from Maun, and you shouldn't have any trouble getting out there as there are Land-Rovers to and from Maun every day. Although everyone has their own favourite, consensus favours Island Safaris and Okavango River Lodge. The former has a swimming pool and films on Wednesdays, Thursdays, Saturdays and Sundays, while the latter probably has the best food. All three provide meals at reasonable prices. The rooms in the lodges themselves are fairly plush, but you can also camp at any one of them for 1.50 pula per night. Rooms at Island Safaris cost 40 pula a single and 45 pula a double for bed and breakfast. Okavango River Lodge is under new management (late 1984) and conveniently situated next to the friendly local village. We've had a few complaints about Joey Graham who, with her husband Tony, own Island Safaris. It seems she's somewhat neurotic, racist in attitude and goes out of her way to make backpackers unwelcome since they don't fit her image of acceptable guests. It also seems she treats local people who work there with contempt and confiscates any tips they make from makuru trips. The owners of Crocodile Camp have come in for the same criticism in the past.

If you decide not to stay at one of these camps but would like to arrange a trip into the delta, contact Sue at *Maun Office Services* and Peter or Russel at *Bushman Curio Shop*, both on the main street in Maun near Barclays Bank.

All three lodges have their own smaller camps further into the swamps where they take visitors on safari. These safaris can be quite expensive, so if you have limited funds, you'll have to content yourself with hiring a *makuru* (canoe) with a poler for two or three days. A good place to enquire is the bottle shop in the village (next to Island Safaris) which should be cheap and where you can be sure that the money you pay goes directly to the local people. On the other hand, some travellers have suggested that cheapest is not best. One traveller who paid for a return flight and a dugout and poler for a day saw virtually nothing but 'reeds, reeds and more reeds.' The going rate for a makuru and poler hired from one of the camps is now 16 pula per day, including the poler's food but not your own. One traveller who spoke to the local people employed by Island Safaris discovered that only 3 pula of this is actually paid to them plus a bag of meali-meal and a can of corned beef. This food is supposed to last them for up to seven days. There is a choice between wooden makurus which take two people in addition to the poler, and fibreglass makurus which cost the same but will take three people and a poler. You might possibly be able to get a makuru for less than this – ask the man who watches the main gate at Crocodile Camp.

If your time is limited or you have no cash problems, it's worth checking out the safaris to **Moremi Wildlife Reserve** offered by the Bushman Curio Shop in Maun beside Barclays Bank. If you take one of these the charges are: return flight (Maun to the Swamps) 60 pula; dugout and poler 20 pula per day; transport from the airstrip to the campsite 5 pula; camping 2 pula per person per night; boatman's camping fees 0.80 pula per night; entrance to Moremi 10 pula per person plus 1 pula for the dugout. Food costs extra and you're advised to take your own. This works out at 125 pula per person for a four-day safari (the dugouts will take up to four people).

You can sometimes get what amounts to a free safari if one of the lodges is moving its overnight safari stop camps – this sometimes happens when either the water gets too low or the swamps flood. They often appreciate help at these times and will take you along for just the cost of your food.

In addition to the lodges mentioned above, there are also some more expensive camps deep in the swamps (such as *Xaxaba Camp*) which visitors normally fly to but which you can get to by makuru in three days from Crocodile Camp – though you won't save that much by going this way. The flights take half an hour and cost 130 pula per plane (or 65 pula per plane if they're also delivering supplies). If you're thinking of staying at Xaxaba Camp, you'll be up for around US$100 per night, all included, but that doesn't mean you necessarily have to stay there. You can take off straight away with a makuru and poler for 16 pula per day (includes the poler's food) plus 1.60 pula per makuru park entry fee, plus 10 pula per week park entry fee per person (or 5 pula per day) and 2 pula camping fees per night. On the other hand, Xaxaba are thinking of combining these rates and the flight costs into an overall package.

Flights over the swamps are available from Maun for US$180 per person in the high season and US$130 per person in the low season – these are return fares. The flights last one hour and are worth every dollar. You can also get a flight from Maun to Chief's Island for 25 pula, one way.

One more place which travellers have recommended is the *Shakawe Fishing Lodge*, where you can camp for 5 pula per night – well worth it for the fantastic location by the river and the only place where you can get a cold beer.

Todilo Hills

These are situated north of the Okavango Swamps up against the border with the Caprivi Strip (Namibia) and are well worth a visit if you have the time and a vehicle. Scattered around here are tribes of Bushmen and many beautiful examples of their cave paintings. Getting here from Maun usually takes at least one fairly long and rough day's journey. Take your own food and water.

Chobe National Park

It's virtually impossible to see this park – or the interesting Xau and Makgadikgadi Pans further south near Nata – without your own four-wheel-drive vehicle. These are not easy to find and are expensive to hire, but you could try *Ad Vriend* in Francistown, who hire Toyota Land Cruisers for 200 pula per week with unlimited mileage. Entry to the Chobe National Park costs 10 pula per week and there's a campsite for 2 pula per night but the only facility is running water. No food is available.

OTHER

Mochudi, the regional capital of the Kgableng tribe north of Gaborone, is an interesting town to visit. It has a good museum – **Phuthadikabo Museum** – which chronicles the history of the Kgableng people. Chief Linchwe II appears to be keeping up his father's campaign to have the dreaded weed legalised (the colonial administration banned it).

If you are interested in indigenous weaving, the Lentswe-La-Udi weavers, some 15 km north of Gaborone, are worth visiting.

Gantsicraft was started up in 1983 as an outlet and training centre for local craft-workers in the Ghanzi area. It was originally administered by a volunteer worker and is a non-profit organisation, all the proceeds on sales going back to those who bring in crafts for sale. A 10% surcharge on articles under 20 pula or a 2-pula surcharge on articles over that covers rent and administrative costs. Because of this, you can pick up traditional craftwork at one-third to one-half the selling price of similar articles in Maun or Gaborone. Gantsicraft offer a wide range of crafts including dyed textile work, decorated bags (4-9 pula), hunting sets (8-15 pula), skirts (12-20 pula), bead or ostrich shell necklaces (2-4 pula), karosses, mats and headgear. The craftshop is situated between the Kalahari Arms Hotel and the post office in Ghanzi.

Burkina Faso

Burkina Faso (or Upper Volta as it was known as until mid-1984) is one of the world's poorest countries and seems locked into a vicious circle which is destined to keep it that way. Not only is much of the land infertile, 'aid' organisations seem unwilling to finance projects appropriate to basic local needs. Instead, they insist on the cultivation of cash crops – principally cotton – which further impoverishes the soil, reduces the amount of land available for food production and does nothing to lay the basis for a more viable rural economy. Most of the country's basic food needs have to be imported. Added to this, Burkina Faso suffered disastrously from the Sahel droughts of the 1970s during which at least a third of the country's livestock perished. Another factor which contributes to its under-development is a long history of labour migration to Ghana and the Ivory Coast. At any particular time the majority of the country's young men will be away working on the plantations and in the factories of those two countries. While this has greatly benefitted the economies of the recipient states, the destructive effects are plainly visible in Burkina Faso.

About half of the population belong to the Mossi tribe whose ancestors were responsible for setting up a number of centralised kingdoms in the area from the 15th century onwards. The most important of these were at Ouagadougou and Ouahigouya, whose kings exercised considerable influence over the course of politics right up to independence. Ouagadougou was taken by the French in 1896 and its king was forced to take refuge in Dagomba country. Only in 1947 were the borders of the country finally defined. Between WW I and WW II, the French colonial authorities put into operation a system of forced labour recruitment among the Mossi to supply the European-owned plantations in the Ivory Coast. The system was abolished in principle by the late 1040s but continued in practice under another name right up to independence in 1960. In order to escape forced recruitment, many preferred to make their way to Ghana; but what awaited them there was in many ways no better than what the Ivory Coast had in store. Instead of being exploited by French plantation owners, the Mossi found themselves exploited by the British counterparts.

When independence was granted in 1960 the first president was Maurice Yameogo, one of the principal figures in national politics since the end of WW II. Though re-elected with an overwhelming majority in 1965, Yameogo's increasingly autocratic style of government and his mismanagement of the economy resulted in his overthrow in a military coup led by Lieutenant-Colonel Sangoule Lamizana in 1966. The military remained in power for four years and was gradually able to put the economy onto a healthier footing. Many of these gains, however, were frittered away by political in-fighting during the four years of civilian government from 1970 to 1974, and the army once again intervened.

Another attempt at civilian government followed a period of military rule, and this was followed by a mixed civilian and military government. One of the most powerful lobbies in the country is the trade unions, which have forced the military to compromise on more than one occasion.

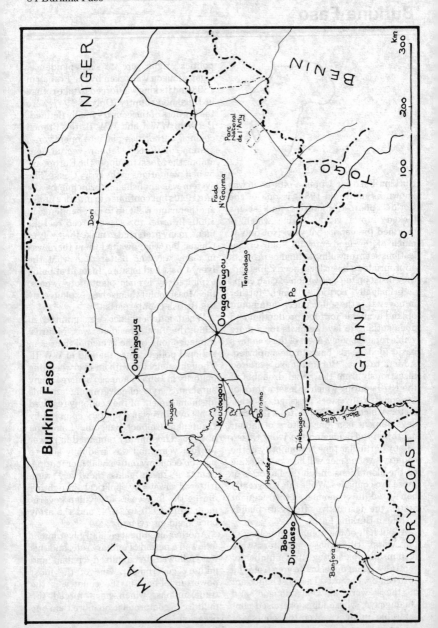

There was recently another military coup, this time headed by Captain Thomas Sankara, but it's too early to say what effect it will have on the country.

FACTS

Much of northern Burkina Faso lies in the Sahel, the fringe of the Sahara desert, where the land gradually dries out into scrub and semi-desert. Only in the south are there significant areas of wooded savannah. Three rivers – the Black, White and Red Voltas – water the plains but settlement in the valleys is very limited because of the incidence of river blindness and malaria. There is a short rainy season between March and April, particularly in the south-west, with the long rains from June to October. From November to mid-February it is cool and dry. Despite the infertility of much of the land, Burkina Faso is one of the most densely populated of the Sahel countries with over 5½ people.

The ancient Mossi kindgoms were effective in resisting the spread of Islam in this area so that today some 65% of the population still follow traditional beliefs. Only some 30% are Moslem.

VISAS

Visas are required by all except nationals of Belgium, France, Germany (West), Italy, Luxembourg and the Netherlands. Visit visas valid for eight days are available to most nationalities and can be obtained either from a Burkina Faso embassy (there are very few of these) or from French embassies (in countries where there are no Burkina Faso consular representatives). Visas usually take 24 hours to issue but in some places can be obtained while you wait.

Exit permits are no longer required.

Benin visas There is no Benin embassy in Ouagadougou and you cannot get a Benin visa at the French embassy, so plan ahead.

Ghana visas Ghanaian visas cost 1000 CFA and take between two and three weeks to issue. They're easier to get in either Abidjan or Lomé.

MONEY

US$1 = 460 CFA
£1 = 550 CFA

The unit of currency is the CFA franc. There are no restrictions on the import or export of local currency.

The airport departure tax is 2500 CFA.

LANGUAGE

French is the official language. The main African languages are More (spoken by the Mossi), Dioula and Gourmantche.

GETTING THERE & AROUND
Air

Burkina Faso, like the Central African Republic, is served by the air charter company *Point Air Mulhouse*, usually known simply as *Le Point*. This company offers the cheapest flights to and from Europe. The flights operate on a weekly basis between Lyon (France) and Ouagadougou and between Lyon and Bangui. The fare between Lyon and Ouagadougou is about US$200 one way and US$320 return (the exact amount depends on which currency you are using and what the prevailing rates of exchange are). Point Air Mulhouse is a travel club so you have to add about US$12 to the fare to cover membership. It's usually necessary to book a month in advance, but you can do this by phone or telex. The company's headquarters are at Point Air Mulhouse, 4 Rue des Orphelins, 68200 Mulhouse, France (tel 89 42 44 61). Its office in Ouagadougou is in the *Hotel Independence* (tel 34186) and the mailing address is BP 127.

Road

Hitching is slow and many of the roads are poor, though there are a couple of good stretches from Ouagadougou to the Ivory Coast and from Ouagadougou to Togo. The road south to Ghana is also in reasonable shape. Regular buses link all the major towns and there are plenty of Peugeot taxis available.

Ouagadougou-Niamey (Niger) In the dry season there are daily trucks for 7500 CFA which normally take about 24 hours but can take two days. There are also buses which leave on Monday, Wednesday and Friday around 11.30 am (or when full) and cost 6100 CFA. They take a full day. You need to book the bus in advance, as there is a lot of competition for seats. The road between these two places can be closed for long periods of time during the wet season, when a series of rain barriers are erected after heavy rain to let the road dry out before traffic is allowed to pass along it.

Bobo Dioulasso-Bamako (Mali) Taxis cost 8000 CFA and can take up to 19 hours, though mostly the ride doesn't take more than 12 hours. The delays are due to road blocks, of which there up to 18! It's a rough road. If you're merely going from point A to B and have spare cash, it's worth considering the *Air Volta* flight which, with student discount, costs 12,000 CFA.

Bobo Dioulasso-Mopti (Mali) A taxi-broussee costs 7500 CFA and takes 10 hours. There are some 18 police checks en route.

Ouagadougou-Lomé(Togo) There is a good paved road all the way from Ouagadougou to Lomé and hitching is easy. A truck will cost 9000 CFA and take about 22 hours. A Peugeot taxi will cost 11,000 CFA and take less time. There are heavy searches at the border. In the opposite direction a taxi will cost 10,000 CFA but it's much cheaper to get a taxi first to Dapango for 3250 CFA followed by another from there to Ouagadougou for 3000 CFA. You need

to get up early (around 6 am) if you're doing the journey in stages.

Ouagadougou-Ghana Taxis don't go over the border but they'll nevertheless attempt to charge you for the journey as far as Bolgatanga. You should pay around 3000 CFA as far as the border. Buy cedis (Ghanaian currency) at the border. There are Ghana state transport buses from the border to Tamale. It's possible to do this in one day – 7 am to 10 pm.

Rail The timetable is the same as the one for the Ivory Coast.

BANFORA
Banfora is situated in a particularly beautiful area of Burkina Faso. You shouldn't miss the **Cascades** about five km from town.

You can sometimes get a room at the *Maison de Jeunes*. Otherwise, try *La Comoe*, which has pleasant rooms for 2000 CFA. You can also camp at the Cascades.

BOROMO
The best place to stay in this town, which is about halfway between Ouagadougou and Bobo Dioulasso, is *Le Campement*. It's good value at 1500 CFA a room and includes a shower and a fan when the generator is running.

BOBO DIOULASSO
This is Burkina Faso's second largest city. The cheapest place to stay here and one which has been popular for many years is the *Foyer de Scouts*, just off the Avenue Guimba Oatara, Quartier Coco. It costs 450 CFA per person in rooms containing four bunk beds. If you arrive by train it's best to take a taxi here as it's a long walk. The *Mission Protestante* also has very clean and quiet rooms for 1500 CFA. The Mission is past the market on the right-hand side near the Hotel de la Paix. Moving up in price a little, there is *Hotel Handabaye*, Rue Alphamdi Dienego

between the Avenue de la République and the Avenue de la Liberté just round the corner from the Gare Routiere, which costs CFA 3000 a double with shower and fan or CFA 3500 a double with shower, toilet and fan. Nearby is the *Hotel de la Paix* just off the Avenue de la République which costs 2000 CFA a single and 3500 CFA a double. Also in the same price bracket is the *Hotel du Palais*. For somewhere even better, try the *Mission Catholique* which costs 4000 CFA a double in clean, quiet rooms with shower and mosquito nets. Meals are available – three-course dinner for 500 CFA. There is a lounge and library and plenty of ice-cold drinks and beer.

Good food is available at the *Café Metropole* next door to the Hotel Handabaye.

Wherever you stay for the night, you must report to Sureté to have your passport stamped. Sureté is on the Avenue Ponty south-west of the market, but there's no sign so you'll have to ask.

The Gare Routiere is on the Avenue de la République north-east of the market.

OUAGADOUGOU

The capital of Burkina Faso, Ouagadougou has a long history as the centre of one of the Mossi kingdoms which was founded in the 15th century. It's worth visiting the **Ethnography Museum** while you are here, as it has an excellent collection of Mossi artifacts. Entry costs 100 CFA.

The Tourist Office is in the foyer of the Hotel Independence, Avenue Quezzin Coulibaly at the junction with Avenue de l'Independence. Point Air Mulhouse also has its office here. Maps of Burkina Faso can be obtained from the Institute du Géographique for 2500 CFA.

Sureté is on the Avenue de l'Independence at Rue Galleni about 100 metres from the Hotel de l'Independence.

The poste restante here charges 150 CFA per letter collected.

It's advisable to keep any camera you have in its case and out of sight unless you're sure that it's OK. Curfews are common so make enquiries.

Places to Stay & Eat

If there is room, you may be able to stay free at the *Casse de Passage des Voluntaires de Progres* (the French VSO). It's on Route de Ouahigouya, which is a continuation of the Avenue Yatenga on our map of the city, behind *Le Natinga Bar*. Tell them you are a VSO if they ask. Another popular place to stay is the *Sougu Noma* (formerly the Hotel La Réfuge) on the Avenue Yennenga near the large mosque about 1½ km from the railway station. It's not particularly clean (in fact, there are times when it gets plain filthy), but you can get a bed here for 1500 CFA. If you don't like the look of it then try the *Restaurant Rialle* a few blocks past the Sougu Noma. It has a few rooms for 1700 CFA per room (sleeps up to six people) or 600 CFA each if you are alone or just two people. You can also buy cheap food here. Similar to the Rialle is the *Bar Royale*. This has a few rooms for 500 CFA. The *Hotel Royale*, opposite the Grande Marche, has quite pleasant rooms for 1500 CFA a single. Two others which have been suggested are the *Hotel Entente* at 2000 CFA a single, and the *Hotel Delwende* which costs 3000 CFA with fan or 4000 CFA with air-conditioning. The latter has an attached bar. Down the Avenue Yennenga about one block past the *Hotel Idéal* are several un-named cheapies (un-named because they don't have enough rooms to require being registered as an hotel). The average cost of these is 2000 CFA a double.

You can camp at *Ouaga Camping* on bus route No 4 for 1500 CFA per person. It's a very good place and run by friendly people.

A little upmarket are the *Pavilion Vert*, which costs 2500 CFA per person; and the *Hotel Yennenga*, Avenue Yennenga, which costs 2500 CFA a single, 3000 CFA a double with fan and shower, 4000 CFA a double with shower and air-conditioning

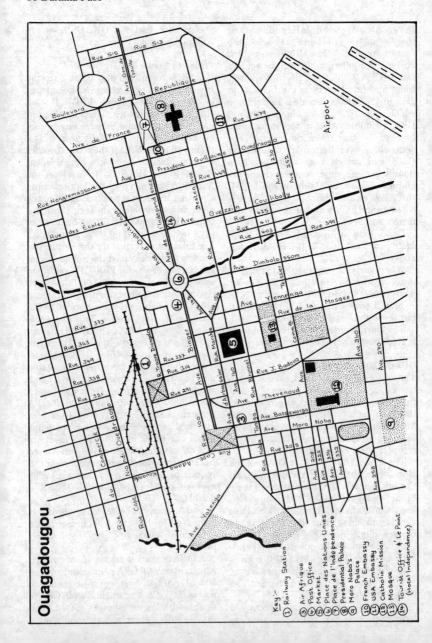

Ouagadougou

Key:-
1. Railway Station
2. Air Afrique
3. Post Office
4. Market
5. Place des Nations Unies
6. Place de l'Independence
7. Presidential Palace
8. Moro Naba's Palace
9. Moro Naba Palace
10. French Embassy
11. USA Embassy
12. Catholic Mission
13. Mosque
14. Tourist Office & Le Point (Hotel Independence)

and 4500 CFA a double with shower, toilet and air-conditioning. The *Hotel Idéal*, Avenue Yennenga near the Sougu Noma, has doubles with air-conditioning and private bath between 4000 CFA and 5000 CFA. Similar in price is the *Hotel de l'Amite*, Avenue Yennenga 400 metres south of the mosque, which costs 3500-4000 CFA a double with fan and shower or 4500 CFA a double with shower and air-conditioning. If you're alone the rooms are 500 CFA less. There's also the considerably more expensive *Hotel Central*, Rue de la Chance on the north-west corner of the market, which normally costs 8000 CFA a single and 9000 CFA a double, but if you have a Point Air Mulhouse ticket then it's 4500 CFA and 5500 CFA respectively. *Hotel Wenud Kunni* has also been recommended. It's a little way out of town but is fairly cheap and has pleasant rooms.

Some good cheap places to eat in Ouagadougou include *La Fourchette Ombu*, Rue Brunnel (very cheap meals – steak for as little as 125 CFA); *Roti Volta*, near the market; *Le Soir Au Village*, about 100 metres down the same street as the Yennenga (big choice, good prices); *L'Escale*, Avenue Yennenga (good food, cold beers – beer is cheap in Bourkinafasso, 130 CFA a bottle); *Café de la Paix*, one block east of the Grand Marche (good food and snacks, salads for 300 CFA), and the *Restaurant du Gare* next to the bus station (*riz gras* for 150 CFA). Another popular place is *Don Camillo* which has steak, chips and salad for 800 CFA.

For an entertaining evening try *Le Maxim* night club or one of the cheaper places, but think twice about the Ghanaian hookers. Locally the 'drips' is known as 'Ghanarrohoea.' If you want to use a swimming pool go to the *RAN Hotel*. It costs 700 CFA on weekdays and 1000 CFA at weekends.

Taxis around town cost 200 CFA per journey.

Burundi

This small but beautiful mountainous country sandwiched between Tanzania and Zaire with magnificent views over Lake Tanganyika has had a stormy history full of tribal wars and factional struggles between the ruling families, complicated by colonisation first by the Germans and later by the Belgians.

The original inhabitants of the area, the Twa pygmies, were gradually displaced from about 1000 AD onwards by migrating Hutu farmers who now make up some 85% of the country's population. In the 17th century, however, migrating Tutsi from Ethiopia and Uganda consolidated their hold on the country and forced the Hutu into economic subjection by introducing a system of feudal land tenure and cattle clientage. By the 19th century the Tutsi had become a loosely organised aristocracy and, although there was a nominal king (the Mwami), in practice the royal princes enjoyed autonomy in their own fiefdoms. Under such a system there was, naturally, a good deal of rivalry between the ruling families.

At the end of the 19th century, Burundi came under the control of the Germans along with Rwanda, but the country was so thinly garrisoned that the Belgians were easily able to oust the Germans during WW II. After the war, the League of Nations mandated the two territories to Belgium. The Belgians ruled indirectly through the Tutsi chiefs and princes, granted a monopoly in education to the Christian missions and set up coffee plantations (coffee is still the country's major export). These colonial policies exaggerated the strains between the two ethnic groups, the Tutsi and Hutu. The Tutsi chiefs were granted wide-ranging powers to recruit labour and raise taxes, powers they were not averse to abusing whenever it suited them. At the same time, the missions concentrated on educating the Tutsi and virtually ignored the Hutu. These developments together with the concentration of wealth derived from coffee in the hands of an urban Tutsi elite resulted in an ever-widening social division.

In the late 1950s a nationalist organisation based on unity between the two tribes was founded under the leadership of the Mwami's eldest son, Prince Rwagasore, but in the run-up to independence the prince was assassinated with the backing of the local Belgian hierarchy who feared their commercial interests would be threatened if he came to power. His assassination provided a convenient pretext for Tutsi fanatics to purge the party of its Hutu representatives.

The early post-independence governments were crippled by rivalry and suspicion and although the Mwami, as head of state, attempted to balance the distribution of power between Tutsi and Hutu, he refused to appoint a Hutu prime minister when candidates of that tribe collected the majority of the votes in the 1964 election. Hutu frustration boiled over a year later in an attempted coup staged by Hutu military and political figures, but it failed and the Mwami fled to Switzerland. A wholesale purge of Hutu from the army and bureaucracy followed, but in 1972 there was a large-scale Hutu uprising in which around 1000 Tutsi were killed. The Tutsi military junta, which had taken over in 1966, responded with what was nothing less than selected genocide.

Any Hutu who had received formal education was rooted out and shot. Some 200,000 lost their lives and well over 100,000 refugees fled to Tanzania. Those refugees are still there and unlikely to return in the near future. Attempts have been made since then by the government to remove some of the main causes of inter-tribal conflict but they've been very half-hearted.

FACTS

Due to its mountainous terrain, much of the country has a mild, pleasant climate with an average temperature of 20°C except on the shores of Lake Tanganyika and along the River Ruzi, where it is hot and humid. The dry season runs from June to September with another short dry spell in December and January. The population of just over four million consists of about 80% Hutu, 15% Tutsi and about 1% Twa pygmies. Europeans – mainly Belgians – number some 6000. About half of the population is Christian (mainly Catholic) while the rest follow traditional beliefs. Communications are poor and only a very small part of the road network is surfaced.

VISAS

Visas are required by all. Nationals of South Africa are not admitted. If you arrive at Bujumbura airport without a visa you're liable to be deported on the same or the next available international flight regardless of its destination, so make sure you get a visa beforehand. On the other hand, we had a report recently which said that two-day transit visas can be obtained on arrival by boat. They cost BFr 300 and take two days to issue. Immigration keeps your passport until the visa is issued. One-month visas cost BFr 1000 and require three photos.

Rwanda visas In Bujumbura visas cost BFr 1000 and take 48 hours to issue. They're valid for two weeks from the date of issue.

Tanzanian visas Avoid getting these in Bujumbura if at all possible. They cost BFr 300 and require two photos and a letter of recommendation from your own embassy, and they keep your passport for one week! The embassy is opposite the post office. Letters of recommendation from the British consul (next to the Librarie Biblique) cost BFr 300.

Zaire visas Single-entry visas valid for a stay of up to three months cost BFr 1790 plus a letter of recommendation from your own embassy. A multiple-entry visa costs BFr 2090. Be warned, however, that the embassy staff are very unfriendly and unhelpful and may refuse to give you more than 15 days initially. Also, if you're travelling on a British passport you can expect difficulties getting the letter of recommendation. The honorary consul in Bujumbura is a Belgian with an oversized ego who isn't going to lift a finger if he can help it to assist 'riff-raff' like travellers. Be persistent and expect to pay BFr 300 for the letter.

MONEY
US$1 = BFr 125

The unit of currency is the Burundi franc (BFr) = 100 centimes. There are no limits on the import of local currency but export is limited to BFr 2000. There is a very open black market where you can get US$1 = BFr 140 (sometimes 160) depending on who you change with and how much you change. Dealers will sometimes take traveller's cheques (BFr 140) as well as cash but they're harder to find. You can also buy the currency of neighbouring countries at good rates. Tanzanian shillings, for example, can be bought in the market at Bujumbura at the rate of US$1 = Tan Sh 80 with Indian traders, though the usual rate is Tan Sh 75.

There are large commissions charged for changing traveller's cheques in some banks – up to BFr 100 plus 6½% – so make

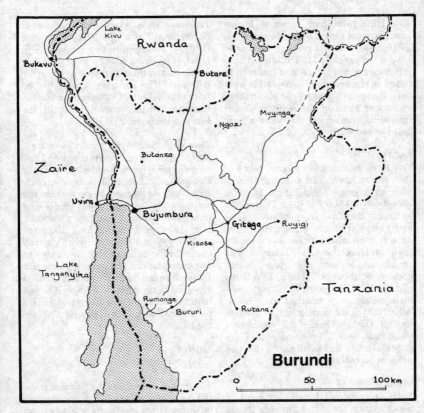

Burundi

0   50   100km

---

sure you change at the Banque de la République du Burundi or at the airport in Bujumbura where no commission is charged. It's possible to buy hard currency at the Banque Commerciale du Burundi, but commission is charged and you must know someone who has an account there.

The airport departure tax is BFr 1000.

LANGUAGE
French and Kirundi.

GETTING THERE & AROUND
Public transport has finally become a reality in Burundi and the minibuses are new, clean and in good working order. Roads are generally in pretty bad shape – dusty or muddy depending on the season, and pot-holed – but there are good sealed roads from Bujumbura to Kigoma (Tanzania) and Kigali (Rwanda). Recent travellers have warned that it's virtually impossible to get overland into Tanzania as there's so little traffic. Much the same applies going to Rwanda. First take an early morning bus to Kayanza (BFr 300) and then a *matatu* (share-taxi) to the border (BFr 100). After that the wait begins! You may be lucky and get a ride from the border to Butare but you'll most likely have to negotiate a price with a truck passing through or with a local motorcyclist

who will take you there for RFr 500! You can, of course, walk–it's beautiful walking country.

The best point of entry is from Bukavu (Zaire) to Bujumbura via Uvira on Lake Tanganyika. There are trucks from the Marche Mama Mobutu in Bukavu to Uvira for Z30 which take about five hours with many stops en route.

Note This road loops briefly into Rwanda and although only a few km are involved, you must have a transit visa for Rwanda. If you haven't, then it's going to be an expensive day because the Rwandan border officials will demand up to RFr 500 or, if you have no Rwandan francs, up to US$10 (The charge varies between US$7 and $10.) Since you also leave Zaire and then, you'll need a multiple entry visa for Zaire.

Get all this sorted out before you set off. From Uvira to the border there are taxis for Z10. Crossing the border is no major hassle but the officials are liable to ask a lot of questions and will want to see how much money you have. From the border to Bujumbura there are vans for BFr 100 which stop en route to give you a chance to change money.

Bujumbura-Nyanza Lac There are buses along this route for BFr 400 but you can also hitch. This is part of what has become a very popular way of getting into Tanzania.

Lake Tanganyika Ferry Service
The main ferry service is operated by Société Nationale des Chemins de Fer Zairois (SNCZ) which connects Zaire, Burundi, Tanzania and Zambia. There are two boats which service the lake ports, the *MV Liemba* and the *Mwongozo*. The former is the more comfortable boat though it's the oldest. The *Liemba* departs Kigoma on Sunday at 10 pm, arrives Bujumbura on Monday at 7.30 am, departs at 5 pm, arrives Kigoma on Tuesday at 8 am, and departs on Wednesday at 4 pm, after which it calls at all ports further south during Thursday and arrives at Mpulungu on Friday at 8 am. It departs Mpulungu on Friday at 5 pm and then calls at all ports going north, arriving in Kigoma on Sunday at noon. The timetable for the *Mwongozo* is the reverse of that for the *Liemba*. It leaves Mpulungu on Tuesday, arrives at Kigoma on Thursday, leaves Kigoma on Thursday afternoon and arrives Bujumbura on Friday morning. It then leaves Bujumbura either on Friday afternoon or early Saturday and arrives in Kigoma the following morning. It leaves Kigoma on Sunday evening and arrives at Mpulungu on Tuesday morning.

The fares from Bujumbura to Kigoma are BFr 1840 (1st class), BFr 1480 (2nd class) and BFr 745 (3rd class). From Bujumbura to Mpulungu the fares are BFr 8000 (1st class), BFr 4000 (2nd class) and BFr 2013 (3rd class). First class is a two-berth cabin, 2nd class is a four-berth cabin and 3rd class is the deck. In Bujumbura tickets for the boat can be bought from Sonaco, Rue des Usines off the Boulevard du 1er Novembre (near the Boulevard du Port). If you're heading for Zambia then you can reduce the cost of this trip considerably by initially only buying a 3rd-class ticket as far as Kigoma (Tanzania) with Burundi francs. On arrival in Kigoma, get off the boat, go through Tanzanian customs and immigration and then buy another ticket (this time in Tanzanian shillings) from the shipping agent at the railway station about 100 metres from the port. This way the cost works out at around US$7.50 instead of US$30. You can't buy a ticket on the ferry itself if there is a company office or agency in the port where you boarded the ferry. You won't encounter this problem if you're heading north from Zambia because there's no ticket office in Mpulungu, so you might as well buy a ticket for the whole journey in Mpulungu on the ferry itself. However, you can only pay in Tanzanian shillings or in Burundi francs. Remember that there is a BFr 200 departure tax from Burundi.

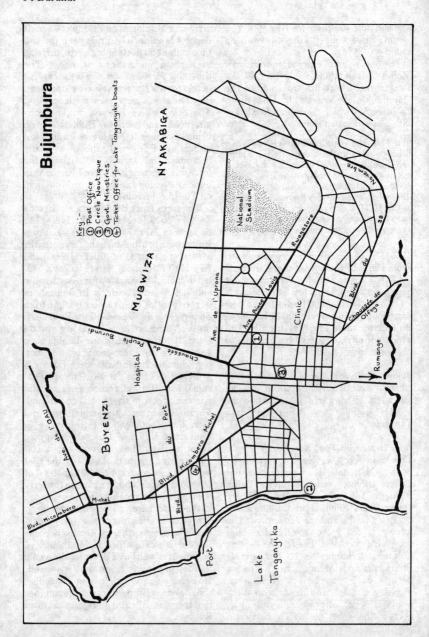

Bujumbura

If you don't want to get off the boat at Kigoma and hassle around for another ticket, go to Kigoma via Nyanza Lac (see below).

Third class on the *MV Liemba* isn't usually overcrowded and you can use the showers in 2nd class. There's a good, clean restaurant on board where you can buy three-course meals for Tan Sh 80 and coffee for Tan Sh 5.

A cheaper way of getting to Tanzania and one which has become very popular over the last few years is via local ferries from Nyanza Lac (the last village in southern Burundi) to Banda (another village on the Burundi/Tanzanian border), and from there to Kigoma. There is no departure tax payable going this way. First take a bus (BFr 400) or truck from Bujumbura to Nyanza Lac. From there, a daily boat to Banda departs between 4 and 5 pm; it takes about three hours and costs Tan Sh 50. You'll arrive after dark and will have to walk about one km to the Tanzanian side (no formalities). It's best to get a local guide to go with you. On the Tanzanian side you take another boat to Kigoma which departs at 10 pm and arrives at 8 am. The fare is Tan Sh 40. The fares on both these boats are payable in Tanzanian shillings (if you haven't got any when you leave Bujumbura you can buy them in Nyanza Lac). Immigration formalities are at Nyanza Lac and Kigoma, but in the latter place you'll have to hike round town to find them as they won't be around when the boat arrives.

PLACES TO STAY

Except in the capital, Bujumbura, there are neither hotels nor rest houses of any kind so you'll have to camp or ask around in the villages for somewhere to stay.

BUJUMBURA

Located on the shores of Lake Tanganyika, Bujumbura is a pleasant city with a population of some 100,000. Most of the hotels in the centre are pretty expensive, being geared towards businesspeople.

The Tourist Office is on Avenue de l'Uprona near the Rue de la Mission. The Banque de la République du Burundi is on Avenue du Gouvernement. The post office (PTT), Sabena, Air France and the Tanzanian embassy are all on Avenue Patrice Lumumba near the Rue du Commerce. The moneychangers are in the Place du Marche. The Banque du Crédit Bujumbura will accept Eurocredit cheque cards. Buses leave from the Place du Marche near the Avenue du Marche, Rue du Commerce and the Avenue Prince Louis Ragasore. The airport is out on Route National No 5 (11 km). To get there, head out on Boulevard du 1er Novembre (Micombero Michel). It's fairly easy to hitch.

The majority of travellers find a welcome at the *Vugizu Mission* (ask for 'Chez M Johnson'), which is attached to the Wheaton College, Illinois, USA. It's a Christian fundamentalist mission run by Mr and Mrs Johnson, who have been here for 35 years. They have a two-bed caravan and a two-person tent in the garden for travellers' use plus space for people who want to put up their own tent. You must comply with the rules about noise and hygiene and dress modestly, but it's free. Good breakfasts are available daily and occasionally other meals too. The people who run it can be very helpful about visas if you're having problems. Please do your best to keep a low profile and to help out where possible at this place. These people have been very hospitable to a lot of travellers and deserve to be treated with respect. A minibus (BFr 20) from behind the market will take you there or you can hitch from the INSS building. The Mission moved in April 1985 but we've had word that travellers are still welcome at the new place.

Other than the Vugizu, try the *Au Bon Accueil*, Avenue du Peuple Burundi, which costs BFr 800 a single and BFr 1500 a double. To get there, go down the Avenue du Peuple Burundi as far as the BP station and then turn right 150 metres.

Also relatively cheap is the *Panama Guest House* on the street before the Au Bon Accueil and then right 300 metres. It costs BFr 650 a single and BFr 750 a double. Other cheapies in this area include the *Hotel New Bwiza*, the *Hotel Escottise* and the *Au Chateau Fort*. The *Alliance Protestante* near the post office has also been suggested. It costs US$5 but is often full. Other cheapies can be found in the Bwiza quarter but there are no street names in this district so you'll have to hunt around. It's about one km from the centre. Going upmarket a little, there is the *Hotel Central*, Place de l'Independence near the Avenue de l'Uprona, and the Avenue du Peuple Burundi, which costs BFr 1200 a single.

Most of the other hotels will cost at least US$25 a single and they will add on an extra 25% for two people of the same sex sharing a room.

One of the cheapest places to eat is the *Protestant dining room* near the French embassy, which is open from 6 to 10 am and noon to 2 pm. You can also get food, milk and tea at the *Boulangerie/Patisserie*. Another very cheap place to eat is *Les Delicieuses*, a patisserie right on the central roundabout where a full meal should cost no more than US$8. There are also a number of cheap cafés in the Bwiza neighbourhood. There are no small cafés in the market, but other than that it's an excellent market for all sorts of things and cheaper than Kigali. Be careful of pick-

pockets here. They are not only numerous but skillful. Licencing hours (for buying spirits, beer, etc) are from noon to 2 pm and from 5 to 10 pm (the Poms will appreciate this!).

There's a reasonably good bar at the *Cercle Nautique*. If you go there in the evenings you may see the hippos come up out of the lake. Cercle Nautique also serves very good food.

ELSEWHERE IN THE COUNTRY

There are very few hotels outside Bujumbura and you'll have to rely on missions or camp.

At Gitega there is quite a lot of choice. Also, the Catholics have a huge place which is often free if you approach them in the right manner. While you're in Gitega you should pay a visit to the **National Museum** just outside of town – entry is free.

At Kilemba try the *Swedish Mission*, which charges BFr 150 for a bed in a room without private bathroom and BFr 500 for a private room with attached bath. About 16 km from Kilemba are hot springs and a waterfall with a very deep pool. You can swim here.

At Rutavu, seven km from the pyramid marking the southernmost possible source of the Nile, you can sleep at the *Catholic Mission*. There is a tariff for the rooms here but you may not be asked for any money.

Cameroun

If Zambia is Africa's most geographically artificial country, then Cameroun is its most socially artificial. Never at any time were its diverse tribal and linguistic groups united, and the history of the Cameroun since independence has been dominated by the intense and often brutal drive towards unification. Before the area was colonised, the south and east of the country were inhabited by Bantu peoples organised along patrilinear or matrilinear lines, while on the central Bamileke plateau there existed a number of well-organised and independent chiefdoms. The northern part of the country was peopled by a complex mix of Negroid, Hamitic and Arab-related societies which formed the border areas of the empires of first Bornu, then Mandara and finally Sokoto. By the late 19th century, the whole of the north was ruled by the Emir of Yola, who was himself a vassal of Sokoto. These different areas developed more or less independently of one another largely due to the different trade links which they enjoyed with areas further afield. The coastal peoples, for instance, like the rest of coastal West and Central Africa, were strongly influenced by the slave trade to the Americas until well into the 19th century when local products began to replace slaves as the main export.

Though the Portuguese first made contact here at the end of the 15th century, no attempt was made to colonise the area until the 19th century.

A commercial treaty was signed between one of the chiefs of Douala and the British in 1856, but when the latter showed no interest in a subsequent request by the chiefs to declare a protectorate over the area, the chiefs turned to Germany. The Germans set up their protectorate in 1884. By WW I, most of the country had been 'pacified' and the Moslem chiefs of the north brought into subjection. Railways were constructed and the beginnings of the school system were established. After WW I the area was divided between the British and French under League of Nations mandates. This arrangement was reconfirmed by the United Nations after WW II.

Nationalism began to take root firmly in the 1950s and elections for a legislative assembly in the French part of the country took place in 1956. They were contested by four parties, only two of which could claim support from all areas of the country. It was the Union Camerounaise led by Ahmadou Ahidjo, representative of the north, however, which picked up the bulk of the seats. Domination by the north naturally was resented by the peoples of the centre and south, and rebellion was a constant feature of the late 1950s. Even as independence was granted to the French part in 1960, a full-scale rebellion was raging on the Bamileke plateau. It was suppressed with extreme ruthlessness over an eight-month period by French troops and a squadron of fighter bombers. Thousands lost their lives and only in 1975 did the government lift the ban on visits to the Bamileke and Sanaga Maritime areas of the country without a special pass.

The British-administered part of the country was granted independence in 1961 and the two halves united by referendum the same year. The president from independence until late 1982 was Ahmadou Ahidjo. This made him one of

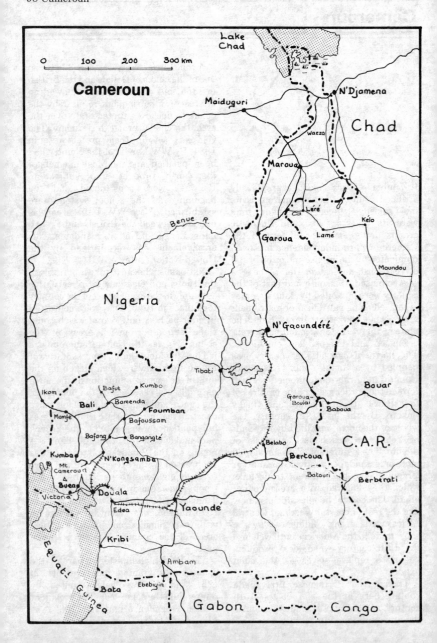

Africa's longest-serving elected presidents. But despite Ahidjo's moderating influence and the great strides that have been made towards unification, the early years of rebellion have left their mark on the country. The government has armed itself with all manner of legislation which can be used to suppress dissidence. Strikes are banned and the press is totally effete. Journalists are constantly harassed and, according to Amnesty International, there are still hundreds of people detained without trial though the government will only admit to 50. The abuse of power is commonplace and corruption is rife, yet the country still manages to project an image of stability – something which cannot be denied when comparisons are made with neighbouring countries.

Yet even Ahmadou Ahidjo, it seems, wasn't content to retire from politics gracefully, and in April 1984 he attempted a coup from outside the country. It failed but severely shook the government and led to a purge of northerners from the government (Ahidjo was a northerner and had seen to it during his tenure as president that northerners secured the most desirable jobs in the government, army and civil service). It also led to a renewed suspicion of foreigners; recently we've had many letters from travellers commenting on the hard time they've been given by the security forces in this country. You'd be well advised to keep as low a profile as possible until things quiet down again. You can expect to be interrogated at least once on suspicion of being a spy.

There has been much improvement in the agricultural sector in recent years, but the bulk of the population is still engaged in growing subsistence crops. Much of what surplus is produced is bought by businessmen in Douala and transported to Libreville, Gabon, where high prices are fetched. This practice continued even when near-famine conditions hit the north recently; the famine was only averted by massive imports of grain from America.

Efforts are being made to encourage greater self-sufficiency, and a large area of irrigated and non-irrigated land in Yagoua, Mbo and Ndop has been planted with rice – a staple food of most Camerounians. There is some heavy industry – mostly concerned with aluminum – and factories are being set up to manufacture consumer goods. Foreign investment in industry is being encouraged, and the government has used overseas aid to begin the construction of a modern communications network.

FACTS

There are great differences in climate and geography in this long, wedge-shaped country ranging from the near desert of the north to the dense tropical forests of the south. The centre is largely upland savannah. A chain of volcanic mountains runs from the coast along the border area with Nigeria until it peters out on the plain of Maroua. Some of the most beautiful country is to be found north and north-west of Douala, where there are mountains rising to 2000 metres and more. The cool freshness of the atmosphere here, the fine waterfalls and attractive villages make it one of the most popular areas of the country to visit. There are also some spectacular waterfalls along the Sanaga and Nyong Rivers.

Travel in the north is best from November to February. Many roads become impassable during July and August because of flooding. Moslem traditions in this area are still very much alive and the people, on the whole, are very friendly. The western part of the country is also a major draw, being the centre of Bamoun culture with its many festivals and feast days which are celebrated with music and dancing. Foumban is an excellent place to see these.

VISAS

Visas are required by all. You cannot get a visa on the border or at an airport if you arrive by plane. Also note that if you arrive by air, you must leave the same way. Entering overland, you may well be asked to show sufficient funds, but otherwise there is no fuss.

If you arrive by plane you may be asked for an onward ticket. If you don't have one, among the cheapest you can buy is Douala-Malabo (Equatorial Guinea) at US$60. Make sure your vaccination certificates are up to date because they will check them.

If you're coming from Nigeria you can get a Cameroun visa either at Lagos (4 Elsi Fermi Pearse St, Victoria Island) or Calabar (6 Ezuk Nkapa St.). The visa costs Naira 7.50 and takes 24 hours to issue. It's valid for a stay of 20 days.

Visa extensions can be obtained in any regional capital and cost CFA 3500 plus CFA 300 for a letter requesting the extension. They usually come through without a fuss but some travellers have waited up to two weeks for them. A lot depends on who processes your application.

Benin visas There is no longer an embassy in Yaounde so if you're heading up from the Central African Republic, that leaves Lagos as the only possible place where you can get a visa.

Central African Republic visas The embassy in Yaounde is situated in the Bastos district close to the Greek cathedral. Visas cost CFA 10,000 (!!), require one photo for a 10-day stay and are issued in 24 hours.

Chad visas In Yaounde a 15-day visa costs 4000 CFA and takes one hour to issue. The man who deals with applications is one of the friendliest people you will meet in Africa.

Equatorial Guinea Visas The cost is CFA 3000 in Douala and CFA 5000 in Yaounde. You get a 15-day visa which is issued in 24 hours.

Gabon & Congo Brazzaville visas In Yaounde these both cost CFA 2500 and they're issued in 24 hours without fuss.

Nigerian visas These cost CFA 3500 and are issued in 24 hours. If you're travelling on a British passport they are supposed to be free. Tell them you understand this to be the case but don't count on it working. All Nigerian border posts have computer printouts of everyone who enters Africa via South Africa or who has visited that country, so they'll know if you've been there regardless of whether your passport bears any indication of the fact or not. If you have, expect a hassle.

Sudan visas All visa applications have to go to Kartoum for approval and you'll find it can take up to six weeks to come through.

Zaire visas The embassy is in the Bastos district (Bus No 20). Visas cost CFA 8000, require three photos and a letter of introduction from your own embassy, and take four days to come through (they have to telex Kinshasa).

If you have a camera, then get hold of a photography permit as soon as possible from the Ministry of Information and Culture in any regional capital. Travellers with cameras have been befriended by people who turned out to be plain-clothes police and who either arrested them or confiscated their cameras. Some travellers have even had to take refuge in their embassies from over-zealous, armed police. A photography permit won't keep these people at bay and you may still have film confiscated, but it will keep you out of jail. Don't take photographs of public buildings, industrial installations, railway stations or army bases.

We've been getting a lot of negative feedback lately about the Camerouns. This extract from a letter typifies the sort of hassles you're likely to encounter:

This place is a nightmare at the moment for foreigners. Any jerk in a uniform uses the right given by his gun to hassle you and make you turn out rucksacks totally. We took a bus from a town called N'Gaoundal to catch a train to Yaounde. After two hours in a police station we were allowed to catch the train and had our passports, etc checked every hour of the 14-hour journey by various people – army, gendarmes, police, railway staff, railway police ad nauseam.

Other travellers have written in to say that in the south and centre of the country they were searched and interrogated in every town they stopped in, but that this sort of treatment petered out in the far north. Keep a low profile.

MONEY
US$1 = CFA 454

The unit of currency is the CFA franc. Import/export of local currency is allowed up to 75,000 CFA. The Société Cameroun de Banque is recommended for money changing but banks won't accept Nigerian naira. If you have any of these you may be able to change them with traders but the exchange rate won't be anything to write home about. West African CFA can be changed on a one-for-one basis with Central African CFA at banks. If you're having money sent to you, you need permission from Customs to receive it in foreign currency; otherwise you'll be paid in CFA. The BICIC is the best place to have money sent to, but it will still take about two weeks to come through.

There are no banks in Banyo, Tibati, Kalaldi or Lokiti. The bank nearest these places is in N'Gaoundere. There is now a bank at Garoua-Boulai (Cameroun/CAR border). It's on the main street but is closed on Saturday and Sunday.

You may well be subjected to a shoes-off body search for CFA before leaving the country but this isn't always the case.

LANGUAGE
French and English are the official languages but there is also a wide diversity of African languages spoken.

POST
Douala is a better post office to use than Yaounde if you're having letters sent to you, but they only keep letters for two weeks.

GETTING THERE & AROUND
Road
Hitching can be slow and can involve long waits, especially in the wet season when roads and bridges get washed out or damaged. During this season a system of rain barriers are erected in an attempt to protect the surface of the roads. It makes a lot of sense to arrange lifts the night before at the truck park – this applies particularly in the north. Few lifts are free.

There are few buses; public transport is usually by shared taxi ('remassage') or truck. In theory, taxi and bus fares are fixed at around CFA 7.50 per km for long-distance rides plus extra luggage charges which are based on weight. Up to 10 kg should be free but this isn't always the case. Ten to 20 kg should cost 200 CFA but can cost up to 700 CFA on some runs. Backpacks are often free in the north but rarely in the south. The prices are fixed by a society called SETRACAUCAM (PB 4222, Yaounde); it publishes a list of current fares which you can buy for CFA 3000 but it doesn't really count for much – you still have to ask others what they are paying. Also, in the wet season prices double and triple depending on the state of the road (eg in the dry season Bamenda-Mamfe costs CFA 1500; in the wet season it can be CFA 6000 to 8000!). Also in this season you can expect to get out and push in waist-high mud when your car gets stuck.

Whatever form of transport you take, journey times can be long because of the numerous police checkpoints where they look for people evading taxes and illegal immigrants. Carry your passport with you at all times.

In the cities taxis usually cost CFA 50 per journey, though fares to and from airports and night journeys naturally cost more.

Despite a lot of investment in roads over the last few years, most roads in Cameroun are either gravel or dirt. There are very few sealed roads (Bafoussam to Yaounde is an exception – recently completed). Expect uncomfortable journeys.

Some examples of transport costs around the country are as follows:

Mamfe-Kumba A taxi costs CFA 3250 and takes 4¼ hours. The road is unpaved but usually in good shape in the dry season. In the wet season buses may only take 'strong men' – in other words, those who can push hard enough or even carry (!) the bus over the rough patches. There is beautiful countryside all the way – high mountains, lush jungle and picturesque villages – so try to do the journey during the day.

Kumba-Limbe (Victoria) A taxi costs CFA 750 plus CFA 250 for baggage and takes about two hours. There are superb views of Mt Cameroun en route.

Buea-Kumba Costs CFA 1500 plus CFA 500 for luggage.

Buea-Douala Costs CFA 750.

Limbe (Victoria)-Douala A taxi costs CFA 750 plus CFA 400 for baggage and takes about one hour.

Douala-Bafoussam Costs CFA 2700.

Bafoussam-Bamenda Costs CFA 1000 plus CFA 200 for a backpack in a shared taxi and takes two hours along a sealed road.

Bamenda-Douala Costs CFA 3500 in shared taxi plus CFA 300 for luggage. It's a good sealed road.

Bafoussam-Yaounde Costs 2400 to 2750 CFA plus 250 CFA for a backpack and takes about 10½ hours along a rough road. There's also a ferry crossing which may delay you for up to two hours.

Yaounde-Douala Costs CFA 2500 and an extra CFA 500 for baggage. It's a dirt road.

Douala-Foumban Costs CFA 2500.

N'Gaoundere-Garoua A bush taxi costs CFA 2275 plus CFA 225 for each piece of luggage depending on the weight. The trip takes about five hours. These bush taxis resemble 'bread trucks' and are packed tight full of people, making them very uncomfortable. If you want to wait as little time as possible at the autogare, try to be there between 6.30 and 7 am as this is when the majority of people do their travelling.

Garoua-Maroua A bush taxi costs CFA 1600 plus baggage charges. The journey takes about three hours along a good sealed road.

Maroua-Mokolo 'Bread truck' bush taxis delivering 31 human loaves cost CFA 650 per loaf. The journey time is about 1¼ hours along a sealed road. Going in the opposite direction, the best days to find a taxi are Wednesday and Friday at about 6.30 to 7 am. On other days of the week you may well find yourself waiting a long time.

Garoua-Maroua Costs CFA 1600 and luggage is usually free.

Maroua-Waza Buses cost CFA 900.

Maroua-Kousseri Costs CFA 2100 and luggage is usually free.

Maroua-Nigerian border Before you set off it's wise to check that the border will be open. 'Bread truck' bush taxis cost CFA 1000 or you can get a Peugeot station wagon for CFA 1500. From the border there are Peugeot 504s for Naira 6 plus baggage charges or vans for Naira 4 plus baggage.

Rail

The main line runs from Douala to N'Gaoundere via Yaounde, with a branch line from Douala to N'Kongsamba. There's also a short track between Victoria and Ekona via Buea. The schedule is as follows:

Route & Train No	Departure Station	Time
Ligne Ouest		
Douala-N'Kongsamba (No 161)	Douala	7.30 am
Douala-Kumba (No 165)	Douala	3.00 pm
M'Banga-Douala (No 162)	M'Banga	7.55 am
N'Kongsamba-Douala (No 166)	N'Kongsamba	8.24 am
Ligne Transcam 1		
Douala-Yaounde (Omnibus 3)	Douala	8.30 am
Douala-Yaounde (Autorail 1)	Douala	12.00 noon
Douala-Yaounde (Express 101)	Douala	8.30 pm
Yaounde-Douala (Omnibus 4)	Yaounde	7.30 am
Yaounde-Douala (Autorail 2)	Yaounde	12.00 noon
Yaounde-Douala (Express 102)	Yaounde	9.00 pm
Douala-Edea (Express 103)	Douala	4.00 pm
Ligne Transcam 2		
Yaounde-N'Gaoundere (No 11)	Yaounde	7.45 am
Yaounde-Belabo (Autorail 13)	Yaounde	3.50 pm
Yaounde-Belabo [Express 111)	Yaounde	7.10 pm
Belabo-Yaounde (Autorail 12)	Belabo	6.00 am
N'Gaoundere-Yaounde (No 14)	N'Gaoundere	7.00 am
N'Gaoundere-Yaounde (No 112)	N'Gaoundere	7.20 pm

On the Douala-Yaounde line the fares are CFA 7000 (1st class sleeper), CFA 6000 (1st class express), CFA 4950 (1st class ordinary), CFA 3485 (2nd class express) and CFA 3065 (2nd class ordinary). First class is very comfortable with linen, blankets and pillows being provided. If you take 2nd class then beware of thieves. Reservations can be made at 9 am on the day of departure. The journey takes six hours by express train.

From Yaounde to N'Gaoundere the trains depart daily at 7.45 am (arriving at 6.30 pm) and 7.10 pm (arriving at 8.30 am the next day). The trains can be up to four hours late. The fares are CFA 12,050 (1st class couchette – two-bed cabin), CFA 11,845 (1st class couchette – four-bed cabin), CFA 10,340 (1st class – seats only) and CFA 6380 (2nd class – seats only). Reservations for the couchettes must be made in the morning on the day of departure. Reservations for the day train

are not necessary – get your ticket on arrival at the station. Don't count on there being a 1st-class car on the day train. Second class is 'colourful' – hot, noisy, crowded, smelly and uncomfortable. Bring your own water. There are plenty of vendors selling food through the train windows at each stop.

If you're coming into Cameroun from the Central African Republic via Garoua-Boulai and want to catch the night train to Yaounde, then once over the border, take a bus to N'Gaoundal (not N'Gaoundere) and get the train from there. This is much more convenient than going all the way to Belabo to get the train, but you must arrive at Garoua-Boulai early in the day to do this.

To/From Nigeria

Since Nigeria closed its land borders you can now only fly in. *Air Afrique* and *Cameroun Airlines* each have three flights per week to Abidjan (Ivory Coast). All the flights stop in Lagos, two of them stop in Lomé and another two stop in Cotonou. There is no charge for stop-overs. Yaounde-Abidjan costs CFA 93,500 and Douala-Abidjan costs CFA 86,000 plus tax one way. If and when the borders open up again the most popular overland crossing between the two countries is via Ikom and Mamfe. The Nigerian customs at this border are both efficient and officious. The road from the border to Mamfe is bad and a Land-Rover will cost CFA 3000. Mamfe to Kumba costs CFA 1500 in the dry season and up to CFA 4000 (including luggage) in the wet season. Again the road is bad. From Kumba to Douala along a good road costs CFA 1400 (including luggage) by minibus.

An alternative route between the two countries is by boat from Idua Oron, south of Calabar, to a small port in Cameroun not marked on the maps. The boats leave Oron daily at about 8 pm and arrive about 8 am next day. The fare is Naira 20. You can forget about sleeping on the boat as there's usually too much arguing, quarrelling and whinging going on. Don't bother going to the Immigration Office in Calabar for an exit stamp – this is all fixed up in Oron. A taxi from the boat landing to Kumba costs CFA 1000. The route is temporarily suspended while the Nigerian border is closed, but we're including it in case the borders open again, in which case the schedule and fares will probably be much the same.

To/From Equatorial Guinea & Gabon

If you're going to Bioko (Fernando Poo) you must fly. There are flights at least once a week and sometimes three times per week with *Air Cameroun* from Douala to Malabo which cost CFA 29,000 return. If you haven't already got a visa, these are issued on arrival for CFA 2000. If you're going to the mainland half of Equatorial Guinea (Rio Muni) or to Gabon you can go overland. Head south from Yaounde to Ambam. Here the road branches, one branch going to Rio Muni and the other to Gabon. For Rio Muni you head for Ntem, cross the river by ferry or canoe and then take a pick-up to Key-Ossi. From there to Ebebeyin, the first town in Equatorial Guinea, it's a one-km walk. If heading for Gabon, take the Ambam-Oyem road which will eventually take you to Ndjole and Libreville.

To/From Central African Republic

The main crossing point here is at Garoua-Boulai (not to be confused with Garoua on the Bertoua-Bouar road). You have the choice here of going by train from Yaounde to Belabo (CFA 3815 in 2nd class – three trains daily) and then on to Garoua-Boulai by road, or doing the entire journey by road. There is a bus from Yaounde to Garoua-Boulai for CFA 4500 which takes 15 to 18 hours, or you can go first to Bertoua on the same bus for CFA 2600, after which you take trucks, buses or taxis to the border (bus costs CFA 2000). If you prefer, you can arrange a lift on a truck the whole way to the border for around CFA 4200. If you take the bus it's worth paying an extra CFA 1000 to have a seat up with the driver, as the lengthwise benches in the rear are absolute torture. It's a dirt road and you should allow two days to get from Yaounde to the border if you go by truck. From Garoua-Boulai there are daily buses to Bangui stopping overnight in Bouar for CFA 7700, and buses to Bouar for CFA 2300. There are many police checkpoints en route so expect delays, but it's a good road from Bouar to Bangui. In the wet season the journey from Yaounde to Bangui can take at least a week.

To/From Chad

The pirogues across the river from Kousseri to N'Djamena are CFA 100.

BAFOUSSAM

The cheapest place to stay here is the *Foyer Evangelique*, 100 metres from the taxi park, which offers beds at CFA 1500 per person including use of shower. If it's full try the *Hotel Frederick* at CFA 2500, or the *Auberge de la Mifi*, which has a variety of rooms for CFA 3000, 3800 and 5000. Two places that have been recommended for the food are the *Restaurant Familiare* at the top of the hill, and the *Riz Restaurant* near the market and taxi park.

BAMENDA

Bamenda is a beautiful and popular resort town in the highlands north of N'Kongsamba with friendly people and a good market. It also has an excellent, though very small, museum and an artisans' co-op where you can find bargains in craftwork – you must bargain hard.

Probably the best place to stay in terms of location and price is the *Presbyterian Mission*. It is on top of a hill just outside town (ask for the 'church centre,' not the main church, as they're a long way apart) and offers dormitory accommodation for CFA 2000 per person. Clean sheets, showers and toilets are provided. If there are enough people staying they will cook meals for you. Lockers are available for gear. If it's full or you don't want to stay in a dormitory, try the *Savannah*, off the main street, which costs CFA 1500 a single, or try the *Mezam National Hotel*, Commercial St. The latter has a variety of rooms including breakfast for CFA 1750, 2250 and 2500. The more expensive rooms have their own bathroom. Another place which has been recommended in the past is the *Ring Way Hotel*.

For good, cheap food try the *Ideal Park Hotel and Restaurant* which is close to the market and has good views over the town. You can eat here for CFA 1000. It also has rooms but they're more expensive than those mentioned above. Another place to try is the *Commercial Eating House* on the main street near the market where you can get a two-egg omelette for CFA 75. For something to do, try the *People's Palace*, *Monte Cristo*, *Queens Valley*, or the *Ideal Park*, where people go dancing.

While you're in Bafoussam you should make a trip to **Bafut**, a beautiful village 20 km north where there is an interesting palace built in the early 20th century for the Fon's 75 wives. People still walk around this area with flintlock rifles. On 18 December there is a huge feast and festival when all the local Fon's masks and costumes are bought out. Make sure you see it if you're in the area at the time. Good ebony and other woodcarvings can be found if you ask for 'Mr Peter.'

BAFANG

The *Auberge du Haut Nkam* here offers accommodation at CFA 1500 a double. The showers are none too clean. Simple but comfortable rooms have also been available in the past at Michel Djimai's place opposite the BICIC bank (Michel is a tailor).

BANGANGTE

You may be able to find accommodation in the *Protestant Mission* in this small village east of Bafang. If they won't let you in then try the *Centre Touristique*, two km out of town. It has doubles for CFA 2000, but the staff are not very friendly.

BANSO (also known as KUMBO, NSU & KINBO)

The *Presbyterian Mission* here has one room for free; otherwise try the *Baptist Mission Rest House* (very comfortable with cooking facilities and meals by arrangement), the *Tobin Tourist Home* (meals by arrangement), or *Kilo's Rest House*. All offer relatively cheap accommodation.

The Banso tribes who live in this area are worth a visit and the local ruler, the Fon of Banso, is a friendly chief who speaks English. Don't shake hands with these people or cross your legs in front of them, as these are regarded as insults.

BELABO

This small town on the railway line between Yaounde and N'Gaoundere can be used as an overnight stop either on the way to N'Gaoundere or to the border crossing point of Garoua-Boulai (there are buses from Belabo to Bertoua and others from there to Garoua-Boulai). A good place to stay here is the *Auberge Maria Bassa*, also known as Mama Maria's. The woman who runs it is the sister of the stationmaster and the hotel is located straight down the street leading from the station to the village, on the right-hand side after you go through the shopping area. You can eat here but there's no electricity or showers – you're given a pail of water to slosh over yourself. It costs CFA 2000 per night (less if you bargain hard) and all meals cost CFA 500.

BERTOUA

The *Catholic Mission* here doesn't like backpackers but there are several cheap hotels in the town for around CFA 1500 per room.

BUEA

Buea is located on the lower slopes of Mt Cameroun (4070 metres; 13,352 ft) and is a good base for climbing the mountain. You don't need any special equipment to climb to the top and there are a series of huts that you can stay in en route. It's advisable to pay for a guide to take you to the first hut but after that the route is obvious. It will take about half a day to the first hut, a full day to the third hut and another day to the top and back down again. You may well meet officials who will attempt to charge you CFA 3000 for the privilege of climbing the mountain, but many travellers have written saying this is definitely an unofficial charge. Mt Cameroun is the highest mountain in West Africa but it's a much less strenuous climb than either Mt Kilimanjaro or Mt Kenya. If you decide to climb this mountain, remember to do the following things: (1) Register with the police. (2) Ask around town for a guide and bargain for the rate. A man called Anthony who lives in the village charges CFA 4000 per day (the 'rainy season rate'). The dry

season is from November to March. (3) Wear the right clothes – sturdy boots and waterproof clothing. Bring a change of dry clothes, camping gear, food, water and warm clothes. It's a steep but steady climb over muddy trails.

For somewhere to stay in Buea, try the *Hotel Mermoz*. It is clean and costs CFA 3000 a double. Avoid eating in the restaurant here as it's expensive. There is also the *Parliamentarian Flats Hotel*, which looks as pretentious as it sounds but is not too expensive at CFA 4500 a double or CFA 4800 a double with hot water. It's clean, quiet and comfortable. The restaurant serves delicious food but it's expensive at CFA 2000 for a dinner of chicken and fries or steak and potatoes, green beans, melon and hot chocolate. Breakfast (omelette and fries) costs CFA 1000. If you'd like to stay in the area for a while, enquire about renting a house in the country nearby – there are quite a few of them.

DOUALA

Douala is the largest city and the industrial centre of Cameroun. It isn't a particularly pleasant place: mosquitoes and muggings are both problems at night, so watch out. Even during the day you may well find suspicious-looking people following you around waiting for the right opportunity. The worst area is between the railway station and the Cathedral.

The **Artisanat National** – a craft/souvenir market – is worth a visit if you're interested in ivory, ebony and malachite jewellery and carvings, musical instruments or leatherwork. You must bargain hard! It's located across from the Cathedral.

Useful Addresses

American Express
    Cam Voyages, 15 Avenue de la Liberté,
    PO Box 4070, Douala (tel 42-31-88)
Thomas Cook
    Transcap Voyages, 8 Rue Ivy (off Boulevard de la Liberté)

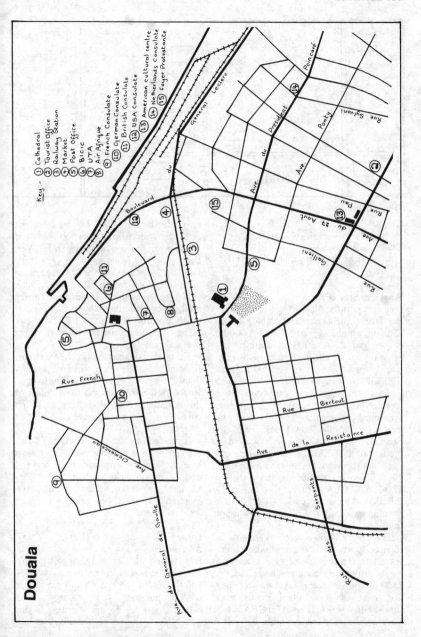

Douala

Key:-
1. Cathedral
2. Tourist Office
3. Railway Station
4. Market
5. Post Office
6. B.I.C.I.C.
7. UTA
8. Air Afrique
9. French Consulate
10. German Consulate
11. British Consulate
12. USA Consulate
13. American cultural centre
14. Netherlands Consulate
15. Foyer Protestante

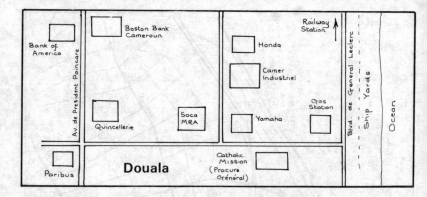

German Consulate
 Boulevard de la Liberté at Rue Pau
UK Consulate
 21 Avenue de General de Gaulle, PO Box
4006, Douala

Places to Stay & Eat

One very popular place to stay is the *Foyer des Marines* (Seamen's Mission), 2 Rue Gallieni, which has rooms for CFA 6500 a single and CFA 8000 a double. It's centrally air-conditioned and each room has its own toilet. It can sometimes be difficult to get into unless you can convince the management that a member of your family is a seafarer. There is a swimming pool here. There's also the *Foyer Protestante*, one block from the Seamen's Mission, which has accommodation at CFA 3000 a double and excellent three-course lunches from CFA 1500. There are cheaper rooms (only two of them) for CFA 2000 but they're always full. Breakfast is served for CFA 400 but evening meals are not offered. Beware of theft here.

The *Centre Baba Simon*, Avenue de la Liberté, has been recommended by many travellers. It's very friendly and clean and has hundreds of dormitory beds at CFA 2500 per person and good showers. They also have air-conditioned rooms with three beds, a sink and bidet for CFA 5000. Very good meals are available here. It's

opposite the Cathedral not far from the railway station (turn left as you come out of the station if you arrive by train). You can't miss the place as it's a very large building. Another Catholic Mission known as the *Procure Generale*, Rue Franqueville, is also recommended. It has a swimming pool, air-conditioning, a beer machine and meals available. The cost is CFA 2500 per night. You can leave baggage here perfectly safely.

Up-market there is the *Hotel Beausejour*, Rue Joffre and Rue Pau, which costs CFA 9000 a single; and the *Hotel Kontchupe*, Rue Alfred Saher just off the Boulevard du Président Ahmadou Ahidjo, which costs CFA 6000 a single and CFA 8000 a double.

If you're not eating at any of the above, then try the street vendors for cheap snacks. They come around 10 pm and sell coffee, sandwiches, kebabs etc. The *Moritz Café*, three blocks up from the Seamen's Mission, has relatively cheap steak and salad.

Other

All the airlines are on the Avenue de la Liberté and the Boulevard de la Liberté.

A shared taxi to the airport costs CFA 1000. Around the city shared taxis cost CFA 90 per journey. Buses around the centre cost CFA 45 per journey. If you want to get to the airport cheaply, take bus

No 1 from the Central Post Office to the market and then bus No 11 from there to the airport.

FOUMBAN

Foumban is an interesting place with many old traditional houses in the surrounding countryside and the German-built **Fon's Palace**. The latter has no entry fee but is presently closed for restoration work. There's also an excellent **museum** here (CFA 200 entry) and a good **market**.

It's no longer possible to stay at the *Catholic Mission* in Foumban even though they do have four rooms with showers. The cheapest hotels are at the southern end of town and you can expect to pay around CFA 4000 per night.

GAROUA

This is the commercial centre of the north and there are many foreign residents living here. There is a market on Saturday, and plenty of cheap *auberges* across from the bus station. One which has been recommended is *Chambres de Passage* which costs CFA 1000 – there's no sign so ask at *Restaurant de la Benoue*. The *Mission Catholique* sometimes takes guests but they're not very friendly. It costs CFA 500 per night if you can get in. If you'd like something better then try the *Relais de St Hubert* (air-con and non-air-con rooms), the *Relais Korman* (air-con and non-air-con rooms) or *Hotel Boulai*. The Relais de St Hubert is pleasant and costs CFA 7500 a double with dinner at CFA 2000. It's often full by early evening.

Avoid the rip-off *Hotel Pacifique* which will cram up to four of you in a dingy little room meant for two and charge you 2000 CFA each.

For cheap food try the stalls in the autogare. Yogurt, hard-boiled eggs, fruit and bread are available for breakfast.

GAROUA-BOULAI

Garoua-Boulai is a small, dusty village (in the dry season) 400 metres from the CAR border on the road between Bertoua and Bouar. It's possible you may be stuck for a lift here and have to spend the night, but try to avoid it if possible. The *Catholic Mission* has good double rooms for CFA 4000. It's beside the petrol station in the truck and bus park area. The management are friendly. You may also be able to camp here. There's also the *Auberge Central* for CFA 1500 a double.

KUMBA

The cheapest places to stay here are the *Motor Lodging Hotel*, close to the truck park, which is clean and costs CFA 1000 a double; the *Harlem City Hotel*; and the *Meme Central*. Other cheapies which have been recommended in the past are the *Playfair, Authentique, Monte Carlo* and *Congo*. If you're looking for something slightly up-market, try the *Meme Pilot Hotel* behind the bus station which costs CFA 3500 a double with shower, sink, toilet and fan. It's good value ('one of the cleanest hotels in Africa') and the staff are friendly. The tiny restaurant next door has good, cheap food – large plates of rice and sauce for CFA 75, fried plantain for CFA 50 per slice, beans for CFA 50 and two eggs for CFA 150.

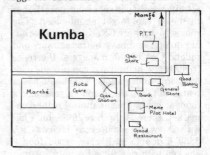

LIMBE (formerly VICTORIA)

You can camp free in the Botanical Gardens near the Miramar and Atlantic Beach Hotels, but beware of thieves. One of the cheapest places to stay is the *Mansion Hotel*, where you can get a room for CFA 1500 a double. The rooms are

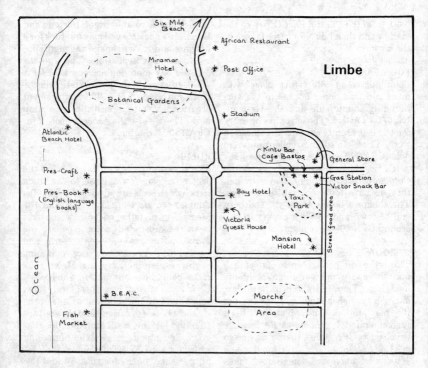

clean and have fans but the toilets outside are dirty, and if you get a room near the bar then you can forget about sleep. The rooms upstairs are CFA 1800 a double but are quieter and have better showers and toilets. One of the managers, Pierre, is friendly and helpful and can provide a lot of useful information. The hotel has a restaurant but the menu is generally a figment of the imagination. Further up-market, there is the *Bay Hotel*, on a hill with a view and sea breezes. It costs CFA 3850 a double and serves good food – chicken with rice for CFA 950. *Victoria Guest House* next to the Bay Hotel also costs CFA 4000 a double. More expensive still are the *Miramar Hotel* on the ocean-front, where doubles cost CFA 3900-8000; and the *Atlantic Beach Hotel*, also on the oceanfront, which costs CFA 8000 a double. Both these last two hotels have

good *boites*. The one at the Miramar has no admission fee on weekdays if you just come to dance, but if you sit down at a table you must buy a drink – CFA 1000 for Cokes, CFA 600 for beer. At weekends the admission charge is CFA 1000 but this includes a drink. It's sometimes possible to get a bed at the *Presbyterian Youth Centre* for CFA 1500, but they only have two beds. It's a great place and the people there are friendly. To get to it from the taxi park, turn right when you reach the main road and it's only 150 metres from there.

For cheap food, try the tiny omelette stand between the *Kintu Bar* and bakery on the same street as the Bay Hotel. It's open all night (4-5 pm till 8-9 am) and you can get an omelette for as little as CFA 150. Look for the sign that says *Café Bastos*. Corn, fish and chicken are sold on the street near the Mansion Hotel. If you just want to hear music while you have a beer (CFA 400) then try the *Victor Snack Bar*. The *Honolulu Restaurant* has also been recommended – they serve good meals at reasonable prices but don't go there just for a cup of tea, as they'll charge you CFA 200 for that.

Six Mile Beach is a popular spot, though quite a way out of town. On weekdays you'll have the place to yourself but on weekends the hordes come down from Douala. There's a CFA 200 'gate fee' for which an attendant will guard your possessions while you swim. There's nowhere to stay (camping is dangerous because of thieves) and the restaurant is only open at weekends so bring food and drink with you. The cheapest way to get there is by taxi from in front of the stadium near the post office. From here it will cost CFA 150, but from anywhere else in town it will cost CFA 1000 or more. Forget about the beaches near town, as they're polluted and often crowded. One traveller said he came out of the sea at Limbe 'feeling like a Torrey Canyon seagull.'

For craftwork go to *Prescraft* – they have an unusual and interesting collection of things at very reasonable prices.

MAMFE

One of the best places to stay here is the *African City Lodging House* which has friendly staff and cooking facilities and costs CFA 2000 per room. The *Great Aim Hotel* also has clean double rooms at CFA 2000. Slightly more expensive are the *Inland Hotel* at CFA 2500 a double and the *Mamfe Hotel* at CFA 3000 a double. Meals at the last place cost CFA 1500. There are no facilities for changing money at the border, so plan ahead.

MAROUA

The *Mission Baptiste* next to the SGBC bank has a number of small houses here which cost an incredible CFA 100 per night! Otherwise try the *Campement Harade* (pronounced Har-day) which

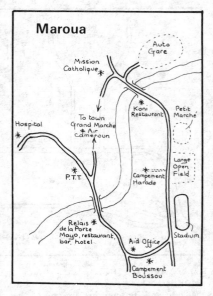

costs CFA 2500 a double. Look for a small sign with a picture of a grass hut on it which says, 'Votre escale de plaisir.' Turn off here and the place is off to the right. Similar is *Campement Boussou*, which has tree-shaded, circular mud-brick huts for CFA 2500 a double. The *Relais de la Porte Maya* also has air-conditioned, circular mud-brick huts for CFA 5300 a double. There is a good bar and restaurant but you have to run the gauntlet of souvenir sellers outside. *Chez Pierrot* can sometimes arrange cheap, basic rooms though it's mainly a restaurant.

For fairly good African food at CFA 1000-2000 try the *Restaurant Koni*. Moderately priced European food is available at the *Relais de la Porte Maya*. Street vendors selling chicken, brochettes, beef, lamb, bread, fruit, hard-boiled eggs and the like can be found in the streets around the *Grand Marche*.

The **market** on Sundays at Mora, on the way to the Waza National Park, is worth a visit. Many primitive people come down from the hills to barter goods here.

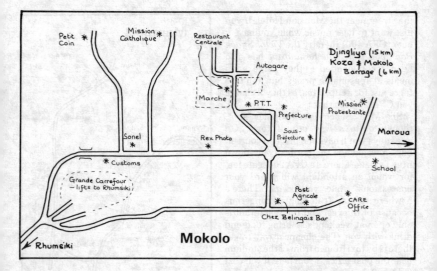

Mokolo

MOKOLO

Mokolo and its environs are one of the most fascinating areas of Cameroun. Superb mountain country with huge volcanic plugs (eg at Rhumsiki), colourful markets (try Tourou on Thursdays where the women wear wooden calabashes on their heads like army helmets, or Mora on Sundays where you may see the bizarre spectacle of bare-breasted mountain women sitting next to Moslem women shrouded from head to foot, both selling their wares) and interesting villages (try Ziver). During the tourist season (December to April) it's easy to get rides to many of these places. Otherwise there are bush taxis along the following routes: Mokolo-Rhumsiki (50 km, transport every day or every other day from the autogare or 'grande carrefour'); Mokolo-Koza (20 km, market on Sundays); Djingliya (15 km, on the road to Koza); Mokolo-Tourou (market on Thursdays); Mokolo-Mora (market on Sundays). It's also possible to rent mobylettes for around CFA 1000 per hour or bicycles from the Marche.

In Mokolo you can stay at the *Mission Catholique* which costs CFA 800 per night. It has electricity and running water. The mission bell rings early in the morning. There's also the over-priced *Hotel Flamboyant* for CFA 7000.

At Rhumsiki there is the *Campement* for CFA 7000 per night but it's possible to arrange to stay the night with local people for a small fee. At Djingliya there is the *Cas de Passage* which costs CFA 3000 for a room with two beds and enough space on the floor for another two people – no problems with the management if you want to do this. At Waza there's the super-expensive *Campement* for CFA 14,000, though you can find accommodation with local people for much less. There are also a lot of Peace Corps volunteers in the area. You might be lucky.

N'GAOUNDERE

The cheapest place to stay here is the *Mission Protestante* which costs CFA 1500 per night, but they go to bed early. The *Hotel Hauts Plateaux* in the centre of town (about three km from the railway station) has some rooms for CFA 3000, but most of them cost CFA 5500 a double with own bathroom and hot water. Avoid the *Hotel Transcom* if possible, as its least expensive rooms go for CFA 7700, though most of them are CFA 11,500 a double. However, it does have a branch hotel where you can get rooms for CFA 4000 – be sure to ask about it. During school holidays it's worth trying the *College Mazenot*.

Cheap food is available from the stalls at the autogare – bread, hard-boiled eggs, avocados, etc.

N'KONGSAMBA

The *Protestant Mission* here may well be able to provide you with a bed for CFA 400. If you're unsuccessful, then try the *Central Hotel* which has relatively cheap rooms.

YAOUNDE

This is the capital of Cameroun – a clean, modern city which is hilly and picturesque and has a refreshingly cool climate. It has a huge indoor market, two museums, seven cinemas, several large bookshops and lots of other interesting shops.

The **Artisanat** at the Place Kennedy is similar to Douala's and has ivory and malachite for sale.

Places to Stay & Eat

The place where most travellers stay and one of the cheapest in the city is the *Presbyterian Mission* (also known as the *Foyer Internationale* and the *Mission Protestante*). It's situated some distance from the centre of town in the Djongola district between the city centre and the embassy district of Bastos (bus No 4 from the centre or take a taxi). A bed in a dormitory costs CFA 2000 per person. Breakfast and lunch are available on request. You can also camp here for CFA 300. Watch out for thieves.

Near the Mission is the *Hotel Aurore*, which costs CFA 3290 a double with breakfast available for CFA 400 (omelette and French bread). Other hotels recommended are the *Hotel des Nations*, which is clean and has rooms for CFA 2000 to 2500 a double and is close to the Mission; *Hotel Flamenco*, which has rooms for CFA 1500 to 2000 (they will allow several people to share a double room); and *Hotel Le Progres* near the Mokolo taxi park across from the market, which charges CFA 3500 a single.

Accommodation can sometimes be found at the *Faculté de Théologie*, but you can give the unfriendly Catholic Mission a miss. American nationals are allowed to camp in the grounds of the *International School* – ask for permission at the school.

If you're staying in the Hotel Aurore, try the food at the *Restaurant Extra Moderne*, which is very good. The *Pizzeria* three doors down from the *Capitole Theatre*, Avenue du Marechal Foch, is good (CFA 1800 for a rather small pizza). So is the *Marseillaise* on the second floor across the road from the Theatre; their large menu includes Chinese food and for CFA 1750 you can get chicken, frites, green beans and a Coke. There are also the usual street stalls. If you get to the African quarter try the *Club l'Année 2000*. It's a long way from the centre of town and you'll have to take a taxi, but the food is excellent. The *American Recreation Camp Club* has good, but expensive, hamburgers and salads.

Other

Public buses cost CFA 45 but are incredibly crowded in the rush hours. Bus No 2 is the one to take for the CAR and Zaire embassies. Taxis within town are CFA 90. Bus No 9 goes to the airport every half hour or so.

The Bank of Credit and Commerce (Cameroun), Avenue J F Kennedy, charges no commission for changing traveller's cheques.

Useful Addresses

Canadian Embassy
    Immeuble N Stamatides, Avenue de l'Independence near the City Hall and Chase Bank

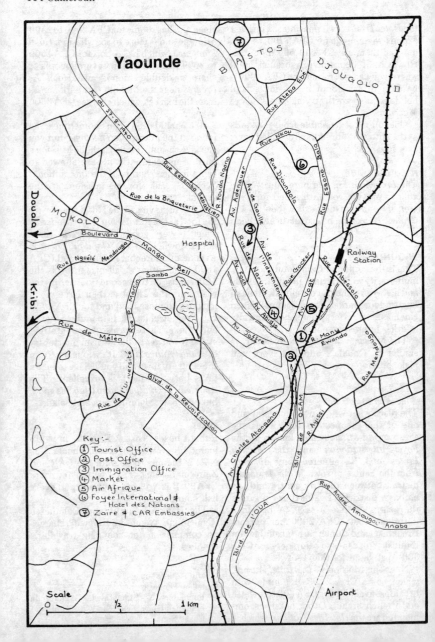

French Embassy
   Avenue des Cocotiers Douala, PO Box 1071
Ivory Coast Embassy
   The embassy is in Nlongkak near Bastos at the traffic circle (bus No 4 terminus). From here take the Route du Bastos and then the first left. This becomes a dirt road strewn with abandoned cars, but right at the end is the embassy.
Nigerian Embassy
   To get there head up Avenue Vogt to the Camerouns Airlines office and then down the side street to the Renault and Mercedes dealers.
UK Embassy
   Winston Churchill Avenue (near the Hotel Independence)
USA Embassy
   Rue Nachtigal, PO Box 817
Note There are also Benin and Togolese embassies in Yaounde but there is no Niger embassy.
British Council
   Les Galeries, Avenue J F Kennedy
American Cultural Centre
   Boston Bank Building near City Hall on Avenue de l'Independence

WAZA NATIONAL PARK

This is the most famous of Cameroun's national parks. Here you can see elephant, giraffe, hippo, ostrich, antelope, gazelle, lion (February is the best time for these) and many different varieties of birdlife. There are no vehicles for hire at the park so you need your own transport; otherwise you'll have to try your luck hitching tourist cars at the park entrance. There is a bus from Maroua to the park entrance for CFA 750 plus CFA 400 for your baggage. You can stay either at the *Campement* for CFA 5790 per room (three beds) or camp for a small charge near the park entrance. Entry to the park costs CFA 2500 but this allows you to visit as many times as you like in one year. A guide is compulsory in each vehicle and costs CFA 1500 (some people have been charged CFA 2500 and others CFA 3500). The park is only open during the dry season – November to March.

LAKE CHAD

Being one of the few but also the largest natural body of water in West Africa, Lake Chad certainly has a romantic quality about it but it's a sensitive area and you may find that it is essentially out of bounds. One traveller who attempted to go there recently got only as far as the village of Makari (about 15 km from the lake). As soon as he stepped off the bus he was told in no uncertain terms by both a tribal chief and an army officer to get out double quick – and they made sure he did just that by putting him on the first vehicle going south. Maybe you'll have better luck?

Cape Verde

The Cape Verde islands lie some 600 km off the coast of Senegal and are one of the smallest and poorest of the African nations. Earlier uninhabited, the islands were colonised by the Portuguese in 1462, the labour and the majority of the population being slaves taken from the West African coast. The racial mixture which developed – mainly mulattos, some blacks and a few whites – remains much the same today, and the language – a Cabo Verdian Creole – is the result of a melding of Portuguese and various West African languages.

Even though there is evidence of an earlier, richer vegetation, much of the land is now barren and, like most of West Africa south of the Sahara, the islands have borne the brunt of the Sahel drought throughout the '70s and '80s. The local staple food, maize, grows under very precarious conditions and is correspondingly unreliable. Fruit and vegetables (bananas, manioc, beans, sweet potatoes) are only available in small quantities. All the same, a start has been made in many places to counteract the effects of the drought under the 'green barrier' scheme, though food supplies and the largest contribution to the national wealth continue to come from the sea, which teems with fish. Also of some significance is salt mining on the islands of Sal and Maio.

The importance of the islands for the Portuguese lay not so much in any inherent wealth they may have possessed, but in their strategic placement between Africa, America and Europe. Cape Verde was long one of the most important slaving stations of the region. Even when the Portuguese were forced to drastically curtail their slaving activities as a result of British navy intervention in the 19th century, the islands continued to flourish as the centre of the slave trade between West Africa and the Spanish Antilles.

With the advent of the ocean liner, the harbours of Mindelo/Sao Vicente became important victualing stations where ships took on supplies of coal, water and livestock. Those who made the most of this were not so much the colonial authorities as the emerging northern European economic powers – chiefly Britain. The Portuguese, however, despite the fact that they were incapable and unwilling to care much for the welfare of the Cabo Verdians, clung on stubbornly to their control of the islands though they did make certain concessions, particularly in the cultural realm. While Portugal continued to neglect the economic and political development of its mainland African colonies, Cabo Verde, with its

Cape Verde Islands

light-skinned population, was regarded as a special case and efforts were made to keep it separate from Africa and bound more closely to Portugal. It was the first Portuguese colony to have a school for higher education, and though education was available only to a small minority, this led to the growth of a rich indigenous literature which found expression in the magazines *Claridade*, *Certeza* and *Suplemento Cultural*, among others.

The ideas expressed in these magazines, however, gave evidence of a growing sense of identity with the African nations, which accelerated after WW II and eventually led to the formation of the African Party for the Independence of Guinea and Cabo Verde (PAIGC). Under the leadership of Amilcar Cabral, PAIGC began to pressure the colonial authorities to grant independence. The fascist regime in Lisbon was in no mood to come to terms with these demands and reacted with increasing violence and repression, forcing the PAIGC to adopt guerrilla tactics from 1961 onwards. In Guinea-Bissau they were relatively successful so that by 1973 it was possible for a unilateral declaration of independence to be made. Guerrilla warfare in the jungle is one thing, however. On barren islands in the middle of the Atlantic it is quite another, and Cabo Verde had to wait until Salazar was toppled in Portugal before independence was granted in 1975.

One of the aims of PAIGC was the union of Cabo Verde and Guinea-Bissau. Between independence and 1980 efforts were made to achieve this, but they were dashed in 1980 when the Guinean President, Luiz Cabral, was overthrown in a coup by the prime minister, Joao Vieira. Since then, Cabo Verde has gone its own way under the African Independence Party of Cabo Verde (PAICV).

Though Marxist in orientation, PAICV follows a very pragmatic course, and with the generous assistance of international welfare agencies and corporations life on the islands has improved considerably.

Being only too familiar with the harshness of the climate and the need to make the most of the limited resources available, the government is doing its best to see that all is divided equally. The threat of starvation has been removed, illiteracy is being eradicated (a sixth of the population now attend school) and health facilities have been considerably improved.

Nevertheless, independence has brought no immediate prosperity to the islanders and every time the east wind blows they look abroad for their future. In the last 100 years over half a million Cabo Verdians have emigrated, nearly half of them to the USA.

For many years we heard of no one going to the Cape Verde islands, and although this changed recently with the arrival of two quite detailed letters, they are unlikely to become a popular destination. Cape Verde isn't an exotic tropical paradise. It's a small land which makes its impression subtly through its cultural independence, pleasant atmosphere and friendly people.

FACTS

The islands, which cover some 4000 square km, are of volcanic origin and consist of 10 islands and eight smaller islets, nine of which have been settled in the course of time. They fall into two groups depending on their relation to the wind: Barlavento (the windward islands), comprising Santo Antao, Sao Vicente, Santa Lucia, Sao Nicolau, Sal and Boavista; and Sotavento (the leeward islands), comprising Maio, Santiago, Fogo and Brava.

The main towns are the capital, Praia (Santiago) and Mindelo (S Vicente). The population is around 300,000, a third of whom live on Santiago.

VISAS

There are Cabo Verdian embassies in the following countries: Angola, Algeria, Argentina, Guinea-Conakry, Italy, Netherlands, Portugal, Sao Tome e Principe,

Senegal, USSR and USA. Portuguese speakers can apply direct to the Ministerio de Negocias Estrangeiros, Direccao de Immigracao, Cabo Verde. If you can't speak Portuguese, most Portuguese embassies will assist you in filling in the necessary forms and will process your application if there is no Cabo Verdian embassy in the country where you apply. You need two photos, an onward ticket and an International Vaccination card for cholera and yellow fever. The embassy in Senegal is at Rue du Relais, off Avenue Ponty, Dakar. Visas there cost CFA 2000 and take about three weeks to come through.

There are no duty-free allowances of anything (tobacco, alcohol, perfume, etc).

MONEY

US$1 =   78 Escudo
DM1 =   30 Escudo

The unit of currency is the escudo = 100 centavos. There are no restrictions on the import of local currency but export is limited to 6000 escudos.

Currency declaration forms are issued on arrival and strictly checked on leaving to make sure that all transactions have gone through a bank (receipts must be shown).

LANGUAGE

Portuguese is the official language but Cabo Verdian Creole is the everyday language of virtually everyone.

GETTING THERE & AROUND

Probably the most useful flight for travellers is the direct Dakar-Praia flight which goes on Tuesday (by *TACU* – the Cabo Verdian airline) and Saturday (by *Air Senegal*). The fare is US$110. All other international flights land at Amilcar Cabral airport on the island of Sal.

There is a network of internal flights to all the islands with the exception of Brava (airport under construction here). Praia to Mindelo (S Vicente) costs US$20. There's also a boat which costs US$8 but the schedule is irregular. Brava can be reached from S Filipe (Fogo) by boat. Travel on the islands themselves is by bus or truck. Taxis are generally very expensive.

PLACES TO STAY

Every island has something of interest, but by and large the pace of life is slow. Santiago, for instance, is very African and it's here that the majority of black people live. The markets are very colourful and it's worth making enquiries about the dates of local festivals in honour of various deities. Music is an integral part of these festivities.

The town of Mindelo (S Vicente) is very reminiscent of a deserted Portuguese provincial town. The small bars in and around the harbour have their own special atmosphere and are well worth a visit. Because of the rocky coastline, there are only a few beaches. The most beautiful is at Tarrafal (Santiago), reached by bus from Praia (about 80 km). There's a small, cheap house for rent there. Another is the black volcanic sand beach on the west coast of Fogo south of S Filipe, the main town on the island. The volcano on this island also offers spectacular views. The beaches are anything but over-run and the water is warm all the year round (between 20°C and 27°C). During the winter months, however, strong north winds make bathing unpleasant.

There are few fairly good hotels in the middle price range at Praia, Mindelo, Sal and S Filipe. Other than these, cheap *pensao* can be found in most places. Average prices are 300 escudo a single and 450 escudo a double. In Praia, try the unnamed *pensao* on the corner of the *Café Portugal* or the *Hotel Felicidade* which costs around US$7 per night. In Mindelo, try the *Chave d'Ouro*. On Sal try the *Pensao Dona Angela* which is in the small village near the international airport (within walking distance even with a rucksack). It's cheap, interesting and has great food and drink.

Food is available in most hotels and *pensao*; a good meal should cost around 100-160 escudo. The local dish, *cachupa* (maize and beans), is generally available in small bars and the like. There's a wide variety of alcoholic drinks – beer, wine, local spirits, punch – but non-alcoholic drinks tend to be quite expensive.

If you have any health problems here, ask to see Andreas Kalk, the German doctor at the hospital in Mindelo (S Vicente).

If you'd like more information about Cabo Verde, contact the Secretario de Estado de Comercio Turismore Artesanato, CP105, Praia, Sao Tiago, Cabo Verde.

Central African Republic

This area of Africa has been raped for centuries and the process is still going on. As a result, the CAR is an underdeveloped, fragmented and poverty-stricken country, but with an enlightened government it could be relatively prosperous. Unfortunately, that isn't an event which is likely to occur for quite some time, not only because of the rapaciousness of its own rulers but because of the influence of foreign interests. Despite the fact that the country has important deposits of uranium, copper, tin, iron, chromium and diamonds and could export significant amounts of cotton, timber and textiles, precious little of the wealth which is – and could be – generated ever seeps down to the population at large. Most of it is frittered away by a tiny elite on luxury items. Even the country's independence, which supposedly dates from 1960, is a charade. The Central African Republic remains, to all intents and purposes, a French colony; and the current president, David Dacko, is merely a French puppet. The nation's economy, likewise, is heavily dependent on French aid.

The area's undoing came with the slave trade to the Americas. Despite archaeological remains which indicate extensive settlement in the region long before the rise of ancient Egypt and, later, an advanced culture whose artisans were coveted from far afield, organised society here gradually collapsed when not only hundreds of thousands of people were dragged in chains to the West Coast for transportation to the Americas but Islamic conquerors swept down from the north to institute their own trade in human flesh. Even as recently as the 19th century about 20,000 slaves from this part of Africa were being sold every year on the Egyptian market.

Into this scene of devastation came the French and Belgians in the 1880s, the former bent on rivalry with the British in the Sudan. The territory passed to France, which quickly parcelled it out to private enterprise. The concession agents and managers who were brought in to exploit the country proved to be nothing less than murderous psychopaths, and the French colonial authorities were little better in their treatment of the indigenous population. Thousands lost their lives as forced labourers or as a result of torture and execution for supposed misdemeanors and desertion. This kind of treatment naturally generated resentment, and although the Africans resisted the onslaught on their independence, the backbone of the resistance movement had been broken by the 1930s as a result of French military action, famine and epidemics.

The first signs of nationalism sprang up after WW II in the form of Boganda's Mouvement d'Evolution Sociale de l'Afrique Noire. The party was to be instrumental in forcing the French to grant independence, but before it did so Boganda died in a mysterious plane crash in 1959. The leadership was taken over by David Dacko, who became the country's first president at independence in 1960. Dacko's rule quickly became highly repressive and dictatorial, and in 1966, amid an atmosphere of political rivalry, impending national bankruptcy and a threatened national strike, he was overthrown by the army commander, Jean-Bedel Bokassa (a close relative of Dacko). So began 13 years of one of the most sordid and brutal regimes Africa has ever experienced. Even the pretence that the country enjoyed some sort of democracy was swept aside as Bokassa progressively took over all the important government portfolios and snuffed out opposition wherever it raised its head. The slightest hint of dissent was sufficient for offenders to be publicly clubbed to death – often with the personal involvement of Bokassa himself. One particularly shocking display of barbarity which aroused international condemnation was the massacre of school children who had taken to the streets to protest against Bokassa's demand that they all buy uniforms from one of Bokassa's own clothing factories. Again, Bokassa was personally involved. Yet France, covetous of the uranium deposits at Bakouma and the exclusive big game hunting grounds near the Sudanese border (patronised by former French President Giscard d'Estaing) continued to bail out the economy and pander to Bokassa's every whim. Loans were negotiated from such diverse sources as South Africa and private US banks using the country's mineral resources as the carrot, but virtually all this money was squandered on prestige projects, many of which were never completed.

Then, in 1976, Bokassa embarked on his final and silliest fantasy – to have himself crowned 'Emperor' of a renamed Central African Empire. The coronation took place in December 1977 and despite the worldwide derision which the event provoked, the French agreed to finance almost the entire operation. A more cynical misuse of funds (which amounted to virtually all of the GNP of the Central African Republic for a whole year) would be hard to imagine in one of Africa's poorest countries. Bokassa's time was obviously running out, and when news of the massacre of Bangui school children surfaced France began to plot his removal with Dacko as its protege. Plans for a coup were formalised in September 1979 when France abruptly ended its aid to the

'empire.' This predictably sent Bokassa off to Libya to beg for support. Within hours of his departure, Dacko arrived in Bangui aboard a French Air Force plane along with 1000 French troops flown in from Libreville, Gabon and N'Djamena, Chad.

Bokassa eventually turned up at Orly Airport in Paris, begging for political asylum, but the French refused to let him leave the plane. Meanwhile, Dacko's takeover wasn't being greeted with quite the enthusiasm that he and his backers had hoped for and he came to rely increasingly on the presence of French paratroopers. That not a lot has changed or is likely to do so can be gleaned from the fact that Dacko has announced he intends to keep a French military presence in the country for the next 10 years and is going to exchange ambassadors with South Africa.

FACTS

The Central African Republic has a population of around two million, many of whom still lived a traditional lifestyle in villages in the bush until Bokassa forcibly relocated them near the main roads. Very few travellers seem to take time to explore this country, particularly east of Bangui, the capital, but those who have suggest that it's well worth the effort. The country is one immense plateau varying in height between 600 and 700 metres with three distinct climatic zones. The south is tropical, with high humidity and temperatures gradually changing to a 'Sudan-Guinea' type of climate in the centre with abundant rainfall. The north is dry scrub and forms part of the Sahel. The main rainy season is from May to November.

VISAS

Visas are required by all except nationals of France, Germany (West), Israel and Switzerland.

In Lomé, Togo, visas are obtainable from the French embassy for CFA 1200. You need one photo. The visa takes 48

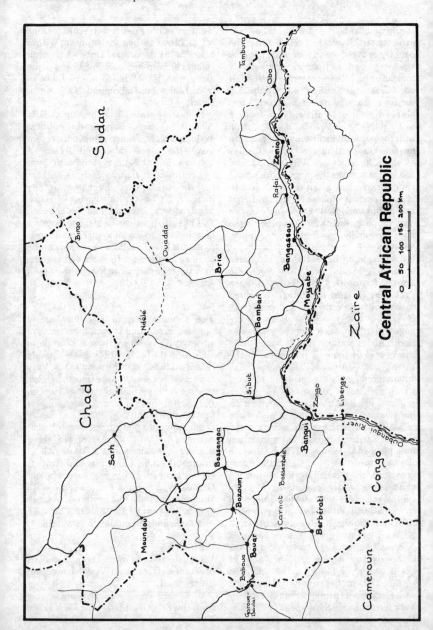

Central African Republic

0 50 100 150 200 Km

hours to issue and is valid for 30 days. In Brazzaville, Congo, a visa costs CFA 1500, one photo is necessary, and it is valid for a stay of 10 days. In Yaounde, Cameroun, a visa costs CFA 10,000(!) and you need one photo. It is valid for a stay of 10 days and takes 24 hours to issue.

Avoid applying for your visa in Paris, as the man in charge of issuing visas has been described as 'a right bastard' and you could be kept waiting for weeks even if you have a booked flight.

Separate entry and exit permits are necessary for Bangui. If you're on your way into Bangui from Cameroun, the entry permits are issued at PK12 (a police checkpoint on the outskirts of Bangui). Before leaving Bangui for Zaire you have to get an exit permit from the Immigration Office in town. This is also where you must get an entry permit if you're coming in from Zaire. (If you're coming from Zaire the entry and exit stamps for Bangui can be obtained at the same time.)

Visa extensions cost CFA 2000 for a further 10 days, CFA 2500 for a further 15 days and CFA 4000 for a further 21 days. The fee must be paid in tax stamps and the extensions are generally issued the same day you apply. You may also need to write a letter setting out why you want to stay longer; you're advised to use plenty of honorifics ('Your esteemed Excellency,' 'Your humble servant,' etc) if you want your application to be successful. The letter must be written in French.

Cameroun visas In Bangui, these vary in price and length of stay allowed. Typical would be 1500 CFA for a visa of 21 days issued in 48 hours, but some people have paid CFA 1000 for a 20-day visa which is issued in 24 hours. Others have paid CFA 2000 for a 10-day visa which is issued in 48 hours.

Chad visas The embassy in Bangui is on Rue de Bongada. Visas cost CFA 3000 for a stay of less than 30 days and CFA 4500 for a stay of 30 days. They are issued while

you wait, and although a lot of questions are asked, the ambassador is very friendly.

Nigerian visas Seven-day stay permits are free and issued while you wait.

Sudan visas The embassy in Bangui is on Avenue de l'Independence. All visa applications have to be referred to Khartoum and it will be up to eight weeks before you get a reply.

Zaire visas The embassy in Bangui is on Avenue de l'Independence. The price of visas varies considerably. A four-month, single-entry visa issued in 24 hours costs CFA 6400 plus two photos. Three-month, multiple-entry visas issued in 24 hours cost CFA 12,800. The one good thing about the embassy here, however, is that it is one of the very few Zairois embassies that do not demand a letter of introduction from your own embassy.

MONEY
US$1 = CFA 460

The unit of currency is the CFA franc. Import/export of local currency allowed is up to CFA 75,000.

There is a good black market for Zairois currency in Bangui; if you're going that way it would be a good idea to stock up there rather than in Zongo across the river. Check with travellers coming from Bangui on what the current rate is. Sometimes it's better to change in Zongo, but this doesn't appear to be the case at present. The bank in Zongo won't accept traveller's cheques and will only change amounts of cash in excess of US$50. The moneychangers know this and lower their rates correspondingly. Hide your zaires very well, as the customs search is usually very thorough. The moneychangers prefer CFAs to US$ if you're buying zaires.

There are no banks between N'Gaoundere and Bangui. If you are stuck for money in Bouar try the *Maison Murat*, which will usually take both cash and traveller's cheques. It is sometimes possible to buy US dollars at the BIAO bank in Bangui but don't count on it. However, this bank is very efficient if you want to change traveller's cheques into CFA, and there is no commission.

Airport departure tax for West Africa, Sudan and Zaire is CFA 1200 (single ticket) or CFA 2400 (return ticket). For other destinations it is CFA 3500 (single ticket) or CFA 7000 (return ticket).

LANGUAGE
French is the official language and Sango is the national language. Very little English is spoken.

POST
The Poste Restante in Bangui charges CFA 100 per letter. Check the letters very carefully, as they're all lumped together in the one box.

GETTING THERE & AROUND
Air
Bangui has recently become a starting/returning point, especially for French people, since there's a very cheap charter flight operated by a company called *Point Air Mulhouse*, or simply *Le Point*. It flies between Lyon in France and Bangui, from November to April. Tickets cost French francs 2750 return for less than 30 days and French francs 3150 return for more than 30 days or French francs 1800 one way. There is a French francs 300 supplement going south during July. The planes leave Lyon on Tuesday on alternate weeks and on Wednesday on the other weeks. The flight takes six hours. The office in Bangui is on the Rue de la Résistance at Avenue David Dacko, in the same building as the Peace Corps. Office hours are 8 am to 1 pm. The same company operates an even cheaper flight between Lyon and Ouagadougou, Bourkinafasso, which costs US$250 one way. You'd be hard-pressed to find a ticket as cheap as this to the heart of Africa anywhere else.

Road
There are no railways in the Central African Republic but, at least in the western part of the country, there is a well-maintained network of roads. East of Bangui as far as the border with Sudan the roads are terrible, as there has been no maintenance since 1973. Abandoned road graders litter the sides of the road and the jungle is beginning to take over again. Hitching is easy in the west and many travellers have been given free lifts recently. Garoua-Boulai (Cameroun border) to Bangui shouldn't take more than two days, and in the right vehicle can take only a day. In the opposite direction, the minibuses from Bangui to Bouar leave daily between 6 and 7 am from the Gare Routiere, though the cruising for more passengers and the paperwork generally delay departure until 9 am. The fare is 5500 CFA and the journey takes 15 to 20 hours. From Bouar to Garoua-Boulai the minibuses leave daily at 6 am, cost 2300 CFA and take about six hours. Where lifts have to be paid for, they will cost about CFA 10 per km. Buses cost CFA 15 to 20 per km. Most are 18-seater minibuses which often squeeze in 24 people.

To/From Cameroun
The crossing point which most people use is Garoua-Boulai on the road between Bouar and Bertoua. There are direct buses, usually daily, between Bangui and Garoua-Boulai for CFA 7700, as well as buses from Bangui to Bouar for CFA 5500 which take 15 to 20 hours and then from Bouar to Garoua-Boulai for CFA 2300 which take about six hours. This stretch is easy to hitch and it's often possible to get a free lift. If hitching from Bangui, take a bus or taxi first to checkpoint PK12 and then hitch from there. There are trucks all day and lifts cost about CFA 7000.

If you intend to catch the train once you get into Cameroun, then instead of heading for Belabo, which is where many people pick it up, get a bus from Garoua-Boulai to N'Gaoundal (not N'Gaoundere) and pick up the overnight train to Yaounde from there. You need to arrive at Garoua-Boulai early in the day to do this.

To/From Chad

An interesting route to take into Chad is from Bangui to Sarh via Damara, Sibut, Dekoa, Kaga Barboro and Kabo (640 km in total). Get a taxi from the centre of Bangui and start hitching from PK 12 (the police checkpost on the outskirts of Bangui). You may get a direct lift to Sarh from there, but it's more likely you will have to village-hop as there's not much traffic. Expect to have to pay CFA 7000 to 10,000 for the journey. If you're offered a lift to Batangafo, get off at Kaga Barboro as the former is off the main road and you could be stuck for days. The Chad customs are located at Maro and you can expect a very heavy search. They turn out *everything*! And the process is repeated five times before you reach Sarh!

To/From Sudan

In the dry season there are trucks which ply the route between Bangui and Nyala, but in the wet season (August to December) you will have to go by camel train or hire donkeys and a guide. If you make use of the camel trains then you're in for a very interesting trip. Travellers who have done this have all spoken enthusiastically about it, saying it was one of the highlights of their trip. Further details are in the Sudan chapter.

To/From Zaire

To get to Zaire you simply take the ferry across the Ubangui River from Bangui to Zongo. It costs CFA 100 plus CFA 50-100 for a backpack or Zaire 10. Don't cross the river at weekends, as the Zaire customs don't work then and you'll have to hang around in Zongo until Monday morning. If the ferry isn't working – it breaks down occasionally – take a motor boat or pirogue. If you're taking a vehicle across this river you not only have to pay for the ferry (CFA 6000) but also for the vehicle platform (CFA 12,000). Make enquiries first at the Port Captain's office. If you have traveller's cheques there is now a bank at Zongo (Banque du Peuple).

Another crossing is possible by ferry from Bangassou. If you have your own vehicle and want to get across the river here, it's going to be an expensive day. Nine times out of ten the ferry will be across the other side of the river and the ferry man will demand CFA 500, five litres of diesel and a loan of your battery to get his ferry started. Add on US$20 plus a tip for the canoe boy before he'll consider taking you to the other side. Make sure the ferry is securely tied up at either end before you drive your vehicle on or off. Some travellers have ended up with broken springs and trailer couplings because the ferry started to drift off. One unlucky bunch of travellers even had to promise to give the ferry man a lift to the first town in Zaire (150 km) after the ferry lost its drive shaft in mid-river and he had to pole it the rest of the way! If you're on foot or have just a motorbike, you can go across by pirogue.

BANGASSOU

You can camp free at the *Mission Protestante* or on the grounds of the *Tourist Hotel* for a small charge. Apart from these two places there is the very exclusive *Hunting Hotel-Restaurant* where you may well get to rub shoulders with French cabinet ministers and even Giscard d'Estaing out there on shooting holidays. Watch out for thieves if you are camping.

BANGUI

The capital of the Central African Republic, Bangui is a pleasant, shady town full of military personnel. You're advised to cross the road rather than walk past anything with an armed guard. If you're stopped, just look blank and pretend you don't speak French.

The **Boganda Museum**, Rue de l'Industrie between Avenue Boganda and Avenue de

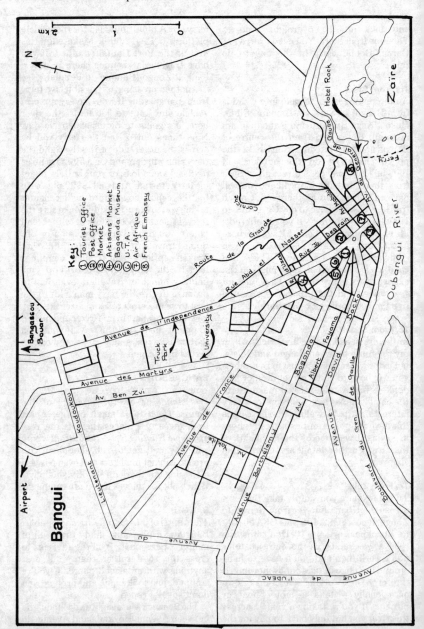

Bangui

Key:
1. Tourist Office
2. Post Office
3. Market
4. Artisans' Market
5. Boganda Museum
6. U.T.A.
7. Air Afrique
8. French Embassy

l'Independence, is well organised and well worth a visit. One of the most interesting collections is of musical instruments from the area, and you're allowed to try them out. There are also good displays on the pygmies and their culture. Admission costs CFA 200 or CFA 150 if you have a student card. The museum is close to the Cameroun and Nigerian embassies.

The **artisans' market** is also worth a visit. There are some exquisite malachite bead necklaces for sale here. The only other places you will find them in Africa is in certain places in Cameroun and southern Zaire. Prices in this market are more or less fixed, so bargaining won't get you too far. Avoid the market at Km 7. It seeths with thieves who will attack even large groups of travellers in broad daylight with knives.

Information
The Tourist Office is on Avenue Bartholomew Boganda. The agent for Thomas Cook here is Bangui Tourisme.

The Immigration Office is two blocks west of the market at Rue Joseph Degrain and Avenue du Président Senghor, in a dilapidated old house with no sign. It's easy to walk right past it unless you ask.

The BIAO bank, Place de la République, is efficient and makes no charge for changing traveller's cheques. It's open from 7 to 11.30 am.

Useful Addresses
Belgian Embassy
  Place de la République
French Embassy
  Boulevard de General de Gaulle, BP 784
British Consulate
  c/o Diamond Distributors, Avenue Bartholomew Boganda about one km from the centre. It's only open between 8 and 9 am during the week.
Cameroun Embassy
  Off the Avenue Boganda near the Boganda Museum
Chad Embassy
  On the Avenue Boganda two to three km from the centre

Congo Brazzaville Embassy
  On the Avenue Boganda close to the city centre
Nigerian Embassy
  Between Avenue Boganda and the Avenue de l'Independence near the Boganda Museum and the Cathedral
Sudan Embassy
  On the Avenue de l'Independence two to three km from the centre and before the Gare Routiere
USA Embassy
  Place de la République, BP 924
Point-Air Mulhouse
  Rue de la Résistance at Avenue David Dacko (same building as the Peace Corps). Office hours are 8 am to 1 pm.

Places to Stay
One of the most popular places in the past was the campsite below the Hotel Roc, but this has now been closed down. The *Catholic Mission* is very friendly and will allow you to camp there for a small donation. Facilities include hot showers and a bar with cold beer. It also has rooms to rent but they're expensive. There are no cheap hotels as such, but two of the cheaper ones are the *Minerva Hotel*, Avenue du 1er Janvier 1966 two blocks from the Place de la République, and the *Palace Hotel*, Place de la République (Avenue Boganda and Avenue de l'Independence). The Minerva costs 11,270 CFA a double. The Palace has large, airy rooms with bathroom for CFA 9500 a double, and also has its own bar and restaurant. At the same price as the Minerva is the *Independence Hotel*, Avenue David Dacko two blocks from the Place de la République. The *Hotel Roc* is well upmarket at CFA 12,000 a double minimum. All the rooms are air-conditioned and have their own bathrooms. There is a bar, restaurant, swimming pool, dancing room and even a bowling green.

Many people stay at the *Centre d'Accueil Touristiques* (Tourist Welcome Centre) (tel 611256), which is at Km 7 on the old road to M'Baiki. To get there, take a service taxi out along the Avenue Boganda to the Km 5 market (where the paved road ends) and then walk two km along the same road. It costs CFA 500 to camp, CFA 1000 a single and CFA 2000 a double. There's also a CFA 5000 deposit to pay which is refundable when you leave. The rooms vary. Some have mosquito nets and doors with locks. Others have no nets and just plastic cartons for doors. The place has its own restaurant – the *Kirite* – and prices are reasonable but service is very slow. There are also plenty of cafés just down the road. Nothing is safe at this place so don't leave gear hanging around, and if you have your own vehicle then don't park it alongside the fences, as thieves will cut a hole in the fence and use the vehicle as cover while they break in.

If you're looking for something to do in the evening, try the bar of the *Hotel Safari* – once the most expensive hotel in Bangui but now somewhat run-down. It has a superb location on an isthmus which juts out about halfway across the river. You can see hippos here. Beers are sold at normal prices– CFA 200 for a large chilled bottle.

Other

There are service taxis along all the main routes which cost 90 CFA (before 9 pm) and 125 CFA (after 9 pm) per journey. To the airport they cost 150 CFA (before 9 pm) or 200 CFA (after 9 pm). These are shared taxis. If you hire the whole cab they cost 700/900 CFA in the city and 900/1500 CFA to the airport. Minibuses are even cheaper and there are also infrequent buses.

The minibuses to Bouar (for Cameroun) leave from the Gare Routiere about four km out along the Avenue de l'Independence early in the mornings between 6 and 7 am. They first cruise along the Avenue du Lt Koudoukou to the Km 5 market and back to the Avenue de l'Independence looking for more passengers before leaving. They can also be caught at PK 12, where the paperwork usually delays them until 9 am.

Warning Watch out for thieves and pick-pockets in Bangui, especially at the markets and down by the Hotel Roc. There are plenty of them.

BIRAO

Birao is a small, interesting town near the Sudanese border in the far north-east of the CAR. You can stay here free at the *Catholic Mission*, but water is in short supply and often dirty. Avoid using the village well or you'll make yourself very unpopular.

Travellers who have been through Birao recently report that there is only one person in the whole town who is willing to change money, and his rates are very poor. Unless you bring in CFAs, it's going to be an expensive place to pass through. If you have your own vehicle this can be a serious problem – head on for Ndele and try the Catholic Mission there.

BOUAR

Bouar is a small town on the road from the Cameroun border to Bangui and is the country's largest French military base. The cheapest place to stay here is the *Foyer de la Jeunesse* on the main road into town. A bed in the dormitory costs CFA 950. The bathrooms are excellent and the director is a very friendly person. If it's full, try the *Hotel Moura*, which has four comfortable, clean rooms at CFA 1500 a double. *Hotel des Relais* has also been recommended. Forget about the missions here as they don't welcome travellers.

NDELE

Ndele is a small, interesting town near the Chad border in north-central CAR. You can stay here free at the *Catholic Mission*.

NATIONAL & GAME PARKS

A start has been made to train rangers for a number of projected national parks to the east of the country but, according to expatriates working on the scheme who wrote to us, when the areas eventually become open to tourists all the game will have been wiped out. The amount of poaching which goes on is incredible and includes gangs from Chad and the Sudan as well as local entrepreneurs and CAR officials – in fact just about everybody. It's so bad in the east that a Sudanese gang gunned down a local mayor and several other people over a dispute about shooting game. It appears that the Sudanese are highly organised, use automatic weapons and shoot down virtually everything that moves. Sounds just like the Australian outback!

A few people have written in to recommend a visit to the waterfalls at **Boali** about 80 km north-west of Bangui.

They've been described as the second most impressive waterfalls after Victoria Falls. There is a campsite there with a bar. Equally impressive if not more so are the falls at **Kembe** west of Bangassou on the Bangui-Bangassou road. There is an area cleared for campers at Kembe which is free but there's no bar.

OTHER

Jobs If you're skilled or professionally qualified it's fairly easy to get a job in the Central African Republic. One man from Australia even got himself a job as a park warden because he'd spent time shovelling shit in a zoo in Australia.

Chad

Ever since independence from the French in 1960, Chad has been torn apart by violent conflicts in which thousands have lost their lives. Far from bringing anything nearer to resolution, independence has brought the exact opposite. At various times Christians have been pitted against Moslems, northerners against southerners, tribe against tribe and one political faction against another. Arms, cash, training camps and headquarters-in-exile have been provided at various times by France, Libya, Egypt, Gabon and the Sudan to one group or another depending on their political colour or military fortunes. Both France and Libya have intervened directly with their own regular troops on more than one occasion. Alliances between various factions have been formed and broken with bewildering regularity, and all attempts at mediation by neighbouring countries, the OAU and the UN have failed miserably. N'Djamena, the capital, has been besieged by fierce fighting on several occasions despite agreements to demilitarise the area around it.

Working out who's who in this tragic mess isn't easy, and keeping up with events here is even more difficult. What is fairly clear, however, is that throughout the 1970s Chad became a battleground in the struggle between France and Libya for control of the country. At present a stalemate exists, with the country partitioned roughly in half. The north is held by Goukouni's forces backed by regular units of the Libyan armed forces, and the south is held by Habre's forces backed by French paratroopers with air support. Neither is willing to give an inch, nor are the two backing powers willing to risk an all-out confrontation.

The latest conflict came about as a result of the Libyan invasion of the Tibesti – the mountainous area of northern Chad – in late 1980. At that time, 3000 Libyan troops backed by tanks, artillery and war planes gradually fought their way south to N'Djamena where they defeated the troops of Hissene Habre, the leader of one of the strongest factions. The remnants of Habre's forces fled east towards the Sudan after destroying their headquarters and ammunition dumps while Habre took refuge in Cameroun. Shortly after this, President Goukouni made an official visit to Libya where it was announced that the two countries would work towards full unity. The announcement was greeted with consternation not only by the French but by many other black African countries which viewed it as an annexation of Chad by Libya. Their fears were probably genuine. Qadafi is renowned for his aborted attempts at 'union' with other countries – Egypt, Syria, Tunisia and, most recently, Morocco – but Chad was in a different league, being politically, economically and militarily weak. Not only that, but it was no secret that Chad had important deposits of uranium, wolfram and cassiterite in the Tibesti, gold in Mayo Kebbi, and gold, uranium, iron and bauxite in the eastern part of the country. It also grows a considerable amount of cotton in the south.

To understand the factionalism that has split this country, it's necessary to appreciate that the imposition of French colonial rule on this area reversed the traditional balance of power. Before the arrival of the French, the Moslem kingdoms of Kanem and Baguirmi dominated the area and based their economies on the slave trade. The slaves were procured by raiding the black peoples of the south who could offer little resistance because of their decentralised political structure based on the lineage system. The northern kingdoms fought long and hard against the French and it wasn't until 1916 that the French brought the area largely under their control. Even then, fighting continued until 1930.

In the south, on the other hand, the French quickly established their control, introduced cotton, and encouraged the development of a market economy which led to the breakdown of the old social order. The cultivation of cotton led to modest investments, the building of schools and the training of the local population. Nothing of this nature took place in the north until the 1950s. As a result, the educated people of the south were in a much better position to assume leadership of the nationalist movement after WW II.

The first nationalist movement, the Parti Progressiste Tchadien (PPT), set up in 1947, based its struggle around the slogan, 'No more cotton, no more chiefs, no more taxes.' Since this struck at the heart of the colonial system, France switched allegiance to the feudal Moslem forces of the north, but after the PPT abandoned this stance in 1950 and integrated itself into the colonial structure the French were able to install a compliant territorial assembly, known as the Loi Cadre. This body assumed responsibility for the country's internal autonomy, granted in 1956. All this took place in the era of De Gaulle and his attempts to make all French colonies into overseas departments of metropolitan France.

The Loi Cadre only had limited support and in 1958 the Union Nationale Tchadienne (UNT) was formed by trade unionists, students and intellectuals. It demanded complete independence, the ousting of the French-installed regime and the withdrawal of all foreign troops. When independence was granted in 1960,

Francois Tombalbaye became the first Head of State. Intent on making himself into a dictator, Tombalbaye purged the government of supporters of its previous leader (Gabriel Lisette), declared a one-party state (the PPT), and arrested the leaders of the UNT. The arrests provoked a series of conspiracies which Tombalbaye conveniently used to bolster his own personal power.

Opposition to Tombalbaye's rule and the exorbitant taxes which he imposed was met with violent repression. Against this background the Chad National Liberation Front (FROLINAT) was formed at Nyala in Sudan in 1966. FROLINAT was an alliance between UNT and the Chad Liberation Front (FLT). The latter was a regional, conservative Moslem movement which already controlled resistance forces in the east of the country. The resistance movement spread quickly, especially in the north and centre, because of the harassment and contempt shown towards traditional leaders by the central government – the Derde, father of one of FROLINAT's leaders, went into exile in Libya in 1966. By mid-1968 the situation was serious and Tombalbaye was saved only by the intervention of France, which dropped paratroopers into the northern provinces and deployed a further 2500 troops in the country the following year. Tombalbaye was unable, however, to undermine FROLINAT, which began to receive substantial aid from Libya after 1971 until power struggles within the Front and the effects of thousands of arrests began to split the movement. Sudan cut off aid to FROLINAT early in 1972 and at the end of the year Libya did likewise, following a secret deal with Tombalbaye in which Libya was allowed to occupy a part of northern Chad (the 114,000-square-km Aouzou Strip) in return for 23,000 million CFA in aid.

Tombalbaye managed to alienate even further the support he had left by seeking to erase the memory of French colonialism. All French street and place names were

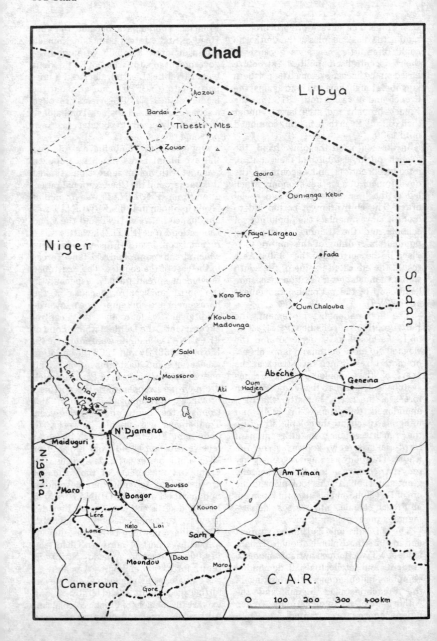

changed in favour of traditional names, Christian names were banned and all government officials, civil servants and ranking military officers were forced to undergo the *yondo* initiation rites of Tombalbaye's tribe. He was assassinated in a *coup d'etat* in 1975 and the government was taken over by General Malloum, whom Tombalbaye had imprisoned two years earlier on charges of plotting against him.

FROLINAT, however, was suspicious of a man who had once led Tombalbaye's troops against it and refused to lay down arms. Libya resumed its support of the Front in 1976 and after successful offensives in 1977 and 1978 a fragile truce was put together with Goukouni Oueddei assuming the leadership of the Front. The truce didn't last long and was complicated by intensified French military involvement, which led to the setting up of a so-called Government of National Unity with key posts distributed equally between the supporters of Malloum and Hissene Habre. (Habre had been dismissed from the leadership of FROLINAT in 1976 for his opposition to the Libyan occupation of the Aouzou Strip and had gone on to form his own army.) A power struggle between Malloum and Habre was inevitable and broke out in 1979. Thousands of civilians were massacred in N'Djamena and the south of the country, and the conflict quickly took on a decidedly regional and religious colour with the north pitted against the south and the Moslems against the Christians.

In the meantime, FROLINAT was having its own problems with power struggles, so that by the time another truce was arranged in late 1979 there were at least five armies in existence: FAN (Habre), FAP (Goukouni), FAT (Abdel-kader Kamougue), FACP (Abba Said), and FAO (Moussa Medela). Again the truce didn't last, and renewed fighting broke out in 1980 in which Habre's FAN, well supplied with arms from Egypt, was pitted against the rest, who in turn were supported by Libya. Habre's forces held their ground for quite some time, but when Libya made a renewed effort to oust them by throwing in units of its regular troops in 1983 this provoked France to intervene yet again.

FACTS

Chad, like the Sudan, stands at an ethnic crossroads where Arab Africa meets Black Africa. Unlike in the Sudan, however, the black Africans are in the majority here and dominate the government and civil service. The north is populated by people of Arab descent as well as nomadic Tuareg and Toubou.

Landlocked Chad is one of the world's poorest countries and development is hampered by insufficient and primitive communications as well as by political turmoil. The Sahel drought which has continued more or less through the 1970s and early 1980s has probably affected Chad more than any other country by destroying centuries-old patterns of existence and cultivation.

The country has three distinct climatic zones. The south is tropical, with as much as 1000 mm of rain per year. The centre is a mixture of scrub and desert and is the location of Lake Chad – the world's 11th largest lake. The north forms part of the Sahara desert and includes the Tibesti mountains, which are some of the highest in North Africa (the highest peak is nearly 3500 metres). The dry season runs from November to May in the south, and while temperatures usually range from 20° to 25°C, they can rise to 40°C just before the rains arrive.

VISAS

Visas are required by all except nationals of Andorra, Monaco and West Germany. In Bangui (CAR) a visa costs CFA 3000 for a stay of less than one month and CFA 4500 for a stay of over one month, and is issued while you wait. A lot of questions are asked but the ambassador is very friendly. The embassy is on Rue de

Boganda. In Yaounde a visa costs 4000 CFA for 15 days and is issued in one hour. the official who deals with visa applications is one of the friendliest people you're likely to meet in Africa. There are also consulates in Garoua and Kousseri (Cameroun).

You must register with immigration on arrival in N'Djamena and Sarh unless you entered Chad via the ferry from Kousseri to N'Djamena, in which case the entry stamp is sufficient. An exit stamp must be obtained before leaving. If you're taking the ferry across the Chari River from N'Djamena to the Cameroun, you can get the exit stamp at the boat terminal.

Until recently any travel east or north of the capital was forbidden. The same applied to Lake Chad, but you could travel anywhere south of N'Djamena without a special permit. The long closure of the Nigerian border throughout much of 1984, however, radically changed the situation, and the withdrawal of both French and Libyan troops from Chad in November 1984 is likely to ease travel restrictions considerably. The only thing you need these days in order to travel around the country is a *laissez-passer*. You get this by collecting a letter from the Ministry of Tourism near the Hotel Tchadienne, and then taking it to the Ministry of the Interior about 400 metres down the road behind the PTT. ('It's like an American Express Gold Card – you don't even have to produce your passport with this letter!') To get the letter you have to specify your itinerary and the licence number of your vehicle. If you're travelling by public transport then write 'en camion particulaire.' The Minister of the Interior himself signs the paper you get from the latter place and he's a friendly fellow who is always keen to meet travellers. The whole process may take a day or two, so get it in motion as soon as you arrive in N'Djamena.

There are very heavy searches on the CAR/Chad border at Maro. They turn out *everything* and even leaf through books,

etc. This is repeated no less than five times before you reach Sarh.

If you have a camera, you are strongly advised to get a photography permit. These are obtained from the Ministry of Tourism near the PTT just off the Etoile in N'Djamena (look for the new building with no bullet holes in it). The man who issues them may try to extract CFA 5000 from you for the permit. Smile, thank him for his time and head for the door. You'll get it for nothing 'because you're a student' or some similar face-saving phrase. You then have to get the permit stamped by Surete about 200 metres away in the same building as Immigration. There are even bullet holes in the filing cabinets here as well as in the walls and ceilings!

MONEY
US$1 = CFA 460

The unit of currency is the CFA franc. There are no restrictions on the import of local currency but export is limited to 10,000 CFA.

Airport departure tax for international flights is CFA 1200 on one-way tickets and CFA 2400 on return tickets to West Africa, Sudan and Zaire. It is CFA 3500 on one-way tickets and CFA 7000 on return tickets to all other destinations.

LANGUAGE
French is the official language but there are more than 50 local languages.

GETTING THERE & AROUND
The most usual overland points of entry are by ferry across the Chari River to N'Djamena from Kousseri in northern Cameroun (costs CFA 50) or by road from Bangui (CAR) to Sarh via Maro. It's also possible to enter from Cameroun at Lere and go by road to Sarh via Pala, Kelo, Moundou and Koumba. This road carries much more traffic than the Sarh-N'Djamena road and is an important route to northern Nigeria. There's also a new route opened

up between Chad and Niger along the top of Lake Chad.

Internal Transport
Air
There are no civil aircraft. The only planes are military DC4s and the light planes of SONASUT (sugar industry) and COTOTCHAD (cotton industry). If you're in Sarh it's well worth asking SONASUT pilots for a lift to Bangui (CAR) – said to be easy – Yaounde, Garoua and N'Djamena. Most of the flights are free. You can also get free rides on the military DC4s, though these have been known to be shot out of the air on occasion.

Road
As far as the roads go, the best time to travel is between November and May. During the rest of the year roads are often impassable because of flooding and deep mud. There are almost no sealed roads and there is no public transport system (buses, etc). From Sarh to N'Djamena there is at least one truck daily (ask in the market). The journey takes a day and a half and costs CFA 7500. The road is a dirt one with patches of potholed tarmac. You must get a stamp in your passport at Guelengdenl en route. A truck from Sarh to Lai costs CFA 5500.

Overland travel in Chad can be quite an adventure. Here's one account of the journey from the CAR to Sarh:

This road's great! Babies burst into tears at your horrible, deformed face (it's white). Crowds of kids gather when you arrive and run away when the terrible white apparition speaks, saying, 'Ca va!' Gradually they all return. I beckon them to come and shake hands. They approach and then run away again four times in all. Finally one plucks up the courage to shake hands and runs away again as soon as he touches. After that, one by one, they come up to shake hands beaming with pleasure. The younger ones are lifted up to shake hands by their sisters – just incredible. In another village I produced a camera and 50 kids ran into the picture wanting to be photographed. As you leave they all cheer. Totally undeveloped. No shops, not even the wooden suitcase sardines, bubble gum and cigarettes you get anywhere else in Africa. Just little round thatched huts with huge piles of cotton everywhere. Very picturesque.

Because of the long closure of the Nigerian land borders throughout much of 1984, a new route opened up across the top of Lake Chad direct to Niger. All you need in order to take this route is a *laissez-passer* from N'Djamena (see under 'Visas'). You first take a Land-Rover from the Parc Mao in N'Djamena to Mao for 10,000 CFA. From there you take another vehicle to the small village of Baga Sola for 5000 CFA. (Since Lake Chad hasn't filled up since 1975, there is an alternative route via Massagnet, Massakory and Bol to Baga Sola.) Baga Sola is full of friendly people and the police are very likely to provide you with accommodation until transport arrives to take you to Liwa. From Liwa you take another Land-Rover to N'Guigmi (Niger) for a further 5000 CFA. This journey involves driving across the dry lake bed of Lake Chad, which consists of thick sand; a four-wheel–drive vehicle with high clearance is necessary. Expect heavy but civil searches on the Niger side of the border. From N'Guigmi there are minibuses to Zinder for 6000 CFA along an excellent road.

Petrol is expensive in Chad. Expect to pay 350 CFA per litre in N'Djamena and up to 700 CFA per litre north of Lake Chad.

N'DJAMENA
The *Catholic Mission* costs 2000 CFA for bed and breakfast if they'll let you stay. The rooms are very pleasant and clean with fans, showers and mosquito nets. Meals are available at 1400 CFA each. Other than the Mission, the only cheap hotel in town is the *Hotel l'Hirondelle* very close to the market and the large modern mosque. It has a selection of rooms available for 2500 CFA, 3000 CFA and 3500 CFA.

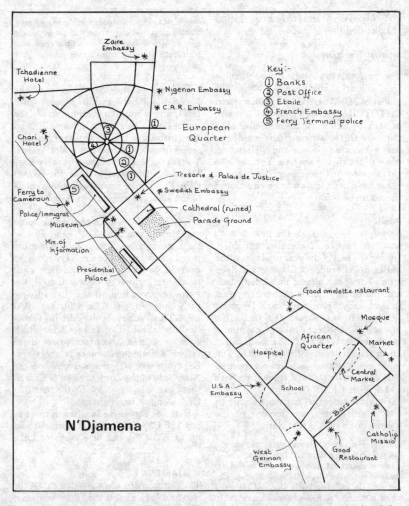

Key:-
1. Banks
2. Post Office
3. Etoile
4. French Embassy
5. Ferry Terminal police

Zaire Embassy

Tchadienne Hotel

Nigerian Embassy

C.A.R. Embassy

European Quarter

Chari Hotel

Tresorie ∗ Palais de Justice

Swedish Embassy

Ferry to Cameroun

Police/Immigrat.

Museum

Min. of Information

Cathedral (ruined)

Parade Ground

Presidential Palace

Good omelette restaurant

Mosque

African Quarter

Market

Hospital

Central Market

U.S.A. Embassy

School

Bars

N'Djamena

West German Embassy

Good Restaurant

Catholic Missio

An excellent place to eat is the *Etoile du Tchad*, Avenue Charles de Gaulle, which serves excellent steak and chips for 1250 CFA as well as luxurious fruit milk-shakes for 250 CFA each. The staff are friendly too. It's near the mosque.

If you need to cool off, go along to the *Hotel Tchadienne* and use their pool. It costs 500 CFA per day.

Literally every building outside of the African quarter is riddled with machine-gun fire and shell holes. Many buildings are totally destroyed. Our correspondent (Mark Pitt) came across a complete machine gun with fully-loaded belt and tripod standing in a breach in the walls of what was left of the Presidential Palace. A little further on he found a helmet with a bullet hole through it and graffiti on the wall showing a man with a machine gun wishing everyone a 'Happy New Year.' He heard gun shots at night but was told it was just drunken soldiers letting off steam. Forget about the museum here, as it was looted.

SARH

The *Catholic Mission* here will take you for CFA 500 per night plus CFA 1000 to eat, but the pastor is very unfriendly and will probably only let you stay for one night. Other private accommodation is available. There's also an American couple about seven km from town who run a *Baptist Mission*. They apparently welcome travellers.

There is a free **museum** near the Catholic Mission which is small but of interest. Also, there's an excellent **workshop** run by artisans which is very interesting. It's on the road to the airport and has some of the best crafts in this part of Africa.

Comoros

The Comoros consist of four main islands – Grande Comore, Moheli, Anjouan and Mayotte – as well as a number of islets. They lie between the northern tip of Madagascar and the African mainland. Like Madagascar, they were originally settled by people of Malay-Polynesian origin around the 6th century AD. Since then, the population has become much more racially mixed as a result of successive waves of immigration by Africans and Arabs, and particularly by Shirazi refugees from the Persian Gulf and the Red Sea between the 10th and 15th centuries. The latter were responsible for setting up a number of rival sultanates in the islands whose wealth was based on the slave and spice trades. France became interested in the islands in the mid-19th century and the rivalry between the sultans contributed to the ease with which the French assumed control. The first step in this direction came when the sultan of Mayotte sold his island to the French for a guaranteed annual payment; the rest came after several naval bombardments.

Despite numerous peasant revolts, the French maintained an iron grip over the islands for well over a century. Political organisations and newspapers were banned and revolts were suppressed with unrestrained military efficiency. No one was allowed into or out of the islands without the approval of the colonial authorities. The islands were officially declared a colony in 1912 and a form of internal autonomy was granted in 1961.

Seven years later, however, a strike by local students led to mass demonstrations and the French were forced to allow the formation of political parties. Numerous parties were formed representing various factional interests ranging over the full spectrum from those demanding immediate and unconditional independence to those who vigorously opposed independence.

Political tension between the various parties grew steadily over the next few years and, in an attempt to contain it, the French staged a referendum in late 1974. Overall, 94% of the population was in favour of independence, though in Mayotte some 64% voted against it. Less than a year later Ahmed Abdallah announced a unilateral declaration of independence while Mayotte's deputies cabled the French government requesting French protection. The Comoros – minus Mayotte – were admitted to membership of the OAU barely two weeks later.

Several weeks later Ahmed Abdallah was deposed in a coup led by Ali Solih, who favoured continued association with France and a more restrained attempt to bring Mayotte into the fold. Mayotte, however, refused to be drawn in and in 1976 became a 'territorial community' within the French republic. Despite this

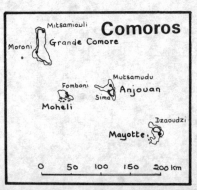

setback and the withdrawal of French aid, Ali Solih set to work to radically transform the islands with the help of the Jeunesse Revolutionnaire. French citizens were expelled and their property nationalised; feudal institutions were attacked; women were unveiled; the traditionally elaborate and costly arrangements which were part of marriages and funerals were abolished; and the privileges of ancestry based on dubious claims of belonging to the Prophet's immediate family were likewise attacked. The economy continued to deteriorate and was made worse by the need to re-settle about 20,000 Comorans who poured in from Madagascar after well over 1000 of them had been killed in rioting in Majunga in December 1976. In order to consolidate his power, Ali Solih also banned all political activity.

Many of Solih's ideas were doubtless well-intentioned but, like most movements of this nature which attempt to overturn centuries-old traditions in a matter of weeks or months using raw youth as the enforcing agency, many excesses were committed. The alienation which set in cost Ali Solih a great deal of his popular support. In May 1976 he was overthrown in a coup led by the French mercenary, Bob Denard. Ahmed Abdallah was invited back from exile in France to become the country's president, and the name of the country was changed to the Federal Islamic Republic of the Comoros. A few days after the coup, Ali Solih was shot dead while under house arrest. He has since acquired something of the status of a martyr among the youth of the country.

Bob Denard himself was expelled from the islands some time later, but his associates continue to operate there. Many of those who took part in the coup are members of the Presidential Guard, while others own hotels and control the Société Maritime des Comores. This has not gone unnoticed in places like Madagascar, the Seychelles and Tanzania, which remain very suspicious of the Comoros regime. Perhaps naturally, French aid to the islands has been resumed, but Mayotte continues to be a French colony in all but name.

Despite all these heavy politics, recent travellers to the islands report that they're well worth visiting. People are polite, friendly and honest. You can walk around anywhere unmolested. Each island is quite different from the others and all have their interest. There are white coral sand beaches with not a tourist in sight (the south side of Moheli is beautiful and great for snorkelling), picturesque old Arab-style town centres (Moroni and Mutsamudi), luxuriant vegetation and even an active volcano (Karthala on Grande Comore).

Use malarial tablets and take care with tap water.

VISAS

Visas are required by all, but the only way you can get into the Comoros at present is by air, and all travellers arriving by air are admitted with or without a visa. You must, however, go to Immigration in either Moroni (Grande Comore) or Mutsamudi (Anjouan) as soon as possible afterwards in order to get your visa. Mayotte is still effectively a French colony and you won't find anyone on the other islands who is willing to commit themselves about visas to and from Mayotte, but it seems that a visa for the Comoros is also valid for Mayotte since travellers arriving in Moroni on charter flights from Mayotte don't pay visa fees. They merely fill out the usual arrival and departure cards. You must have an onward ticket on arrival.

MONEY
US$1 = CFr 428

The unit of currency is the Comoran franc, which is linked to the French franc on the basis of CFr 50 = Fr fr 1. There are no limits on the import or export of Comoran francs and there is no black market.

The airport tax for international flights is CFr 3000.

LANGUAGE

French and Arabic are the official languages, but most people speak the Comoran variant of Kiswahili.

GETTING THERE & AROUND

Air

There are twice-weekly flights on Wednesday and Thursday by *Air Mauritius* and *Air Madagascar*, which take the following route: Nairobi-Grande Comore-Antananarivo (Madagascar)-Reunion-Mauritius. *Air France* flies every Saturday (in each direction) from Paris to Grande Comore via Keddah and Dar es Salaam. *South African Airways* flies from Lilongwe (Malawi) in either direction on Monday. There are no flights from Tanzania. *Air Comoros* handles internal flights.

If you're flying from Australia to Africa, there is an interesting possibility which covers the route: Mauritius-Reunion-Mayotte-Anjouan. Use *Air Mauritius*, *Reunion Air Service* or *Air Comores*.

The internal air schedule is as follows:

Monday
    Moroni (dep 8 am)-Moheli (arr 8.25 am; dep 8.40 am)-Anjouan (arr 9 am; dep 3.55 pm)-Moheli (arr 4.15 pm; dep 4.35 pm)-Moroni (arr 5 pm).
Tuesday
    Moroni (dep 10.30 am)-Anjouan (arr 11.05 am; dep 11.30 am)-Dzaoudzi (arr noon; dep 3 pm)-Anjouan (arr 3.30 pm; dep 3.55 pm)-Moroni (arr 4.30 pm).
Wednesday
    Moroni (dep 8 am)-Anjouan (arr 8.35 am; dep 8.55 am)-Moroni (arr 9.30 am).
Thursday
    Moroni (dep 8 am)-Anjouan (arr 8.35 am; dep 8.55 am)-Moroni (arr 9.30 am; dep 10.30 am)-Moheli (arr 10.55 am; dep 11.15 am)-Anjouan (arr 11.35 am; dep noon)-Dzaoudzi (arr 12.30 pm; dep 2.30 pm)-Anjouan (arr 3 pm; dep 3.25 pm)-Moheli (arr 3.45 pm; dep 4.05 pm)-Moroni (arr 4.30 pm).

Saturday
    Moroni (dep 9 am)-Moheli (arr 9.25 am; dep 9.40 am)-Anjouan (arr 10 am; dep 2.55 pm)-Moheli (arr 3.15 pm; dep 3.35 pm)-Moroni (arr 4 pm).

An excursion fare Grande Comore-Moheli-Anjouan-Mayotte-Grande Comore is possible for under US$100 but must be flown in that order. A return flight from Moroni to Anjouan costs CFr 25,000. The flights are often full so you need to book in advance and reconfirm at each step. The *Air Comores* office in Moroni is in the terminal building at the old airport directly opposite the Hotel Karthala. The new airport is at Hahaya north of Moroni. Taxis from here into Moroni (about 20 km) will charge what they think they can get out of you, but the correct fare should be CFr 4000-5000 depending on how far you go. Taxi drivers will hotly deny that there is a bus into town, but there is one. It's an *Air Comores* green-and-white minibus which costs CFr150 and goes right into the centre. It's mainly for airport staff but passengers can use it. There's an airport bus on Anjouan Island.

Road

Land transport on each island is by taxi-brousse (Peugeot 404s). They're fairly frequent and serve most of the villages on all the islands.

Boat

There is no regular sea transport to or from the Comoros at present. There are no boats at all to Madagascar, but there are irregular boats to the African mainland. Enquire at the port in Moroni.

There are irregular inter-island boats, though they're usually crowded. The fare from Anjouan to Grande Comore is around US$14. Many boats which ply around the islands take passengers. Enquire locally.

GRANDE COMORE

This island is quite pretty, being 65 km

long with a large volcano (Mt Karthala – 2361 metres) on the southern end as well as several cones over 1000 metres high at the northern end. Most of the coast is raw black lava with semi-submerged coral on the outer edge of that. At the northern tip of the island is a more extensive coral reef and a beach. There are also regular stretches of coral down the east coast. The vegetation is an interesting mixture of coconut and pandanus palm, bananas and baobab trees that project their skeletal forms over the top of the palms. Further up there are plantations of ylang-ylang whose trunks resemble overgrown grape vines, and further up still is rain forest fed by constant cloud. There's surprisingly little birdlife but many bats and spiders. The bats – up to one metre across – fly around even in broad daylight. You may also catch sight of mongeese.

Outside of Moroni the villages get more down-to-earth and many of the houses are made of coconut palms surrounded by manioc plots. You may find that a lot of the older people are very anti-European, so be extremely discreet with cameras if you have one.

MORONI

The first thing that will strike you about Moroni is its small size. The most obvious parts cluster around the tiny harbour and are painted white, glowing with a peculiar soft light that seems to be characteristic of the place. This is the Arab town, mildewed with tortuous alleyways and miniscule courtyards. The waterfront itself is more Mediterranean than African, with solid rock jetties enclosing a small area where large wooden boats are tied up in parallel. These boats are worth seeing on their own. Each rib is hand-hewn and each plank hand-fitted. They serve as cargo dories to the ships which call at the island.

If you're prepared to hunt around, there are some very cheap places to stay, but until you find one try the *Hotel Karthala*, which costs about US$15. It's being renovated, so by the time you get there prices may have increased. The other hotels here – *Hotel Itsandra*, seven km from Moroni right on the beach, and the *Hotel Coelacanthe*, which has 12 bungalows, a restaurant and bar and diving equipment for hire – are considerably more expensive and well out of the reach of budget travellers. Expect to pay CFr 18,500 for a single 'demi-pension,' CFr 13,500 per person in a double 'demi-pension,' CFr 22,000 for a single 'pension complete,' and CFr 17,000 per person in a double 'pension complete.' These prices include transport to and from the airport. There may be a chance of finding accommodation at the *Catholic Mission*, but don't count on it.

Restaurant prices are generally reasonable. Try the *Café du Port*.

There is only one bank which will change traveller's cheques, but it apparently keeps strange hours.

It's possible to rent cars if you have the funds. A Renault 4 would be the cheapest at 9000 CFA per day, but you must also pay for petrol and that is not cheap. Most of the roads are sealed and you can drive around the island in one day.

MOHELI

Ask for M Legrand, who has a room or two to rent right by the airstrip. The charges are very reasonable and he serves good, cheap food. There is also the *Relais de Moroni*, but it costs about US$25 per room.

ANJOUAN

Try the *Hotel Al Amal*, which has a bar estaurant and a swimming pool but costs about US$25 per room.

MAYOTTE

Try the *Hotel du Rocher* in Dzaoudzi which costs around US$25 per room.

TOURS

Comores Services-Tours & Safaris (BP 974, Moroni, Grande Comore, tel 23 36 airport and 24 06 bureau) offers various tours around the island and is well worth considering if your time is limited. Tours include:

Grande Comore

1) *Ville de Moroni*. A half-day tour of the capital including a visit to the National Museum. Cost is CFr 1500.

2) *Mitsamiouli*. A full-day tour which includes visits to the ancient capital at Itsandra (fortress, royal tombs and mosque), the hot sulphur springs at Lac Sale, various beaches (where you can have a swim) and other tombs and mosques. Cost is CFr 2500.

3) *Southern Circuit*. A full-day tour which visits Iconi, a 14th-century village; Mbachile, a fishing village; a ylang-ylang distillery (this perfume is one of the Comoros' most valuable exports – defiant ex-hippies please note); a swimming beach; and Foumbouni, once the site of the sultan's palace. Cost is CFr 3350.

4) *Karthala Volcano*. A two-day tour which includes a trip to the crater rim and a visit to the Nioumbadjou Forest. Cost is CFr 6000.

Moheli

A full-day trip around the major centres of the island, including a boat trip to some of the smaller, inhabited islands just off the coast. Cost is CFr 7500.

Anjouan

As with Moheli, a full-day trip around the island taking in picturesque Mutsamoudou with its beautiful Arabic architecture; Domoni, the ancient capital; and one of the island's colourful markets. Cost is CFr 10,500.

Mayotte

Again, a one-day visit around the island which takes in the island capital of Dzaoudzi, itself built on a small islet off the coast; the coral reefs off Kadidjou; and a folklore dance at the town on Mamutsu. Cost is CFr 9500.

Congo

Since independence from France in 1960, the Congo was for a long time the only unreservedly Marxist state in Africa, with its closest neighbours all more or less ideologically opposed to it. Since then, of course, it has been joined by all the former Portuguese colonies, Ethiopia and Zimbabwe. Most of the time it has maintained a non-aligned foreign policy while supporting African struggles for national self-determination, apart from a brief period in the early years of independence when the Youlon regime effectively supported Tshombe's attempted Katangan secession in return for promises of economic aid. The radicalisation of its people goes back a long way and is rooted in the exploitation it was subjected to first by the slave trade and later by the French colonial authorities. The slave trade resulted in the establishment of a number of small independent kingdoms along the coast, the capital of each being a trading post. For the slavers, this was a very convenient arrangement since milking the interior for a regular supply of slaves was done by these local rulers. All the slavers had to do was turn up at one of these trading posts and take the slaves on board. The loss of population to which the present-day countries of Congo, Zaire and Angola were subjected is nothing short of staggering and has been estimated at 13,500,000 over the course of three centuries.

When the slave trade was finally abolished, the coastal kingdoms gradually collapsed and the stage was set for the next attempt to milk the area for everything it had got. In the 1880s the French explorer Savorgnan de Brazza floated a plan to divide up the whole of the Congo territory (which then included Gabon and the Central African Republic) between concessionary companies which would exploit the area. By expropriating the land from the local people, Brazza intended to force them into becoming wage labourers for the companies he had in mind. The scheme was only partially successful but resulted in dislocation of a large part of the population followed shortly by famines brought on as a result of the French conquest. The most accessible areas taken over by the French were bled white and it's estimated that the population was reduced by a factor of two-thirds between 1914 and 1924. As though that were not enough, what remained of the population was subjected to yet another form of exploitation by the construction of the railway to Pointe Noire between 1924 and 1930. In order to secure sufficient labour for the project, the French authorities mounted what were virtually man-hunts and, since even the most elementary of safety precautions were ignored during the railway's construction, thousands lost their lives.

Because of such conditions, anti-colonialism quickly took root. In the early years it took the form of Matswanism, a quasi-religious movement named after Matswa, one of the first resistance leaders. By the end of WW II, however, Congolese youth, student and trade union movements had become closely connected with developments in the communist world, and resistance to the French took on a more stridently political colour. By the time independence was granted in 1960, the mass movement had become a strong, well-organised political force. Such a movement naturally represented a threat to continued French interests and control, and so the colonial authorities attempted to groom a generation of moderate politicians to lead the country after independence. They found them in Youlou and Opangault, but the only points on which the two could agree was on their opposition to 'communist plots.' They failed to appreciate that these were the earliest manifestations of the mass movement started by the youth, students and unions. Thus, some three years later, when Youlou attempted to break the power of the unions by arresting its leaders, he was deposed by Massembat-Debat.

Youlou's overthrow, however, was only the beginning of the struggle since the forces of repression inherited from the colonial era – the army, police and gendarmerie – remained unpurged. Massembat-Debat's presidency was marked by violent conflicts with these forces as well as with the popular militia and civil defence groups which had been created after the 1963 revolution. The latter groups were assisted by a sizable Cuban contingent. In an attempt to bring the youth movement and the civil defence under his control, Massembat-Debat introduced into them the same ethnic divisions which dominated the army, but the plan backfired. By 1968, the army and the civil defence had reached a stalemate and a coup was staged in which Massembat-Debat was replaced by Captain Marien Ngouabi, a left-wing army officer from the north. The coup resulted in the integration of the army and civil defence forces but with the latter retaining its own officers. The Congolese Workers Party (PCT) was also formed at this time.

In 1972, there was a badly organised attempt at a coup but it failed and resulted in Ange Diawara, the former head of civil defence, taking to guerrilla warfare. Diawara was eventually forced to take refuge in Zaire but was handed over by Mobutu to the Congolese army chief of staff, Yhombi-Opango, and shot. From this point on, Ngouabi's political base

came to rest on the middle ground among those who were in the direct pay of the French, and Yhombi's ascendancy was assured.

In the mid-70s, with the MPLA gradually moving towards victory in Angola, Ngouabi came under pressure from the French and other European interests to organise the partition of Cabinda with Zaire (Cabinda is the Angolan enclave sandwiched between the Congo and Zaire and is rich with oil). He failed to bring this about mainly because of massive street demonstrations in support of the MPLA, but his failure cost him the support of the French. In 1977 he was assassinated.

The running of the country was taken over by a military commission headed by the army chief of staff, Yhombi. The PCT was eclipsed and the government took a decided turn to the right, though it still used the language of the left. The idea behind Ngouabi's assassination had been to upset the balance between the people and the army in favour of the army, but the exact opposite happened. With their long history of struggle, the Congolese people were not to be fobbed off with such a transparent attempt to deprive them of power. Popular opposition to Yhombi began to break out all over the country, particularly in the form of strikes and, in early 1979, after a series of street demonstrations organised by the trade unions federation, the PCT met to reassert itself.

Yhombi was ousted, the military commission dissolved and its powers handed over to the central committee of the PCT. Later that month, Colonel Sassou-Nguesso was named the new head of state and Yhombi was arrested for embezzlement of several billion CFA francs, 400 million of which had been a loan from Algeria for the construction of water supplies to the people of the impoverished Bateke plateau. It subsequently came to light that in the matter of corruption Yhombi had surpassed even the excesses of Youlou.

With the removal from power of Yhombi and his group, the army had finally been purged of pro-western agents and power centred firmly in the popular movement. The new government included, for the first time, a number of younger ministers who were untainted by the corruption and opportunism of the previous generation of politicians. Some of these ministers were known to have close links with the USSR but the country was not about to become a Russian puppet state; a French delegation attending the centenary celebrations in Brazzaville in late 1980 were given the red-carpet treatment, much to the displeasure of the Soviet delegation.

FACTS

The narrow coastal plain is low-lying and dry, with grassland vegetation. Further inland there are the Mayombe and Chailou highlands and plateaux which are forested and deeply dissected with gorges and valleys. The northern part of the country is equatorial rain forest with an average rainfall of 1100 mm. The rainy season lasts from October to May, with a brief dry spell around the end of December. Temperatures average between 21° and 27°C. Road conditions are pretty poor. There are no sealed roads outside of Brazzaville, the capital. Roads are frequently closed during the rainy season to protect the surface.

The main tribal groups are the Vili, Kongo, Teke, M'Bochi and Sanga. There are sizable minorities of Gabonese and Europeans (mainly French).

VISAS

Visas are required by all except nationals of France and West Germany. At least that's the official position, but travellers who have been through the Congo recently have warned that everyone must have a visa regardless of what Congolese embassies might tell you to the contrary. French travellers entering at Moussogo on the Gabon/Congo border have been sent back to Libreville for a visa – this despite a notice on the wall at customs stating that French and West Germans don't need them. They argued all day but to no avail.

Depending on your nationality and where you apply for your visa, you may be given only five days, though 15 days is the usual with a fixed date of entry. It will be hard going to get through the country in that time. Two Australians who recently got their visa in Kinshasa were given five days, but on arrival in Brazzaville by ferry they were refused entry and no reason was forthcoming.

Visas in Libreville, Gabon, cost 5000 CFA, require one photo and can be got in 24 hours, though it's best to allow 48 hours. Officially an onward ticket is required but no one has mentioned having to produce one.

Visa extensions are not available.

There are police checkpoints every 25 to 30 km in the countryside where you will be stopped and asked for your passport and vaccination certificates. These stops will take up to half an hour at a time while they study all the stamps. By the time you get through the country, several pages of your passport will have been taken up with various stamps and half-page essays in ball-point pen. Sometimes these stamps can attract a 'fee.' At Kibangou, for instance, expect to pay 600 CFA to get your passport back plus 2000 CFA if you have your own vehicle.

Make sure you don't miss any of these The police posts are rudimentary to say the least, so you can always say that they didn't give you a stamp though you checked in there.

the posts are rudimentary to say the least, so you can always say they didn't give you a stamp though you checked in there.

You must register with Immigration at Loubomo, fill in a form and hand across two photos.

Avoid discussing politics with strangers in this country. There are many plain-clothes policemen in the towns and cities. You'll find anyone who doesn't belong to the police or the military, however, to be very friendly.

Zaire visas You can certainly get these in Brazzaville, but you're advised not to. In order to take the ferry between Brazzaville and Kinshasa you need, in addition to your visa, a *laissez-passer* issued by the Zaire embassy. They will only issue this if you obtained your visa elsewhere. A lot of travellers have been caught out on this one and have had to take the flight, which is an outrageous rip-off at around £200!

MONEY
US$1 = 300 CFA

The unit of currency is the CFA franc, on a par with the CFA franc of Gabon, Cameroun and the CAR. It is not inter-changeable with the CFA of the West African countries. Import of local currency is unrestricted but export is limited to 10,000 CFA. Inflation is high.

GETTING THERE & AROUND
The two points of entry are from Gabon and Zaire. The normal route from Gabon is by road from N'Dende to Kibangou and from there to Loubomo, where there is a choice of road or rail to Pointe Noire (on the coast) or Brazzaville.

Road
There are occasional trucks and jeeps south from N'Dende to the border, but most of them don't cross. It's reported, however, that there is a beer truck from N'Dende to Loubomo on Tuesday and Friday which stops at every bar en route and takes one or two days. It costs 6500 CFA. If you get dumped at the border it's a two-km walk from there to the first Congolese village – Moussogo – where you can stay in a room behind the general store for 500 CFA per person (bed and mosquito net). From Moussogo there is a twice-weekly beer truck which goes as far south as Kibangou, stopping at every village en route and taking two days. Every stop involves a celebration and you'll be too drunk to notice the passage of time! Once you get to Kibangou there are plenty of trucks and taxis available to take you further south (the journey from Kibangou to Loubomo is particularly beautiful and the people friendly and unassuming). Many people find they have to do a lot of walking between N'Dende and Kibangou.

Rail
The railway runs between Brazzaville and Pointe Noire. There are daily trains in either direction. The trains which have 1st and 2nd class are faster if there are no complications, and take between 12 and 24 hours. The trains which have only 3rd class take between 20 and 24 hours. Student reductions of 50% are available on the fares. Derailments are frequent and can often put the system out of action for weeks at a time, so don't rely on it. The fares from Brazzaville to Pointe Noire are 9485 CFA (1st class), 6325 CFA (2nd class) and 3160 CFA (3rd class). Loubomo

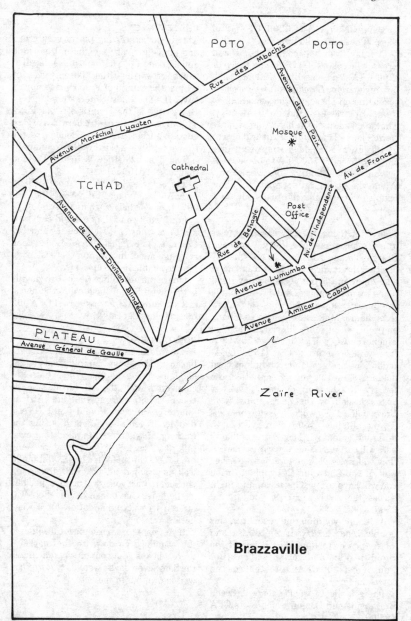

Brazzaville

to Pointe Noire costs 3200 CFA (2nd class). These are full fares.

The day train between Loubomo and Brazzaville costs 2500 CFA (2nd class) and 1700 CFA (2nd class) for students. The fast night train, L'Eclair, offers 1st-class couchettes on Tuesday, Friday and Sunday from Brazzaville and on Monday, Thursday and Saturday from Pointe Noire. There is a 1000 CFA supplement for this. Buy your tickets a day in advance and pay the extra 250 CFA to book a seat or you will be standing the whole way. When the gates are opened to allow people to board, all hell breaks out.

Boat

Apart from flying, the only way to get to or from Zaire is by ferry between Brazzaville and Kinshasa. It goes hourly in either direction between 8 am and noon and 2 pm and 5 pm. The journey itself takes about 20 minutes, but if you include the bureaucracy at each end, then allow three hours. Make sure you go to a bank and get a currency declaration form whichever way you go. It costs 2500 CFA (one way or return); 33% (1500 CFA) reductions are available to student card holders. However, you can only take the ferry to Kinshasa if you have a laissez-passer issued by the Zaire embassy in Brazzaville. They will only issue this pass if you obtained your Zaire visa at a different embassy. The Zaire embassy here will certainly issue you with a visa but they will not give you a laissez-passer as well. If you find yourself in this position you will have to fly. The 10-minute flight across the river will cost you around £200!

Assuming you don't get caught in this double bind, take your Zaire visa and laissez-passer to Immigration left of the Hotel de Ville and get an exit visa for Congo (costs 300 CFA). After that you can catch the ferry.

There is also a weekly ferry between Brazzaville and Bangui which costs CFA 85,000.

BRAZZAVILLE

This is an interesting place, very green and sprawling with a cathedral, mosque and markets and a national museum, all of which are worth visiting. The city was, for a time, the capital of Free France during WW II. The most interesting part of Brazzaville is the suburb of Poto Poto. The arts and crafts centre here is also very good. Ten km from Brazzaville are the Congo rapids – a worthwhile excursion.

The Tourist Office is in the Plateau district (tel 810953).

The only hotel which is remotely cheap is the M'Foa, Avenue du 28 Aout 1940, BP 297. It, nevertheless, costs CFA 8000.

For food, two of the best and cheapest are Chez Charton (Vietnamese) and Les Caimans. The Safari Snack has also been recommended. In addition there is cheap food available in the markets.

One of the best things about Brazzaville is the nightlife and the local music dives.

Taxis around Brazzaville cost CFA 500 per journey (flat rate).

POINTE NOIRE

It's hard to find accommodation here because the town simply hasn't got enough hotels to house all the expatriates connected with the oil business. The cheapest hotels are in the Cite (African quarter) and cost around 7500 CFA a double. If you're thinking of using the Catholic Mission, bear in mind that even this place costs 7000 CFA for bed and breakfast. On the other hand, you might well meet someone who will offer you a cheaper room if you ask around, especially in the bars. One bunch of travellers was offered free accommodation for a week here.

If you want to catch some local colour in the evenings, go down to the market – there's heaps going on: music, dancing in the bars seven days a week. Try Parafifi, a well-known bar in the Cite.

Djibouti

Previously known as the French Territory of the Afars and Issas, Djibouti was the last French colony on the African mainland to gain its independence (in 1977). It consists of little more than the port of Djibouti and a sliver of semi-desert hinterland. The population of just over 250,000 is made up largely of Afars – ethnically a part of Ethiopia – and Issas whose links are with Somalia. There are also sizable minorities of Somalis, French and Yemenis as well as about 30,000 refugees who fled there as a result of the Ogaden war. The country's income comes almost entirely from port dues and the Addis Ababa-Djibouti railway – Ethiopia's most important outlet to the sea – but these are totally inadequate to finance the trappings of a modern state. Djibouti remains heavily dependent on French aid to the tune of US$200 million a year, US$130 million of which is spent on the maintenance of the 5000-strong French garrison.

The French moved into this area in the middle of the 19th century to counter the British presence in Aden on the other side of the Babel-Mandeb Straits. Agreements were made with the sultans of Obock and Tadjourah which gave the French the right to settle in the area, and in 1888 construction of Djibouti was begun. At the end of the 19th century another treaty was signed with the emperor of Ethiopia which designated Djibouti as the 'official outlet of Ethiopian commerce'; this led to the construction of the Addis Ababa-Djibouti railway. The railway has been of vital strategic and commercial importance to Ethiopia ever since and is one of the reasons why that country has refused to compromise over the question of sovereignty of the Ogaden with Somalia. It also explains why Ethiopia is hostile to any suggestion of a merger between Djibouti and Somalia.

The country's borders were established without any consideration being given to ethnic links, language, trading patterns or even traditional grazing rights, and these issues continue to dominate politics. As early as 1949 there were anti-colonial demonstrations by the Somalis and Issas who were in favour of the British attempt to reunite the territories of Italian, British and French Somalia. Hostility toward the French continued to grow and induced the colonial authorities to switch their allegiance to the Afars in 1958 in an attempt to hang onto the territory.

As a result of this switch, the French placed Ali Aref and his friends in control

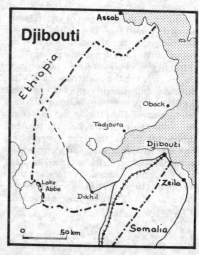

149

of the local government council. This didn't stifle opposition, however. There were serious riots in 1966 during the visit of General de Gaulle and again after the 1967 referendum which produced a 60.4% vote in favour of continued rule by France. The vote in favour of France was achieved partly as a result of the arrest of opposition leaders and the massive expulsion of Somalis. Many of those who were expelled went to join the Somali Coast Liberation Front, which increased its terrorist activities within the colony during the early 1970s.

In the end, Ali Aref's position became increasingly untenable, and after huge demonstrations in support of the opposition African People's League for Independence (a moderate inter-ethnic party led by Hassan Gouled and Ahmed Dini) and pressure by both the Arab League and the OAU on France, Aref was forced to resign in 1976. The French again switched allegiances, but in order to retain some control through setting up a government which would remain on favourable terms with them, they reluctantly conceded that granting independence was the only remaining option.

Independence has not bought tribal harmony to the former colony. Hassan Gouled seized on the initial Somali successes in the Ogaden war as an opportunity to remove Afars from key posts in the administration and security forces. When Ethiopia struck back with Russian and Cuban support, he was forced to reinstate many of those who had been removed from their posts as well as to seriously readdress himself to Afar grievances. Since then the government has signed new trade and commercial agreements with both Somalia and Ethiopia, and Gouled has added his voice to those attempting to get the two warring countries to agree to a truce and negotiated settlement.

VISAS
Visas are required by all except nationals of France. A visa d'escale (transit visa) or a 10-day entry visa can be granted on arrival to nationals of Belgium, Denmark, Finland, Germany (West), Italy, Japan, Luxembourg, Netherlands, Norway, Sweden, UK and USA. No extensions of the 10-day visa are possible. Nationals of Israel and South Africa are not admitted.

If you arrive without a visa, you have to buy a transit visa on arrival. This costs US$12 for a three-day stay. You must have an onward ticket to get into Djibouti; if you don't have one they'll force you to buy one before issuing you with the transit visa. The cheapest is Djibouti-Hargeisa (Somalia) for US$70. Customs will stamp it 'non-refundable.' You can buy the ticket at the airport.

MONEY
US$1 = 175 Djibouti francs

The unit of currency is the Djibouti franc. There are no restrictions on the import or export of local currency.

You cannot buy Somali shillings in Djibouti at the banks, but moneychangers on the street will do it. The rate is 3 Djibouti francs = 1 Somali shilling (equivalent to US$1 = 58 Somalian shillings. The official exchange rate inside Somalia is US$1 = 17.38 shillings, so it's obviously worth buying Somali shillings in Djibouti if you have the chance).

LANGUAGE
Arabic is the official language but French is widely used. Afar and Somali are also spoken.

GETTING THERE & AROUND
These days, Djibouti is just a glorified truck-stop for tourists and travellers en route to somewhere else by air. Because of this, everything is geared to taking as much money from visitors as possible. It's a very expensive place and you're advised to give it a miss unless you are heading for northern Somalia or you want to drop a heap of cash for nothing in particular.

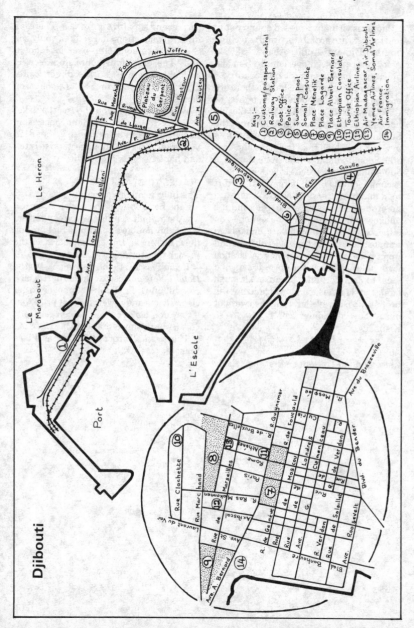

Djibouti

Key:-
1. Customs/passport control
2. Railway Station
3. Post Office
4. Police
5. Swimming Pool
6. Somali Consulate
7. Place Menelik
8. Place Lagarde
9. Place Albert Bernard
10. Ethiopian Consulate
11. Tourist Office
12. Ethiopian Airlines
13. Air Madagascar, Air Djibouti, Yemen Airlines, Somal Airlines, Air France.
14. Immigration

Ethiopia is virtually a closed country still, and tourists are prohibited from travelling on the Djibouti-Addis Ababa railway. Also, you cannot go overland to Somalia unless you have a visa for that country.

If you're heading into Somalia there are minibuses from Djibouti to the border at Loyoda which cost 600 Dj Fr and take one hour. Cross the border on foot. From the Somali side of the border there are trucks to Hargeisa which take two days and cost 300 Somali shillings (the actual price is 500 shillings but truck drivers are quite accommodating if you bargain). It's a dirt road and in pretty poor shape. There are no problems crossing the border and it's unlikely your baggage will be searched on either side. The Somalis are unlikely to want to see how much money you have and won't issue you with a currency declaration form unless you ask for one – it's a good idea to ask for one because although banks in Hargeisa and Mogadishu will probably cash traveller's cheques without one, they certainly won't do so in Kisimaiyo.

Air

Cairo-Jeddah-Djibouti: (first leg *Egypt Air*; second leg with *Air France*). There is a direct connection in Jeddah only on Sunday (two-hour stop-over in Jeddah) and Tuesday (four-hour stop-over in Jeddah). There's also the direct Cairo-Djibouti flight with *Air Djibouti* on Thursday.

Whichever flight you choose, the ticket costs E£ 320 without student concession, but you must buy a ticket with E£ changed at the official rate (not the tourist rate), and bank receipts are required.

PLACES TO STAY

The only relatively cheap places to stay are the bar-hotels in the African quarter. They are about as rough as you can get and invariably double as brothels. Sleeping on the beach near the tennis courts in the French quarter might still be possible.

If you're only staying overnight, try the *Hotel Relais* closest to the airport which costs 6000 Dj Fr. You're supposed to get clean sheets and towels for that price, but if they don't arrive then you can generally get the price down to 3000 Dj Fr.

There is a Tourist Office in the Place Menelik.

Egypt

Egypt, along with Mesopotamia, the Indus Valley and China, was one of the first centres of civilisation in the world. Its recorded history stretches back at least 6000 years, to the time of the Pharoahs. Many of its kingdoms showed remarkable vitality, and the ruined cities and monuments which they left – Memphis, Karnak, the pyramids, the funerary temples and tombs in the Valley of the Kings and Queens, Abu Simbel, Philae and others – are lasting testaments to their skills and inventiveness. Thanks to the dry desert climate, these remains are well preserved, though many of them bear the scars of vandalism which has occurred at various times during the centuries; the Romans were some of the worst perpetrators of this. Certainly the kingdoms fell apart from time to time as a result of decadence, religious conflicts and invasion – the Assyrians, Persians and Macedonians all conquered Egypt in their time – but it's a measure of the strength of the Egyptian culture that it was able to revitalise and absorb conquerers. Even after conquest by the Romans, who finally eclipsed the Egyptian dynasties, the Ptolemys were more Egyptian than Roman.

Until fairly recently, the Egyptian civilisation was regarded as part of the Middle East culture genesis rather than of African origin, but this view is gradually changing. Though Middle East influences were absorbed as a result of trade and conquest, it's now known that the early Egyptian kingdoms had far more contact with Africa than was previously supposed. Evidence has been gathered that they frequently sent trading missions and expeditions to West Africa and as far south as the rain forests of Zaire, and influenced civilisations which were to spring up there later. A fascinating study of the Dogon people of Mali, for example, has revealed that they preserve intact certain aspects of ancient Egyptian religious rites and observances, notably reverence of the dog star, Sirius. A detailed description of ancient Egyptian history is outside the scope of *Africa on a Shoestring*, so before you set off it would be a good idea to browse through some books on archaeology, particularly if you want to deepen the experience you get from the world-famous monuments to be found in this country.

Egypt lapsed into relative obscurity following its conquest by the Romans, and was to remain that way until taken by the armies of Islam following the death of the Prophet. Shortly after this event Cairo became one of the greatest centres of Islamic culture ever to arise, and scholars from all over the known world as well as West and Central Africa came here to study. It's the legacy of this period which today makes Cairo such a fascinating city to explore. Later on Egypt became a part of the Turkish empire which, at its height, included the whole of North Africa, Saudi Arabia, the Middle East, Greece and a large part of Eastern Europe. As the vitality of this empire waned, however, and the sultans took to being virtual recluses inside the Topkapi Palace at Istanbul, Egypt beame autonomous under the rule of the Janissaries – eunuch mercenary troops of the Turks. Corruption, misgovernment and cultural decline set in shortly after this and continued until the government was effectively taken over by the British in the 20th century, following Egypt's inability to finance its foreign debt. The 19th century was a time of rivalry between the British and French for political control and trading concessions in the country, and it was during this century that de Lesseps conceived of and built the Suez Canal. The Canal has been one of the country's biggest money-spinners ever since, though until it was nationalised in the 1950s, the British and French shareholders in the company that managed it creamed off a fair percentage of the income.

The founder of the modern nation was Colonel Nasser, who overthrew the corrupt and effete monarchy in a military coup in the early 1950s. A fervent nationalist and a tough negotiator, Nasser became one of the most prominent politicians of the Third World. By making skilful use of the rivalry between the Americans and Russians, he was able to attract the aid he needed for the construction of the Aswan Dam as well as to acquire the military hardware required for the various wars against the state of Israel. During his time there were numerous attempts at federation or unification with other Arab states – notably with Syria and Iraq – but these fell through, though for many years the name – United Arab Republic – survived as the official name of Egypt until changed recently. Similar mergers have been proposed with Libya and Sudan since then, but nothing has come of them. Indeed, relations with Libya have deteriorated so far at times that war has seemed inevitable. Relations still remain very tense after the Camp David peace treaty with Israel, and Libya misses no opportunity that comes its way of pouring vitriol on the Egyptian regime.

The wars with Israel have had a devastating effect on the country's economy, diverting much-needed funds for development into military equipment. They also resulted in the closure of the Suez Canal for many years and the consequent loss of income as well as the occupation of Sinai (where Egypt's only oil wells are situated) by the Israelis. It

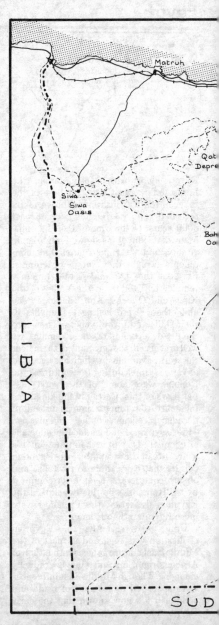

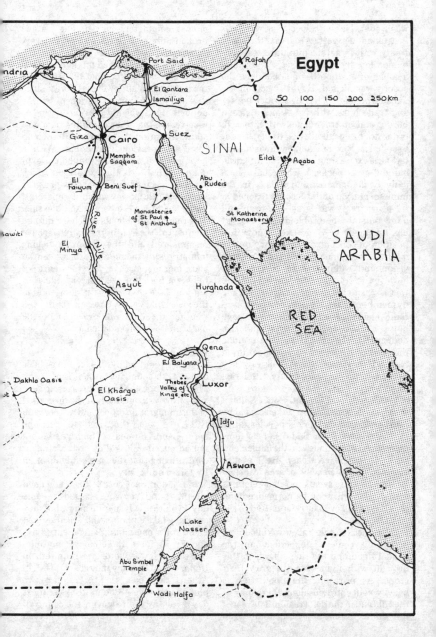

was Sadat, Nasser's successor, who was instrumental in getting together the peace treaty with Israel despite universal condemnation by every other Arab state. Though opposition has abated since the accord was signed, Egypt is now in the unusual position of having an open border and trade links with Israel and a closed border and no trade links with Libya. In order to bring about the treaty, Sadat expelled all Russian military advisors and technical experts and accepted an American aid-and-arms package. There have certainly been disputes and delays in the implementation of the accords reached in the peace treaty with Israel – there are still a few outstanding problems – but Egypt has regained the Sinai and is now in a position to concentrate on sorting out its internal economic problems. Sadat's vision and willingness to compromise, however, eventually cost him his life. He was assassinated during a military parade by members of the Moslem Brotherhood – radical Islamic fundamentalists who have quite a following in Egypt and are dedicated to seeing an Islamic state, along the lines of Khomeini's in Iran, set up in Egypt. If they were to have their way, they would tear up the peace treaty with Israel tomorrow.

Leadership of the country since Sadat's assassination has been taken over by Murbarak, and though his policies differ in some ways from Sadat's, he seems determined to continue with the implementation of the peace treaty. He has also clamped down heavily on the Moslem Brotherhood. It seems too that relations with Jordan will soon be normalised and that Egypt will even be re-admitted to the Arab League.

Ever since the Nile Valley was inhabited, people have been dependent on the annual flood and the rich silt which this brought with it in order to grow their crops. As a result, the population is heavily concentrated along the banks of the Nile and in the delta region. The rest of the country – some 95% of the total – is an almost completely barren, flat plateau broken only by a few scattered but very substantial oases. The building of the Aswan Dam has stopped this annual flood and it may be, in time, that the fertility of the lower Nile Valley will deteriorate since the soil is no longer enriched by the deposit of silt which it previously used to receive. On the other hand, the dam now allows irrigation of a far larger area of land than was previously possible. With a population of at least 40 million, Egypt desperately needs the extra food which the dam has made possible as well as the hydro-electric power which it generates, but it has proved to be a mixed blessing. The rich sardine shoals which used to be plentiful off the Mediterranean coast have disappeared and the Egyptian fishing industry with them. There has been an alarming increase in the incidence of bilharzia both in Lake Nasser – the 400-km-long lake created by the dam – and in the lower Nile Valley. It remains to be seen whether the dam will prove to be the panacea it was once hailed as.

VISAS

Visas are required by all except nationals of the Arab countries (except Libya) and Malta. It is possible, in some cases, to get a visa on arrival, but this is at the discretion of the immigration officer and will cost you E£17, so you're advised to get one beforehand. Nationals of South Africa are not admitted unless they hold a student card proving that they are studying at an Egyptian university.

In London visas cost £12.50. You need one photo and they can be issued the same day if you're in a desperate hurry, but they normally take 24 hours. In Paris they cost Fr 60 for a one-month, single-entry visa and Fr 75 for a three-month multiple-entry visa. Two photos are required. In Bonn, West Germany they cost DM 30. In Athens they cost US$14, require two photos and take 48 hours to issue (next day if you say you're leaving the country). In Tel Aviv everyone pays US$10 in cash plus varying amounts of shekels and one photo. The amount of shekels you pay depends on your nationality. Australian and USA citizens pay 150 shekels but New Zealand, Irish and UK nationals pay 560 shekels. Get to the embassy in Tel Aviv well before 9 am if you want to beat the queue. If you do this, you can often pick up your passport the same day. The embassy is at 50 Rehov Basel – take bus No 5 from Tel Aviv central bus station (it's a four-km journey). Whatever else you do, don't get your Egyptian visa in Dar es Salaam. They cost Sh 610 (officially US$40) there!

Most people are given a one-month tourist visa. You can renew these at a cost of E£1.70 for each additional two-week period, but you may be required to change money before they will issue an extension, and they keep the bank receipts – a real nuisance if you intend to buy an airline ticket (you must produce bank receipts when buying airline tickets). You can overstay your visa by up to 14 days without incurring any penalties, so if you don't want to change any more money officially, don't bother renewing your visa. If you want to visit Israel and then return, it's best to get a re-entry permit rather than a new visa in Tel Aviv, but re-entry permits expire one day before your original Egyptian visa expires, so plan ahead. Re-entry permits are obtainable from the Mugamma (Central Government Building, Tahrir Square, Cairo). First go to Room 1, then to Room 17. They cost E£10.50 and are issued on the spot. Holders of re-entry permits do not have to change money when they come back into Egypt.

You have to register with the police at the Central Government Buildings, Tahrir Square, within seven days of arriving in the country. If you fail to do this or if you overstay your visa by more than two weeks, you'll be fined E£6.60.

The biggest bugbear about entering Egypt is that you are required to change the equivalent of US$180 into Egyptian currency at the bank. It used to be possible to get through changing less or even changing nothing at all in some circumstances, but the authorities have now tightened up and there are no exceptions. This applies equally if you're entering Egypt from the Sudan at Aswan. The only exception to this rule is if you're coming in from Israel, and the key to the affair is pre-booked accommodation in a tourist-class hotel in Cairo for a minimum of three nights (one night used to be sufficient but that is no longer acceptable). Both *Egged* and *Galilee* bus companies offer transport/accommodation packages between Tel Aviv and Cairo. Egged costs US$30 for the transport and US$17 a single and US$28 a double for the accommodation. Galilee is slightly cheaper at US$20 a single or US$22 a double. Another company which has been recommended is *ISSTA*, Ben Yehuda St, Tel Aviv, which offers a transport/accommodation package for US$65.

If your stay in Egypt is less than seven days, you are allowed to reconvert any excess local currency up to the amount that you initially changed legally. If you stay more than seven days then you can reconvert up to the amount you initially changed legally less US$30 for each day you have stayed. Other ruses which have been used include going back to the airport the day after arrival and telling them you're about to fly out – you may have to produce a dated ticket to satisfy them, but you can always change this again after you have reconverted. You'll naturally lose the commissions involved in the various transactions, but this will probably be substantially less than 20%. If you're going to Sudan, you cannot reconvert local currency at Aswan, though you can exchange it for Sudanese pounds. Another aspect of this requirement which has been pointed out by a number of travellers is that the most important thing is to get the stamp from the bank on the back of the embarkation card – you get this no matter how much you change. The immigration official who stamps your passport doesn't care how much you changed and wouldn't know unless you tell him.

You do not have to produce bank receipts at the border or the airport when leaving. The only time you have to produce receipts is if you apply for a re-entry permit or a visa extension, or if you want to buy an airline ticket. You cannot buy the latter without bank receipts to the full amount of what the ticket costs. There's only one way round this and that is to go and see a Greek character called George who, for a fixed fee of approximately E£10, will provide you with a workable bank receipt for whatever amount you need. Even for a cheap ticket (say, US$100), the fact that he's saving you about 25 to 30% makes his price a bargain. For obvious reasons we cannot print his address here, but you can find out where he lives by asking either at the Pension Oxford or at the Golden Hotel in Cairo.

Warning If you want to visit Israel and then intend to go to Sudan or any other Arab country, you'll have to buy a new passport in Cairo. The Israeli authorities will willingly put entry and exit stamps on a separate piece of paper which you can throw away when you return to Egypt, but you'll still have the Egyptian exit and entry stamps in your passport. Any careful Arab official who notices these will know that you've been to Israel – and many of them are very astute at this. The Sudanese embassy in Cairo, for example, is very aware of this and will reject your application for a visa. Not only that, but when you go back with a new clean passport they'll reject that too, having made a note of your name. Get that new passport before you apply for a Sudanese visa. The Kuwaiti authorities also recognise those stamps and will deport you immediately on the next available flight regardless of its destination, so if you're stopping off there on a flight to India, for instance, make sure you don't have these stamps in your passport. Most embassies in Cairo are aware of these problems and are helpful about issuing second passports.

Sudanese visas Cairo is full of disgruntled travellers waiting for their Sudanese visas to come through. If that's where you're going after Egypt, then get one before you set off, or plan ahead. Regardless of your nationality, Sudanese visas take about five weeks to issue – but to be on the safe side, you should assume it's going to take six weeks. Since the imposition of Islamic Law in late '83 there has been a resurgence of the civil war in the south and the authorities seem to be actively discouraging tourists by making it a real hassle to get a visa. A visa costs E£10.10 plus three photos, and you must have a letter of introduction from your own embassy (the British Embassy charges E£3.20 for these letters). If your visa hasn't come through after three weeks, it's worth asking your embassy for an official diplomatic reminder. Some people have managed to get their visa in a matter of days by obtaining a letter from their embassy stating that they have urgent business in Sudan and must go there immediately. If you manage to swing one of these letters, you will also have to insist on seeing the consul at the Sudanese embassy. Don't leave it at the desk. Remember that your visa will be refused if there's evidence that you've been to Israel in it.

If you simply haven't got the time to wait up to six weeks for a visa and there's no way you can get one earlier, then you'll have to fly. Cairo-Nairobi costs E£363 with bank receipts.

Ethiopian visas Overland entry into Ethiopia is not permitted. The only way you can get in is to fly into Addis Ababa. If you're stopping overnight you don't need a visa.

The border with Libya is closed so you cannot go overland from Egypt to that country.

MONEY

US$1 = E£1.12 (official tourist rate)
  £1 = E£1.51

The unit of currency is the Egyptian pound = 100 piastres. Import/export of local currency is allowed up to E£20. There is a thriving black market on which you can get US$1 = E£1.25 (E£1.30 for large transactions) for cash and E£1.20 for traveller's cheques, though most street dealers will only give you one for one. Likewise, the £ sterling should fetch £1 = E£1.67. It's very open and you shouldn't experience any problems, but beware of sleight-of-hand tricks and having the cash handed to you in an envelope. Insist on counting out the money yourself before handing over your dollars or whatever. The preferred currency is the US dollar, which earns about 2% more than the other acceptable hard currencies (£ sterling, French francs, Swiss francs, Deutschmarks); and cash earns 2 to 4% more than traveller's cheques. Don't bring in any other currencies; though they may be perfectly respectable in many places and you can change them, the rates are likely to be even lower than the banks' rates. Don't bring Eurocheques or Dutch Postal Money Orders. The best black market rates are to be found in Cairo. The rates in Hurghada are lousy. American Express will change US dollar traveller's cheques into US dollars cash for a 2% commission. Also, if you have an international credit card you can use this to draw US dollars at the Bank of America. On the receipt that they give you, they leave the foreign currency section blank, so fill it in if you need a bank receipt for buying an airline ticket.

If you're heading further south, you may well be able to pick up the currencies of the countries you intend to visit fairly cheaply in Cairo. One place that handles a lot of different currencies is Ragab's Bazaar next to the Café Riche, in the pedestrian alley on Talaat Harb St between the Golden Hotel and Tahrir Square. Ask for Ragab or Rashad. You could also pick up these currencies from travellers returning north – ask around in the budget hotels.

Make sure that you declare all foreign currency (including traveller's cheques) in excess of US$500 on entry; otherwise it may well be confiscated on exit. The US embassy in Tel Aviv has had to sort out eight cases of this in five months. Sometimes they have been successful and the money has been recovered. Others haven't been so lucky.

It's a good idea to bring a bottle of duty-free whisky (you're allowed up to one litre). You'll have no problems selling it for about E£50-60 per litre, but make sure it's Johnny Walker Black Label, Chivas Regal or White Horse. Cognac is also worth bringing in, but duty-free cigarettes are a waste of time.

Try not to have money sent to you in Egypt, but if you can't avoid it, have it sent either to American Express or Thomas Cook. Don't have money sent in the mail.

Twenty-four-hour banking facilities are available at the Nile Hilton, the Sheraton and other large hotels.

Although there are certain exceptions (detailed later), you must buy international airline tickets with local currency bought at the official bank rate (not the official tourist rate), which is US$1 = E£0.82, and you must produce bank receipts for the full amount. Some travellers have also reported that the US$180 you have to change on entry can't be used for this purpose. This means that there are no cheap airline ticket deals available in Egypt.

The departure tax for international flights is E£10.

LANGUAGE

Arabic is the official language but English and French are widely understood. There is also a large Greek minority in the city areas.

POST

The poste restante in Cairo is notorious for its inefficiency, and letters can take weeks to get to the stage where you can claim them. There's also a fee for each letter collected. Use American Express clients' mail instead if you have their cheques or a credit card. Whatever else you do, don't have parcels sent to you here. All parcels are intercepted by the censors, opened, inspected, closed after a fashion, billed and sent to the central parcel office in Ataba Square. You learn – if you're lucky! – of the parcel's arrival by an unintelligible and illegible piece of coloured cardboard that you notice kicking about on the floor of your hotel room or wherever you happen to live. If you know how the system works, or if someone tells you, then you make a time-wasting trek to the dingy parcel office with this piece of card. Someone will duly sift through the shelves of violated and decidedly derelict parcels and, with luck, pick out your parcel. Out will come the *daftar* and you'll be told how much you have to pay. You won't be told what the contents are, nor whether they've been destroyed, censored, thieved or just disappeared. You just have to pay up and take pot luck. Tell your friends to restrain their mailing activities.

STUDENT CARDS & CONCESSIONS

An international student card is very useful in Egypt. You not only get a 50% reduction on rail fares (all classes) but also big reductions on the entry fees to the antiquities and museums. Without a card, those archaeological sites are going to burn a large hole in your pocket – the Valley of the Kings alone costs E£5 without a student card! If you don't have a student card but you do have a Youth Hostels membership card, you can still get the discount on the trains – just show the ticket office your YHA card.

GETTING THERE & AROUND
International Connections
Many travellers fly into Cairo from Athens because there are usually cheap ticket deals available there from one or another of the many travel agents around Syntagma Square. A one-way flight costs between US$85 and US$100 depending on whether you have a student card or are under 26 years old. Recently recommended were *Fantasy Travel*, 10 Xenofontas St (near Syntagma Square), 10557 Athens (tel 3228410). It's run by a friendly and helpful bunch who usually give the under-26 discount regardless of age. *Speedy Ways Travel Agency* on Aristotelous St have also been recommended.

If you buy an airline ticket in Egypt, then nine times out of ten you must show bank receipts at the official bank rate (not the official tourist rate) for the full amount of what the ticket costs. The official bank rate is US$1 = E£0.82 as opposed to the tourist rate of US$1 = E£1.12. An exception is *Yugoslavian Airlines* if you buy your ticket at their office in the Nile Hilton Hotel, Tahrir Square, Cairo. Here you simply pay cash and don't have to show receipts. They fly Cairo-Belgrade-Zagreb-Stockholm-Copenhagen.

Student discounts of 25% may also be available on *Sudan Air* and *Kenya Airways*, but it can take a considerable degree of persistence to get them. Take a photostat of your student card with you when you go to buy a ticket. Cairo-Nairobi with Kenya Airways costs E£363 or E£289 with a student card.

Though not a discount in the strict sense, you can fly from Cairo to Nairobi via Addis Ababa with *Ethiopian Airways* and stop over for one night in Addis with all expenses paid by the airline. You don't need a visa for this – they'll give you one on arrival. This free night of luxury doesn't apply if you stay more than one night. You'll also need a visa if you stay more than one night.

Flights to India cost about US$450 and it's difficult to find a discounted ticket. You wouldn't save much either by flying back to Athens and then buying a discounted ticket there.

If you're thinking of flying back to northern Europe from Egypt, it's worth enquiring first about charter flights from Eilat (Israel) to London. Some travellers have written to say this can cost as little as US$85.

There are no scheduled passenger boats between Egypt and Kenya or Egypt and India. There is a slight possibility of being able to find a free or work-your-passage lift to those places on yachts. Go to Port Said and take the ferry across the Canal to the Yacht Club. Don't listen to anyone who tells you that you need a pass to get into the Yacht Club. All you need is your passport. With luck you may meet someone who is going where you want to go.

To/From Israel

The cheapest way of getting to Israel is to take a combination of local shared taxis and buses. This shouldn't cost you more than E£11 from Cairo to Tel Aviv and you should be able to do it in a day. The quickest way of getting to Israel is to take one of the direct tourist buses from Cairo to Tel Aviv. Depending on which company you go with (*Galilee*, *Isis*, *Egged*, *Emeco*, etc), this can cost up to US$35 but is usually US$25. The journey takes about nine hours. We've had occasional reports of bank receipts being demanded for these tickets, but that would be unusual. There are also cheaper direct daily buses from Cairo to Tel Aviv which leave at 7.30 am from the Sinai Terminal. They cost E£20 and take nine hours. There are also buses from this terminal to Rafah which leave at 7 am daily and cost E£7.

Whichever form of transport you take, you'll have to pay a departure tax of E£5 (this may have gone up to E£10.50 now) and an entry tax of E£2 when you return. Have some Egyptian currency handy for this. The only way you can avoid paying this exit tax is to leave via Taba (the Egyptian/Israeli border near Eilat).

Details of the cheap way to Israel are as follows: Go to Ulali Square (Midan al Ulali) near Ramses Square, Cairo, in the early morning anytime between 4.30 am and 6 am. There you will find service taxis to El Qantara on the west bank of the Suez Canal. Let the taxi driver know you are aware that the fare is E£2 and get in. When it's full it will leave (seven passengers). The journey takes about two hours. When you get to El Qantara, take the ferry across the Canal (free and takes a few minutes). On the east bank you'll find more service taxis which will take you to Rafah (the border). These cost E£3 and take about 2½ hours. On the Egyptian side of the border you go through customs, pay the E£5 departure tax and then buy a ticket for the bus which runs between the two border posts (50 piastres – you are not allowed to walk). On the other side you go through Israeli customs. The time taken to get through both customs varies between 15 minutes and four hours but is usually around two hours. Once through customs you have a choice of shared taxi (US$5-7) or public bus (US$3-4, depart at 12.30 pm and 3 pm) to Ashkelon, where you change for Tel Aviv or Jerusalem. The journey between the border and Tel Aviv is usually about three hours.

Don't take a single taxi between Cairo and Rafah. This is usually more expensive and takes longer than the two-taxi trip because the taxis have to wait (sometimes for hours) for a special vehicle ferry to take them across the Suez Canal. You don't have this problem on the passenger ferry.

Remember the compulsory money change when you return from Israel. If you don't want to go through this a second time, then make sure that you have arranged pre-booked accommodation in Cairo for at least three nights. In the past some travellers have got through without having either of these and telling customs that they only intend to stay in Egypt for a few days or that they simply haven't got US$180 spare, but you'll be extremely lucky to get away with that these days. As a last resort – and certainly if you don't intend to stay in Egypt more than two weeks – you can simply refuse to change US$180. They might equally refuse you entry, but travellers who have done this have been given 48-hour visas. That's all you need because you're allowed to overstay your visa by two weeks without being fined.

You cannot go to Jordan from Israel unless your journey started in Jordan.

To/From the Sudan

The most popular way of getting from Egypt to Sudan is to take the Aswan-Wadi Halfa boat down Lake Nasser. The boats depart Aswan on Saturday afternoon and take two days. The fare is E£5.45 (deck class) and E£21 for a bed in a shared cabin. The cabins are said to be small and rat infested, and the air-conditioning rarely works. Buy tickets at Aswan. If you're going deck class, you need to be at the boat jetty several hours before the boat leaves if you want to have a chance of staking out a patch. Travellers are often waved through customs and so are first on the boat, but you can't count on this. There's no fuss about currency forms at Egyptian customs, and Sudanese passport control is done on the boat. Make sure your vaccination certificates are in order, as they'll be checked. If they have lapsed you'll be given a shot on the boat – the same needle does everyone. You can buy guava juice (35-40 pt) and chicken and *foul* (E£2) on the boat, though many people prefer to take their own food and water with them. If you don't like crowds then go in 2nd or 1st class. Since the fire which sunk one of the ferries in 1983, no stoves or fuel of any kind are allowed on deck. If you're taking a car or other vehicle on this ferry you must empty your tanks.

Currency declaration forms are issued at Wadi Halfa (Sudan customs) and cameras are recorded in your passport. Make sure you get rid of any Egyptian currency before you get on the boat, but only buy enough Sudanese pounds to get you as far as Khartoum because the rates

for hard currency are much better there. In Aswan you can expect E£1 = S£2.20, whereas at the boat jetty in Wadi Halfa you will only get E£1 = S£1.70.

The Land-Rover ride from the boat dock to Wadi Halfa costs S£2.

There's also a Port Suez-Port Sudan passenger ferry which departs every 10 days. It's a three-day journey and costs E£46 (3rd class including food). The boat calls at Jeddah but visas for Saudi Arabia are hard to get. Buy the ticket for the boat at *Egyptian Shipping & Navigation Co*, Talaat Harb, Cairo (next door to the cinema Radio) or in Port Suez. If you're using this boat in the opposite direction (from Sudan) and are prepared to take duty-free whisky and cigarettes through customs on arrival in Suez (where you hand them over to someone who's there to collect them), then the captain of the ship will fix you up with a luxury cabin despite the fact you've only bought a 3rd-class ticket. Those who have taken this ship say it's an exciting trip.

To/From Jordan

There are many shipping lines which operate boats between Suez and Aqaba, most of them Saudi lines. *Egyptian Shipping & Navigation Company* also have boats on this route and they're popular with Egyptian workers going to/returning from Jordan and Iraq where there is work available. As far as travellers are concerned, the existence of these boats presents an alternative way of getting from the Middle East to Egypt without having to go through Israel (and the attendant visa hassles you will experience if you do this). Travellers who have taken this ferry suggest that you buy a cheap deck-class ticket since the captain is more than likely to give you a free luxury cabin right next to his for reasons best known to himself.

Internal Transport
Rail

Trains are the most popular form of transport in the Nile Valley because they are so cheap. Discounts of 50% are available in all classes to those with student cards or Youth Hostel membership cards. Only 1st and 2nd classes can be booked in advance, though 2nd class is often booked up days in advance. Third-class tickets can only be bought on the day of departure. There are two daily trains in either direction between Cairo and Aswan via Luxor. The journey from Cairo to Luxor takes between 12½ and 15 hours; from Cairo to Aswan it takes between 17 and 19½ hours. The evening train from Cairo to Luxor/Aswan departs at 8 pm. From Luxor to Aswan there are three trains daily in the mornings up to 11 am. It's a good idea to book in advance if possible, but as the railway offices only hold the train reservation plans for the next six days, there's no point in trying to book further ahead than that. Examples of fares with student reduction are:

Cairo-Luxor E£4.20 (2nd class air-conditioned)
Cairo-Aswan E£9.85 (1st class) and E£5.50 (2nd class with air-conditioning)
Luxor-Aswan E£1.40 (2nd class with air-conditioning)

Road
The main bus routes of interest to travellers are:

Cairo-Alexandria There are six daily buses in either direction which are very comfortable, air-conditioned and cost E£3. They depart from Tahrir Square in Cairo. Reserve your seat at least a few hours in advance. There are also non-air-conditioned buses which cost E£2.25 but they're not comfortable at all. They leave from the parking lot behind the Hilton Hotel.
Cairo-Hurghada There is a daily non-air-conditioned bus in either direction (at 6.30 am from Cairo and 6 am from Hurghada) which costs E£5 and takes about eight hours. You're advised to book in advance. There is also a daily air-conditioned bus in either direction (at 7

am and 7.30 am from Cairo and 5.30 am from Hurghada) which costs E£8. It can be frustrating trying to find the bus terminal in Cairo, so follow these directions:

Face the railway station in Ramses Square and take the one and only road bridge on the left-hand side that goes over the railway tracks. Once you're over the tracks, take the first set of steps on the right. When you get to the bottom, continue straight ahead for a few hundred metres – through the noise and confusion (stores and buses) – until you get to a green kiosk on the left (no sign). It has a sliding window facing Ramses Station and a slanting roof. Be there at 5.30 am or earlier. Wait in line, and when the man comes between 5.30 and 6 am, make your reservation. He'll give you a piece of paper with the date and your seat number on it. Near this kiosk is a tea shop next to a single tree. The bus will arrive at about 6.30 am. You pay your fare on the bus. Remember to call Hurghada by its Egyptian name of Ghardaka; otherwise no one will understand you.
Luxor-Hurghada There are two buses daily in either direction (at 6.30 am and noon from Luxor) which cost E£5 and take five hours. The buses are air-conditioned. Since the buses go via Qena, you can also pick them up here if there are spare seats. If not, there are three non-air-conditioned buses daily in either direction between Qena and Hurghada (at 4.30 am, 8.30 am and 11.30 am from Hurghada). The fare is E£3 and the journey takes four hours. If you'd prefer a service taxi, these are available all day at either place and cost E£2 per person (seven passengers to a taxi). They take about 3½ hours.

Details about bus services to the Sinai and the Western Oases can be found under those respective headings.

River Nile
One of the things you must do when you're in Egypt is take a *felucca* (Egyptian

sailboat) up or down the Nile between Luxor and Aswan. It's a very relaxing and memorable trip through beautiful countryside. Get a small group together and find a boat. The journey from Luxor to Aswan takes three to five days including stops at villages and antiquities en route. You sleep on the boat at night. In the off-season (summer) you could get one for as little as E£85 with haggling, though the first price quoted is likely to be around E£150. In the high season (winter) it will probably cost you double this. Food for the trip shouldn't cost more than E£2-3 for a four-day trip so long as you don't want meat. The captain will cook for you. Take plenty of water/bottled drinks with you unless you want to drink the water of the Nile. Make sure you stop off at Edfu, Isna and Kom Ombo en route to see the temples and the towns. Don't swim in the Nile – bilharzia is rife. Add to your costs a E£5 per person registration fee which you must pay to the police before setting off. Make sure you pay this. The Nile is well patrolled and there is a fine to pay as well as the fee if you set off without paying. Most *feluccas* take eight to 10 passengers.

ALEXANDRIA

The cheapest place to stay here is the *Youth Hostel*, Port Said St, which costs 90 pt (piastres) per person. It puts on basic meals but there is nowhere you can leave a pack safely, so it may be better to stay somewhere else. Cheap hotels to try are: *Pension St Mark*, 26 Sharia Gorfa Fugaria (tel 806923). This costs E£3.50 a double and offers hot water and the use of a stove and refrigerator.
Hyde Park Hotel, 21 Rue Amin Fikry (tel 35666/7), costs E£4.60 a double including a continental breakfast.
Hotel Ailemma, same address as the Hyde Park Hotel, costs E£5.73 including breakfast.
Gambil, near the East Harbour not far from the Tourist Office, costs E£5.20 including tax.

Hotel Mahaba (formerly the Hotel Majestic), Orabi Square, has been renovated recently and now costs E£11 a double.

Another place you could try outside the city is the *Costa Blanca Hotel* at Agami Beach. A room for four people here costs E£7.60 without breakfast.

Two of the cheapest restaurants in Alexandria are the *Ghad Restaurant* on Mohammed Azni St and the *Foul Mohammed Achmed* on Rue Abd Elfttah el Hadari. Both of them serve excellent *foul* and *falafels*, and the latter makes some of the best sandwiches in the city. The prices are government-controlled. A good place to go for breakfast or for beer and snacks in the afternoon is the *Café Triamon* at Ramel Station. Eggs cost 45 pt, croissants 8 pt and a pot of coffee 25 pt. You can also get good hot and cold drinks including coffee and tea at the *Brazilian Coffee Stores*, 44 Saad Zaghlul on the corner of Nabi Daniel St. Avoid the *Restaurant Ramses* unless you have money falling out of your pockets.

There's not a great deal to see in Alexandria anymore – it no longer lives up to the reputation that WW II troops and Lawrence Durrell (among others) gave it. The **market** area to the south and west of Mohammed Ali Square is worth a visit, however. If you want to go to the **beaches**, bus No 16 goes to the Montazzah Palace and along the Corniche to all the beaches. The palace is now closed to the public and is used for official government guests.

If you need to register with the police here (all visitors have to do this within seven days of arrival in Egypt), go to the office on the corner of Faliky St and Talaat Harb Pasha and collect three yellow cards. Have these stamped by the hotel and return them. If you have the hotel do this for you, they may well charge you up to E£2.

ASWAN

Restrictions on tourist access to most of the sites around Aswan have been lifted so

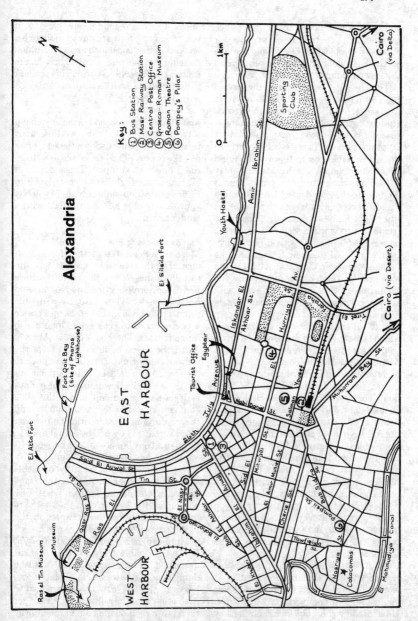

Alexandria

Key:
① Bus Station
② Masr Railway Station
③ Central Post Office
⊕ Graeco - Roman Museum
⑤ Roman Theatre
⑥ Pompey's Pillar

you no longer need apply for police permission. You only need permits for **Kalabsha Temple, Beit El Wali** and **Qartass** on the east bank of Lake Nasser beyond the Aswan Dam.

The cheapest way to get to the **Aswan High Dam** is to take the train from Aswan to Saad el Aali (15 pt with a YH card/ student card), from where you can get a shared taxi across the top of the dam for 60 pt per person. There is a E£1 entry to the dam. While you're there you should visit **Philae Temple**, which costs E£3 entry (E£1.50 with a student card). Tourist boats go to the island on which the temple stands when there are enough passengers (they cost E£2 per person). **Elephantine Island** is also worth a visit. The museum here costs 50 pt entry with student card. Behind it is a Ptolemaic temple and the famous **Nilometer**. On the west bank of the Nile are the **Tomb of the Agha Khan**, the **Monastery of St Simon** (50 pt entry with student card) and the **Tombs of the Middle Kingdom Nobles**. You can make your own way to all these sights, or go on a tour which takes in most of them, or even hire a *felucca* for the day. The local ferry for the Tombs of the Nobles costs 5 pt – set off early in the morning if you intend to walk there. The Youth Hostel offers a four-hour, E£8 tour of the Aswan High Dam, Philae Island and the Obelisk. If you want to hire a *felucca* to see Elephantine Island, the Agha Khan's Tomb and the Tombs of the Nobles, ask around for a man called Bibi Bana opposite the Grand Hotel who owns a boat called *Arabia*. He's been recommended as a very friendly and honest man. It might also still be possible to see all these sights free of charge if you can brazen your way onto the Oberoi launch, but make sure you look like all the other well-heeled tourists or you'll be spotted.

In Aswan town itself, the **mosque** (where 'Old Fort' is marked on the map) is worth visiting. For E£1 a man will show you round and take you up the minaret. He'll hassle you for *baksheesh* on the way

down. There is a good **bazaar** here too if you're looking for bargains in djellabahs, baskets and musical instruments. Nubian dancing can be seen most nights at the **Cultural Centre**, Nile St, which is excellent value for E£1.10 with a student card (E£3 normally).

Abu Simbel There is no longer any cheap way of getting to this world-famous temple about halfway down the east bank of Lake Nasser. The boat which used to go there has been stopped. These days you must take the flight which costs E£55 to E£65 return (depending on where you buy your ticket) plus E£6 entry (E£3 with a student card).

Places to Stay & Eat

Most travellers stay at the *Hotel Continental* on the riverfront, though it's quite run-down these days. It costs 80 pt for a bed in the dormitory (four-bed rooms) and E£2 a single. They also have double rooms. It's a good place to tack up a notice if you're trying to get a group together to hire a felucca. The *Youth Hostel*, Abtal al Tahrir St (three minutes' walk from the railway station and more or less opposite the *Hotel Marwa*), used to be popular but has gone rapidly downhill and these days is described as 'a dump' and 'filthy.' The staff are reported to be unfriendly and there's only one shower. Still, it only costs 60 pt with a YH card. The hostel used to be open all day but now closes between 10 am and 2 pm and after 11 pm at night. There are no cooking facilities or meals available. Another cheapie is the *Hotel Marwa* (*Hotel Malva*?) which costs E£1 per night. It's very clean, the staff are friendly and there's warm water in the bathrooms most of the day.

More expensive are the *Hotel El Saffa*, E£2.90 a double with hot showers but described by one traveller as 'a filthy dump'; and the *Rosewan Hotel* which costs E£5 a single. These two hotels are next to each other near the railway station. To get there, turn right coming out of the railway

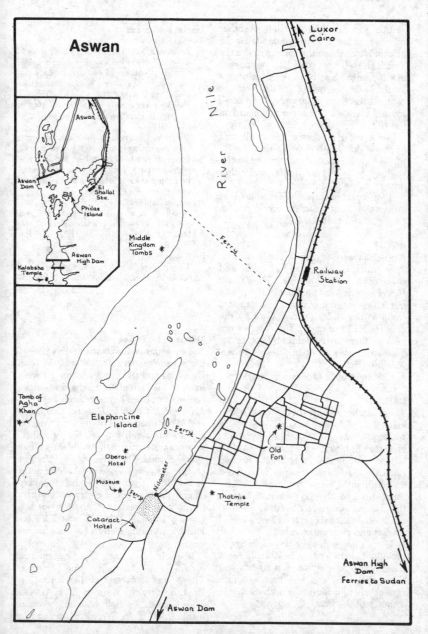

station and take the first left. Another place which has been recommended is the *Miwan Hotel* above the café opposite the Youth Hostel. This costs E£1 per person in a double room with fan. A refrigerator is available for the use of guests. You can camp at the *Hotel Continental* for a small fee and there's a 24-hour armed guard on the site.

For a good meal, try the small café opposite the Youth Hostel where, for 85 pt, you can have a two-egg omelette, yoghurt, honey, bread, butter and either orange or banana juice.

If you want to use the swimming pools at either the *New Cataract Hotel* or the *Oberoi*, it will cost you E£2.

ASYUT

A good place to stay here is the *Hotel Zam Zam* which is clean, has hot water and costs E£3-3.50 a double. The *Youth Hostel* here is very pleasant and friendly but a long way out of town. You can also camp at the *Police Officers Club* by the dam for E£2 per night. The showers are grubby, there are no lights and you're not allowed to have an open fire, but otherwise it's OK.

Visit the **Coptic Monastery** here.

CAIRO

There can be few cities in the world with a history as rich as Cairo's. Where else could you see 6000-year-old pyramids and the Sphinx (some of the world's largest man-made structures), Roman ruins, Coptic churches, exquisitely carved and brilliantly conceived mosques and fortresses from the days when Cairo was the cultural centre of the Islamic world, traditional sailboats on the river, a camel market and even catacombs?

There's an endless variety of things to see and do here – noisy, bustling bazaars packed into narrow winding streets and those thousand and one aromas (both mysterious and foul) which characterise so much of the East.

Useful Addresses
Tourist Office

Located at 5 Adli St, the office has plenty of information on what's worth seeing in Cairo, though this may not be in any language you can read. Others have said it's about as useful as a glass eye. It may not have maps of the city (take a copy of the *Oxford Map of Egypt* with you if you want to be sure).

Tourist Police

are tucked away in an office down a small alley immediately to the left of the Tourist Office. If you have to go here for anything (eg reporting a theft from your hotel room) be prepared for a long haul and to pay for even the most trivial tasks.

American Express

15 Sharia Ksar el Nil, PO Box 2160 (tel 970132). There are branch offices at the Nile Hilton, the Meridien Hotel and the airport.

Bookstore

A good place to pick new and second-hand books in several languages is at 21 Sherif St.

Things to Do & See
The Pyramids of Giza & the Sphinx One of the Seven Wonders of the World, the Giza Pyramids and the Sphinx lie on the west bank of the Nile about nine km from the centre of Cairo. They were built between 2600 and 2520 BC by Cheops, Chephron and Mycerinus, kings of the 4th Dynasty, and are surrounded by smaller pyramids, temples and tombs of the nobles and other court officials. The largest is the Pyramid of Cheops; you're allowed to climb up inside this pyramid to the funerary chamber in the middle. Entry to the site is free, but if you want to climb up inside the Cheops Pyramid this will cost E£3 (or E£1.50 if you happen to have a student card).

It's well worth going to a performance of the *son et lumiere* one evening. There are separate performances in English, French, German and Arabic. The English version is every second night from 6 to 7 pm. Entry costs

E£4 (no reductions), but if you go beyond the pavilion and sit on the wall there, you'll be able to see almost as much as you would by paying for a seat and you'll probably find yourself in the company of many other travellers. Watch out for guards who patrol the area.

Memphis & the Pyramids of Saqqara About 20 km south of Cairo, Memphis was once the capital of ancient Egypt and there's plenty to see. The pyramids here are much older than those at Giza but smaller. The cheapest way of getting there is to take the train to Badrashayn. There's one daily at 10.10 am which costs 8 pt. You can also get there by a taxi-bus combination. First take a bus from Tahrir Square to Giza Square (Nos 900, 904, 108, 124, 8 and others). There are also service taxis for 20 to 25 pt. When you get there, continue on foot for a little further in the same direction and ask for the service taxis for Badrashayn. It should cost about 15 pt and take about half an hour. You can also get to Badrashayn by train – there's one every half an hour which costs 3½ pt with student card. Memphis is close to Badrashayn. From Badrashayn to Saqqara take a service taxi or microbus which will cost around 15 pt and take about 20 minutes. It will drop you about two km from Saqqara, after which you walk along the canal to the pyramids – very picturesque countryside. You can also hire camels and horses to explore this area. Entry to Saqqara costs E£2 (E£1 with student card). There are no hotels at Badrashayn in case you're thinking of staying there overnight.

Egyptian Museum This contains one of the world's best collections of ancient Egyptian artifacts, including the famous mummies and the sarcophagus of Tutankhamen. Don't miss it! The museum is open daily except Friday from 8.30 am to 4 pm and costs E£3 (E£1.50 with student card) excluding the Mummy Room, plus E£10 if you have a camera. The latest reports say that the Mummy Room is now permanently closed (!?).

Islamic Museum This is also excellent and has displays of artifacts dating from the period when Cairo was the cultural capital of the Islamic world. It is open daily from 9 am to 4 pm and costs E£2 (E£1 with a student card).

Other sights worth seeing in Cairo are the **Coptic Museum** (E£1 entry with student card), the **Sultan Hasan Mosque**, the **Abdin Palace**, the **Tombs of the Caliphs & Mamelukes** and the **Citadel** (E£1 with student card and you no longer need to show your passport to get in – it's used partially as a barracks).

The oldest **bazaar** – and the one most visited by tourists – is Khan el Khalily. It's worth spending a whole day wandering around here. Don't forget the side streets and the level above the street where you'll more than likely be welcomed as a friend instead of a brainless tourist throwing money around. One traveller who lived here for a while suggested walking from the bazaar through Old Cairo to the Citadel around late afternoon, in order to see the sun setting over Cairo and its mosques. It's an unforgettable sight. **Muezni-din-Allah**, which runs perpendicular to Al-Azhar St just before Al-Azhar itself, was one of the widest boulevards in the medieval world (four laden horses wide) and still retains much of its traditional character. It offers interesting sights at either end – Bab Zuweila in the south where the heads of undesirables were hung, and the old city walls in the north, one patrolled by Napoleon's graffiti-carving troops.

Another sight worth catching is the **Camel Market** which takes place every Friday morning and sometimes on other days too. Take bus No 99 from Tahrir Square to Suq al Gimaal (the name of the camel market) in Imbaba. You'll see more camels here than you ever dreamed could be brought together in one place, as well

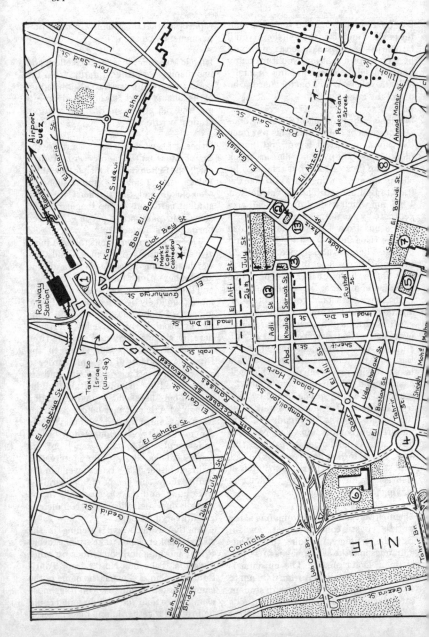

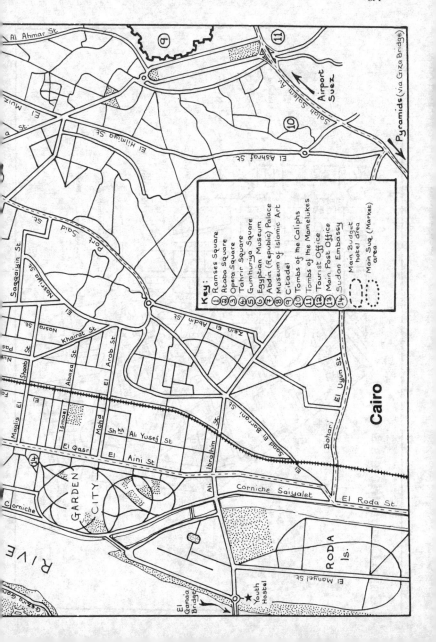

Key:
1. Ramses Square
2. Ataba Square
3. Opera Square
4. Tahrir Square
5. Gumhuriya Square
6. Egyptian Museum
7. Abdin (Republic) Palace
8. Museum of Islamic Art
9. Citadel
10. Tombs of the Caliphs
11. Tombs of the Mamelukes
12. Tourist Office
13. Main Post Office
14. Sudan Embassy
○ ○ Main Budget hotel area
. . . . Main Suq (Market) area

Cairo

RIVE

GARDEN CITY

RODA Is.

Youth Hostel

El Gamaa Bridge

Corniche Saiyalet

El Roda St.

El Manyal St.

Airport
Suez
Pyramids (via Giza Bridge)

Cairo Central (Hotels & Cafes)

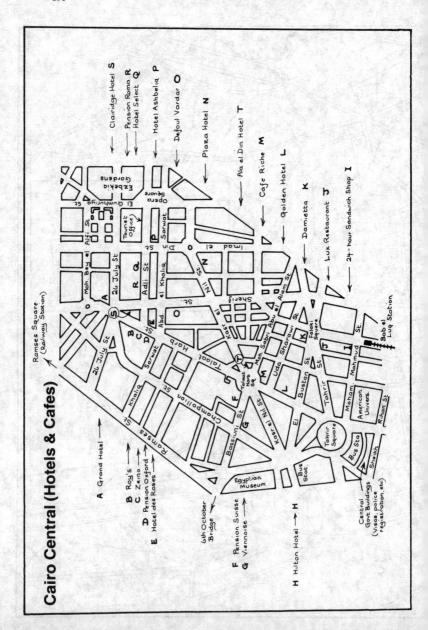

A Grand Hotel
B Roy's
C Zema
D Pension Oxford
E Hotel des Roses
F Pension Suisse
G Viennoise
H Hilton Hotel

I 24-hour Sandwich Shop
K Damietta
L Lux Restaurant
M Cafe Riche
N Plaza Hotel
O Defoul Vardar
P Hotel Ashbelia
Q Hotel Select
R Pension Roma
S Clairidge Hotel
T Ala el Din Hotel

as donkeys and all the accessories which go with them. It's very entertaining. Don't confuse this market with the camel meat market in Al Sayyida where the camels are sold for slaughter.

Another great way to spend a few hours is to take a **Cairo water bus** on the Nile. They're cheap – just 5-10 pt depending on the distance – and you can board them at the Radio & TV building on the Corniche (near the Hilton) or at the southern tip of Roda Island and at other points. You can go all the way to Old Cairo on these buses, or north to the Barrages (Al-Qanatir) where Sadat had a residence. Here you can spend a pleasant day enjoying the gardens (bicycles and horses for hire).

The **Cairo Tower** has also been recommended for a magnificent view over Cairo. The entrance fee is E£1 and is probably worth it if you go in clear weather, but don't be tempted to order a beer up there in the cafeteria as it will cost you E£2.65. Instead, 'Suppress your thirst until you get down, and then have the best *karkade* in town at the open-air refreshment place at the foot of the tower. It costs 60 pt but is so good and strong that you'll have to buy a bottle of mineral water to mix it with.'

Places to Stay

There is a wide choice of cheap and moderately priced accommodation in Cairo, most of it on or off Talaat Harb and between here and Opera Square. One place not in this area is the *Youth Hostel*, which is near the El Gamaa Bridge and opposite Salah el Din Mosque on Roda Island. It used to be a real dump but has apparently undergone a transformation and now has locks on doors, clean bathrooms, meals and is a good place to pick up information from other travellers, though there are still plenty of mosquitoes and cats (better than rats!). At 80 pt per bed (60 pt if you're under 21), it has to be the cheapest place to stay in the city. It's a half-hour walk from Tahrir Square.

In the Talaat Harb area you should avoid the *Golden Hotel*, 13 Talaat Harb near Tahrir Square, and the *Pension Oxford*, 32 Talaab (top floor), unless you're desperate. At one time, both of these were legends among travellers and everyone seemed to stay there, but they've been getting some very unflattering comments lately. Typical are: 'Dirty and overpriced,' 'Bed bugs rife,' 'Water works only infrequently,' 'Notorious for its squalor, bed bugs, the lot.' The Oxford costs 85 pt on the floor, E£1.08 for a bed in the dormitory and E£2.65 a double. It still has a good atmosphere and a friendly Greek owner according to some travellers, but it's very dirty. The Golden is a complete rip-off at E£3 for a bed on the floor and E£6 a double. There's no hot water and lots of bugs (including bed bugs). Another place where you're likely to be eaten alive by bed bugs despite the price is the *Beausite*, Talaat Harb St, which costs E£7.50 including breakfast. The rooms here are pretty grim and often smell of cat piss.

The *Pension de Famille*, Khaliq Sarwat St just off Talaat Harb, has been recommended by many travellers. It's very pleasant and costs E£2.50 per night. Student cards may be available here. The *Plaza Hotel*, 32 Kasr el Nil St (8th floor) next to Galion children's store, is a good clean place with hot water and costs E£3 a single and E£6 a double including breakfast. Similar is the *Hotel Select*, 19 Adli St (8th floor) next to the synagogue. It's clean and friendly and costs E£2.40 a single and E£4.75 a double including breakfast and hot water. It's also possible to get a bed on the floor here for E£2. The *Hotel des Roses*, Talaat Harb near the junction with Abd Khaliq Sarwat St, is also good value and costs E£9.85 a double for the first night and E£7.50 a double for subsequent nights including breakfast. There is hot water sometimes. Other relatively cheap places to stay in this area are the *Pension Suisse*, Bassiuni St near Talaat Harb Square (top floor), which costs E£4 a single and E£6 a double including breakfast; *Hotel Ashbelia*, 16 Adli St (4th floor) (tel 916942), which costs E£2 a single and E£3 a double without breakfast; and *Pension Roma*, Adli St (top floor). The latter has an entrance via a walkway opposite the El Walid clothing store (there's a green painted sign high up). Rooms vary in price but are in the E£6 a double range including breakfast. The *Claridge Hotel* now costs E£5.85 per person. *Hotel Tulipe*, Talaat Harb Square, has also been recommended at E£9.60 a double including breakfast. Also worth trying are the *Plaza Hotel*, next to Libyan Arab Airlines, which costs E£6 a double including breakfast; and the *Bussid Hotel* opposite the Pension Oxford, which has large, clean rooms for E£5 a double including breakfast.

Somewhat out of this area opposite the railway station on Ramses Square is the *Hotel Everest*, which has been enthusiastically recommended by many travellers, especially lately. It costs E£2.55 a single and E£4.50 a double including a good breakfast. The rooms are bug-free and the bathrooms are so clean you could eat your dinner off them. There is hot water and good views over Cairo from the roof. The hotel is on the top floor but there are six lifts so there's always one which is working.

Also out of the main area but excellent value is the *Tiba House Hotel*, 6 Aly Mohammed St, King Faisal Rd, Giza. It's about 10 minutes' walk from the pyramids and nine km from Tahrir Square. This is a new place with 40 rooms (singles and doubles) and each floor has its own toilets and showers. The rooms are all very clean and some have views of the pyramids. The staff are very friendly and there's a small attached restaurant where you can get a sandwich at any time of the day or night. It costs E£5 a single and E£8.90 a double including breakfast. If you stay longer than one week, you can re-negotiate the price (say, E£3 a single excluding breakfast).

Also at Giza there's a campsite available very close to the pyramids. Watch for the signpost indicating a left turn on Pyramids Avenue just before the pyramids themselves. Follow the sign, then turn right down a lane past what must once have been an abattoir or tannery judging from the smell. It costs E£3 per person. The gate is always kept locked and your gear is watched. The campsite offers pleasant gardens, a new, clean shower block and a kitchen area but no stoves.

If you're looking for more comfort than a budget hotel offers, try the *Grand Hotel*, corner of Talaat Harb and 26th July St opposite L'Américain. This is a large hotel and popular with travellers. It costs E£8 a single and E£11 a double including breakfast. It also offers fixed-price lunches and dinners. Similar are the *Hotel Hamburg*, 18 Ela Borsa Tawfikia, which costs E£8.70 a single including own shower (hot water) and substantial breakfast; and the *Hotel Viennoise*, Bassiuni St (2nd floor) just off Talaat Harb Square, which costs E£12.45 a single including breakfast.

In the unlikely event of the above being full, or if you can't find a place you like, there are others marked on the map of central Cairo.

Places to Eat

There are literally thousands of *foul* and *felafa* cafés and teahouses in central Cairo where you can get a meal for much less than E£1, so long as you don't order meat. There are also a lot of fast-food pasta places where you can get a small helping of pasta, rice, lentils, tomato sauce and fried onions for as little as 20 pt. A good hunting ground for these cheap cafés is along the market street between Tahrir St and Mohammed Mahmud St east of Tahrir Square – turn right by the blue footbridge down Tahrir St.

Popular named restaurants include *Felfela's*, Talaat Harb on Talaat Harb Square, which everyone goes to at some time or another. It has cheap sandwiches and other snacks for about E£1.50 but the meals are pricey at around E£4.50 to E£5. The *Zeina Cafeteria*, Talaat Harb near

Abdel el Khaliq Sarwat St, offers vegetarian meals for less than E£1. If you have meat it will cost more. The café is open until midnight. *Roy's Bar and Restaurant*, 42 Talaat Harb, offers very filling meals for between E£2 and E£3. The *Damietta*, Falaki Square (no sign in English), has very cheap meals of *foul*, *taamiya*, lentil soup and yogurt for 20-40 pt.

Other than the local restaurants, it's worth considering the all-you-can-eat breakfasts offered by the large hotels like the *Hilton*, *Sheraton* and the *Meridien*. Although they're no longer the bargain they used to be, they're still fairly good. The cheapest at present is the Meridien, which costs E£3.85 – the dining room overlooks the Nile. The breakfasts at the Hilton cost E£4.50. There is a minimum charge of E£1.50 in the Hilton Coffee Shop.

A good place in which to hang around and have a beer is the *Café Riche* on Talaat Harb Square. It's very popular but you should avoid eating here if you're on a budget. A beer will cost E£2 including service.

If you want a splurge, *El Hatti's* at Midan Halim between the Windsor Hotel on Alfi St and 26th July St has been recommended. It serves great lamb dishes, has heaps of mirrors and chandeliers and is frequented by Arabs from far and near. There is also a new *El Hatti's* beside the Horus Hotel just round the corner, but it doesn't have the atmosphere of the old one.

Getting Around

Local Buses Bus numbers are usually in Arabic numerals, so make sure you are familiar with these. No 400 runs between the airport and Ramses and Tahrir squares 24 hours a day and costs 10 pt. It takes about half an hour at night but up to an hour during the day. Allow four or five hours between setting off from your hotel and boarding your flight. If you're arriving in Cairo by air, this bus leaves from in front of the Departures building (arriving passengers come out of the side of the airport). A taxi to the airport will cost about E£4.

The ordinary buses are often very crowded and slow so it's worth considering the microbuses (converted VWs and Toyota vans) for getting around Cairo. They operate on all the main routes and will stop wherever you want them to. The passengers themselves collect the fares as a rule, so you don't need to haggle like you do with the taxi drivers. Tahrir Square to the Pyramids costs 25 pt; Tahrir Square to Giza costs 15 pt; and Ramses Station to the Pyramids costs 50 pt.

To the Giza Pyramids/Sphinx take No 108 from Tahrir Square. It costs 5 pt. There are also minibuses for 25 pt. Nos 70 and 95 connect Tahrir Square with Ramses Square (railway station). Nos 65 and 80 connect Ramses Square with Ataba Square (GPO). Nos 24 and 25 connect Ataba Square with Ramses Square. No 92 connects Tahrir Square with Old Cairo. No 173 connects Tahrir Square with the Citadel. No 99 connects Tahrir Square with the Camel Market. No 64 connects Attaba Square with Abbasiya Square (for the Sinai Bus Terminal).

Other

Vaccinations Cholera, typhoid and yellow fever vaccinations are available from the *Continental Hotel*, Opera Square, any day between 5.30 and 8 pm for less than E£1 a shot. Bring your passport and health card with you. Remember that your vaccination card must be up to date if you're going to the Sudan.

Jobs There are possibilities of teaching English in Cairo; many Kenyan, Ugandan, Filipino and Americans are doing this. One institute which is always looking for staff either part-time or full-time is the ILLI, Borg el Giza, El Kebly, Giza (tel 720431), which has three branches and is run by a Mr Yakhe. The pay is good by Egyptian standards and you can earn up to E£120 a week. If you want to stay longer than a month, Mr Yakhe can probably arrange a work permit for you. Other jobs are advertised in the English-language daily *Egyptian Gazette*.

The 'Hash Window' Incredible as it may seem, you can actually buy hashish here on a (semi?) legal basis, but it may become an endangered species if Mubarak gets his way. To get to the window take a train from Bab el Luq station and get off at the second stop. Walk to the end of the platform, cross the tracks to the left and go down the alley to the main street. Turn right on the main street and stay on the right until you get to a major intersection. Cross straight over this, continue for another five minutes or so past the vegetable merchant, and go up a little dirt incline into an alley. You'll see the window there with green bars and people queueing. You can either queue there yourself or ask a local to help out. The current price is E£40 for one *irsh* (the *irsh* is a coin). Don't ask for directions from the police if you're going there. What's right for the locals isn't necessarily right for you.

If the above sounds complicated, just wander through the streets of Old Cairo – you'll be able to buy hash on just about every street corner.

EL BALYANA

This town south of Qena is the site of the **Temples of Abydos**. To get there, go to the bus station and get a taxi to Abydos, which should cost 25 pt per person. Entry to the temples costs E£1 with a student card. It is possible to walk there if time and sweat are no object.

Stay at the *Youth Hostel* at Sohaq further downriver (one hour by train). It's a small, very friendly and pleasant place and costs 60 pt per night (45 pt if you're under 21).

EL MINYA

The main attraction of El Minya is the **Hatshepsut Temple** at Beni Hasan further south opposite Abu Qirqus. To get there you take a local bus from El Minya to Abu Qirqus, then the ferry across the Nile (5 pt), and finally walk the remaining three km to the temple.

The best place to stay in El Minya is the *Palace Hotel* – an amazing French colonial-style building with huge rooms, balconies and four-poster beds! It's clean, all the rooms have their own shower and there's hot water. It costs E£3.70 a double. Highly recommended.

HURGHADA

Remember that Egyptians call Hurghada 'Ghardaka,' so ask for the latter when looking for the bus; otherwise they won't understand you. Located on the Red Sea coast more or less due west of the tip of Sinai, Hurghada has become a popular resort with travellers over the last few years. There are plenty of coral reefs around the islands offshore which offer excellent snorkelling and swimming opportunities. In the last edition of this book we uncritically extolled the virtues of this place, and although it's probably still true to say that most people enjoy their stay here, Hurghada has been getting a variable press lately. Typical of satisfied customers' comments are, 'Hurghada is a delightful town, very friendly people and plenty of cheap places to eat.' On the other hand, there are others who take a dislike to the place. One recent acerbic writer put it this way, 'The biggest rock-and-roll rip-off I've had the misfortune to come across on all of my travels to date. This place is really not worth the effort and the money spent getting there. And you mention something about Captain Mohammed being very chatty – well I'm not surprised – he's the front man on the collusive organisation that runs the place. It wouldn't be so bad if the boat trips were good, but they usually consist of as many 25 unsuspecting folks packed on a small fishing boat, allowed half an hour's swimming and fed on frozen mackerel.'

It's true you can't swim on any of the

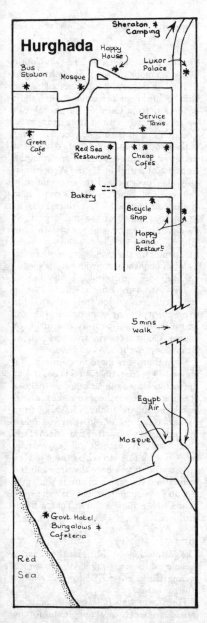

Hurghada

Sheraton & Camping

Happy House

Luxor Palace

Bus Station

Mosque

Green Cafe

Red Sea Restaurant

Cheap Cafes

Bakery

Service Taxis

Bicycle Shop

Happy Land Restaurt

5 mins walk →

Egypt Air

Mosque

Govt. Hotel, Bungalows & Cafeteria

Red Sea

beaches near to town because of the blind mullets (ever been to Bondi?), oil and rubbish, but there is a good beach near the *Sheraton Hotel* about seven km away – take a service taxi (5 pt) from the depot near the Happy House to Ghardaka port and then walk or hitch about 2½ km along the shore road to the hotel. You're supposed to pay E£5 for the 'privilege' of using the Sheraton beach, but the one beside it is almost as good.

Almost everyone who comes here tries first to get a room at the *Happy House* on El Dhar Mosque Square. Captain Mohammed, who owns the place, is a popular man, friendly and very helpful. He also speaks excellent English. His place is clean and pleasant and costs E£2.50 per person. Cooking facilities are provided. If it's full his brother also rents out rooms for E£3 a double. Or there's the *Luxor Palace*, run by Mohammed Unis, which is clean, very friendly and about as popular as the Happy House. It costs E£2 per person. The toilets often don't work and there are a lot of flies. Two other places you might like to try are the *Moon Valley Hotel* between the Sheraton and the town which costs E£3 for bed and breakfast; and the *Sunshine House Hotel* which costs the same. If all these places are full there are plenty of other *locandas* and rooms in private houses available which cost between E£1.50 and E£3 per night. Many of the people who have places to rent will meet you off the bus from Cairo.

In addition to the above, there is a government-owned hotel with bungalows on the beach. The hotel costs E£1.50 in a shared room and E£3 in a private room. The two-room bungalows, each with their own kitchen, are E£10 for as many people as you care to pack in. Meals are available for E£0.50 (breakfast 8 to 9 am), E£1 (lunch 1 to 3 pm) and E£1 (dinner 7 to 9.30 pm). The bungalows are a 10-minute walk from the centre of town. The beach at this point is badly polluted by oil.

If you want to camp, there are two good beaches. The one near the government bungalows is free. The other, more picturesque and isolated, is also free, but you'll need a taxi to get there as it's seven km from town near the Sheraton Hotel. The taxi will cost E£3 shared by up to seven people, or you can rent a bicycle for E£1 per day. There are no facilities at this beach so you need to bring your own food and water with you.

The two best places to eat in the centre of town are the *Happy House Restaurant* (owned by Captain Mohammed) and the *Red Sea Restaurant*. The former offers fish and chips (ah! nostalgia!) for E£1.50 pt; and eggs, bread, butter, jam and tea for 60 pt. The same at the Red Sea Restaurant costs E£3, plus they also offer kebab and a range of side dishes. There's another cheap restaurant in the centre (marked on the map) where you can eat for E£1.10. If you're down at the beach, the fixed-price meals at the government hotel are also good value.

The best way to see the islands and the coral reefs is to take a day-long boat trip. Captain Mohammed's trips have come under fire lately as being overcrowded and breathless, so it might be better to try *Spring Tours*, which a lot of people have recommended lately. The trip is basically the same. You get picked up from your hotel about 8.30 am and are driven to the harbour, where you join the boat which takes you to one of the islands. Masks and snorkels are provided (though usually not as many as one per person) and a fish lunch is included. You return to your hotel between 5 and 6 pm. Both charge E£7 for the trips.

Spring Tours also recently started a ferry service between Hurghada and Sharm el Sheikh on the tip of Sinai. It costs E£22 and leaves once weekly. It leaves at 8.30 am and is scheduled to arrive between 6 and 7 pm, including a stop for a swim off Ras Muhammed. So far, demand hasn't been as good as expected, so they may decide to discontinue the boat. Make enquiries at Spring Tours next to Egypt Air or in the Hurghada Hotel further down the road towards the sea.

Visiting the Monasteries The two Coptic Christian monasteries of St Anthony and St Paul, in the mountains overlooking the Gulf of Suez near Zafarana (about a third of the way from Cairo to Hurghada), can be conveniently visited from Hurghada. You don't need permission to visit either of them, but if you intend to stay overnight then you do need permission from the Coptic Cathedral in Cairo. Women can only stay overnight if they remain fully clothed at all times. St Paul's won't take visitors during Lent. The visiting hours at St Anthony's are 9 am to 5 pm. To get to St Paul's, take the coastal road north from Hurghada and get down when you reach the turnoff for the monastery south of the Zafarana lighthouse. From here it's a 13-km walk on a dirt track across baking desert with very little traffic, so bring water with you and don't rely on being able to pick up a lift. The monastery has a guest house where you can stay overnight, or you can camp in the dry riverbed nearby. Bring your own food.

St Anthony's is more modernised. It's about 45 km from the Red Sea coast, but the monks offer a similar welcome to those at St Paul's. To get there you take the road which goes inland to the Nile Valley from Zafarana and get down when you reach the monastery turnoff. From there it's a 10-km walk. As with St Paul's, you may have to walk this stretch as there is very little traffic. If you have the time and the inclination, it's worth climbing the 1500 feet up the mountain behind the monastery to see St Anthony's Cave. Take a torch with you.

IDFU

The attraction at Idfu is the nearby **Temple of Horus**, which is well worth seeing. Entry costs E£2 (or E£1 with a student card).

The *Samin Amis Hotel* on the main road into town is where most people stay for the night, but you should beware of theft. One traveller had his room broken into recently. It costs E£3 per night. The bathrooms are said to be worse than those at the Youth Hostel in Aswan.

ISMAILIYA

If you have to stay here for the night, there is a kind of *Youth Hostel* in the Sea Rangers' Building about one km from the bus station on the shores of Lake Timsah. There are also a number of good, cheap hotels in the town centre.

LUXOR

Luxor stands on the site of Thebes, the southern capital of the Pharaohs and one of the richest areas in the country for ancient Egyptian ruins and monuments. These include the world-famous Valley of the Kings (where the tomb of Tutankhamen was found) and the Temple of Karnak.

One of the cheapest places to stay is the *Youth Hostel*, though its standard of cleanliness leaves much to be desired. The staff are friendly and it costs 80 pt for a bed. Many travellers prefer to stay in one of the hotels in town.

One of the most popular places is the *New Karnak Hotel* near the railway station. It's clean, has hot showers and costs E£3.50 to E£6 a double including breakfast. It's also a very popular place to eat, as it has a balcony overlooking the railway station. The hotel rents out bicycles for E£1 per day. Nearby is the *Salah el Din Hotel* which is clean, relatively new and costs E£2 for a bed in a four-bed room or E£3 a double. There is hot water and a rooftop restaurant (breakfast of two eggs, bread, butter, jam, cheese and tea or coffee costs 70 pt). Also recommended is the *Khan el Khalily* by the Luxor Temple, which costs E£2.50 a single with sink and balcony. It's noisy, being in a market area and somewhat decrepit, but the beds are clean and comfortable and the staff very hospitable and entertaining. One traveller commented, 'I spent a lazy afternoon in the lobby watching the goings-on – talk about a Le Carre novel co-written by John Cleese!'

Other budget hotels worth considering are: *Radwan Hotel*, next to the railway station, which has a friendly manager and costs E£1.50 per person including breakfast; *Horus Hotel*, also very friendly and comfortable with hot water at E£2.50 a single and E£5-6 a double; *Seti Gordon Hotel*, which is clean, has hot showers, costs E£1.50 per person including breakfast, and offers bicycle rentals at E£1 per day; *Golden Home*, near the railway station, which is pleasant and costs E£3 per person including breakfast; the *Grand Hotel*, which is cheap and clean at E£1 per night (extra for meals) and which rents out bicycles for E£1 per day; and *El Salam Hotel* which costs E£2.50 a double including fan and hot showers. To get to the latter, go straight ahead as you leave the station. Warmly recommended is the *Island Home* near the station and just round the corner from the Sunshine Home. It costs E£1.65 per bed in four-bed rooms, and Mr Hussein, the manager, usually meets the trains coming in from Cairo. The *Sunshine Home Hotel* itself is very good and clean, and the staff are very friendly. It costs E£2.50 per person. As you leave the station, turn left along the main road and take the first street on the left.

There are quite a few new budget hotels being built down the road between the Radwan and the Limpy; turn left when you reach the mosque at the end.

There's a popular campsite here opposite the Luxor Hotel. A man called Babu Hassan will guard your gear for an agreed price, though he lays on the theatricals for more *baksheesh* when you leave.

If you don't want to stay in Luxor itself, there is the possibility of staying on the West Bank. Places to stay here include the *Abul Kasem Hotel*, four km from the river (E£1 by private taxi or 15 pt by shared taxi). The hotel is on top of an alabaster factory where you can watch the workers make their sculptures. The owner fixes his prices according to demand, so sort it out before you take a room. If the place is empty you pay E£1.50. If it's getting full you pay E£3 per person. It's very clean, hot water is available in the shared bathrooms, the rooms have a fan, and meals and cold drinks are available on request. There is also the *Memnon* opposite the Colossi of Memnon which costs E£3 per person, or try the *Habu*.

The New Karnak Hotel has already been mentioned as a popular place to eat, but you can also try *Mensa* on the main street to the right as you leave the station. You can get a meal there for E£1.80. Another place worth trying is *Limpy* (no, not Wimpy) where you can get a three-course meal for E£1.50. A good place for a beer in the afternoon is the *Winter Palace*, an old colonial-style building with a lot of atmosphere. In the evenings, try the bar at the *Nile Casino* on the banks of the Nile opposite the Luxor Temple. Here you can often pick up superb Egyptian folk music played live on traditional instruments, though the drinks will be slightly more expensive on such nights (beers are rarely less than E£2).

If you don't want to risk swimming in the Nile to cool off, the cheapest of the swimming pools at the posh hotels is the one at the *Winter Palace* which costs E£2.

The Antiquities There are so many different archaeological sites in and around Luxor that you're going to wish you had a student card if you haven't got one. There are 11 separate tickets in all for the sites on the West Bank – eight at E£1 plus E£5 for the Valley of the Kings, E£2 for Deir el Bahani and E£2 for Medinet Habu. On the East Bank there are the Luxor Temple for E£3 and the Temple of Karnak for E£3. (These are full-price tickets.) Without a student card you should buy your tickets for the antiquities on the West Bank from the 'Turist Farry' (that's how it's spelt). Student tickets have to be bought from

the 'Inspectorate for Students' near the Colossi of Memnon. You should allow several days to see all the main sites, and you need to work out carefully where you are going to go each day as it gets very hot and you're not going to be able to rush around.

There is a *son et lumiere* which costs E£4 – English version at 6 pm on Monday and Wednesday and at 8 pm on Tuesday. No student discounts are available for this. The new **museum** in Luxor is well worth a visit (E£2 entry) for its striking design and imaginative layout.

Some determined souls walk all the way from Luxor to the Valley of the Kings and the other sites on the West Bank, but you needn't do this as there is a choice of taxi, bicycle or donkey. A taxi to the Valley of the Kings shouldn't cost more than E£1.50 per person (seven passengers), but you need to bargain hard for this price as there may be a lot of well-heeled tourists around depending on the season who will pay virtually whatever the taxi driver quotes. Bicycles can be hired from quite a few hotels for E£1 per day and, in many ways, they offer the greatest flexibility. Donkeys cost about the same as bicycles, but you have to hire a guide with them. They can be picked up on the West Bank or you can arrange a tour by donkey at one or two of the hotels in Luxor. The Salah el Din Hotel offers an eight-hour donkey tour to the Valley of the Kings, Deir el Bahani and the Ramesseum for E£15 all included. Of this tour one traveller commented, 'I though it was too much considering that bikes can be rented for E£1 per day and the guide barely speaks English and is essentially there just to lead you from one site to the next.'

There are two ferries across the Nile – a 'tourist ferry' and the local people's ferry. Take the latter, as it's only a few piastres and bikes are free (at least they are for the locals though, as a foreigner, you'll probably have to pay 10 pt). The operators of the tourist ferry don't like bicycles.

You can buy maps of the Valley of the Kings, Karnak and Luxor from Aboudis tourist shop near the Luxor Temple for 40 pt. If you already have a copy of the *Oxford Map of Egypt* then that is adequate. The *son et lumiere* at Karnak costs E£4 and there are no discounts. Finally, if you come to Luxor in summer (the off season) then it's a good idea to make enquiries about which sites on the West Bank are open. They're sometimes closed at this time of year. Also, some of the sites ban 'big cameras' – presumably movie cameras.

QENA

El Salam Hotel behind the school opposite the post office has been recommended. It's a new place with showers on each floor (hot and cold water) and costs E£1 per person. Take precautions against mosquitoes.

SUEZ

Avoid staying here overnight if possible, as the town has little to recommend it. Hotels around the bus station are usually very expensive – around E£4 for a grotty bed – and often full. There is a *Youth Hostel* about 3½ km from town on Sharia Tariq al Horia which is very friendly and costs the usual price (E£1 for members and E£1.50 for non-members), plus they have group leaders' rooms (very pleasant) for E£1.50 per bed. If you don't want to go all the way out there, try the *San Stefarno*, which is OK and clean and costs E£2 per person.

Buses to St Katherine's leave at 10.30 am from the bus station (E£5.50 with a change at Wadi Feran Oasis).

If you need to change money here, there are quite a few official moneychangers (no black market) but their rates are excellent so shop around. Avoid using the banks for changing money.

THE WESTERN DESERT OASES

Most travellers who come to Egypt don't venture outside the Nile Valley, which is understandable given that most of the antiquities and the cities are to be found there. If you want to see most of them at a leisurely pace, this will take up virtually all of the month that you get on a normal tourist visa. However, you are allowed to overstay your visa by two weeks without incurring any penalty so, if you have the time, it's worth experiencing a different dimension of Egypt. This can be found in the oases of the Western Desert or in Sinai. Travellers who have spent time there have raved about it. Very few tourists get this far, so you'll find people genuinely friendly, curious and hospitable. At Farafra Oasis, for example, two travellers who spent five days there were overwhelmed with hospitality. They were given cups of tea and armfuls of fruit everywhere and the army sent down a jeep every morning to their rest house to pick them up for breakfast.

It's well worth considering making the loop through these oases if you have the time. Please remember, however, that in common with that of all Arab countries, this hospitality is meant to be reciprocated. If you just take without giving, then pretty soon travellers who come after you will find they're being treated with disdain and even contempt. A small gift is all that is necessary. Its material worth is inconsequential so long as it is thoughtful. Of equal importance is your manner of dress – make sure it conforms as closely as possible with what local people would regard as modest and respectable. Don't wear shorts or singlets. This goes for the whole of Egypt, but it's doubly important in the oases.

Getting There

There are regular buses between Cairo and Bahariya Oasis and between Cairo or Asyut and Kharga and Dakhla Oases. There are no buses to Farafra Oasis so you'll have to hitch a ride there. The bus services are as follows:

Cairo-Bahariya There are express buses on Monday, Wednesday and Saturday at

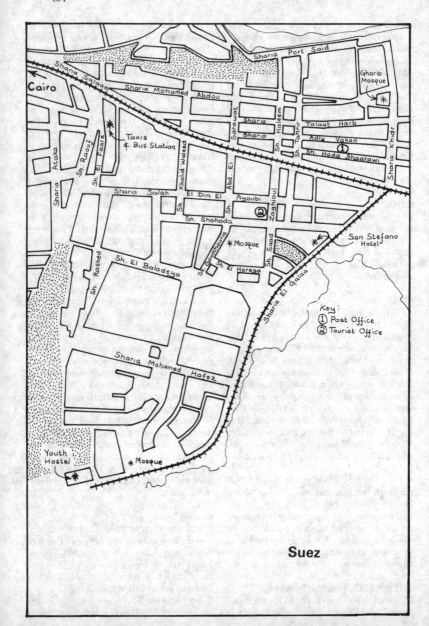

9 am which cost E£3. There are also ordinary buses on Tuesday, Thursday and Sunday at 9 am which cost E£1.85. In the opposite direction, the buses leave from the police station between 6.30 and 7 am daily. The journey takes about seven hours. In Cairo you should try to reserve your seat two days in advance. In Bawiti you can reserve a seat at the police station direction.

Cairo-Kharga There is a daily air-conditioned bus at 10 am which costs E£5. Be sure to reserve a seat at least two days in advance. There are also daily buses from Asyut to Kharga which cost E£2 (air-conditioned) and E£1.60 (ordinary) and take four hours.

Cairo-Dakhla There are buses on Tuesday, Friday and Sunday at 7 am which cost E£5.25 and go via Kharga. Again, you should reserve your seat two days in advance. In the opposite direction the buses leave Mut (the main town in the Dakhla Oasis) from the square behind the one and only hotel at 8 am. The buses go via Kharga, where they stop for an hour, and arrive at Asyut between 4.30 and 5.30 pm. The fare to Asyut is E£2.40.

All the above buses from Cairo leave from 45 El Azhar St. It can be tricky to find this place since it's in a back yard and the sign is entirely in Arabic.

Bahariya Oasis

This oasis is quite a large one and consists of four villages. The administrative centre is Bawiti. There are a number of places to stay in Bawiti but the most popular is the *Hotel Alpenblick* (sometimes known as Laconda Salah) behind the police station, which costs E£1 per night plus an average of E£1 per day for food (there's a hotel 'shop' with food supplies and cooking facilities). If you don't want to cook yourself then meals can be arranged. The owner, Salah, is a great guy who takes his guests to his date gardens and to the nearby hot springs (there's a small charge for the latter). Another possibility is the *Alice Springs* which costs 50 pt in the dormitory. There are no cooking facilities here. A tourist hotel is also being built here.

There are several cafés where you can buy basic meals, but if you want to put your own food together you can get fresh vegetables from street sellers and canned goods from the many stores. A good place to go in the evenings is the *Casino Café*, which has beer among other things. You can also get a game of chess or dominoes there.

There are hot springs in Bawiti and the surrounding area. The largest are five km north-north-east of town near the airstrip. They're excellent for bathing and the area is a potentially good camping site. People who live in this oasis are very friendly, so just take off and wander through the date and citrus orchards and see who you meet. Have warm clothes handy at night as it gets very cold.

If you want to go from here to Farafra Oasis then you need permission from the army. This is just a formality and both the police and the army are very friendly. Get authorisation from the army post in Bawiti. There are no buses from Bawiti to Farafra but the army will generally arrange a lift for you. The journey takes about three hours on a good road and costs E£2.

Farafra Oasis

There is only one place to stay here, the *Rest House*, which is clean but has no cooking facilities and costs E£1 per bed. There are plenty of mosquitoes in this rest house, so bring repellant. If you're coming in from Bahariya it's the first building you see. There are no cafés as such here – people make their own arrangements – though there are two tiny shops which are closed most of the time and have a very limited range of stock. The thing to do is make friends with the army, the police, the school teachers or the doctor. They'll be only too pleased to have your company and to offer you a meal. If you walk around the citrus and date groves here, take a bag with you to carry home all the dates, oranges and sweet lemons which will be thrust into your arms.

Places to visit here include the 'Roman Spring' (an iron-free spring in a garden in the village which bubbles up from a very deep well) and various hot springs. There are several of the latter and they're quite hot – around 36°C. The one in the village has been piped into a concrete tank and is usually full of children, but there is another about six km north-west (called Bir 6) where you can swim undisturbed.

There are also many small oases just a few km away, so spend a day wandering between them. The experience was described by one traveller as 'more rewarding than all the temples and tombs of Egypt put together.'

You must register with the police on arrival. There is electricty from dusk to 10 pm only. Have warm clothing handy at night. Avoid washing your clothes in the hot springs as the iron content of the water will leave them looking decidedly rusty.

There are no buses out of Farafra, so you will have to find a ride. The best place to wait is at the police station, where all vehicles have to stop. There is generally more traffic going south than north. Be prepared to wait a day for a lift. Most drivers will take you free, but others will expect around E£2 to Dakhla (you may need to bargain, as the initial price might be as high as E£5).

Dakhla Oasis

Both Dakhla and Kharga are much larger oases than Bahariya and Farafra and are nothing like the palm-fringed pools that movie-goers expect. Mut is the administrative centre of Dakhla.

There's only one place to stay in Mut and it costs E£1.20 per bed or 45 pt in the common room. It's clean but there are no cooking facilities. There are plenty of cafés here and even a cinema, but the oasis is perhaps not as interesting as the more remote ones. There are a lot of squalid tenement blocks going up and new factories are being built. No doubt this is good news for the local people in terms of employment possibilities, but most travellers don't go thousands of km to look at factories.

There are regular buses between Dakhla and Kharga, and between there and Cairo and Asyut.

Kharga Oasis

There is nowhere to stay cheaply here. The *New Valley Tourist Home* (known locally as the *Hotel Metallco*) costs E£3.20 a single and E£4.60 a double. The other hotel here costs E£7 per night.

While you're in this oasis, make sure you see the **Temple of Hibis** just outside town on the Asyut road. Entry is free. Near the temple is a fascinating **Coptic cemetery** known as Badr-el-Wait. There are also hot springs in the vicinity.

SINAI

The big draws of the Sinai Peninsula are the old **St Catherine's Monastery** near the southern tip of the Sinai Desert, **Mt Sinai** itself, and the resorts of the east coast – **Namaa Bay, Dahab, Nuweiba** and **Taba**.

Getting There

You can get to all the above places by public bus from either Cairo or from Suez. There's now a tunnel under the Suez Canal so there's no need to go to El Shatt across the other side of the Canal any longer.

There are two buses daily from Cairo to Sharm el Sheikh at 7.30 am and 10.30 am. (In the opposite direction they depart from the diving club at Namaa Bay at 5.30 am and 10 am, or from Sharm el Sheikh itself at 6 am and 10.30 am.) They cost E£7 and take six to seven hours. The buses depart from the Sinai Terminal, which is about one km from Abisiyya Square past the army barracks. There's a huge sign in English so you can't miss it. The buses from Suez to Sharm el Sheikh depart daily at 7.30 am and cost E£4. There are also two daily buses in either direction between Sharm el Sheikh and Taba via Nuweiba and Dahab. The bus from Nuweiba to Dahab leaves at 7 am, costs E£1 and takes about two hours. From Dahab to Taba the fare is E£2.50. From Dahab to Sharm el Sheikh the bus leaves daily early in the morning and again at 4 pm and costs E$1.25.

There are two direct buses per day leaving Cairo (Sinai Terminal) for St Catherine's Monastery. The most convenient one leaves at 10 am, makes one stop en route and drops you off at the crossroads about three km from the monastery by 4.30 pm. It costs E£7. There are also buses from Suez to St Catherine's daily at 10.30 am which cost E£5. You can also get to St Catherine's from Sharm el Sheikh by daily bus which departs at 11 am (in the opposite direction at 8 am). It costs E£4 and takes about five hours. Another alternative is to go by taxi between St Catherine's and Nuweiba along the 100 km of dirt track for about E£5 each sharing.

From St Catherine's Monastery to Cairo there are buses twice a day at 6 am and 1 pm except on Saturday, when there is only one bus at 6 am.

St Catherine's Monastery

Although St Catherine's is becoming something of a tourist trap these days, it's well worth making the effort to see this ancient monastery either for its own sake or en route to the east coast resorts. There are still some 17 Greek Orthodox monks in residence there, so please remember that it's not just a museum. There is no entry charge but you are only allowed to see the 'skull room' (full of the bones of deceased monks) and the beautiful chapel. The monastery is only open to visitors between 10 am and 12.30 pm and is closed on Friday and Sunday.

It used to be possible to stay overnight in the actual monastery with prior permission from the Coptic Cathedral in Cairo, but the monks found many of their visitors disturbing so now you can only stay in the hostel next door. This isn't a very friendly place and costs E£5 per night, but it's clean, comfortable and there are cooking facilities and cold-water showers. You must bring your own food. To pay and to get the key you have to go inside the monastery and contact one of the monks.

It used to be possible to stay in the village about two km away where there was a very basic but comfortable and clean hotel and a small restaurant where you could eat mountains of spaghetti for around E£0.25. However, recent reports suggest that it's now illegal for foreigners to stay in the village (this may have been a temporary measure so check it out when you get there). This leaves you with a campsite four km distant with ready-erected tents for E£3 per night and the luxury hotel 20 km away near the airstrip which costs E£47 per night. There are some abandoned huts by the road on the way to the monastery where you can sleep with no worries, but don't make a big show of it; otherwise the police will catch on and that will be the end of the huts.

From St Catherine's you can climb **Mt Sinai**. There are two well-defined routes, one via a series of steps and the other by path. Ask one of the monks for directions if you're not sure where to start. If you go by the path it will take about 2½ hours for the ascent and 1½ hours for the descent. It's best to take the path going up and the steps coming down. There is a tiny mosque on the top (locked) and a small chapel containing beautiful paintings and ornaments, but this too, like the mosque, is locked. If you're fairly robust and have plenty of warm clothing, it's suggested you climb up there for the sunset, camp there overnight and then return as the sun rises. The views are magnificent! It's unlikely you will be rewarded with a burning bush and it's also very unlikely you will be able to find any fuel for a fire. There is a well near the summit but the rope is too short to reach the water (by design?) so take water with you.

The East Coast Resorts

Since the Israelis handed the Sinai back to Egypt a number of resorts have sprung up on the east coast which are attracting more and more travellers each year. They are **Sharm el Sheikh**, **Namaa Bay** (five km north of Sharm el Sheikh), **Dahab**, **Nuweiba** and **Taba** (on the Egyptian-Israeli border). All these resorts have similar set-ups – expensive chalet-type accommodation, bars, restaurants and diving clubs with equipment for hire. A few hundred metres up the beach, however, are colonies of budget travellers living in some form of makeshift accommodation or simply on the beach. This makeshift accommodation is fairly commercialised in Nuweiba and Namaa Bay as local entrepreneurs have moved in, but Dahab is much quieter. Here there are huts scattered along the beach which were built by the Bedouin and then abandoned when they moved to the present village a few km up the coast. In theory, these huts are free but you may well find that various people turn up and ask for rent. Some travellers do pay the 50 pt or E£1 which is asked, but others politely refuse since there's no way of establishing who owns what, so the person who asks might just be out to make a fast buck. Many of the huts are pretty dirty, too, so it might be better to stay on the beach. If you do this, there's a large, empty hotel near the bus stop where you can use the showers and toilet. Snorkelling here is excellent, though some people say it's not as good as at Namaa Bay or Sharm el Sheikh.

There are actually two villages at Dahab – the Bedouin village and Dahab village itself. Food at at the Bedouin village can be as much as 10 times more expensive than in Dahab village itself. At the latter there is a good grocery store and a bakery (a green building on the hill) and you can also buy a limited range of other food (including vegetables). Pitta bread at the bakery costs just 1 pt! The water is brackish but you can buy bottled water for 60 pt per bottle. Fish, rice and salad meals are available for E£1.25-1.50 at the beach restaurants if you have no cooking equipment. The village is about three km from the beach where most people stay. There is also a campsite at the bus station in the village.

Sharm el Sheikh has a good beach with coral reefs about two km east of town – on the way there you pass through a police checkpoint where you will be told you cannot sleep on the beach. In the town itself directly above the bus station there is a *Youth Hostel* which costs E£2 per night but you must have a membership card. It's clean and has cold-water showers, cooking facilities and a small shop for tea, biscuits, chocolate and the like. There are also at least four large blocks of empty flats that can be squatted (they were built by the Israelis). They're unfurnished but described as 'comfortable,' though of course there is no water or electricity. It's hard to say how long these flats will last because they'll probably be re-occupied in time as Egyptians re-populate the town. Sharm el Sheikh has two supermarkets with a limited selection of food, a bakery, a small vegetable market, a gas station, bank and tourist police office.

Namaa Bay is, in effect, an R & R place for American GIs and other soldiers from the multi-national force on weekends when they descend with eskies full of beer and ice. At this time the beach is lit up and cassette players blare away till midnight. There are two expensive hotels here as well as a restaurant and supermarket.

There's a snack bar where you can buy cheeseburgers and iced mango juice. In addition, there are three dive shops where you can hire a windsurfer (E£6/hour) or snorkel gear (E£5/day), or go on diving trips.

There are beach huts for rent for E£1.50 per night but you need your own sleeping bag. The three hotels here cost in excess of E£25 per night.

Equatorial Guinea

Another of Africa's smallest nations, this former Spanish colony is made up of the islands of Biokn (formerly Fernando Poo) and Pagalu (formerly Annabon) and the mainland enclave of Rio Muni. It attained independence in October 1968 under the presidency of Macias Nguema and for a little while enjoyed a period of relatively free democracy. Several months after independence, however, relations with Spain deteriorated rapidly when it was discovered that the country had almost no foreign currency reserves. Nguema accused Spanish businessmen of neo-colonialism in their attempts to renegotiate timber contracts, and encouraged his supporters to intimidate the 7000 Spanish citizens still living in the country. Following a stormy meeting with the Spanish ambassador, Nguema all but ordered the latter to leave. Spain reacted by mobilising units of its army stationed in Equatorial Guinea, which Nguema responded to by declaring a state of emergency. The stage was set for a 10-year dictatorship whose brutality was to surpass even that perpetrated by Amin in Uganda and Bokassa in the Central African Republic.

Macias Nguema began his reign of terror by arresting and summarily executing his foreign minister, Atanasio Ndongo, and Equatorial Guinea's ambassador to the UN, Saturnino Ibongo, along with a number of other prominent politicians who had attempted to defuse the political crisis and stop the attacks on the Spanish citizens. They were accused of plotting against Nguema with the connivance of the Spanish. Over the next 10 years 'plots' and 'conspiracies' were discovered round every corner and many thousands of people were to lose their lives, tortured and executed in the jails of Malabo and Bata or beaten to death in the forced-labour camps of the mainland. At the height of this butcher's madness there were over 28,000 political prisoners in these camps. Almost all of the prominent politicians from the independence period were eliminated and replaced by members of Nguema's family. Intellectuals were personally hunted down by Nguema and either executed or forced to flee into exile. By the time Nguema's regime was toppled in 1979 only one third of the 300,000 Guineans who lived there at independence remained.

Halfway through his reign, Nguema, unable to command either the loyalty or support of his people, was forced to bring in expatriate labour, mainly from Nigeria, but conditions were so bad and wages so low that they led to riots and strikes which were crushed with much bloodshed by the army and police. The shooting of these Nigerian workers led to a crisis with Nigeria and demands by politicians in that country for the annexation of Equatorial Guinea. Finally, after diplomats at the Nigerian embassy in Malabo had been badly beaten up by members of Nguema's youth movement, the remaining 20,000 Nigerians were repatriated. The following year, 1977, Spain broke off diplomatic relations and only a handful of Spanish citizens remained in the country.

But it wasn't just political figures, intellectuals and expatriates who were persecuted. The Catholic Church caught it in the neck too. Priests were arrested and expelled for plots real or imaginary, and in 1975 all mission-run schools were closed, effectively putting an end to formal education in the country. This was followed up in 1978 by the forced closure of all churches in the country. With the country in shambles, bankrupt and all economic activity at a standstill, even Nguema's closest colleagues began to suspect that he was insane, and he was toppled by a coup in August 1979. Along with his bodyguards he fled to his home town of Mengomo on the mainland with every asset he could lay his hands on from the national bank vaults. He was finally brought to heel at Ebebiyin on the Gabonese border. Nguema, the former chiefs of Malabo and Bata jails, Nguema's chief bodyguard and several others of Nguema's clique were executed in September 1979.

The new government is headed by Colonel Teodoro Nguema, reputedly a relation of Macias Nguema. Teodoro Nguema ordered the release of all political prisoners and the lifting of restrictions on the Catholic Church. Relations with Spain and other western countries were resumed and reconstruction begun. It will be a long time, however, before the country gets back on its feet.

Throughout those years of terror, travellers naturally avoided Equatorial Guinea like the plague, but a number of people are once again discovering that it's still an interesting and beautiful place. When Macias Nguema was overthrown people literally danced in the streets, and if you go there now you'll be assured of a very warm welcome, so glad are these people to see faces from outside again.

Equatorial Guinea has had an interesting history. The first part of the country to have contact with Europeans was the island of Pagalu (Annabon), which was visited by the Portuguese in 1470. Portugal subsequently settled Pagalu and the other islands in the Gulf of Guinea – Bioko (Fernando Poo), São Tomé and Principe – until in the 18th century it exchanged Bioko and Pagalu as well as parts of the mainland with Spain for certain regions in Latin America. Bioko itself became an important staging post and slaving base

for several European nations during the 19th century when the rest of West Africa was being colonised. Malabo was founded as a naval base by Britain in 1827 – the first governor of the island appointed by Spain some 20 years later was an Englishman. Britain's interest in the island waned as naval bases were set up on the mainland and control passed to Spain. Cocoa plantations were started on the island in the late 19th century, making Malabo Spain's most important possession in equatorial Africa. The mainland enclave of Rio Muni was largely ignored and the interior wasn't even explored by Spaniards until the 1920s. During the Spanish Civil War, Equatorial Guinea came out in support of General Franco – or rather the Spanish absentee landlords who controlled the plantations on Bioko came out in Franco's support. Macias Nguema was one of the people employed by the colonial administration during this period as well as subsequently. The fascist regime would appear to have been a major influence on his concept of government when he eventually became the country's first president.

FACTS

The most economically important part of Equatorial Guinea, Bioko, is formed from three extinct volcanoes. It's a rugged, jungle-covered island and its main products are cocoa, coffee, bananas and palm oil. It's also here that the nation's capital, Malabo, is situated. The mainland, Rio Muni, has been largely bypassed in the 20th century. Though there are a number of coffee plantations, it's mostly gently rising, thickly forested country with an abundance of wildlife and interesting villages where traditional beliefs survive. The rainy season runs from April to January, during which humidity is high.

The most numerous tribal group is the Fang, who make up about 80% of the population of Rio Muni (240,000). Minor tribal groups include the Kombe, Balengue and Bujeba. Macias Nguema was a Fang.

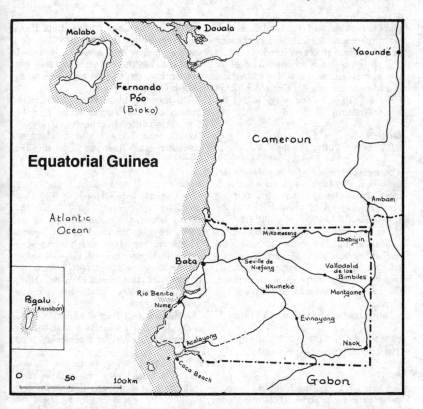

On Bioko the most numerous group was formerly the Bubi, but with the economy in dire straits many Fang have been forced to migrate to the island and they now outnumber the others. There are also a few thousand Fernandinos who are the descendants of freed slaves.

VISAS

Visas are required by everyone. The price of visas and the length of stay given vary widely and are subject to change. In Las Palmas, Canary Islands, they are issued on the spot, cost 1000 pesetas and are valid for an indefinite stay. In Douala, Cameroun, they cost CFA 5000, are valid for a stay of 15 days and an onward ticket is required. In Yaounde, Cameroun, they cost CFA 3000, take 24 hours to issue and are valid for a stay of 15 days. Visas can also be obtained from Madrid (Alonso Cano 27) where they cost 1000 pesetas for a seven-day visa and are issued in 24 hours (no onward ticket required; no questions asked), Libreville, Gabon, and Lagos, Nigeria. Travellers who have arrived at Malabo airport without visas have reported that these are issued on arrival for 3000 bipkwele but are valid for only 24 hours.

Visa extensions are virtually impossible to get. You can expect customs clearance to take a long time on arrival. Everything gets searched.

Malabo has been suggested as a good

place to get visas for Gabon and Cameroun since there's no fuss, no money showing and no onward ticket required.

If you have to buy an onward ticket for Equatorial Guinea, probably the cheapest is a Malabo-Douala *Air Cameroun* ticket for CFA 15,000 (one way) and CFA 29,000 (return).

MONEY
CFA 1000 = 700 bipkwele

The unit of currency is the bipkwele = 100 centimos. The bipkwele is on a par with the Spanish peseta. There is a thriving black market which offers 3 Bk = 1 Sp peseta or CFA 1000 = 1300 Bk. Try Nigerians, Camerounians and Spaniards in Malabo, but beware of old banknotes (called ekuele with Macias Nguema's grinning face on them) as they're worthless. Import of local currency is prohibited. Currency declaration forms are issued on arrival.

International airport tax is 100 Bk.

LANGUAGE
The official language is Spanish.

POST
Try to avoid having mail sent to Malabo – most things never arrive. If you must have mail sent, make sure letters are addressed to Lista de Correos, Malabo (that's the Spanish for 'Poste Restante'). On the other hand, mail from Malabo apparently gets to its destination quickly and postage rates are cheap.

GETTING THERE & AROUND
Air
Air Cameroun flies Douala-Malabo and vice versa at least once per week, sometimes three times per week. The cost is CFA 15,000 one way and CFA 29,000 return. Occasionally private flights are also available from Libreville, Gabon. *Lage*, the local airline, also operates charter flights to Libreville.

An internal flight which may be of interest is the daily Malabo-Bata flight which costs 8000 Bk (about US$15). You can use money exchanged on the black market to buy this ticket. It may take you two or three days to get on the flight, as over-booking is common.

On your arrival in Bata from Malabo, immigration officials can act as if you've flown into a different country and may tell you that your visa isn't valid. Just hang on patiently – they'll let you through in the end.

Road
There are good sealed roads on Biolo, but on the mainland most of the Bioko, but on the mainland most of the roads are unsealed. Hitching is very good. There are very few cars but everyone stops (foreigners are still a novelty after Macias Nguema's regime). Police road-blocks dot the island's roads. Have foreign cigarettes handy to ensure a smooth passage.

A service taxi from Malabo to Luba costs 400 Bk. From Bata to Ebebiyin (Cameroun border) by truck costs 2500 Bk.

If you're heading south for Gabon, there's a truck every two to three days from Bata to Acalayong (Gabon border) for 2500 Bk. From Acalayong there are motorised dugouts to Coco Beach – the cost for this should be around CFA 3000. It takes about 2½ hours depending on the tides. If you're only willing to pay CFA 2000, the boat owner will probably take you one hour downstream to a place where you'll have to a pay a CFA 2000 'exit permit.' Watch out for corrupt army personnel in Acalayong, as they have been known to confiscate items of gear in an attempt to extract bribes from you. They especially like knives.

Boat
There is a boat between Malabo and Bata about once a month; it costs 5.30 Bk in deck class. It's very overcrowded and the trip takes two days.

BATA

This is the principal town on the mainland. There are two cheap hotels here, *Hotel Central* (dirty) and *Hotel Finisterre* (clean) which both cost 2000 Bk a single. The one expensive hotel, *Hotel Panafrica*, faces the sea and has large suites for 8000 Bk. *Club de Tenis* has expensive meals for 2000 Bk. If you arrive by air, a taxi from the airport to the town centre will cost 150 Bk.

EBEBIYIN

Ebebiyin is the first village of any size in Rio Muni as you come across the border from Cameroun. There's no running water and electricity is only available between 7 and 10 pm. The only hotel here is the *Hotel Mbengono*, which costs 1500 Bk. It's dirty and you have to wash in the river. Cheaper but more basic accommodation is available in the bar on the main street.

MALABO

The capital, Malabo, is a beautiful town full of Spanish colonial buildings and open plazas with cloud-capped Mt Malabo as a backdrop. There are, however, no beaches worth mentioning – if you're looking for these go to Luba (the island's second city) where there are some very good, quiet, deserted beaches nearby. There are daily taxi-trucks from Malabo to Luba and if you need somewhere to stay, ask at the *Mission*, 12 km north of town.

It's more than likely that you'll be offered a place to stay by local people before you ever set foot in a hotel here, but if an invitation isn't forthcoming then one of the cheapest places to stay is the *Hotel Flores* close to the GPO. It is very clean and costs 1500 Bk a double. Most of the other hotels are on the expensive side. They include the *Hotel Eureka* and the *Hotel Bahia*, both of which cost 3000 Bk. The latter is the better of the two, being beautifully situated on the Malabo Bay with a bar and restaurant overlooking the sea and a swimming pool. If you have the cash, this place is highly recommended.

A taxi between the airport and the town centre costs 2000 Bk. There are no buses.

OTHER

Since Equatorial Guinea has been virtually closed for years – and because Macias Nguema's regime gave it such a bad reputation – we feel it's appropriate that the country should be put firmly back on the track. The following account of a journey through Equatorial Guinea comes to you from David Bennett of Canada and should help to put the record straight. (Thanks Dave! How about São Tomé and Principe or Mozambique next time?)

TOURIST VISA NO 001

I knew that Equatorial Guinea was off the beaten track, but I didn't fully realise the remoteness of the place until I looked down at my freshly stamped passport. I had just been issued Tourist Visa No 001.

Actually, my presence in the country was quite accidental. My original intention was to travel overland from Cameroun to Gabon, bypassing Equatorial Guinea. Upon my arrival in Cameroun, however, the authorities insisted that I purchase an onward air ticket. Financial considerations and my southward destination made me decide to take the weekly flight to the Guinean town of Bata. My map showed it to be a mere 125 km by road from the Gabonese border.

My outdated guidebook described Bata as a thriving commercial centre with a population of some 30,000 people. I knew, of course, that things had probably changed. Six months earlier, a coup had deposed President Macias Nguema, one of Africa's most tyrannical dictators. During his 10-year rule, many people disappeared, the country's economy collapsed, and half the population was forced to flee. This information didn't fully prepare me for what I found. The centre of Bata was a virtual ghost town. The handsome Spanish colonial buildings were boarded up, and the well-maintained streets were empty of both people and vehicles. I surmised that the refugees had little reason to return here from the relative prosperity of Cameroun or Gabon.

This conclusion did nothing to alleviate my present predicament, however. Knowing there to be no flights, I resigned myself to the possibility of having to walk to Gabon. After about half an hour, I was surprised to come upon an apparently well-populated thatched suburb. I say surprised, but after travelling in Africa for a while, nothing seems that surprising. I therefore did not find it strange to hear the sound of a 15-year-old Beatles' record blaring from a large thatched building. Nor did I find it that strange to enter the building and find a well-stocked bar and about a hundred dancing patrons, 80 of whom were young women. I am sure the most bizarre event to occur that day was the entrance of a lone white man, with a bag strapped to his back.

In any case, I settled down to enjoy a few beers, answer curious questions and gather more information. Amidst many offers of overnight accommodation, I was able to ascertain that a vehicle would be making its weekly journey to Acalayong, the southernmost town, the very next day.

The next morning, a decrepit pickup truck did, indeed, turn up. I thankfully scrambled into the back with sacks of grain, baskets of live chickens and about 15 other passengers. Apart from one small village, there was very little to see during the eight-hour journey. The road was in deplorable condition, practically swallowed up by the dense jungle which closed in tightly on both sides. By the time the truck wheezed into Acalayong, I was alone, my fellow passengers having disappeared into the bush along the way.

Acalayong consisted of 30 huts huddled on the shore of a broad estuary. At the shallow water's edge was beached a flotilla of hollowed-out log canoes, some sporting outboard motors. After intense bargaining, one of the owners agreed to take me across the estuary to Gabon. Soon we were underway, skimming over the water which occasionally surged over the prow of the low-sitting canoe.

We must have travelled a good three hours before the engine sputtered to a halt. The estuary had widened considerably at this point and the change in water colour indicated that we were geographically in the Atlantic Ocean. Apart from a few nearby islets, land appeared to be very far away indeed. I was, therefore, greatly relieved when the current carried us to one of these islets, rather than out to sea.

To be truthful, when we landed I really was surprised. There was a village on this ½-square-km dot of land, and I was surely the first traveller to ever visit it. Not only that, but the friendly villagers considered me to be an honoured guest who had obviously come there to settle. By nightfall, a reed hut had been constructed for me to live in. Then I, and the entire village, sat down to a feast of grilled fish, manioc and copious quantities of palm wine. This was followed by dancing, drumming, and drinking long into the night.

It was very late when I finally staggered to my hut, and I did not have the inclination to reflect on my onward journey. Were I feeling romantic, I may have conjured up a multitude of exotic, Robinson Crusoe-style scenarios. But sleep intervened and I awoke to the reality of a buzzing outboard motor. And so it was, with the entire village enthusiastically waving farewell, that the possessor of Tourist Visa No 001 finally departed Equatorial Guinea.

Ethiopia

Among African countries Ethiopia is unique in that it avoided colonisation (except for a brief Italian occupation shortly before WW II) and has its own home-grown Christian Church going back to the 4th century AD which has successfully resisted the onslaughts of Islam right down to the present day. Whether it will resist the onslaught of doctrinal Russian communism remains to be seen. The prospects don't look bright at present as the country has become, to all intents and purposes, a Russian satellite state. Despite the presence of thousands of Russian and Cuban soldiers, the country is wracked by internal revolt and wars with both the Eritreans and the Somalis. It is virtually a closed country, which is sad since it's very beautiful and has a fascinating culture. The only way of getting in is by air to Addis Ababa; going anywhere other than Addis is hedged with all sorts of bureaucratic restrictions. Unfortunately, Ethiopia is probably a country you'll have to miss for the time being.

The first recorded kingdom in Ethiopia grew up around Axum in the northern highlands during the 3rd century BC, at a time when the Egyptian-influenced state of Meroe was flourishing near what is today Shendi in Sudan. Axum was an offshoot of the Semitic Sabean kingdoms of southern Arabia and soon became the greatest ivory market in north-east Africa. Its king traded with Greeks and even spoke their language. Over the next few centuries Axum gradually encroached on Meroe until the 4th century AD. When Christianity became the state religion, it finally conquered that declining kingdom and forced its rulers to flee to the western Sudan. Axum went on to conquer parts of the Yemen and southern Arabia and was to remain the dominant power in the area until after the death of the Prophet Mohammed. Even when the armies of Islam began to sweep out in all directions from Mecca, Axum remained in control of the western Red Sea coast down to Zeila in Somalia, though the Moslems were able to take advantage of a temporary weakness in the kingdom to capture Massawa and the neighbouring Dahlak Islands.

As Islam expanded, however, Ethiopia was cut off from direct access to its former Mediterranean trading partners and allies, and Moslem merchants gradually replaced the Egyptians, Greeks and Jews in the Red Sea ports. Yet, surprisingly, this didn't result in hostilities between Ethiopia and the Arab armies. Historians believe that part of the reason for this remarkable co-existence, compared with European relations with Islam, is the fact that Ethiopia adopted the so-called Monophysite heresy (condemned by orthodox Christianity in 451 AD). This allowed for a live-and-let-live arrangement between the two religions, similar to that enjoyed by the Egyptian Copts. Under the pact, the Ethiopians were allowed to continue to consecrate their bishops in Cairo and thousands of Christian pilgrims were able to make the journey to Jerusalem in safety without any restrictions being placed on their religious rites and ceremonies. Even Saladin, one of the greatest opponents of the Crusaders, allowed the Ethiopians to maintain their own church in Jerusalem.

The Ethiopians did not, however, have the same relationship with the pagan tribes to the south, and it was from this area that the first major challenge came to their highland empire. Pressure from these tribes eventually forced the Ethiopian emperors to adopt the life of nomadic military commanders living in temporary tented cities and its priests to become monks and hermits in order to keep the religion alive. In time, however, the tribes were pacified and the kingdom recovered sufficiently to take in the provinces of Amhara, Lasta, Gojjam and Damot. At the same time the capital was moved south to Amhara province.

Moslem expansion into Ethiopia began in the 12th century as the number of independent trading kingdoms grew up along the Red Sea coast and gradually began to expand down the Awash Valley following the line of the present-day railway between Djibouti and Addis Ababa. Their wealth was based principally on trade in slaves, ivory and gold which they acquired from the pagan tribes and kingdoms south of the highlands down into the area of the great lakes. But they were not to remain independent for long, being made into Ethiopian vassal states during the 13th and 14th centuries. The largest of these Moslem states – Ifat – was finally eclipsed in 1415 and its people were forced to flee to the Yemen after the king was killed in battle at the capital, Zeila.

Ethiopian fortunes were reversed in the 16th century with the expansion of the Ottoman Empire. The Turks, who succeeded the Mamelukes in Egypt, began to support the various Moslem kingdoms in their struggles with the Ethiopians by providing firearms and artillery, and it was only the intervention of the Portuguese in 1542 which saved the Christian empire from collapse. For a hundred years thereafter, Portuguese missionaries tried unsuccessfully to persuade the Ethiopians to accept the Pope in Rome as head of the Church.

After what was truly a remarkable lifespan the empire broke down into its constituent provinces in the 18th century, and a hundred years of constant warfare between one warlord and another followed.

The shattered empire was eventually put together again by Ras Kassa, who managed to have himself crowned emperor at Axum under the name of Theodore in 1855. He went on to build something approaching a modern army and used this to unite the provinces of Tigre, Amhara and Shoa, but his arrogant treatment of British envoys led to his downfall. A military expedition was mounted by the British under the command of Napier in 1867 which, after much hardship, reached the fortress of Magdala and blockaded it for several months. Abandoned by many of his vassals, Theodore shot himself. His successor, John IV, fought his way to the throne using British arms acquired in exchange for help at Magdala. His success, however, was short-lived and he was forced to accept Menelik, a powerful young vassal king of Shoa, as his heir. While waiting for the throne, Menelik occupied himself building up stocks of European arms, which he used in 1896 to defeat the Italians at Adowa and to expand his empire at the expense of the Afars, the Somalis of Harrar and the Ogaden, and the Gallas of the southwest.

After WW I, Ethiopia became a member of the League of Nations, but this didn't prevent the country from being overrun by Mussolini's Italy in 1936. Though the other western nations condemned the invasion (somewhat hypocritically in view of their own activities in Africa) and although the young emperor, Haile Selassie, made many impassioned speeches pleading for assistance, no help was forthcoming. The Italians remained there until 1941, when they were thrown out during WW II. Ethiopia resumed its course as an independent nation after the war, though the province of Eritrea bordering the Red Sea remained under British administration until 1952 when it was federated with Ethiopia. The federation took no account of the wishes of the Eritreans themselves, and when it was dissolved in 1962 and the province annexed by Haile Selassie, this

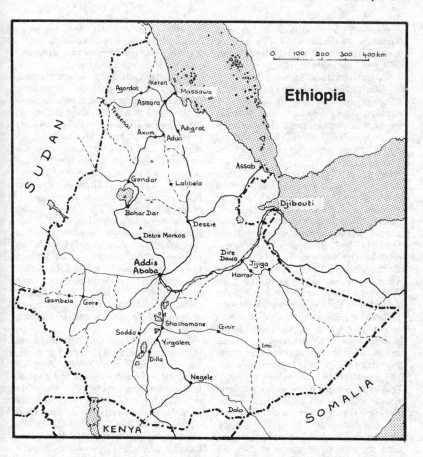

led to the outbreak of guerrilla warfare. The Eritreans were not only Moslems, but had not been a part of Ethiopia for several hundred years, and they regarded the annexation as tantamount to being colonised by another African nation. Many years of inconclusive fighting over this issue under extreme hardship and in remote areas sapped the morale of the soldiers, led to mutinies and increased their awareness of the revolutionary current which was beginning to sweep through Ethiopian society. It was one of the principal factors leading to Haile Selassie's downfall.

Though he had established himself as a national hero during the campaigns against the Italians and had become a respected African statesman instrumental in the creation of the Organisation of African Unity (OAU), Haile Selassie appeared to be unaware of the inappropriateness of medieval feudalism in the 20th century. The constant accumulation of wealth by the nobility and the Church, the hardships experienced by millions of landless peasants, student protests and serious famines in the southern half of the country in which hundreds of thousands of people died, combined with the effects of the war in Eritrea, produced a mass feeling of resentment. The break came in 1974 amid a background of strikes, student demonstrations, army mutinies and peasant uprisings against landlords. Haile Selassie was deposed and held under armed guard in his palace until his death several months later.

Overnight, Ethiopia was plunged into a social revolution it was largely ill-prepared for and ill-equipped to deal with. A clique of junior army officers seized the initiative and imposed a military dictatorship on the country against opposition from trade unionists and intellectuals. Mengistu Haile Miriam, who emerged as the leader of the army officers, threw out the Americans who were associated too closely with the imperial regime, instituted a number of radical reforms which were designed to change the face of Ethiopian society overnight, jailed trade union leaders who were demanding civilian participation in the new government, and appealed to the USSR for economic aid. Months of chaos and excess followed. Thousands of people – many of them sympathetic to the revolution – were massacred in the streets or in their homes by self-appointed vigilante groups. Opposition sprang up everywhere ranging from pro-imperialist groups to ultra-left revolutionary cells. The prisons were full to overflowing and summary executions were the order of the day. As the country slipped further and further into anarchy the Eritreans stepped up their guerrilla campaign and the Somalis, who had waited a long time for such an opportunity, decided to press their claims over the Ogaden Desert and invaded in force. By the beginning of 1978, the Somalis had overrun Jijiga, an important Ethiopian military base, and were threatening to take Harrar and Dire Dawa through which the vital rail link to Djibouti runs. The

military regime in Addis was on the point of collapse, and probably would have, had it not been for the massive intervention of Russian and Cuban troops.

With help from Moscow and Havana, Mengistu was able to throw the Somalis back across the border and recoup some of the losses he had sustained in Eritrea, but even the Russians and Cubans have been unable to break the back of the Eritrean liberation fighters, and the conflict simmers on. Meanwhile, Russian support for Somalia's arch-enemy resulted in the expulsion of all Russian personnel from Somalia and that country's rapprochement with the west. The irony of Cuban troops being committed to fight a war against Eritrean guerrillas whose ideology is essentially identical to that of the Cuban regime has not, however, been lost on Castro, who openly refused to follow Moscow's lead in committing more troops to the Eritrean conflict. Nevertheless, Cuban troop strength in Ethiopia remains at around 12,000. Batista must be laughing in his grave.

Fighting is still going on in Ethiopia and is likely to do so for a long time to come, especially with the consolidation of Mengistu's dictatorship and the endless purges which are conducted to eliminate rivals, real or imagined. There is no doubt at all that the overthrow of feudalism which was the basis of Haile Selassie's regime was of inestimable benefit to millions of landless peasants, but the Kremlin is not noted for voluntarily relinquishing control over its satellites, so Ethiopia is likely to remain off the beaten track for many years to come.

VISAS

Visas are required by all except nationals of Kenya. White nationals of South Africa are not admitted. You must have an onward ticket and at least US$500 to show on arrival.

Transit visas for Ethiopia (maximum of 72 hours – no extensions possible) are available on arrival by air, but if you want to stay longer you must get a tourist visa. This used to be a long and involved process, but the visas are now much easier to obtain. In Khartoum they cost S£15, require two photos and are issued while you wait so long as you have a letter of introduction from your own embassy and an onward ticket. All the same, you may not travel outside Addis Ababa without special permits. The government encourages only the big spenders, so as a general rule, permits are only granted if (1) you are on a pre-arranged tour (2) you are willing to pay for a National Tourist Organisation tour (around US$170 per person per day, or (3) you are willing to hire a car and a 'guide' – very expensive indeed. You can apply for permits at the Tourist Office, Revolution Square, Addis Ababa, or from the Commissioner of Tourism, PO Box 2183, Addis Ababa.

Those are not the only restrictions. You must also stay in government-approved accommodation; you cannot stay just where you like. The accommodation which the government approves is generally considerably more expensive than accommodation you could find for yourself.

That, at least, is the official story. We've had a few letters from sympathetic souls who have taken the revolution to heart and decided that freedom applies to them too. They've attached themselves to international voluntary/aid organisations, taken refuge with influential local people or simply taken off regardless. If you decide to do the latter, we can't promise you anything. If you're picked up, it's probable that you will be deported (this eventuality seems to be negotiable up to a certain extent), though usually they just make sure you get back to Addis double-quick. We've not heard of anyone being jailed even for a short time. You can certainly go to Debre Zeit, Nazareth and Sodere without a permit, but don't try to board the train to Djibouti or go to Eritrea. You'll definitely be off limits. And then the KGB will be in charge.

MONEY
US$1 = 2.07-2.08 birr
£1 = 2.80 birr

The unit of currency is the birr = 100 cents. Import of local currency is allowed up to 50 birr but export is prohibited. There is no black market. It's a good idea to keep receipts for everything (even meals) to avoid any hassles when leaving. Cash and traveller's cheques are carefully counted both on arrival and departure. Don't depend on your hotel being willing to change money even if you're staying there. Some travellers have gone hungry for the night because they haven't had birr on arrival.

Currency declaration forms are issued on arrival. It's not a good idea to attempt to conceal anything, as there are thorough searches of both baggage and your person on leaving (though we have had letters saying the check on exit was slack).

You can re-convert excess birr on leaving, less US$30 per day of your stay.

The airport tax is 8 birr.

LANGUAGE
Amharic is the official language, but Galla is more useful in the south. Arabic, Italian, English and French are also widely spoken among educated people, but not outside the cities. There are significant numbers of Italian speakers in and around Addis and Asmara. Old people and civil servants can often speak academic French. Arabic speakers live mostly along the Red Sea coast and in the north of the country (Eritrea).

Some Amharic
Numerals:

1	ant
2	hulet
3	sost
4	arat
5	amst
6	sidist
7	sabat

8	*simnut*
9	*zutang*
10	*assr*
20	*hya*
30	*salasa*
40	*arba*
50	*hamsa*
100	*moto*

Some useful words

water	*ooha*
tea	*shai*
milk	*wa'tat*
coffee	*buna*
bread	*dabhu*
sour	*dough*
sour bread	*injera*
banana	*mooz*
sauce	*wat*
mincemeat and onion	*kufto*
egg	*uncolal*
please	*bakh*
thank you	*amasagunalhu*
yes	*ow (very breathy)*
no	*idelem*
OK	*ishi*
hello	*tenastele*
expensive	*zerzer*
cheap	*santim*
road	*mungat*
right	*keing*
left	*graa/carmachina*

Some useful phrases

Which is the road to . . . ?
Yetmungat now?
Where are you going?
Wa'dit tehedalhe?
How much does it cost?
Sintenow wagow?

FOOD

In the countryside and most small Ethiopian towns the only thing to eat as a rule is *wat* (also sometimes called *zegeni*) and *injera*. *Wat* is a fiery-hot sauce sometimes containing bits of chicken (if you're lucky), beans and lentils. *Injera* is the national foam-rubber bread made with millet flour mixed with yeast and left to go sour for about three days before being cooked on a clay board heated by a log fire (no firewood and you eat it neat taken from under a dirty cloth covered with flies). Once you get used to this delicacy and the unbearable feeling of your lips being unquenchably on fire, it's quite tasty though of limited nutritional value. Nevertheless, it's cheap. Stay clear of salads as there's a good chance of picking up liver fluke, and DDT is used like water in some areas. Local markets are good for fruit, but peel before you eat. In the larger towns there is a variety of food available – Italian (common), Indian and Chinese in Addis; Italian in Asmara and Massawa.

GETTING THERE & AROUND

The only way you can get into and out of Ethiopia is to fly to Addis Ababa. If you fly *Air Ethiopia* from Cairo to Nairobi via Addis Ababa (or vice versa), you can choose to stop overnight in Addis at Air Ethiopia's expense in a luxury hotel with food included. You don't need a visa for this one-night stop-over. You can also stop over for longer periods but you need a visa for this, and it won't be at Air Ethiopia's expense (though it doesn't increase the price of the ticket).

Internal flights in Ethiopia are not for the faint-hearted. They're all by DC3s and it's like going back 30 years in terms of air travel. Service and comforts are minimal.

The bus from Addis to Gondar costs 23.60 birr and takes 1-1/2 days with an overnight stop. You can only do this if you have a permit, take a 'guide' and pay his expenses. The only other way of getting there is to fly. This costs 88 birr one way and takes 1½ hours.

ADDIS ABABA

Officially, you can only stay in government-approved hotels, and you can be arrested and deported if you stay anywhere else. The cheapest of these is the *Tourist Hotel* (the same as the old Hotel Suisse)

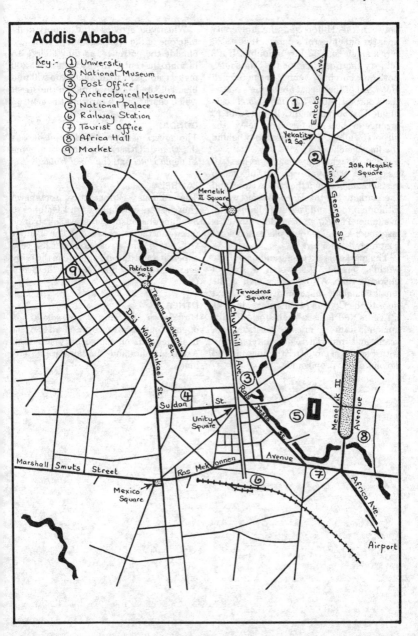

Addis Ababa

Key:-
1. University
2. National Museum
3. Post Office
4. Archeological Museum
5. National Palace
6. Railway Station
7. Tourist Office
8. Africa Hall
9. Market

between the Hilton and the university near the old emperor's palace. It costs 23 birr a single and 33 birr a double. If it's full, try the *Ras Hotel* or the *Nile Hotel*, both on Churchill Avenue, or the *Guenett Hotel*. All of these cost about the same as the Tourist Hotel. The *Hilton Hotel* costs about US$60 per night. If you want to arrange a hotel before you leave the airport terminal, there is an agency behind the luggage check.

Meals bought in hotels cost at least 10 birr, but there are plenty of cheap restaurants between the Hilton Hotel and the market. Try the *Maru Dembia* where Ethiopian food and traditional music are available. The *Elfign* near Bole airport is also good. A meal in these places shouldn't cost more than 5 birr.

The market is excellent and one of the world's largest. It's worth a day of anyone's time. Also worth a visit is the small **Ethnology Museum**, Entoto St next door to the College of Pharmacy. It costs 50 cents and houses prehistoric fossils, ancient statues, musical instruments, crafts and imperial regalia interspersed with displays of modern Ethiopian life and revolutionary propaganda.

When you arrive at the airport don't take one of the cream-coloured taxis just outside the entrance, as they charge 15 birr into the centre. Instead, walk 100-200 metres along the road where you will find blue-coloured taxis waiting on the street which charge only 5 birr into the centre.

GONDAR

The government-approved hotel here is the *Quara*. Other cheap hotels are the *Ethiopia Hotel* and the *Fasil Hotel*.

LALIBELA

The famous 12th-century rock-hewn churches are only open from 1 October to 30 June because the grass airstrip is unsafe in the rainy season. The Tourist Office also runs a road tour but it's very expensive and doesn't operate in the rainy season. The only hotel here is the *Seven Olives*.

OTHER

Dire Dawa and Harrar are sometimes open to tourists who are prepared to fly in. It all depends on the security situation. Axum, Asmara and Massawa are all off-limits.

Gabon

Gabon was once regarded as the economic miracle of equatorial Africa. The nation, which attained independence from the French in 1960, got off to an extravagant start. With the money rolling in from the sale of oil, from possession of some 25% of the world's known manganese ore and from important deposits of iron ore, chrome, gold and diamonds, the country sported a per capita income higher than that of South Africa and only slightly lower than that of Libya. That was before the oil glut, the downturn in the steel industry (the major consumer of manganese) and the recession which, in recent years, all wreaked havoc with the Gabonese economy. But external factors were not the only reason for the change of fortunes. In 1976, an ambitious four-year plan was announced with a budget of US$32 billion which was intended to create a modern transport system, encourage local industry and develop mineral deposits. Most of the money was squandered on misguided projects. Corruption ran rife and Libreville became one of the favourite African capitals for unscrupulous contractors. The railway which was intended to connect the mineral deposits of the interior with the coast, due for completion in 1980, is still only one-third complete. Agriculture, the occupation of some 80% of the population, was completely ignored with the result that local food production accounts for only 15% of the country's needs. Neglect of the agricultural sector has also resulted in a drift of the population to the urban centres. However, not even the recession prevented the completion of the 36,000 million CFA presidential palace, or the staging of one of the most extravagant OAU Summits ever held or ever likely to be held again. On the other hand, from a budget deficit of nearly 600 billion CFA in 1977, Gabon's economy appears to be on the mend.

Gabon has been ruled since 1967 by President El Hadj Omar Bongo (who adopted Islam in 1974). With a personal bodyguard composed of European mercenaries (who included the notorious Bob Denard) and Moroccan troops and the presence of 400 crack French airborne troops as well as numerous French political and military advisors, Bongo has been able to maintain a remarkable image of stability for the country. Since 1968 the country has been a one-party state with lucrative ministerial posts being frequently shuffled between a small number of political faithfuls. Despite the obvious nepotism of the political set-up, Bongo has so far been able to find convenient scapegoats whenever his government has been faced with social unrest. In 1976 Bongo took to making speeches about avaricious foreign companies which expatriated profits, yet almost nothing was done to stop the excesses. (In 1978 French firms controlled 90% of the vital oil sector and the remittances of expatriate workers to foreign banks turned a Gabonese trade surplus into a deficit!) In mid-1978, with the oil industry on the downturn, 10,000 Beninois workers were expelled after President Kerebou renewed his allegations that Gabon had been used as the staging post for the 1977 attempt to invade Benin by air-borne mercenaries. Again, in 1979, an atmosphere of xenophobia was created against refugees from Equatorial Guinea. As you might have gathered, political freedom walks a tightrope in this country. Bongo's attitude to government is dictated by what he once called 'political realism with economic affairs overshadowing political matters.' It's interesting to speculate how these two priorities might be reversed in the event of a threat to Bongo's political survival.

Gabon appears to have been populated originally by pygmies who lived in small family units along riverbanks, but they survive today only in the more remote parts of the country. They were displaced by migrating peoples from the north between the 16th and 18th centuries, principal among whom were the Fang from what is now Cameroun and Equatorial Guinea. Contact with Europeans, starting with the arrival of the Portuguese in 1472, set in motion a train of events which had a profound effect on tribal social structures. The Portuguese largely ignored the place, preferring to base their activities on the nearby islands of São Tomé and Principe, but British, Dutch and French ships called in to trade along the coast regularly for slaves, ivory and precious tropical woods. The slave trade resulted in a staggering loss of population from the interior as well as enhancement of the coastal chiefs' authority.

The capital, Libreville, was established as a settlement for freed slaves in 1849 on the site of a French fort constructed in 1843. French interests became paramount in 1886 with the appointment of a governor whose jurisdiction extended over the whole of the French Congo. The capital of the region was transferred to Brazzaville in 1904 and six years later Gabon became a French colony in French Equatorial Africa. The country became independent in 1960 under the presidency of M'Ba, who died in a French hospital in 1967.

FACTS

Gabon consists of a narrow, low-lying coastal strip which rises to a series of plateaux with peaks over 1500 metres. Tropical rain forests cover three-quarters of the country and deep river valleys dissect the country into small, relatively isolated units. The climate is hot (average temperature is 27°C) and humid. The dry season extends from May to September with a short dry spell in mid-December. The population numbers about one million, most of whom are of Bantu origin with the Fang making up about one-third of these; Europeans number around 50,000. Communications outside the coastal area are very undeveloped.

Probably one of Gabon's most famous personalities was Dr Albert Schweitzer, who worked as a doctor at a mission station near Lambarene on the Ogooue River in the colonial period. I once read a couple of his books years before I went to Africa, and although I'd never suggest that his heart was anywhere except in the right place, the rest of his 'philosophical' embroidery about the 'white man's burden' wore op-shop thin within weeks when I eventually found myself there.

VISAS

These are required by all except nationals of France and West Germany. Gabonese visas are not easy to get and all visa applications have to be referred to Libreville (the government doesn't exactly encourage tourism, especially by shoe-string travellers). Visas cost CFA 4000 and, in general, take one month to five weeks to come through. It helps a great deal if you have a pre-arranged job there. Even if you get a visa you will be refused entry if your passport reflects previous visits to South Africa. Most travellers apply for their visas in Lomé (Togo), Lagos (Nigeria) and Douala (Cameroun), where they are reported to be not too difficult to get. We've had one report from a traveller who got his in Malabo (Equatorial Guinea), where a visa cost 3000 Bk for a one-month stay and took 24 hours to issue. Another person got one in São Tomé and Principe, where it was expensive at US$20 but easy to get. The problem with the latter is getting a visa for São Tomé in the first place.

Gabon refuses admission to nationals of Angola, Benin, Cape Verde Island, Cuba, Ghana, Guinea-Bissau, Haiti, São Tomé and Principe. No home-from-home for those dubious individuals here.

If you're intending to go overland from Gabon to Congo, make sure you get an exit stamp at N'Dende, about 40 km from the border.

On entry and at all times inside the country, make sure you have your papers handy. The gendarmes frequently make a habit of hassling foreigners, especially whites. This is usually mild and they're only looking for beer money. They will often continue asking for various papers until they find one that you don't have.

Generally, this involves a CFA 3000 'fine.' This mild harassment applies equally to expatriates with legitimate jobs there. One correspondent was threatened with jail for not having a WHO card even though he had a permanent visitor's ID card (Carte de Sejour). This resulted in a CFA 15,000 'fine.' Tolerance and patience are invaluable in these situations.

Congo visas In Libreville, these cost CFA 5000, require one photo and take 24 hours to issue. It's more or less impossible to get more than 15 days (with a fixed date of entry).

Zaire visas These cost CFA 4500 for one

month, CFA 8500 for two months and CFA 10,500 for three months, and require two photos and a letter of recommendation from your own embassy. They're issued in 24 hours. If you're heading down to Zaïre, make sure you get your visa here and not in Brazzaville. You can certainly get Zaïre visas in Brazzaville, but unless your visa was issued elsewhere the Zaïre embassy will not issue you with the *laissez-passer* which you must have in addition to your visa to catch the ferry across the river to Kinshasa. That means you'll have to fly, and the cost of the 10-minute flight must be one of the biggest rip-offs in Africa (around £200).

MONEY
US$1 = CFA 460

The unit of currency is the CFA franc. Import of local currency is unlimited; export is limited to CFA 200,000.

The best commercial bank for exchange is the Citi Bank at Trois Quartier in Libreville. Exchange is difficult elsewhere and in some places impossible. Gabonese banks offer lower rates and hotels are the worst.

Inflation is high (around 20%) and most services such as accommodation and transport are outrageously expensive.

Airport tax for domestic flights is CFA 400.

LANGUAGE
French is the official language, although in the interior many local languages are spoken.

PHOTOGRAPHY
Photos are a touchy subject in Gabon. Never take a photo at the airport, nor of any official, building, military vehicle or personnel. If you do, your film and camera will be subject to confiscation. Generally, it's best to ask individuals first if you can take their picture. Be prepared to pay a small amount.

GETTING THERE & AROUND
Entry Points
You can enter Gabon overland from Cameroun, Equatorial Guinea or the Congo (Brazzaville). From Cameroun the route is normally from Ntem to either Libreville or Lambarene via Oyem.

To enter from Equatorial Guinea, head south from Bata to Acalayong on the Equatorial Guinea/Gabon border. From there you need to find a motorised dugout to Coco Beach (the first village in Gabon across the estuary). Insist that the boat owner take you direct to Coco Beach. He'll charge you CFA 3000 for this and the journey should take about 2½ hours depending on the tides. You may be offered this journey for CFA 2000, but avoid accepting it as the boat owner will first take you to a place downriver where you will have to pay a CFA 2000 'exit tax.' From Coco Beach you can get a taxi-brousse to Libreville.

If you're coming south from Cameroun, there are taxis from Bitem (the first town over the border in Gabon) to Oyem for CFA 3000. From there you can get taxis direct to Libreville for CFA 12,000 or a taxi to Ndjole for CFA 9000.

Air
Many places can only be reached by plane or boat. Some sample air fares are: Libreville-Franceville, CFA 32,000; Libreville-Tchibanga, CFA 25,000; Libreville-Omboue, CFA 18,000.

Road
Roads are generally quite good and many are surfaced, but you should be careful of local drivers. More people are killed on the roads in a month than are killed by assorted beasts in those legendary ferocious forests in a year.

If you're heading south towards the Congo, there are daily trucks from Lambarene to Mouila for CFA 4000 and others from there to N'Dende for about CFA 1000. There's also a train twice daily in either direction between Lambarene and N'Dende for CFA 3200. For those in a desperate hurry and with money to burn, there is a bus from Libreville to Loubomo in Congo. From N'Dende south as far as Kibangou in the Congo there is very little traffic. Most of the travellers who have been this way recently have had lifts on beer trucks. One group reported that there is a truck from N'Dende to Kibangou on Tuesday and Friday which costs CFA 6500 (as far as Loubomo). Another group reported a twice-weekly truck from Moussogo (the first Congolese village) to Kibangou. Journey times along this route are alcoholically flexible but usually take about two days. The trucks stop at every bar/village along the way, and every stop is a good enough excuse to get leg-less. You won't have to shout any beers along this route and it's more than likely that accommodation will be laid on too. If you should have to wait in Moussogo, there are rooms for rent behind the general store for CFA 500 (bed and mosquito net).

There are frequent buses and taxi-brousses between the larger cities but they're expensive. Libreville-Lambarene costs CFA 7500; Franceville-Moanda costs CFA 1000; Okondja-Franceville costs CFA 5000.

Rail

The Trans-Gabonese Railway is now open as far as Booue and spurs are being built from there to Franceville in the south and Belinga in the north. There is at least one train daily in either direction between Owendo (Libreville) and Booue. The schedules are available daily in *L'Union*, the daily newspaper (costs CFA 100). The fare from Lambarene to Ndjole is CFA 5000 (2nd class). The trains are very comfortable even in 2nd class and are efficient. Trains are generally on schedule so be at the station early. Buy your ticket in advance, as it costs double if you pay on the train. There are no student discounts. Rail fares are cheaper than the taxi-brousses.

Boat

The boats are far more intersting but are rarely taken by whites, so you'll be treated as a novelty (people are very friendly). Sample fares are: Lambarene-Port Gentil, CFA 10,000; Port Gentil-Omboue, CFA 3000; Port Gentil-Libreville, CFA 10,000. The Port Gentil-Libreville boat is a modern ferry which runs three times a week. The others are river barges which take both passengers and produce. At Ndjole, a 'truck-stop' town on the Ogooue River, there is an oil depot for Mobil. Oil barges run from there to Lambarene and Port Gentil on a semi-regular basis. There are eight to 10 of them and there's generally one each day or so. Enquire at the depot in Quartier Bingoma about getting onto them, though it's generally best to speak directly with the captains. The office may well give you the wrong time and price. The fare to Lambarene should be about CFA 3000 with no baggage charge. The barges make several stops at small villages en route, but Ndjole to Lambarene should take about seven hours. There's plenty to photograph along the way. Take your own food and drink. (There are two stores near the dock in Ndjole where you can buy bread, cheese and groceries of all kinds). Take a mat with you to sit on, as the barges are dirty and there are no cabins.

COCO BEACH

Local people are very friendly and may offer you a place to stay. If not, sleep on the beach or find free floor space at the police/customs office. There is a *Rest House* for CFA 1500 and the *Hotel Restaurant* for CFA 2000 a double. There's an interesting fishing village out of town populated by Nigerians who were once refugees from the Biafran war.

LAMBARENE

This town has an interesting setting on an island in the middle of the Ogooue River. Probably the cheapest place to stay is the grubby *Collective Rurale de Lambarene* at

CFA 1000 a double. Much better are the *Immaculate Conception Mission* or the other *Catholic Mission*. Both are north of the the town centre (a taxi from the centre or the market costs CFA 100). They're both comfortable and quiet places and the sisters are very pleasant and cooperative. The beds in the dormitory cost CFA 1500 per person including the use of showers, and you'll probably have the place to yourself. There are also small private rooms available for CFA 2000. You can have your laundry done here for CFA 1000. In addition to the above there's also a small *case de passage* near the market for CFA 1500 per person. They have no running water but will give you a bucket of water to clean up with. Electricity and a bed are about all you get here.

Restaurants stay open until about 8 pm. The oil barge dock is near the market across the river from the town. The area is full of bars and kebab stalls.

The big attraction of Lambarene is the **Schweitzer Hospital** about eight km from town. A taxi there will cost CFA 200 per person or a pirogue CFA 500 per person. The hospital is still fully functioning and a large new annexe was built in 1981. It's one of Gabon's finest hospitals. Schweitzer's office, home, library, lab and treatment centre are still there although deteriorating. Tours are available (some in English). The museums are now run by a foundation based in Geneva, but they receive 10% support from the government of Gabon. There's also a gift shop with local crafts for sale made largely by people from the leper colony. The selection is excellent. Prices are high and fixed. Better bargains can be found by dealing with individual craftspeople or bargaining with dealers in Libreville. However, all proceeds from the craft shop at the Schweitzer Hospital go to the hospital and most of the stuff sold in Libreville actually comes from West Africa. Although the hospital is not keen on putting up travellers, it is possible to get a room and meals there in exchange for a reasonable donation.

Also available in Lambarene are pirogues into the lake region where hippos and other wildlife can be seen (especially during the dry season). This can be expensive since it takes most of the day to go far enough to see much. A one-hour trip is reasonably priced but you won't see much.

Soapstone sculptures and masks are often for sale in the villages north of Lambarene. If you're interested, ask the pirogues to stop here.

LIBREVILLE

Libreville can be an interesting city if you take the time to get to know it. Each *quartier* has its own character and is loaded with bars and boutiques. Some of the things you might like to visit are: **St Michel** church in N'Kembo – a beautiful building whose entire facade is covered with mosaics and local wood carved to depict stories from the Bible; and the **National Museum** which has numerous examples of indigenous art, musical instruments and masks. Tours are conducted in French.

The beaches north of the city toward the airport are very pleasant. One such place is Cap Esterias and another is Point Denis, the latter across the estuary from Libreville. There is a small hotel and restaurant at Point Denis but it's expensive. Day trips or overnight camping are both possible. Ferry tickets are available from the *Hotel Dialogue* for CFA 3000 round trip. There are several trips daily.

Taxis around the city are CFA 100 per trip and CFA 1000 to the airport. Negotiation is often necessary.

During school holidays ask at the Mission School across from the *Maison Liebermann*, where they'll probably offer you free dormitory accommodation. If you have no luck there then try the bars in N'Kembo (the African Quarter) – you may well meet someone who offers you a place to stay. Expect to pay around CFA 8000 per week after bargaining, but don't expect too much in the way of services

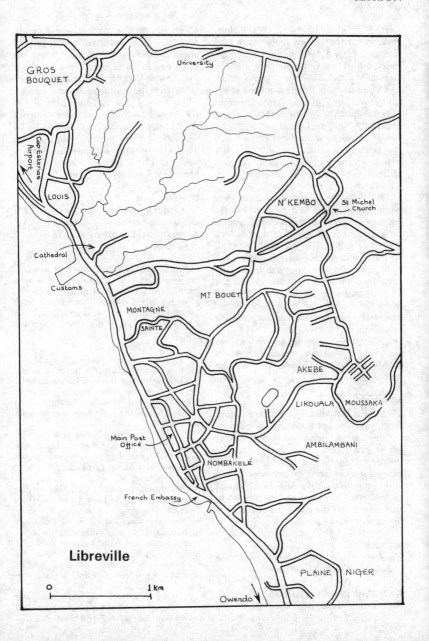

Libreville

0   1 km

(electricity, etc). Otherwise, try the *Hotel Panadou* or the *Maison Liebermann* (the latter costs CFA 1000 per person and is located near the Gare Routiere and the Grande Marche). The French organisation, Les Volunteurs de Progres, at the back of the general hospital, has a limited number of beds which are available to travellers. It costs CFA 2000 per person per night with use of showers and kitchen. There's also the possibility of staying with the UN people who have a house near the airport. Officially, it's only for UN people in transit.

The *Catholic Mission* has some very comfortable, clean and modern double rooms with shower for CFA 4000 (if you're on a very tight budget they may reduce this to CFA 2000). If you want to eat all your meals here, this costs an extra CFA 2500 per day, or you can take just breakfast for CFA 500. To get to the Mission, take the road which forks off from the coast road at the cathedral. Follow this for about two km and then ask again. It's off to the right.

Libreville is a very expensive town (as you might expect) and for budget travellers hotels are more or less out of the question.

N'DENDE

This is the last village of any size before the Congolese border. If you're heading for the Congo, remember that you must get an exit stamp before going on to the border. There are rooms behind the *general store* at CFA 500 per person (bed and mosquito net). The *Mission* isn't keen on visitors. There are no restaurants in this village and the only food available is bread and tinned goods.

NDJOLE

Hotel de la Barriere is good value for Gabon at CFA 3500 a double.

NATIONAL PARKS/WILDLIFE

Because Gabon has so few people, wildlife is still quite abundant in many areas. Elephants, gorillas, chimpanzees, leopards, mandrills and assorted monkeys and antelope are fairly common. Along the coast and in the lagoons there are still a few crocodiles, hippos, manatees and, offshore in the season, humpback whales. There's only one national park – the Reserve de Lope-Okanda in the centre of the country. You can reach this easily by railroad – get off two stops before Booue. This is the best place in the country to see wildlife. There is free accommodation here for a few days.

OTHER

Since so few people venture this way, we'd like to give you an idea of what it's like. Here is a traveller's tale by David Bennett of Canada:

IN THE FOOTSTEPS OF JURGEN SCHULTZ

But you must know Mr Jurgen, he is your brother, said the immigration officer excitedly. I was led into a thatched hut where a large ledger was opened in front of me. 'Voila,' said the officer, pointing to an entry on one of the pages.

It was true. Jurgen Schultz, nationality – German; mode of transport – foot, had indeed crossed the border between Gabon and the People's Republic of the Congo on November 8, 1977. But what connection did this have to me, standing in the same place, nearly three years later?

I looked down at the ledger again. It was a list of all non-African border crossers. There were no entries between Jurgen's name and my own which was now being inscribed. 'Ah, yes,' I nodded, 'Mr Jurgen.'

This wasn't the first indication of the remoteness of my location I had received. Traffic had become increasingly scarce since my departure from Libreville, the Gabonese capital, four days earlier. Although I was on the main international route between West and Equatorial Africa, I had waited all the day for the vehicle which brought me to the border. Now, I faced a 20-km walk to the first Congolese town.

Fortunately, a local who was making the same journey agreed to take me with him. He knew a shortcut that would cut the distance by half. After fording a couple of streams and hacking our way through some dense jungle growth, we finally reached Ngongo, Congo. Ngongo was an almost fairy-tale village consisting of a hundred well-made reed huts set in the midst of a hardwood rainforest. My guide took me directly to the village chief and soon I was shown to a hut. It was mine, for as long as I wanted. I was told the last occupant, a Mr Schultz, had stayed there for more than two weeks.

Later, I was taken to the only stone building in the village, a combination store and bar. As bottles of beer were produced, I reasoned that they must have been delivered by some sort of vehicle. 'It is true,' said the chief. 'The beer truck will come tomorrow.' Reflecting on Jurgen's two-week stay, I realised that the word 'tomorrow' simply meant some time in the future.

I spent two days in Ngongo, where, as an honoured guest, I was treated with warmth and friendliness. On the third day, a dilapidated truck, stocked with cases of beer, wheezed into the village.

'No problem,' said Pierre, the large, jovial driver, 'I can take you 140 km to Makabana. From there you can take a bus to Loubomo in time for the night train to Brazzaville.'

An hour later we set off, myself, Pierre, two helpers and several paying passengers. After a bone-wrenching 10-km ride we reached another village very similar to Ngongo. The arrival of the beer truck was the cause of much festivity. I was an honoured guest in this village also, and two hours and two bottles of beer later, we were underway again.

This scene was to be repeated five times before nightfall. We covered no more than 50 km and the beer had taken its toll. But what else could I do? An honoured guest can hardly refuse hospitality.

Finally, we stopped for the night. 'This is my village,' said Pierre. 'You must meet my wife and children. Come, we'll take some food and drink.'

I awoke the next morning with a crushing headache. It eased as the day became a repeat of the day before. We visited several villages and covered 100 km by nightfall. Unfortunately, I was still not at my destination, as 50 of those km had been side-trips to villages off the main road.

Once again, Pierre took me to visit his wife and children. 'I suppose you have a wife in Makabana, too.' I said jokingly. 'How did you know that?' said Pierre, surprised. Than a glint of recognition came to his face. 'You've been talking to Jurgen, haven't you? He must have told you.'

Now that I understood Pierre's timetable, I awoke the next morning confident of reaching my destination. We travelled quickly until, outside a large town called Kibangou, we were stopped at a police checkpoint. A stern-faced officer perused my passport. 'You didn't get your passport stamped in Lobo,' he said referring to a forgettable village 80 km back down the road. 'You will have to return there to get it stamped.'

My heart sank. Ten minutes of persistent argument proved fruitless. I would have to return to Lobo and God knows how many days that would take. Then I had a sudden inspiration. 'The reason I didn't get my passport stamped,' I blurted out, 'is because Jurgen Schultz told me it was not necessary.' The officer's face lit up and he began to shake my hand vigorously.

After 15 minutes of reminiscences about our non-mutual friend, I was allowed to continue my journey. At the other side of Kibangou, we came to a crossroads. 'Just a quick trip down this side road, and then we can continue on,' said Pierre. Well aware of Pierre's quick trips, I diplomatically suggested I wait at the crossroads in the hope of securing a ride to Loubomo.

A half an hour later, a dusty pickup truck screeched to a halt beside me. The driver, a middle-aged civil servant, was going directly to Loubomo. 'It's 140 km, so we'll be there in two hours,' he said. As I reflected on my good fortune and the 140 km I had just travelled, the man looked over at me. 'A couple of years ago, I picked up another traveller quite like yourself . . . .'

Gambia

Consisting of a narrow strip of territory only 16 to 25 km wide on either side of the Gambia River but nearly 500 km long and surrounded by Senegal, Gambia is a legacy of the rivalry between the British and French for control of trade in West Africa. Small it may be, but it's one of West Africa's most colourful and interesting countries and would still be well worth a visit even if it hadn't been made famous by Alex Haley (of *Roots*) tracing his ancestors back to Juffure. Not only are there numerous tribal groups, all with their own customs, but history has left this country with a treasure chest of relics and ruins ranging from the 12th-century stone circles of Wassu to the forts which dot the mouth of the river. There are unspoilt traditional villages, superb beaches and an endless variety of birdlife.

Gambia's first contact with Europeans came with the arrival of the Portuguese in 1456. They landed on James Island about 30 km upriver from the sea, and although they did not establish a settlement they continued to monopolise trade along the West African coast throughout the 16th century. In those days salt, iron, pots and pans, firearms and gunpowder were exchanged for ivory, ebony, beeswax, gold and slaves. The first settlement was made by Baltic Germans in the service of the Duke of Courland (now Latvia), who built a fort on James Island in 1651. They were displaced by the British in 1661, after which trade and the defence of the island became the responsibility of a Royal Chartered Company with headquarters in London. The settlement was constantly under threat from pirates, the French and the mainland African kings, who would cut off supplies from time to time. Sickness and mutiny also took their toll. The fort was finally taken by the French in 1779 while the British were occupied with fighting the war of independence in their American colonies. Though largely destroyed by the French, the fort was recaptured shortly afterwards but it was soon to lose its strategic importance with the construction of new forts at Barra and Bathurst (now Banjul) at the mouth of the river; these were better placed to control the movement of ships. Nevertheless, Fort James continued to be one of the most important collection points for slaves bound for the Americas until the trade was abolished in 1807.

During the early 19th century the British continued to increase their influence further and further upstream until in the 1820s a protectorate was declared over the area. The new colony was ruled for many years from Sierra Leone, but in 1888 Gambia became a Crown Colony in its own right. Only in 1889 was the boundary between Gambia and Senegal settled following a treaty between the British and French.

The colony became self-governing in 1963, but the British considered independence to be impractical both economically and politically and there was a period of intense activity over the question of whether Gambia should be merged with Senegal. However, although a Treaty of Association was signed, a United Nations team appointed to look into the possibility decided that it was unrealistic at that stage and the country became an independent nation in 1965. Since independence it has been ruled by the People's Progressive Party led by Dawda K Jawara.

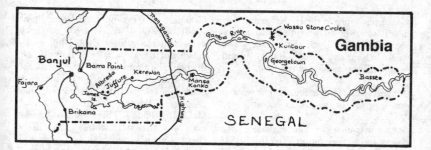

Gambia suffers from a lack of natural resources and its only major export is groundnuts, so it's been an uphill struggle since independence to make ends meet. The country is still heavily dependent on foreign aid – mainly from Libya, West Germany, the People's Republic of China and Britain – and even this has been slow in coming at times. Libya virtually suspended aid when transport (in which they had a 40% stake) was nationalised in 1979. When it was discovered that a Senegalese dissident had persuaded several groups of young Gambians to go to Libya for training as part of his plan to take over Gambia and make it into an Islamic fundamentalist state, diplomatic relations with Libya were broken off and Libyan nationals were expelled from the country. Tourism has also failed to become the money-spinner it was hoped it would be. Most of the tourists who come to Gambia go on package tours, paying for their trip before they arrive. The abortive coup recently also led to a serious decline in the number of visitors. Meanwhile, the population continues to expand but the number of jobs remains static (Gambia is one of Africa's most densely populated countries), so many young Gambians have been forced to leave in search of jobs elsewhere – mainly to Britain and France.

FACTS

Life revolves around the river and there are almost no significant variations in the altitude or the vegetation, which consists largely of savannah and saline marshes. Overgrazing, deforestation and drought have combined to create serious problems in the agricultural sector. The dry season stretches from November to April with the main rains between July and October. Temperature variations from one season to another are slight, averaging around 24°C in winter and 29°C in summer. The population numbers around one million, 90% of whom are Moslems.

VISAS

Visas are required by all except nationals of the Commonwealth countries, Belgium, Denmark, Finland, Germany (West), Iceland, Irish Republic, Italy, Luxembourg, Netherlands, Norway, Spain and Sweden. If you arrive by air you may well be asked for an onward ticket. This doesn't apply if you're coming overland. If you're coming in on the Koalack-Barra road, immigration officials will give you a seven-day stay permit. You can have this extended in Banjul for up to three months but the inspector who deals with these enquiries has been described as a 'surly little shit.' If you get problems, go straight to his superior upstairs. He's much friendlier and will help you out. Visas in Dakar cost CFA 3000 and are issued the same day. The embassy is on Rue Thiong.

Banjul is generally a good place to get visas for other West African countries since it's a small city and very easy to get around on foot. The one exception is Sierra Leone – the person who deals with visa applications at the High Commission here is a sour-faced individual who is more than likely to tell you that it takes two weeks to issue a visa unless you grovel and scrape till you're blue in the face.

Guinea visas The embassy has closed down. Apply for the visa in Bissau.

Guinea-Bissau visas The embassy here has moved to Wellington St by the CUSO office. Visas cost 15 dalasi and are issued while you wait. You may be asked for a letter of recommendation from your own embassy (the USA embassy in Banjul is very reluctant to issue such letters). The ambassador here is very friendly but make sure he fills in your visa correctly – he's sometimes a little careless.

Liberian visas The embassy is on Cameron St. Visas are easy to obtain.

Senegal visas The embassy is on the corner of Cameron St and Buckle. Visas cost 10.10 dalasi, you need three photos and the visa takes 48 hours to issue. You should have no problems here.

MONEY

US$1	=	3.80 dalasi
£1	=	4.00 dalasi
CFA 1000	=	8.00 dalasi

The unit of currency is the dalasi = 100 bututs. There are no restrictions on the import of local currency but export is limited to 75 dalasi. The currencies of Algeria, Ghana, Guinea, Mali, Morocco, Nigeria, Sierra Leone and Tunis are not accepted and cannot be changed in banks. CFA francs are accepted. If you have traveller's cheques it's better to change them into CFA in Senegal and then convert them into dalasi on arrival. This way you gain some 9% more than you would by changing the traveller's cheques directly into dalasi. It's sometimes possible to get up to US$1 = 5 dalasi on the black market, 6.00 dalasi for the £ sterling and

53 dalasi for CFA 5000. At Barra Point you'll be offered dalasi from currency dealers at the rate of CFA 5000 = 45 dalasi, but the rate is better in Banjul itself (it should be about CFA 5000 = 50 dalasi – the same as in Ziguinchor). The black market is fairly open and there are no problems. Try around the GPO and McCarthy Square. There are also tourist taxis and the main hotels. Traveller's cheques are also acceptable.

The departure tax for international flights is 20 dalasi.

LANGUAGE
English is the official language. The African languages of Wolof, Mandinka and Fula are also spoken.

GETTING THERE & AROUND
Air
Student discounts of 40% are available with *Nigerian Air* and, to a lesser extent, *British Caledonian*. Concession forms are available from the Education Offices at the end of Buckle St near MacCarthy Square, Banjul. Banjul-Lagos costs 312 dalasi. Officially, stop-overs aren't allowed, but some travellers have had stops included at no extra cost.

Road
Getting into Gambia from Senegal is simplicity itself. There are two points of entry between Koalack and Ziguinchor. The most westerly route will take you from Koalack to Barra, followed by a ferry across the Gambia River to Banjul. There is a government bus (GPTC bus) from Barra to Koalack and Dakar every day at 9 am. To catch it, take the first ferry of the day from Banjul to Barra at 8 am. It costs 10 dalasi or CFA 1000 to Koalack (two to three hours) and 25 dalasi or CFA 2500 to Dakar (four to five hours). In the opposite direction they depart from the Terminus LeClerc in Dakar on Tuesday, Thursday and Saturday at 10 am. The more easterly route follows the Trans-Gambia Highway which connects Koalack and Ziguinchor.

There is no bridge over the Gambia River on the Trans-Gambia Highway, so a ferry crossing is necessary at Mansa Konko. You can also enter from Tambacounda via Velingara to Basse Santa Su at the eastern extremity of Gambia. Velingara to Basse by pick-up will cost CFA 300 and take about one hour. It's a dirt road. You can change CFA into Dalasi either in Velingara or Basse. There is no border control post at this point so you must check in with the police at some point. Some travellers have said there are no problems about this, but others have said they'll stamp you in only for a limited stay and send you to Banjul to get the full period allowed on your visa/stay permit. If you're on a visa and you don't check in with the police, you could overstay without anyone knowing.

If you're heading south for Ziguinchor and/or Guinea-Bissau from Gambia, first take a VW bus or truck from the taxi park near *Uncle Joe's* in Banjul to Brikama (costs 1½ dalasi plus 50 butut for a pack) or a GPTC bus from Banjul to Brikama (1 dalasi plus 50 bututs for a pack) followed by a pick-up truck or taxi-brousse from there to Ziguinchor (CFA 1550 or 16 dalasi plus 2 dalasi for a pack). The road is sealed most of the way and the journey takes about four hours.

Regarding this road, another traveller had this to say:

If you're crossing the border at Brikama you'll probably have to walk the 15 km to the Senegalese side since there's very little traffic. Do the walk in the evening or at night – it's safe and a night walk is an incredible experience. Sometimes the path is only two metres wide and covered by a canopy of forest. The only animals you'll meet are the occasional Mandingo cattle. Arriving at night on the Senegalese side will assure you a free meal and wine from one of the customs officers and a clean room. The mosquitoes are heavy so have a coil handy to burn or repellant. The customs people are very friendly and if you're heading for Ziguinchor they'll stop any car with a spare seat and tell them to take you. You'll *always* get in the first car with a spare seat.

There is a good, paved road from Banjul to Basse on the south side of the river and three government buses run daily along this route as well as many trucks and pick-ups. The fare from Banjul to Georgetown is 10.50 dalasi plus 7 dalasi for a pack, and the journey takes seven hours. Private companies also do the run but check the state of their vehicles first as many break down and end up taking far longer. Otherwise they cost 10 dalasi with no baggage charge. Banjul to Basse by bus is 17.50 dalasi. Buses are comfortable and reasonably fast. In Banjul they go from the junction of Independence Drive and MacCarthy Square.

Boat

The ferry across the River Gambia between Banjul and Barra departs once every two hours in either direction, takes about 20 minutes and costs 1 dalasi. The first ferry leaves at 8 am and the last at 5.30 pm. There are also 'pack-'em-in' pirogues which will take you across in the meantime. They cost 1 dalasi, plus 50 bututs if you want to be carried to the pirogue from further west along Wellington St. They go when full.

One of the most popular trips to take in Gambia used to be the riverboat which plied between Banjul and Basse via Albreda, Kerewan, Tendaba, Balingho, Yellitenda, Sankwia, Kaur, Kuntaur, Sapu, Georgetown and Bansang. The boat was called the *Lady Chilel Jawara*. Unfortunately, the boat sank on 7 December 1984 and it's not known when or if it will be replaced. If it is replaced, the schedule will probably be the same so we're including the old schedule. It departed Banjul every Tuesday at noon and arrived at Basse the following day. It returned from Basse on Thursdays at 2 pm. Arrival times at intermediate towns depended on cargo traffic. Banjul-Basse cost 21 dalasi in deck class (1st- and 2nd-class cabins were also available). Food on board was reasonably priced and the crew

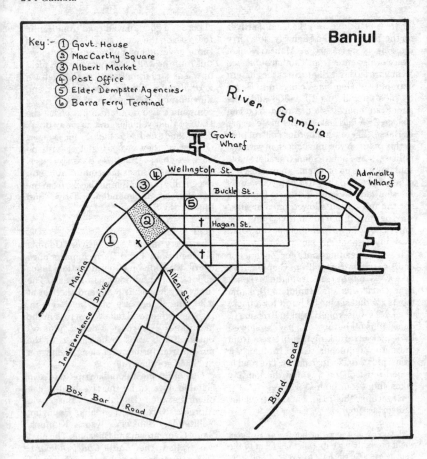

Banjul

Key :-
① Govt. House
② MacCarthy Square
③ Albert Market
④ Post Office
⑤ Elder Dempster Agencies
⑥ Barra Ferry Terminal

River Gambia

Govt. Wharf

Wellington St.

Buckle St.

Hagan St.

Admiralty Wharf

Marina

Independence Drive

Allen St.

Bund Road

Box Bar Road

were friendly. In Banjul, tickets could be bought from the Gambia Ports Authority, Wellington St. If you want to see the ancient stone circles of Wassu, you should get off the boat at Kuntaur.

If you're looking for a passage on a ship to another country, it's worth contacting Mr Dick Parkins, the harbour master. He's friendly and will try to help you out. His office is near the GPA entrance.

BANJUL

After a recent abortive coup, tourism in Gambia hit rock bottom and many of the ritzy hotels were virtually empty, so it was fairly easy to knock the price of a room down to not much more than you would pay in a budget hotel – eg you could get a double room at the *Wadner Beach Hotel* for 45 dalasi and at the *Hotel Palm Grove* for 30 dalasi. However, tourism is beginning to pick up again considerably as the shock waves die down, and you're unlikely to find discounted accommodation during the busier tourist season – October to March.

Of the more rustic hotels, *Uncle Joe's Rest House*, Clarkson St at Dobson, has been popular with travellers for many years and costs 20 dalasi a single or 25 dalasi including breakfast and 30 dalasi a double. The proprietor does also have very tiny rooms without breakfast for 12.50 and 15 dalasi. Another cheapie is the *All City Travellers' Lodge*, 18 Dobson St at Anglesea, which costs 17 dalasi a single and 25 dalasi a double but is part brothel. Be careful of your gear here. Other places which have been recommended are the *Teranga Hotel*, 13 Hill St at Buckle St, which costs 20 dalasi a double with fan; and the *Brikamaba Hotel*, 24 Buckle St at Hill, which costs 30 dalasi a double. The *Apollo Hotel*, 33 Buckle St at Orange, costs 53 dalasi a single and 63 dalasi a double for bed and breakfast, private bath and air-conditioning. It has hot showers and is clean and pleasant. The *Adonis Hotel*, 23 Wellington St at Hill, costs 53 dalasi a single for bed and breakfast, private bath and air-conditioning.

It's possible you might be offered accommodation by VSO or Peace Corps volunteers, but this would be exceptional as they appear to have taken a distinct dislike to travellers over the last couple of years.

If you'd like to stay outside of Banjul on one of the beaches, ask for Alpha in the pub at *Revelations*. He can generally come up with a good place to stay right on the beach at Bakau (15 km from Banjul) for around 12 dalasi per night per person. Taxi vans between Bakau beach and Banjul cost 75 bututs per person. Otherwise, charter a taxi for 15 dalasi and cram it full of people. The *Paradise Bar* on Fijara beach has a happy hour from 5 to 7 pm daily when you can get beers for 2 dalasi.

The *Apollo Hotel* is recommended for an English-style breakfast which costs 2.75 dalasi and for business lunches which cost 3.40 dalasi. For other meals try either the *Restaurant Jobet*, Picton St at the junction with Hagan St, where you can eat for 1 to 4 dalasi, or the *Tropicana Restaurant*, also in the centre of town, which serves fairly good meals. The *Milky Way*, Wellington St, offers great meat and fish pies for 1.50 dalasi. The *Texaco Café* has good Gambian food and is a popular place. Many expatriates hang out at the *Faraja Club* about 15 km from Banjul. If you want to go there it's best to take a taxi. There's no entrance fee and they sell cheap cold beers. The *Bar Texaco* offers good brochettes in pitta bread for 3 dalasi.

It's well worth making a trip to **Fort James** (James Island) while you're in Banjul as well as to Albreda and Juffure. *Wing Afric* in Banjul organises these trips but it's also possible to make your own arrangements and it works out cheaper this way. Get the first ferry from Banjul to Barra at 8 am and then a truck from there to Albreda for 2 dalasi. From Albreda you take a canoe to James Island for 30 dalasi return. The canoe owners wait for you while you have a look around the island. Juffure is a short walk from Albreda and accommodation is available there if you want to stay the night. Beware of tourist touts around Juffure, however, who will offer to take you back to Banjul for 30 dalasi more. You can also make your own way to Juffure and James Island using the Gambia River steamers. Set off early for Juffure on Friday morning by taking the ferry across to Barra, and then take a truck or van to Juffure for 2 dalasi. After midday, make your own way back to nearby Albreda and wait for the *Lady Chilel Tawara* to arrive on its way back to Banjul (if it has been replaced). It normally arrives at Albreda around 3 pm on Friday.

The **National Museum of the Gambia**, next to the Texaco Café in a large white building, is worth a visit. It's open daily.

Useful Addresses
Immigration
  Robson St at Anglesea (1st floor)
Post Office
  Wellington St at Russell (charges 24 bututs per letter collected from poste restante)

Senegal Embassy
    Buckle St at Cameron

Other

If you arrive in Gambia by air at Yundum Airport (the international airport), a taxi to Banjul will cost you 35 dalasi (fixed rate). There are no buses between the airport and Banjul, but the Banjul-Brikama bus passes outside the main airport gate. Take a taxi only to the first bus stop on the main road (about one third of the distance) or to Serrakunda (about one half of the distance), and take the Banjul bus from there.

GEORGETOWN (Makhati)

You'll more than likely be offered a place to stay here, but if you're not then there is a *Government Rest House* for 30 dalasi per person. It's spotlessly clean, has hot and cold water and a lounge and has been described as 'luxury left over from the 1940s.' You'll often have the place entirely to yourself. It's a little expensive but 'worth every butut.' Apply at the police station. There's also the *Educational Centre* rest house at the eastern edge of town which costs 10 dalasi per person. It's clean but there's no electricity or running water.

Georgetown is a good place from which to visit the stone circles at Wassu. Take a bush taxi from here to Kuntaur (1.35 dalasi) and then walk 3½ km from there.

OTHER

If you like a smoke of the dreaded weed, there are minimal hassles in Gambia and it's very easy to find. One recent traveller commented:

In Banjul and Serrakunda the cops will try to book you if you're smoking but the law literally says they have to catch you with the joint between your lips. If that happens, just drop it and squash it and if they book you you just say you weren't smoking.

Ever heard that before? However skeptical you might be, on the other hand, that extract came with a long story which made it all sound very plausible (we can't print that story without identifying individuals – sorry).

Ghana

The area stretching from present-day Guinea to Nigeria has had a long history of civilisation. As early as the 13th century a number of kingdoms arose which were strongly influenced by the Sahelian trading empires such as those of ancient Ghana (present-day Senegal and western Mali), Songhai, Kanem-Bornu and Hausa. The first of these in Ghana itself were the states of Bono and Banda in the northern orchard bush. They gradually expanded south following the course of the Volta River to the coastal grasslands. Penetration of the rain forests didn't take place until the 15th century.

The most well-known and powerful of the kingdoms of Ghana was that of the Ashanti who, by the late 17th century, had conquered most of the earlier states and had begun to turn their attention to controlling the trade routes to the coast. Their capital, Kumasi, was highly organised with facilities and services the equal of most European cities at that time. The ruler, who was known as the Asantehene, employed literate Moslem secretaries from the north to manage trade with the Sahelian kingdoms and to govern distant provinces. As the Europeans became more and more involved on the west coast some of them found employment as advisers to the Asantehene. When the British invaded in the 1870s, for example, a German was engaged to raise and train an army of Hausa troops. Other adventurers involved included a Frenchman who became governor of a province and a

Scots-American who was employed as an economic advisor.

For centuries the focus of trade in West Africa had been away from the coast inland towards the kingdoms which held sway along the Niger River and the edge of the Sahara. Gold, ivory, slaves and salt were the principal elements of this trade, and the dues which cities like Gao, Timbuktu and Djenne extracted from the trans-Saharan caravans carrying these commodities north made them rich and powerful until the 17th century. The event which changed all that and led to these cities' decline was the slave trade to the Americas. Although slaves had been traded along the trans-Saharan routes for centuries, the numbers involved were small in comparison with the vast scale on which the European nations carried it out. In just a short space of time the focus of trade was to be completely reversed so that it centred on the coast and the coastal kingdoms were to grow rich on the proceeds.

Right up until the 19th century there was very little penetration of the interior by Europeans, who relied on the rulers of the coastal kingdoms to deliver their human cargoes to a number of forts which were the collection points. The first of these forts were constructed by the Portuguese in the 15th century and they were soon followed by others built by the British, French, Dutch and Danes. Most were held on a very tenuous basis and depended on good relations being maintained with the local rulers. The forts were frequently overrun and the slavers thrown out or massacred. When slavery was abolished in the early 19th century, however, the Europeans were forced to seek other ways of making profits and this led them to becoming more and more involved in the interior. British interest in the Gold Coast (as Ghana was then known) became paramount after the transfer of the Dutch possessions to the British in 1868.

The British conquest of 'the Gold Coast' was strongly resisted, particularly by the Fante Confederation (an alliance of coastal kingdoms) and the Ashanti and, although Kumasi was sacked in 1874, warfare with that kingdom lasted until 1900. Military conquest didn't, however, extinguish African determination to regain independence, and a number of political parties dedicated to achieving this sprang up in the 1920s and 1930s. Neither these nor the United Gold Coast Convention (UGCC) formed in 1947 were nationally based. They ignored the aspirations of the large numbers of workers attracted to the cities during the boom in public works throughout the 1920s and 1930s. Aware of this, the then-Secretary-General of the UGCC, Kwame Nkrumah, broke away in 1948 to found his own party – the Convention People's Party (CPP), which quickly became the voice of the masses and, for the first time, drew the north into national politics. The slogan of the CPP was 'Self-government now.'

The CPP was an overnight success and Nkrumah's fiery speeches captured the mood of the nation perfectly. Yet rhetoric alone brought no tangible results and Nkrumah, exasperated by the slow progress towards self-government, called for a national strike in 1949. Seeking to contain the situation, the British hauled Nkrumah before the courts and sentenced him to jail. While he was serving his sentence the CPP won the general elections of 1951 and he was released to become leader of the government. Ghana was granted independence in March 1957, the first African country to achieve it from the European colonisers.

Much remained to be done, however, to consolidate the new government's control over the country. Many factional and regional interests surfaced and there was powerful opposition from a number of traditional chiefs and big farmers. A number of repressive laws were passed in

an attempt to contain this opposition and the CPP gradually changed from being a mass party into one which dispensed patronage. Individual and group corruption began to grow. Meanwhile Nkrumah skillfully kept himself out of the fray and became one of the most powerful African spokespeople ever to emerge from that continent. His espousal of pan-Africanism and his denunciations of imperialism and neo-colonialism provided inspiration for other nationalist movements far and wide.

Laudable though his achievements were in that respect, unbridled corruption, intrigue, reckless spending on prestige projects inappropriate to the country's needs, unpaid debts to western creditors, and the expansion of his personal guard into a regiment, were his undoing. In February 1966, while he was in Hanoi, Nkrumah was toppled in a coup led by the army and the police. Describing their coup as essential to save Ghana from a communist dictatorship, the new regime was quickly accorded diplomatic recognition, debts were re-scheduled, emergency aid and supplies were flown into the country and western 'experts' were engaged by the thousand. Three years later the military handed over the leadership to a conservative civilian government headed by Dr Busia. From the start his administration was crippled by the empty treasury, the debts which Nkrumah had left and continuing widespread corruption. It was overthrown in 1972 in another military coup headed by Colonel Achaempong.

The 1972 coup changed nothing. Corruption and mismanagement continued to plague any progress toward economic stability, and continuing civilian exclusion from power began to generate widespread resentment. Instead of going through normal commercial channels, most of the country's cash crops (particularly cocoa) were smuggled across the border into Burkina Faso (then Upper Volta) and Togo. As food shortages became more

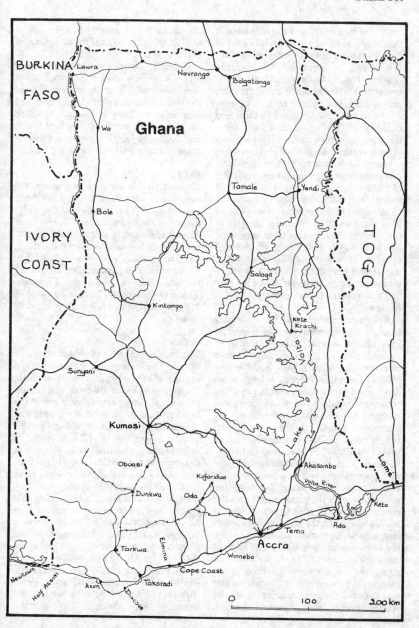

and more desperate and the affluence of the army greater and greater, widespread demonstrations against continued military rule began to break out all over the country. The top brass reacted with all the brutality at their disposal but the reckoning was at hand. Even junior military officers were becoming disillusioned by then, and in May 1979 Flight-Lieutenant Jerry Rawlings called for a confrontation between officers and men in order to root out those responsible for the corruption. Rawlings was court-martialled but his denunciation of the military elite at his trial received widespread publicity and caught the imagination of the country. A week or so later there was a spontaneous uprising of the junior ranks against their superiors. Rawlings was released from his cell and taken to Broadcasting House where he announced that the junior ranks were to take over the government of the country and bring to trial those responsible for its bankruptcy.

Rawling's Armed Forces Revolutionary Council was handed over to a civilian government several months later after general elections, and a major 'house cleaning' operation began. Eight senior officers, including Generals Achaempong, Akuffo and Afrifa, were executed by firing squad and hundreds of other officers and civilian businessmen were tried by impromptu 'people's courts' and sentenced to long periods of imprisonment. The new president, Hilla Limann, was not happy, however, with Rawlings' continued popularity and embarked on a programme of harassing his friends as well as attempting to meddle with the constitution and the composition of the High Court. Detecting a slide back into the old familiar mould, Rawlings began to make speeches warning the population to remain vigilant and not allow the gains of 1979 to be lost. Limann countered by accusing Rawlings of an attempt to subvert constitutional rule and this provoked a second takeover by the Armed Forces Revolutionary Council. Rawlings remains as popular as ever, but it's too early to decide whether he will be able to drag Ghana out of the dire straits it finds itself in.

Ghana's enormous problems were recently made worse by the expulsion of some two million of its nationals from Nigeria in the wake of the oil glut and Nigeria's own financial crisis. Just where all these people will go and where they will find food and jobs is a problem which is going to occupy Ghana for a long time.

FACTS

Most of Ghana consists of wooded hill ranges and wide valleys with a low-lying coastal plain. The damming of the Volta River has created one of the largest lakes in Africa. Humidity is high in the coastal region while the north is hotter and drier. The rainy season stretches from April to September. The population is around 11 million, most of whom are Christian. There are, however, large minorities of Moslems and others following traditional beliefs.

VISAS

Visas are required by all except nationals of the Commonwealth countries, who require Entry Permits (there is little distinction between the two). You cannot get visas or entry permits on arrival at the border, and, because of the continuing political and economic problems in this country, visas can be difficult to get in neighbouring countries too. If you're determined to go to Ghana, try to get your visa before you set off. In London, visas cost £1, you need two photos and they take three days to issue. In Bonn, they cost DM 15 and are issued while you wait. In Lomé, Togo, visas cost CFA 2060; entry permits cost CFA 1030, require four photos and take three days to come through. In Abidjan (Ivory Coast) they cost CFA 2500 and take 24 hours to issue – no fuss. In Ouagadougou (Burkina Faso) they cost CFA 1000 but take two to three weeks to come through. Don't put the word 'transit' on your application form if you want to spend some time in the country; otherwise you'll get three days only (some French travellers were recently given only two days). Also, when you get to the border, tell them you want to stay for as long as your visa says you can stay; otherwise they're likely to knock your stay back down to three days. There is a 14-day limit on most tourist visas and entry permits.

Visa renewals can be obtained from the Ministry of the Interior, near the stadium in Accra. You need two photos and you must either have a letter of invitation from a Ghanaian resident or find someone who knows the immigration officer and is prepared to help you. This isn't as difficult as it might sound. There are a lot of English and German expatriate workers in Ghana who regularly have to go through the same process. Just find one and ask. Don't write 'tourist' on the application form or it will probably be turned down. You can also renew visas at Kumasi, Sekondi and Tamale.

Exit permits are no longer required when leaving Ghana.

There may still be a curfew in force from midnight until 4.30 am daily. There are power cuts every second day from 9 to 6 pm the following night (ie 27 hours on and 21 hours off!). In the north, power can sometimes go off for several days. There are also frequent water stoppages. To compound the difficulties, you never know when the border is going to be closed because of recurring internal crises, and there are also serious shortages of petrol, though the situation has improved recently. In other words, don't expect too much in the way of services. Cameras attract a lot of suspicion and hostility, so you're advised to keep them out of sight.

Ivory Coast visas The embassy is near Danquah Circle. Visas cost 50 cedi, two photos are needed and they take two weeks to issue (the embassy has to telex for clearance). Visas are valid for seven days only.

Burkina Faso visas The embassy is at 2nd Crescent, Asylum Downs. Visas cost US$8 or CFA 2000 – they won't accept cedi.

MONEY

US$1	=	35 cedi
£1	=	50 cedi
CFA 12	=	1 cedi

The unit of currency is the cedi = 100 pesawas. The import/export of local currency is prohibited. Currency declaration forms are sometimes issued on arrival and are supposed to be stamped by the banks when you change money, but they're rarely asked for when you leave. There is a thriving black market despite recent crackdowns on corruption, and everyone seems to be into it. However, be very careful when changing money on the black market, as people are paid to inform and if you're caught they'll throw away the key! Try around Opera Square, the Arts Centre and Makola market. They'll find you. Expect CFA 1000 = 350 cedi but only 320 cedi near the borders, and US$1 = 160 cedi (180 cedi if you're changing US$100).

There are heavy searches at customs so hide well any money you intend to use on the black market. Cedi vouchers have been abolished.

Outside of Ghana, one of the best places to buy cedi is in Lomé (Togo). Depending on where you buy them, you can get up to CFA 1000 = 360 cedi.

As from 1 August 1984, all tourists in Ghana have to pay their hotel bills in hard currency (US$, £ sterling, DM, French or Swiss francs, CFA or Japanese yen). The government has warned hoteliers that if they accept any other currency from foreigners their hotel will be closed down. Nevertheless, taxi drivers, budget hotel owners and traders are still taking cedi, if only because they don't know the value of foreign currencies. Officially, you also have to pay for petrol in hard currency as from the same date.

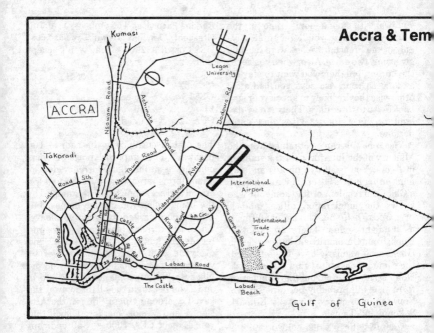

LANGUAGE

English is the official language. The main African languages are Twi, Fante, Ga, Ewe, Dagbeni, Hausa and Nzima.

GETTING THERE & AROUND

Air

If you have too much trouble finding road transport then try flying, which is incredibly cheap if you use money changed on the black market (eg Accra-Tamale for US$6). Current fares are: Accra-Kumasi, 627 cedi return; Accra-Tamale, 1223 cedi return. For international flights, on the other hand, you must pay in foreign currency. Accra-Abidjan costs US$60. If you're looking for external flights, check out *Air India* as they may well offer 30% discounts if you have a student card.

Road

The country is in dire econimic straits; not only have trains ceased to run but even road transport is very difficult to find. You have to stand for hours in bus queues only to miss out when one finally turns up because of bribery and corruption (called *kalabule*). Some examples of fares on state buses are: Accra-Takoradi, 65 cedi; Takoradi-Kumasi, 90 cedi; Kumasi-Busua, 25 cedi; Tamale-Kumasi, 220 cedi; Kumasi-Accra, 180 cedi.

While you're travelling by road there are heaps of police and army checkpoints even along minor routes. Sometimes they just look at your passport, sometimes your luggage (usually not very thoroughly), but occasionally they'll hit you for bribes on some real or invented minor technical infraction of the laws. If this happens pay up or you'll be there all day.

Boat

It is possible to find cargo ships in Tema ar.d Takoradi which are returning to Europe. Expect to pay US$3-4 per day for

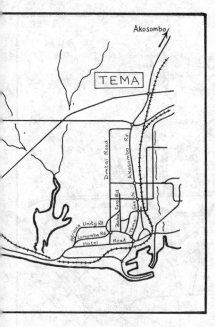

TEMA

Akosombo

Dimtal Road

Akosombo Rd

Batch Farm Rd

Tema South

African Unity Rd

Lumumba Rd

Hotel

Road

a cabin with food included. You'll need time to find a boat.

ACCRA

Mary's House is now closed and both the *YMCA* and *YWCA* are usually chock-a-block with students attending vocational courses. We did, however, receive a letter recently from one of the YWCA's 'World Ambassadors' and she assured us that dormitory space is always set aside for travellers. The charge is 20 cedi per night. The YWCA is on Castle Rd (tel 24700). There are canteen facilities here too. *The Lemon Lodge*, 2nd Crescent next to the Bourkinafasso embassy, has very clean rooms and bathrooms for 180 cedi a single and 220 cedi a double. Meals are available for 100 cedi. Next door is the *Korkdam* which costs 418 cedi a double with own bathroom (hot and cold water). The *Mavis Hotel*, Mango Tree Avenue, costs 180 cedi a single and 200 cedi a double, but is said

to be very dirty and noisy. Other places to try are: *Avenida Hotel*, Kojo Thompson Rd, which costs 480 cedi a double; *Hotel Memorial Nkrumah*, Kojo Thompson Rd, which costs 380 cedi a double but was described by one traveller as 'a hole in the wall'; and the *Crown Prince Hotel*, corner Kojo Thompson Rd and Castle Rd, which costs 120 cedi a single. There's also the *Presbyterian Guest House*, Salem Rd, Kuku Hill, which costs 50 cedi per person. You can cook your own meals here or Dinah will cook for you if you buy the ingredients and the charcoal. If this place is full Dinah knows of another similar place nearby. Similar is the *Methodist Church Headquarters* across from Mobil House; it costs 100 cedi a double.

Information
There is a tourist office on Kojo Thompson Rd but it's more or less defunct.

American Express can be found at Scantravel Ltd, High St, PO Box 1705, Accra (tel 63134/64204).

Taxis around town cost 5 cedi per journey (if you can get one).

The British Council on Liberia Rd has a good reading room and library with current British newspapers and magazines.

Places to Eat
Restaurants are starting to open up again and food can be very cheap depending on what you want to eat – a ball of *fufu* and *banku* costs just 10 cedi. Meat and fish are bought by the piece. *Bus Stop* serves expensive European food most of the week, but on Sundays they have *omo tuo* (rice balls – 10 cedi) and a delicious soup made of fish and meat. The *Sunrise Hotel*, Asylum Downs, also has European food at 200-300 cedi a meal. *Uncle Sam's* has good Lebanese food. There are plenty of cocoa stalls selling bread rolls and cocoa (6 cedi). Many food stalls appear in the evenings which sell very cheap food. There's plenty of choice in the markets if you're putting your own food together.

If you're looking for somewhere to go in

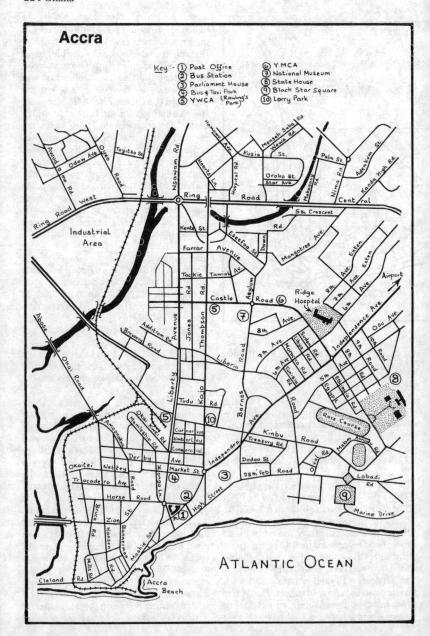

Accra

Key :-
1. Post Office
2. Bus Station
3. Parliament House
4. Bus & Taxi Park
5. YWCA (Rawling's Park)
6. YMCA
7. National Museum
8. State House
9. Black Star Square
10. Lorry Park

ATLANTIC OCEAN

the evenings then try one of the following night clubs: *Le Rev*, near the 'Circle,' has a French owner and Ghanaian prostitutes. *Tip Toe*, also near the 'Circle,' is a dance bar – entry 30 cedi. *Ambassador Hotel* offers live music on Saturday afternoons and costs 30 cedi entry.

KUMASI

Kumasi is the old Ashanti capital and a major cultural centre of Ghana. It was sacked by the British in the late 19th century so don't expect to see it in all its glory. Nevertheless, the **Ashanti Museum** is well worth a visit.

The *Menka Memorial Hotel* has been recommended as a cheap place to stay. It costs cedi 66 per night. Other places which were OK in the past are the *Akuanaba Rest House*, Accra Rd; *Ayigya Rest House*, Accra Rd near the University Hotel; the *Hotel Montana*; and the *Catering Rest House*. The *Presbyterian Church Headquarters* next to the State Transport Yard offers double rooms for 100 cedi. There's also a *YMCA* though it's usually full of students. If you've got time to spare it might be worth visiting the campus of the University of Science and Technology here. You could strike up a friendship with someone who will invite you back – if this should happen, please pay for your keep, as times are very hard for Ghanaian people at present.

NAVRONGO

If you're coming south from Bourkinafasso, this is the first Ghanaian town you will come to. You can usually find accommodation at the *Secondary School* just south of the town.

TAKORADI

Should you find yourself having to spend a night here, try the *Hotel Arvo*. They have rooms for 200 cedi a double but the toilets and showers stink, and the rooms are very dirty and have bed bugs. The *Embassy Hotel* is much cleaner at 120 cedi a single and 150 cedi a double.

OTHER

All the old colonial forts along the coast – **Dixcove, Elmina** and **Pampam** – have been converted into *Rest Houses*. Before Ghana fell on such hard times they were very popular with travellers. They cost cedi 50 per night, but you should make reservations in advance at the West African Museum, Caoe Coast, between Monday and Friday. Elmina has the best facilities. There are no meals available but the caretaker will generally cook a meal for you so long as you provide the food. At Dixcove you can buy shrimp, lobster and tuna from the fishermen. Also, just around the headland from Dixcove at Busua there is a beautiful beach where you can sleep under the coco palms or rent a room in the village. Most of the time you'll have the beach to yourself.

Guinea

Guinea became a French colony in 1891 and was granted independence in 1958 under the leadership of Sekou Toure and his Parti Démocratique de Guinee. For many years, it was one of Africa's most reclusive states and only recently has it begun to open up to the outside world. The reasons for its isolation are largely the result of Sekou Toure's principled stand against French colonialism. Never a man to surrender political objectives for economic considerations, Sekou Toure rejected General de Gaulle's offer of membership in a French Commonwealth as an alternative to total independence, declaring that 'We prefer poverty in liberty to riches in slavery.' He certainly gained the admiration of many other African countries as a result of this stand, but French reaction was swift and vicious. French financial and technical aid was cut off completely, investment in the mining industry ceased, civil archives were destroyed and massive amounts of capital were withdrawn from the country. It's remarkable that the country survived without becoming a Soviet satellite. Yet it did, though the cost was heavy.

After the heady days of independence had worn off, Sekou Toure became more and more obsessed with what he perceived to be opposition to his rule. So-called conspiracies were detected in one group after another, show trials were held, and dissidents and suspects were imprisoned or executed, until by the end of the 1960s there were some 250,000 Guineans living in exile abroad. Toure was never short of would-be counter-revolutionaries, nor did his methods of dealing with them alter very much. At various times he accused both African and other countries around the world of plotting to overthrow him. Among those he accused were the USA, France, the USSR, West Germany and Rhodesia. At least no one could accuse him of undue bias toward any particular power bloc. All the same, while some of the conspiracies were genuine, the majority were merely fantasies, though very useful politically in giving him an excuse to eliminate rivals. Probably the event which had most effect on him was the Portuguese-backed invasion of Conakry by Guinean dissidents in 1970. While the attempt failed, it led to a series of executions and the expulsion of the 100-person West German technical mission – Bonn was accused of amassing a 500-strong group for yet another invasion.

Towards the end of his presidency, however, Sekou Toure was forced to soft pedal in order to attract the capital and technical aid which the country needs to get moving economically and raise its standard of living. His support among the population was also seriously eroded as a result of the witch-hunts of opponents since independence. Relations with France have improved considerably since the visit of Giscard d'Estaing in late 1978 and French aid is now flowing back into the country, but while Toure's policy was one of reconciliation with the west, he was not about to repudiate the east and there are still about 1500 Russian technical experts working in the country.

Since Sekou Toure died and a coup radically altered the composition of the government, Guinea has been accelerating its move back into the western camp. It's now much easier to get into the country and the government is negotiating for entry into the CFA zone.

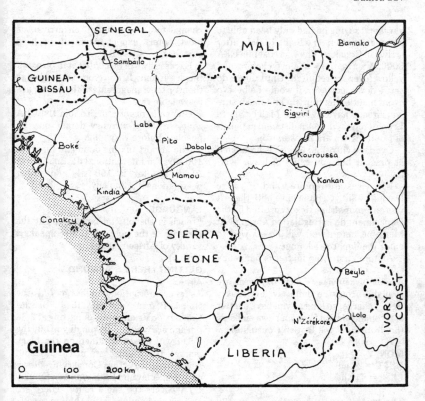

Guinea

0   100   200 km

FACTS

Guinea's geography ranges from humid coastal plains and swamps to the fertile and forested hills and plateaux of the interior. The dry season stretches from November to May, but in the remaining months the country receives up to 430 cm of rain. The majority of the population is engaged in agriculture. There are a number of tribal groups, the most numerous being the Susu of the coastal area, the Malinke and Fula of the centre and north, and the Tenda and Kissi of the east and south. Most of the population is Moslem with only 1% being Christian.

VISAS

Visas are required by all. In the past, most Guinean embassies/consulates demanded a letter of recommendation from your own embassy before they would consider your application. It's now much easier to get visas; indeed transit or tourist visas take just a few hours in Guinea-Bissau. There are consulates at Accra, Algiers, Bissau, Casablanca, Freetown, Lagos, Monrovia and Nouakchott among other places. Visa application experiences still vary quite a lot, but this should sort itself out before very long and become standardised. In Guinea-Bissau transit or tourist visas cost CFA 6000. Most visas have a fixed date of entry. One traveller got a visa in Dakar without much fuss when he explained to the consul that he had to go from Bissau to Freetown (which requires transiting Conakry) and saying he had only been able to get a reservation on a flight 13 days after arrival in Conakry. The visa cost him CFA 3000. Vaccinations against cholera and yellow fever are required. Until things do settle down, however, it would be best to avoid mentioning tourism and make sure you already have a visa for Mali or Sierra Leone if required. Journalists and nationals of South Africa are not admitted.

Overland entry into Guinea is prohibited at present but you can still leave overland.

Exit visas are required and, if you're leaving by air, you must have both the exit visa and your airline ticket certified by the Department de la Regulation Aerienne et Maritime before you will be allowed to enter the departure lounge.

All foreign printed matter is banned.

Guinea-Bissau visas Thirty-day visas are available from the embassy in Conakry free of charge, so long as you have a letter of recommendation from your own embassy (no problem at the British Consulate).

MONEY
US$1 = 24 sily
£1   = 41 sily

The unit of currency is the sily = 100 couris. Import/export of local currency is prohibited. There is a black market for local currency on which you can get CFA 5000 = 2000 sily or US$1 = 250 sily. If you enter from Sierra Leone, you'll find plenty of moneychangers on the border who will offer you 35 sily = leone 1. With a difference of that magnitude you can expect Guinea to be an expensive country if you change at the Mickey Mouse rates offered by the banks.

Currency declaration forms are not issued on arrival.

You have to declare all your foreign currency on entry, and the only convertible currencies as far as the Banque National des Services Extérieurs is concerned are US dollars and French francs. Don't change too much money on arrival, as most hotels expect payment in hard currency.

Excess sily will be confiscated on exit if they're found. If not, you can exchange them on the Senegal side of the border at a reasonable rate.

Guinea is negotiating to join the CFA zone, so these currency details may be obsolete before very long.

The airport tax for domestic flights is 100 sily. For international destinations in Africa the tax is 150 sily. For other destinations it's 200 sily.

LANGUAGE
French is the official language, but the majority of the population also speaks a variety of African languages.

GETTING THERE & AROUND
Air
As far as international flights go, *LIA* (the Guinea-Bissau airline) flies Bissau-Conakry on Friday only, departing at 2.30 pm and arriving at 3.30 pm. If you buy the ticket with pesos obtained on the black market, this flight costs just US$12.50! *Nigerian Airways* flies Conakry-Freetown on Wednesday and Friday, and on Sunday *UTA* covers the same route. There are also air connections with Abidjan, Accra, Banjul, Brazzaville, Brussels, Casablanca, Cotonou, Dakar, Douala, Lagos, Lomé, Monrovia, Moscow, Nouakchott and Paris. From Europe there are cheap flights with *Aeroflot* but it's almost impossible to get a Guinean visa in Europe.

For local flights, *Air Guinee* has one twice a week that connects Conakry with Labe and Sambailo. Conakry-Sambailo costs 3500 sily (one way) and Labe-Sambailo costs 1900 sily (one way). The plane is an Antonov 12 complete with gun turrets. Treat flight schedules as a possibility only, since flights are often cancelled or delayed. The official schedule is as follows:

Wednesday	*Arrive*	*Depart*
Conakry	–	09.45

Sambailo	10.45	11.15
Labe	12.15	12.45
Sambailo	13.25	14.10
Conakry	09.00	-

Friday	*Arrive*	*Depart*
Conakry	–	09.00
Labe	09.40	10.20
Sambailo	10.50	11.50
Labe	12.20	13.20
Conakry	14.00	-

Taxis from Conakry to the Sierra Leone border cost 250 sily and take about three hours. The road is poor but paved, except near the border where it turns into a dirt road. From the border there are buses to Freetown which cost 20 leones and take five to six hours.

Road

Access along the southern route from Guinea-Bissau to Guinea via Cacine and Boke can be problematical, as transport in southern Guinea-Bissau isn't very developed. It's possible to pick up a truck from the truck park at the Medina market in Conakry to Boke for 500 sily or, if you're lucky, a Land-Rover for 900 sily. If you arrive in Boke on Friday, you're in luck as there's a vehicle which goes direct to Bissau on Saturday. If you don't make that connection you'll have to arrange a Land-Rover to Kumbuya for 450 sily. You can get trucks from here to the frontier, but they won't go until they have 50-60 passengers lined up (half the population of the town), so expect several days' delay at least. One traveller was stuck here for what seemed like weeks. He waited for four days and realised that the truck wasn't going anywhere:

On the evening of the fourth day a Land-Rover turned up prepared to do the trip and we set off about 5 pm. Six km down the road it got a puncture and the spare looked as though it wouldn't hold out so we returned for another wheel. This obtained, off we went again. We got four km this time and the carburetor gave up. All attempts at reviving it by jump-starting failed, so we spent the night in the local village and returned to Kumbuya the next morning on foot. I really felt I was destined never to escape from the place. Even so, when the same Land-Rover returned the same morning in working order it was declared unusable in the afternoon.

What saved us in the end was a high-ranking customs official on a mission to the villages right up to the border. He managed to commandeer a very battered Russian-made jeep, at least 15 years old, to do the journey. I doubted if it could ever leave the town but there was no alternative but to risk it. To my disbelief it made it, but what a journey! Eight hours to cover 85 km of rucked and pot-holed road beyond belief, and most of the journey at night as well. Numerous stops both intended and unintended, the former for the official to make his announcements to the bewildered village elders hauled straight from their beds, and the latter due to various mechanical problems.

The frontier here is a river which you get across by dugout whilst being eaten alive by sand flies. The jeep to the border cost 600 sily and the dugout 50 sily.

The northern route is much easier and there are service taxis available from Bafata to Cabu and the Guinean border. You'll probably have to walk from the border to Saidhoboron, the first Guinean town (about 20 km), but from there you'll be able to pick up trucks to Koundara and from there to Sambailo (the latter stretch will cost 50 sily). There are also trucks from Koundara to Tambacounda in Senegal (1250 sily) and to Labe (costs 1200 sily and takes 12 hours – it's mostly a good dirt road).

Rail

The railways also offer limited passenger services. The schedule is as follows:

	Conakry	Kindia	Dabola	Kankan
Tuesday	6.30	10.30	5.50*	10.25*
Friday	7.40*	11.06*	5.15	8.43
	Kankan	Dabola	Kindia	Conakry
Wednesday	4.50	9.40	5.35*	9.23*
Saturday	7.40*	11.20*	5.30	8.39

without * = am
with * = pm

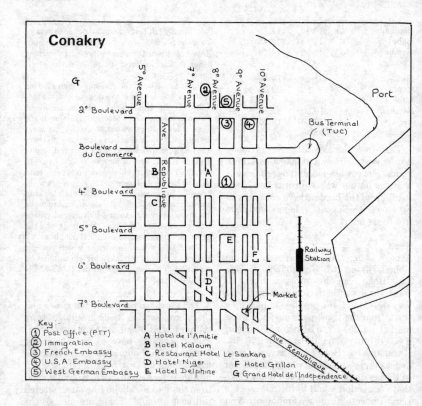

Conakry

Port

Bus Terminal (TUC)

Railway Station

Market

Ave Republique

Key :-
① Post Office (PTT)
② Immigration
③ French Embassy
④ U.S.A. Embassy
⑤ West German Embassy

A Hotel de l'Amitie
B Hotel Kaloum
C Restaurant Hotel Le Sankara
D Hotel Niger
E Hotel Delphine
F Hotel Grillon
G Grand Hotel de l'Independence

The trains are all 2nd-class railcars with buffet service. Take your own food. Conakry to Kankan costs 750 sily one way. The journey can be extremely uncomfortable.

Rail service is offered between Kamsar and Sangaredi north-west of Conakry.

CONAKRY
Whatever you do on arrival here, don't let anyone direct you to either the *Hotel de l'Independence* or the *Grand Hotel de l'Unité*. Both of them charge around US$80 per night. If you have to stay in an expensive hotel, the best place is the *Miriam Makeba* near the airport, but even this will cost you US$30 a night. The Miriam Makeba does have the disadvantage

(?), however, of being noisy – there's music and a discotheque every night.

Finding a cheap hotel (1000-2000 sily) in Conakry can be problematical as most of them appear to be full of semi-permanent residents. Some possibilities near the market and the train station are the *Hotel Niger* (1000 sily); the *Hotel Kalum*; the *Hotel l'Amite* (600 sily); the *Hotel Dolphine*; and a number of bar/restaurants which have a few rooms. If you can't find a cheap room, it's worth asking local people. Someone may rent you a room in their house.

Other reasonably priced hotels which have been recommended are the *Hotel Camayenne* and the *Hotel Gbessia*.

There is an extensive local bus system

in Conakry. Taxis cost 75 sily per journey except to the airport, which costs 300 sily or 600 sily if you are the only person in the cab.

If you have a camera, go to the Office du Tourisme, Place des Martyrs, and get a photograph permit.

For food and entertainment, *Madame Diop's* is almost a national institution and has moderately priced French food. The *Petit Bateau* and the *Escale de Guinee* are both acceptable. The cheapest food (and generally carefully prepared) is to be found in the main market near the Palais du Peuple. The market itself is a very rewarding experience. Local crafts for sale here are more genuinely ethnic than those you will find in Gambia and Senegal. The leather rugs are amazing. Records of Guinean music are very cheap and the music itself incredible. You can hear it any evening in the streets of Conakry, which really come alive at that time of day. You hardly need clubs here – just walk around the streets.

KOUNDARA

This is the Guinea border town with Senegal. Go to the governor's 'palace' here and ask about accommodation. He is a friendly man who will let you stay in one of his rooms for free, though there's no running water. If you need a meal he'll send someone round to take you into town and get a meal for you. There's nowhere else you can stay in this place.

LABE

Hotel de Tourisme at the edge of town on the main road to Conakry costs 450 sily a double but has no running water. Similar is the *Hotel de l'Independence* at the Conakry taxi park (Gare Voiture) which costs 300 sily a single. Again, there's no running water.

SAIDHOBORON

The only possibility here is the *Au Bon Coin*, which has a few beds in the garden for 300 sily per night. It's a very pleasant place.

OTHER

One recent traveller had this to say about the country:

This is a wonderful and very worthwhile, though expensive, country to visit. Try not to be put off by the high prices and bureaucracy. Here more than anywhere else I found a strong African consciousness and I think this country is the kind of Africa most travellers are looking for.

Guinea-Bissau

Guinea-Bissau's long struggle for liberation from the Portuguese was front-page news throughout much of the early 1970s and its political organisation, the Partido Africano da Independencia da Guine e Cabo Verde (PAIGC), provided a model for liberation movements in other parts of the world. PAIGC had its inception in 1956 but it wasn't until 1961 that it resorted to guerrilla warfare in the face of mounting repression by the colonial authorities. Portugal, itself an under-developed nation in comparison with most other European countries, was unable to contain the struggle, so that by the early 1970s about three-quarters of the country had been liberated and the Portuguese armed forces confined to the capital, Bissau, together with a handful of smaller towns and military posts. A network of material and political support was set up for the peasants in the liberated areas and efforts were made to revive the war-ravaged agricultural sector, so that by the time independence was unilaterally declared in 1973 virtually all the necessary preparations had been made for post-independence administration. Although the new government was recognised by most countries around the world, it wasn't until Salazar was toppled several months later that the Portuguese finally withdrew from the country.

Many of PAIGC's leaders actually came from the Cape Verde islands and the party was committed not only to the liberation of Guinea-Bissau and Cape Verde but to

unification between the two. Efforts were being made to bring this about in 1980 when President Luiz Cabral was overthrown in a coup by Prime Minister Joao Vieira while senior army commanders were away in Praia, the capital of Cape Verde. The country has been ruled since then by Vieira and the idea of unification was dropped. The coup also had the effect of replacing the *mestica* (mixed race) leadership with Africans.

Since independence, Guinea-Bissau has slipped into relative obscurity but great efforts have been made to get it back on its feet. It's a slow process but the country has attracted many volunteer workers from various parts of the world, particularly northern Europe. Though all PAIGC's military aid during the war of liberation came from Russia, China and Cuba, the government has largely adopted a non-aligned policy, and, in fact, since liberation its major source of aid has come from the west. Portugal is its largest trading partner by far, taking some 60% of its exports and providing about 40% of its imports. Likewise, the volume of trade with both Sweden and France is about the same as it is with the Soviet Union.

Historically, contact with Portugal was made as early as the 1440s when trading and raiding parties arrived on the coast in search of slaves. As in many other parts of its former empire, Portugal was content for many centuries to control just the coastal area and was only prompted into laying claim to the interior in the latter part of the 19th century when Africa was being carved up between the industrialised nations of northern Europe. Indeed, both the British and French established trading posts on the Guinea-Bissau coast at this

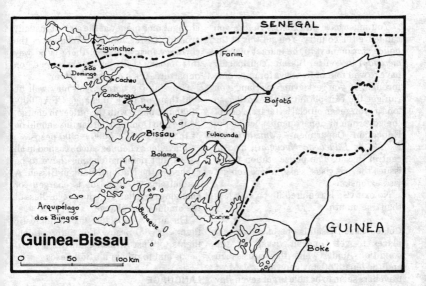

Guinea-Bissau

time and Portuguese claims were not recognised until 1884. Actual control of the interior was not established until 1915 and even then pockets of resistance held out until as late as 1936.

Guinea-Bissau was almost impossible to visit for many years following independence unless you were a member of a volunteer organisation. Tourism was not encouraged. This is now rapidly changing, with visas being easy to obtain in Banjul (Gambia). Nevertheless, you're unlikely to meet many other travellers there.

FACTS

Much of the country is low-lying with numerous rivers, mangrove swamps and rain forest giving way to savannah further inland. Only on the border with Guinea does the land begin to rise. The rest of the country consists of numerous offshore islands. Rainfall is heavy, especially on the coast, and it's generally hot and humid. The coolest months are December and January, and the hottest are April and May. The average temperature is around 20°C.

VISAS

Visas are required by all. It is possible to get visas in some European countries where there is an embassy (eg Portugal and Sweden), but probably the most convenient places to get them are Dakar (Senegal) and Banjul (Gambia). In Dakar visas cost CFA 2000 for a two-week stay and take three days to issue. You must specify the date of entry. In Banjul they cost 15 dalasi and are issued while you wait or within 24 hours. No photos are required. While the ambassador in Banjul is very friendly, he can be a little careless. One traveller was deported to Senegal recently after three days in the country when it was discovered that the ambassador had filled in the visa form incorrectly. The police thought the traveller had falsified the form. Other than this there are no problems.

Three-month residence permits are fairly easy to obtain from immigration. You need to say that you've found a job but are waiting for papers. They take three to six days to come through, require three photos and cost 250 pesos.

You must have an exit visa before you can leave the country. You get this at the police station next to the market place (o mercado) in central Bissau. You usually have to wait four or five days for it to come through. If you're leaving overland you can get the exit permit at the border so long as you get an official letter from one of the government departments such as the Education Department (Ministerio de Estado da Educacao Nacional), also in central Bissau. The police station which issues the exit visas is also where you get visa extensions.

No exit visa is required if you stay less than one month.

Guinea visas Bissau is one of the easiest places to get Guinean visas, but the conditions under which they are issued and the length of stay you get vary. Most travellers seem to be able to get seven-day transit visas which are free and issued the same day, but they have a fixed date of entry. Others have had to pay CFA 5000 for a three-day visa which, like the others, has a fixed day of entry. Don't mention tourism when you apply, and make sure you have visas for Mali or Sierra Leone beforehand if needed. Overland entry into Guinea is prohibited at present.

MONEY
US$1   = 888.2 pesos
CFA 1000 = 239 pesos

The unit of currency is the peso da Guiné-Bissau = 100 centavos. Import/export of local currency is prohibited. There is a black market on which you can get CFA 1000 = 700 pesos in Bissau (ask around in the marche opposite the USA embassy or approach Senegalese people but avoid Mauritanian shopkeepers) and CFA 1000 = 800 pesos in Ziguinchor (Senegal). Ask at the Hotel Balkady or in the Grand Marche in the latter place. Thorough searches of baggage are made on entry but body searches are very rare.

If you arrive by air you will have to change some money at the airport (usually around CFA 20,000). Whatever the currency form may say, there is no way this money will be re-exchanged on departure. It's a one-way system.

Crossing the border, you may well be told that you have to change CFA 3000-5000 into pesos with the officer in charge. At the Sao Domingo border this should be at the rate of CFA 5000 = 900 pesos.

Traveller's cheques can be cashed in all banks, but personal cheques have to be cashed in the National Bank in Bissau. A commission of 25 pesos is charged for changing traveller's cheques regardless of the amount you change.

The airport departure tax for domestic flights is 85 pesos. For international flights to West African countries it's 210 pesos and to others it's 350 pesos.

LANGUAGE
Portuguese is the official language but African languages are also spoken as well as Crioulo. If you want to make a good impression on people here, it helps to speak a shambles of Wolof.

GETTING THERE & AROUND
Air
There are flights from Bissau to Conakry (Guinea) every Friday which cost 6025 pesos. No questions asked.

There are also flights to some of the offshore islands by LIA.

Destination	Frequency	Airline
Lisbon	Wed, Fri	TAP (Portuguese)
Nouadhibou	Fri	Aeroflot (USSR)
Casablanca	Fri	Aeroflot
Dakar	Mon, Sat	LIA (Guinea-Bissau)
	Wed, Fri	Air Senegal
Ziguinchor	Wed, Fri	Air Senegal
Conakry	Fri	LIA
Sal (Cape Verde)	Wed, Fri	TAP

If you're heading to Guinea after

Guinea-Bissau, the *LIA* flight is almost a giveaway at about US$12.50 purchased with pesos bought on the black market. In any case, overland entry into Guinea is prohibited at present.

Road

There are two ways you can enter the country from Senegal: one is from Ziguinchor to Bissau via Sao Domingo, Cacheu and Canchungo (Teixiera Pinto) in the west, and the other is from Sedhiou to Bissau via Farim further east. Along the latter route the road from Sedhiou to the border (Cuntima) is good during the dry season but bad during the wet season.

From Ziguinchor to Sao Domingo there are service taxis for CFA 500. At Sao Domingo there is a daily ferry across the river to Cacheu at noon which costs 150 pesos and takes two hours. If you're leaving Guinea-Bissau for Senegal there is a 2½-peso exit fee at Sao Domingo. From Cacheu there are occasional trucks to Canchungo which cost 50 pesos and take about one hour – you may have to wait around a while for one of these trucks. From Canchungo you take a truck to Safim (75 pesos) where there is a ferry across the River Mansoa. The ferry costs 15 pesos. If the ferry is out of fuel – something which happens quite regularly – then you get across the river by canoe. It's costs the same. From the other side there are trucks into Bissau for 40 pesos.

An alternative to the above route is a bus from Ziguinchor to the Ingore border for CFA 1250, then a walk to Ingore (about one hour). In Ingore you must go to the police to get a *Visto Entrada*. From Ingore you get a truck to the first ferry point and then a taxi-brousse to Bissau. Total fares inside Guinea-Bissau would be 350 pesos.

In Bissau, long-distance taxis and buses leave from the market. The taxis service most of the smaller towns all over the country, depart several times a day and are inexpensive (eg Bissau-Canchungo costs 100 pesos). The buses, which are Volvos manufactured in Norway in 1977

and given to the country by Sweden's SIDA and Norway's NORAD, service the larger towns and are also inexpensive. They usually only have one departure per day, and if you want to be sure of getting on, be at the market by 7 am.

Overland entry into Guinea is prohibited at present so you'll have to take the US$12.50 Bissau-Conakry flight (see above). In case the border opens again in the near future, here are details of how it used to be possible. The southern route into Guinea via Cacine and Boke can be problematical, as transport in southern Guinea-Bissau isn't so well developed. The northern route is much easier and there are service taxis from Bafata to Cabu and the Guinean border. From the border you will probably have to walk the 20 km to Saidhoboron, the first Guinean town, as there's usually only one car or so per week between Guinea-Bissau and Guinea via Buruntuma. From Saidhoboron there are occasional trucks to Konndara and from there to Sambailo (50 sily), Tambacounda in Senegal (1250 sily), and Labe. The road between Koundara and Labe is very bad and can take up to three days by truck. If you don't fancy the trip there is a plane twice a week from Sambailo to Labe and Conakry, which works out to be very cheap if you pay with money changed on the black market (Sambailo-Conakry costs 1120 sily).

Boat

In addition to the ferries on the road from Ziguinchor to Bissau, there is a daily ferry from Bissau to Bolama, the old capital, which costs 150 pesos, takes three hours and leaves at high tide. It's liable to be cancelled without notice if the tide isn't right, as the ferry has to cross a sandbar on the way to the island. Tickets should be bought in advance from the Guinea Mar office, 21A Rua Guerra Mendes near the dock. There are other boats to Bolama from the same place which leave on Monday, Wednesday and Thursday and return on Friday and Sunday.

Between Bissau and Bafata there are ferries which call at many smaller places en route. They cost 120 pesos and take five to eight hours.

Food is in very short supply in many places and is rarely sold 'over the counter,' but the situation has improved a lot lately and the market in Bissau now has bananas, onions and peppers for sale.

BAFATA

You can get accommodation here at the Apartmentos next to the *Pensao Transmontana* for 300 pesos per day. The rooms are good and clean. You can buy meals at the Pensao for 120 pesos.

BISSAU

Bissau, the capital, is a very small town of about 40,000 inhabitants. The simplest way to get around is on foot. The main street is Avenida Amilcar Cabral, which also leads to the marketplace. There's almost no traffic and, because of this, it's one of the most pleasant of all African capitals. Make sure you stop what you're doing and stand to attention when the flag is lowered daily to the sound of the bugle.

If you're planning on staying in Bissau for a while (a week or more), your best bet is to visit the Centro de Informacao e Turismo near the Ministry of Education. They have a list of private houses where you can get board and lodging, which will work out considerably cheaper than staying in an hotel. One traveller who did this recently stayed in a house near the mercado which cost 1000 pesos per week for full board. Doing it this way, you have no problems finding food. The tourist office which arranges these rooms is one of the friendliest in Africa. Don't be surprised if you get coffee and cakes when you call in (all on the house).

Otherwise, the cheapest place to stay is the *Hotel do Portugal*, Praca Che Guevara, which costs 550 pesos but is usually full. Whilst you're here you might meet Manu de Carvalho, who lives in one of the larger rooms on the first floor and is one of the only three bakers in town. If he takes a liking to you he may let you sleep on the floor free of charge. You have more chance of getting a room at one of the following: *Hotel Tamar*, Avenida 12 de Setembro at Rua 3, costs 600 pesos a double for a clean room with a balcony.

Pensao Centrale, Amilcar Cabral near the bank, is 500 pesos including three meals. This is where many volunteers stay until they find a house to rent.

Grand Hotel, Amilcar Cabral behind the cathedral, costs 495 pesos. It's a little bit old fashioned but still good.

Hotel Ronda, Amilcar Cabral opposite the church, charges 300 pesos a double.

There's an unmarked pensao at 23A Amilcar Cabral which costs 300 pesos. The most expensive place in town is the *Hotel 24 de Setembro* at 1650 pesos a double including tax. The swimming pool is filled intermittently, usually only halfway, so don't dive in. A new hotel is under construction in the main street about 100 metres from the cathedral.

Many hotels charge an additional 'service charge' of 5 to 10% which is not mentioned until you leave.

There are a lot of volunteer workers in Bissau as well as in the countryside, and since travellers are few and far between, one of them may well offer you somewhere to stay.

Shortages are still the order of the day, so don't expect too much in the way of food and consumer items.

You're supposed to have a permit if you want to take photos, but you may be given a run-around for this. Travellers have been referred to the Mercado Police Station, who then refer you to the Ministry of Information. It's worth trying to get a permit because Bissau is one of the most attractive towns in West Africa.

There are a number of cheap restaurants, but none of them are marked. One is at the marketplace (*o mercado*). Here you can get fish, rice and hot boiled milk with

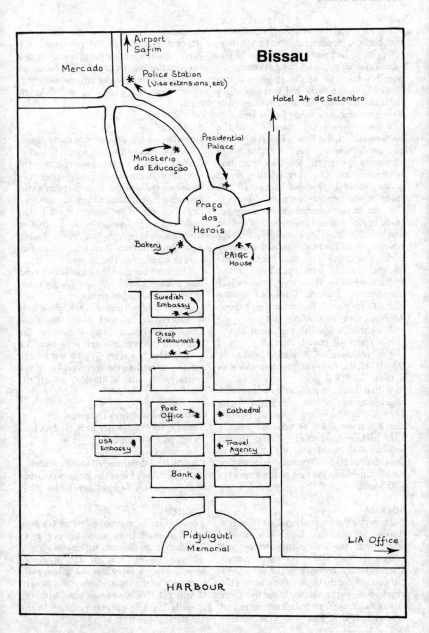

sugar for 30 pesos. Another, situated in the harbour area near the LIA office, offers large fish and as much rice as you can eat for 50 pesos. A third restaurant – possibly the best of the three – is two blocks from the cathedral and one block from the Swedish embassy towards the American embassy. It has fish or veal with rice for 90 pesos. On either side of the bottom end of the Praca dos Herois are two small cafés which serve coffee, small sandwiches, beer and shellfish according to availability. The only trouble about getting one of those scarce beers in Bissau (even at the two un-named litte bars) is that the Russian technicians usually get there before you and reserve six of the six and a half crates for themselves! Beers cost 30 pesos. There's an excellent bakery which has delicious cakes, bread, sandwiches, shrimps, beer and coffee in the Praca dos Herois. Otherwise, you can buy bread at the *Padaria Cashew* near the Hotel Portugal at 5 am and at the *Padaria Africana* near the stadium at 5 pm.

A meal of soup, fish and meat at the *Grand Hotel* will cost 412 pesos.

The **Museum of African Artifacts** in PAIGC House has been recommended as a 'must.'

Within Bissau there is a city bus service which consists of two old buses – one French and the other Belgian. There's also a taxi service. The taxis are usually Faf N'Haye (a small Guinea-Bissau produced Citroen) and are blue. The usual fare is 10 to 50 pesos depending on the distance, but the fare to the airport is 150 pesos.

BOLAMA

Bolama was the original capital of Guinea-Bissau in colonial days. It's now a crumbling, overgrown ruin which will delight those who like such places. There's no accommodation on the island, but you can camp on the beach across the other side of the island from the town (about five km). Your gear is safe here, but beware of the deadly green mamba

dropsnakes which live in the trees. (Recent reports say the government is carrying out a culling programme so that tourists don't get put off.) For food, ask the locals if they know anyone willing to cook you a meal – someone will help you out.

BUBAQUE

One of the outer offshore islands, Bubaque is being developed as the 'tourist island' of Guinea-Bissau. To get there you take the ferry from Bissau which usually goes once a week on Saturdays and returns the following day. It costs 175 pesos one way. If you decide to go straight back to the mainland on the same ferry, it's free as there's nowhere you can buy a ticket. Apart from the ferry there are flights twice a week which cost 250 pesos.

There is a hotel on the island or you can stay at the *Swedish Mission*. Meals at the hotel are reasonably cheap.

The offshore islands are definitely worth visiting if you have the time. Outside of Bolama and Bubaque, the islands are more or less untouched and life is very close to nature. Watch out for the mamba as well as the tree version of the cobra (white with a black motif on the head).

CABU (formerly Nova Lamenga)

There's only one hotel here. It has four rooms so it's often full.

CANCHUNGO (formerly Teixiera Pinto)

If you get stuck here, the large restaurant in the main square has a few beds.

CACHEU

There is no accommodation in Cacheu, and although it is easy to get from Ziguinchor to Bissau in one day, it's difficult to do this in the opposite direction as the ferry leaves Cacheu early in the day so the chances are you'll miss it. If you get stuck you can stay with the friendly US AID workers or camp in the old Portuguese fort.

OTHER

If you want work voluntarily in Guinea-Bissau, ask at the Ministerio da Educacao near the only high school in town. They'll find you a place to live free of charge. If you want to work in Bissau itself you'll probably get an excellent room at the former hotel (*Estabelecimentos Ancar*), 200 metres from the cathedral and 100 metres from the American embassy.

Should you be wondering what Guinea-Bissau is like, this extract from a letter by Tony Nagypal (Norway) who spent two months there recently may interest you:

To me Guinea-Bissau seems to be something quite different from 'French' West Africa (so far I've been to all West African countries). It's much more friendly. It's very poor, but very well organised. Absolutely no corruption, hardly any begging (very few people are as poor as the beggars of Bamako or Ouagadougou). The streets within Bissau are always clean. It's 100% safe to travel in the country and when I was in Bissau and had nowhere to sleep I simply slept on the pavement in the harbour district.

No dope. No prostitution. No Coca-Cola. No police or military road blocks (except one small post in Safim near the ferry).

Another, more recent letter confirmed that the people were very friendly so long as you were not in transit – 'I had quite a rough time travelling through places with just a one-hour stop (no violence) but it was fabulous in the bush' – but suggested that Tony had got a few things wrong:

It's bullshit to say there's no dope or prostitutes in Bissau. I spent many a long night watching thunderstorms from the roof of X completely blown to the very marrow of my bones and brains. Though I admit it's difficult to find and *very risky* – there's a 25-year jail sentence which makes it very doubtful to try unless you know the place and the people very well. Bissau is a big knocking shop contrary to what friend Nagypal stated. Take a 50-peso cab and ask for the 'putas' and they'll take you to a whole street full of whores. Prices range from 100 pesos for a short encounter to 800-1200 pesos for a whole night. Bargaining necessary.

Ivory Coast

The Ivory Coast lives and breathes in the image of Felix Houphouet-Boigny, a doctor and wealthy planter who has been the country's president since independence from France in 1960. Along with a few colleagues, Houphouet-Boigny founded the Syndicat Agricole Africain in 1944 to protest the colonial authorities' preferential treatment of French planters in the recruitment of farm labour. The pressure group soon acquired a broader appeal, leading to mass demonstrations in Abidjan during 1948 to 1949 in favour of greater African participation in the colony's administration. Fifty-two people were killed and over 3000 arrested during those years, but in the face of continued repression by the French authorities, and having gained the commodity price increase his group had campaigned for, Houphouet-Boigny adopted a more conciliatory approach. The change of tack certainly paid off as far as his political career was concerned, but it also led to the Ivory Coast becoming a classic case of neo-colonialism.

There were few contacts between the peoples of the Ivory Coast and Europe before the early 19th century. Most of the trading and slaving took place east of the area. In the 1840s, however, the French embarked on a systematic plan to give French traders a commercial monopoly in the region and a number of treaties were signed with local chiefs. These treaties formed the basis for the French claim to the area in the 1890s when Africa was being carved up by the Western European nations. French colonial policy in the Ivory Coast was based on stimulating the production of cash crops – cocoa, palm oil, timber and bananas – and to make sure there would be a sufficient supply of labour on the plantations established by French expatriates. To implement this a 'head tax' was imposed on the indigenous population in 1903. This measure together with large-scale forced labour used for the construction of roads, railways and public buildings not only led to considerable suffering and social dislocation but to a mass exodus from the Agni region to Ghana. Despite this early set-back, indigenous planters had begun to play an important part in cocoa and coffee cultivation by the late 1930s, though a third of the land under these crops and all of the land under bananas and the timber operations remained in French hands.

Concessions have been made to African aspirations since then – or at least to certain sections of the African population – but precious little else has changed. After a brief flirtation with Marxism, Houphouet-Boigny rejected the ideas of 'revolution' and the 'class struggle' on the grounds that classes did not exist in the Ivory Coast. That may have been true at the time but it certainly no longer applies. Unrestricted reliance on foreign and local private enterprise and the large-scale repatriation of profits has resulted in affluence for a minority but also in a wide gap between those who have and those who have not. The country has also had to face a labour crisis brought on by the government's refusal to subsidise workers migrating from Bourkinafasso and a very serious balance of payments deficit.

The Ivory Coast still continues to support trade and 'dialogue' with South Africa and, until Robert Mugabe took over in Zimbabwe, it maintained quiet trade links with Ian Smith's Rhodesia.

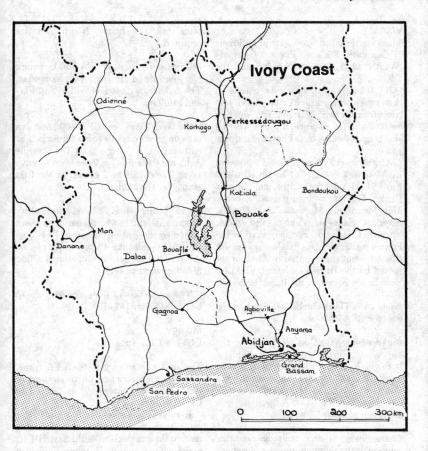

Ivory Coast

Politically, while the Ivory Coast is one of the most stable of African countries, it may be headed for drastic changes. No obvious successor to Houphouet-Boigny has emerged; Phillipe Yace, who was groomed for this position, was recently dumped, having become very unpopular as a result of underhand methods he used to maintain his own and the president's position. Meanwhile, inflation and the effect of oil price hikes have begun to seriously erode the affluence of the elite and make life even more difficult for the poor.

FACTS

There is a marked difference between the north and the south of the country. The south is largely equatorial rain forest with an average temperature of around 27°C and plenty of rain. The dry season in the north runs from November to April. The population stands at about eight million and consists of more than 60 different tribes. In addition to the indigenous population there are large numbers of expatriate workers from Burkina Faso, Mali, Guinea, Benin, Togo and Senegal, plus many French and Lebanese people.

VISAS

Visas are required by all except nationals of Denmark, Finland, France, Germany (West), Italy, Norway, Sweden and the UK.

If you need to apply for a visa extension then make sure you look like you've just come from Yves St Laurent. You won't be entertained, for instance, if you're wearing shorts or a sweaty shirt. They'll just throw you out.

African countries maintaining embassies in Abidjan are Algeria, Benin, Burkina Faso, CAR, Egypt, Ethiopia, Gabon, Ghana, Guinea, Guinea-Bissau, Liberia, Mali, Mauritania, Morocco, Niger, Nigeria, Rwanda, Senegal, Tunisia and Zaire. Visas for Chad and Togo are issued by the French embassy. Visas for Commonwealth countries not represented in Abidjan are issued by the British embassy. Visas for Somalia are issued by the Italian embassy.

Benin visas These can be issued while you wait for CFA 2500.

Burkina Faso visas Don't be put off by the appearance of the embassy in Abidjan. It might look like a chicken farm/wood yard/car-breakers yard, but you can get a visa here in 48 hours if you want more than five days. It will cost CFA 3000 and you need two photos.

Ghana visas Ghana isn't encouraging tourism at the moment and visas are hard to come by. Even a two- to three-day transit visa can take a week to come through and costs CFA 2000. A tourist visa can take up to 10 days to come through. Not only that, but they're a miserable set of bastards in the embassy so expect hassles.

Guinea-Bissau visas These cost CFA 2000, require two photos and take 24 hours.

Liberian visas These cost CFA 4000 and are sometimes issued on the spot but often take 48 hours. No photos are required.

Mali visas These cost CFA 5000, require two photos and are issued the same day. The embassy is closed on Friday, Saturday and Sunday.

Niger visas Visas cost CFA 3000 and can take up to six days to come through. The embassy is in Marcory on the Avenue Achalme (take bus No 00 east on Avenue 16 in Treichville and get off at the first stop after the bridge.

Sierra Leone visas These, and entry permits (Commonwealth nationals), are issued by the British embassy. They cost CFA 3600 and take 48 hours. No photos are required. There is sometimes a fuss about onward tickets.

The addresses of the embassies are to be found under 'Abidjan.'

MONEY

US$1 = CFA 454

The unit of currency is the CFA franc. There is no restriction on the import of local currency, but export is limited to CFA 100,000.

Barclays Bank gives consistently better rates than local banks for exchanging money (in comparison with, say, BICIC and Société General). Barclays Bank is in the tall building named 'SIB.'

LANGUAGE

French is the official language. The main African languages are Dioula, Baoule and Bete.

GETTING THERE & AROUND

Road

Hitching is fairly easy on the main routes, which are generally in good shape and often surfaced, but it's not worth the waiting on minor roads. There is a good network of buses and taxis between the major centres of population as well as to the borders of Mali and Ghana. Going to or from Burkina Faso, most people take the train which connects Abidjan with Ouagadougou. On the other hand, the new luxury buses are fast, clean and only nominally more expensive than the trains.

Abidjan-Man costs CFA 3000 by regular bus or CFA 6000 plus CFA 500 by taxi and takes seven to eight hours. The buses depart from Man at 6 am daily. It's a good sealed road all the way. Both the buses and taxis leave from the Gare Routiere in Adjame early in the morning. Man-Danane by truck costs CFA 1000 and takes about three hours. There are also buses twice a day between Abidjan and Danane which cost CFA 5000 and take about 10 hours. From Danane to the Liberian border there are buses for CFA 600 plus CFA 50 which take 1½ hours. From the border you first take a taxi to Kahnple and from there a truck to Sanniquelle. You may also be able to pick up shared taxis between the border and Sanniquelle for US$1.50-2. Make sure your papers are in order on this border. The officials go through them minutely looking for anything that's wrong or out of date. If they find anything it's going to cost you money.

Abidjan-Bondoukou costs CFA 3000 and takes about nine hours. Transport leaves from the Texaco station at Avenue 8 and Rue 17 daily at 8 am.

There are daily luxury buses from the Gare Routiere in Adjame, Abidjan. Some examples of the fares are: Abidjan-Ferkessedougou CFA 3500; Abidjan-Odienne CFA 5500; Abidjan-Bouake CFA 2500.

To/From Mali

There are two road routes to Mali, one via Man, Odienne and Bougouni, and the other via Ferkessedougou and Sikasso. The first generally takes longer as there is very little traffic and no buses between Odienne and Bougouni. Apart from this, the bridge at Manankaro in Mali is under

water throughout August. If you take the latter route, it's probably better to take the train from Abidjan to Ferkessedougou first and then go by road from there. There is also a once-weekly bus between Bouake and Bamako. Coming from Bamako, this bus leaves on Tuesdays when full, costs CFA 13,925 and takes about 36 hours. Buses between Ferkessedougou and Sikasso cost CFA 7000 and take about 11 hours. If you're hitching along this stretch, there are a number of police checkpoints where you can enlist help in finding a lift.

To/From Ghana

Until fairly recently the usual route to Ghana followed the coast road via Grand Bassam, Assini, Newtown (border), Half Assini and Jewi Wharf. It's still possible to go this way but this involves a lot of messing about and so takes longer. There are daily buses between Abidjan and Grand Bassam (CFA 400) and between Grand Bassam and Assini (CFA 900). From Assini you take a boat (CFA 350 but bargain hard) to the other side of the lagoon and then walk 14 km along a beautiful stretch of beach to the border at Newtown. You then take a bus to Half Assini (30 cedi). The immigration people here may not have a stamp (times are hard even for bureaucrats), in which case they'll go with you to Jewi Wharf by bus (45 cedi). If you get stuck at Half Assini for the night, you could try the Happy Hotel, which is grubby but cheap at 70 cedi. If you don't want to make all the above changes, there's also a boat from Grand Bassam to Jewi Wharf via the lagoons which costs CFA 3000 and takes eight hours. A variation of this coastal route involves going via Aboisso (CFA 900) and others from there to Frambo (border) for CFA 500. From Frambo to Jewi Wharf there are daily ferries for CFA 1500 including the charge for your pack. If you prefer to take taxis along this route, the total cost between Frambo and Abidjan will be around CFA 4500.

Abidjan-Ouagadougou

Train Name/Number & Type

	Rapide No 1	Rapide No 3	Rapide No 5	Express No 11	Autorail No 21	Autorail No 23
Treichville	10.20 am	4.20 pm	5.55 am	2.10 pm	7.00 am	12.30 pm
Abidjan	10.28 am	4.28 pm	6.02 am	2.21 pm	7.08 am	12.37 pm
Agban	10.38 am	4.38 am	6.12 am	2.36 pm	7.20 am	12.48 pm
Anyama	–	–	–	3.05 pm	7.50 am	1.14 pm
Yapo	–	–	–	3.57 pm	8.36 am	1.48 pm
Agboville	11.57 am	5.58 pm	7.31 am	4.17 pm	8.55 am	2.30 pm
Dimbokro	1.32 pm	7.28 pm	9.00 am	6.05 pm	10.28 am	4.28 pm
Bouake	3.45 pm	9.20 pm	11.20 am	8.55 pm	12.55 pm	6.54 pm
Latiola	4.42 pm	–	1.55 pm	10.08 pm	1.55 pm	-
Tafire	6.37 pm	–	2.27 pm	0.36 am	4.05 pm	-
Ferkessedougou	8.05 pm	–	3.55 pm	2.25 am	5.08 pm	-
Ouangolodougou	8.52 pm	–	4.44 pm	3.20 am	–	-
Niangoloko	9.55 pm	–	5.55 pm	4.55 am	–	-
Banfora	10.40 am	–	6.47 pm	5.51 am	–	-
Bobodioulasso	0.40 am	–	8.28 pm	8.40 am	–	-
Siby	3.16 am	–	–	12.08 am	–	-
Koudougou	4.30 am	–	–	1.40 pm	–	-
Ouagadougou	5.45 am	–	–	3.15 pm	–	-

	Autorail No 43	Autorail No 45	Autorail No 61	Autorail No 63	Rapide No 9
Treichville	7.25 am	4.40 pm	–	–	-
Abidjan	7.33 am	4.47 pm	–	–	-
Agban	7.45 am	5.03 pm	–	–	-
Anyama	8.14 am	5.36 pm	–	–	-
Yapo	9.12 am	6.28 pm	–	–	-
Agboville	9.45 am	6.57 pm	–	–	-
Dimbokro	12.32 pm	9.07 pm	–	–	-
Bouake	3.03 pm	–	6.20 am	–	-
Latiola	–	–	7.10 am	–	-
Tafire	–	–	10.10 am	–	-
Ferkessedougou	–	–	11.50 am	6.35 am	8.45 am
Ouangolodougou	–	–	12.43 pm	7.27 am	9.30 am
Niangoloko	–	–	1.55 pm	8.42 am	10.32 am
Banfora	–	–	3.20 pm	9.40 am	11.15 am
Bobodioulasso	–	–	5.53 pm	11.41 am	1.02 pm
Siby	–	–	–	6.27 pm	3.47 pm
Koudougou	–	–	–	7.54 pm	5.05 pm
Ouagadougou	–	–	–	9.32 pm	6.17 pm

Notes

Couchettes are available on train Nos 1, 2, 11 and 12 except on Sunday (No 11) and Tuesday (No 12). Restaurant cars are attatched to train Nos 1, 2, 11, and 12 except on Sunday (No 11).

Ouagadougou-Abidjan

	Train Name/Number & Type					
	Rapide No 2	*Rapide* No 4	*Rapide* No 6	*Express* No 12	*Autorail* No 22	*Autorail* No 42
Ouagadougou	7.35 pm			7.15 am		
Koudougou	8.56 pm			8.58 am		
Siby	10.07 pm			10.30 am		
Bobodioulasso	0.55 am		6.00 am	2.20 pm		
Banfora	2.40 am		7.56 am	4.34 pm		
Niangoloko	3.25 am		8.44 am	5.30 pm		
Ouangolodougou	4.35 am		10.08 am	7.00 pm		
Ferkessedougou	5.40 am		11.23 am	8.17 pm	7.00 am	
Tafire	6.41 am		12.30 pm	9.33 pm	8.08 am	
Katiola	8.36 am			2.50 pm	0.11 am	10.15 am
Bouake	9.50 am	7.00 am	4.00 pm	1.40 pm	11.24 am	12.45 pm
Dimbokro	11.47 am	9.47 am	6.03 pm	4.10 pm	1.35 pm	3.32 pm
Agboville	1.14 pm	10.29 am	7.35 pm	6.03 pm	3.14 pm	6.00 pm
Yapo				6.22 am	3.31 pm	6.32 pm
Anyama				7.14 am	4.21 pm	7.32 pm
Agban	2.36 pm	11.52 am	8.56 pm	7.46 am	4.58 pm	8.01 pm
Abidjan	2.45 pm	12.01 pm	9.05 pm	7.58 am	5.07 pm	8.12 pm
Treichville	2.50 pm	12.06 pm	9.10 pm	8.03 am	5.12 pm	8.17 pm

	Autorail No 40	*Autorail* No 62	*Autorail* No 64	*Autorail* No 20	*Rapide* No 10
Ouagadougou			6.00 am		10.45 am
Koudougou			7.41 am		12.02 pm
Siby			9.08 am		1.17 pm
Bobodioulasso		7.20 am	12.21 pm		4.20 pm
Banfora		8.57 am	3.00 pm		5.37 pm
Niamgoloko		10.34 am	3.55 pm	6.47 pm	
Ouangolodougou		11.50 am	5.00 pm		8.05 pm
Ferkessedougou	12.17 pm	5.48 pm		8.55 pm	
Tafire		2.30 pm			
Katiola		5.50 pm			
Bouake		6.50 pm		7.25 am	
Dimbokro	6.00 am			9.47 am	
Agboville	8.08 am			12.00 pm	
Yapo	8.37 am			12.20 pm	
Anyama	9.37 am	1.16 pm			
Agban	10.08 am			1.44 pm	
Abidjan	10.20 am			1.53 pm	
Treichville	10.25 am			2.00 pm	

These days a lot of travellers are giving the coastal route a miss and going via Abengourou to Kumasi. You can either hitch along this road or go by taxi. A taxi from Abidjan to the border will cost CFA 3000. There is a beautiful stretch of forest between Abengourou and Agnibilekrou.

Ghanaian customs can take a long time, but they're particularly slow along the Assini-Newtown-Half Assini-Jewi Wharf route. It can take up to four hours to get through, though the process has been known to take nine hours! For this reason, try to get to Frambo by early afternoon at the latest, as the last ferry leaves at 4 pm. The ferries have to wait until all the passengers have gone through border formalities.

To/From Burkina Faso

The best way of getting between the two countries is to take the train (twice daily) which connects Abidjan with Ouagadougou. This train is also a very good way of getting to most of the major towns in the interior of Ivory Coast.

Examples of fares on this train are:
Abidjan-Ouagadougou Rapide Nos 1 and 2 cost 15,730 (1st class) plus CFA 3500 for a couchette. Second class costs CFA 13,500. Express Nos 11 and 12 cost CFA 10,575 (2nd class).
Abidjan-Bouake CFA 2350 (2nd class)
Bouake-Ferkessedougou CFA 1950 (2nd class)
Abidjan-Bobo Dioulasso CFA 10,250 on Rapide Nos 1 and 2 (2nd class)
Bobo Dioulasso-Ouagadougou CFA 2895 (2nd class)
Koudougou-Ouagadougou CFA 675 (2nd class)

A meal on the train is CFA 600. Student reductions are available on the above fares. A 1st-class couchette includes a bunk and clean linen.

ABIDJAN

The capital of the Ivory Coast, Abidjan has a magnificent setting but is one of the world's most expensive cities. It's divided roughly into five parts – the Plateau (the modern French quarter), Treichville (the African quarter with heaps of colourful nightlife, cheap restaurants and cafés), Cocody (an exclusive residential suburb), Adjame (another African quarter) and Marcory (another, less select, residential suburb). If you're on a budget then head for Treichville.

The **Ifon Museum** (Ethnology Museum) in Adjame is worth a visit. Most buses from Treichville to Adjame and Plateau pass by the museum.

Be prepared for power cuts in Abidjan. They happen quite regularly.

Information

The Tourist Office is on Boulevard General de Gaulle. It used to have plenty of glossy literature and a map of the city but recent reports suggest it's now a waste of time. Very little English is spoken there.

American Express is in Socopao-Cote d'Ivoire, 14 Boulevard de la République, BP 1297, Abidjan (tel 320211). These people can be very useful. They can even reserve seats on the *Le Point* flights from Ouagadougou to Lyon.

The poste restante here only holds letters for 15 days and charges CFA 200 for each letter collected.

Useful Addresses

British Embassy
  Immeuble Les Harmonica, Boulevard Carde at the Avenue Docteur Jamot. Issues Sierra Leone entry permits and visas.
Burkina Faso Embassy
  Avenue Terrasson des Fougeres at the Boulevard Carde
Canadian Embassy
  Immeuble Trade Centre, Avenue Nogues between Rue 4 and 5
Guinea Embassy
  Résidence Crosson Duplessis No 2, Avenue Crosson Duplessis between Rue 1 and 2
Liberian Embassy
  Immeuble Le General, Boulevard Bertrand Russel at the Avenue General de Gaulle (Rue du Commerce)

Mali Embassy
   Maison du Mali, Avenue General de Gaulle
   (Rue du Commerce) at Rue 1

There are Benin (tel 414414) and Guinea-Bissau (tel 415436) embassies listed in the telephone book, but they're in Cocody, which is a long way from the centre of Plateau.

Most of the West African airlines (except Air Afrique) are on the Avenue General de Gaulle (Rue du Commerce).

Places to Stay

Treichville is the place to head for if you're looking for budget accommodation. *Hotel Haddad*, Avenue de la Reine Pokou, has been popular for years. It's a bit grubby and noisy and there's sometimes no water, but it only costs CFA 3000 a room. One traveller reported it closed in November 1984 (another traveller confirmed this saying it's undergoing renovations). Similar is the *Hotel Treichotel* (formerly the *Hotel Palmyre*), also on Avenue de la Reine Pokou close to the Haddad, which is much cleaner but costs CFA 6000-8000 a double. Close to the Treichotel is the *Hotel Atlanta*, Avenue 15, which has one room for CFA 3000 and others at CFA 4300. The rooms have their own showers and air-conditioning. *Hotel Le Prince*, Avenue 20 near the Treichotel, was renovated in 1983 and should still be pretty clean. It has double rooms with showers and air-conditioning for CFA 4400. *Hotel de la Succes*, Rue 25 between Avenues 14 and 15 opposite the Catholic Mission, doubles as a brothel but is reasonable value at CFA 3500 a double. *Hotel Mandani*, Rue 25, Avenue 7, is another cheapie at CFA 2500 without fan and CFA 3000 with fan for a single.

Two other hotels which have been recommended in the past are the *Hotel Fraternité* (near a cinema) and the *Hotel de la Paix*. They're both in Treichville.

If you're a woman, you could try *Foyer des Jeunes Filles* (Avenue Bachalme), *Mission Biblique*, or *Maison Protestante Edudiante*. These are all in Cocody and the latter takes men as well. The last two only have rooms during vacations but you can camp in the grounds of the Mission Biblique at other times for CFA 500. To get there, take the Bingerville Road and turn right before the École Gendarmerie. The Maison Protestante is behind the Catholic Hospital.

For somewhere cheap in Adjame, try the *Hotel Silva* near the cemetery which is good value and has clean, airy rooms for CFA 3000 a double with shower. In the same price bracket is the *Hotel Liberté*, Avenue 13 just north of the Gare Routiere and about 400 metres south of the Boulevard General de Gaulle, which costs CFA 2600 a single, CFA 3000 a single with shower, CFA 3500 a single with shower and fan, CFA 4000 a single with toilet, shower and fan, and CFA 5500 a single with toilet, shower and air-conditioning. Somewhat up-market from these is the very pleasant *Hotel Le Mont Niangbo*, 25 Boulevard William Jacob about 400 emtres from the large mosque, which costs CFA 7000 a single and CFA 7800 a double with private bath, air-conditioning and balcony. You can sometimes bargain them down to, say, CFA 5000. Similar is the *Hotel Banfor*, Avenue 13 just south of the Gare Routiere (if coming up Boulevard Nangui Abragou turn right at the Dispensary – about 400 metres), which costs CFA 6000 a single and CFA 6500 a double with private bath, air-conditioning and a balcony. Avoid the *Relais d'Adjame* next to the truck park if possible, unless you're fond of open sewers, bus horns and the nocturnal habits of cockroaches. If you do stay there it will cost CFA 3000 for half a day and CFA 4000 for a full day.

Places to Eat

There are plenty of cheap restaurants in Treichville as well as street stalls selling snacks. One of the best restaurants is the *Restaurant Senegalais*, Avenue 21 one block from the Hotel Le Prince. A bowl of soup with buttered bread will cost CFA

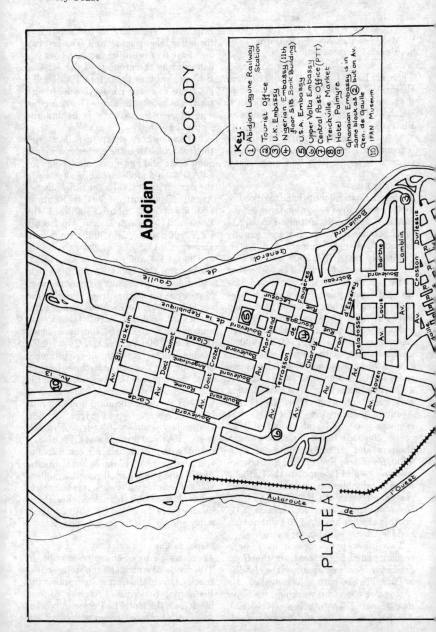

Key:
1. Abidjan Lagune Railway Station
2. Tourist Office
3. U.K. Embassy
4. Nigerian Embassy (11th floor SIB Bank Building)
5. U.S.A. Embassy
6. Upper Volta Embassy
7. Central Post Office (PTT)
8. Treichville Market
9. Hotel Palmyre

Ghanaian Embassy is in same block as ② but on Av. Gen. de Gaulle

10. IFAN Museum

COCODY

Abidjan

PLATEAU

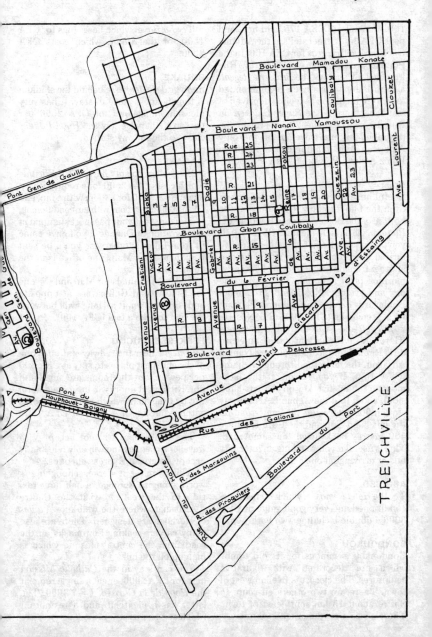

100, an omelette CFA 175, and beef and peas CFA 350. Street stalls at the Adjame truck park sell *riz gras* for CFA 100. In the Plateau area try the *Café Central*, Rue Franchal d'Esperey. The *Brasserie Regent*, also in Plateau, has been recommended for ice cream. If you're feeling deprived of fast food there is the *Super Chicken* on Rue 13 near Avenue 20 in Treichville, described by one traveller as 'the only American-style hamburger restaurant in Black Africa.' He said it was very good.

Other

Useful buses include No 6 to the airport from the bus terminus (Gare Sud) at the bottom of the Boulevard de la République, Plateau, via Treichville (fare CFA 125). If you take a taxi then note that there are two tariffs, one from 6 am to midnight and another from midnight to 6 am. The early-morning tariff is double that during the day and evening. Nos 5 and 25 connect Boulevard de la République, Plateau, with Treichville (CFA 100). Bus Nos 16, 20, 27, 30 and 37 from the bus terminus (Gare Sud) at the bottom of the Boulevard de la République go up Boulevard Nangui Abragou, the main road through Adjame (CFA 100). If you get off at the large mosque (about five km on the left-hand side), you'll find the Agban RAN railway station 500 metres up the same road on the left-hand side and the Gare Routiere 400 metres back down the same road. This is useful if you're taking an inter-city bus or arriving on one.

ABOISSO

Try the *Hotel Bemosso*, which is clean, air-conditioned and very good value at CFA 3000 a double including own bathroom.

BONDOUKOU

Bondoukou is famous for its old tombs which are decorated with figurative sculptures. The closest is five km west of town. There are two others en route to Soffre about 15 km south-east of town. There's also a good market on Sundays.

Try *La Baya*, which has rooms for CFA 1500; or the *Alban*, which costs CFA 2000.

BOUAKE

Auberge de la Jeunesse behind the stadium is the cheapest place to stay. It has very pleasant bungalows for CFA 2000 per person. Otherwise, try the *Hotel Bakary* close to the railway station.

DANANE

A good place to stay here is *Tia Etienne*, which costs CFA 2500 for a room without a fan, CFA 3000 for a room with a fan, and CFA 5000 for a room with air-conditioning.

You must get your passport stamped at Immigration in Danane if you have come in from Liberia; otherwise you'll be sent back here from Man. The office is in the centre of town.

The bus terminals for Man and the one for Liberia and Guinea are at opposite ends of the town. It's a long walk between the two so take a taxi (CFA 100).

FERKESSEDOUGOU

La Gazelle near the railway station is one of the cheapest places to stay at CFA 800 per person, but the rooms are small and hot. Right next door is an un-named hotel run by Ghanaians which has single rooms without fan for CFA 1000 or CFA 1500 with fan.

The banks here will not accept Visa traveller's cheques and will only reluctantly accept American Express cheques.

While you're in Ferkessedougou it's worth going to **Korhogo**, a half-hour taxi ride to the west, to visit the Centre d'Artisanats where the well-known *toiles* of Korhogo are designed. There are also many carvers making Fon masks on the road from the central mosque which is high up on the hill.

You can stay at the *Catholic Mission* here for CFA 2000, or get a single room at the *Hotel de la Gare* for CFA 3000. The latter has a nightclub and a restaurant which serves pizza.

GAGNOA

Hotel Syndicate d'Initiative costs CFA 2000 a double with own shower. It's grubby but the beds are clean.

GRAND BASSAM

Forty-three km from Abidjan, Grand Bassam is the nearest place to the capital for beaches. They're virtually deserted and you can sleep on them, but if you spruce yourself up and ask around, you may find the owner of a beach hut who is willing to let you stay in one free (having someone stay in them helps reduce burglaries). If you can't find anything, try *Chez Antoinette* which costs CFA 3000 a single and CFA 4500 a double. For good, cheap food go to *Le Bon Coin* across the street from the 'Palace.'

MAN

One of the cheapest places to stay here is the *Hotel Mont Dent* near the hospital. Depending on what you want, it has rooms for CFA 1000, CFA 2000 and CFA 2500. Slightly better is the *Hotel Les Montagnes*, which has a range of rooms from CFA 2500-4000 – all with attached shower. Some have fans and others have air-conditioning. Other hotels which have been recommended are the *Hotel Virginia* on the eastern edge of town (CFA 2500 per room); *Hotel Miva* (CFA 3000 per room with meals for CFA 400 each); and *Hotel Fraternité*, 200 metres from the taxi park (CFA 2000-2500 a double with private bath and CFA 3000 with private bath and fan).

Two fairly cheap places to eat are *Restaurant Irannien* near the market which has good chicken and *Restaurant Marie Therese* behind the market which has *foutou avec viande de la brousse* for CFA 350.

If you want to stay outside of town there's the *Mission Catholique Guest House* (Centre Bethanie), which is excellent. It's beautifully located and costs CFA 2000 or CFA 2500 including breakfast. Take a taxi (CFA 250-400 from the town centre), as it's a long walk.

Taxis around town cost CFA 75 for locals but at least double that for tourists. There are three road stations in Man: one for the express buses to Abidjan (and other places), another for the taxis to Abidjan, and a third for the trucks and taxis to Danane.

ODIENNE

If you're heading for Bamako (Mali), there are no buses past this point, and it's also where the tarmac ends. *Le Campement* was renovated recently and is very clean. A double room with shower, flush toilet and fan costs CFA 3000. If you want air-conditioning it will cost you CFA 4000. *La Bon Auberge* across from the Grande Marche has rice and sauce for CFA 150 and steak and French fries for CFA 450.

The bus to Man leaves between 6 and 10 am (when full) from the truck park next to the SNTMVCI (National Transport Office).

OTHER

It's possible to pick up jobs fairly easily if you speak good French. Try asking at the US embassy for a list of companies operating in the country, and then go round to their Abidjan headquarters to see if there's anything going.

Kenya

Unlike pre-colonial Uganda, which saw the rise of several large kingdoms, Kenya was populated by a number of small, dispersed tribal groups, principal among whom were the Kikuyu, Kamba, Luo and Masai. These groups, though they shared the same area, had different origins so that, for instance, the Masai are a Hamitic tribe, the Kikuyu are Bantu and the Luo are Nilotic. There was little penetration of the interior by outsiders until the 19th century, and as a result what was to become Kenya escaped the worst depredations of the Arab slavers, who concentrated their attentions further south. The coastal area, however, formed an important part of the chain of Omani Arab trading posts which stretched from the Horn of Africa all the way down to Mozambique. Lamu, Malindi and Mombasa all had their origins as Arab trading cities. This string of trading posts dealt principally in ivory and slaves and was under the control of the Sultan of Zanzibar.

The gradual eclipse of the Sultan's power began in the late 19th century when both the British and the Germans obtained trading concessions along the coast, the former being allotted what is now Uganda and Kenya and the latter what is now Tanganyika. Administration of these areas quickly became the prerogative of the British and German governments respectively, so that in 1893 Uganda had become a protectorate followed by Kenya in 1895. In the early years, the British were primarily interested in tapping the rich resources of Uganda, and in order to facilitate this a railway was built between Mombasa and Kampala using indentured labourers from India, many of whom subsequently remained to eventually become the substantial merchant class of today. With the arrival of the 20th century, however, the British directed their attention to settling Kenya with white farmers who set up plantations producing crops substantially for export.

In the process of establishing these, many Africans lost the lands they had previously cultivated and were either forced into new – and often inferior – land or into the labour market as a result of hut taxes imposed by the colonial administration. By 1915, the racial segregation of land effectively excluded Africans and Asians from holding properties in the fertile highlands. Other Africans, though not actually dispossessed, lost access to the surrounding uncultivated land which in a sense was their fallow ground. When they moved in the course of shifting cultivation they found themselves rent-paying 'squatters' on ex-appropriated land. The present government is still trying to sort out the legacy of all this, and since independence around 60,000 families have been resettled on land formerly owned by expatriates. Nevertheless, a large proportion of the most important agricultural properties is still owned by expatriates or politicians and much still needs to be done in this direction. Most of the country's employment problems stem from the fact that there is little access to land and that, in any case, only about 7% of the total area receives sufficient rainfall to support viable agriculture. The reconciliation between black and white since independence has undoubtedly been a major political feat (Kenya is one of Africa's most stable and prosperous countries), but it's probably true to say that, having made a few concessions, the white farmers have lost the enthusiasm to make any further concessions.

Not all the various tribes of Kenya were so adversely affected by European settlement. Most of the land taken for plantations came from the pastoral tribes – the Masai, Nandi and Kipsigis – while the numerically larger Luo and Baluyia tribes remained virtually unaffected. Even the Kikuyu, who later came to nurse a particular grievance on the question of land expropriation in the Mau Mau rebellion, were only marginally affected. However, continuing pressure over land, combined with stringent controls over the cultivation and marketing of cash crops by Africans to prevent them from competing with the white settlers, led to the formation of nationalist organisations in the 1920s. Many of the instigators of these movements were Kikuyu and as early as 1929 one of their leaders, Jomo Kenyatta, was sent to England in an attempt to negotiate on behalf of the Kikuyu Central Association.

Political consciousness expanded by leaps and bounds during WW II as a result of many Africans being conscripted into the armed forces. The end result was the formation of guerrilla groups who took an oath of loyalty committing them to the goal of expelling the white settlers from Kenya. By 1952 they had become such a threat to the colonial authorities that a state of emergency was declared and British troops were flown in to crush the rebellion. Despite the outcry in the western press, far more Africans were killed than white settlers. The target of the guerrillas was not only the white settlers but those Africans who collaborated with or benefitted from colonial rule. By the time the Mau Mau rebellion had been crushed in 1956, over 100,000 Africans

had died as opposed to only 30 whites. Not only that, but some 24,000 Kikuyu, Embu and Meru tribespeople had been interned in detention camps including most of the leaders of the Kenya African Union – the successor to the Kikuyu Central Association. The leader of the armed rebellion, Dedan Kimathi, was executed.

The Mau Mau rebellion, though contained militarily, shook the colonial administration and the white settlers to the roots. The restrictions on African cultivation of a whole range of cash crops were lifted and a lot of effort was made to encourage the development of a stable middle class. Events moved quickly from then on until, in 1960, Britain agreed to a conference with African leaders to discuss the future of the colony. The state of emergency was lifted; the Kenyan African Union reformed into the Kenyan African National Union (KANU) and Jomo Kenyatta, transformed from the feared leader of black nationalism into the grand old man of the settlers, was released from prison to become the leader of KANU. In the following year KANU won the elections and decided in favour of a parliamentary system rather than the federal system proposed by the party of the minority tribes, the Kenyan African Democratic Union (KADU). Independence was granted in 1963 with Jomo Kenyatta as the country's first president.

Kenyatta ruled the country from independence until his death in 1978, but his policy of alignment with the west and the continuation of the so-called free-enterprise system earned him many critics. Foremost among them was the vice-president, Oginga Odinga, whose opposition party, the Kenya People's Union, was banned in 1966, when Oginga Odinga was imprisoned. He was only released when he agreed to join KANU. Banning the party, however, didn't stop the steady stream of criticism about Kenyatta's regime (the principal bone of contention was the pace of land reform) and when the powerful Luo government minister, Tom Mboya, was assassinated in 1969 the event led to serious racial riots between the Kikuyu and Luo. In the early 1970s, Kariuki became the main opposition leader until he was assassinated in 1975 during a wave of bomb explosions in Nairobi. This time the government acted quickly to restore order using the army and para-military police.

With the death of Kenyatta, Daniel Arap Moi took over as president. He has so far survived an attempted coup by the Kenyan air force, headed off potential armed conflicts on the one hand from Idi Amin's Uganda which laid claim to parts of western Kenya and on the other from Somalia which laid claim to large parts of eastern Kenya, and begun to diversify the tribal composition of those in positions of authority. Despite an official state visit to Tanzania, however, he has so far not been able to repair the rift with that country. Kenya, Tanzania and Uganda previously belonged to an economic union which covered railways, Lake Victoria steamers, airlines and posts and telecommunications. It was shattered by Kenya's unilateral seizure of the union's assets. The border remained closed for many years and flights between the two countries stopped. This closure seriously affected Kenya's trading relationships with neighbouring countries and was only lifted in 1983. Arap Moi no doubt supported Tanzania's action in invading Uganda, but he was hamstrung by the OAU condemnation of the action.

FACTS

Much of central Kenya consists of mountains and high plateaux including one of Africa's highest mountains – Mt Kenya at 5200 metres high (17,056 feet). The high plateaux are relatively fertile agricultural land but much of the land in the north and east is semi-arid like that in neighbouring Ethiopia and Somalia. The coastal vegetation is largely dry bush. Lake Victoria marks the western bound-aries of the country. In the coastal area it is hot and humid year round, whereas on the plateaux the climate is very pleasant with temperatures ranging from 10°C to 28°C. The main rainy season is from March to June with another short rainy season from October to December. The population stands at about 15 million.

VISAS

Visas are required by all except nationals of Commonwealth countries (Australia being the only exception), Denmark, Germany (West), Irish Republic, Italy, Norway, Sweden, Turkey and Uruguay. All the above can be issued with a visitor's pass on arrival. You can also get a visa on arrival if you fly into the country but it costs US$8. Another traveller reported that visas were available at the border with Tanzania, again for US$8. If you're flying into Nairobi airport you may be asked for an onward ticket and sufficient funds (US$400 is acceptable). The onward ticket requirement has been disputed by some travellers, however. One UK correspondent said that in eight separate visits over three years he had never been asked for an onward ticket and that he was given up to three months' stay on request. This was confirmed by an American traveller. On the other hand, we had a letter from someone who said he was asked for an onward ticket but that when he showed one he was given a stay permit of six months.

In case you do arrive without an onward ticket and immigration demands that you have one, it's been suggested that the best thing to do is ring up *Crocodile Travel* (or any of the other cheap ticket agencies listed in this book under 'Nairobi') and ask them to come out to the airport and sell you a ticket. If you buy one from an airline counter at the airport, immigration may well stamp it 'Non-refundable.' If this happens, go to the main immigration office in Nairobi and politely complain. They may well cancel the stamp so that you can get a refund.

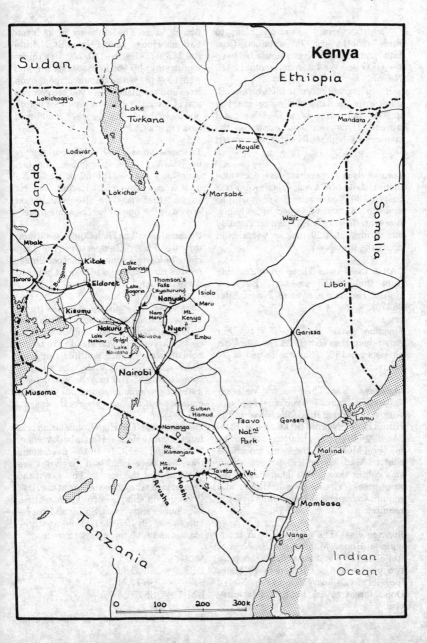

Visa/stay permit extensions of up to three months can be obtained from Immigration in the Nyayo House between the GPO and the Intercontinental Hotel, Nairobi.

If you're given a form to fill in on arrival, don't write the name of a budget hotel on it. Use the name of a five-star hotel instead. This way you minimise the chances of being asked for an onward ticket.

Burundi visas The embassy is in Development House, Moi Avenue, Nairobi. Visas cost Sh 100. You require two photographs and the visa will be issued in 24 hours, however, they are only issued on Tuesday and Friday at 4.30 pm, so you should apply the previous day.

CAR & Chad visas These are obtainable from the French embassy, Embassy House, Harambee Avenue, Nairobi (tel 28373).

Egyptian visas Visa fees vary. For Australians they cost Sh 245 and for USA citizens Sh 135. They are issued in 24 hours.

Malagasy visas There is no Malagasy embassy in Nairobi so you must apply for your visa through *Air Madagascar* in the Hilton Hotel, Nairobi (PO Box 42676; tel 25286/26494). Applications must be made on Monday as the forms have to be sent to Madagascar for approval. Your visa comes through on Thursday of the same week. The visas cost US$24 and require four photos. No onward ticket is required.

Rwanda visas The embassy is in International House, Mama Ngina St, Nairobi (tel 334341). Visas cost Sh 200, require two photos and are issued in 48 hours (possibly in 24 hours if you ask politely). Don't forget to ask for a double entry visa.

Somali visas The embassy is in International House, Mama Ngina St, Nairobi (tel 24301). Visas cost Sh 200 for a three-month stay plus you have to state why you want to go there, the amount of money you have and the place where you are going to stay. Check the dates on your visa before you leave the embassy, as they sometimes make mistakes.

Tanzanian visas The High Commission is in BIMA House, Harambee Avenue, Nairobi. Visas cost Sh 56 or US$4. No photos are required. Recent reports suggest that visas are also available on arrival at the border for the same price.

Ugandan visas The High Commission is on the 4th Floor, Co-operative Building, Haile Selassie Avenue. Visas cost Sh 25, require three photos and take 24 hours to come through.

Zaire visas The embassy is in Electricity House, Harambee Avenue, Nairobi (tel 29771/2). A one-month, single-entry visa costs Sh 160, but you should try to get hold of a three-month, multiple-entry visa which costs Sh 320. Visas take a day to come through. You may be asked for a letter of recommendation from your own embassy but this isn't always the case.

Zambian visas The High Commission is in International House, Harambee Avenue, Nairobi (tel 335972). In the past, some travellers have been told that visas are obtainable at the border. This is not the case so insist they give you one at the High Commission. Single-entry visas cost Sh 24, double-entry visas Sh 50 and triple-entry visas Sh 75. All visas require three photos and take three days to issue.

MONEY

US$1 = Sh 15.35
£1 = Sh 19.50
DM 1 = Sh 5

The unit of currency is the Kenyan

Shilling = 100 cents. Import/export of local currency is allowed up to Sh 100. On the black market you can get up to US$1 = Sh 16.50 and £1 = Sh 23.50, but be very careful of street deals as there have been a lot of robberies recently. The area around the Thorn Tree Café is particularly notorious. Try Zanzibar Curios or Fotomedica on Moi Avenue, Bij Curios on Mama Ngina St, or the C & A Camera Shop, all in Nairobi. Elsewhere stick to Asian shops and merchants. Don't buy Kenyan shillings with US dollars at the Ugandan border as the rate is very poor (US$1 = Ken Sh 14).

There is also a good black market for Ugandan shillings. Using Kenyan shillings, you can get Ken Sh 1 = Ug Sh 27 (this works out at nearly US$1 = Ug Sh 400). If you want to buy Tanzanian shillings there is a good rate in front of the East African Road Service where the Peugeot taxis leave for Namanga. The rate is around Ken Sh 1 = Tan Sh 5 or US$1 = Tan Sh 70. It's possible, of course, to increase this rate to Tan Sh 83 by first changing your hard currency into Kenyan shillings and then buying Tanzanian shillings with the Kenyan shillings.

All banks in Kenya close at 2 pm except for the Commercial Bank of Africa in the lobby of the Hilton Hotel, Nairobi; and Barclays, Kenyatta Avenue, Nairobi. Both of these are open Monday to Friday until 4.30 pm. On the first and last Saturday of every month all the banks are open from 8.30 to 11 am. The commission on traveller's cheques is Sh 1.20 per cheque.

It's possible to get US dollars cash from banks by having a good story and telling them that you will be leaving Kenya within 48 hours. This doesn't always work so you have to be persistent. If they ask for an airline ticket, tell them you are leaving overland. Try Barclays main branch on Moi Avenue or their Union Towers branch. At the latter, tell them you are going to Uganda or Tanzania. One couple who were successful told the bank that they could get a 30% student reduction on a plane ticket to Europe from Bangui, CAR, but only with hard cash. When you buy dollars, however, they will first change whatever currency or traveller's cheques you have into Kenyan shillings and then reconvert into US dollars so you pay commission twice. If you fail, remember that Kenyan shillings are almost as good as hard currency in Sudan, Uganda and Tanzania.

If you're having money sent to Kenya, the ABN Bank in Mombasa should be avoided. They can be very uncooperative about paying out and may insist that you take half of it in Kenyan currency and the rest in hard currency. Barclays in Nairobi are much faster but have been known to stamp the back of traveller's cheques with 'Not negotiable in South Africa.' Two travellers recently had to spend half a day arguing with bank officials about whose money it actually was. They were successful in the end.

The airport tax for international flights is US$10 or £8 and must be paid in hard currency.

LANGUAGE

Swahili and English are the official languages.

Basic Swahili

Vowel pronunciation is as follows: **a** as in f*a*ther
e as in b*e*tter
i as in b*ee*
o as in l*a*w
u as in t*oo*

Double vowels are long. There are no diphthongs and consonants as in English. Swahili is a prefixed language: adjectives change prefix according to the number and class of the noun. Thus mzuri, wazuri, vizuri and kizuri are different forms of the word 'good.' Verbs use a prefix noun:

I	*ni*
you	*u*
he/she	*a*

we	*tu*
you	*m*
they	*wa*

and a tense prefix:

present	*na*
past	*li*
future	*ta*
infinitive	*ku*

Thus you get:

We will go to Moshi
Tutakwenda moshi
Can I take a picture?
Ninaweza kupiga picha?
Juma spoke much
Juma alisema sana

Some useful words in Swahili:

hello*	*jambo or salamu*
welcome	*karibu*
thank you	*asante*
thanks very much	*asante sana*
how are you?	*habari?*
I'm fine, thanks	*mzuri*
what's your name?	*oonitwa nani?*
it is . . .	*ninitwa . . .*
how was the journey?	*habari ya safari?*
goodbye	*kwaheri*
yes	*ndiyo*
no	*hapana*
how much/how many?	*ngapi*
money	*pesa*
where?	*wapi*
today	*leo*
tomorrow	*kesho*
guest house	*nyumba ya wageni*
toilet	*iyoo*
eat	*kula*
sleep	*lala*
want	*taka*
come from	*toka*
is	*ni*
there is	*kuna*
there isn't	*hakuna*
white people	*mazungu*
food	*chakula*

rice	*wali*
bananas	*ndizi*
bread	*mkati*
vegetables	*mboga*
water	*maji*
salt	*chumvi*
meat	*nyama*
goat	*mbuzi*
beef	*ngombe*
chicken	*kuku*
fish	*samaki*
egg(s)	*(ma)yai*
milk	*maziwa*

*There is also a respectful greeting used for elders – 'Shikamoo.' The reply is 'Marahaba.'

Numerals:

1 *moja*
2 *mbili*
3 *tatu*
4 *nne*
5 *tano*
6 *sita*
7 *saba*
8 *nane*
9 *tisa*
10 *kumi*
11 *kumi na moja*
20 *ishirini*
30 *thelathini*
40 *arobaini*
50 *hamsini*
60 *sitini*
70 *sabini*
80 *themanini*
90 *tisini*
100 *mia*
½ *nusa*

HEALTH

You can get vaccinations for cholera, smallpox and yellow fever from the City Hall clinic (ground floor) in Nairobi from 9 am to noon. Each shot costs Sh 20. They are also obtainable from the Central Medical Laboratories, National Bank Building, Aga Khan Walk, Nairobi (tel 335513/4). The latter are by appointment only and each shot costs Sh 40. In Mombasa you can get the same thing from the Public Health Department, Msanifu Kombo St. Shots cost Sh 20.

Bilharzia tests are free at the Mombasa clinic. If you are unfortunate enough to contract malaria, free treatment is available at the Lamu Hospital.

Don't go around barefoot or you might pick up jiggers. Watch out for Nairobi fly which, if squashed on your skin, can cause nasty blistering and a rash.

GETTING THERE & AROUND
Air

Nairobi is one of the best places in Africa to pick up tickets to Europe, India and other places in Africa. There's a lot of competition between travel agents so most of them lean over backwards to give you whatever discounts they can manage. Very popular these days and one for which we've had a lot of recommendations is *Hanzuwan-el-Kindly Tours & Travel*, Rajab Manzil Building (4th floor, room 3), Tom Mboya St (tel 26819/338729). It's run by a man called Fehed A S H el-Kindly though he's known to everyone as 'Eddie.' He's a very helpful person and gives some of the best deals in Nairobi. *Prince Travel*, Kenyatta Conference Centre, has a lot of recommendations, particularly for flights to Cairo. *Crocodile Travel*, Tom Mboya St in the same block as the Ambassador Hotel, used to be very popular and, although they still have cheap tickets, they're no longer as cheap or as helpful as the two mentioned above. They have an office in Mombasa on Moi Avenue opposite the Castle Hotel. Other agents which act as bucket shops are *Tamana Tours, Kambo Travel, Global, Speed Bird, Appel Travel, Let's Go Travel* and *Travel Mart*; we've had a few recommendations for Appel Travel recently.

The cheapest flights to Europe are generally by *Aeroflot* via Moscow and are currently Sh 4600 (Appel Travel), Sh 4800 (Tamana and 'Eddie'), and Sh 5000 (Crocodile Travel) one way. Don't be surprised if your luggage turns up a week late. It does eventually arrive even if they have to sent it by taxi! Nairobi-Cairo costs US$422 (Sh 6060) standard IATA fare, but you should be able to arrange a student discount of 10% at the very least. Prince Travel were selling these tickets recently for Sh 3900 with *Sudan Air* and Sh 4000 with *Ethiopia Air*. A ticket to Bombay should cost around Sh 3200 and one to New Delhi around Sh 3600. Regardless of the discount which any particular company offers, you may well have to produce bank receipts for the full IATA fare if you're paying in shillings. (For instance, you need to produce a receipt for the India tickets of Sh 5200.)

Keep your ears open for stories about airlines which overbook before you buy a discounted ticket. *Sudan Air* are notorious for this and you may be stranded at the airport unable to switch your ticket to another airline.

In addition to *Kenya Airways* – which has flights between Nairobi, Mombasa, Kisumu and Malindi – there are a number of charter flight companies which connect the smaller places as well as do sightseeing runs over the national parks. *Sunbird Aviation* flies from Nairobi to Juba in Sudan. The names and addresses of the charter flight companies are:

Air Kenya
  Wilson Airport, PO Box 30357 (tel 501601/2/3/4)
Coast Air Ltd
  PO Box 133, Malindi (tel 69). They fly to Lamu and the game parks.
Caspair Ltd
  PO Box 30103, Wilson Airport, Nairobi (tel 501421/2/3/4). This company flies to Lamu, Lake Turkhana, Mara and Lake Victoria.
Malindi Air Service
  Lamu Rd, PO Box 146, Malindi
Mombasa Air Services
  Moi International Airport, PO Box 00222. They fly to Malindi and Lamu.

Sunbird Aviation
    Nyerere Avenue, PO Box 87669, Mombasa. This company flies from Nairobi to Juba (Sudan).
Tic Air Charters Ltd
    Lamu Rd, PO Box 146, Malindi (tel 153)
Cooper Skybird
    Another Malindi-based company which flies to Lamu.

Many travellers are using the charter flight companies on the Mombasa-Malindi-Lamu sector since they are relatively cheap. Prices have been fluctuating a little recently but, in general, *Pioneer Airways* and *Cooper Skybird* are the cheapest. Mombasa-Lamu costs Sh 500 one way or Sh 400 on standby. Malindi-Lamu costs Sh 400 one way or Sh 300 on standby. Cooper have two flights daily in either direction (at 10 am and 4 pm from Lamu). Somewhat more expensive is Sunbird Aviation, which does Mombasa-Lamu for Sh 600 and Malindi-Lamu for Sh 375.

Rail

The main railway line in Kenya runs from Mombasa to the Ugandan border via Voi, Nairobi, Nakuru and Eldoret, with branch lines from Nakuru to Kisumu and Nairobi to Nanyuki. There are no through trains to Tanzania on the Voi-Moshi line at present, though these might be resumed now that the border is open normally again. Railway timetables are free at most city railway stations. Trains are sometimes late but they're comfortable if you book a sleeper for overnight trips.

Nairobi-Mombasa Two daily trains run in either direction at 5 pm and 7 pm. The early train takes 14½ hours and the later one 13 hours. The fares are Sh 424 (1st class), Sh 148 (2nd class) and Sh 75 (3rd class). Bedrolls cost Sh 32.50. Dinner on the train (which is highly recommended) costs Sh 60 and breakfast costs Sh 30-35 depending on what you have. You should book 1st and 2nd class berths the previous

day at the latest and further ahead for weekend travel. Second class consists of six berth couchettes. If you're travelling from Mombasa to Nairobi make sure you get up early, as the wildlife can be spectacular.

Nairobi-Kisumu There is one train daily in either direction at 6.30 pm. The fare is Sh 110 (2nd class). Book in advance if possible as 2nd class is often booked up on the day of departure.

Nairobi-Nakuru-Eldoret-Ugandan Border There are trains on Tuesday, Friday and Saturday at 3 pm which arrive between 8 and 9 am the next day. In the opposite direction they leave Malaba (the border town) on Wednesday, Saturday and Sunday at 4 pm. Fares are Sh 158 (2nd class) and Sh 77 (3rd class). Customs are 'a breeze' and, if you need to change money, there's a good exchange rate between the two border posts. The train does not go through to Uganda so you must get down at Mlaba and get a matatu into Tororo. From Tororo there are connecting trains to Kampala at 6 am and 2 pm daily.

Men and women travel in different carriages in 2nd and 3rd classes unless a group book a whole compartment.

Road

Hitching on the main roads, which are sealed and well maintained, is easy and generally free. However, on the minor roads you can wait all day for a lift and still have to pay for it in the end, so you might as well get a matatu or a bus in these places. Hitching to the national parks is generally quite difficult because most people go on organised tours or get a group together and hire their own vehicle.

Taxi There are basically three types of taxis. Matatus are shared vans or small trucks which you can find almost everywhere and which cost about half the price of buses. Peugeot taxis run on fixed routes and cost about 50% more than the buses. This bus-type service generally requires that you book in advance; like matatus the Peugeots are shared. Finally there are conventional taxis and speed taxis – private taxis like the ones you find in most Western countries. The speed taxis are actually something of a con, as no vehicle is officially allowed to travel at more than 100 km per hour – though some companies have a reputation for turning a blind eye to the speedometer.

Taxi and matatu services which cover the same routes as the buses are to be found in the same areas in both cities. *Mombasa Peugeot Services*, for instance, are at the junction of Latema Rd and River Rd, Nairobi, and on Haile Selassie Rd, Mombasa. *Malindi Taxi Service* is on Jomo Kenyatta Rd, Mombasa.

Bus On most main routes there are both luxury buses and ordinary buses. They're faster than the trains, though many have night services to avoid the heat so they're not much good if you want to see the countryside. It's advisable to book a seat in advance.

Other than the country bus station in the suburbs of Nairobi, which caters to buses and matatus going to the more remote parts of Kenya, most long-distance buses have their own terminals in each of the cities. In Nairobi these are scattered around the streets close to the Nairobi River and in Mombasa they are generally to be found along Digo Rd and Mwembe Tayari Rd. The addresses of the main companies are as follows:

Akamba Bus Service
    Lagos Rd near the Fire Station, Nairobi (tel 22027/21779), and Jomo Kenyatta Rd, Mombasa
East African Road Service
    Race Course Rd, Nairobi (tel 23155/ 26155)
Kenya Bus Services
    Mwembe Tayari Rd, Mombasa

Coastline Bus Services
    Corner Accra and Duruma Rds, Nairobi (tel 29494), and Mwembe Tayari Rd, Mombasa (tel 20916)
Goldline Bus Service
    Corner Cross Rd and Riata Rd, Nairobi (tel 25279/21963), and Mwembe Tayari Rd, Mombasa
Tawakal Bus
    Digo Rd, Mombasa
Seaman Bus Service
    Digo Rd, Mombasa
RUP Buses
    Corner Latema Rd and Lagos Rd, Nairobi

Taxi & Bus Fares Some examples of current taxi and bus fares and journey times are as follows:

Nairobi-Mombasa Many departures daily in either direction (mostly in the mornings and late evenings) by Akamba Bus Service (cheapest), RUP, Kenya Bus Service, Coastline Service and Goldline Bus Service. The fare is Sh 90 with Akamba and Sh 100-110 with the others. The journey time is between six and eight hours depending on the bus line (usually 6½ hours). You can also take these buses to get to Voi. To Voi the fare is Sh 90 from Nairobi and Sh 45 from Mombasa.

Mombasa-Malindi Daily departures in either direction by Kenya Bus Service, Coast Bus Service, Tawakal and Seaman Bus Service. The fare is Sh 22-25 depending on the bus line and the journey can take as little as two hours but is generally between three and five hours. You can even get there for as little as Sh 15 with Lotal Bus Enterprises. There are also minibuses for Sh 30-40 and shared taxis for Sh 40 which take about 1½ hours. A lot of travellers use a minibus which leaves from the New People's Hotel, Abdel Nasser Rd, Mombasa. It costs Sh 20.

Mombasa-Lamu Daily buses in either

direction by Tawakal and Seaman Bus Service and by Tana River Service (on Tuesday, Friday, Thursday and Sunday from Lamu). The fare is Sh 95-120 depending on the bus line and the journey takes 8½ hours in the dry season. In the wet season the road between Malindi and Lamu is subject to flooding; at those times the journey can take twice as long and has been known to take three days, though this is exceptional. On all the buses to Lamu you have to pay an extra Sh 7 for the ferry which connects the mainland with the island on which Lamu stands.

Malindi-Lamu The same companies which do this run also cover the Mombasa-Lamu sector, but the *Tana River Bus Service* has been recommended by many travellers. It's a new company and generally has better buses. The office in Mombasa is on Digo Rd next to the New People's Hotel. The fare is Sh 80-95 and the journey takes about seven hours. In Malindi the buses leave from beside the New Kenya Hotel and from the Mobil petrol station which is nearby.

Lamu-Garsen The fare is Sh 55 plus Sh 7 for the ferry. If you want to make Garissa in one day from Lamu, you must get the early bus from Lamu; otherwise you miss the connection at Garsen.

Garsen-Garissa The fare is Sh 70.

Garissa-Madu Gashi The fare is Sh 50. The buses are very crowded.

Garissa-Wajir The fare is Sh 70. The buses are very crowded.

Madu Gashi-Isiolo The fare is Sh 55.

Nairobi-Naivasha A matatu costs Sh 20. If you're heading for the YMCA Youth Hostel, get off at South Lake Rd and walk or hitch the 14 km from there. There are infrequent buses and matatus along this road too.

Naivasha-Eldoret The fare is Sh 50 by matatu and the trip can take up to five hours since the drivers stop frequently to pack as many people as is humanly possible into the vehicle.

Eldoret-Kitale Costs Sh 15-20 by matatu. There is usually one every hour.

Kitale-Lodwar Costs Sh 50-80 by matatu depending on your bargaining powers. The buses are supposed to leave every morning at 8 am, but they generally spend several hours driving round the town finding additional passengers. There's also a daily bus which costs Sh 40 (after bargaining). The journey takes about six hours and the road is sealed all the way so it's fast and comfortable.

Kitale-Nairobi Costs Sh 100 by overnight bus which leaves at 7 pm and arrives at 5 am.

Eldoret-Kisumu Costs Sh 25 by bus, Sh 40 by matatu or Sh 50 by shared taxi.

Nairobi-Nakuru Costs Sh 60 by RUP bus but can be as low as Sh 35 with other bus companies.

Nairobi-Eldoret Costs Sh 125 by RUP buses.

Nairobi-Nyahururu (Thompson's Falls) The best thing to do is go to the country bus station in the suburbs of Nairobi, from which you can get a direct matatu for Sh 60. From the centre of Nairobi you'll first have to take a bus to Gilgil for Sh 60 (eg Mombasa Peugeot Services) followed by a matatu to Nyahururu for Sh 20.

Nairobi-Nyeri Both Mombasa Peugeot Services and RUP cover this route. The fare is Sh 25-35.

Nairobi-Namanga This is one of the services to the Tanzanian border. Akamba cover this route and charge Sh 25. Other bus companies charge between Sh 35 and Sh 45. The journey takes five hours. If you want to go by taxi, these leave from the Esso station at the end of River Rd, cost Sh 50 and take two hours. You can also take a Peugeot or a matatu from the Country Bus Station to Namanga.

Mombasa-Lunga Lunga This is another of the services to the Tanzanian border. There is a daily bus (called *Hora Hora*) which costs Sh 40. The customs here are fairly easygoing. From the border there are matatus to Tanga for Tan Sh 100 (65 km). Remember there are also buses (eg Coastline Buses) which now do the Mombasa-Dar es Salaam run if you don't want to do the journey in stages. The fare is Sh 250.

Nairobi-Malaba This is the service to the Ugandan border. There are buses which travel overnight and cost Sh 100. From Malaba they leave daily at 7 pm and arrive in Nairobi at 5.30 am (there are buses by Tawakal, Akamba and Mawinjo).

Taveta-Mombasa There are daily buses between these two places at 8 am and 10 am which cost Sh 48 and take six hours.

Routes to neighbouring countries

Kenya-Sudan Most trucks and travellers journeying between Kenya and Sudan go via Uganda these days, since connections and road conditions are reliable and it's quicker. It used to be possible to go via Lodwar, Lokichoggio, Kapoeta and Torit to Juba if you could get permission from the Sudanese authorities, but this is a major bureaucratic hassle these days because the civil war in southern Sudan has started up again and they don't want you there. Not only that, there's a very real danger of being ambushed by Toposa bandits in the border region. Avoid the route until further notice. If you do attempt this rough journey, allow at least six days for the trip. We haven't heard of anyone doing it for a long time.

Kenya-Somalia There is a direct bus to Garissa which leaves from outside the Munawar Hotel opposite the Kenya Bus Depot in Eastleigh, Nairobi (a 10-minute matatu ride (Route No 9) from Ronald Ngala St in the centre). The bus leaves at 5 am on Monday, Wednesday, Friday and Sunday, so it's virtually compulsory to stay overnight at the Munawar Hotel. The rate is Sh 60 a double and the hotel has its own restaurant. The bus trip takes about eight hours and costs Sh 80. At Garissa, stay at the *Garissa Highlife Lodging*, Mosque St, which costs Sh 40 a double and has a good restaurant. There are other hotels if this one is full. On the next day the bus to Liboi (border) leaves from the Mobil station (on the road out of town to the north) at 9 am on Tuesday, Thursday and Saturday (in the opposite direction on Wednesday, Friday and Sunday). The actual departure time depends on when the armed escort is ready – there has been trouble with *shifta* in the past but this has decreased since all buses were provided with an armed escort. The bus costs Sh 70 and takes about six hours. A lot of government vehicles cover this route so it's fairly easy to hitch (and usually free) if there are spare seats. When you get to Liboi you must report to the police. The immigration officer here can be a pain in the neck.

The only place to stay in Liboi is the *Cairo Hotel*. Changing money here used to be a good idea, as the rate for Somali shillings was excellent, but the January 1985 devaluation and subsequent float of the Somali shilling has killed the black market. Still, you're going to need some shillings to get you through as far as Kisimayo or Mogadishu. Liboi is an important staging post in the *qat* trade (which is now illegal in Somalia) and at least two light planes a day arrive here from Nairobi, drop their load and return – always empty. It is relatively easy to hitch a ride with them and usually free, but you must be at the airstrip as they don't hang around very long. It's also possible to pick them up at Garissa. If you're returning from Liboi to Garissa by bus, it first makes the 20-km trip to the Somali Liboi and then departs around 9 am when everyone has cleared customs and immigration. Going through Somali customs, you can expect a baggage search. There's no need to report to the police on arrival in Kisimayo. If you're not given a currency declaration form at the Somali customs, ask for one. This will save legwork later, as most Somali banks won't change money without one.

Boat There are no passenger boats to India any longer and there's no chance of getting work on a ship going there. We have, however, heard of a new shipping service which is operating from Dar es Salaam to India. The traveller who informed us didn't know too much about it but did supply the name and address of the company. It might be worth checking out if you want to sail rather than fly. See the Tanzanian chapter for details. Don't do what many travellers still do and turn up in Mombasa hoping to find a cheap ship passage to India. There are none. You have to fly.

The only regular passenger line which connects east coast ports as well as Mauritius and Madagascar with London is the *Baltic Steamship Company*. These are Russian boats and if you're interested you can enquire about them at Etco Travel, Nkrumah Rd, Mombasa.

Dhows ply regularly between Mombasa and Lamu and between Mombasa and Zanzibar when the winds are favourable. The former should take about two days but can take four. You must register with the Harbour Master in Mombasa if you take one of these. However, it's now very difficult to get on a dhow at Mombasa because a couple of *wazungus* drowned recently. It's much easier to get on at Malindi. The trip is not cheap so you can expect to pay around Sh 300-400. Don't pay anything until you get on the dhow. It's also possible at times to find a dhow

going all the way to the Persian Gulf, but the journey would be a long and probably an expensive (though interesting) way of getting there.

Lake Victoria Steamers The steamer service between Kenya and Tanzania has been resumed following the opening of the Tanzanian border. The *MV Bukoba* plies between Kisumu and Musoma and Mwanza. The schedule is as follows:

	Arrive	Depart
Mwanza (Thursday)	-	2 pm
Musoma (Thursday)	10 pm	12 pm
Kisumu (Friday)	2 pm	-
Kisumu (Friday)	-	6 pm
Musoma (Saturday)	7 am	9 am
Mwanza (Saturday)	5 pm	-

ELDORET

You can find cheap accommodation here at the *African Inland Church Training & Conference Centre* about half an hour's walk out of town on the Kisumu road. Singles cost Sh 20 and hot showers are available. There are no double rooms. The *Koringet Hotel*, Arap Moi St, has also been recommended. It has good clean double rooms for Sh 40.

The *Mid-Nite Café* has been recommended for food. It's open 24 hours a day and serves western food like hamburgers, chips, beans on toast.

KISUMU

The *Sikh Temple* here still welcomes travellers but you should leave a reasonable donation. *Hotel Safari* opposite the bus station is quiet and comfortable and costs Sh 35 a single. Also close to the bus station is the *Beograd Hotel*, which is clean and secure though there is a nightclub downstairs and plenty of prostitutes. It costs Sh 60 a double. The *YMCA* has beds in triple rooms for Sh 35 and breakfast is available for Sh 10. The *New Victory Hotel* costs Sh 90 a single. Another traveller recommended the *Guest Lodge* near the Octopus Disco which has rooms for Sh 55 a double. *Sam's Hotel* is a possibility at Sh 40 a single (two people can share a room

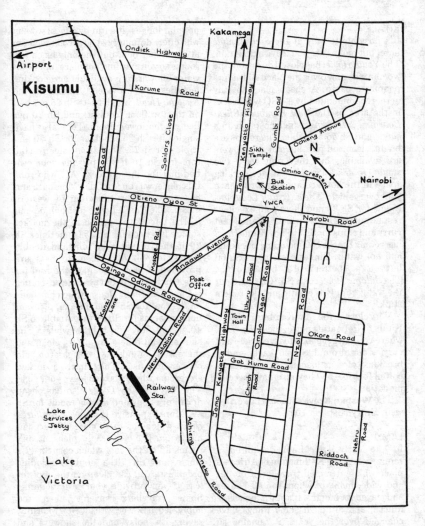

Kisumu

for this price), but it's a bit of a dump. Some travellers have been even less complimentary than that.

Going upmarket, try the *New Victoria Hotel*, which costs Sh 174 a double with own bathroom and includes breakfast. It's a very pleasant place and there are good views over Lake Victoria from the balcony.

The *Mona Lisa Restaurant* is good value. *Aifirose* is a popular place to eat.

The **Kisumu Museum** out on the Nairobi road about 15 minutes' walk from the YMCA is one of the best in Kenya. They even have a tribal homestead with six grass huts, an aquarium, a snake pit and a pit full of copulating tortoises!

KITALE

It's possible to stay at the *Sikh Temple* here, but make sure you leave a donation. The *Youth Hostel* has closed down, but the woman who now owns the place still allows people to camp. A cheap place to stay here, recommended by a VSO who works in the area, is the *New Kamburu Silent Boarding & Lodging*, which costs Sh 35 a single and Sh 55 a double. The rooms are bright, clean and pleasant and hot showers are available, but they only have two single rooms. There's ample parking space in the hotel compound if you have your own vehicle. The *Executive Lodge* has rooms for Sh 30 and there's an excellent restaurant opposite which offers great curry and chips for Sh 30. The *Kitale Hotel* has rooms for Sh 150 including breakfast and hot water. Dinner there costs Sh 60 but you get a better deal at the *Bongo Bar*. The *Salama Hotel* costs Sh 30 a single but the water supply is erratic and the toilets stink.

Very close to the New Kamburu Hotel is Kitale's No 1 eating place, the *Bongo Bar*, where you can get good steak, chicken and curries for around Sh 25 each, and a breakfast of eggs, bacon, sausage, tea or coffee for Sh 15. They also have accommodation.

The **Western Kenya Museum** is worth a visit. Entry costs Sh 10.

LAMU

In the early '70s Lamu acquired a reputation as the Kathmandu of Africa – a place which attracted travellers from far and wide, many of whom rented houses and stayed for months. It's still a travellers' Mecca, and although some things have changed over the years, it remains an exceptionally beautiful place full of old Arab houses dating back to the days when Lamu was an important trading centre and part of the chain of Omani Arab ports strung out down the East African coast. There are plenty of relaxing rustic lodges to stay in.

Mama Nawili's is one of the most popular lodges. It's run by a local woman who offers dormitory-style accommodation at Sh 20 per bed, but she only has a few rooms so you may find her place full. Cold-water showers are available and cooking facilities are provided. Similar is the *Kiswani Hotel*, which costs Sh 25 per bed on the top floor (coolest) and Sh 20 per bed on the lower floors. They also have singles for Sh 35, doubles for Sh 50 and triples for Sh 75. You can still sleep on the roof for Sh 15 if you provide your own bedding (no mosquitoes). Ali, who runs this place, was once a DJ in Mombasa and has an excellent collection of western music. The *Castle Lodge* just behind and to the left of the prison in the market square has beds for Sh 25 (sometimes Sh 20 if they're not very full) and double rooms for Sh 50. Mosquito nets are provided. You can sleep on the roof for less. On the waterfront near the post office is the *Dhow Guest House*, which has beds on the roof for Sh 15 and clean, pleasant double rooms for Sh 50 (negotiable to Sh 40 if you stay for a little while). The showers and toilets are pretty clean and there's a brand-new refrigerator and cooker for use. They have a locked storeroom where you can leave your gear. The *New Century Lodge* also has cheap dormitory beds and double rooms for Sh 40. More expensive is the *New Maharus Hotel*, which has three classes of accommodation. The best are the pleasant, airy rooms up on the roof which cost Sh 47 a single and Sh 73 a double including breakfast. You can sleep on the roof for less if you provide your own bedding. Some travellers haven't been too impressed, however, with the New Maharus, saying it's noisy and the showers and toilets are filthy. The *Bahati Lodge*, two 'blocks' behind the Standard Bank in a small yard, is very pleasant at Sh 50 a double and the roof is a good place to hang out.

Other places which have been recommended in the past are the *Beautiful House* (cheap dormitory accommodation or sleep on the roof), *Zahara Hotel* (double rooms for Sh 50-60), *Kavendoni's* (dormitory accommodation), *Karibuni Lodge, Amu Lodging* and *Kenya Lodging*.

It's possible to rent whole houses with kitchen and refrigerator for about Sh 50 per day. Look around on the waterfront in the buildings near *Pioneer Air Charter*. A bunch of other travellers managed to rent a 17th-century Omani mansion (Kisimani House) at Shelley Beach for Sh 1000 a month. This place is a living museum with a roof garden, plaster frescoes and antiques. It's owned by an Englishman who spends his summers in the UK and his winters in Lamu, so it isn't available all year. Ask the caretaker, Mohammed British, if it's available. Raffel, an Italian who works at the tours and information place (look for the sign) near the wharf, is also worth asking if you're looking for a cheap house to rent.

As you might expect in a place like this, there are a lot of small, intimate restaurants catering to travellers in Lamu. The *Yoghurt Inn*, just behind the Kiswani Hotel, has been popular for years, but though it still has good food (don't miss their prawn masala) and music, it's no longer cheap. Try *Kenya Cold Drinks* instead (shakes cost Sh 10). The *New Star Restaurant* has good food – beef curry for Sh 5 and curried beans or pancakes for Sh 4. They have good spaghetti bolognaise too. Also recommended are the *Olympic Restaurant*, which has good banana pancakes for Sh 6; and the *Lamu Coffee House & Restaurant*, which offers porridge and wild honey for Sh 6 as well as seafood (in the evenings) or steak for Sh 25-40 depending on what you eat. The *Suli Suli Restaurant* has pancakes, wild honey and good yoghurt; and *Ghais* (also known as Guy's) is good for seafood. Two other places you might try are the *Punuwani Restaurant*, just before the Zinj theatre, and the rooftop restaurant at the New Maharus Hotel. A connoisseur of local brews wrote to us saying that the only decent palm wine was to be found at Matondoni village where the school chairperson offers accommodation, food and palm wine at a very reasonable price.

Petley's Inn has the only bar in town. It's a good, laid-back meeting place with a not-too-expensive restaurant upstairs (kebabs are good value and they have excellent mango ice cream). Jambo Hotels, which owns the place, is bankrupt, so Petley's may have to close unless the Texan owner has found a buyer or a new leasee. In between Lamu and the beach is *Peponi's*, which was described by one unimpressed traveller as 'a mandatory watering hole en route to and from the beach but infested with disgustingly rich and brainless tourists.'

The **beach** at Lamu is a 45-minute walk from town, but you can get a boat there for Sh 10 per person.

The **museum** at Lamu is very good and well worth a visit for its interesting collection of tribal crafts. It's located on the waterfront and entry costs Sh 10. If you want to see dhows being repaired, you can do this at Matandoni village – a two-hour walk from Lamu. Don't forget the 14th- and 15th-century Arab ruins on **Manda** and **Pate** islands nearby. Trips to the ruins by motorboat (which takes four people) cost Sh 40 each, plus Sh 15 entry to the ruins themselves.

Dhow trips are easily arranged for about Sh 200 (for the boat) or Sh 80 per person. They normally take you out between 8 am and 4 pm while they do their fishing. The trip usually involves landing on an island around mid-day, where they will cook up part of the catch for lunch (this should be included in the price). Some of these trips go to Manda Island. It's possible to go out at night while they do their fishing by lantern between 7 pm and 2 am. The price is negotiable. Most of the fishermen hang around at Petley's or in the ice cream garden next door. Shariff has been recommended by many travellers. Contact him at the New Star Inn any evening around 7 pm. His boat is called the *Tabassam*.

If you want to stay on Manda Island, try the *Ras Kitau Hotel*, a centre for scuba diving. It has equipment for hire.

The best time to visit Lamu is outside of the tourist season (March to November). It's particularly good to be there on the Prophet's Birthday (most of the inhabitants are Swahili Moslems). At that time there is a week-long festival for which Lamu is famed throughout the area.

There have been reports of a couple of rapes on the beach recently and, as a result, the police are arresting local 'beach boys.' Unfortunately, they've been pretty indiscriminate about this and have been arresting just about any Swahili man they see with a white woman, so be prepared for hassles if you take up with one of the local men.

MALINDI

Malindi is similar to Lamu in that it offers white-sand beaches, coral reefs, surfing, scuba diving and old Omani Arab ruins. However, it's rather more commercialised because of its proximity to Mombasa and because it's much easier to get to. (The road between Malindi and Lamu is poor and subject to flooding in the wet season.)

The *Youth Hostel* (tel 365), opposite the Game and Fisheries Department about one km from the town centre, is clean, comfortable and very friendly, but you need a mosquito net. It costs Sh 30 and there are cooking facilities as well as reading material in English, French, Italian and Punjabi. Someone generally comes round every day to arrange snorkelling trips.

Similar in standard is the *New Kenya Hotel* which costs Sh 25 for a bed, Sh 53.40 a single and Sh 76 a double. Watch your bags here. Also cheap are the *Malindi Rest House*, opposite the market, which costs Sh 25 for a bed in the dormitory or Sh 50 a double; the *New Safari Hotel*, next to the bus station which costs Sh 25 in a shared room, Sh 50 a single and Sh 100 a double; the *Lamu Hotel*, which has good double rooms for Sh 45; and the *Lucky Lodge*, which has rooms for Sh 50 and up. Other recommended places are the *Metro Hotel*, a bit grim but with singles for Sh 30 and doubles for Sh 60, as well as an attached restaurant serving good food; the *Guji Guest House*; and the *Coronation Guest House*.

For food, try *I Love Pizza* beside the Metro Hotel; it has delicious pizzas for about Sh 40. Excellent Indian food can be found at the Hindu restaurant off Kikoi St near the Coronation Guest House and at *Chagga's* on the road leading down to the coast. If you're staying at the Youth Hostel, try the recently opened *Baobab Café* nearby. The food is good and the prices reasonable. The *Matinga* bar behind the hotels is worth a visit and they sell very cheap palm wine. Avoid wandering around Malindi late at night -- it isn't a particularly safe place to do this.

Buses for Lamu leave about 10 am: *Tawakal* from in front of the New Safari Hotel and *Tana River Service* from the Mobil petrol station round the corner.

About two km south of Malindi, *Silver Sands* is still very popular with travellers and costs Sh 15 per person to camp, plus there are a number of bandas which cost Sh 50, 60 and 75 for two people. The more expensive ones are clean and not too dark. The owner, Benghazi, is very friendly and helpful. Water is sometimes a problem here (there's not much of it). There is a small restaurant in the grounds as well as a bar, and cooking facilities are available. Beware of thieves here and on the beach. Food at the *Cold House* next door has been recommended. The *Baobab Café* on the seafront is good for coffee and banana pancakes. Upmarket you might like to try the *Stardust Restaurant*, which has very good seafood.

The village of **Watamu** just south of Malindi has been recommended. Even though there are several large hotels there, the beach is excellent and retains a certain charm. To get there from Malindi, take the Gedi turnoff and follow the road all the way down. For somewhere to stay, try the *Mt Meru Ngamene Guest House* for Sh 60 a double or the *Seventh Day Adventist Youth Camp*. At the latter you can either camp or get a bed in one of the three rooms (each with two to three beds) in the house. The camp is fairly basic and the toilet and shower aren't up to much, but there's a kitchen with a gas cooker (which actually works) and it's close to the beach. The camp is about 10 minutes' walk from the village. It costs Sh 45 per person but the first price quoted is usually Sh 80 (which is definitely overpriced).

You can use the facilities of the large hotels (bar, disco, pool, restaurants) regardless of whether you are staying there (money is money after all). Seeing as the price of beer is fixed by the government, you might as well drink in the large hotels if you feel like it. About half an hour's walk from the village there is the *Seafarer Hotel* where you can go scuba diving. The cost is Sh 350 for a two-hour basic course in the swimming pool plus about one hour's diving on the reef down to six or seven metres. If you've had some experience diving, the cost is Sh 220 for one hour – you don't need a certificate, but they will test you out first in the pool. Each time you go back it costs Sh 10 less. The hotel also has windsurfing facilities here for Sh 100 per hour.

Make sure you don't miss **Gedi**, 16 km south of Malindi, where the ruins of an old city dating back to the 13th century are situated. Tracks have been cleared through the jungle and excavations have unearthed several mosques, a palace, many large houses and wells. It's a good place to visit if you have an interest in archaeological sites. A matatu from Malindi will cost Sh 6-7. Entry to the ruins costs Sh 15.

MOMBASA

Mombasa has been an important port for centuries and many battles have been fought for possession of it. It was taken by the Portuguese in the late 16th century in their quest to destroy the Arab grip over maritime trade in the Indian Ocean. Fort Jesus dates from that time. The Omani Arabs threw them out again a hundred years later and held onto Mombasa until the arrival of the British towards the end of the 19th century. It's still an entrepot for Indian Ocean trade and there are many interesting sights though, regrettably, the dhow careening dock in the Old Harbour is no more.

Note Kilindini Rd has been renamed Moi Avenue, but both names are in use.

Robbery with violence is becoming common in Mombasa. Avoid walking along the streets or the beaches at night alone, and don't carry bags which can be snatched from you by hit-and-run merchants. Forget about sleeping on the beaches. Also watch it around Fort Jesus.

Information

The Tourist Office is on Moi Avenue next to the giant tusks. It's open Monday to Friday from 8 am to noon and 2 to 4.30 pm. On Saturdays it's open from 8 am to noon. Closed Sundays.

American Express has an office at Express Kenya Ltd, Nkrumah Rd, PO Box 90631, Mombasa (tel 24461).

The British Deputy High Commission is in Ralli House, Nyerere Avenue, PO Box 90360, Mombasa (tel 311953).

Most of the bus lines – *Coastline Bus Services*, *Goldline Bus Service* and *Kenya Bus Service* – are on Mwembe Tayari Rd between Jomo Kenyatta Avenue and Haile Selassie Rd. *Akamba Bus Service* is on Jomo Kenyatta Avenue and *Seaman* and *Tawakal* which operate to Malindi and Lamu are on Digo Rd. Taxis going to Malindi are on Jomo Kenyatta Avenue while the other taxi services are on Haile Selassie Rd.

The Likoni Ferry runs at frequent intervals throughout the night and day (every 20 minutes on average between 5 am and 12.30 am; less frequently between 12.30 am and 5 am). The ferry is free to pedestrians.

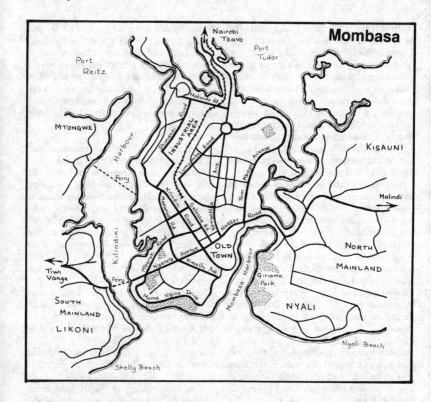

Health

You can get vaccinations from the Public Health Department, Msanifa Kombo St, off Haile Selassie Rd (tel 26791). For yellow fever go there between 8 and 9 am on Wednesday and Friday; for cholera between 2 and 3.30 pm on Wednesday and Friday; and for smallpox between 8 and 9.30 am on Monday, Tuesday and Saturday. All shots cost Sh 20. For a free bilharzia test go to the Control Centre for Communicable Diseases, Mnazi Moja Rd.

Things to See

Fort Jesus, built by the Portuguese in 1593 and taken by the Omani Arabs in 1698 after a 33-month siege, is now a museum with displays of historical relics found on the site as well as artifacts from various other ruins along the coast. It's open every day of the year from 8.30 am to 6.30 pm and entry costs Sh 15.

The **Old Harbour** where dhows come in from the Yemen and the Persian Gulf is still worth exploring, but there is no longer a dhow careening dock there.

The **bazaar**, centred around Biashara St, is particularly good for fabrics and there are plenty of other things from places all around the Indian Ocean and the African interior.

The **Ivory Room**, just off Treasury Square, is now permanently closed.

Places to Stay

Probably the most popular place to stay and the one which gets the most recommendations is the *New Peoples Hotel* at the beginning of Abdel Nasser Rd/Digo Rd. Rooms cost Sh 36-59 a single (latter with own shower) and Sh 61.50-119 a double (latter with own shower). They also have rooms with three to five beds at Sh 25 per bed or Sh 100 for a five-bed room. There's a safe storeroom where you can leave your gear. The *Hydro Hotel*, Digo Rd near the market, has also been popular for many years. It costs Sh 21.85 per bed in dormitory-style rooms and Sh 60-70 a double. There are no single rooms. Reasonably good food is available all day (curries for Sh 15-20). Similar is the *Savoy Hotel*, Digo Rd, which has large, clean, airy rooms for Sh 60 a double. Baggage can be left safely there. The *Mvita Hotel*, Turkana St off Hospital St (which itself is off Digo Rd one block from Kenyatta Avenue) not far from the Hydro, costs Sh 60 a double. It's very clean and bags left here are safe. Towels and soap are provided and there's even loo paper in the toilets. There's a small bar on the ground floor. (Ever seen black-veiled Muslim women drinking beer? A bizarre sight!) Other cheapies which have been recommended are the *Downtown Lodge*, Digo Rd by Hospital St, with doubles for Sh 60; *Al-Egbaal Hotel*, off Jomo Kenyatta Avenue by Mwembe Tayari Rd behind the bus station, which has doubles for Sh 40; *Al-Nasser Boarding & Lodging* at the end of Digo Rd which has doubles for Sh 50; and the *Visitors Inn*, Haile Selassie Rd, which has quiet rooms for Sh 40 a single including breakfast. Bags left at the latter place are secure. Another place recommended by some people who had been living in Zambia for nine years is the *CPK (Church of the Province of Kenya) Guest House*, Box 96170 (tel 451218), opposite the Likoni Ferry. They said it is very clean and excellent value, and the charges for bed and full board are very reasonable. The *YMCA* at Likoni (first street on the left after the ferry) costs Sh 65 for bed and breakfast and Sh 105 for full board.

Going upmarket, there is the *Hotel Rolex*, down a side street off Digo Rd, which has singles for Sh 100 and doubles for Sh 150 including breakfast. It has good, large rooms (four of you can share a double room with shower), and the price of Sh 250 includes breakfast. It's been recommended by several travellers. Opposite the Rolex is the *Select Hotel*, which costs Sh 243 a double. In this same price range is the *Hotel Splendid*, Digo Rd, which is excellent value at Sh 243.50 a double for bed and breakfast, own bathroom and air-conditioning. The hotel has a pleasant rooftop garden and bar. Another in this price bracket is the *New Palm Tree*. More expensive still is the *Castle Hotel*, Msanifa Kombo Rd off Moi Avenue (tel 24799), which has been refurbished and now costs Sh 220 a single and Sh 290 a double including a good breakfast. The hotel is air-conditioned, as is the restaurant. Meals here cost US$20-plus but it's a beautiful old place if you have the spare cash.

A lot of travellers head south or north to one of the beaches where accommodation is available. Just south of Mombasa is **Likoni Beach** where Andy Brow has 'minilets' with cooking and washing facilities for Sh 50. Avoid staying at *Timbwani Camp* as a lot of thieving goes on there. Twenty-five km south of Mombasa is **Tiwi Beach** where you can camp at the *Twiga Lodge* for Sh 15 per person per night. There are good facilities here including showers, toilets, a bar and a restaurant. To get there, don't take the first signposted track to the beach coming from Mombasa but the second one about one km further on. It's much quicker this way. Twenty-seven km south of Mombasa near **Diani Beach** is the popular *Dan Trench's* at the back of the *Trade Winds Hotel*, where you can get a bed for Sh 15 a night or camp. To get there, take a matatu (Sh 10) or a bus from the south side of the Likoni ferry to Ukunda, where you will see a sign for the

Trade Winds Hotel. It's only 50 metres from there to Dan Trench's. The beach is excellent and you can use the facilities of the Trade Winds Hotel (pool, bar, disco) if you are discreet. This place also has an all-you-can-eat breakfast for Sh 35. If you want to splurge, try the lunch at the *Sports Recreation Centre* for Sh 55 (rump steak, baked squid, salad, several dressings, fruit salad and coffee). The outdoor salad bar at the *Jadini Beach* has also been recommended as good value (without the lobster!) and the staff are friendly. There are plenty of cheap restaurants in the vicinity including *James' Restaurant* which offers good, cheap, filling food (chapatti, coconut rice, beans). If you like shish kebab, try the *Bushbaby Restaurant* by the Two Fishes Hotel. Information about scuba diving and snorkelling can be found at the *Barracuda Dive Club* in the Robinson Baobab Hotel at the south end of Diani Beach. Another place which has been recommended for camping is *Nomads* further south than Dan Trench's.

North of Mombasa (25 km), **Kanamai**, where there is a quiet but fairly popular *Youth Hostel* right next to the beach. You can stay here for Sh 20 per night in the dormitory and Sh 60 for a double room. Bags left here are secure. The shop sells only soft drinks and mosquito coils. To get there, take a bus from Mombasa to the village of Majenga (Sh 4). From there the Youth Hostel is signposted and it's a three-km walk. Further along the beach is the *Whispering Sands Hotel* where, if you're discreet and look as though you belong there, you can use the pool without being charged the visitor's fee of Sh 20. They also offer a smorgasbord breakfast for Sh 30 which seems to last most of the day.

Places to Eat

Two very good Indian restaurants where you can eat for around Sh 20 are the *Taj Hotel* and *Singh's Restaurant*. The former is near the Hydro Hotel on a road branching off left from Digo Rd, heading out of town behind the Mobil station. Singh's is beyond the Taj. The Taj serves huge vegetarian curries with parotha at Sh 25. For Swahili cooking try the *Rekoda Restaurant* on Nyeri St parallel to Nkrumah Rd between the Old Town and Fort Jesus. Also recommended are the *Splendid View Restaurant*, Sir Ali St, and *Ashur's*, Jomo Kenyatta Avenue. For good breakfasts, muffins and lime juice try the *Blue Room Hotel* round the corner from the Mvita Hotel. A few minutes' walk from the New Peoples Hotel is the *Ghazel Restaurant*, which offers excellent cheap meals (chicken in coconut or lamb in yogurt for Sh 30 and barbeque kebabs for Sh 8, including as much rice and chapatti as you can eat).

The terrace of the *Castle Hotel*, Moi Avenue, is similar to the Thorn Tree Café in Nairobi – lots of travellers, sailors, prostitutes, local colour – and is a convivial place for a beer in the evenings. Another similar place is the *Istanbul Bar*, also on Moi Avenue. If you feel like venturing out of the centre there are some excellent reggae clubs in the suburbs which are very cheap and great fun – much better than the *Rainbow Hotel* where many people go.

NAIROBI

Nairobi is the capital of Kenya and a very modern city with excellent facilities. It's a good place to get essential business done (banks, telecommunications, visas, etc) and you can always be sure of meeting plenty of other travellers here, some of whom will have been travelling for months and so will be mines of information.

Information

The Tourist Office is on the corner of Moi Avenue and City Hall Way. It's worth calling in here as they have a lot of information, maps and glossy leaflets about both the city and the rest of the country. There's also a free monthly magazine which is worth picking up.

American Express is at Express Kenya

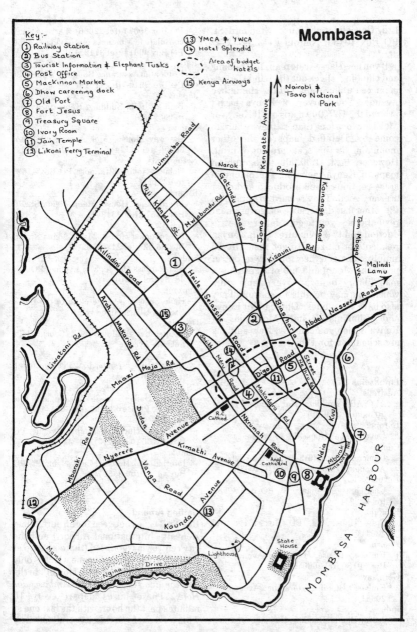

Mombasa

Key:-
1. Railway Station
2. Bus Station
3. Tourist Information & Elephant Tusks
4. Post Office
5. Mackinnon Market
6. Dhow careening dock
7. Old Port
8. Fort Jesus
9. Treasury Square
10. Ivory Room
11. Jain Temple
12. Likoni Ferry Terminal
13. YMCA & YWCA
14. Hotel Splendid
- - - Area of budget hotels
15. Kenya Airways

Ltd, Consolidated House, Standard St, PO Box 40433, Nairobi (tel 334 7277/8).

If you need large scale maps for trekking and climbing, check out the Land Department & Public Maps Office, Harambee Avenue. The Survey of Kenya hasn't printed the 1:25,000 maps of Mt Kenya or Mt Elgon for a long time, so they're hard to come by. Detailed maps of the other mountains on this scale are out of print. However, basic 1:50,000 topographical maps of Kenya including the mountain areas continue to be produced and most are very good. They're hard to obtain, on the other hand, because of government regulations – you need a letter of introduction and two signatures from Kenyan residents or citizens to get them. If you simply can't get them or they're out of print, the Mountain Club of Kenya has a map library built up over many years which you may be able to consult. They also have two guides, 'Guide to Mt Kenya and Kilimanjaro' and 'Mountains of Kenya' which you can buy. New editions are scheduled for 1985.

Embassies

Australia
    AFC/ADC Building, Moi Avenue, PO Box 30360 (tel 334666)
Burundi
    Development House, Moi Avenue
Canada
    Comcraft House (6th floor), Haile Selassie Avenue, PO Box 30481 (tel 334033)
Egypt
    Chai House, Koinange St, PO Box 30285 (tel 22991)
Ethiopia
    State House Rd, PO Box 45198 (tel 23941)
France
    Embassy House, Harambee Avenue, PO Box 30180 (tel 26661)
Germany
    Embassy Building, Harambee Avenue (tel 26661)
India
    Jeevan Bharati Building, Harambee Avenue, PO Box 30074 (tel 22566). There is also a consulate in Mombasa on Kaunda Avenue, PO Box 90614 (tel 311051).
Italy
    Prudential Assurance Building, Wabera St, PO Box 30107 (tel 21615)
Japan
    Bank of India Building, Kenyatta Avenue (tel 332955)
Malawi
    Gateway House, Moi Avenue, PO Box 30453 (tel 21174)
Netherlands
    Uchumi House (6th floor), PO Box 41537 (tel 27111)
Rwanda
    International House, Mama Ngina St, PO Box 48579 (tel 334341)
Somalia
    International House, Mama Ngina St, PO Box 30769 (tel 24301)
Sudan
    Shankardass House, Moi Avenue, PO Box 48784 (tel 20770)
Tanzania
    Haile Selassie Avenue close to the traffic circle at Uhuru Highway
Uganda
    Cooperative Building (4th floor), Haile Selassie Avenue
UK
    Bruce House, Standard St, PO Box 30465 (tel 66369)
USA
    Corner Haile Selassie Avenue and Moi Avenue, PO Box 30137 (tel 334141)
Zaire
    Electricity House, Harambee Avenue, PO Box 48106 (tel 29771)
Zambia
    International House, Mama Ngina St, PO Box 48741 (tel 335972)

Getting Around

Bus No 34 goes between the airport (Jomo Kenyatta International Airport) and the city centre via Ngong Rd (there's a stop at the end of 5th Ngong Avenue which is only 150 metres from the Youth Hostel). In the city the bus starts from the *Ambassador Hotel*. These buses depart every 15 minutes past the hour, with the last one at 7 pm (or 8 pm from the city terminal). The fare is Sh 4. *Kenya Airways* operates a bus every hour on the hour which is willing to drop you at any named hotel in Nairobi. The fare is Sh 40 and the depot in the city is on Koinange St.

Matatus in the centre start from outside the Kenya National Archives across Moi Avenue from the *Hilton Hotel*.

Hitching If you're hitching to Mombasa, take bus No 13 as far as the airport turn-off and hitch from there. You can also take No 109 which drops you on the highway. For Uganda, take bus No 23 from the Hilton to the end of its route and hitch from there. Going to Naro Moru, Nyeri, Nanyuki and Mt Meru, take bus No 45 or 145 from the central bus station up Thika Rd to Kenyatta College and hitch from there, but make sure you get out at the entrance to the college rather than the exit as it's very difficult to hitch from the latter.

Things to See

The **National Museum** has a good exhibition on prehistoric peoples (they have the famous 1470 skull), and the collections of birds, mammals and tribal crafts are quite good. It's open daily from 9.30 am to 6 pm and entry costs Sh 15. **Snake Park** has the same opening hours and entry fee as the National Museum.

A visit to **Nairobi National Park** just outside the city costs Sh 150 for a half-day safari. VW buses leave from outside the Hilton Hotel at 8 am and 2 pm.

The **Bombas of Kenya** where you can see tribal villages and dancing are worth a visit (Sh 40). Get a bus from the station to Langatta.

Places to Stay

Many of the budget hotels are situated on or between Tom Mboya St and Kirinyaga Rd. There are also two very popular places in a different area – Mrs Roche's and the Youth Hostel.

In the main area are the following:
Iqbal Hotel, Latema Rd. This has been a long-time favourite with travellers and has recently been refurbished from top to bottom – new paint, beds, sheets, towels, cupboards with locks, doors with locks, clean toilets. There are even hot showers, a TV lounge and an outside sheltered area, and prostitutes are banned upstairs. The cost is Sh 10 to sleep on the floor, Sh 25 for a dormitory bed and Sh 50 for a double.

Al Mansura Hotel, Munyu St. This is of a similar standard to the Iqbal. It offers cheap dormitory accommodation and doubles for Sh 50. It's fairly clean and there's a reasonable restaurant downstairs.

Mombasa Rest House, River Rd. This place has fairly clean dormitory-style rooms for Sh 23 per bed. You can lock up your baggage here.

Sunrise Lodge, Latema Rd opposite the Iqbal. Like the Iqbal, this was recently refurbished. It's clean and orderly and, although there is a nightclub next door and the hotel doubles as a brothel, the door is always locked. It costs Sh 80 a double including a hand basin. There is hot water all day.

New Kenya Lodge, corner River and Latema Rds. This hotel is good value for Sh 25-27 per bed in the dormitories (four beds per room) or Sh 60 a double. The two men in reception are very friendly and, even if it's full, they'll let you sleep somewhere (Sh 15 on the roof or in the hall). Baggage is safe here.

Sunset Lodge, Latema Rd, costs Sh 45 a single but it's somewhat dingy and doubles as a brothel.

Kambirwa Board & Lodging, Kirinyaga Rd at the junction with Tom Mboya St, has good doubles for Sh 70.

Hotel Gloria, Tom Mboya St at Ronald Ngala St, has rooms for Sh 100 a single and Sh 125 a double including breakfast.

Dolat Hotel, Mfangono St (one street behind Tom Mboya St near River Rd), has very clean rooms with private bathroom and hot water for Sh 81 a single and Sh 117 a double.

Terminal Hotel, Moktar Dada St, across

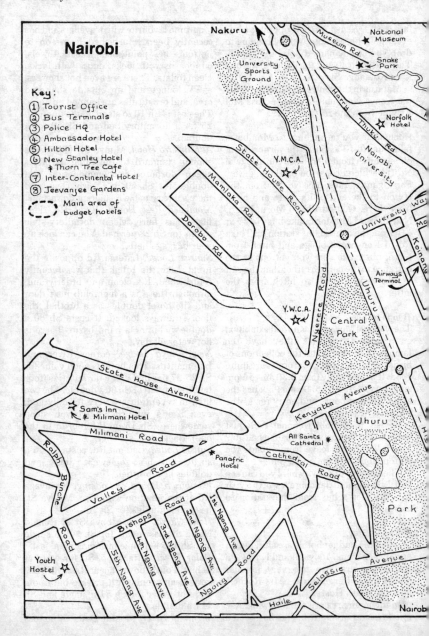

Nairobi

Key:
1. Tourist Office
2. Bus Terminals
3. Police HQ
4. Ambassador Hotel
5. Hilton Hotel
6. New Stanley Hotel & Thorn Tree Cafe
7. Inter-Continental Hotel
8. Jeevanjee Gardens

- - - Main area of budget hotels

Nakuru

Museum Rd

National Museum

Snake Park

Harry Thuku Rd

Norfolk Hotel

University Sports Ground

State House Road

Y.M.C.A.

Nairobi University

University Way

Mamlaka Rd

Dorobo Rd

Nyerere Road

Airways Terminal

Y.W.C.A.

Central Park

Uhuru

State House Avenue

Kenyatta Avenue

Sam's Inn & Milimani Hotel

Milimani Road

All Saints Cathedral

Uhuru

Ralph Bunche Road

Valley Road

Panafric Hotel

Cathedral Road

Park

Bishops Road

4th Ngong Ave

3rd Ngong Ave

2nd Ngong Ave

1st Ngong Ave

Ngong Road

Selassie Avenue

Youth Hostel

5th Ngong Ave

Haile

Nairobi

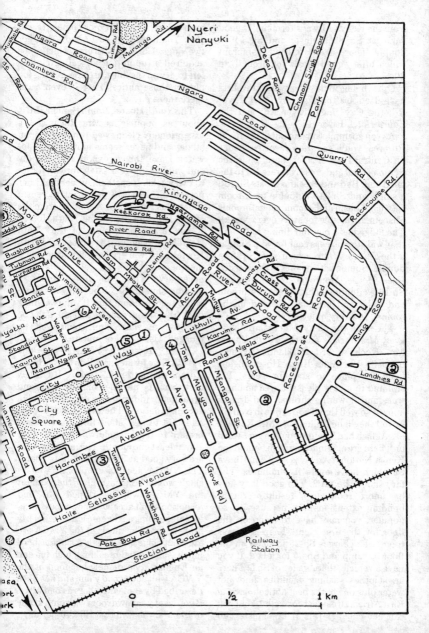

from the Kenya Airways terminal, is good value at Sh 80 a single and Sh 140 a double. There is an attached restaurant which offers good meals for around Sh 20.

Other hotels in this area which travellers have used are the *Sun Ray Hotel*, River Rd; the *City Hotel*, River Rd; and the *Zahra Hotel*, River Rd.

As you go upmarket and out of the River Rd area, you'll see the *Greenview Lodge* off Central Park. To get there, go to the Serena Hotel and cross Nyerere Rd to the dead end. Bed and breakfast costs Sh 130 a single and Sh 240 a double for a room with hand basin and communal bathrooms (discount available for stays over a week). The lodge has a bar and dining room and they will store excess gear for you. Similar is the *Embassy Hotel*, which costs Sh 234 a double. Somewhat cheaper is the *Garden Guest House*, Monrovia Rd, which costs Sh 162 a double including own bathroom and toilet and breakfast (served in the rooms). It's very quiet.

The main travellers' Meccas are, however, *Mrs Roche's* and the *Youth Hostel*. Mrs Roche's, 3rd Parklands Avenue, opposite the Agha Khan Hospital, has been *the* place to stay for years. It's situated in a very pleasant area amongst trees and flowering shrubs. Taxi drivers know it so well that if you arrive in Nairobi by rail they'll be calling out, 'Mrs Roche?' or, 'Agha Khan?' before you can get a word in. There are also matatus from behind the Kenya National Archives on Tom Mboya St which leave every five minutes. The fare should be Sh 2. The good lady now has more room as a result of recent building extensions but, because it's so popular, you may have to sleep on the floor for the first night. There's always room! She charges Sh 25 to sleep on the floor or camp and Sh 35 for a bed. If you have a vehicle, there's a fee of Sh 5. There are clothes-washing facilities and hot water plus one of the best noticeboards in East Africa. Breakfast costs Sh 15 but you can get cheaper (Sh 5) breakfasts 300

metres up the road (two-egg omelette and tea). You'll be pleased to know that her two dogs, Curly and Bruno, which once acquired a reputation for eating clothes left to dry on the lines, are now getting too old for those antics. There's even a cat these days.

The Youth Hostel, Ralph Bunche Rd, is about as popular as Mrs Roche's. It's exceptionally clean, well run, stays open all day and never seems to run out of hot water. Dave, the warden, is very friendly and will lock up gear safely for you for up to two weeks. It costs Sh 30 per night per person plus Sh 5 if you want to rent a sheet. Bus Nos 1, 2, 3, 4, 7 and 8 from the Hilton Hotel all go past the Youth Hostel. If you're not a member of the Youth Hostels Association, the staff at the Youth Hostel here will try to sell you a year's membership for Sh 150. This isn't necessary. You can buy temporary membership for Sh 30 but they're reluctant to tell you about this. If you're coming back from the city centre at night, *don't* be tempted to walk. You could well be mugged. Use a taxi or matatu.

There are three *YMCAs* and one *YWCA*. The former are all on State House Rd and the latter on Nyerere Rd. They cost Sh 76 per person for bed and breakfast (dormitory or share-room accommodation). The YWCA, however, is reluctant to take short-term visitors and prefers to take people who are going to stay at least one month. The monthly rates are very good at Sh 900 including board. The YWCA accepts couples as well as single women. Baggage left in the rooms at the YMCA will be ripped off, and reception won't accept money or passports for safekeeping as the safe is also regularly broken into. The meals at the YMCA are excellent value and include a smorgasbord lunch, substantial breakfast, high tea and an English-style dinner, but food at the YWCA isn't such good value and has been described by some travellers as bad news. If you want your own room with bath at one of the Y's, this will cost Sh 240 per day.

The *Mennonite Guest House* (tel 60264) and the *Mayfield Guest House* (tel 22519) have been recommended by a couple who lived in Zambia for nine years. They say both are very clean and excellent value, and the prices for bed and full board are very reasonable.

Places to Eat

Kenya is well known for its 'all-you-can-eat' restaurants at a set price, and Nairobi has a wide choice of them. Two of the best are the *Supreme Hotel*, Tom Mboya Rd at River Rd, which offers South Indian vegetarian food for Sh 45, and the *Hare Krishna Temple*, River Rd close to the museum, which also offers Indian vegetarian food but only on Sundays. The *Njogu-ini-Rwathia Hotel* round the corner from the Gloria Hotel on Mufangano St is another of these places; the servings are so large that you'll be hard-pressed to eat them even if you just got off a bus from Somalia. The fish-and-chip shop next door to the *Floras Restaurant* has been recommended. This sterling dish will cost you Sh 35.

Many of the five-star hotels offer all-you-can-eat breakfasts and lunches which will keep you going all day. The *Intercontinental Hotel* has really good salad lunches every day for Sh 30, and the *Hilton Hotel* offers a Sunday brunch at a similar price in the restaurant upstairs. It's also worth checking out the *Ambassadeur Hotel* for these sort of deals.

In a place as big as Nairobi there are naturally thousands of restaurants and, of course, everyone has a yen for a particular type of cuisine, but some of the ones which have been recommended are: *Satkar Indian Restaurant*, Moi Avenue near the junction with Latema Rd (good, cheap vegetarian food); *New Flora Restaurant*, just off Latema Rd (excellent chicken); *African Heritage Café*, Banda St (excellent food and live music on Saturdays); *Majah Restaurant*, at the University end of Muindi Mbingu St (good curries from Sh 18 and up); *Eureka Restaurant* in the Heron Court Hotel (good-value Indian food); and the *Trattoria Restaurant*, corner Wabera and Kaunda Sts (not cheap but the best Italian food in Nairobi). The *Bull Café*, 30 metres from the New Kenya Lodge, has very good cheap food and is a pleasant place at which to eat.

The *Mandarin*, Tom Mboya St, is reputedly the best Chinese restaurant in Nairobi. The cost of a meal for two will be around Sh 150. If you're looking for French food then head for the *French Cultural Centre*, Monrovia and Loita Sts – very reasonable prices (a main course costs around Sh 60). A somewhat more expensive Indian restaurant to try if you want a splurge is the *Minar Restaurant*, Banda St. A meal here will cost around Sh 100 per person.

For something out of the ordinary, try the revolving restaurant at the top of the *Kenyatta Conference Centre*, which is the highest building in Nairobi. The views are spectacular, especially at sunset. Lunch or dinner here costs Sh 30-40.

The following places have been recommended but are more expensive: *Angu's Restaurant* (steaks); *China Garden* and the *Pagoda* (Chinese food); the *Tamarind* (seafood); *Tae Kwon Do Restaurant* (Korean food); and the *Pub* on Standard St.

Some travellers have recommended *Giorgio's Italian Restaurant*. The manager here can be quite entertaining. Someone should teach him rap dancing – he'd be even more entertaining.

One of the best places to meet other travellers is the *Thorn Tree Café* under the New Stanley Hotel. It's a wee bit touristy but it's a popular hang-around place and has a very good noticeboard. If you're hankering after some nostalgia or just want a convivial place to enjoy a beer, try the 'olde English pub' in the *Intercontinental Hotel*. Another bar which has been recommended is the *Green Bar* opposite the Iqbal Hotel. It's a wild place, a favourite with *wazungu* and great for just watching people. 'All human life is here,'

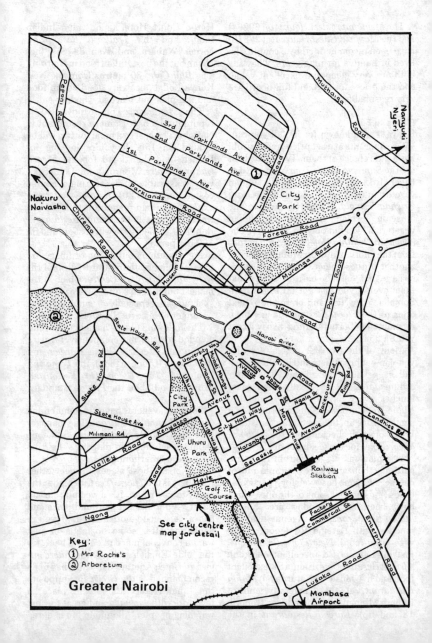

Key:
① Mrs Roche's
② Arboretum

Greater Nairobi

as one traveller put it, and it's open 24 hours a day. For a nightclub, try *Hallians Night Club*, Tom Mboya St (the entrance is the same door as Eddie's travel agency). They sometimes have live bands and you may well be the only *wazungu* there.

Warning In the last edition of this book we warned people against walking round Nairobi at night because of the muggings and robberies that have become common. It seems we put a lot of people off going into the centre at night, so it's time to qualify that warning. It's no worse than any other large city around the world (ever been to New York or Jakarta?). Just one thing, though: don't attempt to walk back to the Youth Hostel (if that's where you are staying) by cutting through Uhuru Park. Instead, take a bus or taxi down Valley Rd.

And there's one more trap not to fall into. It starts off with someone saying to you, 'Help me, I'm a Ugandan student.' Don't believe it. You'll be in trouble if you hang around. Then there is the other which starts off with the 'dropped envelope' apparently full of Sh 50 notes. As one traveller put it: 'Just by chance, so to speak, there's a man behind you who picks it up and joyfully announces that it's a gift from God and he'd like to share his good fortune with you. If you're a greedy pig, you do, but as soon as you've accepted it the man who dropped the envelope returns and demands to look through your wallet and pockets. It probably serves you right if you accepted the money in the first place, but when you get your wallet back you discover that your cash has been replaced by newspaper.' She went on to say, 'Still, a little Yankee ingenuity goes a long way. A Californian acquaintance got to the envelope first, picked it up, crossed the street and dropped it down the drain.' While I might admire the man's pluck, I'm sure it put them off for all of 10 minutes. Newspapers are cheap. Nevertheless: Watch it!

Other
Nilestar Tours close to the Hilton on Moi Avenue run tours to **Nairobi National Park & Animal Orphanage** for Sh 100. The trip lasts four hours. It's easy, on the other hand, to hitch to the national park. The **National Museum** and **Snake Park** are open from 9.30 am to 6 pm. Entry costs Sh 10 or Sh 5 with a student card. The **Railway Museum** (well worth a visit if you're into this kind of thing) costs Sh 4 entry.

A newly developed place in Langatta (south of Nairobi) is the **Langatta Nature Education Centre**, which has Rothschild's giraffes. There is an elevated structure there from which you can see and feed the giraffes at their head height. The giraffes can come and go at will. Worth a visit.

NAKURU
The *Sikh Temple* here generally doesn't take travellers any longer, but if you do manage to get in please leave a reasonable donation. It's roughly 400 metres behind the market on the left-hand side. You can camp in the *Agricultural Showground* for Sh 7.50 a night, but if you're walking back from town at night, make sure you know where your tent is as there are no lights. *Amigo's*, near the market by the round-about, is noisy but secure and very clean. It costs Sh 50 a single and Sh 90 a double. Somewhat cheaper is the *Tropical Lodge* which costs Sh 65 a double. They have hot showers and large clean rooms, and the staff are very friendly. To get there follow Kenyatta Avenue and go to the left at Moi Rd. The *Nakuru Inn*, by the market and Link Rd, costs Sh 50 a double. Two other relatively cheap places to stay are the *Rift Valley Hotel* which costs Sh 30 and has hot

NYERI
The *Central Hotel*, 50 metres from the Clock Tower and post office, is a good place to indulge in a full English-style breakfast. It costs Sh 22 and you get endless tea, toast and coffee as well as newspapers. Stay at the *Central Bar &*

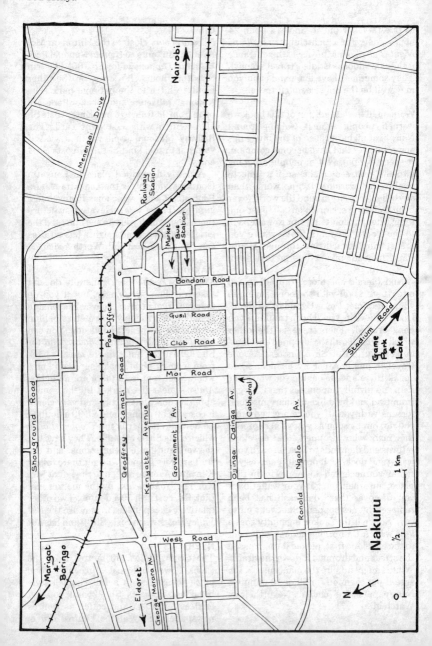

Nakuru

water (but watch your gear), and the *Top Lodge* which costs Sh 100 a double. The latter is somewhat overpriced considering what it offers. You could also try the *3-Ways Hotel*, which costs Sh 40 a single.

Outside of Nakuru itself, Charles Link (an American who has been teaching in Kenya since 1977) and his Somali wife have written to us offering a free place to stay for up to three travellers in their spare bedroom at the school where he teaches. The school is called *Greensteds School* and it's about 16 km before Nakuru town on the new Nairobi-Nakuru road. There's a large sign by the road on the right-hand side as you head into Nakuru from Nairobi.

The *Skyways Restaurant* used to be excellent value for meals, but recent reports suggest it's gone downhill a lot and is now 'very dirty, greasy and expensive.' You can get really good brown bread, sausage rolls and ice cream at the *Rift Valley Bakery*, Gusil Rd, under the hotel of the same name. The *Kenya Coffee Board* shop offers very good coffee but the snacks there are very expensive. The *Tipsy Restaurant*, Gusil Rd, offers excellent curries for Sh 20 and up as well as Western food. The place itself has little character, but the food makes up for it and the two bars are great fun. Another place which has been highly recommended by an expatriate working locally is *Gillanis Restaurant* upstairs from Gillanis Supermarket. The *Railway Restaurant* offers good food but it's very pricey at around Sh 115 for a complete meal. The *Green Hotel* has also been recommended for good food.

NANYUKI

There is a *Youth Hostel* at Emmanuel Parish Centre near the post office on Market Rd (tel 2112). It's good value at Sh 20 for a private single room and the staff are very friendly. The price is the same regardless of whether or not you have Youth Hostel membership.

Some 55 km north-west of Nanyuki is *El Karama Ranch*, run by Guy Grant, where you can hire a tent for Sh 35 per person. He provides firewood, table, chairs, beds and hot water in the mornings, but you must bring your own food. The ranch covers almost 5000 hectares and you can see plenty of game there with the help of a guide. The Kenyan Automobile Association has a sheet showing exactly how to get to this place (office in the Hurlingham Shopping Arcade, Nairobi), but if you haven't got this sheet then take the Thomson's Falls road out of Nanyuki for about 1½ km and turn right down Naibor Rd, then right again on Doldol Rd. When you get to the sign for Ol Jogi Ranch, turn off on the opposite side.

NYAHURURU (Thomson's Falls)

You can stay at *Thomsons Falls Lodge* camp site, or at the *Muthengera Farmer Lodge*. A single room at the latter is Sh 50 and good food is available at reasonable prices. The *Equator Hotel* costs Sh 30 per night and is clean and comfortable with good food. To get there coming from the south, take the first large turning on the left. It's about 150 down there on the left-hand side. There is also the *Nyahururu Hotel Boarding & Lodging* at the north end of town which has clean, comfortable rooms for Sh 45 a single including hot showers. There is a good restaurant attached to the hotel. Others have stayed at the *Nyandarva County Council Hostel* next to the post office which has single rooms only at Sh 45. The beds are very comfortable and there's a restaurant there. The dining room at the *Thomson's Falls Lodge* is exceptionally olde worlde with a superbly elegant, though aged, waiter. Give it a try!

Entry to the falls costs Sh 4, but you'd be very unlucky if anyone asked you for this entry fee. The best time to see them is in the early morning around 7 am, especially in the wet season.

Restaurant for Sh 25 a single, but don't eat there as the food is awful.

TAVETA

Try the *Safari Lodge*, which costs Sh 40 a single and Sh 69 a double.

VOI

Two places which have been recommended here are the *Embassy Hotel*, which costs Sh 87 a double; and the *New Dawida Hotel* at the bus station, which costs Sh 46.80 a single and Sh 76 a double.

NATIONAL & GAME PARKS

Kenya is, of course, the land of game parks, and many of them are world famous. They range from small lakes to vast areas of bush and mountain. Facilities are good and well organised. Many of the smaller parks can be reached by hitching or taking public transport, but to see the larger ones you must have your own vehicle or must join a tour. Neither is cheap, but it's obviously preferable to have your own vehicle. Put money aside for this. After all, how many times are you going to have the opportunity to see the game parks in this part of the world? And what's the point in making all that effort if you can't afford to see them properly when you get there? It's the experience of a lifetime! If you're alone or a couple, there's no problem. There are probably a hundred travellers wanting to link up with others to rent a vehicle at any one time in Nairobi. Try the noticeboards at Mrs Roche's or the Thorn Tree Café in Nairobi. You should know, however, that it's apparently illegal to put up a notice asking for more people to join a safari. We heard that two Dutch tourists were arrested some time ago for doing this and were forced to pay a fine of Sh 1500 each plus the cost of a lawyer. This story has not been confirmed by any other travellers, but the story goes that such notices constitute an 'illegal tourist enterprise' – a tourist visa prohibits you from working or engaging in any business activity. Perhaps this was a one-off because it doesn't seem to have deterred those who put up notices of this kind at the Thorn Tree Café.

If you're renting a vehicle, try to get a Suzuki 4WD rather than a Land-Rover, as they are more economical on fuel (an 800cc 4WD Suzuki two-seater uses about one litre of petrol per 10 km at Sh 8.73 per litre). However, they're also in heavy demand so you need to plan ahead. Some of the places which have been recommended for hiring are *Kimbla Tours*, Market St, Nairobi; *Habib's Cars*, Agip House, Haile Selassie Avenue; and *Oddjobs*. A lot of travellers have plugged for Habib's, and though they're very friendly and fair to do business with, their cars are a bit rough and their rates uniformly higher than Kimbla's. Other companies which have been recommended are *Let's Go Travel*, Caxton House, (first floor), Standard St, PO Box 60342, Nairobi (tel 29539/29540), next to the main post office; and *Capricorn Car Hire*, Prudential Building, Wabera St. A two-week safari through five national parks recently cost a bunch of travellers about US$450 each. This included everything – food, petrol, park fees, camping fees and even a broken windscreen.

A good idea of what it's going to cost you to rent a vehicle can be gleaned from the rates offered by *Let's Go Travel*:

Suzuki Jeep 4WD	*two-seater*	*Sierra four-seater*
Daily	Sh 150 + 2.60/km	Sh 220 + 3.50/km
Weekly	Sh 900 + 2.60/km	Sh 1320 + 3.50/km
Monthly	Sh 6400, 1200 km free, 2.30/km	Sh 8700 + 1200 km free
Unlimited Mileage	Sh 3850/wk	Sh 4900/wk, Sh 3/wk

The above charges include maintenance and comprehensive insurance, except that you are liable for the first Sh 6000 if you have a collision. You can take out Collision Damage Waiver for Sh 70 per day, which will reduce your liability to the first Sh 500 in the event of an accident. You must have a valid driving licence free from endorsements, be over 23 years of age and have held a driving licence for at least two years. If you want to drop the vehicle off anywhere other than Nairobi, it will cost an extra Sh 1000 (Mombasa) or Sh 1400 (Malindi).

On the basis of hiring a two-seater vehicle on the unlimited mileage rates, visiting three parks and covering some 1800 km, the total cost should be in the region of US$450 per week (including fuel).

If you join a safari tour, some of the cheapest are 'The Wildlife Bus' and 'The Turkhana Bus' by *Safari Camp Services*. You'll find it at Koinange St (corner of Moktar Daddah St), Nairobi; and at the Castle Hotel, Moi Avenue, Mombasa. These two buses cost Sh 2700 and Sh 2600 respectively for seven days all-inclusive. The Turkhana trip is popular and done in a large 4WD International two-ton truck, but the pace can be very slow, which means you might not see all the places mentioned in the schedule. The same company also offers a 'Coast Bus' and 'Rift Valley Bus.' The former costs Sh 1050 for three days, Sh 1800 for seven days and Sh 2600 for 10 days. They're good value but said to be overcrowded. *Gametrackers*, Elite Arcade, Kimathi St, Nairobi, run similar safaris. They have a six-day Masai Mara, Lake Bogoria, Lake Nakuru trip for Sh 2150; an eight-day Lake Turkana trip for Sh 2500; a four-day Masai Mara trip for Sh 1800; a four-day Amboseli/Tsavo trip for Sh 1740; and a 14-day 'Grand Kenya' safari for Sh 5600. Also worth checking out is *Bushbuck Adventures* which is run by an Englishman – said to be good value. Also worth checking out is *Best Camping Safaris*, Nanak House, Kimathi St, just round the corner from the Thorn Tree Café. This is a new outfit and their most popular safari is

a five-day tour of the Masai Mara for Sh 1850 (low season) and Sh 2100 (high season). This includes everything except a sleeping bag (which they'll rent for Sh 75). It's well organised, the guides are good and the vehicles are in decent shape, though the groups can be too large for some people (25 people). Tents, too, can be a little small though they usually carry extras.

By comparison, a lot of other companies charge considerably more. Examples are:

African Tours & Hotels (tel Nairobi 336858): Nairobi National Park (Sh 120 – four hours); Tsavo Park via Amboseli (Sh 1800 – two days); Masai Mara National Park (Sh 1950 – 2½ days); Amboseli and Tsavo National Parks finishing in Mombasa (Sh 2800 – four days). *Unique Tours* has an economy camping, four-day safari to Amboseli and Tsavo West for Sh 1600 including tent, sleeping bag, cook and driver.

Entry to the game parks costs Sh 30 plus Sh 30 for a vehicle and Sh 10 per person per night if you are camping inside the park. Student concessions have been abolished.

Amboseli National Park

Situated north-west of Mt Kilimanjaro on the Kenya/Tanzania border, Amboseli is one of the best places for seeing lions, cheetahs, elephants and giraffes due to the flat terrain and the number of tourist minibuses available. Seeing a herd of elephants move across the plain in front of Kilimanjaro has got to be one of the world's most stunning sights. The park is also a Masai reserve. Accommodation, however, is expensive, unless you can get into one of the 'drivers' bandas' near the petrol station, souvenir shop and grocery store. If there's room they'll let you stay there for Sh 30 per person in a three-bed room (the official price for the locals is Sh 25 but it's highly unlikely you'll get a bed for that). If these bandas are full, try *Ol Tukai* bandas which cost Sh 150 per day per person. A refrigerator is provided but you must bring your own food unless you're going to eat at the nearby *Amboseli Lodge*. You can use the swimming pool here if you're a non-resident – the cost is Sh 15. The campsite here has been moved outside the park because the animals were giving the campers a very rough time. It's now about six km past Observation Point and on land owned by a Masai rancher. The charge is Sh 30 per night per person. Sometimes there is no water available.

The road from Namanga to Ol Tukai (70 km) is very badly pot-holed, so it's best to come into the park from the Sultan Hamud turn-off on the Nairobi-Mombasa road.

Lake Nakuru National Park

This was once Kenya's largest bird sanctuary and at certain times of the year it was possible to see flocks of flamingoes numbering over two million as well as considerable numbers of duck and other water birds. Then, a few years ago, because of the rise in the level of the water in the lake, most of the birds moved to **Lake Baringo** north of Nakuru. Recently, however, they've been moving back again to Lake Nakuru so there's a choice of two lakes at which to see them. To get to Lake Baringo, you first take a train to Nakuru followed by a bus to Marigat. There's a daily bus from Nakuru to Lake Baringo at 11 am which returns to Nakuru at 6 am the next day. The bus drops you at the entrance to *Robert's Camping*. It's a good camping site with all facilities and is right next to *Lake Baringo Lodge*. The charge is Sh 30 per person per night in a tent. Also, if you can afford it, there's the *Island Camp* which is a tented campsite on an island in the middle of the lake. It costs Sh 300 a double with full board for Kenyan residents or Sh 600 a double for non-residents. Other travellers have suggested camping at Liboi Gate, where a campsite is under construction. People are very friendly and there are some beautiful hot springs 13 km from the gate. The lake

actually isn't a national park, so you can walk in and camp where you like. There's a beautiful campsite under a cluster of fig trees and another under acacias. There are also hot springs and geysers at the far end of the lake (about eight km).

Mt Kenya National Park

At 5200 metres (17,056 feet), Mt Kenya is one of Africa's highest mountains and very popular with trekkers and climbers. You don't need any special equipment to get as far as Point Lenana (16,355 feet), but beyond that you'll need climbing gear. It will take you about three to four hours to get to Point Lenana from Mackinder's Camp. Don't try to rush the trek up Mt Kenya. A lot of people do and end up with altitude sickness. Ideally, you should give yourself time to become acclimatised by spending three or four days trekking around the lower slopes before you attempt the summit. All the same, it's worth taking aspirin with you. Most people get headaches. This doesn't mean that you're not fit enough – there will be other symptoms if that is the case – and aspirin can make the difference between enjoying and loathing a trip up the mountain. Remember to set off as early as possible on the day you intend to get to the summit, otherwise you'll end up in heavy cloud and miss the magnificent views. You are not allowed to climb Mt Kenya alone – you must go with at least one other person, but it's not compulsory to hire guides or porters.

A good description of the various routes possible together with maps can be found in *Guide to Mt Kenya and Kilimanjaro* and *Mountains of Kenya*. Both of these can be bought from the Mountain Club of Kenya, PO Box 5741, Nairobi, or from the clubhouse at Wilson Airport, Nairobi. These guides are the best available and new editions are in preparation (due out 1985). There used to be a choice of various huts along the way where you could stay for the night, but most of them have now been removed so you should contact the Mountain Club of Kenya before you set off. *Mackinder's Camp* in Teleki Valley is one of the most popular places to stay and costs Sh 100 per night for a somewhat dubious tent, or you can pitch your own for Sh 20. You don't need to book these places in advance – it's a good idea not to unless you know how you will stand up to the altitude. You also need a very good sleeping bag, as the night temperatures can drop to minus 10°C. About one km beyond Mackinder's Camp is the *Rangers' Hut* with accommodation for around 10 people sleeping in one room on comfortable mattresses for Sh 30-40. There are always three rangers there who take care of heating the place with a stove, and they're very friendly people who will usually let you use their stove for preparing food. The other place where many people stay is the *Austrian Hut*, several hundred metres from Point Lenana. Though it's dirty and very poorly kept, there's rarely anyone present to collect the fee (which is Sh 20).

The usual centre from which to explore this national park is Naro Moru on the main Nairobi-Nanyuki road. There are several places where you can stay both in the town itself and outside. You can camp for Sh 10 per night at the *River Lodge*, PO Box 18, Naro Moru, or rent a banda which costs Sh 35 per person per night. These people also handle bookings for *Mackinder's Camp*, a few hours' climbing from the summit. Camping there costs Sh 10 per night plus they also have bandas for Sh 50 per night. The River Lodge is two km out of Naro Moru on the main road away from the mountain. Avoid staying at the *Naro Moru 82 Bar & Restaurant* as the mattresses there often stink of urine. The *Youth Hostel* (tel 2471) is 10 km from town and is a beautiful old converted farmhouse with kerosene lanterns and log fires. It costs Sh 25 per person per night for members and Sh 35 per night for non-members. Cooking facilities are provided and although it's a good idea to take food along, you can buy eggs, milk, carrots and cabbages as well as

prepared food nearby. *Minto's Safaris* is similar. In addition, they have bunkhouses on the far side of the mountain. Accommodation can also be found at the *Meteorological Station* (about 16 km from the Youth Hostel), from which a lot of people start the climb to the summit. It has good, clean, bunkhouse accommodation and cooking facilities for Sh 100 per night, or you can camp there for Sh 20 per night.

Guides and equipment can be hired at many of the lodges in and around Naro Moru, but you need to do some leg work because this can be expensive. The River Lodge hires out boots, coats and sweaters at Sh 20 for each 24 hours, sleeping bags for Sh 25-50 and gas stoves at Sh 10 for each 24 hours (expensive). On the other hand, the lodge is a good place to sell equipment; some travellers say it's even worth buying what you need in Nairobi, using it to go up the mountain, and then selling it when you're through.

Meru National Park

Mt Meru is off the main tourist circuit, which means there are very few minibuses cluttering up the park. The grass gets fairly high, making it difficult to see the big cats, but there are plenty of elephants and buffalo as well as some of the northern animal species like Grevy's zebra, reticulated giraffe, gerenux and oryx. There's a good sealed road to within 15 km of the park and a network of roads within the park which are very well signposted. It's a beautiful place and the bandas at *Leopard Rock* are some of the best you will find in Kenya. They cost Sh 70 per person and include a refrigerator, clean sheets, towels and hot water in the evenings. There are cheaper bandas (Sh 20 per person) at the main public campsite. You can also camp at the site near the Park Headquarters where firewood, running water and showers are provided for Sh 5 per person. White rhino graze in this campsite, so be prepared for the unnerving experience of turning round to find one of these beasts within 10 metres of you! The camp attendants will tell you they're 'tame.'

A visit to Meru is well combined with one to the nearby **Samburu Game Reserve**. If you camp here, pay someone to look after your tent as there have been a lot of rip-offs.

Masai Mara Game Reserve

This park is noted for its wildebeeste migration from Tanzania during July, August and September – an incredible sight! Unfortunately, the park caters mainly to wealthy tourists who like to stay in lodges or luxury tented camps, so there's not much provision for the budget travellers. There is an official campsite at the *Keekorok Lodge* which costs Sh 30 per person. The lodge itself does a good buffet breakfast for Sh 60, though you can also get cheap meals at the drivers' canteen between the campsite and the lodge. Other travellers have managed to camp free by the warden's office, but you have to be careful of roving lions and elephants there. Other places where you can camp in the park itself are by *Sand River gate* (next to the Tanzanian border), up near the *Mara Buffalo Camp*, or near *Governor's Camp*. Ask if the area is safe before you erect a tent. We have had reports of tourists being marched off at gun-point into the bush and robbed.

Nairobi National Park

Only 10 minutes by car from the centre of Nairobi, this small park has a remarkable selection of game. The only one you won't see here is the elephant. At the entrance to the park is the famous Animal Orphanage where young animals which have either lost their parents or have been abandoned are taken. Where possible, these animals are released back into the wild when able to fend for themselves.

Naivasha Lake

This isn't actually a national park but is, nevertheless, a very beautiful area to visit. The *Youth Hostel* (tel 337468) is actually run by the YMCA, which means that your Youth Hostel card is invalid so you'll be charged Sh 5 per night for temporary membership with the YMCA in addition to Sh 14 to camp or Sh 25 for a bed in a banda (or Sh 30 with bedding). The bandas have kitchens but no firewood or charcoal (you can buy this for Sh 4). The hostel is about 10 km out of town on South Lake Rd at the turn-off for Hell's Gate. The small hotels in the village about 30 minutes' walk away have a limited choice of food – usually only mandazi, chapattis, tea and soda. The Youth Hostel office has canned corned beef, cookies and sodas. Cooking utensils are provided free. At *Fisherman's Camp* you can hire a tent for Sh 30 per person. This includes the use of a rowboat for viewing the hippos and pelicans. If you don't stay here you can hire the boat for Sh 10.

The *Safariland Lodge*, six km to the east, offers dinner at 7.30 pm for Sh 90 (very good food). Even if you don't want to go there for dinner it's worth paying a visit. 'It's a rich folks' paradise but closer to heaven you won't get for the price of a pot of tea – peacocks and horses strolling on landscaped lawns, fountains and gardens!' You can camp here for Sh 35 or use the swimming pool free of charge.

If you stay in Naivasha town itself, try the *Top Life Hotel* which costs Sh 45 for two people in a single room or Sh 55 a double. There is hot water.

Hell's Gate, a large, long valley with prolific birdlife and no tourists, is a 35 minutes' walk from the Youth Hostel. You have to sign in with the guard at the entrance on South Lake Rd and then walk through the housing for the Sulmac Ltd flower farm workers. Don't believe the guard who will tell you that the warden doesn't allow people in on foot. Hell's Gate has zebras, Thomson's gazelles, Kongoni antelopes, giraffes, baboons, Lammegayer eagles and one lone male ostrich. The warden, who may walk around with you, will tell you that the buffaloes stay up on the hills and the leopards and cheetahs in their caves during the day. It's a gazetted park and a campsite is planned on one of the bluffs but it's not in operation yet, so there's no charge.

At the entrance to Hell's Gate you will see a large, pointed rock spire and an opening in the walls to the south-east through which you can see the Rift Valley. Turning right (west), you have a 45-minute walk to an area of Masai tribes (who have been ordered out) and Dr Fisher's Tower, a lone 25-metre-high rock outcrop in the middle of the valley. Further on there is a geothermal power project.

Eighteen km or so to the west around the lake from the Hostel is **Green Crater Lake** set in a beautiful small volcanic crater with lush vegetation. Unfortunately, you'll probably have to walk most of the way and you have to cross private land (½ km or so).

Near Naivasha is **Longonot**, an extinct volcano about 3000 metres high. There are superb views in all directions from the summit, which can be reached from the village of Longonot. The journey up to the top, around the crater and back down again takes about six hours.

Tsavo National Park

This is Kenya's largest park and abounds with game of all shapes and sizes. It is particularly famous for its large herds of elephant. In the western half of the park are the **Mzima Springs** inhabited by crocodiles and hippos (you can see the former in a glass-panelled tank there). There are bandas where you can stay just next to the springs; more are located at Ngulia. There's an excellent campsite at the *Chuyulu Gate*, five km from the *Kilaguni Lodge*, where firewood, showers, toilets and a number of thatched roof huts are available to camp under. Make sure you close everything up when you go off; otherwise the baboons will clean the tent out. In the eastern part of the park (one hour's walk from Voi) there is a campsite

and bandas. You can sleep on the floor of the latter for Sh 5 per night. Firewood and showers are available. You can also camp at *Aruba Lodge* inside the park. This costs Sh 5 or you can rent a banda for Sh 50 (sleeps two people) with cooking facilities, toilet and shower. *Crocodile Camp* on the far eastern part is actually five km outside the park, but you can camp here for Sh 60, which includes the crocodile show. There is a restaurant here. There is no campsite at the Manyami Gate, but you can camp outside the gate and use the public toilets.

Lake Turkana

Lake Turkana is well worth visiting and there are plenty of interesting places to visit en route. There are basically two ways of getting there, though the eastern route from Nyahururu via Maralal and Baragoi can be difficult (there's very little traffic). The main route is from Kitale to Lodwar and there's plenty of traffic along it.

There are matatus from Kitale to Lodwar every day which cost Sh 50-80 depending on your bargaining powers. There's also a daily bus in operation which you can get for as low as Sh 40 (bargaining necessary). The main hassle is the time spent picking up passengers in Kitale. This can take up to five hours before the matatu leaves for the six-hour journey to Lodwar! You can therefore expect a two-to three-hour unscheduled 'tour' of Kitale as normal. The road is sealed all the way so it's fast and comfortable.

En route to Lodwar there are a couple of stops worth making. One is at the **Saiwa Swamp National Park** about 15 km north of Kitale to the east off the main road. The entrance fee is Sh 30 and, as the park is very small, you have to walk around it. The main attraction is the shy and elusive Sitatunga swamp antelope. Further north the road passes through the beautiful **Cherangari Hills**. Accommodation is available at Ortum for about Sh 25 per night. This area is one of the great unknown trekking regions in the world. You can climb up to over 10,000 feet (3030 metres) from Ortum and the views are stunning. High up in these hills, the Pokot people are still deeply immersed in their traditional ways of life and at 8000-9000 feet you come across their traditional irrigation and soil conservation terraces built on steep hillside *shambas*. For anyone interested in trekking, this area is a must.

In Lodwar there is a good choice of accommodation. The most popular places are the *Mombasa Hotel* and the *Ngonda Hotel* which both cost Sh 28 a single, and the newly opened *Turkwel Lodge* at Sh 75 a single and Sh 120 a double. The Turkwel is the best place for eating in Lodwar and offers good steak and chips (Sh 24), mixed grill (Sh 28) and beef stew and rice (Sh 20), among other things. Once out of Lodwar the transport and accommodation situation deteriorates rapidly. The main route for travellers is still to the lake shore to either Kalekol (about one km from the lake shore) or Eliye Springs. There is an infrequent matatu service (Sh 25) to Kalekol which will usually be an open-backed Land Cruiser or Land-Rover with bench seats. By Turkana standards, though, this road is quite busy and most people will manage to get a lift if they are prepared to wait around for a day or two. There are VSOs in this area so you may well get a lift with them.

In Kalekol you can stay at the *guest house* (unnamed) across the main street from the Safari Hotel. It costs Sh 28 a single and good, uncomplicated meals are available cheaply. There's also *George's Hotel*, a grass hut with kerosene lamps where you can stay for Sh 25 a bed. The people are very, very friendly and will prepare food for you very cheaply if you ask – subject to what's available. The *Safari Hotel* is a good place to enquire about lifts back to Lodwar. *Lake Turkana Fishing Lodge* at Ferguson's Gulf is definitely for well-heeled tourists at Sh 530 a single and Sh 830 a double with full

board (high season) and Sh 330 per person in the low season (April-June). Lunch at the Lodge costs Sh 50 and will leave you totally bloated and unable to eat for two days afterwards. Sounds like it's worth having lunch there! The food is excellent and based around fish courses – Nile perch and tilapia.

Trips out on the Lodge launch to the **Central Island National Park** are well worth the Sh 150-200, four-hour journey. The island is a dormant volcano and the three crater lakes provide breeding grounds for large concentrations of Nile crocodile and birdlife. It's a stark and arid place and is worth the time if you have the money.

The boat trip across the gulf now costs Sh 40 return, and as most of the local fishermen have wised up to this lucrative income, you won't get it any cheaper than the Lodge boats.

Getting to Eliye Springs is far more difficult so you'll have to rely on lifts in 4WD vehicles, which are a necessity as the road goes through soft sand in places. It's a beautiful place with palm trees, white sand and a blue lake, but the lodge is very run-down and dilapidated these days. You can camp on the beach close to the lodge, but you'll still be charged Sh 40 for this dubious privilege. No food or drink is available, but if you bring your own they have a refrigerator where you can store it, and they'll cook it for you on request.

There are other areas of Turkana well worth visiting, but transport is erratic and unscheduled and accommodation difficult to find. In the far north near Lokitaung the **Lokitaung Gorge** is very wild and beautiful, and accommodation should be possible there if you ask around. West of Lodwar, the **Loima Hills** is an interesting area to explore. They rise up 7000 feet (2121 metres) out of the desert and are topped by cedar forests inhabited by elephant, lion, buffalo and other game. You definitely need your own transport and camping equipment for this trip, and you will need to hire a Turkana guide at the Forestry Camp at the base of the hills.

It's also possible to get boat rides across the lake from Kalekol to Loiyangalani, but the boats are in really bad shape and the prices asked are outrageous (you could fly cheaper).

If you're interested in Turkana handicrafts and artifacts, the best places are in Lokichar (75 km south of Lodwar) and in Lodwar at the Diocesan Handicrafts shop. For basketwork, try either Kalekol or Lodwar, where mats and baskets are for sale along the main streets. Prices are five to six times cheaper than in Nairobi.

If you want to attempt to get up to Lake Turkana from Nyahururu, you must be prepared to abandon the attempt if you can't find transport on the last leg. The first step is a bus from Nyahururu (Thomson's Falls) to Maralal, which costs Sh 45 and takes about 5½ hours. Stay at the *Kariara Lodging* here; it costs Sh 25.50 per person and has hot water in the mornings. Eat at the *Buffalo Hotel* which has 'the last green vegetables you'll see for a while.' Maralal is also where you will find the last bank. It's open only on Tuesday and Thursday between 11 am and 1.30 pm. Next, take a truck to Baragoi which should cost Sh 50 and takes about 3½ to five hours. Look for ostriches, camels and dancing Samburu warriors en route.

Baragoi is a small town which somehow gets rain when everywhere else is dry, so the surroundings are green. During the day, tribal people (Samburu, Turkhana, etc) come to town to talk, sell their goats and necklaces and generally hang out. Their villages made of grass and stick huts surrounded by fences of cacti are all around the town. Stay at *Mt Ngiro Lodging*, which costs Sh 25 a single. It's the first building on the left as you enter the town from the south. Eat at *Hussein Mohammed's hotel* across the street – tea and mandazi for breakfast, meat and potato karanga with rice or chapatti for lunch and dinner. Soft drinks cost Sh 2.50. You can wait in Baragoi for at least a week for a truck going to Lolyangalani (150 km), though it's fairly easy to get to South Horr, the next town en route. The whole area is very untouristed and you'll probably be the only *wazungu* in town. For somewhere to stay in Lolyangalani, try *El Molo Lodge* run by David Wamanda, who is very helpful.

OTHER
Jobs
It's relatively easy to find jobs in Kenya if you have a university or college degree (you need proof of this). There are advertisements in the local papers nearly every week, and there are also a lot of private schools which need teachers and which pay reasonably well. French and German teachers are especially in demand. You do need patience, however, as it can take up to four months to get a job and a work permit as well.

Lesotho

Lesotho came together as a nation in the 1820s, at a time when large numbers of refugees were fleeing from Zulu expansionism. It was put together by a remarkable military and diplomatic strategist, Moshweshwe I, who by the 1850s had built a powerful kingdom which covered the fertile plains of the Caledon River as well as present-day Lesotho. By that time the country had a single language, a unified army and a system of government based on a national assembly of chiefs, each of whom retained a considerable degree of autonomy. Moshweshwe I was able to keep both the Zulu and the Boers at bay until shortly before his death in 1870 when, hard-pressed by Orange Free State commandos, he was forced to accept the loss of the rich grazing lands west of the Caledon as the price of a British Protectorate.

Despite these losses, the chiefs were able to retain their power by loaning cattle to the often destitute newcomers, and they retained their rights to both allocate and evict people from land as well as to demand tribute labour. Yet, at the same time, the country gradually changed from the granary of the high veldt to a mere labour reserve for South African mines and farms. In 1904 alone some 86,000 passes were issued to Swazi labourers for a total population of 350,000. This pattern of labour movement has continued right up to the present.

Nationalist policies got off to a very early start, but it wasn't until the Basuto-land Congress Party was founded in 1952 under the leadership of Ntsu Mokhele that a militant campaign for self-rule was launched. The BCP's radicalism, though not its goal of national independence, was opposed by the Basutoland National Party founded under the leadership of Chief Jonathan in 1958. As a result of the BCP's campaign, the British were forced to grant self-government in 1965 and full independence in 1966, but in the elections leading up to independence it was the BNP which scooped the lion's share of the votes. Part of the reason for this was the massive help given to it by various outside interests. These included the 215,000-member Catholic Church which used its considerable ideological, financial and organisational resources to condemn the radicalism of the BCP and promote the BNP and the South African government of Dr Verwoerd which provided helicopters, trucks and other assistance such as giving the BNP sole access to the 100,000 Basotho expatriate workers inside South Africa. The British colonial administration also threw in its lot with the BNP, though it would have preferred to support a royalist party.

Thus the country became independent in 1966 under the leadership of Chief Jonathan on a platform of friendship and co-operation with South Africa, rabid anti-communism and the muzzling of South African political refugees. Barely two months after independence, Chief Jonathan consolidated the hold of the BNP by forcing King Moshweshwe II to renounce everything but a purely ceremonial role as head of state. The BCP nevertheless remained active, but when it was clearly heading for victory in the elections of 1970 Jonathan staged a coup d'etat, suspended the constitution, arrested opposition leaders, banned all political parties except his own and put the king under house-arrest. Moshweshwe II subsequently went into exile in Holland.

Jonathan's dictatorship, however, was opposed by many sections of the population and so, in 1972, in an attempt to defuse an increasingly tense political situation, he announced an amnesty for political prisoners followed by the creation of an all-party national assembly in the following year. Though there were a few defections from the BCP, the hard-core leaders refused to cooperate in what was a transparent exercise to legitimise Jonathan's dictatorship; and in 1974 serious disturbances broke out including armed attacks on a number of police stations. In the ensuing witch hunt of BCP supporters, at least 250 people were killed by the BNP militia and many more were arrested. Mokhele, along with several other important members of the BCP, fled into exile. Since then Jonathan has attempted to create a one-party state, though with very limited success. Serious disturbances continue to break out, and as recently as 1979 Jonathan's Israeli-trained paramilitary security police were responsible for killing a number of alleged BCP agitators in two separate clashes in the north and south of the country.

Even if Jonathan wanted Lesotho to break out of its status as an economic hostage of South Africa, he would be faced with enormous difficulties. Lesotho's main export is about half its able-bodied men, who work in South Africa under a pernicious migrant labour system which has wreaked havoc with the social stability of the country. There has also been an enormous investment of capital by several South African companies in the search for coal and minerals, including the De Beers company which has sunk Rand 23 million into a diamond mine near Letseng. Then again, there's the very real danger of South African military intervention in one form or another should Lesotho align itself too closely with the revolutionary black African countries. Jonathan has therefore been forced to adopt a style

similar to that of the black 'homeland' leaders in such places as the Transkei and Bophuthatswana while occasionally risking rhetorical outbursts of condemnation of the apartheid regime. He did, on the other hand, refuse to recognise the so-called independence of the Transkei, and when this led to the closure of their common border in 1978 he used it as a gambit to secure substantial loans and emergency aid from various western governments who were not averse to polishing up their anti-apartheid images. At the same time, Lesotho took the opportunity to establish diplomatic relations with Mozambique and Cuba. Nevertheless, the platform on which Jonathan came to power at independence remains basically the same, and when Pieter Botha, the South African premier, met Jonathan in the first-ever meeting between the two in 1980, the latter is widely thought to have sought South African help in dealing with insurgents who cross the border from South Africa.

One of the country's chief aims is to become self-sufficient in food, but it suffers from erosion stemming from overgrazing. The lowlands remain infertile because the lack of tree cover means that animal manure is used for fuel instead of being returned to the soil. The country's most valuable resource – water – is not tapped at all, though there is an old scheme for damming the Orange River which has been shelved many times. If the dam is ever completed, it would provide Lesotho with all the power it needs and allow it to sell the excess to South Africa.

FACTS

Lesotho is one of the world's poorest nations, with few mineral resources, limited agricultural land and a harsh and changeable climate. It makes up for this, however, with its stunning natural beauty and some of the most friendly and generous people you're likely to come across on the continent. While the majority

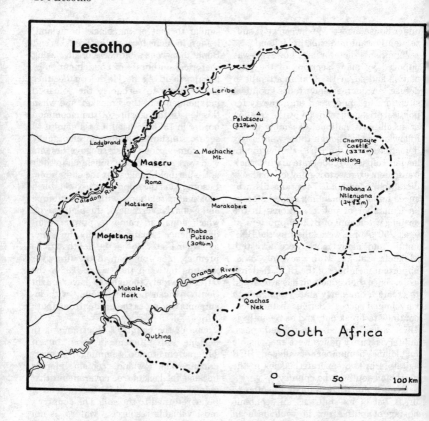

Lesotho

Leribe
Pelatsoeu (3276m)
Ladybrand
Champayne Castle (3375 m)
Maseru
Machache Mt.
Mokhotlong
Roma
Caledon River
Matsieng
Marakabeis
Thabana Ntlenyana (3482m)
Mafeteng
Thaba Putsoa (3096m)
Orange River
Mokale's Hoek
Qachas Nek
South Africa
Quthing

0   50   100 km

of the population lives in the lowlands at around 1500 metres, much of the land is wild mountain country with occasional peaks rising to over 3000 metres. Because of this it is excellent trekking country, though you need to take precautions about the very changeable weather. Never go out into the mountains, even for an afternoon, without a sleeping bag, tent and sufficient food for a couple of days in case you get fogged in. Even in summer it can freeze and thunderstorms are an ever-present danger (quite a few people are killed by lightning here every year). It's generally clear between May and September but cold and windy higher up. The highest parts often register 10 to 15°

of frost at night. Down in the valleys, summer days can be hot with temperatures in the 30°Cs.

There is no trouble finding clean drinking water in the mountains even in the dry season (winter), but if you take water from below a village you must boil it before drinking. You can pick up hepatitis, dysentery and even cholera if you don't do this.

VISAS

Visas are required by all except nationals of the Commonwealth countries, Belgium, Denmark, Finland, Greece, Iceland, Irish Republic, Israel, Italy, Japan, Luxembourg, Netherlands, Norway, South Africa, South

Korea, Sweden and the USA. Where there are no Lesotho diplomatic missions, visas can be obtained from British embassies.

MONEY
US$1 = 0.97 maloti

The unit of currency is the loti (plural maloti) = 100 licente. The loti is on a par with the South African rand. There are no restrictions on the import or export of local currency, but make sure that you change excess maloti back into rand before you leave.

The cost of living is high, especially for such things as food and public transport. Inflation is running at around 15%.

The airport departure tax for international flights is 2 maloti.

LANGUAGE
The official languages are Sesotho and English. Greetings are an important social ritual in Lesotho, so if you want to create a favourable impression on people here, it's useful to know some phrases:

Greetings

for men
Greetings father
Lumela ntate (Du-may-lah n-tah-tah)
Peace father
Khotso ntate (Ko-tso n-tah-tah)

for women
Greetings mother
Lumela 'me
Peace mother
Khotso 'me

for boys
Greetings brother
Lumela abuti
Peace brother
Khotso abuti

for girls
Greetings sister
Lumela ausi

Peace sister
Khotso ausi

When there are two or more people the plural greetings are:
Lumelang bo-ntate or bo-'me or bo-abuti or bo-ausi
Khotsong bo-ntate or bo-'me or bo-abuti or bo-ausi

There are three possible ways to say 'How are you?' They are:

	singular	plural
How do you live?	*O phela joang?*	*Le phela joang?*
How did you get up?	*O tsohile joang?*	*Le tsohile joang?*
How are you?	*O kae?*	*Le kae?*

The answers to these questions are:

	singular	plural
I live well	*Ke phela hantle*	*Re phela hantle*
I got up well	*Ke tsohile hantle*	*Re tsohile hantle*
I am here	*Ke teng*	*Re teng*

The above questions and answers are quite interchangeable. Someone could ask you *O phela joang?* and you could answer *Ke teng*.

When trekking, people always ask *Lea kae?* (Where are you going?) and *O tsoa kae?* or the plural *Le tsoa kae?* (Where have you come from?).

When parting, use the following expressions:

	singular	plural
Go well	*Tsamaea hantle*	*Tsamaeang hantle*
Stay well	*Sala hantle*	*Salang hantle*

You must always add ntate or 'me (or bo for the plural).

'Thank you' is *Kea leboha* (pronounced keya lebowah).
The herd boys often ask for money *(chelete)* or sweets *(lipompong)* (pro-

nounced dee-pom-pong). If you want to say 'I don't have any,' the answer is *Ha dio* (pronounced Ha dee-oh).

GETTING THERE & AROUND

Many people enter Lesotho via the capital, Maseru, which is connected by road and rail to South Africa. The two-km rail link from Maseru to the South African border is the only railway in the country. Once you're in South Africa, there are connections to the rest of the Republic via Marseilles. The border between Lesotho and the Transkei is open to non-Lesotho nationals. If you intend to enter Lesotho in your own vehicle via Sani Pass, make sure it's 4WD. South African customs won't allow 2WD vehicles to pass through.

In the lowlands, minibuses are the usual form of transport. They are cheap and most of the roads are sealed, but they're also dangerous and many people are killed in accidents. These so-called accidents are often the result of drunk driving (alcohol consumption is a real problem in this country and bus drivers are no exception). The Maseru-Roma road is particularly bad. Hitching is easy but you should expect to pay for lifts. In the mountains roads can be incredibly rough and lifts difficult to find, so if you want to get to the heart of this country you need plenty of time and very few expectations. In the more remote areas the only way you'll be able to get around is by walking or either hiring or buying a horse. The few Basotho who own horses regard them as their most valuable possessions and are extremely reluctant to part with them. That being so, you can expect to pay handsomely for one. On the other hand, it is superb walking country and there's no danger of robberies or anything of that nature.

Some examples of bus fares are: Maseru-Morija 1 loti; Maseru-Marakabeis 4.55 maloti; Marakabeis-Qacha turn-off 1.30 maloti; Qacha turn-off to Qacha 2 maloti.

Air Lesotho, the national airline, has a fairly extensive network of internal flights and is worth considering if your time is limited or if you get stuck. Fares are very reasonable:

from	to	
Maseru	Leribe	22 maloti
	Lesobeng	30 maloti
	Mokhotlong	37 maloti
	Nkau's	31 maloti
	Pelaneng	27 maloti
	Qacha's Nek	37 maloti
	Sehongnong	36 maloti
	Sekake's	32 maloti
	Semonkong	25 maloti
	Seshute's	30 maloti
	Thaba-tseka	30 maloti
Leribe	Mokhotlong	32 maloti
	Pelaneng	16 maloti
	Seshute's	21 maloti
Mafeteng	Qacha's Nek	32 maloti
	Maseru	21 maloti
Semonkong	Nkau's	13 maloti
	Qacha's Nek	22 maloti
	Sekake's	13 maloti
Seshute's	Pelaneng	11 maloti
Thaba-tseka	Sehonghong	13 maloti
Nkau's	Sekake's	13 maloti

Since the planes are quite small and most of the airstrips are only grass tracks, cancellations are frequent in bad weather.

There's very little purpose-built accommodation for travellers outside of Maseru, but that doesn't mean you will have any difficulty finding somewhere to stay. People are very friendly, especially in the mountains, and if you ask the village chief for permission to camp he'll not only make sure you get a good spot, if that's what you're looking for, but he'll often fix you up with a rondavel for the night. The government also maintains a series of rest houses in the mountains which range from 0.50 to 2.50 maloti per night. Details are available from the Tourist Office in Maseru, but the rest house in Mokhotlong is closed indefinitely despite what you might be told to the contrary. In the larger places you can try the missions and training centres. There is a Youth Hostels Association (PO Box 660, Maseru), but it only has one hostel at Phomolong (Lancer's Gap), four km from Maseru, which is often closed due to lack of water, and another outside Butha-Buthe. When the Maseru hostel is open, however, it's worth staying there as it's a beautiful place. It costs 2 maloti per night and there are frequent minibuses from the bus station in Maseru to Lancer's Gap which charge about 0.30 loti.

The hostel at Butha-Buthe is very good and costs 1.50 maloti.

The Fraser Group have three lodges (known as *Fraser's Lodges*) at Quaba, Semonkong and Marakabeis which cost 4.75 maloti plus 10% tax. You can make bookings at Fraser's Furniture Store on Kingsway opposite the post office in Maseru or by writing to PO Box MS5, Maseru (tel 050-322601).

MARAKABEIS

Fraser's Lodge is beautifully situated in the mountains outside town. They have rondavels for the usual price and a campsite which costs 1 loti per night per person. There is a small shop where you can buy food, but there is no restaurant. To get to Marakabeis you take one of the daily buses from Maseru which cost four maloti and take four to five hours.

MASERU

The only budget accommodation here is at the *Youth Hostel* at Lancer's Gap, though if you're prepared to pay for your upkeep it might be worthwhile checking out the Peace Corps office on Constitution Rd or the IVS and UN volunteers behind Lancer's Inn. They can usually provide floor space or somewhere to put up your tent. *Lancer's Inn* itself costs 21.50 maloti a double.

The Tourist Office is on Kingsway by the Basotho hat-shaped building. If you're looking for lifts into the interior, check out the CIDA office.

TREKKING

Lesotho offers some of the most spectacular trekking country in southern Africa. Straddling the Drakensberg, which includes the highest peaks in this part of the continent, it is one of the most beautiful areas in the world. Much the same is true of the South African side of this massif. Beautiful it certainly is, but the climate is very changeable and you must prepare for this before you go off trekking into the mountains. Temperatures can plummet to near zero even in summer and thunderstorms are very common. A good book to take with you is David Ambrose's *Guide to Lesotho* (Winchester Press). Good maps can be bought from the Department of Survey behind the Department of Mines, which in turn is behind Barclays Bank in Maseru. They have a large scale map of the whole country (1:250,000) for 5 maloti and section maps (1:50,000) for 2.90 maloti.

Some short excursions in the immediate vicinity of Maseru include **Thaba Bosiu**, a flat-topped hill where the Basotho made an heroic stand against the Boers and where the graves of the chiefs killed in that battle are found. There is a bus most of the way from Maseru. Nearby is the **Ha Khotso Rock Paintings**. Here are some of the best Bushman paintings in the country. To get there, first take a bus from Maseru to Roma. From there, walk to St Michael's at the start of the mountain road and follow this road for about 12 km, after which you take the minor road off to the left for a further six km.

Maraha Bei is a beautiful place to stay and easy to get lifts to as it's on the way to Thaba Tseha. There's a *Fraser's Lodge* here with rondavels at the usual price and excellent cooking facilities, but they won't allow you to camp unless the place is full. The Little Orange River is close by.

The most spectacular area of Lesotho is along the south-east border region between Transkei and South Africa, and if you had two weeks to spare you could walk all the way around this region from Ramanbanta

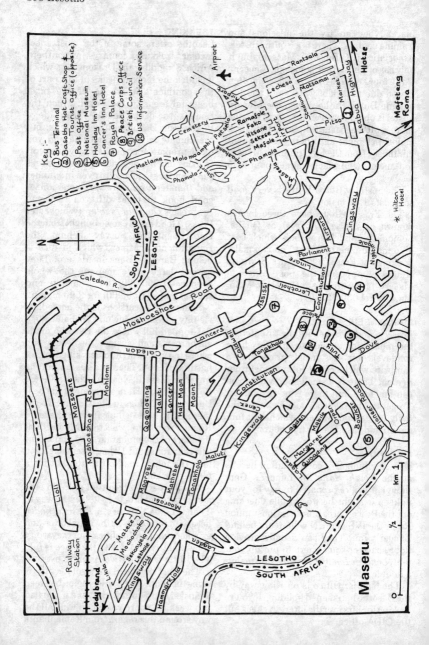

Key:-
1. Bus Terminal
2. Basotho Hat Craft Shop ★
3. Post Office (Tourist office opposite)
4. National Museum
5. Holiday Inn Hotel
6. Lancer's Inn Hotel
7. Royal Palace
8. Peace Corps Office
9. British Council
10. US Information Service

Maseru

to Butha-Buthe via Qachasnek, the Sani Pass, Mokhotlong and the Mont aux Sources. First take a bus from Maseru to Ramanbanta. These depart daily around noon and arrive at 4.30 pm. The fare is 3 maloti. There's also a flight which costs 21 maloti. From Ramanbanta you can either walk to Semonkong (takes about two days) or hitch a ride in a 4WD truck. The latter will cost around 10 maloti between three people and takes about 5½ hours. There are also supply trucks between Ramanbanta and Semonkong which depart daily around 5 pm. There is a *Fraser's Lodge* at Semonkong; otherwise the *Roman Catholic Mission* here will usually offer a bed to travellers for a small contribution. It's run by two French-Canadian priests, Father Latremouille and Father Leo. While you are in Semonkong pay a visit to the **Maletsunyane Falls** (also known as Le Bihan Falls). It's a four-km walk. The falls are some 200 metres high and particularly spectacular in the summer months. There is a small store where you can buy food.

From Semonkong you can either head off to Ha Qaba and then back to Maseru or continue on to Qachasnek and the Sani Pass. If you take the former, it's a three-day walk and you need to take food with you as there are no shops en route except for a very basic store at Thakabanna. It's also difficult to find water along this trail until you're past the halfway mark, so take some with you. From Ha Qaba there is a road to Maseru and it's easy to hitch.

Taking the second route, you head off walking to Qachasnek – or you can get there direct by road from Maseru or Matatiele on the Natal/Transkei border. There's also a flight from Maseru to Qachasnek for 28 maloti. There are a hotel and a store at Qachasnek. From there take the bridle path to Ramatseliso's Gate (Ramatselisohek) – about 1½ days – where there is a store, and then continue on to the **Sehlabathebe National Park**, which takes a further day. There is a lodge at the park for 5 maloti. From here it takes

another two days to climb and walk along the escarpment to the Sani Pass. There are no villages along the way, so take supplies. At Sani Pass there's a shop and chalet with sleeping accommodation. From Sani you can walk to the top of Thabana Ntlunyana, the highest point in southern Africa, in about four hours. The next leg of the route takes you along a ridge and down to Mokhotlong. Here there is an hotel for 6-10 maloti or you can stay at the Agricultural Training Centre for 2 maloti. Ask for Mr Kele-Kele at the latter. There are stores at Mokhotlong and buses to other parts of the country. From Mokhotlong to Oxbow there is a daily bus which costs 6 maloti and takes about 4½ hours. From Oxbow to Butha-Buthe there's a daily bus for 3 maloti.

From Mokhotlong to Thaba Tseka you can walk (takes about five to six days staying at missions en route) or hitch, and there's also a direct flight from Mokhotlong to Maseru for 33 maloti. Mokhotlong is a good taking-off point for the **Mont aux Sources National Park** and down to Butha-Buthe. In Butha-Buthe there is a cheap camping site near the *Crocodile Inn* for 2 maloti and also a *Youth Hostel* outside town. If you want to stay at the latter, ask local people the way to 'Ha-Sechele.' Follow the dirt tracks to this village and then ask the way to Ramakatane's house. There are no signs and the majority of people don't even know that it's a Youth Hostel, which isn't surprising as it's basically an extra room with two beds in a Basotho family house in a typical village. It's beautifully located four km from Buthe-Buthe and highly recommended. It costs 1.50 maloti per night. Take your own food with you, although the family may invite you to eat with them.

PONY TREKKING

This is now really well organised by the Basotho Pony Trekking Centre from their stables and lodge at Molimo Nthuse between the Bushman's Pass and the Blue Mountain Pass on the Maseru-Marakabei road. The road is paved all the way from Maseru to the centre and you should be able to get there within 45 minutes.

There's quite a choice of treks ranging from round-trip one night and two days (40 maloti per person) to four nights and five days (100 maloti per person). Non-return treks range from three nights and four days (80 maloti per person) to six nights and seven days (140 maloti per person). These charges include horses and tackle and a guide, but exclude the cost of overnight accommodation, food and transport to the Centre. You will need to bring your own waterproof clothing, sweaters, sleeping bags and cooking utensils. The Centre prefers groups of between five and 10 people. Trekkers have the choice of using their own tents at overnight stops or renting rondavels from the villagers (usually 5 maloti per person per night). There are also lodges at some places (eg Qaba and Semonkong) where gas cookers and hot showers are available.

Treks must be booked in advance through Basotho Pony Trekking, PO Box 1027, Maseru 100, Lesotho. If you write to this address they'll send you a leaflet containing full details of all the treks, complete with current prices.

If you don't have the time (or the inclination) to plan your own trek with regard to food, accommodation and motorised transport (where needed), you can have all this prepared for you by the Lesotho Tourist Board, PO Box 1378, Maseru (tel 050-322896/323760). Naturally, the treks will cost more this way. For example, a four-day, three-night trek will be 253 maloti and a five-day, four-night trek will cost 315 maloti. These charges are inclusive of all boarding and lodging, a guide, horses and tackle, transport between Maseru and the starting point, and flights (where applicable). You must bring your own sleeping bag, rain gear, warm clothes and eating utensils.

Liberia

Liberia began as a venture by American philanthropists in 1822, the idea being to resettle in Africa freed slaves no longer wanted by the plantations. Not all those who were offered 'repatriation' in this way accepted it. Many regarded it as a humiliation and refused to go. The few thousand who did accept had a hard time establishing themselves, having to contend with the hostility of the indigenous people who resented being alienated from their land and the settlers' attempts to dominate them. Not until 1847 did the new country declare itself to be an independent republic, and even its foster parent, the United States, took until 1862 to formally recognise it.

Ironically, the settlers didn't see any need to extend to the indigenous population the same love of liberty which supposedly had brought them to Liberia in the first place. They saw themselves as part of a mission to bring civilisation and Christianity to Africa and imposed a form of forced labour on the local people, which anywhere else would have gone under the name 'slavery.' This continued for almost a hundred years, and in 1830 both Britain and the USA broke off diplomatic relations for five years as a result of a scandal over the sale of such labour to Spanish colonialists in Fernando Poo. As late as 1960, Liberia was still being condemned for its labour recruitment methods by the International Labour Organisation. Yet, despite the exploitation of the indigenous people, the settlers were never able to develop an independent economic base and were heavily dependent on foreign capital. The country also lost large chunks of its territory to the British and French during the scramble for colonies in the late 19th century.

Early in the country's history, power was monopolised by the True Whig Party and it continued to maintain its grip on the political machinery right up until the 1980 coup. Despite the country's labour recruitment policies, the party was able to project an image of Liberia as Africa's most stable country, and during William Tubman's presidency from 1944 to 1971 this led to massive foreign investment. So eager was Tubman to hand out concessions to foreign companies that Liberia acquired the disparaging tag of the 'Firestone Republic' for a number of years. The huge influx of foreign money, however, soon began to distort the economy and to exacerbate social inequalities, which led to increasing hostility between the descendants of the settlers and the indigenous people. Viewing this development with alarm, Tubman was forced to concede that the indigenous people would have to be granted a measure of political and economic involvement in the country, and one of his concessions was to enfranchise them. Incredible as it may seem, some 97% of the population had been denied the franchise until 1963. William Tolbert, who succeeded Tubman in 1971, was one of South Africa's strongest supporters in its efforts to maintain diplomatic and economic relations with the rest of black Africa.

Tolbert continued with Tubman's policies but, while upholding the values of 'free enterprise,' he sought to broaden the country's contacts. For the first time, diplomatic relations were established with the Communist block and with the People's Republic of China. At the same

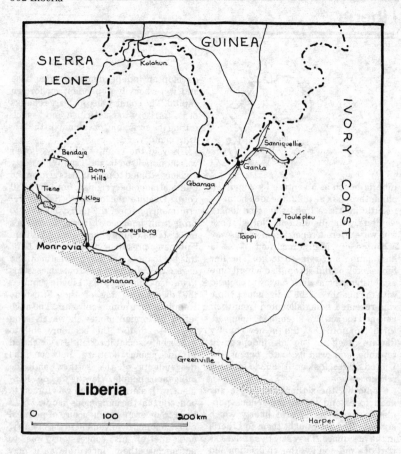

Liberia

time, however, Tolbert clamped down on opposition and brought in harsh laws to deal with anyone considered to be a threat to the regime. Even his staunchest ally, the USA, began to complain about violations of human rights. In the end, the resentment boiled over. Demonstrations against a proposed increase in the price of rice in early 1979 and the shooting of several demonstrators gradually gathered momentum until, in April 1980, Tolbert was overthrown in a coup led by Master Sergeant Samuel Doe. In the fighting which accompanied the coup, Tolbert and many high-ranking ministers were killed and their bodies dumped into a common grave. Of those who survived, the majority were briefly 'tried,' beaten up, and then publicly shot tied to stakes on the beach at Monrovia.

Although the coup gave the indigenous population real political power for the first time since the settlers had arrived, it was condemned by most other African countries as well as by Liberia's other allies and trading partners. Nigeria, for instance, refused to allow the new Foreign Minister, Baccus Matthews, into the country for the OAU economic summit later that year. Since then relations with neighbouring African states have thawed, but the flight of capital from the country following the coup and the basic wage of US$2400 awarded to all workers in the country have put severe financial strain on the economy.

FACTS
Liberia has a warm and humid climate. Temperatures range from 21°C to 32°C. The best time to visit the country is between November and April, which roughly corresponds with the dry season. The population of nearly two million consists overwhelmingly of people of indigenous origin, who are divided into some 16 major tribal groupings.

VISAS
Visas are required by all. White nationals of South Africa are not admitted. There are Liberian embassies in Cameroun, Egypt, Ethiopia, Ghana, Guinea, Ivory Coast, Nigeria, Sierra Leone, Togo and Zaire. Liberian visas in Freetown (Sierra Leone) cost 5 leone and take 24 hours to issue. At the Gbinta (Danane-Sanniquellie) border coming from Ivory Coast they will only give you 48 hours regardless of what your visa says. This means that if you need longer, you'll have to report to a provincial immigration office or the main office in Monrovia to have your visa extended. In Sanniquellie you'll be charged US$5 for this 'service' and told that they're doing you a favour by not charging you US$25. Even if that doesn't happen but you intend to stay in the country more than 15 days, you must report to the Immigration Office, Broad St, Monrovia. Bring two passport photos with you.

There are frequent passport checks on all the main roads.

If you only want to stay 48 hours in the country and are flying in and out of Robertsfield Airport (Monrovia), you can get a transit visa on arrival. However, you must have an onward ticket if you're going to do this.

Ivory Coast visas In Monrovia these cost US$20 (!) and are issued while you wait. Get them elsewhere.

Sierra Leone visas Entry permits are free, require two photos and take 24 hours to issue. You must have a valid vaccination certificate when you apply.

Senegal visas If you apply for this visa here, make sure it goes into your passport and not onto a separate piece of paper. If it goes onto the latter you may well be refused entry at the border of Senegal. This has happened to several travellers recently. For a three-month, triple entry visa they're currently charging CFA 20,000.

MONEY
The unit of currency is the Liberian dollar, which is on a par with the US dollar. US notes and coins are legal tender in Liberia. There is no restriction on the import or export of 'local' currency.

LANGUAGE
The official language is English but a number of African languages are also spoken, especially in the interior.

GETTING THERE & AROUND
Road
There is a schedule of MTA (Monrovia Transport Authority) buses, but it's mostly wishful thinking as they generally leave late and arrive even later. The terminal in Monrovia is at Center and Front Sts. The schedule is as follows:

Ganta-Monrovia Depart daily at 9.30 am and 3.30 pm. The journey is supposed to take four hours.

Monrovia-Ganta Depart at 9.30 am and 2 pm. These buses also serve Gbarnga.

Gbarnga-Monrovia Depart at 9 am and take three hours.

Monrovia-Gbarnga Depart at 4 pm.

Buchanan-Monrovia Depart at 9 am, 2.15 pm and 4 pm, and supposedly take 2¼ hours.

Monrovia-Buchanan Depart at 9 am, noon and 4 pm.

Monrovia-Harper This is a gruelling 26-hour journey so it's worth considering flying with *Air Liberia*.

Boat

A Firestone rubber boat plies between Harbel (near to Monrovia) and Harper (close to the Ivory Coast border) in either direction roughly once a week. It's usually possible to get a free ride if you talk to the captain and buy him a few beers. The journey takes about 36 hours on the open sea.

To/From Sierra Leone

From Monrovia to the border (Bombom) you can take a train, truck (US$3) or taxi (US$6). The route goes through the Bomi Hills. From the border you can get a pick-up to Kenema via Zimi for 42 leone. The trip takes about nine hours along an atrocious road. Kenema is the railhead in Sierra Leone and from there you can get a train to Freetown. A bush taxi from Kenema to Monrovia will cost 70 leones and take all day. The north-eastern route via Kolahun and Kailahun is presently closed (by the Sierra Leone government because too much smuggling was going on).

There are also taxis and minibuses from Monrovia to Mano River Union (border)

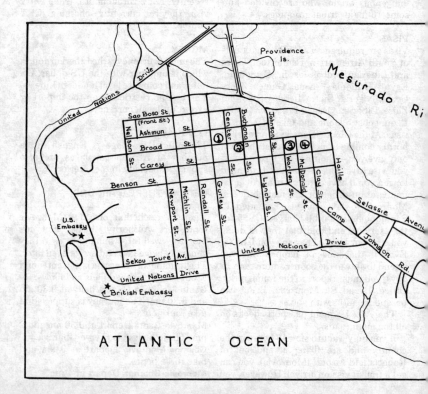

for US$6, to Kenema for US$20 and to Freetown for US$25. It's probably better to take a taxi to the border and then different transport from there, as you can then pay in leones. The taxi/truck park for this transport is on Randall St at Water St, Monrovia. The border closes at 6 pm.

To/From Ivory Coast

The main route into Ivory Coast from Monrovia goes to Man via Sanniquellie and Danane. First take a taxi from Monrovia to Buchanan for US$3.50. From Buchanan there is a daily train which goes to Yekepa/Sanniquellie at 4.50 pm except on Sundays, when it leaves at 6.30 pm. The fare to Yekepa is US$7. Latest reports, however, suggest

that this train is only a cargo train, so you may not be able to use it. If not, there are minibuses from Monrovia to Sanniquellie/Yekepa for US$11 and another from there to the border for US$1. From the border there are taxis to Danane for CFA 600, and others from there to Man for CFA 1200. There are no buses across the border between the two countries on this route.

Alternatively, there are taxis and minibuses between Monrovia and Ganta which cost US$8 and take four or five hours. There is also an *MTA* bus between the two places which costs US$5 plus 25c for your luggage and leaves from the bus stop at Sao Boso St. It takes five to seven hours and is often not very crowded. The road

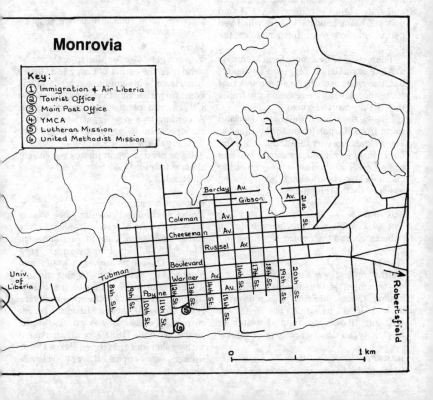

Monrovia

Key:
1. Immigration & Air Liberia
2. Tourist Office
3. Main Post Office
4. YMCA
5. Lutheran Mission
6. United Methodist Mission

Barclay Av.
Gibson   Av.   21st St.
Coleman   Av.
Cheeseman   Av.
Russel   Av.
Boulevard
Tubman   Warner   Av.   16th St.   17th St.   18th St.   19th St.   20th St.
Univ. of Liberia
8th St.   9th St.   Payne   10th St.   11th St.   12th St.   13th St.   14th St.   15th St.
Robertsfield

0   1 km

from Monrovia to Ganta is paved, but between Ganta and the border it's a dirt track. Between Ganta and Sanniquellie there are taxis and minibuses for US$1.50 which take one hour. From there take another truck to Kahnple, and from there a taxi to the border. There are also shared taxis available from Sanniquellie to the border for US$1.50-2. From the border there is a bus once a day to Danane for 600 CFA. Beware of border officials here. They will examine your papers minutely and if there's anything wrong or out of date, however petty, it will cost you money. One traveller had to pay US$20 because his cholera injection certificate was out of date. Also, make sure you get an entry stamp in your passport at Danane – not just an immigration officer's signature and date stamp – otherwise you'll find yourself being sent back there when you get to another town further down the line.

There used to be a route from Monrovia to Abidjan via Ganta, Tappi and Toulepleu, but travellers who have attempted that route recently say there is so little traffic that it's not worth trying.

Finally, there is a little-known overland route from Harper (close to the Liberia/Ivory Coast border) to Tabou. It's a six-hour journey over rough roads by bus and costs US$3. From Tabou you can either continue overland along good sealed roads or fly to Abidjan.

BUCHANAN
The two hotels are the *Sabra Hotel* on Atlantic St and the *Louiza Hotel*.

GANTA
Most people stay at *Sister Rachel's Motel* on the main street. It costs US$15 a double, though you can bargain down to around US$11 as a rule. The rooms are OK but there's no running water or electricity, so they're pretty poor value.

HARPER
Close to the border with the Ivory Coast,

Harper has one of the best beaches in the country. Unfortunately, there's only one place to stay – *The Island* – which costs US$20 a double. For somewhere to eat try *Mary's* under the Plum Tree or *Soul Sister Cookshop*. Both are on Green St.

MONROVIA
Useful Addresses
Cameroun Embassy
    South side of Tubman Boulevard, about 1½ km past 24th St
Guinea embassy
    North side of Tubman Boulevard, about 2½ km past 24th St
Ghana embassy
    11th St at the beach
    Ivory Coast embassy
    North side of Tubman Boulevard, about three km past 24th St
Sierra Leone embassy
    North side of Tubman Boulevard, about 1½ km past 24th St

Visas
You can get a visa for Mali from the street vendor on the corner of Carey and Gurley Sts. He sells Malian handicrafts and will come up with a Malian visa if you give him US$15, two photos and your passport. According to a local expatriate resident, the operation is legitimate (sounds very dubious all the same!).

If you need passport photos you can get them at four for US$2 from street vendors on Randall St.

Places to Stay
Probably the most popular place to stay here and one of the cheapest is the *Lutheran Mission*, 13th St, on the beach. The staff are very friendly and it costs US$10. The rooms are very pleasant and have private bath with hot water and fan. To get here, take a taxi to the Sinkor Shopping Centre. Another popular place is the *United Methodist Mission*, 12th St, corner of Tubman Boulevard, also on the beach, which is US$10 for an apartment with washer and spin dryer! Peace Corps workers are apparently not welcome here.

There's very little choice other than the above if you're on a budget. Some of the cheaper places to stay are the *Park Hotel*, Broad St at Buchanan St, which costs US$13 a single plus 10% tax; the *Palm Hotel*, Broad St at Randall St, which costs US$22 a single plus 10% tax; the *Carlton Hotel*, Broad St, which costs US$25 a single plus 10% tax; and the *Nevada Hotel*, corner of Benson and Gurley Sts, which costs US$25 a double with air-conditioning plus 10% tax, though you can sometimes get rooms here for US$20 a double including tax. In the same price range are the *Hotel Plaza*, Water St at Michlin. There is also a *YMCA*, Broad St at McDonald, where you can get a bed for US$5, but it takes a tussle with bureaucracy to get in. Forget about sleeping on the beaches, as you're likely to get mugged. Muggings are becoming an increasing problem in the downtown areas even during daylight hours.

For food, try the restaurants and rice chop houses on Gurly St off Broad St. Be careful down Gurly St – it's the bar area and muggings are common. The Lebanese restaurant next to the Shelia Cinema, Carey St, offers excellent falafel sandwiches for US$1.50.

Taxis in Monrovia cost 40c per person and there is a zoning system in force. From Monrovia to the airport (Robertsfield Airport is 50 km from Monrovia) should cost US$2 sharing. In the opposite direction the price starts at US$35, but you can bargain this down to about US$20. The taxi stand is near the bridge to Providence Island. The truck park for up-country lifts is on Water St.

Kenema Beach is about the only safe spot to swim around Monrovia. It costs 50c by taxi to get there plus US$1 to get onto the beach. Be careful, as there are riptides and strong undercurrents on all the beaches in Liberia.

ROBERTSPORT

Here you'll find some of the best beaches in Liberia. To get there take a US$4, one-hour truck ride up the coast from Monrovia. There is a cheap US$5-a-night hotel and a number of cheap rice and soup cafés in town.

YEKEPA

Yekepa is a modern mining town which, though located deep in the bush, has incredible facilities. One of the cheapest places to stay here is the *Humble Inn* at US$5 per person. If you can't get into the Humble Inn, try the expatriate bars (there are a lot of British people here). You might get invited back for the night.

OTHER

There is a spectacular two-day river canoe trip up the Sinoe River from Greenville which is sponsored by the Forest Development Agency. It costs about US$35, which includes everything except transport to and from Greenville. On one of these trips you can see monkeys, birds and often crocodiles and hippos. The trips take place from December to March. Enquire at the FDA in Monrovia for details.

Libya

Libya has been conquered and settled at one time or another by the Garamantes, Greeks, Romans, Berbers, Arabs and Turks. The remains of these various periods can still be seen today in the ruined cities along the coast, the Greek remains at Leptis Magna being particularly interesting and some of the best preserved in the world. From the middle of the 16th century until 1911, Libya was part of the empire of the Ottoman Turks and was the empire's last possession along the North African coast. It was taken from them by the Italians in that country's last-minute bid for colonies, but following WW II was placed under United Nations trusteeship until 1951, when Libya became an independent nation.

In 1969 the old King Idris was deposed in a military coup led by Colonel Muammar Qadafi, a man then in his early 30s, deeply religious and inspired by a vision of Pan-Arabism. Qadafi has succeeded in placing the country in the forefront of Middle Eastern and even world politics and drastically changing Libya's former status as a UK-USA client state. His regime is pledged to the equitable distribution of Libya's enormous income from the sale of oil and is currently spending thousands of millions of dollars on roads, schools, houses, hospitals and agriculture. Soon after Qadafi came to power, the British and Americans were ordered to leave the bases they had occupied since WWII, and so were the 25,000 descendants of the Italian colonists.

Some promising moves are being made in the devolution and sharing of political power stemming from Qadafi's *Green Book*. In it he states that the parliamentary system practised in the west is undemocratic since it is used by politicians to take power away from the people, and that a multi-party system is detrimental to political progress, encouraging sterile opposition for opposition's sake while in reality the parties in power pursue much the same policies. Though the book contains some refreshing insights and promising new directions which have revolutionised Libyan society, a fair amount of it is pure eccentric eye-wash.

Almost wholly foreign-owned and controlled at the time of King Idris' overthrow, Libya's vast oil deposits have gradually been taken over by a government determined to return control of the country's natural resources to the people. Despite an attempt to form a cartel to resist such a development, by 1973 all the oil companies had been forced to accept a minimum 51% Libyan participation. The National Oil Corporation began independent operations in 1971, and by 1973, with its own operations and the participation agreements it had wrung from the foreign oil companies, it controlled 70% of oil production. Soon after that it embarked on its own refining, distribution of refined products and the direct export of crude to state concerns. Before these events took place, Libya, despite being one of the world's largest producers of crude oil, was forced to import all of its refined requirements since none of the foreign oil companies had built refineries in Libya. Refined oil is now being exported, often in Libyan-owned tankers, and the natural gas which had been flared in the past is being harnessed to fuel power stations.

Ambitious plans to make Libya self-sufficient in food have brought agriculture into a dominant position in the country, with forestry and fishing following closely behind. Vast areas of land are in the process of reclamation and the government is encouraging farmers to adopt cooperative methods. Dams have been constructed to catch what little water falls, and many novel methods of turning desert back into arable land have been utilised. In Roman times this area and that in adjacent Algeria was known as the 'granary of the empire,' but because of overgrazing, neglect of irrigation systems, lack of planning and wars, the desert has expanded over the centuries, leaving precious little of the country suitable for agriculture.

Libya is well known (some would say notorious) for its support of liberation movements around the world, but in recent years Qadafi's idealism seems to have fallen prey to egotism, and his support of some regimes – particularly that of Idi Amin in Uganda before his downfall – stretches the concept of liberation beyond belief. These days Qadafi seems to be willing to support any bunch of desperadoes so long as they bring him plenty of media coverage and cause as much civil commotion as possible in western and western-oriented countries. This none too subtle change of policy may well have earned him a grudging respect in some circles, but it has also earned him many enemies. His attempts to eliminate exiled Libyan opponents living in various western countries by unleashing death squads in the early 1980s was surely the end of the line as far as his credibility was concerned. Many African countries have also expressed serious concern about Libya's involvement in Chad. When the civil war broke out there several years ago, Libya occupied a section of the northern part of that country and shortly afterwards poured troops and arms into the country to ensure the victory of the faction which it supported. Shortly afterwards, Libya and Chad announced their intention to merge, but this idea was lost in the fighting which engulfed Chad. The fighting eventually reached a stalemate in late 1983 with former President Goukouni supported by 5000 regular Libyan troops in control of the north of the country, and Hissene Habre supported by 3200 French Legionaires in control of the centre and south. Neither the French nor the Libyans wished to risk a direct confrontation. In September 1984, following secret talks between the French Foreign Minister and Qadafi, the two countries agreed to withdraw their troops. It's no secret that Chad has important deposits of uranium, gold, cassiterite and bauxite, especially in the north of the country.

Union with Chad isn't Qadafi's first attempt at pan-Arabism. He has tried it before with Tunisia, Sudan, Syria and Egypt, but the attempts have all come to grief. Indeed, since negotiations with Egypt were broken off, the two countries have twice been on the brink of war, the first time as a result of the treatment of Egyptian workers in Libya (all of whom were subsequently expelled) and then again as a result of the Camp David peace treaty with Israel. Libya has also been implicated in a recent attempted coup against the Sudanese government. Just how long Qadafi can survive this endless string of provocations remains to be seen. Sadat was assassinated for giving peace a chance, yet Qadafi continues to espouse violence. You'll be very lucky to hear an honest opinion about the Libyan regime inside the country, for fear that it might be heard by the wrong ears. Most Libyans will willingly admit that Qadafi has done a lot for the Libyan people since he took over, but his popularity doesn't ride so high any more. There have been a number of attempted coups, though news of them is generally suppressed.

Certainly the income from oil has vastly improved the living standards of Libya's estimated two million inhabitants, but the extremely rapid transition from a largely nomadic existence to a modern consumer society has resulted in many problems.

City streets are full of trash, inflation is rampant and food is not only expensive but scarce. Fruit and vegetables are almost impossible to find, and meat, eggs and butter almost equally so. Not only does Libya have to import about 90% of its food, there are also an estimated one million expatriate workers in the country, many of whom – especially in the oil industry – are indispensable. So indispensable are they that despite American military provocation and the shooting down of Libyan jets in the Gulf of Sirte, they continue to remain there even after diplomatic relations have been severed.

VISAS

Visas are required by all except nationals of Algeria, Malta and Mauritania. Nationals of Germany (West) must get visas from the Libyan embassy in Bonn (visas obtained elsewhere will not be accepted). If you are going to Libya you must have in your passport a translation in Arabic of pages one and two (personal details, place of issue, date of issue and expiry, etc). If you haven't got this, the Libyan embassies won't accept a visa application from you. Most western embassies in North Africa will provide you with such a translation free of charge. Unmarried women under 35 years old are generally refused visas or are made to wait so long (weeks and even months) that it simply isn't worth trying. So much for Qadafi's much-lauded 'liberation.'

Entry into Libya is conditional on you having at least US$500 to show immigration authorities.

Searches at Libyan borders/airports are very thorough. Alcohol, pork products, pornography and anything considered to be anti-Libyan propaganda will be confiscated – paperbacks and cassettes fall into this category regardless of content. 'Marks & Sparks' underwear is definitely suspect. Also, anything vaguely connected with Israel will be confiscated. It's rumoured that radios with short-wave bands will soon be on the list, as the government doesn't like what it hears about itself on the BBC World Service.

You must report to the police station within 48 hours of arriving. Usually your hotel can take care of this, but if not, you'll have to ask someone to help you find a place called Balladia, where you fill in forms and get your passport stamped. You haven't a hope of finding this place or of filling in the forms unless you read and speak good Arabic.

The border with Egypt is closed, and the same may apply to the border with Sudan.

MONEY

US$1 = 0.29 dinar
£1 = 0.48 dinar

The unit of currency is the Libyan dinar = 1000 dirham. Import/export of local currency is allowed up to 20 dinar.

The airport departure tax for international flights is 5 dinar.

LANGUAGE

Arabic is the official language and Qadafi is so keen on promoting its use and discouraging the use of any other language that a phrase book is more or less essential. You'll be very lucky to find a sign in any other language anywhere in the country – including places through which a lot of travellers pass, like airports.

GETTING THERE & AROUND

Because the border with Egypt is closed – which forces you to double back into Tunisia – and because visas are such a hassle to get, very few travellers are going to Libya these days. This means that the information we have is very sketchy. Hitching is easy in the north and lifts are often for long distances, especially between Tripoli and Benghazi – there's very little habitation between these two cities. Lifts are often with expatriate workers and are usually free, though if you're heading down into the desert then you should expect to pay.

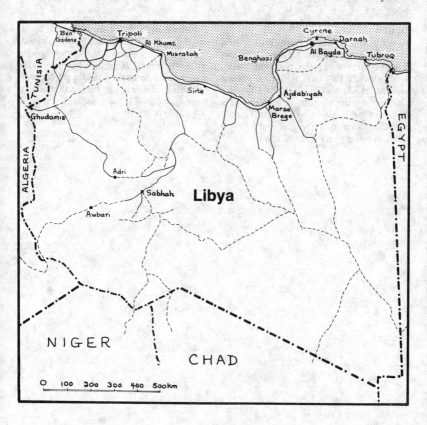

There are fast and efficient daily buses between the main Libyan coastal towns, but you need to buy tickets at least a day in advance as there's heavy competition for seats.

The only effective overland route open at present is from Tunisia along the northern coast road.

TRIPOLI

There's no such thing as a cheap hotel in Tripoli, so be prepared for a shock at the prices that are asked for rooms. Perhaps the best place to try is the *Youth Hostel* situated about 500 metres outside the old city on Sharia Ibn El As (otherwise known as Omar ben Alas). It's just past the cinema on the opposite side of the road. It's comfortable and spacious with clean linen, TV lounge, and hot and cold showers – and sometimes they even have movies. If it's full or you can't find it, try the *Libyan Palace Hotel* not far from the British Embassy which costs 10 dinar a single. It's usually full, but the staff on the desk speak English and might recommend another place.

If you arrive by air, the yellow government taxis will take you into Tripoli for 4 dinar – buy your ticket inside the terminal building. If you take a private taxi, you'll be charged 8 dinar.

OTHER

Even if you're not a ruins buff, you'll thoroughly enjoy a visit to the Greek and Roman ruins along the northern coast. Undoubtedly the best is **Leptis Magna** close to Al Khums (Homs) east of Tripoli. Others worth visiting are **Sabrantha** between the Tunisian border and Tripoli, and **Cyrene** close to Shahhat and halfway along the Benghazi-Tobruk road.

Remember not to take photographs of anything other than the ruins. Libyans are generally very suspicious of foreigners with cameras, if only because the government-controlled media are forever rabbiting on about imperialist-racist enemies of the Libyan people.

Madagascar

Madagascar (or Malagasy Republic as it's officially known) is an enigma in Africa since the majority of its 8½ million inhabitants are descended from Malay and Polynesian migrants. They began arriving from the 6th century onwards, particularly during the 9th century when the powerful Hindu Sumatran empire of Srivijaya controlled much of the maritime trade in the Indian Ocean. These people brought with them the food crops of South-East Asia, so that even today the agriculture of the island resembles that of their origins rather than that of the mainland. It's been suggested that the gradual spread of these crops to the mainland assisted the Bantu tribes of the interior to migrate to the coasts of Kenya and Tanzania. Malagasy agriculture, however, isn't the only factor which distinguishes the island from the mainland. None of the mainland apes, antelopes, poisonous snakes or the lion or elephant are to be found on the island.

A number of different kingdoms came into being side by side on the island, and it wasn't until the end of the 18th century that the Merina kingdom, using weapons and advisors from the European maritime nations, was able to unite the island. During the 19th century a form of the modern state with a trained army and administration, an established church and formal education was created by uniting both traditional and European models of government. The country was invaded by the French in 1895 and was declared a

colony the following year after the Merina queen had been deposed.

Colonisation followed the typical pattern of expropriation of land by foreign settlers and companies, the exploitation of the peasantry through forced labour and taxes, the imposition of an import-export economy (in this case based on coffee) with the construction of roads and railroads to serve it, and the training of an intellectual elite to French standards. Resentment grew on all levels of society and eventually culminated in the insurrection of 1947-48. This was crushed by the French with the loss of several thousand Malagasy lives. In 1960, however, the French, taking advantage of the tensions which existed between the coastal and inland peoples, granted independence on terms very favourable to themselves.

Under the Malagasy Republic's first president, Philibert Tsiranana, French companies were allowed to retain their hold over trade and financial institutions and their military bases on the island. Tsiranana also maintained a 'dialogue' with South Africa and refused contacts with communist countries. His propensity for rigging elections and his brutal repression of an uprising in the south in 1972 proved to be his undoing and he was overthrown in a military coup in that year. General Ramanantsoa took over and initiated a fundamental change in Malagasy policy. Aid agreements with France were renegotiated, all foreign military bases were closed down and there was a return to the collective work system that had been practised in the rural areas before the country was colonised. The new government also severed diplomatic relations with South Africa, Israel and Taiwan and formed new links with China and the USSR.

The closure of the French military bases and Madagascar's withdrawal from the franc zone following abortive negotiations led to a wholesale departure of the French farming community. The exodus was a painful reminder of how dependent the Malagache still were on French capital and technical skills, and major differences of opinion began to surface over the direction of the government's economic policies. Ramanantsoa was forced to step down as a result of this unrest, and was replaced by Colonel Ratsimandrava, who pledged to follow the progressive line of his predecessor but with more vigor. Ratsimandrava was shot to death in his car within a week of taking office, and a rebel group of army officers promptly announced a military takeover. They were routed by officers loyal to the former president and a new government headed by the former Foreign Minister, Ratsiraka, was set up.

Since coming to power, Ratsiraka has pressed ahead with his plan of transforming the island into a socialist society by the year 2000. In 1978 links with the Comoros were cut after the mercenaries' coup and steps were taken to acquire a more sophisticated air force as well as to cooperate more closely with progressive regimes on the mainland – particularly in military terms. Though relations with France have thawed in recent years, there still remains the dispute over sovereignty of several small islands off the northern tip of Madagascar – such as Iles Glorieuses, Juan de Nova and Europa – which the French continue to occupy. No solution is in sight for this dispute, especially as the French have built extensive air facilities on Juan de Nova.

FACTS

Madagascar is set almost entirely in the tropics, but because of the rugged mountain chain which runs down the centre of the island, there are dramatic differences in the vegetation and climate between the west and east sides of the island. The eastern coastal strip is fairly narrow and partly covered with tropical rainforests. The west side of the island has a wider plain of savannah and forest. The south is considerably more arid and features cactus-like vegetation. The mountain chain is dissected by deep valleys. The rainy season stretches from November to March. Cyclones are common along the east coast, with the monsoon between December and March.

VISAS

Visas are required by all. They are valid for a stay of one month. You need to fill in four forms (in French) and provide four photos. The visas cost the equivalent of about US$12 and take up to seven days to issue. There's no hassle about money or onward tickets. There are very few Malagasy embassies. Outside Africa you can find them in Brussels, Bonn, Paris, Rome, Washington and Tokyo. A visa in Paris costs French francs 200 (about £18!) for a single-entry visa and French francs 300 for a multiple-entry visa. The embassy says it will return passports sent in by post, but it doesn't always do this – one correspondent had to go to Paris from the UK to collect his!

In Africa you have the following choice of embassies:

Algeria
    22 Rue Aouis Bologhine, Algiers
Mauritius
    6 Sir William Newton St
Tanzania
    Magoret St, Dar-es-Salaam

There is no longer a Malagasy embassy in Nairobi, but you can apply for the visa through *Air Madagascar* at the Hilton Hotel, PO Box 42676, Nairobi (tel 25286/26494). They only take applications on Mondays, as the forms have to be sent to Antananarivo for approval. You get the visa on Wednesday of the same week.

If you arrive from continental Africa you must have valid cholera and yellow fever vaccinations.

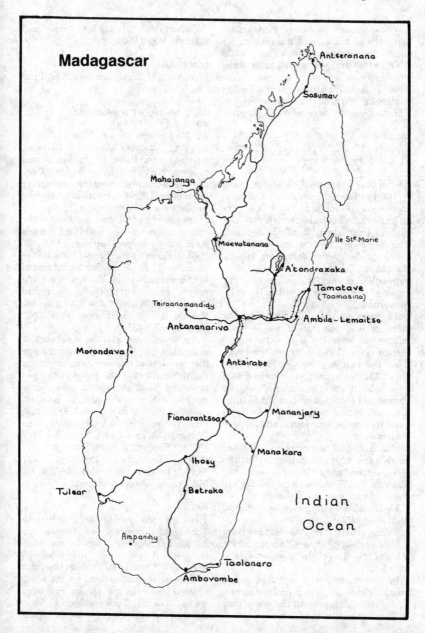

Visas are easy to extend in Antananarivo at the Ministry of the Interior for up to two months more. The cost is MFr 15,000 and you must supply three photos, a photocopy of your *visa d'entrée* and a short letter in French explaining why you want an extension. They take three days to come through.

MONEY

US$1 = MFr 422
£1 = MFr 650

The unit of currency is the Malagasy franc = 100 centimes. Import/export of local currency is prohibited. There is a very strict currency control on arrival and your cash will be checked down to the last cent. The same happens when you leave. Currency declaration forms are issued. Plan ahead. Malagasy francs are almost impossible to get rid of outside the country. (They are officially non-convertible.)

The black market is difficult to find, but more or less essential if you're on a budget, as everything is expensive – though since Madagascar left the Franc Zone the currency has depreciated by about 35% so it's not as expensive as it used to be. It's best to meet a Malagache abroad and change with him (up to twice the bank rate). Inside the country you could try approaching Indian and Chinese traders.

The cost of living is high and many goods are only available in limited quantities and at exorbitant prices on the black market. These include cooking oil, paper, bread, soap, toothpaste.

Fashionable western clothes, electrical goods and calculators sell well.

Average costs: A double room in a hotel is MFr 3000-5000. A meal in a restaurant is MFr 1200. A meal in a 'transport café' is MFr 500.

In the markets you will find prices quoted in piastres, ariary, drala or parata. These units all represent the same thing and are equivalent to MFr 5.

Airport departure tax for international flights is MFr 1500.

LANGUAGE

French and Malagasy are used. Very little English is spoken.

GETTING THERE & AROUND
Air

Air Madagascar flies to Nairobi, Dar es Salaam, Comoros, Mauritius, Reunion, Seychelles and Paris. This airline is fond of appearing to be fully booked, so if you can't get a confirmed seat (on domestic or international flights), try standby. It often works. Be sure to reconfirm flights – it's best to have a confirmed flight out of the country; otherwise you could find yourself staying there longer than intended.

From Europe the cheapest fares are the discounted *Aeroflot* flights from London to Antananarivo via Moscow for £420 return. From Africa there are return excursion fares from the following places: Nairobi (US$402); Reunion (US$326); Mauritius (US$353).

Air Madagascar also has a network of internal flights. If you're thinking of using their services extensively, enquire about the Air Tourist Pass which allows unlimited travel for fixed periods of time. Some sample airfares *ex* Antananarivo are: Antseranana (Diego Suarez) MFr 50,450; Fianarantsoa MFr 25.450; Mahajunga (Majunga) MFr 29,150; Nossi Be MFr 46.750; Taolanaro (Fort Dauphin) MFr 46,750; Toamasina (Tamatave) MFr 18,300; Toleara (Tulear) MFr 46,750. Air Madagascar always overbook.

Rail

There are railways from Antananarivo to Toamasina (Tamatave) on the coast via Ambila-Lemaitso, and from Antananarivo north to A'tondrazaka and south to Antsirabe. There is also a short line from Fianarantsoa to Manakara on the coast which is scenically spectacular. Rail fares are based on MFr 5 per km. Journey times are slow because of the difficult terrain and the narrow gauge track. On Nossi Be there are 60-cm-gauge plantation trains which you can ride free.

Antananarivo-Toamasina (Tamatave) Daily trains except Sundays. Trains are comfortable and relatively fast but you need to make reservations in advance. The fare is MFr 2690 (2nd class) and the journey takes 12½ hours.

Antananarivo-Antsirabe There are two trains daily which cost MFr 1150 (2nd class) and take four hours.

Fianarantsoa-Manakara There is at least one train daily (some days there are two) and the journey time is six hours.

Road

Road transport is slow, expensive and infrequent. The only reliable bus service in Madagascar is operated by the railways. They cover the Antsirabe-Fianarantsoa route in 7½ hours for MFr 1000. Avoid coming here in the rainy season if possible, as many roads are impassable. Regardless of the type of transport you take, be prepared for very uncomfortable journeys and breakdowns – Fianarantsoa-Taolanaro (Fort Dauphin) can take up to five days even in the dry season! Take warm clothes if you're travelling in the mountains during winter. The locals wear up to four blankets in some areas. Hitching is a joke as there are so few vehicles and you pay for rides anyway. There are four categories of public transport. The 'taxi-be' is the quickest and most comfortable but expensive. Next best is the 'taxi-brousse' which is fast but uncomfortable and seats about 15 people. Next is the van-type bus which seats 25 to 30 people. This is more uncomfortable than the taxi-brousse and makes more stops, but is quite tolerable. Last are the buses proper, which seat over 30 people. You're advised to give these a miss as they're slow and don't handle the Malagasy roads very well (most of the

island's roads are unsealed). Always book transport in advance. All transports stop for meals. Bus stations have *hotelys*, which are restaurants where you can buy hot meals for MFr 300-500. Unless you want a large meal, it's best to order a *demi-plat*. These are smaller and usually MFr 50 cheaper than the larger *plat*.

There are bandits in the south, but public transport is probably safe.

It helps to know when market days are in neighbouring towns; otherwise you can get stuck in a place for days because there's no transport available.

Examples of road transport are:

Antananarivo-Tulear Taxi-brousse costs MFr 15,000 and takes about 24 hours.

Antananarivo-Taolanaro (Ft Dauphin) Costs MFr 20,000.

Antananarivo-Antseranana (Diego Suarez) Costs MFr 20,000.

Toleara (Tulear)-Taolanaro (Ft Dauphin) A taxi-brousse costs MFr 10,000, but they only go once a week on Fridays at 4 am.

If you intend going to the National Park at Joffreville (near Diego Suarez), you need prior permission from the Ministre de Forestiere et Eaux in Diego Suarez. It's free but you're expected to tip them.

There is a boat from Hell-Ville (on Nosy Be Island) to Mahajunga every three to four days. It's a good trip and costs only MFr 7000 (as opposed to MFr 20,000 by land). There is no firm departure time. There is also a boat between Toamasina and Nosy Boraha.

Ferries operate between Hell-Ville and Antsahampano and between Mahajunga and Katsepy.

Places to Stay

Accommodation prices at lodges are per room – you pay the same whether you're on your own or travelling with others. You can always find cheap hotels by asking the

Malagasy. Small lodging places can cost as little as MFr 500 per bed or MFr 1000 for a room, but beware of bed-bugs and body lice (the latter are a real pest in Madagascar).

TOAMASINA (Tamatave)

Hotel Plage opposite the football stadium has been recommended. It costs MFr 5000. A cheaper place is the *Fiadanamanga* which costs MFr 2800. For food, try *Restaurant Vietnamien*, Rue Aviateur Goulette 16 off Boulevard Joffre, or one of the many 'soupe Chinoise' restaurants which lay on cheap soup.

ANTANANARIVO (Tananarive)

Good accommodation in the capital is expensive, though there are a number of cheap places to the right as you come out of the railway station. To find a room there you need to be early. They include the *Hotel Lapan'ny Vaniny* and the *Hotel Ivarivo*. Both are dirty. If you're looking for something better, there's a good choice of places under US$10. One of the cheapest is the *Hotel Select*, Avenue 18 de Juin next door to Alitalia. A small room here costs MFr 4500-5500. It's very clean and conveniently located. Similar to it is the *Hotel Terminus*, Avenue de la Libération (tel 20376) just by the railway station, which costs MFr 3500 a single, and the *Hotel Glacier* which costs MFr 5000. Others are the *Acropole*, 71 Avenue Lenine (tel 23380), which also serves good Malagasy and French food; the *Lido*, Avenue 26 Juin 1960 (tel 23848); and the *Mellis Hotel* (tel 123425) in the centre of town. If these are full, try the *Hotel La Murzille de Chine* (tel 23013), which costs MFr 6000-8000 for a room with a private bath. Lastly, there is the *Hotel-Restaurant Pavillion de Jade*, 20 Rue Emile et Juliette Ranarivelo (tel 22690), which one traveller described as the best in Antananarivo. It only has eight rooms but it serves excellent Chinese food and has a laundry service, both of which are half-price to guests. If you're thinking of staying at the *Lido*, you should know that it's run by an Evangelical who won't allow two men to share the same room.

For food, most of the hotels in the station area have daily fixed menus for MFr 1500-3000 for a five-course meal. One restaurant which has been recommended for good food is the *Restaurant Fiadanana*, Avenue Adrianampoinimerina 12 – first street left from the station.

For an evening out, try the disco at *Le Cellier*, 8 Rue Ingereza (tel 22060), but be wary of the prostitutes who are better at picking pockets than anything else.

There is a public bus to and from the airport and the railway station area during the day. This is the cheapest way of getting there. Air Madagascar also runs a daily bus service along the same route which costs MFr 800 (or MFr 1000 after 8 pm) plus MFr 100 for excess luggage. A taxi to the airport will cost MFr 2000-4000 and double that at night once the buses have stopped running.

Zuma is the big market in Antananarivo held every Friday. It is supposedly the second largest in the world and people flock to it from all over the island. Beware of pick-pockets and muggers. Don't go there alone and don't carry bags.

Also worth visiting are the **Rova** or Royal Village, the **Zoo** and the **Botanical Gardens**.

There is a Tourist Office, Place d'Abohij-Atavo, Tsimbazaza, opposite Aeroflot, and the zoo can sometimes be quite helpful.

It's suggested you stay off the streets at night in this city, as they're not particularly safe.

TAOLANARO (Fort Dauphin)

This town has a really fine location and was the scene of much colonial rivalry between the French, Portuguese and Dutch. Parts of the actual fort are still in existence, though it's now occupied by the Malagasy army. About 15 km away by road and canoe is the remains of the fort built by the Portuguese. The area is noted for its wide variety of carnivorous pitcher plants (*Nepenthes* species) and spectacular orchids. If you have an interest in them, it's worth visiting the **Mandona Agricultural Centre** at Sainte-Luce Bay. This bay is one of the few places where you can swim safely and there's delicious seafood available.

There is only one reasonable place to stay here. It's the *Hotel de France* and costs MFr 2500. There's also a good beach where you can camp.

It's difficult to get into or out of Taolanaro during the rainy season, during which it can rain for four or five days nonstop and be very cold and miserable, so bear this in mind.

HELL-VILLE

The only good place to stay here is the *Hotel Saloon*, which costs MFr 3000 a single.

AMBOSITRA

The main attraction of Ambositra is the woodcarving cooperative whose work is famous throughout the island. The originators of this craft are the Zafimaniry families. The best way to visit them is to contact the Jesuits, many of whom work around here. If you're lucky enough to be taken along with them to these peoples' villages, you'll probably be offered a glass of *toaka gasy*, the local firewater, often distilled to 125° proof. Whether you're a hard drinker or not, refusal offends – but expect violent headaches within 24 hours.

The *Zakarandaha* (tel 71272) has seven rooms and costs MFr 2500 a night. It's clean and has good Malagasy food. There is also the *Grand Hotel* with 15 (often empty) rooms and an indifferent reputation; it's expensive at MFr 12,000 per night.

ANTSERANANA (Diego-Suarez)

This is one of the most cosmopolitan towns in Madagascar, with a mixture of Arabs, Indians, French, Malagasy, Reunionais and Africans. It also has one of the island's most stunning harbours, but the road to Antseranana is only open between July and October. Twenty-four km south of the town is the **Ambre Nature Reserve**, which is famous for its lemurs.

There are only two reasonable places to stay here. They are the *Tropical Hotel*, which has 17 rooms and costs MFr 3500; and the Indian-run *Hotel la Racasse*, which costs MFr 2800 per room and has good vegetarian curries for MFr 300.

ANTSIRABE

The lake and the hot springs are what draw people to this place (which was founded by two Norwegian missionaries), but one traveller described it as 'the worst kind of European-inspired hotch-potch.' Hotels tend to be expensive here. One of the cheapest is the *Hotel Baobab*, Avenue de l'Independence, which costs MFr 4000 and serves reasonable Malagasy food.

FIANARANTSOA

Fianarantsoa is regarded as the intellectual capital of Madagascar. Not only that, it's a Christian centre (unusual on this island) and the main wine-producing area. Getting around the town can be perplexing, as there are three distinct levels.

The *Hotel des Voyageurs* here costs MFr 3000 per night and has an excellent cosmopolitan menu.

One hour by taxi from Fianarantsoa is **Ambalavao**, known throughout Madagascar as the 'home of the departed.' In a country where ancestors are periodically exhumed as a mark of respect, this place is of great spiritual importance. Nearby are **Ambondrome crag**, said to be the paradise of all Malagasy ancestors; and **Ifandana crag**, the site of the mass suicides of 1811. If you visit the latter place it's important to observe the *fady* (taboo) of the local people. (In the past tourists have apparently attempted to take away the bones that are still very much in evidence – unbelievable, isn't it!)

Ambalavao is also a crafts centre where you can find *antaimoro* paper, made by arranging patterns of flower petals in the wet pulp; and *lamba arindrano*, a hand-woven silk rectangle with geometric patterns.

If you want to stay in this town there's only the *Hotel Verger*, which has eight rooms. You can reserve a room here from Fianarantsoa by ringing Ambalavao 5.

MAHAJANGA (Majunga)

This town is a large port on the estuary of the Betsiboka River (Madagascar's largest), but its main attraction is the shark-free beach. There are road connections here between July and October by bush taxi from Antseranana. The journey can be interesting since it goes through the Mahajamba Valley, famous for its fossils and forests full of lemurs.

For a place to stay, try the Vietnamese-run *Chez Lolo* which has good rooms for MFr 3000 a night plus excellent food. There's also the *Hotel de Bretagne*, Avenue de la République, which is reasonable at MFr 3200 a night.

NOSY BE

Nosy Be island is the Zanzibar of Madagascar. Here you will find the plantations which provide the perfume industry with its raw materials – macassar oil (or ylang-ylang as any self-respecting hippie will tell you), lemon grass and patchouli – as well as vanilla which even Reagan eats from time to time. There are also sugar-cane plantations with miniature railways so, if you're from northern New South Wales or Queensland and are feeling nostalgic, here's balm for your eyes. If you're a history buff there's a ruined Indian village 11 km east of Hell-Ville which dates from the 17th century, when there was a wave of immigration from that sub-continent.

Road connections with Nosy Be are impossible outside of the dry season (July to October), though the ferry to and from the mainland operates all year round. If you want to go there during the rest of the year you'll have to consider flights – there are connections from Antananarivo, Mahajanga and Antseranana.

There are plenty of places to stay here (including a *Holiday Inn*), but if you're on a budget then try the *Hotel de la Mer* in Hell-Ville which costs MFr 5200 a night, or *Les Cocotiers* at Dzamandzar which costs MFr 4500 per night.

TOLEARA (Tulear)

This town has some good colonial architecture and excellent beaches but otherwise isn't that interesting.

The only reasonably priced hotel here is the *Tropical Hotel* which costs MFr 3500.

Malawi

Malawi consists of a thin sliver of densely populated territory running the whole length of beautiful Lake Nyasa (Lake Malawi) and a southern extension which dips down deep into Mozambique, almost cutting the latter country in half. Before the arrival of Europeans it was settled by various Bantu tribes who traded their small agricultural surplus and ivory with Portuguese merchants from the coast. European interest in the area was kindled by David Livingstone's travels, and it wasn't long after his return to Britain that Scottish missionaries began to arrive in the country in considerable numbers. Employing the well-tested policy of 'divide and rule,' the missionaries were able to overwhelm the warlike Ngoni and Yao tribes, suppress slavery, open up missions and begin to make inroads on traditional agricultural practices by establishing estates. Following the declaration of a Protectorate in 1891 (over what was then known as Nyasaland by the British) and the introduction of coffee, the number and size of these plantations began to grow rapidly.

As more and more land was expropriated, and when a 'hut-tax' was introduced and traditional slash-and-burn methods of agriculture were discouraged, increasing numbers of Africans were forced to seek work on the white settler plantations or become migrant workers in Zimbabwe and South Africa. Already by the turn of the century some 6000 Africans were leaving the country, and by the 1950s this number had grown to 150,000. Opposition to colonial rule surfaced early in the southern highlands but didn't become a serious threat until the 1950s, when the Nyasaland African Congress was formed to oppose federation with Northern and Southern Rhodesia and what had become intolerable colonial interference in traditional agricultural methods. Its support, however, remained limited until Dr Hastings Banda was invited to return home and take over the leadership (Banda had, by that time, spent 40 years abroad in the USA and Britain studying and practising medicine). Banda was so successful in whipping up support that just one year after he took over, the colonial authorities declared a state of emergency, threw Banda and other leaders into jail and went on a rampage of suppression in which 52 Africans were killed.

Nevertheless, opposition continued and in 1961 the colonial authorities were constrained to release Banda and invite him to London for a constitutional conference. In the elections which followed, Banda's Malawi Congress Party swept to victory. Shortly afterwards the Federation was dissolved and Malawi became independent in July 1964.

Despite his fierce oratory, however, Banda was no radical, and when major political differences began to surface between him and his ministers, Banda demanded they declare their allegiance to him. Rather than do this, many resigned and took to violent opposition. Drawing his support from the peasant majority, Banda was quickly able to smash opposition and drive the leaders into hiding or into exile, where they have remained ever since. With the opposition muzzled, Banda has continued to strengthen his dictatorial powers by having himself declared 'President for Life,' banning the foreign press, outraging the OAU by

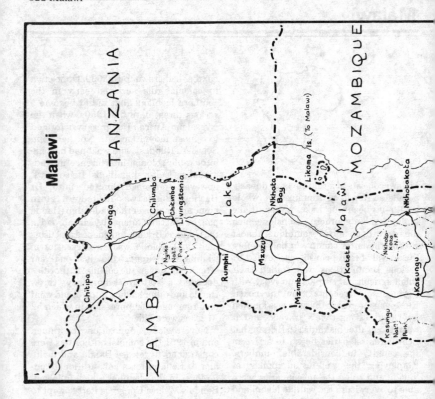

refusing to ostracise the South African regime (for which he has been handsomely rewarded financially), and waging pogroms against any group he regards as a threat. Although there was a slight liberalisation attempted in 1977 where about 2000 detainees were released (many of whom immediately fled the country), thousands more continue to languish in jail and it's virtually impossible to discuss politics with a Malawian. Spies and informers abound.

Typical of Banda's dictatorial powers is his control over the largely rubber stamp parliament, whose function is not to discuss the merits of his policies but to decide how best to implement them. Criticism is regarded in the same light as treason and is as likely as not to result in dismissal and imprisonment. In 1978, in the only general election to be held since independence, Banda personally vetted everyone who intended to stand as candidates, demanded that each pass an English examination (thereby precluding 90% of the population), and even re-instated supporters who were defeated.

Banda's control over the country isn't just political, however. Foreign capital investment, particularly from Britain, Israel, Taiwan and the USA, is actively encouraged. So, too, are government ministers encouraged to acquire land, start businesses and grow cash crops. Thus land is becoming more and more concentrated in the hands of the Malawian

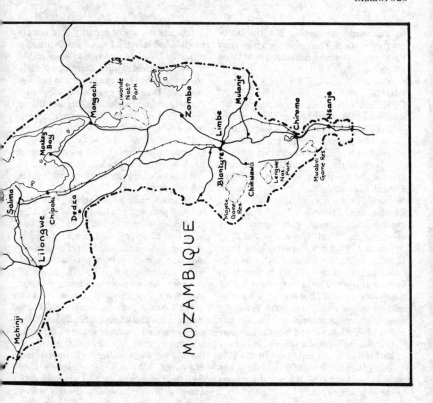

elite, with the peasants being forced to move onto land that is largely unsuitable for agricultural use. Managements of these estates is often placed in the hands of white expatriates from what was Rhodesia. Banda himself owns all but one of the 5000 shares of Press Holdings, a conglomerate of companies with wide interests including an agricultural subsidiary, which accounts for an estimated 30% of the country's economic activity. This is in complete contrast to the situation in Zambia and Tanzania, where ministers are banned from business activities. At the same time, education and medical facilities are a low priority in the allocation of development funds, while roads and railways serving plant-ations and prestige projects like the new capital at Lilongwe are given precedence.

Just how long Banda will be able to remain in power with a system like this in operation isn't clear. Already groups committed to the military overthrow of Banda have been formed in Tanzania and Zambia but they have, as yet, to show their teeth.

Warning
Banda doesn't like criticism, and because of what was written about him in the previous edition of this book, it now enjoys the dubious status of being banned. That being so, it's likely to be confiscated on entry if found, although this hasn't happened to everyone. A possible solution

to this might be to tear out the introductory section. You could then point out that the book contained nothing offensive.

FACTS

Of Malawi's total area of just over 94,000 square km, 20% is taken up by the waters of Lake Malawi. The only other country having sovereignty over part of the lake is Mozambique. High plateaux rise up from the shores of the lake and there are some spectacular mountain areas in the north around Livingstonia (Nyika Plateau National Park) and in the south near Zomba and Mulanje. The climate is healthy and pleasant, with temperatures averaging around 20°C in winter and 27°C in summer. The rainy season lasts from October to April, though much less rain falls along the shores of Lake Malawi than in the highlands. The population stands at nearly six million, but up to a quarter million of the adult males are generally absent at any one time, working in the mines of Zimbabwe and South Africa or on the tobacco farms of southern Zimbabwe. Lake Malawi is the only lake in the Rift Valley generally free of bilharzia – the main exception to this is around Karonga in the extreme north.

VISAS

Visas are required by all except nationals of the Commonwealth countries, Belgium, Denmark, Finland, Germany (West), Iceland, Irish Republic, Luxembourg, Netherlands, Norway, Portugal, South Africa, Sweden and the USA.

Those who don't require visas are given 30 days or less on arrival, depending on what sort of front they put up.

Extensions are free of charge and available at Lilongwe, Blantyre, Zomba, Monkey Bay, Mzuzu, Karonga and any other regional police station. If you think you might be staying for more than 30 days, you can apply for an entry visa (as opposed to a tourist visa). They're free of charge but you need two photos.

Despite the use of scantily-clad female models in Malawi's tourist literature, it's officially illegal for women to wear either trousers or skirts which don't completely cover the knees (except at certain holiday resorts). Likewise, men with long hair (loosely defined as hair falling in bulk to the collar) or flared trousers are barred from entry. And they mean it!

If you enter Malawi via Lilongwe International Airport, you may be asked to show an onward ticket.

A valid cholera vaccination certificate is also required.

Clearing customs on arrival can be a lengthy process. It's likely that you'll be subjected to two separate and detailed searches of your baggage and possibly your person. Communist literature, girlie magazines and this book are banned and will be confiscated if found. A lot of travellers have been specifically asked if they have this book. It seems we still haven't been forgiven for certain comments in the 2nd edition, even though they were removed from the 3rd edition in an attempt to bring an end to all the strife at the border as travellers' cherished and dog-eared 'bibles' were brusquely torn from their sweaty palms and ignominiously dumped in the trash can. Surely we've earned a reprieve by now? Fortunately, most travellers get through without being deprived, but it would be a good idea to back the book in plain brown paper.

South African visas These are free and issued while you wait at the embassy in Lilongwe near the Capitol Hotel.

MONEY
US$1 = Kw 1.50
£1 = Kw 1.78

The unit of currency is the kwacha = 100 tambala. Import/export of local currency is allowed up to Kw 20. Currency declaration forms are issued on arrival and you may be asked to show how much foreign cash and traveller's cheques you are bringing with you. The same might well happen when you leave. There is a black market on which you can get US$1 = Kw 2 and £1 = Kw 3 (£ sterling are preferred to US dollars), but it's difficult to find. Ask Asian shopkeepers. If you are going to Zambia you can usually exchange the kwacha of both countries on a one-for-one basis with bus conductors, but the rate varies from time to time.

Changing money at banks can be a major bureaucratic hassle. The commission on traveller's cheques is 3% plus 36 tambala at the District Commissioner's Treasury office in Chitipa, but only 1.5% in Nkhotakota. There are no permanent banks north of Mzuzu. Towns north of here have a system of 'roving banks' which operate on one or two days of the week only. In Nkhata Bay it's on Friday; in Chilumba on Monday and Thursday.

If you have a Eurocheque card, you can cash personal cheques at the National Bank of Malawi in Lilongwe, Blantyre, Mangochi and Mzuzu. The bank tellers are familiar with this and you get a better rate than for traveller's cheques.

You can reconvert up to Kw 20 per day of your stay back into hard currency at the banks. This transaction is often not recorded on your currency form, so it's possible to visit several banks.

The only permanent banks north of Mzuzu are at Karonga. The bank day at Rumphi is Thursday. Livingstonia gets the mobile bank on the first and third Monday of each month.

Airport departure tax for international flights is Kw 10.

LANGUAGE

English and Chichewa are the official languages. There are a number of other African languages spoken.

The following words in Chichewa could be useful:

hello	*moni*
how are you	*muli bwanji*
I'm fine	*ndili bwino*
good/fine/OK	*chabwino*
thank you/excuse me	*zikomo*
thanks very much	*zikomo kwambiri*
goodbye (to person leaving)	*pitani bwino*
goodbye (to person staying)	*tsalani bwino*
please	*chonde*
to eat	*kudya*
water	*madzi*
milk	*mkaka*
chicken	*nkuku*
meat	*nyama*
fish	*nsomba*
lake perch	*chambo*
eggs	*mazira*
potatoes	*mbatata*
father = man (polite greeting)	*bambo*
mother = woman (polite greeting)	*mayi*
women (polite greeting)	*amai*
yes	*inde*
no	*iyayi*
where?	*kuti?*
here	*pano*
over there	*uko*
in there	*umo*
house	*nyumba*
to sleep	*kugona*
how much?	*mtengo bwanji?*
I want	*ndifuna*
I don't want	*sindifuna*

On toilet doors, *akazi* means women and *akuma* means men.

GETTING THERE & AROUND
Air

Air Malawi flies to Harare, Johannesburg, Lusaka, Mauritius and Nairobi. *UTA* (in conjunction with Air Malawi) flies from Paris via Libreville and Lusaka. Other airlines servicing Malawi are *SAA*, *Zambian Airways*, *Air Tanzania*, *KLM* and *Kenya Airways*.

All international flights go through Kamuzu International Airport, 27 km north of Lilongwe.

Road

Roads have been considerably improved over the last few years and the main north-south highway is now sealed all the way to Karonga. Hitching is OK in the south and especially along the Blantyre-Lilongwe road, but elsewhere you should be prepared for long waits as there's little traffic. Pick-up trucks and council trucks are not supposed to take passengers, but they often do anyway in order to supplement their income. At weekends, white expatriates living in Blantyre and Lilongwe make a bee-line for Monkey Bay and Cape McLear, so it's easy to get a lift there on Fridays. It's equally easy to get a lift in the opposite direction on Sundays. If you're going to Livingstonia, you will probably have to walk up the escarpment to the town from the main north-south highway as there is no public transport and the road is too steep for buses. There is a short cut through the hair-pin bends but it's very steep and, in the wet season, slippery. It will take you about four hours to walk up. If heading to the **Nyika National Park**, you may be lucky and connect with the mail Land-Rover which comes from Rumphi three times a week on Monday, Wednesday and Friday. It leaves Rumphi at 9 am and arrives at Livingstonia at 11 am. It then leaves Livingstonia at 11.45 am and arrives at Rumphi at 1.45 pm.

Most travellers prefer to use the Lake Malawi steamers to get around, but there is also a network of public buses which you will find useful. If using the buses, make sure you ask for the 'express' bus. They're much faster since they don't stop every 100 metres or so. Some examples of routes, fares and journey times are as follows – but enquire locally about schedules as they change from week to week:

Blantyre-Zomba There are buses daily in either direction which cost Kw 1.70.

Blantyre-Lilongwe There are at least three express buses daily at 6.30 am, 9 am and 1.30 pm which cost Kw 10.55 and take about six hours. You can book in advance.

The 9 am bus goes all the way to Kamuzu International Airport for the afternoon flights.

Blantyre-Salima There are buses on Wednesday, Friday and Sunday which cost Kw 2.35.

Blantyre-Monkey Bay There are two to three buses daily in either direction at 5 am and 10 am from Blantyre and at 9 am, noon and 5.30 pm from Monkey Bay. The fare is Kw 5.65. Another bus is operated by the *Yanu Yanu Bus Company*, which goes as far as Liwonde and costs Kw 4.

Blantyre-Karonga There is one 'express' bus daily in either direction (at 1.30 pm from Karonga) which calls at many places en route such as Mzuzu, Nkhotakota and Nkhata Bay. It costs Kw 25 and takes about 24 hours. It's usually overfull.

Lilongwe-Salima The fare is Kw 2.65 and the journey takes three hours. From Salima the bus leaves at 7.30 am.

Lilongwe-Chipata There is one bus daily at around 8 am which costs Kw 3.20 and takes about eight hours.

Lilongwe-Mzuzu The fare is Kw 13.05 and the journey takes about 10 hours. The bus leaves Lilongwe at 6.30 am.

Mzuzu-Karonga There are two 'express' buses daily which leave Mzuzu at 7.30 am and 8 pm, calling at Ekwendeni, Enukwoni, Rumphi, Mzakata, Chitewa, Chitimba, Uliwa, Chilumba and Nyungwa and arriving at Karonga at 12.35 pm and 1.05 am respectively. The fare is Kw 7. It's a very spectacular journey.

Mzuzu-Nkhata Bay Costs Kw 1.20 by ordinary bus, Kw 1.40 by express bus and Kw 1.50 by minibus. The trip takes about two hours. The bus leaves Mzuzu at 6.30 am.

Karonga-Chitipa There are buses on Monday, Tuesday, Thursday and Saturday. They depart around 1 pm and arrive at 5 pm. In the opposite direction they leave at 8 am and arrive at 11 am. The fare is Kw 2.40.

Rail

There is a train which connects Limbe with Salima via Blantyre, Nsanje and with Salima via Blantyre, Nsanje and Chipoka with a small branch line to Zomba, but it's unlikely that anyone other than a railway buff would use the line; not only are the trains very slow, second class is more expensive than the buses. There is a daily train in either direction which leaves Blantyre at 5 am and costs Kw 8.32 (2nd class) and Kw 3.93 (3rd class) as far as Chipoka. There is very little difference between 2nd and 3rd classes. Both are equally overcrowded.

Boat

Lake Malawi Steamers There are two boats, the *MV Ilala* and the *MV Mtendere*. The latter has only 2nd and 3rd classes and 3rd class is below the deck (very crowded). Second class is at deck level with a large promenade area around it. Above this are the crews' quarters, a bar and another open area for the use of 2nd-class passengers. There's plenty of room to sleep up here and the crew are very friendly (they'll often lock up your bags for you during the day). Third-class passengers regularly get chased off the promenade deck back downstairs. The *Ilala*, on the other hand, is a much older boat and has room for only 10 1st-class-cabin passengers who have the exclusive use of two-thirds of the boat. This means that about 800 2nd- and 3rd-class passengers are cramped into the remaining one third. Second class on the *Ilala* is worse than 3rd class on the *Mtendere*, and as tickets are hardly ever checked it's not worth paying the extra for 2nd class. First-class tickets are checked regularly and if you're on the wrong deck you'll be removed. It's worth enquiring about cheaper 1st-class tickets without a cabin (sleep on the deck).

If you want a cabin (1st class), book as far ahead as possible (especially during South African school holidays) by writing to the Marine Traffic Manager, Box 5500, Limbe (tel 640 844).

Good food is available on the boats (and regardless of which class you are travelling in, you can eat in the 1st-class dining room) at Kw 4 for breakfast, Kw 6 for lunch and Kw 7 for dinner. Notify the staff in advance if you want a meal. Otherwise you can buy fish, eggs and fruit from local people who come out to the boats to sell these things. Tickets for the *Mtendere* are only sold when the boat is sighted, so queueing tends to start about a day before it's due to arrive. On the other hand, there's no question of anyone being refused – it just gets filled up, and up, and up! Schedules for the boats should be taken as approximate, but they generally leave earlier rather than later.

On the *Mtendere* you are not allowed on the deck except when the boat docks. This appears to apply specifically to the upper decks – there is a promenade deck around the 2nd-class level.

There are occasionally nasty storms out on the lake, so watch out.

MV Mtendere

Port	Arrive	Depart
Monkey Bay	-	10.00 Tue
Chipoka	12.30	22.30
Nkhotakota	05.30	06.30 Wed
Likoma Island	12.00	13.00
Chizumulu Island	14.00	14.30
Nkhata Bay	17.30	06.00 Thu
Mangwina Bay	07.00	07.30
Usisya	09.00	09.30
Ruarwe	10.30	11.00
Charo	11.30	12.00
Mlowe	13.30	14.30
Chilumba	16.30	06.00 Fri
Kambwe	09.30	10.30
Kaporo	11.30	12.30
Chilumba	17.00	06.00 Sat
Mlowe	08.00	08.30
Charo	10.00	11.00
Ruarwe	12.00	13.00
Usisya	13.30	14.30
Mangwina Bay	15.30	16.30
Nkhata Bay	17.30	02.30 Sun
Chizumulu Island	05.30	06.00
Likoma Island	07.00	08.00
Nkhotakota	13.30	14.30
Chipoka	21.30	06.30 Mon
Monkey Bay	09.30	

On the northbound sector there is a connecting train which arrives at Chipoka on

Tuesday at 12.48 pm. Second class is available. On the southbound sector, the connecting train arrives at Chipoka at 5.42 am. No second class is available on this train.

MV Ilala

Port	Arrive	Depart
Monkey Bay	-	08.00 Fri
Chilinda	10.00	10.30
Makanjila	12.30	14.00
Chipoka	17.00	22.00
Nkhotakota	05.30	06.30 Sat
Likoma Island	12.30	13.30
Chizumulu Island	15.00	16.00
Nkhata Bay	19.30	04.00 Sun
Usisya	06.30	07.30
Ruarwe	08.30	09.30
Mlowe	11.30	12.30
Chitimba	13.30	14.30
Chilumba	16.00	04.00 Mon
Chitimba	05.30	06.30
Mlowe	07.30	08.30
Ruarwe	10.30	11.30
Usisya	12.30	13.30
Nkhata Bay	16.00	03.00 Tue
Likoma Island	08.30	10.00
Nkhotakota	16.00	21.30
Chipoka	05.30	09.00 Wed
Makanjila	12.00	13.00
Chilinda	15.00	15.30
Monkey Bay	17.30	-

The 2nd-class fares (in kwacha) from Monkey Bay are as follows:

Chilinda	1.15
Makanjila	1.80
Chipoka	2.09
Nkhotakota	7.88
Likoma Island	9.68
Chizumulu Island	10.66
Nkhata Bay	12.82
Usisya	14.76
Ruarwe	15.34
Mlowe	16.67
Chitimba	17.28
Chilumba	17.78

On the northbound sector there is a connecting train which arrives at Chipoka on Friday at 3.02 am. Second class is available. On the southbound sector the train arrives at Chipoka at 6.08 am on Wednesday.

To/From Zambia

There are two points of entry – via Chipata on the Lilongwe-Lusaka road in the centre of the country, and via Chitipa on the Karonga-Nakonde road in the extreme north of the country.

Buses from Lilongwe to Lusaka depart at 7 am on Monday, Wednesday, Thursday and Saturday, cost Kw 16.80 and take between 18 and 21 hours. There are likewise four buses per week in the opposite direction. The border can be very slow and there are several police checks. It's advisable to book the buses in advance. There is a shortage of tyres in Zambia and bus companies often do not provide their buses with spare tyres (the drivers apparently sell them to supplement their incomes). This means that if you get a puncture which cannot be repaired, you'll be stuck where you are until another bus comes through with a spare from Lusaka. There are also daily buses in either direction between Chipata and Lusaka which cost Kw 14.70.

The other route between Chitipa and Nakonde should not be attempted at weekends or during bad spells in the wet season, as there will be no buses or other traffic at those times. During the week there are usually buses at 7 am on Monday, Wednesday and Friday from Nakonde to Chitipa, though some only go as far as the Zambian border (Nyala) and you must walk from there. In the opposite direction there are buses usually on the same days which leave Chitipa at 2 pm. The fare is Kw 2.90. If you decide to take a taxi, this will cost at least Kw 6. The two border posts are about three km apart, and if there is no transport available you'll have to walk. Some travellers have suggested it's a bad idea to walk this stretch on your own as you might be robbed, but if you're in the company of a lot of local people who have got off a bus at the border, just follow them through the clearly marked paths across the fields. There should be transport from the Malawi border post to Chitipa, but if there is none it's about 1½ km to Chitipa downhill all the way.

To/From Mozambique

There are buses and trains (latter cost Kw 8.65 – 1st class only) all the way to Beira, though you may have to wait a day for a connection at Sena. It's a beautiful journey but the railway line is occasionally blown up by guerrillas of the Mozambique Resistance Movement (RNM), so make enquiries before you set off. Take food and cigarettes with you on this journey, as both are scarce in Mozambique.

To/From Tanzania

A new direct route between Malawi and Tanzania has opened up recently and it's getting to be the preferred route between the two countries (rather than via Nakonde and Chitipa). Take one of the twice-daily buses for Kw 16 from Karonga to Kapora along the new road. Beyond the town is the Malawian customs and immigration (very easygoing). From there you must hitch 20 km to the actual frontier, which is the bridge over the Songwe River. Tanzanian customs sometimes man their end of the bridge between 10 am and 3 pm; otherwise they'll be at the main office in Kyela. The security guard may let you go on to Kyela if customs are not there, but he may also demand that you wait there for them to arrive. If you get stuck at the border you can ask the customs officials for a ride at the start or finish of their shift. From Kyela there are buses to Mbeya.

To/From Zimbabwe

If you don't want to go via Zambia into Zimbabwe, there is an alternative route through Mozambique via Tete. A lot of trucks use this route from Blantyre to Harare from Monday to Friday, so finding a ride is easy. The road through Mozambique is sealed and customs are no hassle. Convoys of up to 60 trucks drive through to Harare under Zimbabwean army escort (in case of attacks by NMR guerrillas). The journey through the Mozambique sector takes about six hours and they go as fast as they can. Going this way you save about 1000 km, as opposed to going via Lusaka. If you like, and if your visa allows, you can stop off in Tete.

In almost every town there is either a *government rest house* or a *district rest house* or both. The latter are cheaper and generally more crowded but usually clean. They cost between Kw 2 (a single) and Kw 7 (a double) and sometimes have dormitory-style accommodation for as little as 75 tambala. The government rest houses are generally of a higher standard and you should expect to pay around Kw 15 to Kw 17 for a double including breakfast, but you can pay up to Kw 27.50 for a double (Likoma Island, Mzuzu and Nkhata Bay for instance). You can generally camp at either type of rest house, but the charge varies considerably.

BLANTYRE

Blantyre is the main commercial and industrial centre of Malawi and has a population of around 250,000. It stretches for about 20 km, but most of the places of interest and importance to travellers are well within walking distance of the rest house.

The *district rest house* (also known as the *Travellers' Rest House*), Chikka Rd opposite the bus station, has three classes of accommodation costing Kw 3 a single and Kw 4.50 a double. VIP suites cost Kw 6.75. The management are friendly and the rooms are good value. The restaurant here has a surprisingly varied menu but stocks only a fraction of the foods listed, though what it has is usually good. Don't confuse this place with the other rest house about one km out of town on the Limbe road. Just opposite the district rest house is *St Michael's Mission*, which has a beautiful guest house in the grounds for Kw 5 a single. It's clean and quiet, and meals can be provided if ordered in advance. There's a rest house in Limbe if these are full. It has a restaurant and the accommodation charges are the same as at Blantyre. Buses run frequently between Blantyre and Limbe.

If you wish to camp, however, it's well

worth paying the Kw 1 per day temporary membership fee for the *Blantyre Sports Club*, since this not only allows you to camp free on the gravel car park but lets you in on the swimming pool, film nights, darts match nights and the bar. This place, which is at the bottom of the main street, has become very popular recently.

If you're looking for somewhere luxurious, try the *Mt Soche Hotel* which costs Kw 42.50 a single.

One of the best restaurants here is the *Melting Pot Restaurant*, Haile Selassie Rd near the rest house, which offers Indian and continental food and steaks. Nothing is priced over Kw 6. There are quite a few other restaurants along Glynn Jones Rd around the bus station or next to the Malawi Arts and Crafts Centre; you can get fish and chips for 60 tambala. The *Creme Centre*, Main St, has been recommended as having reasonable food, or there's the somewhat more expensive *Hong Kong Restaurant*. You can even get fairly cheap food at the ritzy *Mt Soche Hotel* if you order carefully (delicious vegetable curry for Kw 2.50). It's worth checking out *El Brazil* café on Victoria St if you're looking for lifts, cheap accommodation and other information. It's a hangout for local groovers.

The **National Museum** is situated midway between Blantyre and Limbe just off the main highway. Entry costs 10 tambala. The British Council has an excellent reading room and library. There are three second-hand clothes stores near the Central Bookshop where you can pick up cheap second-hand books.

The bus to the airport leaves from outside the Mt Soche Hotel and costs Kw 5.50.

CHITIPA

You will inevitably pass through this town if you're going to or from Zambia. Chitipa is five km from the border (Nyala), and although there are usually three buses a week to Nakonde, you may have to walk.

If you need to stay here for the night, there is an excellent *rest house* which costs Kw 4 a double, or you can sleep on the verandah for just 20 tambala. Mosquito nets are provided in the rooms. It's best to stay here rather than Nyala, as at the latter place there is no place to stay and no place where you can buy food. Other travellers have recommended the *Javet Rest House* run by Mr Suali. It costs Kw 4 a double, but if you have no kwacha he'll let you eat and sleep there on credit until the banks open.

There is a roving bank which operates on two days of the week, but if it's not there you can change up to US$20 at the District Commissioner's office. If you're reconverting money into hard currency here, there's a limit of Kw 20 worth.

KARONGA

Try the *Kankununu Guest House* behind the market to the right. It costs Kw 3 a single and Kw 5 a double for a very basic room. There is an attached restaurant which serves good, cheap food and lots of it.

LIKOMA ISLAND

It's well worth staying here between steamers if you have the time. The enormous two-bedroom *government rest house* on the beach is a great place to stay but costs Kw 22 a single and Kw 27.50 a double (they let four people use a double room for that price). The cook's services are free and there's a refrigerator (BYO beer). Bring all your own food with you except fish. Cheaper is the *Akuzike Rest House*. It's pretty cramped but costs only Kw 10 per room. They have a restaurant and bar (subject to beer being available). You can also camp which, of course, is much cheaper.

Swimming in the crystal-clear water which teems with fish is excellent. You should also visit the amazing **Anglican Cathedral** 15 minutes uphill from the beach.

LILONGWE

The new capital of Malawi is still being constructed, but most of the embassies and government departments have already moved here. It's a pleasantly landscaped city but otherwise of limited interest. All the travel agents, embassies, banks, the National Parks and Wildlife office and a PTC supermarket are clustered around the city centre.

The South African embassy is in the Impco Building (tel 730 888) and the Zambian High Commission up the hill across Convention Avenue (tel 731 911). *Air Malawi* is in Gemini House and *Air Tanzania* is on City Square. Manica Freight Service is American Express's agent but they don't cash traveller's cheques. The National Parks and Wildlife office is upstairs in the arcade along with all the travel agents. It's open from 8 am to noon and 1 to 4 pm and has plenty of good information.

The large blue-and-white UTC City Line buses make a 'City Circular' run which takes you from the main bus station by the rest house to the city centre, passing the Peace Corps headquarters on the way.

If you have a tent or a Combi van, one of the best deals here is the *Lilongwe Golf Course* almost opposite St Peter's Church, which has been recommended by many travellers as well as resident expatriates. For Kw 3 per day you can pitch a tent on the golf course/cricket ground and have access to the bathrooms (which are clean and have toilet paper and soap), the restaurant, bar and swimming pool (latter costs 20 tambala extra). The *council rest house*, Malangalanga Rd opposite the bus station, costs Kw 3.50 a single and Kw 7 a double, plus they have an overcrowded dormitory for 25 tambala. This rest house isn't particularly good as it is badly maintained and has heaps of mosquitoes, but they do have a restaurant offering good meals (30 tambala to Kw 1.50) and a bar. They have a baggage storeroom where you can leave gear for 10-20 tambala per bag per day depending on the size. *St Peter's Church*, on the opposite side of the river from the bus station, offers good accommodation for Kw 7 a single and Kw 10 a double. If the above are full then try *Kholowa's Rest House* on the other side of the market from the bus station. It costs Kw 7 a single and Kw 10 a double but is nothing special. There's also a choice of fairly cheap hotels lining the short lane near the market.

You can get good, clean rooms at the *Golden Peacock Restaurant* near the old post office for Kw 5. It's run by an Indian family and they serve very good meals.

For something more luxurious try the *Lilongwe Hotel* which costs Kw 30 a single and Kw 44 a double, or the *Lingadze Hotel* which costs Kw 30 a double.

The *Indian restaurants* in the area around the bus station (Area 3) are recommended for good, cheap food. The Indian shops in this area are recommended for changing money. A good middle-priced restaurant is the *Causerie Restaurant* in the city centre on City Square, which has an excellent menu with café tables outside. Sizzling chicken costs Kw 3.25, Portuguese steak Kw 4 plus there are European dishes. Avoid eating inside; the prices are higher.

Lilongwe City Market adjoining the bus station is quite good for fruit and vegetables, and snacks are available.

If you're looking for action, the street next to the market has a row of bars and restaurants. In the evening, street sellers offer fried chicken and the like. The *Msungama Bar* at the end of the street by Kholowa's Rest House has non-stop music and dancing.

There is a bus to the airport which calls at various hotels and costs Kw 4.

If you need dental treatment, go to the Seventh Day Adventist Dental Clinic, which is staffed by American dentists and has the latest equipment. People come from as far as Lusaka to get their teeth fixed here. A filling will cost around US$16.

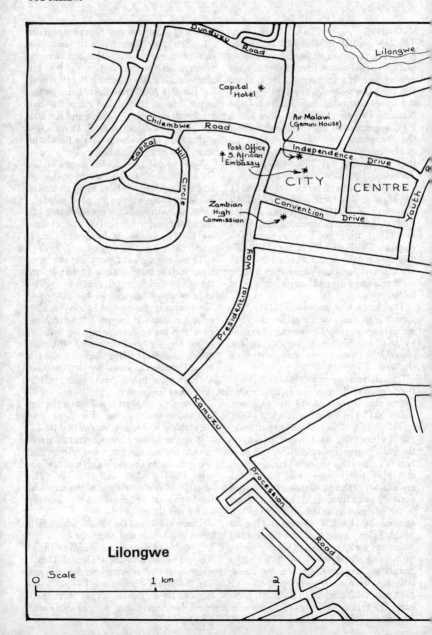

Lilongwe

Scale
0   1 km   2

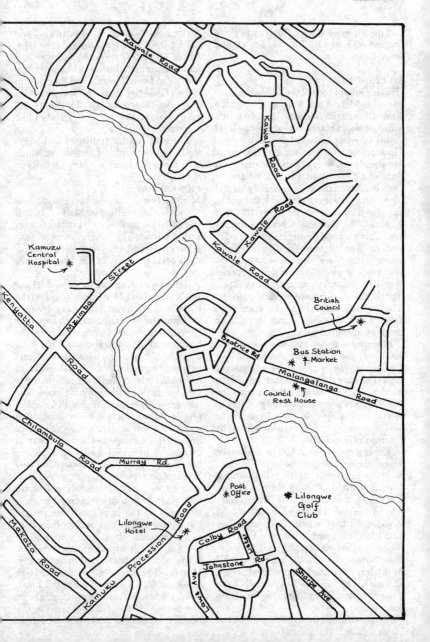

The **Lilongwe Nature Reserve** is three km out on Kenyatta Rd near the capitol area. Entry is free.

LIVINGSTONIA

This is probably one of the most attractive places in Malawi and was founded by the Free Church of Scotland in 1894. It's situated about 800 metres above the level of the lake on the top of the Livingstone Escarpment and has some of the most spectacular views in Africa. The place still exudes a colonial air and is a centre for Irish Presbyterians who are usually helpful about lifts – there is no public transport to the town from the main north-south highway. The technical school has a truck which goes up and down almost every day and charges 40 tambala. On the down journey they are usually heading for Karonga. They usually come down between 9 and 10 am and go up about 4 to 5 pm. There are also occasional ambulances. The walk up there from the main road takes about five hours and three back down again with a pack.

Manchewe Falls, 100 metres off the road down the Escarpment and about four km from the rest house, are over 60 metres high. The caves behind the falls were once used by Phoka tribesmen hiding from the Ngoni slavers some 100 years ago. They're worth a visit, as is the **Museum** in Livingstonia (get the key upstairs from the Overtoun Grocery).

The *rest house* about 500 metres down from the clock tower is the best in Malawi and has hot water, flush toilets and a friendly warden. It's very clean and costs Kw 4 per bed. If it's full they'll reluctantly let you sleep on the verandah for Kw 1.50 if you don't have a tent. Generally, they won't let you camp here. Food is very limited so take some with you if possible. If you haven't done this, ask the manager if he will buy a chicken from the local people and cook it up for you. They usually have good rice porridge available for breakfast too.

If you get stuck waiting for a lift at the Livingstonia/Chitimba crossroads and need a feed, walk back towards the lake. About 50 metres from the highway is a family living in the bush hut who will make a very good meal for you. And they do it in style – table and chairs, tablecloth, china and even silverware! The local kids will take you down to a beach on the lake too if you want to go there.

The only regular transport to Livingstonia is the hospital Land-Rover which goes down to Chitimba every Thursday.

MONKEY BAY

Monkey Bay is a weekend watering hole for expatriates living in Malawi and, if you're lucky, you may be invited to stay with someone. The beach, however, isn't up to much, and most travellers head for **Cape McLear**, about 18 km from Monkey Bay.

Before you even get to Cape McLear you'll hear about *Mr Stevens'* place on the travellers' grapevine, since it's become very popular over the last few years. 'Mr Stevens' is actually two remarkably similar brothers (George and Ernest). They have a range of variously priced beach huts here starting at Kw 2.50 a single and Kw 5 a double without own bathroom and Kw 10-15 a double with own bathroom. The huts are very pleasant. Almost all travellers give Mr Stevens' a rave recommendation and it's the sort of place people go back to time and time again. Cape McLear is certainly a beautiful spot with a pebble beach and warm lake water, and the Stevens' place is very easygoing. You help yourself to beers, Cokes, etc and write what you take into an old exercise book. It all works on the honesty of the people staying there. The restaurant offers fish, salad, rice and chips, but you need to order a meal hours in advance and be prepared for the restaurant to close early. Meals cost between Kw 0.90 for fried fish or an omelette to Kw 2 for a full meal. George has a boat which you can use to row across to the island opposite the beach. It takes eight to 10 people at a time.

Mr Stevens (or rather one of them) generally meets buses and boats arriving at Monkey Bay and takes people out to Cape McLear in the back of his truck for Kw 1.

You can stay at the *Golden Sands Holiday Resort* right by scenic Otter Point, about 1½ km past Mr Steven's, for Kw 9.10 a double or Kw 13.65 for a rondavel. They have meals and a nice bar, and there's good diving and snorkelling available.

In Monkey Bay itself there is the *district rest house* next to the bus station and 15 minutes' walk from where the boats dock. It costs Kw 4 a single and Kw 5 a double. You can also sleep in the common room for 75 tambala. Good meals are available here. Or you can rent a room or camp at the more expensive *government rest house*.

Offshore from Monkey Bay is the quiet nature reserve of **Thumbi Island**, which has birds and reptiles and where you can camp free. You should bring food with you from Monkey Bay, though fishermen often come across in the afternoons to sell you fish.

MULANJE

The town of Mulanje is situated at the foot of Mt Mulanje and is the centre of the tea-growing area. It's also a popular mountain-climbing and bushwalking area. If you're interested in doing some of the treks, get hold of *Guide to Mulanje Massif* by Geoffrey Eastwood. It's also worth contacting the Mt Mulanje Mountain Club in Blantyre, since they frequently do a trip to the top and they have huts on the mountain where you can stay for the night for Kw 1.50. Some of the members may tell you that it takes as little as three hours to get to the top, but you should take this with a pinch of salt. If you're very fit and interested in doing nothing but getting to the top, you might do it in 5½ hours. At a more leisurely pace you should allow 7½ hours. Avoid climbing after dark unless you can handle leopards and poisonous snakes – as one correspondent did, who lived to tell the tale! It's said you can see the Indian Ocean in clear weather from the 3000-metre summit. Porters and guides are available for Kw 1.50 a day plus 75 tambala for food (more if you stay out overnight, in which case you must provide blankets). The porters appreciate small extras like cigarettes. There are many different climbs and walks available which range from easy to difficult. Woodcarvings made from local fallen cedar are available in the villages around the base of the massif.

MZIMBA

The cheapest accommodation here is the *council rest house* next to the market, which costs Kw 2 per bed. Also cheap is a private guest house at the left on the main road from the bus stop, which costs Kw 4 a single. It's clean and there's food available. There is a *government guest house* near the police station, with good facilities.

MZUZU

The *council rest house*, Mtwala Rd, is very clean and costs Kw 6 a double.

NKHATA BAY

Although some of the beaches further south are very pleasant (eg Cape McLear), they're somewhat commercialised as they're popular with expatriates. Nkhata Bay is much quieter (as is the beach at Chikale, south of Nkhata Bay, where you can camp free). These beaches are practically deserted except for a few travellers and when the fishing boats come in at dusk to sell their catch. If you like fresh fish, buy it directly from the boats and take it to the rest house, where they will cook it for you. In the town itself, all the stores and bars are situated around a central 'meeting place.' Dancing goes on just about all the time in the bars. Simply stroll in whenever you feel like it.

The *council rest house* here costs Kw 2.50 a room or 20 tambala on the floor, but it's suggested you avoid this place as it is noisy, dirty and the sanitation is appalling. There is a private *rest house* behind the PTO superette and Southern Bottlers wholesalers, which is better value at Kw 4 a double but the toilets are filthy. Another cheap place here is the *Heart Hotel*, where you can camp for 50 tambala. The owner, Phillip, is an excellent cook and turns out the most amazing meals from an open fire, but as you might expect, it's slow. There's a pit toilet but no running water, though they will heat up a tub of water so you can wash behind a bamboo screen. To get there you turn left past the prison and police station and continue on for another 500 metres.

The *government rest house* is of a much better standard but costs Kw 27 a double including breakfast for one person (just what the other person is supposed to do isn't clear). The place is very clean and breakfast costs Kw 2. You can camp at this rest house for Kw 4.50.

The Barclays Bank Land-Rover arrives on Friday if you need to change money.

NKHOTAKOTA

This is reputedly one of the oldest market towns in Africa and was once the centre of the slave trade in this part of Africa. There's a Chinese agricultural mission here which has been very friendly in the past towards people interested in their work. The town itself is about one km from the lake, whereas the post office, banks and other government buildings are clustered together about two km from the lake. Buses for Lilongwe and Salima leave from the bus station opposite the Pick & Pay Rest Housemarket, but you're advised to book ahead as they're often full. The *district rest house* is situated on the beach by the boat jetty and was once an amazing place made out of parts of old boats, trucks and cars. There are still windows made from car doors. It's somewhat run-down these days and has no restaurant, no electricity and warm beer, but it's pretty clean and has a beautiful second-storey terrace overlooking the lake, so it's much

breezier than town. Dormitory beds cost Kw 1.75 and you may well have the place to yourself. They also have interior doubles for Kw 4 and two cell-like rooftop doubles for Kw 8. Smokables are easy to come by. The *Pick & Pay Rest House*, run by Philip Banda opposite the bus station, is very friendly, very clean and good food is available (fish, meat, rice and salad for Kw 1.50) but the place is often full. It costs Kw 4 a single and Kw 5 a double. The *Linga Rest House* next door isn't quite as good but charges Kw 4 for singles and Kw 5-6 for various doubles with a fan. Another place you could try is the *A R Chewe Afa Restaurant* opposite the market which has some rooms for Kw 4 a double. There are several other places to stay but they're not such good value.

RUMPHI

Rumphi, between Nkhata Bay and Livingstonia, is a good starting point if you want to get to Chelinda in the **Nyika National Park**. The *government rest house* in Rumphi is located about one km from the market. There's no electricity there and you need to take your own food, but they do have hot showers. It costs Kw 22 a single and Kw 27.50 a double. The *district rest house* next to the market near the bus station is more convenient and costs Kw 2.50 per person. It has pit toilets and good showers. There's also the *Universal Rest House*, which has friendly staff and costs Kw 2 a single.

If you have your own transport, there's the *Simphawaka Inn* several km before you get to Rumphi. It's quiet, clean and costs Kw 4 a single and Kw 10 a double. Meals cost Kw 1.50 and there's a bar.

There's good nightlife in the bars of Rumphi, and women come round selling fried chicken, liver and beef.

Getting to the national park can be problematical without your own transport. It's best to contact the District Commissioner on the edge of town and ask if there's any chance of getting a lift. He's a friendly man who will probably radio through to the park headquarters and ask when the park truck is coming down for supplies and wages (it does both regularly). The road is rough and in the wet season may require 4WD. Failing all else, you may be able to hire a vehicle from the store owners in Rumphi.

The *lodge* at Chelinda itself consists of one large building with four double bedrooms and four separate bungalows. Whichever section you stay in, the cost is Kw 9 per person, which includes shower facilities, a cook and as much wood as you need, but you should take as much food as possible with you as there is very little stocked there. Men can get a bed in the *Drivers' Hostel* for 50 tambala if it's not full (it consists of only one small room). They don't take women. There's also the possibility of sleeping on the floor of the *Reception Centre* if you're short of funds. The town is quite high up so you need warm clothes at night.

The *Zambian Rest House* charges Kw 6 a single (part of the park is in Zambia). It's run-down but has a pleasant atmosphere. Nearby is the **Chowo Forest**, the last remnant of natural forest in the park. There are walking trails through it.

The park is noticeably different from those further north – rolling hills and mountains covered with a mixture of natural forest and artificial pine plantations. There are large herds of deer and antelope as well as leopards, and the rivers and streams are rich in trout if you're interested in fishing. Because of the altitude it gets very cold here in June and July, so have warm clothes handy. Unlike in many other game parks, you are allowed to walk around this one.

SALIMA

The town is about 15 km from the lake and is where most people stop off for the night before heading down to the beach. There is actually a choice of three *council rest houses* here. The one opposite the bus station is very clean and has doubles for Kw 3 as well as dormitory accommodation.

The other two are both 1½ km back along the main road to town and then 100 metres off to the left. They both cost Kw 3-4 a double and have a good restaurant. The *Evergreen Restaurant*, opposite the bus station, has good food and double rooms for Kw 4.40.

Down at Senga Bay is the *Grand Hotel* which, although it's somewhat of a misnomer, is very friendly and good value. The cheapest double rooms here are Kw 16.50 including breakfast. Meals at the restaurant cost Kw 8, but you can also get very good meals on the verandah or at the bar for Kw 1.80-4. If you have your own tent, the Grand has an excellent campsite with facilities which include showers, toilets and firewood. The charge is Kw 1.50. There are reasonably well-stocked stores at Senga Bay and Salima, and you can buy smoked fish and other food in the village at the camping end of the Grand Hotel. You can change money and buy postage stamps at the Grand. The nearest bank is in Salima itself.

It's well worth visiting **Lizard Island** while you are in Salima. It's a beautiful national park and home to a wide variety of eagles and huge lizards. The whole island is spattered white with cormorant droppings and stinks, but don't let that put you off. Rowboats (Kw 2 per hour) and motorboats (Kw 4 per hour) are available to get you there.

ZOMBA

Zomba is the old capital of Malawi and a good place from which to explore the 2000-metre-high Zomba Plateau.

The *Municipal Rest House* opposite the bus station is pretty good and costs Kw 4 for a private room (single or double occupancy) and 75 tambala in the dormitory. It also has a good restaurant. The *Welcome Inn*, round the corner, costs Kw 2.50 a single and Kw 5.50 a double but is 'pretty seedy' and there's loud bar music to put up with. Up on the Zomba Plateau there is the *CCAP Rest House* – book in advance at the Zomba Theological College.

Also up here is a *campsite* run by the Forestry Department which has hot showers, etc. While you're up on the plateau, visit the *Kuchawe Inn* for tea. There are beautiful views from here. Remember to order individual trays of tea for each person (90 tambala); otherwise you'll get the same size of pot for two people but you'll pay double because they give you two cups!

If you're going to visit **Chingwe's Hole** (reputedly so deep that no one has ever been able to measure its depth), there is a good campsite for 50 tambala per day at the nearby hotel. Facilities include hot showers and toilets, but you should bring your own food as meals at the hotel are very expensive.

MARKETS

Virtually every town has a market selling vegetables, rice, peanuts, fruit, dried fish and utensils. A few have local crafts for sale such as ebony carvings and bracelets, ivory necklaces, reed and raffia baskets. The further north you go, the cheaper things get. Market traders, as a rule, don't hike their prices for travellers. Bargaining is certainly possible in some places, but it often doesn't secure a reduction in the original price asked. The Zomba market is outstanding.

NATIONAL PARKS & GAME RESERVES

Malawi has five national parks, each protecting certain species of animal and their habitats. All but Lake Malawi National Park have government-run accommodation available. Booking for accommodation in the national parks should be made through The Chief Game Warden, Department of National Parks & Wildlife, PO Box 30131, Capital City, Lilongwe 3 (tel 730 944), except for the Kasungu National Park (see below).

All parks and game reserves have an entry fee of Kw 1.50 per person per day plus Kw 4.50 per day per vehicle (under 2000 kg) and Kw 6.50 per day (over 2000 kg).

Kasungu National Park

This park has rolling *miombo* woodlands and there is excellent game viewing available late in the dry season when fires have burned off the tall grass. The wildlife roads are open from mid-June to early January, and at those times you can see elephant, buffalo, zebra, antelope and many others. A game-viewing vehicle is sometimes available. Guides cost Kw 2 per trip and are compulsory for walks. There are Bushman paintings to be seen. The park is closed during March.

The park entrance is 38 km from Kasungu town. Fourteen km inside the park is the *Lifupa Lodge* overlooking a small lake. It has twin-bedded rondavels with showers, toilet and electricity for Kw 30 a single and Kw 35 a double. Meals cost Kw 7 for lunch and Kw 8.50 for dinner, plus there's a bar. There are also seven tents with three beds each; they are provided with linen, the use of a kitchen and a cool room. These cost Kw 12 per person – camping in your own tent costs Kw 10 per person. Make your booking through Hertz/Hall's Car Hire.

Lengwe National Park

Some 75 km from Blantyre (the last nine km on dirt), Lengwe's woods and thickets are home for nyala antelope and other ungulates as well as a large and varied bird population. You can view game from the 'hides' at artificial water holes. The best season to visit is during the dry (May to December).

There are four chalets, each with double rooms and hand basins, fully equipped kitchens and refrigerators, but you must bring your own food.

For permission to visit the **Majete Game Reserve** north of Lengwe or the **Mwabvi Game Reserve** to the south, check with the Wildlife Management Officer, Lengwe NP, PO Box 25, Chikwawa (tel 0-1203). Majete has elephant, kudu, sable antelope and waterbuck. There's only one chalet which costs Kw 8 regardless of how many people stay there.

Mwabvi has hills, sandstone ridges and rocky gorges with black rhino, leopard, hyena and antelope. There are two rondavels which cost Kw 4 regardless of how many people stay there.

Liwonde National Park

Fifty-six km north of Zomba on the Shire River, this park includes part of Lake Malombe and the eastern Upper Shire plain. Hippos and crocodiles live in the river and there are about 300 elephants. The birdlife is very varied. The second half of the dry season is the best for game viewing because the animals congregate along the river at that time. The park roads are closed in the wet season.

At the *Mvuu Camp* on the Shire River are adequate twin-bedded rondavels. There are pit toilets and you get water from the river, but you must bring your own bedding, cooking utensils and food. Firewood is provided. In the wet season you can get there by boat.

Nyika National Park

This was the first of the Malawian national parks to be established. It encloses a beautiful montane plateau over 2000 metres high and covered in moor-like open rolling grassland that is completely treeless so it's very easy to see the animals. Trees only grow in occasional islands in the valleys. During the rainy season when the grass grows on the plateau you can see herds of zebra, eland, roan antelope, reedbuck, bushbuck and warthog without even moving from the Chelinda Camp. You may also be lucky and sight leopard from the camp.

Due to the absence of lions and elephants, you may walk anywhere in this park, and there are trails where you may camp on walks taking up to five days, escorted by a game scout. The best game-viewing times are between November and May, though you will miss the wildflowers which flourish at that time. You may fish for trout in the streams the whole year or in the dams from September to April.

Thazima Gate, where the park headquarters is located, is 67 km from Rumphi and about 10 km north of the Rumphi-Katumbi road. Without your own vehicle it can be problematical getting to the park. There are several possibilities. First try contacting the District Commissioner in Rumphi (on the edge of town) and ask him if there is any possibility of getting a lift. He's a friendly man and he will probably radio through to the park headquarters and ask if there is a park truck coming down for supplies and wages. They do this regularly. Alternatively, you can take a morning bus from Rumphi or Katumbi to the park turn-off, but from there you'll have to hitch or walk to Thazima, where there may be a park vehicle going to 60 km to Chelinda Camp. You may well have to wait a day for this – maybe more. If nothing comes through, the park staff have government-issue sleeping bags and will let you sleep in the gatehouse. If you'd like to know with more certainty what your chances are, you can telephone either Chelinda Camp (tel Chelinda 1) or the Thazima headquarters (Rumphi 50) and find out what day a park vehicle will go. Every Thursday is bank day in Rumphi, so the vehicles often come down to get funds/do banking and they'll give you a lift back.

Chelinda Camp is beautifully situated on the edge of a pine forest overlooking a small artificial lake and the rolling grass hills. It has six double rooms with one bathroom per two rooms; the bathroom is equipped with a bathtub (no showers) and hot water. The bedrooms each have a fireplace. There's a fully equipped kitchen/dining room with wood stoves. These double rooms cost Kw 9 per person (even if you occupy them singly). In addition, there are four chalets, each with two bedrooms, a huge living room, bathroom, fireplace and kitchen. There's electricity in the evenings. The chalets cost Kw 36 per chalet, but in the off-season you can book them for Kw 9 per person. There is also a campsite nearby with pit toilets, running water and picnic shelters. It costs Kw 3 per person.

The *Drivers' Rest House* consists of two small buildings with beds and kerosene lamps and an outside toilet and shower shack. You can use the kitchen at the bedroom block. The park office will tell you that you can't stay here but that's not true – just tell them you're very short of money. It costs Kw 1.50 per person. The rest house is right next to the shop which sells beer and few basic canned goods. You need to bring most of your own food with you.

If you have your own transport, you have the choice of the *Juniper Forest Cabin* 45 km south-east of Chelinda Camp, on a dirt track road in the most southerly part of the park. It consists of one rustic cabin with four bunk-beds, blankets and some kitchen equipment, but there's no electricity or running water. It costs Kw 6 per person.

Lastly, there is the *Zambian Rest House* just off the road to Chelinda and about 40 km from the Thazima Gate in the Zambian part of the park. There's no customs or immigration and you don't need a Zambian visa to go there. It costs Kw 6 per person. Nearby is **Chowo Forest** – the last remnant of natural forest. There are walking trails through it.

Mali

The area occupied by the modern states of Mali and parts of Niger and Senegal was one of the most important trading centres of the entire Islamic world in medieval times. The reputation of some of its trading cities – like Djenne, Timbuktu and Gao – as centres of wealth and cultural brilliance became world-famous and surrounded by a mystique which has endured through the centuries right up to the present day. Others, famous in their day, like Kumbi and Audagost, are now ruins on the edge of the Sahara. The development of these places owed much to the spread of Islam, which became the religion of trade in those days. However, the religion itself made little impact on the peoples of the Sahel until the 15th and 16th centuries, except insofar as it was commercially convenient. Throughout this time the traditional beliefs continued to be of paramount importance and still survive today among peoples like the Dogon, Songhay and Mossi.

The wealth of these trading cities was based primarily on the taxes levied on the transport of West African gold to North Africa and the Middle East, and of salt from the Saharan oases to West Africa. So important was West African gold in those days that there would have been no general use of the metal as a medium of exchange in medieval times otherwise. Monarchs as far away as England struck their coins in gold which had originated in West Africa. The long series of powerful medieval empires which grew up and

collapsed in this part of the world from the 9th to the 16th century only came to an end following invasion from Morocco and the breaking of the Moslem monopoly on trade in Africa and the Indian Ocean by the European maritime nations.

Berber traders who plied the trans-Saharan routes west from Morocco through Mauritania and south through the Fezzan to the Middle Niger and Lake Chad had been important during Phoenician and Roman times, but for a long time after, this trade was disrupted by the invasions of the Vandals, Goths and Visigoths and was not to be revived until the advent of Islam. Islam brought with it an accepted system of law and order which enabled trade to thrive once again. Ghana, the first empire to spring up among the Soninke people in the area of the Upper Niger and Senegal rivers, came into being in the 9th century. By that time the Soninke had come to dominate all the important relay stations along the western trade routes and had established their capital, Kumbi, 200 km north of modern Bamako. Like the wealth of all the empires which were to grow in this part of the world, their wealth was principally based on the movement of gold and ivory from West Africa to the Mediterranean and Middle East, and on the movement of salt from the Saharan oases to West Africa. It also encompassed copper and cotton, fine tools and swords initially from Arabia and later from Italy and Germany, horses from Morocco and Egypt and kola nuts and slaves from southern West Africa. The empire of Ghana was, like most early medieval empires, based almost exclusively on the personal rule of the king and his immediate companions. There was no system of bureaucracy or civil service as was to be developed by the later empires of Mali and Songhay. None of Ghana's kings converted to Islam; instead they retained

their traditional beliefs based on a community of the ancestors, the living and the still-to-be-born.

After nearly 500 years of existence, Ghana was finally destroyed by the invading Moslem Berber armies of the Almoravids from the plains of Mauritania in 1076 – the same people who also took possession of Moorish Spain. The Almoravids were unable to hold onto power, being restless raiders, and what was left of Ghana struggled on until 1230 when the capital, Kumbi, was taken by people from the Tekrur area in northernmost Senegal. Shortly afterwards a new empire arose among the Mandinka under

the leadership of Sundiata Keita, who converted to Islam as a gesture of friendship to the trading partners to the north, but also to take advantage of the efficiency and organisation which allegiance to Islam brought with it. Nevertheless, Sundiata owed his political success as much to the exploitation of traditional religion as to Islam, and also to the fact that the Mandinka were the most successful cultivators of the Gambia and Casamance rivers. This new empire of Mali, with its capital at Niani, covered its greatest territory under Mansa Musa (1312-1332) when it stretched from the Atlantic to the borders of present-day Nigeria. It was about this time that trans-Saharan trade reached its peak, and so wealthy was the empire under Mansa Musa that when he passed through Egypt on his pilgrimage to Mecca he ruined the value of the Egyptian gold-based dinar for several years by his lavish gifts of the precious metal.

Musa's reign was a period of stability and prosperity; it was during this time that Timbuktu and Djenne's long career of scholarship and cultural brilliance began. Musa brought back architects from Arabia to construct new mosques in these cities and improved his administration by making it more methodical and literate, but the advent of an actual civil service had to wait until the rise of Songhay.

The Songhay still survive as a group of some 750,000 people living as farmers, fishermen and traders along the banks of the Niger River, stretching from the borders of Nigeria to the lake region west of Timbuktu. It is their villages, especially around Bandiagara near Mopti, which are the major attraction for travellers in Mali other than the old trading cities of Gao, Timbuktu and Djenne. Though originally vassals of Mansa Musa, by 1375 the Songhay had founded a strong city-state based on Gao and were able to throw off Malian overlordship and make a bid for empire themselves. By 1400 they were strong enough to raid the Malian capital of Niani, and in 1464, under the leadership of Sunni Ali, finally embarked on a systematic conquest of the Sahel which was to eclipse the Malian empire. The final collapse of Mali came under Ali's successor, Askia Mohamed Ture, who came back from Mecca with the authority to act as Caliph of Islam in West Sudan. Ture pushed his armies west towards the Atlantic coast and east as far as Kano, overrunning the Hausa states in the process. Following these successes the armies turned north to take the Tuareg stronghold of the oases of Air, establishing a community of Songhay settlers there whose descendants still survive today.

Like the rulers of Mali, those of Songhay converted to Islam but took care to preserve and respect the traditional beliefs of the peasants of the countryside. Where Songhay excelled over Mali was in the creation of a civil service controlled by provincial governors on long-term appointments, a professional army and the beginnings of a professional navy on the Niger River. The sympathies and power base of the early rulers of Songhay lay in the peasants of the countryside, but gradually this was transferred to the Moslem-dominated trading cities. In this lay the basic weakness of the empires in this region. Such an arrangement was fine as long as the rulers could rely on the Islamic system of beliefs and government for promoting centralised rule and long-distance trade and credit, but in times of crisis these town-based empires were an easy prey to collapse. This was the main reason Songhay was rapidly eclipsed in 1591, following an invasion from Morocco and the ensuing internal revolt of subject people. On the other hand, even had Songhay been able to withstand the invasion from Morocco, it's doubtful that the prosperity of the Niger trading cities would have lasted long once the European maritime nations had found a means of circumventing their middle role by trading directly with the primary producers along the West African coast and further south. With the rise of European naval hegemony, the trans-Saharan trading routes lapsed into relative obscurity, though even as late as the 1950s caravans were still transporting salt from the Saharan oasis of Bilma (in Niger) south to Nigeria.

Towards the end of the 19th century, Mali became a French colony and its people were gradually forced into cultivating cash crops – mainly groundnuts, cotton and gum arabic – initially through a system of forced labour and later by taxation. As in neighbouring Upper Volta (now Burkina Faso), the leagacy of the emphasis on cash-cropping and the neglect of food crops has continued to plague the nation's agriculture.

Mali became independent in 1960, though for a few months it was federated with Senegal. Modibo Keita, the first president, quickly put his country on a socialist road to development and opposed French imperialism. The French were required to vacate their military bases in the country and, in 1962, Mali left the Franc Zone and set up its own currency (though the country did return to the Franc Zone in 1967). State corporations were set up and industrialisation was encouraged. However, some four years later, mismanagement and excessive bureaucracy forced the government to announce austerity measures which the general public were very reluctant to accept since there was a lot of obvious profiteering going on. Keita was overthrown in a bloodless military coup in 1968 and the country has been ruled by the leaders of that coup ever since. The military are not particularly popular and the regime has been challenged on a number of occasions by student and labour organisations. The death in detention in 1977 of Modibo Keita, in particular, provoked spontaneous demonstrations throughout the country.

Being a part of the Sahel, Mali suffered disastrously from the droughts of the 1970s. The drought turned enormous areas of once marginal grazing and crop-raising land into desert and resulted in massive losses of crops and livestock. It also spelled the end of a centuries-old way of life for many desert nomads, who now crowd the cities of Mali as refugees.

FACTS

Only in the extreme south is rainfall sufficient to permit cultivation without irrigation. Cultivation depends largely on the flooding of the Niger and its tributaries, but rearing livestock remains the predominant occupation of most of the peasants in the countryside. Resources are so limited that many Malians are forced to migrate into neighbouring countries in search of work. The rainy season in the south lasts from June to September and sometimes October. The dry season stretches from October to February. The population of about 6½ million consists mainly of Bambara. Minority groups include the Songhay, Malinke, Senoufou, Dogon and Fulani. The north is populated mainly by Tuareg.

VISAS

Visas are required by all except nationals of France. There are very few Malian embassies/consulates around the world, so you need to plan ahead. You cannot get a visa at the border, so bear this in mind if you are driving your own vehicle into Mali from Algeria via Jessalit; if you don't have a visa, the border guards will refuse you entry. Since you won't have enough petrol or diesel to get back to Adrar, you'll be forced to sell the vehicle – and guess who to? Of course, if you sell your vehicle a concession can be made regarding your lack of a visa. Remember that Sahelian countries have traditionally made money from the trans-Saharan routes.

Avoid buying a visa in your home country, as they generally cost far more than those bought en route. In West Germany, for instance, they cost the equivalent of US$30. In Paris (embassy at 89 Rue de Cherche Midi, Paris 6e) they cost Fr fr 100, require two photos and are issued while you wait, but they are only valid for a stay of seven days.

Algiers seems to be a good place to get visas for Mali. You can get a two-month visa here for 150 dinar plus two photos. They are issued in 24 hours. One-week visas in Dakar (Senegal) and Abidjan (Ivory Coast) cost CFA 1000, require three photos and take 48 hours to issue. There is now an honorary Malian consulate in Niamey (Niger) close to the Grand Marche. Visas here cost the same but are generally issued the same day. There are no Malian embassies in Burkina Faso or any of the West African countries east of Ghana. French embassies cannot issue Malian visas.

Some years ago Malian bureaucracy rivalled that of India; you had to report to the police in every place you stayed for the night, and the stamps you collected in your passport by doing this would take up six or seven full pages. Not just that, but if you happened to be staying in a small town where they had no rubber stamp, they'd just write a half-page essay in your passport instead. These days they've eased up and you no longer have to report to the police in the place where you stay overnight.

To avoid any hassles with police, there are number of things you should do immediately on arrival in the first main town you come to (eg Bamako, Gao, etc). First buy a tourist card which costs CFA 500 (these don't all look the same – it depends where they're issued). Next, if you have a camera, get a photo permit which costs CFA 2500 plus CFA 100 tax. Lastly, apply for a visa extension if you need one. These cost CFA 2500 per month plus CFA 100 tax.

Visa extensions are available at varying prices depending on where you apply for them. In Bamako you must first obtain the necessary forms from the SMERT office near the mosque on Boulevard des Peuples. They cost CFA 2500 for a four-week extension plus CFA 100 tax, require two photos and take 24 hours to issue. In Gao (where they are said to be cheaper) you must apply at the Commissariat de Police near the market. You can also get extensions in Mopti for CFA 3000 (which includes CFA 1000 'tourist tax').

If you overstay your visa, the police in Bamako will oblige you to pay for it in the form of a new visa which will cost CFA 2500 per week.

Exit visas are no longer required.

Senegal visas There is no Senegalese embassy in Bamako, so you may be in for a few problems if you're going there by rail or road without a visa (where required). This applies particularly on the train. Some people have been turned back.

Most travellers seem to get through.

MONEY
US$1 = CFA 460
£1 = CFA

The unit of currency is the CFA franc (until May 1984 Mali retained its own currency – the Mali franc – but this was phased out shortly afterwards). There are no restrictions on the import or export of local currency. West African CFA are generally acceptable (Fr fr 1 = CFA 50), but Central African CFA will usually be refused.

Allow at least one hour for changing money in the banks.

LANGUAGE
French is the official language but Bambara is more widely spoken. Senoufo, Sarakolle, Dogon, Tuareg and Arabic are spoken in various areas.

GETTING THERE & AROUND
Air
Air Mali flies to most of the places you might want to visit in Mali, but you must treat their schedule with a pinch of salt. Flights are often cancelled.

Mopti to Timbuktu costs CFA 13,000 and there are normally three flights per week.

Road
Most roads in Mali are pretty rough at the best of times, and when it rains they often get washed out completely. At these times barriers are erected to prevent the roads being churned up more than they usually are. Hitching is generally a waste of time. You should arrange lifts the day before with truck drivers, or take a taxi. If you intend going north from Gao on the Route du Tanezrouft to Adrar in Algeria, you may have to wait around for up to a week before you find a truck going that way (there are generally no more than five or six vehicles crossing the border between the two countries per day). A truck

between Gao and Tamanrasset should cost around 200 French francs (CFA 10,000) including food and water, though you're advised to take some food and water along with you. The journey takes about four days (and nights) and it's very hot during the day. Further west, the road between Bamako and Dakar is rarely used. Most people and the bulk of goods go on the train between the two countries.

Examples of local road transport, costs and journey times are as follows:

Bamako-Mopti There is a choice of trucks, buses and taxis along this route. Buses cost CFA 3750 and Peugeot taxis CFA 4200. The journey takes 10 to 12 hours. Bring food and water with you. Trucks and taxis now depart from Sogo Niko, which is a MFr 500-1000 taxi ride (six km) from the centre of Bamako, and if you want to be sure of finding transport you need to get there early in the morning before 8 am. If you decide to take a taxi, you'll also have to pay a luggage charge (about CFA 500 for a rucksack).

Bamako-San From the autogare in Bamako (CFA 50 plus CFA 50 for a pack by shared taxi from the Gare Routiere near the Grand Mosque) you can get a taxi-brousse for CFA 2500 plus CFA 250 for a pack. The journey takes about 10 hours including tea and prayer stops. There are numerous police checkpoints en route.

San-Djenne There are taxi-brousses only on Sundays (in preparation for the Monday market at Djenne). They cost CFA 1250 plus CFA 250 for a pack and CFA 50 for the ferry to Djenne.

Mopti-Gao Trucks between these two towns charge around CFA 5000 but they can take a long time to find. You could wait up to three days for a ride. The best place to ask is at the Somimex sign near the boat terminal. This journey was recently described as 'three days of hell and endless delays even by African standards.'

Timbuktu-Mopti Land-Rovers between these places cost CFA 7500. You also have the choice of a flight between these two places for CFA 12,500.

Timbuktu-Bamako A truck between these two places will cost CFA 12,500 (CFA 15,000 in the cab) and takes about two days. Be sure to bring enough water with you.

Mopti-Djenne A taxi between the two will cost CFA 1500 if the taxi is full or CFA 1750 if it is not full. The journey takes all day. Access to the town is quite difficult as it's situated in the swamp area south-west of Mopti on the River Bani, which joins the Niger at Mopti. There is a ferry which operates most of the year and costs CFA 25, but it is generally suspended in the middle of the dry season, as the water in the river gets too low.

Mopti-San A taxi costs CFA 1750 plus CFA 250 for a rucksack.

San-Koutiala Pick-ups charge CFA 1250.

Koutiala-Sikasso A taxi along this stretch costs CFA 1500 plus CFA 200 for baggage.

Bamako-Sikasso By taxi this journey costs CFA 2500 plus CFA 250 for baggage and takes six to seven hours along a paved road.

Bamako-Bougouni The trip costs CFA 1300. It's easy to find transport from here to the Ivory Coast.

Examples of international road transport, costs and journey times are as follows:

Bamako-Bobo Dioulasso (Burkina Faso) There are regular buses along this route which cost CFA 5000 plus CFA 1000 for baggage and take about 19 hours. A taxi will cost CFA 6250. You can also do the journey in stages. Bamako to Sikasso by taxi will cost CFA 2500 plus CFA 250 for baggage and takes six to seven hours along a paved road. Sikasso to Bobo by taxi will cost CFA 2500 or by pick-up CFA 2250 plus CFA 200 for baggage, and takes five to seven hours along a dirt road. If there is a curfew in force in Burkina Faso (between 11.30 pm and 5 am), the taxi or bus will probably have to stop at the border overnight and complete the journey early the next day. The Bamako-Segou-Koutiala-Bobo route is the best one to take in terms

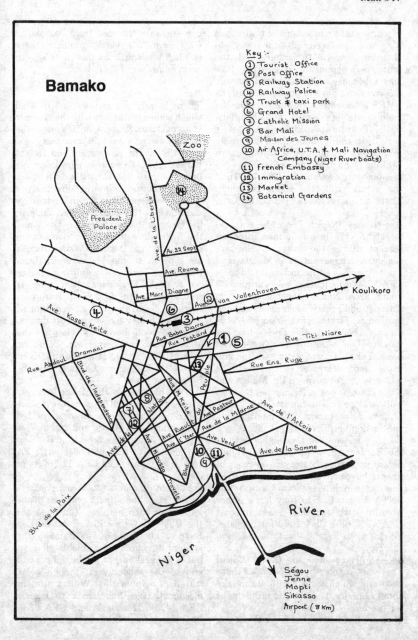

Bamako

Key:-
1. Tourist Office
2. Post Office
3. Railway Station
4. Railway Police
5. Truck & taxi park
6. Grand Hotel
7. Catholic Mission
8. Bar Mali
9. Maison des Jeunes
10. Air Africa, U.T.A. & Mali Navigation Company (Niger River boats)
11. French Embassy
12. Immigration
13. Market
14. Botanical Gardens

Zoo

President Palace

Ave. de la Liberté

Av. 22 Sept.

Ave. Roume

Ave. Marr Diagne

Ave. van Vollenhoven

Koulikoro

Ave. Kasse Keita

Rue Baba Diarra

Rue Testard

Rue Titi Niare

Rue Abdoul Dramani

Blvd. de l'Indépendance

Rue M Keita

Rue Ens. Ruge

Pey Jale

Ave. de l'Artois

Ave. Pasteur

Ave. de la Marne

Ave. Nation

Ave. Ruault

Ave. Verdun

Ave. de la Somme

Ave. l'Yser

Ave. M Boussa Travele

Ave. la

Blvd. de la Paix

River

Niger

Ségou
Jenne
Mopti
Sikasso
Airport (8 Km)

of journey time and volume of traffic, and it's now surfaced all the way to Ouagadougou. On the other hand, the route via Bougouni and Sikasso may take longer because of the unpaved stretch, but you don't have to put up with all the SMERT bullshit at the border. On the main route via Segou and Koutiala, SMERT can be a pain in the neck. There's very little traffic along the other route from Mopti to Ouahigouya. If you want to get from Bobo to Mopti via San, there are taxi-brousses available for CFA 7500 and the journey will take about 10 hours. There are no less than 18 police checks en route!

Gao-Niamey (Niger) There is a twice-weekly *SNTN* bus in either direction (except during the worst of the wet season) which leaves Gao on Monday and Friday between 10 am and noon and costs CFA 5250. The journey takes around 30 hours. From Niamey the bus leaves on Tuesday and Friday. Make sure you book in advance. Tickets for the Monday bus go on sale as soon as the Friday bus has departed on a first-come, first-served basis. Take plenty of water with you and expect long delays at the border. The buses overnight between the Malian and Niger customs posts. Remember that you will need sufficient funds (US$500), a return air ticket and a valid international vaccination certificate to get into Niger. Baggage is searched thoroughly both at the border and a further three times before you reach Niamey. A number of private buses cover this route, but their depots are in different locations from the SNTN buses. In Gao they leave either when full or when the boat gets in, and cost CFA 4500 plus CFA 1000 for baggage. You need to haggle about the baggage charge.

Sikasso-Ferkessedougou (Ivory Coast) There are regular buses between these two towns which cost CFA 3500 and take about 11 hours. There are no problems at the border.

If you're heading for the Ivory Coast you can also take the road from Bamako to Odienne and Man via Bougouni, but there is much less traffic on this route so you must be prepared for delays.

Rail

There is only one railway line in Mali which connects Bamako with the Atlantic coast at Dakar, Senegal, but it's one of the country's most important transport links. Virtually all the passengers and freight between the two countries pass along this line. The road link is hardly used at all. There are two trains in either direction per week. They depart Bamako on Wednesday and Friday at 11.30 am. However, although the fares on the two trains are the same, the Senegalese train (from Bamako on Friday and from Dakar on Wednesday) is far superior to the Malian train (from Bamako on Wednesday and from Dakar on Friday). The Senegalese train is comparable with any West European train. It's clean, pleasant, air-conditioned and has a buffet car serving soft drinks, beer and good food. First class on the Malian train, by comparison, would be called 4th class in any other country. Even the insects prefer going 1st class! Take the Senegalese train.

If you have to take the Malian train, get to the station several hours before it's due to leave. It can be unbearably overcrowded even though seats in 1st and 2nd classes are now reserved. The fares from Bamako to Dakar are CFA 27,600 (sleeper), CFA 18,500 (1st class) and CFA 11,700 (2nd class).

Student discounts (30%) are available on the fares, but only for that part of the journey through Senegal. You must see the Chef du Gare (Station Master) in Bamako about these. In Bamako the student discounts are available all year, but in Senegal only at the beginning and end of the school year, though some travellers dispute this. With a student discount the fare from Bamako to Dakar is CFA 14,955 (1st class) and CFA 9865 (2nd class). In addition to the above two trains there are daily trains between Bamako and Kayes.

If you feel like treating yourself and have had a gutful of overcrowded buses and trains, go to Kati, a few km west of Bamako. From there, a lot of freight trains go to Dakar and if you speak with the drivers they may agree to take you with them for a very reasonable price. The freight trains work out a lot cheaper and pleasanter than the ordinary trains.

Beware of robberies on the passenger trains, especially at night.

Boat

There are three river boats which ply up and down the Niger River between Mopti, Timbuktu and Gao, but at the present time, because of the Sahel drought and the lack of water in the Niger River, none of them are operational. The situation may change, so keep your ear on the grapevine. Normally, between September and December the boats cover the whole route between Bamako and Gao, but between December and February they only ply between Gao and Mopti. During July and August they only ply between Bamako and Kabara (Timbuktu). The *Mali* and the *Soumare* are the older boats (they are as near as you're likely to get to Noah's Ark), but they cost about one-third the price of the new boat regardless of the class you travel in. The new boat is called the *Kanga Moussa*. The trip is well worthwhile in any of the boats, but if you want anything approaching basic amenities and comfort then you'll have to travel 2nd class. Food can be bought on the boats or at the stops en route, but take as much water as possible with you. The journey from Mopti to Gao takes five days on average but can take 10 days even in August (engine trouble and getting stuck on sandbars are the most common reasons for delays). Timbuktu is no longer on the river – it's changed course over the centuries – so if that's where you're heading you must get off at Kabara (11 km from Timbuktu). Taxis are available

from Kabara to Timbuktu. If there is a lot of cargo to unload at Kabara then you may have time to take a taxi there, have a look around and return in time for the boat. If not, you may have to stay in Timbuktu for up to a week waiting for the next boat to come along. Or you may have to take a motorised pirogue, arrange for a lift by road (not easy), or fly out.

Between Gao and Mopti the fares on the *Kanga Moussa* are CFA 120,000 (1st class), CFA 30,000 (2nd class), CFA 15,000 (3rd class) and CFA 5250 (4th class). The two older boats cost CFA 21,000 (1st class), CFA 18,500 (2nd class), CFA 10,050 (3rd class) and CFA 3750 (4th class). Between Gao and Timbuktu the fares are CFA 17,700 (1st class), CFA 23,050 (2nd class) and CFA 7700 (3rd class). The three boats work on a two-week cycle and are scheduled to leave Gao on Monday and Thursday the first week, and on Tuesday the second week, but don't count on this as they are almost always a day or two late.

First class consists of two-berth cabins and includes food; 2nd class is a four-berth cabin with food; and 3rd class is either an eight-berth or 12-berth cabin with food. Fourth class is just deck space without food. Fourth class was recently described as 'utter swill – it is too crowded to pick your nose, it smells like a burning pig farm and there are more screaming babies than at the Bellevue Hospital Maternity Ward.' Third class allows you to sleep on the upper deck, which is much less crowded, much nicer and a pleasant place to hang out during the day. You should bring some of your own food, as what is offered in 3rd class is bland and boring. You will also need your own bowl and fork. Soda, beer and mineral water can be bought on the boat, though they sometimes run out.

If you're thinking of going on the above boat trip and are in Niamey, Niger, you can find out the current position of the boats by making enquiries at *Air Mali* in Niamey before you set off.

If you don't want to take a large boat (or can't because of the level of the river), motorised and non-motorised pirogues are available between Timbuktu and Mopti. The trip in a motorised pirogue should cost about CFA 4500 including your pack, but you'll only get this price after hard bargaining. The starting price might well be CFA 10,000 excluding pack (the locals pay CFA 3500). You need to take lots of food and water with you and, if you want to eat on board, donate a couple of handfuls of rice to the meal; you'll be rewarded with a share of the communal bowl of fish and rice (plus the odd CFA 100 for fish and salt, etc). There's very little food you can buy on the way.

The journey time between Mopti and Timbuktu varies from six to 15 days depending on the amount of cargo carried, the size of the pirogue, the water level in the river and whether the pirogue is motorised or not. You should expect delays when the boat owner goes off to see friends and family on the riverbank – often for up to half a day at a time.

If it doesn't rain sufficiently in the latter part of 1985, even the motorised pirogues will be unable to negotiate the river and you'll be down to the smaller variety, which have to be hand-poled. The motorised pirogues are already having difficulty in places (sacks have to be unloaded and the boat pushed, etc).

There are somewhat more predictable pirogues between Mopti and Djenne, primarily for local people taking produce to various markets. They generally leave Mopti on Friday and Djenne on Monday and Tuesday mornings. The journey takes about nine hours and the fare should be around CFA 1000. If you're starting from Djenne you must get to the Bani ferry point, from which the pirogues depart. A taxi there from Djenne costs CFA 300 (shared), or you can get there by truck for CFA 125.

BAMAKO

Hotel accommodation in Bamako is generally quite expensive, but paying a lot of money doesn't always guarantee a good room so it's worth checking out the missions before you try the hotels.

The *Centre d'Accueil des Soeurs Blanches*, corner 130th and 133rd Sts, has a dormitory for 12 people which costs CFA 1000 per person and has showers, mosquito nets and clean toilets. Baggage left here is generally secure (though they did have an armed robbery on 15 January 1985 – but it's the first and last time it's ever happened!). You can cook your own food here in the courtyard if you have your own stove. The *Conseil Diocesian des Religieuses* (Foyer de Bko-Koura, BP 298) is a pink building near the Vox Cinema. It's a kind of mission with spotless rooms and attached showers for MFr 2000 per person. It also provides hammocks in a dormitory for the same price. There are laundry facilities and a pleasant garden, and it's safe and friendly.

If you can't get in at any of the above, try the *Hotel Majestique*, Avenue de Fleure, which has rooms for CFA 3125 a single and CFA 4300 a double. If you want air-conditioning, it's CFA 5940 a single and CFA 7190 a double. For the price, the Majestique isn't half as good as the Centre d'accueil, and it lacks mosquito nets. Another place to try is *Chambres de Passage* at the Gare Routiere in Sogoniko, which has rooms for CFA 2250 a double or CFA 3000 a double with ceiling fan. A taxi from the train station to the Gare Routiere will cost CFA 225-300 depending on the amount of luggage and the time of day. Avoid staying at the *Bar Mali* near the Vox Cinema if you can. It used to be popular with travellers but is now 'a filthy bordello with over-priced food' and costs CFA 3300 a single and CFA 6000 a double. *Restaurant Au Bon Coin*, Avenue de la Nation, has recently been recommended as having good, cheap food as well as rooms to stay which cost only CFA 4000 for up to five people.

Other good places to try for food are the *Istanbul* (formerly the Chez Jean Restaurant) near the large market; the *Bambou*, which has good food for CFA 450-600; *Chez Aminah*, behind the Catholic Mission; *Restaurant Mikado*, which has good Vietnamese food at reasonable prices; *Snack Bar Hanoi*, with pleasant surroundings and steak and chips at CFA 750, Cantonese rice at CFA 1000; *Restaurant Centrale*, which you get to by turning first right past the *Mali Hag* (formerly the Printania) supermarket; and *Le Gonole*, Avenue de la Nation, which has good French and Lebanese food.

Popular expatriate hangouts are the *Berry Bar* (also good for making contacts for lifts), *Les Trois Caymans* and the *Bar Centrale*. You might meet Peace Corps volunteers here who may offer you a place to sleep for the night. The Peace Corps office is on El Hadja Samba Kone, Quartier Niarella, near the Hotel Dakan. It's open Monday to Thursday from 7.30 am to 3 pm and on Friday and Saturday from 7.30 am to 12.30 pm; tel 24 479. The office isn't really open to outsiders, so if you're interested in seeing what they get up to in the villages, you'll have to make personal contact with a volunteer.

Information

The Tourist Office is opposite the mosque and has free maps of the city. You can also get free maps of the city from the first floor of the building opposite the Texaco pump near the Hotel Majestique.

The Institute Géographie National is worth checking out if you're thinking of doing some walking trips around Mali, especially in the Dogon country. To get there, take the road that has the Banque du Commerce on its right and follow it for about one km. It's open Monday to Friday from 7 am to 1.30 pm and on Tuesday and Thursday from 3.30 to 5.30 pm.

If possible, avoid using Bamako as a poste restante address, as the post office isn't very efficient.

The truck park is known as Sogo Niko and is about six km from the city centre.

Rue M Keita is now called the Avenue de Fleure. Avenue Van Vollenhoven should be below the Rue Testard.

If Bamako is the first city you arrive at in Mali, go through the bureaucratic mill as soon as possible. Buy a tourist card (CFA 500) from SMERT, Boulevard du Peuple near the Grand Mosque, and a photo permit if you have a camera. The photo permit requires one photo and costs CFA 2500 plus a CFA 100 *timbres fiscal* from the Treasury (near the Hotel Majestique) or a post office. Collect it in 24 hours. Also, if you need a visa extension, fill in the forms at SMERT, buy a CFA 2500 and a CFA 100 *timbres fiscal* and take these with one photo to Immigration, just off Avenue de la Nation. A one-month extension will be issued in 24 hours.

Things to See

The **National Museum** on the road to the zoo is very well laid out and interesting, especially as far as weaving and Dogon artifacts are concerned. The **Zoo** itself costs CFA 100 (CFA 50 for students). There are artisans' workshops worth visiting near the Grand Mosque. If you'd like a good view of Bamako and the Niger Valley, walk along the road which leads out of town above the zoo and take one of the paths that go off to the left. If you continue to follow these paths for some four km, you'll end up returning to Bamako from the west.

BANDIAGARA/DOGON COUNTRY

This area south-east of Mopti is one of the most fascinating in North Africa and has been the subject of many anthropological and archaeological studies. Islam made very little impact on these people, so that today most of their traditional beliefs based on the dog-star Sirius survive intact. The Dogon number about 250,000, distributed over some 700 villages built in pairs along the 200-km Bandiagara Plateau. The design of their houses is unique and very characteristic. There are two basic types. The first is the plateau type built on flat rock outcrops between arable fields, while the second and most spectacular are erected on the steep slopes of the escarpment itself. Each house, collectively built and made of rock and mud-brick, consists of a number of separate rooms surrounding a small yard and interlinked with stone walls. Roofs are flat and families will sleep there during the hot, dry season. The granaries, on the other hand, have conical straw roofs which are assembled on the ground and then lifted into place.

Unfortunately, the Dogon villages are so picturesque that the more accessible of them have become over-touristed. This is particularly true of Sangha. A lot of insensitivity on the tourists' part has been shown towards the Dogon belief that cameras steal the soul – some people have even taken pictures of funeral ceremonies despite local protests – and, as a result, antipathy towards visitors can be uncomfortably high in the escarpment villages. This feeling hasn't yet spread to the villages of the plateau, so you're likely to be given a much friendlier welcome there. Also, because this area has become over-touristed, it's money that speaks these days. There's now a price for everything. It's not that you don't expect to have to pay your way, but once a price has been agreed on for something, you have to deal with all the demands of cadeaux from all interested parties and many others who have nothing to do with what's going on. SMERT, the Mali tourist organisation, has also got in on the act and is beginning to demand money from visitors or force them to take a guide. They're not much in evidence on market days, but you're advised to keep out of their way on other days. One American was asked for CFA 6000 by SMERT before they would allow him to go onto the escarpment. Another, who actually speaks the Dogon language and had spent nine days exploring the villages on his own, was picked up by SMERT and hassled for CFA 25,000. When he refused to pay, they threatened him with jail.

The best thing to do is go first to Bandiagara, but don't hang around there for too long as it has been spoiled by tourism. There are numerous possibilities. You should be able to arrange either a moped and/or a guide to take you around some of the villages. Neither will be particularly cheap; you should expect to pay around CFA 3000 per day for the moped and CFA 3000-4000 per day for the guide. One good person to contact is Mamadou, who will arrange visits to some of the most beautiful and remote of the Dogon villages such as Kanicombole, Djiguibombo, Tegourou, Diombolo and Teli. You can find good handicrafts in many of these villages. Mamadou hangs about in Le Conseil in Bandiagara. The owner of the Bar Kansaye in Bandiagara also can arrange tours of the villages. Another possibility is to go to Dini village (close to Bandiagara) and ask there for Ogo (Ogotemelon Dolo) or his younger brother, Amatigue Dolo. They will put you up – usually on the roof – as well as cook for you and act as guides. They've been very helpful to travellers in the past and won't charge you an exorbitant amount for a tour. In Bandiagara itself there are a few places to stay while you arrange for a guide. Le Campement, across the other side of the river, costs CFA 2000 a single. The Bar Kansaye has rooms for CFA 600 per night. Le Conseil is unmarked – it's on the river bank to the right before you cross the bridge to Le Campement. You can stay on the roof here for CFA 1000 per night.

Market day in Bandiagara is Monday. A covered truck from Mopti to Bandiagara presently costs CFA 800.

Instead of going to Bandiagara, you can take a taxi (CFA 1500 plus CFA 250 for a pack) from Mopti to Bankas. The journey takes about five hours. In Bankas, stay at Le Campement for CFA 1000 per person. The people are friendly, the bar is reasonably priced, and they're happy to provide you with tables and chairs if you want to cook your own food. Cheap food and coffee are also available in the café in the marketplace. At *Ben's Bar* you can sleep on a mat on the floor for CFA 1000 per person. Ben is very friendly and aware of travellers' needs. Enquire either at the Campement or at Ben's about a horse and cart (the cartmen will generally double as guides) and, if you don't want to stay at the Campement, about private accommodation – usually at CFA 500 per person per night. Avoid hiring a guide as soon as you get here. Many young Dogon speak French these days, so a guide isn't really necessary. The horse, cart and driver will cost about two-thirds as much again as a guide alone. There is a market in Bankas on Monday, good for buying blue Dogon cloth.

From Bankas there are many South Falaise villages which you can visit via horse and cart. Konikombole is four hours' walk or a two hours' ride by horse and cart. From here you can climb up the cliff face to Djuigibombo (1½ hours). If you like, you can hire a local youth to take you there for CFA 500, which includes a tour of the village. In the same area it's worth seeing Teli, a beautiful old village high up on the falaise (fee to visit the village is negotiable), and Endi, which has a market on Saturday mornings. You can stay in the latter place with villagers for CFA 500 per person, but people here have experienced a lot of tourism so expect to pay for even the smallest service and to be hassled for *cadeaux* by the local kids.

Villagers in the above places will generally prepare food for you (around CFA 400 per person) if you bring food from outside to contribute. Otherwise, put your own together.

If you have your own vehicle, the SMERT office in Mopti may attempt to charge you CFA 1000 per person for permission to drive to Bandiagara.

DJENNE

Djenne is a city full of legends. It's possibly the oldest and most impressive of the trading towns which once straddled the lucrative trans-Saharan caravan routes. Precious little has changed here for centuries; in fact, the town remains much as it was when the opening of direct sea links between West Africa and Europe put paid to the trans-Saharan caravanserai. It's a mud-brick town right down to the famous mosque here. The Djenne of today dates from around 1400 AD and had its heyday during the 15th and 16th centuries. Old Djenne (Jenne-jeno), a few km upstream, has its origins around 250 BC and was a thriving city by the 9th century AD. It was abandoned around 1400 AD for reasons which are not clear, though it's thought that the Moslem elite considered the city too contaminated by pagan practices. A lot of travellers miss this place because it isn't easy to get to, but it's worth the effort.

The Monday market is very interesting, though there tend to be a lot of overland expedition tourists here. The rest of the week it's very quiet. Make sure you visit the mud-brick mosque. You can get onto the roof (price negotiable) for an excellent view of the town and of the market below (on Monday). The narrow alleyways of the town are also well worth exploring.

Old Jenne-jeno is a four-km walk from Djenne. Walk out to the last village you passed on the way into Djenne, turn right and head for the rise with trees on it. All this area is part of the abandoned city. Pottery fragments are everywhere.

While you're looking around for somewhere more interesting to stay (or if you only have a couple of days to spare), *Le Campement* has beds for CFA 1000 and double rooms for CFA 2000. The beds are flimsy and only some of them have mosquito nets. There are good showers and toilets but no running water, and the management are very reluctant to fetch more water from the well in town when the water pots are empty. There is erratic electricity from 6 to 10 pm. Good food is available but it's expensive at CFA 1500 and, according to many travellers, inedible.

The rotisseries in the main square are excellent for food. Charcoaled goat meat costs CFA 500. Get there by 5 pm to select your cut and watch it cooked; otherwise all the 'best' cuts will have been reserved. The café to the left of the post office in the main square is worth visiting too. Coffee and bread will cost CFA 100. Street food is especially easy to find on market days.

If you're staying more than one night, make sure your papers are in order and register with the Commissariat de Police (the police won't give you a stamp unless you have a tourist card and, if you don't have one, they'll demand that you first buy one from SMERT). It takes half an hour and there's no fuss or charge. If you don't have a tourist card, photo permit, etc, then SMERT may well demand that you pay to see the town.

GAO

Like Djenne, Gao was another prosperous Sahelian trading city which flourished during the 15th and 16th centuries. It's been more affected by the 20th century than Djenne, but it's still very interesting. Make sure you visit the curious tomb of Askia and the associated mosque, the two good markets and the river area (pirogues, sand dunes, cultivation patterns and people washing clothes).

One of the most entertaining places to stay is *Camping Dominique*, which costs CFA 500. Meals are available for CFA 750. It's about 1½ km from the centre of town, near the SNTN. A French couple run the place. The woman speaks good English and is a normal human being, but the man frequently goes off his tree and has been known to hurl legs of meat around the place, burn magazines regardless of who they belong to or their contents, and hit out and shout at all and sundry. It's supposed to be because the kids put diesel on the fire to make it burn and that doesn't do much for his *haute cuisine*. Regarding those kids, don't allow them to do your washing for you. Clothes get 'lost' and you'll have to pay another kid to 'find' them apart from the laundry charge. Other than this, possessions are safe here.

The only hotel here is the *Hotel Atlantide*, where the cheapest rooms are CFA 2500 a single and CFA 3700 a double including taxes and an excellent breakfast (bread and jam plus three cups of strong coffee). They also have more expensive, air-conditioned rooms. The water supply is somewhat erratic, as is the electricity supply, but the toilets are kept as clean as is possible. You can also camp here for CFA 500 per person or rent a Tuareg-style tent with mats on the floor for CFA 750 per person with use of the hotel's shower and toilet facilities. If you stay in the latter, have your gear locked up in the main building while you're out. Meals are available here but they're not cheap. Expect to pay CFA 1300 and up.

Other places which have been recommended in the past are *Le Village* (local-style huts) and *Chez Yarga*, which is a 40 minutes' walk out of town. The latter offers mats on the floors of rooms without doors as well as showers and well water for CFA 750 per person after negotiation. The caretaker of the *Government Rest House* offers double rooms with mats on the floor for CFA 3000. There are shower and toilet facilities, and the doors lock. Accommodation in private houses is also available – expect to pay around CFA 750 per night.

Street food is pretty good in Gao. CFA 500 will buy you enough grilled filet of lamb or beef for two people. The usual goat meat is available, as are spicy sausages for CFA 125. The *Toure al Husseini* and *Oasis* restaurants have been recommended. Good, cheap African food can be found at the *Sahel Vert* near the police station. It's got a nice atmosphere and you can get rice, steak, coffee and bread at very reasonable prices. A café called the *Blackpool*, which is hard to find, does good omelettes. *Café Sportif* is a pleasant place to hang out. It's got a

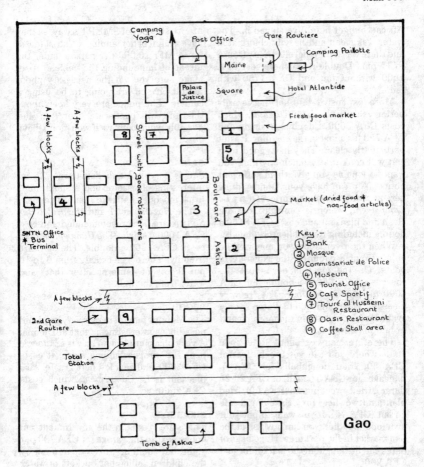

Camping Yaga

Post Office

Gare Routiere

Camping Paillotte

Mairie

Palais de Justice

Square

Hotel Atlantide

Fresh food market

A few blocks

A few blocks

Street with good rotisseries

⑧ ⑦

④

Boulevard Askia

③

②

Market (dried food & non-food articles)

SNTN Office & Bus Terminal

Key :—
① Bank
② Mosque
③ Commissariat de Police
④ Museum
⑤ Tourist Office
⑥ Cafe Sportif
⑦ Touré al Husseini Restaurant
⑧ Oasis Restaurant
⑨ Coffee Stall area

A few blocks

2nd Gare Routiere

⑨

Total Station

A few blocks

Gao

Tomb of Askia

garden where you can sit around and relax with ice-cold drinks or tea/coffee and tapes of Bob Dylan and Simon and Garfunkel.

The bank in Gao is only open from 8 to 11 am and charges CFA 500 commission to change traveller's cheques.

KAYES

If you have to spend the night here, try the *Hotel du Rail*, which costs CFA 3600 a double.

MOPTI

Hotel Bar Mali in the old part of town has been a very popular place for many years, but opinions vary widely about it. Some travellers dismiss it with comments like, 'A dirty bordello but with good food,' or 'A ghastly place – OK for a beer but awful to stay.' Another described it as a 'brilliant place. A maze of corridors and passageways. Small terraced area with plants. Good cold showers, clean toilets. A brothel, but so was virtually every other

African budget hotel I've stayed in. The water was clean and heavily chlorinated and there was (sporadic) electricity from 6 to 11 pm.' Double rooms here cost CFA 1500 without fan and CFA 1750 with fan.

More expensive but not necessarily better value is the *Hotel Oriental*, which costs CFA 3000 a double or single and CFA 750 for a bed in the corridor. It isn't particularly clean. They have good food and will cook pretty much anything you want so long as you give them sufficient notice. You can have your laundry done here at a very reasonable price. Or try *Le Campement*, which is centrally located, clean and pleasant and costs CFA 8150 a double including two (obligatory) meals.

When the river is low you may well be able to rent a cabin on the Niger ferry boats. On the most modern boat the charges are CFA 5000 a double and CFA 6000 for a cabin for four. They're very pleasant, clean and quiet. Water is only available for one hour in the morning and from 6 pm onwards.

There are many excellent street food stalls where you can get brochettes for CFA 50, fried doughballs for CFA 5, pancakes for CFA 5 (small) or CFA 20-25 (large), fried sweet potato (CFA 50), fried plantain (two slices for CFA 25) and café au lait (CFA 75). If you want to put your own food together, you can buy fish at the fish market in the port area. Huge bags of dates can be bought in the market for just CFA 200.

As far as restaurants are concerned, you can get good food at the *Lebozo Restaurant* at the end of the harbour, though it isn't particularly cheap and the service is very slow. Make sure they know exactly what your order is. A bunch of travellers recently ordered two plates of fish and 1½ hours later were brought four salads! Another place which serves good food is *Les Nuits de Chine*. If you want a touch of fading French elegance, try the wine and cheese at the *Welcome Hotel*.

If you're driving your own vehicle in Mopti, stay out of SMERT's way, as they have a habit of demanding a 'tourist fee' of up to MFr 10,000 per person under the threat of impounding the vehicle. Also, make sure you get the necessary photo permits if you are going to be using a camera. The police are very keen about this and will confiscate your film and possibly your camera if you don't have one.

SAN

San is a typical Sahelian town with an interesting old sector and a small mud-brick mosque similar to that at Djenne.

The *Bazani Hotel* and the *Hotel Bar Sangue* are both recommended and cost CFA 1000 a single. The *Campement* here costs CFA 2500 a double. The staff are friendly. There's electricity from 6 to 10 pm (kerosene lanterns after that) and water from the well.

SEGOU

The Monday market here is very good and possibly as interesting as that at Djenne. A very pleasant place to stay is *L'Auberge* near the pirogue landing stage. It costs CFA 3500, and gear left here is safe. Also pleasant is *Le Campement*, which costs CFA 2500.

SIKASSO

There are rooms in the government-run house next to the garage for CFA 700 per night, but you'll be woken up at 5 am by the children selling hot buckets of water for CFA 50. *Hotel Solo Khan* at the Gare Routiere has rooms for CFA 1500 a single.

The Gare Routiere is about one km out of town on the road to Ferkessedougou, just past the Bobo Dioulasso turn-off. A taxi from the centre of town should cost you CFA 80. Transport for Bobo, however, does not leave from there but from the centre of town.

TIMBUKTU

Few places in the world have a legend as

enduring as Timbuktu. Although the realities are a little frayed at the edges these days, it would be a strange traveller indeed who, having got as far as Mali, didn't feel compelled to go there. From humble beginnings in the 11th century as a trading post of the nomadic Tuareg, it had grown by the 15th century into one of the most famous centres of Islamic scholarship in the entire Moslem world. Its wealth, like that of many other Sahelian towns straddling the trans-Saharan trade routes, was based on gold and salt, the two being considered of rlmost equal value. Its decline set in after it was captured and sacked in 1591 by the armies of Sultan Mansour of Marrakesh, but this by no means eclipsed its import-ance and it continued to be fought over

and ruled right up until the 20th century by a variety of peoples ranging from the animist Bambara kingdom of Segou to the French who took it in 1894.

Today, it is a typical desert town of low, flat-roofed mud-brick buildings, yet it still retains its famous Djingerebur and Sankore mosques which, although partially restored from time to time, essentially date from the 15th century. The Sidi Yahaya mosque is also worth seeing. Do spend some time wandering around the narrow streets – there are numerous heavy doors studded and ornamented with metal and surrounded with ornate frames – and even plaques to various western explorers who came through here, eg Rene Caillie (1828) and Alexander Gordon Laing (1826). Even such 20th-century intrusions as

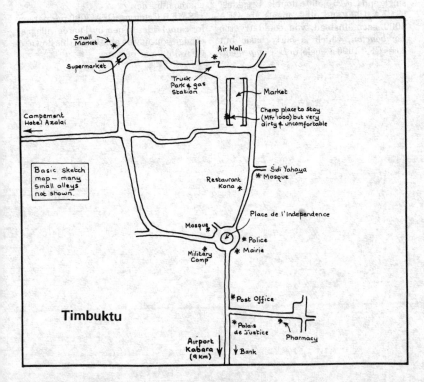

Timbuktu

trucks and planes haven't entirely put a stop to traditional means of transport and sources of income. A salt caravan, often consisting of over 3000 camels, sets out for Taoudenni twice a year in March and November.

If you're interested in reading more about Timbuktu, there was an excellent and very detailed description of the place together with some beautiful colour photographs in the March-May 1984 edition of the Australian magazine *Earth Garden*. You can get hold of copies of these from Earth Garden, PO Box 378, Epping, NSW 2121, Australia, for A$2.50 plus postage.

A new 42-room luxury hotel, the *Azalai* (built by Air France), has been completed but is very expensive at CFA 12,000 a single and CFA 15,500 a double. Breakfast is CFA 1000 and other meals are CFA 3000 each. Instead, you could try the *Tombouctou*, which is fairly basic but costs CFA 1000 a single; or *Le Campement*.

which costs CFA 3500-5125 a double. They also have singles and more expensive doubles depending on the facilities. Breakfast is included in these prices, but other meals cost CFA 2400. *Babo's Restaurant* is now closed – Babo unfortunately died recently. However, there's a new restaurateur called Arafat in the marketplace, who offers rooms in his house. Initially he'll offer what isn't a very good room for CFA 3000 a double, but if you persist he will generally move his stuff into the room he offered you and give you his own room for CFA 2250 a double. It's got a comfortable bed and a lock on the door. He's a friendly person and coffee is available (CFA 100). Arafat offers meat and pasta dishes fairly cheaply. If you prefer to make your own, he'll loan you a charcoal burner.

SMERT charges CFA 5000 per person for camel rides to nearby Tuareg villages, though you may be able to get this down to CFA 3500 per person.

Mauritania

Much of Mauritania forms part of the Sahara desert – a region of shifting sand dunes, rugged mountain plateaux and rocky outcrops. Only in the oases and along a narrow strip bordering the Senegal River can food crops be grown. The country exists almost entirely on the export of iron ore from the deposits around Zouerate, which until recently provided some 80% of the country's income. Recently, however, the fishing industry has taken over as the country's largest provider of income.

Mauritania may be dry and inhospitable these days, but through it once ran one of the most lucrative of the trans-Saharan trade routes from West Africa to the Mahgreb. So rich were the pickings in gold, slaves and salt along this route that the Almoravid dynasty in Morocco sought to control the trade. In 1076 they defeated the empire of Ghana, which held sway over what is today Senegal and parts of Guinea and Mali. The Almoravid commanders who had taken part in the campaign quickly asserted their independence from Morocco and their descendants were to rule over this area until defeated by the Arabs in 1674. The conquest resulted in a rigid caste system which has survived largely intact to the present. Incredibly, it was only in July 1980 that slavery was officially abolished in this country, and even then it depended on compensation for the former owners! It's estimated there are still over 100,000 slaves in the country.

Very little interest in Mauritania was shown by the European nations until the 19th century, when France took over the area. Even then Mauritania was little more than an administrative appendage of Senegal, and it wasn't until 1934 that sporadic resistance to French rule came to an end. Self-government of a sort was granted in 1957 under the Loi Cadre, and independence in 1960 under the presidency of Mokhtar Ould Daddah. Nevertheless, the French maintained a stranglehold over the economy. In fact, one of the reasons why they were prepared to grant independence was to prevent the area's absorption by Morocco, which maintained that it had an historical claim to the area and refused to recognise Mauritania until 1969.

In the early years of Mokhtar Ould Daddah's regime, opposition came first from the black people of the south who resented his decision to make Arabic, along with French, an official language. The next challenge came from the trade unions who objected to the racial inequality in the mining community at Zouerate (the 3000 expatriates there earned a staggering two-thirds of the country's entire wage bill). Ould Daddah survived that challenge by nationalising the mines in 1974 and withdrawing from the Franc Zone, but the event which led to his overthrow was his signing of the tripartite agreement between Spain, Morocco and Mauritania. This resulted in the partition of what was the Spanish Sahara between Morocco and Mauritania, against the wishes of the people of that colony. The Mauritanians took the largely worthless southern third of the colony and the Moroccans took the phosphate-rich northern two-thirds of the colony.

Both countries immediately found themselves fighting a vicious war with the guerrillas of the Saouarhi POLISARIO

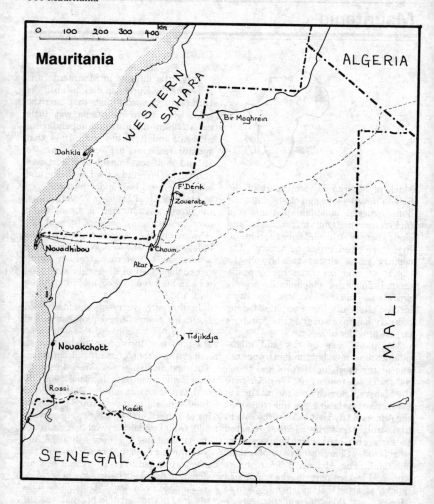

Front who were supported by Algeria, Libya and Cuba. Mauritania was totally incapable both military and economically of fighting such a war. Its weak spot was the railway line between the iron mines of Zouerate and the port of Nouadhibou, and the guerrillas knew it. They repeatedly sabotaged the track as well as conducted daring bombing raids on the capital of Nouakchott. Though Ould Daddah attempted to reinforce the Mauritanian army of 1800 men with a further 15,000 (at enormous cost), they proved to be no match for the guerrillas. Even with Moroccan troop reinforcements and French air-power, he was still unable to contain the guerrillas and in 1978 he was overthrown in an army coup.

The new regime dithered for over a year about what to do to extricate Mauritania from the war. Eventually, however, renewed guerrilla attacks and demonstrations by the black population of the south against the increasing Arab influence forced the regime to renounce all territorial claims to the Western Sahara. The guerrillas have now ceased to attack Mauritanian targets, but Morocco has annexed the whole of the Western Sahara and the war continues.

Ould Daddah was deposed in a coup by Maidalla shortly after the country renounced claims to the Western Sahara; Maidalla in turn was deposed in a coup on 12 December 1984. The present head of state is Colonel Maouya Sid Ould Taya.

As a result of the war between Morocco and POLISARIO, the trans-Saharan route (Route du Mauritanie) from Algeria to Senegal via Mauritania has been a no-go area for travellers for many years and remains so. The only way to get to Mauritania is either from the Canary Islands, Mali or Senegal. Except from Senegal, most possible routes into Mauritania are both rough and inconvenient, and as a result very few travellers go there these days – we've only heard from two in the last three years.

VISAS

Visas are required by all except nationals of France and Italy. The nearest Mauritanian embassies are in Dakar, Rabat and Madrid. There is a Vice-Consulate in Las Palmas (Canary Islands) at 'Pecheurs Mauritaine.' It's in a poorly marked office in Calle Raffael Cabrera, but visas take a long time to come through here as your passport has to be sent to Madrid. Other travellers report that visas are easy to obtain in Paris (the embassy is in the same building as the Mali embassy).

In Dakar visas cost CFA 2600, require two photos and take 24 hours to issue, plus you will probably have to get a letter of recommendation from your own embassy. The British embassy will charge you CFA 1800 for a visa, but will give it to you the same day if you ask politely.

There are heavy searches at the border. One traveller who went there recently said his baggage and his papers were checked five times between Rosso and Nouakchott.

There is no British embassy in Nouakchott. If you are British and have problems, the American embassy may help.

MONEY

US$1 = 66 ouguiya
£1 = 86 ouguiya

The unit of currency is the ouguiya = 5 khoums. There are no restrictions on the import of local currency so long as you declare it, but export is prohibited. Currency declaration forms are issued on arrival and the authorities are very strict about them. You may be stopped inside Mauritania by the police and searched. If they find you have more foreign currency than you declared on arrival, they will confiscate the extra. Take this seriously, as many people have been caught out.

If you're arriving from Senegal, there is a bank at Rosso on the Mauritanian side of the border where you can buy ouguiya. It's closed between 12.30 and 3 pm.

Banks are closed on Friday and Saturday.

Airport departure tax for domestic flights is 70 oug. For international flights to African countries it is 220 oug. Elsewhere the tax is 560 oug.

LANGUAGE

French and Arabic are the official languages. The Moors speak an Arabic dialect known as Hassaniya, whereas the black people of the south speak Pulaar, Soninke and Wolof.

GETTING THERE & AROUND
Air

There are two flights daily between Nouakchott and Nouadhibou which cost 3800 oug one way.

Road

Ever since Spain handed over the Western Sahara to Mauritania and Morocco and the guerrilla war began with the POLISARIO Front, the most westerly trans-Saharan route – the Route du Mauritanie from Algeria to Senegal – has been out of service. The only way of getting into Mauritania now is from Senegal or perhaps by ship from the Canary Islands. As very few people go there anymore, we have little recent information except for a few sketchy notes which a traveller sent us; he took a ship from the Canary Islands to Nouadhibou and then went by road to Senegal via Nouakchott. Some other travellers entered from Mali via Nioro to Ayoun el Atrous. It's possible that things may change now that Mauritania has withdrawn from the Western Sahara, but the prospects don't look good as the guerrilla war against Moroccan occupation continues and there are frequent hot-pursuit raids by Moroccan armed forces into Mauritanian territory.

There are only two roads as such in Mauritania: Nouadhibou to Rosso (Senegal border) via Nouakchott, and the Route du Mauritanie from Nouakchott to Tindouf (Algeria) via Atar, Choum, F'Derik and Bir Moghrein. Rosso to Nouakchott by truck will cost 450 oug including your rucksack. A truck between Nouakchott and Nouadhibou will cost 1500 oug including food and tea, and takes about 29 hours. The trucks start out from the market in the Cinquienne part of Nouakchott. There's another possible route from Mali via Nioro to Ayoun el Atrous. The road between Nouakchott and Nema is sealed as far as Ayoun el Atrous.

Fares on road transport are determined by frequency of use rather than distance (the less competition, the dearer they are), and you should expect to pay for your baggage. A Peugeot 404 pick-up from Ayoun el Atrous will cost 1200 oug, and Nouakchott to Rosso should cost 250 oug. Find out what the local people are paying before you hand over the fare.

Rail

In addition to road transport, there is one railway line which runs between Nouadhibou and Zouerate, where the iron ore mines are located. The trains which travel along this route are among the longest in the world – often three km long! As you might expect, they consist of open-topped ore bogies which make no concessions to comfort and are slow and filthy, but they're free. You just choose your wagon. They run two to three times daily in either direction and take about 12 hours to cover the 540 km. It's a bone-shattering experience and, if you're coming from Nouadhibou, the train doesn't stop until it gets to Choum. You should try to get a wagon up near the front as there is generally less dust to contend with there. Some travellers have spoken with the engine driver and managed to get a lift in the cab with them. The difference in comfort and the standard of refreshments is incomparable, so make the effort. There's a baggage car right at the end, but you have to pay to ride in it.

Boat

It is possible to get lifts on boats between Nouadhibou and Las Palmas, Canary Islands, but you may have to wait up to one month. On the other hand, it only costs 8000 oug by plane one way.

NOUADHIBOU

There are a number of hotels in the town, but they're not cheap so ask at the *Catholic Mission* for a place to stay. They're quite friendly and will generally let you stay free. If you're coming in from the Canary Islands, bring some whisky with you – the priest's friend, the French doctor, will readily buy it from you at a reasonable price.

For a quiet drink and something to eat, try the *Cabanou* about 12 km from Nouadhibou beyond the airport.

There are some beautiful deserted beaches to explore in this region on both sides of the peninsula. A traveller who was there recently said he had no problems crossing the border between Mauritania and Morocco. There were no guards, police or any other officials in sight.

It's sometimes worth a visit to **Port Mineralier**, 15 km from Nouadhibou, where the ore is loaded onto ships. You may meet up with bored crew members off European cargo ships who will take you back to their ship for a weekend of inebriation and high living. They may even offer you a lift back to Europe or further south.

NOUAKCHOTT

Nouakchott is the capital of Mauritania.

Ask first at the *Catholic Mission* for a place to stay. They're very friendly people who will often allow you to stay free. The cost by taxi from the centre is 10 oug. If the mission can't take you, stay at the *Hotel Adrar*, which is 700 oug a single. It doubles as a brothel but is otherwise clean and relatively quiet. The *Hotel Oasis* has an expensive bar, but next to it are toilets with toilet paper, soap and a mirror. A good place to eat is the *Restaurant Sindibad*, opposite the market. There are plenty of other cheap restaurants where you can get a rice plate for 25-30 oug and an omelette for 50 oug.

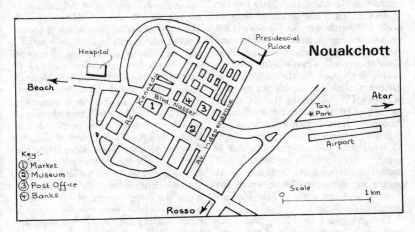

Mauritius

Almost 2000 km off the east coast of Africa, this independent island group consists of Mauritius, Rodrigues and two smaller groups of islands and reefs to the north and north-east. All the islands are volcanic in origin, are surrounded by coral reefs and have a sub-tropical climate. They're not really a part of Africa and the people don't consider themselves to be African, though the country is a member of the OAU. Most of the islands' multi-racial population of about one million is descended from Indian immigrants and contract labourers (both Hindu and Moslem). The main source of income is sugar, though tourism is becoming of increasing importance. Probably most people will remember Mauritius as the home of the now extinct flightless bird known as the dodo.

Though visited by Malay and Arab mariners before the arrival of the Europeans, Mauritius remained uninhabited until the end of the 16th century. The first Europeans to call there were the Portuguese under the command of Pedro Mascarenhas, after whom the island group is named. The Portuguese laid no claim to the island and it wasn't settled until the Dutch landed a party there in 1598. The island subsequently became an important port of call for Dutch, French and English trading ships; and it was from here that the Dutch captain, Tasman, set off on the voyage which was to lead to the discovery of Australia.

The Dutch colonial period saw the introduction of sugar cane and slaves to work it, the decimation of the ebony forests and the extermination of the dodo and other indigenous birds. Their settlement lasted until 1710, when it was abandoned. Five years later the island was claimed by France and its name was changed to Ile de France. The French imported large numbers of slaves from the African mainland, Madagascar and India and set up extensive plantations for the cultivation of sugar, cotton, indigo, cloves, nutmeg and other spices. They also used Mauritius as a base from which to harass English merchant ships on their way to and from India as well as to mount invasions of Britain's Indian colonies. It remained a thorn in the English side until 1810, when the French forces were defeated by a British naval squadron which launched its attack from the island of Rodrigues. At the end of the Napoleonic Wars the island was ceded to Britain, though under the terms of the treaty the French way of life, its religion, customs, language and laws were safeguarded.

Under British rule, life continued in much the same way until 1835 when, despite strident opposition from French *colons*, slavery was abolished. Most of the freed slaves left the plantations and settled in the coastal towns, which resulted in a labour crisis. It was solved by importing indentured labourers from India, mostly from Bihar and the southern provinces. At the end of their contracts most of the Indian labourers chose to remain on the islands; by 1860, out of a population of some 300,000, two-thirds were Indian. The sugar plantations continued to thrive until competition from European-grown sugar beets began to make large inroads on the market. The importance of Mauritius as a port of call declined further with the opening of the Suez Canal.

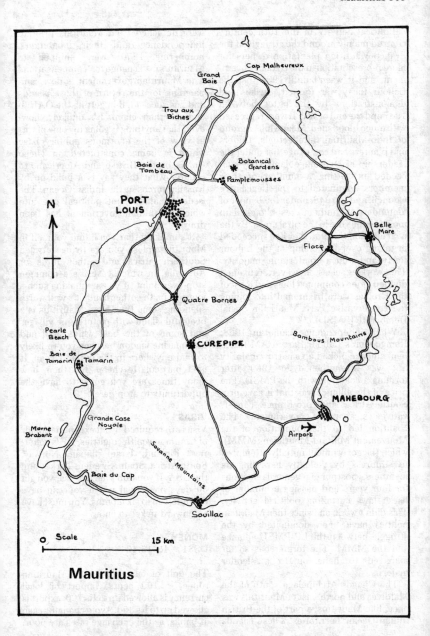

Mauritius

N

Political activity in the 19th century centred mainly around the struggle of the Franco-Mauritian plantation owners for more representation in the colonial government, and it wasn't until 1936 that the Labour Party was formed. Strikes and demonstrations by the latter between 1937 and the end of WW II were repressed with much bloodshed. Meanwhile, a group of Indo-Mauritian intellectuals, traders and planters had come together under the leadership of Dr Ramgoolam. They succeeded in getting a number of their members nominated to the Legislative Council, and in 1948, under the banner of 'defenders of Hindu interests,' picked up most the vote in the rural areas. By the next elections in 1953 they had succeeded in taking over leadership of the Labour Party and won a comfortable majority. The working class, however, remained divided along communal lines and most of the Creoles were frightened into joining the conservative Parti Mauricien Social Democrate (PMSD).

When independence came in 1968, Ramgoolam's Labour Party-CAM (Moslem) alliance picked up a narrow majority but was strengthened in 1969 after forming a coalition with the PMSD. The price of the alliance was that it gave pro-South Africa and pro-France conservatives a share of government. The coalition led to the foundation of the Mouvement Militant Mauricien (MMM), which the government initially attempted to suppress by violently harassing its members, postponing general elections for four years and passing a number of harsh laws curtailing political activity. This didn't work, and since then Mauritian politics have been dominated by the struggle between the LP-PMSD alliance and the MMM. The former has so far managed to hang on to a slender majority.

The Chagos Archipelago south of the Maldives and north-east of Mauritius was once, like Mauritius, a part of the British Indian Ocean Territories. These islands were detached from Mauritius prior to independence and their inhabitants, numbering 1200, were shipped to Mauritius in exchange for 'compensation.' The Mauritian government is now campaigning for the return of those islands and has succeeded in getting the OAU to endorse their claim. It's unlikely, however, that anything is going to come of this in view of the enormous military base which is being constructed on Diego Garcia by the British and Americans to counter what they say is a build-up by Russian forces in the Indian Ocean. The issue remains a hot political one into which the Indian government has been drawn.

It's unlikely that you'll find yourself in Mauritius unless you are flying between Southern Africa and either India or Australia, in which case it's a common stop-over point. If you are making such a journey, on the other hand, it's well worth spending some time here. Mauritius is a beautiful island with picturesque villages and some of the best white sand and aquamarine lagoon beaches you're likely to find anywhere in the Indian Ocean. It isn't particularly cheap, but then, how many times are you going to have the opportunity to stop here?

VISAS

Visas are required by all except nationals of Commonwealth countries, EEC countries, Finland, Israel, Japan, Norway, South Africa, Spain, Sweden, Turkey and the USA. If you don't need a visa, you get 30 days on arrival which you can have extended up to six months. You must have an onward ticket to enter.

MONEY
US$1 = Rs 15.40

The unit of currency is the Mauritian rupee = 100 cents. Import of local currency is allowed up to Rs 700: export is allowed up to Rs 350. Avoid changing cash at banks, as the exchange rates are poor.

The rates for traveller's cheques is much better. There is no black market.

Airport departure tax is Rs 100 for international flights. There is an 11% government tax on all airline tickets bought within the country.

LANGUAGE

English and French are the official languages, but many people don't speak the former. About 80 to 90% of the people speak Creole (a French-Bantu-Malagasy mixture) which is, in effect, the lingua franca. Many of the Indo-Mauritians speak Bhojpuri (derived from Bihar), but they also speak Creole.

GETTING THERE & AROUND

Air

British Airways, Air France, Air India, Lufthansa, Air Malawi, South African Airways and *Zambia Airways* are among the airlines which call at Mauritius. Most allow a free stop-over here.

La Plaisance International Airport is situated near Mahebourg in the south-east corner of the island. It is 43 km from the capital, Port Louis. There is a Tourist Office here, but travellers who have been to Mauritius recently say it's useless. There is, however, a Chamber of Commerce and Industry 'accommodation desk' which is helpful and will book you a hotel room, guest house or apartment anywhere on the island. You must pay them a deposit of 20% of the first night's rent, but this is then deducted from your hotel bill. There is a bank at the airport which opens when flights arrive. Make sure you reconfirm your onward flight.

A taxi to Mahebourg will cost Rs 40-50, but there are also public buses from the airport to Mahebourg (Rs 1.50) and Curepipe (Rs 4). Ask a policeman or a security guard where the buses stop (there's no sign). The conductors speak French and English and they won't charge you for luggage. Other people on the bus can be very helpful about telling you where to get off.

Road

Roads around the island are good and sealed. There's an excellent bus service to most places, though the last buses to most places leave at 7 pm or even earlier. The only drawback to the buses is that there are so many private bus lines that you may have to change buses several times to get from one place to another, but they're often more convenient than hitching. You may be charged extra for luggage. From Mahebourg to Curepipe costs Rs 4 and takes one hour, while from Curepipe to Port Louis costs Rs 3.50 and takes one hour.

Boat

People from nearby Réunion often visit Mauritius and vice versa; they may help out with transport between the two (boats and light planes).

PLACES TO STAY

There are good campgrounds around the beaches if you have a tent, but the best deals are the self-catering apartments and bungalows near the beaches where you can do your own cooking and chill your own fruit and drinks. These apartments are often cheaper than the *pensions de famille*, and radically so if you can get a group together to share a two-bedroom apartment. *Pensions de famille* cost Rs 45-100 and over depending on facilities and quality, and also on the season and whether you're a tourist. There are a few cheap hotels, but they're mostly in the cities and not at the beaches. Hotels fill up quickly once a plane arrives, so don't waste time getting there. You can also camp anywhere on the island free of charge. Curious local people may visit you and invite you to eat with them.

MAHEBOURG

Mahebourg is a sleepy little town but convenient for the airport or if you arrive in Mauritius late in the day. It's worth visiting the **Historical Naval Museum** out on the highway towards the airport. The museum is housed in an old French colonial 18th-century house and has displays of old ships' bells, cannons, charts and furniture. It's open daily from 9 am to 4 pm except on Tuesday, Friday and public holidays.

If you're a woman travelling on your own, the best place to stay is the *Pension Notre Dame*, Souffleur St (tel 71 587), which is run by nuns. It's very good, is quiet, and costs Rs 50 a single and Rs 80 a double with common bath and without breakfast, or Rs 100 for a private room with breakfast and lunch or dinner (cheaper without meals). A refrigerator is available. Our correspondent said, 'Soeur Anette is dynamite!' but didn't elaborate. Also recommended is the *Auberge Diane* (tel 71 695) on the waterfront a few blocks south of the bus station. It's a pleasant place and has singles for Rs 75 and doubles for Rs 150, including breakfast. There are sinks and showers in some of the rooms but toilets are communal. Apart from this place, try the *Blue Lagoon Hotel* on the beach at Blue Bay. It costs Rs 80 for a private room with bath, including breakfast. Government tax is Rs 8. Lunch or dinner costs Rs 45. There are buses to and from Blue Bay only in the morning and afternoon.

Outside of Mahebourg there is the *Blue Lagoon Hotel* (tel 71 529) at Blue Bay, which charges Rs 90 a single and Rs 180 a double including breakfast. They also have one self-catering bungalow with two beds for Rs 150 (no breakfast). Meals at the hotel are quite expensive (Rs 50).

The *Monte Carlo Bar & Restaurant* is well worth going to if you're looking for some action or a drink and a meal. It's popular with local people and offers excellent curries (turtle, fish, chicken, etc) with rice for Rs 20. They have egg dishes as well.

PORT LOUIS

There are plenty of cheap hotels and pensions around the bus stations. One of the cheapest places to stay in Port Louis is the *Hotel President Tourist*, which is very friendly and costs Rs 75 a double including breakfast (there are no singles and no reductions for single occupancy). The *Tandoori Hotel*, Victoria Square across from the southern routes bus station (tel 20 031), has rooms with shower and toilet for Rs 75 a single and Rs 100 a double including breakfast. It has a restaurant serving Indian and local dishes. *Le Grand Carnot* (tel 08 3054) has rooms for the same price with shower and toilet and including breakfast. If you intend to stay for a week or so, it's better to look for a *pension de famille*. Highly recommended is the one run by Mme Jean Louis at 13 Avenue des Capucines, Quatre Bornes, which costs Rs 350 a week including a tin of Nescafé, excellent breakfasts and a hot meal on Sundays. The owner is a 76-year-old woman who really enjoys the company of travellers. The pension is centrally located.

Mauritian food is usually curry with rice or noodles, or curry with *roti*. Curries with many different spices are known as *daube*; those with fewer hot spices and more tomatoes are known as *rougaille*. For local food at its cheapest, try the food stalls lined up on Poudriere St between the Natural History Museum and Company's Garden park where you can sit and eat. They feature *roti*, fried rice or fried noodles (*mine frit*) with curries of octopus (*ourite*), fish, chicken and beef for Rs 4-7. There are also egg dishes, desserts and drinks for sale.

Le Café de la Cité, Place de la Cathedrale, offers a more elaborate cuisine in a pleasant setting. Lunches cost from Rs 20 including pork chops, steak and chips, curries and blood sausage (*boudin*). The *Underground Restaurant & Snack*, Bourbon St between Leoville l'Homme and Remy Ollier Sts, serves Chinese and Creole dishes from around Rs 25. They have great *daubes* and a good sound system.

Just about everything in Port Louis closes between 5 and 6 pm except for

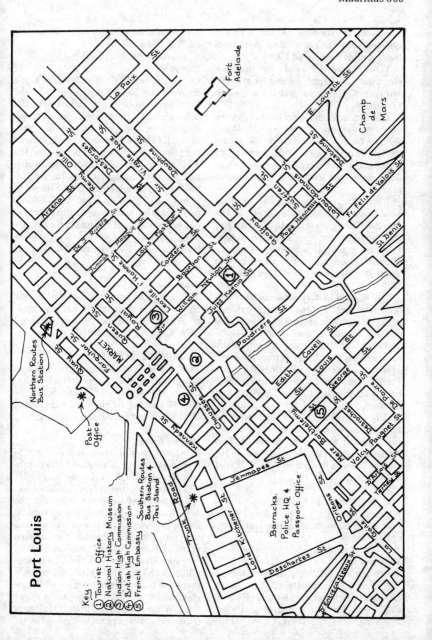

Port Louis

Key:
1. Tourist Office
2. Natural History Museum
3. Indian High Commission
4. British High Commission
5. French Embassy

Northern Routes Bus Station

Post Office

Southern Routes Bus Station
Taxi Stand

Fort Adelaide

Champ de Mars

Barracks, Police HQ, Passport Office

some street vendors in the Chinese quarter. You can get a filling meal from these people for around Rs 10.

The Tourist Office is in the new Registrar's Building, William Newton St, but recent reports suggest it's not worth visiting.

The Indian High Commission is on the 5th floor, Bank of Baroda Building, William Newton St near Royal Rd. Hours for visa applications are 9.30 am to 12.45 pm Monday to Friday. Visas take two to three days, cost Rs 57 and require three photos.

There are two bus stations in Port Louis, one for buses going north to the beaches (Immigration Square Bus Station) and another for the southern routes (Victoria Square Bus Station). They are about 10 blocks apart. There are buses to Tombeau Bay from Port Louis for Rs 1.25.

The **Natural History Museum** has been recommended, if only to see the exhibits of the extinct dodo and the museum's view on the origin of the earth, which is certainly different from the normally accepted version. Entry is free. It's open Monday, Tuesday, Wednesday and Friday from 9 am to 4 pm and on Saturday from 9 am to noon. Closed Thursday and Sunday.

Other interesting places to visit are the **French Government House**, built in 1738; the **Jummah Mosque** on Royal St; **Fort Adelaide**, built in the reign of William IV; and the **Chinese Pagoda** on Volay Pougnet St in Chinatown.

THE NORTHERN BEACHES

If beaches are what you're looking for, the best of them are on the north-western tip of the island.

Tombeau Bay

There are two relatively cheap places to stay here: *Le Clapotis* (tel 37 724), which has rooms with common bath for Rs 95 a single and Rs 115 a double including breakfast; and the *Hotel Capri*, which offers bed and breakfast for Rs 90 a single and Rs 130 a double.

Pereybere

One of the best of the beaches. Try *Etoile du Nord* (tel 038 303) just opposite the Pereybere public beach and close to the bus stop. It offers small, self-catering apartments equipped with kitchen, fan, etc for Rs 150 a single or double. It's one of the cheapest in the area. There is also the *Sivayon Peramal* (tel 038 558/182), which has self-catering apartments for Rs 100 (one or two people) and Rs 125 (three to four people). You can get air-conditioned, two-bedroom apartments with kitchen, balconies and maid service for Rs 200 per day. Tel 083 570 or ask for Stephen Boutique in Pereybere. Camping is permitted here.

Grand Baie

This is another popular beach with a wide choice of accommodation, but it's somewhat touristy. Many yachts are anchored here. Camping is permitted.

RODRIGUES ISLAND

This small (108 square km) volcanic island with a population of around 30,000 lies about 650 km east of Mauritius and is only 18 km long by eight km wide, but it offers excellent hiking and camping.

Getting There

If your time is limited, you can get to Rodrigues on *Air Mauritius* Twin Otters and HS 748s for Rs 1398 one way or Rs 2517 return excursion fare (15-30 days).

The best deal, however, is to take the *MV Mauritius*, which sails there every 20 days or so, staying for five to six days and then returning to Port Louis. The passage takes 36 hours and the fares are Rs 175 (covered deck), Rs 300 (bed in a dormitory with 10 to 18 beds per dormitory – there are two of these) and Rs 630 (1st-class cabin, two beds). These are one-way fares. While the ship lies in Port Mathurin (Rodrigues) the captain will generally let you keep a 1st-class cabin for Rs 75 per person per day. You need to book this ship as far in advance as possible, as it fills up quickly. Write or call Rogers & Co, Rodrigues Service, 5 President John Kennedy St, PO Box 60, Port Louis (tel 086 801 ex 239).

Places to Stay

In Port Mathurin try the *Ciel d'Ete Pension de Famille*, Jenner St (tel 587), which is run by a Chinese family.

Some 10 minutes from town on the oceanfront at Anse aux Anglais is the *Pensionnat les Filaos* run by Mr Begue. Bed-and-breakfast rates here are Rs 75 a single and Rs 150 a double, with half board costing Rs 125 a single and Rs 250 a double.

At Pointe Venus, east of Port Mathurin, is the *Relais de Pointe Venus* which costs Rs 155 for a room without meals, Rs 205 for bed and breakfast and Rs 325 for half board.

OTHER PLACES OF INTEREST

The **Trou au Cerfs**, an ancient crater close to Curepipe, is worth a visit for the fantastic views over the whole island. There are buses to close by. Another place worth visiting is the **Carela Bird Park** close to Tamarin Bay. Apart from the Mauritius pink pigeon, it has two Bengal tigers. A barbeque is available there for Rs 80; this entitles you to free entry to the park. Otherwise you pay Rs 30 on weekdays and Rs 20 at weekends. The **Aquarium**, one km from Trou aux Biches on the road towards Pointe aux Piments, is well worth a visit for its eels, sharks, turtles, rays, octopi and tropical reef fish. It's open every day from 9 am to 4.30 pm. Entry costs Rs 27.50. **Pamplemousses Botanical Gardens** is a large garden with ponds and cages full of 100-year-old tortoises. The Garden's headquarters is an old colonial house which used to be the governor's residence.

Many thanks to Jan King and Tom Harriman (USA) for providing the bulk of the information in this chapter.

Morocco

Morocco, unlike other North African countries, is still largely populated by the descendants of its original Berber settlers who came to this area thousands of year ago and at one time controlled all of the land between Morocco and Egypt. Little is known about the origin and history of these early Berbers, other than that they were occupying Mahgreb in the New Stone Age period. (Rock carvings in the Saharan regions and a Cromlech – circle of stone – at Larache date from around this time.) But there is indication that Morocco was settled even earlier than this. Several fragments of fossilised human remains with the characteristics of Neanderthal Man of Paleolithic times have been found near Rabat, Casablanca and Tangier. However, there are no written records of the history of these early people, nor is there any evidence that links them with the original Berbers. What we do know about the latter is that they were never

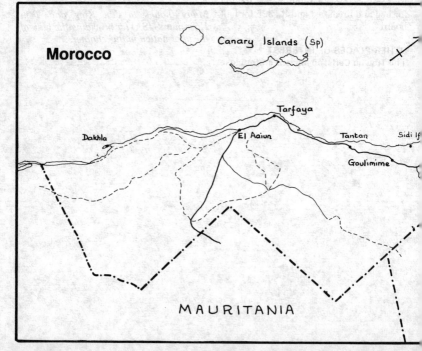

united except for brief periods when expediency dictated such an arrangement to face a threat from a common enemy. And even today the various tribes in Morocco jealously guard their independence. Berber society is based on the clan and village, each village being autonomous and ruled by a council of adult males. Sometimes villages will come together in a loose kind of confederation to better administer something of mutual concern, but the autonomy of each village is always respected. This entrenched unwillingness to forfeit their independence has muted the effects of various conquerors who have come and gone over the centuries, and has resulted in the preservation of one of Africa's most fascinating and colourful cultures through the 20th century. It has understandably been a travellers' mecca for many years, though excessive tourism is beginning to spoil many of its unique features.

The Berbers' language is different from that of the Arabs, who began arriving here in the wake of the Moslem expansion after the death of the Prophet Mohammed, and who have their own script. Arab horsemen failed to penetrate the mountains of the Rif and Atlas; as a result, these areas remain firmly Berber, though a considerable amount of intermixing has gone on in the cities and on the plains. Examples of the art and buildings left by the many brilliant cultures and empires which have grown up here can still be seen today, ranging from the Roman city of Volubilis to the Moslem kingdoms which had their capitals variously at Marrakesh, Fez, Meknes and Rabat.

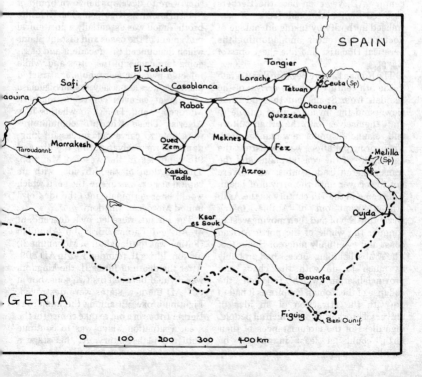

The Berbers first come into recorded history as the merchants who traded with the Phoenician coastal cities by virtue of their control of the trans-Saharan gold and ivory trade. They were never much influenced by the urban culture of the Phoenicians, though they sometimes allied with them to fight the Romans if this paid in terms of trade. Likewise, when the Romans finally established themselves here, the Berbers were willing to trade with them – even fight for them if it paid – but were unwilling to give up their independence, so that Roman rule was at best tenuous in this part of North Africa. All the same, Roman rule ushered in a long period of peace and prosperity during which many cities were founded and Berbers of the coastal plains became city dwellers. Christianity arrived in the 3rd century AD, yet even here the Berbers asserted their traditional dislike of centralised authority by taking advantage of doctrinal differences and adopting the heretical Donatist line like the Copts of Egypt.

The Roman Empire began to disintegrate in the 5th century with the arrival of the Vandals from Spain, but the end came slowly and the invaders were unable to graft themselves onto the urban culture and relaunch it under new management. Their principal effect was to disrupt the agriculture of the coastal plains and the trans-Saharan trade routes, which were not to recover until the arrival of Islam. This came in the 7th century as the Arab armies swept out of Arabia, taking Byzantine Egypt and then moving west to conquer the whole of the north African coast and eventually much of Spain too. The Arabs' lightning success had probably as much to do with the chaos and provincialisation which followed the collapse of the Roman Empire as it had to do with the attraction of an idea of universal brotherhood in which all people, regardless of the circumstances of their birth, could (at least in theory) be members of a new and broad community based on equal dignity and worth. In this respect the Arab conquest was markedly different from that of the Romans, but although they couldn't have been as successful as they were without delivering some of the goods, the reality was a long way from the Utopia. Once the initial flush of enthusiasm had subsided, the basic tribal divisions and animosities began to reappear. As with the Christians, there grew up doctrinal differences based on the interpretation of Mohammed's teaching and disputes over where power should reside in the Islamic community. It is from this time that the basic schism between Sunnis and Shi'ites dates.

The Berber tribes were not slow to see these schisms as a convenient way of expressing their independence while at the same time remaining Moslems, and they were to develop their own brand of Shi'ism known as Kharijism. The Kharijite brotherhood was essentially a puritanical movement of the oases and distant plains which denounced the decadent and easy-going tendencies of the cities and, while rejected by Islam as a whole, it attracted many followers, especially around Sigilmasa –the great caravan centre in southern Morocco – and Tahert in what is now Algeria. These Kharijite communities were able to carve out successful kingdoms for themselves during the 8th and 9th centuries in the western Mahgreb. The kingdom of the Idrisids, with its capital at Fez, was to sow the seed which would later germinate into the idea of a united Moroccan kingdom.

The Idrisids were led by a descendant of Ali and Fatima Idris ibu Abdullah (Fatima was the daughter of Mohammed); his son, Idriss II, founded Fez in AD 809. After the death of Idriss II, the kingdom was divided between his two sons, but in 921 AD the new states were destroyed. Fighting broke out among the numerous Berber tribes in a bid to take control of the area, a situation which was to continue until the 11th century. At this stage a second Arab invasion took place, much of

North Africa was plundered, and many peoples took up a nomadic way of life.

Out of this, another fundamentalist movement got under way among the Berbers of the plains of Mauritania and Morocco; it was enthusiastically supported by the peasant people of this area. The Almoravids, as they became known, quickly overran Morocco and Moslem Andalusia, and then turned south to destroy the power of the kingdom of Ghana in the Western Sudan, which had expanded to a point where it had succeeded in imposing tribute on Audaghost, the principal southern trading centre of the Berbers. The Almoravids went on to found Marrakesh and build a rich and prosperous empire over the western half of the Mahgreb, but in doing this they gradually lost the simple faith, military energy, and cohesion of their desert days. A revolt among the tribes of the Moroccan Atlas Mountains led to their overthrow and replacement by another dynasty, the Almohads.

Under these new rulers a professional civil service was set up and the cities of Fez, Marrakesh, Tlemcen and Rabat reached the peak of their cultural development. To pay for all this as well as a professional army and navy, the Almohads had the land throughout their empire surveyed and taxes levied according to its productivity. In doing this they came up against the age-old problem of tribal rivalries by intensifying an already apparent distinction between the confederation which had overthrown the Almoravids (who were now the rulers) and the rest. Discontent spread among the 'excluded' tribes which, together with the threats posed by the Christian armies in Spain and the advancing Bedouin from the east, forced the Almohads to divide their administration. One of these – the Hafsids of Tunis – became so successful that, after defeating the Bedouin, they declared themselves independent of Marrakesh and began trading directly with European nations.

Some time after this, Almohad prestige suffered a drastic setback with the resounding Christian victory of Las Nevas de Tolosa in Spain, and the empire began to disintegrate into its constituent tribal parts. During the confusion the Bedouin seized the opportunity to overrun much of what is now Tunisia and Algeria. Morocco itself continued to be held together after a fashion by a succession of small kingdoms, but gradually lost Spain to the Christian armies in the 15th century. Nevertheless, neither the victorious Spaniards nor the Ottoman Turks, who conquered the rest of North Africa in the 16th century, were able to take Morocco. In time, a new period of cultural brilliance was born under the Saadid dynasty from which the present ruler, King Hassan, is descended.

The Saadids reached the peak of their power after victories over the Turks and Portuguese in the late 16th/early 17th centuries, and thereafter took advantage of dissensions within the empire of Songhay in the Western Sudan to attack that too. Though the attack on Songhay was successful and led to its disintegration, the Saadids were unable to govern what they had taken and there was chaos on the trans-Saharan commercial routes as well as in the cities of Timbuktu, Gao and Djenne. Another group took over from the Saadids in the mid-17th century, the Alawite Sharifs. Under Moulay Sharif the Alawite Sharifs subjugated and pacified Morocco, reoccupied Tangier (evacuated by the British in 1684) and made their capital, Meknes, into a sort of Moroccan Versailles. However, on the death of their leader, the country reverted to chaos – yet again. A kind of fragile order and unity was restored under Moulay Shinan (1792-1822), but strong, internal organisation was seriously lacking. The country remained medieval, the trading cities of Western Sudan never regained their former influence and the primary trading routes were shifted further east, which left Morocco a commercial backwater.

Morocco managed to retain its independence throughout the 19th century as Tunisia and Algeria became French colonies, though less through any effort on its own part than because of the mutual jealousies of the European nations. It was not until 1912 that the country was partitioned between Spain and France. The fiercely independent mountain tribes, however, were not fully 'pacified' until the mid-1930s. During Morocco's brief period as a French colony, 400,000 French went to settle there as farmers, but when independence came in 1956 all but 90,000 abruptly returned to France. This was a severe blow to the country's economy, which has taken many years to recover. The Spanish renounced their Moroccan possessions shortly after the departure of the French, but hung on to Ifni in the south and the Mediterranean ports of Ceuta and Melilla. Ifni was handed back to the Moroccans in 1969, but the two Mediterranean ports remain Spanish to this day.

King Hassan II, the present ruler, has several times been threatened with attempted coups, but he remains to all intents and purposes a despotic ruler with the prerogatives attached to absolute monarchy. A lot of political repression within the country is designed to keep things that way, with troops and police very much in evidence along main roads and in towns. The former leader of the opposition party, Ben Barka, was abducted and murdered whilst living in exile in Paris in 1965, following his alleged complicity in the conspiracy against Hassan in 1963. Subsequent French investigations into his murder led to the issue of arrest warrants for several high-ranking members of Hassan's government, including the Minister of the Interior. This led to a temporary break in diplomatic relations with the French.

Recalling Morocco's historical claims to the Western Sahara, Hassan organised several hundred thousand men, women and children to walk over the border into Spanish Sahara in 1975 in an attempt to force Spain to hand over the territory. There was a great deal of diplomatic and military sabre-rattling at the time, but in the end, Spain, unwilling to get embroiled in a colonial war, agreed to hand over the territory to Morocco and Mauritania for partition between the two – much against the wishes of the indigenous Saouarhis, who wanted independence. The result was a guerrilla war fought by the Saouarhi POLISARIO Front supported by Algeria, Libya and Cuba, against Mauritania and Morocco. This has on several occasions brought Morocco and Algeria very close to war. The Mauritanians eventually withdrew, having had their economy virtually wrecked by the activities of the POLISARIO Front, but Morocco refuses to budge an inch and has taken over the part vacated by the Mauritanians. There is little doubt that one of the reasons underlying Morocco's interest in the Western Sahara is based on the fact that the territory contains the world's largest deposits of phosphate ore. Morocco is already a major supplier of this mineral, generally used as a fertilizer, so with control over the Saharan deposits they will secure a virtual monopoly. The war is still being fought, and its effect on travellers has been to put a large part of southern Morocco and the trans-Saharan Route du Mauritanie out of bounds for a while. The continuing bad relations between Algeria and Morocco mean that only the overland crossing between Oujda and Tlemcen is presently available, and even that is sometimes closed. Keep your eye on the political situation if you're going that way.

FACTS

The principal crops are cereals, dates, olives, citrus fruits and grapes. There is a good deal of market gardening for vegetables – principally tomatoes. In the mountains large flocks of goats and sheep are reared.

A prominent characteristic of rural life is the weekly market or *souk,* normally held on a traditional site and located about 30-50 km from each so that tribespeople can visit the nearest one and return home within a single day. The traditional means of travel is on foot, though buses and cars have changed this pattern somewhat in the last few years. Local produce is exchanged for imported or manufactured articles such as household hardware, tea, coffee and cloth, while the services of tradespeople and skilled workers such as cobblers, bankers, tinkers and blacksmiths are available. There is also an itinerant 'doctor' who treats minor ailments.

Native Moroccan towns are generally overgrown villages and three distinct functional sectors are commonly discernible: the *medina* – the traditional huddle of houses comparable to the villages; the *mellah* – mainly occupied by the Jews who have long been active in the commercial life of Morocco and the rest of Mahgreb; and the *kasbah* – the Arab quarter. In some cases a fourth has been added – the European quarter or the Ville Nouvelle, situated a short distance away from the main town and more spaciously laid out.

VISAS

Visas are required by all except nationals of West European countries (with three exceptions, Belgium, the Netherlands and Portugal), Australia, Brazil, Canada, Chile, Japan, Mexico, New Zealand, Peru, Philippines, USA, Venezuela and most Arab countries (Jordan and Libya are exceptions). Nationals of Israel and South Africa are not admitted. Visas cost US$2 or the equivalent and are valid for a stay of 90 days with a maximum of two entries. If you fit into the category of what Moroccan immigration officials regard as 'hippies,' it's just possible you might be refused entry, but we haven't heard of this happening to anyone for several years.

If you intend to stay more than three months, you must make an application for this within 15 days of arrival. Nationals of France and Spain are allowed unlimited stay so long as they report to the police within three months of arrival.

If you're bringing your own vehicle in from Algeria, the Moroccan customs at Oujda will impound it and hold it until they get a letter from your embassy in Rabat confirming that you are going to take it out of Morocco again and not sell it inside the country. It's best to arrange this yourself; otherwise it will take days and days.

Although you cannot cross the Moroccan-Algerian border between Oujda and Tlemcen on foot, the Moroccan officials won't stop you from walking to the Algerian side, where you will be refused entry. It's probably their idea of a joke. You can only go across this border in a car. If you get a lift, have the driver put your rucksack in the boot of the car. If you have no car or can't find a lift to take you across, you'll have to go down to Figuig/Beni Ounif and cross there.

Algerian visas If the Algerian embassy in Rabat is closed, visas can be obtained from the United Arab Emirates embassy. There is an Algerian consulate in Oujda.

Egyptian visas These cost Dr 67.50 and are issued while you wait. There's no fuss or money-showing.

MONEY

US$1 = Dr 9.90
£1 = Dr 10.60

The unit of currency is the dirham = 100 centimes. Import/export of local currency is prohibited. There is a currency black market, but the rates are not much better than what is offered in the bank. You should beware of rip-offs when changing money on the street – all the usual tricks are employed to relieve you of it. If you are going to Algeria, however, it is worthwhile buying Algerian dinars in Ceuta, Melilla or Oujda before you go there. You can get US$1 = 10 to 15 dinar and Dr 1 = 2 dinar.

There are plenty of moneychangers doing the rounds in Oujda. Don't accept any 500-dinar notes, as they've been withdrawn from circulation and are now worthless.

There is usually no commission charged on traveller's cheques in banks. You can reconvert up to 50% of your dirhams on leaving, so long as you have bank receipts to cover the amount.

Petrol costs about £2 a gallon in Morocco, so if you're coming in from either Ceuta or Melilla, stock up as it's only £1.20 a gallon there.

LANGUAGE

Moorish Arabic, French and Spanish are the main languages. English is also spoken in many places. Spanish is more common in the north and French in the south.

GETTING THERE & AROUND

For many travellers Morocco will be their first taste of Africa, the other common points of entry being Tunisia and Egypt. The cheapest way to get to Morocco from Europe is to take one of the ferries from Spain to Tangier, Ceuta or Melilla. Details of these are to be found in the Getting There chapter.

Air

If your time is limited and you want to see as much of Morocco as possible, it's worth occasionally considering the internal flights offered by Royal Air Maroc. If you're 26 years of age or under, it works out particularly cheap as they offer 40% 'youth fare' discounts on the normal prices.

Road

Hitching is OK but demands a thick skin and considerable diplomatic expertise in the north, due to aggressive hustlers who simply won't take no for an answer or who feign outrage if you express lack of interest in whatever it is that they're trying to sell you – usually drugs. It's particularly bad on the road between Tetuan and

Tangier. In the south you can only go by road as far as Goulimime because of the war with POLISARIO in the Western Sahara. There are numerous army and police road-blocks where vehicles are searched for arms, though foreign-registered vehicles are often waved through. Also, because of tension between Morocco and Algeria due to the former's occupation of the Western Sahara, there are now only two possible crossing points between the two countries – Oujda/Tlemcen in the north and Figuig/Beni Ounif in the south. If you're driving your own vehicle, you can cross at either point. If you're on foot, you can only cross at Figuig/Beni Ounif. If you have a lift in a car which is crossing the Oujda/Tlemcen border, the date of your Moroccan entry stamp must be the same as that of the driver's. Algerian immigration check this, and if it's not the same then you'll be sent back and will have to go down to Figuig/Beni Ounif.

Make sure you have a valid 'Green Card' if you're driving your own vehicle. Police can fine you Dr 35 on the spot if you can't produce one.

There is a good network of buses all over the country, and departures are frequent. CTM (Compagnie de Transports au Maroc) is the main company. Between the main centres of population they generally offer luxury and 1st-class buses plus 2nd-class buses along some routes. On minor routes the buses are usually 2nd class. CTM buses are generally slightly more expensive (about 20%) but no faster than those of the smaller companies such as SATAS, Maroc Express and Schwartz. CTM generally have their own separate bus terminals in the various cities, often situated in the Ville Nouvelle – though not always.

A complete CTM bus timetable is outside the scope of this book, but a precis of the main routes follows:

From Casablanca

Casablanca-Rabat There are 16 buses daily in either direction. From Casablanca the first is at 5.45 am and the last is at 5 pm. From Rabat the first is at 3.30 am and the last is at 4 pm. The journey time is usually 1½ hours.

Casablanca-Rabat-Meknes-Fez There are seven to eight buses daily in either direction, plus several others which cover the shorter sector from Rabat to Fez. From either end the first is at 6 am and the last at 7 pm. The journey time is five hours.

Casablanca-Meknes-Ifrane-Azrou There are two buses daily in either direction at 6.30 am and noon from Casablanca, and 7.30 am and 1 pm from Azrou. Another bus which covers the Meknes-Azrou sector departs Meknes at 6 pm and Azrou at 9 am. The journey time is six hours.

Casablanca-Tangier-Tetuan-Ceuta On the Casablanca-Tangier sector there are five buses daily in either direction. From Casablanca the first is at 5.45 am and the last is at 11.30 pm. From Tangier the first is at 5.30 am and the last is at 11.30 pm. The journey time is 6½ hours. Between Casablanca and Ceuta (Sebta in Arabic) there is one bus daily in either direction at 9.30 pm. The journey time is 8¼ hours. This last bus branches off at Larache and does not go via Tangier.

Casablanca-Marrakesh-Agadir There are five buses daily in either direction between Casablanca and Marrakesh. From Casablanca the first is at 6.45 am and the last is at 7.30 pm. From Marrakesh the first is at 6.30 am and the last is at 8.50 pm. The journey time is four hours. Only one of these five buses completes the whole circuit (Casablanca to Agadir). From Casablanca it is the 3 pm bus and from Agadir it is the 4 pm bus. The journey time for this bus is 8¾ hours.

Casablanca-El Jadida-Safi There are seven buses daily in either direction. From Casablanca the first is at 5.45 am and the last is at 7.15 pm. From Safi the first is at 5 am and the last is at 4 pm. The journey time is 4¼ hours. There are other buses which travel only between Casablanca and El Jadida.

Casablanca-Essaouira-Agadir-Tiznit There are two buses daily in either direction which do the whole sector. They leave from either place at 5.30 am and 5.30 pm. The journey time is 12½ hours. Another bus (at 9 pm from Casablanca and 8.30 pm from Agadir) covers the Casablanca-Agadir sector. Finally, another bus goes only as far as Essaouira (at noon from Casablanca and 7 am from Essaouira).

From Fez

Fez-Marrakesh There are two buses daily in either direction at 6.30 am and 9.30 am from either place. The journey time is 8½ hours. The buses go via Beni Mellal, Kasba Tadla, Khenifra and Azrou.

Fez-Oujda There are two buses daily in either direction. From Fez they leave at 7.30 am and 12.30 pm. From Oujda they leave at 5 am and 11 am. The journey time is six hours.

Fez-Rabat There is one bus daily in either direction at 8 am from Fez and 6.30 am from Rabat. The journey time is 3½ hours.

Fez-Tangier There are two buses daily in either direction at 7.30 am and 6 pm from Fez and 8 am and 6 pm from Tangier. The journey time is 5½ hours. These buses go via Meknes, Souk El Arba, El Ksar and Larache.

From Meknes

Meknes-Rabat There is one bus daily in either direction at 7.30 am from Meknes and 4 pm from Rabat. The journey time is 2-1/2 hours.

From Marrakesh

Marrakesh-Agadir There are two buses daily in either direction at 6.30 am and 6 pm from either place. The journey time is 4¼ hours. The buses go via Chichaoua and Imintanout.

Marrakesh-Essaouira There is one bus in either direction daily at 1 pm from Marrakesh and 6.30 am from Essaouira. The journey time is 4½ hours and the fare is Dr 16.90.

Marrakesh-Zagora There is one second-class bus daily in either direction at 5.45 am from Marrakesh and 5 am from Zagora. The journey time is 10 hours.

From Tetuan

Tetuan-Tangier There are eight buses daily in either direction. From Tetuan the first is at 5 am and the last is at 5.15 pm. From Tangier the first is at 6.30 am and the last is at 8 pm. The journey time is 1½ hours and the fare is Dr 5.

Tetuan-Ceuta (Sebta) There are 10 buses daily in either direction. From Tetuan the first is at 5 am and the last is at 5.30 pm. From Ceuta the first is at 7.30 am and the last is at 8 pm. The journey time is 1½ hours and the fare is Dr 5.

Tetuan-Melilla There are two buses daily in either direction at 5 am and 7 pm from Tetuan and 7 am and 5 pm from Melilla. The journey time is 12 hours. The buses go via Chaouen, Bab Taza, Ketama, El Hoceima and Nador.

From Oujda

Oujda-Melilla There are four buses daily in either direction. From Oujda they are at 7 am, 10 am, 1 pm and 3.30 pm. From Melilla they are at 5 am, 7 am, 8 am and 2 pm. The journey time is about 4½ hours.

Oujda-Figuig There are three buses per week in either direction. From Oujda they leave at 6 am on Tuesday, Thursday and Sunday. From Figuig they leave at 6 am on Wednesday, Friday and Saturday. The fare is Dr 38.20 and the journey time is 7½ hours. The buses go via Bouarfa.

From Agadir

Agadir-Tiznit-Goulimime There are two buses daily in either direction at 6 am and 2 pm from Agadir and at 6 am and noon from Goulimime. The journey time is five hours. These buses are operated by SATAS.

Rail

As with the bus system, there is a good network of railways connecting all the main centres of population, but through services to Algeria were suspended many years ago because of political tension between Morocco and Algeria over the war in the Western Sahara. Trains are slow but cheaper than the buses if you go third class. There are first, second and third classes. Third class is quite an experience. It's often like a mobile farmyard.

Railway timetables are prominently displayed in the stations.

PLACES TO STAY

You can camp anywhere in Morocco so long as you have the permission of the owner, but there are a large number of official campsites which vary in price depending on the facilities provided. Tourist offices have details of their location. There are quite a number of Youth Hostels (Auberges de Jeunesse) in Morocco and, if you're travelling alone, they are among the cheapest places to stay. If you're travelling with a companion, it's often just as cheap to rent a simple room in a Berber-style hotel. The charge is usually Dr 10 per night with a Youth Hostel card or Dr 12.50 without. If you buy a Youth Hostel card in Morocco it will cost you Dr 35. Meals are not generally available at hostels and you have to pay extra for hot showers (cold showers are free). If you haven't got a Youth Hostel membership card, you can buy one for Dr 25. There are hostels at Asni, Asrou, Casablanca, Chaouen, Fez, Ifrane, Marrakesh, Meknes, Mohammadia and Rabat. Where there is no Youth Hostel, there is usually a Centre de Sportif/Jeunesse where basic accommodation can be found for a small charge. Sometimes it's just floor space, other times a bed. A cheap hotel will cost in the region of Dr 15 a single and Dr 20 a double.

If you stay with Moroccan friends in a private house, make sure that you never tell police or border officials, as it could lead to their arrest.

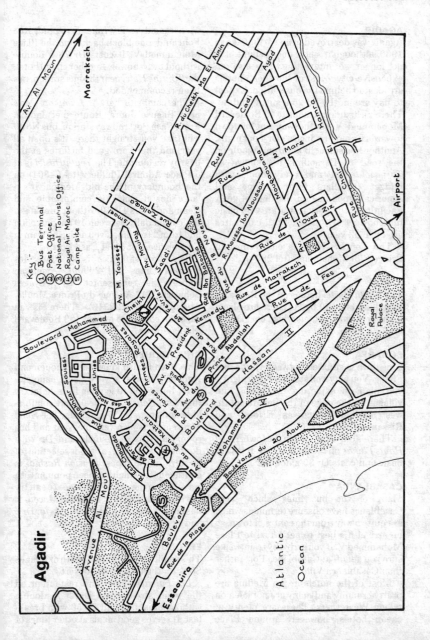

Agadir

Key:-
1. Bus Terminal
P. Post Office
N. National Tourist Office
H. Royal Air Maroc
S. Camp site

Marrakech

Essaouira

Airport

Atlantic Ocean

Av. Al Moun

Boulevard Mohammed

Av. M Youssef

Rue Mantar Souissi

Rue Nations Unies

Avenue Al Moun

Boulevard

Rue de la Plage

Boulevard du 20 Aout

Boulevard Mohammed

Rue du Gen Ketani

R. des Forces

Av. du Changui

Av. du President Kennedy

R. du Prince Abdallah

Hassan

Rue de Fes

Rue de Marrakech

Av. de l'Oued Ziz

Rue du Mongon 2 Mars

Rue du

Rue de Al Moussa Ibn Noussar

Rue Ibn Batouta 18 Novembre

R. Moulay Saadi

Rue Zaitoga

Cheikh

Rofales

Fevrier

Rue du Cheikh Ma El Amin

Cadi

Agad

Hamra

Rue Chair

Royal Palace

AGADIR

Agadir was destroyed in an earthquake in 1960; although it's now been rebuilt, it is no longer so interesting. It's also an expensive city. Most of the cheap hotels are located behind the bus station. Expect to pay around Dr 20-25 a single and up. There's a luxurious campsite off Boulevard Mohammed V on the way out of town towards Essaouira. It costs Dr 4 per night. Another lies some 20 km from Agadir on the road to Essaouira; it's known as *Tarhazoute Plage* and is very popular with budget travellers from Europe and America depending on the time of year. Facilities at the Tarhazoute are very basic (no showers or toilets). Both campsites are open all year.

The Tourist Office is on Avenue du Prince Sidi Mohammed (tel 2894).

AZROU

The *Youth Hostel* here is on the Route du Midelt and has 40 beds. There are also a number of cheap hotels which cost Dr 20-30 for a room.

BOUARFA

This town is situated between Oujda and Figuig. You may well stay here overnight if you plan on exploring the towns and villages on the edge of the Sahara south-west of here, such as Erfoud and Rissani.

There's only one hotel in the town, *Hotel Hauts Plakas* on the main street. It is very basic and costs Dr 30 a double.

CASABLANCA

Many of the bus lines which serve Casablanca have obscure terminals which are quite a way from the centre of town, so on arrival it's best to get a taxi to Place Mohammed V. If you arrive by train, make sure you get off at Casablanca Port rather than Casablanca Ville.

Most of the hotels in the Medina are pretty crummy and many are not keen on taking Westerners. There are plenty of cheap hotels, however, around Place Mohammed V. Try *Hotel Perigauld*, Rue Foucauld, one block back from the Place Mohammed V. It costs Dr 28 a double without own shower. Another cheap hotel, the *Touring Hotel* near the bus station, has been recommended.

The campsite here is *Camping Oasis* near Beause Jours, Route d'el Jadida. From Casa Port railway station, bus No 30 will take you straight there. It's open all year and there are good facilities at the nearby restaurant. The *Youth Hostel* is at 6 Place Admiral Philbert (tel 74301) on the boundary of the old Medina. It's a large hostel which is comfortable and clean and costs Dr 10 without breakfast. It's closed daily between 10 am and noon and from 2 to 5 pm. If you arrive by train in Casablanca, get off at Casa Port.

The Tourist Office is at Place des Nations Unies (tel 20909). American Express is represented by Voyages Schwartz, 112 Avenue du Prince Moulay Abdallah (tel 222946). There is an Algerian consulate here at 159 Boulevard Moulay Idriss.

CHECHAOUEN

This town is also known as Chaouen and Xauen. There's a very good campsite here, but if you're looking for a hotel try the *Hotel Sahra*. It's clean and comfortable and costs Dr 17 a double. The *Hotel Mauretaine* is also very pleasant and has rooms for Dr 10 a single and Dr 20 a double. They have a good selection of western music tapes. *Pension Rashidi* is another hotel which has been popular with travellers in the past. For a place to eat, try the restaurant next to the *Hotel Macou*. It has good couscous for Dr 6, salads for Dr 2 and desserts for Dr 1.

ERFOUD

This small town is located south of Ksar es Souk on the edge of the desert.

Les Palmiers hotel and restaurant on the main street costs Dr 25 a double without breakfast and Dr 50 with breakfast. It serves good meals at other times of

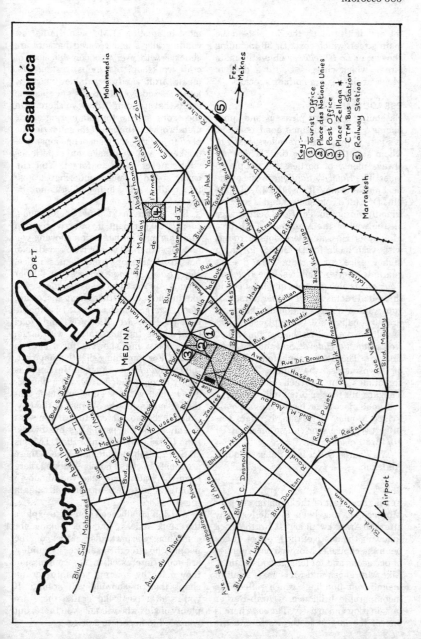

Casablanca

Key:-
1. Tourist Office
2. Place des Nations Unies
3. Post Office
+ Place Zellaga
5. Railway Station

the day. If it's full, try the *Ziz*, also on the main street, which costs Dr 30 including shower; or *La Gazelle*, again on the main street, which charges Dr 30 a double. Meals at the Ziz are nothing special.

ESSAOUIRA

Essaouira is a very pleasant and quiet fishing village with some good beaches. It's very popular with travellers, many of whom stay there a long time. There are always plenty of parties and people to meet. The *Hotel d'Atlantique* is one of the best places to stay. It costs Dr 22 a double plus Dr 1 for a cold shower and is run by a friendly Moroccan. The *Hotel Beau Rivage* on the wall of the Medina at 14 Prince Moùlay el Hassan offers double rooms with wash basin for Dr 25-35. Paying a higher price for a room here doesn't guarantee better facilities. The *Hotel du Tourisme* is also pleasant and has beds in three-bed rooms for Dr 10 per person. If you want a single or double they cost proportionally more. Other places recommended in the past are the *Des Amis Hotel, Hotel Majestic, Hotel du Sud* and the *Hotel Tangaro*. The latter is about four km south of town across the dunes. You can sometimes rent a beach hut near the Tangaro but they're often full.

A good place to eat here is the café at 23 Prince Moulay el Hassan. It offers set-price two/three/four course meals at Dr 10/15/20 respectively.

The Tourist Office is on Sahaat Moulay Abdallah.

FEZ

Fez is the oldest of the imperial cities of Morocco, having been founded shortly after the Arabs swept across North Africa following the death of the Prophet. It has been the capital of Morocco on a number of occasions and for long periods of time. Like Marrakesh and Meknes, it's full of magnificent buildings which reflect the incomparable brilliance of Arab-Berber imagination and artistry. The *souk* here is one of the largest in the world and the most interesting in Morocco. Its narrow winding alleys and covered bazaars are chocker with every conceivable sort of craft workshop, tea shops, restaurants, meat, fruit and vegetable markets, mosques and dye pits. But it's not just the sights that are going to draw you here. Add the exotic smells, the hammering of the metalworkers, the call of the muezzin, the need to jostle past a team of uncooperative donkeys, and you have an experience you're never going to forget. You can easily spend a week wandering through this endless labyrinth and still not be ready to leave.

The *Youth Hostel*, Rue Chefchaouen, costs Dr 10 per night. If you arrive by train there's a map in the station showing you how to get there. If you arrive by road, take bus No 19 six stops from the post office. *Hotel Savoy* is good value at Dr 20 per room – you can fit as many people as you like in one room. Other cheap places are *Hotel Atlantic*, which costs Dr 16 a double plus Dr 1 for a cold shower; and *Hotel CTM* above the bus station, with large, airy rooms and showers for Dr 27 a double. For something slightly upmarket, the *Hotel du Pacha*, Avenue Hassan II, is highly recommended at Dr 40 a double. The trouble with the above places is that they're not inside the old part of the city, which is the most interesting. If you want to stay in the old part, get a bus or taxi from the railway station or the CTM bus station to Bab Bou Jeloud, where there are plenty of cheap hotels. Walking there from the station will take you about 45 minutes. There are plenty of small cafés in this area too.

You don't really need a guide to explore the souk unless you are looking for something in particular. Most of the people who offer their services as 'guides' are more interested in the commission they make by steering you into certain shops than in showing you around. If you're after particular crafts, there are plenty of kids who will take you there, but you need to negotiate a price.

The National Tourist Office is on Boulevard Hassan II (tel 234 60). There's a Syndicat d'Initiative on Place Mohammed V (tel 247 69).

FIGUIG

The *Hotel Sahara* costs Dr 15 a double. You can buy good food cooked by 'Mohammed the Berber' for Dr 10 (couscous) or Dr 15 (tajine and tea). You'll meet plenty of other travellers, but there is no black market. If you find yourself here during Ramadan, make sure you do what the natives do and don't eat in public during the day. You'll be arrested otherwise, and dealt with according to Islamic Law.

GOULIMIME

The best time to come to Goulimime is in July for the annual camel fair, but it's worth visiting any time of year. Small caravans depart for the Sahara virtually every week. The weekly market is on Saturday. There is a good campsite here, but most people find accommodation on the roofs of cafés.

MARRAKESH

There can be few travellers who have not heard of Marrakesh. During the 1960s and 1970s it was the traveller's mecca, along with Istanbul and Kathmandu – and rightly so! This turn in the fame and fortunes of Marrakesh is only the most recent of the city's ups and downs. Sitting against the snow-capped backdrop of Morocco's highest mountain, the city has a scenic setting that would be hard to surpass. Once one of the most important artistic and cultural centres in the Islamic world, Marrakesh was founded in 1062 AD by Yussef Ibn Tashfin, who was responsible for introducing the underground irrigation canals which still supply the city's gardens with water. The city was razed by the Almohads in 1147, but was rebuilt shortly afterwards in the Omayyad style and became the capital of that empire until its collapse in 1262. For the next 300 years the focus of Moroccan brilliance in the arts moved to Fez, but after the defeat of the Merinids by the Saadians in 1520 Marrakesh once again became the capital of the empire. In time, decadence set in and Morocco was taken over by the Alaouites, who made Meknes their capital, but Marrakesh regained some of its former prestige when Moulay Hassan was crowned there in 1873.

Expect a lot of hassle from touts in Marrakesh, especially around the main square.

The focal point of Marrakesh is **Djemaa El Fna**, a huge square in the old part of town where many of the budget hotels are. The bus station is just outside the Medina walls at Bab Doukala, a 25-minute walk or Dr 5 taxi ride from the Place Djemaa El Fna. If you arrive by train you'll have to take a bus or taxi to the centre, as it's quite a long way out. Three hotels recommended in this area are the *Hotel Sahara, Hotel de France* and the *CTM Hotel*. The Hotel Sahara is very clean and costs Dr 30 a double or triple; the Hotel de France is Dr 15 a single; and the CTM Hotel facing the Djemaa El Fna is both clean and cheap. The letter has a flat roof which is perfect for watching the activity in the square below.

There is a *Youth Hostel* here which costs Dr 10 a night, but it is inconveniently located well out of town at Terrain de Camping Gueliz in the Quartier Industrielle, and the warden is renowned for being incapable of keeping his roving hands off women. Others have said that the hostel has bed bugs too.

The best place to eat in the evening is the *Djemaa El Fna*, which comes alive with food stalls and cafés. Avoid the *Snack Hippy*, which serves greasy, dirty omelettes.

The Tourist Office is on Place Abdelmoumen Ben Ali (tel 30258), but the staff are not very friendly. American Express is represented by Voyages Schwartz, Rue Mauritanie, Immeuble Mouataouakil No 1 (tel 33321).

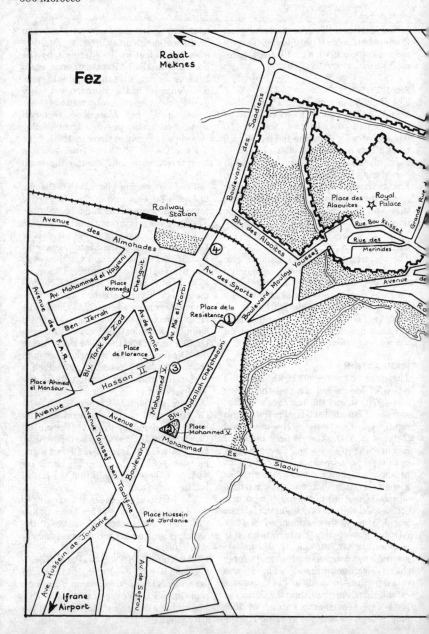

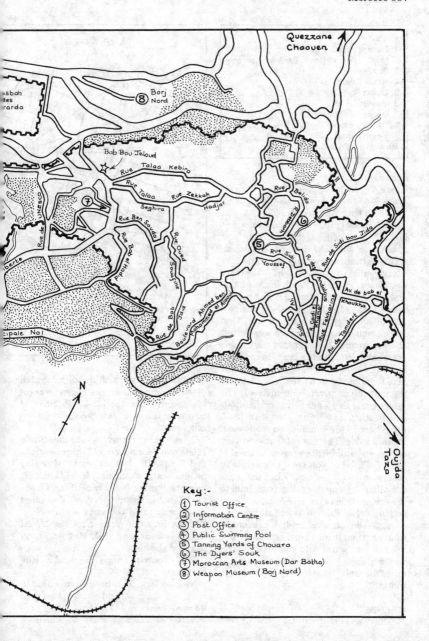

Key :-
① Tourist Office
② Information Centre
③ Post Office
④ Public Swimming Pool
⑤ Tanning Yards of Chouara
⑥ The Dyers' Souk
⑦ Moroccan Arts Museum (Dar Batha)
⑧ Weapon Museum (Borj Nord)

Key
1 Place Jemaa El Fna
2 Medina Post Office & Bank of Morocco
3 Bus Station
4 Royal Palace
5 Gueliz Post Office
6 Tourist Office
7 Gueliz Bus Station
8 Railway Station
9 Youth Hostel
10 Municipal Campsite

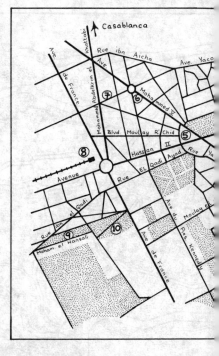

Excursions from Marrakesh

There is an incredible **donkey market** every Monday at nearby Ourika. Take a bus there from Marrakesh.

Mt Toubkal (4165 metres) is Morocco's highest mountain. Getting there from Marrakesh will take you through spectacularly beautiful countryside. First take a bus from Marrakesh to Asni – they leave every hour. There is a *Youth Hostel* at Asni if you want to stay there. From Asni you take a taxi to Imlil, where there is also a sort of hostel; but bring your own food unless you are happy with omelettes, cheese, bread and oranges, which you can get in Imlil. You can buy maps in Imlil and hire hiking boots. You can hire a guide here too, but you don't really need one to the first refuge (over 3000 metres). The refuge costs Dr 17 per night and has beds and heating, but bring your own food. From here to the summit you really need to hire a guide. There are streams virtually all the way up, but the water in them is fairly polluted so you need to sterilise it; otherwise you'll get sick. Also, there are two villages along the valley from Imlil to the refuge. One of them is Avenid, where you may be able to purchase bottled drinks. The other is Sidi Chamanoux, where bottled drinks are a certainty. You need to take water with you in summer if you're going up to the top, though you might be able to get away with this in winter.

MEKNES

Meknes was the capital city of the Alaouite dynasty, which grew after the fall of the Saadians, whose centre was at Marrakesh. Like the other old cities of Morocco, it has an extensive and fascinating souk.

The *Youth Hostel* is at the Stade Municipal near the *Hotel Transatlantique* and costs Dr 10 per night. Cooking facilities are available. *Hotel Volubilis* near the bus station is friendly and costs Dr 17, but it has no showers. Two other hotels which cost the same are the *Hotel Touring* and the *Hotel Excelsior*. *Hotel Regina* is also cheap at Dr 10 a single and has cold showers.

The Tourist Office is at 12 Rue Bouameur (tel 30508).

Meknes is a good base from which to visit the largest and best preserved **Roman ruins** in Morocco. They are situated at **Volubilis** some 63 km from

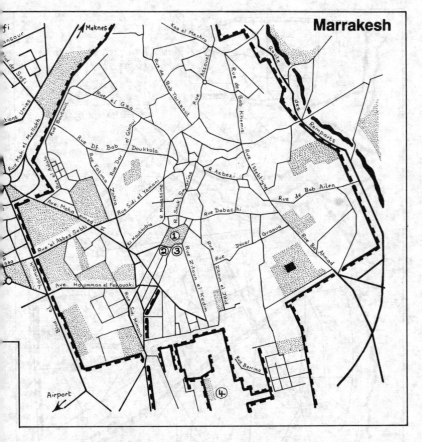

Marrakesh

Meknes. The ruins date from the early 1st century AD. To get there, you must first take a bus to Moulay Idriss (30 km). From there you'll probably have to take a taxi, unless you can find a lift with tourists who are going there.

OUARZAZARTE
This is a very interesting and large desert town over the pass through the Haut Atlas from Marrakesh.

There are plenty of hotels to choose from here. The *Hotel de Saada* has been recommended. It's next to the cinema on the Rue de la Poste and costs Dr 16 a single, Dr 27 a double and Dr 33 a triple. There are plenty of cafés along the Rue Mohammed V.

OUJDA
Oujda is the last Moroccan town before the Algerian border. There is an Algerian consulate here if you need a visa.

Hotel Royal is good value at Dr 53 a double, though a little expensive. Avoid staying at the *Café Hotel Hassania*, Rue de Casablanca, if at all possible. It's one of the filthiest hotels you will come across in

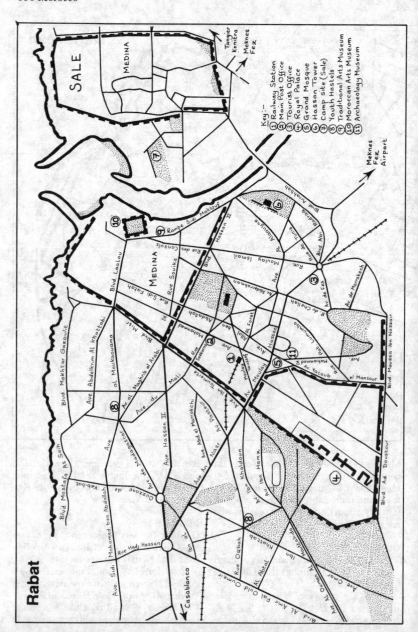

Rabat

Key:-
① Railway Station
② Main Post Office
③ Tourist Office
④ Royal Palace
⑤ Grand Mosque
⑥ Hassan Tower
⑦ Camp Site (Sale)
⑧ Youth Hostels
⑨ Traditional Arts Museum
⑩ Moroccan Arts Museum
⑪ Archaeology Museum

Morocco, and yet it still costs Dr 30 a double. There's a primitive campsite at Parc Lalla and rumour has it that there's now a *youth hostel* here.

RABAT

Rabat has only been the capital of Morocco for a relatively short time, but it has a history going back as far as Roman times. The Islamic city has its origins in the 12th century.

There is a campsite at *Sale Beach* which is open all year. Facilities include showers, toilets and a shop. The *Youth Hostel*, Boulevard Misr just outside the city walls, is a new place and costs Dr 10. Most of the cheap hotels are in the Medina off Avenue Mohammed V near the CTM bus station. Two which have been recommended are the *Hotel du Centre* (in the first alley on the right after the Medina walls) and the *Hotel Marrakesh*. *Hotel de France* opposite the CTM bus station is also popular. A good place to eat here is the *Restaurant Jamahiriya*, Avenue Mohammed V well inside the Medina. It has excellent food such as chicken for Dr 8.

The Tourist Office is at 22 Avenue d'Alger (tel 21252). There is a Syndicat d'Initiative on Rue Patrice Lumumba.

Embassies

Algeria
    46 Bd Tarip Ibnouzaid (tel 255 91)
Egypt
    31 Zankat El Jazair (tel 318 33)
France
    Avenue Mohammed V (tel 204 21)
Mauritania
    64 Zankat Oum Errabia (tel 709 31)
Senegal
    11 Avenue de Marrakech (tel 260 90)
Tunisia
    6 Avenue de Fez (tel 256 44)

The Algerian embassy may still be closed, so if you need a visa you must get it from the United Arab Emirates embassy, 8 Zankat Ifrane (tel 309 17) near the USA embassy. A one-month visa costs Dr 22 and takes two to three days to issue.

TANGIER

Tangier has been coveted for centuries as a strategic site for a fortress commanding the Straits of Gibraltar. The area was certainly settled by the ancient Greeks and Phoenicians and has been fought over ever since. Among those who have occupied it at one time or another are the Vandals (5th century), Byzantines (6th), Arabs (8th), Berbers (8th), Fatimids of Tunis (10th), Almoravids (11th), Almohads (12th), Merinids (13th), Portuguese (15th and 16th), Spanish (16th), British (17th), and the French (19th). In the 19th and early 20th century it was the object of intense rivalry between the French, Spanish, British and Germans, and this led to it being declared an international zone in 1923. Tangier retained that status until after WW II, when it was finally reunited with Morocco. All the various peoples who have settled here at one time or another have left their mark on the city, so it has an atmosphere which is markedly different from other Moroccan cities as far as architecture is concerned. The advent of tourism has wrought a completely different change – you can now no longer take one step without being besieged by someone who wants you to visit his shop, buy something, see something or whatever. It's total over-kill.

There are numerous cheap pensions along the Rue de Portugal and the Rue de la Plage as well as around the Petit Socco inside the Medina, especially along the Rue des Postes. Some which have been recommended are the *Hotel Chouan* (very basic), *Hotel Marrakesh* and *Hotel Miami*. Another good place is the *Hotel de Bretagne*, which costs Dr 18 a double. It's suggested you avoid the *Pension Monaco*, as there have been a lot of reports of rip-offs and women being molested. There is a *Youth Hostel* at 39 Rue San Francisco close to the Grand Socco.

Useful Addresses

Tourist Office
    29 Boulevard Pasteur (tel 39453)

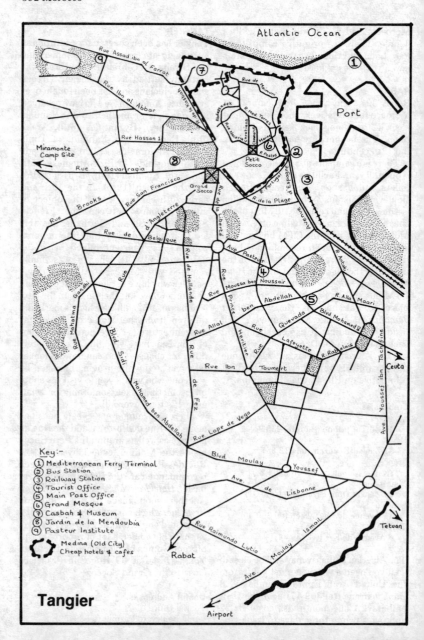

Tangier

American Express
    Voyages Schwartz, 76 Avenue Mohammed
    V (tel 33459)
Transmediterranea Ferries
    31 Rue Quevado (tel 34101)
Royal Air Maroc
    Place de France (tel 21501)

TETOUAN

There are quite a few cheap hotels in the
Medina. The best way to find them is to
ask one of the children who hang around
the bus station to show you where they are
(they'll want Dr 1-2 for this service).
Recommended are *Hotel Navarre* (good
value at Dr 10 a single), *Hotel Seville* and
Hotel Marrakesh. Be prepared for hustlers
in this town – there are lots trying to sell
dope.

OTHER

Here are a couple of travellers' tales from
this magic land to give you an idea of the
atmosphere you can expect if you decide
to stay for some time with local families.

THE MAGIC MOONS OF MOROCCO or GRAND-FATHERS ARE ALL THE SAME

Every night we sit on the roof to watch the sun
go down and the moon rise. The old man is
always there before us. He is lying on a
flattened brown sheepskin rug, his head
supported by one gnarled bony arm, his free
hand holding a long-stemmed pipe, carved in
concentric swirls of wood. Blue smoke drifts so
slowly from its small red clay bowl that it
appears to hang still in the air – until he begins
to speak. The harsh, guttural sound of his voice
scatters the smoke into thin strands of grey
which disappear over the rim of the roof into the
night sky. He must speak quite loudly, to
overpower the noise of his pink plastic, battery-
operated radio, acquired recently from Spain.
The thin, toneless screeching renders Arabic
and Spanish songs into raucous, exhausting
cacophony. He welcomes us 'La bas' (no harm),
and motions us to sit down. Mylie, my five-year-
old daughter, takes up her usual place, curling
up on her sleeping bag beside him, to watch him
smoking and talking. The pipe finished, he
expertly spits the glowing red ball of consumed
tobacco on to the concrete, places the pipe
reverently on the sheepskin and starts stroking
her hair, muttering and crooning a half-forgotten
lullaby. Her eyes close, their pale lashes
fluttering on to her freckled cheeks, quite
visible in the moonlight. His black eyes smile
and he starts talking to us again, pointing to
himself and her. 'Grandfather ... grand-
daughter,' he says over and over again.

'Yes,' we nod, smiling back, pleased that this
ancient Berber has so easily and naturally
assumed this role, one which transcends
language and cultural differences. Tomorrow,
he will play with her all day, teaching her the
finer points of 'cat's cradle' and 'jacks,' and
then, sitting in a rickety chair in the sun, watch
her ride her bicycle in the courtyard in front of
our adjoining houses. He will warn her of the
dangers of the well and of the huge black bees
which congregate around its dilapidated stone
walls. I know I need never worry about her while
he is in charge.

The moon is rising higher in the sky and the
stars in the Milky Way seem to merge into
liquid silver. Every now and then a shooting
star flashes into existence and burns itself out,
leaving a pale, vaporous after-image in the sky.
It is almost too bright to look.

The old man starts to tell us more about his
life. In Arabic, Spanish, fragmentary French
and even more explicitly with his face and
hands. Tales of the Spanish Civil War, guns,
people dying in the heat, the stench, Franco. He
is so graphically clear and concise that even the
murderous weapon of the radio seems to fade
into obedient silence. He pauses to light
another pipe, passes it with great ceremony to
my husband and begins again. His son, he
informs us, is studying medicine in England. It
hardly seems possible that this is so. The old
man, an illiterate peasant living here, in a tiny
fishing village in Morocco, and his son in a
hospital in London! He notices our raised
eyebrows – and hastily embellishes his story
with facts and figures. How many hectares of
land he sold, how many goats and chickens went
towards the educational fees and even how
many litres of milk had to be sold to obtain a
passport!

The mint tea arrives. Grandmother Berber
joins us for a moment to lay down the silver tray
and teapot and serve the first round in small
glasses. She cackles and laughs at the old man,
showing a mouth devoid of all but two teeth.
Her chin is marked with strange tattoos. She is
swathed in a multitude of red, white and blue
striped shawls and wears a huge belt of red
cotton around her waist. She suddenly dives

her hand into the belt, searching in the folds to produce, magically, a small brown paper parcel. For Mylie, she tells us, pointing and smiling – when she wakes up. I know what it is, a little mound of pink solidified sugar – *haloua,* which all Moroccan children love and which probably explains the state of their teeth! Grandmother vanishes down the stairs, leaving us to drink the sweet, sickly tea and to eat cakes made of honey and almonds.

It is very quiet now. I can hear the faint sound of the sea in the distance and the occasional clucking of a chicken, disturbed in its roost. The old man begins to doze. It is time to go. I pick up Mylie, sleeping so peacefully near her grandfather, and tiptoe down the stairs.

DAY-DREAMING IN MOROCCO

In 1976 my mother came to Morocco. I had been living there for almost 18 months and had quite accepted the fact that I was 'here,' not 'there,' a condition of being which always takes time. It requires an establishment of a routine of daily living in the same place of residence, the same faces becoming more familiar day by day, and a certain familiarity with the languages and customs of the country, before this state can be achieved.

My mother, however, straight from a North Shore suburb of Sydney, her first time away from home, never achieved this feeling, even after several months. Her first words were 'Why are all those men wearing bandages on their heads, dear?' Comments like these made me suspect that for her, the whole ordeal – as it sometimes was – of living in Morocco never progressed beyond a fantasy state, a wonderful and easy way of 'managing' in such a strange and foreboding culture. Often, while we were sitting around the table at night, in the gloom of the kerosene lamp, she would persevere with her embroidery and regale me with tales of what my family were doing in Sydney, the superb commodities they had bought at Grace Brothers and what my old aunt had said on the occasion of her 90th birthday. She talked as if they were 'there' for her, or so close that they were just outside the mud walls of the house, or at the very least within easy reach of a telephone call, not thousands of km away on some different planet, eons away in time, place and thought.

One of *my* fantasies, one I can call forth at will, is to revisit Morocco. I go to the small towns I know so well; retrace my steps along familiar alleyways; drop into shops, hotels,

cafés. I walk along river banks, revisit historical sites, hear conversations ... always about money and goods! In some ways these fantasies are better than the real thing. For instance, there is no fear – in this fantasy – of an arm appearing sneakily from a dark and pokey shop, grabbing me round the neck, and pulling me inside for whatever purpose – innocent or ill-intentioned. There is no problem with intense heat; no problem of finding a quenching drink, a drink without the possibility of wiping me out instantly with some form of hybrid cholera; no problem of persistent tiredness, unrelieved from exhausting attacks of fleas, mosquitoes and bed bugs; no problem of smells that twist the nostrils and dry out the mouth with their rancid intensity. I can float freely and absorb the myriad of colours which assail me from every angle. Remove the pain of travelling with one easy dream!

I think I'll go to Chaouen now, a small town of not many people, not far from Tetouan. In my fantasy I have the same choices I would in reality. The difference is that everything is easy. I can walk there following the river; take the bus with all the Berber women and their chooks and goats; or drive my little old Deux Chevaux and go bumping along the stony road, following the signposts, so often spelt in different ways – Chauen, Xauen, Chechauen, all English phonetic interpretations of the Arabic word. I arrive, neither footsore nor weary, no hassles like flat tyres or mechanical problems to frustrate or worry me. I follow the main road into the town square. I know that I will not stay in the hotel on the left of the square, as I had an unpleasant encounter (about money of course) with the manager last time – so I make straight for the one on the right-hand side, down a small side street. In Chaouen all the buildings are whitewashed regularly inside and out. The whitewash is so strong it is almost blue, so the houses resemble ice-blue meringues. I take my shoes off, walk inside and my feet are immediately covered in white powdery residue. It is so cool. I sit on the red rug in the middle of the floor, and look at the white footprints I have made on the carpet. The mint tea arrives instantly. I sip its sugary sweetness and listen to the jabbering Moroccans outside the door – their voices only just penetrating my consciousness, like a quietly buzzing swarm of bees in a field of wild poppies. I sit very still for a long time, waiting for the heat of the day to pass.

I leave my precious bag of belongings (in my

fantasy no-one will steal it) and wander back to the main square where the shadows of the few large trees are already lengthening. Behind the square there is a small path which will take me up the mountain. Effortlessly I glide along its stony way until I reach a small house about three-quarters of the way to the top. Abdullah the nightwatchman lives here, a nuggety brown man with arms and legs knotted with muscles and sinews. His job is to watch over the town and guard it. From whom? From what? I don't know. As always, he is at home, sitting on a small stool on the whitewashed floor, a large board on his knee and a lethal-looking knife in his hand. He looks up when he sees me and smiles. La bas! La bas! We greet one another. He is still chopping the *keif* (marijuana) on the board – deftly, quickly, years of practice in his technique, parting the seeds from the head. When he has enough seeds on the side of the board he calls to his lone white chicken which, comb flapping crazily over one eye, comes gyrating towards the dish where he has thrown the seeds. 'Chbeni jdad,' he says, 'the old chook. Hamuk,' he laughs, 'She's mad.' No wonder, when her diet is so strange!

Once again he tells me that he is the fastest walker in the whole of Morocco. Of how he used to walk to Marrakesh in less than a day and call in at Fez on the way back. I listen and nod sagely, praising his achievements. While he is speaking I look at Chaouen spread out below, an occasional green door floating in the white-blue ice. I drink more tea and leave him just before nightfall. Slowly I walk down the path; the sounds of the call to prayer floating up from the valley below. The song, amplified by a loudspeaker, is so clear, so pure. I imagine the thousands of Moslems, all over Morocco, kneeling on their prayer mats as they face Mecca and pray with the utmost concentration. It grows louder as I approach the town. Yet everything else is strangely quiet. I will go back to my room and wait for the night.

– Lyssa Hagen

Mozambique

Although the Portuguese first arrived here in the late 15th century, their early activities were restricted to setting up a number of trading enclaves and forts along the coast which acted as collection points for the gold, ivory and slaves derived from the interior. The African principalities of the interior remained independent and conducted vigorous trading systems of their own. Not until the late 17th century did colonisation begin in earnest with the setting up of privately owned agricultural estates on land granted by the Portuguese crown or obtained by conquest from African chiefs. Later in the 19th century, when the country's borders were defined during the European scramble for colonies, huge concessions were granted to foreign character companies which remained virtually autonomous until Salazar came to power in Portugal in the 1920s. A protectionist policy was introduced then in an attempt to seal off the colonies from non-Portuguese investment and to tie the colonies' economies in more closely with that of Portugal. The outbreak of the liberation wars in the 1960s, however, forced Portugal to abandon this policy and to lean again on its international allies.

Portuguese colonialism was a particularly backward and unbalanced affair. In the early days it relied heavily on slave labour, and when that was abolished in the 19th century forced labour took over. Every man was compelled to do six months' unpaid labour a year, and in the south most of the work force was sent to the mines of South Africa in exchange for the routing of a part of South Africa's transit traffic through Mozambican ports. There wasn't even a pretense of social investment in the African population, so that at independence 90% were illiterate and after the large-scale exodus of Portuguese specialists there were only 40 doctors left in the entire country. In the towns a sprawling service economy generated parasitic classes, and only towards the end of the colonial era did the large bureaucracy begin to take in Africans at its lower levels.

Resistance to colonial rule coalesced in 1962 with the formation of Frelimo, the Mozambique Liberation Front. It was made up of exiled political groups, radical intellectuals and underground organisations which had begun to operate inside the country. Frelimo launched its first military campaigns two years later and by 1966 had driven the Portuguese army out of much of the two northern provinces of Cabo Delgado and Niassa. But the Front wasn't just a guerrilla army. In the areas which it liberated, a socialist economy was put into operation and essential services were provided so that by the time the Portuguese were overthrown in 1975 Frelimo had accumulated a lot of experience in organising production and devising participatory structures. This guaranteed that the post-independence government would be committed to a policy of radical social change and not merely the Africanisation of the existing colonial structure.

Nevertheless, when independence was won in 1975, Frelimo was faced with an enormous task made even worse by the wholesale exodus of Portuguese skilled labour and capital, and by the looting and random destruction of machinery, heavy

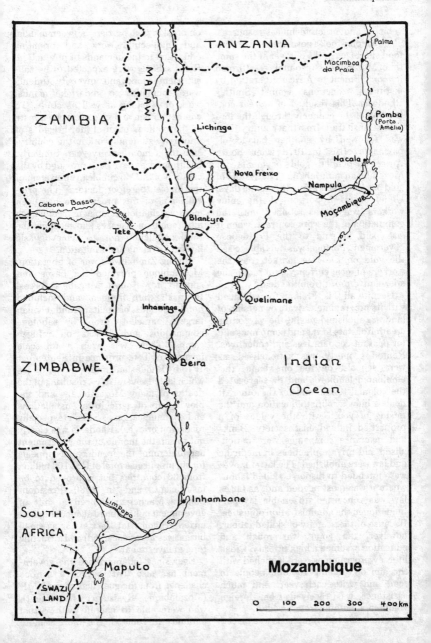

Mozambique

vehicles and other technical resources. The economy took a nose-dive and serious food shortages broke out, yet at the same time, Mozambique resolutely re-affirmed its commitment to African liberation by instituting sanctions against Smith's Rhodesia. This resulted in a great contraction of the economy through the loss of the transit trade from that country. This was followed by another balance-of-payments crisis in 1978 when South Africa suspended gold payments for Mozambican mine labour. (The system of gold payments was set up in colonial days. Under it, a proportion of the mine workers' wages was retained until the completion of the work contract, when it was paid in gold to the Portuguese government. Portugal was thus able to sell the gold on the free market, pay the workers in local currency, and retain the speculative profit from the deal.)

Despite all this, Frelimo forged ahead with its programme. Private ownership of land was abolished, paving the way for the creation of state farms and companies and for peasant cooperatives and collectives. Rented property was nationalised, as were schools; on the one hand, this eliminated landlords and de-segregated the colonial towns, and on the other, it dealt a blow at elitist education and the raising of youth with the values of a propertied individualist society. Banks and insurance companies were nationalised and private practices in medicine and law were abolished. The latter moves were intended to disperse skilled labour where it was most needed and, as far as law was concerned, to enable lay participation in the administration of justice. Because of the scarcity of skilled labour, however, the going was rough and education assumed a high priority. Crash literacy programmes were launched with the aim of teaching 100,000 people to read and write each year, and much assistance was received from foreign volunteers, notably from Sweden.

At the same time, emphasis was placed on breaking the barriers between manual and intellectual work and orienting education to the demands of production. Rural schools were expected to be self-sufficient in food, and university students were compelled to undertake manual work or teaching as well as study. To combat elitism and give everyone a taste of the realities of rural life, brigades of university students work in the countryside for a month every year. Similarly, health services have been provided by the creation of the Mozambican equivalent of the Maoist 'barefoot doctors.' The principal aim of this programme has been mass vaccination campaigns against the most common diseases and teaching the rural population how to achieve basic levels of hygiene and sanitation.

During Zimbabwe's war of liberation, Mozambique provided the bases and support for Robert Mugabe's forces. Reprisals were frequent and included bombing raids of military and civilian targets, parachute drops by sabotage commandos and attacks on refugee camps. There was even a full-scale invasion of Tete province in September 1979 by Rhodesian ground and air forces which lasted several days, resulting in the deaths of many Mozambicans and the blowing up of agricultural installations and communications systems (especially roads and bridges). Rhodesia was clearly out to sap the morale of the government and undermine the economy. UN appeals for aid produced a total of US$102 million from 33 countries but it proved to be insufficient, and in 1980 President Samora Machel announced a shift of government policy aimed at encouraging a mixed economy (at least as far as small businesses were concerned) and attracting foreign investment.

Ever since independence the government has also had to face a serious challenge from the guerrillas of the NMR (Mozambique Resistance Movement), who were able to operate with virtual impunity in some of the more remote provinces. They were responsible for blowing up bridges, oil pipelines and railway lines as well as occasionally planting bombs in Maputo itself. There was strong evidence that they were supported by the South African regime, though naturally the latter denied this. Machel's support for exiled members of the ANC (the banned South African black movement) also brought retribution in the form of an air-borne raid by the South African air force. In this raid a jam factory on the outskirts of Maputo (which the South Africans claimed was being used as an ANC headquarters) was destroyed.

Machel claims that since independence, pressure – both direct and indirect – from South Africa has cost the country US$333 million and caused the destruction of 900 rural shops, 495 primary schools, 86 health posts and 140 communal villages. In the end this became intolerable, and with the country's economy on the brink of collapse Machel was forced to negotiate with the South Africans. In early 1984, an accord was signed whereby Machel promised to cut off support for the ANC if the South Africans ditched the NMR and provided Mozambique with substantial aid. Although some members of the white regime suggested at the time that there were no real benefits in the accord for South Africa, it was an obvious diplomatic coup. It must also have been obvious to them that, in terms of lives and cash, it's much cheaper to control a neighbouring country through a network of economic relationships than to destabilise it (though, of course, they did that anyway as part of the softening-up process).

Since the reconstruction effort which faced the new government was so vast, Mozambique has not encouraged tourism and until recently visas were very difficult to get. This is beginning to change and, though it's still not easy, quite a few travellers are going there these days. If you decide to go, be prepared for very limited services – suspended road and rail connections, sporadic electricity and water supplies. Food is scarce and many shops are closed. Many hotels are often full of residents.

FACTS

There are many different tribal groups in Mozambique, including the Shona, the main tribal grouping in Zimbabwe, but the largest group is the Makua-Lomwe, which accounts for some 40% of the population. The land consists of a wide coastal plain rising to mountains and plateaux on the Zimbabwean, Zambian and Malawian borders. Two of Africa's major rivers – the Zambesi and Limpopo – flow through the country. The huge Cabora Bassa dam is sited on the Zambesi. The dry season runs from April to September, during which time the climate is pleasant. In the wet season it's hot and humid with temperatures ranging from 27°C to 29°C on the coast but cooler inland.

VISAS

Visas are required by all. They can be obtained in Dar es Salaam (Tanzania), Lusaka (Zambia) and Mbabane (Swaziland). There are also embassies in the USA and Portugal. There is an embassy in Harare (Zimbabwe), but visas are only issued there for Zimbabwean residents and nationals (the embassy is at 152 Rhodes Avenue). In Lusaka the embassy is near the university and one-month tourist visas cost Kw 6. There's no fuss, but you must state the provinces which you intend to visit. Some travellers received visas the next day; others have had to wait for three days. The embassy staff are friendly but they have no information on the country. Visas are also reputed to be easy to get in Dar es Salaam, though they may take seven days to come through. In Mbabane (embassy near the Highland View Hotel) you have to fill in two forms, provide three photos and the name of a person you will be staying with or confirmation of a hotel booking. Visas can take two weeks to issue.

You can, if you have a certain amount of determination, apply for your visa direct either by registered mail (Ministerio de Negocias Estrangeiros, Caixa Postal 290), Maputo) or by telex (6374). The formidable list of details you need to supply are: your full name (and maiden name if a married woman); your father's and mother's full names; the country, place and date of your birth; nationality; sex; marital status; your passport type, number, place and date of issue and validity; permanent home address; profession; name of your firm or organisation and the position you hold there; what type of work your firm does; whether you have ever been to Mozambique before and, if so, the dates of entry and departure; whether you have ever been a resident in Mozambique and, if so, your residential address and the firm or organisation which you belonged to; the names, addresses, telephone numbers, nationalities and relationships of any friends or relatives in Mozambique; your proposed length of stay and proposed dates of entry and departure; the address of the place you intend to stay; the name of any religious or associated organisation to which you belong; the reason for your proposed visit; and the address to which a reply should be sent.

If you think that's a bit rude you might be right, but the reason there is such a poor success rate for visa applications by post is that not enough information is provided. Telexes in Portuguese are sometimes dealt with immediately. The response to telexes in English normally takes a day or two.

Don't take photographs of public buildings or soldiers. They're naturally very sensitive about things like that.

So long as your visa is in order, there is no problem crossing the border at Mutare (Zimbabwe). The baggage search going in or coming out is usually cursory. You are supposed to change some money at the bank on entry, but it's usually only a small amount (US$20-30 is generally acceptable).

Entry formalities at the international airport in Maputo are much stricter.

MONEY

US$1 = 40 metacal (official rate)

The unit of currency is the metcal (plural metacal) = 100 cents. Import/export of local currency is prohibited. Customs officials are usually very strict about this and you may be thoroughly searched. Others have said that customs and immigration are among the most easy-going on the continent. There is a lively black market for hard currency, but you need to be very discreet when changing as there are heavy penalties. Asian traders are the best people to approach. The current rates are US$1 = 800-1000 metacal (that's not a printing mistake!). There is a smaller market for Zimbabwean dollars in Beira, (Z$1 = 500-600 metacal). Rands would also be acceptable.

Currency declaration forms are not issued at the land borders.

The airport tax for international flights is 350 metacal. The tax for internal flights has been abolished.

LANGUAGE

Portuguese is the official language but there are many African languages and, in the more remote provinces, you may not find many people who speak Portuguese.

GETTING THERE & AROUND
Air

Due to the current exchange rate, flying is incredibly cheap and the obvious answer to long-distance travel. Most of the main towns have an airport and both Beira-Maputo and Beira-Pemba cost well under 4000 metacal, plus you even get a semi-decent meal on the flights. Flights are frequently delayed or cancelled, so it's advisable to get to the airport well in advance as overbooking is common. Book your tickets as far in advance as possible, as there is heavy demand for them. There are daily flights in either direction between Beira and Maputo (3850 metacal, takes one hour). To other towns (Quelimane, Tete, Lichinga, Nampula and Pemba) the service is less frequent, though usually it's offered two or three times per week. Bank receipts only have to be shown for international flight tickets.

Road

Hitching is good despite what people might tell you. Drivers will stop and offer you lifts even over short distances, and will often go out of their way to help you. Between the Zimbabwean and Malawian frontiers and Beira, however, you may be in for a long wait (days) since there is so little traffic, and the buses which do exist are in bad shape and very unreliable. Treat all schedules as a figment of the imagination.

From Malawi & Zimbabwe

The railway lines between Beira and the Malawian and Zimbabwean frontiers are probably the best bet if you're entering from the north, but services can be disrupted for weeks on end due to sabotage by the NMR (the threat should lessen following the accord between Mozambique and South Africa, and a recent report suggested that Frelimo and the rebels have also reached an agreement).

The Chicualacuala crossing between Zimbabwe and Mozambique is closed even though there is usually a daily train between there and Maputo. Also, the road between Beira and Maputo is presently off-limits due to terrorist activity (this may change in the near future).

If there are no problems with sabotage, there is generally a bus from Milanje (Malawi/Mozambique border) to Quelimane on Tuesday and Saturday. From Quelimane to Caia there is a daily bus, and from Caia to Beira there is a daily train (if it's not a passenger train you're likely to get a free ride on a freight train).

There is a daily train from Beira to Mutare (Zimbabwe/Mozambique border) when the line is intact. Sabotage normally takes place on the upper sections of the track. Enquire in Harare before you set off. If the train is not operating, there is a bus between Manica (on the Mozambique side of the border from Mutare in Zimbabwe) which is supposed to go daily but breakdowns are frequent. It costs 179 metacal.

From South Africa

If you're coming in from the east, the best bet is to take the train between Johannesburg and Maputo via Ressano Garcia. There is a daily train in either direction which leaves Johannesburg at 6.15 pm and Maputo at 4.35 pm. The journey takes about 17 hours and costs Rand 34.20 (1st class), Rand 23.10 (2nd class) and Rand 10.25 (3rd class).

From Swaziland

There are twice-weekly buses between Mbabane (Swaziland) and Maputo operated by *Oliveiras Transportes e Turismo*. They leave on Friday and Sunday from Maputo, but hitching is easy too. Customs and immigration at Namaacha are very easygoing (one traveller had no bank receipts, no currency form and his visa was out of date but there were no problems).

From Zambia

From Zambia the best point of entry is Chanida/Cassacatiza just south of Chipata. A new road has been built between the two border towns. If you come this way you must be prepared for long waits, as there is very little traffic. The customs people are friendly and may let you stay with them while you wait for transport. There used to be three buses per week from Cassacatiza going south, but don't rely on them.

To Tanzania

If you're thinking of heading north to

Tanzania, here is one possible route which a young Australian woman travelling alone took:

The first leg was a flight from Beira to Porto Amelia (Pemba), which cost 3400 metacal. There is no bus service. In Pemba, ask for the Swedish teachers at the local high school. They'll put you up for 250 metacal but prefer food in kind. Next she took a bus from Pemba to Mocimboa da Praia for 150 metacal. The bus takes all day. There's only one *pensao* in town which costs 140 metacal per night. From Mocimboa da Praia there are no buses going north and she hitched to Palma (85 km) – very little traffic. She stayed at the *Palma Hotel* on the beach there for 200 metacal per night including two basic meals (fish and rice). The staff at the hotel were very friendly, as were the immigration officials who helped her find a guide for the 50-km walk to the Tanzanian border. The guide charged 200 metacal plus a few gifts like cigarettes and a bar of soap. On the other side of the River Ruvuma there is a village (Mwambo) where you can arrange transport to Mtwara. From Mtwara there are buses and flights available to Dar es Salaam.

We've heard of a partial alternative route to the above which will take you as far as Mocambique town. First take a flight to Nampula and go by rail to Lumbo, changing at Rio Monapo. The rail fare is 74 metacals (2nd class). At Lumbo there is a connecting bus to Mocambique operated by *CFM* (Caminhos de Ferro de Mocambique). There are also buses from Nampula to Mocambique – try your luck at the Rodoviaria.

BEIRA

This is one of Mozambique's most important ports and the terminal of the oil pipeline and railway line to Zimbabwe and Malawi. There are some beautiful beaches and you'll rarely meet another traveller here.

One of the cheapest places to stay is the *Estoril Hotel*, which, despite its price, is said to be better than the more expensive Dom Carlos. A single here costs 250 metacal per night and the hotel is a good place for meeting people. The food is excellent (prawns, pork, chicken, fish) and there's always plenty of beer. For most of the day there is no running water, but each of the rooms has a bathroom, a refrigerator and a gas cooker (though there's no gas available). There is a self-service restaurant at the hotel where you can get a meal for 200 metacal including a beer. Most of the people at reception speak English.

Hotel Dom Carlos is along the beachfront to the north of town near the lighthouse. Bus No 3 to 'Macuti' will get you there if you don't want to take a taxi. It costs 1500 metacal a double and includes an egg for breakfast. A meal here costs 480 metacal (three courses) or a bit less if food is in short supply that day. Beer is rationed to one bottle per person per meal and costs 45 metacal (large bottle). It's worth going for a meal here at weekends, as they serve Portuguese wine on Saturday and Sunday evenings.

Hotel Mocambique closer to the centre costs 470 metacal a single and 1200 metacal a double, but breakfast consists of 'two dry rolls and rubbery, powdered egg and costs an extra 150 metacal.' The lift works only occasionally and all the cooking is done on a wood fire outside the hotel (the Portuguese apparently destroyed the kitchens). Lunch or dinner here costs 350 metacal and consists of noodle soup followed by fish and noodles (it's the same every day).

Hotel Embaixador costs 1400 metacal a double. There is hot water all day, only one of the lifts works some of the time, the food is said to be poor, there's often no beer and the place has heaps of cockroaches. Only one of the people at reception speaks any English and he's often not there.

There are a number of smaller hotels and *pensao* but they're often full and, in any case, you need to be in an hotel which provides food. Otherwise you are limited to food bought from the foreign currency shop, where goods have to be paid for in hard currency (expensive). If you do decide to plump for a cheap place, try either the *Messe dos Trabalhadores* one block from the Hotel Embaixador, or the *Pensao Imperio*. They both cost around 100-200 metacal a single.

The *Voleiro* by the roundabout at the coast has been recommended as a good restaurant if you like pork and meali meal. They also have good bread.

There are two nightclubs here which are worth visiting if you're looking for some action or want a beer without having to buy a meal. The *Oceana* near the Grand Hotel is open every night except Monday from 9 pm to 4 am and every day for lunch. Entry costs 500 metacal. If you intend to go at night you must reserve a place the day before. Good prawns are available here at night, and beef (sometimes) at lunch.

The market has a good selection of vegetables but there are no other food shops in Beira except for bakeries and the *Interfranca* shop where you must pay in hard currency. They take traveller's cheques (including Zimbabwe dollar cheques but not cash) and give you change in US dollars and rand.

There are a few public buses and an even smaller number of taxis around town, but they're not worth waiting for as schedules are erratic and the buses very overcrowded indeed. Hitch-hike instead; it's very easy.

The beaches are open for a fair stretch to the north and a little to the south of town. They get cleaner as you head north (the one close to the Hotel Dom Carlos is good), but you can't go too far north as they are closed off by the army.

INHAMINGA

Try the hotel near the station which costs 420 metacal a double.

MAPUTO

Maputo is the capital of Mozambique. If you have an old map with you, it may still be marked as Lorenco Marques (the old Portuguese name). I even have one edition of a Bartholomews map which marks it as Can Phumo, though I suspect they got that one mixed up with one of their South-East Asian maps!

Hotel Cordoso is very pleasant and privately run. It's more expensive than the ordinary run-of-the-mill place, though you can still pay in metacal. The only disadvantage is that it's a long way from the centre. The *Pensao Central*, Avenida 25 Julho just above Independence Square (tel 24476), is still popular and good value at 660 metacal a double including breakfast, lunch and dinner! There is hot water and the place is clean. The food served here is better than that at some of the more expensive hotels. It's run by 'a bossy Portuguese woman.'

The other hotels here are government-run and cost 900-5000 metacal a double. *Hotel Tourismo* charges 1030 metacal a single with own bathroom, hot water and telephone room service. The food is quite good and if you get there early you have the choice of meat or fish, otherwise only the latter. The problem with this hotel is that it has 12 floors (the dining room is on the 11th floor) and the lifts often don't work. It's possible to telephone Europe (or elsewhere) from your hotel room for around 500 metacal – a bargain! Others include *Hotel Mozambicano* and *Hotel Tivoli*. A few travellers have suggested you avoid the *Hotel Polana*, as you have to pay in hard currency (which makes it expensive); and the *Hotel Santa Cruz*, which is said to be 'awful.'

The cheapest food in Maputo is to be found at the *Self* restaurant at the University of Eduardo Mondlane. The best Mozambican food is at *Matchedje*, Avenida Mao Tse Tung. The *Coxemira*, Avenida Ho Chi Minh, offers good, cheap East African and Asian dishes. The restaurant at the airport does superb

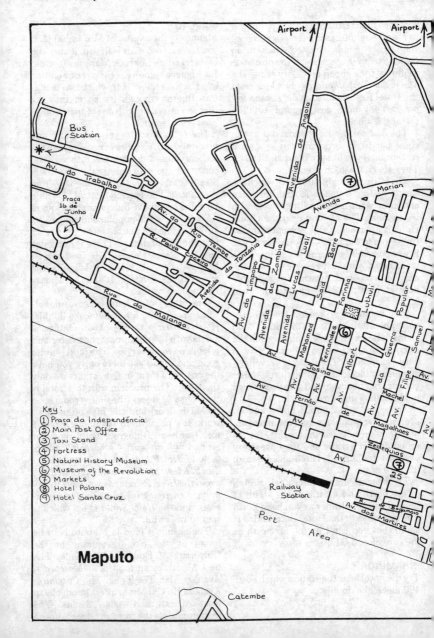

Key:
1. Praça da Independéncia
2. Main Post Office
3. Taxi Stand
4. Fortress
5. Natural History Museum
6. Museum of the Revolution
7. Markets
8. Hotel Polana
9. Hotel Santa Cruz

Maputo

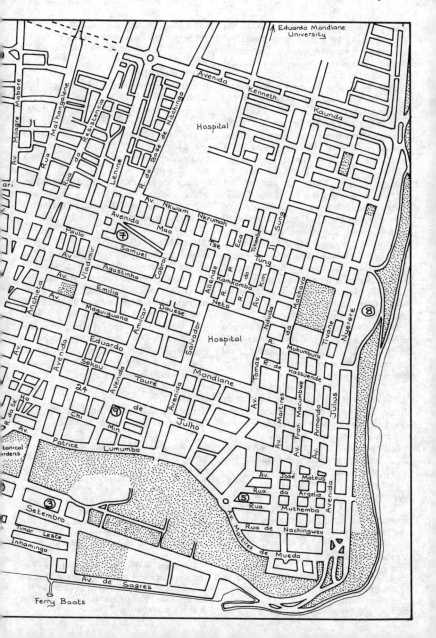

pizzas. At many of the other restaurants you may have to queue for a meal, but beers aren't rationed here like they are in Beira. Matches, however, are almost impossible to find.

If you're looking for some music or you want to buy seafood, take the early morning boat across the harbour to Costa del Sol (about five km north). There are good beaches there and a good cosmopolitan restaurant where you can get a meal for about 150 metacal. There is live music at weekends. The fishermen sell straight from the boats here and you can get two dozen prawns for about US$4. Another good place to visit is the island of Inhaca, a four-hour boat ride (50 metacal) from Maputo. The island is visible from Maputo. It's suggested that if you want to stay there, you make prior reservations at the only hotel on the island through the Mozambique Information Agency, PO Box 896, Maputo (tel 30795). The hotel isn't cheap and you must pay for full board, which costs 2000 metacal.

Don't sleep on the beaches unless you want to get arrested and interrogated as a suspected spy. The island has a good nature reserve and a well-kept marine biology museum.

In Maputo itself you might like to visit the **Museum of the Revolution**, Avenida de Julho. It costs 10 metacal entry, but you really need to go with a guide unless you can read Portuguese. A lively and colourful place to visit is the **market** on Avenida 25 de Setembro – fruit, vegetables, spices and basketwork.

Bus Nos 22, 13 and 14 go to the airport.

The beaches in Maputo are very dirty and it's difficult to get buses south where the better beaches are located.

Useful Addresses
Tourist Office
    1179 Avenida 25 de Setembro (tel 5011). Helpful with out-of-Maputo hotel bookings and information.
Banco de Mocambique

    Avenida 25 de Setembro 1695
LAM terminal (Mozambique national airline)
    Avenida 25 de Setembro 1747 (tel 26001)

MOCAMBIQUE
If there's any possibility of getting to this town, you should do so. It's a fascinating place full of mildewed 17th– and 18th-century mosques, churches, palaces and Portuguese colonial buildings. If you like these sort of old relics and the time-warp atmosphere which goes with them, don't miss this place.

Stay at the *Posada de Mocambique*, which costs 250 metacal a single and serves meals for 50 metacal each. It's highly recommended.

QUELIMANE
This is a small port north of Beira. The cheapest place to stay here is the *Hotel 24 de Julho*, Avenida Samuel Magaia 216, which charges 100 metacal for a bed in the dormitory. Otherwise there is the *Hotel Chuabo*, with rooms for 1000 metacal. The Chuabo has one of the port's few restaurants. It's normally only open to residents but no-one is going to refuse you. A meal there costs 160-200 metacal and the food is good.

OTHER
Regarding the availability of goods, two travellers had this to say recently:

Mozambique makes Tanzania seem like a prime holiday resort. It's one thing having metacal to spend, quite a different thing finding something to spend them on! Great if you like *perri perri* sauce, furniture polish or wooden buttons. There are some very nice carvings available but it's impossible to post them home from Mozambique, as you need a permit to send anything other than a letter out of the country. Maputo was a great place for international telephone calls.

There are two foreign currency stores – one small one in Beira and a large one in Maputo called the *IF* (Interfranca) in 24 Julho up the hill from the Pensao Central. The one in Beira is near the post office.

Namibia

In the carve-up of Africa among the European powers towards the end of the 19th century, Namibia became a German colony except for the enclave of Walvis Bay which the British had annexed for the Cape Colony in 1878. The indigenous tribes – the Herero, Nama and Ovambo – vigorously attempted to preserve their independence. When it became clear by 1904 that this couldn't be done by peaceful means, the Herero rose in rebellion, to be joined later that year by the Nama. The colonial authorities responded with over a year of open genocide in which some 60% of the black population of the south and centre were wiped out, including 75 to 80% of the Herero. The Ovambo were luckier and managed to avoid conquest until they were decisively beaten by Portuguese forces in 1915. In that same year the Germans surrendered to a South African military force, and at the end of WW I South Africa was given a mandate to rule the territory by the League of Nations. Namibia continues to be occupied by South Africa to this day despite UN condemnation and numerous attempts to set up an independent government there. Meanwhile, the guerrilla war mounted by SWAPO (South West Africa People's Organisation) continues to escalate. This had led to the stationing of 50,000 South African troops there, as well as a number of full-scale invasions of southern Angola by those troops on the pretext of wiping out guerrilla bases there.

South African intransigence over Namibia is based on its fears of having yet another antagonistic government on its doorstep and on losing the income which it derives from the mining operations there. The country is rich in minerals such as uranium, copper, lead and zinc and is the world's foremost source of gem diamonds. These are all mined by South African and other western multi-national companies under a very generous taxation scheme which enables them to export up to third of their profits every year. The labour is supplied by black Namibians, who work in bad conditions at rock-bottom wages and are recruited under what is, to all intents and purposes, a forced-labour system. Forced labour has been the lot of the Namibians ever since the Germans arrived, and was one of the main factors which led to mass demonstrations and the development of nationalism in the late 1950s.

Having secured a mandate over the country, South Africa proceeded to extend its own racist legislation and practices over Namibia. By the 1960s, the bulk of the country's viable farming land had been parcelled out into over 6000 farms owned by white settlers. Black workers and their families were restricted to their place of work by pass and labour laws, and 'desertion' was treated as a criminal offence. The rest – women and children, the elderly, the sick and the unemployed – were dumped in reserves which they could only leave with a work-seeker's pass. The more populous Ovamboland in the north was sealed off and left to stagnate while a pernicious labour contract system was imposed on migrant labour. Under this system a worker has no choice of employer, no say over wage rates or the length of the contract period and no right to give notice. Even tribal leaders in the reserves were appointed by the South Africans regard-

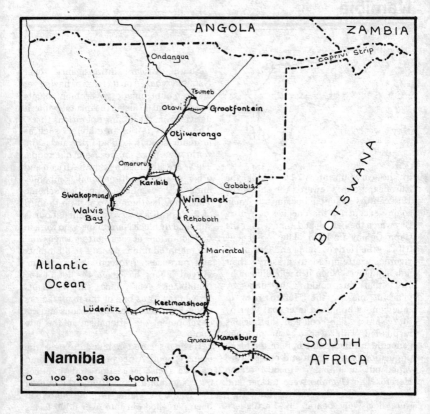

ANGOLA ZAMBIA

Ondangua

Tsumeb

Otavi Grootfontein

Otjiwarongo

Omaruru

Karibib Gobabis

Swakopmund Windhoek

Walvis Bay Rehoboth

Atlantic Ocean Mariental

BOTSWANA

Lüderitz Keetmanshoop

Grunaw Karasburg

Namibia

SOUTH AFRICA

Caprivi Strip

0   100   200   300   400 km

less of whether they had any popular support or not.

Opposition to South African rule began to grow rapidly in the 1950s. A number of political parties were formed, strikes were organised (not only among workers in Namibia but also among contract labourers who had been sent to work in South Africa), and support was sought from the United Nations. By 1960 most of these parties had merged to form SWAPO, which took the issue of South African occupation to the International Court of Justice. The proceedings there were inconclusive and in 1966 the UN General Assembly voted to terminate South Africa's mandate and set up a Council for

Namibia to administer the territory. At the same time, SWAPO launched its campaign of guerrilla warfare.

The South African government reacted with its typical mixture of arrogance, deceit and brutality. Casting aside international opinion, security forces fired on demonstrators, arrested thousands of activists, tortured many of them and banished the rest to the reserves. At the same time they began to pump funds into white and compliant black organisations which would pave the way for a unilateral exercise in self-determination. In this way they hoped to upstage the UN and discredit SWAPO by presenting to the world what appeared to be a representative government which enjoyed support from all sections of Namibian society. In terms of stalling for time and currying the favour of the five western members of the UN Security Council who continued to veto sanctions against South Africa, it was a major success. It lost credibility, however, when Dirk Mudge – the leader of what became known as the Turnhalle government – made it known that SWAPO's participation would be severely limited and that defence and foreign affairs would remain under the control of South Africa. South African interests stretched far beyond Namibia's boundaries, on the other hand, and the breathing space was used to mass troops and equipment on the border with Angola. In 1975 the South Africans launched a full-scale invasion of southern Angola in support of UNITA with the aim of crushing the MPLA. The attempt was a failure and by March 1976 the troops had been withdrawn.

The MPLA victory considerably inspired SWAPO and even while South African forces remained inside Angola a major guerrilla campaign was launched in Ovamboland. By late 1977 SWAPO had not only established semi-liberated zones complete with a parallel administration but had begun to mount attacks on fixed South African military positions. Meanwhile the five western members of the UN Security Council took the initiative of trying to bring the two sides together in the hope of getting an agreement which would lead to independence. The three main bones of contention were the withdrawal of South African security forces, the status of Walvis Bay, and UN control of the transitional period up to independence. SWAPO surprised the South Africans by accepting the presence of a reduced South African garrison. This meant that in order to maintain the appearance that they were negotiating in good faith, South Africa was forced to compromise on that issue. Walvis Bay – Namibia's only deep-water port through which most of Namibia's exports and imports pass – proved to be more difficult. Basing their claim on the British annexation of 1878, the South Africans claimed that Walvis Bay was part of South Africa, even though it had been administered from Windhoek since 1922 (it was transferred back to Cape Province in late 1977). Both sides agreed to shelve the issue until after independence. By mid-1978 it appeared that agreement had been reached in principle on the transition process which would take Namibia to independence.

The optimism quickly proved ill-founded. Only days after accepting the western plan, South Africa launched a massive air raid on the SWAPO refugee camp at Kassinga in southern Angola, killing over 850 and wounding hundreds more. At the same time they began a unilateral registration of voters in preparation for an internal election which was duly held in December of that year despite all protests. Predictably, it was the Democratic Turnhalle Alliance which swept up the majority of votes, though it was joined a year later by two black organisations – the Namibian National Front, a rag-bag of small regionalist and neo-colonial parties, and the SWAPO-Democrats, a party formed by ex-SWAPO leader Andreas Shipanga.

Since then South Africa has continued to play a double game. While it is careful not to reject UN initiatives entirely, it also clearly has no intention of allowing a SWAPO-dominated government to take over in Namibia. Meanwhile, the war of attrition between SWAPO and the South African security forces has continued to escalate. From time to time virtually the entire national branch leadership of SWAPO is rounded up and interned for months on end. Others considered to be more subversive are incarcerated on notorious Robben Island. The torture of detainees is both routine and widespread and, because the area north of Windhoek is now effectively under martial law, open political activity has become very dangerous. The South Africans have also created a 'free fire' zone along the Namibian/Angolan border as well as mounted a number of invasions of southern Angola in an attempt to destroy SWAPO training camps there. Given this sort of South African intransigence and prevarication, a peaceful settlement in Namibia seems as far away as it ever was.

VISAS

As for South Africa. Permits are necessary for visiting the 'Homelands.' These are available from the Ministry of Bantu Affairs in Windhoek.

MONEY

As for South Africa.

LANGUAGE

English, German and Afrikaans are the official languages, the latter being the most widely used. African languages fall into two groups – Khoisan and Western Bantu.

GETTING THERE & AROUND
Road

More and more travellers are going to Namibia these days and it's getting easier all the time. You don't even need 4WD unless you plan to go right out into the desert, as the roads are excellent. An ordinary 2WD car will do – road signs will tell you where 4WD is needed. There is a good network of sealed roads and railways which connect all the main towns and cities. Even the gravel tracks are well maintained. Hitching is slow because there are so few vehicles, but when one comes along it almost invariably stops and you'll often be offered accommodation. You shouldn't, however, attempt to hitch off the tarred roads, as it's almost impossible to find lifts. It's also possible to pick up hire-cars in Windhoek and drive them down to Cape Town for just the cost of fuel, especially during November and December.

If you're heading for Botswana it's possible to arrange lifts from Windhoek to Ghanzi.

Rail

A single rail line connects South Africa with Namibia. The route is De Aar-Prieska-Upington-Karasburg-Keetmanshoop-Windhoek. The schedule is as follows:

Station	Frequency		
	Suidwester		
	Tues	Tues	Daily ex Tues
De Aar	10.30 pm	5.00 pm	6.00 pm
Prieska	2.21 am	9.26 pm	10.18 pm
Upington	7.10 am	3.45 am	5.05 am
Karasburg	1.20 pm	10.35 am	12.05 am
Keetmanshoop	7.05 pm	4.35 pm	6.15 pm
Windhoek	7.00 am	5.40 am	7.35 am

Station	Frequency	
	Suidwester	
	Mon	Daily
Windhoek	11.30 am	8.20 pm
Keetmanshoop	11.15 pm	10.10 am
Karasburg	4.40 am	4.45 pm
Upington	11.30 am	12.15 pm
Prieska	3.40 pm	6.26 am

De Aar   6.45 pm   10.50 am

The Suidwester takes only 1st– and 2nd-class passengers. On all trains there is an hour's stop (approximately) at both Upington and Keetmanshoop.

From Windhoek there are branch lines west to Walvis Bay and north to Tsumeb and Grootfontein. From Windhoek there are branch lines west to Walvis Bay and north to Grootfontein. From Keetmanshoop there's a line to Luderitz:

Windhoek-Tsumeb-Windhoek

Station	Frequency		
	Sun, Thurs, Fri	Mon, Thurs, Fri, Sat	Tues, Wed
Windhoek	20.10 pm	–	–
Kranzberg	2.15 am	–	7.35 am
Otjiwarongo	7.42 am (arr)	–	3.10 pm
–	11.50 am (dep)	10.10 am	–
Otavi	4.25 pm	2.15 pm	–
Tsumeb	6.18 pm	–	–

The 10.10 am train from Otavi to Otjiwarongo continues on to Grootfontein. The 7.35 am train from Kranzberg to Otjiwarongo originates in Grootfontein.

Station	Frequency		
	Wed, Fri, Sat, Sun	Wed, Fri, Sat, Sun	Mon, Tues
Tsumeb	7.00 am	–	–
Otavi	9.25 am	11.37 am	–
Otjiwarongo	1.34 pm (arr)	3.18 pm	–
–	6.30 pm (dep)	–	6.55 am
Kranzberg	12.14 pm	–	2.23 pm
Windhoek	5.30 am	–	–

The 11.37 am train from Otavi to Otjiwarongo originates in Grootfontein.

Walvis Bay-Usakos-Windhoek-Walvis Bay

Station	Frequency	Station	Frequency
	Daily		Daily
Walvis Bay	6.25 pm	Windhoek	7.00 pm
Swakopmund	7.50 pm	Karibib	11.39 pm
Usakos	12.17 pm	Kranzberg	12.55 pm
Kranzberg	1.30 am	Usakos	1.45 am
Karibib	2.05 am	Swakopmund	6.06 am
Windhoek	6.50 am	Walvis Bay	7.20 am

Otavi-Grootfontein

Station	Frequency	Station	Frequency
	Mon, Thurs, Fri, Sat		Wed, Fri, Sat, Sun
Otavi	2.15 pm	Grootfontein	7.30 am
Grootfontein	6.10 pm	Otavi	10.55 am

Keetmanshoop-Luderitz

Station	Frequency	Station	Frequency
	Fri, Sun		Fri, Sun
Keetmanshoop	7.00 pm	Luderitz	6.30 pm
Seeheim-Noord	8.04 pm	Aus	11.25 pm
Aus	2.09 am	Seeheim-Noord	5.05 am
Luderitz	6.30 am	Keetmanshoop	6.20 am

The other branch line from Windhoek to Gobabis is for freight only.

PLACES TO STAY

There's a whole range of accommodation available in most of the places of interest. Prices are R 5-18 for a bungalow (two to six beds) and R 2.50-6 for a campsite (for up to eight people and two vehicles). Facilities are excellent. Before you go to Namibia, get hold of the small but comprehensive booklet 'SWA Accommodation Guide for Tourists,' which lists virtually all the campsites, bungalows and hotels in the country with their prices, facilities and seasons (where applicable). You can get these booklets from either the Directorate of Nature Conservation, Private Bag 13267, Windhoek 9000, Namibia (tel 36960), or from South West Africa Tourist Commission, New Street North, Johannesburg, South Africa (postal address: PO Box 11405, Johannesburg 2000). The Nature Conservation Office, in particular, is very helpful and it's well worth calling in at their Windhoek office.

GROOTFONTEIN

Apart from the official campsite, you can erect a tent at the rugby stadium, Rundu Rd, free of charge.

KEETMANSHOOP

The campground here costs R 1.50 for one or two people. Extra people cost R 0.30 each. This is the only campsite between the South African-Namibian border and Windhoek.

A good place to eat is the *German pub* 100 metres down the road from the campsite. It has an excellent bar.

LUDERITZ

Luderitz is an interesting German colonial town well worth a visit. The desert is slowly encroaching on the town and some of the outlying houses are already partly covered with sand. The diamond mining ghost town of Kolmankoop nearby is also worth seeing.

The *government bungalows* cost R 5 for two people. In addition, there is the *German School* which costs R 3. The facilities include hot water. Camping is available in the town or by the lighthouse.

One traveller described Luderitz as the 'crayfish capital of the world' and suggested splurging on a meal of them at the café opposite the museum. Six tails cost R 14.50 – a superb meal. If you're stuck for somewhere to stay, it's worth asking here.

MARIENTAL

Stay at the *Hardap Recreation Resort* while you are here.

SWAKOPMUND

This is another nice old German colonial town with an interesting local history museum. The *government rest camp* charges R 7.50 for two people and there is a campsite for R 6 for up to eight people. Accommodation can be difficult to find during December and January, as that is when settlers from the inland areas come here for their holidays. If you can't find anywhere to stay, ask at *JJ's Restaurant*, which is also a good place to pick up a cheap meal.

From mid-December until the end of

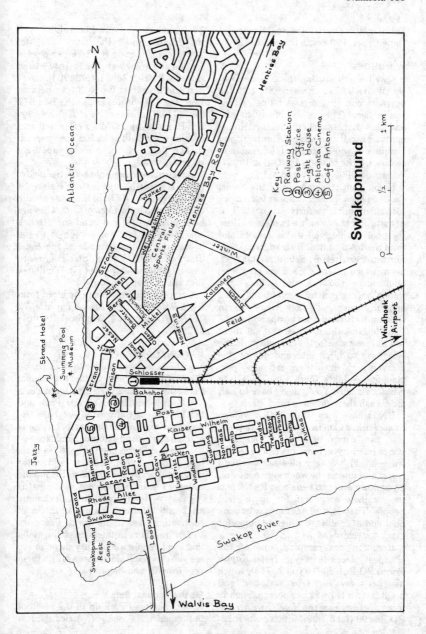

Swakopmund

Key:-
① Railway Station
② Post Office
③ Light House
④ Atlanta Cinema
⑤ Cafe Anton

February you can visit the Seal Reserve at Cape Cross, 120 km to the north.

WINDHOEK

It's well worth visiting the Nature Conservation Office, Kaiser St (at the opposite end to the post office), whilst you're here. They're extremely helpful and they have excellent detailed information as well as maps of Windhoek and Namibia. If you'd like this information in advance, write to them at PO Box 13267, Windhoek 9000 (tel 061 29251).

If you want to camp, avoid the *Safari Caravan Park*. It might appear to be more convenient but it's a dirty site, costs R 10 per site and they won't let you use either the pool or their van which goes to and from the town centre. Instead, try *OASE Caravan Park* (tel 061 62098), 15 km from town, which offers a good grassed site, immaculate showers and toilets (hot water) and is run by very friendly and helpful owners. To get there go to Okahandja Rd and head north. Follow the signs to Brakwater. When you get there you will see a sign for the caravan park. It's very easy to hitch into and out of this caravan park since there are many permanent residents there who drive into Windhoek daily. You'll never have to wait more than three minutes for a lift.

If you have a car there's *Dan Viljoen Game Park*, 24 km from Windhoek, where you can camp or rent a bungalow surrounded by zebras, oryx, kudus and springbok. It's a very pleasant weekend resort and during the week very peaceful. Bungalows with two beds cost R 7.50 and the campsite costs R 5 for up to eight people. There's a restaurant, swimming pool and a small lake which is home for many waterbirds.

If you're not camping, one of the cheapest places to stay is *Hotel Kapp's Farm*, PO Box 20946 (tel 29713), which has beds for R 14-18 and bed and breakfast for R 18-22 per person. Slightly more expensive are the *Hotel Grossherzog*, PO Box 90 (tel 37026), which costs R 20-24 per person for bed and breakfast; and the *Hansa Hotel*, PO Box 5374 (tel 23249), which costs R 22-26 per person for bed and breakfast. The *Privat Pension Handke*, PO Box 20881 (tel 34904), offers bed and breakfast for R 20 per person. Both the *Continental Hotel*, PO Box 977 (tel 37293), and the *Hotel Kaiserkrone*, PO Box 208 (tel 37520), offer bed and breakfast for as little as R 22 per person, though they both have more expensive rooms as well.

A nice place to hang out is the *Schneider Café*, Hepworth Arcade (off Kaiser St across from the GPO). In the same arcade and also good is the *Central Café*. They are both inexpensive and good for a quick snack or a coffee. For a beer go to the beergarden in the grounds of the *Hotel Thuringer Hof*, Kaiser St. There are several fish-and-chip places in Windhoek that are all pretty good.

Camping equipment can be hired from *SWA Safaris* or from *Budget* car hire, 72 Tal St, PO Box 1754, Windhoek (tel 061-28720).

NATIONAL PARKS

Namibia is well endowed with game parks, the main ones being Etosha National Park, the Skeleton Coast National Park, the Namib-Naukluft National Park and the Fish River Canyon. If you have the time they're all worth getting to, but many of them close during October and November due to the rains and the heat. Namibia has some of the weirdest and most wonderful landscapes in the world and the country I would compare it with most is Afghanistan though, of course, the people are totally different. It's one of the most captivating areas in the world. There are so few travellers in this part of the globe that local people will be very surprised to see you and you'll almost always find them very friendly and helpful.

Etosha National Park

Etosha National Park up in the north of the country is one of Africa's most

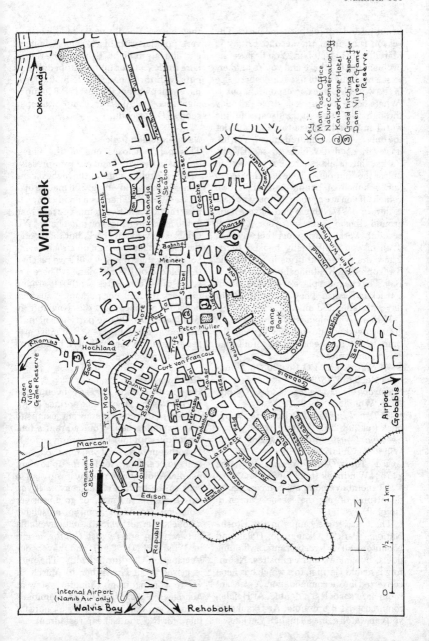

Windhoek

Key:-
① Main Post Office
Nature Conservation Off
② Kaiserkrone Hotel
③ Good hitching spot for
Daen Viljen Game
Reserve

beautiful and interesting game parks. The season runs from the second Friday in March to 31 October. You'll have no problem getting there and you're unlikely to see anything quite like it anywhere else in the world. As one correspondent put it, 'Where else could you drive all day through the bleakest landscape in the world and suddenly see three oryx under the only tree for a hundred miles?' You do, however, need a vehicle to see Etosha Park – hitch-hikers are not allowed in unless they happen to have been invited to join a bunch of people with their own vehicle. If you are a group, it would be best to hire a 4WD vehicle and have a look around these parks on your own. It certainly works out cheaper this way than if all of you individually booked tours. There are car rental firms in Windhoek, Swakopmund, Keetmanshoop and Walvis Bay. The cheapest place at present to rent a truck is *Budget*. They charge R 32 per day with unlimited mileage.

If there's no chance of you getting a group together and you haven't got the time to hitch, check out the following safari companies:

SWA Safaris Ltd, PO Box 20373, Windhoek (tel 37567/8/9)

Springbok-Atlas Safaris Ltd, PO Box 2058, Windhoek (tel 24252)

SAR Travel Bureau, PO Box 415, Windhoek (tel 298-2561/2/3)

Skeleton Coast Safaris, PO Box 2195, Windhoek (tel 37567/8/9)

Africa Tours/Okuti Safaris, PO Box 21754, Windhoek (tel 27668)

All the above companies have regular departures during the season (March to October).

There are three camps in the Etosha National Park at Okaukuejo, Halali and Namutoni, all with restaurants, swimming pools, bungalows and campsites. Namutoni is an old German fort which has been converted into accommodation. A pleasant room here costs R 5 a double. At Halali a room costs R 6 a double. At Okaukuejo you can watch game all night if you like, as they have a floodlit water-hole which is very popular with black rhino, elephant and lion late at night. Tents can be rented here for R 7.50 for up to four people and huts with three beds for R 8.50. If you have your own tent the cost is R 6 for up to eight people. Another camp will open soon at Otivasandu.

Namib-Naukluft Park

This park encloses one of the oldest deserts in the world and offers impressive sights, including some of the highest sand dunes in the world – up to 300 metres high (at Sossusvlei). There is a good campsite near the dunes at Sessreim. You may read in the brochures that you must have 4WD vehicles to visit this park, but that's only the case if there's a sign on a road saying so, and by that time you will have reached the middle of the red dunes. There are seven other campsites scattered around the park (R 1.50 per person). You must book in advance for the Naukluft in Windhoek, as only one party per night is allowed at the campsites. You must also get a permit to visit this park before you set off from Sessreim.

Fish River Canyon

Here is the second largest canyon in the world. Nearby are the hot springs of Ai-Ais where there is a restaurant, campsite and swimming pool. You can rent a tent for R 7.50 with four beds, a caravan for R 10 with four beds or, if you have your own tent, you can camp for R 6 for up to eight people. Allow about one day if you plan to walk to the bottom of the canyon. If you stay there for the night or go downriver when you get to the bottom, you must have a special permit which is only available between May and August. Get the permit in Windhoek (R 2.50) and have your Vaccination Certificate handy. The park is closed from November to March. If you're coming from Upington, stay at **Augrabies Falls**, another of Namibia's little-known wonders. There's a campsite there for R 5 and a cheap restaurant.

Brandberg/Twyfelfontein

Otherwise known as **White Lady**, this area
has some very interesting rock paintings
and a petrified forest not far away. The
whole area can be explored from Khorixas,
where there are bungalows (R 12 for four
beds) and a campsite for R 1.50 per
person. You can camp on the ground at the
beginning of the trail to the rock paintings.

Skeleton Coast Park

This is a wild and lonely stretch of
windswept coast with very cold water. It's
good for fishermen and you may come
across the occasional old wreck. There is a
simple campsite at Torrabay (R 2) and a
larger one at Terracebay (R 25 per person
including all meals). North of Terracebay
the coast is closed to the public.

Northern Namibia/Caprivi Strip

The following letter comes to you from a
traveller who recently spent some time in
this area:

The northern areas of Namibia along the
Angolan border and the Caprivi Strip are not
out of bounds as many people believe and as
South African authorities would like you to
believe. I had no trouble travelling through the
area except for minor hassles at road blocks
with soldiers waving sub-machine guns. This is
no different to Zimbabwe or Mozambique.

For travel along the Caprivi Strip between
Bagani Bridge and Kongolo a military permit is
required. This is easily obtained by fronting up
at local army headquarters. If travelling from
east to west, apply at the Katima Mulilo
headquarters or, if starting in the west, apply at
Sector 20 headquarters at Rundu. Travel in all
northern areas after sunset is prohibited and in
any case extremely unwise. If traversing the
Strip, the journey can be broken overnight at
Popa Falls – a very pleasant rest camp a few km
south of Bagani Bridge. There are camping
facilities or, for a few rand, a bed at one of the
rest-camp tents. Reservations shouldn't be
necessary but you can book in advance at the
Dept of Agriculture & Nature Conservation,
Private Bag 13267, Windhoek 9000 (tel
29251).

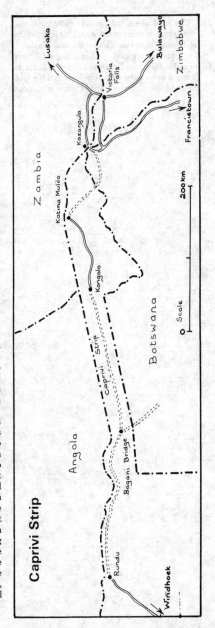

The road along the Strip is quite good and even bitumen some of the way. This is by far the best route between Zimbabwe and Namibia, the only alternative being the nightmare journey through Botswana from Maun to Buitpos across the northern Kalahari. In fact, the road through the Caprivi Strip is so good that quite a few people do it in ordinary saloon cars. You can always find out where petrol is available – no problem.

Entry into Angola is no problem for the determined. Extensive tours of the country are readily arranged for you upon enlistment in the South African army.

Niger

Like the other countries of the Sahel belt, Niger suffered horrendously from the droughts of 1969 and 1972-74. At least 60% of the livestock was lost, there were no food harvests for two years, and many rural dwellers were forced to leave the land for good and migrate to the cities. The effects of the drought might not have been so catastrophic had there not been an ill-considered and rapid expansion of stock-breeding in the north during the 1960s which had already overburdened the delicate ecological balance of the pastures. What saved Niger from economic disaster (though perhaps not the rest of the world from ecological disaster) were the uranium mines at Arlit. So valuable were deposits that Niger's trade balance actually went into surplus by 1976 and the country is no longer dependent on French financial subsidies. By 1980 uranium accounted for 75% of the country's exports and is due to rise to 90% by the mid-1980s. Uranium has not proved to be a universal blessing, however, as it has led to high inflation and social discontent among students and trade unionists over the disparities in income levels caused by it.

Long before the country was colonised by the French, a number of prosperous and well-organised states occupied all, or part of, the Niger republic as it stands today. They included the Songhai empire in the west, the Hausa kingdoms in the centre and the empire of Kanem-Bornu in the east around Lake Chad. The wealth of these states was based on control of the trans-Saharan trade routes which were of vital importance to West Africa and the countries bordering the Mediterranean. The principal commodities were slaves, gold and salt. The wealth of Sahel empires diminished rapidly during the 18th and 19th centuries as a result of the European maritime nations' increasing trade directly with the West African coastal kingdoms. Even so, trans-Saharan trade has never actually ceased even today. Until quite recently, annual caravans consisting of thousands of camels were loading up with salt at the oasis of Bilma and heading south for Nigeria and Cameroun.

Islam was introduced into the area during the 10th and 11th centuries, but it remained the religion only of the aristocracy and the wealthy urban elite right up to the 19th century. The rural population continued to follow traditional beliefs, and when Islam began to make headway with these people in the 19th and particularly the 20th century, it did not undermine traditional beliefs. Pagan rituals are not only practised alongside Islam but are accepted without question. Niger has preserved a good number of its pre-colonial traditions and institutions and these can carry far more weight in social relations than the country's constitutional laws. Even urban dwellers rarely question traditional values.

Despite the fact that the British were the first to explore the upper reaches of the Niger beginning with the Scotsman, Mungo Park, who disappeared in the area in 1806, it was the French who colonised it between 1891 and 1911. The country was not fully 'pacified' until much later, however, and there were a number of resistance movements which severely tested the mettle of the colonial authorities. The most serious of these was the siege of Agadez by Tuaregs in 1916-17.

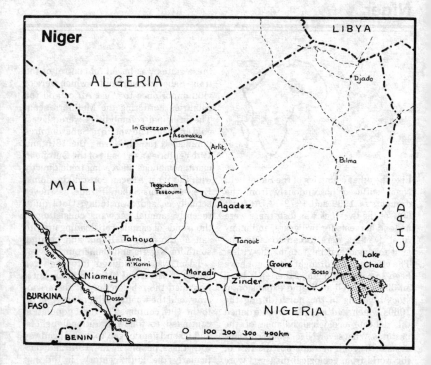

Niger suffers from poor soils; this, together with the fact that most crops are watered only by rain, makes the production of food entirely dependent on the hazards of the climate. These factors hampered the development of the colony for a long time until groundnuts were introduced in 1930. These quickly became the country's most important export and, along with cattle, remained so until uranium took over in the 1970s.

Independence was granted in 1960 under the presidency of Hamni Diori. The earlier years were troubled with insurgency from Sawaba commandos until an agreement reached in 1965 with Algeria, Ghana and China put an end to their aid to the opposition. Sawaba, a communist/radical left political grouping, had gone into exile when it failed to win control of the government in elections prior to indepen-

dence. The drought of 1973, however provoked severe economic and social upheavals which Diori was unable to control. He was overthrown in a coup the following year by Lieutenant-General Seyni Kountche, who has remained in power ever since.

FACTS

A good part of Niger's 480,000 square miles lies in the Sahara Desert, with most of the remainder lying in the Sahel. The climate is hot and dry except for a brief rainy period in July and August. November and January are the coolest months, when the Hamattan blows off the desert. Vegetation in the north is sparse or nonexistent, gradually merging into scrub in the Sahel and lightly treed grassland in the extreme south. Most of the country's land mass receives less than 500 mm (20 inches) of rain per year. Even so, millet and sorghum fields are found in some of these drier areas. The only permanent river is the Niger, which flows parallel to the south-west border. The only permanent lake is Lake Chad on the south-east border. Though most of the country is a vast plain, the Air Mountains (pronounced 'Eye-ear') in the north rise to 2000 metres. The population of Niger is estimated at 6½ million. Population densities range from .007 people per square km in the north to 40 people per square km in the heavily populated agricultural areas in the south. The annual rate of increase is close to 3.2% – one of the world's highest. Average life expectancy is 43 years. Eighty percent of the population is sedentary, living either in cities, urban areas or farms, while 20% remains nomadic. There are five principal ethnic groups: Hausa, Djerma-Songhai, Peuhl/Fulani, Tuareg and Kanuri/Beri-Beri. The Hausa represent half of the total population and the Djerma-Songhai a further quarter. Each ethnic group has its own language and customs but the Hausa language is the one most widely spoken. Ninety-eight percent of the population is Moslem.

VISAS

Visas are required by all except nationals of Belgium, Denmark, Finland, France, Germany (West), Italy, Luxembourg, Netherlands, Norway, Sweden and the UK.

There are very few Niger embassies around the world, so you need to plan ahead. In Africa you can obtain visas in Abidjan (Ivory Coast), Accra (Ghana), Addis Ababa (Ethiopia), Algiers (Algeria), Cairo (Egypt), Cotonou (Benin), Dakar (Senegal), Freetown (Sierra Leone), Kano (Nigeria), Khartoum (Sudan), Lagos and Kano (Nigeria), and Monrovia (Liberia). If you are coming down from the north and need a visa, make sure you get one in Algiers (Algeria). There is no Niger consulate in Tamanrasset. French embassies are sometimes empowered to issue Niger visas where there is no Niger embassy, but this is not always the case so don't rely on this. In Liberia and Sierra Leone the Ivory Coast embassy deals with Niger visas. In Sudan it is the Chad embassy.

In addition to a visa (where required), everyone entering Niger must show at least US$500, an International Health Card with yellow fever and cholera vaccinations, and either an onward ticket or a document from an established bank guaranteeing repatriation by confirming that funds are available if they are needed. This latter document must be translated into French. These requirements (including the onward ticket) apply equally whether you are on foot or driving your own vehicle. Don't turn up at the border unless you have all of these – especially at the Assamaka border (Algeria/Niger). We've been receiving a lot of horror stories from travellers who were stuck for weeks at Assamaka. This extract from a letter sums it all up:

There was a big problem when we arrived (at Assamaka) in that the authorities had started to demand onward tickets. Many people were unaware of this and were stuck, many unable to return to Algeria due to lack of a visa, fuel or whatever. Some were running out of food and drinking water, having been stuck for up to two weeks. There's nothing at Assamaka and the water is foul. The military treated them like shit, not allowing them to sit under the only tree, saying it was a military zone and occasionally giving them scraps of food. We were fortunate to arrive at the same time as an English film crew that had a typewriter on which we forged a bank guarantee of repatriation (the only acceptable alternative to an air ticket). This got us through eventually, but the only solution for many people was to give money to travellers who got through to buy tickets from the *Air Niger* office in Arlit, some hundred miles south, which they could then give to people coming north to give to the stranded travellers. Various explanations were given for the situation, one of them being a directive from the government due to pressure from the French who were sick of having to repatriate their citizens. It was noticeable that the French were given a particularly hard time.

Expect border formalities to take at least 24 hours on both sides. Heavy searches are common. There is a lot of petty bribery going on at the Assamaka border, so if you have problems it's worth discreetly dropping a few dollars here and there. Rumour has it that the officials here make so much money out of this sort of bullshit that the staff is changed once a month.

You must report to police in each town where you stay overnight. The stamps you get will use up quite a few pages of your passport if you stay any length of time, but it's important to comply with this. You may have problems otherwise, although some travellers ignore the requirement here and there by saying they were stranded in a broken-down truck overnight, etc. Make sure your story is convincing, however, as some travellers have been sent back all the way from Niamey to Arlit for failing to do this.

Exit visas are no longer required if you're going to either Nigeria or Benin, but it would be a good idea to confirm this with other travellers or with Immigration for the moment. The stamp you get in your passport from the Sureté National in Niamey doubles as both an entry and exit stamp.

If you intend to use a camera, you must get a photography permit. These cost CFA 5000! In Agadez you can get one at the Tourist Office, but it's only valid for that particular department. The ones issued in Niamey are valid for the whole country. To get it you must buy a CFA 5000 *timbre fiscal* from the Prefecture, corner Rue du Souvenir and Rue du Président Luebke near the Tourist Office. You then take this stamp to the Ministere de l'Intérieur, Avenue Charles de Gaulle, where they will attach the stamp to the photo permit. It generally takes about 1½ hours. No photos are necessary.

If you intend to travel to Chad or anywhere east of Zinder, you need a special letter of authority from the Ministry of the Interior. To get this you need to write a grovelling letter in French asking the honourable Minister to grant you special permission to travel to the Chadian frontier. With luck, the letter will be ready the same day.

Algerian visas These cost CFA 3500 and take 24 hours to issue in Niamey.

Benin visas A seven-day, double-entry visa costs CFA 1000 and is issued the same day. The people at the embassy are friendly. Extensions are possible in Cotonou. The embassy in Niamey is a long way from the centre, so take a taxi (CFA 100).

Burkina Faso visas These are obatinable from the French embassy. A 90-day visa costs CFA 3000, requires two photos and is issued in 24 hours. The visas are multiple entry.

CAR visas Obtainable from the French embassy. A 48-hour visa costs CFA 3000 and is valid for two months.

Chad visas Obtainable from the French embassy. A 90-day visa costs CFA 3000 and is issued in 24 hours.

Mali visas There is now a Malian consulate in Niamey in an obscure little office on the left of the Grand Marche. Visas cost CFA 5000, require two photos and are issued the same day.

Nigerian visas These cost CFA 1200, require one photo and take 24 hours to issue. The staff are very hostile but there are no problems as long as you do not have any South African stamps in your passport.

Ivory Coast visas Obtainable from the French embassy in Niamey. They cost CFA 1500 and are issued in 24 hours.

Togo visas These are obtainable from the French embassy, cost CFA 1000, require two photos and take 24 hours to issue. The political situation there has eased up considerably, so they will even consider applications for a three-month visa these days.

You can also get visas for Egypt, Liberia and Morocco in Niamey. Other than embassies for a few West European countries, Saudi Arabia, Pakistan, People's Republic of China, USA and USSR, there are no other embassies or consulates in Niamey.

MONEY

US$1 = CFA 460
£1 = CFA 563

The unit of currency is the CFA franc. There are no restrictions on the import of local currency, but export is limited to CFA 25,000. Banks in Arlit and in some other towns around the country (eg BIAO in Niamey) charge CFA 750 commission on traveller's cheques.

On the Niger/Nigerian border money-changers offer CFA 10,000 for Naira 56.

If you're driving your own vehicle, in Birni N'Konni you can buy cheap petrol smuggled from Nigeria. It costs CFA 120 per litre (official price is CFA 220 a litre). The petrol should be dyed red and you need to check for added water. Black market diesel costs CFA 75 per litre, but stock up here if you are going to Nigeria, as it is even cheaper there (though this might change soon if the military junta accept IMF demands to abolish the fuel subsidy).

Petrol is expensive in Niger – CFA 230 per litre – but near the Nigerian border (in places like Birni N'Konni and Maradi) you can buy it for almost half that price on the black market. You should be careful though, as some people have complained about finding water in black market petrol.

LANGUAGE

French is the official language but the main spoken languages are Hausa, Zarma, Fulani, Tamachek and Kanuri.

POST

If you are collecting mail in Niamey, be sure to check not only the Hotel des Postes near the Sureté National but also the larger and older main post office. There is a charge of CFA 80 for each letter collected.

GETTING THERE & AROUND
Road

A few years ago, roads in Niger – where they existed – used to be dreadful and you'd get off at the end of a journey bruised and battered from head to toe. This is still true of the road between Zinder and Agadez, but everywhere else money has been poured into surfacing roads, primarily to improve access to the uranium and other mineral mines in the Air Mountains. There are now good, sealed roads all the way from Niamey to Arlit via Tahoua and Agadez and between Niamey and Zinder (the road is the same for these two routes as far as Birni N'Konni).

Because of the improvement in the roads there is now a fairly good network of buses between the main centre of population in Niger. They generally cost much the same as trucks over the same distance, but they're often very crowded so you may prefer to go by truck anyway. Try to arrange a lift by truck in advance (say, the night before) and don't hand over any money (even a deposit) until you are on the truck. This includes giving money to people who are touting for passengers.

Some examples of transport costs and journey times along the main routes are as follows:

Arlit-Agadez There are daily trucks for CFA 2500 and a once-weekly bus by *SNTN* which costs CFA 2265.
Agadez-Zinder Daily trucks and buses run

twice a week. The trucks cost CFA 3700 and take up to 20 hours. The buses cost CFA 5200 and take 12 hours, but you must book them two days in advance. The road is as rough as hell. Trucks generally stop between 2 and 6 am so that everyone can catch some sleep.

Agadez-Niamey There are daily trucks along this route and a *SNTN* bus three times per week in either direction (on Monday, Wednesday and Friday at 4 pm from Niamey). The bus costs CFA 12,000 and takes one day on average. It used to make an overnight stop at Tahoua but this town is now closed to foreigners. The trucks are slightly cheaper at CFA 10,000. The bus leaves Niamey on Thursdays and the terminus is upriver from the Hotel Gaweye. There are 10 police checkpoints to go through on this journey.

Agadez-Tahoua There are trucks most days of the week in either direction throughout the dry season; they cost CFA 5000. There are also Peugeot taxis for CFA 3500 including baggage.

Birni N'Konni-Dosso There is a daily bus for CFA 2000 including baggage.

Niamey-Gaya A daily bus leaves at 9 am and costs CFA 2250.

Niamey-Maradi The *SNTN* buses run in either direction three times per week on Tuesday, Thursday and Saturday from 7 to 9 am and cost CFA 6500. Bush taxis leave from the autogare by the Grande Marche early every evening and cost CFA 4000 including baggage charge. They take about 14 hours.

Niamey-Tahoua There is an *SNTN* bus on Monday, Wednesday and Friday which costs CFA 6000.

Zinder-Niamey An *SNTN* bus runs three times per week in either direction (at about 7 am on Tuesday, Thursday and Saturday from Niamey). The journey takes one day and the fare is CFA 8825. There are also trucks and Peugeot taxis along this route.

To/From Algeria (Route du Hoggar)

There are no buses between Agadez and Tamanrasset (Algeria) except for the occasional bus between the Algerian border post and Tamanrasset (usually once per week), so you'll have to arrange a lift on a truck. Fares are more or less standardised and you should expect to pay CFA 15,000 on the back and CFA 20,000 in the cab. Food and water are usually included, but you should confirm this before you pay the 'fare.' The journey usually takes three days but can take five depending on breakdowns/punctures. There are two routes from Agadez to the border: one goes via Arlit (sealed road from Agadez to Arlit) and the other goes via Assaours and Tegguidam Tessoumi. The trucks usually take the latter route. On the truck route you can only get water at Tegguidam and at In Guezzam (Algerian border post). There is water at Assamaka (Niger border post), but it comes from a sulphur spring and tastes really foul. One traveller suggested it was 'palatable' if you dished in a couple of water-purifying tablets (desperation breeds resourcefulness!).

If you can get a group of 10 people together, you have the option of chartering a Land Cruiser which will cost CFA 20,000 per person but will only take a day and a half if the border times and the guards who staff them are congenial. The price may or may not include food, so don't forget to confirm this before you set off.

There is another possibility, too, but you shouldn't be in a hurry if you're thinking of trying it. Between August and December Algerian date trucks come down to In-Gall west of Agadez, dump their loads and then return to Algeria empty. You might well be able to get on one of them. A bush taxi from Agadez to In-Gall should cost about CFA 2000 and the truck from there to Tamanrasset should be about CFA 10,000 (cheaper than Agadez-Tamanrasset). The journey should take four to five days once your ride is found.

To/From Benin

There are daily *SNTN* buses from Niamey to Gaya which leave early in the morning and take about four hours. The fare is CFA 2250. You can either stay overnight in Gaya (eg at *Amir Asmir's hanger*) or continue on into Benin. There are bush taxis from Gaya to the border (Malanville – eight km) for CFA 500. From the border you can take an *STB* bus to Parakou which costs CFA 1800, takes seven hours and leaves between 9 and 10 am (when full); or you can take a Peugeot taxi, which will cost CFA 2500. Between Parakou and Cotonou there are trains twice daily in either direction which leave Parakou at 9.20 am and 10 pm. The fare is CFA 5350 (1st class) and CFA 2450 (2nd class), and the journey normally takes about 10 hours but has been known to take 16. Drinks are available on the train and food is sold at stations en route (turkey tails or *dindon*, coconut balls, bananas, oranges, maize wrapped in leaves, even cooked rat!).

To/From Burkina faso

There are both buses and trucks between Niamey and Ougadougou which cost CFA 3150 and take up to 30 hours, including a sleep stop for several hours en route. The buses (which are sometimes suspended) only go three times per week and leave when full, so there is no definite departure time. A taxi between the two places costs CFA 4200 and takes about 25 hours (less if there's no curfew in Bourkinafasso). Fruit, bread and coffee are available along the way. This road is often closed during the rainy season.

To/From Mali

There are irregular trucks from Niamey to Gao which leave from the Gare Routiere next to the Camping Touristique and cost CFA 3500. *SNTN* buses leave at noon on Monday, Wednesday and Friday and arrive the next morning at about 9 am. They cost CFA 5700 plus CFA 35 per kilo of baggage (the weight meter starts off at 10 kg with nothing on it!). Try to book this bus in advance. The journey takes two days with generally a stop at the border. One traveller reported recently that 'failure to take the anti-cholera pills will result in you being sent back to Niamey.' (Pills?! What are they doing? Optimistically dousing everyone with antibiotics?) If you're in a hurry, there is an *Air Mali* flight which leaves Niamey on Thursday and costs CFA 18,000.

To/From Nigeria

The three main routes into Nigeria from Niger are Birni N'Konni-Sokoto, Maradi-Katsina/Kano and Zinder-Kano. There are usually daily trucks between Zinder and Kano, but the best days to find a lift are Thursday and Friday, as there are a lot of trucks which do the run on those days after loading up with supplies from the Zinder market. On the Birni N'Konni route there are taxis for CFA 1000 to Sokoto. If you're going via Maradi there are *SNTN* buses from Niamey to Maradi on Tuesday, Thursday and Saturday between 7 and 9 am. The fare is CFA 6500.

Note Throughout much of 1984 the Nigerian land borders were closed. It's unlikely this situation will continue but, as a result, new possibilities have opened up which involve bypassing Nigeria altogether by going direct from Niger to Chad over the top side of Lake Chad. If you don't want to go through Nigeria, it's worth enquiring about this route.

AGADEZ

Agadez is certainly a welcome sight after the desert and an interesting town to explore, though its character is changing as more and more tourists go there and the wealth from the uranium mines at Arlit filters down the line. The old town is a maze of narrow alleyways, rarely more than three metres across, which weave between the single-storey, mud-brick buildings. It's a market town where the nomadic Tuareg and their former slaves, the Bouza, come in from outlying areas to

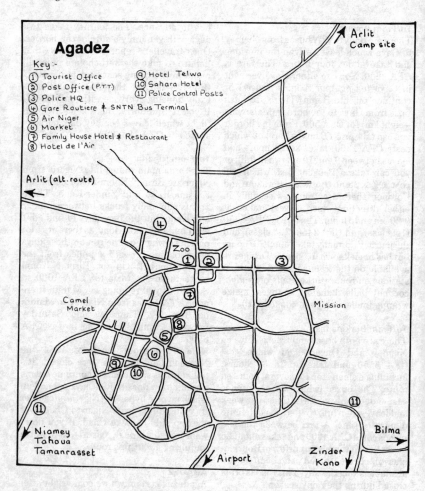

Agadez

Key:-
1. Tourist Office
2. Post Office (P.T.T)
3. Police HQ
4. Gare Routiere & SNTN Bus Terminal
5. Air Niger
6. Market
7. Family House Hotel & Restaurant
8. Hotel de l'Air
9. Hotel Telwa
10. Sahara Hotel
11. Police Control Posts

Arlit Camp site

Arlit (alt. route)

Zoo

Camel Market

Mission

Niamey
Tahoua
Tamanrasset

Airport

Zinder
Kano

Bilma

barter their goods for those of the Hausa traders from the south.

The two most popular hotels are the *Hotel de L'Air*, which is CFA 4500 for a room without shower, CFA 6000 for a double with shower or CFA 1000 to sleep on the roof or the terrace with a mattress; and *Hotel Telwa* (formerly the Hotel Atlantide), which is now government-run and costs CFA 3400-6000 per room regardless of whether you are alone or want to share a room. At the latter, the rooms all have air-conditioning, are clean and pleasant and have their own shower. There is a bar and restaurant. Even if you don't stay at the Hotel de L'Air, it's worth visiting for its architectural qualities and the view of the mosque from there. Other travellers have recommended the *Hotel Sahara* opposite the market; it offers double rooms for CFA 1500, 2000 and 2500.

A popular campsite is *L'Oasis* (formerly Joyce's Garden), which is eight km from town on the Arlit road and costs CFA 500 per person per night plus CFA 500 if you have your own vehicle. It's a beautiful site and there's a good swimming pool as well as ice-cold beer and orange juice for CFA 500 (twice what you will pay in Agadez). The food, like the beers, is expensive, so bring your own. The showers are erratic and the toilets are often filthy. If you are using water from the well, make sure you purify it before drinking, as there are bats around and they're none too fussy about where they shit. There is another camp-site about five km out of town on the new Arlit road past the police roadblock. It has showers, toilets, a bar and restaurant. It's illegal to camp out in the bush anywhere within five km of Agadez.

In addition to the above places, you may be offered rooms in private houses by local children. If you find one you like, bargain madly.

There are many small restaurants in the market area serving rice and sauce; these are about the cheapest places to eat. The *Restaurant Senegalaise* in the centre of town is popular with travellers. It has a friendly young crowd and is a good place to ask around for lifts. Other watering holes include the *Bar L'Ombre du Plaisirs* and the *Agreboun* (formerly the Family House Restaurant). The former is a good place to hang around in the evenings, as local musicians play there and cheap maize beer is available. *Restaurant Islamique* in the market has been recommended for inexpensive, hearty meals.

If you are changing money here, the BDRN Bank near the market is very slow.

Remember to register with the police and get a stamp in your passport. Don't neglect to do this or you may be sent back from as far away as Niamey.

Make sure you stock up on water before leaving Agadez, whichever way you are going.

ARLIT

Arlit is the uranium mining town in the Air Mountains north of Agadez and is often the first overnight stop in Niger if you're coming south from Algeria. It isn't marked on Bartholomews maps but it is on the Michelin maps. There are now two campsites in this town, one to the south near the beginning of the tarmac road, and the other between Arlit and the Somair mine just off the improved road. Both of them are OK and cost CFA 500 per night per person plus CFA 500 if you have a car. Food is available though quite expensive, and showers cost an extra CFA 250.

A popular watering hole is the *Cheval Blanc*, where you can get ice-cold beers for CFA 350 per litre. If there is music on that evening there will be an entry charge of CFA 500. Try the *Ramada* near the PTT in the centre of town opposite the main bakery for a reasonably cheap meal (around CFA 500). There are also the more expensive *Sahel Restaurant* and the *Tamesna*. You can get good steak at the latter for CFA 600.

You must report to the police immediately on arrival and leave your passport with them. If you need to change money, you'll have no problem getting it back temporarily. There are two banks in Arlit but they charge heavy commissions for changing traveller's cheques, so you have some French francs handy.

DOSSO

There is only one hotel here – the *Djerma* – which is very expensive at CFA 5200 a double but very good, and the rooms are air-conditioned.

MARADI

Maradi is one of the main commercial and industrial centres of Niger. The present town is only some 40 years old but the original settlement at Sohongari in the lush Maradi valley dates back to about 1790 and was founded by the animist Barki. At that time it was part of the territory controlled by the rulers of

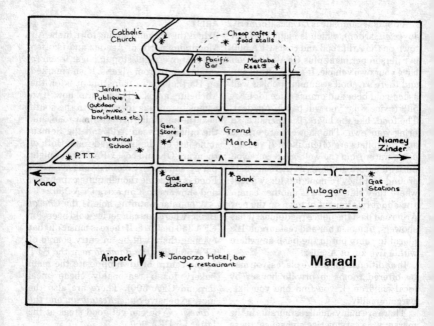

Katsina whose regional governor, known as the *maradi* (chief of the fetishers), gave his name to the town. Maradi was a way station on the traditional caravan routes between the Air Mountains and northern Nigeria and, consequently, there was a lot of fighting for its control. These conflicts eventually led to the city's decline in favour of Kano. When colonisation by the European nations began in earnest in the late 19th century, the city was originally taken by the British in 1902 but was ceded to the French a year later at the London Convention.

The main industrial products are peanut oil, tanned hides, blankets and bricks made of traditional indigenous materials. The Maradi market is held twice a week on Monday and Friday, when it is filled with local people as well as those from the outlying villages of Sofo, Soura, Madarounfa, Guidan Roumdji and Dan Issa. Bicycles are available for hire and if you want to explore this city it's a good idea to use one because Maradi is very spread out.

Hotel Niger has been recommended for an overnight stay. It costs CFA 2500 a single and CFA 3000 a double. Both types of rooms have a shower and fan. There is also *Le Campement*, located between the new city and the old town down in the valley.

There are numerous bars and two cinemas. The cinema *Vox* shows films which come from Maradi, whereas the *Jan Gorzo* shows English-language films which come from Nigeria.

NIAMEY
Niamey has been the capital of Niger since administration moved from Zinder in 1926. It's grown rapidly in recent years and now has a population of over a quarter of a million, yet in 1940 there were still only 2000 people living there. It has most of the amenities you would expect to find in a modern capital city.

Information

The Tourist Office is opposite the Grand Hotel and near the Nigerian embassy.

The agents for Thomas Cook are Transcap Voyages, Immeuble El Nasr (tel 733 234).

The Algerian embassy is on Avenue du Président Luebka (tel 733 251). The Malian consulate is in an obscure little office to the left of the Grand Marche.

For changing traveller's cheques, the Bank of Development of Niger has been recommended as offering a good exchange rate, being efficient (15 minutes) and charging only 1% commission. If you need to change money outside bank hours, go to the *bureau de change* at the Hotel Gaweye near the Pont Kennedy. If you need to exchange Central Africa CFA for West African CFA, go to the Banque Centrale des États de l'Afrique Ouest. You can get a straight swap here without commission.

Medical supplies (drugs, etc) are cheapest at the *Pharmacie Populaire* and the *Pharmacie Soni Ali Ber*. If you can't find what you want there, try the *Pharmacie Centrale*, which has the widest range of stock but is expensive. Photographic supplies can be bought from *Mouren* in the Bata Arcade (Kodak); *Studio Kap* (Agfa and Polaroid); and *Optique Photo*, across from the Vox cinema (Kodak and Polaroid as well opticians' services). *Photo Niger* does passport photos if you need them. For books and magazines *Camico-Papeterie* and *Burama* are best. Both also stock stationery and art supplies.

If you need medical treatment, the Clinic Gamkalley (tel 732 033), by the river about two km east of town, has been recommended but it is not cheap – CFA 6500 per consultation.

Taxis are plentiful and cost CFA 100 per journey in the main part of town. If you go outside of town then the fares increase. A taxi to the American embassy, for instance, will cost CFA 200. To the airport a taxi will cost CFA 1000. Expect to pay about CFA 50 for a pack.

The Grand Marche burned down about two years ago and was moved to Wadata along with the Gare Routiere. This is where the trucks and buses depart from these days.

The Petit Marche has a good variety of shops and products and is open all day, every day. Bargaining is essential. The majority of the shops are closed from noon to 4 pm and open again until 6.30 pm. Artisan shops sell jewellery and crafts at more-or-less fixed prices (reasonable). Many of the items are made by those who exhibit their wares at the museum and are particularly well crafted.

If your personal belongings are stolen in Niamey and you need an official declaration (for insurance purposes), you may well find the police uncooperative, so be persistent. Don't go there at lunch hour or you'll be wasting your time.

Things to See

The **National Museum** is well worth a visit and, like those in Accra and Kampala, is structured differently from most European-conceived establishments so that it can play a vital role in the life of a developing country. While it has the usual exhibits of local costumes and implements, it has gone beyond this to incorporate an extensive zoo with examples of all of Niger's birds and animals; an area featuring the characteristic dwellings of the country's main ethnic groups, authentically constructed and furnished; and an active artisanal section where craftspeople skilled in traditional metalwork, weaving and leather are busy at work. The sale of articles made by these craftspeople helps fund ambitious outreach projects as well as academic and vocational courses for underprivileged children. Entry is free and the museum is open daily except Monday from 8 am to noon and 4 to 6 pm.

The **Franco-Nigerien Cultural Centre** is also worth a visit. It generally has some kind of exhibition on as well as films, a craft workshop and a library.

Niamey

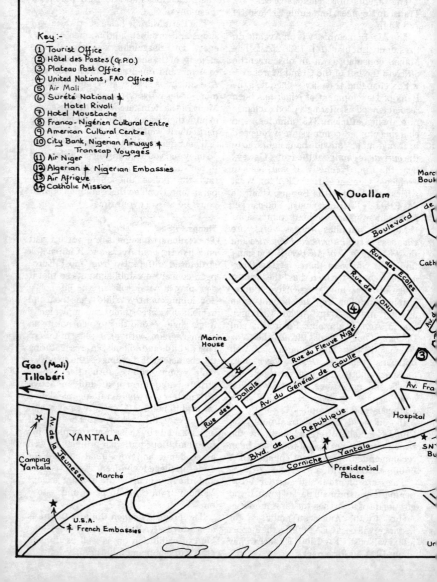

Key:-
1. Tourist Office
2. Hôtel des Postes (G.P.O.)
3. Plateau Post Office
4. United Nations, FAO Offices
5. Air Mali
6. Sureté National & Hotel Rivoli
7. Hotel Moustache
8. Franco-Nigérien Cultural Centre
9. American Cultural Centre
10. City Bank, Nigerian Airways & Transcap Voyages
11. Air Niger
12. Algerian & Nigerian Embassies
13. Air Afrique
14. Catholic Mission

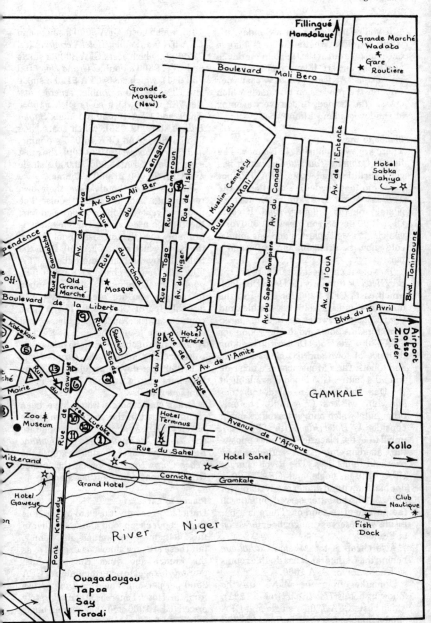

Fillingué
Hamdalaye

Grande Marché
Wadata
Gare
Routière

Boulevard Mali Bero

Grande
Mosquée
(New)

Muslim Cemetery

Hotel
Sabka
Lahiya

Av. Soni Ali Ber
Av. de l'Arewa
Rue du Senegal
Rue du Cameroun
Rue de l'Islam
Rue du Mali
Av. du Canada
Av. de l'Entente

Rue de Gandatche
Old
Grand Marché
Mosque
Av. de

pendence
off.
Boulevard de la Liberté

Rue du Tchad
Rue du Togo
Rue du Niger
Av. du Niger

Av. du Sapeurs Pompiers
Av. de l'OUA
Bld. Tanimoune

Blvd. du 15 Avril
Airport
Dosso
Zinder

Rue Kobakain
Stadium
Rue du Stade
Hotel
Ténéré
Rue du Maroc
Rue de la Libre
Av. de l'Amité

GAMKALE

Mairie
Rue du Gaweye

Zoo
Museum
Rue de Pres. Luebke
Hotel
Terminus
Avenue de l'Afrique

Kollo

Mitterand
Rue du Sahel
Hotel Sahel

Hotel
Gaweye
Grand Hotel
Carniche
Gamkale

Club
Nautique

Pont Kennedy

River Niger

Fish
Dock

Ouagadougou
Tapoa
Say
Torodi

If you're in Niamey on a Sunday, it's worth enquiring whether there is a horse or camel race out at the **Hippodrome** on the way to the airport. If you can't make this, no worries. At least you can feast your eyes on the procession of camels which crosses the **Kennedy Bridge** every evening at sundown laden with firewood.

Places to Stay

There are two campsites in Niamey. The first is *Camping Touristiques*, which has good facilities and costs CFA 750 per night (no tent needed). The other is the *Yantala* about five km north-west of Niamey on the Tillabery road. It costs CFA 1000 per person plus CFA 500 for a vehicle. It's well guarded and has toilets, cold showers, drinkable tap water and a bar.

Two of the cheapest hotels here are the *Bar/Hotel De* (formerly the Hotel Domino), which costs CFA 2200 for a bed in the dormitory and CFA 3600 a double; and *Chez Moustache*, which has beds in shared roms for CFA 2500 and double rooms for CFA 5300. The Hotel De is within walking distance of town and has clean showers and toilets. Chez Moustache is a taxi ride from the centre. Good food is available at the De – half a chicken, salad, tomatoes and chips will cost CFA 1500. The only other hotel which budget travellers might consider is *Hotel Rivoli* (tel 733 849), uphill from the Place de Kennedy opposite the Canadian embassy. It is often used by overland tour buses. The Rivoli charges CFA 5150 a single and CFA 5700 a double. Lunch and dinner are available for CFA 2500, the latter served outside on the pavement restaurant. There is a bar inside which serves draught beer (*pression* in French).

Also cheap is the *Mission Catholique* behind the Cathedral. It has double rooms with showers for CFA 1000.

Upmarket from the above are the following hotels: *Hotel Sahel* (tel 732 231), which costs CFA 7700 a single and CFA 8300 a double; *Les Roniers Hotel* (tel 723 138), which costs CFA 8000 a single and CFA 8700 a double; *Hotel Terminus* (tel 732 692), which costs CFA 8000 a single and CFA 9800 a double; *Grand Hotel* (tel 732 641), which costs CFA 9150 a single and CFA 10,050 a double; *Tenere Hotel* (tel 732 020), which costs CFA 9150 a single and CFA 10,050 a double; *Sabka Lahiya* (tel 732 933), which costs CFA 9150 a single and CFA 10,050 a double; and *Hotel Gaweye* (tel 733 400), the most expensive at CFA 18,000-19,000 a single and CFA 20,000-21,000 a double.

All the above hotels have their own restaurants and swimming pools. The pools are generally open to non-residents; the fee for use varies. The cheapest is probably the Olympic-sized pool behind the Sahel which costs CFA 250. Both the Sabka Lahiya and the Tenere charge CFA 500. The Gaweye charges CFA 800. The pool at the Terminus is really only open for people who are prepared to pay a monthly fee of CFA 4000. If you have contacts at the American embassy you may be able to use the pool at the Les Roniers free of charge with the manager's consent. The pool at the *Grand Hotel* (CFA 500 per day) is popular with many travellers and is a good place to make contacts for lifts.

Other cheap hotels which have been recommended in the past but which we haven't had news about for some while are the *Hotel Nigerienne* and *L'Elephant Blanc*. It's no longer possible to stay at the *Peace Corps Hostel* between the former Grand Marche and the Rue Salaman.

Places to Eat

Until fairly recently it used to be possible to get good, cheap food at one or other of the Vietnamese restaurants in Niamey, but these are now almost as expensive as the French and other European restaurants (expect to pay a minimum of CFA 2500 per person). The *Nam Dinh* across from the Hotel Tenere is still moderately priced (CFA 1000-2500 per person) but is only open for dinner (7 to 10 pm) and is closed on Wednesday. In the same bracket is *L'Ermitage*, which offers steak and frites dinners in the outdoor beer garden. There is an air-conditioned bar inside and occasional live music on Saturday. The *Epi d'Or* snack bar is reasonably priced and popular with local people and expatriates after the cinema. It has a French café/bar atmosphere. The *American Recreation Centre* snack bar (open from noon to 8 pm daily) is definitely inexpensive for hamburgers and meals. Although officially only open to members, guests and Peace Corps volunteers, in practice it's open to all and the pool is free. Non-members just have to pay more for food and drink, but the Nigerien barmen can easily be made to believe that you are a Peace Corps volunteer and (therefore) a member. Otherwise you can buy temporary membership for CFA 1200 per month. Apart from the pool, there is a tennis court and table tennis.

Other restaurants which have been recommended by travellers include *Restaurant Marhaba*, down the last side street on the right-hand side off the Rue de Gaweye before the junction with the Boulevard de la Liberté (slow service but good cheap food); and *Restaurant Islam* in the Soui Al Ber district (all the taxi drivers know this place).

The other restaurants in Niamey are expensive and only worth considering if you feel like a splurge. They include the *Lotus Blue* (Vietnamese food, dinners only, pleasant garden setting, closed Tuesday); the *Oriental* (Middle East cuisine with daily specials, dinners only, closed Wednesday, return taxis difficult to get); the *Vietnam* (Vietnamese and European dishes, dinners only, closed Monday); *La Cascade* (French and Italian cuisine, dinners only refreshing atmosphere, closed Tuesday); *Chez Nous* (excellent French cuisine, dinners only, air-conditioned, closed Sunday); and *La Flottille* (Russian cuisine, lunch and dinner, closed Sunday).

Most of the main hotels have their own restaurants, and some of them are no more expensive than the restaurants mentioned above. They include the *Tenere Hotel* (French cuisine, lunch from the menu at around CFA 2500, dinner a la carte, open daily); *Terminus Hotel* (French cuisine, lunch and dinner, open daily); *Sahel Hotel* (fair French cuisine and good salads plus pizza in the evenings, lunch – CFA 2200 from the menu – and dinner, open daily, outdoor portion has a superb view over the Niger River but you need to have mosquito repellant handy); *Sabka Lahiya* (Tunisian cuisine, lunch and dinner, open daily, off the airport road near the Wadata Market); *Les Roniers Hotel* (French cuisine, lunch and dinner, open daily, located on the old Tillabery Road past the American embassy); *Rivoli Hotel* (steaks and brochettes with a menu for CFA 2500, lunch and dinner, open daily); *Grand Hotel* (mediocre French cuisine but very good omelettes, lunch and dinner, air-conditioned dining room, menu for CFA 2500, open daily, attractive terrace overlooking the Niger River, good for breakfast); and the *Gaweye Hotel* (two restaurants serving excellent French cuisine, lunch and dinner, attractive setting, excellent pizzas on Friday nights at 9 pm by the pool for CFA 2500).

If you're looking for some action in the evenings, one of the most popular places is the *Marine House* next door to the Tunisian embassy which is open to the public on Monday, Wednesday and Friday nights (and sometimes on Saturday too). They have a bar and swimming pool (the latter can be used every day of the week) and show movies on Monday and Wednesday nights. Entry to the movies cost CFA 300-500. The movies start at 8 pm though most people get there earlier – it opens at 6 pm. The place is run by the boys of the US Marine Corps who guard the embassy, but they're a good bunch of guys.

There are a number of nightclubs/discotheques which open early but really only start moving about 11 pm and go on till the wee hours. They're all relatively expensive, but the best is probably the *Fo-Fo Club* in the Sahel Hotel which plays African music. Few Europeans go there and drinks cost CFA 1000. Others include the *Hi-Fi* (drinks CFA 1000); the *Satellite* (drinks CFA 1000); and the *Kakaki* in the Gaweye Hotel (drinks CFA 2500).

TAHOUA

Tahoua is closed to foreigners at present and has been for some time. You will have to bypass the town.

It's possible to camp in the grounds of *Le Campement* for CFA 150 per person, if and when it opens up. Otherwise, ask at the *Maison de Jeunes*. If it's a room you want, you'll have to stay at Le Campement, as this is the only hotel in town.

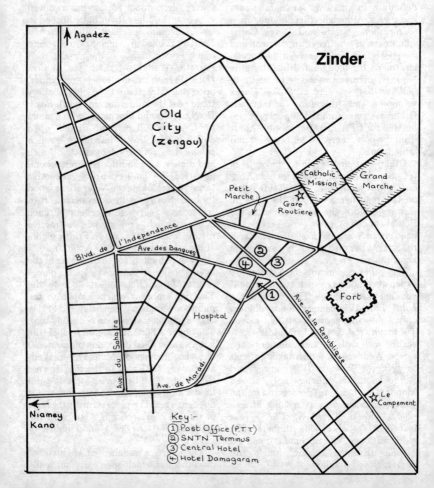

Zinder

Agadez

Old City (zengou)

Catholic Mission

Grand Marche

Petit Marche

Gare Routiere

Blvd. de l'Independence

Ave. des Banques

② ④ ③

①

Ave. de la Republique

Fort

Hospital

Ave. du Sahara

Ave. de Maradi

Niamey Kano

Le Campement

Key :-
① Post Office (P.T.T)
② SNTN Terminus
③ Central Hotel
④ Hotel Damagaram

ZINDER

Like Agadez, Zinder is one of the traditional market towns of Niger and was the capital until 1926. Don't miss the beautiful large **market** here which takes place on Thursday. There is a lot of good quality leatherwork. The market is also a good place for securing lifts to Kano with Nigerians who come up for the market.

Hotel Central, across the street from the post office, is probably the best place to stay. It has huge rooms with their own shower and toilet and even air-conditioning (when it works). The cost is CFA 4000 a double, and you can get as many people as you like into a room so long as you're discreet about it. The *Peace Corps Hostel* might still be worth checking out, as they sometimes put people up. It's near the Maison de Jeunes. The *Catholic Mission* no longer takes travellers.

Two cafés which offer good, cheap food are *Restaurant Senegalaise* and *La Liberté*. You can also get cheap food at the Gare Routiere.

AIR MOUNTAINS

If you're not madly intent on heading south out of the desert, it's worth considering a visit to the Air Mountains east of Arlit or north of Agadez. One recommended place which isn't too hard to get to is **Iferouane**. The world wildlife centre there is built in traditional style without the use of wood. Unfortunately, our correspondent didn't say much else about the place (where are you Jo Hanson?).

Nigeria

Nigeria is Africa's most populous state and one of its wealthiest. It consists of a fascinating collection of different peoples, cultures, histories and religions. Never united at any period in the past, today it is trying to find a sense of nationhood out of the rivalries and bloodshed which bedevilled the country for years after independence. Its diversity is a powerful attraction to travellers, but there is another, rather negative, side to the country. This is the unbridled and often ill-considered 'development' that has taken place, particularly in the cities, which was fuelled by what appeared to be an endless source of easy money through the sale of oil. As a result, most Nigerian cities have been transformed beyond recognition. Overcrowding, pollution, noise and traffic chaos, soaring crime rate, and inadequacy of public utilities combine to make most urban centres hell-holes. Rapid development has also led to massive migration from the country to the cities, and consequently a decline in agricultural production. This in turn, has meant more and more importation of food. Inflation has also taken its toll. Nigeria is now a very expensive country and many travellers are being forced to rush through as quickly as possible. But if you come to the conclusion that things have got out of hand, at least you won't be alone in thinking that. Many Nigerian workers are finding it increasingly difficult to cope and the government threw out about three million (!) West African expatriates who thought they could make big money from the oil boom.

The first recorded state which grew up in this part of Africa was Kanem, located north-east of Lake Chad. Its wealth was based on control of one of the most important trans-Saharan trade routes from West Africa to the Mediterranean. On the strength of this, it was able to raise a powerful army and extend its control over neighbouring areas. Islam became the state religion quite early on in the empire's history. Like other empires in the Sahel, it occasionally fell on hard times and in the 14th century was invaded and forced to move south to Borno. In time, however, the empire regained its vigour and reconquered the area it had originally occupied. Meanwhile a number of Islamic Hausa states flourished between the 11th and 14th centuries, based around the cities of Kano, Katsina, Zaria and Nupe.

In the south-west a number of Yoruba empires grew up between the 14th and 15th centuries, centred in Ife, Oyo and Benin. These three cities became important trading and craft centres. Goods produced there and from the area under their control were much in demand in Morocco and the other Islamic Mediterranean states. The political systems of these states rested largely on a sacred monarchy with a strong court bureaucracy and, unlike the states to the north, they retained their traditional pagan religions. Islam made very little headway here until the late 18th century. The Obas (kings) of these states still survive today though, of course, their influence has declined considerably. In the south-east the Ibo and other peoples never developed any centralised empires but instead formed loose confederations.

The first contact between the Yoruba states and the Europeans came in the

15th century with the Portuguese. They began trading in pepper, but this was later supplanted by slaves. Commerce was increasingly directed towards the coast, in contrast with the northern Islamic states which continued to trade principally across the Sahara and remained untouched by Europeans until well into the 19th century. The Portuguese were gradually displaced by the Northern European maritime nations throughout the 16th and 17th centuries and the slave trade expanded dramatically. It's estimated that up to 40 million West Africans were dragged off in chains to the Americas while this sordid trade continued, but human misery wasn't the only result. The internal effects of the trade were catastrophic, resulting in continuous wars, political instability and the neglect of agriculture and other avenues of possible trade. By the time slavery was abolished in the early 19th century, the coastal kingdoms had become so dependent on the trade and so inured to the decadence it engendered that they were unable to make the transition. By that time, however, the British had begun to lay the foundations for direct political control of the hinterland in order to protect their trade monopoly from being challenged by the French. Another change of importance which took place towards the end of the slave trade era was a revolutionary upheaval in the Hausa kingdoms of the north. This led to the replacement of Hausa kings with Fulani and the setting up of the Sokoto caliphate.

Once military conquest was completed, the British were content to rule indirectly through local kings and chiefs, as they were in most other places in their empire. This was not only less costly but guaranteed a stable environment from which economic surplus could be extracted without undue disruption. The policy worked quite well in the north but much less smoothly in the south-west, where none of the traditional rulers had ever extracted taxes. The imposition of these taxes led to widespread resentment among the Yoruba. In the south-east the policy was even less successful, largely because the British did not understand that there had never been any centralised authority in this part of the colony.

As the demand for independence gathered force after WW II, the British attempted to put together a constitution which would take into account the interests of the three main areas of the colony – the north, mainly Moslem with an ethnic majority of Hausa and Fulani; the east, Catholic and mainly Ibo; and the west, mixed Moslem and Anglican and mainly Yoruba. It proved to be an extremely difficult task. The northerners feared that the southerners had an educational advantage that would allow them to dominate politics and commerce, and demanded 50% representation in any central government. There was likewise considerable mistrust among the southerners, the result of fierce competition for jobs in the civil service and for business contracts. The British favoured appeasing the north since the more conservative leaders of this region were seen as the best way of safeguarding British interests after independence and so, in the end, each region was given its own civil service, judiciary and marketing boards (the main earners of foreign exchange). Thus, when independence was granted in October 1960, Nigeria was essentially three nations.

The first six years of independence were disastrous. National politics degenerated into a vicious power game, corruption became rampant and the elite took to accumulating wealth by any means at their disposal. With their interests ignored and faced with extortionate rents and rising food prices, the workers organised a general strike in 1963. This was followed by another strike in 1964 after the government had totally rejected a commission of enquiry's recommendation for an increase in the minimum wage. Their grievances finally exploded in

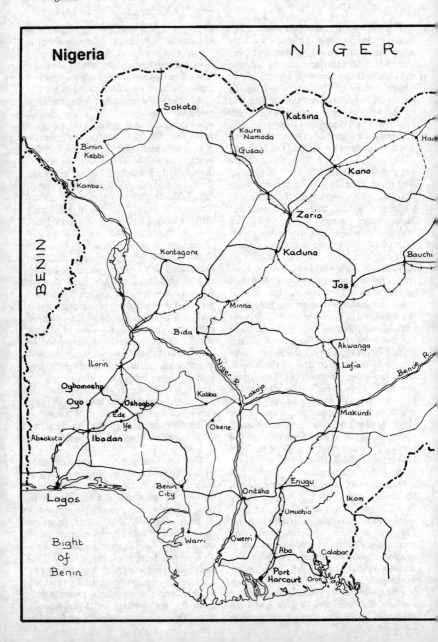

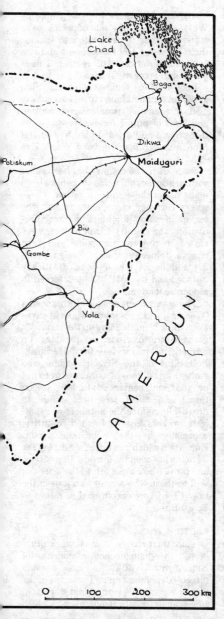

an orgy of looting and violence which swept the country following blatantly rigged elections in the western region in 1965. It was obvious that something had to give, and in early 1966 a group of army majors, most of whom were Ibos, attempted a coup. The prime minister, the premiers of the west and north, and most of the senior army officers were assassinated, but the coup failed when General Ironsi, himself an Ibo, managed to rally the army. What was left of the cabinet hurriedly agreed to hand over power to the army.

Ironsi's accession to power was welcomed by many sections of the Nigerian public, but his regime had no sense of direction nor any idea of how to sort out the disastrous political situation. A few months later he was toppled in a coup staged by a group of northern army officers after anti-Ibo riots had broken out in the north. Ironsi and a number of Ibo officers were killed in the coup and a new regime was set up under the leadership of Lieutenant-Colonel Yakubu Gowon, a Christian officer from a minority group in the north. The coup was viewed with horror in the east and the military commander of the area, Lieutenant-Colonel Ojukwu, refused to recognise Gowon as the new head of government. His antipathy to the new regime was sealed when large-scale massacres of Ibos took place in the north, triggering a return to the east by thousands of Ibos from all over the country. In May 1967, Ojukwu announced the secession of the east and the creation of the independent state of Biafra.

Biafra was recognised by only a handful of African countries, and the civil war dragged on for three years as the Ibo forces fought tooth and claw for every inch of territory which the federal forces took back. By late 1969, however, Biafra faced famine and its forces were compelled to capitulate. Despite the hatreds which had been fanned by civil war, reconciliation was swift and peaceful. Gowon was careful not to treat the Ibo as a vanquished people. Unfortunately, he was unable to use the same degree of imagination to get the economy moving again, and corruption once more grew to intolerable proportions. He was overthrown in a peaceful coup by General Murtala Muhammad while attending an OAU summit meeting in Kampala in 1975.

The new government set a brisk pace and launched a cleanup of the civil service, the judiciary and the universities. Some 10,000 officials were sacked or forced to retire and a start was made on trying to break up the antagonisms between the various regions by creating seven more states – four in the north and three in the south. A decision was also made to move the capital from Lagos to Abuja in the geographical centre of the country. Muhammad was assassinated in an attempted coup in early 1976, but the other members of the regime survived and continued implementing his policies until power was handed back to a civilian government following elections in 1979. The new civilian regime of President Shagari appeared to have its act together and pursued conservative economic policies in an attempt to control inflation and pay off debts. It also adopted increasingly radical policies regarding interference in its internal affairs, particularly by the British.

One of the regime's most dramatic acts was the expulsion of millions of 'illegal' West African expatriate workers, including an estimated two million Ghanaians. Throughout the 1970s people from all over West Africa flocked to Nigeria in the hope of participating in the booming oil-based economy – Nigeria is Africa's largest oil producer with Libya a close second. The oil glut of the early 1980s and the price-cutting which resulted forced the Nigerian government to drastically pare back its expenditures and put in mothballs any project which had not been started. The result was a decline in the demand for labour which forced the government to act, though, of course, the sudden influx of hundreds of thousands of unemployed workers into neighbouring West African states (all of which were suffering from the recession to various degrees) was a traumatic event and one from which they are still reeling. This is particularly true of Ghana.

Like previous regimes, however, Shagari's government failed to make headway against economic problems, corruption and theft of public funds. He was overthrown in a military coup led by General Mohammed Buhari on New Year's Eve 1983.

Since then, the country has been ruled with an iron fist, but bold moves have been made to get the country together. There was a currency changeover to halt the export of naira (for black market speculation), the country's land borders were closed to prevent smuggling and have remained closed ever since, foreign spending and imports have been drastically reduced and the IMF has been forced to moderate its demands.

The government has also introduced a 'War Against Indiscipline' which involves everything from cleaning up the country's garbage-strewn cities to queueing up properly (a major feat for Nigerians!). Politicians of the Shagari regime who embezzled millions of naira have been put on trial and sentenced to long prison terms. An effort has been made to drastically reduce the numbers of expatriate workers from developed countries, especially in the education sector. Education which was once free during the oil boom has seen the introduction of fees, and those who cannot afford these fees as well as those who cannot find jobs in the towns are being encouraged to return to agriculture.

FACTS

Despite the revenue from oil, agriculture is still the main economic mainstay of Nigeria with 70-80% of all male workers directly dependent on it. The crops of the north are mainly groundnuts, cotton, sugar cane, rice, wheat and tobacco, which reflect the comparatively short rainy season in that area and the use made of riverine lands flooded during the rains. In the south the most important crops are cocoa, rubber, palm oil and kola nuts. From the central area comes beniseed, ginger and yams. The Fulani of the north keep large herds of cattle, sheep and goats.

The comparatively high wages paid in the oil sector and in the towns has encouraged large-scale migration from the countryside to the towns. The result has been increasing reliance on food imports and high prices which agricultural workers have been unable to cope with.

The climate is hot and dry in the north and hot and wet in the south. The rainy season in the north is between April and September while in the south it is from March to November. A long dry season stretches from December to March when the cooling Harmattan blows off the desert. The coast is an almost unbroken line of sandy beaches and lagoons running back to creeks and mangrove swamps. It's very humid here most of the year. The population is estimated to be around 93-100 million.

VISAS
Visas are required by all. Nationals of South Africa are not admitted. You can expect a lot of hassle getting a Nigerian visa these days. Far from encouraging people to go there, Nigeria is actively throwing them out – by the millions. Depending on where you apply, you may have to show them sufficient funds (US$60 per day is acceptable) and a letter of recommendation from a Nigerian citizen together with his/her passport! These are not the only complications. The price of a visa varies considerably from place to place and on your nationality. They're supposed to be free for British people (and possibly other Commonwealth nations too), but this doesn't seem to have stopped certain embassies and consulates from charging for them.

One of the best places to get a visa appears to be the British embassy in Tunis, where they are free irrespective of your nationality and take 24 hours to come through. In Niamey, Niger, a one-month visa costs CFA 4000 and takes 48 hours to issue. In Douala, Cameroun, they cost CFA 3500 and take 24 hours to issue. You can't get visas at the border.

If there's any indication in your passport that you have visited South Africa, you'll be refused entry. If you're Australian, they'll know whether you've been regardless of what is stamped in your passport. It seems there has been some collaboration between immigration departments somewhere along the line, as all Nigerian border posts have a computer printout with details of all Australians who have visited South Africa. Now who would have done that?

Cameroun visas There are consulates in Lagos (4 Elsi Fermi St, Victoria Island) and Calabar (Ezuk Nkapa St). Visas cost naira 7.50, require three photos and usually take 24 hours to come through, they are sometimes issued the same day. Visas are valid for a stay of 20 days.

MONEY
US$1	=	naira 0.76
£1	=	naira

The unit of currency is the naira = 100 kobo. Import/export of local currency is allowed up to naira 50. Between 24 April and 5 May 1984, Nigeria closed its land borders to effect a currency change operation which involved all old naira notes being exchanged for new bills. The idea was to catch out tax evaders, hoarders and black marketeers. It hasn't made much difference to the availability of naira on the street in Cotonou or Lomé, however, but you do need to be able to recognise the old and new notes – the old notes are now worthless. The design on the new notes has not changed but the colour has. Here's what to look for:

Value	Old Notes	New Notes	
		Front	Back
naira 1	green	red & green	olive green
naira 5	»	blue & crimson	crimson
naira 10	»	red & orange	red
naira 20	»	blue & green	green

The 50-kobo notes remain unchanged.

Black market rates for the currency are US$1=naira 3 (cheques) and US$1-naira 4 (cash).

Banks charge heavy commissions for changing traveller's cheques. This can be as high as naira 2 for each transaction. In general, banks will not accept CFA so you must change them on the street. Try not to end up with a surplus of naira when you're ready to leave. Even if you got them at a bank and have a receipt to prove it, the banks at the airport will not reconvert into hard currency unless you originally changed your money there. Even if you did, it can take up to half a day to get your money.

In Lagos the place to change money officially and quickly is either at the airport or at the First Bank around the corner from the Canadian High Commission. Both charge only a nominal commission.

Nigeria is a very expensive country, so if you're on a budget then get through as quickly as possible.

The airport departure tax for internal flights is naira 2. For international flights the tax is naira 5.

LANGUAGE

English is the official language. The main African languages are Hausa (in the north), Yoruba (in the south-west) and Ibo (in the south-east). There are also large numbers of Edo and Efik speakers.

GETTING THERE & AROUND

Nigeria's land borders are closed so overland travel is impossible. You must fly into the country. There have been rumours suggesting the borders may open again soon, but nothing is definite. Keep your eye on the newspapers and your ear on the travellers' grapevine.

Air

You must pay for international flight tickets with either hard currency or with naira accompanied by a bank receipt, but the bank receipt is not taken from you when you buy a ticket, so you can use it to buy as many tickets as you like. There might be a possible snag, however. Usually currency declaration forms are just given a cursory glance, but if you were questioned about where you got the money to buy the ticket, you'd have to come up with a convincing story or pay a bribe. This is totally acceptable at Nigerian customs and is generally a share of the money you saved buying the ticket.

And that isn't the only problem. When you're taking a flight in Nigeria, either domestic or international, get to the airport hours in advance. Planes are often overbooked by double and even triple.

If you're flying into Lagos, make sure you're not the last off the plane and make sure all your papers are in order; otherwise you can expect to start handing out the bribes.

Some sample fares are:
Lagos-Cotonou: naira 30
Lagos-Lomé: naira 50
Lagos-Abidjan: naira 120
Lagos-Douala: naira 60
Lagos-Nairobi: naira 350 (excursion fare, one month naira 405 return.

Buy your tickets at the racecourse in Lagos.

Road

The roads in this country are very good and most are sealed, so journey times tend to be relatively short and predictable compared with those in some of the neighbouring countries. Hitching is usually easy, especially in the north, and you will be offered quite a few free lifts. All the same, you should ask about this when you get into a car because if the driver didn't intend to give you a free lift and you haven't agreed on a price, you're likely to end up paying twice what the locals pay.

Apart from hitching, one of the best forms of road transport are the 'passenger transport cars,' which are Ford Transit vans or shared taxis. They're fast and leave when full. Check out what the other passengers are paying before you get in; otherwise the drivers will ask for as much as they think they can get away with. Taxi drivers are pirates and the fares posted on cab windows are merely a joke.

A few large bus companies run buses between the main centres of population.

Some examples of fares and journey times follow:

Lagos-Ibadan Naira 5 by taxi; takes about one hour.

Ibadan-Kaduna Naira 12 by *Hiace* minibus; takes 12 to 13 hours.

Kaduna-Kano Naira 5; takes about three hours.

Maiduguri-Kano Buses cost naira 5.50, minibuses naira 7 and Peugeot taxis naira 12. The journey takes 5½ to 6 hours.

Lagos-Owerri Naira 15 by taxi.

Owerri-Umuahia Naira 2 by taxi.

Umuahia-Enugu Naira 5 by taxi.

Lagos-Benin City Naira 5 by bus; naira 12 by taxi.

Lagos-Onitsha Naira 15 by bus.

Benin City-Onitsha Naira 2 by bus.

Onitsha-Ikom (Cameroun border) Naira 12 and takes all day.

Onitsha-Enugu Naira 2.

Enugu-Abakaliki Naira 2.

Abakaliki-Ikom Naira 4.

Ikom-Mfum (Cameroun border) Naira 1 to 2 by taxi.

Aba-Calabar Naira 4 by taxi.

Calabar-Ikom Naira 7 by taxi.

Gambaro-Maiduguri This northern border crossing route between Cameroun and Nigeria costs naira 2 by minibus or naira 3 by Peugeot taxi.

Maradi-Kano This is one of the three possible routes from Niger to Nigeria. A taxi will cost CFA 2500 and takes about five hours. When you get to Katsina don't be surprised if the driver pulls into the truck park, grabs your bags and walks away without a word. Drivers sometimes transfer passengers from one vehicle to another for the remainder of the journey to Kano. You don't pay extra if this happens.

Rail

There are two main railway lines which run north from the coast. The first starts in Lagos and goes to Kano via Ibadan, Oyo, Ogbomosho, Kaduna and Zaria. The other starts in Port Harcourt and runs to Maiduguri via Aba, Enugu, Makurdi and Jos. The two lines are connected between Kaduna and Kafanchan. There is also a branch line from Zaria north to Gusau and Kaura Namoda. Trains are the cheapest way of getting around, though they are definitely slower than the buses and taxis. Third class is crowded and uncomfortable – it's best to travel 2nd class.

Kano-Port Harcourt There is a daily train in either direction (at 11 am from Kano). If you're only going as far as Aba (en route to Calabar/Oron and then the boat to Cameroun), the train arrives in Aba at 4 pm the next day. The fare as far as Aba is naira 43.90 (1st class – private compartment, sleeping berth, toilet and fan) and naira 11.20 (2nd class – seats only). Along this same route there is also the *Daily Express* bus which leaves from Sabon Gari in Kano around 5.30 to 6 am, costs naira 15 and takes about 12 hours. It isn't as safe as the train.

Boat

A popular way of getting to Cameroun from Nigeria (or vice versa) used to be to take a boat from Idua Oron near Calabar to a small place near Limbe (formerly Victoria) which isn't marked on the maps. This is now illegal because of the border closure. Should the route open up again, however, the possibilities will probably be much the same as they were previously. If that's the case, there will be a choice of boats, but the cheapest are the open fishing boats which leave daily around 8 pm and cost naira 25. They take 12 to 14 hours. Although these boats are safe, they're often very crowded and there may be up to 150 people on a 15-metre-long boat! Forget about sleep, as there's too much whingeing, arguing and quarrelling going on all night. The other boat is a speedboat known locally as the *Flying Boat*; the fare is CFA 10,000 and the trip takes three hours. The speedboat leaves daily at 10 am, which means you'll have to stay overnight in Oron, as the ferry from Calabar doesn't arrive in time to connect with it. There are very few hotels in Oron so expect to pay naira 40 a double. This makes it an expensive trip, so if you're not thinking of taking the fishing boats then it's worth considering the *Air Nigeria* flight from Calabar to Douala which costs naira 35.

The ferries from Calabar to Oron are somewhat unpredictable. The first one leaves between 8 and 9 am, the second around 2.30 pm and the last around 8 pm. The last boat usually stays in Oron overnight.

To/from Niger

The main route between these two countries is from Kano to Zinder, but you can also go from Birni N'Konni to Sokoto and from Maradi to Kano via Katsina. There is plenty of transport in either direction along the first route, but it tends to be expensive (expect to pay around naira 20) and bargaining doesn't get you very far. If you're hoping to find a free lift, Tuesday and early Wednesday are the best from Kano to Zinder, and Thursday is the best in the opposite direction. At least 30 trucks do the run to pick up produce from the Zinder market which takes place every Thursday.

Between Maradi and Kano there are trucks and taxis, the latter costing CFA 2500 and taking five hours. You may have to change vehicles in Katsina, but this doesn't cost extra.

To/from Benin & Togo

If you like, you can get a Peugeot taxi all the way from Lagos to Lomé (Togo), but these can cost up to naira 25 plus a charge for your baggage. The time taken for this run depends very much on border formalities rather than on the distance (it's quite a short run). Taxis doing this run leave from Lagos Island at the end of Carter Bridge. It's probably cheaper to do the journey in stages. First get a taxi from Lagos to the border (naira 2), then a second from there to Cotonou (CFA 2000) and a third from there to Lomé (CFA 1500).

To/from Cameroun

One of the most popular routes has already been covered under 'Boats.' The usual road route is between Ikom and Mamfe. You can get to Ikom from Enugu (naira 6) or from Calabar (naira 7 by Peugeot taxi). From Ikom you take another taxi to Mfum (the Nigerian border village) for naira 1 or 2. Unless you have through transport, it is a one-km walk from Mfum to Ekok (the Cameroun border village). From Ekok there are taxis to most of the towns in western Cameroun via Mamfe.

There is also another crossing in the far north between Maroua and Maiduguri.

To Lake Chad

If you want to visit Lake Chad, make sure you go about it the right way. The only place you can get a permit (and you must have one) is from the Maiduguri military base. Don't zip through Maiduguri and expect to get permission from the Mile 4 military base in Baga near the lake. Two travellers who attempted to do this a while ago were arrested by a psychotic commander there who accused them of being mercenaries and spies. He took them under military escort to Maiduguri where they were interrogated all day. When the travellers asked why they would be so stupid as to go to a military base to ask for a permit if they were spies, they were accused of making fun of the military and of plotting to kill the commander's driver and steal the truck! When those in charge of the interrogation got bored with asking questions the two were transferred to a military barracks and guarded by 30 fully armed soldiers. The next day they were taken to the police, asked what tribe they were from (!!), had their bags searched and were finally allowed to go. What a farce! All the same, get that permit in Maiduguri.

A Peugeot taxi from Maiduguri to Baga via Dikwa costs naira 7. There are also minibuses for naira 5. From Baga to the lakeside transport costs 50 kobo. This last stretch of the road is very rough.

PLACES TO STAY

Accommodation in Nigeria is ridiculously expensive. Even a small, very basic room will often cost you naira 40 per night, while in Lagos most places charge naira 100. In the past, many travellers tried to get onto one of the expatriate circuits (construction industry, universities and volunteer organisations) in the hope of being offered accommodation in exchange for a little help here and there. These days this is very difficult, not only because Nigeria has cut down drastically on new projects and expatriate labour, but also because the expatriates themselves have become very unfriendly towards travellers. We've had a number of letters from these people complaining about our past suggestions that travellers might be able to find overnight accommodation with them. I agree that if accommodation is offered, those who benefit from it ought to cover any expenses involved; however, I also feel that there's an element of whingeing in these complaints. Travellers turn up all the time and stay in my humble shed and I've yet to turn anyone away.

ABA

You might be able to find a bed at the *Catholic Mission* here. Father Peter is friendly but please make sure you leave a donation. For food, try the *Etona Restaurant* (in the Etona Hotel) which has excellent, reasonably priced food for 50 kobo (soup, chicken, vegetables, chips, fruit salad and bread). It's open from 7 pm.

BENIN CITY

Benin is one of the old Yoruba capitals. A highlight of a visit is the **museum**, with its very interesting collection of artefacts from the kingdom which flourished here for centuries before the advent of colonialism. It's also possible to visit the **Oba's Palace**, but you need to make arrangements in advance. Try to do this in Lagos.

One of the cheapest places to stay is *Tommy's Guest House* near the Seven Sisters' Hotel. It costs naira 10-15 a double with fan, radio, toilet paper, towels and clean sheets daily. The guest house is very clean, bucket showers are available and there's a good bar. Other places which have been used in the past are the *Seven Sisters' Hotel*, a whorehouse with character but no running water at naira 20 per night; and *Hotel Crispo*.

CALABAR

The *Catholic Mission* and the *Methodist Mission* are worth trying before you resign yourself to an hotel. One of the cheapest hotels is the *Ropsop Guest House*, 91 Palm St near the Cameroun consulate, which costs naira 15 per night. A *CUSO* hostel may be opening up soon, so ask around. (CUSO is a Canadian volunteer organisation. They don't appreciate travellers dropping in on members' homes, but their hostels are open to all).

The Cameroun consulate is difficult to find and taxi drivers generally don't know where it is. It's at 6 Ezuk Nkapa St (though a recent letter said it was at 50 Main St on the second floor). There is a side entrance which is not at all obvious. Visas cost naira 6.50 and take 24 hours.

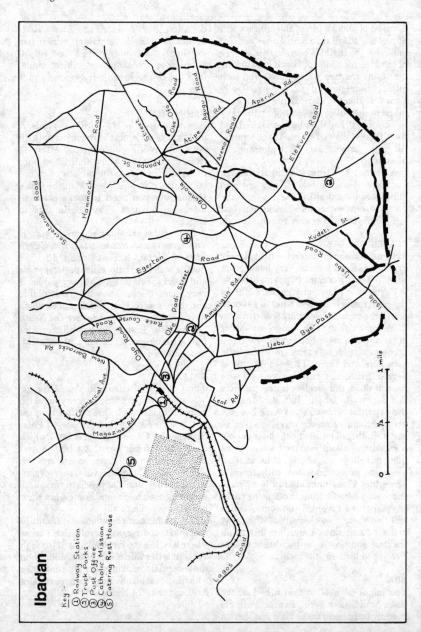

Ibadan

Key:-
① Railway Station
② Truck Parks
③ Post Office
④ Catholic Mission
⑤ Catering Rest House

ENUGU

Enugu was one of the principal centres of resistance during the Biafran war, but it has now fully recovered and is a very green and prosperous-looking city with extremely friendly people.

For a place to stay, try either *St Helen's Guest House* or the *Palm Beach Hotel*.

IBADAN

Ibadan is as large as Lagos but is much easier to get around. It also has one of the largest markets in Nigeria – the Dugbe Market – next to the post office (No 3 on the street map).

The best place to stay here is the *CUSO* hostel. You can pick up the key to this place at the office at 836 Adelabu Rd (tel 414032), which is a short walk from the hostel. To get to the office take a mini-van from Dugbe Market to 'Ring Challenge' and get yourself dropped off at 'Joyce B' pharmacy. From there it's 200 metres' walk down the street running beside Joyce B (look for the small CUSO signs).

There are some Lebanese restaurants in Ibadan where you can get excellent food, though they're a little pricey. If you want some real luxury (after the desert, for instance), you can bluff your way into IITA (Institute of Tropical Agriculture), where you can go for a swim and eat at the subsidised restaurant. They will hardly question you at the front gate, but have an expatriate name handy (any will do) and prefix it with 'Dr' if asked who you want to see. IITA is a luxurious research station staffed mainly by high-priced expatriate scientists.

IFE

Ife is one of the centres of traditional Yoruba culture. The university here is the home of the national carver of Nigeria – Burmadele. It's also a centre of batik dying. There's a small but pleasant museum which is free of charge. If you're interested in carving, seek out Gabriel Alaye across from the *Mayfair Hotel* or visit St Joseph's Workshop at Inisha (a half-hour taxi ride north of Oshogbo), where there are many carvings on display. You can camp there too (beautiful grounds).

The best way to find accommodation is to befriend an expatriate or a Nigerian who is either studying or teaching at the university. If unsuccessful, you can camp at the *Catholic Mission*, St Peter & Paul Church on the main road.

IKOM

This is the last main Nigerian town on the southern route into the Camerouns. Depending on when you arrive, you may have to spend the night here. If so, try the guest house opposite the bus park. It's nothing to write home about, but it only costs naira 6 a double.

JOS

After the steamy mayhem of Lagos, a trip to Jos might well be the highlight of a visit to Nigeria. It's cool all year round because of the high plateau on which it sits, and there's even plenty to see.

There are two or three church missions to stay at. Two of them are the *ECWA* and the *CBM* missions across the road from each other behind the Challenge Bookshop. They both have rooms for naira 10 each including breakfast. Rooms at the CBM come complete with a kitchen.

Within walking distance of the missions are the **Jos Museum**, **Railway Museum** and the **Zoo**. The most important attraction, however, is the **Museum of Traditional Nigerian Architecture**. Here you can see a series of life-size reproductions of historic buildings in Nigeria which are either run-down or demolished, or to which entry is prohibited. They include the Kano wall, the Kano mosque and the Zaria mosque as well as traditional huts and villages of the various tribes in Nigeria. Well worth a visit and free of charge.

KANO

Kano is the largest city in northern Nigeria and one of the country's most interesting.

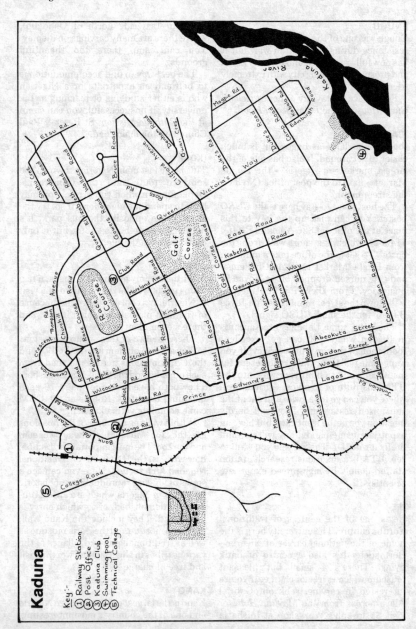

Kaduna

Key:-
① Railway Station
Ⓡ Post Office
Ⓚ Kaduna Club
⊕ Swimming pool
⑤ Technical College

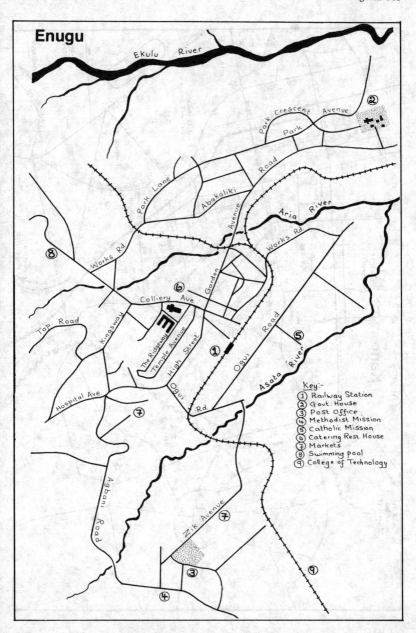

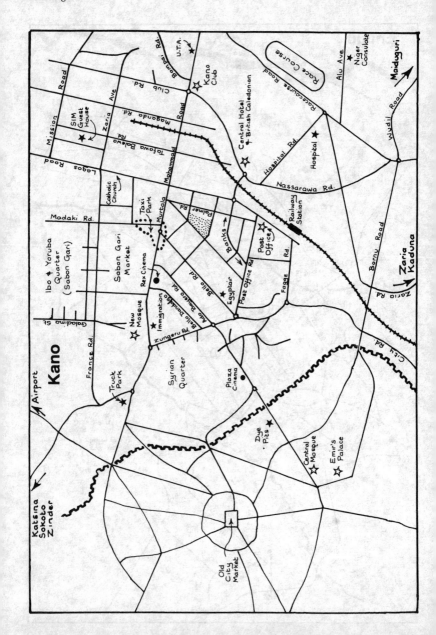

It has a history going back a thousand years and was once a very important trading centre and a crossroads of the trans-Saharan trade routes. The old city consists of thousands of narrow, winding streets enclosed by an impressive city wall which remains largely intact. On the surface, little has changed here for centuries, though outside the city walls oil money has naturally made a major impact. Inside the old city are the famous **dye pits** (Kofar Mata) which are still used to this day and are said to be the oldest in Africa. There is also the **Emir's Palace** (an outstanding example of Hausa architecture), the **Central Mosque** (or Grand Mosque) and the **Gidon Makama market**.

The cheapest place to stay here and just right for travellers is the *CUSO* hostel, off State Rd and opposite Baba's Restaurant. It costs naira 2 per night and has cooking facilities. The next best place is the state government *Kano Tourist Camp*, State Rd (tel 2341), between the Central Hotel and the Kano Club. It costs naira 3 per night for a bed in a room containing eight beds (there are three such rooms), naira 6 for a double private room, or you can camp with your own tent for just naira 2. If you have a vehicle this will cost an extra naira 2. Facilities here are excellent and include mosquito nets, a common room with TV, fridge and air-conditioning, a tennis court, indoor games, bar and restaurant. Meal prices are naira 2 for breakfast, naira 4 for lunch and naira 4.50 for dinner. Also in much the same price bracket is the *SIM Guest House*, between Zaria Avenue and Mission Rd near the SIM Eye Hospital.

Most of the other places to stay are quite pricey and are going to cost between naira 20-25 a single and up to naira 40 a double. The only exceptions to this are: *Challenge Guest Inn*, 87 Yoruba Rd, Sabon Gari (tel 7719), which costs naira 10 a single and naira 13 a double; *Universal Hotel*, 86 Church Rd, Sabon Gari, which costs naira 15 a single (no doubles); *Hotel de France*, 54 Tafawa Balewa Rd, a small place with 12 rooms each with private toilet which costs naira 12 a single and naira 15 a double with meals available at naira 4 (breakfast) and naira 5 (lunch and dinner); and the *Criss Cross Hotel*, 2A Church Rd, Sabon Gari (tel 3305), which costs naira 18 a single and naira 30 a double plus meals for naira 3.50 (breakfast), naira 4.50 (lunch) and naira 5.50 (dinner). The latter has a choice of air-conditioned and fan-cooled rooms.

Upmarket from the above are: *Duniya Hotel*, 12 Festing Rd, Sabon Gari (tel 8754/8398), which offers air-conditioned rooms at naira 22 a single and naira 28.50 to 40 a double; *Akija Hotel*, 13 Murtala Muhammed Way (tel 3514/5327), which has air-conditioned rooms for naira 23 a single and naira 30 a double; *Usman Memorial Hotel*, 288 Kurmawa Quarters, which costs naira 20 a single and naira 27 a double; and the *J Heman Hotel*, Sarkin Yaki Rd, Norman's Land, Sabon Gari, which has rooms for naira 20 a single and naira 25 a double. All the above hotels have their own restaurants.

For food, *Baba's Restaurant*, State Rd near the High Courts building, has cheap, filling food (rice and gristle or nam nams and meat) for naira 1.50. Don't order chicken here or you'll get three bones floating in a bowl of sauce for naira 2. If that sounds pretty mean, it should be tempered with the opinion of a Canadian volunteer who worked in Nigeria for several years. He considered the meals here to be 'excellent.' The *Shangri-La* has pleasant Indian food, including vegetarian dishes at reasonable prices. If you're looking for American-style food, go to the *Topper Restaurant* which is at the back of a building on Amadou Bello Way round the corner from the Shangri-La. There is a small sign out front with a top hat painted on it. The prices are reasonable. At other restaurants in town you should expect to pay a minimum of naira 5 (and up to naira 15) for a meal.

A popular watering hole for expatriates and others is the bar at the *Central Hotel*, Club Rd (tel 3051/5141). Similar is the

Kano Club, junction of Bompai Rd and Murtala Mohammed Way (tel 4041). The latter has sports facilities (golf, squash, tennis, badminton, table tennis, snooker), a swimming pool, nightly films, a bar and a restaurant which has a la carte menus from 8 am to midnight. To get in you have to take out a week's temporary membership which costs naira 6 for one person or naira 10 for a couple. There are many other clubs (listed in the Kano State Hotel Guide) if you're looking for somewhere to go in the evening. They're all open to the public, charge naira 2-5 'gate fee' and offer disco, bar and snacks.

The Tourist Office is in the Ministry of Home Affairs and Information building, New Secretariat, Zaria Rd (tel 2341). There is an information kiosk at the airport.

The Niger consulate is on Alu Avenue near the racecourse.

LAGOS

Although a new capital city is being constructed at Abuja near the geographical centre of Nigeria, Lagos remains, for the time being, the capital. Oil money and the lure of getting rich quick have turned this city into a hell-hole. The traffic, noise and pollution are beyond belief. There are piles of garbage everywhere and the public utilities – electricity, water and sewerage – are simply incapable of coping with demand. The same could be said, of course, about Calcutta (India), except that there people take all this in their stride and accept it with stoical indifference. In Lagos there is fierce competition for space, speed and anything else that you might regard as normally available in a city. Rush hours are simply incredible. Most travellers get out fast or simply avoid going there in the first place. Even Nigerians agree that it's a hell-hole. Even so, amongst all this chaos are some beautiful old colonial-style suburbs with rolling lawns and flowering trees. What a contrast!

Information

The Tourist Office is at 47 Marina, Lagos Island. This place and most bookshops in Lagos stock the booklet, 'Guide to Lagos,' which contains lots of information and maps. It's worth getting hold of if you have things to do in this city.

Thomas Cook are at Transcap Voyages, Wesley House, 20/21 Mariba, PO Box 2326, Lagos (tel 415410). There are branches at Apapa, Kaduna, Kano and Port Harcourt.

Useful Addresses

American Express
    Mandilas Travel Ltd, Mandilas House, 96/102 Broad St, PO Box 35, Lagos (tel 663220)
Algerian Embassy
    26 Maitama Sule St, S/W Ikoyi
Australian High Commission
    Investment House (4th floor), 21/25 Broad St (tel 25981/2)
British High Commission
    11 Eleko Crescent, Victoria Island (tel 51630/1/2). There are branches at Ibadan and Kaduna.
Belgian Embassy
    Block B, 12th Floor, 8-10 Broas St
Cameroun Embassy
    4 Elsi Permi Pearse St, Victoria Island. There is a branch at Calabar.
Canadian High Commission
    4 Idowu Taylor St, Victoria Island
Central African Republic Embassy
    108 Awolowo Rd, Ikoyi
Egyptian Embassy
    81 Awolowo Rd, Ikoyi
French Embassy
    1 Queen's Drive, Ikoyi
German Embassy
    15 Eleko Crescent, Victoria Island (tel 58430)
Ghana High Commission
    21/22 King George V Rd
Kenyan High Commission
    25 Queen's Drive, Ikoyi (tel 22024)
Netherlands Embassy
    Western House (12th floor), 8-10 Broad St
Senegal Embassy
    14 Kofo Abayomi Rd, Victoria Island

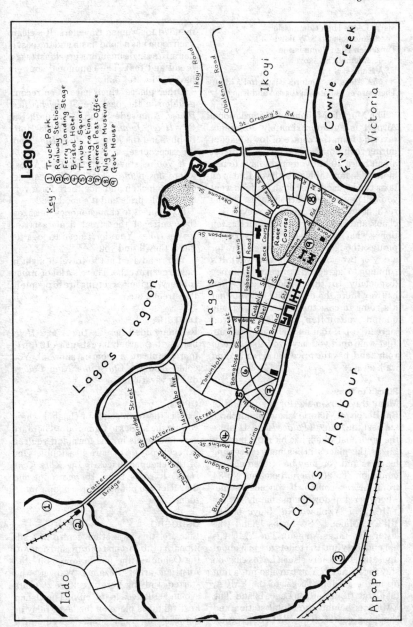

Lagos

Key:-
1. Truck Park
2. Railway Station
3. Ferry Landing Stage
4. Bristol Hotel
5. Tinubu Square
6. Immigration
7. General Post Office
8. Nigerian Museum
9. Govt House

Ikoyi

Five Cowrie Creek

Victoria

Ikoy Road

Obalende Road

St Gregory's Rd.

King George V Rd.

Okesuna St.

Simpson St.

Lewis St.

Igbosere Road

Race Course

Catholic St.

Campbell St.

Broad Street

Lagos

Lagos Lagoon

Bamgbose St.

Takunboh St.

Izumagbo Ave

Victoria Street

Gt Bridge Street

Carter Bridge

St Martins St.

Balogun St.

John Street

Broad Street

Marina

Lagos Harbour

Iddo

Apapa

Sierra Leone High Commission
  29 Ademola St, S/W Ikoyi
Tanzanian High Commission
  45 Ademola St, Ikoyi
USA Embassy
  15A Aleke St, Victoria Island (tel 57320).
There are consulates in Ibadan and Enugu.

The Murtala Mohammed International Airport is an approximately 20-minute taxi ride from the centre of town (except during rush hours). The taxi should cost about naira 20 but you might have to pay more. The fare tables which you find in all taxis can be used as a rough guide to what you will pay outside of rush hours. During rush hours and at night, however, it's chaos, and fares can rise by as much as ten times what is normal. Taxi drivers are pirates (though after you've been here for a day or two you'll understand why). It's common to 'agree' on a price for a journey (especially to the airport), and then halfway there the driver will tell you that it's going to cost the figure he originally quoted you (often double what you 'agreed' to). If that happens, don't argue. Just wait until you have your baggage in your hand, pay the price you agreed to and walk away.

Places to Stay

Many travellers make for the far end of Bar Beach on Victoria Island, about three km past the *Federal Palace Hotel*. Despite the holocaust which has hit most parts of Lagos, this place still has many redeeming features and you may be offered accommodation. To get there, take bus No 84 from the racecourse. If you need somewhere to camp down immediately, try the *YMCA*, 77 Awolowo Rd, Ikoyi; or the *YWCA*, Maloney St, Lagos Island (the latter only takes women). The YMCA is hot and dirty and the toilets are just about unusable, but where else in Lagos can you stay for naira 10? You can also put a tent up in the garden. To get to the YMCA, take a bus from Keffi on Lagos Island. The YMCA is behind the Mobil station and shopping centre. The YWCA is recommended for women travellers. It's clean, each room has a hand basin and the cost is naira 15 a single including breakfast (eggs, bread and tea). The communal showers have cold water only.

Other places which have been recommended in the past are *St Helen's Rest House*, Aninwede St off Edinburgh Rd; *City Hotel*; *Jubilee Hotel* near the Hotel Bobby; and the *King's College Hotel* near the racecourse.

If you're staying at the YMCA, ask where *Josephine Lodge* is. You can get curried chicken and rice there for a very reasonable price and it's good food.

If you need to change money in Lagos, the centre of the street dealers is the *Bristol Hotel*. You don't need to look for them; they'll find you.

You're advised not to travel at night in Lagos even in cabs. There's a lot of armed robbery, vigilantes setting fire to people in the streets, etc.

ONITSHA

Recommended here is the *A P 2 Hotel* behind the market. It costs naira 10 (up to four people to a room is allowed). You could also try *Christ the King College* during vacations.

ORON

This is the town south of Calabar where you get the ferries to Cameroun. There are very few hotels in this town and you can expect to pay up to naira 40 a double. One of the cheaper places is the *King Kong Hotel*. It costs naira 10 per room and they'll let you put up to three people into a room.

OSHOGBO

Like Ife, this is another centre of traditional Yoruba art and culture and home of the Oshun Shrine (made famous by the Austrian artist Suzanne Wanger who started studying Yoruba culture 20 years ago and still lives in the city). The Oshun Festival takes place on the last Friday or Saturday in August and is well worth getting to if you're in the area at the time.

SOKOTO
The cheapest place to stay here is the *SIM Mission Guest House*, which is not easy to find (even the taxi drivers generally don't know where it is), but it only costs naira 2 per night. There is also a government rest house, but it costs considerably more than the SIM Guest House.

Réunion

About 650 km off the east coast of Madagascar and close to Mauritius lies the volcanic island of Réunion. It is one of France's last colonies or, more correctly, an Overseas Department of France administered by a prefect with an elected local council which sends three deputies to the French National Assembly.

The island has a history very similar to that of Mauritius and was visited, though not settled, by Malay, Arab and European mariners. It was first claimed by the French East India Company in 1664, who put in French settlers and Malagasy slaves. Until 1715 they were content to provide only for their own needs and those of passing ships, but when coffee was introduced the island's economy changed dramatically and demanded the large-scale use of slaves – this despite the company's rules specifically forbidding the use of slave labour. As a result of bad management and the rivalry between France and England in the 18th century, government of the island passed directly to France in 1764. In the late 18th century there were a number of slave revolts, and those who managed to escape made their way to the interior. They organised themselves into villages run by democratically elected chiefs and fought to preserve their independence from the colonial authorities.

While the Mascarenes (Réunion, Mauritius, Rodrigues, etc) remained French colonies, Réunion had the function of providing the island group with good food while Mauritius made the profits in the form of sugar exports, but when Mauritius was ceded to the British after the Napoleonic Wars, sugar was introduced to Réunion. The change took place to the detriment of food crops and quickly became the only agricultural activity. It resulted in the dispossession of many small farmers who were forced to sell out to those with capital to invest in the new monoculture, and in the migration of those small farmers to the interior. Like Mauritius, Réunion experienced a labour crisis when slavery was abolished in the first half of the 19th century and, in exactly the same way, the crisis was 'solved' by the importation of contract labourers from India. Many of those imported in the 19th century were Hindus; they remain largely distinct from the Moslem Indians who arrived in the early years of the 20th century.

With competition from Cuba and sugar beet from Europe, Réunion's economy stagnated and resulted in a further concentration of land and capital in the hands of a small French elite. Since then the situation hasn't essentially changed. A left-wing group, the Comité d'Action Démocratique de Sociale, was founded in 1936 on a platform of integration with France, but when the island eventually became a Department after WW II they turned against it because of the obvious futility of it all. The conservatives who initially opposed this integration with France for fear of losing their privileges as colonialists eventually did an about-face too, since they realised that independence would release the resentment of those who had been dispossessed for so long and they would have to face it without French police or military protection.

Like Mauritius, Réunion is populated by descendants of French plantation owners, African slaves and contract

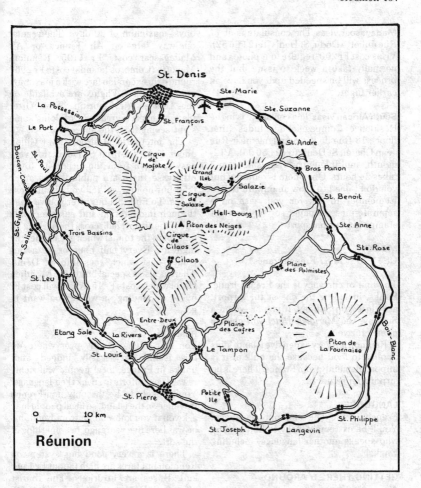

Réunion

labourers from India, but with the addition of about 20,000 Chinese.

Réunion has lush forested mountains, picturesque villages and good hiking trails which rival those in Hawaii, though the beaches are a little disappointing.

VISAS

These are required by all except nationals of Western European countries, North and South American countries (Central America excepted), Australasian countries, Japan and South Korea.

You must have an onward ticket to get into Réunion; an MCO is not acceptable. Also, you might have difficulties at the airport on arrival if you cannot name a place where you intend to stay. If you haven't made up your mind where you are going to stay, Immigration will consider *La Loggia* acceptable. It is at 31 bis Bd Doret (tel 21 59 77).

Madagascar visas The consulate is at 77 Rue Juliette Dodu, St Denis (tel 21 66 52). Visas cost Fr 200, require four photos and normally take a week to issue, but the process will be speeded up if you have an earlier flight.

South African visas The consulate is in the Résidence Compagnie des Indes (first floor), 18 Rue de la Compagnie near Rue Jean Chatel, St Denis (tel 21 50 05). A 12-month, multiple-entry visa is free and takes 24 hours. One photo is required but you don't need to show an onward ticket. Remember to ask for your visa on a separate piece of paper so you don't get stamps in your passport.

MONEY
US$1 = 8.87 French francs

The unit of currency is the French franc. Banks, including the one at the airport, are closed on Sunday. If you arrive on a Sunday, the *Meridien Hotel* will change money for you.

Réunion is a very expensive island. This applies to food because the bulk of it is imported, mainly from France! There is no airport departure tax.

LANGUAGE
French is the one and only language. You'll be extremely lucky to find anyone who speaks another language, including English.

GETTING THERE & AROUND
Air
UTA, *Air France*, *Air Madagascar*, *South African Airways* and *Air Mauritius* operate international flights to Réunion. The French charter company, *Le Point*, has 707 flights from Lyon, France to Réunion for Fr 4800 return. This works out far cheaper than taking the regular airlines.

Réunion-Antananarivo (Madagascar) can be done for Fr 1790 return on an excursion ticket – minimum stay of six days, maximum of 30 days. The regular one-way fare on Air France or Air Madagascar costs Fr 1195. Réunion-Mayotte (Comoros Islands) costs Fr 2960 round-trip excursion fare with a maximum stay of 23 days. Flights are available on the 16-seat Air Mauritius Twin Otter planes; this is a great way of doing some sight-seeing from the air.

The international airport is at Gillot, about eight km from St Denis. It's very easy to hitch from the airport to town; otherwise there are public buses at Fr 6.50 but no one will tell you about these buses. To find this bus after you've been through immigration and customs, walk out of the airport hall, cross the parking lot and get to the tunnel which goes under the highway. Every half hour or so a bus comes past which goes into St Denis. There is also a special bus to the Meridien Hotel which costs Fr 15. A taxi will cost Fr 50-70 depending on where you want to go.

Road
You can hitch virtually everywhere on this island very easily indeed and, unlike in France, local people will richly reward your efforts to speak their language. You're likely to be the only non-French traveller on the island, so local people may ask you if you know 'John from London – he was here five years ago' or something of the sort.

There is a very good bus system on Réunion but fares are high (about Fr 1 per km). Buses are luxurious. The tourist office in St Denis hands out a booklet with maps of the various towns on which are marked the bus stations.

PLACES TO STAY
Hotels and *pensions de famille* are very expensive on this island. Not only that, the relatively cheaper *pensions* are often permanently full (St Denis) or are in towns of little touristic interest (Tampon). There are, however, some cheap accommodation possibilities such as the *Youth Hostel* in

Hell-Bourg, the seven camping sites around the island, the 12 mountain huts (*gites de montagne*) on the hiking trails, the three government-run vacation villages and a few cheap hotels detailed later. Another interesting and inexpensive form of accommodation is the *chambre d'hôte*. This is generally two to three guest rooms in houses which offer *tables d'hôte* – traditional meals of local produce served family-style. Bed and breakfast at these places generally costs Fr 70-100 a double. Meals cost about Fr 45-60 per person including wine and coffee. For a list of these places, contact the office at 2 Avenue de la Victoire, St Denis, one block from the Tourist Office (tel 20 31 90). This office also has information about *gites ruraux*, which are country houses for two to 12 people and which cost Fr 550-1550 per week.

There are municipal campsites at St Gilles les Bain, St Leu, Etang-Sale, Grand 'Anse and Bois Court. A new one is due to open in Cilaos. These sites cost Fr 25 per day plus Fr 3 extra if you want electricity. Water is available on site. You need your own tent to make use of these sites. The one at Etang-Sale is quite small (75 metres wide) and sandwiched between the main St Denis-St Pierre highway and the black sand beach. There are showers, (dirty) toilets, a restaurant and a shop about 200 metres away.

The Creole cuisine on Réunion is a combination of influences from India, Madagascar and France. Spicy curry is the most common dish, usually of chicken, beef or goat (*cabri*). Two speciality curries are turtle (*torture*) and octopus (*zourite*). *Bredes*, a delicious green vegetable somewhat like spinach, is often served. *Rougail*, usually of tomatoes, is a hot sauce similar to Mexican salsa that accompanies most meals.

Regional specialities include the famous lentils and homemade sweet wines of Cilaos, the trout of Hell-Bourg and turtle supplied by the turtle farm in St Leu.

Locally distilled white rum is very cheap and popular. Try *rhum arrange*, which is aged rum flavoured with vanilla, orchid, aniseed and cinnamon. The local beer, *Biere Dodo*, is quite good; otherwise you can drink *pastisse* like many local people do.

Finding cheap or even reasonably priced restaurants in Réunion is very difficult. If you want to keep costs down you will almost always have to order the *plat du jour*, which can be shared between two people because of the amount of bread and rice usually served. Other than this, the best bet is to buy bread, cold cuts, cheese, paté, yogurt, fresh fruit, vegetables and wine (one litre for Fr 8) in the supermarkets and shops. Since you can cook in the Youth Hostel, vacation villages, *gites de montagne* and the campgrounds, you can reduce the high cost of eating out. Nevertheless, the food is delicious and beautifully prepared in the local restaurants.

ST DENIS

You will probably find that many of the *pensions de famille* are full in St Denis, so you may initially have to do a lot of walking around to find a bed. One of the cheapest places is the *Pension Hik*, 12 Rue Labourdonnais (tel 20 05 08), which costs Fr 25 for a bed in the dormitory and Fr 90 for a double room. Another popular place run by very friendly people is *Madame Roche*, 39 Rue General de Gaulle, which costs Fr 85 a single and Fr 170 a double. Meals cost Fr 20 and are excellent. Other travellers have recommended the *Pension Bourbon*, 58 Rue General de Gaulle, which costs Fr 75 per person per night including breakfast, plus Fr 45 for each extra person. Others worth trying are *Madam Smith*, 100 Rue Roland Garros, tel 21 36 19 (Fr 30-40 per night); *Madame Techer*, 18 Rue Sainte-Anne (Fr 50 per night); and *Euro-Pension*, 21 Rue Felix Guyon, tel 21 53 70 (Fr 25-70 per night). Another pension de famille which has been recommended is that of *Madame Moulan*, 4 Rue de la Batterie near the bus station, St

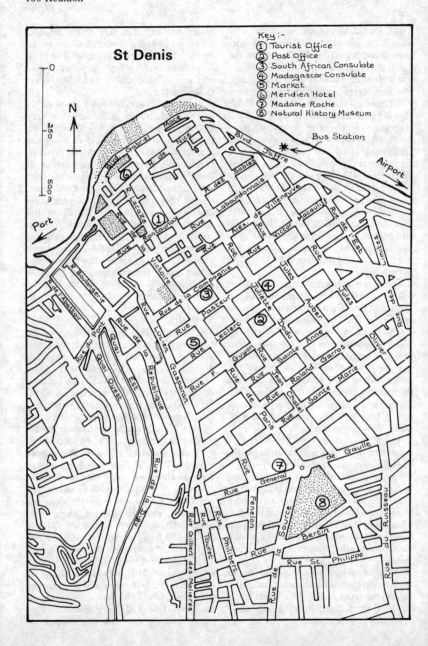

St Denis

Key:-
1. Tourist Office
2. Post Office
3. South African Consulate
4. Madagascar Consulate
5. Market
6. Meridien Hotel
7. Madame Roche
8. Natural History Museum

Denis. It has cooking facilities and costs Fr 50 a double.

The hotel *La Loggia*, 31 bis Bd Doret, off Bd de la Providence (tel 21 5977), has been recommended. It has private rooms from Fr 105 per night and a dormitory where students stay for Fr 40 per night. Many petty officials stay here.

The 'Indian Ocean's first takeaway fast-food outlet' has opened in St Denis. It is *Dan's Hamburgers*, 34 Rue Juliette Dodu. A hamburger, chips and Coke cost Fr 23.40 – said to be the cheapest meal on the island though you can buy *samoussas* (vegetables and herbs fried in batter) from street sellers.

The Tourist Office is at 4 Rue Rontaunay (tel 21 24 53). The people there are very friendly and speak English 'with the Peter Sellers accent.'

The post office here has a good poste restante, but you must pay Fr 2.10 for each letter you collect.

It's worth visiting the **Leon Dierx Art Gallery** on Rue Paris which is open from 10 am to noon and 3 to 6 pm every day except Tuesday. The gallery has a good collection of French Impressionists. The **Natural History Museum** in the Jardin de l'État is also worth a visit. It's open Wednesday, Saturday and Sunday from 8 am to noon and 2 to 5 pm.

HELL-BOURG

Hell-Bourg is in the Salazie Cirque, the most beautiful and verdant of the three *cirques* on Réunion. (A *cirque* is a large, volcanic cul-de-sac valley surrounded by high mountains.) There are some amazing waterfalls in the vicinity, especially **Le Voile de la Mariee** between Salazie and Hell-Bourg which you can walk to. There are many streams where you can bathe.

The best accommodation deal here is the 20-bed *Youth Hostel* (Auberge de la Jeunesse), Rue de la Cayenne, Maison Morange, 97433 Hell-Bourg (tel 23 52 65). It costs Fr 30 per person and is in a beautiful old colonial building built in 1938 in the centre of town. You must have

a Youth Hostel card to use the place (if you don't have one then you can buy membership for Fr 100). There is a huge, well-equipped kitchen, dormitories and private rooms, hot water, patios, pretty grounds and good views as well as plenty of food shops nearby. If you plan to come here direct from the airport, hitch or take a bus to St André (30 km). From there you can get another bus to Hell-Bourg – a beautiful 25-km run.

If the Youth Hostel is full, there is the *Relais des Cimes* hotel two blocks away which costs Fr 165 a double, including breakfast.

While you're here it's worth a visit to the **Trout Farm** (tel 23 50 16) run by Paul Irigoyen and his wife. It's just a short walk from the Youth Hostel. You can buy freshly caught trout here for Fr 50 a kg and cook it at the Youth Hostel.

The nearby village of **Grand Ilet** is worth a day trip from Hell-Bourg. It's famous for its *tables d'hôte* – country-style, several-course set meals. People worth checking out here are *Madame Grondin* (tel 23 59 29), *Madame Nourry* (tel 23 51 27) and *Madame Boyer* (tel 23 52 81), all of whom serve these meals for Fr 45-60 including wine and coffee.

Hiking in the Cirque de Salazie is one of the main attractions of the area and an excellent way of taking in all the best of what Réunion has to offer. Ask for the YH brochure which has a map and a description of several local day-long hikes. You can also use Hell-Bourg as a base for longer hikes, resting in the *gites de montagne*. One such hike would be to the **Piton des Neiges**, the highest point on the island (3069 metres) and then back to Hell-Bourg via Grand Ilet. Another would be up to the same point and then down to Cilaos.

CILAOS

Cilaos is in a beautiful mountainous area and once famous as a refuge for runaway slaves. It's 113 km from St Denis and at a height of 1220 metres. Hitching the 113 km from St Denis to St Louis is easy, but it's hard to get out of St Louis and you may well have to take the bus from there to Cilaos (Fr 17, 36 km).

There is a campsite here if you have the gear. Otherwise, one of the cheapest places to stay is the *Marla Hotel* (tel 27 72 33), which has doubles with common bath for Fr 100. Double rooms with own shower and bidet but common toilet cost Fr 125. The Marla is a very pretty, friendly place and has the cheapest Creole restaurant in town. Breakfast here costs Fr 15 and set-meal lunches and dinners cost Fr 45. Rabbit, goat, lentils and sausages are specialities. One *plat du jour* is quite adequate for two people.

If the Marla is full, try the *VVF Fleurs Jaunes* (tel 27 71 39), which costs Fr 150 per person with full board.

Cilaos is famous for its **hot springs** (Les Thermes) where you can get a private tub for Fr 15. To get to them you take a short hike down into a river valley from town. They're open from 6.30 to 11.30 am and from 1 to 4.30 pm. Swimming in the river is also good. It's possible to go wine-tasting in homes and shops which sell the locally made sweet wines – look for signs saying 'Vin a vendre.'

The **Cirque de Cilaos** is noted for its fine hiking possibilities and splendid views. Two popular day hikes are to **Le Bras Sec** (14-km round trip) and to **Ilet a Cordes** plateau (22-km round trip). You can plan longer treks using the *gites de montagne* to Cirque de Salazie and Cirque de Montagne.

BEACHES
St Gilles, St Leu & Etang-Sale

Although you might expect Réunion to have good beaches, there are only 30 km of beaches out of a total of 207 km of coastline, and these are mostly shallow coral going out to the reef.

St Gilles is probably the best of them. Right on the best swimming and surfing beach is the *Hotel Surf* (tel 24 42 84) at Roches Noires. It costs Fr 128 a single and

Fr 145 a double with private bath, including breakfast. It also has a cheap restaurant for beer and snacks. The hotel is often full, especially at weekends. In town on the main road is *Hotel Loulou* with rooms for Fr 150 a single or double for bed and breakfast. Four-person bungalows are Fr 200 (air-conditioning and TV). South of the river on Rue General de Gaulle across from the bus stop is *Hotel Nenuphars* (tel 24 43 89), with large double rooms for Fr 168 a single and Fr 191 a double including breakfast, air-conditioning and a swimming pool.

If you have the gear, the municipal campsite costs Fr 24 per night plus Fr 3 for electricity.

Just south of St Gilles on the beach and again 16 km south of St Leu on the beach are two *Villages Vacances Familiares*, which have new studio apartments with fully-equipped kitchens and complete bedding for two to four people for Fr 118 per apartment per weekday night and Fr 140 at weekends, but they're usually full on Friday and Saturday. Before you can use the VVFs you have to pay an annual family membership fee of Fr 45, good for all VVFs in Réunion and France. For information and reservations contact tel 24 47 47. The VVFs also serve good family-style lunches for Fr 27.

Two km north of St Leu is the **Corail Turtle Farm**, which is free and worth a visit. The farm supplies the island's turtle meat and shell, but due to export restrictions is facing bankruptcy. If you'd like a meal of turtle meat prepared in the local style, try the beachfront restaurant across from the VVF in St Leu.

OTHER

Hiking To really see this island you must go up into the mountains. There are some 12 *gites de montagne* (mountain cabins) you can use for overnight stays; they are maintained by the tourist office in St Denis. They're all situated on one or other of the 600-km network of maintained hiking trails. The cabins have from 10 to

38 beds, two blankets per bed (bring sheets), cold water and fireplaces or wood stoves for cooking but no electricity. They cost Fr 35 per night and there's a two-night limit at any one cabin. You must make reservations in advance at the Tourist Office in St Denis (tel 21 24 53 or 21 65 23).

If you're thinking of hiking along the popular GRR1 trail which goes to all three *cirques* (Salazie, Cilaos and Mafate), get hold of a copy of the book *GR1 Le Tour du Neiges* for Fr 34 from the Tourist Office. They also sell the excellent Institut Geographique National 1:25,000 topographical maps. No 4405 R covers the *cirques* (Fr 50).

A Must One of the 'musts' on this island is a visit to the still-active volcano. To see it you must go on a tour which takes two days and costs Fr 50. The tour takes you up to the edge of the crater where you can watch the 'bubbling and gurgling and the flaming inferno and, if you're lucky enough, witness a minor eruption.' The landscape is strange and moon-like.

Thanks to Jan King and Tom Harriman (USA) for supplying the bulk of the information and the maps for Réunion.

Rwanda

As in neighbouring Burundi, the original inhabitants of Rwanda, the Twa pygmies, were gradually displaced from 1000 AD onwards by migrating Hutu tribespeople who, in turn, came to be dominated by the Tutsi from the 15th century onwards. The Tutsi used the same methods for securing domination over the Hutu as in Burundi, namely, the introduction of a feudal land system and a master-client relationship with regard to the ownership of cattle, which represented wealth. (The Hutu were agriculturalists whereas the Tutsi were stock-raisers.) The similarities with Burundi, however, end there. The Rwandan king's (Mwami's) authority was far greater than that of his opposite number in Burundi and the system of feudal overlordship which developed here was unsurpassed outside of Ethiopia.

Not only was the Rwandan Mwami an absolute ruler in every sense, with the power to exact forced Hutu labour and to allocate land to peasants or evict them from it, here Tutsi overlordship was reinforced by ceremonial and religious observances. Military organisation, too, was the sole preserve of the Tutsi. Rwanda, however, was more intensively farmed than Burundi, and in the process of growing food crops on all available land the Hutu eventually denuded the hills of tree cover. This resulted in the loss of good soil (and of wood for fuel), which, combined with competition for land by the Tutsi pastoralists, frequently threatened the Hutu with famine. Indeed, in the 20th

century alone there have been no less than six famines in Rwanda.

Faced with such a narrow margin of security, something was bound to give sooner or later among the Hutu, but it wasn't to come until the end of the colonial period. In 1890 the Germans took over Rwanda and held it until 1916 when the colony was taken over by the Belgians, who ruled it until independence in 1962. Throughout that time the power and privileges of the Tutsi were increased. They were not only trained to run the bureaucracy but had a monopoly on the educational system operated by the Catholic missionaries. In the meantime the conditions of the Hutu peasantry deteriorated even further and led to demands for urgent radical reforms in 1957. Instead of seeing the writing on the wall, a ruthless Tutsi clan seized power when Mwami Matara III died in 1959 and set about murdering Hutu leaders. Their actions resulted in a massive Hutu uprising, a great deal of bloodshed and the flight of the new Mwami into exile.

Faced with an explosive situation, the Belgian colonial authorities were forced to introduce political reforms, and when independence was granted in 1962 it brought to power the Hutu majority party under the prime ministership of Gregoire Kayibanda. Certain sections of the Tutsi, however, were unwilling to accept the loss of their privileged position. They formed a number of guerrilla groups which mounted raids on Hutu communities, but this only provoked further Hutu reprisals on the Tutsi. In the bloodshed which followed, thousands of Tutsi died and tens of thousands of their tribespeople fled to Uganda and Burundi. Things have since cooled down, though there was a resurgence of anti-Tutsi feeling in the early 1970s when Hutu tribespeople were being massacred by the tens of thousands in

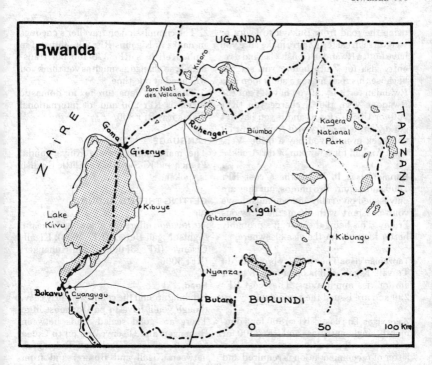

Burundi. Disturbances in Rwanda during this period prompted the army commander, Juvenal Habyarimana, to oust Kayibanda. He has ruled the country ever since.

FACTS

Sandwiched between Uganda, Tanzania, Burundi and Zaire, Rwanda, like Burundi, is a mountainous country, though perhaps not as beautiful because of the deforestation which has been going on for the last few centuries. It does, however, offer the extensive Kagera National Park which covers much of the eastern border area with Tanzania and has one of the few gorilla sanctuaries in the world. Rwanda also has frontage on beautiful Lake Kivu, which it shares with Zaire.

Over 90% of the population is Hutu. The remainder comprises Tutsi, Twa pygmies and various European minorities.

The climate is generally cool and pleasant, with an average temperature of 23°C. The rainy season runs from January to May and October to December. The population is nearly five million.

VISAS

Visas are required by all except nationals of West Germany. In East Africa you can get your visa in Nairobi (Kenya), Kampala (Uganda), Dar es Salaam (Tanzania) and Bujumbura (Burundi), but you can no longer get them in Goma (Zaire). Visas cost about US$10 (depending on where you get them), require two photos and usually take 48 hours to issue. In most places, except Nairobi, you also need a letter of recommendation from your own embassy. You cannot get a visa on the border.

If there is any possibility you might be

using the road from Bukavu to Uvira or vice versa in eastern Zaire, make sure you have both a Rwandan transit visa and a re-entry visa for Zaire before you set off, because this road makes a short loop into Rwanda territory. If you haven't got the Rwandan visa, they'll charge you (RFr 750) or US$5-7 for it, and if you haven't got a Zairois re-entry visa they won't let you back in until you pay a bribe. Very neat! And all for a few km of dirt track!

Burundi visas In Kigali these cost RFr 1000 and require two photos, but they are only issued on Friday and you must leave your passport with them the previous Friday. This being the case, it's probably better to apply for the visa elsewhere.

Tanzanian visas The embassy is on Rue du Travail, Kigali, and is open from 8 to 11 am for visa applications. They cost RFr 290 and are issued the same day.

Zaire visas The cost is RFr 1800 for a one-month, single-entry visa and RFr 2400 for a three-month, multiple-entry visa. No letter of recommendation is required and the visas are issued in 24 hours. The embassy is staffed by 'offensive petty bureaucrats,' so keep your cool.

MONEY
US$1	=	RFr 104
£1	=	RFr 131

The unit of currency is the Rwandan franc = 100 centimes. Import/export of local currency used to be restricted to RFr 5000, but recent reports suggest the restrictions have been lifted. There is a black market of sorts, but most of the time it's hardly worth the bother as the banks often offer better rates. However, depending on who you meet, you may get up to US$1 = RFr 123. In Ruhengeri the banks often offer better rates than the black market, so it's worth checking before you change money. You can't change traveller's cheques on the black market.

The commission on traveller's cheques in banks in Kigali is RFr 250-350 and in Ruhengeri it is RFr 370-400 per transaction, so change as much as you think you will need at one time.

The airport departure tax for domestic flights is RFr 250 and for international flights it is RFr 800.

LANGUAGE
The main languages are Kinyarwanda, French and Ki-Swahili. Very little English is spoken.

GETTING THERE & AROUND
Air
Air Rwanda offers the following domestic flights: Kigali-Butare (RFr 3000); Kigali-Gisenye (RFr 3500); Kigali-Ruhengeri (RFr 3000).

Road
Hitching around the country is fairly easy, though you'll have to pay for most lifts. There are good sealed roads between Ruhengeri and Gisenye and on to Goma (Zaire); between Kigali and Ruhengeri; between Kigali and Butare; and from Kigali to the Tanzanian border. There's also a brand-new sealed road between Kigali and Kabale (Uganda) via Byumba. The new roads are the result of a joint West German-Chinese aid programme. If hitching, watch out for the licence plates, which will tell you where the vehicles are likely to be going: AB for Kigali; CB for Butare; HB for Ruhengeri; and GB for Gisenye. If you are not hitching, there are plenty of buses, pick-ups and taxis (unlike in Burundi), but they're generally ridiculously overcrowded and relatively expensive at around RFr 3 per km.

Some examples of internal transport are:

Kigali-Ruhengeri Costs RFr 400 by taxi or minibus and takes about two hours. Daily government buses between these two places cost RFr 355 and take about 4½ hours. They're often packed but the trip is lovely if you can see out of the windows.

Kigali-Butare There are taxibuses every 15 minutes. The fare is RFr 400.

Ruhengeri-Gisenye Costs RFr300 by taxi or minibus and takes one to two hours.

Gisenye-Cyangugu There used to be a boat between these two places which cost RFr 768, but the latest reports suggest it's been suspended indefinitely.

Cyangugu-Butare Costs RFr 400 by bus and takes about six hours.

Boat

Lake Kivu Steamers *La Vedette* plies between Goma and Bukavu via Gisenye, Kibuye and Cyangugu. It goes up the lake one day and back the next, making three trips per week, but it's often out of order so make enquiries. *La Vedette* usually goes south from Gisenye on Wednesday and Saturday and north from Cyangugu on Monday and Thursday. Goma to Bukavu costs Z 62.50 (1st class). Kibuye to Gisenye costs RFr 215 and takes about three hours. Gisenye to Cyangugu costs RFr 768.

To/From Tanzania

There are buses twice a week between Kigali and Mwanza via the Tanzanian border village of Rusumu. They depart Kigali on Monday and Thursday in the morning and take about 49 hours. The bus stops twice so the driver (and everyone else) can sleep. If you pay for the whole trip in Kigali, it will cost RFr 2000. It's better, however, to pay for the fare in two stages, first from Kigali to Rusumu in Rwandan francs and then Rusumu to Mwanza in Tanzanian shillings. This works out a lot cheaper if you buy your shillings on the black market (Rusumu to Mwanza costs Tan Sh 200). The buses are operated by *H Rahemtullah & Co* and the Kigali terminus is on the corner of Rue du Travail and Rue de Burera, three blocks from the post office.

It's also possible to find trucks direct from Kigali to Mwanza for around US$20; the trip takes about 26 hours.

If you want to do this journey in stages, you must first take a bus or hitch to Kibungu from Kigali (daily buses at 7 am which take about two hours). From Kibungu you take a Peugeot taxi to the Rwandan border. From the Rwandan border to the Tanzanian border is a few hundred metres' walk. There is transport from Rusumu to other parts of Tanzania.

To/From Uganda

You should avoid having to cross this border at weekends if possible, as the Ugandan customs and immigration officials go home to their families so you'll have to wait there or go looking for them. You can, if you want, go to the police in Kisoro, who will stamp your passport and then send you across the road to the District Commissioner. This man processes all immigration from both Rwanda and Zaire, but he doesn't have any currency forms.

The best way to get between the two countries is along the Ruhengeri-Kidaho-Kisoro road. Kidaho is the Rwandan border village. There are daily microbuses between Ruhengeri and the border which cost RFr 80, but there are no buses between there and Kisoro. A taxi from Ruhengeri to the border should cost about RFr 100 if you share it. You'll probably have to walk the three km from Kidaho to the Ugandan border (Cyanika) and possibly even as far as Kisoro (about 11 km in all), but even if you have to walk all the way from Ruhengeri to the Ugandan border it's only 28 km.

If you get stuck in Kidaho, enquire at the town hall for somewhere to stay. They'll usually fix you up with something free of charge. You can use Ugandan shillings between Ruhengeri and the border, as many Rwandans go shopping in Kisoro.

BUTARE

A pleasant place to stay here is the *Procure de Butare* opposite the Cathedral. It is very quiet and relaxing, but they only have single rooms at RFr 400 – 'worth it' according to a number of travellers. The place is run by nuns, and excellent evening meals (three courses, all-you-can-eat) are available for RFr 200. There are no signs for this place so you must ask directions. The *Mission* is said to be very unfriendly, but if you can get in they have single rooms with hot showers for RFr 450. Other than the above, there is *Hotel Weekend* next to the market and petrol station (where the minibuses start from). It costs RFr 600 a single and RFr 1000 a double. There are two other very plush hotels opposite the bank on the main street, but if you are looking for a double room they're not much more expensive than the Weekend.

The new Artisans' Cooperative beside the bank here is worth a visit. Prices are better than in Kigali.

GISENYE

Except for a couple of hotels up the hill around the market where you can get tiny, clean rooms for RFr 500 a double, most hotels here are prohibitively expensive. Many travellers stay at the *Presbyterian Mission* three blocks in front of the Pentecostal Church; it is run by pleasant Swedish people. They have a trailer which can accommodate four people comfortably at a cost of RFr 150 per person. It's an excellent place to rest up for a couple of days and you can cook your own food, though electricity is intermittent. A kindly Belgian man who lives opposite the border post and who grows herbs and keeps bees will let you sleep in his garden free. Camping is officially forbidden anywhere, so be discreet if that's what you want to do.

At **Nyundo**, 10 km from Gisenye, you can stay in the 'home' at the *Catholic Mission* for RFr 100 per bed (dormitory rooms). It's worth the effort of getting here, as the dinners (which cost a mere RFr 75) are enormous and the food excellent. Breakfast costs the same but isn't such good value, seeing as it consists only of bread, butter, jam and tea. A good craft workshop here sells things at very reasonable prices.

Also outside of Gisenye (about 10 km), overlooking Lake Kivu, is the *Kigufi Guest House*, which costs RFr 1600 plus 10% service charge per person for full board. It's very quiet and the birdlife is prolific. To get there, take the road past the Bralirwa brewery and then ask for directions. You need to book ahead if you want to stay there at weekends because it's very popular.

KIBUYE

The place to stay here is *Home St Jean* next to the Catholic Church in a really beautiful spot overlooking Lake Kivu. Accommodation costs RFr 50 in the dormitory, RFr 450-650 a single, RFr 800 a double, RFr 800 a triple and RFr 1000 for a four-bed room. Meals are good and servings generous though a little expensive at RFr 200 for the main course with meat or RFr 280 for a three-course meal. A simple vegetarian meal is available for RFr 80. Breakfast costs RFr 130. If you don't want to eat here, there are some cheap restaurants in the town where you can get a meal of beans and potatoes for around RFr 60. Home St Jean has been recommended by many travellers.

KIGALI

In October 1983, the government issued orders prohibiting missions from accommodating travellers, but we continue to get letters from people who have stayed in one or another of them so it seems to have taken little or no effect.

The *Presbyterian Church 'Auberge'*, Avenue de Rusumo, has accommodation for RFr 300 in the dormitory, RFr 550 a single and RFr 1000 a double. The *Catholic Mission* has beds for RFr 400 but it may take some effort to get them to accept you, and you must be able to speak French. Excellent cheap breakfasts are available. *CCF Bornefonden* (Scandinavian Fonds pour Enfants), down the hill by the bank on Rue Paul VI, has a very friendly director who may give you a room to sleep in for the night free of charge if you show

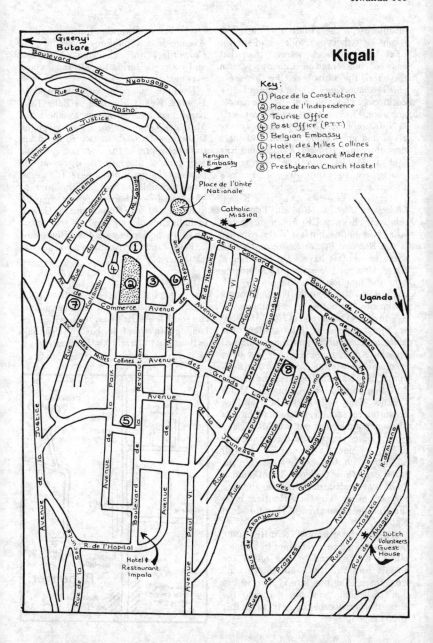

Kigali

Key:
1. Place de la Constitution
2. Place de l'Independence
3. Tourist Office
4. Post Office (P.T.T.)
5. Belgian Embassy
6. Hotel des Milles Collines
7. Hotel Restaurant Moderne
8. Presbyterian Church Hostel

an interest in the Children's Fund. The rooms have their own toilets and shower ('I've had cold beers warmer than that shower!' commented one Canadian woman traveller), the sinks leak, the floors are concrete and there are large, inquisitive cockroaches for company – but the people are great. The *Centre d'Accueil*, Avenue de la Nutrition near the main church, is very clean and good value at RFr 150 for a dormitory bed, RFr 350 a single and RFr 500 a double. If you're looking for somewhere to camp, try *St Andrews College*.

Hotels can be very expensive in Kigali. *Lodgement Metrole*, Rue du Travail, is relatively cheap at RFr 550 a single and RFr 750 a double, but it is 'filthy.' Similar is the *Bonjour Bar & Restaurant*. Both these two hotels have very few rooms. *Hotel Moderne*, Avenue du Commerce near the junction with Rue du Travail, costs RFr 750 a double. The bathrooms are grubby but hot water is available.

You can get good food at *Hotel Moderne* at the government bus station, the *Mabenga Restaurant* and the *Restaurant Impala*. Another place which has been recommended is the *Eden Garden Restaurant*, Rue Kalisimbi between the Avenue du Commerce and the Avenue des Milles Collines. They sell snacks, beer and ice cream at reasonable prices and have a pleasant patio looking out over Mt Kigali.

Air France is opposite the Banque de Kigali, Avenue du Commerce. *Sabena* and *Ethiopian Airlines* are located in the *Hotel des Milles Collines*. The Ugandan embassy is on Rue de l'Epargue opposite the post office. The Gare Routiere is on the Rue du Commerce at Rue du Mont Kabuye.

A taxi to the airport will cost RFr 1000, but you can get there cheaper by taking a bus to Kabuga and getting off at the airport turn-off. It's a 500-metre walk from there. The bus fare is RFr 30 but don't tell them you are going to the airport; otherwise they often try to get RFr 1000 off you.

The Franco-Rwandan Cultural Centre, Avenue de la République near Rue de la Concorde, is worth checking out for films and concerts during the afternoons and evenings.

If you're looking for lifts on trucks to Uganda, Kenya, Burundi or Zaire from Kigali, go out to *magerwa* (short for Magasins Generaux du Rwanda) in the Gikondo suburb about two to three km from the centre of the city. You can have your pick of hundreds of trucks at the customs clearance depot here. It's sometimes possible to get all the way to Mombasa free (otherwise expect to pay up to RFr 5000) or to Bujumbura for US$10 including meals and maybe a few beers. To get to the depot, walk down Boulevard de l'OAU and turn right when you see the sign.

RUHENGERI

The most popular place to stay here is the *Centre d'Accueil*, a kind of government-run youth hostel. It's easy to miss if you're coming into town from Kisoro (Uganda), as there is no sign and it's surrounded by a

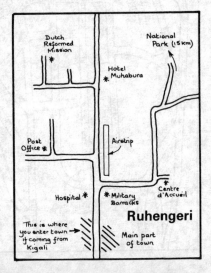

three-metre-high hedge, but it should be easy to find from the accompanying map. Accommodation here costs RFr 200 in eight-bed dormitories, RFr 350 a single and RFr 500 a double. Good meals are available. The *Catholic Mission* has similar accommodation for about the same price. If you want somewhere to camp, ask at the *Dutch Reformed Mission*. The *pere* is very friendly. A room at the *Un Deux Trois Hotel* will cost you RFr 650 a single.

If you need to change money, the best people to approach are the merchants on the main street near the south edge of the business district, across the street and south of the Pharmacie Ramji.

Air Rwanda has an office at the *Hotel Muhabura*, Avenue du 5 Julie opposite the Banque Commercial du Rwanda.

The Saturday market in Ruhengeri is well worth a visit if you are in town at that time.

PARC NATIONAL DES VOLCANS & THE GORILLA SANCTUARIES

Very few gorillas remain in the wild, so this is probably the only opportunity you will have of seeing these magnificent animals in their natural surroundings. It's possible to see them on the Ugandan side of the border near Kisoro, but the chances are nowhere near as good as in Rwanda. The sanctuaries are on the slopes of Visoke and Muside volcanos north-west of Ruhengeri in the Parc National des Volcans.

Until recently there were just three families of gorillas. The guides who take you can generally find them within a few hours. The gorilla families are known as Groups 9, 11 and 13 and there are different booking regulations attached to the various groups. For Groups 11 and 13 you must book in advance at the Office Rwandais du Tourisme et des Parcs Nationaux (ORTPN), BP 905, Kigali. The office is open Monday to Sunday from 7 am to 11 pm including public holidays. For Group 9 you must book at the park headquarters near Kinigi village the

afternoon before you intend going. The reason for this is that Group 9 moves around a lot so no one can be sure in advance what your chances are of seeing them. The headquarters is two km from the village and about 18 km from Ruhengeri. Maximum group size for all the above is six people.

Other than the three groups mentioned above, a new group was sighted in September 1983. It has been named 'Susa' after the river near where they were seen. Getting to see this group (maximum of six people) is a more rugged trip and takes two days with an overnight stop in a metal hut at 3000 metres. You need to take warm clothes, food for two days, cooking utensils, a sleeping bag, foam mattress, waterproof clothes and a torch. Charcoal (RFr 50) and water (RFr 100) are both provided at the camp. The gorillas of this group are still very wild and not accustomed to humans, so don't get too close. The gorillas of the other groups (9, 11 and 13) are now so used to humans that they'll let their babies sit on your lap!

The park entrance fee is RFr 1000 (which covers you for four days) and the gorilla viewing fee a further RFr 3500 (including guide fees). For the 'Susa' group there's a RFr 1000 park entrance fee plus RFr 2500 gorilla viewing fee. The rules say that the permit for the park is valid for four days, but only for one attempt at seeing the gorillas. If you miss them on any particular day, it's entirely up to the discretion of the park authorities whether you can try again free, try for a reduced additional fee, or pay again in full.

On the day of the visit you must turn up at the Kinigi park headquarters between 7 and 8 am to pay fees and have your permit checked. After that you go by vehicle to the various departure points: 'Point 9' for Group 9, 'Parking du Visoke' for Group 11, and 'Karandagi' for Group 13. The guides meet you at the departure points at about 9 am. It's hard going on the slopes

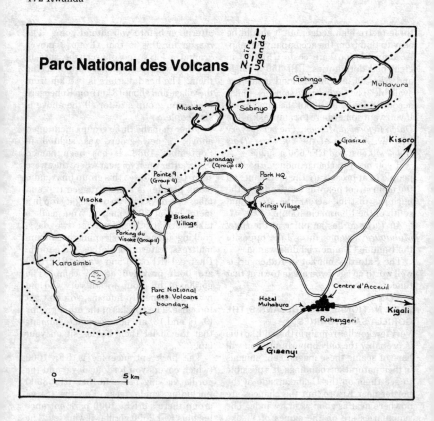

Parc National des Volcans

Muside · Sabinyo · Gahinga · Muhavura · Kisoro · Gasiza · Karandagi (Group 13) · Park HQ · Pointe 9 (Group 9) · Kinigi Village · Visoke · Bisate Village · Parking du Visoke (Group 11) · Karasimbi · Parc National des Volcans boundary · Centre d'Acceuil · Hotel Muhabura · Ruhengeri · Kigali · Gisenyi · Zaire/Uganda

0 — 5 km

and the vegetation is very dense. The following extract of a letter will give you some idea of what you are in for:

Don't underestimate either difficulty or the expense of getting to go on a mountain gorilla safari. The groups can be very heavily booked – whole planeloads of tourists are coming in and certain groups can be booked out six months in advance. Getting transport to Kinigi early, or to the staging areas at all, is a real hassle. Who is there to hitch with? The tourists sure don't want to pick you up, and no one else seems to be going there. The return journey in the evening is especially difficult. Tell people to bring gloves. It is not only that you are pulling yourself up and down incredible brush heaps, but every time you grab something to keep from falling it is always a stinging nettle and you will be in pain for days afterwards. Your shoes and pants will end up soaked through, so bring waterproof hiking boots if possible. If you're into photography then you need high-speed film – it is dark and rainy in the mountains and the gorillas like to fade into the undergrowth.

Nevertheless, the experience is incredible. And if you're on a tight budget, don't be on a tight schedule; otherwise you might well have to hire a car to get you from Ruhengeri to the park headquarters in Kinigi on the morning you are due to see the gorillas. (The Madame at the Mahabura Hotel in Ruhengeri can arrange a car for a mere US$80 return or you can hire them elsewhere for about US$50 return.) Give yourself plenty of time instead, and hitch. One group of people camped in their tent on the lawn of the park headquarters. They bought wood for a fire/cooking for RFr 100, eggs (delivered in the evening) and fresh cow's milk from the dairy next to the headquarters for RFr 32 per litre. Another couple who didn't have a tent were allowed to sleep in the park headquarters office overnight. In other words, if you have some initiative it can be both cheap and enjoyable. We've had other letters, too, which have said you can hire a tent at the park headquarters for RFr 500 per night or a metal hut at the 'Parking du Visoke' for RFr 250 per person per night.

If you have the time and the inclination while you're in this area, there are quite a number of treks you can go on. One of the most popular is a climb to the top of Visoke volcano (3711 metres). It will take you six or seven hours to get to the top and back again. There's a beautiful crater lake at the top and magnificent views to the north-east over the Parc National des Virunga in Zaire. **Lac Ngezi** is another crater lake immediately to the east of Visoke. It stands at 3000 metres and can be visited in three to four hours there and

back. A longer trek – two days there and back – can be made to **Karasimbi** (4507 metres) south of Visoke. The first day involves a five– to six-hour trek to a metal cabin on the slopes of the mountain where you can stay the night. (The keys to this hut have to be collected from the caretaker of the 'Parking du Visoke.') Next day you set off for the summit, which you should reach within four hours. The rest of the day you spend returning to the base of the mountain.

There are also excursions you can make to the summit of **Sibinyo** (3634 metres – five to six hours there and back); to **Gahinga** (3474 metres); and to **Muhavura** (4127 metres). The last two are taken as one trek and require two days. A guide is included in the price of the entry fee to the park, but it's advisable to give him an additional tip if you want to get on well together. Porters can be hired at RFr 300 per day plus RFr 500 for each night spent away from the departure point.

KAGERA NATIONAL PARK
This covers a sizable area of Rwanda along the border with Tanzania. The main attraction here is **Rusumu Falls**. Entry to the park costs RFr 1000.

São Tomé e Principe

Remote islands have always been a magnet for travellers; these two some 320 km off the coast of Gabon are no exception. They constitute one of Africa's smallest countries and you could easily be forgiven for thinking that this chapter has somehow escaped from a guidebook to South America. The two volcanic islands, with a population of only 80,000, are a legacy of the Portuguese empire and achieved independence only in 1975. The capital, the town of São Tomé, has a population of only 4500! It's not easy to get there, but the few travellers who have made it describe the islands as among the most beautiful in the world.

Unlike in Portugal's other African colonies, independence here gave birth to a moderate government, but events soon forced it to take a sharp turn to the left. The principal factor was the fear of a Comoros-type invasion or the one which nearly happened in the Seychelles. The fears were not entirely unjustified since many Sáo Toméan opposition figures, including the former health minister, Carlos da Graca, live in exile in Gabon (a staunch pro-western country) and un-identified ships and planes were sighted frequently in São Tomé's territorial waters and air space during 1978. The invasion never took place but resulted in the dispatch of 1000 Angolan troops to the islands to augment the 140 or so Cuban soldiers and advisors already there. Since then the country has strengthened its ties with the Marxist

regime of Angola; and President Manuel Pinto da Costa, along with other leaders of the party, has made official visits to Cuba, East Germany and the USSR.

The islands' position in the Gulf of Guinea off the coasts of oil-producing Nigeria and Gabon is of more than passing interest to the outside world despite their relative obscurity. Nevertheless, they remain economically aligned with Europe. The principal trading partners are still Portugal and the Netherlands (a traditional market for São Tomé's cocoa), though politically the country looks increasingly towards the communist world and 75% of the islands' skilled labour is provided by Cuba. Much of the remaining labour force, in the form of teachers, technicians and agricultural experts, is provided by Portugal. Relations with Gabon remain tense as a result of President Bongo's support of da Graca, but this is treated with a degree of latitude rarely to be found in other Marxist-leaning regimes.

The rugged, forested islands were first sighted by Portuguese navigators between 1469 and 1472, and São Tomé was established in 1485. Principe was not settled until 1500. The islands quickly became the largest sugar-producing country in the world, but in 1530 a black revolt scared the plantation owners off to Brazil. However, slavery, on which the brief sugar boom had been built, remained the cornerstone of the colony's economy and São Tomé and Principe became staging posts for the slave trade between West Africa and the Americas. The coffee and cocoa plantations which were set up in the 18th and 19th centuries likewise depended on slave labour. Even when slavery was abolished in 1875, it was replaced by a system of forced labour with minimal wages.

The people of the islands, including

those brought in to work the plantations from Angola, Mozambique and Cape Verde, fought the Portuguese on numerous occasions in a bid to win their freedom. Each time the revolts were put down bloodily by the colonial forces, the worst example being the notorious massacre of 1953 when over 1000 plantation workers were gunned down by Portuguese troops on the orders of Governor-General Carlos Gorgulho, in an attempt to suppress a strike. Despite the repression, the spirit of nationalism continued to grow. A liberation headquarters was set up in Libreville, Gabon, under the leadership of Pinto da Costa, and from there further strikes were organised. With the fall of Salazar in Portugal in 1974, followed shortly afterwards by a mutiny of black troops, the colonial authorities were finally forced to come to terms with the liberation forces. A transitional government was set up in December 1974 to steer the country to independence, yet even at that late date the Portuguese governor-general, in an attempt to ensure that a moderate post-independence government came to power, undertook a purge of radical elements, particularly those who had advocated nationalisation of the cocoa estates and the disbanding of the colonial army. It was a pointless exercise. When independence was declared in July 1975 there was a mass exodus of the 4000 or so Portuguese settlers who feared reprisals – just as they did in their other African colonies.

The European exodus left the country with virtually no skilled labour, a 90% illiteracy rate, only one African doctor and many abandoned cocoa plantations. An economic crisis was inevitable. Da Costa, up until then a moderate, was forced to concede to many of the demands of the more radical members of his government. The majority of the plantations were nationalised four months after independence, laws were passed prohibiting anyone from owning more than 100 hectares of land, and a people's militia was set up to operate in the workplaces and villages.

Since then the government's priorities have been to revive the cocoa industry (which previously provided 90% of total GNP – US$40 million in 1978) and to diversify into other areas.

VISAS

Visas are required by everyone. Officially, 'tourists' are forbidden; to get a visa you must be on an 'official mission' and have references inside the country. One traveller who made it suggested that you make up a Portuguese name, give it some kind of important position and then use it as a 'reference.' You should expect considerable delays before a visa is issued. If you're successful, the visas are valid for a stay of two months, cost CFA 1750 (in Libreville) and must be used within four months of issue. There are embassies in Lisbon, Conakry (Guinea), Libreville (Gabon) and Luanda (Angola). It's suggested you apply at one of the first three, since getting into Angola itself is quite a feat. Another traveller who got there suggested applying direct by registered letter to the Ministerio de Negocias Estrangeros, São Tomé. If you do it this way, you need to supply the following formidable list of details: Full name (and maiden name if a married woman); country, date and place of birth; nationality; sex; marital status; father's and mother's full name and nationality; passport number, type, date and place of issue and validity; your permanent home address; profession; which employer/organisation you work for and your position; the nature of the business which your employer/organisation is involved in; if you have ever been to São Tomé before and, if so, the dates when you entered and left and your residential address there; the names, nationalities, relationship, address and telephone number of any friends or relatives you have in São Tomé; your proposed date of entry, departure and length of stay; proposed place where you will stay and the address; the name of any religious or associated organisation which you belong to; the reason for your proposed visit; and the address to which a reply should be sent. If you think all that is excessive, you might be right, but the main reason for the poor success rate of visa applications by post is that not enough information is provided.

If you are granted a visa, you can pick it up on arrival. You must have a yellow fever vaccination before they'll let you in.

Before leaving the country you must get an exit permit.

Travel round the island of São Tomé is no problem, but travel to Principe is subject to all manner of special provisions.

The islands are full of Russian, Cuban, East German and North Korean advisors, and the regime is very paranoid about 'imperialist' infiltration. The fears of invasion have still not subsided, so use some discretion when wandering around the islands. It's forbidden, for instance, to walk along the boulevard next to the sea in São Tomé town at night smoking a cigarette. You could well be suspected of sending messages to submarines. Also, when the flag is raised you're supposed to stand still even if you can't see the flag but can hear a remote trumpet.

MONEY

CFA 1000 = 130 dobra (official rate)

The unit of currency is the dobra. There is no black market. While there are no restrictions on the import of local currency, export is limited to 30,000 dobra.

GETTING THERE & AROUND

The only regular air services to São Tomé are the weekly flights from Luanda (Angola) and Guinea-Bissau. A return excursion fare from Luanda with *Deta*, the Angolan airline, costs about US$225. There are no boats. There are plans to establish a regular service to and from Libreville (Gabon), but this may take some time. Representatives of organisations like the UN and the World Bank usually rent small planes in Libreville to take

them to and from São Tomé. This is the most convenient way of getting there. Ask around in Libreville at the offices of the UNPD or the European Development Fund. If you don't have any luck there, try the offices of *Air Service* and *Air Affaires*. If there's a spare seat going, it's more than likely you'll get on and it's unlikely you'll have to pay. When you want to leave the island, ask around at the same offices in São Tomé or try the Russian, East German and Chinese embassies.

Around São Tomé Unlike many other parts of Africa, all the roads here are sealed and there's a good network of buses to almost everywhere. Buses are cheap at around 1 dobra per two km. Hitching is simplicity itself.

SAO TOMÉ

The island is extremely beautiful. It's full of strange remnants of extinct volcanoes which look like huge pillars, some rising 600 metres straight up out of the jungle. The north of the island is drier with rolling hills and baobabs. The coasts are ringed with beautiful, deserted beaches of white sand fringed with palms and the water is turquoise. The town of São Tomé itself is a picturesque little place full of Portuguese colonial buildings and shady, colourful parks, and it's very, very clean.

There's only one hotel, the *Boa Vista*, about 20 km from town, but it's often full (there are only 10 rooms) and it's expensive at 600 dobra per night. More than likely, one of the few western volunteers (Portuguese, Dutch and French) will invite you to stay with them, as they never see any tourists there.

Food can be a minor problem. The many once-filled shops are empty except for sardines and toilet paper. There's no bread, meat, soft drinks or cigarettes. On the market you can buy breadfruit, manioc and sometimes tiny tomatoes and pineapples. There are two restaurants in São Tomé, the *Omstep* and *Club Nautico*. The former has meals for 100 dobra, the latter for 120 dobra. You can only get one meal (usually rice or breadfruit with fish). Be sure to get there by 7 pm or there will be nothing left. Beer and coffee, when available, are very cheap. The Club Nautico has a free swimming pool.

Senegal

Senegal has been inhabited for many thousands of years, as testified by the neolithic stone circles to be found in the country (and in Gambia). However, its recorded history began when part of it was ruled by the Ghana Empire between the 8th and 11th centuries. The rest of the country came under the control of the Tekrour Empire which grew up here in the 9th century and was converted to Islam shortly after as a result of Almoravid raids from Morocco. As these empires waned a new kingdom arose – the Djolof – during the 13th and 14th centuries, in the area between Cape Verde and the Senegal River. It was with this kingdom that Europeans had first contact.

Initial contact was through the Venetian, Cada Mosta, who in 1455 was employed by the Portuguese prince, Henry the Navigator, to explore the coast of West Africa. Fifty years later a Portuguese explorer spent four years travelling through the country, and on the basis of his reports the Portuguese established a monopoly of trade with the Senegalese coastal kingdoms which was to last until the 16th century, when they were displaced by the British, French and Dutch. What these last three nations hoped to do was gain control of St Louis and Gorée Island, which were strategic points where slaves bound for the Americas could be collected. After changing hands several times, St Louis was finally secured by the French and a fort was built there in 1659. Although slaves formed the bulk of the trade, gold, ivory, leather and gum arabic were also purchased.

When slavery was finally abolished in the 19th century and the trade in gum arabic was on the decline, France turned to cultivating cash crops such as indigo and cotton, but the venture was unsuccessful because of the hostility of the inhabitants. The expansion of the colony was largely the work of Louis Faidherbe, who was appointed governor in 1854. It was he who undertook the systematic conquest of the Senegal basin and developed the cultivation of groundnuts as the dominant cash crop of the area. His successor destroyed the rising power of al-Hajj 'Umar, a Tucolor, who, on his way back from Mecca, had married a daughter of the Sultan of Sokoto and raised a *jihad* (holy war) against the French and what he regarded as the decadence of his Islamic neighbours. By 1863 'Umar had raised an army of 2000 and created an empire stretching from the land occupied by the French to Timbuktu. His downfall, however, was not so much due to French military superiority as to the penchant of his troops to plunder, which alienated the people who had been conquered and led to their uprise against him.

The conquest of Senegal by the French was completed in the last decade of the 19th century and Dakar was built up as the administrative centre and showpiece of France's West African empire. Roads, railways and port facilities were constructed and a university was opened. As early as 1848 Senegal had sent a deputy to the French parliament, but it wasn't until 1914 that the first black deputy, Blaise Diagne, was elected to the position. The franchise was limited to the citizens of the four communes of St Louis, Gorée, Rufisque and Dakar. Diagne was soon to lose the support he had previously enjoyed as a result of his collaboration

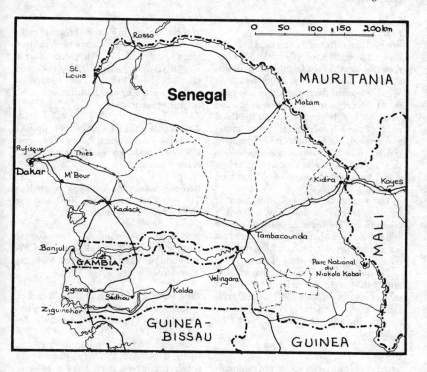

with French interests in the colony. A new generation of black politicians came to the fore, led by Lamine Gueye and Leopold Senghor. They campaigned for the granting of French citizenship to the colony's subjects, the abolition of forced labour, a general improvement in the standard of living, and against the right of the colonial authorities to hold in detention without trial anyone deemed subversive.

In the run-up to independence, Senegal joined French Sudan to form the Federation of Mali in early 1959. The Federation became independent in 1960, but only two months later Senegal seceded and declared itself independent as the Republic of Senegal under the presidency of Leopold Senghor. Since then Senegal has followed a very moderate course and is one of the few black African states in favour of 'dialogue' with South Africa. It is apparent that not everyone is happy with the political set-up, as from time to time student unrest explodes and leads to violent demonstrations in the streets of Dakar. The government has managed to contain most of their grievances until now, but a new source of opposition emerged recently when farmers refused to plant groundnuts because of drought and falling prices on the world market. The World Bank also uncovered a racket whereby the state organisation responsible for the groundnut crop had been underpaying farmers for their crops.

At the end of 1980, Senghor stepped down as president and his place was taken by Abdou Diouf, but he remains head of the party which rules Senegal.

FACTS

Senegal has suffered a great deal from the droughts which have affected the Sahel recently. North of the Gambia River much of the country is barren and unproductive. Wind erosion and increasing salinity have made the problem worse. Few crops can be grown in this area except on the flood plain of the River Senegal, where millet and groundnuts are cultivated. Irrigation projects now underway may help alleviate this problem and allow rice to be grown there, but it could also lead to increased salinity.

The best time to travel in Senegal is between December and May, when it is cool and dry. However, at this time of year you should be prepared for the Harmattan – a strong, dry wind which blows off the desert for lengthy periods of time.

The population is around five million, an eighth of whom live in Dakar. The main groups are the Wolofs (36%), the Fulani (18%) and the Serer (17%). Nomadic groups include the Moors and the Bassaris.

VISAS

Visas are required by all except nationals of Belgium, France, Germany (West), Italy, Luxembourg and the Netherlands. Nationals of South Africa and Zimbabwe are not admitted. Visas can be obtained from French embassies where there is no Senegalese embassy (eg Mali). You are officially required to have an onward ticket but this is rarely enforced. You can sometimes get into Senegal without a visa (where one is required). This is true of the Senegal/Mauritania border at Rosso. Other travellers have made it from Mali on the Bamako-Dakar train, but you can expect a lot of hassle. There is no Senegalese consulate in Bamako (Mali), so you'll have to get one (where required) in Algiers, Tunis or Niamey. If you get one in the latter place make sure the consul stamps the visa in your passport instead of onto a loose piece of paper; otherwise you'll have problems at the border unless you can explain (in French) how that came about. Some travellers have been refused entry because of this. Senegalese visas in Banjul (Gambia) cost 10.10 dalasi and take three hours to issue. They're good for a three-week stay and multiple entry. No photos are required.

Cape Verde visas The embassy is on Rue du Relasis, off Avenue Ponty. Visas cost CFA 2000 and take two to three weeks to come through.

Gambian visas The embassy is on Rue Thiong. Visas cost CFA 3000 and are often issued the same day.

Mali visas The embassy is on Avenue Lamine Gueye. One-week visas cost CFA 5000 and you need three photos. Visas are issued in 48 hours.

Zaire visas The embassy is on Rue Leo Frobenius in the Fann suburb (take bus No 7 from the Place de l'Independence for CFA 70). One-month visas cost CFA 3500. A three-month, multiple-entry visa costs CFA 5300. Three photos are required and you must have a letter of introduction from your own embassy.

Other visas you can get in Dakar are:

Algeria CFA 900, four photos
Bourkinafasso CFA 3500, three photos
Egypt CFA 1220, one photo
Gabon CFA 2500, two photos
Gambia CFA 3000, two photos
Ghana CFA 1400, three photos
Guinea-Bissau CFA 3000, two photos
Guinea CFA 5000, two photos
Ivory Coast CFA 3500, three photos
Kenya CFA 2600, one photo from the British embassy
Liberia CFA 500, one photo
Mauritania CFA 2600, two photos. A letter of recommendation from your own embassy may be required. The British embassy charges CFA 1800 for these.
Morocco CFA 2500, two photos

Niger CFA 500, four photos
Nigeria CFA 1500, three photos
Sierra Leone CFA 2400, three photos
Togo CFA 1500, three photos

MONEY
US$1 = CFA 460

The unit of currency is the CFA franc. There are no restrictions on the import of local currency. Export is limited to CFA 20,000. There is no black market.

Opening hours vary from bank to bank but are usually from 8.30 am to noon and from 2.30 to 4.30 pm. You can change money on Sunday in Dakar at the Chamber of Commerce office. Although there are banks in all the large towns, don't rely on being able to change traveller's cheques in the banks in smaller places.

If you're heading for Gambia, you can buy dalasi on the street in Ziguinchor at the rate of CFA 5000 = 45-50 dalasi (the same as in Banjul).

LANGUAGE
French is the official language. Wolof is the most widely spoken African language.

GETTING THERE & AROUND
Air
There are no ferries to the Cape Verde Islands. The only way to get there is to fly. *Air Senegal* flies on Saturday and *TACV* (the Cape Verde airline) on Tuesday. The flights cost US$110 and the planes land on São Tiago Island.

Road
The main routes through Senegal run north-south from the Mauritanian border at Rosso to the Guinea-Bissau border at São Domingo via St Louis, Dakar, Kaolack, the Gambia River and Ziguinchor; and west-east from Dakar to Kayes in Mali via Tambacounda. There are good networks of buses, taxis and trucks on these routes, though it's unlikely you'll take road transport if heading for Mali, as the train is much more convenient.

Below are some examples of transport on the north-south route:

Dakar-Ziguinchor There is a choice of a bus which costs CFA 2750 or minibus (25 seats). Both usually take about eight hours but can take up to 14 hours. A taxi costs CFA 4000 and takes seven hours. Just how long the trip is depends on the state of the ferry at Mansa Konko on the Gambia River. If you're coming up from Ziguinchor and arrive at Mansa Konko for breakfast, there is a large open-air cafe by the ferry pier.

Dakar-Barra Point (Gambia) Direct taxis are available for CFA 3500 plus CFA 500 for a rucksack and take about five hours. *GPTC* (Gambia Passenger Transport Corporation) buses run between the two places usually daily, but at least three times per week from LeClerc bus terminal. From Barra Point there are ferries to Banjul which cost 50 batuts and take 20 minutes. The ferries leave from either side every two hours throughout the day (last at 8 pm).

Dakar-Joal Bus is CFA 700.

Dakar-M'Bour Minibus costs CFA 600.

Joal-M'Bour Taxi costs CFA 350.

M'Bour-Kaolack Minibus costs CFA 800 plus CFA 100 for baggage.

Kaolack-Barra Point (Gambia) Taxi costs CFA 1300 plus CFA 100 for a rucksack.

On the above routes there are two possibilities between Kaolack and Ziguinchor. The direct road takes the Transgambian Highway, which cuts across the centre of Gambia. (There is still no bridge across the Gambia River so you have to take a ferry.) The other route goes via the capital of Gambia, Banjul, and requires taking the ferry across the Gambia River from Barra Point to Banjul. If you are coming up from the south there are buses from Ziguinchor to Banjul for CFA 1500, including baggage.

From Ziguinchor you can either go south to Guinea-Bissau or north-east to Tambacounda. Ziguinchor-São Domingo by taxi costs CFA 600, while Ziguinchor-

Kolda by truck is CFA 1700 or CFA 2200 by taxi including baggage. To go to Kolda-Velingara by taxi you'll be up for CFA 1340 plus CFA 100 for rucksack. Velingara-Tambacounda by taxi costs CFA 1140 plus CFA 100 for a rucksack. You can get a direct taxi from Kolda to Tambacounda for CFA 2050 plus CFA 300 for a rucksack. From Tambacounda you can take the train to either Dakar or Bamako (Mali), but this isn't a particularly good place to get on because the train will be packed to the gunwales by then and there are a lot of thieves about.

Rail
Dakar-St Louis There is one train in either direction daily along this line. It leaves Dakar at 1.40 pm and St Louis at 6.30 am. There's another from Dakar to St Louis on Saturday at 9 am. The fare is CFA 1125 (2nd class) and the journey takes seven hours. Make sure you're at the station at least an hour before the train is due to leave if you want to have any chance of getting a seat.

Dakar-Bamako (Mali) There are two trains in either direction along this line. They depart Dakar on Wednesday and Friday at 10.30 am and Bamako on Wednesday and Friday at 11.30 am. The journey takes between 30 and 36 hours (12 hours to Tambacounda and 24 hours to Kayes). The fare from Dakar to Bamako is CFA 27,600 (sleeper), CFA 18,500 (1st class) and CFA 11,700 (2nd class). From Dakar to Tambacounda the fares are CFA 14,515 (sleeper), CFA 7315 (1st class) and CFA 4420 (2nd class). From Dakar to Kayes the fares are CFA 19,435 (sleeper), CFA 12,235 (1st class) and CFA 7000 (2nd class). If you're going 2nd class, get to the station by 7 am if you want to be sure of getting a seat. These days there are two queues, one for women and one for men, so it's not the melee it used to be.

There is a vast difference between the Senegalese train and the Malian train. The Senegalese is comparable with trains in any West European country. Second class is no problem – the carriages are really clean and there's a dining car which serves food and beer. The Malian trains, by comparison, are a disaster. Even first class is filthy, full of insects and often crowded. Do yourself a favour and take the Senegalese trains (from Dakar on Wednesday and from Bamako on Friday).

Student discounts (30%) are available for that part of the journey through Senegal, but not any more for the Malian part. These discounts are available all year if you're travelling from Mali to Senegal, but in Senegal they appear to be available only at the start and the end of the school year (15 July to 15 August and 1 to 31 October), though other travellers have disputed this. If you get a discount, this makes the fares CFA 14,955 (1st class) and CFA 9865 (2nd class). In Dakar see the Chef du Gare (Station Master) about these.

Passports are collected on the train before you get to the Senegalese border. You have to get off at the frontier station and collect them from the police who will be standing around somewhere on the platform. The passports will again be collected when you've crossed the Mali frontier. You have to get off at Kayes and collect them from the Police Speciale, which involves going out of the station and to the right about 50 metres.

You can also get on the train at Tambacounda, but it's not advised as the train arrives there packed-out at 10 pm and there's no chance of getting a seat. There are also a lot of thieves who take advantage of the dark.

Dakar-Kaolack There is a daily train at 5.20 pm.

Boat
Dakar is a major West African port and many ships call here. You can get ships from France, Spain, Morocco and the Canary Islands but none of them are cheap or cater to budget travel.

Even the cheapest fares will cost you more than the price of a flight.

DAKAR

The capital of Senegal and a major West African port, Dakar is a large modern city where an eighth of the country's population lives. It's an expensive place to stay and it gets a variable press. Some travellers don't like it and consider it to be dangerous because of incidents of robbery with violence. While this has been on the increase, it's no worse than in any other large city around the world. You certainly need to exercise discretion about going back to a house alone or wandering down small alleyways, and you should definitely stay away from the beach at night. Other than that, Dakar seems a welcome sight to most travellers, especially after they've been roughing it in the desert. One traveller had this to say:

It was a treat to go to real city with real stores and indoor restaurants and, best of all, the ocean. I loved the ferryboat ride to and from Gorée Island. Enjoyed shopping there too and found some really nice things – especially batiks and batik-dyed fabric – in the market at reasonable prices. Like any city, it takes money to enjoy, but if you resign yourself to that ahead of time it can be a nice break from roughing it. I had enough of that last year and after two years in the desert I'm ready for comfort!

Another traveller who liked the place had this to say:

Almost alone among sub-Saharan African countries (I've been to most), the Dakar area has a pleasant, Mediterranean-type climate from October to May. The city is built on a volcanic peninsula which extends westwards in the maritime tradewinds and has a seafront area reminiscent of the south of France, making it one of the more pleasant cities anywhere in the world. There are sometimes young street scam artists who try to talk you out of your money in the Petite Corniche area, but I have never heard of them being anything but laughable. I have heard of people alone at night on the beaches being mugged but, excepting

this, the sleazy bars in the port area are the only parts of the city where I would not feel particularly safe. I'm a native of New York so I know. Dakar is certainly the favourite African city of the foreigners resident there who have knowledge of the rest of the continent. It has a number of sidewalk cafés along the Avenue Pompidou as well as inexpensive restaurants and hotels.

Contrast those impressions with this:

Dakar – Wuuugh! Disgusting, unfriendly, rotten, fucking sordid place with heaps of unfriendly, bastardish, rude, dangerous, mother-fucking assholes either hassling you with their shit or looking for a fight. Dakar is pure, sheer rot. I HATE the place. What a load-ff!

You couldn't get much more abusive than that! And the man would normally speak in French or Walloon, coming from Belgium.

Information

The Tourist Office is on the Place de l'Independence.

The poste restante at the main post office charges CFA 100 per letter collected.

The French embassy is at 1 Rue El Haji Amadou Assane Ndoye at Rue Mage. Visas for Bourkinafasso here cost CFA 3000, require three photos and take 24 hours. The Mali embassy is at 46 Boulevard de la République near Avenue Lamine Gueye. Visas cost CFA 5000, require two photos and take 24 hours to issue.

A public bus runs between the airport and the city centre; it costs CFA 80. If you take a taxi it will cost up to CFA 4500. Bargaining madly can reduce this price but not by much. Taxi rides in the city should be CFA 100 (cabs are metered). Be sure the meter clicks on. 'Tourist taxis' run the meter five times faster than they are supposed to, so if it reads 500 CFA before you turn the corner, get out and find another taxi.

Note these street name changes: Rue Thiers is now Rue El Haji Amadou Assane Ndoye; Avenue Ponty is now Avenue

Pompidou; Rue de Bayeux north of Avenue Ponty is now Rue Raffenal.

Things to See

The **Ifan Museum** is well worth a visit. It has a superb collection of West African masks, furniture and royal paraphernalia. Entry costs CFA 200 (CFA 100 with student card). It's open 8.30 am to 12.30 pm and from 2 to 6 pm; closed on Monday.

One of the 'musts' in Dakar is a visit to **Ile de Gorée** by ferryboat. An old fortified slaving station, the island was one of the very first French settlements on the African continent. There is an excellent historical museum on the island, slaves' houses, old colonial mansions and a marine zoo. Entry to the museum is CFA 200 (CFA 100 with student card). The House of Slaves is CFA 100. There are ferries every two hours from Dakar; the fare is CFA 500 return. The museum here is closed on Monday. Cheap beers are available at *Chez Michou*, a small shop behind the museum.

There are two markets, the **Sandaga** and the **Kermel**. The Kermel is the more expensive of the two but you can find bargains if you hang around long enough. The Sandaga is notorious for pick-pockets, so be careful. The Mauritanian silver-workers are through Sandaga to any alley at 69 Avenue Blaise Diagne. Turn left there – lots of silver at fair prices.

The **Artisans' Village** is really just a hyped-up tourist craft market that charges high prices, so stay away.

For a great view of the city, go to the top of the Hotel de l'Independence.

Places to Stay

Among the cheapest and most popular places to stay here are:

Hotel du Coq Hardi, 34 Rue Raffenal (not marked on the map but between Avenue Lamine Gueye and Rue de Bayeux). This is a long-time favourite which has singles for CFA 3500. There is no restaurant here any longer.

Hotel St Louis, 68 Rue Felix Faure. Many of the cheaper rooms at this hotel (CFA 3000 a single) are booked out weeks in advance, so you may have to take one of the more expensive ones at CFA 5300 a double. It's clean but there's only water between the hours of 10 pm and 8 am. Offers good French-style meals for CFA 2500 (set four-course meal).

Restaurant l'Auberge Rouge, corner Rue Blanchet and Rue Jules Ferry. The small hotel attached to this restaurant has only seven rooms but they're clean and cost CFA 5800 a double. There are no showers but you can store baggage here.

Hotel Metropole, in front of the PTT, is a brothel but has cheap triple rooms for CFA 4500.

Hotel de la Paix, 38 Rue El Hajj Amadou, has rooms for CFA 3500.

Hotel Central, Avenue Ponty, has rooms for CFA 5000 a triple.

Hotel Provencal, just off Place de l'Independence, costs CFA 3500 a single and CFA 4000 a double.

Hotel de Prince, 49 Rue Raffenal, costs CFA 3000 a double with shower and CFA 3500 a double with shower and air-conditioning. It's said to be dirty these days and they have problems with the water. There are also no keys to the doors.

Hotel Mon Logis, down an unmarked alley off the Avenue Lamine Gueye three blocks from the Sandaga market and opposite the Marche Video-Cassette, used to be popular but it has now changed its name and is under different management. It costs CFA 3000 a single with own shower. The toilets are clean. You can no longer sleep on the roof.

If you're looking for something up-market, try the *Atlantic Hotel*, Rue de Dr These one block off the Place de l'Independence. A comfortable single room with air-conditioning and private shower will cost CFA 4500 and a double CFA 7200. The *Hotel Pavilion* has also been suggested. It costs CFA 7100 for a double room.

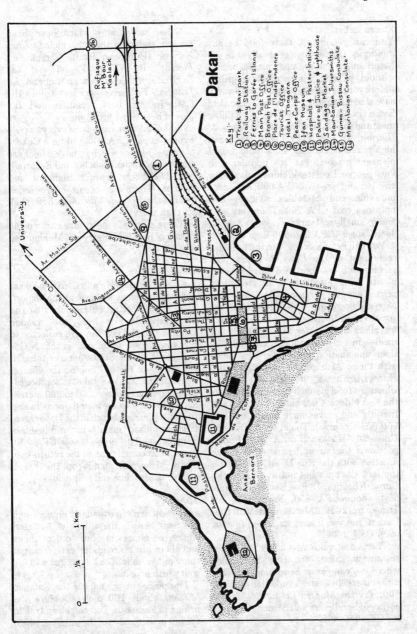

Dakar

Key:-
1. Truck & taxi park
2. Railway Station
3. Ferries to Gorée Island
4. Main Post Office
5. Branch Post Office
6. Place de l'Independence
7. Tourist Office
8. Hotel Tangara
9. Peace Corps Office
10. Ifan Museum
11. Hospitals & Pasteur Institute
12. Palace of Justice & Lighthouse
13. Sandaga Market
14. Mauritanian Silversmiths
15. Guinea–Bissau Consulate
16. Mauritanian Consulate

Places to Eat

You can get cheap, tasty food at any *dibitterie*. These are generally run by Mauritanians and are small places, usually without a sign, where meat is grilled before your eyes. You take the grill away in a twist of newspaper. Eaten with a hunk of bread (available everywhere), it's a filling meal and the cost is minimal. The *Gargotte Diarma*, 56 Rue Felix Faure, has been highly recommended as a cheap and pleasant place to eat. It's popular with local people. Beefsteak, chips and salad or chicken and rice cost CFA 600; entrecôte plus chips and vegetables or kidneys and potatoes cost CFA 700. There are also many small restaurants along Avenue Jean Jaures (CFA 250-500 for a meal).

You can get a good meal in the open-air restaurant at the *Hotel St Louis*. The restaurant is in a courtyard full of hanging plants. The atmosphere is great and prices are very reasonable. The *Keir Ndeye Restaurant*, Rue Vincens, serves superb traditional Senegalese food (some travellers disagree) for CFA 500-1000 per meal – but check your bill carefully, as their imagination sometimes runs away with them. Also good is *Restaurant des Plates Africaines*, 95 Rue de Bayeux, which has food at much the same prices as the Keir Ndeye. *Chez Lutchea* is clean and friendly and serves huge meals for CFA 750 (main course). To get there, find the University Bookshop on Avenue Ponty, go down the street beside it past the junction with the Rue Diouf, and it's on the left. Cheaper but not as good is the *Daron-Khoudes*, 13 Rue Escarfait. Meals cost about CFA 250. For pizzas try *Travestere*, 26 Rue Mohammed IV off Rue Carnot, but you'll have to pay quite a lot (over CFA 2000).

There are quite a number of cheap restaurants along the Rue Sandiniery where you can get *riz Senegalais* for CFA 200 and excellent steak and salad for CFA 500. Try the *Modern Restaurant* on the corner of Sandiniery and Blanchot – meals for CFA 150-500.

Other restaurants which have been recommended in the past include *Chez Nanette* (European food); *Gargotte du Plateau*, Rue Felix Faure; and the *Gargoutier* (delicious cheap dinners). *La Latticia Patisserie* across from the Cathedral has been recommended. It's closed between 1 and 3 pm.

Soft drinks are expensive everywhere – expect to pay CFA 300-500 for a Coke.

Cheap bars in which to have a beer are *Bar Nana*, corner Blanchot and Escarfait; and *M'Bellache*, corner Blanchot and Carnot. There's a cheap beer garden behind the *Hotel de Ville* (and they speak English there).

There's a really good *jazz club* on the corner of Rue Jules Ferry and Mohammed V.

Other

A pleasant weekend excursion from Dakar is to the beach at **N'Gor** near the airport. Take bus No 7 (CFA 80) from the Place de l'Independence or from the Avenue Lamine Gueye. Tell the fare collector to let you know when you reach N'Gor Village. Walk about 200 metres through the village to the bay behind the village. From there you can take an outboard-powered dugout canoe 200 to 300 metres across the bay to the island opposite and the most pleasant beach in the Dakar area. It's patronised mainly by middle-class Senegalese. The canoe fare is CFA 300, payable on completion of the return trip. There are small stands on the beach selling sandwiches and soft drinks.

JOAL

Joal itself isn't particularly interesting, but near here is the village of **Fadiouth** where the houses are built out of shells and there are no roads or cars. You get there either on foot or by pirogue and it's well worth a visit.

The place to stay here is the *Catholic Mission* about 100 metres before the bridge to Fadiouth. You can sleep free in the hut in the garden of the mission, which is run by nuns. For food, apart from the very expensive *Relais 114*, there are two very small restaurants offering cheap food at the place where the trucks pick up the fish.

KAOLACK

One option for accommodation here is the *Hotel Napoleon*, Avenue Cheikh Ibra Fall one block from the Cathedral and three blocks east of the market. It costs CFA 3000 a double with own bathroom or CFA 5000 a double with own bath and air-conditioning. Otherwise try the *Catholic Mission* or the *Peace Corps Hostel* behind the Dakar taxi rank, which is about one km along Avenue Van Vollenhaven until you cross the railway tracks. Continue one km to the right along Avenue Diogoye Senghor. The taxi park for Tambacounda and Banjul is on Avenue John Kennedy at Avenue Ababacar Sy (Gare Routiere).

M'BOUR

M'Bour is a typical package holiday village in the high season (November to April), but during the rest of the year it's all yours. There's a good beach here.

The *Centre Touristique de la Petite Cote*, Avenue Diogoye Senghor near the Prefecture, costs CFA 4500 plus CFA 400 tax a double with private bath, and CFA 5500 plus CFA 400 tax a double with private bath and air-conditioning.

RUFISQUE

If you don't like Dakar, head off for Rufisque and stay there – take bus No 100 from opposite the *Hotel de l'Independence* and in front of the Sabena office in Dakar.

There's a cheap CFA 1000-per-room hotel which doubles as a brothel and, near the market, several cheap, small restaurants which ask CFA 250 for a meal and a drink. They're unnamed. If you're obviously short of money, you may be invited to stay with a local family. Money would be welcome to some (indeed some are very greedy), but to others it would an

offense. If you stay with a family for a month or so, buying them half a sack of rice wouldn't be too much (CFA 6000).

Rufisque is a nice place with open-air bars and two cinemas, though the quality of the films is generally poor. Friendly people everywhere.

ST LOUIS

Like Ile de Gorée, St Louis was once a fortified collection point for slaves bound for the Americas. It's the oldest French settlement on the continent.

The best of the cheapies here is *Hotel Maimaido*, which costs CFA 4000 per person. Good meals are available for CFA 400. Another place which travellers use is the *Hotel Battling Siki* (formerly the Hotel St Louis). It only has seven rooms and according to the latest reports they were dirty, smelly and noisy. It costs the same as the Maimaido. If you're looking for something better, try the *Hotel de la Résistance*. Rooms here cost CFA 4000 a single and CFA 6700 a double. Finally, there is the *Hotel de la Poste*, which is somewhat more expensive at CFA 5000.

About three km south of the city is an excellent beach for swimming.

While you're in St Louis it's worth visiting the nearby **National Parks of Djoudj** (to the north) and **La Langue du Berberie** (18 km south of St Louis near the village of Gandiol). You should visit these parks in winter, as you'll see very little birdlife during the summer months. Entry to the latter costs CFA 2000, plus you'll have to pay CFA 2000-3000 for a pirogue to take you to the sandbar. Both parks close at noon, so get moving early in the day.

TAMBACOUNDA

The *Catholic Mission* has very clean single rooms, each with its own shower, but it's very unfriendly these days (in contrast to other places in Senegal). You can definitely find a cheap place to stay either at the *Maison de Jeunes* (CFA 500-1000), which is very run-down; or with the *Voluntaires*

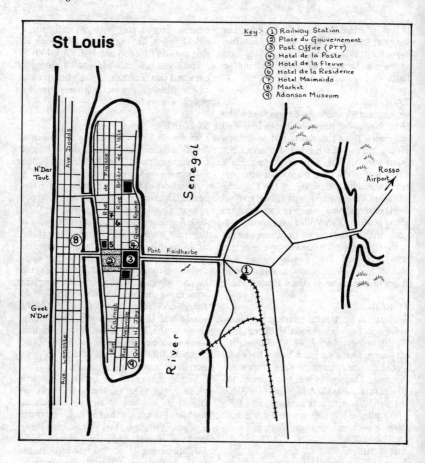

St Louis

Key :-
① Railway Station
② Place du Gouvernement
③ Post Office (PTT)
④ Hotel de la Poste
⑤ Hotel de la Fleuve
⑥ Hotel de la Residence
⑦ Hotel Maimaido
⑧ Market
⑨ Adanson Museum

du Progres, a French organisation which has a good hostel near the *Hotel Asta Kebe* for CFA 500 including breakfast. The hotel itself is very expensive.

If you want to visit the **Niokolo Kabai National Park** south of Tambacounda, it can be very difficult to get a lift right into the park. There are occasional trucks for CFA 2050 plus CFA 200 if you have a rucksack, but you'll probably have to hitch first to Dar es Salaam at the park entrance and then radio Siminti from there for transport to *Le Campement* (costs CFA 5000 return plus park entry fee of CFA 2000, which allows for a three-day visit). The park lays on a jeep and guide for 4½-hour safaris for CFA 4000 per person. You can camp at *Le Campement des Leons*, nine km from Siminti, free of charge, or rent a bungalow. The beautiful site overlooks the river and is immaculately kept. Food is expensive there, so bring your own if possible.

ZIGUINCHOR

The best place to stay here is *Hotel*

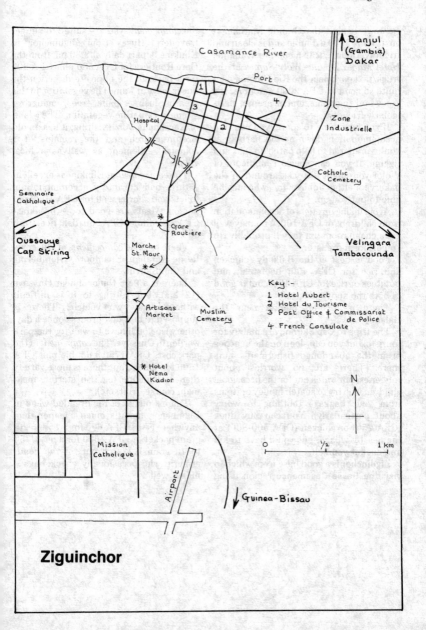

Ziguinchor

Key:-
1 Hotel Aubert
2 Hotel du Tourisme
3 Post Office & Commissariat de Police
4 French Consulate

Balkady behind the Grande Marche. It costs CFA 2000 a double and is clean and friendly. Good, cheap meals are available. *Hotel Mama Djanke Waly Sames* at the truck/taxi park near the Rio Cinema isn't quite so good at CFA 2000 a double. It's noisy and the management are not particularly friendly.

If you have time to spare, you can find accommodation down at the harbour if you're prepared to help patch up sails and rigging. If you can speak a modicum of Wolof you might also ask around in the bakery for either John or Joe, who may be able to put you up.

Avoid taking up offers of accommodation from children for CFA 100. You may well get a cheap room but they'll probably rip you off for more later.

Food is best at the Balkady (chicken and rice for CFA 400; beefsteak and potatoes or rice for CFA 400), but is good in both the above places.

There is a **craft market** near the Balkady.

The trips to **Cap Skirring** are mainly for tourists, but you can sleep on the beaches or in the abandoned fishermen's huts there. There are no worries about robberies, but watch out for the occasional children who try to snatch money or items from your baggage (nothing to worry about particularly). You can buy duck (CFA 750) or chicken (CFA 500-800) at the nearby village, but you'll have to kill and cook it yourself.

Ziguinchor is a good base from which to visit the **Basse Casamance** region using the *campement* system – suited to budget travellers. Buses from Ziguinchor to Elinkine depart daily at 2.30 pm from the Gare Routiere for CFA 580 plus CFA 200 for a pack. In the opposite direction the buses leave at 7 am. The vegetation in this area is lush – palm trees, mangrove swamps, estuarine vegetation. The island of Karaban is worth visiting; it has an old Breton church and the remains of a colonial settlement as well as a local village.

The *campement* at Elinkine is excellent – three-bed dormitory accommodation, toilets and showers, all for CFA 1000 per person. Meals are good too – breakfast CFA 500, dinner CFA 950 (fish, rice, fruit, etc).

There are also *campements* at Oussoye, Ile de Karaban, Enampore, Djembering and Cap Skirring.

There is a **Parc National** near Oussoye (12 km), but getting to it is difficult without your own vehicle. There is supposed to be a taxi-brousse once a day; otherwise you'll have to wait for the park warden in Oussoye. The *campement* in the park costs CFA 1750 a double plus CFA 1500 for a meal, but there is more variety than at Elinkine (eg fish starter, meat main course, fruit, etc).

There's plenty of the dreaded weed in Ziguinchor and it's much cheaper than anywhere else – CFA 600 for a 15- to 20-gram packet or CFA 1500 for a *pasul* (50 to 75 grams). Watch out for the gendarmerie who occasionally check bags – hide it well.

Seychelles

If you're looking for that unspoilt tropical paradise thousands of miles from anywhere, where you can lie on palm-fringed beaches, go swimming in warm, crystal-clear seas and relax among friendly, easygoing people, then the Seychelles fit the bill. Scattered over a vast expanse of ocean but with a total land area of only 440 square km, the Seychelles lie some 1500 km east of the African mainland and about 3000 km west of India. There are 87 islands in all, 38 of them granitic (the only mid-oceanic group of granite islands in the world) and the remainder coralline. Since they remained uninhabited until fairly recent times, a unique assembly of plants and animals were able to develop on these tiny fragments of land. As a result, they're of immense botanical and zoological interest and the government is intent on keeping them that way. Conservation is a major consideration and all development is carefully regulated and controlled to protect the natural beauty of the islands.

Some 80 species of indigenous trees and plants have been discovered in the Seychelles, ranging from the giant Coco-de-Mer to a tiny insectivorous pitcher plant. The double nuts of the Coco-de-Mer are the heaviest seeds in the plant kingdom and can weigh over 27 kg! The seed-nut takes seven years to mature and a year to germinate, and many of the 30-metre-high palms on which it grows are estimated to be 800 years old. Long before the Portuguese rounded the Cape of Good Hope, the empty nuts were found

on the shores of lands surrounding the Indian Ocean and gave rise to cults which attributed mystic powers to the fruit. Since no one had ever discovered their origin, the tree was thought to grow under the sea – hence the name. But it isn't just strange plant life which the Seychelles support. The lagoons team with marine life: giant tortoises are a common sight on some islands, and there are many unique frogs, geckos, chameleons and flying foxes to be seen, all of them harmless. As you might expect, snorkelling and scuba diving are popular here.

The islands were sighted by Vasco da Gama, the Portuguese navigator, at the beginning of the 16th century, but no settlement was attempted until French planters and their slaves arrived in the 1770s. They introduced cinnamon, cloves, nutmeg and pepper, but the British took control of the islands in 1810 and administered them from Mauritius until they were made a Crown Colony at the beginning of the 20th century. Political organisations didn't surface until 1964, when two rival parties were formed: the Seychelles People's United Party (SPUP) led by France-Albert Rene and the Democratic Party (SDP) led by James Mancham.

The SPUP stood for complete independence while the SDP wanted association with Britain. The first full elections in the colony resulted in a stalemate between the two parties, but in 1970 the SDP won a majority. However, Mancham was unable to persuade the British authorities that association would be better than independence, which was granted in 1976. The first post-independence government was a coalition between the SPUP and the SDP, with Mancham as president and Rene as prime minister. Mancham remained in power only a short time. His flamboyant style

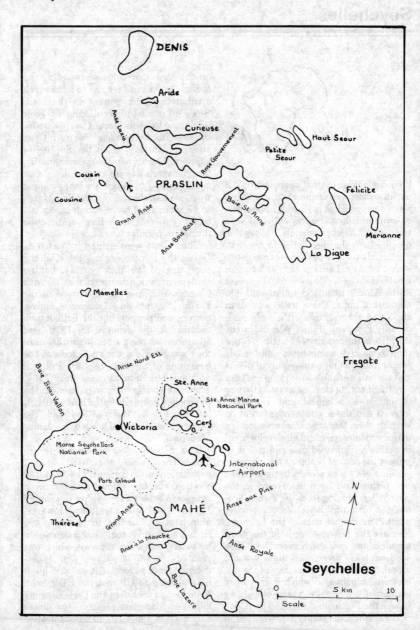

DENIS

Aride

Anse Lazio

Curieuse

Haut Seour

Petite Seour

Anse Gouvernement

Cousin

PRASLIN

Cousine

Felicite

Grand Anse

Baie St. Anne

Marianne

Anse Bois Rose

La Digue

Mamelles

Fregate

Anse Nord Est

Baie Beau Vallan

Ste. Anne

Ste. Anne Marine
National Park

Victoria

Cerf

Morne Seychellois
National Park

International
Airport

Port Glaud

N

Anse aux Pins

MAHÉ

Thérèse

Grand Anse

Anse à la Mouche

Anse Royale

Baie Lazare

Seychelles

0   5 km   10

Scale

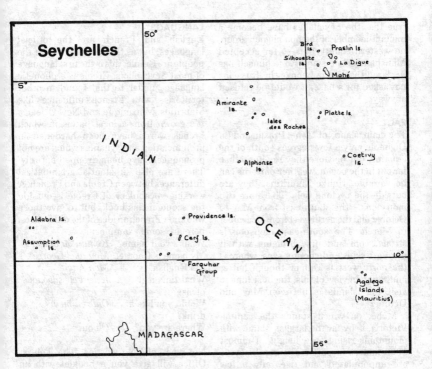

and his plans to make the Seychelles into a tax haven for the rich and powerful were completely at odds with Rene's commitment to social change, so when Mancham was away attending a Commonwealth Conference in London in 1977 a coup was staged and the presidency was assumed by Rene.

Rene is well aware of the ease with which a well-armed group of mercenaries could take over a scattered island group such as his with such a small population (about 65,000). The perfect example was provided by the coup in the nearby Comoros Islands in May 1978. Since then, an effort has been made to provide the islands with a degree of security. The measures have included setting up a regular army backed by a 3000-strong militia and joint manoeuvres with Tan-

zanian and Malagasy forces. Nevertheless, this didn't prevent a group of mercenaries (including some of the most notorious in Africa) from attempting to do the very thing Rene most feared. The attempt took place in 1982 and very nearly succeeded, but its cover was blown when an airport customs officer discovered a sub-machine gun in the baggage of what appeared to be a party of businessmen on holiday. A gun battle ensued at the airport, and while some of the most notorious mercenaries managed to escape by hijacking a plane and flying it to South Africa, many others were arrested.

Mancham and his supporters, meanwhile, have continued to lobby for western support in toppling Rene, painting him as a communist who is about to offer a site for a military base to the Russians. While it is true that the Seychelles have become a militant member of the non-aligned group, no western country has so far accepted Mancham's claims and Rene himself has declared that not only have the Russians not asked for a base, it would be refused anyway.

FACTS

The main islands of Mahe, Praslin and La Digue lie only a few degrees south of the equator, but because they're situated so far out in the ocean, weather patterns can be variable. Unlike Mauritius, they are outside the cyclone belt. There are two monsoons – the south-east from May to October and the north-west from December to March. The south-east monsoon is strong, cool and dry, bringing with it overcast skies and choppy seas, whereas the north-west is calmer though hotter and rainy. In view of this, the best time to visit the islands is between May and October.

Mahe, on which stands the capital, Victoria, is by far the largest island, with mountains rising to a height of almost 1000 metres in parts. The coral islands are unpopulated and rise only a few metres above sea level.

VISAS

Visas are not required by anyone. A one-month visitor's pass is issued on arrival subject to your possession of an onward ticket or sufficient money to pay a returnable 'security bond.' You must have a valid cholera vaccination certificate if arriving from Africa. Customs are very thorough. Visitor's passes can be renewed up to one year.

MONEY

US$1 = Rs 7.24

The unit of currency is the Seychelles rupee = 100 cents. There are no restrictions on the import of local currency, but export is limited to 100 rupees. There is no black market.

LANGUAGE

English and French are the official languages, but as the vast majority of the people are Creole, this is the first language of most Seychellois. Creole is a phonetic language similar to that found in other territories with French influence like Mauritius, Martinique and New Orleans. It's grown from a local patois in which French words have been hardened in pronunciation and syllables which are not pronounced have been dropped entirely. There are also substantial grammatical differences between Creole and French. A working vocabulary of Creole is outside the scope of this book, but to give those who know French an idea of the differences, here are some examples:

What's your name? *Koman ou apele?*
My name is George. *Mon apel George.*
I'm English. *Mon Angle.*
What time is it please? *Keler i ete silvouple?*
Would you like a drink? *Oule en bwar?*
Where are you? *Oli ou?*

Not easy, eh? No worries. The Tourist Office will give you a booklet with an extended list of phrases on arrival. Make sure you ask for it.

GETTING THERE & AROUND
Air

Air France, *Air India*, *British Airways*, *Kenya Airways* and *Air Seychelles* all fly to the Seychelles, so you can get there from any one of the following places: Europe (London, Paris, Frankfurt, Zurich); Asia (Jeddah, Bahrain, Colombo, Bombay, Hong Kong, Tokyo); and Africa (Djibouti, Nairobi, Johannesburg, Réunion, Mauritius). Nairobi to Mahe costs US$370 return. Air Seychelles (a British Caledonian DC 10) flies once a week London-Frankfurt-Seychelles and return.

Air Seychelles has several daily flights between Mahe and Praslin (Rs 135 one way and Rs 270 return) twice a day, seven days a week, and the same to Fregate. Bird and Denis Islands are served by charters. Enquire about flights in the office across from the Tourist Office in Victoria.

Road

Mahe and Praslin are the only two islands with sealed roads and a regular bus network. On Mahe the buses operate between 5.30 am and 7 pm and cost Rs 3-5, making taxis expensive and unnecessary. A bus from the airport to Victoria costs Rs 3. The bus stop is directly across from the airport parking lot on the road in front of the gas station. Taxis are available on both these islands at rates fixed by the government. On the other islands the roads are gravel, and about the only form of transport is the ox-cart. Bicycles can be rented on most of the larger islands. Hitching is excellent.

Boat

Cruise ships and cargo vessels call at Mahe, but there is no regular passenger ship calling there these days. For several years there have been no passenger boats between India and Africa.

Ferries connect the islands of Mahe, Praslin and La Digue on a regular schedule. Details are as follows:

Mahe-Praslin-La Digue

Ferry	Days	Depart	Arrive	Price
La Belle Praslinoise	Tue	Praslin 6 am Mahe 1 pm	Mahe 9 am Praslin 4 pm	Rs 25
	Wed	As above	As above	
	Fri	As above	As above	
Louis Alfred	Mon	Praslin 6 am Mahe 1 pm	Mahe 9 am Praslin 4 pm	Rs 25
	Wed	As above	As above	
	Fri	As above	As above	
La Bellone	Mon	Praslin 6 am Mahe 1 pm	Mahe 9 am Praslin 4 pm	Rs 25
	Thu	As above	As above	
Aroha	Mon	La Digue 6 am Mahe 1 pm	Mahe 9.30 am La Digue 4.30 pm	Rs 25
	Wed	As above	As above	
	Fri	As above	As above	

Praslin-La Digue

Ferry	Days	Depart	Arrive	Price
Silhouette	Daily	Praslin 10.30 am La Digue 11.30 am Praslin 2.30 pm La Digue 3.30 pm	La Digue 11 am Praslin 12 pm La Digue 3 pm Praslin 4 pm	Rs 25
Ideal	Daily	La Digue 7.30 am Praslin 10.30 am La Digue 3.30 pm Praslin 5.00 pm	Praslin 8 am La Digue 11 am Praslin 4 pm La Digue 5.30 pm	Rs 25

The port of call/departure point in Praslin is Baie Ste Anne.

PLACES TO STAY

It's suggested you avoid the high seasons if possible – July and August and again in December and January – as the price of accommodation rises and it's often difficult to find somewhere to stay.

There are hotels, guest houses, self-catering apartments and beach bungalows on Mahe, Praslin and La Digue. You can get a full list of them from the Tourist Office, Independence House, Independence Avenue, Victoria, Mahe (closed Sunday). They're very helpful and will telephone free of charge to check room availability and prices. This can save a lot of hassle. Off-season prices can be as little as half the high-season prices, so do bargain if you're there in the off-season. Most places offer full board, but you're advised to take half board because it's hot during the day and you generally don't feel like eating much more than a piece of bread. Dinners are enormous in most restaurants – average costs are Rs 80 (dinner) and Rs 50 (lunch).

The high-season price of hotels and guest houses is in the following range:

One Star Rs 90-175 single and Rs 165-240 double for bed and breakfast. Rs 140-220 single and Rs 245-330 double for half board.

Two Star Rs 150-270 single and Rs 210-365 double for bed and breakfast. Rs 200-320 single and Rs 300-465 double for half board.

In addition to hotels, guest houses and beach bungalows, accommodation is offered by some local families. This is mostly in the same price range as the One Star hotels and guest houses.

Camping is frowned on so you're advised not to do it unless you can find a truly remote spot like Anse Matelot on Praslin.

Seychellois food is a blend of French, Indian and Chinese influences. Most meals consist of fish or a curry served with white rice and salad or fruit. Octopus (usually curried and very tender) is a common local delicacy, as is grilled bourgeois (red snapper) and becune (mackerel). Other favourites are *rougaille* of local sausage cooked with green pumpkin; *daube* of pork with potatoes and tomatoes; and chicken, beef or fruit bat curry. Desserts include mashed bananas mixed with sugar and nutmeg, and yams in coconut milk. Drink *calou*, the local toddy sold in bamboo containers.

MAHE
Things to See

The **Botanical Gardens** in Victoria are well worth strolling through to see the Coco-de-Mer palms, orchids and giant tortoises. There's no charge for entry, but the Orchid House costs Rs 10. The **National Museum** opposite the Pirates Arms Hotel is open Monday to Friday from 10 am to 6 pm. It's free and is worth a visit.

Some excellent walks are possible into the interior of the island where there are forests, coconut, cinnamon and vanilla plantations as well as magnificent views of the smaller islands and the coastline. There's a small colony of giant tortoises on Therese Island off the west coast. Off the east coast opposite Victoria are the five small islands of St Anne, Cerf, Long, Round and Moyenne which together make up one of the **Marine National Parks**. Glass-bottomed boats and snorkelling equipment are available for hire.

For scuba diving go to the *Seychelles Underwater Centre* at the Coral Strand Hotel, Beau Vallon. You can go diving here for Rs 150, which includes all the equipment. Two dives on the same day would cost Rs 230. This makes it cheaper than *Le Diable de Mer* at the Northome Hotel.

Places to Stay

Eureka Guest House, La Louise (tel 44349). The high season tariff here is Rs 160 a single and Rs 300 a double for bed and breakfast (though depending on the season you may be quoted Rs 175 a double for bed and breakfast). alf board is Rs 250 a single and Rs 400 a double. The cuisine is excellent and the owners, France and Rosemary Adrienne, are very friendly and hospitable.

Bel Ombre Holiday House, Bel Ombre (tel 23616). This whole house can be rented for Rs 280 (four people) or Rs 380 (six people) in the high season, or for Rs 150 (two people) in the low season. It's clean, pleasant, close to the sea and has good bus connections.

Beau Vallon Bungalows, Beau Vallon (tel 47382). These are very pleasant and beautifully situated. Single rooms in the owner's house cost Rs 100 for bed and breakfast. The regular rooms cost Rs 125 a single and Rs 225 a double for bed and breakfast.

Madame Michel's Les Mangiers, Machabee near North Point, (tel 41455). These three houses overlook a beautiful cove and come complete with equipped kitchens, towels, all bedding, fans and

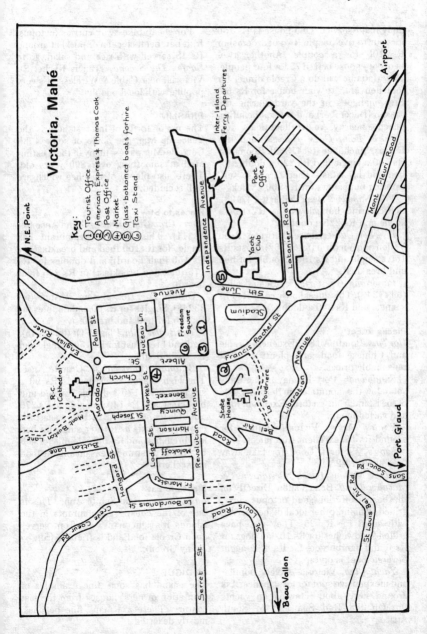

Victoria, Mahé

Key:
1. Tourist Office
2. American Express + Thomas Cook
3. Post Office
4. Market
5. Glass-bottomed boats for hire
6. Taxi Stand

daily maid service. One house is Rs 150 for four to five people (two bedrooms) or Rs 100 for a couple. Another two-bedroom house is Rs 175 for four people. The Madame will do a Creole dinner for four delivered to your house for Rs 60. Free mangoes in the yard during the season (December) and several beautiful beaches nearby. An excellent deal.

North Point Guest House, Fond des Lianes, Machabee (tel 41339). Rooms for Rs 150 a single and Rs 220 a double for bed and breakfast. There are also self-catering bungalows for Rs 700 a week.

Villa Napoleon, Beau Vallon (tel 47133). Self-catering bungalows for Rs 125 a single and Rs 225 a double.

Lè Niol Guest House, between Beau Vallon and Victoria (tel 23262). Costs Rs 150 a single and Rs 195 a double for bed and breakfast.

Panorama Guest House, Beau Vallon (tel 44349). This guest house costs Rs 175 a single and Rs 240 a double.

Places to Eat

Hoi Tins, Pointe Au Sel. Excellent Creole and Chinese food, and plenty of it at reasonable prices.

Sundowner, Port Launay. Beautifully set below the mountains on the other side of the island from Victoria. Excellent food and varied menu.

Pirates' Arms, Victoria. Lunch for around Rs 15; excellent fruit juices.

Sony's, Victoria. Good for take-away food at Rs 12-25.

Beau Vallon Beach Restaurant & Macquerel Pub, Beau Vallon. Directly on the beach, offering good octopus curry, grilled fish and other local dishes served with salad for Rs 25. They also have grilled sandwiches for Rs 10, hot dogs for Rs 6 and hamburgers for Rs 8. Draught *Seybrew* beer is on tap.

Yacht Club, Victoria. A very popular and inexpensive spot for local dishes. Ask around here about crewing on yachts through the Red Sea and to South Africa.

For cheap take-away curries (octopus, fruit bat, beef, chicken or pork) at around Rs 18 served with rice and salad, go to *Confex The Second*, Francis Rachel St, Victoria, near Cable & Wireless. It's very popular with local people.

PRASLIN

The major focus of interest here is the **Vallee de Mai**, the home of some 4000 Coco-de-Mer palms, many of them estimated at something over 800 years old. There also plenty of beaches which are well secluded.

Places to Stay

Merry Crab Guest House, Grand Anse (tel 33311). This bar and restaurant has singles for Rs 100 (bed and breakfast) or Rs 150 (half board), and doubles for Rs 175 (bed and breakfast) or Rs 275 (half board).

Orange Tree House, Baie St Anne (tel 33248). Singles for Rs 90 and doubles for Rs 175 for bed and breakfast.

The Beach Villa, Plage d'Or (tel 33445). Bed and breakfast for Rs 150 a single and Rs 204 a double.

Britannia Guest House, Grande Anse. The high season tariff here is Rs 90 a single and Rs 170 a double for bed and breakfast, and Rs 140 a single and Rs 270 a double for half board. In the low season it can cost as little as Rs 60 a single for bed and breakfast and Rs 200 a double for half board. It's clean and pleasant and the food is excellent.

Places to Eat

Lost Horizon, Baie Sainte Anne. This is one of the cheapest restaurants in the islands. It's right on the waterfront, serves good Creole food and is friendly (run by Jenny Green).

LA DIGUE

The island has some fine examples of plantation owners' houses from the last century. There are many fine beaches, mostly deserted.

Places to Stay

Chateau St-Cloud This beautiful old plantation house is five minutes' walk from the boat jetty. Maston, who runs it, charges only Rs 100 per person for half board. Bicycles can be rented for Rs 30 per day.

Choppy's Bungalow, Anse Reunion (tel 34224). Costs Rs 105 a single and Rs 182 a double for bed and breakfast.

Bernique Guest House, La Passe (tel 34229). Bed and breakfast costs Rs 100 a single and Rs 150 a double. Half board costs Rs 175 a single and Rs 250 a double.

Cabanes Des Anges In the high season the cost is Rs 270 a single and Rs 365 a double for a bed and breakfast, and Rs 320 a single and Rs 465 a double for half board. In the low season it can cost as little as Rs 250 a double for half board. It's a great place right on the seafront, offering delicious food and run by friendly people.

SILHOUETTE

If you'd like to get some idea of what the Seychelles were like last century, take a boat to Silhouette from either Victoria (two hours) or Beau Vallon (one hour) on Mahe. Only group tours depart from Victoria, but you can charter boats individually for US$1 at Beau Vallon. Before you visit the island, however, you must first get a permit from the government. There are no vehicles on this beautiful island with a population of only 450. The planter's house is one of the finest examples of wooden Seychellois houses.

COUSIN, BIRD & ARIDE ISLANDS

Those who have an interest in birdlife should make a point of visiting one or more of the islands where they are most numerous – Cousin, Bird and Aride. Cousin Island is administered by the International Council for Bird Preservation and can be visited on Tuesday, Thursday and Friday in groups of no more than 20. The trip there takes 1½ hours by boat from Mahe or half an hour by boat from Praslin. Getting to Bird Island requires more time. Boats take six to eight hours from Mahe (they depart Mahe at 9.15 am and 11 am and Bird Island at 10.30 am and 3.30 pm). There's also a plane which takes 30 minutes. A lodge on the island costs Rs 495 a single and Rs 705 a double for half board. Aride Island is owned by the Society for the Promotion of Nature Conservation and is the home of the greatest concentration of seabirds in the entire region. Tours can be arranged through local travel agencies in Victoria but they only run from 1 October to 30 April.

Sierra Leone

Sierra Leone owes its origins to a convergence of interests between British philanthropists seeking to establish a homeland for freed slaves and commercial concerns in the country wanting to expand trade links with West Africa. The first 411 settlers (who included 100 whites) landed at Freetown in 1787, but three years later their numbers had dwindled to 48. The next batch of 1200 freed slaves landed in 1792 and were soon augmented by another 550 brought from Jamaica. The colony was initially governed by the Sierra Leone Company, but financial problems forced the British government to take over in 1808. Over the next 60 years the settlers were joined by about 70,000 West Africans liberated from slave ships intercepted by the British navy and by tribespeople migrating from the interior. This Freetown comprised a very mixed population divided by religion, language and economic status. The result was the development of largely separate ethnic communities with their own leaders and internal organisation.

The colonial authorities naturally favoured those settlers who identified with British culture and values, but there was very little friction between the different communities right up until the late 19th century. The event which changed all this was the imposition of a hut tax in 1898. The result was war between the indigenous population and the settlers, and many of the latter were killed. The xenophobia which this produced has not entirely subsided even today and in the run-up to independence in 1961 one group of Creoles actually petitioned against the granting of independence – it was obvious that political power would be monopolised by the indigenous groups since the Creole community numbered less than 2% of the entire population.

In the last years of the colonial regime two parties emerged: the Sierra Leone People's Party (SLPP) led by Milton Margai, which identified with the Mende of the south; and the All People's Congress (APC) led by Siaka Stevens, which represents the interests of the Temne in the north. With Creole support, the SLPP won the elections prior to independence and Milton Margai took over as the country's first prime minister. He died in 1964 and his place was taken by Albert Margai. Ever since the 19th century the Creoles had monopolised positions within the civil service and Albert Margai set about replacing them with people from the southern provinces. Alarmed at seeing their hold on power eroded in this way, the Creoles threw weight behind the APC in the 1967 elections, and although the party gained a majority, it was prevented from taking its place by a military coup. This was followed two days later by a second coup led by Brigadier Juxon-Smith, who ruled the country for a year. Siaka Stevens, meanwhile, went into exile in Guinea and there raised a guerrilla army in preparation for invading Sierra Leone. As it turned out, this wasn't necessary as another coup in 1969 re-established civilian rule and Stevens was able to take his place as the country's new prime minister.

The return to civilian rule, however, did not bring peace. The country remained under a state of emergency, large numbers of SLPP supporters were tried for treason,

Sierra Leone

```
0        50       100      150 km
```

political parties were banned and inter-tribal rivalries led to violence. At one point Guinean troops were flown into Freetown to support the government. Things have cooled down considerably since those dark days, and the APC has gone on to win two further elections. In the process the country has become a republic and, since 1978, a one-party state. Siaka Stevens became the country's first president.

FACTS

Approximately half of the country consists of a flat belt of coastal lowland up to 120 km wide. Behind it the country rises to mountainous plateaux on the borders with Guinea. The climate is hot and humid with heavy rainfall along the coast – up to 3250 mm per year. Most of the rain falls between June and September, but it can extend for two months on either side of that period. The population stands at around 3½ million, of which some 30% is composed of Temne and Mende peoples. There are significant minorities of Europeans, Lebanese and Indians.

VISAS

Visas are required by all except those who are entitled to an entry permit. Entry permits are available to nationals of Commonwealth countries, Belgium, Denmark, Greece, Irish Republic, Iceland, Italy, Luxembourg, Netherlands, Norway, Spain, Sweden and Turkey. Entry permits are free. A single-entry visa costs leone 5 (or the equivalent) and a multiple-entry visa costs leone 20 (or the equivalent). Most visas and entry permits are for a one-week stay, but they'll give you longer if you ask for it. On the other hand, regardless of what your visa or stay permit says, Immigration at the border, on entry, will probably give you 48 hours to get to Immigration in Freetown. On the form you fill in at the border, it's best to put an expensive hotel in Freetown as the place where you are going to stay. Extensions up to a total of six months can be obtained from Immigration, Wellington St, Freetown. White South Africans are not admitted.

Burkina Faso visas These are obtainable from the French embassy. They cost leone 15.50, require one photo and take 24 hours.

Liberian visas The embassy is by Siaka Stevens Stadium. Visas cost leone 11.50, require three photos and take 24 hours to come through.

MONEY

US$1 = leone 2.50
£1 = leone 3.80

The unit of currency is the leone = 100 cents. Import/export of local currency is allowed up to leone 20. The street rate for the leone hovers between US$1 = leone 6-8 and up to leone 7.50 for the £ sterling. You can also buy leones in the large bank on Ashmun St in Monrovia, Liberia for close to the prevailing black market rate. (They won't, however, buy leones from you.) At the Sierra Leone/Liberian border you can buy Liberian dollars for leone 5.50 each. Be discreet if you are changing money on the street in Sierra Leone.

Currency declaration forms are issued on arrival at the airport, but there is no check on how much you actually have either coming in or going out. Customs at Kambia en route to Conakry (Guinea) don't even collect the form. There are large signs in all the hotels in Sierra Leone saying that foreign guests must pay either in hard currency or with leones bought at a bank (a bank stamp on your currency form is necessary to prove you obtained the leones at a bank) but, in practice, only the expensive hotels enforce this.

It's possible to buy air tickets for destinations within Africa using leones without bank receipts. For other destinations you must produce bank receipts. If anyone stops you at the airport and asks for proof that you have bought leones at a bank, just tell them you weren't issued with a currency declaration on entry by road. That's acceptable (if you did indeed enter by road).

You may find that local people quote prices in pounds. If this happens, remember that one pound is equal to two leones.

The airport departure tax for international flights is leone 10.

GETTING THERE & AROUND

Very few travellers go to Sierra Leone, largely because it usually involves a lot of back tracking to get out. Apart from the road between Conakry (Guinea) and Freetown, communications with neighbouring countries are poorly developed.

Air

If you can't handle the overcrowded bush taxis and trucks, it's worth considering flying. Quite a few travellers have recommended the flights in this country because the planes fly low enough for you to see all the detail of what's below. *Sierra Leone Airlines* flies from Hastings Airport to Bonthe (US$10) and Kenema (US$20).

If you fly to Monrovia from Freetown,

the fare is US$48 (or leone 581 using money bought on the black market).

Road

Hitching is slow even along the main routes, and there are many police and army checkpoints where your baggage will be searched and papers scrutinised. A reasonably good bus service operates between Freetown and all the larger centres of population such as Bo, Kenema, Makeni and Sefadu. The buses are fast and fairly cheap, but be there well before they're due to leave if you want to be sure of getting on (they are as cheap as private vehicles but much more comfortable, so there is a lot of competition for tickets). Some examples of fares are as follows:

Freetown-Makeni Leone 7
Makeni-Kabala Leone 6-8
Makeni-Bo Leone 8
Bo-Kenema Leone 3
Freetown-Kenema Leone 11, twice a day

Passenger cars called *poda poda* are the main means of transport other than the buses. They're crowded, uncomfortable and at times hazardous – up to 24 people are crammed inside a VW-sized mini-bus or Toyota pickup. A cheap taxi service (leone 5, one hour) is available between Bo and Kenema along the excellent German-built highway (the best road in the country). A taxi between Bo and Freetown costs leone 14 and takes about four hours (it's a poor though paved road).

There are no buses to Conakry (Guinea) from Freetown any longer, but there are buses to the border from Free St daily at about 8 am which take five to six hours and cost leone 20 plus leone 2-4 for baggage. If you prefer through transport, there are still trucks which cover this route. You can find them at the truck park on Free St at Regent Rd. They cost leone 40.

There used to be two routes you could take to Liberia, but the route via Kailahun in the north-east has been closed because a lot of smuggling was going on. This means that the only route open at present

is the one via Kenema, Zimi, the Mano River and Monrovia via the Bomi Hills. There are taxis through from Kenema to Monrovia for US$20 or leone 120. Expect to have to deal with hassles and bribery at at least 10 checkpoints en route. If you want to do the journey in stages, there are taxis from Freetown to Bo for leone 14 which take about four hours; taxis from Bo to Kenema for leone 5 which take about an hour; a pick-up or truck from Kenema to Zimi for leone 12 that takes about three hours; and pick-ups or trucks from there to the border (Mano River Union) for leone 30 that take up to six hours along an atrocious road. From the Mano River Union you can get a pick-up to Monrovia for US$6. The Mano River Union border closes at 6 pm daily. You can just about get from Freetown to Monrovia in one day during the dry season, but not during the wet.

Rail

The railway between Freetown and Kenema shown on most maps of Sierra Leone has been out of operation since 1971.

PLACES TO STAY

Until recently there were no hotels outside of Freetown and Bo, but there are now a number of small boarding houses/hotels in the provincial towns such as Kabala and Kenema. They usually charge around leone 3 per night. The Peace Corps operate a number of hostels in outlying towns such as Kenema. You might be able to stay in one of them for the night for a small charge if they have room. In other places you'll have to ask around – someone will generally help out if you're willing to pay for your keep.

FREETOWN

As one traveller put it recently, 'Freetown has a steamy, run-down decadence and is thoroughly enjoyable.' It did, however, benefit from Siaka's chairmanship of the OAU conference held here in 1980, when

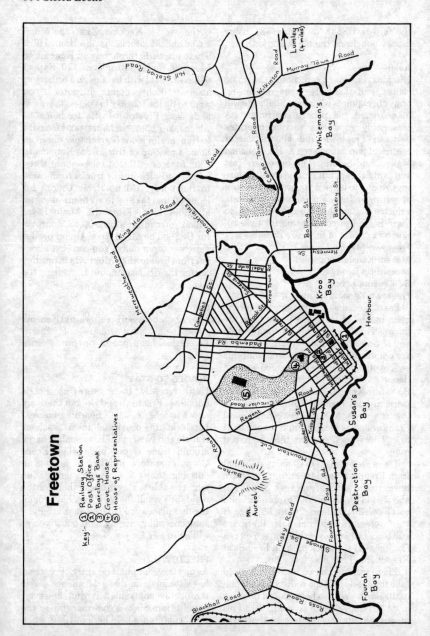

Freetown

Key:—
① Railway Station
® Post Office
③ Barclays Bank
④ Govt. House
⑤ House of Representatives

new ferries were purchased, roads were widened and improvements were made to the public transport system and street lighting.

It's possible to sleep on the floor at the *Christian Youth Centre*, Garrison St, for leone 1.50. The *Canadian Volunteers Hostel* (CUSO), Siaka Stevens St, has a few beds for leone 3. There is a *YMCA* on Fort St where you can stay for leone 22 in air-conditioned doubles (leone 19 for Peace Corps volunteers). The *City Hotel*, Lightfoot Boston St at Gloucester St, has fairly cheap rooms for leone 8 a single and leone 12 a double as well as 'shades of Graham Greene.' It's none too clean and has lots of mosquitoes, but it does have plenty of character. Slightly upmarket is the *Lido Hotel*, Garrison St at Charlotte St, which costs leone 15 a single and leone 20-30 a double including breakfast. More expensive still are the *Lamar Hotel*, Howe St just up from Siaka Stevens St, which costs leone 33 a single with private bath, air-conditioning and breakfast; and the *Leone Hotel*, Regent Rd one block up from Kissy St, which costs leone 45 a single and leone 55 a double. You may be able to stay at the *Peace Corps House* for leone 10 a night.

It's probably best not to sleep on the beaches south of town towards the Milton Margai Teachers' College because of the danger of being mugged. On the other hand, all except Lumley Beach are unspoiled by tourism or day-trippers – and even Lumley is hardly touched. Take bus No 3 to get there.

A good place to try for food is the *Q Café* in the quadrangle behind McCarthy Square. The *Yum Yum* and the *International*, both on Rawdon St, have also been recommended. In addition to the above, there are plenty of cheap chop-houses.

Taxis within town cost leone 1 per journey; poda poda costs 25c. To Lumley Beach from Short St will cost 25c. To Aberdeen will cost 50c. To the airport there is a Sierra Leone Airlines bus from the *Paramount Hotel* for leone 12, but you can do it cheaper by taking a taxi to the ferry terminal for leone 1, crossing by ferry for 50c and then taking another taxi to the airport for leone 1. International flights depart from Lungi Airport. Domestic flights depart from Hastings Airport, which is much closer to the city and does not involve a ferry crossing.

The government bus station in Freetown is in Rawdon St at Wallave Johnson St in the old railway station. You may be offered places in the queue by small boys, but it's generally not worth it. Private buses leave from Dan St or Fyabon or from the Shell station in Kissy St. These buses are usually very crowded and uncomfortable. The truck park for trucks going to Conakry (Guinea) is on Free St at Regent St.

Useful Addresses

Immigration
    Siaka Stevens St at Rawdon St. Count on spending some time there.
Barclays Bank
    Siaka Stevens St at Charlotte St. They charge leone 5 commission on each traveller's cheque!
American Express
    22 Siaka Stevens St

KENEMA

The *Travellers' Lodge* at the Mobil Station has been recommended and costs leone 10. More luxurious is the *Eastern Motel* on the main street which costs leone 20.

Somalia

Until fairly recently, very few travellers visited Somalia largely because of the difficulty of getting visas and the lack of communications, but with visas becoming more freely available a trickle of more intrepid travellers are beginning to filter in. If you have a yen to see a beautiful land of camels, sand, thorn scrub, endless beaches and interesting villages completely unspoiled by tourism, this is the place to head for. It's well worth the extra effort required. Visas are now easy to get in Nairobi and Cairo. There's still a lingering feeling of political suspicion about foreigners (and outright hatred of the Russians for their support of Ethiopia in the Ogaden War), but most of the people you meet will be very friendly. Also, Islam here is a much mellower version than elsewhere so women travellers should experience no problems.

The Somali coast once formed part of the extensive Arab-controlled trans-Indian Ocean trading network. Its ports of Mogadishu and Brava were part of the East African chain which stretched through Malindi, Mombasa, Zanzibar and Kilwa as far as Sofala in Mozambique. The prosperity of these ports and indeed the trading network itself were largely destroyed by the Portuguese in the early 16th century following the latter's discovery of a sea route to India and beyond via the Cape of Good Hope. Somalia lapsed into obscurity, ignored by European traders because of its lack of exploitable resources.

In the 19th century much of the Ogaden Desert – ethnically a part of Somalia – was annexed by the empire of Ethiopia during Menelik the First's reign. This loss has never been accepted by the Somalis, and has not only poisoned Somalia-Ethiopian relations for over half a century but has led to war on more than one occasion. Throughout the 1970s Somali guerrilla organisations dedicated to recovering the Ogaden were supported by the Somali government and at one point had succeeded in not only throwing back regular Ethiopian army troops from the desert area but in taking Jijiga and almost capturing Harrar and Dire Dawa – the major towns in southern Ethiopia. They were eventually pushed back over the Somali border only with massive Russian and Cuban assistance following Moscow's switch of allegiance from Mogadishu to Addis Ababa in the wake of Haile Selassie's overthrow and the Marxist takeover in Ethiopia. Somalia also claims parts of northern Kenya which were detached during the late 19th century by the British, though these claims are on a much lower key than those relating to the Ogaden.

At the turn of the century, Somalia was divided between the British, who took the northern part opposite the South Yemen, and the Italians, who took the southern part alongside the Indian Ocean, but the two parts were reunited when independence was gained in 1960. Nine years later a military coup brought current president Mohamed Said Barre to power on a ticket of radical socialism which has resulted in enormous changes in Somalian society. The government places great emphasis on self-reliance and on the use of teamwork; many roads, houses, hospitals and agricultural projects have been created by such methods, paralleling similar redevelopments in Maoist China.

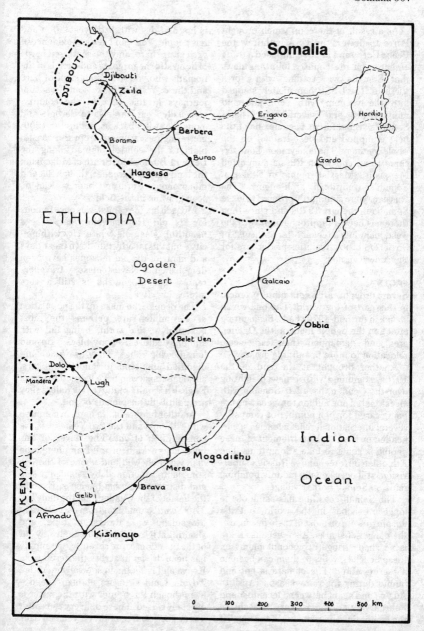

As a result of the coup which brought Barre to power, the USA withdrew the Peace Corps and in 1970 imposed a trade embargo on the country following news that Somalia was trading with North Vietnam. The USSR immediately stepped into the vacuum with economic and military aid and several years later Somali's armed forces became one of the best equipped and best trained on the whole continent. The honeymoon, however, came to an end when Russia supported Mengistu's Marxist regime in Ethiopia, Somali's traditional arch-enemy. The Russians were summarily ordered to leave Somalia in the late 1970s and since then there has been a rapprochement with the west, including a recent offer of the use of Soviet-built port facilities at Berbera for the American navy.

FACTS

Severe droughts are a continuing problem in this part of the world. The one which struck in the mid-1970s had a devastating effect on the people living in the Ogaden area and demanded their large-scale relocation to more favourable areas.

Another drought at the end of the 1970s, combined with renewed fighting over the Ogaden, have left Somalia with an estimated one million refugees who are being cared for in a number of camps by several international relief agencies spearheaded by the UN. Resettlement of these people is going to take a long time. The Ethiopian airforce, under Russian supervision, still occasionally mounts bombing raids on Somali border villages.

The Somali coastline has some of the longest beaches in the world, but it's unsafe to swim on most of them because of the danger of sharks. Also, because there is no shady fringe of coconut palms on these beaches, visits to them can become a searing affair. The climate is hot and humid during the rainy season (April to August and again between December and February) but otherwise very pleasant. In the mountains and plateaux of the north it is hot and dry with little vegetation and few people. You won't see any evidence of agriculture here, only the scattered herds of domestic sheep, goats and camels of the nomads who you will catch sight of here and there. You can make some beautiful journeys in this part of the country, especially from Hargeisa to Berbera and along the switchback ascent up the 1000-metre-high escarpment from the coastal plain to the central plateau along the Berbera-Burao road. South of Mogadishu the land becomes greener, though flat and monotonous. Corn and bananas can be seen growing in the fields.

Mogadishu, the capital, was once famous for its old Hammawein quarter – a beautiful, gleaming white city-within-a-city – but this is sadly run-down these days and many of the old mosques have been demolished. Nevertheless, travellers report that Mogadishu is still a very interesting city.

The people who make up the population of 4½ million are perhaps the most beautiful in the world, being tall with aquiline features, ebony-black skin and long flowing robes. They are quiet and dignified and tend to ignore strangers, although those who have learned to speak English are quite ready to talk unless you are politically suspicious of you.

Another feature of life here, in common with Ethiopia and the two Yemens, is the consumption of *qat*. The leaves of this bush give a kind of mild amphetamine high when chewed and is one of the few stimulants sanctioned by Islam. Its sale and distribution is big business. Even at the height of the Ogaden War the daily DC 3 *Air Somalia* qat flight from Dire Dawa to Mogadishu was always on time, and shooting at it by either side was strictly out of the question. More recently, the supply has been driven in across the scrub from Kenya and Ethiopia in specially modified Toyota Land Cruisers at high speed – even though the border with the latter is officially closed! These delivery runs offer a very good source of lifts if you can hack the punishing your head and kidneys get along the rough desert roads. Qat is now officially illegal in Somalia but the supply continues to pour in nevertheless. Sound like something else you might have come across?

VISAS

Visas are required by all and are now much easier to obtain. In Nairobi, Kenya (embassy in International House, Mama Ngina St), a three-month visa costs Ken Sh 200 and requires two photos. In addition, you have to state why you want to visit Somalia, how much money you have and where you intend to stay. Check the dates on your visa before you leave the embassy, as they sometimes make mistakes. In Cairo, Egypt (embassy just west of Dokki St, 10 minutes on foot north of 6th October St) they cost E£21.70 and require three photos plus a letter of recommendation from your own embassy. No onward ticket is required and the visa is issued in 24 hours. The visa is valid for one month and must be used within one month of issue. Visa applications are accepted on Wednesday, Saturday and Sunday between 10 am and noon. You can also get visas easily in Djibouti. You cannot get a visa at the border or on arrival by air.

You must have valid vaccination certificates for entry, including one for yellow fever. If you arrive in Mogadishu by air without a yellow fever vaccination certificate, they may well insist on vaccinating you there and then. Get it done before you arrive. Malaria is also a serious problem in Somalia, and even if you are taking chloroquine you might still get a light bout that will knock you off your feet for a few days. If this happens, go to the nearest refugee aid centre rather than a Somali hospital. It's well to remember also that although WHO claims smallpox has been wiped out, you shouldn't take this for granted if you're going near any refugee camps. It's a good idea to have a smallpox vaccination beforehand, just in case. Tap water in Mogadishu is said to be all right for drinking, but elsewhere it should be avoided because of the risk of hepatitis.

Those with cameras must have a photography permit. These cost Sh 22, require three photos and take four days to issue. For permits contact the NRC in Mogadishu and tell them you are interested in the refugee situation. They might even issue you with an NRC card if you are convincing. Even with a photography permit you should be discreet about taking photographs. Many people object to it.

MONEY

US$1 = Som Sh 36 (official)
Som Sh 80 (floating tourist rate)

The unit of currency is the Somali shilling = 100 cents. Import/export of local currency is allowed up to Sh 200. In January 1985, the government announced a major devaluation and a two-tier exchange rate – a fixed official rate (Sh 36) and a floating tourist rate (against the US dollar). It's envisaged that the two rates will converge at some point in the future. These measures have put an end to the black market. The US dollar is the easiest currency to change into shillings, with the £ sterling a poor second. Apart from the Saudi ryal, any other currency is a waste of time. (It's estimated that about two million Somalis work in Saudi Arabia.) Credit cards, likewise, are a waste of time.

If you arrive by air, you must buy a currency declaration form for Sh 12. Make sure you declare everything they're likely to find during a thorough search; otherwise you could find yourself spending a week in jail and deported afterwards. At Liboi (the land border with Kenya) and Loyada (the land border with Djibouti), currency forms are not normally issued, but it's worth asking for one anyway to avoid hassles later. If you try to change money at a bank inside the country without a currency form, for instance, you may well be referred first to customs. This can soak up time.

The devaluation has made Somalia a very reasonable place to visit in terms of costs. For the while, too, international phone calls are very cheap and the service is efficient (you'll never have to wait more than one hour).

The airport departure tax is Sh 80 in Mogadishu and Sh 30 in Hargeisa.

LANGUAGE
Somali is the official language. It's usually possible to find someone who can speak reasonable English even out of the crowd on the back of a truck. Here's a basic English-Somali vocabulary:

Numerals

1	*kaw*
2	*laba*
3	*sader*
4	*afar*
5	*shan*
6	*leh*
7	*todoba*
8	*sided*
9	*sagal*
10	*toban*
20	*laba tau*
30	*sodon*
40	*afar tan*
50	*koh tan*
100	*bogol*
200	*laba bogol*
1000	*kuhn*

Useful Phrases & Words

Good morning
  Subah wanaqsan
Good afternoon
  Galab wanaqsan
Good evening
  Habeen wanaqsan
How are you?
  Iska waran?
I'm fine
  Ficaan

Thank you
  Mahatsini
Where do you come from?
  Hage ka timio?
I come from . . .
  Wahan ka imid . . .
What is your name?
  Maga?
My name is . . .
  Maga aniga . . .
How much . . . ?
  Waa imissa . . . ?

yes	*ha*
no	*maya*
I	*aniga*
you	*adiga*
he	*isaga*
she	*iyada*
we	*anaga*
they	*iyaga*

On the Road

Is this truck going to (Erigavo)?	*Baaburr ke tagaya (Erigavo)?*
How much?	*Imisa?*
How many km?	*Imisa km?*
How many hours?	*Imis sa'adood?*
Where do you go?	*Hage u so'ofa?*
Where?	*Hage?*
When?	*Mahrki?*
Who?	*Kuma?*
before	*qor*
now	*had*
maybe	*lege yaba*
far	*fuq*
fast	*degdeg*
slow	*tartip*
big	*wean*
small	*yahr*
road	*djit*
town	*magalo*

Food

water	*beeyu*
milk	*anno*
meat	*hillip*
camel	*gil* (hard 'g')
goat	*ari*
liver	*ber*

rice	baris
bread	roti
vegetable	kudar
tea	shah
spaghetti	basta
lobster	argosto
fish	khallun

GETTING THERE & AROUND

Air

There are two flights per week in either direction between Nairobi and Mogadishu on Sunday by *Kenya Airways* and on Wednesday by *Somali Airlines*. The fare is normally about Ken Sh 950, but if you have Mogadishu added to another ticket (say, from Nairobi to Cairo), the extra stop-over should cost Sh 550. It's common practice for someone to go through your baggage at Mogadishu and remove anything of value before it gets to you – film, cassettes, cameras, etc. Rucksacks which don't lock are a gift, but even 'hard' luggage (lockable) isn't safe.

Be prepared for a major search upon leaving Mogadishu.

Somali Airlines flies Mogadishu-Hargeisa daily except Friday for approximately Sh 1000. There are also flights from Hargeisa to Djibouti.

If you're travelling south down through Africa and want to see northern Somalia without having to back-track, it might be worth considering the flights from Cairo to Djibouti (see Kjibouti chapter).

Road

There is now a regular network of buses between the main centres of population in the south but very few in the north. Most of them travel at night to avoid the heat of the day. There are sealed roads between Mogadishu and Kisimayu and, except for a few stretches of desert track, between Mogadishu and Hargeisa. Elsewhere the roads are gravel or just tracks through the bush. In the dry season (September to March – but considerably longer at present because of the drought) the unsealed roads and tracks are no

problem and you'll get from one point to another quickly. In the wet season, however, the stretch between Kisimayu and Garissa (Kenya) alone can take up to two weeks! The road between Hargeisa and Djibouti gets into a similar state but it isn't quite so radical. One traveller who went along the latter in the wet described it as the only road he'd come across in Africa where you could be covered in dust and bogged in the mud at the same time.

You cannot go overland into Ethiopia at present. Toyota Land Cruisers on the *qat* run do it every day, but unless you're in the game, you're *persona non grata*.

Examples of current bus fares and schedules are as follows:

Liboi (Kenya/Somalia border)-Kisimayu There is usually one bus per day, either direct or via Afmadu. The cost is Sh 300 (plus there might be a baggage charge) and the trip takes about 10 hours.

The 'road' is just a sandy track through the scrub. There are numerous security checks which involve 'everybody off/baggage search/document check/everybody back on.' They're mainly concerned with Somalis smuggling goods in from Kenya. Officials are generally courteous to western travellers.

Kisimayu-Mogadishu Daily buses leave about 7 am (be there are 5 am if you want a about 7 am (be there at 5 am if you want a seat) from in the square next to the police nine hours. Trucks cost about the same.

Mogadishu-Erigavo You'll have to ride a truck along this route. They cost Sh 500 and take about 2½ days.

Erigavo-Burao Trucks cost Sh 400 and take all day.

Burao-Berbera Trucks along this paved road cost Sh 200 and take about four hours.

Berbera-Hargeisa There is a minibus available along this paved road which costs Sh 150 and takes about three hours.

Hargeisa-Loyada (Djibouti border) Trucks along this unpaved route usually cost Sh

500 (though drivers will often reduce the price to Sh 300 if you bargain – local people pay Sh 500). It's a two-day journey.

Apart from buses, lifts with one of the relief agencies are relatively easy to get. This is a cheap way of getting around the country. The vehicles which these agencies run are officially for relief workers only, but if you are interested in the work they do then chances are that they'll give you a lift. One of the best places to try is the United Nations High Commission for Refugees (UNHCR) in Mogadishu on the 'Volag' (voluntary agencies) noticeboard. There are many 'lifts offered' notices here. The Anglo-American Beach Club, Lido Rd, Mogadishu, is a good place to ask around for lifts, as are the Finnish TB Centre (Finnish medical aid) and the GTZ Bureau near the German embassy (enquire there).

To/from Kenya

There are two possible routes, one from Kisimayu to Garissa via Liboi and the other in the extreme north from Lugh to Garissa via Mandera. The route via Liboi is the most predictable as far as transport and road conditions go, and a full description of it can be found in the Kenyan chapter under 'Getting There & Getting Around.' The route via Lugh requires more initiative. There are some trucks along this route, but usually you will have to find a lift in a Toyota Land Cruiser on the *qat* run. Ask around in any of the border towns about these, but remember that they drive very fast and you'll feel like a piece of jelly at the end. On the other hand, it isn't that difficult to find a lift.

You must first have permission from the District Commissioner before crossing the border from Lugh. If you start from Kisimayu and are heading to Kenya via Liboi, you must get an exit stamp from the National Security Service before setting out.

To/from Djibouti

Regular trucks travel this route. The trip is short but it can take two days. The landscape is stunning and well worth the discomfort. First check with the UNHCR in Hargeisa for any refugee vehicles that might be going that way. If you are travelling in the opposite direction, the best place to find a lift is at the Somali border post around mid-afternoon – ask the drivers as they stop at the border. Get a visa for Djibouti (where required) at the embassy in Mogadishu near the UNDP compound, as they are cheaper here than at the border and there's a lot less hassle if you already have one. You must have an onward ticket to get into Djibouti.

Boat

The Russians virtually killed the dhow trade while they were in Somalia, so there are now very few boats plying up and down the coast. However, if you have time, it is worth making enquiries down at the old port in Mogadishu or in the small port at the end of Kisimayu Beach. In the latter place, ask for Rachid (a dhow captain) in the marketplace. If you go with him he'll also arrange the exit stamp for you at immigration. The price to Lamu is usually Sh 1000 including food and, if the wind is favourable, the journey should take about four days. The dhows which do go south to Kenya only do so at certain times of the year (November to March). At other times of the year the wind is blowing in the wrong direction and it can take two weeks to get from Mogadishu to Lamu!

PLACES TO STAY

Outside of Mogadishu and Kisimayu there are few hotels to choose from. All are of a very basic standard with considerable variation in cleanliness. Expect to pay Sh 25-30 for a shared room and up to Sh 40 for a single in these small places. If you sleep out in the desert (as part of a truck ride from one place to another), you need a sleeping bag or warm clothes. It gets quite cold at night.

The staple diet everywhere is rice, macaroni or spaghetti with a splash of sauce for Sh 15-20. A joint of sheep or goat costs Sh 20-25 and the endless cups of tea you will drink cost a standard Sh 2. In the Mogadishu market there is a fair choice of food such as tomatoes (Sh 25 per kg), bananas (Sh 2 each), grapefruit (Sh 5 each), bread rolls (Sh 2 each), onions and peppers. Cheese can be bought in certain shops for about Sh 45 per 100 grams. The standard breakfast throughout Somalia is fried liver (of sheep, goat or camel) with onions and bread for Sh 25 – very tasty if you like liver.

BAIDOA

There are plenty of cheap hotels here in the Sh 20-25 range. The *Bar Bekin* at the start of town coming from Mogadishu has been recommended as a good place to meet people and have cold drinks.

HARGEISA

The *State House* two km outside of town is a good place to stay. The staff are friendly and you can camp in the park. There are smaller, more basic, hotels closer to the centre.

KISIMAYO

The cheapest place to stay here is the *Hotel Kisimaiyo*, which costs Sh 60 but is a 'real dive.' It's suggested you only stay here if you are fond of mosquitoes, cockroaches and the smell of kerosene. Probably the best place to stay is the *Hotel Quilmawaaye*, which is spotlessly clean and costs Sh 80 a double. The manager, Ali, speaks English and is very helpful. *Hotel Wamo* is past its prime but still costs Sh 320 a double. It is, however, a good place to meet expatriates and locals, especially if you are looking for a lift to Mogadishu and elsewhere. A taxi from the

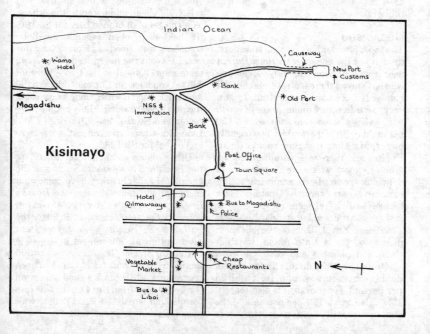

town centre to the Wamo will cost Sh 30-40.

One traveller suggested it might be worth asking at the ARABCO compound, which is an expatriate hangout. Someone there might offer to put you up for the night. Take some western cigarettes and whisky with you and leave them as a contribution to your keep.

LIBOI

This border town is a fascinating little place. Local people bring in their camels, goats and cows for water at the borehole. There's one mud-brick lodging house for Sh 50 a room (double or triple). Food is limited to chai, chapati, boiled goat and a few tomatoes in the market under the tree, but this is usual all the way to Kisimayu, where there is more variety. Cafés hardly ever serve vegetables. Normally it's just meat, spaghetti and *mofu* (local bread that resembles a chapati but would be better used as a cushion – it's thick and rubbery).

MOGADISHU

The most popular hotel among travellers, though not the cheapest, is *Hotel Dalsan* near the American embassy. Everyone who has stayed there has recommended it highly. It has about seven clean, bright, cockroach-free, airy rooms (some of which have a view of the ocean) and costs Sh 100 per night or Sh 150 a double. The friendly owner, Ms Alina Bus Bus, speaks fluent English and there is a restaurant on the ground floor where tea, coffee and delicious roast beef sandwiches (inexpensive) are served. Upstairs is a lounge with a refrigerator for use by residents. Of a similar standard is *Hotel Zeno* near Km 4. One of the cheapest places to stay is *Hotel Muna*, which is clean and pleasant and costs Sh 75 a single and Sh 150 a double (if you share a double room with someone else it is Sh 65 per person). *Hotel Scebeli* is also reasonable value at Sh 150 per person and the staff are friendly, but some of the rooms

are gloomy and have cockroaches. Another cheapie mentioned in the past is *Hotel Hargeisa* near the Scebeli Hotel.

The *Juba Hotel*, opposite the post office, is quite pricey at Sh 300 a single and Sh 600 a double including breakfast, and you must pay in hard currency. The rooms are pleasant enough but the staff aren't particularly friendly. Of a similar standard is the *Croce del Sud Hotel*, which costs Sh 250 per person including breakfast. Avoid the *Alruba Hotel*, which is expensive and has bad plumbing.

You can find breakfast at both the Juba and Scebeli hotels. Also, don't forget the snack bar at the Dalsan Hotel. One of the cheapest restaurants is the *Torino*, which has good service and food. Spaghetti with sauce costs Sh 30 and Russian salad Sh 20. For lunch or dinner there is a good choice of places to eat. Many people have recommended the Chinese restaurant *Ming Sing* near Fiat Circle and the Dalsan Hotel; it is one of the best in town and relatively cheap compared to the others. You can get a lot of food here for Sh 100. (It has even been recommended by someone who lived in Hong Kong for years.) Avoid the overpriced *Hong Kong* restaurant. A meal at the Croce del Sud will set you back Sh 130, and although the food is good and the surroundings pleasant, the portions are small. Many people have recommended the *Anglo-American Club*, Lido Rd, where you can get a western-style meal for Sh 120.

Other places you might like to try are the *Pakistani Restaurant* (Sh 25 for the cheaper meals plus they have somewhat higher-priced seafood); and the *Hassan Restaurant*, which is also very pleasant but somewhat more expensive at Sh 80 for the buffet meal. *Hazzam's Roof Top Restaurant* offers all-you-can-eat Italian-style buffets for Sh 100. The *Pizzeria* some 300 metres from the *Lido Night Club* has been recommended. There is a good bakery on the beach road from Km 4 on the way into town which is painted pink. Follow your nose for excellent bread rolls.

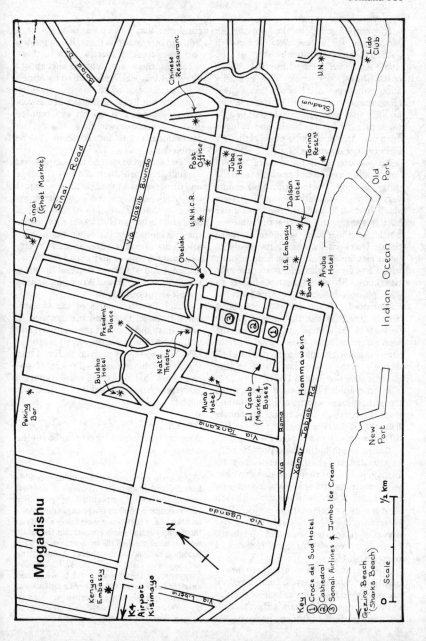

Mogadishu

Key:
① Croce del Sud Hotel
② Cathedral
③ Somali Airlines   ⚹ Jumbo Ice Cream

Scale

0   ½ Km

N

If you're going to be staying in Mogadishu for a few days, it's worth getting temporary membership at the *Anglo-American Club*, Lido Rd, which costs Sh 140 per week. This not only allows you to get in, it lets you take a guest along except on Friday. The bar is a very popular spot with expatriates and people working at the various aid and refugee agencies. Another similar place is the *UN Club* further down the road.

All working expatriates here have a 'booze allowance' which they get from the duty-free shop. The local rum has become very expensive recently (about Sh 60 for a small bottle), but when beer (Sh 80 per bottle) is scarce this can cost the same per bottle, so the choice is yours at those times. There is a disco on Thursday nights in the last building along the Lido, usually with a live group who sing western music. Entry costs Sh 30 and there is a bar. It's a good place to meet people. One traveller commented, 'If you go as a couple, a Somali guy may ask the man if he can dance with the woman and then thank the man afterwards and have a chat without uttering a word to the woman concerned!' There's also a popular disco in the basement of the Alruba Hotel.

Photographic permits and authority to travel to refugee camps can be obtained from the NRC at Km 4 round the corner from the USAID building. The UNHCR is 50 metres south of the post office.

Gezira Beach is the most popular with expatriates and Somalis, especially on Friday, but to get there you need to have your own transport or know someone who has. There is a hotel there with a beach supposedly protected from sharks. The restaurant here is reasonably priced and serves fish, lobster, rice and spaghetti. Lunch for two with fish and tea should come to Sh 150.

Further along the coast there are a number of isolated coves, though not all are protected from sharks (one of them is appropriately called Shark's Bay, though the name is derived from a shark-shaped coral reef that juts up out of the water). You can buy fresh fish there. It's suggested you do not take a local woman to these areas, as there are military checkposts along the way which are staffed by armed soldiers, most of whom are 'young lads.' They are not likely to behave in the way you might want. Keep an eye out for sharks if you go swimming. It's not an uncommon event for someone to be gobbled up.

Taxis around town tend to be expensive, partially because there is a fuel shortage and drivers are rationed (at present to just five litres per day – you don't get many fares on that!). Fares are negotiable but are rarely less than Sh 250 per ride (inside the city limits). On the other hand, there are plenty of public buses around the city which are frequent and cheap (Sh 5 per journey) and which run along all the main roads. Flag them down. When you want to get off shout out, 'Jojii!'

Buses to other parts of the country leave from El Gab, the big expanse of sand, dust and chaos at the southern end of Lido St. The cheapest way to get to the airport is to take a pick-up to Km 4 and then walk the remaining 1½ km. If you can't hack that, a taxi will cost around Sh 100 (though they may ask for considerably more).

OTHER

A recent traveller had this to say about the country:

The Somalis were, without exception, incredibly friendly and hospitable, although it was not uncommon to be surrounded by genuinely curious onlookers when trying to get directions and the like. Travellers are certainly a rarity in the country and it's only natural that the locals wonder what the hell these creatures are with bloody great bags on their backs. As usual, the kids were especially curious but an adult would always shoo them away, which we found amazing since they were not even a nuisance in the first place! Little English is spoken throughout the south (we didn't go north of Mogadishu), but the ones who do know some are eager to talk and learn something about other people and places. The hospitality in the villages was often embarrassingly overwhelming, with people inviting you into their huts to drink chai and eat boiled goat. This sounds OK until one sees the conditions under which food is prepared, but it's difficult to refuse without causing offence.

Another traveller who came down from Djibouti through northern Somalia had this to say:

Almost everywhere I went, I was warmly welcomed and received. If otherwise, people were not cold, only aloof – due, I believe, to the infrequency of foreign travellers along much of my route (between Zeila and Mogadishu over a period of 10 days I did not encounter another white face). I seldom paid for a cup of tea and often a Somali fellow passenger would insist on paying for my meal as well. Until I reached Mogadishu, where there are many foreign workers of international aid organisations, I was never harassed by children or approached by adult beggars. Usually at least one person of the 10 or 20 people on the back of the lorry could speak reasonable English and was happy to talk with me. On a couple of occasions it was made abundantly clear that hatred of the Russians runs very deeply because of their support of the Ethiopians in the war in the Ogaden. I maintained as low a profile as possible with regard to officials and met with no hostility from them.

And finally, a third had this to say:

Women, you'll like Mogadishu. You can walk around in the evenings shopping or watching the ocean with no fear for your personal safety. To avoid being pursued by ardent young men, a simple *Waan leyahay niin* (I have a husband) cuts short any advances. Somalis are particularly friendly to anyone who makes any effort to speak Somali, although Italian can be useful. Many shopkeepers know English.

South Africa

The Cape of Good Hope had been known to Europe since the early Portuguese mariners pioneered the sea route into the Indian Ocean towards the end of the 15th century, but it wasn't until the mid-17th century that any attempt was made to colonise this part of Africa. Up until then South Africa was populated by three main groups of people. The oldest of these were the !Ke (Bushmen) who lived in the mountains of the southern Cape area. They were hunters and gatherers organised into small family units without any centralised tribal authority. Further east along the Cape coast lived the Khoi-Khoi (Hottentots). The remainder of South Africa was inhabited by various Bantu tribes: the Sotho and Venda in the Transvaal; and the Tsonga, Nguni, Swazi, Zulu, Thembu and Xhosa strung out along the coastal area south of the Drakensberg. Both the Khoi-Khoi and the various Bantu tribes were primarily pastoral and tribal. They held the land in common, undertook some form of agriculture in addition to stock-raising and traded by barter.

The first European settlement was planted in 1652 by the Dutch East India Company at the Cape. Its purpose was not only to establish a supply point for Dutch merchant ships on their way to or from India and the East Indies, but to find slaves, raw materials and precious metals to fuel the expanding merchant capitalist economy of Holland. Over the next century and a half, the Dutch colonists gradually spread east, taking land from the indigenous people who were, in the process, wiped out, enslaved, or forced into working on the Dutch farms. Meanwhile, slaves were imported from the East Indies, Madagascar, Mozambique and West Africa. The 'coloured' people of South Africa are the descendants of intermarriage between the Dutch, the indigenous peoples and the imported slaves. They are quite distinct from the 'Indians,' who are descended from contract labourers imported from India and Malaya during the 19th century to work the sugar plantations and vineyards.

While the Dutch were expanding eastwards, the Bantu of the Natal coastal areas were likewise multiplying and expanding northwards and westwards in search of new land. The traditional Bantu solution to overpopulation had been to hive off small groups and send them in search of new lands, but their ability to do this became more and more limited as time passed. The Dutch had already crossed the Orange River by 1760 and the stage was set for the inevitable confrontation. It came in the 1770s when the eastward expansion of the Boers (the Dutch-Afrikaans farmers) was stopped by the Xhosa. This first so-called Bantu War was one of many which would be fought with great bitterness by the two opposing groups, and in them lie the roots of apartheid. It's claimed by pro-apartheid historians that the wars represented the clash of two irreconcilable cultures (hence the creation of separate 'homelands' over the last decade), but this is merely an attempt to gloss over the rapacious attitude of the Boers, who systematically robbed the indigenous peoples of their land, destroyed their economic independence and forced them to accept the status of wage labourers in a society based on the private ownership of land and the means of production. There has never been any genuine attempt to come to terms or compromise with a society based on a different set of assumptions. Racism arose from, and is sustained by, the economic system on which white South African society is based. It has its parallel in the treatment of the Aborigines by white Australian society.

The Boers, however, were not the only people to rob the Bantu of their lands. During the Napoleonic Wars in Europe, the Dutch East India Company, bankrupted by the transition from mercantile to industrial capitalism, was forced to cede the colony to the British. A few years later, a British expeditionary force drove some 20,000 Xhosa from their land in the eastern cape and brought in 5000 British settlers. The event which really sealed the fate of the remaining independent tribes, however, was the banning of slavery by the British authorities in 1834. Despite the fact that the order was hedged with measures binding former slaves to their previous owners as contract labourers, the Boers found the interference intolerable. This gave rise to the Great Trek across the Orange and Fish rivers in the same year. But if the Boers found British interference intolerable, the Bantu found the pressure from the Boers even more so, and this led to profound political and social changes among the tribes of the Natal areas.

The changes were spearheaded by Dingiswayo, a chief of the Mtetwa, who reorganised and unified his tribe into a military nation along European lines. The commander of his regiments, Shaka, discontinued the traditional Bantu methods of conducting warfare based on ritualised single combat and the ransom of fallen champions, substituting rigorously trained soldiers who fought in formation – to the death if necessary – and were intent on annihilating their enemies. So began the many grim years of intertribal warfare that left a scene of carnage and devastation previously unknown in this part of Africa

and created an impression in the minds of Europeans who came across it that this was the normal state of affairs. It also led to the wholesale migration and dispersal of defeated tribes. One such migration, led by Mzilikazi who had quarrelled with Shaka, even got as far as Lake Tanganyika, destroying in the process the effete Rozwi empire based on Great Zimbabwe and Khami. Other groups fled south and west over the Drakensberg, clashing with settled tribes there and leaving similar scenes of devastation. The genesis of both Swaziland and Lesotho and, to some extent, Botswana, dates from these struggles.

It was into this scene of fanatical Zulu militancy that the Boers came in search of new lands. Not far behind them were the British, who were settling in ever-increasing numbers in Cape Province and Natal. The spears and shields of the Zulu, however, were no match for the guns of the Europeans, and the Zulu were eventually forced into submission. Relations between the Boers and the British, meanwhile, remained tense and frequently led to armed conflict, particularly after the formation of the autonomous Boer republics of the Orange Free State and the Transvaal. Nevertheless, when diamonds were discovered in 1867 and then gold in 1886, the Boer republics needed to attract British capital in order to develop the deposits. Capital poured into the republics and the demand for labour soared. The wars of conquest had created the ideal labour pool and many Africans, unable to feed themselves or pay colonial taxes, were forced to seek work in the mines. The supply of labour, however, was never equal to the demand and in the early years the African workers were able to turn this to their advantage by demanding higher wages or deserting when it was not forthcoming.

Against this background the British, along with other industrialised European nations, were in the process of grabbing what was left of Africa. Bechuanaland was

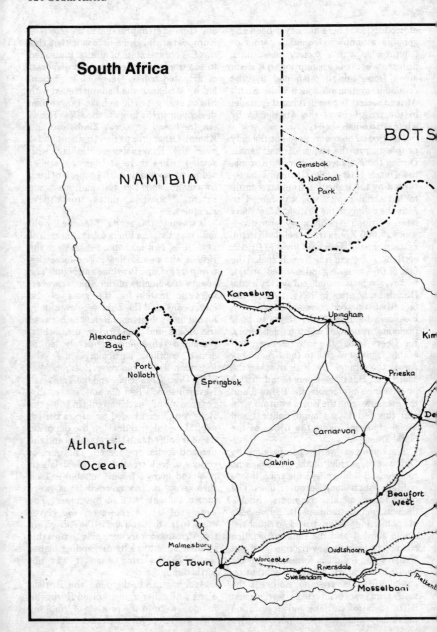

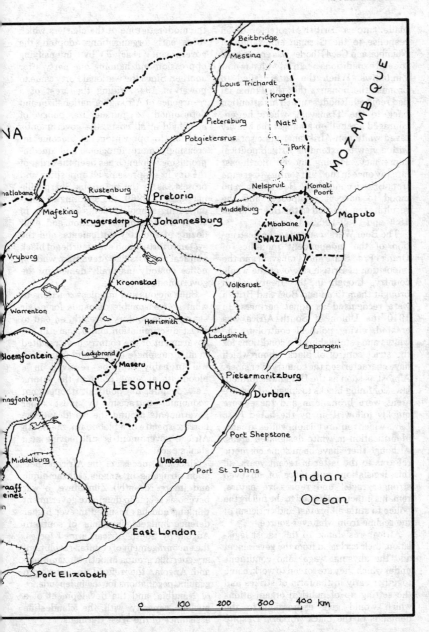

made into a British Protectorate in response to the German annexation of Namibia, and Cecil Rhodes was encouraged to send expeditions north into what is now Zimbabwe. When the latter failed to promise the bonanza that the Transvaal had realised, Rhodes turned his attention back to the Transvaal, where he encouraged a rebellion amongst the heavily taxed white non-Afrikaaner mineworkers with a view to extending British political supremacy. Having moved north-east already once in the 19th century to escape from British control, the Boers were in no mood to have it reimposed, and the resulting tensions led to the Boer Wars of 1890 and 1899-1902.

The Boer Wars resulted in the destruction of the independent republics of Orange Free State and Transvaal and the imposition of British rule over the whole country, though in the treaty which brought them to an end Boer and British were recognised as equal partners. In 1910 the Union of South Africa was created, giving political control to the whites and establishing the conditions for the strict control of black labour which have characterised the country ever since. Almost as soon as the Union was formed, laws confining blacks to specified reserve areas were brought in and these were quickly followed up by the hated Pass Laws which require all non-whites to carry identification in white-designated areas. Although there have been some cosmetic reforms to the latter in recent years, all this legislation, and more of an even stronger racist and repressive nature, remains intact and is used to the full by the police to stifle all protest and criticism of the regime from whatever source.

African resistance to this racist legislation, their exclusion from the government and the abysmal wages and conditions under which they are forced to work, came together early in the form of strikes and the setting up of political organisations which would give expression to the demands of the black workers. Despite the moderate tone of the charters which these early organisations adopted, the government reacted by intensifying oppression and banning one party after another. Since the National Party came to power in 1948, riding the crest of a resurgence of Afrikaaner nationalism and determined to pursue its policy of apartheid at all costs, the government's reaction to opposition has become increasingly more ferocious and uncompromising. Violence has been the order of the day in suppressing all opposition and protest, as in the notorious Sharpeville massacre of 1960, the shooting of demonstrating school students in Soweto in 1976, the forcible evacuation and bulldozing of squatter settlements, and the systemic torture and even murder of black political activists like Steve Biko while in police custody (naturally denied by the government).

Such vicious and mindless reactions to what are reasonable demands for a fair share of the country's wealth, an end to racist discrimination and a share in the government of the country have resulted in an atmosphere of hate and fear which will probably only be resolved in a bloodbath at some point in the future. Yet, despite its political (though not economic) ostracism by most other governments around the world and the horrific spectre of a bloodbath, the South African government is still moving at a snail's pace.

Since the success of the African liberation struggles in Angola, Mozambique and (more recently) Zimbabwe, a war psychosis seems to dominate government thinking and has resulted in ever higher defence budgets, invasions of southern Angola by South African armed forces, the encouragement of counter-revolutionary guerrilla groups in both Mozambique and Angola, the refusal to enter into genuine negotiations for the independence of Namibia, and the development of a nuclear capacity with the clandestine assistance of the West Germans.

On the other hand, during the '70s South Africa was assisted in shoring up white supremacy by the political opportunism of certain ambitious black leaders who made possible the creation of the so-called independent black homelands of Transkei, Ciskei, Bophuthatswana and Venda. One of the effects of this was to temporarily hive off black militancy. It was pure window-dressing and universally recognised as such even by those African countries which exchange ambassadors with South Africa. In order to maintain its 'independence,' the Transkei, for example, depends on South Africa for 75% of its income, has up to 55% of its adult male population working as migrant labour in the Republic at any one time and retains such pillars of apartheid as the Mixed Marriages Act and the Immorality Act (which outlaw marriage or sexual relations between whites and blacks). It also maintains separate schools for the 11,000 whites remaining there. Not only are the so-called 'independent' homelands convenient labour pools for the Republic (labourers coming from there are naturally denied citizenship rights of the Republic and can be deported back there at the slightest sign of militancy), but they are also convenient dumping points for blacks who don't have a pass enabling them to stay in white-designated areas. The latter are often the wives and children of black labourers who do have a pass. That the sycophants who have been installed in these homelands are only too willing to bend over backwards to accommodate the South African government was demonstrated recently when the 'illegal' squatter camp at Crossroads in the Western Cape – one of the oldest and best organised of such camps – was broken up and many of its residents were dumped in Bophuthatswana. Only when the damage had been done did the government decide to soft-pedal over the issue.

Yet it isn't just the social and political issues which make a mockery of the 'independence' of these homelands. The convoluted physical borders alone are sufficient to do this. Bophuthatswana consists of no less than seven separate enclaves, all of them land-locked and all but one of them completely surrounded by South African territory. The Transkei consists of three separate enclaves, and between Venda and Zimbabwe in the extreme north-east corner of Transvaal runs a thin sliver of South African territory, the reason for which doesn't require any great feat of the imagination.

Yet despite their apparent successes even the die-hards couldn't have it all their own way. Towards the end of the 1970s South Africa was rocked by one of the biggest scandals ever to surface when it was disclosed that tens of millions of dollars had been pumped into a secret propaganda scheme to improve South Africa's image abroad. Not only had newspaper proprietors, reporters and other prominent media personalities been bribed with substantial payments, but there had been attempts to acquire majority interests in various influential publications. The disclosures led to the enforced resignations of Drs Vorster (prime minister), Mulder (minister of information and the heir apparent to the prime ministership) and Diederichs (minister of finance) as well as a number of lesser figures. Dubbed as 'Muldergate' by the press after its erstwhile American parallel, the full truth never came out and the present leaders have yet to rid themselves of the suspicion that they too were a party to the conspiracy.

The scandal did, however, have its constructive aspects in that it resulted in a slightly more liberal government which seemed prepared to address itself to some of the more outstanding grievances of the black population. Progress has been slow because of the political need to appease the hard-liners who would have none of it, and much of what has been done has been cosmetic, but at least something is happening.

In March 1984, an accord was signed

with Mozambique whereby that country would withdraw its support for the African National Council and clamp down on their activities within Mozambique. In turn, South Africa would withdraw its support for the MNR – the guerrillas fighting for the overthrow of Machel's Marxist regime. The MNR were initially sponsored by the Smith regime of Rhodesia and then later by South Africa. It's estimated that their activities cost Mozambique US$333 million over an eight-year period, and included the destruction of rural shops, schools, health clinics and communal villages.

Many South African publications suggested there were no benefits for South Africa other than security in this accord, but they forgot to mention that it's much cheaper to control a neighbouring country through a network of economic relationships than it is to destabilise it. The accord also gave Pretoria's international standing a boost, with photographs of Pik Botha shaking hands with Samora Machel being wired around the world. In addition, it legitimised to some extent the trade links between South Africa and black Africa. The latter have been regarded as politically repugnant but also as economically necessary for a long time (South Africa claims it trades with 49 African countries, most of whom vote for sanctions at the UN). The accord was a well-timed diplomatic coup. Even the 'Frontline States,' which desperately need peace and stability, were forced to concede that it was a constructive step.

Later on that same year, the government announced that it was to set up separate legislative chambers for the Asian and 'coloured' sections of the population, though it soon became clear that real power would remain in the hands of the whites. There was a massive boycott of the elections to these two new chambers early in 1985, but the white government (naturally) claimed they were a success and the chambers were duly set up. If the aim was to drive a wedge between the so-called moderates and militants, and

between them and the black population, it appears to have been successful. But, like most other moves, it is essentially a holding operation. Even more recently, there has been talk of repealing the Mixed Marriages and Immorality Acts. A book published by a professor at a Cape Province university, which suggests that probably most Afrikaner families have some black blood in their veins dating from the early days of settlement, has provoked some very acrimonious exchanges – and even violence – in the white parliament and a great deal of mirth outside South Africa.

Meanwhile the shootings, whippings, torture and repression of the black population continue with no franchise in sight. Nevertheless, apartheid is on the run. Nobel Peace Prize winner Bishop Tutu of Johannesburg, though eschewing violence, has been speaking out against the system on every possible occasion, and the US government appears to be moving towards a policy of disinvestment in South Africa. Even the South African government has deemed it expedient to offer Nelson Mandela – the acknowledged leader of the black population held in Robbin Island prison for over a decade – freedom on the condition that he will not be involved in political activities. Such conditions are an insult to a man of Mandela's stature and he has refused to acquiesce.

You might be interested to know that the Information Attaché at the South African Embassy in Australia wrote to Lonely Planet objecting to a similar introduction to South Africa in the last edition. The man described the introduction as inflammatory, irresponsible and blatantly inaccurate. Under different circumstances we might be vaguely flattered by such high-level attention, but he betrayed his origins and his paymasters with comments such as, 'The white South Africans, who by an historic inheritance have had the responsibility of assisting the various non-white nations to develop, have never regarded these people (the blacks) as animals. In fact, the black peoples of South Africa have flourished, advanced and grown in population as nowhere else on the continent.' And if that load of arrogant crap doesn't make you squirm with embarrassment or anger then this surely will: 'Every adult, male, female, black, white, coloured or Indian has a franchise, not in the boiling pot of a unitary state, but in a constellation of national states whereby the 'beautiful country with a diversity of peoples and cultures' will be able to retain those beautiful qualities without being swamped by the strongest tribe.'

So now you know.

VISAS

Visas are required by all except nationals of Botswana, Irish Republic, Lesotho, Seychelles, Swaziland, Switzerland and the UK. Visas are free to nationals of Australia, Austria, Belgium, Canada, Denmark, Finland, France, Greece, Israel, Luxembourg, Mauritius, Netherlands, New Zealand, Norway, Spain, Sweden, USA and West Germany. For anyone not in the above categories, visas cost R 2.50. Most people are issued with a three-month, triple-entry visa which allows you to visit Lesotho and Swaziland without having to apply for another visa. If you don't get a multiple-entry visa, you must get one before you visit these two countries. Re-entry visas can be obtained from the Department of the Interior, Civitas Building, Corner Struben and Andries Sts, Pretoria 0002 (Private Bag X1114), or from similar offices in Johannesburg, Cape Town, Durban, Bloemfontein, Port Elizabeth, East London and Kimberley.

The South African authorities are very strict about the onward ticket requirements, especially if you arrive by air or via Beit Bridge. At Jan Smuts Airport, Johannesburg, for instance, they won't accept any excuses. If you haven't got an onward ticket you may well have to deposit up to R 1200 (refundable on exit). Even if you fly in with a return ticket, it may well be stamped 'non-refundable,' making it impossible to cash in. You're advised to look clean and tidy on entry. A return air ticket from Nairobi to London is not acceptable.

If you had to pay a deposit (through not having an onward ticket) and are leaving via Ramatlhabama (South Africa/Botswana border), go to the South African 'embassy' in Mafikeng (officially in Bophuthatswana) first. They'll take the deposit to the border with you and give it back to you at that point.

We have heard a few other stories from time to time concerning difficulties for travellers coming into South Africa. One was from a British passport holder who was resident in Swaziland. He was returning to Swaziland from Zimbabwe in a Swazi-registered car via Beit Bridge, and was asked to show an air ticket back to the UK before before entering. It took all day to make the officials see sense. This sort of thing only used to happen at the Beit Bridge crossing, but the authorities have now also tightened up at Ramatlhabama on the Botswana/South African border. We've had reports of travellers without onward tickets having to pay R 1000 deposit at this crossing. Many South African businesspeople go through the Tlokweng Gate, as this is the shortest route from Gaborone (Botswana) to South Africa. Reports suggest that officials here are still fairly easygoing.

The biggest problem with South African visas, however, is that once you have one of their stamps in your passport, you've got big problems getting into most other countries in Africa, and you may even be refused entry to quite a few. (Zambia and Tanzania are two where this is most likely to happen.) Travellers who wouldn't otherwise need a visa have been refused entry at borders because of South African stamps in their passport, and have been sent back to the nearest capital city to get a visa. Normally, South African immigration officials are aware of this and will, if you ask, insert a loose card in your passport with the stamps on that. When you leave, you throw the card away. It's not unknown, however, for sharp Tanzanian officials to pick up on, say, Swaziland or Lesotho stamps or even Zimbabwean and Botswanan exit stamps picked up at borders with South Africa and pointedly ask you how you came to get them. You naturally took a flight or were refused entry at the South African border. But it can take half a day to convince them.

There's a further complication these days because of the creation of the so-called homelands – Transkei, Bophuthatswana, Ciskei and Venda. Unless you specifically want to go there, you can get round them all except if you're travelling direct from Cape Town to Durban (through Transkei) or coming from Botswana between Gaborone and Mafikeng (through Bophuthatswana).

Entry requirements for the 'homelands' are:

Bophuthatswana No visas required for a visit up to 14 days so long as you have a valid passport and a South African visa (where required). If you're planning on staying longer, visas can be obtained from the Embassy of Bophuthatswana, 39 Glyn St, Colbyn, Pretoria 0001 (tel 436001); or from the General Consulate, Nedbank Mall, 145 Commissioner St, Johannesburg 2001 (tel 001-215931).

Ciskei No visas required.

Transkei Visas required by all except South African nationals. They can be obtained from the Transkei Consulate-General, 164 Commissioner St, Kariba House, Johannesburg 2001 (tel 011-215935). There are consulates in Durban, Port Elizabeth, Bloemfontein, Cape Town and East London. Tourist visas cost R 2.50 and are issued while you wait.

Venda No visas required.

If you need a visa for any of the above 'homelands,' you will also need a South African re-entry visa. You can avoid this by getting a multiple-entry visa for South Africa in the first place. This applies equally if you're going to visit Lesotho and Swaziland.

The above are official requirements. In practice, you may find that at many crossing points between South Africa and the various 'homelands' there are no customs/immigration posts so you simply drive through (or ride undisturbed on the train). The same may apply when you re-enter South Africa. On the other hand, there are all sorts of permutations on this theme. You may be stamped in as leaving South Africa but not stamped for entering, say, Transkei. You may be stamped leaving, say, Transkei, but not stamped as entering South Africa. It's generally true to say that if you don't have a visa for a 'homeland' (where required), it can be obtained on the border. This is invariably true if you're travelling by train. We've only had one report of a traveller being fined for not having a Transkei visa (he entered by road and was fined R 40). As with South Africa, officials on these borders will put stamps on a separate card in your passport, though we did have one report of the officials at Kei Bridge (Transkei) north of East London insisting that stamps went directly into the passport.

Lesotho & Swaziland visas Neither of these countries maintains diplomatic relations with South Africa. Visas must be obtained from the British Consulate-General, Nedbank Mall, 145 Commissioner St, Johannesburg 2001 (open Monday to Friday from 9 am to 2 pm), or from British consulates in Cape Town and Durban. The British Embassy in Pretoria does not issue visas.

MONEY
US$1 = R 1.10

The unit of currency is the rand = 100

cents. Import and export of local currency is limited to R 50. There is no black market.

If you've got money to throw away, try breaking the speed limit or carry *dagga* or both. You'll find the fines incredibly high.

LANGUAGE
Afrikaans and English.

INFORMATION
The South African Tourist Corporation (Satour) maintains offices in many large cities in America, Western Europe, Australasia and Japan as well as a number of other places. If you're planning on spending any length of time there, it's worth writing to them for information before you set off, as they turn out some excellent literature – maps, accommodation and transport digests, and booklets containing detailed descriptions of the national parks, game reserves, hiking trails and just about everything else you're likely to want to see.

Inside the country itself there are Tourist Offices at Bloemfontein, Cape Town, Durban, East London, George, Jan Smuts Airport, Johannesburg, Kimberley, Nelspruit, Port Elizabeth and Pretoria.

There is a network of Youth Hostels and you can get full details of these by writing for the brochure published by the South African Youth Hostels Association, PO Box 4402, Cape Town 8000 (tel 43 5693); or ask at any Satour office.

An interesting magazine put out by the Educational Wildlife Expeditions, in association with the Wilderness Trust, has articles by travellers not only on South Africa but other places on the continent. It's worth getting hold of. The subscription address is: Great Outdoors Magazine, PO Box 84436, Greenside, 2034, Johannesburg.

GETTING THERE & AROUND
Air
You can fly into South Africa direct from many places around the world, but unless you're coming from South America or Australasia, it's more than likely you will start a trip through South Africa from the north of the continent. The main connections from Australia are *South African Airways* from Perth to Johannesburg and *Qantas* from Perth to Harare, with an immediate connection on *South African Airways* to Johannesburg. Perhaps the cheapest flights out of South Africa to Europe are with *Luxavia* to Luxembourg. The carrier is a non-IATA member, but the flights generally work out cheaper than what you are likely to find on Hillbrow noticeboards in Johannesburg. Check out these flights at 87 Rissik St, Johannesburg. More details about these flights can be found in the introductory section of this book.

If you're coming from Zimbabwe by air, some of the cheapest flights are with *Air Zimbabwe* on their 'Skycoach' Viscount flights from Bulawayo to Johannesburg on Friday and Sunday.

If you fly into South Africa, you are entitled to buy a VIRSA fare for R 274 which allows a 28-day unlimited excursion on *South African Airways* within South Africa and Namibia, but you can only visit the same city once.

There is a 30% reduction on internal South African Airways flights if you go standby, but this is usually only possible on certain flights – usually the first and the last of the day.

Road
Overland travellers have a choice of two main border crossing points – Beit Bridge (Zimbabwe/South Africa) or Ramatlhabama (Botswana/South Africa). Both have road and rail connections with the Republic. Ramatlhabama is by far the easier of the two crossings. Officials at Beit Bridge are well known for their strictness regarding onward tickets, sufficient funds and the like.

South Africa is one of the easiest countries in the world to hitch through – if you're white. So easy, in fact, that most travellers rarely use the bus and train networks, but you must get out of the suburbs before you start (most cities sprawl for miles). Johannesburg to Durban should take about a day, and Johannesburg to Cape Town about three days with long waits here and there en route. One route which can be very slow is from Mafikeng to Vryburg, and you may well have to take to public transport along this stretch. Your country's flag on the front of your pack is a great help in securing lifts. South Africa's roads are excellent but they have one of the highest accident rates in the world. Many of these accidents involve heavy trucks; one reason appears to be complete lack of control over drivers' hours.

The majority of people who pick you up will be extremely friendly and hospitable – so friendly that many travellers don't see the inside of a hotel room from one end of the country to the other. Depending on who you meet, however, you may have to put up with long lectures on the virtues of apartheid. Afrikaans speakers are generally keen on this, English speakers much less so. You will also probably be told about the 'dangers' of hitching in the black homelands and the possibility of being murdered there. You can safely ignore this warning. We get letters from travellers all the time who have hitched through and met nothing more sinister than hospitality, curiosity and friendliness.

The licence plate system works on the basis that the first letter indicates the state (C, O, N, T) and the subsequent letters indicate the city/town, eg, CA – Cape Town, CB – Port Elizabeth. Transvaal plates end with T but don't indicate the town.

There are very few long-distance buses (only coach tours) – at least for whites. For others, however, there are plenty of such services as well as a range of local buses.

Rail
South Africa has an extensive network of railways, but remember that if you're white, third class is off-limits; you can only travel first or second class. A list of schedules and fares follows – abbreviated to the main stations only. If you want the full schedules, get hold of a copy of *Intercity Train Time-Table* from any office of the South African Railway Travel Bureau (R 3 plus sales tax). The addresses of these bureaus in the main cities are:

Bloemfontein
   FVB Centre, Shop 29, 40 Maitland St (tel 7-6352)
Cape Town
   Travel Centre, Station Building, Adderley St (tel 218-2391/2282)
Durban
   Trust Ban Centre, 475 Smith St (tel 310-3376/3363/3371)
East London
   Southern Trident House, 56-58 Terminus St (tel 2-3952)
Johannesburg
   Intown Centre, corner Rissik & Kerk Sts (tel 713-5541/4941/4163)
Pietermaritzburg
   Capital Towers, corner Commercial Rd & Prince Edward St (tel 55-2461/2)
Port Elizabeth
   Fleming Building, Market Square (tel 2-2922/2233)
Pretoria
   African Eagle Life Centre, 236 Vermeulen St (tel 294-2222/3/4)

One thing you must know about the railways is that if you've been in South Africa less than three months, you're entitled to a 40% reduction on the fares – ask for it!

Pretoria-Johannesburg-Bloemfontein-Cape Town (38 hours)

Station	Frequency
	Tues, Thur, Sat, Sun
Pretoria	7.15 pm
Johannesburg	8.30 pm
Kroonstad	12.19 am
Bloemfontein	3.55 am
Springfontein	6.07 am
Noupoort	10.05 am
De Aar	2.15 pm
Beaufort West	7.38 pm
Cape Town	9.05 am

Station	Frequency	Frequency
	Tues, Thur, Sat, Sun	Daily
Cape Town	9.00 pm	-
Beaufort West	8.10 am	-
De Aar	4.10 pm	-
Noupoort	6.45 pm	-
Springfontein	10.10 pm	-
Bloemfontein	1.16 am	7.25 am
Kroonstad	-	12.15 pm
Johannesburg	-	5.20 pm
Pretoria	-	-

Pretoria-Johannesburg-Kimberley-Cape Town (26-29 hours)

Station	Frequency				
	Trans-Oranje	Trans-Karoo	Blue Train		
	Tues, Fri	Tues, Thur, Fri, Sat, Sun	Varies	Tue, Thu, Fri, Sat, Sun	Daily
Pretoria	-	6.45 am	10.00 am	1.40 pm	5.10 pm
Johannesburg	-	9.00 am	11.30 am	3.30 pm	7.30 pm
Klerksdorp	-	12.08 pm	2.29 pm	6.53 pm	11.35 pm
Kimberley	12.45 am	4.47 pm	6.51 pm	12.10 am	7.55 am
De Aar	4.33 pm	8.25 pm	10.19 pm	3.55 am	2.15 pm
Beaufort West	8.49 pm	12.53 am	2.19 am	8.08 am	7.38 pm
Worcester	3.08 am	7.13 am	8.25 am	3.07 pm	4.45 am
Cape Town	6.32 am	10.45 am	11.40 am	6.40 pm	9.05 am

Station	Frequency				
	Trans-Karoo	Blue Train		Trans-Oranje	
	Tues, Thur, Fri, Sat, Sun	Varies	Tue, Thu, Fri, Sat, Sun	Mon, Fri	Daily
Cape Town	9.00 am	10.30 am	3.30 pm	6.30 pm	9.00 pm
Worcester	11.55 am	1.13 pm	6.37 pm	10.25 pm	12.29 am
Beaufort West	6.20 pm	7.46 pm	1.21 am	4.06 am	8.10 am
De Aar	10.35 pm	12.02 am	5.35 am	8.15 am	1.50 pm
Kimberley	2.00 am	3.35 am	9.25 am	12.05 pm	6.55 pm
Klerksdorp	6.30 am	7.45 am	2.25 pm	-	1.24 am
Johannesburg	10.35 am	11.20 am	7.02 pm	-	5.30 am
Pretoria	11.56 am	12.30 pm	8.23 pm	-	-

Both the Trans-Karoo and the Trans-Oranje carry only first and second-class passengers. The Trans-Karoo does not take passengers getting off at intermediate stations between Pretoria and De Aar on the journey south; nor does it take passengers getting off at intermediate stations between Cape Town and Kimberley on the journey north. Passengers travelling from Pretoria/Johannesburg to Cape Town (or vice versa) have preference over those wanting to go only part of the way. The Blue Train consists of special, deluxe, air-conditioned carriages only, and a separate fare schedule applies to it. The Blue Train does not run every day, so you need to refer to the SA Railways timetable for the schedule. The unnamed trains convey all classes of passengers.

Pretoria-Johannesburg-Bloemfontein-Port Elizabeth (22 hours)

Station	Frequency	
	Daily	Tues, Thur, Sat, Sun
Pretoria	3.25 pm	7.15 pm
Johannesburg	5.30 pm	8.30 pm
Kroonstad	8.59 pm	12.19 am
Bloemfontein	12.23 am	3.55 am
Springfontein	2.45 am	6.07 am
Noupoort	5.45 am	9.10 am/ 7.10 pm (change)
Port Elizabeth	2.30 pm	6.55 am

Station	Frequency
	Daily
Port Elizabeth	5.00 pm
Noupoort	1.25 am
Springfontein	4.23 am
Bloemfontein	7.15 am
Kroonstad	10.19 am
Johannesburg	1.50 pm
Pretoria	2.57 pm

The 7.15 pm train from Pretoria to Port Elizabeth involves a change at Noupoort and a 10-hour wait for the connecting train.

Pretoria-Johannesburg-Bloemfontein-East London

Station	Frequency
	Daily
Pretoria	1.20 pm
Johannesburg	2.50 pm
Kroonstad	6.32 pm
Bloemfontein	9.56 pm
Springfontein	12.07 am
East London	11.00 am

Station	Frequency
	Daily
East London	3.00 pm
Springfontein	1.20 am
Bloemfontein	4.25 am
Kroonstad	7.29 am
Johannesburg	11.00 am
Pretoria	12.21 pm

Pretoria-Johannesburg-Pietermaritzburg-Durban (15 to 22½ hours)

Station	Frequency		Drakensberg		Trans-Natal
	Mon, Wed, Fri, Sun	Daily	Fri	Daily	Daily
Pretoria	-	8.35 am	4.12 pm	4.43 pm	5.40 pm
Johannesburg	8.00 am	10.15 am	5.45 pm	6.05 pm	6.30 pm
Volksrust	11.43 am	4.58 pm	9.45 pm	11.41 pm	10.31 pm
Ladysmith	3.03 pm	10.40 pm	1.29 am	4.16 am	1.54 am
Pietermaritzburg	6.29 pm	3.10 am	4.55 am	7.43 am	5.29 am
Durban	9.06 pm	7.00 am	7.45 am	10.30 am	8.15 am

Station	Frequency		Drakensberg	Trans-Natal	
	Mon, Wed, Fri, Sat	Daily	Sun	Daily	Daily
Durban	6.30 am	11.45 am	5.45 pm	6.30 pm	8.00 pm
Pietermaritzburg	8.30 am	2.31 pm	8.03 pm	8.38 pm	10.49 pm
Ladysmith	11.55 am	6.48 pm	11.29 pm	12.07 am	4.17 am
Volksrust	3.17 pm	11.13 pm	3.10 am	3.45 am	9.15 am
Johannesburg	7.26 pm	4.59 am	7.35 am	8.15 am	3.40 pm
Pretoria	-	6.08 am	8.16 am	9.24 am	5.37 pm

All the above trains except the Trans-Natal involve a change at Johannesburg. On the Trans-Natal no intermediate passengers are allowed between Durban and Standerton going north or between Johannesburg and Mooirivier going south. The Drakensberg consists of special, deluxe, air-conditioned carriages for which a separate fare schedule applies. Passengers travelling from Johannesburg to Pietermaritzburg/Durban or vice versa are given preference over those wanting to go only part of the way.

Cape Town-Worcester-Mosselbaai-Port Elizabeth (38 hours)

Station	Frequency
	Daily ex Sat
Cape Town	3.45 pm
Worcester	7.55 pm
Ashton	10.13 pm
Riversdale	5.25 am
Mosselbaai	8.25 am
Oudtshoorn	2.00 pm
Port Elizabeth	6.07 am

Station	Frequency
	Daily ex Sat
Port Elizabeth	6.40 pm
Oudtshoorn	10.20 am
Mosselbaai	3.34 pm
Riversdale	7.29 pm
Ashton	2.03 am
Worcester	4.00 am
Cape Town	8.30 am

There are also trains on Saturdays at the same times during December and the first week in January.

Cape Town-Beaufort West-De Aar-Noupoort-Queenstown-East London

Station	Frequency	
	Sun	Tues, Thu
Cape Town	6.45 pm	9.00 pm
Worcester	10.25 pm	12.29 am
Beaufort West	6.18 pm	8.10 am
De Aar	2.00 pm	2.00 pm
Noupoort	4.12 pm	4.12 pm
Rosmead	5.35 pm	5.35 pm
Stormberg	9.30 pm	9.30 pm
Queenstown	12.12 am	12.12 am
East London	5.30 am	5.30 am

Station	Frequency
	Tue, Thu, Sat
East London	4.00 pm
Queenstown	11.00 pm
Stormberg	1.54 am
Rosmead	6.07 am
Noupoort	7.55 am
De Aar	10.55 am
Beaufort West	4.12 pm
Worcester	12.55 am
Cape Town	5.23 am

On the train from East London to Cape Town white passengers must change at De Aar. Passengers for stations between Bellville and Cape Town must change at Bellville.

Cape Town-Bloemfontein-Kroonstad-Ladysmith-Pietermaritzburg-Durban

Station	Frequency	
	Trans-Oranje	
	Mon, Fri	Tues, Thur, Sat, Sun
Cape Town	6.30 pm	9.00 pm
Worcester	9.20 pm	12.29 am
Beaufort West	4.06 am	8.10 am
De Aar	7.45 am	1.20 pm
Kimberley	12.05 pm	-
Noupoort	-	6.45 pm
Bloemfontein	3.05 pm	1.16 am arr/ 8.35 am dep
Kroonstad	6.10 pm	-
Ladysmith	1.29 am	12.30 am
Pietermaritzburg	5.09 am	5.00 am
Durban	7.45 am	8.30 am

Station	Frequency	
	Trans-Oranje	
	Mon, Thu	Mon, Wed, Fri, Sun
Durban	5.30 pm	7.30 pm
Pietermaritzburg	7.47 pm	10.10 pm
Ladysmith	11.16 pm	2.55 am

Kroonstad	6.15 am	-
Bloemfontein	9.40 am	6.50 pm arr/
		10.10 pm dep
Kimberley	12.45 pm	2.22 am arr/
		8.35 am dep
De Aar	4.33 pm	2.15 pm
Beaufort West	8.49 pm	7.38 pm
Worcester	3.08 am	4.45 am
Cape Town	6.32 am	9.05 am

Passengers getting off at intermediate stations between Cape Town and Kimberley are not allowed on the 6.30 pm Trans-Oranje from Cape Town.

Johannesburg-Pretoria-Pietersburg-Messina-Beitbridge

Station	Frequency
	Daily
Johannesburg	7.05 pm
Pretoria	8.50 pm
Pietersburg	2.35 am
Louis Trich	6.57 am
Messina	12.00 (ch)
Beitbridge	12.42 pm

Station	Frequency		
	Daily ex Sun, Fri, Sat	Daily ex Fri, Sat	Fri, Sat
Beitbridge	1.30 pm	-	-
Messina	2.10 pm	2.58 pm	2.58 pm
Louis Trich	-	7.07 pm	7.35 pm
Pietersburg	-	11.29 pm	12.35 am
Pretoria	-	5.45 am	7.18 am
Johannesburg	-	7.10 am	8.50 am

On the journey going north you must change trains at Messina. The incoming train arrives at 10.43 am and the connecting train leaves at 12 pm.

Johannesburg-Zeerust-Mafikeng (7½ hours)

Station	Frequency		
	Sat	Thu	Daily
Johannesburg	9.00 am	1.30 pm	8.03 pm
Koster	12.17 pm	4.17 pm	9.46 pm
Groot-Marico	1.43 pm	5.32 pm	12.22 am
Zeerust	2.41 pm	6.25 pm	1.42 am
Ottoshoop	3.30 pm	7.09 pm	2.22 am
Mafikeng	4.26 pm	7.50 pm	3.10 am

Mafikeng-Zeerust-Johannesburg (7½ hours)

Station	Frequency		
	Wed	Sun	Daily
Mafikeng	6.30 am	9.15 am	11.25 pm

Ottoshoop	6.59 am	9.52 am	11.56 pm
Zeerust	7.47 am	10.46 am	12.44 pm
Groot-Marico	-	11.36 am	1.31 am
Koster	9.41 am	1.07 pm	2.45 am
Johannesburg	12.35 pm	4.35 pm	6.00 am

International Rail Connections
South Africa-Botswana-Zimbabwe
De Aar-Kimberley-Mafikeng-Gaborone-Bulawayo

Station	Frequency				
	Tues	Daily	Sat	Daily ex Sat	Mon, Wed, Fri, Sun
Bulawayo	11.45 am	1.30 pm	-	-	-
Plumtree	2.05 pm	4.20 pm	-	-	-
Francistown	3.51 pm	6.26 pm	-	-	-
Mahalapye	8.45 pm	12.50 am	-	-	-
Gaborone	1.30 am	6.10 am	-	-	-
Lobatse	3.25 am	8.26 am	-	-	-
Ramatlhabama	5.00 am	11.09 am	-	-	-
Mafikeng	5.30 am	11.45 am	3.15 am	6.40 am	7.24 pm
Vryburg	-	-	8.55 am	11.35 am	12.28 am
Warrenton	-	-	1.00 pm	3.25 am	4.15 am
Kimberley	-	-	2.19 pm	4.54 pm	5.42 am
De Aar	-	-	-	-	-

The 11.45 am train from Bulawayo takes only first– and second-class passengers, and if you're heading for Johannesburg you need not change trains at Mafikeng. Several connections are possible between Kimberley and De Aar, including the Trans-Oranje (departs Kimberley 4.47 pm daily except Monday and Wednesday; arrives De Aar 8 pm), the Blue Train (departs Kimberley 6.56 pm, arrives De Aar 10.01 pm), plus a daily train at 7.55 am (arrives 12.49 pm) and another on Monday, Wednesday, Friday, Saturday and Sunday at 12.10 am (arrives 3.40 am).

Station	Frequency					
	Daily ex Sun	Sun	Mon, Wed, Fri, Sat, Sun	Mon, Wed, Fri, Sun	Daily	Thu
De Aar	-	-	5.35 am	-	-	-
Kimberley	6.55 am	12.08 pm	9.25 am	9.45 pm	-	-
Warrenton	8.40 am	1.40 pm	10.21 am	11.27 pm	-	-
Vryburg	12.21 pm	5.23 pm	-	2.57 am	-	-
Mafikeng	4.50 pm	10.05 pm	-	7.51 am	2.00 pm	9.00 pm
Ramatlhabama	-	-	-	-	4.10 pm	9.30 pm
Lobatse	-	-	-	-	5.40 pm	10.40 pm
Gaborone	-	-	-	-	7.57 pm	1.04 am
Mahalapye	-	-	-	-	1.00 am	5.15 am
Francistown	-	-	-	-	6.55 am	9.56 am

Plum-tree	-	-	-	-	10.05 am	12.09 pm
Bula-wayo	-	-	-	-	12.45 pm	2.10 pm

The Thursday train from Mafikeng to Bulawayo takes only first-and second-class passengers. There are other connections between De Aar and Kimberley than those indicated above. They include the Blue Train (departs De Aar 12.02 am, arrives Kimberley 3.11 am), the Trans-Karoo (departs De Aar 10.35 pm daily except Monday and Wednesday, arrives Kimberley 1.45 am), the Trans-Oranje (departs 8.15 am Tuesday and Saturday, arrives 11.25 am), and a daily train (departs 1.50 pm, arrives 6.32 pm).

South Africa-Mozambique
Johannesburg-Pretoria-Komatipoort-Maputo (17½ hours)

Station	Frequency		
	Daily	Daily	Daily ex Tues
Johannesburg	6.48 am	4.45 pm	6.15 pm
Pretoria	8.38 am	6.30 pm	7.53 pm
Middelburg	1.05 pm	10.43 pm	11.00 pm
Nelspruit	7.25 pm	5.03 am	3.55 am
Komatipoort	10.32 pm	9.13 am	6.10 am
Ressano Garcia	–	–	8.20 am
Maputo	–	–	10.26 am

Station	Frequency		
	Daily	Daily	Daily ex Wed
Maputo	–	–	4.00 pm
Ressano Garcia	–	–	6.24 pm
Komatipoort	5.00 am	4.50 pm	9.26 pm
Nelspruit	8.07 am	8.15 pm	11.54 pm
Middelburg	1.31 pm	2.23 am	4.17 am
Pretoria	6.10 pm	6.32 am	7.49 am
Johannesburg	8.10 pm	8.15 am	9.30 am

The 8.20 am train from Ressano Garcia to Maputo and the 4 pm train from Maputo to Ressano Garcia take only first– and second-class passengers.

South Africa-Namibia
De Aar-Prieska-Upington-Karasburg-Keetmanshoop-Windhoek

Station	Frequency		
	Suidwester		
	Tues	Tues	Daily
De Aar	10.30 pm	5.00 pm	6.00 pm
Prieska	2.21 am	9.26 pm	10.18 pm
Upington	7.10 am	3.45 am	5.05 am
Karasburg	1.20 pm	10.35 am	12.05 pm
Keetmanshoop	7.05 pm	4.35 pm	6.15 pm
Windhoek	7.00 am	5.40 am	7.35 am

Station	Frequency	
	Suidwester	
	Mon	Daily
Windhoek	11.30 am	8.20 pm
Keetmanshoop	11.15 pm	10.10 am

Karasburg	4.40 am	4.45 pm
Upington	11.30 am	12.15 am
Prieska	3.40 pm	6.26 am
De Aar	6.45 pm	10.50 am

The Suidwester takes only first - and second-class passengers.

PLACES TO STAY

South Africa has a network of Youth Hostels in all four states. At an average cost of R 3 per night, it's the cheapest accommodation you're likely to find, so it's worth having a membership card. If you haven't got one with you from your own country you can join for R 3. The National Office is at 606 Boston House, Strand St, Cape Town 8001 (tel 42 5693).

House-Sitting If you intend to stay for a month or more in any of South Africa's larger cities, the cheapest form of accommodation is house-sitting. This is very efficiently organised by *House Sitters Service*, who have offices in many cities and put out a quarterly newsletter called *House Sitters*.

The sort of people they look for generally need short-term accommodation for a few weeks to a few months. They prefer couples without children, but this doesn't necessarily exclude single people. Twenty-five is considered a reasonable lower age limit, though this isn't rigidly applied (they're looking for people with sufficient experience in looking after a home and its contents). Sitters are expected to undertake basic maintenance of the house, garden and swimming pool if there are no servants. Three hours of watering and one hour of mowing per week is regarded as a reasonable stint if required. Current fees for sitters are: Daily fee – R 3 plus R 1.50 per person in excess of two, or R 150 per month for sits over three months long, and a refundable deposit of R 100. Electricity, water and servants' costs are normally paid by the owners subject to negotiation if the sit is over two months.

If you're interested, get in touch with the following offices:

Cape Town
28 Lympleigh Rd, Plumstead, 7800 (tel 77 4972)
Durban
12 Canal Drive, Westville, 3630 (tel 86 1547/86 5010)
East Rand
33 Albu Rd, Meadowbrook, 1610 (tel 53 7135)
Johannesburg
5 Conrad Drive, Blairgowrie, Randburg, 2194 (tel 787 3901/787 4212; after hours 787 9203)
Pietermaritzburg
7 Carbis Rd, Scottsville, 3201 (tel 62943)
Windhoek (Namibia)
PO Box 3362, Windhoek 9000 (tel 22090)
Zimbabwe
18 Percy Fynn Rd, Belvedere, Harare (tel 82721)
UK
5 Ridgeway House, The Crescent, Horley, Surrey (tel 2934 72154)

CAPE PROVINCE

Cape Province has the following Youth Hostels:

Stan's Halt, The Glen, Camps Bay, Cape Town 8001 (tel 48 9037), located next to the Round House Restaurant. It's a popular place with travellers and has hot water and cooking and laundry facilities. The hostel is closed from 10 am to 5 pm. To get there from Cape Town, take a train to Camps Bay. From the station turn left into Adderley St, then take the Kloof Nek bus to the terminus (47c) and walk down Kloof Nek Rd to the hostel (about one km).

Port Rex Youth Hostel, 128 Moore St, Eastern Beach, East London 5201 (tel 0431-52855). A traveller once described this place as 'Run by a tyrannical old lady, who, underneath it all, has a heart of gold.'

Abe Bailey Youth Hostel, corner Maynard and Westbury roads, Muizenberg, Cape Town (tel 88 4283). The hostel has hot water and laundry facilities and is run by a very friendly and easygoing couple.

Kimberley Youth Hostel, Bloemfontein Rd, Kimberley 8301 (tel 0531-28577), about four to five km from the centre of town.

The hostel in Port Elizabeth is now closed.

BEAUFORT WEST

If you're on a tight budget, try the *Catholic Mission* across the bridge; Father Muller may find floor space or a couch for you to sleep on. Otherwise, try one of the following hotels, all of which are in the lower price category:

Donkin House, 14 Donkin St (tel 4287). A room costs R 6 per person or R 7 with bath. Additional 6% tax.

Royal, 20 Donkin St, (tel 3241/2).

Park Rooms, Danie Theron St (tel 3878).

Young's Halfway House, 143 Donkin St (tel 3878).

Safari Tourist Rooms, Pritchard St (tel 2439). A room costs R 6.

Meals and/or bed and breakfast are available at all these places.

CAPE TOWN

Apart from the Youth Hostels there are the *YMCA*, 60 Victoria St (tel 41 1848), which costs R 4.50 per night; and the *YWCA*, 20 Belleview Rd (tel 221886), which costs R 6.60-7.50 per night. Another good cheap place which has been recommended is *Bergheim*, 12 Constantia Rd, Tamboerskloof, on the Table Mountain Cableway bus route. It is run by Mr and Mrs Schafer, who are very friendly and eager to help. They charge R 4-7 per night including the use of communal cooking facilities. If you're short of money, ask for Father Doolley at the Salesian College for Boys. He may find space for you but don't stay more than two nights.

Among the cheapest hotels in the central area are:

Café Royal, 23 Church St (tel 22 9047), which costs R 10 a single and R 16 a double for bed and breakfast.

City Hall Hotel, 50 Darling St (tel 46 59 47), which costs R 7.50 a single for bed and breakfast.

Tudor, Greenmarket Square (tel 41 0196), which costs from R 16.50 for bed and breakfast.

Other hotels in the budget range include the *Castle Hotel*, 42 Canterbury St (tel 466306), which costs R 10 per bed; *Good Hope Hotel*, 87 Loop St (tel 223369), which costs R 15 for bed only; *Stag's Head*, 71 Hope St (tel 454918), which costs R 12 for bed only; and *Mrs B Mayer*, 6 Upper Orange St, Oranjezicht, which is 'a veritable museum of a guest house' – every room being full of trinkets, nativity scenes, etc. If you're a single woman, Mrs Mayer will wait up for you every night until you get in! On the same street is the similarly priced *Lennox Lodge*.

Information

The Tourist Office is on the third floor, Broadway Centre, Heerengracht (tel 021-216274). American Express is in Greenmarket Place, Greenmarket Square, PO Box 2337, Cape Town 8000 (tel 22 8591).

The Transkei Consulate is at 42 Strand near the station. Visas cost 50c for up to three days or R 2.50 for longer, and are issued while you wait.

For good coverage of local events, cultural activities, exhibitions and what's on generally, get hold of a copy of the monthly publication *Cape Town Diary*. You can pick it up all over Cape Town.

Things to See

In a city the size of Cape Town and with such a spectacular setting there are endless things to see and do. The following are things you won't want to miss.

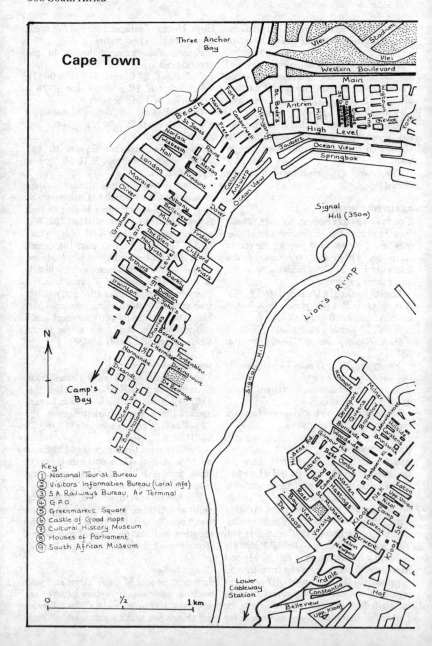

Cape Town

Key:
1. National Tourist Bureau
2. Visitors' Information Bureau (Local info)
3. S.A. Railways Bureau, Air Terminal
4. G.P.O.
5. Greenmarket Square
6. Castle of Good Hope
7. Cultural History Museum
8. Houses of Parliament
9. South African Museum

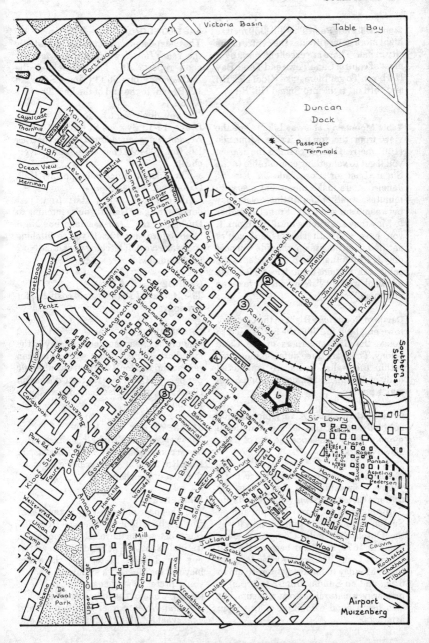

Signal Hill View Point This hill (350 metres high) more or less divides the centre of the city in half. There are excellent views over most of central Cape Town and Table Bay Harbour. To get there, take Kloof Nek Rd and turn off right into Signal Hill Rd.

Table Mountain Cableway Like to see the view from the top of Table Mountain (1067 metres)? In Africa this is the nearest you'll get to something comparable to the Sugar Loaf or Corcovado in Rio de Janeiro. Cars make the ascent every 30 minutes, weather permitting, every day between 9 am and 6 pm. From December to May they keep going until 10.30 pm. If you have a Youth Hostel card you're entitled to a concession; the ride will cost only R 1.50 (otherwise R 3). To get to the cable car station from Kloof Nek bus terminal, walk up Tafelberg Rd or take the minibus (20c).

Castle of Good Hope Right in the centre of town and built in 1666, the castle used to house the first governors of the Cape colony. There are three different museums within the walls. Tours are conducted daily at 10 am, 11 am, noon, 2 pm, 3 pm and 4 pm.

Greenmarket Square A very picturesque cobbled square, this is now a national monument and was once the site of Cape Town's market.

Museums There are several of these, but if you're a museum buff don't miss the **Cultural History Museum** (open Monday to Saturday from 10 am to 4.45 pm and on Sunday from 2 to 4.45 pm). Initially it was the Dutch East India Company's slave lodge in 1679, and later became the Old Supreme Court. The **South African Museum** (open Monday to Saturday from 10 am to 6 pm and on Sunday from 2 to 6 pm) is primarily a natural history museum but also has a good exhibition of Bushman artefacts.

EAST LONDON

The cheapest place to stay is undoubtedly the *Youth Hostel*, which gets consistently good reports. It's located behind the *Holiday Inn* – bus No 11 (Moore St) or No 12 (Beach) to the end of the line. The fare is 25c.

If you don't want to go there, try *Kei Lodge*, 13-15 Symons St (tel 2 8105); or *Newlands Accommodation*, 12 Fitzpatrick Rd, (tel 2 0548). They are both relatively cheap.

The Tourist Office is in the City Hall, Oxford and Argyle Sts.

All city bus routes start from just outside the City Hall. If you're hitching to Durban or the Transkei, take bus No 8 (Abbotsford) for 40c. If you're hitching east, take No 3. If hitching west, take No 2 (Collingdale).

GEORGE

The *Municipal Tourist Camp* costs R 5 for a rondavel.

GRAAF REINET

One of the cheapest places to stay is the *Urquhart Tourist Camp* where you can rent a rondavel for R 6.50 per day plus 50c per person. Otherwise try the *Caledonian Chambers*, which has beds for R 8 per person.

JEFFREY'S BAY

Just west of Port Elizabeth, Jeffrey's Bay has accommodation at *Smith's Rooms*, 50 Diaz Rd, for R 5. Another place opposite the post office charges R 4.

KIMBERLEY

The cheapest place to stay is the *Youth Hostel* about four or five km from the centre of town, on the road to Bloemfontein (tel 0531 28577). The warden is very strict but it's a good hostel and there are bicycles for hire and a swimming pool. If you'd prefer to stay nearer the centre of town, try one of the following places:

Grand Hotel, corner Southey St and Transvaal Rd, (tel 2 65251/2/3). Bed and breakfast R 27.50.

Cresent Hotel, Darcy St. Bed and breakfast R 11.

Queens Hotel, off Stockdale Rd (tel 2 3299). Bed and breakfast R 10.

Halfway House Hotel, corner Main and Egerton Sts. Bed and breakfast R 12.

Information

The Tourist Office is in City Hall, Market Square.

Things to See

Kimberley is the site of the world's largest man-made hole – known as **The Big Hole**. In 1871 diamonds were found on what used to be a hill here. From then until 1914, the hill was not only completely dug away, a huge crater covering 15 hectares and 756 metres deep was gouged out of the earth. Thousands of people came to seek their fortune and quite a few of them made it. Of the 28 million tonnes of earth removed by hand, some three tonnes of diamonds were found worth R 94 million. Next to the Big Hole is a museum where the streets of Kimberley as they were in Victorian times have been reconstructed; there's a diamond exhibition as well. The museum is open daily from 8 am to 6 pm and costs R 1.50 entry with a Youth Hostel card.

Diamond mining has now moved to the other side of town in the shape of the **De Beers Mine** and, in time, it promises to rival the Big Hole in terms of size. There's an observation platform where you can watch the workings below.

KNYSNA

The campsite by the lagoon on the east side of town is popular and costs R 6.42 for two people.

MAFIKENG

It's unlikely you'd stay here overnight unless you were looking for the ghost of Baden Powell, but if you do, try either *Caravan Park* or *Hotel Welkom*, which costs R 10 per night. There's a campsite

just before the railway bridge on the right which costs R 4.50 per night (pula are acceptable).

MOSSEL BAY

Try the *ATKV Camp* at Hartenbos Beach, 10 km east of the town, which costs R 2 for a rondavel.

OUDTSHOORN

Try *NA Smit Tourist Camp*, where you can get a rondavel for R 3.

Don't miss the **Cango Caves** north of here.

PLETTENBERG BAY

Located about a third of the way from Port Elizabeth to Cape Town near Knysna, Plettenberg Bay has one of the finest beaches in the Republic. If you stop off here, try *Archerwood Student Rooms*, which cost R 12 per night. The rooms are two-bedroom 'flats' with hand basin and communal hot showers. Meals are available at the motel.

PORT ELIZABETH

The Youth Hostel has been closed, but there is a *Municipal Camping Ground* at Humewood which has rondavels (three beds) with bath for R 6, or singles for R 7 and doubles for R 13. No bedding is provided. To get there take bus No 2 to Humewood from stand 5.

Some of the cheaper hotels are: *Belle Aurora*, 58 Kirkwood St, North End (tel 58 1415); *Canadia Accommodation*, 50 Belmont Terrace (tel 2 4832); *Central Lodge*, 12 Western Rd (tel 2 8831); *Cuylerholme*, 42 Western Rd (tel 2 9032); *Hornby Holiday Accommodation*, 39 Beach Rd (tel 2 5120); *Inchkeith*, 7 Havelock St (tel 2 6216); *Laurel Lodge*, 6 Fort St (tel 2 8870), with rooms at R 6.50; *Richly House*, 80 Cape Rd, (tel 39 1570); *St Croix*, 10 Havelock St (tel 2 2614); *Town House*, 81 Cape Rd (tel 33 1072); or *Valhill Accommodation*, 17 Prospect Hill (tel 2 4700).

There is a *YMCA* at 31 Havelock St (tel 2 3913) which costs R 29.50 per week. A

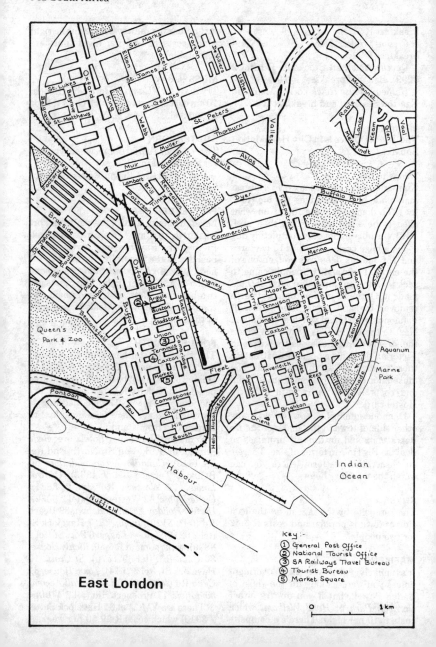

East London

Key :-
① General Post Office
② National Tourist Office
③ SA Railways Travel Bureau
④ Tourist Bureau
⑤ Market Square

0   1 km

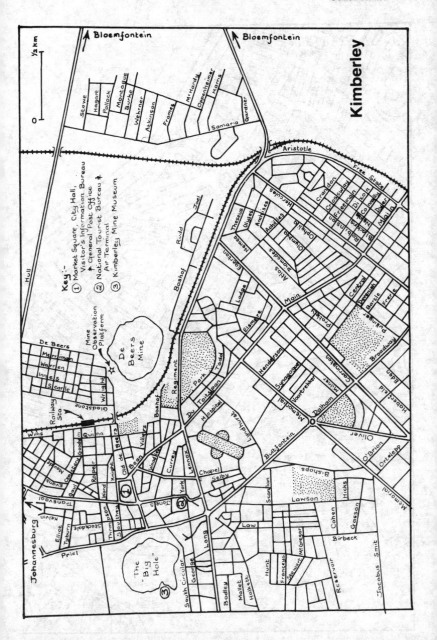

Kimberley

Key:-
① Market Square, City Hall, Visitor's Information Bureau
② General Post Office
   National Tourist Bureau
   Air Terminal
③ Kimberley Mine Museum

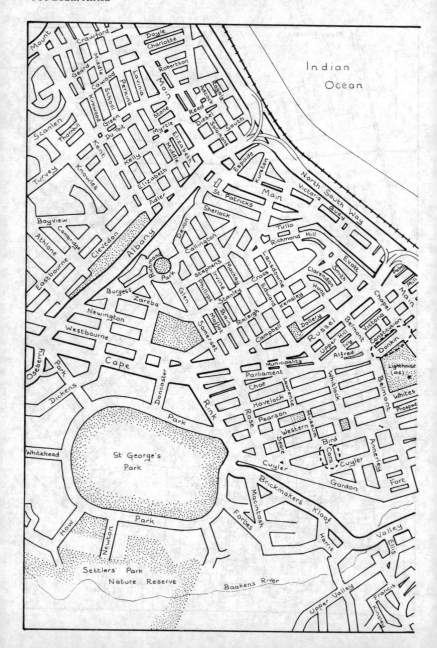

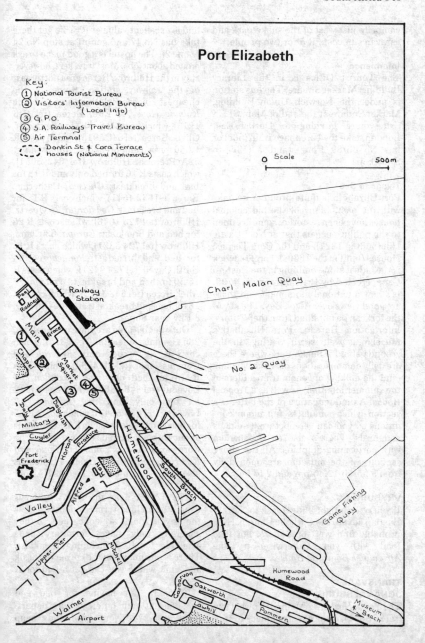

Port Elizabeth

Key:
① National Tourist Bureau
② Visitors' Information Bureau (Local Info)
③ G.P.O.
④ S.A. Railways Travel Bureau
⑤ Air Terminal
- - - Donkin St & Cora Terrace houses (National Monuments)

0 Scale 500m

Railway Station

Charl Malan Quay

No. 2 Quay

Peel
Rodney
Main
Grace
Chapel
Market Square
Dalgleish
Military
Cuyler
Horton
Produce
Fort Frederick
Alfred
Hall
Humewood
South Beach
Valley
Upper Pier
Mitchell

Game Fishing Quay

Carnarvon
Oakworth
Lawhill
Pommern
Humewood Road

Walmer
Airport

Museum & Beach

campsite just west of the snake park and caravan site costs R 5 for two people.

Information

The Tourist Office is in the Library Building, Market Square. The bus station is under the Norwich Union Building, Market Square at the end of Main St.

If you're hitching to Durban/East London, take the Uitenhage train (60c) or bus No 86/89 from stand 7 (53c) to Swartkops.

Things to See

Port Elizabeth is quite proud of its links with the past. Many of the old colonial houses have been restored; some are open to the public, such as that at No 7 Castle Hill (built in 1827), and the Cora Terrace Houses (built in the 1830s). **Fort Frederick** is the oldest stone building in the Eastern Cape, erected by British troops in 1799. It's now a national monument and there are good views over Algoa Bay. The key to the fort can be obtained from the Visitors' Information Bureau. Port Elizabeth's **Museum** is well worth visiting. In the grounds stand a **Snake Park** where there are daily demonstrations of snake handling (and the milking of venom from adders in the summer months), as well as a **Tropical House**. A unique feature of the latter is a section which simulates full moon conditions so you can see nocturnal animals and birds! There's also an **Oceanarium** with performing dolphins. All the above sections of the museum are open daily from 9 am to 12.45 pm and 2 to 5 pm.

VRYBURG

If you're on a tight budget, ask for Father Bastian next to the Catholic Church. He'll probably find you somewhere, but take food with you. Otherwise, try the *Afrikaaner Boarding House*.

TRANSVAAL
JOHANNESBURG

The *Youth Hostel*, 32 Main St, Townsview (tel 26 8051), is the cheapest place to stay

and is excellent value at R 3. To get there take bus No 47 and get off at stop No 24 (Zone 2). The hostel is a good place to ask around about jobs. Most travellers, however, stay in the Hillbrow/Berea area north-east of the railway station. Some of the cheapest places in this area include *Kolping House*, 4 Fife, Berea (tel 643 1213), which costs R 6.50; *Hawthorne*, 45 Olivia, Berea (tel 642 5915), which costs R 12.50 for bed and breakfast; *Ambassador*, 52A Pretoria, Hillbrow (tel 642 5051), which costs R 16 for bed only and R 18 for bed and breakfast; *Chelsea*, Catherine, Berea (tel 642 4541), which costs R 18 for bed and breakfast; *Constantia*, 35 Quartz, Hillbrow (tel 725 1046), which costs R 25 for bed and breakfast; *Europa*, 63 Claim, Hillbrow (tel 724 5321), which costs R 12 for bed and breakfast; *Rondebosch*, 24 Edith Cavell (tel 724 9421), which costs R 18.50 for bed and breakfast; *Whitehall*, 8 Abel, Berea (tel 643 4911), which costs R 18 for bed and breakfast; and the *Odyssey*, 8 Lily near Soper.

Outside this area are the *Cosmopolitan*, 285 Commissioner (tel 614 3315), which costs R 20 for bed only; *Federal*, 180 Commissioner (tel 29 4584), which costs R 13 for bed only; *East London*, 54 Loveday (tel 836 5862), which costs R 12 for bed only; and the *Gresham*, 13 Loveday (tel 834 5641), which costs R 25 for bed and breakfast. The East London is about to be renamed, but we've had no word yet of the new name. The *Boulevard Rest House* next to the Chelsea Hotel has also been recommended. It costs R 12 per bed.

The *YMCA* near the train station is usually full of long-term residents as far as the private rooms are concerned, so they generally only have dormitory beds available for R 7 including breakfast. There is an annexe on the corner of Rissik and Smit where you can get a bed for R 5.

If you're not paying for bed and breakfast at your hotel, *Jo'burg* department stores do very good and cheap breakfasts for early shoppers; you can get a full English-style breakfast with coffee for around 90c. For a meal at other times of the day, try the *Kasbah Steak & Snack*, Katze St, Hillbrow. For action in the evenings, two good hangouts are the *Chelsea Theatre* under the Chelsea Hotel on Catherine (very good bands and pleasant atmosphere); and *Lucky Luke's*, Pretoria (friendly manager called Steve). Both are in the Hillbrow area. *Plum Crazy*, also in Hillbrow, has good jazz on Sunday afternoon.

A word of warning about the Hillbrow area. There has been an alarming increase in mugging here recently. It's usually at night, but incidents do take place in broad daylight.

The Tourist Office is in Suite 4611, Carlton Centre, Johannesburg 2000, and there's an American Express office at Merbrook 123, Commissioner St, PO Box 9395, Johannesburg 2000 (tel 37 4000).

There's a very useful noticeboard in the lobby of the *Highpoint Apartment Complex*, Kotzee St, Hillbrow. Categories include airline tickets for sale, lifts and camping gear. Most of the airline tickets advertised are the return halves of APEX tickets. The sellers will go out to the airport with you and check in the bags, as the tickets will be in their name. It's a cheap way of getting back to Europe/USA/Australia.

For cheap safaris check out the travel shop, *Game Trails*, in the Hillbrow area.

If you'd like to see the surface workings of a gold mine while you're here, there are tours on Wednesday and Friday mornings for R 4. You should try to make a booking at least two weeks in advance through the Public Relations Adviser, Chamber of Mines of South Africa, PO Box 809, Johannesburg 2000 (tel 838 8011). If you're not going to be around that long, there are tours of the historic **Simmer and Jack Gold Mine** in Johannesburg from Monday to Saturday at 8.30 am. The 3½-hour tour includes surface and underground workings, a museum and a Ndebele village. The tour costs R 8 and should be booked two days in advance at Simmer & Jack Gold Mine, PO Box 192, Germiston, 1400 (tel 51 8571). The **Gold Mine Museum**, Alamein St by Kimberley Freeway, is also worth a visit. Entry costs R 12 and includes an underground tour.

The fares on local 'white' city buses are based on zones – Zone 1 is 45c, Zone 2 is 60c, Zone 3 is 70c and Zone 4 is 80c. You can buy 10-trip vouchers (usable by more than one person) from the main bus terminal for R 2.60 (Zone 1), R 3.90 (Zone 2), R 5.20 (Zone 3) and R 6.40 (Zone 4).

South African Airways run a bus between the centre and Jan Smuts International Airport for R 2.20.

If you're hitching to Kimberley (Route 29) or to Bloemfontein and Cape Town (National 1), take bus No 55 (Ridgeway) to the end of the line (Zone 2) and then walk about 1-1/2 km to the Golden Highway (Route 29). Buses run direct to the Golden Highway, though less frequently; they are Nos 52 (Mondeor), 56 (Kibler Park) and 57 (Power Park), all in Zone 3.

If you want to go to **Soweto** you first have to apply for a permit at the West Rand Administrative Board, Albert and Delvers Sts. It's free, though you'll need to find someone who is willing to take you round. There are pricey organised 'tours' for R 18.

PRETORIA

Some of the cheapest places to stay are the *Belgrave*, 22 Railway St (tel 3 5578); the *Louis*, 599 Schoeman St (tel 44 4238); the *Pretoria*, 611 Schoeman St (tel 42 5062); and the *Republique*, 47 Schoeman St (tel 3 2025).

The *YMCA* has a number of Youth Hostel-type beds which cost R 2.

The Tourist Office is in Frans du Toit Building (3rd Floor), Schoeman St, Pretoria 0001.

American Express is in the SAAU Building, 308 Andries St, Pretoria 0001 (tel 2 9182).

If you want to see a working diamond mine, there are tours of the Premier

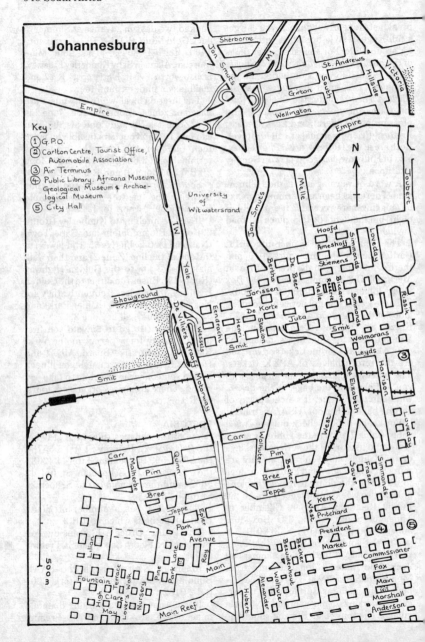

Johannesburg

Key:
① G.P.O.
② Carlton Centre, Tourist Office, Automobile Association
③ Air Terminus
④ Public Library, Africana Museum, Geological Museum & Archaeological Museum
⑤ City Hall

Diamond Mine, 40 km north-east of Pretoria, Tuesday through Friday at 9.30 am and 11 am except on public holidays. You need to make reservations in advance with the Public Relations Officer, Premier Diamond Mine, PO Box 44, Cullinan 1000 (tel 368). The Tourist Office will advise you about transport to Cullinan.

Two places worth visiting in Pretoria are the **National Cultural History Museum** and the **Fort Klapperkop museum**. The former is devoted mainly to the black tribes of the Transvaal and has a collection of prehistoric rock paintings, but there are also sections on the cultural history of the European population and Voortrekker furniture. It's open Monday to Saturday from 8 am to 5 pm and on Sunday from 10.30 am to 5 pm. Fort Klapperkop was built in 1898 and has been converted into a museum of the military history of the Republic from 1852. It's open Monday to Friday from 10 am to 4 pm and on Saturday and Sunday from 10 am to 6 pm.

If you're hitching to Johannesburg (Route 28 changing to National 1), go down Potgieter to the start of the freeway about 750 metres from the railway bridge.

NATIONAL PARKS & GAME RESERVES
The national parks are South Africa's main attraction, and because of the abundance of wildlife and, in some, the spectacular mountain scenery, you should make an effort to spend time in at least one of them – preferably more than one. They all have rest camps that offer a wide variety of accommodation from cottages and rondavels to dormitory huts. If you prefer, you can camp (R 6 per night per person). Most of the camps have restaurants and shops, and equipment is usually for hire. Very popular are the Horse-back and Wilderness Trails, which you take on foot through areas where cars and other vehicles are banned. Accommodation and trails should be booked in advance with the National Parks Board,

PO Box 787, Pretoria 0001 (tel 44 1194). The parks are very popular during the school holidays, so if you propose to go there then you should book as far in advance as possible.

Probably the best way to go to the parks is to get a small group together and rent a vehicle; otherwise you'll have to hitch, relying on someone else to take you to a rest camp and to drive you around those sections of the parks where vehicles are allowed (most South Africans are very helpful when it comes to things like this). All the parks in Natal are now multiracial and the same is gradually happening to those in other parts of the Republic, though attitudes haven't necessarily kept in step with this development – we had one letter from a mixed party who said they were so harassed by the other campers they had to leave.

In addition to the national parks and game reserves below, there are a number of others which are smaller or less well known. Details can be obtained from the National Parks Board office in Pretoria.

Kruger National Park
This huge park virtually all the way along the Transvaal border with Mozambique is one of the largest in Africa and the largest in the Republic. It's claimed to have the greatest variety of animals in any game park in Africa, and includes lions. leopards, cheetahs, elephants, giraffes and many varieties of antelope. There are a total of 11 rest camps, the largest of them situated in the heart of the park. Others are located at four of the seven entrance gates. All types of accommodation provide mattresses, bedding, towels and soap. Lamps are provided in those camps where there is no electricity. Reservations can be made up to a year in advance or, during school holidays, for more than five nights at any one camp. When accommodation is fully booked, only a limited number of day visitors are admitted. Accommodation includes cottage with kitchenette, two double bedrooms and bathroom (R 28 for

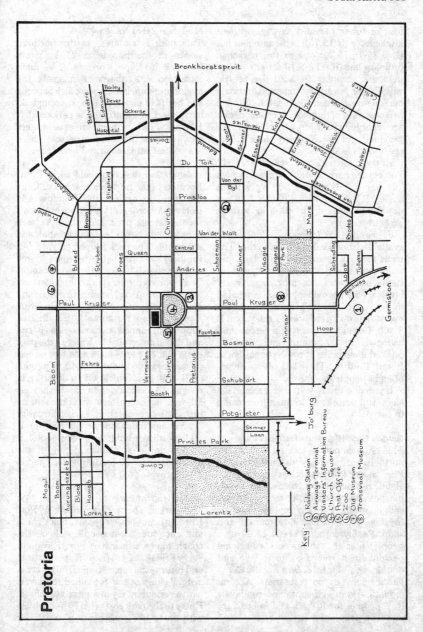

Pretoria

Key:
- ① Railway Station
- ② Airways Terminal
- ③ Visitors' Information Bureau
- ④ Church Square
- ⑤ Post Office
- ⑥ Zoo
- ⑦ Old Museum
- ⑧ Transvaal Museum

four or fewer persons); cottage without kitchenette (R 19.75); self-contained hut (R 9.45-10.75 for one or two persons); ordinary hut (R 6.25-8.10 for one or two persons); camping (R 1.90 per vehicle with five or fewer passengers. Additional persons are charged 30c each). Additional persons in any of the above accommodation are charged R 2.50 where beds are provided and R 1.25 where there are no spare beds available.

Entry to the park costs R 1.90 per visit. Vehicle fees are: R 1.20 admission plus 70c per day if under 1500 kg without trailer; R 2.40 admission plus R 1.20 per day for vehicles up to 4000 kg with or without trailer.

Three-day Wilderness Trails are available from Skukuza Rest Camp. The trails are led by experienced black and white rangers and all necessary equipment (tents, rucksacks, sleeping bags, water bottles, etc) is provided. Food is included in the cost of the trail. Trails commence every week on Tuesday and Friday, cost R 67.60 (excluding park entry fees and transport to the camp), and must be booked in advance at the National Parks Board, Pretoria. There is a set maximum of eight people in a group.

If you don't have your own vehicle, it's easy (and permitted) to hitch from camp to camp.

Golden Gate Highlands National Park

This national park is located close to the northern border of Lesotho in the Orange Free State. Its main attractions are the eland, red hartebeest, black wildebeest, blesbok and springbok. There are two rest camps within two km of one another. *Brandwag Camp* has a restaurant and shop. Family cottages are R 15.60 (two people) plus R 2.30 for each additional person; single rooms go for R 8.85 and double rooms for R 13. *Glen Reenan Camp* has a shop but no restaurant. Accommodation is in self-contained rondavels (two people) for R 9.35, and in ordinary juts (two people) for R 7.80.

Mountain Zebra National Park

This park is situated on the northern slopes of the Bankberg, 27 km from Cradock in Cape Province. The main attraction is, as the name suggests, the mountain zebra, but there are also baboons and herds of eland, gemsbok, springbok, hartebeest, etc. Entry to the park costs R 1.10 per vehicle with up to five passengers plus 30c for each additional person. There is a communal kitchen and barbeque.

Kalahari Gemsbok National Park

Located in the northern reaches of Cape Province up against the Namibia and Botswana borders, this is South Africa's second largest park. Animals to be seen here include lion, cheetah, gemsbok and springbok. The park is open all year, but the best time to visit is between March and October. There are three rest camps: *Twee Rivieren*, the park headquarters; *Mata Mata*, on the Namibian frontier; and *Nossob*, 139 km north of Twee Rivieren. There are no restaurants, but limited supplies of canned goods as well as petrol and diesel are available. Entry to the park costs R 3.30 per vehicle with five or less passengers and under 2000 kg in weight, or R 4.50 per vehicle up to 3000 kg in weight. Accommodation costs are as follows: family cottage with kitchenette (up to four people), R 16.15; hut with shower and toilet (one or two people), R 10.70; ordinary hut (one or two people), R 5.75. Additional people in any of the above cost R 2.30 (bed provided) and R 1.15 (provide your own bed).

Addo Elephant Park

The park is about 72 km north of Port Elizabeth and has elephants, black rhino and antelope. Most people visit on the coach tour which leaves Port Elizabeth every Friday at 2 pm (weather permitting) and returns the same evening, but there is a small camp of self-contained rondavels with a restaurant if you want to stay there. Entry to the park costs R 1.10 per vehicle with up to five passengers plus 10c for each additional passenger. Accommodation costs R 9.35 per hut (one or two people) plus R 2.25 for each additional person.

Zululand Game Parks

There are five main game reserves in Zululand (northern Natal) – Hluhluwe, Umfolozi, Mkuzi, Ndumu and St Lucia. Accommodation in the reserves is in two-bed and four-bed self-contained huts which cost R 5 per person, with a minimum charge of R 8 for the four-bed huts. A number of larger, self-contained cottages at Hluhluwe cost R 6 per person with a minimum charge of R 12 for a four-bed cottage and R 18 for a six-bed cottage. Reservations, which can be made up to six months in advance, must be made at the Game and Fisheries Preservation Board, PO Box 662, Pietermaritzburg 3200, Natal (tel 5 1514). There are no restaurants or stores at these reserves so you must take your own provisions. Petrol and diesel are available and cooking and eating utensils are provided. The kitchen staff prepare all meals. Admission to the parks costs R 3 per vehicle plus 50c per passenger.

Hluhluwe This reserve is famous for its rhino, but there's also a large variety of other game, including buffalo.

Umfolozi Umfolozi is primarily a sanctuary for the 'white' rhino, although there are many other species of game to be seen. One of the features of Umfolozi is the three-day Wilderness Trail. Trips take place throughout the year, but reservations must be made in advance with the Game and Fisheries Preservation Board, Pietermaritzburg. If you plan to take part in one during May to August, you're advised to book ahead as far as possible. The trail costs R 50 per person or R 200 for a group of six people (six is the maximum for a group). You must provide your own food, clothing, soap and towels, but sleeping bags, tents and cooking and eating utensils are provided. Transport of food,

bedding, camping gear, etc is by pack animal.

Mkuzi This is mainly a waterfowl reserve, but you may also see the timid suni antelope. If you want to camp, there is a site outside the entrance which costs R 1.20 per person. Reservations must be made in advance with the Officer-in-Charge, Mzuki Game Reserve, PO Mzuki, 3965, Zululand (tel Mzuki 3).

Ndumu Located right on the Mozambique border, Ndumu is another reserve mainly for waterfowl. Tours are available around the pans with one of the rangers.

St Lucia The reserve consists of an island-studded bay almost 72 km in length and from two to eight km wide. It was established primarily as a fishing reserve, but also contains buck, hippo and crocodile. There are two camping areas and two hut camps. *St Lucia Estuary* offers camping (reservations to The Ranger-in-Charge, PO St Lucia Estuary 3936, Zululand (tel St Lucia 20). *Charter's Creek* has huts available. *Fanies Island* offers camping and huts (reservations to The Camp Superintendent, Fanies Island, Private Bag X7205, Mtubatuba 1431). Camping costs R 1.20 per person (minimum charge of R 1.80).

Five-day Wilderness Trail trips are available from Charter's Creek under the supervision of a ranger every week between April and September. They cost R 50 per person. Those who go on the trail are taken 24 km up the lake to the wilderness area by boat. The same conditions apply as for the Wilderness Trail in the Umfolozi Reserve. Reservations for the huts in this reserve and for the Wilderness Trail must be made with the Parks Board Office in Pietermaritzburg.

There are special launch tours of the St Lucia Estuary and Charter's Creek when tidal conditions permit.

Giant's Castle Game Reserve

Located on the eastern face of the Drakensberg up against the Lesotho border, this park is a must if you're in the area. It's the home of 12 species of antelope and two rare species of eagle. Horseback trails of two to six days' duration can be arranged with the Parks Board Office in Pietermaritzburg. Two-bed and four-bed bungalows as well as larger, self-contained cottages are available for rent. Prices and reservations are the same as for the reserves in Zululand.

Royal Natal National Park

The Royal Natal is one of the smallest of South Africa's national parks, but in terms of landscape it's the most spectacular. Right up against the Lesotho border, the Drakensberg here forms an eight-km-long wall of rock known as the Amphitheatre, behind which is the Mont-aux-Sources summit where both the Orange and the Tugela rivers originate. The area is well watered by countless streams and has forests of cypress, cycad and sagewood as well as a profusion of both birdlife and wildflowers. Entrance to the park costs 60c, a map of the park R 1.07 and camping is available for R 5 per night including hot-water showers.

VISITING THE HOMELANDS
Transkei

It's probably not worth the trouble of getting a visa before arrival, as these are issued at the border at Umzimkulu and Kei Bridge for 50c (Transit) and R 2 (Tourist), but some travellers have said it's best to have one beforehand. Three-month, multiple-entry visas cost R 2.50. Entry via a road without a border gate is officially illegal for a foreign passport holder. Transkei officials usually aren't too concerned about this (though we have heard from one traveller who was fined R 40 for not having a visa), but South African officials can be difficult. There's a lot of paperwork to get through at the borders, so bear this in mind as it soaks up time.

A simple rule to observe: If you enter on a road with a border gate, leave on a road with a border gate (eg the main Pietermaritzburg-East London road). If you enter via a road without a border gate (34 to choose from), keep your mouth shut and leave the same way.

There's an unspoilt and very beautiful beach which rarely has anyone on it at Port St Johns. The *Second Beach Camp* there has fully equipped rondavels for R 10 per night, or you can camp for R 5. It's an idyllic spot, but watch out for sharks if you go swimming. (This applies all along the Wild Coast.)

In Umtata there is a somewhat basic campsite with showers on the edge of town. It costs R 4 per site. To get there take Alexandra Avenue towards the hospital and turn left. The *Grosvenor Hotel* is a good place to stay since, if you ask, the manageressa will more than likely offer you the 'hiker price' of R 8.50 a room, including an enormous breakfast. If they're full, however, you may have to pay R 23 per person and even up to R 50 depending on what rooms are available. A lot of commercial travellers stay at the Grosvenor, so lifts to East London, Durban and Port St Johns are easy to find here.

Mazeppa Bay and the **Dwesa Game Reserve** have also been recommended as good places to visit.

Bophuthatswana

We have hardly any information about Bophuthatswana (which, absurdly, consists of no less than seven separate enclaves, all but one of which are completely surrounded by South Africa) or the more recently created homeland of Venda. It seems few travellers are going there, or if they are, they're just passing through en route to somewhere else. We did have one letter from a volunteer health worker some time ago, which said the people in Bophuthatswana were incredibly friendly once you had broken through the old black-white barrier. He said people were dying for a chance to be friendly and to invite you into their homes despite their poverty. It's just that they're suspicious at first that you're going to push them around like most of the Afrikaaners do. If you're not camping, there's almost nowhere to stay except in the homes in a few of the larger villages with Afrikaaner hotels, but they are very dreary places and the atmosphere is heavily apartheid. There's not much to see either, apart from the huge maize plantations run by Afrikaaner farmers and lots of squalid little settlements where the Tswana people from Johannesburg and Cape Town were dumped after the homeland was created in 1976. Infectious diseases are apparently rife in these places, since no one in any position of authority really cares.

OTHER

Jobs If you're skilled in some aspect of electronics, there's a staggering amount of work going and you have a choice of umpteen jobs. There's also a fair amount of work for draughtspeople and linguists. Getting a work permit involves very little fuss if you have a skill in demand. You just need a letter from your prospective employers, after which the permit can come through in as little as 24 hours. If you don't have a skill in demand, getting the permit can be more difficult and you may be required to deposit R 1000 and show an onward ticket. On the other hand, it's fairly easy to get casual part-time work at most restaurants and the pay is pretty good.

Pay is better in Johannesburg, but the cost of living is high. It's the other way round in Cape Town.

Real Ale Freaks Here's good news for all CAMRA cognoscenti. If you pass through the small town of Knysna, about halfway between Cape Town and Port Elizabeth on the coast, ask for Mr Lex Mitchell. This man brews his own stout, bitter ale and lager using imported barrels and taps from the UK. It's all above board and fully licenced. Our source didn't give the man's address, so it might require a little persistence to find him!

NATAL PROVINCE
DURBAN

The cheapest place to stay is the *Youth Hostel*, 15 Cadogan Place, Durban North (tel 842050), run by Mrs D A Griffiths. It costs R 3 per night but only has two beds! To get there take bus No 2 from the centre or No 22 from the railway station.

Also very cheap is the *YMCA*, Beach Walk, Esplanade (tel 324441), which costs R 5.50 for bed and breakfast.

If you don't want to stay at the Youth Hostel, the best place to go looking for cheap hotels is Gillespie St. The prices of virtually all accommodation in Durban doubles during the high season and it's very difficult to find any accommodation at Christmas, Easter and during the summer school holidays.

One of the cheaper places along Gillespie St is *Impala Holiday Flats*, Marine Parade (tel 32 3232), which costs R 10 per day for a fully equipped small flat or R 20 in the high season. Others worth trying along this road are the *Hilton Heights Holiday Flats*, 5 Gillespie St (tel 37 1535), which costs R 10 a double in the low season; *Sea Breeze Hotel*, 55 Gillespie St (tel 37 8696), which costs R 9 per person for bed and breakfast; *White Hotel* which costs R 10.70 per bed in the low season; *Killarney*, which costs R 16.50 for bed and breakfast in the low season; *Casa Mia*, which has beds for R 15 in the low season; *Miramar Hotel*, next to the Sea Breeze Hotel, which costs R 13 for bed and breakfast; and the *Beachsider Holiday Rooms*, 14 Rochester St, which costs R 12 a double.

If possible, avoid the *Blenheim Hotel*, 37 Gillespie St (tel 37 4066), as not only does it cost R 15 a double, it has bed bugs and roaches and isn't very clean. Another place which has been recommended is the *Outspan Hotel* (or, as one traveller described it, 'Gasworks View'). Nevertheless, it offers air-conditioning and very good food for just R 10 for bed and breakfast, with no seasonal increase.

There's also the *White House*, which offers bed and breakfast for R 10.75-11.75. One other place worth trying, although it's a bit sleazy, is the *New City Hotel*, Russell St. You can get bed and breakfast for R 8.

A good place to eat is the small dining room beside the *Balmoral Hotel*, Marine Parade. It serves the same food as the main dining room, but at much lower prices, and you can order course by course. A soup and main course should cost about R 1.50 (ask the waiter if you want a bigger helping). *XL Café*, Marine Parade, is also worth considering. It's a bit seedy but it's open all night and has a good atmosphere and videos.

The Tourist Office is at 320 West St (3rd floor), tel 6 7144.

American Express is at 3 General Building, Field St.

The Transkei Consulate is in the Commercial City (3rd floor), Commercial St, not far from the GPO. Visas cost R 2.50 and are issued while you wait.

The Ciskei Consulate is at 320 West St (4th floor).

If you're looking for something to do in Durban, pay a visit to the **Snake Park** on the beachfront. It has a good collection of snakes – mainly poisonous – from South Africa and many other parts of the world, and is a major producer of serum for the southern half of the continent. It's also worth visiting the **Old Fort**, an important bastion of the British forces during the war with the Boers in 1842. The fort is open daily except Saturday and public holidays from 10 am to noon and 1 to 4 pm.

For an uncrowded beach in Durban, go to **Umhlanga Rocks** (pronounced 'Umshlun-ga') north of the city. The scenery is fantastic, and out of season there are long, almost deserted beaches. Buses there run all day long during the week from downtown Durban outside the Metro Theatre – the Tourist Office has the schedule. Other travellers have suggested a trip to Port St Johns (Transkei). A bus there from Durban costs R 9 and departs at 7.30 am, arriving at 3 pm. The route is wild and beautiful, with plenty to see on the way. (The bus is a 'black' one but it also takes whites.)

PIETERMARITZBURG

One of the cheapest places to stay is the *Youth Centre* (tel 69252), which costs R 10 per night. At the same price is the *YMCA*. There's a campsite near the freeway for R 2 per night. Otherwise, try one of the following reasonably priced places: *Cosy*, 456 Church St (tel 2 3279), which costs R 7.50 for a bed only; *New Watson*, corner Church and West Sts (tel 2 1604), which costs R 15 for bed and breakfast; and the *Norfolk*, 23 Church St (tel 2 6501/2).

While you're in Pietermaritzburg it's worth visiting the **Voortrekker Museum** on Boshoff which contains, among other things, one of the ox-carts used by the pioneers and a chair carved from an ironwood tree for the Zulu chief, Dingaan. The museum is open Monday to Friday from 9 am to 1 pm and 2 to 4.30 pm, and on Saturday from 9 am to 12.30 pm. The **Natural Museum** is also worth a visit. It has sections on ethnology, natural history, paleontology and ornithology as well as a reconstruction of a Pietermaritzburg street of the 1870s. The museum is open daily from 9 am to 4.30 pm.

ORANGE FREE STATE
BLOEMFONTEIN

Two of the cheapest places to stay are the *Capitol*, 126a Maitland St (tel 7 7711), which costs R 18.50 for bed and breakfast; and the *Oranje*, 62 Andrews St (tel 7 9849), which costs R 15 per person for bed and breakfast.

The Tourist Office is on the ground floor, FVB Centre, Maitland St.

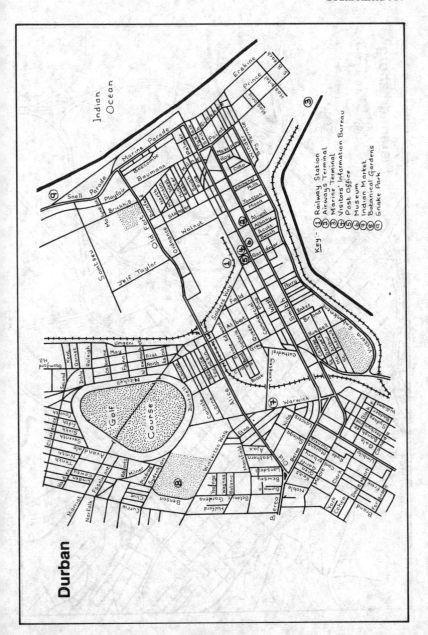

Durban

Key:-
1 Railway Station
2 Airways Terminal
3 Marine Terminal
4 Visitors' Information Bureau
5 Post Office
6 Museum
7 Indian Market
8 Botanical Gardens
9 Snake Park

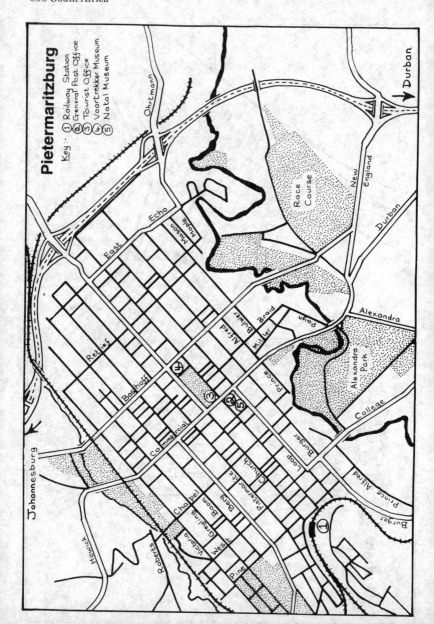

Pietermaritzburg

Key:-
① Railway Station
② General Post Office
③ Tourist Office
+ ④ Voortrekker Museum
⑤ Natal Museum

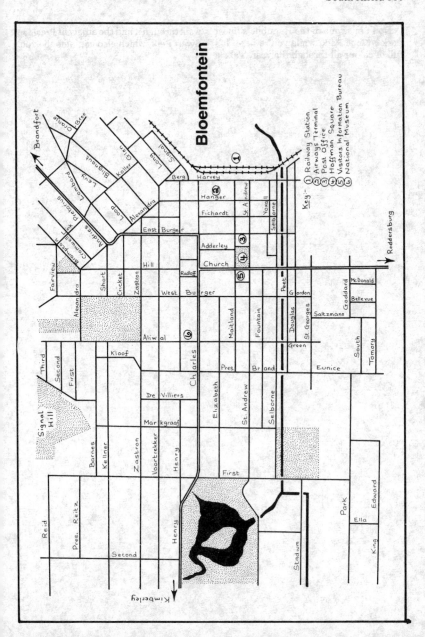

Bloemfontein

Key:-
1. Railway Station
2. Airways Terminal
3. Post Office
4. Hoffman Square
5. Visitors Information Bureau
6. National Museum

Don't miss one of the Republic's finest parks, **Kings Park,** while you're here. It's full of colour all through the year. Take a walk through it and the adjacent **President Swart Park,** which also contains the zoo.

Spanish North Africa

All that remains of the Spanish colonies in Africa are the two tiny enclaves of Ceuta and Melilla on the northern Moroccan coast and the tiny islands of Alhucemas, Chafarinas and Peñon de la Gomera just off the coast. Ceuta and Melilla are two intensely Andalusian cities which came under Spanish control in the 15th century at a time when the Moslem armies were gradually being pushed out of Spain and Portugal. They remained under Spanish control when Morocco gained its independence in 1956. Both are administered as city provinces of Spain. About 90% of the inhabitants are Spanish and the cities' main function is to supply the Spanish troops stationed there and to service the NATO base and other calling ships. Fishing and the export of iron ore from the Rif Mountains are the other main activities. The Moroccan government occasionally campaigns for the provinces' return to Morocco.

These places interest the traveller beacuse the cheapest ferries between Spain and Morocco operate through them, and because customs tend to be easier going than at Tangier.

VISAS

Visas aren't required by nationals of any West European country including Yugoslavia; any country in the Americas including the Caribbean; Japan; South Korea; Philippines; Singapore; and in Africa, Gambia, Kenya, Mauritius, Morocco, Seychelles, Sierra Leone and Tunisia. Nationals of Australia, Israel, New Zealand and South Africa require visas.

MONEY
US$1 = 150 pesetas

The unit of currency is the Spanish peseta.

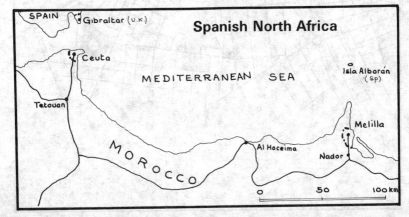

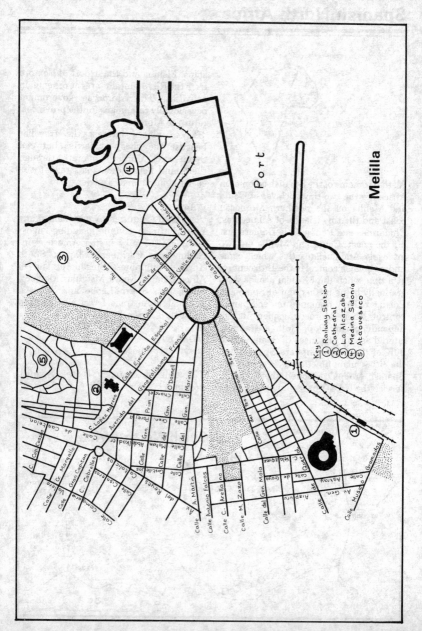

PLACES TO STAY

Very few people stay in Ceuta or Melilla since they are only pocket-sized enclaves; you may as well continue on into Morocco. If you arrive on a late boat from Spain, however, there is a *Youth Hostel* in Plaza Vieza in Ceuta which costs 295 pesetas. This is close to the stop for the bus from the ferry. There is an attached bar and cafeteria.

There are frequent buses to Tetuan from the main square for Dr 5 and taxis for Dr 10.

OTHER

If you are going to Algeria from Ceuta or Melilla, buy a bottle of whisky (semi-duty free). You can keep costs down in Algeria by selling it later on.

Both places have Algerian currency for sale at reasonable rates – though these may be slightly below what you can get inside the country.

Petrol is duty-free here, so if you're driving to Morocco (and Algeria), stock up.

Sudan

Sudan, Africa's largest country, stretches from the deserts of Nubia to the equatorial rainforests and swamps of the Sudd, just north of the great lakes and the source of the Nile. Like neighbouring Chad, it straddles the dividing line between two distinct cultural traditions – those of the Arab north and the black south – and, like Chad, the country was torn by civil war between the two groups for many years after independence. The conflict ended in the late 1970s with the granting of a large measure of autonomy to the south. This was one of former leader Jaafar el-Nimeiry's greatest achievements, allowing the country to concentrate on social and economic developments – especially in the more primitive south. It was, therefore, hard to believe when Nimeiry unilaterally scrapped autonomy for the south and decreed Islamic Law over the whole country in 1983. As a result, Sudan is once again torn by civil war and there is no end to the conflict in sight.

The worldwide fame of Egypt's exceptionally long and rich cultural heritage has tended to overshadow that of the Sudan, yet this country's history has been just as interesting. As early as 2300 BC the Pharaoh kingdoms had begun to extend south, and by 1000 BC Nubia had become an Egyptian colony and the empire's most important source of gold – it's estimated that at its height it was producing 40,000 kg per year. Further south lay a whole series of Egyptian towns, the most important near what is today Merowe, just

below the fourth cataract of the Nile. Out of this town grew the independent kingdom of Kush around 1000 BC, whose rulers conquered Egypt in the 9th century BC and made their capital, Napata, one of the most important centres of the ancient world for a time. After the sacking of Thebes by the Assyrians in 666 BC, the kingdom retreated even further south into what was then well-wooded country, and established a new capital at Meroe near present-day Shendi. Here it survived virtually untroubled for centuries, while Egypt was overrun by the Persians, Macedonians and Romans. The legacy of this Egyptianised kingdom can still be seen today in the temples, tombs and other ruins scattered on the banks of the Nile all the way from Wadi Haifa to Khartoum.

The kingdom's wealth was based on the export of ivory, slaves, rare skins and ebony, but after the 1st century AD it gradually came under pressure from the rival trading state of Axum in Ethiopia. The end came in the 4th century, when Meroe was sacked by the Christian rulers of Ethiopia and Meroe's rulers were forced to flee west to Kordofan and Darfur, where they eventually set up a successor state. From there, Egyptian influences spread far and wide over the centuries and have been traced as far as Mali and Zimbabwe by archaeologists and anthropologists.

After the destruction of Meroe, a Christian kingdom grew up in Nubia with its centre at Dongola. It was sufficiently powerful to stop the advance of the Arab armies which seized Egypt from the Byzantine Empire in 641 AD. Ten years later, however, Dongola was bombarded and the Nubians were forced to sign a treaty with the Arabs that guaranteed Moslem traders freedom of access and worship in return for the Arabs' respect

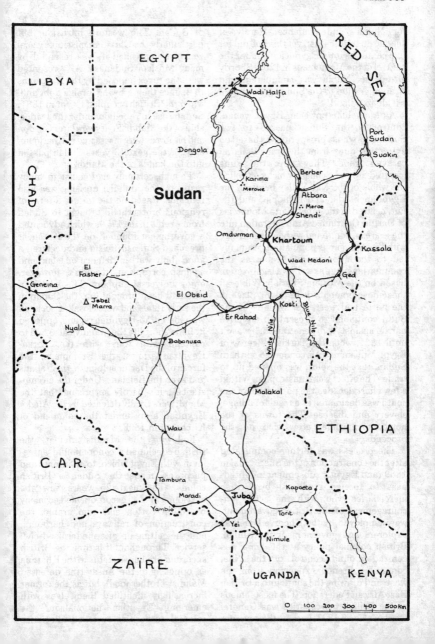

for Nubia's independence. Rarely, it seems, do treaties last, yet this one did for five centuries until Egypt came under the control of the Mamelukes in 1250. Shortly afterwards Nubia was conquered, and Arab migration to the Sudan grew from a trickle to a flood.

As Mameluke power in Egypt waned, control of the Sudan passed to two Sultanates whose prosperity was based on extracting dues from the trans-Saharan caravan trade. They were the Fung (centred around Sennar), which controlled the whole of the Nile Valley between the Egyptian border and Ethiopia; and the Fur, centred in the Jebel Marra Mountains of Darfur. Continued Arab migration into these areas, combined with intermarriage with the indigenous population, gradually led to the adoption of Arabic as the common language as well as a legal system based on the Moslem Shariah. While all these developments were taking place in the north and west, the swamps of the Sudd continued to present an effective barrier against Arab penetration. It wasn't until 1821, when the Turkish Viceroy of Egypt, Muhammad Ali, conquered northern Sudan, that the south was opened up to trade. The effect was catastrophic. Within a few short decades the population of the south was decimated as a result of pillage, slavery and disease. The towns of the north, meanwhile, grew rich on the proceeds.

The process was further complicated after the construction of the Suez Canal in 1869 (and Egypt's subsequent indebtedness to foreign creditors) by British mercenaries who, with the active encouragement of the British government, were employed by the Khedive Ismail as explorers and governors of the Sudan. British colonial policy at this time was centred around control of the Nile, containing French expansion from the west, and drawing the south into a British East African Federation. The most famous of the British mercenaries was General Gordon who, in 1877, became the governor of Sudan. The western intrusion, but particularly the Christian missionary zeal which accompanied it, was resented by many Moslem Sudanese. Also resented were the taxes imposed by the Egyptians to finance their growing foreign debt and, when the British occupied Egypt in 1881, Sudan rose in rebellion under the leadership of the Mahdi. Five years later Gordon and his forces were massacred at Khartoum, and for the next 13 years Sudan passed into the hands of the Mahdi.

Though certainly nationalist in many respects, the Mahdist uprising was also religious. Based on the *tariqa*, a form of religious brotherhood brought to Sudan from Arabia in the 1770s which advocated a government founded on the Koran, it preached Sufi asceticism and declared a *jihad* (holy war) in defence of Islam and against corruption. It didn't, however, enjoy universal support. The Khatmia, who had been brought into the Sudan in the early 1800s and were closely associated with the Turko-Egyptian regime, opposed it. In its short life the Mahdiya also had to contend with wars with the Turko-Egyptian armies, the Ethiopians, the forces of the Darfur sultanate, the Italians and even the Belgians. Under the circumstances, it's hardly surprising that the Mahdi were finally defeated by the Anglo-Egyptian army under the command of Kitchener in 1898.

Following the Mahdist defeat, the British concluded a 'condominium' agreement with Egypt which, to all intents and purposes, made the Sudan a British colony. The next 25 years saw the development of an export-oriented economy based on cotton and gum arabic, the construction of railways and harbours, and the setting up of a modernised civil service. Throughout this time the British accorded privileged status to the Khatmia as opposed to the Ansar (the defeated Mahdist brotherhood), but as the former increasingly identified themselves with emerging Egyptian nationalism, the colonial authorities switched allegiance and rehabilitated the Mahdi family. The Mahdi quickly re-established themselves as a semi-feudal aristocracy advocating independence from Egypt as a way of safeguarding their economic interests.

At the end of WW II, two political parties had emerged in Sudan. They were the Ashiqqa Party, formed by educated supporters of the Khatmia and which was eventually to become the National Union Party (NUP); and the Umma Party formed by the Mahdists. Both of these parties were soon to be rivalled by the Sudanese Communist Party, which drew its support from factory workers – particularly those who worked on the state-owned railways. The SCP was one of the best organised Communist parties ever to emerge in Africa or the Middle East, and played a decisive part in Sudanese politics until the abortive coup by pro-Communist army officers in 1971. At its height, it had the support of almost half a million members. Yet when the British were forced to acquiesce to demands for independence in Sudan after the 1952 revolution in Egypt which ousted the effete monarchy, it was with the Umma Party that negotiations were conducted, not the broad nationalist front formed from the NUP, CP, the student unions and the Sudanese Women's Union. As things happened, it probably wouldn't have mattered who negotiations were conducted with, since the south, disappointed by the rejection of its demands for secession or at least federation, exploded in 1955. As the British departed, the country sank into a bitter civil war which lasted for 17 years and by the late 1960s was consuming 30% of the national budget.

The leaders of the Anya-nya ('snake poison') secessionists were largely anti-Moslem, anti-Communist, Christian missionary-educated officers who were supported by the tribal chiefs. Their bid for independence, combined with the declining prices for cotton on the world market (Sudan's principal export), were the main reasons for the military takeover by General Ibrahim Abdoud shortly after independence. They also proved to be the junta's undoing in 1964. Sudan could ill-afford the expense of fighting such a never-ending war and the dislocation that it was causing; the junta's failure to end the war led to a general strike in 1964, in which the Communist Party played a leading role. In the elections which followed, the Communists won a number of seats in parliament, but the Umma-NUP coalition refused to allow them in and the party was forced underground. Sadiq al-Mahdi, the great-grandson of Muhammed Ahmed, emerged as the leader of the coalition. Though he had a large popular following, his manipulation of government money into schemes designed to benefit his kinspeople, his inability to bring the war in the south to a conclusion, and the disastrous fall in the price of cotton on the world market led to Sudan's US$260 million foreign debt by 1969. In May of that year the country was taken over in a coup led by Colonel Jaafar el-Nimeiry with Communist Party support. A year later 11,000 armed supporters of Sadiq al-Mahdi were killed in a confrontation with the forces of the military regime and al-Mahdi was sent into exile.

Nimeiry ruled over the Sudan for the next 16 years and survived a number of attempted coups – first by pro-Communist army officers with Libyan support in 1971, and then by the National Front (an alliance of the Moslem Brotherhood, Umma and the National Union Party) in 1975 and 1976. The latter were put down with Egyptian military assistance. Nimeiry was forced to make many twists and turns of policy in order to outflank his opponents and keep his major aid donors sweet (particularly Saudi Arabia), but the one major achievement which guaranteed him widespread support was the ending of the civil war. He achieved this by granting the south a wide measure of autonomy. He subsequently attempted a reconciliation with the opposition by releasing political prisoners and allowing Sadiq al-Mahdi to return from exile as well as promoting the leader of the Moslem Brotherhood, Abdullah Turabi, from political prisoner in 1977 to attorney-general in 1979. On the other hand, he came down hard on the Communists. A widespread purge of known members was encouraged after the riots by high school students against food price hikes in Khartoum in late 1979. Towards the end Nimeiry also had to contend with about 400,000 refugees from Ethiopia and Uganda. Of the 280,000 Ethiopians, most are Eritreans and many of them are skilled workers. As these people join the work force in increasing numbers, resentment is growing among the Sudanese because of what they see as lost job opportunities. There have been moves to try and confine the refugees to camps, but this hasn't happened as yet.

In late 1983, however, Nimeiry, either through overconfidence or, as some suspected, senility, abruptly scrapped the autonomy accord with the south in favour of 'regionalisation' and imposed Islamic Law on the whole country. Reports soon began to trickle out of Sudanese courts ordering multiple amputations for such crimes as robbery, and public flogging for possession of alcohol and for real or imagined adultery. Foreigners were not exempt either, as several discovered to their detriment. Just why Nimeiry adopted such a provocative stance isn't clear, but many of his experienced lieutenants were dismissed at the time and their places were taken by a gaggle of mystics and Islamic fundamentalists who became his closest advisors. Not only did this provoke widespread disaffection in the north, it was anathema in the south and led to a resurgence of the civil war. Within a couple of months the central government virtually lost control of the south as the railway was sabotaged, the Kosti-Juba Nile ferry was blown up and roads were mined. At the same time, Qadafi announced his support of the rebels (now known as Anya-nya 2).

Nimeiry reacted by declaring a state of emergency which suspended the constitution and banned all strikes, public gatherings and demonstrations. Shortly afterwards, Omdurman was bombed by a plane whose origin is still the subject of controversy. The government accused the Libyans but, as it was the opposition leader's house which sustained the most damage, and as the bombing took place when he was under house arrest, others have suggested that the government itself was to blame and that the reason was to secure a renewal of the US$287 million in military and economic aid provided by the American government. This aid was in danger of being withdrawn because of complaints in Congress about the increasing repression and violence in the Sudan.

Nimeiry was deposed in a coup in early April 1985, a month before the 16th anniversary of his rise to power while he was on his way home from a visit to Washington. He remains in Cairo. The new military regime headed by General Abdul Rahman Swareddahab, the former defence minister, set about purging all those associated with the former regime and sacked the chief justice, who had a reputation for being a Moslem fundamentalist and a strict interpreter of the Shariah. At the same time they announced a moderate domestic and foreign policy. The new regime was swiftly recognised by most countries having diplomatic relations with the Sudan, including Egypt, which has a mutual defence treaty with the Sudan.

Shortly afterwards the Anya-nya 2 unilaterally announced a seven-day cease-fire and called on the new leaders to announce a specific timetable for a return to civilian rule. It remains to be seen, however, whether the new leaders will be able to bring peace to the country, but the signs are encouraging. It seems that Islamic Law may soon be repealed; if that happens it will not only be seen as a major concession by the people of the south but will diffuse widespread opposition in the north as well. In that event, the Sudan may well open up again and restrictions on travel may be lifted.

FACTS

With a population of nearly 17 million, Sudan is one of Africa's poorest and least developed nations. To the north and west are vast areas of desert which support little life, while in the east is the semi-desert of Nubia. Rain hardly ever falls in these areas, and when it does it creates raging torrents in the *wadis* (dry river beds) which can cut communications for days on end. In the summer months there are frequent dust storms. The only areas which support crops of any size are the Gezira, between the Blue and White Niles south of Khartoum, and a small area south of Suakin on the Red Sea coast. Elsewhere in the north, life centres around the date palm, camels and stock rearing. The desert gradually gives way in the south, first to savannah and then to the rain-forests on the borders of Uganda and Zaire. Very few sealed roads exist and communication is largely over desert tracks or via the Nile steamers and the railways. Travel can be slow and un-predictable, but this is more than comp-ensated for by the incredible hospitality found everywhere – not just from ordinary people but from government officials and the police as well. This is something experienced by every traveller. We've received countless letters raving about the friendliness and hospitality of this country.

Sudan is well on the way to completing one of the largest irrigation projects ever attempted in Africa. This is the Jonglai Canal, which is being cut through the swamps of the Sudd from Bor to Malakal. The idea is to drain off much of the water which normally flows into the swamps and is lost by evaporation, and increase the amount of water joining the Nile further north. The extra water will be used for irrigation. A number of voices have been raised to suggest that the scheme may backfire by destroying the ecological balance of the area. The swamps are a natural habitat for large herds of buffalo, elephant and hippopotami, and they're also essential for the cattle-raising activities of the indigenous tribes. The scheme is being monitored by a UN ecology unit, but the effect of taking 20 million cubic metres of water per day from the swamps still remains to be seen. The latest news is that the scheme has been (temporarily) abandoned because of the resurgence of the civil war in the south.

Rainfall in the north – where it occurs – usually takes place between July and September, but is rarely more than 100 mm per annum, often less. In the south, annual precipitation can exceed 1000 mm and usually occurs between April and November. Temperatures are generally high and can exceed 38°C in Khartoum in the summer months.

VISAS

Visas are required by all. Nationals of Israel and South Africa are not admitted. If your passport contains Israeli stamps or Egyptian stamps from the Egyptian/Israeli border (at Rafah), then you will be refused a visa. The only way around this is to buy a new passport, but if you applied on your old one and were refused, there's no point in reapplying again at the same embassy with the new passport.

Sudanese visas take up to six weeks to issue, and even then you cannot be absolutely certain of getting one. Cairo is full of travellers waiting for Sudanese visas. At the embassy in Cairo, visas cost E£10.10 and require three photos and a letter of introduction from your own embassy (the British embassy charges E£3.20 for these letters). Some people have managed to get a Sudanese visa in a matter of days by obtaining a letter from their embassy stating that they had urgent business in the Sudan and had to go there immediately. The American embassy routinely issues such letters plus a signed calling card for its citizens to take to the

Sudanese embassy. Don't count on this, however, as the Sudanese authorities have tightened up considerably and we've had quite a few reports saying that these letters don't make a scrap of difference. On the other hand, we've had letters from as far afield as Kathmandu and London, written by travellers who managed to get a Sudanese visa in just 24 hours. In one case an American woman got a letter of introduction from the US embassy in Kathmandu, took it to the Sudanese embassy in New Delhi and was issued a visa in 24 hours. In African countries, however, you can generally expect to wait up to six weeks. There is no longer an embassy in Athens.

If you need a visa extension, once you get to Sudan apply for it at the Ministry of the Interior in Khartoum. They cost S£3 and take three days to come through.

Officially you need additional permits to go anywhere south or west of Khartoum, but permits to go from Kosti to Juba (or vice versa) are impossible to get at present (unless you have an airline ticket to Juba) because of the resurgence of the civil war there. However, this may change if the new regime brings an end to the civil war. Permits for Nyala and the Jebel Marra mountains in the west are still being issued, however. That, at least, is the official story. In practice, many police in the provinces are apparently unaware of these regulations or don't care, and the further you get from Khartoum or Juba the more so this applies. We keep getting letters all the time from travellers who were unable to get permits for overland travel in Khartoum, so they took off without them. Most reached Juba without mishap. One or two were told to go back to Khartoum, but we haven't heard of anyone getting deported or thrown in jail. Even the permits which are presently available may be withdrawn if the civil war gets any worse, so you need to keep your ear close to the travellers' grapevine to find out how things stand. The rebels in the south have already blown up the

railway line to Wau and the Kosti-Juba Nile ferry as well as sabotaged the roads south of Kosti. Apply for permits at the Ministry of the Interior in Khartoum or from a provincial police station. More details about this are under 'Getting There & Getting Around.'

If you have a camera you need a photo permit. You can get one free of charge from the Tourist Office in Khartoum.

MONEY
US$1 = S£3.50

The unit of currency is the Sudanese pound (S£) = 100 piastres. Import/export of local currency is prohibited, though if you're coming south from Aswan on the Lake Nasser ferry, no one is going to say anything about you bringing in sufficient local currency to see you through to Khartoum. There used to be a thriving black market for hard currency in Khartoum and Juba, but this has now been taken over by official exchange houses which give receipts, so there's generally little point in hawking around the streets. It's sometimes worth approaching expatriate workers, as they get paid in Sudanese pounds and are keen to convert (usually at the rate of US$1 = S£4.20). The best time to do this is March and April (the end of the school year).

Banks charge 75 pt commission for all traveller's cheque transactions.

Although the selling price of a bottle of whisky has rocketed to S£100 since Islamic Law was declared, there's no point in attempting to bring one in. Indeed, if you're caught with alcohol you face being publicly flogged. Islamic Law applies to foreigners as well as to local people, as one Italian man discovered recently. He was caught drinking whisky and was given 60 lashes! When Islamic Law was declared, the authorities went through all the big hotels, confiscated all alcohol and threw it into the Nile or simply smashed the bottles. You're in for a dry time. The revolution hasn't changed this.

Airport tax is S£30 for international flights.

LANGUAGE

Arabic is the official language and is spoken by about half the population – mainly in the north and the centre. Nilotic and Nilo-Hamitic languages are spoken in the south. Darfur is spoken in the west in the province of the same name. English is widely spoken among government officials.

FOOD

Local food is mainly *fasulia* (a bean stew) served with bread and *dura* (cooked maize or millet). There are several varieties of meat dishes which are known as *kibda* (liver), *shoya* (charcoal barbequed meat) and *kabab* (fried meat). Along the Nile you can find dishes of Nile perch (fish). Mangoes, dates, figs and bananas are plentiful and cheap, as are tomatoes and grapefruit in the south.

GETTING THERE & AROUND

Whichever route you take through the Sudan, you'll end up having to use an sting collection of trucks, riverboats, trains, international agency jeeps, mail vans and even the occasional free flight in a light plane. Apart from flights, all travel is slow and many routes are impassable during the rainy season from June to September, so allow plenty of time to get through this country. In the more remote areas of the south it can take a week to find transport going in the direction you want to go. This is particularly true between Wau and Juba and between Juba and Lodwar (northern Kenya). There are, however, daily trucks between Juba and the Ugandan border, and this is now the preferred route rather than the much rougher route into Kenya via Torit, Kapoeta, Lokichoggio and Lodwar.

Moreover, it isn't just road transport which is slow. The trains, too, are notoriously slow and subject to long delays. This extract from a letter by two people who visited Jebel Marra, Nyala, Khartoum, Kassala and Port Sudan gives you some idea of what to expect:

You need lots of time to see Sudan. The transport is diabolical and expensive. We took three months to see these few places. Most of the time was taken up being transported or waiting for transport. An example is when we left Jebel Marra with Ramadan starting. It took three days to do 65 km on a lorry in the rain, and then when we arrived in Nyala we missed the train by half a day so we had to wait a week for the next one. This was then five days late for no apparent reason. When it finally arrived, it sat for ages in the station and then finally got moving. After 16 hours it stopped for 24 hours while the engine went back to get a train-load of cars. We couldn't believe it! Other delays entailed waiting for sand to be dug off the track; travelling at less than walking pace because the rain had washed away the foundations of the track; four hours going backwards to pick up the last carriage that had fallen off; derailments; mechanical failures and stopping to pick up people who had fallen off the roof. This was additional to waiting hours at little stations in the middle of nowhere. We eventually reached Khartoum 6½ days after we left Nyala. The 1000-km journey between Jebel Marra and Khartoum had taken about three weeks. It was fun though!

Air

If you buy airline tickets in Sudan you must produce bank receipts to show that you changed the money officially. This makes the tickets quite expensive. Khartoum-Nairobi costs US$370; Khartoum-Entebbe costs US$320; Khartoum-Kilimanjaro costs US$390 and Khartoum-Dar es Salaam costs US$430. Student discounts of 25% are sometimes available from *KLM*, but neither *Sudan Air* or *Air Ethiopia* will give you one. On the other hand, if you fly with Air Ethiopia you can stop off in Addis Ababa overnight at the airline's expense.

Because the direct route down the Nile valley (Khartoum-Kosti-Juba) is no longer permitted, many travellers are flying between Khartoum and Juba. This costs S£160 (or US$130), but book in advance as flights are heavily booked.

Road

There are very few sealed roads. The main one is the Khartoum-Wad Medani-Gedaref-Kassala-Port Sudan road. Most 'roads' are just a set of tyre tracks in the sand, dust or mud, or a dirt-track through the forest. Trucks frequently get bogged down in bull-dust (or mud in the south) and everyone has to get off and start digging. This can be immense fun (at least after the event) and is a good way of getting to know your fellow travellers, but it doesn't always happen at convenient times of the day and night. Many 'roads' in the south are closed for months on end during and after the rains, as they get washed out. If possible, try to do your travelling between February and April. Protect yourself from the sun when travelling on top of trucks during the day, or you may get sunstroke. You should also take plenty of water with you when travelling through the desert; otherwise you will have to rely on wells and waterholes and you may end up with hepatitis or dysentery. Free lifts are rare but 'fares' are more or less standardised, and it's unlikely you will have to pay more than the locals. Travelling inside the cab generally costs about double what it does on top of the load.

Petrol shortages are fairly common and can result in delay or cancellation of your lift. Punctures and mechanical problems are another source of delay. Everyone has their own story about these. Try to arrange lifts the day before you want to go, but don't pay until you get on the truck. As in most African countries, trucks generally leave either from the marketplace or from a truck park nearby early in the morning. In Khartoum there are two truck parks – one in Khartoum north and the other in Omdurman. Trucks heading west generally leave from Omdurman.

Rail

There's a good network of railways in the Sudan connecting Wad Halfa with Khartoum, Atbara with Port Sudan, and Khartoum with Sennar. At Sennar the line branches, one going east to Kassala and Port Sudan, the other going west to Kosti and Babanusa where it branches again, one line going to Nyala and the other to Wau. The branch from Babanusa to Wau is not operational at present because of sabotage by the rebels in the south. It's also very difficult to get travel permits to go there. Even if you do get as far as Babanusa, the police will probably turn you back.

Student reductions on train fares have been abolished.

There are three classes on the trains but, unless you're particularly robust, it's suggested you avoid 3rd class, which can sometimes turn into a nightmare on long journeys. If you do go 3rd class, make sure you buy the slightly more expensive tickets for the carriages with padded seats rather than the cheapest ones for the carriages with slatted wooden benches. Trains never run on time, so expect long delays. Where a train originates from a particular station, you should be aware that while it is parked beyond the platform the local boys board all the 3rd-class carriages and 'reserve' seats for every man and his dog, so that by the time it gets to the platform it's 'full.' Either join the local lads or pay one of them to 'reserve' you a seat.

Boat

Lake Nasser Steamers These boats from Wadi Halfa to Aswan have already been covered in the chapter on Egypt.

Nile Steamers In the past, one of the most popular ways of getting between Kosti and Juba (or vice versa) was to take a Nile steamer. This service has been suspended until further notice because of military action by the Anya-nya 2 rebels of the south (they shot at and sunk one of the steamers in February 1984). Foreigners are, in any case, prohibited from using this route at present.

Red Sea Steamers The Egyptian Steamship and Navigation Company has steamers which connect Port Suez with Port Sudan and Jeddah. For more details see the chapter on Egypt.

Routes through the Sudan

Because of the resurgence of the civil war in the south following the declaration of Islamic Law, you officially need special permits to travel anywhere south or west of Khartoum and, at present, overland travel between Kosti and Juba along the Nile valley is off-limits to foreigners. This means that the only way to get south overland is to take the long loop through western Sudan. Permits are still available for this route via Wau and for the even longer loop via Nyala, Buram, El Fifi, Kafia Kingi, Raga and Wau. If you take the latter, you cannot get a single permit in Nyala to cover you for the entire journey to Juba. Instead, you have to get permission at each place to go to the next large town.

In Khartoum you can sometimes get permits the same day you apply, but this isn't always the case. A few travellers who were put through the waiting game decided to ignore the regulations and set off without permits. Typical of these was a very determined 20-year-old English-woman from York who was travelling alone and who sent us a very long letter detailing how she did this from Khartoum to the Ugandan border. Disregarding official requirements about special permits, she nevertheless managed to travel all over western and southern Sudan – Nyala, Jebel Marra, Wau, Yambio and Juba. She hitched trucks virtually the entire way (spending many days under thorn bushes in the desert as a result of breakdowns) and slept in or on whatever was available at the time. She missed being sent back to Khartoum, jailed or even deported by the skin of her teeth on a few occasions, but she did make it. She met quite a few other European and Australian travellers who had decided to do just the same (and some of those made it too), so her report wasn't just a one-off. She spent 1-1/2 days in the cab of a truck with a policeman at one stage and was even offered accommodation with his family at the end of the journey!

When this Englishwoman finally got to Juba, several expatriate workers warned her of dire consequences, but she simply walked up to the police there and applied for a permit to go overland to the Ugandan border. After several fruitless days of waiting and being put off, she set off regardless yet again and, although it was touch and go with customs and police at the border, she made it.

You certainly need determination to do this, as well as plenty of time. It's not for those in a hurry or those who worry. On the other hand, her experiences were not a one-off. She met a lot of other travellers en route who were doing the same thing. You need to talk to travellers who have just come from the Sudan to find out exactly what is happening before you set off with high hopes.

That's the situation as far as the south is concerned, but you can still travel extensively in the north of Sudan without problems.

Wadi Halfa-Khartoum-Kosti-Juba-Uganda border

The Kosti-Juba section of this route is off-limits to foreigners at present.

The cheapest and quickest (but the most uninteresting) way of getting between Wadi Halfa and Khartoum is by train. If you're coming through from Egypt on the Lake Nasser steamer, the trains from Wadi Halfa connect with the arrival of the steamers so there's generally no need to spend the night at Wadi Halfa. If you're heading north from Khartoum, the trains depart on Wednesday and Sunday at 7 am. The journey can take as little as 24 hours, but often takes up to 35 hours. The fare is S£12.80 (ordinary 3rd class) and S£14 (special 3rd class). It's a long, dusty journey. These trains north don't always connect with the boats down Lake Nasser, so you may have to wait a day or two in Wadi Halfa.

If you'd prefer to follow the course of the Nile and visit the antiquities (of which there are hundreds), first take a truck from Wadi Halfa to Kerma. This should cost about S£15-20 and take about 1½ days. It's as rough as hell and the nights are very cold, so take plenty of warm clothes. Next take a shared taxi from Kerma to Dongola for S£5, about 2½ hours. There are also direct trucks from Wadi Halfa to Dongola. One traveller got a lift on these for just S£5. From Dongola there are trucks to Karima, but most people take the boat. The Dongola-Karima steamer leaves every Thursday and Sunday, takes three days and costs S£9 (3rd class) and S£14 (2nd class). The schedule can be erratic if supplies of diesel for the boat don't arrive on time. Those who have done this trip recommend it highly. You can get off the boat at villages and towns en route and have a look around – there are plenty of interesting souks. Bean soup and tea are available on the boat. Once you get to Karima, you can take the train to Khartoum. There are trains every Wednesday and Sunday which take about 20 hours and cost S£12 (3rd class). If you just want to go as far as Atbara, the fare is S£5 (3rd class). If you're coming up from the south rather than down from Egypt, first take the train from Khartoum to Karima.

Between Khartoum and Kosti you can take either the train which costs E£3.50 (3rd class) and takes about 20 hours, or an express bus which costs S£7 and takes six to eight hours. The express buses leave three times per day. Remember that you need a special permit for travelling south of Khartoum, so get this before you hop on the train or bus.

Travel south of Kosti – either on the Nile ferry or by road – was prohibited towards the end of Nimeiry's regime, but this route may again open up if the new rulers successfully bring an end to the civil war. Keep your ear to the tracks. At present the only overland route open is to head out west and then south.

In case the government lifts the prohibition on taking the Kosti-Juba Nile steamer, we're including the schedule and fares as they were before the civil war flared up again. It will probably be different but should give you a good idea of what to expect. The old steamer was sunk by the rebels from the south in 1983 so the new boats Juba and Nimule are used. They only have 1st and 2nd classes, but they do the journey in far less time than the old boat used to take. Upstream should take about six to eight days and downstream as little as four. The fares are S£55 (1st class) and S£40 (2nd class). If you want a berth then you must book in advance. There won't be any spare berths on the day of sailing. Meals can be bought on the boat but they're not cheap – S£1.65 for lunch and S£1.75 for dinner. If you want to keep costs down, take some food of your own and a portable stove (putting your own food together helps pass the time). Water comes straight from the Nile and is not boiled. You will also need insect repellant. The toilets get sluiced down once a day but they don't stay in that condition for very long. There are departures two or three times a week in either direction.

If you're heading north from Juba, it's worth hanging around the harbour for a while to talk to the crew members of boats docked there. Some travellers have managed to get free lifts as far north as Malakal. You can save a lot of money this way, as boats from Malakal to Kosti cost S£15 (2nd class) or S£19 (1st class).

Depending on how you take to slow boats, this journey can be interesting – there are plenty of tribal villages and wildlife to be seen en route – or boring. If it turns out to be the latter, you could always pass some time by writing us a letter and telling us about the latest developments. Be careful about taking photographs of tribespeople on the river banks. Many travellers have had film ripped from their cameras; the boat crew are especially sensitive.

Going south from Juba, you have a choice of crossing into Uganda or Kenya. Until Idi Amin was deposed in Uganda, the main route south went directly into Kenya via Torit, Kapoeta, Lokichoggio and Lodwar. It's still possible to go this way if you're looking for a rugged trip, but you should allow at least a week for the journey, and if it's the rainy season then you can forget about it. The Lodwar-Kapoeta section was being upgraded but the civil war has probably put an end to this.

Most travellers these days take the road into Uganda via Nimule. To do this trip you need a permit, which is obtainable in Juba. There are trucks most days from Malakia, two km from Juba, which go to Kenya via Uganda. They cost Ken Sh 300 or S£20 (the drivers prefer Kenyan shillings but they will also accept US$ and £ sterling). The journey takes about 1½ days and there are many army/police checkpoints en route where you will be thoroughly searched. Ugandan army and police will pressure you into giving them certain items of your baggage. A polite but firm refusal and a little bit of humour generally does the trick. It's best to go through in the morning, as they're more likely to be sober then. There are also daily buses between Juba and Nimule which cost S£3.05 and take about six hours.

Khartoum-Kosti-Wau-Yambio-Juba

If you have the time, it's well worth taking the long way round, especially if you make a side trip to the Jebel Marra Mountains (over 3000 metres and the highest mountains in Sudan). The first part of the journey involves taking the train from Khartoum to Wau with a change at Babanusa. Departure times are unreliable and depend on what sort of delays and breakdowns are being experienced further down the line. The journey takes about eight days and costs S£20 (3rd class),

though it is possible to ride on the roof free. Guerrilla fighters of the south were attacking this train in 1984, so it now has a military escort and only runs during the daylight hours. The nights are spent at military posts. You'll see several burnt-out villages en route – the army decided they harboured guerrillas so they drove the people out and razed the houses.

To give you some idea of this journey, we're including a description by David and Heather Bennet at the end of the chapter. It should keep you amused for a while.

The Babanusa-Wau train was no longer running in late 1984 but there were still trains from Khartoum to Nyala once a week, leaving Khartoum on Monday. The fares are S£94 (1st-class sleeper), S£56 (1st class), S£44 (2nd-class special), S£37 (2nd class), S£24 (3rd-class special) and S£18 (3rd class). The roof is free. The journey can take anywhere between 3½ days and three weeks depending on breakdowns, sand on the track, track washed away, waiting for other trains, derailment and general Sudanese inefficiency. You need to book a seat a month in advance!

If you don't fancy the train, there are trucks from Khartoum to Nyala which will cost S£30 on top and S£60 in the cab.

From Wau to Juba there is really only one practicable route. What appears to be the direct route on the maps – Wau-Rumbek-Juba – is almost impassable these days and there's virtually no traffic along it. Apart from that, it goes a little too close to the fighting, and the Anya-nya 2 guerrillas have warned that they will kill all white people on sight. The road you must take is the Wau-Tambura-Yambio-Maridi-Yei-Juba one. You'll need to get rides on trucks from Wau to Yei, but from Yei to Juba you have the choice of truck or bus. There are daily buses in either direction between Yei and Juba. They depart Juba between 6 and 7 am. The total cost of lifts from Wau to Juba shouldn't be much more than S£20. The Wau to Tambura stretch is pretty bad, but the Germans have been busy building a new road from Juba to Yambio so this section is much better. There are incredible views into the Nile and Zaire river basins along the Maridi-Yei section. The best people to approach for lifts along this route are the international aid agencies like UNICEF and FAO, Sudanese government departments and the Sudanese Council of Churches. If you find yourself stuck in Wau, there is a mail truck which leaves every Monday for Juba and takes three to five days – but there's a lot of competition for seats.

To/From Central African Republic

Between August and December there are no trucks between Nyala and Bangui due to the rains, and the police will refuse to grant travel permits to head west at this time. This doesn't mean that you can't make it. If you choose to ignore the permit regulations, there are trucks as far as Rahad el Bhirdie from Nyala for around S£15 which take about 12 hours. You can stay at the police station in Rahad. Ask around here for a guide and animal transport to take you to Umdafog, the border town. Camel trains are the usual transport and the 'service' should cost about S£5 for your bags plus S£30 if you want to ride as well. The 160 km is very hard going through shallow swamps and coarse grasses, but you should be there within five days. Donkeys and guides are available for about S£50.

At Umdafog you can stay at the police station. Food is available at a café.

The journey from Umdafog to Birao (the Sudanese often refer to this town as Daba) takes another 1½ days and involves fording five deep wadis and staying with nomads herding their cattle. You can hire camels – two camels and a guide should cost S£25 per person. These nomads are usually very hospitable and helpful. You eat with them – prime steak, fresh milk and yogurt – and, if you're lucky, they may treat you to some of their tribal music. In Birao you can stay at the *Catholic Missions*, though the people there are not particularly friendly and the mosquitoes are ferocious. There are no cafés in Birao and only limited supplies are available from the market. Shop owners may put meals together for you – such things as meat and spaghetti for CFA 200. There's only one moneychanger and his rates are very poor.

In the wet season there is no transport from Birao to Bangui except flights. The commercial flight costs almost CFA 4500, but the French military regularly fly between Bangui and Birao with supplies for the latter place and return empty. A lot of travellers have managed to talk their way onto a free flight. If you do have to take the commercial flight, don't change money for it in Birao. Instead change when you get to Bangui, and then pay for the flight.

PLACES TO STAY

Hospitality in the Sudan can be incredible and you may well find that half the time you have no need of hotels. Only rarely will you board a train or get a lift on a truck and get off at the other end without an invitation to stay with someone. Offers of money towards your keep will probably be politely refused, but it's important to offer. A thoughtful gift or help doing something, on the other hand, is a different matter, and is the correct way to show your appreciation of the hospitality you have been given. If you neglect your obligations as a guest, these people will start to assume that travellers are a bunch of uncultured yobs and this will reflect on those who come after you. Please keep it sweet. There are very few places like the Sudan left in the world.

ABU HAMED

Next to the railway station there is a *government rest house* with a huge verandah. It costs S£1 per person with use of showers, but to stay here you first need authorisation from the police station, which is about 500 metres from the mosque.

ATBARA

Hotel Astoria, about 500 metres from the railway station, burned down in 1984, but there's a small hotel next to its former site which costs 50 pt per night. It's clean but there are lot of mosquitoes. *Hotel Atbara* has also been recommended. If you're short of money, enquire at the police headquarters, where you may be provided with a bed for the night. Cheap, basic meals can be bought here.

DONGOLA

El Din Hotel costs S£1 per night. A somewhat better place is *Hotel El Minna*, which costs S£2.50 per bed. Good, cheap food is available in the cafés opposite the market.

EL OBEID

Try *John's Hotel*, which has reasonable prices. If you're camping they'll let you use their showers.

JUBA

A lot of people who have been brought up on the romantic Hollywood nonsense of Gordon of Khartoum or Kitchener's campaigns in the Sudan approach Juba with the expectation of seeing something similar to a film set in the Nevada desert. It isn't like that. Juba is definitely a 'one-horse town,' though many people do grow to like it.

For many years the most popular hotel has been the *Hotel Africa*, but it's often full. It costs 85 pt to S£1.25 per bed or 50 pt to sleep on the floor. Because of its popularity, however, the management have got slack and allowed the place to run down. It was recently described by one traveller as 'no better than the boat.' Another traveller drew attention to the 'cholera-style toilets.' The hotel serves food which is good but certainly not the cheapest in town. If you don't like the Africa or can't get in, try the *MTC* (Multi-Service Training Centre or Medical Training Centre), which has 10 beds for S£1.50 each, or you can sleep on the floor for 50 pt. It's behind the football stadium. If you need something more comfortable, try the *Juba Hotel*, which costs S£30. You may be able to stay on the verandah of the Immigration Office free of charge.

For food, go to the *People's Restaurant* or the *Greek Club*. The latter has been recommended by many travellers. Also very popular is *Unity Garden* on May St.

Most of the tap water in Juba comes straight from the Nile and is not filtered. If you drink it you'll get sick.

You must register with the police on arrival in Juba (this costs 10 pt for a revenue stamp). If you're heading south, you must get an exit permit before you leave. These permits are obtainable from Immigration in the same building as the police. They cost 25 pt. Get this permit before you start looking for a lift. Photography permits can be obtained at the Ministry of Information, but they have to be counter-signed by the police.

Outside of Juba, south of Torit, are the **Imetong Mountains**, which were developed as a hill station by the British colonial authorities. If you have time for a detour, it's worth making your way to the *Gilo Guest House* at Gilo which, although it was looted in the civil war, still retains a lot of olde worlde charm. There are no mosquitoes or tsetse flies up there and it's cool. You can forget about this place in the rainy season, however, as the road is impassable.

Malakia, two km from Juba, is where the truck park is located. It's a traditional village and is where much of the life of Juba actually takes place. The market is well worth a visit, especially if you're about to take the boat north to Kosti. Among other things, you can buy portable stoves at S£1-2 and charcoal at 25 pt.

KARIMA

There is a small hotel near the hospital which costs S£1. The restaurant in the

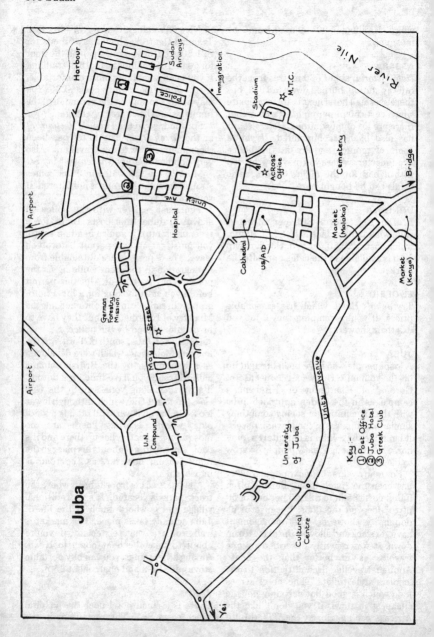

Juba

main square has good food. There are some very interesting ruins nearby (pyramids, etc) which you should visit if you have time. Entry is free.

KASSALA

Since it's no longer possible to enter Ethiopia overland, very few travellers come by this way, but it's a nice place to visit with its sugarloaf mountains and extensive orchards of mango, banana, grapefruit, tangerine, pomegranate and guava. There's an interesting *suq* (market) where you can catch sight of the highly decorated women of the Rashida tribe.

The three cheapest hotels used by most travellers are the *Salim Hotel*, *El Watania Hotel* and the *Bahrain Hotel*. They all cost S£1.50 per night. The first two are close to the market. Others which have been recommended are *Hotel Shark*, near the Ethiopian consulate, *Hotel Abu Tayara* and *Hotel Africa*. The latter costs S£7 a double, but they also have some cheaper beds if you're prepared to share a room with two or three others.

There are plenty of good meat restaurants and cafés where you can sit around and have tea or coffee.

KHARTOUM

If you're coming to Khartoum on the train from Wadi Halfa, it's likely you will be adopted by a Sudanese student on the way and invited to stay with him. If you don't make such a connection, one of the cheapest places to stay is the *Student House* (sometimes called the Youth Hostel). The cost is S£1.80 per night in the dormitory. It has cold-water showers and is easygoing, though the management are sometimes tiresome and you should keep an eye on your baggage. The Student House is open all day. No meals are available.

The *Port Sudan Hotel*, Killiyet At Tibb St, five minutes' walk from the railway station, has become very popular with travellers and has clean, airy and comfortable rooms for S£2 or dormitory beds for

S£1.80. Similar is *El Nahrein Hotel* on El Nahrein St.

Upmarket from these are *El Khalil Hotel*, opposite the bus station, which costs S£3 a single and S£5.30 a double (it's clean and a good place to meet students); *Hotel Lido* at S£7-9 a double; and the *Asia Hotel*, on the side of United Nations Square opposite the mosque, which costs S£4.35 per bed in four-bed rooms, or S£8.70 a double, but only has cold-water showers. The Lido is good value and you can leave gear there safely while you visit other places in Sudan. More expensive than these but very pleasant is *Hotel Shark*, Gamhouriya St east of most of the shops and near Abu Sina St (it has a large sign so you can't miss it). The cost is S£15 a double with own hand basin and shared bathrooms. The new owner, George, is very friendly and helpful.

One of the most popular places for breakfast is the *Araak Hotel* in the middle of town; it has an all-you-can-eat buffet for S£9. Get there early, as they start clearing it up around 10 am. Similar is the *Meridien Hotel*, but they don't like non-residents eating there, so look like you belong. *El Khalil Hotel* and the snack bar across from the American embassy have also been recommended. The *Athenae Café* in the small square behind the British embassy is a popular meeting place and has excellent meat dishes and good sandwiches as well as yoghurt, grapefruit juice and the like. There is an excellent pancake shop around the back of the Araak Hotel and a beefburger place as well. The restaurant next to the Asia Hotel is very good and cheap for breakfasts and lunches. The *Sudan Club*, a sort of hangover from the days of the British Empire, is all right if you can get yourself signed in by a member (S£3 per day). Otherwise it's no longer a viable proposition for travellers, as you have to buy a month's temporary membership to use the facilities and this costs S£40. If you do manage to get in for a day, there's a swimming pool, hot showers

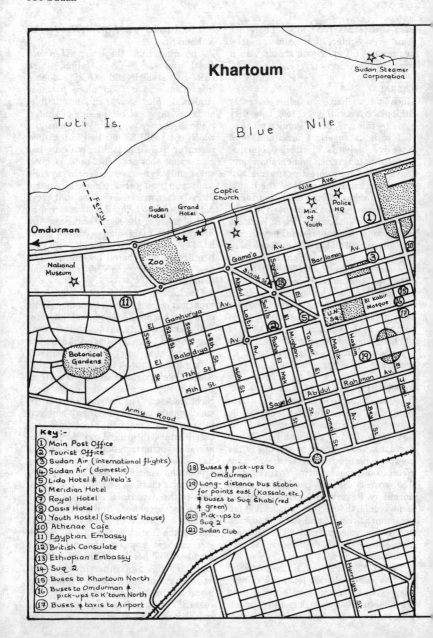

Khartoum

Sudan Steamer Corporation

Tuti Is.

Blue Nile

Omdurman

Nile Ave.

Coptic Church

 Min. of Youth

Police HQ

Ferry

Sudan Hotel

Grand Hotel

National Museum

Zoo

Barllaman Av.

El Gamhuriya Av.

Botanical Gardens

El Balaldiya Av.

Army Road

El Kabir Mosque

U.N. Sq.

Key:-
1. Main Post Office
2. Tourist Office
3. Sudan Air (international flights)
4. Sudan Air (domestic)
5. Lido Hotel & Alikela's
6. Meridian Hotel
7. Royal Hotel
8. Oasis Hotel
9. Youth Hostel (Students' House)
10. Athenae Cafe
11. Egyptian Embassy
12. British Consulate
13. Ethiopian Embassy
14. Suq 2
15. Buses to Khartoum North
16. Buses to Omdurman & pick-ups to K'toum North
17. Buses & taxis to Airport
18. Buses & pick-ups to Omdurman
19. Long-distance bus station for points east (Kassala, etc.) & buses to Suq Shabi (red & green)
20. Pick-ups to Suq 2
21. Sudan Club

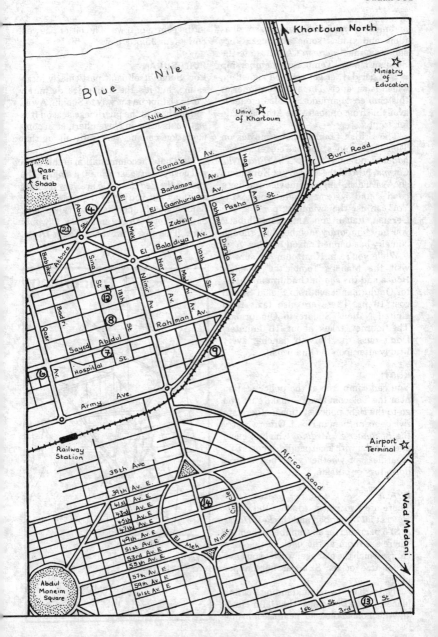

and meals at reasonable prices as well as films and videos some evenings. Very similar is the *American Club* close to the Student House. Temporary membership is S£2 per day, or get yourself signed in, which is cheaper. The average dinner at this club costs around S£5. Ice cream is available from opposite the Athenae Café for 75 pt.

The British Council shows movies on Tuesday evenings, and has current newspapers and magazines. The *Blue Nile Cinema*, beyond the Ministry of Education, shows English-language movies and has a good sound system. A show costs S£1. You can use the swimming pools at the German, Italian and American Clubs if you buy temporary membership, though Nimeiry has banned mixed bathing.

While you're in Khartoum, be sure to visit the **Mahdi's Tomb**, the **Khalifa's House** and the *suq* in Omdurman. Buses for Omdurman leave from Sinkat St and cost 10 pt. There are also taxis from United Nations Square to Omdurman. The journey takes about 10 minutes. Don't miss the Dervish dancing every Friday afternoon in Omdurman.

KOSTI

You can camp free at the police station near the Telecom tower – make sure you go to the right police station as there are five or six of them in Kosti. Otherwise try the *Lokander El Medina*, which is clean and popular with local people. It costs S£3 regardless of whether your bed is in a dormitory or outside.

NYALA

There are two places to stay, the *Dafur Hotel* at 50 pt per bed and the *Rest House* at S£5 per room for any number of people. There's a room at the back of the Rest House which the manager will let you have either free or for S£1 per person per night.

Nyala has two outstanding eating places, *Camp David* near the Dafur Hotel and the 'hole in the wall' near the mosque in the centre of town. The latter has veal cutlets for 95 pt a pair.

PORT SUDAN

Port Sudan itself isn't particularly interesting, but it's the first place definitely worth visiting on the way to Suakin. Avoid coming here in the pilgrimage season (the last boats leave in November), as accommodation can be very difficult at that time.

Most hotel accommodation in this town will cost you at least S£5.50 a single. The staff at the *Red Sea Club* are very friendly and may put you up in their rest house. Some of the cheaper places to try are *Hotel Sinkat*, *Hotel Africa* and *Hotel Olympia Park*. There is, however, a *Youth Hostel*

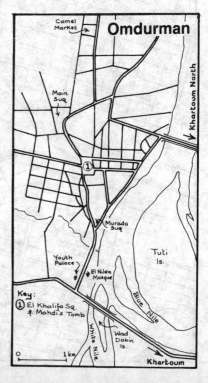

outside of town at Salabona where you can get a dormitory bed for 80 pt per night. Catch a red bus from town to get there. Salabona has an excellent area of shack-type restaurants which sell fried fish, salads, *foul* and banana fritters. Yoghurt is also widely available.

The only place to eat in Port Sudan is the Red Sea Club. Temporary membership costs S£3 and entitles you to use the swimming pool and snooker tables.

The Tourist Office here are very friendly and helpful.

Buses for Suakin depart from Diem Suakin, but it's fairly easy to hitch along the tarmac road.

SENNAR
Hotel Tourism behind the market and opposite the cinema costs S£4 and is very clean but is certainly not the cheapest.

SUAKIN
Before the construction of Port Sudan, Suakin was Sudan's only outlet to the sea. It was abandoned by the British in the 1930s and is now full of decaying coral houses. It's a fascinating place to wander through and, because very few people come this way anymore, you'll probably have the place to yourself. Before you come here you need to get a special permit from the Red Sea Province headquarters in Port Sudan regardless of whether you have already done this in Khartoum. You'll be sent back to Port Sudan if you don't have this.

There is a government rest house in Kitchener's old headquarters, but the story goes that a bunch of Germans had a 'drug-crazed party' there some time ago so they don't take foreigners any more. You can still camp free in the ruins.

The mainland village opposite Suakin is worth visiting.

WADI HALFA
There are two small hotels at the far end of town which cost 50 pt per night. They're pretty basic but all right for a night.

WAU
You can sleep free in the police station yard so long as you don't mind bedding down in the dust along with the mosquitoes and a bunch of interesting criminals. Otherwise try the *Catholic Mission*, which sometimes dispenses a little Christian charity; or the *Youth Hostel*, which costs S£1 per night – no membership card required. For relatively cheap accommodation try *El Nilein Hotel* or the *Riverside Hotel*.

The best place to eat here is the *Unity Restaurant*, where you can get good meals for S£1.50.

YAMBIO
You can stay at the beautifully located *Protestant Mission* for S£2 per night. You can cross the border into Zaire via the market village of Gongura. From the latter place trucks are possible to Isorio.

YEI
Ask at the *Agricultural Research Station* for a place to stay.

JEBEL MARRA MOUNTAINS
Nyala is the jumping-off point for a visit to the Jebel Marra, the highest mountain in Sudan and an extinct volcano with lots of rivers, orchards and good, hilly walking country. No two people's experiences here are the same, but everyone would agree that the hospitality is second to none and the trip is likely to be one of the most memorable you'll ever make. Food and water are no problem and it's very unlikely you will get lost. Local people will insist that you visit their houses, fill your arms with fruit and point you on the right track.

To get there, take a truck from Nyala to Nyatiti and then start walking towards the mountains. Halfway to Quaila, just past the first village, is an excellent waterfall and pool where you can camp and swim. From Quaila you walk to the hot springs, then up to the crater of Jebel Marra; you then go halfway round the rim and down

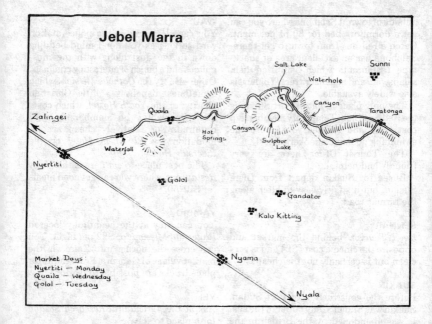

Jebel Marra

Zalingei

Nyertiti

Quaila

Waterfall

Golol

Hot Springs

Canyon

Salt Lake

Waterhole

Sulphur Lake

Canyon

Sunni

Taratonga

Gandator

Kalu Kitting

Nyama

Nyala

Market Days:
Nyertiti — Monday
Quaila — Wednesday
Golol — Tuesday

again to the crater floor. From there you walk out through the canyon to Taratonga, where there is a weekly truck to Nyala. From Taratonga you can visit nearby villages if you have time; Sunni in the north or Gandator and Kalu Kitting in the south-west are some worth visiting. From the latter place you can get back to the tarmac at Nyama, where there is a camp for the German construction gang who have been building the road. They often have transport going to Nyala, and some travellers have been allowed to use their swimming pool. In Quaila the schoolteacher may find accommodation for you and point you in the right direction for the crater.

It's possible to go in the opposite direction, as the sketch map in the 'tourist office' in Nyala suggests. The exact route you take will naturally depend on your inclinations and the time you have, but to give you a good idea of what's possible here's one route:

First you take a truck from Nyala to Menawashi (S£4), which is little more than a truck stop; it does have plenty of food vendors but no rest house. You can sleep in the food vendors' huts. From Menawashi it's a two-hour walk to Marshing over flat scrubland; there you should ask the local schoolteacher about where to sleep (there's usually an empty hut). Food is available at a café here – soup and bread S£1 and tea for 25 piastres. There is a market here on Wednesday and Sunday. A five-hour walk from Marshing will bring you to Melemm, which is a beautiful, fairly large village with a rest house next to the police station. The police are very friendly and will probably supply you with firewood, water and other necessities. There is a market here on Monday and Friday.

From Melemm to Deribat it's an all-night truck ride (S£4-5) through beautiful hills, some of which are so steep it may be necessary to winch the truck up! There's no rest house in Deribat but there are several tea houses, a café and a Monday market. A two-hour walk from Deribat will take you to Jawa, where you should stay in the huge new hospital. It's empty and not used, but there is one bed. The market day is Thursday. About 1½ hours away is Sunni, one of the Jebel Marra's most scenic settlements. A large old rest house there has four beds which cost S£1.50 each. There's no *suq*, but a small shop sells rice, nuts, dates, cigarettes and the occasional chicken. Don't forget to visit the 35-metre-high waterfall behind the power station.

From Sunni it's a five-hour walk/scramble to Lugi with beautiful views, but it gets cold and there are only a few huts in the fields along the way. There's no rest house or market at Lugi, but there is a small store with basic supplies. Next you walk to Taratonga (2¼ hours) through a landscape similar in some ways to the Scottish lowlands – conifers and heather. Taratonga is very picturesque and set on wooded, grassy slopes. There's a market on Saturday and a shop which sells basic supplies. The rest house is in bad repair and it's better to look for an empty hut if you're there in the rainy season. The schoolhouse is another possibility (the teacher speaks English and can put you in touch with guides to the crater).

It's a good idea to get a guide up the crater; otherwise it could take you a lot longer than necessary (three hours instead of five to eight). The same applies between the crater and the next village of Kronga (also known as Kuela). With a guide this should take about five hours (it can take a long time if you get lost).

From Kronga it's a 1½ hour walk to Khartoum (Saturday market) and then another 3½ hours from there to Nyatiti with its well-stocked market, cafés, rest house and transport back to Nyala.

If you don't fancy walking or you have no camping equipment, it's possible to buy donkeys (about S£20) and sell them again when you're ready to leave.

OTHER

If you have mechanical/engineering skills, it's pretty easy to find work in Sudan. Ask around in the engineering and construction companies in Khartoum to see what's on offer. Most of their offices are in Suq 2 or Amarat. Teaching posts at private schools are very easy to get if you have your university/college papers with you – the subject doesn't particularly matter. Rates of pay differ considerably. There's no point, however, in trying to get jobs in government schools. They insist that you apply through their recruiting offices abroad. Don't get too enthusiastic about jobs in Khartoum. It may well be fairly easy to find one, but rents are extortionate.

SLOW TRAIN TO WAU

The Wau (pronounced 'wow') Express covers the 480 km of track between Babanusa and Wau in a little over three days. 'When,' the reader may ask, 'will I ever have occasion to take the Wau Express?' The answer is probably never, unless you are prone to seasickness, detest mosquitoes and are in a 'hurry' to get from Khartoum to Juba overland on the way to Nairobi. In that case the two– to three-week riverboat journey up the Nile to Juba is out and the Wau Express is for you.

Actually, the train trip is only a small part of the journey to Juba. Before it you have to get from Khartoum to Babanusa. This is accomplished by taking a fairly comfortable and punctual train from Khartoum via Kosti. At Babanusa you change trains and board the Wau Express – if it is there and running, of course.

Heather and I were lucky; the train was standing in the station ready to go. It looked as if it were built about the same time as the railway, the early 1900s, and consisted of a steam locomotive and about 25 decrepit carriages. We were told it would leave in an hour's time at 9 pm. Feeling extravagant, we decided to splurge $5 on a couple of 2nd-class tickets (there was no 1st class that day). This entitled us to a comfortable, reserved seat in a six-seat compartment. The compartment was empty when we boarded and, expecting the train to leave soon, we bedded down for the night hoping that no one else would enter. No one else did, but then since the train was still sitting in the station the next morning, this was understandable. Around 7 am, eight Sudanese, who also had the wisdom to travel 2nd class, crowded into our compartment and the train chugged out of the station.

Although initially annoyed about the over-booking of the compartment, we were pleased with our choice when we saw the conditions in the 3rd and 4th classes. Third class consisted of a carriage filled with wooden benches. The benches were jammed and every square cm of floor space was covered with squatting people and their baggage. The luggage racks were filled with children. Fourth class, a cattle car, was beyond description.

The corridors of the 2nd-class carriages were crammed with people, making passage impossible. We were therefore forced to use the window to enter and exit our compartment. This would have made it difficult to get to the dining car when the train was moving but, as someone had forgotten to attach the dining car, this was of no great consequence. On the roof of the train there must have been about a thousand people. They were the lucky ones as far as space was concerned, but that must have been outweighed by the intense heat of the day and the cold of the night. 'Why are there so many people?' I asked my fellow passengers. I was told that the twice-weekly Wau Express was making its first trip in three weeks.

So the journey began. The train travelled very slowly to start with. Later we came to the bracing realisation that it was travelling at top speed: 12 km per hour. Every 25 km or so the train would stop at a station for an hour or two. This was so the engine could be watered and rested. Each time, many of the passengers would disembark. Fires were built, pots produced and food cooked. Children and clothes were washed and five times a day Mecca was faced in prayer. A quick blast of the whistle and the train was off again with hundreds of people scrambling to get back on.

We actually welcomed these delays because they gave us the opportunity to stretch, cool down and go out for food and water. Water was usually available, but food was limited to boiled eggs, bananas and raw beans. These were sold by scores of vendors who would appear from nowhere at even the most remote stations.

Halfway to Wau, in the middle of an uninhabited, roadless desert, the train suddenly stopped yet again, this time for no noticeable reason. Mechanical failure, we were told soothingly. After a few hours we began to get a little uneasy. Was the engine beyond repair? If so, would we have to complete our journey on foot? Happily the answer to both questions was no. Eight hours later the problem was apparently solved and we were again on our way. During the last hundred or so km a number of extra stops were made. These were due to the antics of the playful Dinka tribe, who enjoy placing large boulders on the track.

Finally, over three long days, thoroughly sick of our monotonous diet and crowded sitting and sleeping arrangements, we wheezed into Wau station. Heather and I looked at each other, flushed with the special relief that accompanies great endeavors. 'Wau!' we said.

Swaziland

Swaziland is one of the only three monarchies remaining on the African continent and until King Sobhuza II died at the end of 1982 he was the world's longest-reigning monarch. The country, like Lesotho, had its origins in the early years of the 19th century when the Zulu nation was expanding. Swaziland's first king, Sobhuza I, was able to merge refugees fleeing from the Zulu with his own people and create a powerful military nation which withstood Zulu pressure. By the time he died in 1839, Sobhuza ruled over an area twice the size of the present country. It was whittled down to its present area by the Boers between 1840 and 1880, and after a protracted period of rivalry between the British and the Boers for political control over what remained of the country, it became a British Protectorate. The king's powers throughout the colonial period were restricted to internal civil matters.

The loss of sovereignty wasn't the only thing that happened, however. In the land rush of the 1880s virtually all the natural resources were placed in the hands of concession hunters, and in 1907 all but 38% of the land was expropriated from the Swazi peasantry. The land which was taken was distributed among concessionaries and the monarchy in about equal amounts, but the majority of the Swazi crown's land had been sold off to white settlers by 1930. British interest in the colony was minimal right up to independence, and the development of cash cropping on small holdings by the Swazi peasantry was actively discouraged by white farmers and mining concerns, who preferred to have a pool of labour available for manual work. The arrangement suited the monarchy in many ways, since the growth of a system of Swazi small holdings would have threatened the Swazi king's traditional rights over the land and his subjects. The king was entitled to demand an annual tribute in the form of labour or crops and also to allocate land to peasants or evict them from it as the case may be. Since independence, however, Sobhuza pursued a policy of buying back concessionary land and converting it to Swazi Nation Land for the use of the nation as a whole.

There was a brief flirtation with a constitutional monarchy after independence, but in 1972 – when the parties of urban workers and intellectuals collected sufficient votes to begin to erode what had, until then, been the overwhelming dominance of the Imbokodvo (traditionalist party) – the king suspended the constitution, dissolved all political parties and declared a state of emergency which has remained in force ever since. Sobhuza then banned trade union meetings. The country is now governed by tribal assemblies, who handle the affairs of state in the traditional manner in the Royal Cattle Kraal at Lombamba outside of Mbabane. The king and his ministers sit, in traditional dress, on the ground facing the sacred hills across the valley; and the audience, regardless of rank, sits in front of the king while measures are debated and the king issues decrees. Critics of this ancient form of government are answered with the claim that direct rule by the monarchy has resulted in Swaziland being one of Africa's most stable countries. While this is undoubtedly true, popular resistance is surfacing in many quarters.

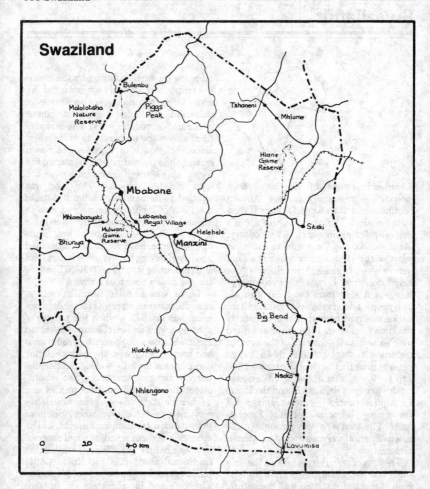

In 1975, striking railway workers marched on Lobamba only to be dispersed with tear gas. Some 400 teachers did the same thing in 1977, which resulted in the banning of the National Teachers' Association. Further demonstrations by school and university students with parental support took place later in the year. These were broken up by baton charges and tear gas, but in the rioting which followed, a lot of government property sustained considerable damage. There has also been discontent among professional and white-collar workers.

Certainly the post-independence government of Mozambique didn't think much of the Swazi political system, and condemned it as western-orientated and capitalist. Relations between the two countries were tense in the late 1970s but have since improved, if only because Swaziland, in order to maintain some degree of economic independence from South Africa, needs the cooperation of Mozambique. The railway line from Mbabane to Maputo carries a large proportion of Swazi exports to the outside world. Yet while Swaziland cultivates friendship with Mozambique, the growth of its security forces in recent years has been dramatic. The Swazi regular army now numbers over 5000, with several thousand part-timers in reserve. These troops have generated widespread resentment both in rural and urban areas by their undisciplined behaviour at roadblocks. There is also a more disciplined para-military Mobile Police Unit numbering several thousand as well as armed Security Police suspected of collaboration with their South African opposites. Both these units are under the control of the prime minister, General Maphevu Diamini, a staunch royalist who is also the army and police chief. Under the state of emergency which has been in force since 1973, a 60-day detention-without-trial law has been freely used to jail or muzzle political dissidents.

King Sobhuza II died in late 1982 and, in keeping with Swazi traditions, a strictly enforced 75-day period of mourning was announced by Dzwelie (Great She-Elephant), the most senior of the king's 100 wives. No soil could be tilled, no harvest reaped, cattle could be milked and tended but not slaughtered, and only commerce essential to the life of the nation was allowed. Sexual intercourse was banned under pain of being flogged. These devout observances, however, didn't stop the first stirrings of a power struggle within the inner circles of the monarchy. The choice of a successor wasn't easy. Sobhuza, through his many wives, had fathered over 600 children, some 200 of them princes and, in theory, contenders for the throne. The first choice was an 18-year-old student at an American university, but this was quickly scotched as a result of a whispering campaign within the harem. The second choice was a 14-year-old boy named Makhosinvelo. In order to protect him from palace intrigues and to train him for the responsibilities he will have to assume in due course, he has been removed to a secret hideaway behind barbed-wire security fences and heavily armed police and army guards. Here he will be educated in Swazi customs and traditions by royal counselors, tribal elders, soothsayers and others appointed by the Great She-Elephant. He will also be taught by selected western tutors and will eventually attend an overseas university to complete his education. In the meantime, the Great She-Elephant will act as regent and govern the country with the help of the *liqoqo*, a traditionalist governing council appointed by Sobhuza a few months before he died.

Though Swaziland leans heavily on tradition in some areas of life, it has been developed with skill and has a healthy economy. The Japanese built the Mbabane-Maputo railway in 1964, and it now carries 80% of the country's exports. Pineapple and citrus orchards have been established and large areas have been irrigated for the cultivation of rice, sugar cane and bananas. Diamond mining has been going on since the early 1970s; the De Beers company of South Africa has pumped in large amounts of capital in search of the stones. Relations between the 9000 white farmers (who own much of the best farming land – 37% in total) and the monarchy are cordial. In contrast to this, political refugees from South Africa are barely tolerated because of fears that they will radicalise potential and possible military action by South Africa should the country become a base for their activities.

The main reason for Swazi cooperation with the South African regime is that over 80% of the foreign capital invested in the country comes from South Africa and the country is part of the Rand Monetary Unit. As a result, all Swaziland's imports, exports and industries are virtually controlled by Pretoria. It's sometimes said that South Africa looks on Swaziland as its most successful 'homeland.' Indeed

Swaziland is presently negotiating to obtain KaNgwane, the South African 'homeland' for Swazis who live in the republic. If this happens, South Africans of Swazi descent will automatically loose their South African citizenship and become nationals of Swaziland.

FACTS

Surrounded on three sides by South Africa and on the other by Mozambique, Swaziland sits on the edge of the southern African escarpment. Beautiful rugged mountains in the west descend to low-lying plains in the east. Abundant rainfall in the mountains falls principally during the summer months (October to March). Ninety percent of the population is Swazi, the remainder being Zulu, Tonga, Shangaan and European.

VISAS

Required by all except nationals of Commonwealth countries, Belgium, Denmark, Finland, Iceland, Irish Republic, Israel, Italy, Luxembourg, Netherlands, Norway, Portugal, South Africa, Sweden and the USA. If you intend to stay longer than two months, you must apply for a Temporary Residence Permit from the Chief Immigration Officer, Box 372, Mbabane. Where there are no Swazi embassies or consulates, visas can be obtained from British embassies (eg in Johannesburg).

You must have a valid cholera vaccination certificate for entry.

Visas for Mozambique are obtainable from the embassy in Mbabane (near the *Highland View Hotel*). They cost E 5 and take about a week to come through. Refusals are many, but people do get visas and the embassy staff are friendly, so it's worth trying.

MONEY

US$1 = E 0.97

The unit of currency is the lilangeni (plural emalangeni) = 100 cents. The lilangeni is on a par with the South African rand, which is also legal tender in Swaziland. However, Swazi currency is hard to get rid of in South Africa – banks there will discount it by 10% if you want it changed into rand. There are no restrictions on the import or export of local currency.

LANGUAGE

The official languages are SiSwati and English. SiSwati is very close to Zulu and the two speakers can understand each other. Until the early 1970s, school children learned Zulu instead of SiSwati because there were no textbooks in SiSwati. All education is supposedly in English for other subjects, so any Swazi who has been to school will know at least a little English.

Some helpful phrases in SiSwati:

hello	*sawubona*
yes	*yebo*
how are you	*unjani*
I'm fine	*ngikona*
thank you	*siyabonga*

Sawubona literally means 'I see you.' *Yebo* is sometimes said as a greeting and sometimes as the response.

It is the custom to greet everyone you meet. Often you will also be asked, *U ya phi?* (Where are you going?).

FOOD

Traditional Swazi food is cornmeal porridge and stew. Swazis are great lovers of meat – meaning beef. The closest you get to real Swazi food is in one of the innumerable cafés, where you should order either stew and porridge or curry and porridge. You can find these cafés everywhere. You might want to try 'bunny chow' – a dish from the Indians of South Africa. It consists of half a loaf of bread with the inside torn out so that the crust forms a bowl with stew inside.

There are many inexpensive Portuguese restaurants. If you go to one of them and want to splurge, try the chicken *peri-peri* or, better, the famous Mozambique prawns. For an inexpensive lunch, ask for a *prego*.

Fast-food addicts will be pleased to know that there are *Kentucky Fried Chicken* outlets in both Mbabane and Manzini!

GETTING THERE & AROUND

Air

Royal Swazi Airways flies to Blantyre (Malawi), Lusaka (Zambia), Madagascar and Mauritius as well as to Johannesburg and Durban.

Road

There are regular and punctual buses all over the country. Where roads are sealed the buses are quite comfortable. On dirt roads you should expect a bumpy and dusty journey, especially towards the end of the dry season. Most buses are modern vehicles with fares averaging around 3½c per km. Mbabane-Manzini costs E 1.45. The bus from Lavumisa to Manzini departs daily at 7.30 am and costs E 4.45 (on the route coming up from Natal).

Hitching is easy even in remote areas. You must be determined though. Swazis will jump out in front of a vehicle to get a lift. Most rides are free. If you're going to hitch to Swaziland, bear in mind that many people from Johannesburg go there on Friday for the weekend and come back on Sunday. Hitching anywhere along the road to Benoni (just outside Johannesburg) on Fridays is a 'snap.' It's a large, well-travelled motorway. At other times the traffic can be pathetic and it will take you ages to get there. The two main points of entry are Bulembu (via Baberton), open from 7 am to 4 pm (nowhere to stay but a picturesque route); and Oshoek, the main crossing point, open from 6 am to 10 pm.

If you're heading to Durban and other parts of Natal, try hitching from Helehele, about eight km from Manzini where the road to south-eastern Swaziland and Natal forks from that going to Maputo.

Rail

The railway line from Mbabane to Maputo is for freight only, but some travellers have managed to get lifts on it by speaking to the driver or the guard. There is a connection by a twice-weekly bus in either direction between Mbabane/Manzini and Maputo via Namaacha. From Maputo the first bus leaves on Friday at 9 am and Sunday at 11 am and costs 200 metacal (sometimes there's a bus on Tuesday as well). From Lomohasha (on the Swazi side of the border – a two-km walk from the Mozambique border) there is a bus at 1.30 pm which costs Rand 3.50 and reaches Manzini at 5 pm. South African railways (SAR) also run buses between the republic and Swaziland. Enquire at the SAR office, Coventry Crescent, Mbabane.

Border

All the border posts with South Africa are now staffed on both sides. The smaller border posts close at 4 pm while the larger ones, including Mahamba, Oshoek and Lavumisa, remain open until 10 pm. If you go through Oshoek on Friday evening (from South Africa) or Sunday afternoon (from Swaziland), expect delays as the weekend tourist traffic is heavy at those times. Other border posts are quiet all the time so there are no delays. No customs duties are payable on anything you bring into the country, but don't bring fresh meat, fruit or vegetables. (One traveller turned up at the border with about Rand 400-worth of booze in his car, but the only concern of the customs officer was whether he had any oranges!)

PLACES TO STAY

Travellers on a tight budget could do worse than ask the principal of a school for a classroom for the night, particularly in rural areas. Swazis are very friendly and hospitable, and few would refuse. You would probably get a brick-built room and some sort of toilet and water supply, almost certainly clean.

You may be able to find somewhere for the night with Peace Corps volunteers. Many of them are teachers at local schools, so it might be an idea to enquire there. Although most PVCs are willing to help out, they exist on very little money so you must be prepared to supply your own food and contribute to meals, and don't overstay your welcome.

You can camp anywhere, but it's important to introduce yourself to people living nearby to reassure them that you're not a danger to them and that you have not come to steal their cattle. Be careful with water as there is a lot of cholera and bilharzia about.

Hotels are expensive, though there are a number of smaller ones which don't cost too much and are clean and comfortable. Forget about the Holiday Inns, which are even more expensive than their South African counterparts. However, they do have regular special events when you pay a fixed price and then eat vast quantities of food – they don't appear to mind how many times you go back to the buffet.

Apart from the towns described at length later, the following places offer relatively inexpensive accommodation:

Hlatikulu

Assegai Inn (tel 16). Dinner, bed and breakfast from E 7.80. Good bar and plenty of local colour.

Mankayane

Inyatsi Inn (tel 12). Dinner, bed and breakfast for E 11.50 a single and E 23 a double.

Nhlangano

Robin Inn (tel 160). Bed and breakfast for E 8.40 a single and E 14.90 a double.

Lavumisa

Lavumisa Hotel (tel 7). Bed and breakfast for E 7.35 a single and E 14.70 a double, both with attached bath.

Siteki

Stegi Hotel (tel 26). Dinner, bed and breakfast for E 12.10 a single and E 22 a double. There is a good bar. Even cheaper is the *Bamboo Inn* next to the Stegi Hotel; it's very inexpensive.

Pigg's Peak

Highlands Inn (tel 12). Bed and breakfast for E 10.50 a single and E 20 a double, both with bath.

MBABANE

The capital of Swaziland, Mbabane is a small, pleasant city though heavily South-African influenced. South Africans flock here in droves at the weekends to see films banned by their own censors, to visit the brothels and to gamble at the Holiday Inn's casino. The same kind of thing happens in Manzini, the second largest town, but to a lesser extent. Because of this, hotel accommodation is geared to affluent weekenders and it's difficult to find cheap places to stay.

It's advisable not to wander round alone or even in small groups at night because of gangs known as *sidlani*. They are named after the question which they ask – *Utsi sidlani?* (What do you think we eat?).

One of the best places to stay is the *Thokoza Church Centre*, Mhlanhla Rd (tel 42805), which is non-denominational and run by Mennonites. A nice clean room with hot showers costs E 3.50; a double costs E 10. Meals are available at reasonable prices. If the place is being used for a conference, you may have to stay in a dormitory (E 2) instead of a private room. It's a good place to meet Peace Corps volunteers and VSO. The Centre is behind the police station and near Mater de la Rosa High School; from Allister Miller St turn onto Walker St and go past Johnston St and Markett St. Go over the bridge, turn left at the police station and then keep left along a dirt road up the hill for about 10 minutes. It's signposted. Another cheap place to stay is the *Mbabane Youth Centre*, Msunduza (tel 42176), which costs E 4.50 per person. From the police station turn right (south) and go down about one km.

More upmarket is the *Jabula Inn*,

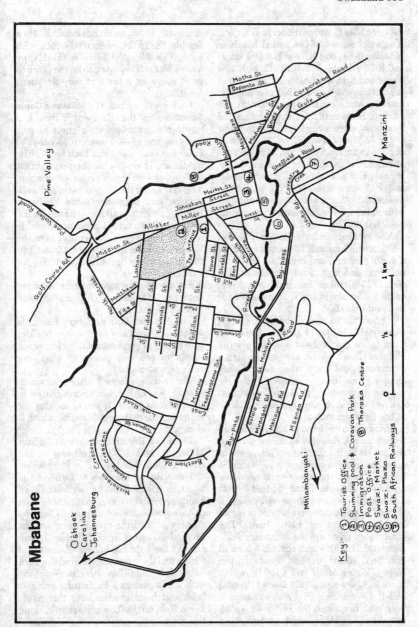

Mbabane

Key:-
① Tourist Office
② Swimming pool ✱ Caravan Park
③ Immigration ⑧ Thoroza Centre
④ Post Office
⑤ Swazi Market
⑥ Swazi Plaza
⑦ South African Railways

Allister Miller Drive, next door to Wimpy's. It's the cheapest of the actual hotels in Mbabane and good value at E 8.50 a single and E 16 a double without bath, or E 10 a single and E 18 a double with bath. There is a restaurant, and the bar is a popular place for white-collar workers. The *Studio 21* disco rages until 2 am on weekdays and 5 am on weekends. Slightly more expensive is the *Highland View Hotel* (tel 42461), about one km from the town centre on the Manzini road overlooking Ezulwini Valley. It costs E 9 a single (E 13 at weekends) and E 19 a double (E 27 a double at weekends). All the rooms have their own bath. There are a restaurant, swimming pool, bar and disco.

Also in Mbabane is the *Tavern Hotel* (tel 42361), which costs E 13 a single and E 26 a double for bed and breakfast (charcoal grill, bar and nightclub). The *Swazi Inn* (tel 42235), three km from Mbabane, costs E 15 a single and E 20 a double for bed and breakfast.

If you want to camp, *Timbali Caravan Camp* (tel 61156) is 11 km from Mbabane (turn off at the Midway Spar before the Holiday Inn). There are rondavels, a swimming pool and a shop here. Other camping facilities, A-frame family-size cabins, a swimming pool and restaurant can be found at *Smokey Mountain Village* in the Ezulwini valley.

Many of the weekend or holiday visitors from South Africa stay at one or other of the hotels in the Ezulwini Valley, about nine km from town where the casino is located. None of these places come anywhere close to being budget hotels and, unless you have some well-pressed, snappy gear, chances are you're going to look pretty out of place here. The cheapest of them are the *Mantenga Falls Hotel* (tel 61049), which costs E 8 for bed only or E 10 for bed and breakfast; the *Happy Valley Motel* (tel 61061), which costs E 8.50 a single (E 11 at weekends) and E 13 a double (E 17 at weekends), both with bath; and the *Diamond Valley Motel* (tel 61041/2), which costs E 10 a

single (E 15 at weekends) and E 12 a double (E 18 at weekends), both with bath. The *Why Not Disco* at the Happy Valley Motel is reported to be the place to go if you want a taste of very decadent Swaziland.

On the other hand, the **Mlilwane Game Sanctuary** in the Ezulwini Valley has rondavels, dormitory-style guest houses and camping sites. You must pay first to enter the sanctuary, and then for accommodation. There is a barbeque (you must bring your own meat) and a small shop. You can watch the hippos being fed each evening and there are some Bushman paintings within walking distance of the accommodation area. Horses are available for rent. Game isn't as plentiful as in the Kruger National Park (South Africa), but the landscape is beautiful. Tel 61037 for details and prices.

For cheap, Portuguese-style food try *Lourenco Marques* at Gilfilliam St and Allister Miller.

The Tourist Office, Swazi Place, is worth visiting. They offer a free booklet with plenty of good suggestions for walks, things to see and places to visit (hot springs, waterfalls).

The Swazi **market**, although worth visiting, has high prices and is geared to the weekend trade. If you're looking for crafts, try the market at Manzini, which is cheaper.

There is a British Embassy on Allister Miller St, and a USA Embassy in the Central Bank Building.

The **National Museum** at Lobamba is worth a visit, with its well-displayed handicraft exhibits, explanations of Swazi culture and historical displays. Close by along the 'Lozitha' road (turn left at Lobamba coming from Mbabane), you can see the light blue dome of the **Royal Palace** and the mountains behind it, where Sobhuza is said to have been buried along with a live goat and his faithful retainer (who had been groomed for this ritual death from birth). The university is along this road.

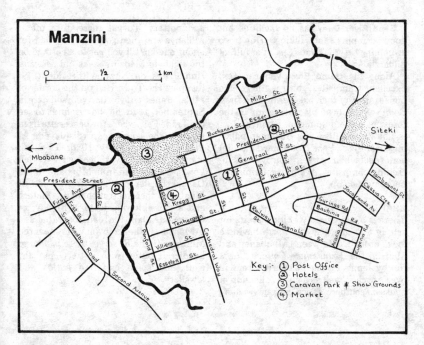

MANZINI

The cheapest places to stay here are the *Highway Motel* (tel 506113), about seven km east of Manzini, which costs E 9.50 a single and E 12.50 a double (restaurant, bar and nightclub); and *Uncle Charlie's Hotel* (tel 52297), opposite the show-grounds on the edge of town, which costs E 7.85 a single and E 13.70 a double for bed and breakfast. Another place worth trying if you want to stay for a week or more is *Mrs Smith's* boarding house on Meintuust St past the Mozambique restaurant, over the bridge and on the left at the corner. If you prefer to camp, *Paradise Camp Site* is seven km from Manzini on the Mbabane road near Matsapha and the university.

If you're looking for something up-market, try the colonial-style *George*.

For cheap, Portuguese-style food try the *Mozambique* on Meintuust St or the *Gil Vincente*.

An absolute 'must' is the **market** on Thursday and Friday mornings. Get there as early as possible (at dawn if possible). The rural people bring their handicrafts to sell to retailers.

CAMPING & TREKKING

Since most people in the rural areas of Swaziland walk for transport, there are trails all over the country. As long as you observe local customs and don't camp near houses or graveyards, and as long as you ask the chief's permission to camp, you are limited only by your imagination.

Mbuluzi Game Sanctuary past Simunya has camping facilities, water, showers and marked trails for hiking along the mountain ridges and along the river bed.

Hlane Game Sanctuary on the road to Simunya has camping facilities and 'a friendly giraffe who likes to have his photo taken.' Other game includes rhino and buck.

Sand River Dam has no facilities but good camping and hiking. Don't go swimming in the water as it's full of bilharzia.

Along the **Usutu River** you can find excellent campsites, but if there are houses nearby then ask permission first. Some of the best places are up in the forest past the pulp mill at Bhunya.

The **Komati River** has Bushman paintings near Pigg's Peak (you'll need a guide) and spectacular gorges nearby with incredible campsites. Again, ask permission before you camp.

CRAFTS

There is a wide variety of local crafts for sale in Swaziland so it's worth having a look around. Between Mbabane and Manzini the *Tishweshwe Cottage Crafts* run by Jenny Thorne has curios from all over Africa as well as a good collection of books on southern Africa, mohair sweaters and pottery. To get there, turn off at Mhlanya and then go down the road for about one km till you get to a cottage on the right. In Manzini check out *Manzini Handicrafts* on Ngwane (President) St just past the Town Hall on the corner of Mhlakurane St. If you find yourself here in September, go to the showgrounds to see the Trade Fair, where the best crafts from all over the country are displayed. At Pigg's Peak there are 10 or 12 small stands selling Swazi carved wooden bowls. On the road from Mbabane to the Oshoek border post (14 km outside of Mbabane) there is a mohair rug factory and a glass-blowing factory. Finally, at **Mantenga Falls** on the road from Mbabane to Manzini, in the Ezulwini Valley near the Mlilwane Game Reserve, there is a large handicraft outlet with pottery, mohair, cloth and some imported curios and jewellery.

Tanzania

Tanzania came into existence as a result of the political union between mainland Tanganyika and the offshore islands of Zanzibar and Pemba. The two halves of the union attained independence from Britain separately, the mainland in 1961 and Zanzibar in 1963. Penetration of the interior by Europeans was delayed until the 19th century, though the coastal area had long been the scene of rivalry, first between the Portuguese and Arab traders, and later between the various European maritime nations. The mainland was first taken over by the German East Africa Company in 1885 but was administered directly by the German government from 1891 until WW I, when the League of Nations mandated the territory to Britain. Britain continued to administer the country until independence, after the mandate was renewed by the United Nations. Zanzibar, once the centre of the East African slave trade and ruled by sultans of Omani extraction, became a British Protectorate in 1890. The union between the two independent nations came about a year after the independence of Zanzibar, following the toppling of the Sultan and his replacement by a Revolutionary Council formed by the Afro-Shirazi Party. The country is now a one-party state headed by Julius Nyerere – the president since independence and undoubtedly one of the most sincere and inspiring leaders ever to emerge from Africa. That he remains popular has been amply demonstrated in the presidential elections of 1975 and 1980, when he was picked by 92% and 93% of the vote respectively. None of his party colleagues have come even close to matching this performance, as witnessed by the large numbers of ministers and MPs who lost their seats in the various general elections held since independence.

Nyerere is perhaps best known for his individual brand of socialism based on the Ujamaa village – a collective agricultural venture run along traditional African communal lines. The villages were intended to be socialist organisations created by the people and governed by those who lived and worked in them. Basic goods and tools were to be held in common and shared among members while each individual had the obligation to work on the land. Nyerere's proposals for education were seen as an essential part of this scheme and were designed to foster constructive attitudes to cooperative endeavour, stress the concept of social equality and responsibility for service, and counter the tendency towards intellectual arrogance among the educated. Nyerere also sought to ensure that those in political power did not develop into an exploitative class by banning government ministers and party officials from holding shares or directorships in companies and from receiving more than one salary. They were also prohibited from owning houses which were rented out. Though all has not been plain sailing and it can hardly be said that corruption has been wiped out, the country does seem to suffer much less from it than other African states.

The Ujamaa villages have undergone considerable transformation since their inception. In the early days, progressive farmers were encouraged to expand in the hope that other peasants would follow their example, but this resulted in little improvement in rural poverty and the enrichment of those who were the recipients of state funds. This approach was abandoned in favour of direct state control of planning, organisation, and the resettlement of peasants into well-planned villages with the object of modernising and monetising the agricultural sector of the economy. The settlement schemes were well provided with all the necessary requirements for healthy living and modern husbandry such as drinkable water supplies, rural health schemes, educational facilities, fertilisers, high-yielding seed and, where possible, irrigation. The new approach was again a failure. Many peasants were hostile to what they regarded as compulsory resettlement, lack of consultation in the decision-making process and continuing corruption. The schemes also proved to be beyond the country's means – Tanzania is one of the world's poorest countries. Prior to independence, Tanzania's economy was one of subsistence, with only sisal and groundnuts making any contribution to export earnings. Mechanisation of agriculture affected less than 5% of the 4½ million hectares under cultivation. Since then, droughts, poor harvests, massive increases in the price of oil and the cost of the Ugandan expedition have all contributed to Tanzania's woes.

With the failure of the second scheme, a third was adopted based on persuading the peasants to amalgamate their small holdings into large, communally owned farms using economic incentives and shifting the emphasis onto self-reliance. In this way the benefits reaped by members of such Ujamaa settlements were a direct reflection of the dedication of those who lived there. Despite its critics, this scheme has been very successful and has prompted the government to adopt a policy of compulsory villagisation of the entire rural population. Only by doing this has it been able to head off economic disaster, since rich western nations have been very tardy about providing funds for investment despite

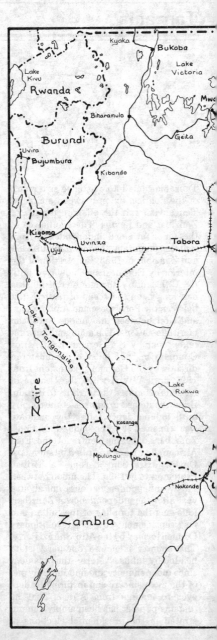

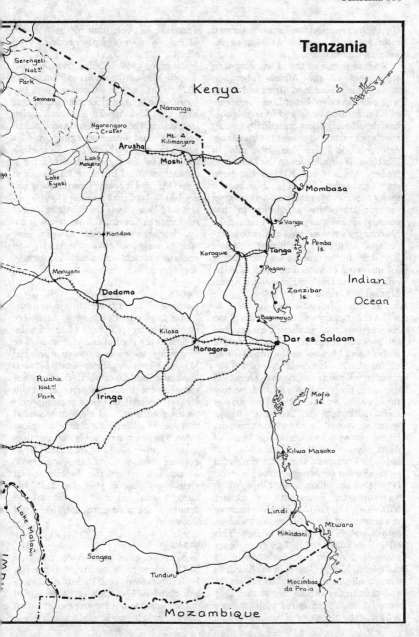

their verbal support for Tanzanian armed intervention to oust Idi Amin in neighbouring Uganda.

Nyerere is one of the most outspoken supporters of the African liberation movements in southern Africa and, along with other so-called Front Line Presidents of Zambia, Botswana and Mozambique, has played a large part in gradually forcing the Smith regime to accept the inevitable and concede black majority rule in Zimbabwe. His influence on the Zimbabwe leaders, Mugabe and Nkomo, has been considerable and has doubtless been a major factor in Mugabe's moderate stand towards the white population in that country. He has also powerfully influenced his country's non-aligned stance in international affairs – the Chinese People's Republic, for instance, were responsible for financing and building the TAZARA railway from Dar es Salaam to Kapiri Mposhi in Zambia.

The most dramatic recent event to affect the country was the invasion of the Kagera district of northern Tanzania and the bombing of the Lake Victoria ports of Bukoba and Mwanza by the armed forces of Idi Amin. Tanzania responded by invading Uganda with the object of deposing the dictator who had by that time become an international embarrassment. Although the Tanzanian troops were welcomed with open arms by Ugandans who had borne the brunt of Amin's years of virtual genocide, and although Tanzania's action was applauded by most other countries around the world (a notable exception being Libya, which was supplying Amin with his military hardware), the OAU refused to endorse the action and Tanzania was left with an estimated bill of US$500 million. This effectively wiped out its foreign currency reserves. Nyerere certainly assisted his old friend, Milton Obote, in the elections which took place subsequently in Uganda, and though few would doubt that they were fair and even fewer wish to see a return to the atrocities of Amin's regime,

Tanzania has been denied the financial assistance it so urgently needs to keep afloat.

Relations with Kenya remain cool despite Moi's official visit to Tanzania in 1979. The border between the two countries has been closed for years, ever since the East African Economic union (comprising Tanzania, Kenya and Uganda) split up amid bitter wrangling over its assets in the early 1970s. Tanzania's involvement in Uganda has become a delicate political dilemma for Kenya at the OAU, and it seems that the issue will not be resolved for a number of years yet. It would be a pity if one of Africa's most moderate and reasonable post-independence leaders were to be cast aside for mere lack of funds to cover the cost of an operation which was almost universally applauded.

FACTS

Because of the large variation in altitude, Tanzania's climate ranges from the languorous tropical heat of the coastal region to the cool of the highlands. The long rainy season is between April and May, with another shorter season between November and December. Tanzania has some of the most extensive and well-stocked national parks and game reserves on the continent, and it's recommended that you set aside plenty of time to explore them. They're considerably cheaper than those of either Kenya or Zambia as far as accommodation costs are concerned. Mount Kilimanjaro can be climbed at almost any time of year outside of the rainy season, but the best months are January, February, September and October.

VISAS

Visas are required by all except nationals of Commonwealth countries, Denmark, Finland, Iceland, Irish Republic, Norway and Sweden. Nationals of South Africa are not admitted. All visitors must get an entry permit before arrival, though this is usually obtainable at the border or at the airport on arrival by those holding passports of Commonwealth countries.

A three-month, multiple-entry visa costs Sh 100 in Nairobi, Kenya, and is issued on the spot.

If you have South African stamps in your passport, these are going to cause a lot of problems and may result in you being sent back to the nearest capital city to get a visa (regardless of nationality). Any evidence in your passport or elsewhere that you have worked in South Africa will result in refusal to let you enter. Some of the border officials recognise Botswana and Zimbabwe exit stamps issued at the borders with South Africa and will assume that you have been there even if you don't actually have any South African stamps in your passport. If that happens, expect trouble. We had one letter from a British national who had to get a new passport in Swaziland from the British High Commission there. When he got to Tanzania they refused him entry even though he reasoned with them all day and despite the fact that there were no South African stamps in the passport. They were also very unpleasant towards him. If you think you will encounter any problems like this, visit a Tanzanian embassy before you arrive at the border and get a visa or entry permit.

Visas and entry permits can be renewed at any immigration office in large towns and cities while you wait. There is no fee and no photos are required.

You may be asked to show an onward ticket and/or sufficient funds (usually US$400) at the border on entry, but most people get through without any problems in this respect. Officials at the Tunduma (Zambia/Tanzania) border are heavy duty according to most travellers. (The more florid description of them used in the last edition apparently upset them, according to one traveller who spent most of the day talking to them. He wrote saying they were a bunch of very pleasant guys underneath the official facade.)

Dar es Salaam is a good place to get visas for other countries because of the exchange rate on the black market.

Note The border between Tanzania and Kenya is now open normally. Permission is no longer required to cross it.

Burundi visas These cost Sh 200, require two photos and are issued in 24 hours. Visas are valid for a stay of one month. There is an embassy in Dar and a consulate in Kigoma.

India visas These cost Sh 16, require three photos and take 48 hours to issue.

Kenya visas These are issued at the High Commission, Home Affairs Building (ground floor), corner Ghana and Ohio Sts, Dar, in the mornings only up until 11.30 am. They cost Sh 50. No photos are required.

Rwanda visas These cost Sh 200, require two photos and are issued in 24 hours. They are valid for a stay of two weeks.

Uganda visas Visas and entry permits are obtainable from the Liaison Office, corner Samora Machel Avenue and Maktaba diagonally opposite the British High Commission. They cost Sh 22.50, require three photos and take 48 hours to issue.

Zaire visas These cost Sh 250, require three photos and take 48 hours to issue. They are usually valid for one month and are single entry, so if you need a three-month, multiple-entry visa make sure you specify this on the application form. There is an embassy in Dar and a consulate in Kigoma.

Zambia visas If you're from the USA, try to get this visa somewhere other than Dar. We've had reports that the embassy was making it very difficult for Americans by taking up to one month to issue visas.

MONEY

US$1 = Sh 17.91
£1 = Sh 23

The unit of currency is the Tanzanian shilling = 100 cents. Import and export of local currency is prohibited. Currency declaration forms are issued on arrival and you're strongly advised to keep them in order as well as to keep any bank receipts for money changed at the banks. If you go to any of the game parks (especially Serengeti and Ngorongoro Crater) you will be asked for the currency form. If they find any currency on you in excess of what you declared on arrival, it will be confiscated, so if you do have any then make sure it's well hidden. By the time you get there you should also make sure that the form looks convincing by changing something officially at a bank and getting a stamp on the form. It's best to assume that your currency form will be scrutinised at the border when you leave, but we've has a lot of reports saying they don't bother to collect it at the Namanga crossing (Kenya/Tanzania border) and that the Kaporo/Kyela (Malawi/Tanzania border) is pretty easygoing. Tunduma (Zambia/Tanzania border) and Lunga Lunga (Kenya/Tanzania border) can be very tough.

Many travellers are doctoring their currency forms, for instance, by changing $30 or $40 in a bank and adding zeros in the appropriate places to make it appear that they have changed $300 or $400. However, you cannot alter bank receipts in this way, as the amount exchanged is written out in words. So if you do this you must 'lose' the corresponding bank receipt. The authorities are alert to this trick and will not admit people to the national parks if they don't see bank receipts to accompany the currency form. No worries. It is easy to purchase bank receipts on the black market showing that you have exchanged cash. It's more difficult and time-consuming to purchase bank receipts showing that you have exchanged traveller's cheques. Think about this before you turn up at the border. It obviously makes sense to declare plenty of cash even if you don't have it. Buying bent bank receipts generally takes the form of a lower exchange rate – say, Sh 55 to the dollar. Arusha is a good place to buy bank receipts. The man who used to do them is now being watched closely by the police so he may no longer be in business, but you can generally count on finding someone by asking around.

If you are considering doctoring your currency form and/or buying bank receipts and going on a safari, it's a good idea to pay for transportation alone initially (you need to show your currency form and bank receipts to pay for this). When you get to the game lodges in the national parks, they only check the currency form to see whether you exchanged enough money to pay for the lodge. They ignore the means by which you paid for the transport. In July 1985, however, park fees were raised to US$15 per day (or Sh 240 with a bank receipt to prove you changed officially).

If your currency form and/or bank receipts are stolen, make sure you report this to the police; otherwise you may have major problems when you want to leave.

You cannot buy airline tickets with local currency unless you can back it up with bank receipts and a duly stamped currency form. The same goes for accommodation at the game parks. If you buy an airline ticket in Tanzania, the airline will probably keep the bank receipt. Air Kenya certainly does. This is going to cause hassles when you leave, so make a photostat of the receipt and insist that they take that and not the original.

The Tanzanian shilling is ridiculously overvalued, and the Mickey Mouse rates you get at the banks make everything about twice as expensive as Kenya. It's not surprising under these circumstances that there is a flourishing black market on which you can get up to US$1 = Sh 90 depending on how much you change. The best rate is to be found in Dar. Elsewhere it's less. Asian shopkeepers are the best people to approach. Be careful when changing money on the black market, as the penalties are very high. Local people are often reluctant to do it. You can also change Kenyan shillings on the black market, as they hold their value well. Expect Ken Sh 1 = Tan Sh 5.50. If you're heading into Zambia, get rid of your excess shillings at Nakonde, where the exchange rate is Tan Sh 20 = Kw 1 (this is a far better rate of exchange than a straight swop from US dollars into Kwacha).

You can only re-exchange up to Sh 400 on exit regardless of the number of bank receipts you have – and even then they're reluctant to do it.

There are serious shortages of basic commodities in Tanzania, especially fuel and even water. This frequently leads to the cancellation of trains, buses and boats.

You can sell virtually anything in Tanzania – T-shirts, Levis, pens, calculators, canned butter, whisky. New T-shirts will go for at least Sh 150, and Levis and calculators for Sh 800. This goes for the Masai as well if you're interested in buying local artifacts (T-shirts and Levis are the most sought-after items).

The airport tax for international flights is US$10.

LANGUAGE
Kiswahili and English are the official languages.

GETTING THERE & AROUND
Air
Dar-Zanzibar There are flights two to three times daily by *Air Tanzania*. The fare is Sh 270. Advance booking is necessary – the office in Dar is at Luther House, City Drive.

Dar-Kigoma There are flights on Monday, Wednesday and Friday which cost Sh 1530 plus Sh 40 airport tax.

Road
Since the war with Idi Amin's Uganda, there have been severe petrol and diesel shortages and a scarcity of spare parts for buses. Road maintenance has been neglected because of lack of government funds. These factors have all wreaked havoc with the road system and public transportation, especially along minor routes. Buses are often cancelled, and when they do arrive there's always an enormous backlog of people wanting to get on them. In other words, if you're planning on getting around Tanzania by bus, allow plenty of time. Only those vehicles with special licence plates are allowed to use the roads between 1 pm on Sunday and 6 am on Monday.

Because buses are frequently cancelled due to shortages of petrol or spares (or whatever), there is fierce competition to get on one that's running. It's a question of fighting, pushing, elbowing and clawing your way on board. You can't do this and get your backpack on the roof at the same time, so it makes a lot of sense to travel in groups. There are heaps of pickpockets at Tanzanian bus stations too, so be very careful. Arusha and Moshi are particularly bad.

Current possibilities, fares and journey times along the main routes are as follows:

Dar-Moshi There are several daily buses in either direction from the Morogoro Rd terminal. Luxury coach costs Sh 95 or Sh 150 and takes 11 to 16 hours. One company covering this route is the *Imam* bus line. Their ticket office in Dar is on the corner of Mosque and Jamhuri Sts, but the buses themselves depart from the corner of Libya and Morogoro.

Moshi-Arusha There are frequent daily buses in either direction which cost Sh 33 and take about 1½ hours.

Arusha-Namanga (Kenyan border) When a bus runs, it leaves at 7.30 am and costs Sh

20. A matatu along the same route will cost Sh 100. The journey takes about 1½ hours.

Moshi-Marangu Marangu is the starting point for climbing Mount Kilimanjaro. There are buses in either direction daily which cost Sh 10 and take about 1½ hours.

Dar-Tanga There are several buses daily in either direction. Cost is Sh 300.

Kigoma-Arusha The most reliable route between these two places is via Dar, but if you don't mind the risk of getting stuck here and there, it's possible to go direct. First take an overnight sleeper on the train from Kigoma to Tabora. This usually arrives in Tabora around 5.30 am. If you're told at Kigoma that there are no 1st or 2nd-class sleepers available, get on the train anyway. It's more than likely that the ticket collector will find you a berth, as they tend to save places for people getting on in Tabora.

Once in Tabora, you take a bus to Nzega for Sh 30 and then another bus from there to Singida for Sh 100, arriving at the latter place around 6 pm. There are plenty of small hotels near the terminal where you can stay for the night. The following morning you catch a bus or truck to Arusha. You should get there the same day. The cost is around Sh 100. In the opposite direction, the railways run a bus from Arusha and Moshi to Dodoma. It leaves on Wednesday and Saturday morning, costs Sh 280 and must be booked in advance. If you miss it, get a local bus first to Singida for Sh 300 (the official price is Sh 220 but everyone has to pay the extra Sh 80). From Singida you can get a bus to Manyoni. From either Singida or Dodoma you can pick up the trains to Kigoma.

Moshi-Mwanza There are usually four buses per week in either direction (petrol being available) by *Tanganyika Bus Service*. They cost Sh 150 and take about 23 hours. The road is very bad. Try to book the bus in advance, as it will be full on the day of departure. You may also be able to pick this bus up in Arusha. The fare from Arusha is Sh 140.

Mwanza-Musoma There is one bus daily in either direction (at 5 am from Musoma) and you need to book the ticket in advance the previous morning – get there by 6 am as demand is high. It's possible to use this bus to get to the Serengeti National Park. Some 18 km south of Bunba along this route is the Ndabaka entrance to the park, but you'll have to ask fellow passengers where to get down, as the gate is about 200 metres from the road and you may miss it otherwise. The fare to here is Sh 27 and the journey takes about four hours. There's very little traffic from the gate to Seronera village, so you may have to wait around for a long time. As the journey to Seronera takes about three hours and you have to be there by the latest at 7 pm, the park officials won't let you set off after 4 pm. You can sleep at the gate, where water is available, but bring your own food.

Dar-Mbeya The *Kwatcha Bus* leaves Dar daily at 7.30 am and Mbeya daily at 10 pm. The fare is Sh 135 and the journey takes around 20 hours. The *Kamata Bus* also covers this route, departing Dar at 2 pm and arriving at Mbeya between 4 and 6 pm the next day.

Rail
Trains are perhaps the most reliable form of transport in Tanzania and certainly the most comfortable over long hauls because of the state of the roads. There are three main lines of interest to travellers. Student reductions of 50% are available on the trains, though some degree of effort is usually required to get them. First you must get a form from the Pugu Rd railway station in Dar and then take it to the Ministry of Education to get a stamp of approval. Don't forget to take your

international student card with you. The Ministry of Education is beside State House. Another traveller said the procedure was to pick up a form which you can only get at the TAZARA station/office on Kilimani Rd. It's a huge building which you can't miss – take a bus from Posta bus station by the seafront (junction of Kivukoni and City Drive) to Uwanja ya Ndege or Chagombe. Book a couple of weeks in advance and pay for your ticket five days before departure.

If at all possible, you should try to buy your tickets for 1st or 2nd class four or five days in advance. Third-class tickets can only be bought on the day of departure.

Dar-Moshi/Arusha & Tanga via Karogwe There are trains from Dar to Moshi on Tuesday, Thursday and Saturday, and from Moshi to Dar on Wednesday, Friday and Sunday at 4 pm. The journey takes 16 to 18 hours. Advance booking is advised, especially for the Sunday train. The fares are Sh 220 (1st-class sleeper) and Sh 142 (2nd-class seats). 'Third class is like a zoo,' according to one traveller.

Moshi to Arusha costs Sh 15 (3rd class).

Moshi to Tanga costs Sh 78 (2nd class) and Sh 36 (3rd class).

Dar-Mwanza & Kigoma via Tabora There should be a daily train between all three places, but fuel shortages generally reduce it to three times per week. The journey takes 36 to 42 hours between Dar and Kigoma or Dar and Mwanza. First and 2nd classes are often booked up weeks in advance – buses from Kigoma to Dar are rare. Sometimes an extra 2nd-class carriage is added. If that happens, tickets go on sale at 11 am on the day of departure. Queue early! The carriages were bought new from the UK in 1980 but there's been no cleaning or maintenance done since then. Both 1st class (two-berth compartments) and 2nd class (six-berth compartments) are single sex unless you take up the whole compartment. The fares

from Dar to Kigoma are Sh 509.90 (1st class), Sh 276 (2nd-class sleeper) and Sh 98.30 (3rd class). There's often no food or drink available in the buffet car or at the stations en route.

Dar-Kapiri Mposhi (Zambia) via Tunduma/ Nakonde Built by the Chinese in the 1960s, this TAZARA railway is still a very important link between Tanzania and Zambia, but it no longer operates anywhere near as efficiently as it did when it first opened. From two express and two ordinary trains per week in the early 1970s, the service has now been reduced to just two ordinary trains per week although there is still the occasional express train. Most of the cancelled trains are a result of fuel shortages. Delays are frequent.

In theory, there are ordinary trains which depart Dar on Monday, Wednesday, Thursday and Saturday at 10.45 am (in practice this is generally reduced to Wednesday and Saturday only). They arrive at Nakonde at 2.20 pm the next day and Kapiri Mposhi at 8.40 am on the second day. You must change at Nakonde. In the opposite direction they depart Kapiri Mposhi on Monday, Wednesday, Thursday and Saturday at 4.30 pm (in practice this is reduced to two trains per week). They arrive in Nakonde at 11.45 am the next day and Dar at 5.20 pm on the second day.

The express trains are scheduled to run from Dar on Tuesday and Friday at 4.30 pm. They arrive in Nakonde at 1.10 pm the next day and Kapiri Mposhi at 12.20 pm on the second day.

The fares from Dar to Nakonde are Sh 490 (1st class), Sh 320.30 (2nd class) and Sh 132.10 (3rd class). From Dar to Kapiri Mposhi the fares are Sh 904.20 (1st class), Sh 607.90 (2nd class) and Sh 250.40 (3rd class).

As with other trains in Tanzania, 1st and 2nd class are single sex unless you take up the whole compartment. Meals in the buffet car are good – breakfast at Sh 20 and lunch/dinner at Sh 50 – but they often run out of food so it's best to take some along with you.

Absolutely do not take any photographs on this train unless you have discussed what you want to do first with the police. There are always a number of undercover agents on board, and spy phobia runs high. If you're seen taking pictures you can expect to get into a lot of trouble with the police or army, and your film will most likely be confiscated.

If you intend to get off at Nakonde (for Malawi), it's much quicker to get off instead at Tunduma and walk across the border; it can take up to four hours of shunting to move the train between the two border towns, despite the fact that the distance is only a couple of km. Also, the Zambian officials who check out the train are adamant that you change money with them rather than with those who staff the road crossing (cash only and often below the official rate). There are often personal and baggage searches between Tunduma and Nakonde.

Boat

Lake Victoria Steamers The service between Kenya and Tanzania has been resumed.

Lake Tanganyika Steamers These ferries are covered in this section under 'To/From Burundi & Zaire.'

Getting to Zanzibar & Pemba Islands

You can get to either of these islands by plane or boat. If you go by plane, it's a good idea to book three days in advance.

If you prefer to go by boat, the *MV Mapinduzi* sails between Dar and Zanzibar. Petrol and diesel shortages have been playing havoc with the boat's schedule, but it usually departs once a week on Wednesday and sometimes twice a week on Tuesday and Saturday. From Zanzibar it returns on Friday and Monday. The journey takes five hours. Book your ticket at the office on Morogoro Rd near the technical college in Dar (marked on

Tourist Office maps as 'CCM Youth'). Women always go to the head of the queue. The fares are Sh 180 (1st class), Sh 140 (2nd class) and Sh 110 (3rd class) one way.

The other ferry, the *MV Mandeleo* sails between Tanga, Pemba and Zanzibar once every two weeks. It leaves Tanga on Tuesday at 3 pm, arrives at Wete on Pemba at 6 pm, stays there overnight and then arrives Zanzibar at 1 pm the following day. The fare from Tanga to Zanzibar is Sh 170 (3rd class – reclining upholstered seat), Sh 90 from Tanga to Pemba, and Sh 100 from Pemba to Zanzibar.

To/From Kenya

As the border between Kenya and Tanzania is now open normally, you can cross at Isebania (on the Kisii-Musoma road), Namanga (on the Nairobi-Arusha road), Taveta (on the Voi-Moshi road) and Lunga Lunga (on the Mombasa-Tanga road). If you take the Isebania crossing you may have difficulty getting a connection into Tanzania (coming from Kenya), and if you arrive late in the day you'll probably have to stay in one of the hotels in no-man's land. There is supposed to be a bus from the border to Musoma early in the morning. If it doesn't arrive you'll have to find a matatu for the 10-km trip to Tarime (or walk). There is a bus from Tarime to Musoma at about noon, but it's usually overcrowded.

If you're heading for Mombasa, there are buses from Moshi to Himo for Sh 5, buses from there to the border for Sh 10, and buses from Taveta (two km from the border – walk or matatu for Sh 10) to Mombasa.

Heading into Tanzania from Mombasa via Lunga Lunga, you can take a matatu from the Likoni ferry in Mombasa to Lunga Lunga. They leave early in the morning. At the border make sure you only declare foreign currency/cheques and enough Tanzanian currency to get you to Tanga (non-Kenyan citizens are not allowed to take out Kenyan shillings). There is no bank at Lunga Lunga and no accommodation available. Pick-up trucks and vans are available for the six-km trip to the Tanzanian customs in the mornings (it might be possible to hitch at other times). Tanzanian border officials will expect you to have plenty of money or a return ticket or an MCO (though we haven't heard of anyone being refused entry). A bus is available in the morning from Tanzanian customs to Tanga and from Tanga to Dar at about 9 am.

Arusha to Namanga costs Sh 50 by bus or Sh 100 by matatu.

Passenger train services between Kenya and Tanzania are to resume shortly.

The Lake Victoria steamer service between Kenya and Tanzania has been resumed. The *MV Bukoba* now plies between Kisumu and Musoma and Mwanza on the following schedule:

	Arrival	*Departure*
Mwanza (Thursday)		2.00 pm
Musoma (Thursday)	10.00 pm	12.00 am
Kisumu (Friday)	2.00 pm	
Kisumu (Friday)		6.00 pm
Musoma (Saturday)	7.00 am	9.00 am
Mwanza (Saturday)	5.00 pm	

To/From Malawi

Until recently, in order to get from Malawi to Tanzania it was necessary to first go to Zambia via Chitipa, Nyala and Nakonde and then over the border to Tunduma. This is no longer necessary following the completion of a bridge between Kaporo and Kyela. The bridge has lately become the preferred crossing between the two countries, since the Tanzanian customs at Tunduma are notoriously heavy. It's also better if you're one of those unfortunate

people who would otherwise need a double-entry visa for Zambia (eg USA).

From the Malawian customs post at Kaporo you must either hitch or walk to the Tanzanian border. There is a daily bus from Kaporo to the last Malawian village (Iponga). In the opposite direction there is a bus from Iponga to Karonga via Kaporo which leaves daily at 6 am and arrives Karonga at 8.30 am. The fare is Kw 1.15. From Kaporo, the bridge is 20 km away. Police at the bridge will want to see your exit stamp from Malawi. Once over the bridge, you are in Tanzania but the customs post is two km east of Kyela village. The new road comes across about 10 km west of Kyela so you have to backtrack 12 km to get a stamp. There are buses between Kyela and Mbeya.

Watch out for the Malawian border guards on this crossing, as they're keen on confiscating this book.

To/From Uganda

The most usual crossing point is from Bukoba to Masaka, but there are no direct buses. The road was dug up in the campaign to oust Idi Amin from Uganda and it still hasn't been repaired, so you may have to walk the 30 km from Kyaka (the last Tanzanian village of any size) to the Tanzanian border, and then a further nine km to the first Ugandan village (Mutukula). If possible, try to do this trip on a Saturday, as that is market day in Kyaka and there's a good chance of getting hold of lifts (cost about Sh 30). If you're heading down from Uganda to Tanzania, there are buses from Kampala to the Ugandan border village on Monday, Wednesday and Friday at 10 am. The fare is Ugandan Sh 750 and the journey takes about eight hours. In the opposite direction the buses depart on Tuesday, Thursday and Saturday very early in the morning.

To/From Rwanda

Although there is a road between Mwanza and Rulenge (about 70 km from the border) and another from there to the

Rwandan border and Kigali, the latter is practically deserted and it's very difficult to find a lift. Travellers have waited for days without success. The Mission people at Rulenge go to Kigali once every two weeks and may offer you a lift. Most people find that it's easier to get between the two countries via south-western Uganda along the Kabale-Kisoro-Ruhengeri road.

To/From Burundi & Zaire

There are no direct land connections between Tanzania and Zaire. To go from one to the other, you take a boat along Lake Tanganyika from Kigoma. Between Tanzania and Burundi you have a choice of road or lake transport.

A very popular route to Burundi these days involves the use of two local ferries and a bus journey. You first take a local ferry from Kigoma to the Tanzanian border (no customs or immigration facilities there). They leave every day in the morning except Sunday from the beach, which you get to by following the railway tracks for a few hundred metres. The cost is Sh 40 (another letter said Sh 100) and the trip takes 10 hours. From the Tanzanian border you then have to walk about one km to the Burundi border village of Banda, where you pick up another local ferry to Nyanza Lac. They leave every day, cost Sh 50 and take about three hours. From Nyanza Lac there are daily buses to Bujumbura for BFr 400, or you can hitch.

A scheduled steamer along Lake Tanganyika, the *MV Liemba*, connects ports in Burundi, Tanzania, Zaire and Zambia. The main ports of call are Kalundu (Uvira), Bujumbura, Kigoma, Kalemie and Mpulungu. The boat generally calls at each of them at least once a week, but the schedule varies so you'll have to play it by ear. At present, the boat generally leaves Kigoma for Bujumbura on Thursday and Sunday at 6 pm. The fares are Sh 257 (1st class), Sh 203 (2nd class) and Sh 93 (3rd class), plus there is a Sh 40 'departure

tax.' First class is a two-bunk cabin, 2nd class is a four-bunk cabin and 3rd class is the deck. Dinner on the boat costs Sh 75.

To/From Zambia

The most usual route into Zambia from Tanzania is along the main Dar es Salaam-Lusaka road via Tunduma/Nakonde or on the TAZARA railway. Details of the rail link can be found under 'Rail.'

There is also the possibility of using the *MV Liemba* steamer along Lake Tanzania. It connects Kigoma with Mpulungu via Lagosa, Kibwesa, Ikola, Karema, Mtakuja, Kipili, Wapembe, Kala and Kasanga (all in Tanzania). The boat schedule varies, but it usually leaves Kigoma for Mpulungu on Wednesday at 4 pm. The fares are Sh 451.30 (1st class), Sh 358.20 (2nd class) and Sh 162.60 (3rd class).

PLACES TO STAY

Hotel rooms can be an expensive commodity in this country, especially in Dar es Salaam, but it's generally acceptable for two people to share a single room (one sleeps on the floor or they both sleep either intimately or uncomfortably on the single bed). The word 'hotel' here usually means a restaurant, so if it's a bed you're looking for then ask for 'lodgings.' Many Sikh temples still take travellers, and though your stay is usually free do make sure that you leave a reasonable donation. Otherwise, travellers who come after you will find themselves being turned away.

During the months of April and May the Tanzanian Tourist Corporation offers half-price accommodation at its hotels in Arusha, Moshi, Ngorongoro Crater and Lake Manyara.

ARUSHA

There are a lot of hotels in Arusha so you shouldn't have much problem finding a relatively cheap place to stay for the night. Try the *Central Guest House*, Market St on the corner of Uhuru St, which costs Sh 180 a double and is popular with travellers. If it's full – often – then round the corner is the *Malaika Guest House* at Sh 100 a double. It's very clean and has hot water. A cheaper alternative is the *Friends Corner Guest House*, Sokoine St, which costs Sh 50 per person but only has cold water. Also popular with travellers is the *Greenland Hotel*, which is clean and costs Sh 90 per bed or Sh 180 a double. Joseph, the manager, is friendly and will sometimes let you sleep on the floor free. Another good place is the *Uziri Guest House*, which is Sh 60 a double. Quite a few people have recommended the *Lutheran Centre* near the clocktower, which is very modern and clean and has rooms for Sh 80 a single and Sh 160 a double, but they're apparently getting fussy about who they take. You could try the *Catholic Mission Mt Theresa* in the park beside the Greenland Hotel; it has beds for Sh 50, double rooms for Sh 100 and floor space for Sh 25.

Other cheapies are *Mount Meru Guest House*; the *Continental Hotel* behind the market, which costs Sh 60 a single and Sh 80 a double; *Amigo Guest House*; the *Flamingo Hotel*; *Tinga Guest House*; *Ruby Guest House*; and *Salami Lodge* just past the pink-and-grey mosque. The *YMCA* costs Sh 120 per person including breakfast. The *Miami Beach Hotel* is good value at Sh 100 a double.

The *Sikh temple* here no longer takes travellers. The same applies to the *Christchurch Anglican Guest House*. We received a tartly worded letter from the reverend gentleman who runs the latter place, saying that it's 'not for those who wish to scrounge cheap accommodation as they travel around the world, but for missionaries from the bush.'

There are several campsites in the Arusha National Park on both sides of Mount Meru and at Momela Lake (book by phoning Arusha 2335). There's also a site at Lake Duluti, 13 km from Arusha on the south side of the Moshi road; you can book it c/o A Czerny, Box 609, Arusha. Regarding camping in Arusha, we've had a lot of mail recently about thefts from sites.

Don't assume that because you've locked up your vehicle, it's safe. There are plenty of thieves wandering around with skeleton keys. Avoid camping behind the *Equator Hotel*. Tents, vans and trucks all get ripped off even in broad daylight. 'Even when you're watching the slimy buggers get in – and you're watched constantly. You're never alone and they're devastatingly professional. Everybody gets something stolen. Our wing mirrors were removed while we were inside the police station for five minutes!' wrote one traveller.

A good place to eat in Arusha is the *Cooperative Union Building* (*Ushirika* in Swahili). It serves European-type food. There is a good beer garden at the *Equator Hotel* and the *New Arusha Hotel*.

BAGAMOYO

The hotel most popular with travellers is the *Badeco Beach Hotel*, which costs Sh 35 a single and Sh 70 a double. The water supply is erratic and the place is somewhat run-down, but the excellent beach compensates for all that.

BUKOBA

The best place to stay is the *Nyumba Na Vijana* (Youth Centre) of the Evangelical Lutheran Church on the road to the hospital. It costs Sh 30 and is clean and secure. There are also many cheap hotels around the bus station. The *Catholic Mission* offers a place to stay for Sh 30 per night. If you don't mind spending over the odds for a really pleasant place, head for the *Lake Hotel* or the *Coffee Tree Inn*, about two km from the town past the police station and council offices. They're both very clean and typical colonial-style hotels. The Lake Hotel costs Sh 190 a double for bed and breakfast. Dinner is Sh 40 per person. If you arrive in Bukoba by lake steamer, the jetty where the boats tie up is about 2½ km from town.

DAR ES SALAAM

Finding a cheap room in Dar is no easy

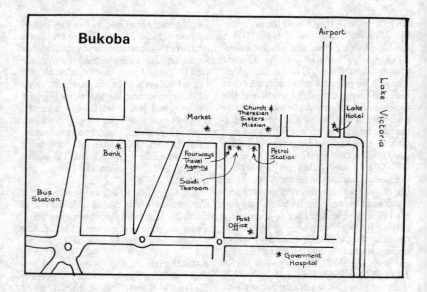

task. Most of the budget hotels are more or less permanently full. Even at check-out time in the morning you won't necessarily find a vacant room. A lot of stealing from hotel rooms goes on, so be very careful. The 'guard' at the YMCA is said to tip off thieves while you're out! Most of the more expensive hotels want to see your currency form. There are shortages of just about everything, including water, which generally runs out during the day regardless of where you stay. As a result, you'll find many restaurants closed in the evenings. If you're travelling alone, you can expect to pay the full price for a double room (Luther House is an exception).

The *Sikh temple* on Livingstone St is one of the best (of the Sikh temples) and has rooms for Sh 20 a night, but we've had reports that they're turning travellers away these days, so don't count on it. Behind it is the *Sikh Association*, which has a guest house with self-contained rooms, but it only takes Indians. Other than these, one of the cheapest places to

stay is the *Danish Volunteer Hostel*, which costs Sh 80 per person with cooker and refrigerator provided. Its only drawback is its distance from the city centre – half an hour's walk. To get there, head for Selender Bridge and turn left just before you get to it. After that, take the first road on the right-hand side. There's a sign so you shouldn't have any difficulty finding it.

Some of the most popular budget hotels around the city centre are:
Florida Inn, Jamhuri St, costs Sh 75 a single and Sh 150 a double for bed and breakfast. Almost always full.
Windsor Hotel, Nkrumah St very close to the clocktower, has been popular with travellers for many years but is usually full. It costs Sh 90 a double, plus they have singles. Many of the rooms are small and stuffy and the plumbing was designed by John Cleese.
Clocktower Guest House, Nkrumah St, is similar to the Windsor and often full. It costs Sh 120 a single and Sh 150 a double.

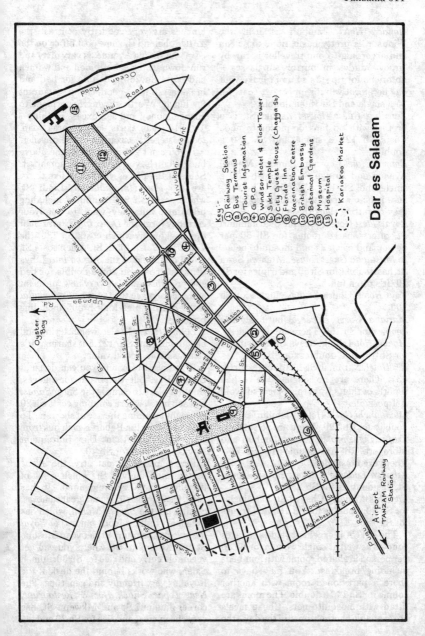

Dar es Salaam

Key:-
① Railway Station
② Bus Terminus
③ Tourist Information
④ G.P.O.
⑤ Windsor Hotel & Clock Tower
⑥ Sikh Temple
⑦ City Guest House (Chagga St)
⑧ Florida Inn
⑨ Vaccination Centre
⑩ British Embassy
⑪ Botanical Gardens
⑫ Museum
⑬ Hospital
◠◞ Kariakoo Market

Holiday Hotel, Jamhuri St near the Windsor, is pretty basic, none too clean and according to one traveller is run by 'groovy dudes in mirror sunglasses – notorious for rip-offs so don't leave your bag here or it will disappear.' It costs Sh 75 a single and Sh 150 a double.

Zanzibar Guest House, Zanaki St, is a brothel with no fans or mosquito nets. Costs Sh 120 a single and Sh 180 a double.

Emm's Hotel, corner Samora Machel Avenue and Bridge St, costs Sh 100 a single and Sh 175 a double. The restaurant below used to be quite good but they're getting slack these days.

Royal Guest House, Mosque St at Jamhuri St, offers shared rooms for Sh 80 per person and has fans and mosquito nets.

Al Mustapha Guest House, Mtaa wa Sewa St, has doubles for Sh 50 and triples for Sh 60. It's often full.

Keys Hotel, Uhuru St, has singles for Sh 200.

Mariana Guest House, Uhuru St, has doubles for Sh 150. There are no singles.

Mbowe Hotel, Makungaya St, has singles for Sh 150 and doubles for Sh 300.

Rex Hotel, Nkrumah St, has doubles for Sh 337. There are no singles. We've had reports of thefts from this place, so avoid it if possible.

Mwananchi Guest House, Jamhuri St, has doubles for Sh 120. There are no singles.

Traffic Light Motel, corner Jamhuri and Morogoro Rd, has doubles for Sh 200. There are no singles.

Kibodya Lodging & Guest House, Uhuru St, has doubles for Sh 250.

City Guest House, Chagga St, has singles for Sh 80, doubles for Sh 160 and triples for Sh 180.

The *YWCA* is excellent value and takes couples as well as single women for Sh 80 per person in shared rooms with four beds including breakfast. You may have to share a partitioned room with another couple for Sh 140 a double. The rooms are fitted with mosquito nets. Cheap meals are available at other times of the day – the lunches are very good. By contrast, the *YMCA*, behind the new post office on the corner of Ghana Avenue, is very dirty and run-down. It takes both men and women and costs Sh 260 a double for bed and breakfast. It has a good, cheap restaurant for lunch. 'Worth staying for a night to change money and sell excess clothing – T-shirts, jeans, skirts, scarves, bras, soap, toothpaste, etc,' according to one traveller.

If you can't get in at any of the above budget hotels, you'll have to go upmarket. Some of the places you might like to try are the *Hotel International*, Lindi St, which costs Sh 260 a double including breakfast, but they want to see your currency form; the *Delux Inn*, Uhuru St at the clocktower, which costs Sh 280; the *Tamarine Hotel*, Lindi St, which costs Sh 250 a double; and the *Jambo Inn*, Libya St, which costs Sh 250 a double for bed and breakfast and is a very new, pleasant and secure place to stay. The *Continental Hotel* has doubles for Sh 506 including breakfast.

Luther House is also worth trying and has rooms for Sh 127.50 sharing. It's clean, safe and good value.

If you want to camp, you can do so at Oyster Bay, but watch out for thieves. Another place to camp is the *Silver Sands*, a beach hotel, where camping costs Sh 20 per night including the use of showers. To get there, take the Bahari Beach bus from Kariakoo Market in Dar (infrequent service) or a taxi for Sh 40.

For a place to eat, try the *Naaz Restaurant*, Jamhuri St, which a lot of travellers have recommended. It has good, clean Indian food and great samosas. Similar are the *Sheesh Mahal*, which has excellent Indian food; and the *Royal Restaurant*, Jamhuri St between Mosque St and Kitumbini St, where you can get vegetable curry and rice for Sh 30. Jumah Saleh, who works behind the desk at the Royal, is very friendly and generous. The *New Topaz Snack Bar & Restaurant*, corner Jamhuri St and Mkwepu St, has very cheap meat and rice for Sh 20 and tea

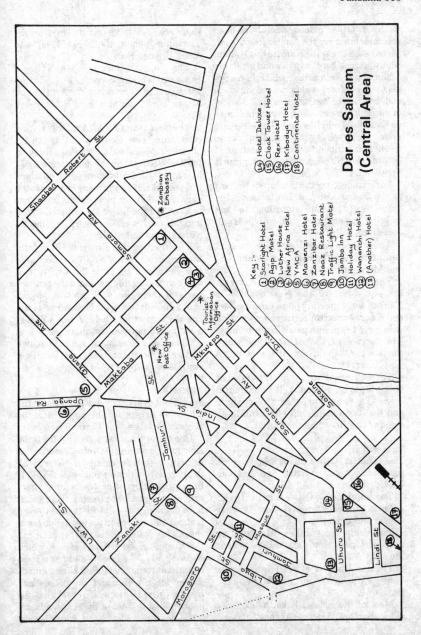

Dar es Salaam (Central Area)

Key:-
① Starlight Hotel
② Agip Motel
③ Luther House
④ New Africa Hotel
⑤ YMCA
⑥ Mawenzi Hotel
⑦ Zenzibar Hotel
⑧ Naaz Restaurant
⑨ Traffic Light Motel
⑩ Jambo Inn
⑪ Holiday Hotel
⑫ Wananchi Hotel
⑬ (Another) Hotel

⑭ Hotel Deluxe
⑮ Clock Tower Hotel
⑯ Rex Hotel
⑰ Kibodya Hotel
⑱ Continental Hotel

for Sh 4. Other places which have been recommended are the *Nawaz Restaurant*, Msimbazi St near the Kamata bus station, where you can get cheap rice and meat; the *Salamander Restaurant*, which is particularly good for breakfasts and lunches; and the *Chinese Restaurant* in the basement of the multi-storey NIC Investment House on Samora Machel Avenue. The little café under the *Motel Agip* is excellent value, clean and efficient. Chicken and roast potatoes are Sh 85, soup is Sh 25, pizza is Sh 40 and coffee is Sh 8.

For a splurge try the rooftop restaurant at the *Twiga Hotel*, which is where the 'elite meet to eat' according to one traveller. A very good meal with beer will cost around Sh 150.

A tea shop serving excellent cookies and buns is on the corner of Jamhuri St and Morogoro Rd.

The *New Africa Hotel*, Oyster Bay, is the equivalent of the New Stanley in Nairobi and a meeting point for travellers and others on the terrace, but they will only serve beers with meals in the evening. The terrace of the *AGIP Motel* round the back of the New Africa is much pleasanter.

Take a stroll down to the waterfront at about 5 pm on a Sunday. It's a colourful scene. There are food sellers everywhere and the Asian community turns up in its Sunday best to watch the sunset.

Information

The Tourist Office is at Maktaba St between Samora Avenue and Sokoine Drive.

The Immigration Office is in the Home Affairs Building, ground floor, corner Ghana and Ohio Sts.

The main post office Maktaba St between Upanga and Jamhuri Sts, next to the YWCA.

Thomas Cook is at AMI Ltd, corner Samora Machel Avenue and Mkwepu St, Box 9041.

Most of the airlines have their offices along Samora Machel Avenue, though there are a few more on City Drive (eg *Air Tanzania* behind Luther House) and along Upanga Rd.

The national bus company's depot (*Kamata*) is on the corner of Pugu Rd and Msimbazi St. The buses for Arusha and Moshi leave from Morogoro Rd by Libya St.

The bus to the TAZARA railway station runs from the Cenataph, City Drive, Uhuru St, Msimbazi St and Pugu Rd (look for 'Univ/Ndege' on the destination sign). The fare is Sh 1.50-5 depending on which bus you take. If you're using city buses, be very careful about pickpockets and other thieves. All the buses are jammed to the gunwales so it's easy to have a bag slashed without your knowledge.

The international airport is 13 km from the city centre. Bus No 67 connects the two, but if you get on at the airport then make sure it's going right into the centre – some of them don't. There's an airport shuttle bus between the New Africa Hotel and the airport for Sh 45. A taxi will cost Sh 175-230 but you can share.

There is a free paperback exchange service at both the USA and Canadian embassies.

KIGOMA

Just about everything in Kigoma is on the Ujiji road except for the post office, the Railway Hotel and the Burundi consulate.

One of the cheapest places to stay is the *Kigoma Community Centre*, which has dormitory-style accommodation for Sh 25 per person and double rooms for Sh 50. It fills up quickly after trains and boats arrive, so if you want to stay there you'll have to make a bee-line for it. The Centre is about 150 metres on the left as you leave the railway station. Other places to try are the *Kigoma Hotel & Guest House*, which costs Sh 137.50 a double and has a good restaurant (breakfast for Sh 25 and lunch/dinner for Sh 45); and the *Mapinduze Hotel & Guest House*, which costs Sh 130 a double. Just in front of the Kigoma Hotel is the new *Lake View Hotel*, which is very pleasant. It costs Sh 105 a single and Sh 135 a double without own bathroom and Sh 175 a double with own bathroom. The restaurant here isn't that good, however. To get to the Kigoma Hotel or the Lake View Hotel from the station, walk straight up the road towards the market and they're on the left-hand side. *Safari Lodging* has rooms at Sh 105. There are plenty of other guest houses up near the top of the hill. The *Railway Hotel*, 500 metres on the right from the railway station, is an old colonial-style hotel with heaps of atmosphere and is a hang-out for expatriates and volunteers. If you take a fancy to it, make sure you have some money. A single costs Sh 270 and a double with attached bath costs Sh 490. You can get a good dinner and cold beers here at reasonable prices.

Immigration is about five km out on the Ujiji road. The bus ride there costs Sh 2 – ask the conductor to point it out, as there's no sign. Customs (for currency forms) is near the railway station, 100 metres on the right. The Burundi consulate is about 50 metres off the road by the market. There's also a Zaire consulate here.

The **Gombe Stream National Park** north of Kigoma is well worth a visit. It is a chimpanzee sanctuary and the site of Jane Goodall's research station set up in 1960. There are some 50 chimpanzees here and a group come down almost every day to the research station at 3 pm. Local boats will take you there in about two hours for Sh 100 (these are same boats which go to the Burundi border). They leave every morning except Sunday between 9 and 10 am and return daily.

Entry to the park costs Sh 40 per day. You can camp here or rent a cabin (five double rooms available) 50 metres from the lake shore for Sh 50 per night. Bring your own food. Firewood, a wood stove and pots are provided. To see the chimpanzees and baboons, you can either wait till they come down to the station or hire a guide for Sh 50 per day. The park has been warmly recommended by the few

travellers who have been there. All have said it's an interesting and worthwhile experience. Also, you'll probably be the only visitor. There's a nearby beach where, according to Dutch volunteer workers, it's safe to swim. The Michelin map marks the park slightly off (it actually goes down to the lake shore), and the road marked as going through the middle doesn't exist.

Just south of Kigoma is **Ujiji**, one of Africa's oldest market villages and the place where all the 'Dr Livingstone, I presume?' business started (Stanley met Livingstone here and there's the inevitable plaque). The village is well worth visiting and a good deal more interesting than Kigoma. You can get a taxi or bus there by road (20 minutes by bus) or take one of the 'water taxis' down the lake. Boat building and repairs go on by the lake shore. If you need a meal whilst in Ujiji, the *Kudra Hotel* has good food and fruit salads.

MBEYA

Until recently very few travellers stayed here overnight, but since the opening of the new road and bridge direct to Malawi via Kaporo, Mbeya has become a busy overnight stop. One of the cheapest places to stay is the *Moravian Youth Hostel* near the radio tower which costs Sh 84. It's very clean and the staff is friendly. Breakfast costs Sh 15 and dinner Sh 50. The *Mbeya Hotel*, opposite the football stadium, run by the Tanzanian Railways Corporation, has also been recommended. It's very colonial and items are available which you can't get for love nor money elsewhere in Mbeya. Pleasant rooms with clean sheets, mosquito nets and very hot showers cost Sh 175 a single including breakfast.

MOSHI

You can no longer stay at the *Sikh temple*, but you can get floor space at the *Mwariko Art Gallery* for Sh 20 per night. The floor is concrete so you really need an air mattress. Other relatively cheap accommodation can be found at both the *Anglican* and

Lutheran guest houses (latter opposite the post office) if they have room.

The *YMCA*, near the clocktower, takes both men and women and is a very popular place to stay. It has good rooms with electricity all day and hot showers in the evenings, and the new manager has cleaned up and refilled the swimming pool. You can swim there between 10 am and 5 pm for Sh 20. Rooms cost Sh 140 a single and Sh 280 a double for bed and breakfast. A three-course meal costs Sh 75 but 'it's worth it.' Be careful here. We had a report recently that three Dutch men were mugged at knifepoint in broad daylight.

Other relatively cheap places are:
Amani Guest House, Kiusa St, costs Sh 120 a double.
Njaei Hotel, recommended by many travellers, is clean and costs Sh 55 a double.
Tafia Hotel, on the same street as the Sikh temple, costs Sh 105 a double.
New Family Guest House has clean, pleasant rooms for Sh 150 including breakfast.
Liberty Hotel, an Indian-owned hotel, has rooms for Sh 80-150.
Greenview, near the station, has doubles for Sh 200.

There is a campsite about two km out of town on the main road to Arusha adjacent to the playing fields. It's a good site and there are showers.

If you're not eating at your hotel, try the *KUC Hotel* near the clocktower. A vegetarian curry and rice will cost around Sh 50. This place has rooms but they're quite pricey.

Rather than stay in Moshi, many travellers head out to **Marangu**, the starting point for treks up Mount Kilimanjaro. The hotels are not cheap but they both offer organised treks up the mountain which cost almost the same as what you could get together yourself, though with considerable more leg-work. The *Marangu Hotel* has an 'idyllic' location and costs Sh 390 for full board per person. The *Kibo Hotel*, surrounded by a beautiful flower garden and very 1920s in style, costs Sh 690 a double including breakfast and dinner (the latter is a huge four-course meal).

MUSOMA

Most people stay at the *Mennonite Centre*, which is very cheap, clean and friendly. Its only drawback is that it's a long way from the boat terminal. If you find it inconvenient, try the *Sensera Hotel*.

Good food is available at the *Railway Hotel*. Lunches cost about US$1 depending on what you have. The building is new and has rooms for Sh 230 a double.

MWANZA

There are many cheap hotels around the bus station, but they're mostly small, dingy places and often full. The *Sikh temple* will take travellers, but the *Catholic Mission* only takes those of like persuasion. The *Mutimba Guest House* is a popular place to stay. It's clean, provides fans and mosquito nets and costs Sh 150 a double. On the same street is the *Capitol Guest House*, a friendly place with the same facilities as the Mutimba; rooms cost Sh 120 a double and Sh 135 a triple. To get to both of these, go down Nyerere Avenue until you get to the mosque. Go down the street opposite the mosque, take the first left and then turn left again. Other relatively cheap places which have been recommended in the past are the *Lion Lodge* near the bus station; the *Shinyanga Guest House*, Lumumba St, a few blocks from the bus station; and the *Hotel Victoria*, which is clean and has rooms for Sh 150 a double including own bathroom.

Shar's African Restaurant, just down Lumumba St from the Shinyanga Guest House across Nyerere Avenue, has been recommended for food. It isn't the cheapest at Sh 60 for a meal, but the food is very good.

Fifteen km east of town is the **Sukuma Museum**, which has an excellent drum

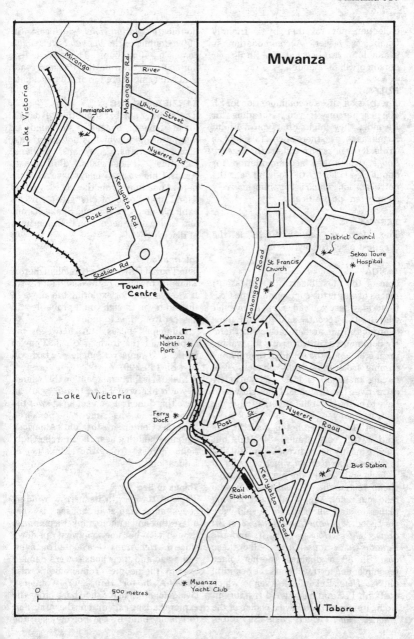

Mwanza

Lake Victoria

Mirongo

Makongoro Rd.

River

Immigration

Uhuru Street

Nyerere Rd.

Kenyatta Rd.

Post St.

Station Rd.

Town Centre

District Council

St Francis Church

Sekou Toure Hospital

Makongoro Road

Mwanza North Port

Lake Victoria

Ferry Dock

Post St.

Nyerere Road

Kenyatta Road

Bus Station

Rail Station

Mwanza Yacht Club

0   500 metres

Tabora

collection put together by a friendly Quebeçois father. Accommodation is available in two-bed huts for Sh 60 per person or Sh 80 a double.

RULENGE

The *Mission* offers accommodation for Sh 40 per person. If you're heading for Rwanda, they might offer you a lift to Kigali, as they go there once a fortnight as a rule. If the mission is full, try the *Rulenge Lodge*, which has accommodation for about US$1. Or try the lodging near the petrol station, which is very informatively signposted 'post office.'

TABORA

The *Moravian Church Hostel* is the cheapest place to stay.

TANGA

One of the most bizarre (but pleasant) places to stay is the compound of the *CSP Convent*, where you can camp. A traveller who did this recently said that the nuns even invited him to share meals with them. He commented, 'It was really fun waking up at 5.30 am to the sound of their hymns coming from the nearby chapel. Also, having meals in silence was curiously attractive. The first meal I thought would have to be the last, but I ended up enjoying their company.'

Most of the cheap hotels near the bus station will cost around Sh 100, but they're mostly noisy dives. You might like to try the *Majestic Hotel*, which costs Sh 40 a single and Sh 50 a double. They have a cheap restaurant. A local resident who read our book suggested the following places to stay, all of which he said were very good: *Mpakani Guest House*, 21st St; *Sunset Guest House*, 19th St; and the *Equator Guest House*, 5th St. All of these cost Sh 80 a double. Another place recommended by travellers is the beautiful old *New Hotel*, Eckenforde Avenue, which costs Sh 170 and has a good restaurant. Going upmarket, you have a choice of the *Mkonge Hotel*, which costs Sh 400 a

double; the *Marina Hotel*, which costs Sh 350 a double; or the *Baobab Hotel*, which costs Sh 350 a double. The latter is five km south of town on the Pangani road. You can camp there for Sh 20 per night.

ZANZIBAR ISLAND

The name 'Zanzibar' doubtless evokes a lot of romantic images in the minds of many travellers, which is not surprising. The Sumerians, Assyrians, Indians, Egyptians, Phoenicians, Portuguese, Arabs, Chinese and Malays have all come here at one time or another. It's from this island that some of the great African explorers such as Burton, Speke, Grant and Livingstone set out on their journeys of discovery.

Information

The Tourist Office has an excellent map of Zanzibar town and of the island for Sh 10. It's very useful for exploring the alleys of the old town, though you'll probably still get lost from time to time.

Municipal buses run between the airport and the town at Sh 3. They're marked 'Uwanja wa Ndege.' A taxi will cost Sh 150-200.

Malaria is fairly rampant on this island. If you'd like your blood tested, you can have this done free and get an answer the same day at the American-sponsored Malaria Center in the old American embassy building near the Starehe Club, right across from the Ministry of Education.

Things to See

The old town, with its narrow winding alleys and Arab-style houses, is very interesting and a photographer's paradise, though it has become somewhat run-down since the rich Arabs were booted out a few years ago and their houses were handed over to 'the people.' You shouldn't miss **Beit-el-Ajaib** (or House of Wonders); **Livingstone House**, the base for the explorer's last expedition; the **Arab Fort** (originally built by the Portuguese); the

Zanzibar

Nungwi

Mkokotoni

Mangapwani
Slave Caves

Kinyasini

Kiwengwa

Prison
Island

Kibweni
Palace

Uroa

Zanzibar

Dunga

Airport

Chwaka

Chukwani
Palace

Bwejuu

Fumba

Paje

Muungoni

Uzi
Is.

Jambiani

Kizimkazi

Makunduchi

0   10 km

Cycling to various places around the island is highly recommended. Bicycles can be rented from a shop near the Malindi Guest House and from an old man named Isaac near the Air Tanzania office. The charge is usually Sh 10 per hour or Sh 60 per day. **Mangapwani**, 15 km north of Zanzibar, is well worth a visit to see the old slave caves and to enjoy the beach. If you don't want to pedal all the way and back, you can get a bus (No 2) from the market to within one km of the place. The fare is Sh 10 for you and Sh 5 for the bicycle on the roof. Local people are very warm and friendly. Smiles seem to be an epidemic on the island and are always accompanied by the popular greeting, 'Jambo! Habari!'

Another excursion worth making is to **Prison Island** about five km off the coast east of Zanzibar town. The cost of getting there depends on your bargaining prowess with the *nahodna*. On the island is a prison which was never used, a disused hospital, a beautiful beach and a bunch of wild tortoises large enough to ride (though they doubtless don't appreciate this).

Places to Stay

One of the problems about visiting Zanzibar is that all hotels and guest houses insist that you show bank receipts from the People's Bank of Zanzibar when paying for hotel accommodation. Shillings bought legally on the mainland and backed up by bank receipts are not acceptable. It used to be possible to get around this silly situation in some of the cheaper guest houses, but such is the power of the commissars that this is becoming increasingly difficult. Also, in the most expensive hotels, you must now pay in hard currency. The other bit of compulsory lunacy is that you must change US$30 per day of your intended stay if you arrive by air. There is no such requirement if you arrive by boat. All this makes a trip to Zanzibar somewhat of an expensive excursion.

The most expensive hotel is the

Shirazi Mosque, which dates back to 1107 AD; the **Old Slave Market**; the **National Museum**; and the **Slave Caves** at Mangapwani, some 15 km north of Zanzibar town. The new town itself is an unbelievably ugly contrast with its anonymous East German-designed and built housing blocks.

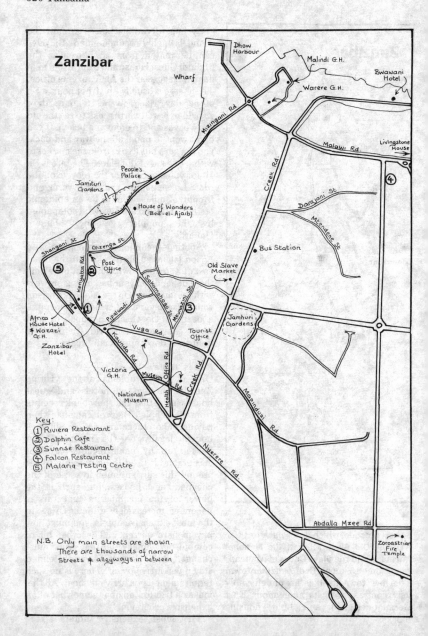

Zanzibar

Dhow Harbour

Malindi G.H.

Bwawani Hotel

Wharf

Warere G.H.

Mizingani Rd.

Malawi Rd.

Livingstone House

Creek Rd.

People's Palace

Jamituri Gardens

④

House of Wonders (Beit-el-Ajaib)

Darajani St.

Shangani St.

Chizenga St.

Mtendeni St.

Kenyatta Rd.

② Post Office

⑤

Bus Station

Sokomohogo St.

Old Slave Market

Pipalwadi St.

Mkunazini St.

①

③

Africa House Hotel ₩ Wazazi G.H.

Vuga Rd.

Jamhuri Gardens

Zanzibar Hotel

Kaunda Rd.

Tourist Office

Victoria G.H.

Museum

Health Office Rd.

Creek Rd.

National Museum

Mapinduzi Rd.

Key:

① Riviera Restaurant
② Dolphin Cafe
③ Sunrise Restaurant
④ Falcon Restaurant
⑤ Malaria Testing Centre

Nyerere Rd.

Abdalla Mzee Rd.

N.B. Only main streets are shown. There are thousands of narrow streets & alleyways in between

Zoroastrian Fire Temple

Bwawani Hotel, which is currently under British management. The cheapest rooms are Sh 600 a single and Sh 750 a double. They also have 'executive,' 'deluxe' and 'presidential' suites ranging from Sh 1300-1800. There is a swimming pool but it's for the use of residents only. The hotel's European-style discotheque is open (to non-residents too) on Thursday, Saturday and Sunday in the evening. Somewhat cheaper is the *Spicey Hotel* near the town market. Rooms with a fan cost Sh 380 a single and Sh 460 a double plus Sh 100 for an extra bed in the room. Air-conditioned rooms cost Sh 480 a single and Sh 560 a double.

In the middle range, there are the *Zanzibar Hotel* and *Africa House Hotel*, both of them owned and operated by Furaha ya Visiwani Ltd (the Afro-Shirazi Party). Bed and breakfast at the Zanzibar Hotel costs Sh 234 a single, Sh 417 a double and Sh 572 a triple without own bathroom; and Sh 268 a single, Sh 488 a double and Sh 633 a triple with own bathroom. Rooms at Africa House cost Sh 243 a single, Sh 416 a double and Sh 557 a triple without own shower; and Sh 259 a single, Sh 475 a double and Sh 590 a triple with own bathroom. Both these hotels offer meals to non-residents and residents alike (breakfast Sh 75, lunch or dinner Sh 150), but they're not recommended. Africa House, however, is a good place to go for a drink in the evening and watch the sunset. It has a bar on the first floor with a terrace overlooking the ocean. The building is the former 'British Club.' It still has the billiard table and the bathrooms marked 'Ladies Powder Room' and 'Gentlemens Cloak Room'!

Cheaper still are the *Malindi Guest House* and the *Warere Guest House*, both located behind the Cine Afrique near the port. They have singles for Sh 183 and doubles for Sh 260. The Malindi includes breakfast, though one could hardly call it that, seeing as it consists of just a cup of tea and two *mandasi*.

The least expensive guest house is the *Wazazi*, which has singles for Sh 74 and doubles for Sh 140. It can be difficult to find. As you face Africa House, go right and take the first alley on the left. Then, roughly five metres from the corner above a dark doorway, you'll see the sign with the words 'Wazazi Guest House.' The manager may tell you it's full when it isn't. Perseverence helps if this is what you are told.

Probably the best place to stay for budget travellers, however, is the *Victoria Guest House*, Victoria Rd halfway between the Majestic Cinema and the Soviet consulate. It's usually full but well worth trying. Clean rooms with a fan and shower cost Sh 90 a single and Sh 166 a double. The price includes a good breakfast of omelette, bread, pastry and all the tea you can drink. If you want to visit the clove plantations and take a look at all kinds of local fruits, spices, etc, contact a man called Mitu. He will take you on a six-hour taxi tour for Sh 800. He's a mine of information and very friendly.

There are five excellent *Tourist Bungalows* on the east coast of the island which can be rented from the Tourist Office in Zanzibar town. Travellers who have stayed in one or another have recommended them highly. They're relatively primitive as far as services go – only Jambiani has running water and none of them have electricity. You either have to carry water from a well three to five km away or pay a local boy or girl to fetch it for you. Usually only seafood and coconuts are available at the villages on the east coast, so take anything else you might need with you. If you don't want to cook yourself (primus stoves can normally be rented if you do), the local people may offer to do so for you, and prices are very reasonable – around Sh 60 per day per person. Jambiani is probably the best of them all. A traveller who stayed there recently for 10 days said, 'I loved every minute of it. Fresh fish and lobster every day and a beautiful deserted beach less than six metres from the front step!'

You don't need bank receipts to pay for these bungalows, but this could change any time. The bungalows are priced on the basis that five people will stay in them (there's no reduction if there are fewer than five of you), but they'll sleep six. Prices are: Bwejuu, Sh 183.50; Chwaka, Sh 224 (large house) and Sh 183 (small house); Jambiani, Sh 306; Makunduchi, Sh 229; Uroa, Sh 229. Each additional person over five is charged an extra Sh 50 per night.

You can get to all of them in the same day from Zanzibar town by public transport. Jambiani is three to four hours by bus along a very rough road.

It's usually possible to get the local fishermen to take you out in their boats during the day. You need to bargain for this. Prices may start around Sh 200 but can drop as low as Sh 80.

Places to Eat

There are a number of restaurants where you can find good food. One which has been popular for years is the *Dolphin Restaurant*. Similar is the *Sunrise Restaurant* on Mkunazini St. The *Riviera*, a new restaurant which opened recently, serves excellent food at reasonable prices in a clean and comfortable atmosphere. It's on Kenyatta Rd about 300 metres up from the Dolphin and right across from Africa House. Another new restaurant, the *Falcon*, off Malawi Rd near the new apartments, has relatively good food and a pleasant terrace where you can sit and watch the people walk by.

Apart from the above restaurants, do make sure that you go to *Jamituri Gardens* (People's Park) on the waterfront near the Beit-el-Ajaib (House of Wonders) in the evening. The townspeople gather here at that time to socialise, talk about what's happened and watch the sun set. Vendors sell spicy curry, roasted meat, maize and cassava, smoked octopus, sugar-cane juice and ice-cream at extremely reasonable prices. The Gardens is one of the cheapest places to eat in Zanzibar.

If you want a splurge, try the *Bwawani Hotel* on Saturday evening for their all-you-can-eat buffet. It's a sting at Sh 250, but the food is absolutely superb.

PEMBA ISLAND

Unlike Zanzibar, Pemba has few visitors so local people tend to be very hospitable. It doesn't have the same degree of Arab influence as Zanzibar, and the beaches are very difficult to get to. Most of the cloves on the offshore islands are grown here. There are only three towns on the island and three hotels, all of them government-owned and identical. They cost Sh 70 per person plus Sh 20 for breakfast. If you want full board, this will cost Sh 140. In theory the hotels have air-conditioning and a TV, and the rooms have private showers and toilets, but don't count on this. Travellers who have stayed here recently said neither the hotels at Wete nor Mkoani had electricity, and the one at Mkoani had no running water either. The other hotel is at Chake Chake in the centre of the island. The main harbour is at Wete; this is where the ferries from Tanga and Zanzibar dock. You can occasionally pick up dhows going to Mombasa and Lamu from Wete.

NATIONAL PARKS & WILDLIFE REFUGES

Tanzania has some of Africa's most famous game parks – the Serengeti and Ngorongoro Crater among them – as well as the highest and possibly most beautiful mountain in Africa – Kilimanjaro. They are undoubtedly the main attraction of the country, so set aside sufficient time and money to see them properly.

The entrance fee for national parks is US$15 per day (half that for children between the ages of three and 16) in cash dollars or other hard currency, or Sh 240 per day with a bank receipt to prove you changed the money officially. Per day, motor vehicles cost Sh 100 (private) or Sh 200 (commercial) under 2000 kg weight, and Sh 400 (private) or Sh 800 (commercial) over 2000 kg. Camping on established sites costs Sh 40 per person per day (Sh 20 for children between the ages of three and 16); at other sites it costs Sh 60 per person per day (Sh 30 for children between the ages of three and 16). In many parks a guide is compulsory. The fee for a guide is Sh 50 per day or Sh 125 if you go off the beaten track. There are no student concessions.

Make sure your currency declaration form is in order and that no one is going to find undeclared money on you before you enter any national park. Your form and currency will be checked thoroughly (often by officials with calculators) and if they don't match up, you're in for trouble.

Hiring Vehicles & Tours

The cheapest vehicle to hire for a tour of the national parks is a VW Combi microbus. They take up to seven people and will cost Sh 250 per day plus Sh 8 per km. If you want something more rugged, a Land-Rover (which also takes up to seven people) will cost Sh 250 plus Sh 11 per km. Anything better than these gets pricey: Range-Rover (Sh 400 per day plus Sh 14.50 per km); Peugeot 504 (Sh 400 per day plus Sh 8.50 per km); Ford Transit (up to 13 people at Sh 400 per day plus Sh 15 per km); 25-seater bus (Sh 400 per day plus Sh 18 per km).

One company which has been recommended is *Subzali Tours and Safaris*, PO Box 3061, Arusha (tel 3681). Their charges include a driver.

For tours (as opposed to hiring a vehicle), try *Arumeru*, PO Box 730, Arusha (tel 2780) on the street perpendicular to Uhuru Rd across from the Metropole cinema. For Sh 3800 per person they'll take you on a four-day, five-night tour of Serengeti, Ngorongoro Crater, Lake Manyara and Olduvai Gorge. Each tour takes seven people and the price is all-inclusive (accommodation, meals, park fees, vehicle, guides, driver, etc). They also have three-day tours to

Ngorongoro Crater and Lake Manyara for Sh 6800 shared between six people, which includes accommodation, food and park fees (but not park fees for the vehicle). *Star Tours*, AICC, Ngorongoro Building, 1st floor, Rooms 139 & 140, PO Box 1099, Arusha (tel 3181 ext 2202), now charge Sh 3500 per person but the price only includes vehicle, fuel and driver. You pay extra for accommodation, meals and park fees. Their itinerary is the same. They also offer a three-day, two-night tour of Lake Manyara, Ngorongoro Crater and Gibb's Farm (a coffee farm with waterfalls) for about US$25 each.

Serengeti National Park

This large park in north-east Tanzania lies adjacent to the Masai Mara National Reserve over the border in Kenya and offers some of the most spectacular sights in Africa. The best time to see the wildebeest, zebra and other herd animals is from December to May, when they mass on the plains in the southern part of the park. After this they move away to the north and the east, where there is permanent water. They head back down south with the arrival of the short rains in November. Unfortunately, it isn't as easy as it used to be to get to camping and other accommodation in Seronera village in the middle of the park, as the bus which used to run between Musoma and Arusha via Seronera is very unreliable. You may well have to get there by truck or try to find someone with a vehicle in Moshi, Arusha or Musoma who intends going there and with whom you can share expenses. This being the case, it makes a lot of sense (as in Kenya) to get a group together and hire a vehicle.

Land-Rover trips are available through the park with park rangers but, again, this can be expensive unless you're part of a group. The trips cost Sh 80 per km (minimum 65 km). It's a good idea to take a guide along with you. They charge Sh 50 per trip and can be hired at the park headquarters.

There are a number of campsites in the park, though initially you'll probably find yourself staying at the one located several km from Seronera village (costs Sh 40 per person per day). If you have no camping equipment, there is a hostel at Seronera village itself with dormitory-style rooms, cold-water showers and toilets which costs Sh 50 per person per night. Bring your own bedding. Candles and a torch are also very useful, as there's no electricity. You can eat at the hotel in the village but the quality of the food is poor. The *Seronera Lodge* about one km from the village is an expensive place designed for well-heeled tourists. Both the campsite and the hostel are within 20 minutes' walk from the Lodge, though not in the same place.

There is a lodge and camping at Ndutu on the border between Serengeti and Ngorongoro Crater parks.

If you like, you can book ahead for the campsites and lodges at the Tanzanian National Parks, PO Box 3134, Arusha, but it isn't really necessary. Make sure you ask for and get a receipt for any lodging you take; otherwise you'll be given a hard time when you get to Ngorongoro Crater.

Ngorongoro Crater

If Serengeti is spectacular, Ngorongoro is unreal. This vast plain in the crater of an extinct volcano (which, at 20 km across and 700 metres deep, is the world's second largest) is world famous for its immense herds and just about any other wild animal you would expect to see in East Africa. It's a microcosm – though on a large scale – of all the national parks in this part of the world, and if you can only afford to see one, this is the place to visit. Entry to the park costs Sh 50 and officials at the entrance are hot on currency forms.

As with Serengeti, it can be very difficult to get to Crater Village at the entrance to Ngorongoro with public transport. *Shaz Bus Co* is supposed to run a bus here from Arusha, but it's always breaking down. It used to be possible to get to Crater Village on the same Arusha-Musoma bus which passed through Seronera village; however, it's very unreliable so you'll probably have to hitch. Even this will take time, but the big disappointment will come if, when you get there, the park vehicles which take people on trips down into the Crater have no petrol.

If you don't want to risk this, it's worth thinking about arranging a tour in Arusha. You need a group in order to share the cost. *Star Tours & Safaris*, AICC, Ngorongoro Building, 1st Floor, Rooms 139 & 140, PO 1099, Arusha (tel 3181 ext 2202), has been recommended by some travellers. Others have said that the company's vehicles are not that well maintained (so you get numerous breakdowns), that the drivers try their best to cut down on game-viewing times, and that they try to get the passengers to pay for the vehicle and the guide's costs for Ngorongoro Crater (their safaris are supposed to be all-inclusive). They offer a three-day, two-night tour to Ngorongoro for Sh 11,900 (or Sh 16,000 for four days) including driver. Up to seven people can share the cost of this. It might be better to check out the following two companies, which offer exactly the same safari at the same price: *Arumeru Tours & Safaris*, PO Box 730, Seth Benjamin St opposite the Metropole cinema, Arusha (tel 2780); and *Himat Tours*, Conference Building, PO Box 7008, Arusha (tel 1300).

If you do decide to make your own way and there's no Arusha-Musoma bus available, then first hitch to Karatu. If you get stuck there you can stay at the *Kirway Guest House* for Sh 60 a single in good, pleasant rooms; or at the *New Safari Guest House*, which costs Sh 40 a single but isn't as good as the Kirway.

Only 4WD vehicles are allowed into the crater; you have a choice of going down in what is effectively a public 4WD bus or hiring a vehicle of your own. The latter will cost Sh 1000 for half a day and Sh 2000 for a full day. *State Travel* hire out Land-

Rovers with a driver for Sh 1250 per ½ day which can be shared between seven or eight people. Even if you see a lot in half a day, you'll wish you'd booked the whole day. A guide is compulsory and you must produce your currency form before you can rent a vehicle. If you're not hiring a vehicle, the tour buses leave from Crater Village every morning at about 8 am and arrive on the crater bottom about ½ hour later.

Most people stay in or around Crater Village. A popular place is *Simba campsite* at Crater Rim about two km from the village. It costs Sh 40 and has hot showers, toilets and firewood. The camp is now guarded, as the local Masai were beginning to steal things from the camps. There are two other campsites down in the crater for those with their own vehicles; these cost Sh 75 per person per night, but if you want to stay in one of them then you must have a ranger with you at all times. This will cost Sh 120 per day. If you have no camping equipment, there is a simple lodge about two km from Crater Rim. It's run by the Ngorongoro Consumers Co-operative Society and costs Sh 50 a single and Sh 100 a double. Bring something warm to sleep in, as only one blanket is provided. Keep an eye on your gear because the rooms don't lock. Meals of rice and meat are available nearby for Sh 15, and you can get a drink at either the cooperative store or at the market stalls.

At Crater Village itself there's a simple lodge where workers and drivers normally stay. You can get a double room here for Sh 50. They offer cheap, simple food.

Ask about rooms at these places at the *Ushirika Co-op Restaurant*, which offers good, cheap food.

If you're in need of comfort or don't mind a splurge, try the *Crater Lodge*. It costs Sh 600 a double plus tax for bed and breakfast and Sh 1200 a double plus tax for full board. It's expensive but has been built on a tremendous site. Similar is the *Forest Lodge*, five km from Crater Village. It's possible to camp here.

If you're putting your own food together, you can buy most of the staples you're likely to need at Crater Village (bread, cabbage, onions, dried beans, tomatoes, etc).

If you have the opportunity en route to Ngorongoro, call off and stay for the night at *Gibb's Farm* – a coffee farm run by an English couple who offer superb lunches for Sh 150 (soup, roast pork/beef, quiches, flans, salads, rhubarb crumble with cream and coffee!).

Lake Manyara National Park

West of Arusha, this is one of the smallest and most beautiful of the national parks. Its main attractions are the herds of elephant and the prolific birdlife. April to September is a good time to visit, as the storks and pelicans are nesting, but other travellers have recommended Christmas, when the park teems with a wide variety of animal life.

To see the park properly you need your own vehicle, as there is no public transport inside the park and you're not allowed to walk in there.

This park is considerably easier to get to than most of the other national parks because it's virtually on the main Arusha-Dodoma road. A bus from Arusha to Mto Wa Mbu (the village one km from the park entrance) costs Sh 60. Occasional buses run from the YMCA in Moshi when the demand warrants it.

There are several campsites near the entrance to the park which you should, if possible, book in advance through the Tanzanian National Parks, PO Box 3134, Arusha. Campsite No 2 has been recommended – self-help bandas under huge fig trees with running water, toilets and firewood. Beware of greedy baboons. The sites cost Sh 40 per person and the bandas Sh 150 a double. If you have your own transport, the campsite up on the plateau near the *Manyara Hotel* inside the park itself is recommended, though you'll have to pay the Sh 40 daily entrance fee as well as the charge for the site. There is a *Youth*

Hostel on the right-hand side after you enter the park gate, but it appears to close from time to time; some travellers have reported it to be empty when they've turned up. Others, however, have had no such problems and have got a bed there for Sh 40 per night.

If you don't want to camp or you haven't got the equipment, stay at the *Rift Valley Hotel* in Mto Wa Mbu. This costs Sh 85 a double. They have a Land-Rover for hire which costs Sh 700 for four hours. There's a supermarket in the village and a local open market which is a good place to see Masai tribespeople.

Mount Kilimanjaro

Climbing Mount Kilimanjaro is one of the star attractions of a visit to East Africa. Anyone who is reasonably fit will make it to the top. No special equipment is required, but you do need to take plenty of warm clothing with you for the last section of the climb as it's very cold at night – Kilimanjaro is 5895 metres high (19,340 feet). The main path is well trodden and easy to follow, and you can stay for the night in a series of huts. You need to take all your food with you, and a portable cooker is very useful. (How else are you going to cook those dried packet soups that warm you up when the sun has gone down?) You will need a water container, as there is no water beyond the second hut. If you need to hire anything, you can do so in Arusha, at the YMCA in Moshi, at the hotels in Marangu, or at the park entrance, but the equipment at the park entrance is limited and of poor quality. One traveller who rented equipment from the park gate commented, 'The boots were too small, had no laces and no tongue – I was provided with a piece of string and the explanation 'Tanzanian shoelaces'; the sleeping bag was ripped and the zipper didn't work; the sweater was patched in five or six places; the jacket was too small and soaked from the previous user. I had no complaints about the gloves or the hat.'

The climb starts at 1800 metres (6000 feet). The first day is a hard slog but the second and third days are much easier. The first hut (Maraba) is at 9000 feet and is set in a small clearing from which there is a spectacular view over the valleys, plains, lakes and forests all the way to the horizon. The climb goes through forest which often forms a canopy over the trail, and there are numerous streams to cross. The next day up to Horombo hut (12,000 feet) first goes through dense forest, eventually comes out above the treeline and then continues over more rocky terrain with sparser vegetation. If your clothes are soaked by the time you get to Horombo, don't assume you'll be able to dry them there, as all available firewood is generally reserved for cooking. You may also have to cope with a lack of bunks at this hut, as it's the stop-over for people coming down the mountain. Meals are generally done in shifts.

Early on the third day you clear the rocky terrain and get onto the saddle. From here on it's a barren moonscape surface and you can see Kibo hut from a long way off. When you get there you'll be at 4650 metres (15,500 feet). The porters don't go beyond this point so you'll have to carry any gear you need with you. It's a very good idea to stay for two nights at the third hut to rest and acclimatise rather than carry straight on to the top. If you don't do this and aren't used to these altitudes, you'll probably have a thumping headache and won't enjoy the trip at all. You might not even make it to the top. Headaches at this altitude are a normal reaction. They don't necessarily mean you have altitude sickness. If you do get the latter, you'll have a lot of other symptoms too (in which case you'd better head down fast). Arranged tours normally only have you stay at the third hut for one night, so get them to change this to two nights.

Whether you stay one night or two at Kibo hut, guides will begin waking you between midnight and 1 am for the final ascent. It's very steep and cold and slow going because of the thin air, but you should reach Gilman's Peak before sunrise. From here you can see the crater's interior and the glaciers surrounding the edges, though rolling cloud may obscure the view. Unless you have boots with cleats, you will not be allowed to continue on to Uhuru Peak through the ice and snow – another two hours' slow walk away. You need plenty of warm clothes up at the top. Don't skimp or you'll freeze to death. The upper reaches of the mountain are clothed in cloud after 9 am.

The two-day descent is considerably easier and you should be back at Marangu gate around noon.

Most travellers these days go on a tour, since you don't save much by attempting to do it all on your own. Most of the fees are standard anyway regardless of who you go with, and a guide is compulsory. Organising your own tour involves a lot of running around, so most people find they haven't got much energy left for cooking by the time they reach the huts. If someone is doing that for you, it makes a lot of difference.

Most travellers take the Marangu trek; though there are two other treks, they don't have the same facilities (huts, etc), so considerably more organisation is needed on these. The other two routes start from villages nearer Moshi, but don't go through the national park or you'll be subject to the fees.

The standard fees on the Marangu trail (whoever you go with) are as follows:
Entrance: US$15 per day (or Sh 240 with bank receipts)
Hut: Sh 70 per night (or Sh 40 for camping)
Rescue: Sh 80 (covers expenses up to Sh 2000)
Guides and porters: Sh 400 for the guide, Sh 350 for the assistant guide and Sh 300 for a porter per five days/four nights. Porters will carry up to 15 kg of your baggage plus five kg of their own.
Guides and porters' hut: Sh 80 per night per person

A quick calculation will tell you that the absolute minimum for this trip excluding food, cooking equipment, utensils, hire of extra clothing and transport to the park will be Sh 1850 and will not include an extra day at the last hut for acclimatisation. (This day will cost an extra Sh 390 excluding the same things.) However, discounts seem to be available, as the prices below indicate.

Knowing the above, you are in a position to compare costs of the tours being offered. Many travellers take the tour organised by the YMCA in Moshi. It costs Sh 2250 for one person alone, Sh 1755 each for two people and Sh 1700 each for more than two people. This includes park fees, guide, porters, and cooking utensils. It does not include equipment rentals, food (average cost Sh 400) and transport to the park gate (usually Sh 1200 shared with whoever else is going). Book through the Secretary, Travel Service, YMCA, PO Box 85, Moshi, Tanzania (tel 2362/4734).

The *Marangu Hotel* in Marangu, charge Sh 3000 and the *Kibo Hotel* charges Sh 2900, but these charges include transport to the gate and all necessary equipment (except boots). Many travellers have commented that their guides and porters are more professional than those with other tours and that the food is amazingly good.

The national parks also organise tours. Their price for a five-day/four-night tour is Sh 3112, which includes everything except extra clothing and transport to the park gates. They hire extra equipment/ clothing at the following rates: sleeping bags (Sh 100); boots (Sh 100); sweaters (Sh 80); raincoats (Sh 60); goggles (Sh 50); gloves (Sh 50); dacron jackets (Sh 80); long johns (Sh 66); water bottles (Sh 10); socks (Sh 50); balaclavas (Sh 60); rucksacks (Sh 120); rain trousers (Sh 60). And they even have hang-gliders for hire – Sh 1500!

All the hotels and organisations (including the national parks) which organise tours also lay on transport from various points (such as Moshi, Arusha and Marangu) to the park gate, but it's not cheap. If you want to reduce costs, take public transport. There is a local bus from Moshi to Marangu for Sh 10. The bus goes to the foot of the dead-end road which leads to the park entrance. It's a four-km walk from there. You can generally leave extra baggage at your hotel.

If you're bringing your own food, it's a good idea to buy it in Arusha or Moshi. The selection at Marangu is limited.

Officially you must pay for the above tours either in hard currency or with local currency backed up by bank receipts. There is scope for negotiation here, but (as one irate traveller commented) it would be an act of almost criminal naivete to name names!

Guides and porters expect a handsome tip at the end of a climb. Sh 100 or a T-shirt is normally expected.

There's a good choice of places to stay before you climb Kilimanjaro. Both the YMCA and the national parks have hostels near the park gates. Per person, the latter charge Sh 60 per night (cold-water showers only) and Sh 80 per night (hot-water showers); camping is possible. The park hostel has an excellent cook who turns out delicious meals at Sh 60-70 for either lunch or dinner,

If you need comfort or you don't mind splurging, try the *Marangu Hotel*, which costs Sh 375 with full board; or try the *Kibo Hotel*. Both are in Marangu village and are good value but the former is generally more popular with travellers.

Arusha National Park

The main attraction here is Mount Meru which, at 15,000 feet, is a smaller version of Mount Kilimanjaro. Quite a few travellers climb this mountain first in order to get acclimatised for the trek up Kilimanjaro. The climb takes three to four days and there are huts at 8000 feet and 11,500 feet. As for Kilimanjaro, you must take a guide but porters are optional. Currency forms are demanded when paying for services.

There are campsites in the park and at *Momella Lodge*.

Mikumi National Park

On the road from Dar to Mbeya, this is a delightful small park with large herds of buffalo, elephant, lion and other animals. If you're lucky you might catch sight of giraffes in herds of over 50 and lions in prides of 20 or more. Check out the hangar at the airstrip, as this seems to be one of their favourite haunts. If possible, visit during the week (rather than the weekend), as it's very quiet then. To get there, you can take the luxury bus from the railway station in Dar; it will drop you off on the main road right by the tented campsite and less than a two-km walk from the lodge. The lodge costs Sh 400 for a double with breakfast (other meals cost Sh 100 for a three-course meal). Its swimming pool is beautifully situated above a waterhole. Through the lodge telescope you can see lots of game – the elephants come in really close at night.

Togo

Like Gambia further to the west, Togo is another idiosyncratic legacy of 19th-century European colonialism. This narrow sliver of a country encompasses people from very different cultural and linguistic backgrounds, yet they have been welded together to form a modern nation without any discernible tribal rivalry. On the other hand, there has been a good deal of political opposition to the military regime of Major-General Etienne Eyadema which has ruled the country since 1967, but most of the leaders live in exile in Paris. The Rassemblement du Peuple Togolais, the only legal party and one of Eyadema's creations, has been active for many years rooting out opposition at a grass-roots level and subjecting former trade union radicals to brutal repression. As a result, many Togolese have sought political asylum abroad. At the time of independence, incorporation into Ghana would have made a lot of sense, especially as the border between the two countries cuts through the Ewe heartland. But although a referendum in 1962 came out in favour of integration with that country, it was blocked by Sylvanus Olympio, the country's first president. The opportunity to bring this about now seems to have passed.

Togo became a German colony in the 1880s, but it wasn't until 1902 that 'pacification' was completed. The Germans set about establishing plantations and building a communications network, but they were overtaken by WW I, after which the colony was divided between the British and French under a League of Nations mandate. The division of the Ewe people was not to their liking, and when nationalism developed shortly after WW II, it centred around unification of the territory. This was never to occur, since not only were the French colonial authorities violently opposed to the idea, but in 1956 a plebiscite was held in the British part which resulted in its incorporation into Ghana, then about to be granted independence. The French part gained its independence in 1960 under the leadership of Sylvanus Olympio.

Not long after independence, however, major differences of opinion arose between Olympio, a member of a powerful trading family and director of the United Africa Company (controlled by British capital), and the Juvento, the youth arm of his political party Comité de l'Unité Togolaise. The Juvento had played an important part in 'the radicalisation of the nationalist movement and was not to be taken lightly. Nevertheless, Olympio attempted to suppress it but was overthrown in a military coup in 1963. His place was taken by Grunitzky, who was brought back from exile in Paris, but he too was overthrown in a military coup in 1967. Eyadema, who led the coup, has ruled the country ever since.

One of the ironies of Togo is that the north could produce sufficient millet, rice and yams to make the country self-sufficient in these foodstuffs, but there is an acute shortage of labour due to long-term and seasonal migration into Ghana. It is estimated that at any one time there are as many as 200,000 to 300,000 young Togolese men working in Ghana.

FACTS

Although it has a coastline of only 56 km, Togo stretches inland for some 540 km.

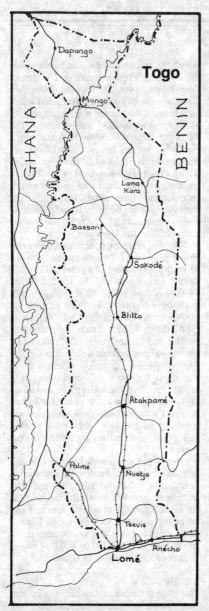

The centre of the country is mountainous and forested with deciduous trees, whereas the north and south are savannah. The main rainy season lasts from April to July and there is a short rainy period from October to November. Togo is densely populated with over 2½ million inhabitants. The largest tribal groups are the Ewe and Kabre.

VISAS

Visas are required by all except nationals of Belgium, Canada, Denmark, France, Germany (West), Italy, Luxembourg, Netherlands, Norway, Sweden and the USA. Where there is no Togolese embassy, visas can generally be obtained from the French embassy.

Visa extensions can be obtained from the Sureté National in Lomé but they take three days to issue and the bureaucracy can be a headache.

You must get an exit visa (Permit d'Embarquement) from the Sureté National if you stay in Togo more than 10 days. These cost CFA 1500. You must apply 48 hours before you intend to leave.

The French consulate (not the French embassy – this is in another building) in Lomé issues visas for Burkina Faso, the Central African Republic, Chad, Djibouti, Ivory Coast, Mauritania and Senegal. Each one of them costs CFA 3000, requires two photos and is issued within 48 hours. The visas are valid for a stay of three months.

Benin visas There is no Benin embassy in Lomé and you cannot get your visa from the French consulate. However, the Benin government has finally woken up to the fact that this makes it very difficult for travellers going from Togo to Benin, so you can now get visas at the border (Ouidah) on the Lomé-Cotonou road. A one-month visa costs CFA 1000 and is issued while you wait. This is the only exception for getting Benin visas at the border.

Ghana visas A visitor's pass costs CFA 1030 and a visa costs CFA 2060 for a visa. Four photos are required and the visa takes three days to issue. You need the name and address of a Ghanaian resident when you apply for the visa if you want any hope of getting the maximum time (14 days). Many people get only five-day transit visas. Embassy officials often will not accept a hotel address on a visa application form.

Nigerian visas The embassy is on the Boulevard Circulaire. Visas take three days to issue and two photos are required. Prices depend on your nationality (French, CFA 1600; German, CFA 4500).

Other Embassies These include Egypt, Gabon (visas cost CFA 4000 and take one month to issue – all applications have to be referred to Libreville), Ghana and Zaire.

MONEY
US$1 = CFA 425

The unit of currency is the CFA franc. Import of local currency is allowed up to CFA 25,000. Export is limited to CFA 50,000.

Lomé is the black market capital of West Africa and a very good place to buy the currencies of other West African countries (except the CFA zone), especially those of Ghana and Nigeria. Be careful with street dealers, as they're very good with sleight-of-hand tricks. Count all the bills you're handed one by one and then give them your money. Ghanaian cedi are freely available at the rate of CFA 1000 = 340 cedi (the official rate is CFA 3500). If you're buying naira (CFA 1100 = naira 10 or US$1 = naira 7), watch out for old naira notes which are worthless (Nigeria called in all old naira notes in April/May 1984 and issued new ones – see the Nigerian chapter for more details).

The airport tax for international flights is CFA 2500.

LANGUAGE
French is the official language. The major African languages are Ewe and Kabre.

GETTING THERE & AROUND
Air
Air Afrique has a youth fare (12-29 years old) which offers 45% discounted air fares on intra-African flights. They also offer 30% discounts on seven– to 30-day round trips within Africa regardless of age.

Air Afrique, *Air Gabon* and *Air Zaire* all offer flights from Lomé to Libreville (Gabon). Flights cost CFA 76,000-78,000. Air Zaire is very liberal about excess baggage.

There is a black market for airline tickets in Lomé. They're usually of the 'via Lagos' variety but customs officers in Nigeria have been known to confiscate them if you have no Nigerian currency. (Just why they do this wasn't clear from the letter we received.) Before you buy one of these tickets, read about similar schemes in the Benin and Nigeria chapters. It seems that a discreet bribe is all that's necessary if you encounter problems. Whatever you do, don't hand over money until you have the ticket in your hand. Ask around at Alice Place, Ramatou or Robinson Plage if interested.

Road
Except in the extreme north, roads are very good and sealed all the way to the Burkina Faso border. Hitching is fairly easy but becomes progressively more difficult the further north you go (traffic thins out).

There is an excellent network of mini-buses which cost about the same as pick-up trucks but are more comfortable and usually much less crowded. A rucksack can cost up to CFA 100 extra depending on the distance. Some examples of the fares are:

Lomé-K'Palimé CFA 600
Lomé-Atakpamé CFA 800
Lomé-Dapango CFA 2950 or CFA 3250 by Peugeot taxi

Lomé-Lama Kara CFA 2025
K'Palimé-Atakpamé CFA 500
Atakpamé-Sokodé CFA 950
Atakpamé-Lama Kara CFA 1800 or CFA 2200 by Peugeot taxi

Journey times depend a lot on how many police checkpoints you have to go through – they occur every 30 km or so along most roads, though they are slowly being phased out.

Minibuses and taxis are available to Benin and Nigeria from Lomé. According to the board at the taxi park near the Grand Marche in Lomé the prices are as follows:

Lomé-Grand Popo CFA 700 by minibus
Lomé-Ouidah CFA 1000 by minibus
Lomé-Cotonou CFA 1200 by minibus and CFA 1500 by taxi
Lomé-Porto Novo CFA 1500 by minibus
Lomé-Lagos CFA 2500 by minibus and CFA 3000 by taxi

Baggage charges are additional to the above fares.

If you're heading towards Ouagadougou (Burkina Faso), it's cheaper to do the journey in stages. You need to get up early if you're going to do this. First take a minibus (CFA 2950) or a Peugeot taxi (CFA 3250) to Dapango. Another taxi from there to Ouagadougou costs CFA 3000. If you get a direct taxi from Lomé to Ouagadougou, it will cost you CFA 10,000.

Rail

The main line runs north from Lomé to Blitta via Atakpamé. There are also branch lines from Lomé to K'Palimé and Lomé to Anecho. On the Lomé-Blitta line the train departs Lomé daily about 5.45 am and arrives between 1 and 1.30 pm. It then turns around and goes back to Lomé, arriving about 9 pm. The fare is CFA 2210 (1st class – comfortable) and CFA 1000 (2nd class – crowded). On the Lomé-K'Palimé line there are two trains daily in either direction at 6.30 am and 2 pm from

K'Palimé. The journey takes at least six hours and costs CFA 475 (2nd class). Take food and water with you on the trains. Fruit can be bought at stations en route.

ANECHO

Try the *Hotel Oasis*, which costs CFA 3000 without air-conditioning and CFA 5000 with air-conditioning. The rooms are good value, but eat elsewhere as the food is expensive. For cheaper food try *As des Picques*. The staff are friendly.

ATAKPAMÉ

A popular place to stay is the *Relais des Plateaux*, 500 metres to the right from the bus station. It is very pleasant and has double rooms for CFA 2500 including shower and fan, and CFA 3500 with shower and air-conditioning. The owners are French. The *Rock Hotel* has rooms for CFA 2000 (single or double). Another cheap place recommended in the past is the *Relais du Sorad* on the road into town. The *Bar Solidarité* is a good place to eat and you might well meet Peace Corps volunteers.

Other travellers have recommended *Hotel Alafia*, a very good hotel with a bar and restaurant. The Alafia is in Hiheatro, a village about two km out of Atakpamé on the K'Palimé road. You can get a room here for CFA 1000.

DAPANGO

Try the *Hotel l'Union* opposite the *douane* in town. It has good rooms for CFA 1500 and an attached restaurant. Otherwise there is the *Cercle de l'Amitier*, which costs CFA 2500 a double and CFA 2000 a single. It's a very clean place. Another hotel further from town than Le Campement is very pleasant and costs CFA 2000 a double (the correspondent didn't say what it was called). Le Campement itself charges CFA 3500 for a double or a single. In the evening the best place to meet local people is the *Relais des Savannes*, a pleasant bar.

KANDÉ

Le Campement on the main road costs CFA 1500 without fan or CFA 2000 with fan.

LAMA KARA

A nice place to stay and popular with travellers is the *Hotel Sapaw*, which costs CFA 2000 a single and CFA 2200 a double. To get there go down the Rue de l'Hotel Kara (the expensive hotel) about 400 metres from the main road to the Wax Restaurant; then go left about 100 metres down a dirt road. You'll see a sign there. Eat at the *Mini-Rizerie* opposite the post office. It serves excellent food and you may meet Peace Corps volunteers here. Another good restaurant is the *Wax*.

The village of Ketau is well worth visiting on Wednesdays for its huge market – the second largest in Togo.

K'PALIMÉ (formerly Palimé)

Most people stay at the *Delima Bar*. It's a good place and costs only CFA 1200 a double. The owner will cook you an omelette and chips if you ask. Otherwise, *Hotel Solo* is a bargain at CFA 500 a single and CFA 800 a double for rooms with a fan. The *Hotel Concordia* has rooms for CFA 1500 a single and CFA 2500 a double. The attached restaurant serves good food and the bar has lots of local colour but the music can be very loud. Another place to stay is *Le Campement* at Kloto, about 12 km from K'Palimé.

LOMÉ

Information

The Tourist Office is next to the Garage Renault between the Rue du Commerce and Boulevard de la République, about one km east of the centre.

The Sureté National is two blocks directly south of the railway station. Before you apply for an embarkation permit/exit visa, get an *attestation* from the airline first to confirm that you have a ticket. You don't need a permit if you have stayed less than 10 days. Permits are free,

no photos are needed and they are issued in 48 hours.

The address for American Express is STMP, 2 Rue de Commerce (tel 6190).

The poste restante charges CFA 100 per letter. Letters are often misfiled.

Most of the airlines have their offices on the Rue du Commerce, Rue du Grande Marche and Route d'Atakpamé.

French Consulate This consulate (not the embassy, which is in a different building) handles the visas for Bourkinafasso, Central African Republic, Chad, Djibouti, Ivory Coast, Mauritania and Senegal. To get there from the Hotel Benin on Boulevard de la République, go up Avenue Général de Gaulle for one block. A small road angles off to the right there and the consulate is half a block up this road. It's only open from 8.30 to 11.30 am Monday to Friday.

Ghana embassy The embassy is situated off the Route de Palimé (it's signposted), about two to three km from the centre. Hours are 8 to 11 am Monday to Friday.

Mali visas There is no Mali embassy in Lomé, but embassy staff are supposed to visit the *Air Mali* office on Thursday, Friday and Saturday; the hours are irregular so it's hit-and-miss whether you find them. If you do catch them, it should be possible to get a Mali visa. If not, you'll have to go elsewhere – eg to Accra, Ghana.

Health

Vaccinations are obtainable from the Institute of Hygiene one block east of Avenue Sarakawa (about halfway along). It's open Monday to Friday from 7 am to noon and 2.30 to 5.30 pm. The Institute can supply cholera vaccine (CFA 900) but you will have to bring other vaccines with you. The best place to get them is *Pharmacie Pour Tous* near the Café de Chine on the Route de K'Palimé. *Togopharma* and the *Pharmacie de Boulevard*

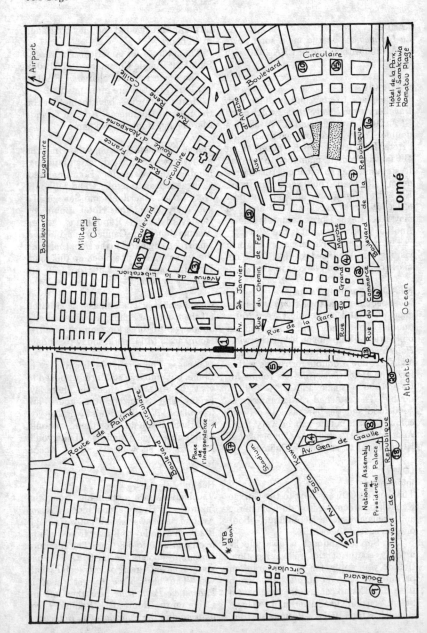

don't usually stock vaccines. There is a charge for the injection itself – CFA 450 is usual.

Places to Stay

In town there are a number of places are popular with budget travellers. One of the cheapest is *Hotel Atlantique* behind the Customs building, which has beds for CFA 1500 but there are no fans in the rooms. Good food is available in the evening for CFA 200-350. *Hotel de la Plage*, junction of Boulevard Circulaire and Boulevard de la République right on the seafront, has rooms for CFA 2500-3200 a double with shower and fan (the more expensive rooms have a toilet). They also have doubles with air-conditioning, shower and toilet for CFA 5000. It's excellent value. *Hotel La Refuge* is a friendly place with its own restaurant and has rooms for CFA 2000 a double with shower but no toilet, CFA 2500 a double with shower and toilet, and CFA 3000 a double with shower, toilet and mosquito nets. *Hotel Paloma* is centrally located but is grubby and often has no water (in which case you have to fetch it from the well). It costs CFA 2500 a double.

Out on the Route K'Palimé, very close to the Chinese embassy, is the *Agni*, which has become popular of late and costs CFA 2000 a double. On the same road but six km from the Cathedral is the new *Hotel Todman*, which has very pleasant doubles with fan and shared toilets and showers

for CFA 3500. It has a cosy attached restaurant.

Other places which have been recommended in the past include *Hotel Boulevard* (CFA 3500 a double), *Hotel Ahoudikpé Eboma* (CFA 3000 a double with fan and CFA 5000 a double with air-conditioning), the *Foyer des Marins* (from CFA 3000 per room) and the *Continental Hotel* (CFA 3000 a single with fan, CFA 4000 a single with air-conditioning and CFA 5000 a double with air-conditioning). Meals are available at the Ahoudikpé.

If you're looking for something very much upmarket, try *Hotel Le Benin*, where the cheapest rooms are CFA 10,000. You can buy steak and chips by the swimming pool for CFA 1600 or prawn kebabs at the same price. There are cheaper dishes too.

Beach Accommodation Few travellers stay longer than a couple of nights in Lomé itself. Almost everyone heads out east of the city to one or other of the beach spots – *Robinson Plage*, *Campement Ramatou* or *Alice Place*. They're all close to one another, about 9½ km east of Lomé. Both Robinson Plage and Ramatou are good but the first is probably the best of them all because it's right on the beach. Alice Place has been described as 'a shit heap with no showers, disgusting toilets and CFA 500 to pitch a tent with no sea views.' Ramatou is about 100 metres from the sea, has good toilets and showers and

---

Key
1. Railway Station
2. Cathedral
3. Main Post Office
4. Grand Marche
5. Surete National & Police
6. Air Afrique & UTA
7. United States Embassy
8. French Embassy
9. British Embassy & Hotel de la Plage
10. Nigerian Embassy
11. Mosque
12. Restaurant Senegalaise
13. Hotel Atlantique
14. French Consulate
15. Zaire Embassy
16. **Tourist Office**
17. Hotel 2 Fevrier
18. Hotel Benin
19. BIAO Bank
20. BCCI Bank

costs CFA 500 to camp or CFA 2000-3000 for a *paillotte* (a wooden beach hut). There is a restaurant with prices similar to those at Robinson Plage. Robinson Plage itself is under new management (a French couple who are very friendly and easy-going). It costs the same as Ramatou, but it's on the beach under the palms and has a lovely terrace with good sea breezes. The *paillottes* take four to eight people – you pay for the hut rather than the number of people sleeping there. The toilets and showers are good. Excellent meals are available for CFA 2700-3000 exclusive of drinks (lobster is CFA 3500). Beers and soft drinks are somewhat pricey at CFA 200 for a small bottle. Keep an eye on your belongings in all these places – theft is on the increase.

House Rental If you want or have to stay in Lomé for two or three months, it's worth looking round for a house to rent. During the months of June, July, August and, to some extent, September, many European expatriates go home to Europe on their annual holidays, leaving their homes unoccupied. Many of these people (the majority of whom are French and German) look for 'house-sitters' before they go. If you build up a few contacts with Euro-peans working here, you may be able to rent a house in this way. Some ask for rent (CFA 5000-10,000 per month); others let you stay rent-free so long as you pay for gas and electricity and leave a deposit to cover possible damages.

Places to Eat
One of the most popular places in town and the one most expatriates rate highly as far as quality and price go is the *Relais de la Poste*, 50 metres from the PTT. The food is excellent though it costs a little more than at the cheapest places. *Escale*, at the market on the Boulevard; and *Bopato*, in front of the BIAO bank, offer some of the cheapest meals in town. Typical prices would be: *pressions* CFA 60; soda (½ litre) CFA 90; beer (½ litre)

CFA 60-100; spaghetti and meat CFA 200; *pommes frites* with bread CFA 200; omelette with bread CFA 200; steak CFA 300; half a chicken CFA 250; rice with sauce CFA 300. The *Amitie* on the Rue Grand Marche is also popular but a little more expensive. Expect to pay, on average, CFA 500 for a meal. *Restaurant Senegalaise* is similar. The *Jungle Bar* is said to have the cheapest drinks and kebabs in town. For an all-you-can-eat breakfast at CFA 1100, go to the *Hotel Sarakawa*. A new snack bar, *La Rabile*, recently opened at the junction of Route d'Atakpamé and the Boulevard Circulaire. They offer good sandwiches for around CFA 450.

Whilst you're in town go along to the *Bar Panoramique* on the 35th floor of the *Hotel 2 Fevrier*. It's worth the CFA 1200 fruit cocktail just for the views (if the air is clear). For more earthly pleasures try the *Seemannsheim/Foyer de Marins*, which is always crowded with lots of European seamen and whores. There's a swimming pool and air-conditioned bars. If that doesn't appeal, try one of the open-air night spots on the Route d'Atakpamé north of the Boulevard Circulaire.

There is both an *American Cultural Centre* and a *French Cultural Centre*. The American one is in front of the embassy. It offers a library and free movies on Friday evenings. The French one has a library and daily movies for CFA 200-400. It's on Avenue 24 Janvier close to the main post office. Both centres are worth visiting if you're looking for something to do. Entry is free.

If you are English or you can speak English, you may well come into contact with the English staff at the refinery. According to the impression you create, you may be invited to their private bar (snooker, darts, videos, BBC news, etc) in the evenings or to their swimming pool during the day. You might meet them at Robinson Plage or on your way from there or Ramatou to Lomé between 7 and 8.30 am, in which case they're more than likely to give you a lift whether you are hitching or not. They're extremely friendly people and enjoy talking with travellers.

Taxis around town cost CFA 175 per journey, though they're more expensive at night. A taxi from the centre of town to the airport will cost CFA 1000.

Detailed maps of Lomé can be obtained from the *Service Topographique et Cadastre* near the junction of Rue Marechal Joffre and the Avenue Albert Sarraut between the station and the sea.

The supermarket *Goyi-Score* stocks European products at prices more reasonable than elsewhere in Lomé or Niamey (Niger).

The market *La Marche-Be*, four km from the centre in the Quartier de Be, has all the normal stuff which markets sell plus a voodoo and fetish section – skins, bones, love potions, etc. It's well worth a visit and there are very few or no tourists.

SOKODÉ

You can either stay at the *Hotel Kododji*, which is clean and costs CFA 2000, or at *Le Campement* next to the *douane* on the road to Lomé. If you're looking for company, try the *Bar Sans Souci*, which is a Peace Corps hang-out.

TOGOVILLE

The north side of the Lac Togo is the centre of the fetish cult in Togo. You'll be lucky to find anywhere to stay, though you might be able to persuade the *Catholic Mission* to help out – it's an advantage if you're a Jesuit. Most people stay at Agbodrafo on the south side of the lake, where there are some very good hotels. The *Swiss Castle Club-Hotel* costs CFA 3000 a double. It's fairly flash, quiet and is more or less hidden behind a beautiful flower garden. *Hotel du Lac* is more expensive at CFA 5000 a double but has a beautiful terrace, a swimming pool and facilities for sailing and windsurfing. Pilots and nightclub owners stay here.

Tunisia

The smallest of the three Maghreb states, Tunisia has a rich cultural and social heritage stemming from the many empires which have come and gone in this part of the world ranging from the Phoenicians through the Romans, Byzantines, Arabs and Ottoman Turks to the French. In addition, there have been substantial numbers of immigrants from Spain, Italy and Malta, and many Jews are still numbered among the population. Because of the thoroughness of the Arab invasions, the original Berber population now forms only 1% of the total, confined mainly to the dry and inhospitable south of the country. In this respect Tunisia differs from the other Maghreb states of Algeria and Morocco, which still have very substantial Berber populations.

Phoenician staging posts were established very early on throughout the length and breadth of the Mediterranean, but remained relatively unimportant until the mother cities along the Syrian coast lost their independence in the 6th century BC and Greek colonies began to be planted in Cyrenaica (eastern Libya) from the 7th century BC onwards. As a result of these events, Carthage, a few km from Tunis, grew rapidly into the metropolis of the Phoenician world and, at its height, had a population of about a half million people. The Phoenicians, who were principally maritime traders, had a profound effect on the native Berbers by introducing them to advanced agricultural methods and urban living. The Jews too, many of whom were involved in trade, helped spread the idea of a monotheistic religion among these pagan tribes.

Carthage eventually fell to the Romans, who literally ploughed the city into the ground but were quick to appreciate the value of the settled Tunisian plains as a granary for the empire and began to erect their own cities here. The remains of many of these cities stand today and are among the country's principal attractions, though Roman Carthage itself is somewhat of a disappointment, much of its stone having been carted away to erect the later Arab cities. The most significant Roman contribution to this part of Africa, however, was largely incidental – that of opening up North Africa to the spread of Christianity. In the centuries following Roman conquest, Carthage became the greatest of Christian centres, second only to Alexandria, and produced one of that religion's central figures – St Augustine, a Libyan Berber educated in Carthage. Roman rule here was never popular and opposition to it found expression in religious doctrinal differences and the adoption of Donatism, regarded by the orthodox Byzantine Church as a heresy. Persecutions launched by Byzantium as a result alienated much of the population, but the many centuries of influence, first of Judaism and then of Christianity, paved the way for the rapid adoption of Islam, which had the advantage of not being associated with the imposition of foreign rule.

The Arabs first arrived in 670 AD and established a base at Kairouan, but they lost this after a disastrous attempt to conquer the lands further west and were not able to establish their control until the end of the century, when the Byzantine navy had been defeated and could not cut the Arab lines of supply to Egypt by landing troops in Libya. Even then they had to contend with a confederacy of

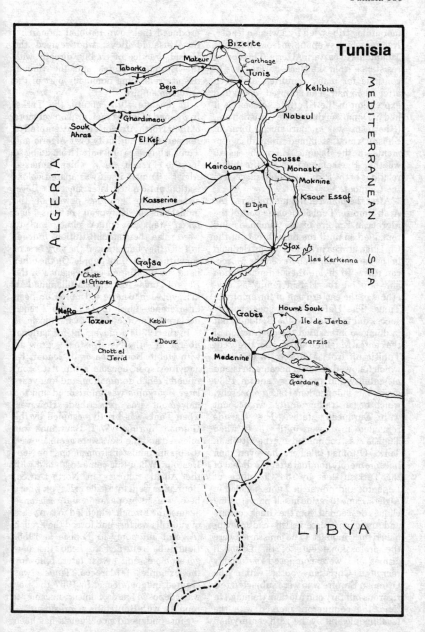

marauding tribes, led by a woman leader, Kahina, which swept down from the Aures Mountains in eastern Algeria. This sort of resistance from the Berber tribes was to continue for many centuries, and even after Islam had been adopted was to find expression in the Kharijite schism, as it had in Donatism during the Christian era. (Kharijism was a puritanical form of Sh'ism which stemmed from disagreements in the Islamic Hierarchy as to whether the companions or the blood relations of the Prophet should succeed to the Caliphate.)

After the political fragmentation of the Arab Empire, Tunisia became part of the Moroccan Empire of the Almohads and remained so until the dual threats of the Christian armies in Spain and the Bedouin in the central Maghreb forced the Moroccan rulers to divide their administration and appoint the Hafsid family as governors of the eastern half of the empire in Tunis. The Hafsids were spectacularly successful in defeating the Bedouin, but in doing so intensified the destruction of the central Maghreb and so effectively cut Tunisia off from Morocco. In the years which followed, Tunisia became an island of stability and prosperity and in 1230 created its independent Hafsid monarchy, which began trading on its own account with European states. The Hafsids remained in power until 1574, when Tunisia was conquered by the Ottoman Turks. Ottoman rule here, however, soon became merely nominal after the defeat of the Turkish fleet by the Christians at Lepanto; and power in Tunis, as also in Algiers, came to reside in self-perpetuating cliques descended from the Greek corsairs and Anatolian janissaries who had accomplished the conquest. (The janissaries were the professional elite of the Ottoman armies and were composed of forcibly recruited Christian youths within the Ottoman Empire who were subjected to a rigorous military and Moslem training.) In time, the conquerors merged with the local people and by the 18th century had produced their own national monarchy, the Husainid Beys, who revived the Hafsid practice of trading directly with the European states and the Sudan, despite remaining nominally part of the Ottoman empire.

In the late 19th century, the Turks, frightened of losing their grip on yet more of their North African lands, attempted to reassert their authority over Algeria and Tunisia but were prevented from doing so by the French navy which annexed Algiers. Tunisia itself was spared colonisation until much later since its Beys, aware of the growing power of the industrialised European nations, had taken steps to outlaw piracy and to westernise their administration. Indeed, in 1857 they had granted the very first of constitutions to their people. On the other hand, the continued extravagance of the Beys of Tunis – like that of Muhammed Ali in Egypt – led to more and more European interference until in 1881 the French declared a 'protectorate' over Tunisia.

In the 1930s a movement for national liberation – the Neo-Destour – grew up with Habib Bourguiba as its leader. Its activities soon became a threat to continued French domination, and four years later Bourguiba was imprisoned and the movement was proscribed. However, when Tunis was briefly occupied by the Germans during WW II Bourguiba was released and the Beys were again allowed to appoint ministers from among the Neo-Destour. When this came to an end with the Allied victories in North Africa, Bourguiba went into exile in Egypt, where he organised propaganda and resistance against the French, which led to two years of guerrilla warfare and forced the French to grant autonomy to Tunisia in 1955. Bourguiba returned to head the new government, and a year later, following the example of Morocco, Tunisia was granted independence. In 1957 the Bey was deposed and Tunisia became a republic with Bourguiba as president.

Since independence Tunisia has been

one of the most stable and moderate of the Arab countries and, as such, its friendship has been cultivated by the USA and West Germany, which supply the bulk of foreign aid. A union with Libya resulted from a number of hurried negotiations between Qadafi and Bourguiba some years ago, but it collapsed almost as soon as it had been announced. There were strained relations between Tunisia and France and Italy in the 1960s due to the expropriation of European-owned farms, but this was eventually patched up with the offer of compensation. Tunisia is rapidly becoming one of the major Mediterranean tourist attractions and yearly draws millions of northern Europeans to its shores, so it is now fairly expensive for the budget traveller.

VISAS

Visas are required by all except nationals of Western European countries (except Holland), Canada, Japan, Korea (South) and the USA. If you're one of those nations who require a visa (eg Australia and New Zealand), you can get them on arrival at the border (cost 1 dinar) so long as you only intend to stay one week. If you want to stay longer, get your visa before arrival, because getting visas extended is a very time-consuming process. Visas cost 2 dinar or the equivalent, require two photos and are generally issued while you wait. Nationals of Israel and South Africa are not admitted.

A visa extension involves a lot of running around and can take up to 10 days to come through (though this would be exceptional). In order to get one you need bank receipts (which they keep), a receipt (*facture* in French) from your hotel, photos and a *timbre fiscal* for 2.50 dinar (which you may be able to buy from a tobacconists, but if you can't then you'll have to go to the government finance office at 21 Rue d'Angleterre). Take these to the Ministry of the Interior and fill out the forms there. The building is diagonally opposite the Tourist Office on Avenue Habib Bour-

guiba. It's the third entrance on the side street, Rue Abderrazak, and is on the 1st floor.

Algerian visas In Gafsa these cost 3 dinar, require four photos and are issued while you wait. They're valid for one month and are good for one month's stay. In Tunis, visas are free of charge and are issued in ½ hour.

Libyan visas Before you apply for a visa, you must have your passport details translated into Arabic. They won't entertain you otherwise. You can get this done at your own embassy in Tunis and sometimes at the passport office in your own country. The visas costs 2.80 dinar and take several days to come through. The Libyan embassy is at 48 Rue du 1er Juin.

Nigerian visas Tunis is a very good place to get visas, in contrast to many other capital cities further south where they're a real hassle to get hold of. They're issued in 24 hours by the British Embassy, 5 Place de la Victoire. Visas remain valid for three months and there's no fuss.

MONEY

US$1 = 0.53 dinar
£1 = 1.00 dinar

The unit of currency is the dinar = 1000 millimes. Import/export of local currency is prohibited. You can re-exchange up to 30% of the dinars you bought back into hard currency on departure up to a limit of 100 dinar, but you must do this at the same bank and branch where you originally changed your money.

There is a currency black market but you would have to be Tunisian to find it, as it's very unlikely anyone will offer.

You must produce a *bon de passage* when buying airline tickets. These are obtainable from a bank by showing them bank receipts for money changed. If you need to apply for a visa extension, get the *bon de passage* before you go for the extension, because when you apply for the latter they will take your bank receipts off you.

Algerian border guards have no objections to you bringing Tunisian currency into the country. There is a black market for it in El Oued, so if you want to take advantage of it, don't enter your dinar on the currency form. You cannot change dinar in a bank, however.

LANGUAGE
Arabic and French are the main languages, though English, German and Italian are quite common in places.

GETTING THERE & AROUND
Air
Fifty percent reductions are available on fares to Cairo from Tunis if you are under 24 years old. Enquire at *Atou-tours* in Tunis. The normal fare is 165 dinar.

Road
Hitching is particularly easy down the coast to the Libyan border and as far south as Gafsa, even for two people, and you'll probably never have to pay for lifts. Up in the north it isn't quite so easy because the area is overrun with tourists. Don't expect lifts to come too easily on minor roads, however, because of the lack of traffic.

An excellent network of regular and cheap buses throughout the country links all the major centres of population as well as many small ones besides. An alternative to the buses is the *louage* – a large taxi with seats for five passengers. They're a little bit more expensive than the buses but generally more comfortable and faster. These taxis leave when full and cover much the same routes as the buses, as well as many smaller places. Some examples of bus fares are:

Tunis-Tabarka Daily departures about 1 pm. The fare is 1.70 dinar and the journey takes three hours.
Tunis-Kairouan The fare is 1.40 dinar.

Sousse-Kairouan The fare is 0.60 dinar.

Rail
Tunisia has a good network of railways which connect all the major centres of population. There are through services to Algeria via Tebessa and Souk Ahras. The trains are good value, fast, comfortable and efficient. Tunis to Sousse costs 1.36 dinar and Tunis to El Fahs costs 900 millimes.

Boat
Ferry Tunisia is one of the possible gateways to Africa if you take the ferry from Sicily to Tunis. For more details about this ferry, see under 'Mediterranean Ferries' in the Getting There chapter.

There is a ferry between Sfax and the Iles Kerkenna which leaves twice daily in either direction and costs 250 millimes one way.

Every 20 minutes there is a ferry in either direction between Jorf and Djerba Island from 5 am to 7 pm. The fare is 50 millimes. As an alternative, you can get to the island by driving between Zarsis and Djerba over the Roman causeway.

To/From Algeria
There are three main border crossings, though these are not the only ones.

Tabarka-Annaba via El Kala (Le Calle) This is the most northerly of the routes and follows the coast road. Very few travellers use this route and there are few cars along it, so be prepared to walk part of the way if you are hitching. Daily buses link Tabarka with El Kala during the daylight hours.

Ghardimaou-Souk Ahras This is quite a popular route but not the most scenic, and hitching between the two places can be difficult because of the lack of villages between the two border posts. If you want to be sure of not getting stuck, take the train from Tunis to Souk Ahras (daily in either direction).

Gafsa-Nefta-El Oued The most scenically attractive and interesting, this route passes by the salt lakes (Chotts) and along the edge of the Grand Erg Oriental (sandy desert). You can go as far as Tozeur by train; there are also regular buses as far as Nefta and the border. *Louages* run from Nefta to the border for 500 millimes. The border is at Hazoua/Bou Aroua, about 40 km west of Nefta, and the border posts are four km apart. There is an Algerian consulate at Gafsa if you need a visa.

To/From Libya
The best route is the coast road from Gabes to Tripoli via Ben Gardane and Ras Agedir. It's pretty easy to hitch along this road and the chances are that you'll get a ride going a long way – at least as far as Tripoli and sometimes as far as Benghazi. There are buses twice a week in either direction between Tunis and Tripoli; they take two days but are pretty expensive. The buses leave Tunis on Monday and Thursday.

You can safely ignore anyone who tells you there is no public transport along this route (as the customs people at Ben Gardane are fond of telling people).

PLACES TO STAY
There are few campsites with any facilities worth talking about, but you can pitch a tent anywhere so long as you have the permission of the owner of the land where this might apply. Purpose-built campsites can be found about 1½ km south of Hammam-Plage on the road to Hammam Lif (follow the signs for *Hotel Salwa*, Nabeul (L'Auberge des Jasmins), Hammamet (L'Ideal Camping), Sousse and Tozeur (Belvedere).

The cheapest places to stay if you're not camping are the Youth Hostels and Youth Centres. You should have a Youth Hostel membership card if you intend to use these places. Most hostels are quite good and meals are available, but they're in heavy demand during school vacations. The nightly charge is 800 millimes. There

are Youth Hostels or Youth Centres in Ain Draham, Ain Soltane, Beja, Borj Cedria, Bizerte, Chebba, Dermech, Gafsa, Gabes, Kairouan, Kasserine, Kelibia, Le Kef, Menzel, Temime, Nabeul, Monastir, Rades (Tunis), Rimel, Sfax, Sousse and Zarsis.

BIZERTE
The Youth Hostel is on the Route de la Corniche (tel 02 31608).

DJERBA
Djerba Island is one of Tunisia's beauty spots and was even a recreation area in Roman times. It's a flat, palm-covered island surrounded by clear turquoise sea and white sandy beaches. At least that's how it used to be until 1984, when many travellers reported that thousands of palm trees had died, the beaches were covered in dead palm fronds, and the sea was a murky brown topped with thick grey foam. (Fancy saving up all year for a two-week package holiday of this!) Djerba is a handicraft centre and the weaving here is especially good. Avoid the island during the summer months, as it's a favourite with tourists from northern Europe.

The *Youth Hostel* is on Rue Abdelhamid El Kadhi off Avenue Habib Bourguiba, just before the harbour in Houmt-Souk. If you don't want to stay there, try *Hotel El Arischa*, which is quite cheap and has lots of atmosphere.

GABES
This is an oasis town on the southern coast surrounded by palms and fruit trees. Gabes is a good place from which to explore the nearby oases by horse-drawn carriage. The famous troglodyte dwellings of **Matmata** are south-west of Gabes. Here you will find a whole town made of underground houses carved out of the rock – it's quite a sight since there's nothing at ground level to indicate that the town exists at all! If you'd like to stay in one of these dwellings, contact the *Marhala Touring Club*. They'll fix you up

Kairouan

Key:-
1. Tourist Office
2. Post Office (P.T.T.)
3. Mosquée de la Rose
4. Mosquée Zeitouna
5. Mosquée el Maalek
6. Mosquée el Bey
7. Mosquée des Trois Portes
8. Museum

Scale 0 500m

for 2 dinar per night. There are similar places at Ben Aissa, Techine, Bled-Matmata and Hadeje.

Halfway between Gabes and Tozeur is the Berber village of **Douz** where an annual camel festival is held between 26 and 29 January. During this time there are camel races, dancing, folk songs and displays of craftwork. Daily minibuses run between Gabes and Douz, or you can take the Gabes-Tozeur bus and get off at Kebili. Douz is a short taxi ride from there.

There is a *Youth Hostel* in Gabes on Avenue Fahrat Hached opposite the railway station, and a campsite at the *Centre de Formation de Jeunesse*. To get to the latter, take the road from the main market down past the Agip station, then over the bridge and through the iron gates on the left-hand side. If you want a hotel, try *Hotel de la Poste*, which is a small place next to the mosque. It's very pleasant, friendly and clean but there are no showers. The cost is 2 dinar a single – or you can sleep on the roof during the summer. More expensive but very pleasant is *Hotel Regina*, which costs 6 dinar a double. It's clean and has hot showers and a patio in the middle of the hotel where you can have breakfast. Similar is *Hotel Nejib*.

KAIROUAN

The old walled city of Kairouan is Tunisia's most historic spot, and the **Grand Mosque** is one of the most important in the Islamic world. The *souk* is among the best in Tunisia, so put aside time for exploring it.

You can stay at the *Youth Hostel* on the outskirts of town to the south-east for 1 dinar per night; or try *Hotel Barrouta* in the Medina on the main thoroughfare for the same price (though there are no showers at the latter). The nearby hammam costs 550 millimes for a shower but you can't sleep there. If you want something slightly upmarket, try either *Hotel Sabra*, which costs 6 dinar a double; or *Hotel Marhala* for 2.50 dinar a single.

NABEUL

The *Youth Hostel* is right on the beach about two km from the centre of town. It's clean, has cold showers and your gear is safe. Full board costs 1.70 dinar or you can get bed and breakfast for 800 millimes. In the town itself the two cheapest places are the *Pension Les Roses* and the *Pension Les Oliviers*.

SFAX

Sfax is a resort town and the place where you catch the ferries to the Iles Kerkenna. There is a *Youth Hostel* at the usual price. You can also try *El Habib*, Rue Borj Ennar; *Le Maghreb*, Rue Borj Ennar; or *Hotel Paix*, Rue Alexander Dumas.

SOUSSE

Sousse is another resort town which has undergone a lot of redevelopment in recent years, but it still retains its large and interesting walled *souk*. There are often more tourists in there than local people.

The *Youth Hostel* is north of town on the Plage Boujaafer, a 10-minute walk from the centre, and costs 1 dinar per night. Many travellers, however, prefer to stay at *Camping Belvedere*, three km from town (ask for directions). Here there are palm-frond huts to stay in, a broken pipe 100 metres down the road with warm water pouring out of it to shower in, a sand WC and large bonfires at night around which everybody gathers and 'either bullshits or eats meals that everyone has contributed to and which Abdullah's (the owner) son, Mabrook, has cooked up. All this for 400 millimes a day. It's a great place to hang around for a while,' according to a traveller.

If you want to stay somewhere in town, try *Hotel Ahla*, Place de la Grande Mosquee, which costs 7 dinar a double. You can also try the *Mabrouka* and the *Messaounda*. Further upmarket is *Hotel Claridge*, Avenue Habib Bourguiba, which costs 3.50 dinar for bed and breakfast.

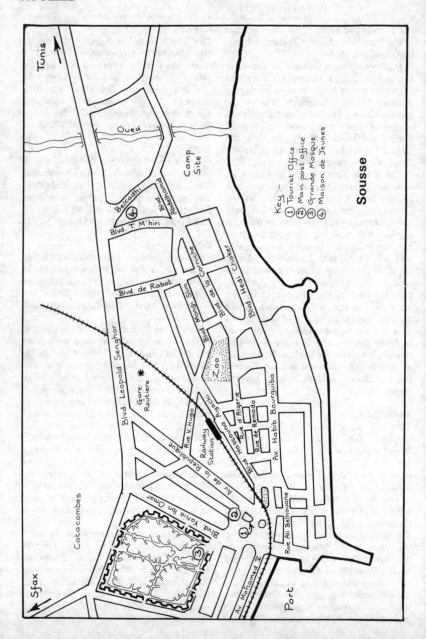

Sousse

Key:-
① Tourist Office
② Main post office
③ Grande Mosque
④ Maison de Jeunes

TOZEUR

Tozeur is an oasis town sandwiched between the two enormous salt lakes of **Chott el Jerid** and **Chott el Gharsa**. Stay at the *Belvedere* campsite, one of the best in Tunisia. There are bathing places employing the natural hot springs, a good bar and small huts to sleep in.

TUNIS

The capital of Tunisia, Tunis is a major gateway to Africa. There's plenty to do and see so it's worth staying a few days.

Useful Addresses

Tourist Office
    Place de la Victoire (tel 244 142)
American Express
    Carthage Tours, Avenue Mohammed V
Thomas Cook
    65 Avenue Habib Bourguiba (tel 242 673)
Algerian Embassy
    136 Rue de la Liberté
British Embassy
    5 Place de la Victoire (tel 245 100)
Egyptian Embassy
    16 Rue El Sonyouti, El Menzah
French Embassy
    Place de l'Independence
Libyan Embassy
    48 Rue du 1er Juin
USA Embassy
    144 Avenue de la Liberté (tel 282 566)
Tirrenia Line
    22 Rue de Yougoslavie (ferries to Italy)

Getting Around

If you arrive by air, blue bus No 35 runs between the airport and the city centre every half hour. Arriving by boat from Italy, you will dock at La Goulette on the

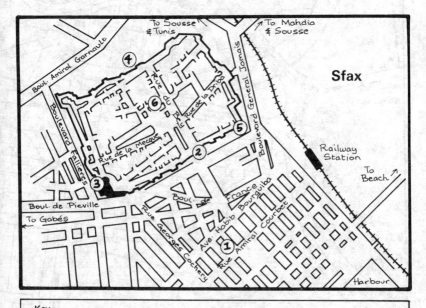

Key

1 Town Hall (Roman mosaics)
2 Bab Diwan (main Medina gate)
3 Kasbah
4 Bab Djebli
5 12th century Fort
6 Great Mosque

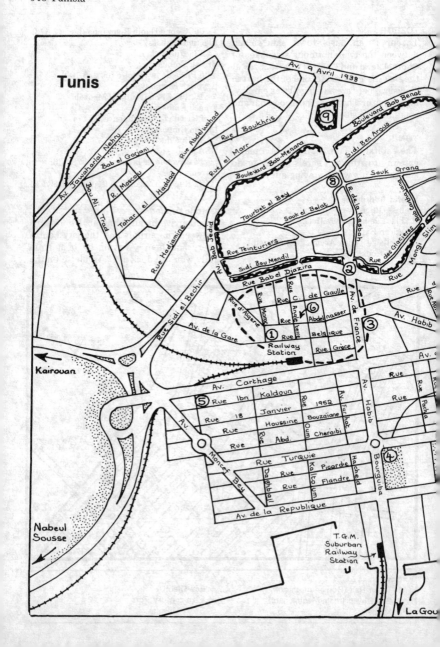

Tunis

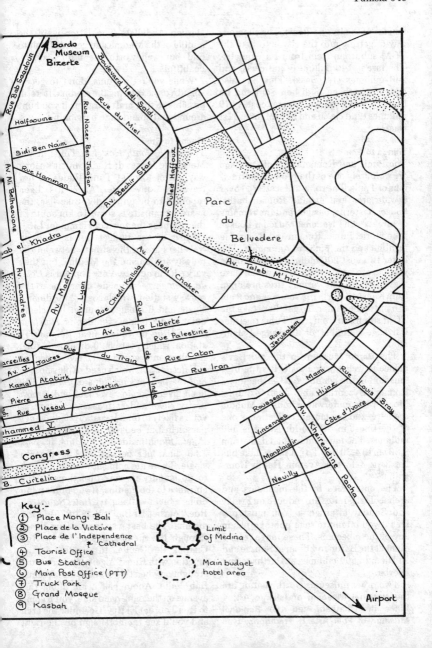

Key:-
① Place Mongi Bali
② Place de la Victoire
③ Place de l'Independence
    ✝ Cathedral
④ Tourist Office
⑤ Bus Station
⑥ Main Post Office (PTT)
⑦ Truck Park
⑧ Grand Mosque
⑨ Kasbah

Limit of Medina

Main budget hotel area

far side of the Lac de Tunis. The cheapest way of getting into the city is to take the TGM suburban train from La Goulette. The fare is 140 millimes (2nd class) and 240 millimes (1st class). This line also goes to Carthage, Sidi ben Said and La Marsa. Tunis to La Marsa costs 170 millimes (2nd class) and 270 millimes (1st class).

Things to See

The Punic and Roman ruins of **Carthage** are definitely one of the principal attractions of Tunis. The ruins are scattered over a wide area and include Roman baths, houses, cisterns, basilica and the remains of streets. The **National Museum** houses prehistoric, Punic, Roman and Byzantine exhibits and the **Baths of Antoninus**. The latter two cost 200 millimes entry unless you have a student card, in which case they are free. The various sites are open from 8 am to 6 pm in the summer and 9 am to 5 pm in the winter. To get there take the TGM suburban train from Tunis to either Carthage-Hannibal or Carthage-Salammbo.

The **Bardo Museum** in the old Bey's palace is well worth a visit. It's the best museum in the country for Carthaginian, Roman, Byzantine and Arab exhibits. Most of the underwater finds at Mahdia are here, and the mosaic collection is one of the finest in the world. Entry is 500 millimes. The museum is open daily from 9.30 am to 4.30 pm. To get there, take bus No 3 or 4 to the Avenue Habib Bourguiba.

The entry fees to the museums and archaeological sites are reduced on Friday and Sunday afternoons. You must pay fees if you intend to take photographs in any of the museums. These range from 2 dinar at the Bardo to 1 dinar at Sousse and El Djem to 500 millimes at Carthage and Djerba.

Two other museums worth visiting are the **National Museum of Islamic Art**, 4 Place de Chateau, and the **Regional Museum of Folk Arts & Traditions**, Rue Darben Abdallah. The latter is in the middle of the Medina and very difficult to find but well worth the effort, as it's beautiful.

While you're in Tunis, don't forget to spend a day exploring the medina. It's still possible to find craft bargains if you hunt around and spend time bargaining.

Places to Stay

There is a *Youth Hostel* in Tunis at the Maison de Jeunes de Rades, but it's a long way out of town at Tunis-Rades so few travellers stay here. Also, it's been reported to be unfriendly. Likewise, the nearest campsite is some 15 km south of the city near the town of Hammam Lif.

Most of the budget hotels used by travellers are in the streets between the railway station and the Medina, but they vary a lot in quality. Very popular is *Hotel de Bretagne*, 7 Rue de Grece near the railway station, which costs 2.50 dinar a single and 6 dinar a double. It's clean, quiet and friendly. Similar is *Hotel de Suisse*, Rue de Suisse near the railway station, which costs 5.90 dinar a double. It's clean and very friendly. Even cheaper is *Hotel de Lion*, which used to play host to half the bedbugs in Tunis but which has been given a major overhaul and is now pretty clean and as pleasant a place as you're likely to find. It costs 1.20 dinar per person in four-bed rooms. Fairly similar is *Hotel Milano* inside the medina; it costs 1.50 dinar per person or 2.50 dinar a single. There are cold showers and a sink to do laundry in. Ask directions at the entrance to the medina. If you don't mind doing a bit of walking, try *Hotel Sabra*, 83 Rue Tourbet El Bey (tel 494 875) in the medina. The best way to get there is not through the medina but to follow Rue Charles de Gaulle, turn right at the junction with Rue d'Algerie and continue straight on when this changes into Avenue Bab Jedid. About half a km along this avenue on the right-hand side, you'll come to Rue Tourbet El Bey. Go under the arch and you'll see the hotel sign on the right about 100 metres down. The hotel is clean, the management is friendly and it costs just 1.30 dinar a single. You may be invited to share a meal with the manager at no extra charge.

Somewhat more expensive are *Hotel Riadh*, Avenue Mongi Slim near the British Embassy, which is clean and has showers and costs 3 dinar; and *Hotel Victoria*, 72 Avenue Farhat Hached (tel 241 894), across the square from the railway station. It's very friendly and costs 4 dinar a single including breakfast. There are no showers but there is hot water in the rooms after 8 pm. Another which has been recommended is *Hotel Nouvel*, Place Mongi Bali, near the railway station (tel 243 379), which costs 4 dinar a single. It isn't such good value as the others since it's a bit grubby, there are no showers and no hot water, and the price doesn't include

breakfast. One or two travellers have suggested *Hotel de la République*, 14 Rue du Maroc (tel 241 979).

Avoid *Hotel Tranquillité* if possible, as it's dirty and there are no showers. The price, though, is only 2 dinar per person.

Places to Eat

There are several good restaurants in the Rue Ibn Khaldoun off Avenue Habib Bourguiba, including the *Miranda*, the *Cosmos* and the *Barcelona*. They all offer good French cuisine as well as local specialities. A large fillet steak would cost you about US$2.90, couscous about US$2.60 and a whole fish about US$3. You can get excellent local dishes at small stand-up cafés for less than a dinar (a souvlaki-type sandwich would cost about 80c). French rolls cost around 7c and bottled water about 15c.

Uganda

Uganda is still in the process of picking up the pieces after a decade of brutality, fear and misrule unmatched anywhere else on the African continent and, if recent reports are anything to go by, it will have even more pieces to pick up following the overthrow of Obote. In his single-minded pursuit of absolute power by each and every means at his disposal, Idi Amin brought this once prosperous and socially cohesive country to its knees. By the time he was overthrown in 1979 the country was bankrupt, virtually all industrial and agricultural activity had ceased and many hundreds of thousands of people had lost their lives – most of them as a result of arbitrary measures dictated by Amin.

The war of liberation, though necessary to rid the country of this tyrant and his henchmen, contributed to the devastation, and the signs are visible everywhere even today. It will be a long time before the wounds are healed. Travellers are once again flocking to this country and their reports are full of praise for the friendliness of the people and the beauty still to be found there. You may hear the occasional burst of gunfire in the cities at night, and the Karamoja province is still out of bounds as a result of diehard military activity, but it's now quite safe to travel in most areas. Go and see for yourself.

Despite the fertility of the land and its capacity to grow surplus crops, there were virtually no trade links between Uganda and the coast until the area was colonised by the European powers. The area was left to develop on its own without interference from outside. A number of traditional kingdoms came into being from the 14th century onwards, among them the Buganda, Bunyoro, Toro, Ankole and Karagwe, with Bunyoro initially being the most powerful. Through centuries of alternating rivalry and cooperation, Buganda eventually assumed the mantle of the dominant kingdom and it was during the reign of King Mwanga of the Buganda in the mid-19th century that contacts were finally made with Arab traders and European explorers. However, neither the kings of Buganda nor of Toro were too enthralled with the activities of either the Moslems or the Christians and, as a result, there were wholesale executions of the followers of these two faiths. The British reacted to these executions by deporting King Mwanga to the Seychelles.

Following the Anglo-German treaty of 1890, which defined areas of influence in Africa, Uganda became a British colony along with Kenya and the islands of Zanzibar and Pemba. The British adopted a policy of indirect rule giving the traditional kingdoms a considerable degree of internal autonomy. By the time independence arrived, the kings were loath to hand over their power to an elected central government, and the legacy of this is still around today.

Unlike Kenya and Tanzania, Uganda never experienced the wholesale expropriation of land by foreigners. The peasants were encouraged to grow cash crops for export through their own co-operative organisations. A a result of this, nationalist organisations were much later arriving on the scene than in neighbouring countries; it wasn't until 1952 that the first multi-tribal political party was formed. In 1958, Milton Obote, who has

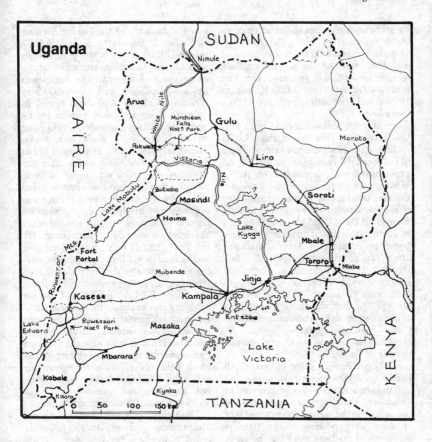

spent six years in politics in Kenya, became the most forceful spokesperson in the Legislative Council. In the run-up to independence in 1962, he forged an alliance between his own party and the traditionalist Kabaka Yekka to safeguard the interests of the King of Buganda. Obote became the newly independent country's first prime minister, with the king of Buganda as the head of state.

It wasn't a particularly propitious time for Uganda to come to grips with independence. Civil wars were raging in neighbouring southern Sudan, Zaire, Rwanda and Burundi, and refugees streaming into the country added to its internal problems. The most important of these problems was the struggle between the nationalists, who wanted a unitary form of government, and the traditionalists, who were bent on preserving the powers enjoyed by their semi-autonomous local governments. After a series of events which included a mutiny of the fledgling Uganda army (and the subsequent promotion of Idi Amin) and a scandal in which both Amin and Obote were accused of assisting anti-Mobutu insurgents, Obote began to resort to arbitrary measures in an attempt to stem criticism of his government. A number of cabinet ministers were arrested and Amin stormed the Kabaka's Palace allegedly in search of an arms cache. The raid resulted in the flight of the Kabaka to Britain and his death in exile there three years later.

Another scandal surfaced in 1969 with the revelation that more than US$5 million in funds allocated to the Ministry of Defence could not be accounted for. An explanation was demanded of Amin. When it was not forthcoming, his deputy, Colonel Okoya, and a number of junior officers demanded his resignation. Shortly afterwards Okoya and his wife were shot to death in their Gulu home and rumours began to circulate of Amin's imminent arrest. It never came. Instead, when Obote left for Singapore to attend the Commonwealth Heads of Government conference in January 1971, Amin staged a coup. The British, whose investments had been partially nationalised under Obote's socialist policies, leapt in to recognise the new regime. Obote returned to exile in Tanzania.

So began Amin's reign of terror. All political activities were quickly suspended and the armed forces were empowered to shoot on sight anyone suspected of opposition to the regime. In the process of crushing all opposition, some 100,000 soldiers and civilians were butchered in the first few years of Amin's rule. Prime targets of the dictator's death squads were the Acholi and Langi, who were decimated in a wave of massacres. Then, in 1972, Amin gave all Asians in the country 90 days to leave. They were allowed to take virtually nothing with them except the clothes they stood in. When the last of them had gone, Amin grabbed the US$1000 million booty they had been forced to leave behind.

The assets were quickly squandered on new toys for the army, luxury items for Amin and his henchmen, and wholesale corruption. Meanwhile, most industrial activity ground to a halt. The British were singled out as the next targets and in 1973 nearly US$500 million worth of investments in tea plantations and other industries were nationalised. The booty was again squandered, and as the country sank into anarchy Amin was forced to delegate more and more powers to the provincial military governors, who became virtual warlords in their own areas. Something had to give. Discontent began to spread in the lower ranks after the Treasury was unable to meet soldiers' payrolls. At the same time, international condemnation of the sordid regime was reaching new heights as more and more news of massacres, torture and summary executions leaked out of the country. By this time, Amin's only source of support was coming from Libya under the increasingly idiosyncratic leadership of Qadafi (always a sucker for psychotic shit-stirrers and killers). Libya bailed out the Ugandan economy and began an intensive drive to equip the Ugandan armed forces with sophisticated weapons. It didn't stop the rot, however, and in an attempt to divert attention from domestic problems and to teach Tanzania a 'lesson' for supporting anti-Amin dissidents, Amin invaded northern Tanzania and bombed the Lake Victoria ports of Bukoba and Musoma.

The action backfired, since not only did Tanzania unexpectedly launch a full-scale counter-attack, it brought together the many disparate groups opposed to Amin. The Ugandan forces were quickly pushed back across the border and then routed on their own territory as the Tanzanians continued their drive into the heart of the country. By the end of April 1979 organised resistance had effectively collapsed and Amin had fled to Libya.

The Tanzanian action was criticised – somewhat half-heartedly – by the OAU at the time, but it's probably true to say that most African countries breathed a sigh of relief to see Amin thrown out. All the same, Tanzania was forced to foot the bill for the war – estimated at US$500 million.

This was a crushing blow for an already desperately poor country, and it has so far failed to get any contributions towards the bill.

Some 12,000 Tanzanian troops remained in the country to assist in reconstruction, but they have now been withdrawn. Under the aegis of the Uganda National Liberation Front, Usefu Lule was installed as president but was voted out after only 68 days in power. He was replaced by Godfrey Binaisa amid riots in Kampala in favour of Lule. Binaisa quickly came under pressure to set a date for general elections and a return to civilian rule. Although this was done, he found himself at odds on ideological, constitutional and personal grounds with other powerful members of the provisional government, particularly over his insistence that the old political parties in existence before Amin's coup not be allowed to contest the elections. The strongest criticism of this came from two senior members of the army, Tito Okello and David Ojok, who were supporters of Milton Obote. Fearing a coup, Binaisa attempted to dismiss Ojok but the latter refused to step down and instead placed Binaisa under house arrest. The government was taken over by a military commission which set elections for later that year. Obote, meanwhile, returned from exile to an enthusiastic welcome in many parts of the country. Later that year he was victorious in the elections, which Commonwealth observers described as generally fair and honest.

The honeymoon with Obote, however, proved to be relatively short. Like Amin, Obote began to heavily favour certain tribes; and large numbers of civil servants, army and police commanders belonging to the tribes of the south were replaced by Obote supporters belonging to tribes of the north. Tension began to rise and reports leak out of atrocities and the discovery of mass graves unrelated to the Amin era. At the time this seemed merely an attempt by Obote's opponents to discredit his regime, but all became horribly real once Obote was overthrown in a coup in mid-1985 and the truth was exposed. The coup, however, didn't make anywhere near a clean sweep of the old guard. General Tito Okello, its leader, was himself one of Obote's closest military aides for some 15 years, and the new prime minister, Paulo Mwanga, was Obote's vice-president and minister of defence. The latter has many enemies in Uganda's political circles.

The country faces an enormous reconstruction task. Not only was the Treasury bankrupted by Amin and the civilian administration all but destroyed, but in the war of liberation an estimated million people lost their homes, particularly in the south of the country. Looting by isolated pockets of Amin's troops remained a threat long after the main fighting had ceased and goes on today, especially in the Karamoja province (north-east Uganda). This province is largely unsafe to travel in because of sporadic fighting. Now, following Obote's ouster, there will be even more political and tribal feuds to sort out, except that this time the sorting can't be done under the umbrella of a disciplined Tanzanian army of occupation (which maintained law and order after Amin's defeat). It will have to be done against the background of an undisciplined Ugandan army, and that can only lead to an upsurge in the already high level of violence in Uganda. Resettling a million refugees meanwhile seems to be on the back burner. The light at the end of the tunnel will be a long time coming.

However, as far as travelling goes, it's now relatively safe to travel in most parts of Uganda and you shouldn't be too apprehensive about visiting this country. Nevertheless, it would be a good idea to talk with other travellers who have been there recently and with embassy staff in neighbouring countries (remembering that the latter tend to be over-cautious). As a rule of thumb, if there is transport running to a place, then it's probably safe enough to visit. Avoid army units wherever possible. They're often drunk and very aggressive.

One more thing travellers report is that since well-heeled tourists long stopped coming to Uganda because of the political climate, the tourist offices have seen only backpackers and are consequently oriented to assist these sorts of travellers. It makes a refreshing change from the 'tour the game parks' mentality of Kenya.

FACTS

Uganda lies beside Lake Victoria and the White Nile, which passes through the country and makes it one of the best watered areas of Africa. The land ranges from the lush and fertile areas around the northern shores of the lake to the snow-covered and mysteriously spectacular Ruwenzori Mountains in the west which separate it from Zaire. The mountainous south-west along the border with Rwanda is also particularly beautiful. The tropical heat is tempered by the altitude, which averages over 1000 metres. The rainy season runs from March to May and from October to November. The population is about 12½ million.

VISAS

Visas are required by all except nationals of the Commonwealth countries, Denmark, Finland, Germany (West), Iceland, Irish Republic, Italy, Norway, Spain, Sweden and Turkey. However, all except those who are flying into Entebbe must get a Visitor's Pass before arrival at the border. These cost Sh 25 at the High Commissions in both Nairobi and Dar es Salaam. No photos are required and they're generally issued while you wait. Some people get a one-month pass, others get two weeks, but if you do get one month, you may well find that this is reduced to two weeks at the border for no apparent reason.

Visa and visitor's pass extensions are easily obtained at the Immigration office in Kampala.

Uganda used to be a good place to buy visas for other countries because of the very favourable street exchange rate which made visas paid for in Ugandan shillings very cheap. However, there is now no cost advantage, as most embassies demand payment in hard currency (eg Egypt US$20; Zaire US$24).

Burundi visas The embassy is near the National Museum beyond Makerere University and next to the Kenyan High Commission. Visas cost Sh 3000 and take three hours.

Rwanda visas The embassy is in Baumann House, Obote Rd, near the British High Commission. Visas cost Sh 3400, require three photos and take 24 hours to issue.

Sudan visas All visa applications have to be referred to Khartoum and it's very unlikely that your visa will come through in less than six weeks.

Tanzanian visas The High Commission is in Nile Mansions, Shimoni Rd at Mackinnon and Kintu Rds. Visas cost Sh 250, require three photos and take 24 hours to come through. The High Commission closes at 12.30 pm. Be prepared to show money and answer a lot of questions.

MONEY
US$1 = Sh 480-550 (fluctuates)

The unit of currency is the Ugandan shilling = 100 cents. Import of local currency is prohibited but no one bothers to check. There is a thriving black market on which you can get up to US$1 = Sh 1100-1200 (Uganda/Kenya border), Sh 1000-1100 (Kampala) and Sh 800-900 (Kabale). You can also get good rates for Kenyan shillings. Expect around Ken Sh 1 = Ug Sh 42.

Currency declaration forms are issued to most people on arrival. If you're not given one, then ask for one because you will need it if you don't want to pay in hard currency at any of the Uganda Hotels Corporation hotels and game lodges (there are a lot of these).

Because of the very favourable exchange rates (especially on the black market), Uganda used to be a cheap place to visit, but the prices of such things as hotels, telecommunications, transport and airline tickets are being brought into line with those prevailing in Kenya. Food is still relatively cheap, however.

You must pay for airline tickets in hard currency. Not even *Ugandan Air* will accept shillings with or without bank receipts.

If you're coming in from Kenya via Malaba, you can change money between the two border posts. There are men walking around here with large wads of bills asking everyone who comes across if they want to change money. The average rate is Ken Sh 1 = Ug Sh 42.

Inflation is high so expect prices to change rapidly.

The airport departure tax for both domestic and international flights is Sh 1000.

LANGUAGE

English and Luganda are the official languages, but many localised languages are also spoken. Kiswahili is not used much in Kampala.

GETTING THERE & AROUND
Air

It's no longer possible to buy airline tickets with Ugandan shillings. Not even *Ugandan Air* will accept them. All tickets have to be paid for in hard currency, so that's the end of cheap air fares in Uganda. On the other hand, Ugandan Air still offers excursion fares which are approximately half the price of other airlines. Some sample fares are: Entebbe-London/Koln £360, Entebbe-Rome US$415, Entebbe-Cairo US$360.

Road

Hitching is generally very easy. The best place to find a lift is at a police roadblock, and there's usually one on every road just outside of most Ugandan towns. Tell them where you want to go and they'll get your lift for you. Army roadblocks tend to be less friendly but they're usually not troublesome. Forget about hitching after 8 pm. Apart from the fact that there's hardly anyone on the roads after that time, it can be unsafe to be out on the open road in some areas at night. Lifts are often free, but if that's what you are looking for then make sure that it's understood before you get in. Drivers may assume that you're willing to pay if you don't say anything to the contrary.

There's a good transport network of matatus, buses and trucks. Matatus only cost marginally more than the buses and are often preferable if you're not hitching, as the buses tend to be very crowded. There are sometimes shortages of fuel, and the first casualties when that happens are the buses.

Whichever form of road transport you take, be prepared for a frustratingly slow journey because of the numerous army checkpoints. There ae 30 of these between the Kenya/Uganda border and Kampala alone! The soldiers who staff them are normally very polite to tourists, but the locals get fleeced for cash – lots of it. If you want to avoid roadblocks, travel by train.

Some examples of road transport are as follows:

Malaba-Tororo There are pick-up trucks between Malaba (the Kenya/Uganda border) and Tororo which cost Sh 200 and take ½ hour.

Tororo-Jinja Bus costs Sh 700. Shared taxi costs Sh 1400 but you need to bargain.

Jinja-Kampala Bus costs Sh 500 and shared taxi Sh 700.

Kampala-Tororo Bus costs Sh 1200. There are several buses daily in the mornings between 8 and 9 am. They leave from behind the Uganda Bus Service station near the football stadium in Kampala. By shared taxi the journey will cost Sh 2000.

Kampala-Gulu Costs Sh 900 by bus and Sh 1000 by truck.

Kampala-Masaka-Mbarara The bus along this stretch costs Sh 800 as far as Masaka and Sh 2000 to Mbarara.

Kampala-Kabale Bus costs Sh 3000.

Mbarara-Kabale Bus costs Sh 1000.

Kabale-Kasese Bus costs Sh 2000.

Kabale-Kisoro Pick-up trucks between these two towns cost Sh 1200. There is also a daily bus at around 2 pm which costs Sh 450 and takes six hours. From Kisoro to the Rwandan border there are other pick-ups for Sh 300. If you walk from Kisoro to the border, it will take you about three hours.

Rail

Trains are a relatively cheap and comfortable way of getting around Uganda and you also avoid the numerous army checkpoints. Most of the railway carriages are new. There are two classes: upper class, which consists of compartments with six berths similar to Kenyan 2nd class; and lower class, similar to Kenyan 3rd class. On some trains there are more expensive upper-class compartments with just two berths. In lower class, men and women are put into different compartments unless you request otherwise when buying your ticket.

Kampala-Tororo One train daily in either direction at 9 am from Kampala and 10 am from Tororo. The fares are Sh 950 in upper class (another letter said Sh 800) and Sh 400 in lower class. The journey takes six hours. If you're coming in from

Kenya, the train from Nairobi to the border town of Malaba gets in at 8 am. You must get off the train here (there are no through trains) and take a matatu to Tororo.

Kampala-Gulu This costs Sh 2000 in upper class and takes at least 26 hours.

Kampala-Kasese There is a daily train in either direction at 4.30 pm but it's often late setting off. The fares are Sh 3700 for a two-berth sleeper, Sh 1800 in upper class and Sh 800 in lower class. The journey takes 15 hours. If you want a berth, you must buy your ticket the previous day. If you're a couple, tell them you are married. That way you may well get a cabin to yourselves. There is no bedding or food available on the train (but fresh fruit, hot local dishes, tea and bread are available at stations en route), and there are no lights at night (bring candles). There are two army checkpoints en route where you may be hassled for money. You should politely refuse.

To/From Kenya

You can get to the border either by road or rail, but there are no through trains between the two countries. If you're coming by rail, there are trains from Nairobi to the border town of Malaba on Tuesday, Thursday and Sunday which arrive between 8 and 9.30 am the next day. (In the opposite direction there are trains from Malaba to Nairobi on Wednesday, Saturday and Sunday at 4 pm.) The fares are Ken Sh 153 (2nd class) and Ken Sh 77 (3rd class). There are also buses daily from Malaba to Nairobi at 7 pm which cost Ken Sh 100 and arrive in Nairobi the next day between 5 and 6 am.

To get from Malaba to Tororo (where the Ugandan rail system starts), you must take a matatu (Ug Sh 200). It's an easy border to cross and there are no problems. Change money between the two borders – there are plenty of dealers.

To/From Rwanda

You can cross into Rwanda from Uganda at two points. The main route is the Kabale-Gatuna-Kigali road and there's plenty of traffic on this road so it's easy to hitch. There are also pick-ups available from Kabale to the border (Gatuna) in the mornings; they cost Sh 300. From the border there are microbuses to Kigali hourly during the morning.

The other route is the Kabale-Kisoro-Cyanica-Ruhengeri-Kigali road. This is the one preferred by many travellers since it gets you direct to Ruhengeri, the starting point for a visit to the Parc National des Volcans and the gorilla sanctuaries. The only trouble with this route is the scarcity of traffic, so you should be prepared to do some walking. There are usually daily buses operated by the *Uganda Transport Company* in either direction between Kabale and Kisoro; these cost Sh 300 and take about 4½ hours. If not, there are pick-ups which charge Sh 1200. From Kisoro to the border (Cyanica) you may be able to find a matatu or hitch a ride with the occasional car or truck, but if not, you'll have to walk (12 km). You may also have to walk from the border to the first Rwandan village (Kidaho), which is another three km. From Kidaho there are daily taxi-vans to Ruhengeri at around 7 am for RFr 100. If you have no Rwandan francs, you can use Ugandan shillings all the way to Ruhengeri.

Avoid crossing the Ugandan/Rwandan border on weekends, as the customs and immigration officials go home to their families at this time, so you'll either have to wait or go looking for them.

To/From Tanzania

There's now only one border crossing point between the two countries; it is on the Masaka-Bukoba road. You cannot cross south of Kikagati anymore. There are no through buses between the two countries and you will probably have to walk between Mutukula (the Ugandan border village) and Kyaka (the Tanzanian border town). It's about 30 km. There are buses, usually daily but sometimes only on Monday, Wednesday and Friday, at 10 am from Kampala to Mutukula via Masaka; the trip takes about eight hours. In the opposite direction the buses depart very early on Tuesday, Thursday and Saturday. You'll probably have to stay in Mutukula overnight. There's no immigration officer at Mutukula, only a police post, and they don't ask for your currency form. Although the rate isn't up to much, it's advisable to change any excess Ugandan shillings here. Otherwise you won't be able to get rid of them until you get to Mwanza. Tanzanian immigration and customs are at Kyaka. Currency declaration forms are issued here. There are daily buses from Kyaka to Bukoba, or you can hitch.

To/From Zaire

The main crossing points are between Kabale and Rutshuru via either Kisoro or Ishasha, between Lakes Kivu and Edward (Adi Amin Dada) and between Kasese and Beni via Kasindi. There's not much traffic on any of these routes, so be prepared for long waits or walking – beautiful countryside! A truck from Kabale to the Ugandan/Zaire border will probably cost you around Sh 1000.

PLACES TO STAY

Many places were damaged or destroyed in the war to oust Idi Amin and, because of the country's financial problems, not a lot of maintenance or repair has gone on since then. Water and electricity supplies can be erratic even in the more expensive places, so don't expect too much. At all the hotels and lodges run by the Uganda Hotels Corporation you will have to produce your currency form to prove that you've changed money officially at a bank. If you can't do this, they'll demand that you pay your bill in hard currency. If you have a tent, it's worth enquiring at local police stations or at the Gombolola headquarters for a place to camp. From time to time, many travellers have been offered not only a site but even a room and bathing facilities.

ENTEBBE

Try the *Lodging House No 139* near the market. A bed in a basic room costs Sh 400 per night. There's also a campsite on the road to Kampala just outside of town where you can camp free. From the signpost on the main road the walk is 1½ km.

Make sure you visit the **Botanical Gardens** while you're in Entebbe. They're really well kept and have a wide variety of tropical trees. It's safe to walk around here.

FORT PORTAL

One of the cheapest places to stay is the *Top Travellers Lodge*, where you can get a room for Sh 450 a double. The *Mountains of the Moon Hotel* has also been recommended. It's one of the Uganda Hotels Corporation places and costs Sh 825 a single and Sh 1160 a double. A notice in reception says that non-Ugandan residents have to pay in foreign currency, but there are usually very few guests so they'd generally rather see you pay in local currency than have you not stay there at all.

GULU

Two places which have been recommended are the *New Gulu Restaurant*, Pakwach Rd, which costs Sh 400 a single; and the *Luxxor Lodge*, opposite the truck park, which costs Sh 550. If they're both full, ask around among the truckies, who are very friendly and usually know where you can find a cheap room. If you're looking for something better, try the *Acholi Inn*. It's another of the Uganda Hotels Corporation places and costs Sh 1000 a double. You must produce a currency form unless you want to pay in foreign currency.

JINJA

Jinja is a low-key but alive market town with attractive and extensive lake frontage. The market day is Saturday and you can find almost anything you want, including fresh fish and curry powders. A railway ferry from here to Mwanza (Tanzania) on Tuesday has space for 30 passengers.

The *Belle View Hotel* has been recommended at US$4 a double. It has clean rooms but no hot water. Cheaper and just as pleasant is the *Lake Victoria Hotel*. Other possibilities are the *Market View Hotel* and the *Blue Cat Hotel*.

Eat at the *Mango Bar/Restaurant*, where there's a variety of good, cheap food around lunchtime as well as an outdoor garden with music.

KABALE

This town is situated in a particularly beautiful area of Uganda described by many travellers as 'the Switzerland of Africa.' A suggested walk is to Lake Bunyonyi; it will take you all day to walk there and back. The road between here and Kisoro is also pretty spectacular but in a bad state of repair.

You may well be met by Mr Singhi, the tourist officer, on arrival in Kabale. He's very friendly and keen on finding you the cheapest accommodation as well as explaining what there is to do in the area – mountain climbing or visits to the pygmies and the copper mine, for example.

A good place to stay and one of the cheapest is *St Paul's Training Centre & Hostel* behind the church, between the market and the police station. It costs Sh 1320 a double. Water supplies can be a problem but baggage left there is safe. Cheaper is *All Saints Hostel* next to the police station, which has double rooms for Sh 550. Double rooms at the same price can also be found at the *Paradise Hotel*. More expensive but good value is the *Highland Hotel*, on the main street at the west end of town about 300 metres from the UTC bus station. Rooms here cost Sh

500-600 a double. There is a bar and restaurant where you can get a meal for around Sh 800-1000. Breakfasts aren't such good value at Sh 1200.

Two other places which have been recommended are the *Sky Line Motel* and the *White House Inn*. The latter is just outside of town on the terraced hillsides and is part of the Uganda Hotels Corporation chain. Rooms there cost about the same as at the Highland Hotel and you must pay in hard currency unless you have your currency form with you, but travellers who have stayed there say it's a much better deal than the Highland.

A good place to eat if you don't take meals at your hotel is the *Kabale Coffee House*. A breakfast of eggs, meat, chips and coffee costs Sh 450. The *Rubanza Restaurant* opposite St Paul's Hostel is also good. Rice, chicken and vegies cost Sh 900.

KAMPALA

Kampala is the capital of Uganda and a good place to meet other travellers. It has a pleasant atmosphere despite the occasional bursts of gunfire; many travellers find themselves staying here much longer than they intended. If you have a camera, be very discreet about taking photos. There are a lot of plainclothes police roaming the streets as well as uniformed police and army personnel – and the one thing that gets up their nose is people taking photographs. There are numerous reports of travellers being arrested, and while you won't be subject to rough treatment if this happens to you, it can be a hassle getting out. Other than this, foreigners have little trouble here.

Information

The Tourist Office is in the Ugandan Hotels Building (ground floor) next to the Metro Café. They're very helpful but they have no maps or information sheets. If you need maps of the Ruwenzoris, you can only get them from the Map Office in Entebbe for Sh 500 each.

A good place to go for information on the Ruwenzoris is the Ministry of Tourism and Wildlife, Obote Avenue (formerly Parliament Avenue). Ask for their very useful *Notices of the Ruwenzoris*.

If you're looking for handicrafts, there's an excellent selection in the *UNICEF* shop on Bat Valley Rd.

Useful Addresses

Belgian Embassy
  2c Kampala Rd, PO Box 7043, Kampala (tel 43060)
British High Commission
  10/12 Obote Avenue, PO Box 7070, Kampala (tel 47057)
Burundi Embassy
  Off Kila Rd near the National Museum, beyond Makerere University
Egyptian Embassy
  Corner of Shimoni and Speke Rds (5th floor)

Things to See

While you're in Kampala, make sure you visit the **Kabaka's Palace** (the seat of the Kings of Buganda before Idi Amin forced the last king into exile during Obote's first term as president in the early 1960s). It's located past Makerere University – just ask, everyone knows where it is. En route is **Bat Valley**, aptly named as you can see hundreds of thousands of bats hanging from trees along the main road. It's a very weird sight! You should also see the old Bugandan **graveyard** near the Kabaka's Palace. It has fantastic old huts of the type you can read about in *White Nile*. The ancient tombs here are tended by what appear to be equally ancient local people.

Places to Stay

It used to be possible to stay at one or the other of two *Sikh temples* in Kampala, but the latest news suggests they no longer take travellers. One of the most popular places to stay is the *Tourist Lodge*, Kampala Rd near the railway station. This place wasn't too badly looted in the war, so it has running water and reasonable furniture. It costs Sh 4000 a double. They

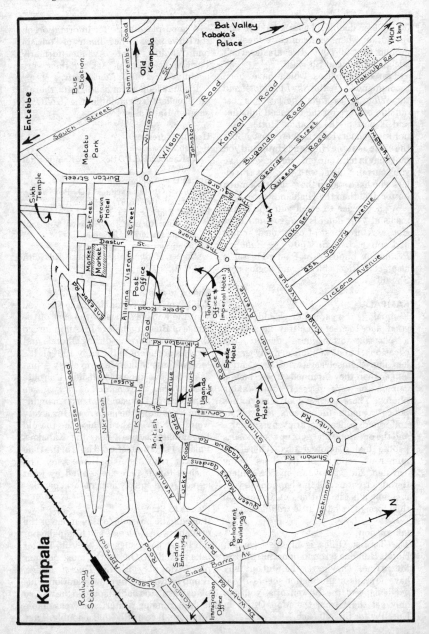

Kampala

won't let people sleep on the roof anymore, but it's a good place to meet other travellers and the management are very friendly. The Lodge has its own restaurant.

Also popular are the *New Star Shelly Apartments*, on the left-hand side as you leave the railway station; and the *Namirembe Guest House*, run by the Church of Uganda and situated near the Anglican Cathedral about 1½ km west of the city centre. The New Star costs Sh 4000 a double. It's sometimes raided by the police for no apparent reason, so you may find yourself spending a night in a cell only to be let out in the morning. The Namirembe is somewhat cheaper (US$1 per person) and they'll always find room for you even if it's just a mattress in the dining room. To get to the Namirembe, take a matatu – it's a long walk from town with a backpack.

Another recent recommendation was the *West End Hotel* on the left-hand side of Williams St walking away from the centre (about three cm off our map of Kampala). It's clean and friendly and costs US$3.50 a double. Also cheap is the *Trust Inn*, South Rd opposite the Esso petrol station, which costs Sh 2500 a double. It's pretty basic 'but quite good fun – there are 30-odd bar girls working here,' according to a traveller.

Other places where travellers stay are the *Blue Room* near the bus station, which costs Sh 1000 a single and Sh 1500 a double but there's no hot water; the *1980 Hotel* which costs Sh 3500 a double (but demands payment in hard currency – don't pay for the breakfast in advance as 'the hotel hasn't seen an egg since 1952'); and the *Serown Tourist Hotel*, which costs Sh 4400 a double but has problems with the water supply.

Also recommended by a lot of travellers is the *Mukwano Lodge*, Plot 27, Nakivuso Place. To get there, turn left out of the railway station and follow the road for about one km – it's directly opposite the gates of the market next to the large soccer stadium. A bed costs Sh 600 and a double costs Sh 2000. Your gear is safe here and the downstairs restaurant serves good food (meat soup and bananas cost Sh 1250).

The *YMCA* is being used as a school but the people are very friendly and have mattresses for Sh 700. However, you must be out between 7.30 am and 5 pm. You can leave your gear safely in the office during the day and use their bathroom facilities.

Two other places to try are the *Rubaga Training Centre* (matatu for Sh 50 from the main stand), which costs Sh 700 per bed including breakfast and a good dinner; and the *3 Star Hotel & Restaurant* near the railway station, which has singles for Sh 2000 and doubles for Sh 4000. The 3 Star is very clean, has reliable hot water and the lunches are good and reasonably priced for Kampala – but it seems to be temporarily closed.

Finally, you can find relatively cheap rooms (around Sh 3300 a double) in the restaurant-bars around the large market.

Places to Eat

The cheapest eats are to be found at the stalls around the big market due west of the clock tower. Here you can get *matoke* (plantain), beans, fish stews and the like for Sh 50-100 per meal. There are also stalls selling coffee and tea spiced with ginger. In the same area are a number of local restaurants which make pilau, chicken, steaks, *ugali* and rice, but they're more expensive and not all that clean. Look for them around the stadium and bus station.

There are several good, cheap cafés on the left-hand side of Williams St west of the junction with South St. For Indian food, try the *Step In Restaurant*, Kampala Rd opposite the Centre Cinema. Western-style meat dishes can be found at the *Tender Pot*, Market St near the Hindu temple. The *3 Star Hotel* is recommended for breakfast, which costs around Sh 500 depending on what you have. The *Serown Tourist Hotel* is recommended for lunch – again around Sh 500. The *Uganda Coffee Shop* used to be a good place for samosas, bananas and coffee, but the latest reports suggest that it's closed.

A three-course meal at the *Speke Hotel* costs Sh 1500 if you want to splurge.

KASESE

Most people stay at the *Saad Hotel* on the road from the station to the town centre. The management are friendly and the cost is Sh 4400 for double rooms with toilet and shower (hot water is usually available). Good food is available in the hotel's restaurant – lunch here will cost Sh 450. Similar to the Saad is the *Hotel Kaghesera*, which costs Sh 2200 a double. It's clean, has hot water and serves food. The owner is trying to organise tours to the Ruwenzoris and may have this together in the near future. Two other cheapies are *Moonlight Lodgings*, which costs Sh 1200 a double and has running water and electricity; and *Highway Lodging*, though the latter is a bit grim.

Upmarket there is the *Hotel Margarita*, one of the Ugandan Hotels Corporation chain. It costs US$45 a double (hard currency only) with own bathroom and hot water. Most of the rooms have good views of the mountains and the food is excellent (lunch costs Sh 700). Have your currency form handy if you don't want to pay in hard currency.

KISORO

Like Ruhengeri in neighbouring Rwanda, Kisoro was once a place where you could hire a guide to take you to see the gorillas in the mountains on the border between Uganda and Rwanda. Unfortunately, very few people have seen any gorillas on this side of the border recently, though they have occasionally come across their lairs. Bear this in mind if you hire a guide to take you out. Even if you don't see any gorillas though, it's well worth going on a trek just to take in the beautiful countryside. Zacharia is a well-known guide who will take you out on a long day's trek for Sh 1000 each. He sets out early – before dawn – but you can camp at his place overnight

(take your own food). Contact him through the Travellers Rest, as he lives about seven km above the hotel.

Most people stay at the *Travellers Rest*, which is part of the Uganda Hotels chain. The management (friendly) usually only accept hard currency in payment for bills regardless of whether you have a currency form, but they seem to be relaxing this rule lately. This place is situated where the road out of town forks for Rwanda and Zaire. It costs Sh 3300 a double and good food is available (meals cost Sh 700). The hotel has its own generator. If you'd prefer to stay somewhere cheaper, there are lodgings for Sh 400 per bed on the right-hand side on the road from the Travellers Rest to the market.

MASAKA

This town was flattened by the Tanzanians in the closing stages of the war against Idi Amin. Most of the remaining lodges are on the main street and cost Sh 3000. A cheaper one known as the *Musaka Lodge* costs Sh 2000 a double and is very clean. There is no sign so ask at the Blue Hotel for directions. It's about three minutes' walk from the bus station.

Another suggestion by travellers was to go about 20 km due east of Masaka to Lake Nabugabu and stay at the *Church of Uganda Holiday & Conference Centre*, where there are bandas for Sh 6000 per night including food for one person. The proprietors are very pleasant. There's also a beautiful campsite here.

From Masaka you can visit the **Sese Islands** in Lake Victoria. First get a matatu from Masaka to Bukakata in time to catch the daily (except weekends) ferry from there to the islands. It leaves at 8 am and costs Sh 150. If you miss the ferry, there are huts at the Bukakata ferry jetty where you can stay free if you ask the local people. There are two or three buses per week from the boat jetty on Sese to the main town on the island, Kalangula. If there's no bus when you get there, you'll have to hitch a ride on a bicycle. In

Kalangula ask at the missions for a place to stay, or take a room in a lodge.

MBABARA

A good place to stay is the *New Ankole Hotel*, on the main road past the police station, which costs Sh 5000 a double with no currency form hassles. It has hot water in most rooms, a pleasant dining room and beautiful grounds.

There is a cinema and a nightclub with live music every Saturday. The nightclub is round the corner from the cinema.

MBALE

Just north of Tororo, this town is located at the foot of a lush green mountain with plenty of waterfalls. There is a surfaced road to the top and various footpaths from the waterworks at the far end of town. It's a good base from which to go trekking up Mt Elgon in neighbouring Kenya.

Stay at the *Tower Lodge* or *Sharif's* near the market. The *Sikh Temple* may still take travellers.

MBARARA

Stay at the *Church of Uganda Hostel*, which is just up the road from the bus station. A bed in the dormitory costs Sh 330.

MOROTO

Nestling under beautiful Mount Moroto, which is nearly 3000 metres high, Moroto is a very pleasant place to stay. For Sh 220 you can spend a night or two at *St Philips Mission Guest House*, where the warden is not only very friendly but a mine of information.

TORORO

A good place to stay is the *Prince Pot Hotel*, which has large double rooms for Sh 1100 but no running water.

NATIONAL PARKS & GAME SANCTUARIES

Uganda's national parks suffered very badly during Idi Amin's regime, par-

ticularly when his undisciplined troops fled north in the face of the Tanzanian offensive. Troops went on the rampage with automatic weapons, killing just about everything that moved, particularly elephants, big cats and rhinos. The Tanzanian troops which remained after Idi Amin was ousted behaved in no better fashion and contributed to the slaughter. It will take decades of careful management and protection to re-stock these parks with their former variety and numbers of game. Fortunately this is already happening, though big game is still scarce in some parts. Don't let this put you off visiting the national parks, however, as the landscape – especially in the Ruwenzoris – is breathtaking and there's plenty to see and do.

Entry fees to the national parks are Sh 200 per day per person plus Sh 300 per visit for a vehicle. Hire of a Land-Rover or minibus (fuel permitting) costs Sh 75 per km plus Sh 100 per day for a guide. Still cameras attract a fee of Sh 1000 per visit and movie cameras Sh 5000 per visit. The parks are open from 6.30 am to 7.15 pm.

Kidepo National Park

This park on the Sudanese border covers some 1200 square km and is not as well known as the other two in the west. It has plenty of big game, including several rare species of the greater kindu, Bright's gazelle and Chandler's reed buck. Unfortunately, entry to this part of Uganda at present is restricted, as there are pockets of Amin diehards in the area.

Murchison Falls National Park (Kabalega National Park)

There are two main lodges in this park – one at Paraa and the other at Chobe. The one at Paraa suffered badly in the war but is supposedly the better of the two. Both are run by the Uganda Hotels Corporation, so you need to have your currency form handy if you don't want to pay in hard currency. Both cost Sh 1100 a single and Sh 2000 a double. Meals are available but expensive. If you're trying to save money, you might be able to find a place on the floor at Chobe for Sh 100 (try the museum) or at Paraa in the *Education Centre* for Sh 200 including the use of cooking facilities. Chobe has a beautiful setting overlooking the river, and you can see hippos, elephants, giraffes, crocodiles, warthogs and buffalo.

There is a launch which will take you to Murchison Falls (a spectacular sight), but it supposedly costs Sh 25,000! If you don't want to pay, it's a 25-km walk through the park – local people walk through it so presumably it's safe to do so. You can rent one of the ranger's vehicles with a guide/driver for around Sh 150 per km if petrol is available, which isn't always the case. Petrol shortages affect the boat to the falls as well.

You can get to Chobe Lodge fairly easily from Gulu, but there are several ways of getting to Paraa. It's possible to get lifts direct from Masindi but there's not much traffic and you may have to go via Gulu and Pakwach. If you take the latter route, there is a lodge where you can often pick up a lift with a ranger going into the park. The other way of getting to Paraa is to take a bus or matatu from Masindi to the lakeside town of Butiaba, and a boat from there to Paraa. Check with the Tourist Office in Kampala as to whether this boat is still running.

Ruwenzoris National Park (Queen Elizabeth National Park)

This is one of the most spectacularly beautiful areas of Africa and one you shouldn't miss. The Ruwenzoris (or Mountains of the Moon as Ptolemy named them 2000 years ago) form the border between Uganda and Zaire. You can, of course, explore them from either side, but communications are better on the Ugandan side. Game has become much more numerous here since Idi Amin's stragglers were pushed out. The park entrance fee is Sh 1200.

There are three types of accommodation in the park: the *Mweya Lodge*, the *Ecological Institute* and the *Student Camp* (otherwise known as the Educational Centre). The latter two offer cheap dormitory-style beds (Sh 1000 per person), but the Mweya Lodge is a Uganda Hotels Corporation place and considerably more expensive at Sh 6600 a double, plus you need a currency form if you don't want to pay in hard currency. The lodge offers a three-course dinner to both residents and non-residents alike.

It's more or less essential to have your own transport to tour the national parks unless you're going trekking. You can hire vehicles in the park, but the cost is high and only worth considering if there are a group of six or more of you. Much the same applies to the boats which can be hired at Mweya to go out on Lake Edward (Idi Amin Dada), since they cost Sh 10,000. If you are interested in doing the boat trip, it is best to go on a Saturday or Sunday as you can then join a group and share the cost.

Many travellers come here to go trekking in the mountains. There are a number of routes available, but you'll need a guide and porters. John Matte has been taking groups of trekkers into the mountains for years now, and judging from the reports we get, he is the best person to contact. You can get hold of him at the *Mountain Club*, PO Box 276, Kilembe, Uganda. To get there, take the Kasese-Fort Portal road and turn left after about 10 km on the road signposted to Ibanda. He provides accommodation for Sh 150 on the floor or Sh 250 for a bed. Guides cost Sh 600 per day and porters Sh 300 per day. John Matte can arrange all the food and any equipment you might need. If you're heading this way from Kampala, it's best to go on Tuesday or Wednesday so that you arrive in Kasese for the Friday market. If you do this, you're much more likely to find a local taxi or bus going to Ibanda for the Saturday market there (the bus should be Sh 150).

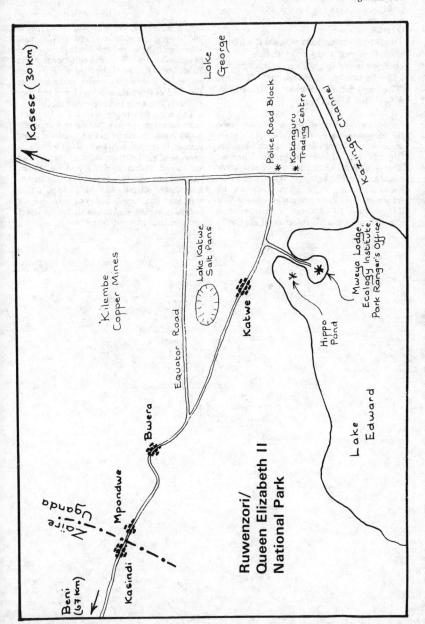

Ruwenzori/
Queen Elizabeth II
National Park

OTHER

To give you some idea of what it's like to walk (but not trek) around this border area, we leave you with an extract from a letter by two travellers who set off to see 'The Impenetrable Forest' south of Lake Albert (Idi Amin Dada):

From Kabale we wanted to go to Inshasha to see the Impenetrable Forest. We caught a slow, scenic bus to Kisoro around Mount Mubbura (Uganda's second highest mountain). There we discovered that the map lied and we must cross into Zaire for 100 km or so. We walked seven km to the border at Boroguna. There was no transport on the Zaire side either, so we walked for two days to Rutshuru – an interesting experience I wouldn't recommend anyone to repeat unless they enjoy playing Pied Piper to 100 ragged individuals chanting 'Wazungu! Wazungu!' There are *bakkis* from Rutshuru up to Inshasha, which is a small settlement still in Zaire. Inshasha River in Uganda is only a police post with a crowd of bored soldiers. They searched us three times in two hours and they still didn't find our hidden money stash.

This was a frustrating period. The Impenetrable Forest was proving to be totally impenetrable. We were unable to find transport going through it, and the police would not let us walk because of all the tree-climbing lions. Instead we walked 10 km to Kihihi and caught the hospital bus at 6.30 am the following day to Kasese. The dilapidated vehicle had no brakes and four flat tyres, but we were quickly becoming accustomed to this kind of transport and it at least gave our feet a rest.

Zaire

The Amazonia of Africa, this vast country is the archetypal explorer's dream. In the heart of the tropics, Zaire is covered with endless jungle, enormous rivers, mountains, volcanoes, prolific wildlife and even wilder people, as well as one of the most diabolical transport systems in the world. In short, it has everything that adds up to genuine adventure. Any traveller who has been there will entertain you for hours with the most improbable stories you're ever likely to come across. There's certainly no rushing through this place – even if you wanted to – and whichever route you choose, it's going to take a long time before you reach the other side. Politically, the country is a daunting one, as anyone with even a vague interest in armed conflict in Africa will know, but you're unlikely to come face-to-face with any of this, and you'll find village people some of the friendliest in the world. Don't pass up what will be one of the most memorable trips of your life because of impressions you may have formed about the country through reading newspapers reporting one armed conflict after another.

The earliest inhabitants of Zaire were bands of hunters and gatherers who lived in the densely forested areas without a social structure or kinship system, much as the pygmies of today still do. In time, however, settled communities sprang up along the rivers and at the edges of the forest, surviving by fishing and a kind of farming. As they gradually improved their agricultural techniques and grew into more complex societies, these communities were able to increasingly dominate the pygmies and extend their areas of control until, by the 14th century, the first great kingdoms had come into being. Foremost among these was the kingdom of Kongo which, through a combination of conquest and matrimonial alliances as well as an elaborate political structure, controlled a large part of the coastal area around the mouth of the Zaire River. Governors appointed to subject states over a wide area were responsible for collecting tribute in the form of ivory, cloth and slaves. Further south emerged a similar pattern of feudal states whose power was based on the control they exercised over long-distance trade. The most important of these kingdoms were the Luba, Kuba and Lunda.

Into this scene came the Portuguese in 1482. Their arrival marked the beginning of new networks of exchange and trade which gradually undermined the power of the Kongo kingdom. Above all else, it was the Portuguese demand for slaves which led to the eclipse of the kingdom. Before the arrival of the Europeans, slavery had constituted only a small part of the wealth on which the Kongo based its power, but by the 17th century the Portuguese demand for slaves to work its Brazilian plantations had far outstripped the numbers which could be supplied by traditional methods. In order to procure sufficient numbers, Portuguese raiding parties and the kingdoms further south quickly began to undermine the economy of the Kongo, and war was declared in 1660. The Kongo was disastrously beaten by the superior fire-power of the Portuguese, and the kingdom went into rapid decline. The kingdoms of the interior, however, continued to grow by trading slaves and ivory for firearms, cloth and luxuries with the Portuguese. Their power was enhanced in the 19th century by the arrival of other slavers from Zanzibar – mostly Arabs – who used Bagamoyo, on the Tanzanian coast, and Ujiji, on Lake Tanganyika, as their main trading posts.

Despite the many centuries of trade with European powers, there was no direct penetration of the interior until the 19th century. One of the most famous of those to explore this area was, of course, David Livingstone, whose chronicles inspired both Catholic and Protestant churches alike to dispatch missionaries by the thousands to Christianise and bring 'civilisation' to the poor benighted 'savages' of 'darkest Africa.' They weren't the only people to become interested in the area, however. This was the era when Africa was being scoured for minerals and suitable land on which plantations could be established.

It was the American newspaper reporter, Stanley – who had originally gone in search of Livingstone (whom he met at Ujiji) before turning his attention to exploring the area himself – who finally paved the way for the colonisation of this part of Africa. After returning from one of his exploratory trips, Stanley was met at Marseilles by representatives of King Leopold of the Belgians and, as a result, became the king's personal representative. Employing Stanley's knowledge of the area, Leopold laid claim to a vast area of central Africa and was successful in getting the other European powers to ratify his claims at the Berlin Conference in 1884-85. Leopold's personal empire became known as the 'Congo Free State.' The use of the word 'free' must have been one of the most cynical to which it has ever been put. While Leopold remained the sole owner of this vast territory, its inhabitants were subjected to among the most brutal and ruthless forms of colonisation ever to disgrace the face of the earth. When news of the worst atrocities leaked out, Leopold was forced to hand over the territory to the Belgian government.

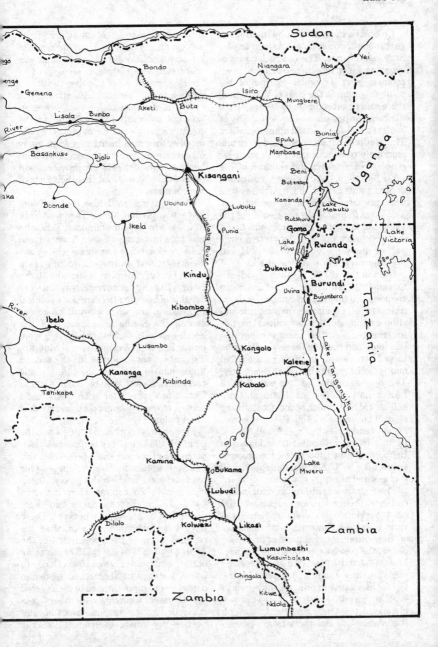

Colonial administration by the Belgian government, however, was to lead to very little real change. The old racist stereotypes remained intact, 'pacification' programmes were a regular feature of the colony right up to the start of WW II, and there was no attempt whatsoever to train Africans for positions of responsibility or leadership in the colonial administration. The Catholic Church retained a virtual monopoly over education, with the best schools reserved for the children of the white settlers, and higher education denied to all except those Africans who were prepared to enter the priesthood. The years following the depression of the 1930s saw a phenomenal economic boom in the country which underwrote a large part of the war effort during WW II, but they saw no political reform at all.

Only in the 1950s, with independence movements sweeping other African colonies, did the Belgian authorities deem it time to relax their paternalistic rule and allow a number of African political parties to emerge. Yet the change came too suddenly and too late for any unity to be forged between the many disparate tribal and regional groups in this huge country. The only exception to this was Patrice Lumumba's Movement National Congolaise (MNC), which stood for a strong central government, able to resist secessionist tendencies by more locally based parties. Riots in Kinshasa (then known as Leopoldville) in 1959 shook the colonial authorities so badly that independence was granted abruptly the following year.

The country was ill-prepared for independence, though Patrice Lumumba tried hard to maintain cooperation between the various parties. However, within a matter of days after the granting of independence, the governor of Katanga Province, Moise Tshombe, declared the secession of his province. Lumumba appealed to the UN for assistance in bringing the rebels to heel, but on returning from New York was dismissed by the president, Joseph Kasavubu, with assistance from a powerful army commander, Mobutu. Lumumba was eventually delivered into the hands of his arch rival, Moise Tshombe, and was murdered. The Katangan secession was finally crushed after massive UN intervention in another country's affairs. The return of Katanga to the fold, however, was not to result in a solution to the country's problems. Kasavubu was soon faced with armed insurgency from many quarters, including supporters of Lumumba, governors of the eastern provinces and plain would-be war lords in other parts of the country.

In an attempt to defuse the situation, Kasavubu invited Moise Tshombe back from exile to be prime minister. Tshombe was able to secure western financial and military assistance (including white mercenary troops) and use it to impose a crude kind of control over virtually all the Congo. But neither he nor Kasavubu were capable of inspiring the necessary political confidence, and when a revolt broke out among the Simba tribespeople of the north-east in 1965, both were swept from power in a coup led by General Mobutu. Tshombe went into exile for the second time, but in 1967 a chartered plane carrying him was forced to land in Algeria. There, two years later in an undisclosed prison, it was announced he had died of heart failure.

Mobutu has continued to rule since the coup of 1965, but his regime has been plagued by the same kind of economic and political upheavals which dogged his predecessors, and with power being increasingly concentrated in his own hands he has become more and more dependent on his western backers. There have been attempts to popularise his regime – some of them cosmetic like the Africanisation of names (in 1971 the name of the country was changed from Congo to Zaire, Katanga to Shaba; and Christian names were dropped, much to the anger of the Catholic Church), and others less cosmetic like the announcement of 'amnesties' for dissident leaders in exile (many of whom have subsequently been arrested and executed or simply murdered on arrival) – yet none of these attempts have essentially changed the autocratic nature of Mobutu's regime. The strongest challenge to his position came in 1977 after the price of copper had plummeted to almost half its former price, resulting in a foreign debt of US$300 million – the world's highest per capita at the time. In that year some 5000 guerrillas of the Front de Libération Nationale du Congo invaded Shaba province from Angola and got as far as the important mining town of Kolwesi. That Mobutu's soldiers were no match for the FLNC became quickly obvious, and they were only expelled with the aid of 1500 regular Moroccan troops, French transport planes and military advisers, Egyptian pilots and other military assistance from Belgium, Britain, West Germany and the USA as well as food supplies from the People's Republic of China. A year later the same thing happened. Mobutu's troops were once again shown to be inadequate and the insurgents were only repulsed with the aid of French and Belgian paratroopers.

By this time Mobutu had become an embarrassment for his western backers in terms of international credibility. After the second defeat of the FLNC some 250,000 civilians had fled to Angola. Pressure was put on Mobutu to liberalise his regime. A result of this was a rapprochement between Zaire and Angola in which Mobutu agreed to end assistance to anti-MPLA groups fighting to overthrow the Marxist government of President Neto in return for Neto's agreement to disarm the FLNC guerrillas and remove them from the border area with Shaba province. Since then a number of rivals and former dissidents – particularly Nguza Karl I Bond who was condemned to death after the first Shaba war – have been reinstated in the government and efforts have been made to restore its diplomatic and economic credibility. Nevertheless, under Mobutu's autocratic regime, discontent continues to grow, particularly in the east and north-east (the Zairois army and security services are firmly controlled by members of Mobutu's own tribe, the Ngbande). In 1980, an Amnesty International report said that several hundred prisoners held indefinitely without trial had died while in detention between 1978 and 1979. And that's just the tip of the iceberg. Many travellers have reported incidents of Zairois army personnel dragging people off trains or buses and beating them to death on the spot. When you are days from the nearest telephone, you can perhaps understand the agony these people have to go through in order to keep their mouths firmly shut. So far we haven't heard any reports of this happening to travellers.

FACTS
The greater part of the country consists of a huge, flat basin through which the rivers Zaire and Oubangui flow to the Atlantic Ocean. Most of this region is covered by lush tropical rainforest. Further south in Shaba province, the forest gives way to savannah. The country's eastern borders run the length of the Rift Valley, taking in Lakes Mobutu Sese Seko, Kivu, Tanganyika and Mweru. Here the land rises into a string of mountains, some of which top 5000 metres in height, particularly in the Ruwenzori Range. Temperatures vary between 20°C and 30°C in the central forest area and between 15°C and 25°C on the high plateau. Humidity is high at all times. The best time to visit is from June to September south of the equator and from November to March north of the equator. These periods correspond to what might be called the 'dry' season. The population stands at about 26 million and consists of up to 200 different ethnic groupings, several of which straddle the borders with neighbouring countries. The pygmies, who have spurned all attempts to integrate them into modern life, live mainly in the forests of the north-east.

VISAS

Visas are required by all. The cost of a visa and the conditions attached to their issue vary considerably from place to place. Most Zaire embassies demand a 'letter of introduction' from your own embassy (the embassy in Bangui, Central African Republic, is an exception) before issuing a visa, but they don't normally ask for an onward ticket. When you apply for your visa, make sure you ask for a three-month, multiple-entry visa. If you don't, you'll be given a one-month, single-entry visa and will have to mess about getting an extension later. Some embassies are reluctant to issue multiple-entry visas. If you come up against this, tell them you will be going by road from Bukavu to Uvira. This road loops briefly into Rwanda, so you need not only a Rwandan transit visa (bought at the border) but also a multiple-entry visa for Zaire in order to get back in again. At some embassies the application form you fill in for a visa may state, 'Entry through Kinshasa only.' This doesn't get stamped on your passport, so don't worry about it.

Extensions are fairly easy to get in Bukavu for up to three months more. In Lubumbashi they officially take eight to 10 days, but with luck they can take as little as two days. They cost Z 75 and require two photos. There is usually no fuss about onward tickets or sufficient funds. You can also get extensions in Kinshasa and Kisangani. In Kinshasa they take four to five days, cost Z 600 for two months, and require two photos, a letter from your own embassy and sometimes a letter from a doctor. Immigration is on Avenue Tombalbye.

If you enter Zaire through Kinshasa from Brazzaville (Congo), you need, in addition to your visa, a *laissez-passer* issued by the Zaire embassy in Brazzaville. This takes 24 hours and is free, though others have had to pay CFA 1000. Even though Zaire visas can be obtained at this embassy, they will not issue the *laissez-passer* unless you got your visa elsewhere. Many travellers have been caught out here and, if you are one of them, you'll have to fly across the river. The 10-minute flight will cost you £200 or the equivalent! Sometimes travellers have got around this by buying an onward ticket, but don't count on it. If you have to buy an onward ticket in order to get the *laissez-passer*, you can buy a Kinshasa-Yaounde ticket and then cancel it when you have the letter, at a loss of about US$7.

If you have a camera, then officially you must have a photography permit issued in Kinshasa, but you can also get these at border posts (eg Kasindi on the Zaire/Ugandan border for Sh 400). It's a good idea to keep cameras out of the sight of police and army personnel, and don't take photographs near transport terminals or government buildings. Some people have had film confiscated, while others were arrested and interrogated.

Burundi visas In Kinshasa these cost Z 65, require two photos and are issued in 24 hours. An onward ticket is required. There's a Burundi consulate in Bukavu as well, where a one-month visa costs US$10 and takes 24 to 48 hours to issue.

Congo (Brazzaville) visas These cost Z 300 and require two photos and a letter of introduction from your own embassy. French nationals must apply for a special permit which costs Z 280. When you apply for the visa, you must tell them which day you intend to cross the river. The people at the embassy are not at all friendly.

Rwanda visas You can get these in Kinshasa at the usual price (about US$10), but they are no longer issued in Goma. All applications for visas have to be approved in Kigali, so they can take a week to come through.

Zambian visas In Lubumbashi a double-entry transit visa valid for three months can be obtained the same day you apply.

However, the border between the two countries was closed in June 1984 because of a border dispute which led to clashes between the armed forces around Kasumbalesa south of Lubumbashi. It probably won't be closed for too long, but make enquiries before you set off.

MONEY
US$1 = Z 40
UK£1 = Z 47

The unit of currency is the zaire = 100 makutas. Import/export of local currency is prohibited. Currency declaration forms are issued at some points of entry (eg at Kinshasa airport and Zongo across the river from Bangui, Central African Republic), but not at others. Even at the places where forms are issued, they often won't bother to give you one if you tell them you only have traveller's cheques. It's a good idea, however, to insist that you are issued with a form, because there are certain places where you will run into trouble if you don't have one. The worst place is the immigration office at the ONATRA riverboat landing stage in Kisangani. A lot of travellers have been 'fined' here for not having a currency form. Others have been put through an inch-by-inch search at Buta and 'fined' US$50 because they didn't declare their coins on entry (pennies, cents, etc). Any undeclared notes found in the search will be confiscated regardless of the amount. The currency forms issued at Zongo are handwritten and don't look very official, but it's a good idea to keep them in order (by whatever means you like) and keep undeclared cash hidden. If you have to change money in the banks, *BCZ* bank is the best.

Allow plenty of time for changing money in banks. It's a major bureaucratic exercise! Most banks charge Z 10 commission per transaction for changing traveller's cheques. Watch out for the common practice of giving you huge piles of small bills (say, Z 5). You'll not only need a wheelbarrow to take it all away, but with such heaps of money you won't count it all, and inevitably there will be a few missing here and there. They do have larger bills, so insist on getting them.

The zaire was devalued by 500% in 1983 and, as a result, the black market rate isn't that much higher than the bank rate, but many travellers prefer it because of the time it takes to change money at a bank. The street rate continues to fluctuate a lot depending on the country's economic circumstances, and varies considerably from one place to another. It generally improves as you go from west to east, so you should be able to get up to £1 = Z 52. You can also get CFA 1000 = Z 95 in Kisangani. If you buy your zaires in Bangui, Central African Republic, beware of the trick of handing you 50 makuta notes instead of Z 1 notes.

If you do get caught with undeclared money, you can expect a hassle and have to pay a bribe. There is an immigration office at the ONATRA riverboat pier in Kisangani where you may be strip-searched and your baggage pulled apart when you get off the boat. This happened to some travellers recently, and vast amounts of undeclared dollars were discovered. Only after hours of talking and negotiating and paying a large bribe were they allowed to leave. Even if everything otherwise is OK but you don't have a currency declaration form, you may be charged Z 20 to Z 50 for one to be issued.

Corruption is endemic in Zaire, though quite a few travellers get through without coming up against it. If you find yourself being hassled, act friendly, joke, make complimentary comments about the president – but steadfastly refuse to give them money. And carry your passport at all times. Soldiers at roadblocks outside of Kinshasa get more and more insistent about cigarettes and money as the night wears on, so avoid travelling at those times. At Kinshasa airport, everyone – from the customs people to the bag rummagers, ticket collectors and police –

will threaten and harass you for money. They go so far as to take things out of your baggage and tell you they will be keeping it. If you're leaving by way of Kinshasa airport, don't attempt to take any zaires with you. Once you've been through check-in they won't allow you back into the reception area again, so you'll end up having them confiscated.

LANGUAGE

French is the official government language, but Lingala is the official language of the armed forces. Other major languages spoken in certain areas are KiSwahili, Tshiluba and Kikongo. Very little English is spoken. A short vocabulary of Lingala follows:

hello	mbote
what's new?	sangonini
nothing new	sangote
go	nake
depart	kokende
where?	wapi
where are?	okeyi wapi
why?	ponanini
OK/thanks	malam
very far	musika
tomorrow	lobi
house	ndako
home	mboka
to eat	kolia
to drink	komela
things to eat	biloko yakolia
water	mai
manioc	songo
bananas	makemba
rice	loso
beans	madeso
salted fish	makaibo
fresh fish	mbisi
meat	niama
peanuts	injunga karanga
market	nazondo
strong	makasi
a lot	mingi
new	sango
dog	mbwa

FOOD

There are chronic food shortages in certain parts of the country so food prices vary widely even over short distances. The state of the roads also affects food prices. If you want to keep costs down, eat what grows locally.

POST

Poste restante at post offices charges Z 7.50 for each letter collected.

GETTING THERE & AROUND

Getting around Zaire is an exercise in initiative, patience and endurance. It also promises some of the most memorable adventures you're ever likely to experience. To enjoy it to the full, you need to forget all about such fetishes as how long it takes to get from A to B, the sort of food you will be eating and the standard of accommodation you're likely to find. Nothing can be guaranteed, nothing runs on time, and in the wet season you could be stranded waiting for a lift for weeks. Not only that, but apart from the riverboats on the Zaire and Kasai rivers and the railways in the east and south-east of the country, the only way of getting around the country is to hitch lifts on trucks. There are very few public buses in this country.

With few exceptions, the roads are diabolical so you'll probably end up at your destination covered in mud, bruised, battered and thoroughly exhausted. Free lifts are the exception rather than the rule unless you meet the occasional Kenyan or Somali driver. The price of lifts often reflects the difficulty of getting there rather than the distance. You don't have to go by truck, though. If the spirit of adventure runs in your veins, you can get through this country in all manner of weird and wonderful ways. Some travellers have literally walked from Kisangani to the Rift Valley, staying in pygmy villages along the way, and have encountered the most disarming hospitality at every stop. Others have haggled for pirogue (dugout canoe) in Bangui, Central African Republic, got the price down to CFA 10,000 after three days of haggling, and sailed it down to Kwamouth at the junction of the Zaire and Kasai rivers. After selling it there, they struck out down the Kasai River and eventually reached Lubumbashi. Whichever way you go, it's going to be an adventure!

As far as reasonably predictable transport goes, there are certain routes to choose from in getting from one end of the country to the other. In the west the starting points are either Kinshasa, the capital, (coming from/going to Congo Brazzaville); or Bangui/Zongo (coming from/going to Central African Republic). In the east there are Aba/Yei (coming from/going to Sudan); Beni or Rutshuru (coming from/going to Uganda); Goma/Gisenye and Bukavu/Cyangugu (coming from/going to Rwanda); Uvira/Bujumbura (coming from/going to Burundi); and Kalemie/Kigoma (coming from/going to Tanzania). In the south the route is Lubumbashi to Chingola, Kitwe or Ndola (coming from/going to Zambia). The border with Angola is effectively closed. The main cross-roads of all the above routes are Kisangani, Kabalo and Kamina.

Don't take any road marked on a map as anything other than a possibility. Sometimes it won't even exist any longer. The Bartholomews maps commit some serious errors by confusing the small eastern towns of Komande and Komanda along the borders with Uganda. The Michelin maps are better in this respect.

Routes through Zaire

The most popular route through Zaire is from Bangui/Zongo on the Central African Republic/Zaire border to Goma/Bukavu/Uvira on the Uganda/Rwanda/Burundi/Zaire borders. The main reason it's so popular is because it's one of the only feasible routes between the game parks and mountains of East Africa and the countries of West Africa. It also recommends itself because you're likely to meet other travellers en route, so by exchanging information you can get a pretty good idea of the state and possibilities of the transport further along your intended route as well as a lot of other useful information such as accommodation possibilities and currency exchange rates. You can, of course, come up from Lubumbashi (Zambia/Zaire) or Kalemie (Tanzania/Zaire across Lake Tanganyika) but, unless you're going Lubumbashi-Kinshasa via Ilebo, all these routes converge on Kisangani. This city on the banks of the Zaire River is the main 'bottleneck' where you can be sure of running into other travellers and where you are presented with a choice of which direction to head in next.

If you're heading east from Kinshasa, you have the choice of going east along the Zaire River to Kisangani and taking it from there, or heading south-east to Lubumbashi and into Zambia.

Depending on how much time you want to spend in Zaire, you can come up with a combination of these possibilities to suit your inclinations – Lubumbashi to Bangui/Zongo or Goma to Lubumbashi, for example.

This section has been organised to treat Bangui/Zongo to Goma/Bukavu/Uvira as the basic route, and then to deal with the alternative routes separately and to incorporate them (where appropriate) into the basic route. This way duplication of information will be avoided.

Since the possibilities of accommodation on many of these routes are very limited, it makes sense to include them along with transport information. The only cities excepted from this are Kinshasa, Kisangani and Lubumbashi.

Finally, I've had quite a few letters from travellers who were heading east to west or south to north and complained about the west-to-east or north-to-south bias in the last edition. I've done my best to make this information intelligible to travellers moving in either direction, so if you're in the minority, I apologise. Just read it backwards!

Bangui/Zongo-Goma/Bukavu/Uvira

The ferry across the Oubangui River from Bangui to Zongo costs CFA 100 plus CFA 50-100 for a rucksack. It's not always in operation, in which case you'll have to take a motorboat or pirogue across the river. This might cost a little more, since in those circumstances it's a sellers' market. If you want to ferry your own vehicle across the river, you will have to hire the whole ferry and, if the engine is 'under repair,' you'll have to hire a tug as well. The owner of each vehicle has to pay the full amount regardless of how many vehicles are on the ferry. Hire of the ferry costs CFA 3500. The tug, if necessary, will cost CFA 3850. Don't cross the river on Saturday or Sunday, as the customs people don't work at weekends and you'll just find yourself hanging around in Zongo until Monday morning. Stock up on Zaire currency in Bangui and hide it well. If you only have traveller's cheques there are banks in Zongo, Gemena and Bumba.

From Zongo it's possible to get free lifts to Gemena (eight to nine hours), or you can get a truck for Z 60. The road isn't too bad. From Gemena a truck to Akula costs Z 50 and takes about five hours. Between Akula and Kinga there is a ferry across the Mongala River. It may be out of operation. If that's the case, take a pirogue for Z 2. Binga to Lisala by truck will cost Z 50 and take five to six hours. From Lisala it's possible to get free lifts as far as Bumba and even Buta. You must report to Immigration in both Bumba and Buta; they're very thorough with baggage, money and anything else. You'll have to pay Z 50 'administration fee' and probably a 'gift' of Z 100 or US$10 if you don't want major hassles or your visa cancelled.

It's definitely worth waiting for the *ONATRA* Zaire river steamer at either Lisala or Bumba if you have the time, though it's rarely on schedule. Waiting for up to a week wouldn't be unusual. Bumba is a better place to wait than Lisala. This is the same steamer which runs between Kinshasa and Kisangani. The fares from Bumba to Kisangani are Z 1603 (1st class), Z 603 (2nd class) and Z 430 (3rd class) including food – tickets which don't include food are not available. Recent reports suggest that substantial student reductions are available on the fares, but you need a letter of attestation obtainable from the local education officer. In Lisala his office is on the hillside above the port towards the post office (don't go to the mission school headmaster for these attestations, as the port officials will tell you).

In 1st class you get three substantial meals a day which are basic but edible and mainly western-style meat and vegetable. In 2nd and 3rd class there is only one meal per day and your ticket is stamped when you collect each meal. The food is filling and consists of heaps of rice with sauce and a good quantity of fish, chicken or pork plus beans and sometimes manioc or spinach. In the past the food left much to be desired, but according to recent reports it's improved tremendously. Water comes from the river and isn't filtered. You can, of course, put your own food together; the boat calls at plenty of places where food is available or where you can buy fresh fish, meat and fruit. Local people will come alongside the boat in their dugouts and sell the food to you. It's also possible to buy meals in the 1st-class dining room for Z 100.

These boats are a classic African experience and not to be missed. Together with six barges, they make up a virtual floating city, with up to 1500 people on board. Any discomfort you might experience is quickly mitigated by the friendliness of the people, the marijuana, the beautiful river vistas and the camaraderie which develops among fellow travellers on a long journey. There's lots of loud music, bars, beers and everything else an African heart needs to enjoy life.

First-class cabins are basic, with two bunks and a metal cabinet, but they have their own small shower and toilet. You can find a cabin with three bunks for four people in 2nd class, though the usual is nine people sharing four bunks with all manner of baskets full of smoked fish, live tortoises, dead crocodiles, hens, pots, pans and you name it! If your group occupies a whole cabin, it's possible to rent a lock for the duration of the journey. This is worthwhile, as there are always a lot of thieves on board. Deck space is dirty and very limited on 3rd class, so the best places to sleep are on top of the barges or on the restaurant floors. Conditions resemble a Hollywood biblical production with a cast of thousands.

When buying 1st or 2nd class tickets, it's important to make sure that the cabin number is written on the ticket; otherwise it will be almost impossible to find an empty cabin. Even so, because of chaotic organisation there's no guarantee you'll have a cabin straight away. Military personnel are allowed to get on the boat and occupy cabins without tickets, so no one knows what space will be available at any time. If you paid for 2nd class and find yourself out on the gangway, ask to see the captain. He'll generally arrange something for you even if it means cramming you into a cabin with lots of other people.

Forget about smuggling your friends into your cabin to sleep, as there are nightly ticket checks in all classes and the boat stops every evening for two hours whilst a search for stowaways is conducted – there are always two to three hundred of these but they only catch a few.

The best place to enjoy the views (and some space, too) is on the barge roofs. Primitive river-water showers up there are operated by the boat engine. This is the only way you can get a decent wash apart from in 1st class.

Watch out for Immigration on arrival at Kisangani. They process all westerners one at a time, and if you haven't got a currency form then you're up for a 'fine' (usually a few dollars). There's no point in complaining that you weren't issued a form on arrival. It's Catch 22.

If you're strapped for time, you can find out when the boat is expected to arrive, as the ferry people in Lisala and Bumba make a radio call daily to find out where it is on the river.

The usual journey time between Lisala and Kisangani is three days, but expect delays.

If you don't fancy the boat or if it isn't due for days, there's the possibility of persuading the captains of cargo barges to take you to Kisangani. The easiest way to get on is to buy them a few beers. These cargo boats are usually a number of barges linked together and pulled by a tug. They're much slower than the steamer (average time between Lisala and Kisangani would be nine days), but they're infinitely more spacious than 3rd class on the steamer and cost about the same. Expect to spend a lot of time stranded on sand banks.

The alternative is to consider going overland through Buta and Isiro and then down to Nia Nia and Epulu (Station de Capture d'Epulu). The railway line between Bumba and Isiro is said to be 'out of order' indefinitely, but this may not be the case. Certainly there is no point in asking at the station in Buta, because they haven't a clue what's going on. Instead, go to what is known as the 'triangle' about three km out of town. Freight trains leave from there and you may be able to get on one of them. They certainly take local people but the guards are hesitant to take whites. Take along a few beers or a good line in Lingala.

If you have to go by road from Bumba to Isiro, it can take a week – you can spend two to three days waiting for a vehicle to come through along this road. If you get stuck, try *Sotexco* between the centre and the Protestant mission in Buta. They sometimes have trucks which go direct to Isiro. These trucks won't be cheap, but even if you find other trucks you'll be lucky to get away with less than Z 100. From Isiro you can usually hitch free to Mungbere.

If you are heading for the Sudan

(difficult at present because of visa and special permit difficulties), there are occasional trucks to Faradje which cost Z 150 and take about two days. Faradje to the border (Aba) you may have to walk. The distance is about 70 km but villagers along the way are very friendly and you'll never be without food or a place to stay. There used to be a bus line along this last stretch called *Tulla Tulla* – aptly named since in Lingala this means 'couldn't care less.' Their schedule is about as reliable.

Places to Stay along the Way

Aba There are no hotels or cafés but you may be able to find accommodation at the *Catholic Mission*, but don't count on it.

Bumba This town has a good choice of hotels ranging in price from Z 60-90, but there are very few restaurants. *Hotel de la Paix*, close to the supermarket, has clean, basic rooms and good service for Z 91 a double. There are no singles. There is a bar but no restaurant, though a local woman will cook for you if you advance the money. Z 150 a day would be sufficient for up to six people.

Binga This is a small but busy market town with several cheap hotels costing about Z 50 per person. If you need to change money, ask at the Catholic Mission.

Buta Stay at the *Protestant Mission* about four km out of town. It's run by very friendly Norwegians.

Dingila A small town about 25 km northeast of Bambesa, Dingila is on the Michelin maps but not on the Bartholomews maps. The cheapest place to stay is *Hotel Disco*, which has rondavels for Z 15. Good food is available here; otherwise there are very few places to eat in town in the evening. There is also *Hotel Bas-Vele*, where a room costs Z 35.

Faradje The *Catholic Mission* will reluctantly put you up.

Gemena The *Catholic Mission* is extremely reluctant to help out with accommodation, but there is another mission some three km out of town which isn't quite so unwelcoming. If you can't get in at either, try the soap factory, which usually has floor space and may even fix you up with a lift.

Isiro Ask at the *Tennis Club* if you can either sleep on the verandah or camp in the grounds. It's guarded at night and they have a swimming pool as well as a relatively cheap bar, but no food is available. Otherwise, try *Hotel Sport* by the football pitch, which is reasonable value at Z 100 a double. Don't bother trying the *Catholic Mission* – they won't even give you a drink of water. There are hotels here but they're almost all expensive. You can find reasonably cheap food in the evenings at the cafés at *Mon Village* market. There are usually Somali, Sudanese and Ugandan traders here who you can change money and arrange lifts with.

Lisala The *Catholic Mission* no longer takes travellers, but you may be able to camp free in the garden of the *Protestant Mission*, three km down the river from Lisala. Other travellers have suggested going to the Portuguese compound, where you can find accommodation, discreetly change money and buy cheap government petrol (if you have your own vehicle).

Apart from that there is the *Complexe Venus*, which has rondavels in the town for Z 95 a double. For a cheap hotel room try the *Hotel du Marche*, which costs Z 50 a single. The *Hotel Montagne* has been recommended in the past but it is not cheap.

The Protestant Mission (Americans) will change small amounts of money (at the bank rate) if the bank is closed.

Zongo There are a number of cheap places to sleep around the immigration office for Z 50.

Kisangani-Goma/Bukavu

The main route between Kisangani and the eastern border with Uganda and Rwanda is along the Kisangani-Beni/Bunia road via Bafwasende, Nia Nia, Epulu, Mambasa and Komanda. Another possibility is the less-used route between Bukavu and Kindu further south. There are no railways or riverboats over this stretch, so the only way to cover it is to hitch rides with trucks, walk or take a flight. If you fly, *Air Zaire* offers 75% student discounts to people under 26 years who have a student card.

The road from Kisangani to Bafwasende is relatively good and shouldn't take more than a day. After that you're on to some of the most diabolical roads in Africa. The worst stretches are between Adusa and Komanda, Mambasa and Komanda, Butembo and Lubero, and Goma and Bukavu. Work is being done on the last stretch so it may be considerably better by the time you read this. You can expect the journey from Kisangani to Goma to take up to six days in the dry season (though some have done it in three days) and up to 14 days in the wet season. Add on another two days at least between Kisangani and Bukavu. The roads running along the border area between Uvira and Bunia via Bukavu, Goma and Beni pass through spectacular countryside, including the fabled Ruwenzori mountains. The sights to be seen here will more than compensate for the bruising and battering you have to put up with. There's also plenty of traffic in this part of the country because it's an important coffee and tea growing area.

To find lifts from Kisangani, it's best to contact the Belgian man mentioned under the Kisangani accommodation section. He can generally organise a truck all the way to Beni or even beyond. Otherwise, you have to go out to Kibibi about six km from the centre. Take either the *Air Zaire* shuttle bus from the Palace Hotel or find a ride at the market. The fare should be about Z 10. It's often possible to find lifts going all the way to Goma from Kibibi, but don't count on it. Some examples of rides available follow:

Kisangani-Komanda Expect to pay around Z 500 for a truck between these two places. You may be able to do this journey in 2½ gruelling days, but that would be exceptional.

Komanda-Beni This costs Z 100 in a pick-up truck and takes around six hours. Trucks generally take longer – reckon on at least 10 hours.

Beni-Kasindi Costs Z 180 and takes about four hours. The best day to find a lift is Thursday, as there's a market near the border then. The road is OK in the dry season. Kasindi is on the Zaire/Uganda border and is a possible crossing point if you're headed for Kasese. The Ugandan customs post is three km down the road from Kasindi, after which it's another three km to Bwera, where you can find accommodation.

Beni-Butembo The cost should be around Z 60 depending on what sort of transport you find. The trip takes about two hours. Taxis leave Butembo for Beni twice daily as a rule, around 8 am and 3 pm.

Butembo-Goma A bus leaves on Monday and Thursday in the early morning. It should cost Z 185 and takes about 14 hours. Advance booking is advisable. A truck will cost about Z 150. The Butembo-Lubero section is virtually impassable in the wet season.

Butembo-Kayna Bayonga Trucks should cost around Z 60, though they may start at Z 90. The journey should take about 13 hours.

Goma-Rutshuru There are pick-ups between these two places which cost Z 25 and take about two hours. It's a good road.

Rutshuru-Inshasha This is another of the

possible crossing points into Uganda, but there's hardly any traffic along the road and a lot of it has been dug up in an attempt to prevent coffee smuggling. You'll probably have to walk the whole way. There are plenty of cheap lodging houses in the first Ugandan village.

Goma-Bukavu Trucks cost Z 100 and take 12 hours-plus (assuming no stops) over a badly rutted road, but there are spectacular views all the way. Take food with you because the cafés en route usually only have tea and bread despite the variety of vegetables for sale everywhere. The prices in these cafés are also high.

Bukavu-Uvira Trucks cost Z 80 and take about five hours. The road between these two places loops briefly into Rwanda for a few km and this fact is conveniently exploited by the Rwandan authorities to fleece you of US$7 for a transit visa. You don't have to pay this if you already have a visa, of course, but you can't get them anymore in Goma. You will also need a visa to get back into Zaire, which is why, when you apply for the Zaire visa, you should make sure you get a multiple-entry one. If you don't have a multiple-entry visa you will have to pay a bribe to get back in.

Uvira-Burundi border There are taxis between the two places for Z 10.

Lake Kivu Steamer Instead of going by road between Goma and Bukavu, you can take the steamer. It's quicker and cheaper than going by road. The steamer, the *Vedette*, plies between Goma and Bukavu via Kibuye and Cyangugu (the latter two are in Rwanda) twice a week in either direction. From Goma to Bukavu takes six hours and costs Z 105. Tickets must be bought at 7 am the day before sailing or at 7 am on Friday for the Sunday boat. Don't count on getting a ticket, as they're often bought out by people with inside connections before they even go on sale.

Departures are often cancelled due to lack of fuel. There's also a barge once a week which takes 24 hours and costs around Z 35.

The alternative route between the Zaire River and the eastern border (Bukavu-Kindu) takes somewhat more effort and initiative than the main Kisangani-Goma route. Between Bukavu and Kamituga there are two to three trucks every day. Most of them charge Z 300-350. The road is not too bad and basic commodities are available en route. The journey will take two or three days. West of here it's difficult to find bread, candles, soft drinks, beer and most fruit and vegetables until you get to Kampene. Between Kamituga and Kitutu the number of vehicles decreases to one every two to three days and you'll probably have to do a lot of walking. The villages en route are friendly and you can always find food and a bed for the night.

At Kama, 12 km from Lusenge, on the main road, is an American missionary named Mr Vinton. He's an amazing character who must be touching 90 years old and has been there since 1928. He's known locally as 'Baba Vee.' If you're a Christian, it's worth stopping off here for the delicious food and hot showers.

The direct road from Kama to Kampene isn't marked on the maps, but it's slightly quicker than via Itabatshi and should take about two days to walk. When you get to Kampene, go to the *Entriaco* offices just outside town. They have several daily trucks to Kindu. Ask at the transport office and they'll give you a free pass. The journey takes one to two days and the roads get better all the time.

Places to Stay along the Way

Beni There are several cheap hotels within 300 metres of the roundabout at the end of the main street, and others where the roads to Mambasa and Komanda start. One of the cheapest places is the *Jambo Hotel*, which costs Z 50 a single and Z 70 a double. To get there, go down the main street to the roundabout, turn left and the hotel is 30 metres down on the left. Other relatively cheap places are the *Lodge Sina Makosa*, which costs Z 110 a single; *Hotel Busa Beni*; and *Hotel Isale*. The latter costs Z 100 a single and Z 150 a double and is clean. All are clean and friendly and have good views of the Ruwenzoris. Another which has been recommended in the past is *Hotel Bashu* near the small market. Give *Hotel Beni* a miss if you're on a budget. It's expensive and geared to cater for well-heeled tourists.

For somewhere to eat, try *Restaurant Bismallah* on the roundabout at the north end of the main street. It offers rice and meat for Z 16. *Restaurant Sukisa* next door to the Hotel Sina Makosa offers good, cheap food so long as you're willing to send your food back several times to make it *moto sana* (they don't speak English or French). A friendly Somali restaurant about half a km down the Kasindi road offers good, cheap food and has rooms for Z 50 a single. If you feel like a splurge then you could go for dinner at *Hotel Beni*. It will cost you about Z 50. The local intoxicant is made from sorghum and bananas and is very cheap at around Z 1 per bottle.

Bukavu Most of the cheapies are on the road west of the Place du 24 Novembre near the Mama Mobutu market. *Hotel Joli Logi*, Avenue Industrielle near the market, costs Z 62 a single and Z 90 a double including own bathroom. The *Ruzivi Hotel* (also known as the *Canadian*) near the cathedral has large rooms with private bath for Z 70-90 per night. Another cheapie which doubles as a brothel is *Hotel de la Victoire*, which has singles for Z 150 and doubles for Z 200. *Hotel La Fregate*, on the main street, is somewhat expensive but has pleasant, clean, airy rooms for Z 426 a double. Others recommended are *Hotel Taifa*, which costs Z 110 a single and Z 165 a double and has a bar with a busy nightlife, *Hotel Bana Zaire* and *Hotel de la Groupe de*

Kalemie. You may also be able to stay at the *Bereeme Mission* next to the prison up the steps from the Place Novembre 24. Ask for the missionaries Mr and Mrs Crumley.

You can find a cheap breakfast at the market near the junction. A two-egg omelette, onion, tomato, bread, margarine and tea should cost around Z 15. For a good, solid meal (Z 80), go to the *Hotel Taifa*, which has a very good restaurant and bar. It almost always has beer and 'the steak and chips taste like heaven after several days of slopping through the jungle mud.' The *Patisserie de Kivu*, Avenue President Mobutu, is good for tea, *kahawa* and *mkate*.

The *Pharmacie de l'Avenue*, Avenue President Mobutu, is a good place to go if you need medicines for which you'd need a prescription in many other countries.

There is a **gorilla sanctuary** about 20 km from town in the **Parc National du Kahuzi-Biega**. Entry costs Z 600, which includes a guide and cutters. Buy tickets either from the gate or at the Tourist Office.

Bunia Try the *Chez Tout Bunia* hotel and restaurant, which has singles for Z 70. Rooms are also available for Z 50 further down the hill.

Butembo Many of the cheapies are near the market, but if you have the money it's worth spending a night at the *Oasis Hotel*. This colonial-style hotel is a delightful example of 'deteriorating elegance.' It's owned by an old Belgian man and costs Z 300 for a room, but you might be able to get it down to Z 200 if you show the owner his name in the book. The dinners here are excellent (soup, meat, bread and butter, coffee) and cost Z 60. A cheaper place to stay is *Hotel Butembo* on the main road. It's also owned by a friendly Belgian man and offers excellent food. The *Restaurant Bismallah* has cheap rooms, but you should avoid idle talk about Idi Amin here, as many of his exiled henchmen use it as a hangout. Another place which has been recommended is *Hotel Brise Soleil*. For something a little more upmarket, try *Hotel Semiliki*, which costs Z 220 a double and has a good restaurant.

Epulu (Station de Capture d'Epulu) You can camp at the *Station de Capture* for Z 50 per person; it's a beautiful site. Some travellers have been offered a place on the verandah free.

The pygmy villages in this area are getting fairly touristy and you will be hassled for food, presents and other gifts as well as charged for photographs.

Inshasha There is a quiet lodge called the *Mapendo* which costs Z 60 a double.

Goma It used to be possible to camp free at the *Cercle Sportif*, but they now charge Z 200 per night! One of the cheapest hotels is the *Chambres Aspro* (!) which costs Z 100 a single. It's run by a very friendly Rwandan family. Other places to try are the *Centre d'Accueil*, which costs Z 50 and is clean; *Hotel Macho Kwa Macho*, which has single rooms for Z 45; *Hotel Amani*, which costs the same as the Macho; and the *Chambres Aspro* across the street from the Macho. Other travellers have stayed at the mission, known as *Chez les AFI*, next to the *Hotel Turkano*, which is clean and good value at Z 60 a double including breakfast. *Hotel Elegance* is another possibility. It's a very inelegant brothel but clean and run by a friendly gay man. It costs Z 60 a double. More expensive places include *Hotel Rif* at Z 85 a double including breakfast; and *Hotel Haute Zaire*, which costs Z 155 a double.

For food try the *Hotel Restaurant de Confiance*, where omelette and tea will cost Z 12. Another good place is the *Restaurant Stade des Volcans* between the market and the Hotel Haute Zaire.

Goma has acquired a reputation as having the most undisciplined police force in Zaire. If you don't want to tango with them, stay indoors at night.

It's no longer possible to get Rwandan visas here. That means if you haven't already got one and are going by road from Bukavu to Uvira, you'll have to pay US$7 for a transit visa.

Komanda Ask around for two Anglican women who run a small guest house (it's not a mission). Hot water is available and you can camp as well. *Restaurant Makesate* has rooms for Z 30.

Mambasa The *Catholic Mission*, on the road towards Beni is a possibility but bring your own food. Don't expect any favours and keep a low profile.

Mount Hoyo Thirteen km off the Beni-Komanda road and 12 km from Komanda is the *Cascade des Escaliers de Venus* (a waterfall), grottos and pygmy villages. They're getting very touristy these days but perhaps are still worth visiting if you're passing through. You can camp for Z 12. Water and toilets are available, but the electricity sometimes doesn't work because of fuel shortages. Rooms cost Z 50 and chalets Z 250. Meals are fairly expensive even for a simple breakfast. You can rent equipment and a guide at the lodge to go up to the top of Mount Hoyo. It's a two-day walk there and back.

Nia Nia If you're lucky you might be offered a room at the *Catholic Mission*. It's run by two Italians; the old *pere* is somewhat eccentric.

Rutshuru The *Catholic Mission* has purpose-built accommodation where you can get a room for Z 35, dinner for Z 30 and breakfast for Z 20. Camping is possible. The *Katata Hotel* is very clean and costs Z 70 a double including hot showers. *Hotel du Parc* costs Z 50 a double but often has no running water.

Uvira Hotels tend to be expensive. The cheapest is *Hotel Babyo La Patience*, Avenue Bas-Zaire near the mosque, which costs Z 70 a single.

Make an effort to look like a normal tourist and avoid taking photographs. People feel an intense paranoia concerning mercenaries.

You can change zaires for Burundi francs at an excellent rate here. It is Z 100 = BFr 385.

Kisangani-Lubumbashi & Kisangani-Kalemie

The first part of this journey involves getting to Kindu, from which there is a railway all the way to Lubumbashi with a branch line to Kalemie on Lake Tanganyika from Kabalo.

The train from Kisangani to Ubundu is supposed to run twice a week on Tuesday and Saturday, but it's always getting cancelled because of fuel shortages and derailments. You may well have to wait up to 10 days. The journey generally takes 16 to 20 hours but has been known to take 30! There are three classes, but 3rd class is a test of endurance as it's always crammed to the gunwales with a writhing, perspiring mass of bodies. Third class costs Z 30 plus Z 10 for the ticket collector and Z 10 for a seat. Take food and water with you, though food can be bought at stops on the way – groundnuts, rice, corn, elephant meat, caterpillars and beer.

When you get to Ubundu you may be lucky and connect with the riverboat down to Kindu. This only runs every so often so you'll probably find yourself waiting around again. There are two kinds of boat – a barge and an ordinary boat with three classes. Organisation is virtually non-existent in 3rd and 2nd classes, so if you want a bunk you'll have to move fast. Good food is available in the 1st-class dining room, but the boat stops frequently at wayside ports so you can buy rice, manioc, nuts, oranges and bananas as a rule. The boat takes between four and six days. When things run more efficiently (which is rare), it's possible to buy a combined rail/boat ticket for Z 259 which covers you for the Kisangani-Ubundu and Kindu-Kamina trains and the Ubundu-Kindu riverboat.

If something goes wrong with either the Ubundu train or the boats and you get sick of hanging around, you can attempt to get to Kindu by road – but it's not easy. There's very little traffic after Lubutu, and the Lubutu-Punia stretch is in really bad shape. Many travellers who attempted this road had to walk the part from Lubutu to Punia (145 km). If you have to do this, it should take about five days. There's plenty of friendly villages along the way, but stay clear of the Yumbi police post. Once you get to Punia you'll find plenty of transport going south to Kindu.

At Kindu there is a train all the way to Lubumbashi with a branch from Kabalo to Kalemie on Lake Tanganyika. It departs once a week on either Friday or Saturday but is often delayed. The journey can take as little as 2½ days, but if there are problems it can take up to five days. Student concessions of 50% are available if you have a student card and authorisation. Try not to travel on this train alone, especially if you're a single woman. We've had reports of gangs of thieves terrorising passengers with the connivance of the railway staff. There are also many drunks on it who can get violent, so keep a low profile. From Kamina there are trains to Lubumbashi for Z 456 (2nd class).

If you're heading for Tanzania, change trains at Kabalo and take another which leaves on Sunday heading east for Kalemie. At Kalemie you can take the Lake Tanganyika steamer to various ports in Burundi, Tanzania and Zambia. The steamer is often delayed but the official schedule is as follows:

Kalemie-Bujumbura

	Arrive	Depart
Kalemie		4 pm Sun
Kigoma	7 am Mon	2 pm Mon
Kalundu	7 am Tues	9 am Tues
Bujumbura	10 am Tues	

Bujumbura-Kalemie

	Arrive	Depart
Bujumbura		12 pm Tues
Kalundu	1 pm Tues	4 pm Tues

| Kigoma | 7 am Wed | 4 pm Wed |
| Kalemie | 7 am Thurs | |

If you're travelling in the opposite direction (from Tanzania to Lubumbashi), you can buy a railway ticket all the way from Kigoma to Lubumbashi. The cost on the *rapide* is Z 1800 (1st class ordinary) and Z 1555 (2nd class).

Places to Stay along the Way

Kindu One of the cheapest places to stay is *Hotel Lusa*, two blocks parallel to the main street, which costs Z 31 a single and Z 46 a double. Be careful about people breaking into your room whilst you are sleeping. If you don't like this place, try *Hotel Maniema*, which costs Z 60 for a large, clean double room with own shower and toilet; or *Hotel Relais*, which charges Z 119 a double. Don't bother going to the *Catholic Mission*, as they're very unfriendly.

Ubundu The *Catholic Mission* might provide you with free accommodation. If not, there is a small hotel where you can get a bed for Z 20 a night.

Kinshasa-Kisangani

The only way to get between these two cities other than flying is to take the *ONATRA* river steamer. It's a fantastic journey and a 'must' in this part of Africa. For a graphic description of the conditions on the boat, read the section on Bangui/Zongo-Goma/Bukavu/Uvira. The journey from Kinshasa to Kisangani is supposed to take 10 days, but two weeks should be allowed. The fares are Z 5362 (1st class) including three meals a day, Z 2062 (2nd class) and Z 1479 (3rd class). Second- and 3rd-class tickets include one meal per day for a maximum of eight days. This isn't sufficient for a two-week journey, but there are usually plenty of people cooking on board who will either give or sell food to you. There's another way round the food problem. The meals you get in 3rd class are as large as the container you give them,

so if you're a group of two or more, take turns to go to the kitchen with a large bowl (tickets are stamped every time you get a meal). This way, even if there are only two of you, you'll end up getting at least one meal a day. Believe it or not, beer is cheapest in the 1st-class bar (Z 15) and no one minds you hanging around there even if you're travelling 3rd class.

If you just want to go from Kinshasa to Lisala, the fares are Z 3642 (1st class), Z 1386 (2nd class) and Z 1017 (3rd class).

The staff at the Gare Fluvial in Kinshasa are very helpful but the cabin numbers on your ticket mean nothing.

Kinshasa-Lubumbashi

The first part of this trip involves getting to Ilebo. The direct way is to take the *ONATRA* river steamer down the Kasai River from Kinshasa to Ilebo. It goes in either direction once every two weeks (sometimes only once per month), taking six days. The fares are Z 3642 (1st class – cabins with two beds and three meals per day), Z 1438 (2nd class – cabins with six beds and two meals per day), and Z 1017 (3rd class – dormitory beds and one meal per day).

If you don't want to take this steamer, there are plenty of cargo barges you can pick up either in Kinshasa or Kwamouth which go to Mangai, about one day's ride by truck from Ilebo. In the opposite direction there are plenty of barges from Ilebo to Kinshasa. It's fairly easy to get a free ride on one of these barges. Courier boats do the Kwamouth-Ilebo run too, but they cost Z 150.

The third possibility is to take a bus from Kinshasa to Kikwit with *Compagnie Sotraz*, which has a depot close to the GPO in Kinshasa. Their luxury buses leave daily between 7 am and noon and between 3 and 6 pm. The fare is Z 480, but at either end you must buy your ticket at the bus station at 4 am! The road is surfaced to Kikwit. From there, trucks leave daily at around 6 am for Idiofa. From there it's no problem to get a lift first to

Brabanta (now called Mapangu) and from there to Ilebo. Between Kikwit and Ilebo there is a river to cross by a ferry service, which only operates twice per day. The ferry times are variable but the boat usually makes the crossing between 9 and 11 am and between 3 and 4 pm. If you're hitching, either wait at the river crossing or at Hotel Los Palmos on the road down to the river. All trucks must pass this hotel and it's a pleasant place to wait (bar and friendly management). If buses don't appeal, there are trucks from Kinshasa to Ilebo virtually every day, even in the rainy season; they take two days and cost about Z 700.

From Ilebo you can go all the way to Lubumbashi by train. The ordinary train leaves on Tuesday and the *rapide* on either Saturday or Sunday. The former takes six days and the latter four. In the opposite direction, the ordinary train leaves Lubumbashi on Saturday and the *rapide* on Thursday. Fares are Z 2675 (1st class deluxe *rapide*), Z 2225 (1st class), Z 1965 (2nd class *rapide* – compartment with six bunks) and Z 1670 (2nd class ordinary). Third class has bench seats only. The fare from Kananga to Lubumbashi is Z 1632 (1st class). Student concessions of 50% are possible if you have a student card and authorisation from the railway staff.

This is a pretty rugged train trip – millions of screaming kids, pots, pans, vast amounts of luggage, dried fish – and it stops frequently in the middle of nowhere so that ticket inspectors can eject ticketless passengers (there are always plenty of them). The *rapide* has a buffet car and bar but the food is very expensive, so take enough to last you until Kamina, after which there are plenty of hawkers selling food at the stations. There is rarely any water on the train so take your own. If you want to head north to Kisangani or east to Lake Tanganyika, change trains at Kamina.

From Lubumbashi to the Zambian border you can go by truck, pick-up, taxi or train, but there are no through passenger trains to Zambia. The train goes only as far as Sakania and then only once a week at 9 am on Wednesday. All road transport from Lubumbashi leaves from the 'Zone Kenya.' Trucks from here to Chilabombwe (Zambia) cost Z 20-40. Otherwise, get a taxi (Z 35) or a pick-up (Z 25) from the Zone Kenya to Kasumbalesa, a minibus from there to Chilabombwe (Kw 1), a bus from there to Chingola (Kw 0.50), and finally another bus from there to Kitwe (Kw 1.80). From Kitwe there are trains south to Lusaka. If you take the train from Lubumbashi to Mokambo there is a bus from there direct to Chingola for Z 40.

Places to Stay along the Way

Idiofa There is a hotel opposite the *carrefour* (the truck park), but it's pretty expensive at Z 125. It also serves good food. There are cheaper places for about Z 55 – ask the local people.

Ilebo There is a mission three km from town on the Lubumbashi road; it's worth trying if you want cheap accommodation. Otherwise, there are *Hotel Frefima* at Z 70 a single and Z 105 a double; and *Hotel du Palme*, which costs Z 295 a single.

Mapangu Ask for the *Maison de la Passage*, owned by PLZ (Plantations Lever Zaire). It's a rest house for the use of PLZ employees but very rarely used. You can get accommodation for Z 15 per person. Good meals are available.

Kananga With a population exceeding half a million, this is one of Zaire's largest cities. You can sometimes find accommodation with the *Protestant Missions* – there are two of them – or with the Peace Corps, but don't count on it. Otherwise try *Hotel Palace*, where you can get a room for Z 30; or *Hotel Musube*, which has rooms for Z 45.

Kananga has a good **museum** if you are interested in local craftwork. Entry costs Z 1.

Kikwit Try *Hotel Mutashi* opposite the beer garden of the only large hotel on the main road to Ilebo. It costs Z 120 a double.

Kinshasa-Matadi

If you want to take the train from Kinshasa to Matadi, a *rapide* leaves Kinshasa at 7.15 am on Monday, Wednesday and Friday and arrives at Matadi the same days at 2.30 pm. From Matadi to Kinshasa it leaves at 8.30 am on Monday, Thursday and Saturday. The fare is Z 213 (1st class) and Z 185 (2nd class). There are also ordinary trains (2nd and 3rd classes), but they take about twice as long. In addition,

SOTRAZ buses run between the two places for Z 256.

Kinshasa-Zongo

When the river is high enough there are boats all the way from Kinshasa to Zongo. You can pick up boats from Brazzaville to Bangui at the same time.

LUBUMBASHI

The capital of Shaba province, Lubumbashi is in the heart of the copper belt. Formerly called Elizabethville, it's a pleasant city with large numbers of Lebanese, Greek and Italian expatriates. Good places to stay here include:

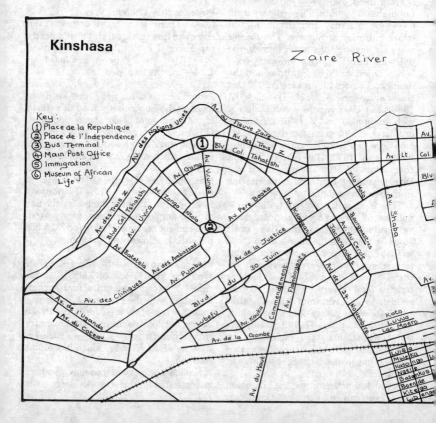

Kinshasa

Key:
① Place de la Republique
② Place de l'Independence
③ Bus Terminal
④ Main Post Office
⑤ Immigration
⑥ Museum of African Life

Hotel Globe in front of the railway station, which has excellent rooms with shower and toilet for Z 200 a double.

Hotel Wagenia, which has clean, quiet and comfortable rooms for Z 70 a double.

Hotel de la Paix, close to the hospital, which doubles as a brothel and has rooms for Z 150 a double.

Hotel du Shaba, 486 Avenue du Mama Yemo, which has clean rooms for Z 50 a single and Z 65 a double. It's owned by a friendly Belgian man. The hotel has its own restaurant.

Hotel Silver House, situated near the SNCZ Hotel, which has rooms for Z 55.

The hotel has a mixed bar.

Hotel Silver Star, which has rooms for Z 215 a single and Z 350 a double.

Hotel Macris, near the Silver Star, which has rooms for Z 270 a single and Z 320 a double. It's Greek run and has a good restaurant.

For cheap food try the cafés opposite the market where you can get beans and meat; or try the *Restaurant Zaire* near the Hotel Globe.

KINSHASA

The rest of Zaire may be pretty wild and untamed, but Kinshasa, the capital, is a pleasant, modern city with wide, tree-

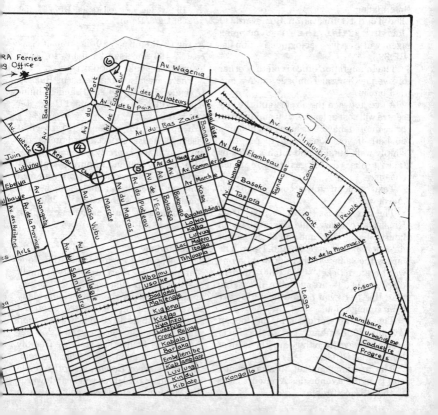

lined boulevards, parks and lots of friendly people. The *cité* is the most interesting and lively part of the city to stay in, with its live bands, bars and clubs.

Make sure you carry your passport at all times. If you get stopped at night without it, you'll probably be hauled before the army for questioning. Unless you're with friends who can go and find your passport, you may be slapped with a large 'fine' – they won't allow you to go back to wherever you left it. You can also expect a visit from the security forces at your hotel between 3 and 4 am to check passports and baggage.

Information

The Tourist Office is on Boulevard 30 Juin (tel 22417). There is a mapping agency at Service Géologique Nationale, BP 898.

The Immigration office is on the corner of Avenue General Tombeur and Avenue de Plateau.

A taxi between the airport and the city centre will cost at least Z 200 and the first price quoted may be as high as Z 800 (it's 29 km). If you don't want to pay this, simply walk outside and hitch a truck or take a bus (Z 10), as they're much cheaper.

Taxis around town cost Z 20 per journey.

The ferry across the Zaire River from Kinshasa to Brazzaville operates on an hourly basis day and night in either direction except at 7 am and 1 pm. The fare is the same whether you want a one way or return ticket – CFA 1800. Student discounts of 33% are available. In order to take this ferry you need a *laissez-passer* from Immigration.

The railway station is at the foot of Avenue 30 de Juin. The Zaire River steamers leave from the Gare Fluvial near the Tourist Office.

The artisans' market (for malachite, etc) is on the Avenue des Aviateurs close to the USA consulate.

Embassies

Belgium
  Place 27 Octobre, BP 899
Burundi
  Avenue de la Gombe 17 near the university (tel 31588)
Central African Republic
  Avenue Pumbu 11
Cameroun
  Boulevard 30 du Juin near the Maison Royale
France
  3 Avenue Republique du Tchad, BP 3093
Germany
  201 Avenue Lumpungu, BP 8400
UK
  9 Avenue de l'Equateur (5th floor), BP 8049 (tel 23483/6)
USA
  310 Avenue des Aviateurs, BP 697 (tel 25881/2/3/4/5/6)

At the CAR embassy 10-day transit visas cost Z 400 and take 24 hours to issue. Tourist visas take four days.

There are also consulates in Bukavu (Avenue Mobutu, tel 2594) and Lubumbashi (1028 Boulevard de l'Ueac, tel 2324/5).

If applying for a Congo (Brazzaville) visa in Kinshasa, expect a hard time at the embassy. They're pretty unfriendly there. Visas cost Z 300 and require two photos and a letter of introduction from your own embassy. French nationals also need a special permit which costs Z 280. It's more or less the same as a visa except in name.

Places to Stay

The cheapest area to stay is the Zone Matonge, where there are plenty of small, obscure cheap places. Expect to pay around Z 100 per room per night. Many travellers stay in the *Hotel Yaki*, 28 Avenue du Stade du 20 Mai, which is good value but not the cheapest at Z 250 per room for 24 hours. The staff are friendly and there are good views from the roof. Cheaper is *Hotel Sanda*, just off Avenue Kasavubu on the left as you head towards the Matonge area, where you can get a room with own shower for Z 60 a double. Similar is *Hotel Kita Kita*, Avenue Croix Rouge, which costs Z 80. Locks are available. Another place which has been recommended is *Hotel Mini Kapi*, Rue Sundi 88. It has a friendly staff and costs Z 40 per night. Many of the small places in the Matonge area are badly marked and nearly all are brothels. Walk around and have a look at a few. The *Protestant Mission*, Avenue Kalemie, also has accommodation but it's fairly pricey at Z 250 per room.

A good place for bread with peanut butter and coffee in the morning is the small market next to the Hotel Yaki. For beans or fish and rice, try the stalls by the roundabout opposite Big Steak not far from the Yaki – an enormous bowl of beans and rice costs Z 15.

A good place to escape from the sometimes oppressive atmosphere of Kinshasa with a few cold beers is the bar of the *Kinshasa Inn*, Boulevard du 30 Juin.

Although Kinshasa is a much bigger city than Brazzaville, many things are harder to get here than across the river. This includes medicines, technical items of all kinds (water purification tablets, vehicle and bicycle parts). You'll have to pay more for them too, since they have to be smuggled across the river.

KISANGANI

Formerly Stanleyville, Kisangani is the main city on the middle reaches of the Zaire River. There are many Greek expatriates here as well as travellers on their way through Zaire.

Most travellers stay at *Hotel Olympia*, a Greek-owned place where you can camp for Z 40 per person, though they're pretty slack about collecting the money. Rooms vary in price depending on what you get. They start at Z 150 and go up to Z 400 a double with air-conditioning. Watch your gear; as one traveller commented, 'Three British fellows who'd just come overland on a camel train from Cairo had all their underwear stolen.' That's desperation for

you! The food tends to be on the expensive side but it's good. In the Zone de Chopo, *Hotel Baninga* has some very cheap rooms. Also recommended are *Hotel des Chutes* near the river, which is a pleasant old colonial-style hotel with double rooms for Z 245. The *Wagenia Hotel* is considerably more expensive at Z 400 a double. Neither the des Chutes nor the Wagenia have their own restaurants. At the top end of the market is the *Zaire Palace Hotel* above Air Zaire which costs Z 1000 per person. It has a good bar and restaurant.

Most of the restaurants are Greek-owned and the food is expensive. The only cheap Greek restaurant is on the top floor of the four-storey building round the corner from the post office. The *Ali Baba* close to the Zaire Palace Hotel and the *Transit Café* are both good. The latter place has a blackboard listing the arrivals of airplanes, trains and boats, and is a good place to meet other travellers. It's about halfway between the Olympia and Wagenia hotels.

There's a sort of Mr Fix-It in Kisangani who's the person to see for all manner of things – changing money, arranging lifts, buying and selling cars. He's a Belgian man and his wife is Zairois. Both of them are very reliable. Find out where they live by contacting Eugene, who works for him.

If you don't go through the Belgian man, be careful when arranging lifts. There are one or two rip-off merchants in this town who work hand-in-glove with the police. You may be told, for instance, that there is a truck going to Goma (or wherever) at 5 am in the morning. While you're being led to it, the police stop you, take your passports and refuse to hand them back unless you give them money. All this time, the man who is taking you to the truck is urging you to settle up or you'll miss the truck. After you've handed over money and finally got to where the truck is supposed to leave – bingo! – there's no truck.

Allow plenty of time if you're changing

money in the banks. The best one to go to is the Commercial Bank down by the river, though even here it can take half a day. The other bank charges exorbitant commission on traveller's cheques. We heard one story recently of a woman who wanted to change US$20 and was told she owed them money!

A good place for souvenirs is the Catholic Mission.

NATIONAL PARKS
Virunga National Park
Stretching from Goma to north of Beni and encompassing Lake Edward, this park is one of the most beautiful in the world. It has snow-capped mountains (including the Ruwenzoris or 'Mountains of the Moon,' as Ptolemy called them), volcanoes, lush rainforests and plenty of wildlife, though it appears that the elephants are being shot by park wardens on the payroll of a Kisangani politician who has a nice line in ivory going and an expanding waistline. His flatulence fortunately doesn't reach as far as Virunga, where the high altitude makes for a very agreeable climate.

The major attractions in the southern end of the park between Goma and

Rutshuru are the two volcanoes, Nyiragongo and Nyamulgira, both of which can be climbed. Nyiragongo erupted only a few years ago and from time to time molten lava can still be seen in the crater from the rim in the evening, though the fireworks are nowhere near as spectacular as they were shortly after the eruption had ceased. Don't build up your hopes too much, though, as some nights there is no activity. The view next morning compensates for any disappointment you might feel if this happens. The volcano can be climbed in about five hours. To get there, find a ride to Kibati, 13 km north of Goma. You can either arrange a guide (compulsory) and porters at Kibati or head for the park entrance and fix things up there. The park entry fee is Z 400 for a week-long permit, and though it is supposed to include the cost of the guide, you won't get much cooperation without an additional and substantial tip. If you plan on using porters, they charge Z 50 per day. The park officials may attempt to charge you a photo permit fee if you have a camera. Officially there is no fee except for movie cameras, but most people end up paying the extra Z 50.

Most people stay in the hut just below the crater rim overnight and return the next day. Take a torch with you if you don't want to break your leg returning from the rim to the hut after dark.

Climbing the other volcano, Nyamulgira, takes three days, and you have to take all your own supplies as nothing can be bought on the way. Nyamulgira has no boiling lava like Nyiragongo, but the views over the steaming rainforests below are unforgettable. Once again, a guide is compulsory on this trek, though if you paid the park entry fee to climb Nyiragongo you don't have to pay again. To get to Nyamulgira, go first to Ruga, 24 km from Goma. The best time to visit the volcanoes is during December, January and June. At other times of the year they tend to be shrouded in cloud.

Further north between Rutshuru and Lake Edward, the main attraction is the herds of game – lion, elephant, hippo, giraffe, antelope, hyena and many others. The major centre is the lodge at Rwindi. Trucks there from Goma take about five hours. The lodge is situated in the middle of a treeless plateau and consists of a 100-room hotel and a number of thatched cottages. A room at the hotel costs Z 43 a single and Z 50 a double. The food is relatively expensive. If you don't have the money, ask about a room in the truck drivers' section at the back of the main hotel. The rooms are much cheaper and yet have much the same facilities as the hotel rooms.

Whilst you're here it's worth making a trip to the small fishing village of **Vitshumbi** on the shores of Lake Edward.

The northern section of the park east of Beni encompasses the Ruwenzoris, which rise to a height of over 5100 metres. If you'd like to climb these, head for Mutwanga (taxis from Beni for Z 100) where you can make arrangements for a guide (compulsory) and porters (recommended) at the lodge. The lodge is deserted most of the year so you'll certainly get a room. If you're on a tight budget, however, walk a further two km to Musoma, where there is a small army base and the park headquarters. You can get a bed there for Z 160 a double. Allow four or five days to climb the Ruwenzoris, and make sure that the guide you hire is willing to take you all the way. Some of them refuse to go as far as the third hut, thus cutting the trip down to three days. Trying to get a refund for the other two days (which you naturally have to pay in advance for) is a waste of time. No special equipment is needed. The fee for the park (if you haven't paid it already) is Z 600 plus Z 50 per day per person for the use of the huts. Porters charge Z 50 per day plus Z 50 per day for food.

The ascent is an incredible experience, if only for the changes of vegetation. You begin on grassy plain, pass into lush rainforests followed by deciduous forest, and finally emerge onto an eerie, rocky landscape of twisted, leafless trees and bright yellow heather. Shortly afterwards you come to the snowline, where mosses, lichens and giant wildflowers grow. If the sky is clear the views are incredible. This climb can be very difficult in the rainy season. Before you return to Beni, visit the fishing village of **Ishango** on the shores of the lake. If you feel like staying overnight, there's a pleasant lodge at which to stay.

Kahuzi-Biega National Park

This park is situated about 35 km north-west of Bukavu and is one of the last sanctuaries of the gorilla. To get there, hitch from the Place de 24 Novembre to the cross-roads seven km from the park entrance (you may get a free lift but expect to pay Z 30). The last stretch to the park entrance is difficult to hitch and you'll probably have to walk. Alternatively, you can get a taxi from Bukavu to the park entrance for around Z 700 with lots of bargaining. The journey takes about half an hour. Get to the park entrance by 9.30 am at the latest, as that's when the guides begin organising groups.

A guide is compulsory; you'll need one anyway if you want any hope of sighting the gorillas. The fee is Z 400 per person plus Z 50 for a camera, which is good value – it's shared between four men who hack their way through the bush ahead of you. You can safely assume those men are going to appreciate you shouting a round of beers at the end of the day. Either that or a reasonable tip. It's often possible to get a lift back to Bukavu with tour groups. You can be fairly certain of seeing the gorillas by noon and arriving back in Bukavu by early afternoon. This means it's considerably easier and cheaper to see gorillas in Zaire than in Rwanda.

There's no need to arrange guides in advance at the park warden's office in Bukavu. It can all be done at the park entrance.

OTHER

The dreaded weed Congolese grass is world famous and needs little further comment. You buy it here in small banana-leaf rolls. Z 1 will buy you heaps of the stuff, especially in the pygmy areas of eastern Zaire.

Zambia

This strangely shaped country is one of Africa's most absurd legacies of colonialism. Its borders correspond neither to any single or complete tribal (or even linguistic) area nor to the boundaries of any kingdom which existed here prior to the arrival of the Europeans. As a result, regionalism constantly threatens to tear the country apart, is deliberately exploited by politicians to further their own ends, and has made it all but impossible for the Zambian leadership to generate any sense of national identity. It has also forced – or, depending on your point of view, been used as a convenient excuse by – the president, Kenneth Kaunda, to declare a one-party state and to consolidate his supremacy over the political machinery of the country. Zambia certainly has an elected government but its powers are considerably limited. Kaunda is not only head of both the government and the party but also commander of the armed forces, with the power to order the arrest and indefinite detention of anyone he regards as a threat. It is Kaunda who makes all major policy decisions, and the function of his government is not to debate the merits of these decisions but merely how best to implement them. He has, on the other hand, been a consistent supporter of African liberation movements and always willing to support genuine diplomatic initiatives to prevent bloodshed.

Zambia (or Northern Rhodesia as it was known before independence) was largely the creation of Cecil Rhodes' British South Africa Company which laid claim to this part of Africa in the 1890s in the last-minute scramble by various European nations to annex what was left of the continent. Rhodes' purpose in coming here was to search for minerals and recruit cheap labour for South African mines and Rhodesian mines and plantations. Though a railway had been pushed through the territory to the copper mines of Katanga by 1910 and a lead and zinc mine opened up at Kabwe, the new colony was slow to develop. Then, in the late 1920s, vast deposits of copper ore were discovered on the Katangan border and by 1940 the mines were employing 30,000 workers. Migrant labour thus became a major feature of the country and, for families in the centre and south of the colony, almost obligatory with the imposition of taxes and the setting up of commercial farms by white settlers on land appropriated from the local people.

The colony was put under direct British control in 1924 and it was not long after that that the white settlers began to agitate for federation with Southern Rhodesia (Zimbabwe) in order to consolidate their political control over the country. The federation didn't actually come about until 1953, but when it did, it was seen clearly by African nationalists for what it really was and led to mass demonstrations. Considerable pressure was put on the British government to end federation and grant independence, but it took 11 years to bring this about. That the colonial authorities and their supporters were none too keen to see this happen can be gleaned from the fact that by the time of independence the British South Africa Company had extracted some US$160 million in royalties from 'ownership' of the mineral resources while the British Treasury had collected about US$80

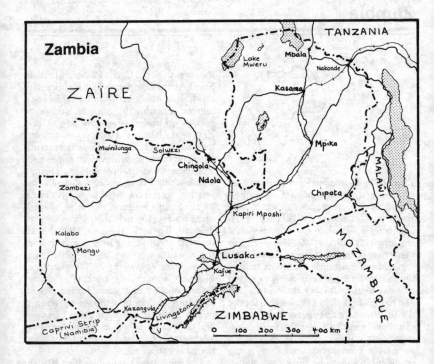

million in taxes, yet spent only US$10 million on the colony. At the same time, some US$200 million of wealth created by Northern Rhodesia had been spent or invested in Southern Rhodesia in the 10 years of federation. Zambia still suffers from the effects of this staggering loss of capital and lack of investment.

Kaunda, however, refused to allow the country's poverty or its total reliance on the transportation systems of Rhodesia (and, later, Zimbabwe-Rhodesia), South Africa and colonial Mozambique and Angola to compromise his commitment to the liberation of white-ruled territories. The Mozambique liberation front, Frelimo, was the first of such groups to be given bases and assistance. Others have included SWAPO (the Namibian liberation front) and both wings of the Zimbabwe Patriotic Front (ZAPU, led by Nkomo; and ZANU,

led by Mugabe). At the same time, Kaunda has kept a close eye on the activities of these liberation fronts and has insisted on their cooperation whenever a diplomatic initiative is launched. In the event of their refusal he has not been above withdrawing support or even deporting them. Thus, in 1971, ZAPU militants opposed to Nkomo were deported back to Rhodesia (and the Smith regime's prisons), while in 1975 ZANU guerrillas opposed to any diplomatic settlement with Smith were jailed and the organisation banned from Zambia (Mozambique subsequently became ZANU's operational base). The more radical members of SWAPO have been subjected to similar constraints and in 1975 Zambia actually intervened in Angola to aid the South African– and US-assisted forces of Savimbi's UNITA.

Zambia's support for these liberation movements has many times threatened it with financial ruin and brought the country to the brink of famine. It has also led, on occasion, to serious internal security problems. At the height of the conflict in Zimbabwe it was estimated that there were more ZAPU guerrillas under arms in Zambia than there were members of the Zambian army. The most serious threat, which nearly brought the country to its knees, came from the Smith-Muzorewa regime which, in October 1978, began a determined campaign of sabotage and military intimidation. Virtually all the roads and railways (except one through Zimbabwe) on which Zambia depended for exporting its copper and bringing in supplies had been knocked out. The final turn of the screw came with the announcement that 300,000 tonnes of maize which had been bought from South Africa to head off what was to all intents and purposes a threatened famine could not be transported through Zimbabwe-Rhodesia until Kaunda stopped supporting ZAPU. A massive air-lift was mounted by various western nations but the situation was really only saved some months later in April 1980 with the settlement in Zimbabwe.

Although Kaunda has finally been able to take his country off a war footing, all those years of sacrifice, fears of armed intervention, saboteurs and spies have left their mark. The economy totters on the brink of collapse; foreign exchange reserves are almost exhausted; there are serious shortages of food, fuel and other basic commodities; and both the crime rate and unemployment are rising sharply. Many travellers have begun to report unpleasant experiences there so you're advised to keep a low profile, especially with police and military personnel. Don't do anything which might even vaguely be regarded as suspicious.

This kind of letter is not at all unusual:

Watch out for soldiers and policemen – some are incorruptible and you get into some real shit for peanuts. People are rough along the usual tourist-trail but very friendly once you get up north, and hospitality there can be unique. Some advice: don't wear khaki clothes, baggy pants or anything that looks military; don't take pictures of post offices, railway stations, etc; don't make any arrangements to meet people in front of a post office or railway station in the evening. You're arrested for nothing here. I was writing a postcard to a girlfriend – in French – and a soldier arrested me and took me to the police station where I was accused of spying. They told me I was to be shot and left me scared shitless but later let me go, though the police officer kept my postcard, saying, 'We're keeping this as evidence against you.' It wasn't over yet. Going back to the station, I found it locked and when I tried to open it to get on to the platform I heard someone calling behind me. When I turned round I had a gun in my belly and the same fucking soldier shouting, 'You filthy spy!' Back to the police station where they searched through my backpack. I had a close shave when they narrowly missed the hard currency I hadn't declared at the border. They let me out after two hours. I must say my South African stamp in my passport didn't help matters. A friend of mine got a butt in the face, another one was beaten up and a third arrested when he took a picture of the sunset near a border post. I also had a friend who offered a cigarette to two soldiers, who arrested him because he was walking around in camouflage trousers near a post office. They beat him up and then left him on the pavement when they discovered his passport.

These sorts of letters are almost always about encounters with police and military personnel. Most are at pains to point out that ordinary people you meet are quite different and that if you keep out of the way of police and soldiers you can have a really good time here.

Warning Crime – particularly robbery with violence – is on the increase in Zambia mainly because the economy is in such a mess and unemployment is really bad. We've had reports of hitch-hikers being held up at gunpoint by truck drivers. This isn't to say that you won't meet friendly people, but be careful.

FACTS

Zambia sits on a gently undulating plateau between 900 and 1500 metres high, studded with lakes and covered with a mixture of deciduous forest, savannah and marshland. Except for one feature, it's geographically unremarkable, but that feature – the Victoria Falls – is one of the natural wonders of the world and no-one within striking distance of it would want to miss such a sight.

There are three distinct seasons – cool and dry from May to August; hot and dry from September to October; and rainy from November to April. Average temperatures are 16°C in winter and 24°C in summer.

VISAS

Visas are required by all except nationals of Commonwealth countries, the Irish Republic, Romania and Yugoslavia. If you have South African stamps in your passport (even if you're one of those nationals who don't need a visa), this can cause problems and might even result in you being refused entry. Check with a Zambian embassy or consulate before turning up at the border. Zambian visas in Nairobi can take just a few hours to be issued, or they can take one month depending on what's been happening inside the country or who's in charge of issuing them.

If you're coming in from Zaire at Kasumbalesa or Mokambo, get your visa at the Zambian consulate in Lubumbashi. Ask for a transit visa which allows double entry, costs Z 15 (about US$1) and is issued on the spot. When you get to the border, the immigration official will ask you how long you want to stay and is more than likely to stamp you in for two weeks despite anything it says on the transit visa about you only having 48 hours! A tourist visa at the same consulate costs Z 60 and takes 24 hours to be issued.

Visa extensions are very easy to get at Immigration in Lusaka, on Cairo Rd next to the post office.

Tanzanian visas The High Commission in Lusaka is on Independence Avenue near the Intercontinental Hotel. You need two photos for a visitor's pass which costs Kw 2.50 and is issued while you wait, but you would be wise to allow a couple of days as there's only one person there – and he often isn't! The Tanzanians are even less keen on South African stamps than the Zambians so you're in for a lot of trouble if you have one in your passport.

If you're thinking of crossing the Zambia/Tanzania border near Mbala you may have problems if you're white. The official who controls the border there has a fertile imagination and suspects every white person of being a spy.

MONEY

US$1 = Kw 2.00
UK£1 = Kw 1.85

The unit of currency is the kwacha = 100 ngwee. Import/export of local currency is allowed up to Kw 10. Don't change more money into kwacha than you need, as they're virtually impossible to change outside the country. There is a thriving black market but it only operates in certain places. It's fairly easy to find in Livingstone (ask around among the Asian traders) but difficult to find in Lusaka and Victoria Falls. In Lusaka you could try the Asian traders on Freedom Way – we can't be any more specific than that for obvious reasons. On the black market you can get up to Kw 6 for the US dollar (only Kw 4 in Livingstone) and Kw 8 for the £ sterling, but the rates in Nakonde are lousy. Be careful when changing money on the black market, as it's not particularly safe. Also, corruption is rife and customs officials specialise in stand-over tactics. Care is needed in dealing with these people.

Currency declaration forms are issued on arrival, so if you want to use the black market, declare less hard currency than you actually have and hide the difference. Keep all bank receipts. Be careful of the Zambian customs at Nakonde – they'll make you account for every last cent. They're also quite keen on currency forms at the Chipata border, but forms are generally not asked for at Victoria Falls and Kazungula. Traveller's cheques attract whopping rates of commission – Kw 6 per cheque at the Standard Bank in Lusaka; Kw 3 at the Zambia National Commercial Bank and at Barclays Bank. No commission is charged at Barclays if you have VISA traveller's cheques.

You must show currency declaration forms and bank receipts when buying airline tickets for domestic or international flights. There's no way round this anymore.

Airport departure tax is Kw 8 for domestic, and Kw 10 for international.

At the official rate of exchange Zambia is a very expensive country and inflation is fierce.

LANGUAGE

English is the official language. The tribal languages of Bemba, Lozi, Nyanja and Tonga are common in certain parts of the country.

GETTING THERE & AROUND
Road

Except along the Lusaka-Lubumbashi road, hitching is relatively easy in Zambia and you shouldn't have much trouble finding lifts. Many of the truckies are Somalis. Some charge for lifts, others don't. There's only one drawback to hitching in this country and it's called drunkenness. Drunk drivers are a real problem here. The roads are littered with stoved-in trucks and cars. If you don't want to end up one of the corpses at the side of the road, be very careful whom you accept a lift with.

Rail

There are two lines of interest to travellers. One is from Kitwe to Lusaka and on to Livingstone; the other is from Kapiri Mposhi to Dar es Salaam (known as the TAZARA railway).

TAZARA Kapiri Mposhi-Dar es Salaam The journey takes about 60 hours. Buy your ticket in advance at the TAZARA Office, Cairo Rd, Lusaka (next to the GPO). There are 50% student reductions for international student-card holders, but sometimes they won't give them to you in Lusaka. If this happens, it's suggested you take the train to the next station and try again there (the train generally stops long enough for you to have the time to do this). Full fares are Kw 64 (1st class), Kw 40 (2nd class) and Kw 17 (3rd class).

There are two trains per week. One departs Kapiri Mposhi at 4.15 pm on Wednesday, arrives in Kasama at 6.13 am on Thursday, arrives in Nakonde at 1 pm the same day, arrives in Mbeya at 7.30 pm the same day and arrives in Dar at 5 pm on Friday. The other departs Kapiri Mposhi at 4.15 pm on Saturday, arrives in Kasama at 6.13 am on Saturday and continues on to Dar, arriving at 5 pm on Monday.

Fares from Kasama

	1st class	2nd class	3rd class
Nakonde	Kw 13.15	Kw 8.90	Kw 3.65
Tunduma	Kw 13.70	Kw 9.30	Kw 3.75
Mbeya	Kw 20.05	Kw 13.50	Kw 5.60
Dar	Kw 64.95	Kw 43.75	Kw 18.00

Be very careful of Tanzanian officials at the border. Searches are generally thorough. Some people get strip-searched.

Kitwe-Lusaka-Livingstone There are two trains per day in either direction – the express (standard-class carriages only) and the ordinary train (economy-class carriages only). If they're running on time, the ordinary train departs Lusaka for Livingstone at 5.30 am and the express at 3.30 pm. The express takes about nine hours and the ordinary train about 12 hours, but the latter often runs very late. If you're coming south from Kitwe, the express departs at 7 pm. The fares from Lusaka to Livingstone are Kw 16.30 (sleeper), Kw 11.60 (standard) and Kw 8.10 (economy). There are 50% student reductions for those with international student cards except on Saturday and Sunday.

The Lusaka-Kitwe trains are the same ones you must first take to get to Kapiri Mposhi in order to connect with the TAZARA railway. The fares from Lusaka to Kapiri Mposhi are Kw 6.80 (sleeper), Kw 4.80 (standard) and Kw 3.40 (economy class).

Boat

Lake Tanganyika There are two boats – the *Liemba*, the older, more comfortable boat; and the *Mwangozo*, newer though less comfortable. However, it's a matter of luck which one arrives when you want to go. From Mpulungu (Zambia) you have to pay in Tanzanian shillings the equivalent of Kw 70 (1st class) and Kw 25 (3rd class) from Mpulungu to Bujumbura. You cannot pay for the boat ticket in Zambian kwacha. Tanzanian shillings are easy to find in Mpulungu. In the opposite direction, if you start from Bujumbura (Burundi), you must pay in Burundi francs, which makes it very expensive – BFr 8000 (1st class), BFr 4000 (2nd class) and BFr 2000 (3rd class). Get around this by buying a ticket only as far as Kigoma (Tanzania) in Burundi francs. Get off the boat, go through Tanzanian customs and immigration, and buy a ticket for the rest of the way in Kigoma using Tanzanian shillings exchanged on the black market. You cannot buy a ticket on the boat if the town where you board it has a ticket agency on shore. This means that only in Mpulungu can you buy your ticket on board. You can pay for anything you buy on board in Tanzanian shillings. Food on the *Mwangozo* is 'awful', so it's best to take your own together with a few bottles of wine to pass the time. Third-class travel isn't recommended (unless you have a tent you can erect on board!). If you're coming up from Mpulungu and don't have a Burundi visa, you will not be allowed to get off the boat at Kigoma to get a visa (from the Burundi consulate there) if you have South African stamps in your passport.

To/From Tanzania

The majority of roads are badly potholed in Zambia, particularly the one between Lusaka and Chipata, and the breakdown rate is high with both government and private buses. There's a shortage of tyres for buses in Zambia and bus companies won't provide their buses with a spare (the drivers apparently sell them off). As a result, you can expect long delays due to flat tyres (which are common), since the buses have to wait for their opposite number to come past and take a message to Lusaka requesting a spare. Now that takes some beating!

The border crossing is Nakonde/Tunduma. Most travellers enter on the TAZARA railway from Dar es Salaam to Kapiri Mposhi (details later), but you can also come by road using buses or hitching trucks. There are direct buses between Nakonde and Lusaka which cost Kw 10.90 and take about 24 hours. They generally depart Nakonde around 8 am. If you don't want to go all the way to Lusaka, there are buses between Nakonde and Kapiri Mposhi which cost Kw 9.75 and take about 21 hours. There are several buses per day in either direction between Lusaka and Kapiri Mposhi. The best are the UBZ express coaches which leave from near the old bus station in Lusaka at 8 am, 10 am and noon. They cost Kw 4.45 and take three hours. Book in advance if you can. Other buses do this trip from the new bus station, but they're said to be unreliable.

It's virtually impossible to get across the Zambia/Tanzania border north of Mbala if you're white.

You can get to Tanzania via Mpulungu on the Lake Tanganyika ferry to Kigoma. Further details below.

To/From Zaire

From Lusaka to Lubumbashi you have a choice of crossing the border either between Chilabombwe and Kasumbalesa or between Chingola and Mokambo. Most travellers first take the train from Lusaka to Kitwe (details later) and then a combination of taxis, buses and trucks from there to Lubumbashi. There are no direct trains even though the two railway systems are linked and Kitwe is the last station for passenger traffic coming up from the south. Crossing either border is no problem, but you should expect baggage and body searches in Zambia because there is a lot of diamond smuggling.

It is not easy to hitch on the road from Lusaka to Lubumbashi because of bandits. Robberies are quite common. Any *mzungu* driver who sees someone standing by the side of the road will simply speed up to pass rather than risk stopping and getting robbed. It's also not a good idea to be in Chilabombwe at night. Again, robberies are common. Chingola is a safer place to stay for the night.

Kitwe-Chingola Buses are available for Kw 1.80. If you're heading for Mokambo there is a bus from Chingola for Z 40 (or the equivalent). Between Mokambo and Lubumbashi there is a passenger train once per week (it departs Lubumbashi on Wednesday at 9 am). If you don't want to go this way, take the bus from Chingola to Chilabombwe; it costs Kw 0.50. It's sometimes possible to pick up trucks from here going all the way to Lubumbashi for around Z 20-40 (they terminate in the 'Zone Kenya' in Lubumbashi). Otherwise, take a mini-bus from Chilabombwe to Kasumbalesa for Kw 1 and from there either a taxi (Z 35) or a pickup (Z 25) to Lubumbashi. You can change spare kwacha into zaires (and vice versa) very easily at Chilabombwe (Kw 1 = Z 6).

To/From Malawi
If you're coming up from the south, there are direct buses from Lusaka to Lilongwe three times per week for Kw 16.50. The buses leave the central bus station in Lusaka at 7 am and arrive at about 10.30 pm. There are also daily buses in either direction between Chipata and Lilongwe for Kw 2.40 (they depart from the market in the old town, Lilongwe at 6.30 am). There are several buses daily between Lusaka and Chipata in either direction. The fare is Kw 11.90 to Kw 13 (usually the latter).

Coming south into Zambia from Tanzania, there's another popular route into Malawi from Nakonde to Chitipa. *Zambian National Bus Co* (based in Nakonde) makes the journey from Nakonde to Chitipa three times a week at 7 am on Monday, Wednesday and Friday; however, this varies due to breakdowns, tyre and petrol shortages. The trip takes three to four hours and costs Kw 2.90. Don't attempt this during a bad spell in the wet season, as there are no buses and no other traffic at those times. Sometimes the bus only goes as far as the Zambian border (Nyala) and you must walk the 10 km from there to Chitipa. Try not to walk this stretch alone, as robberies have been reported. Buses to the border cost Kw 1.50. If you have to take a taxi it will cost about Kw 5. The two border posts are about three km apart, and if there's no transport between the two, simply follow everybody else along the clearly marked path through the fields. From the Malawi border post there should be transport to Chitipa but you may have to walk (about a further six km).

To/From Botswana
This essentially follows the same route as the one from Zimbabwe through Victoria Falls, except when you get to Livingstone you have to branch off west a short way by road to Kazungula. Here you take the ferry across the Zambesi River and go by road to Kasane.

To/From Zimbabwe
Although there are direct buses five times per week from Lusaka to Harare, they're of little interest to travellers since taking

one would involve missing the Victoria Falls! Most travellers take the train from Lusaka to Livingstone (details later); there are also two daily buses which depart Lusaka at 7.25 am and 4.30 pm, cost Kw 9.50 and take about 10 hours. There are daily bus and train connections from Victoria Falls to the rest of Zimbabwe.

PLACES TO STAY

Most of the hotels in Zambia are expensive and you'd be well advised to give them a miss if you're trying to keep costs down. Even ungraded hotels cost between Kw 7.50-9.45 a single for bed and breakfast plus a 10% service charge and 10% government tax. Somewhat cheaper are the government rest houses, of which there are a few, though most are not in towns where you're likely to be staying. The ones of interest to travellers are at Chipata, Livingstone and Mbala. In the national parks there are a series of 'catering' and 'non-catering' lodges. Some of these are open all year whereas others are only open during the dry season. None of them really cater to budget travellers (ie they're not cheap), which is a great pity as Zambia has some very extensive national parks with plenty of wildlife in them.

Whatever else you do, don't attempt to sleep in a railway station unless you want to be woken up by the police or the army indiscriminately wielding rifle butts.

CHIPATA

Try to get into the government rest house *Luangwa House* near the hospital; it costs Kw 10 a double with own bath, hot water, sunroom and full board. Or try the *Kapata Rest House*, Kapata Avenue opposite the bus station. There are also two expensive hotels in town. Another possibility is the friendly *seminary* run by Irish expatriates along the 10 km of no-man's land between Chipata and the border.

KACHALOLA

This is an overnight truckies' stop between Lusaka and Lilongwe. If you don't want to sleep out, there is the *Comfortable Lodge* which costs Kw 16 a double for bed and breakfast.

KAPIRI MPOSHI

The best place to stay is the *Unity Motel*, which is good value at Kw 16.50 a double with own bathroom. The only other hotel in town is the *Kapiri Inn*, but it's run-down these days and costs Kw 20 a double. The new station for the TAZARA railway is about 1½ km from the centre of town.

KITWE

The two hotels in the centre of town, *Hotel Edinburgh* and the *Nkana Hotel*, are four-star and two-star respectively and not for budget travellers. Try to get to the *Buchi Hotel*, about six km out of town, which costs around Kw 7.50 a single.

LIVINGSTONE

Livingstone is the Zambian town nearest Victoria Falls and, as such, sees a lot of travellers who come to soak up some of the magic (and the spray!) of one of the world's most magnificent sights. The town is about seven km from the falls and there are frequent buses between the two for Kw 0.40 or taxis for Kw 4. You can also hitch with ease.

The cheapest place to stay is the *government rest house*, which costs Kw 1.60 to sleep on the floor or Kw 2.75 for a double room. It's often full, but sometimes they pretend it's full when it isn't, so it's best to book first at the Tourist Office. The *Windsor Hotel* now costs Kw 19.60 a double including breakfast but, like the rest house, is often full. If you want to camp, you can do so between the two big hotels at the falls themselves. The site costs Kw 3 per person and has excellent facilities. Camping may also be possible at the *Rainbow Lodge* at the falls for Kw 2 per person per night. The Rainbow has singles for Kw 22, doubles for Kw 33 and triples fo. Kw 44 as well as very pleasant rondavels for Kw 23 a double including a

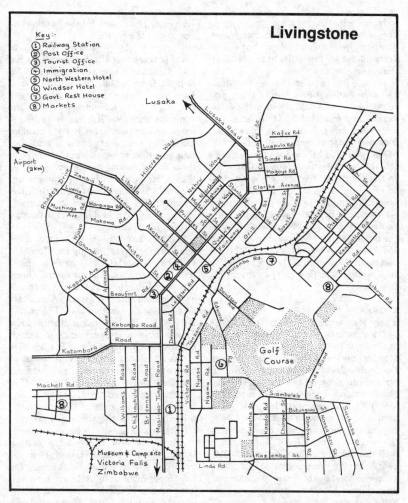

Livingstone

Key :-
1. Railway Station
2. Post Office
3. Tourist Office
4. Immigration
5. North Western Hotel
6. Windsor Hotel
7. Govt. Rest House
8. Markets

Lusaka

Airport (2km)

Golf Course

Museum & Camp site
Victoria Falls
Zimbabwe

good breakfast, but watch your gear. The Rainbow puts on good dinners for Kw 9. Another good place to buy meals at about the same price is the huge *Musi-O-Tunya Intercontinental Hotel* which, despite its intimidating name, offers excellent food at cheaper prices than the Rainbow Lodge except for the weekend buffets which cost Kw 15.

If you want to splurge, the Musi-O-Tunya charges Kw 107 a double including continental breakfast. That's about US$15 using kwacha bought on the black market. Here's your big chance to stay in an 'intercontinental' hotel. Two travellers commented recently that although this place still has pretensions, it's 'a rundown dump.' The buffets are good though.

If you're looking for somewhere to go in the evening, try the bar in the *North-Western Hotel*, which is an expatriate hang-out; or try the buffet at the Musi-O-Tunya.

If you'd like to go on a tour of the **Musi-O-Tunya National Park** (white rhino and antelope), it will cost Kw 8 and can be booked at the hotel of the same name. You can also book boat rides down the Zambesi (hippos and elephants) here. Whilst you're in Livingstone town, have a look at the **Livingstone Museum** adjacent to the Tourist Office. It charges Kw 0.50 to see an interesting archaeological collection and Livingstone paraphernalia – letters, etc. The **Victoria Falls Museum** costs Kw 0.10 entry. There are buses to the border from the bus stand on Kabompo Rd (Kw 0.50). A taxi to the falls costs Kw 6 (set rate). You can cross the border for day trips without fuss (border open from 8 am to 6 pm).

LUSAKA

There is no accommodation near the bus or train stations. It's still possible to stay at the *Sikh Temple*, but you can normally stay for only two nights. To get there take the double-decker bus to the showground. Or you can sleep on the verandah of the *Salvation Army* in the centre of town free. The *YWCA*, opposite the hospital, takes men as well as women and costs Kw 13 per bed, or you can sometimes crash down in the common room for Kw 4. The campsite on Kafue Rd, two to three km from the city centre, is very run-down and most of the people who stay there are permanents. The shower block has been vandalised and there's no hot water and sometimes no water at all. It costs Kw 1. Close to the airport at Chamba Valley is the *ECZ Guest House* (tel 253569), which is self-catering and costs Kw 6 per night. If you want to stay closer to the centre of town, it's worth trying the *Hubert Young Hostel*, which is mainly for teachers. It costs Kw 4 a single including three meals and is about 2½ km from the bus station next to the

Ridgeway Hotel. Ask for the hotel, as no one knows the hostel.

Upmarket from the above is the *Lusaka Hotel* (a three-star affair) which costs Kw 30 a single and Kw 36 a double plus Kw 25 deposit (returnable). Not all the rooms have their own shower. If you have a hammock you can sling it up in the campsite on Kafue Rd, two to three km from the city centre, for Kw 1 per night. Look after your gear. There is a total of four government hostels but you have to do a lot of talking to be accepted, as they're supposed to be only for government officials. *Longacres*, near the Intercontinental Hotel, is one of these hostels and costs Kw 10 a double with full board – but the food is awful.

Outside the city itself, a lot of travellers head for the hostel run by the Zambian Council for Social Development which, until recently, was known as the *Dutch Volunteer Hostel* (tel 714412) or sometimes as the 'Dutch Farm.' It's run by Alex and is a very pleasant place to stay. The cost is Kw 6.50 for a bed in the dormitory and Kw 22 a double including breakfast. Lunch costs Kw 4 and dinner Kw 6. The hostel is about 10 km out of the city. Also out of town about six km on the Kitwe road are the *Zani Muone Hotel* and the *Hill Top Hotel*, both which cost Kw 13 a double, but food there is expensive. Unfortunately, the only way of getting there is by taxi (Kw 10 after a long hassle) or pick-up.

Accommodation is available with a farming family, Mr & Mrs Bland, *Yielding-tree Farm*, Botha's Rust Rd, Lusaka, for Kw 15 per night or in exchange for some work around the farm. It's about 10 km west of Lusaka. They appreciate you going to church on Sunday, but that's not compulsory.

For somewhere to eat in Lusaka, try *Zamby's*, Chachacha Rd (good curries etc, for Kw 3); or try the snack bar behind UTA Airways for good, cheap snacks. For fast food try the *Rooster* on Cairo Rd.

For crafts, try the *Ridgeway Hotel* or the *Cultural Village* on Burma Rd.

Information

The Tourist Office is at the NIEC Supermarket, Cairo Rd, but it isn't worth visiting. Whatever your enquiry, the staff will tell you to visit a travel agent.

Black's Travels are about the only travel agents in Lusaka who don't ask for bank receipts when you buy an airline ticket (or, if they do and you say you've forgotten to bring them along, they don't care).

If you stay in Lusaka for any length of time, it's worth getting hold of a copy of *The Peugeot Guide to Lusaka* published by the Zambian Geographical Association is available from bookstores or from the Pamodzi Hotel for Kw 4. The guide contains a map of central Lusaka and a description of points of interest as well as the history and geography of the city.

If you need other maps of Zambia, visit the Map Sales Department in the Department of Lands, Mulungushi House, Independence Avenue. This is the building near the red-and-white chequered water-tower.

The sole cycle shop in Lusaka is *C S Cycles*, Chachacha Rd, but they don't have anything in the way of light-weight bicycles and stock only Indian and Chinese models.

There is a duty-free shop opposite the post office on Cairo Rd which has cheeses and cheap whisky at US$5.50 a bottle. The whisky might make a very nice present, as otherwise it costs Kw 47 if it's available at all. The shop only accepts credit cards after lunch, but will accept cash, traveller's cheques and cards in the morning.

Beware of walking round Lusaka at night. The chances are you'll get mugged. Keep your eyes open for pick-pockets at all times.

Be careful with traveller's cheques in Lusaka. If you lose them or if they are stolen, American Express can take up to a week to issue another set.

The airport is 14 km from the city centre.

Useful Addresses

Automobile Association of Zambia
  Dedan Kimathi Rd (tel 75311)
Zambia Airways
  Haile Selassie Avenue (tel 74213)
Air Malawi
  Heroes Place, Woodgate House, Cairo Rd
  (tel 72541)
East African Airways
  Chester House, Cairo Rd (tel 75891)
Botswana High Commission
  2647 Haile Selassie Avenue (tel 25084)
British High Commission
  Independence Avenue (tel 21 6770)
Kenya High Commission
  United Nations Avenue (tel 21 2531)
Tanzania High Commission
  United Nations Avenue (tel 21 1422)
USA Embassy
  United Nations Avenue (tel 21 4911)
Zimbabwe High Commission
  building next to Findeco Tower

Tanzanian visas cost Kw 2.50, require two photos and are issued while you wait. Kenyan visas cost Kw 5.10 and take 24 hours (no photos). The Kenyan High Commission is only open in the morning and is closed on Thursday, Saturday and Sunday.

MBALA

There's a good *government rest house* here. If it's full you can get a bed in a dormitory in a private rest house opposite the bus station for Kw 2. If they're both full, try the *Arms Hotel*, which costs Kw 7.50 a single. Camp free at the *Outward Bound School* 10 km from town on the Mpulungu road, or stay in the dormitories and eat with the staff, who are very friendly. There is no charge but donations are appreciated – Kw 10 per day including all meals. There is a swimming pool.

Whilst you're in Mbala, visit the **Moto Moto Museum**, which is a personal collection put together by Father Corbell over his 40 years in Zambia. It relates largely to the Bemba tribe. The collection has been given to the government, with exhibition halls built by the Daines. You'll be pressed to see it all in one day.

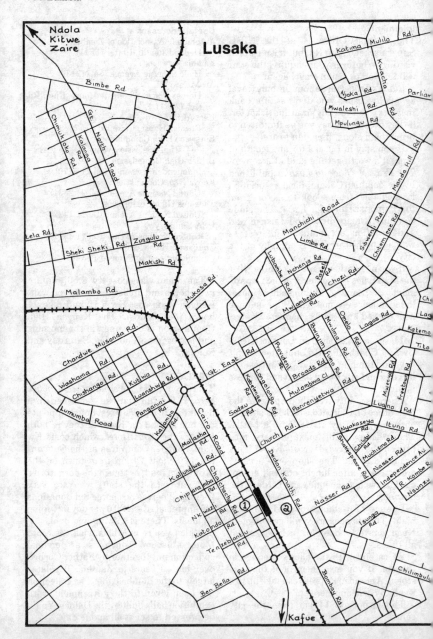

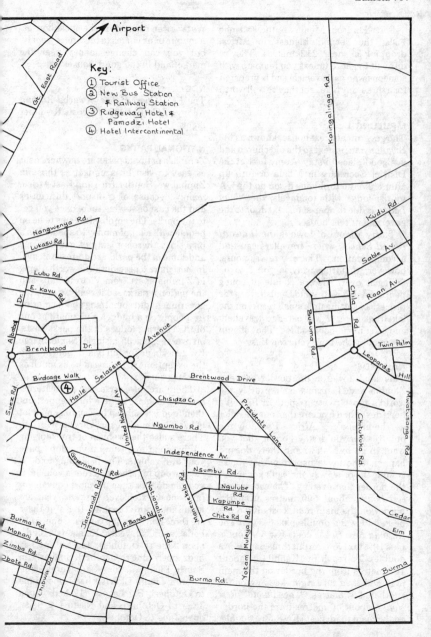

Airport

Key:
1 Tourist Office
2 New Bus Station
‡ Railway Station
3 Ridgeway Hotel ‡
Pamodzi Hotel
4 Hotel Intercontinental

Forty km from Mbala are the **Kalambo Falls**, the second highest in Africa, dropping a sheer 212 metres. They're difficult to get to unless you team up with someone who has a vehicle and is prepared for a three-day hike, but they're well worth it.

MPULUNGU

The government rest house, known as the *Bwananyina*, is next to the old church and is a good place to stay. Apply first at the District Secretary in Mbala or turn up after 5 pm (no problems if you do this). A tourist lodge with rondavels, the *Nkupi Lodge*, is due to open soon next door to the government rest house.

Thirty km out of town is the *Outward Bound School*, where travellers can find accommodation. There are rumours, however, that the army is going to be taking it over. Also, a couple of young people named Kathy and Denish are in the process of setting up a small resort on the lakefront here; it will cater to travellers and offer home-cooked food. They should be open by the time you read this.

NAKONDE

This small town on the border between Zambia and Tanzania isn't exactly the world's most riveting spot. In fact, it's been described by more than one traveller as 'the arsehole of Africa.' Probably the only reason you'd stay here is that you want to go to Malawi and there doesn't happen to be any transport, or that you're coming the other way and can't get across the border that evening. The *government rest house*, about 500 metres from the border on the main road, costs Kw 5 per bed and Kw 9 a double plus 6% tax. The *Kalinda Rest House* costs Kw 6 a double plus 10% tax (you can put three people in a double). To reach the Kalinda go about 100 metres from the border on the main road and then turn right, keeping on for another 50 metres. The *Ikumbi Rest House*, about 50 metres from the border on the main road, costs Kw 8.50 a double.

Water often runs out in the guest houses. A mobile bank comes to town once weekly, but you can change money near the market and in the guest houses.

NDOLA

The *ECZ Guest House*, Kwacha Rd and Anonya Zulu (tel 82851), costs Kw 6 per night.

NATIONAL PARKS

Zambia's national parks are nowhere near as easy to visit on a budget as those in Zimbabwe, South Africa and East Africa, mainly because of transport difficulties and the cost of staying there once you get to the parks. The emphasis seems to be on people with a lot of money to spend. It's a pity since there's plenty of game to see and some of the parks are quite extensive. In fact, there's precious little worth seeing in Zambia apart from Victoria Falls and the national parks, so it really is time the government did something about catering for people on a budget. Full board at one of the catering lodges in the parks costs, on average, Kw 35 a single. Some charge Kw 29 a single for full board, but they are the exceptions. Others can be as much as Kw 50 a single.

There are, of course, the non-catering camps which are quite a bit cheaper, but then food isn't cheap in Zambia and a lot of basic commodities are very hard to find. There's also the problem of transporting all that food to a camp if you don't have your own vehicle. The best thing to do is get a group together and rent a vehicle. If you can do this, then the most convenient (and most extensive) parks to visit are **Kafue** and **South Luangwa**. In Kafue there are three non-catering camps: Chunga (10 beds, open all year); Kalala (six beds, open June to October); and Lufupa (six beds, open June to October). Similarly, in South Luangwa there are three non-catering camps: Lion (six beds, open June to October); Big Lagoon (12 beds, open June to October); and Nsefu (12 beds, open June to October).

Entry to the national parks costs Kw 2 per vehicle plus 75 ngwee per person. Further details are available from the Tourist Office in Lusaka, Livingstone or Ndola.

If you want to stand any chance of visiting Kafue Gorge, you must get permission first from ZESCO headquarters in Lusaka. This is because the hydro-electric power station there is a sensitive installation and the government is paranoid about spies and saboteurs. If you just get permission from ZESCO in Kafue and from the Kafue police, you will be sent back.

The botanical and zoological gardens of Munda Wanga at Chilanga on the road to Kafue are well worth a visit. The staff are helpful and there are not too many people during the week. Entrance is Kw 2 plus Kw 1.50 if you have a camera. It's only a short journey from Lusaka. Some of the animals are free-range, such as antelope, baby elephants, camels, crested cranes and storks.

THE COPPER BELT

It used to be possible to tour one or another of the mines in the copper belt along the border with Zaire, but these are difficult to get permission for these days. You must first make a written application to the Director of Public Relations, ZCCM Ltd, 74 Independence Avenue, PO Box 30048, Lusaka, make sure that you stress some particular interest or experience, and give them at least three weeks' notice. It's better to tell them that you will arrange your own transport and accommodation. If you want to take photos, make sure you request permission in the letter, because permission for anything has to come from the top in this country, especially photography.

Zimbabwe

Zimbabwe finally joined the ranks of Africa's independent nations in April 1980 under an internationally recognised black majority government headed by Robert Mugabe. The settlement ended 14 years of rebellion by the white Rhodesian Front government of Ian Smith and many years of bitter guerrilla warfare carried on by the two wings of the Patriotic Front – ZANU, based in Mozambique and led by Mugabe; and ZAPU, based in Zambia and led by Joshua Nkomo.

The roots of the conflict between black and white go back to the last years of the 19th century, when the country was taken over by Cecil Rhodes' British South Africa Company, but it didn't come into sharp focus until after the 1922 referendum in which the whites chose to become a self-governing colony rather than be included in the Union of South Africa. Though the colony's constitution was, in theory, non-racial, the franchise was based on financial considerations and this effectively excluded most blacks from the vote. White supremacy was further enhanced in 1930 by a Land Act which excluded Africans from ownership of the best farming land in the country and by a labour law in 1934 which prohibited black people from entering skilled labour. The effect of these two measures was to force Africans onto the labour market, from which they could be drawn to work on white farms, mines and factories at mere subsistence wages.

The abysmally poor wages and con-ditions naturally led to the gradual radicalisation of the African labour force so that by the time Southern Rhodesia, Northern Rhodesia and Nyasaland were federated in 1953, local and foreign mining and industrial concerns were in favour of the creation of a more racially mixed middle class as a counterweight to the more radical elements in the labour force. White farmers, skilled workers and businesspeople, however, regarded such moves as a threat to their privileged position and when Garfield Todd, the Federation's prime minister, attempted to satisfy some of the more moderate African demands, he was thrown out. The same thing happened to his successor in 1962, after the approval of a new constitution which envisaged some sort of vague African-European parity at a very distant point in the future. Even this was too much for the white farmers and workers.

While all this was going on, African impatience with the prospects of constitutional change coalesced into a number of political parties as well as found its expression in sporadic acts of sabotage. Foremost among the parties was the Zimbabwe African People's Union (ZAPU) under the leadership of Joshua Nkomo; it was soon joined by the Zimbabwe African National Union (ZANU), a breakaway group under the leadership of Ndabaningi Sithole which was dissatisfied with the pace of progress under Nkomo's leadership. In the aftermath of the Federation's break-up in 1963 – which paved the way for the independence of Northern Rhodesia (Zambia) and Nyasaland (Malawi) – both ZAPU and ZANU were banned and most of the leadership was imprisoned. Meanwhile, in response to Britain's refusal to grant independence to South Rhodesia until an accommodation could be worked out between black and white, Ian Smith had taken over leadership of the white Rhodesian Front party in an atmosphere where there was overwhelming white support for a unilateral declaration of independence. In the election of May 1965, Smith's party picked up every one of the 50 seats in the government and UDI was made in December of the same year.

Britain reacted by declaring Smith's action illegal and imposed economic sanctions in an attempt to bring him to heel. The UN eventually voted to make these sanctions mandatory in 1968, but with South Africa openly assisting Smith and Mozambique still under colonial rule, the loopholes were enormous and the sanctions were ignored by most western countries, including Britain. What was intended to bring Smith to the negotiating table within weeks rather than months was an almost complete failure. In fact, under laws which were passed to restrict the export of profits and impose strict import controls, the Rhodesian economy actually started to grow with the rapid expansion of import substitution manufacturing. Under such circumstances Smith was in no mood to concede anything, and this became patently obvious in the various attempts made by the British government to get him to revoke UDI and accept black majority rule.

Given such intransigence, both ZANU and ZAPU opted for guerrilla warfare. ZANU took the initiative in 1966, but it wasn't until Frelimo had liberated substantial areas of neighbouring Mozambique that they were able to set up bases there and escalate the conflict. ZAPU, in the meantime, set up its bases in Zambia. The guerrilla raids which gradually struck deeper and deeper into the country with ever-increasing ferocity led to an alarming increase in white emigration from Rhodesia and the abandonment of many white farms in the eastern part of the country, but the single most important event which was to totally alter the balance of power in

the area was the overthrow of the fascist regime in Portugal in 1974 and the independence of both Angola and Mozambique in the following year. This event forced both the USA and South Africa to completely reappraise their attitude towards southern Africa if they were to protect their economic and political interests.

Both countries quickly changed their tack and began to pressure Smith into somehow accommodating the nationalists. With assistance from Zambia's Kaunda, the various nationalist groups were persuaded to come together under the united front of Muzorewa's African National Congress, and Smith was persuaded to release from detention the most important leaders of the nationalist movement – Nkomo, Sithole and Mugabe among others. As far as Smith was concerned, it was just an exercise in window-dressing and the talks broke down amid an atmosphere of recrimination between Smith and the nationalists on the one hand, and between the various nationalist leaders on the other. Mugabe, meanwhile, made his way to Mozambique where he replaced Sithole as the leader of ZANU.

A number of other attempts were made to bring the two sides together, notably at Geneva. For the purposes of this conference Nkomo's ZAPU and Mugabe's ZANU were induced to form an alliance known as the Patriotic Front while Sithole and Muzorewa led separate delegations. Again the talks were a failure, and though the Patriotic Front survived in name, the disunity between the two factions was as strong as ever. Not long after the Geneva conference, Smith, faced with wholesale white emigration and a collapsing economy, was forced to try a new ploy. This was an 'internal settlement.' Both Sithole and Muzorewa were induced to join a so-called transitional government in which the whites were to be guaranteed 28 out of the 100 seats in the government plus a veto over all legislation for the next 10 years; a

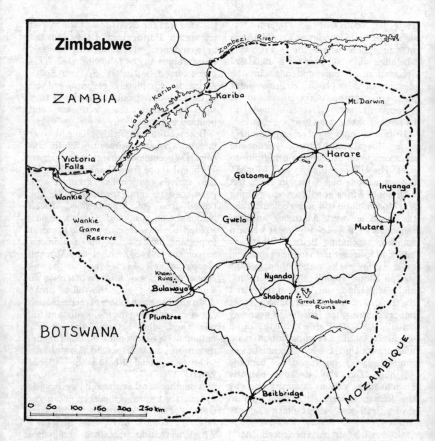

guarantee for all white property and pension rights; and white control of the armed forces, police, judiciary and civil service. An amnesty was also declared for Patriotic Front guerrillas. The effort was a dismal failure. Indeed, the only thing which happened was an intensification of the war. To salvage the settlement, Smith entered into secret negotiations with Nkomo, offering to ditch both Sithole and Muzorewa, but Nkomo didn't take the carrot.

Finally, with support for Smith waning among the white population and the destruction of the country's largest fuel depot (17 million gallons) by guerrillas of the Patriotic Front, Smith was forced to call a general election of both black and white sections of the population and hand over leadership of the country to Muzorewa, but on much the same conditions as the previous transitional government. Diplomatic recognition of the new government of what was now called Zimbabwe-Rhodesia was withheld by all but a tiny handful of countries. That didn't, however, prevent the Rhodesian armed forces from mounting devastating raids on suspected guerrilla and refugee camps in both Mozambique and Zambia. Indeed, 'invasion' would be a more appropriate word.

The Commonwealth conference in Lusaka in 1979 eventually paved the way for a black majority government when an agreement was reached between British Prime Minister Thatcher, Kaunda of Zambia and Nyerere of Tanzania. The deal was a conference to be held in London between the two leaders of the Patriotic Front – Nkomo and Mugabe – and the leaders of Zimbabwe-Rhodesia – Muzorewa and Smith. Kaunda and Nyerere were to lean on the Patriotic Front and Thatcher was to lean on Smith. After 14 weeks of talks an agreement was reached whereby 20 seats in the new government would be reserved specifically for whites (far out of proportion to their numbers) and the remainder for blacks. In the carefully monitored elections which followed, Mugabe's ZANU picked up 57 seats, Nkomo's ZAPU 20 seats, and Muzorewa's UANC only three seats.

Despite the long and bitter struggle, Mugabe, a committed socialist and Marxist thinker, displayed remarkable restraint in dealing not only with the white section of the population but also with his rivals in the ZAPU. Nkomo was made Minister of Home Affairs (though Mugabe retained command of the armed forces), and two whites were given portfolios as Minister of Commerce and Industry and Minister of Agriculture. Since then, however, things have taken an alarming turn for the worse, fuelled by the resurgence of the rivalry between ZANU and ZAPU. After armed conflicts between ZANU and ZAPU supporters, Mugabe ordered the arrest of five prominent Nkomo supporters in 1980 and demoted Nkomo in 1981. Another event which inflamed tension was the arrest of the Minister of Manpower Planning, Edgar Tekere, for the alleged murder of a white farmer and, though he was eventually found not guilty, he has not been offered another cabinet post.

More recently, Nkomo has been accused of plotting to overthrow the government and there has been a resurgence of guerrilla action in Matabeleland, the area from which ZAPU draws the bulk of its support. In early 1983 Mugabe sent in the North Korean-trained Fifth Brigade to quell these disturbances, but from all accounts they appear to have gone berserk. Over 1000 people were reported dead in an orgy of killing in which whole villages were gunned down and prominent members of ZAPU were systematically eliminated. It would be tragic if such actions were to result in a civil war between the Shona (largely ZANU supporters) and the Matabele (largely ZAPU supporters). Part of the reason for the tension between the tribes is that people who were educated in the eastern part of the country (and therefore often ZAPU supporters) find it extremely difficult to get jobs. Not only that, but it has become a definite disadvantage to be an ex-combatant when looking for a job. School students are being encouraged to emulate businesspeople rather than the freedom fighters who liberated them.

Zimbabwe has had a long history of civilisation, as attested to by the massive stone structures at Great Zimbabwe, Khami and Dhlo-Dhlo. The first of the major civilisations to establish themselves were the Mwene Mutapa (or Monomatapas as the Portuguese called them). By the mid-1440s, King Mutota had welded together an empire which included almost all the Rhodesian plateau and large parts of what is today Mozambique. The empire's wealth was based on agriculture and small-scale industries like textiles, gold and copper mines, and iron-making. Trade was conducted with Arab and Swahili merchants along the coast and these people were regular residents of the empire's trading towns. The arrival of the Portuguese in the early 16th century destroyed this trade and led to a series of wars with the Europeans which gradually weakened the empire to the point where it was in rapid decline by the beginning of the 17th century. While this was going on, another empire, the Rozwi to the west of the Monomatapas, was gradually expanding and taking advantage of the Monomatapa decline to gain control of external trade. By 1690 they had driven the Portuguese off the plateau and taken over much of the land once controlled by the Monomatapas. The next two centuries were peaceful and prosperous, and it was during this time that the centres of Great Zimbabwe, Khami and Dhlo-Dhlo received their greatest enlargement.

The Rozwi empire met its end in the mid-19th century as a result of the turmoil in the Transvaal and Natal. Mzilikazi, one of the military commanders of the expansionist Zulu state, quarrelled with Shaka, and in order to get out of the reach of the latter's vengeance led his splinter group north over the Limpopo River and into Matabeleland. The Rozwi were no match for the Zulu and the empire was shattered. Mzilikazi set up his capital near present-day Bulawayo and was succeeded in 1870 by his son, Lobengula. Lobengula proved to be the last of the Ndebele rulers as a result of increasing pressure from European settlers. In 1888 a treaty was signed with the British South Africa Company, allowing them to mine gold in the kingdom. Having got a foot in the door, however, the company began to send in large numbers of settlers and war broke out with the Ndebele in 1893. White immigration began in earnest despite further risings of the Ndebele, so that by 1904 there were some 12,000 settlers in the country and double that number by 1911.

FACTS

Zimbabwe sits on a high plateau between the Limpopo and Zambezi rivers, with a range of mountains in the east along the border with Mozambique. It has an exceptionally healthy climate; temperatures range from 22°C on the plateau to 30°C in the Zambezi valley during the summer, and from 13°C to 20°C in the winter. The two main ethnic groups are the Shona in the centre and the east, and the Ndebele in the west. The population is about seven million.

VISAS

Visas are required by all except nationals of Commonwealth countries, Belgium, Denmark, France (including French Overseas Departments and Territories), Greece, Iceland, Irish Republic, Luxembourg, Netherlands, Norway, Sweden, Switzerland and the USA.

Immigration are very strict about onward tickets, though if you have one they rarely ask to see how much money you have. MCOs are not acceptable. The only way you can get into Zimbabwe without an onward ticket and sufficient funds is by rail from Botswana. At any other point of entry, if you don't have an onward ticket then you either have to buy one on the spot or leave a returnable deposit in cash or traveller's cheques; the deposit varies but is rarely less than US$1000. If you do have to leave a deposit, don't count on getting it back in the currency you paid. Some people have been given Zimbabwe dollars just before they were due to leave – and that's bad news! We've had quite a few reports of travellers who were turned back at the Zambia/Zimbabwe border because they had not enough funds or no onward ticket. The Chirundu post is particularly bad. Even travellers with a Eurocard and a letter from a bank manager or US$900 to show have been refused entry. Patient and friendly persuasion can sometimes overcome this, but don't count on it. An airline ticket with Johannesburg as the starting point is acceptable. If you're coming from South Africa, a return Johannesburg-Bulawayo/Harare ticket with *Express Motorways* (Z$117) may well do.

If you want to avoid red tape, don't write 'journalist' on your entry form, otherwise they'll give you 24 hours to get a temporary employment permit. On the other hand, this could be quite useful. The 14-day visa/work permit is no trouble to get (takes about two hours), plus you're issued a press card – all for Z$4!

Immigration is on the 7th floor, Linguende House, Baker St. They're very efficient and pleasant people.

You can go into Zambia for the day at Victoria Falls without a visa – just show your passport. On returning, however, Zimbabwean customs may give you a hard time – the usual story of onward tickets, money, etc – so if you haven't got these it might be a good idea to think twice about going over to Zambia for the day. One American couple were recently given a hard time here even though they had Bulawayo-Mafeking rail tickets, a South African visa and US$2000. The official wanted to see return air tickets to the USA! They assured him they had left them in Bulawayo. Also, remember not to take more than Z$20 with you; otherwise you'll contravene currency regulations.

Kenyan visas High Commission, 95 Park Lane, Harare. Visas are issued the same day.

Mozambique visas Embassy, 152 Rhodes Avenue, Harare. Visas cost Z$6, require three photos and take three days to come through, though some travellers report they are only available to Zimbabwe residents.

Nigerian visas High Commission, 36 Samora Machel Avenue, Harare. Entry permits are free but you need one photo and they take three days to come through.

South African visas Diplomatic Mission, Temple Bar House, 39 Baker St, Harare. It's very busy here so arrive early in the morning.

Tanzanian visas High Commission, Ujamaa House, corner Blakiston and Baines Avenue, Harare (tel 21870). Visas take two days, cost Z$15, require two photos and must be used within three months. Your passport will be checked for South African stamps and you may well be asked where your 'other' passport is!

Zaire visas Embassy, 5 Pevensey Rd, off Enterprise Rd about eight km from the centre. Visas cost Z$10 but are only for single entry.

Zambian visas High Commission, 6th Floor, Zambia House, Union Avenue near Julius Nyerere St (tel 790851). Tourist visas which Americans supposedly need take five to six weeks but most travellers are being told they are obtainable at the border. This is true, but how long you get depends on how much money you show (one to two weeks is normal).

Border Post Hours

Beitbridge: 6 am to 8 pm daily.
Plumtree, Victoria Falls, Kariba, Chirundu, Mutare, Nyamapanda, Kazungula: 6 am to 6 pm Monday to Friday and 8 am to noon on Saturday.

WARNING

It can be dangerous to travel at night and even during the day between Bulawayo and Victoria Falls because of ZAPU guerrilla activity. You're advised to use public transport along this stretch and not hitch-hike. The bodies of a group of western travellers in an overland truck who were kidnapped and killed by guerillas in 1982 were found in bush graves in 1985. (The kidnappers were eventually executed in 1986.)

On the other hand, travellers who have been there recently and resident workers and volunteers have reported that the situation has now calmed down considerably and that there is nothing to worry about when travelling in western Zimbabwe.

Travel in Matabeleland is restricted to daylight hours.

MONEY

US$1 = Z$1.10 (official)

The unit of currency is the Zimbabwe dollar (Z$) = 100 cents. Import/export of local currency is allowed up to Z$20. If you only have traveller's cheques then you won't be issued with a currency declaration form on arrival. If you're bringing in cash, however, then insist that they issue you with one. Without this form you are only allowed to take out US$20 in foreign notes when you leave. Though there is a black market, the transaction isn't as simple as it is elsewhere. If often involves using up a resident's Zimbabwean dollars held in a bank account. You repay them in hard cash (US$ or rand). They often use the hard currency you give them for vacations abroad (there is a limit of US$350 every two years which a resident can get from the banks officially to use outside the country). On this basis it's possible to get up to Z$4 for £ sterling and Z$3 for the US dollar. The best rates are in Harare.

It used to be possible to bring in Krugerrands and sell them for 2½ to three times what you paid for them in South Africa (buy for Rand 500 in South Africa, sell for Z$1300 in Zimbabwe), but this is now officially illegal so you have to be careful who you approach if you're going to do it. Kenyan shillings are not accepted for exchange at the banks, but Barclays Bank will exchange traveller's cheques for cash US dollars. However, they only cash up to US$20 and make an entry in your passport, so you can only do it once.

You must produce bank receipts when buying airline tickets (but not train tickets) even for Botswana or South Africa. You can reconvert up to Z$100 into hard currency when leaving the country if you have sufficient bank receipts to cover that amount.

There's an 18% sales tax on all commodities including airline tickets but excluding raw foodstuffs. A bottle of whisky is useful for trading in Zimbabwe and can be bought cheaply in Botswana. Petrol costs Z$1.04 per litre but you cannot buy it on Sunday.

LANGUAGE

English is the official language. African languages are Ndebele and various Shona dialects.

Useful Words & Phrases

English	Shona	Ndebele
how are you	makadii	linjani/kunjani
good/very well	ndiripo zvangu	skhona/ngiyaphila/siyaphila
bad	handisi kunzwa zvakanaka	angiphilanga kuhle
thank you	ndatenda/mazvita	ngiyabonga/siyabonga kakulu
please	ndapota	uxolo
goodbye	chisarai zvakanaka	lisale sesihamba/lisale kuhle
welcome	titamberei	siyaalemukela
danger	ngozi	mingozi
friend	shamwari	mngane/umngane
sorry	ndine urombo	uxolo
excuse me	pamusoroi	uxolo/ngixolela
good morning	mangwanani	livuke njani
good afternoon	masikati	litshonile
good evening	manheru	litshone njani
what time is it	dzava nguvai	yisikhati bani
now	zvino	khathesi
morning	mangwanani	ekuseni
evening	manheru	ntambama
afternoon	masikati	emini yantambama

English		
today	*nhasi*	*lamhia*
yesterday	*nezuro*	*izolo*
tomorrow	*mangwana*	*kusasa*
time/hour	*nguva*	*isikhati*
night	*usiku*	*ebusuku*
day	*kwakachena*	*emini*
one	*potsi*	*okukodwa*
two	*piri*	*okubili*
three	*tatu*	*okuthathu*
four	*ina*	*okune*
five	*shanu*	*okuyisihlanu*
six	*tanhatu*	*okuyisithupha*
seven	*nomwe*	*okuyisikhombisa*
eight	*tsere*	*okuyisitshiyangalo mbili*
nine	*pfumbamwe*	*okuyisitshiyangalo lunye*
ten	*gumi*	*okuli tshumi*
Monday	*muvhuro*	*umvulo/ngumvulo*
Tuesday	*chipiri*	*ngolwesibili*
Wednesday	*chitatu*	*ngolwesithathu*
Thursdays	*china*	*ngolwesine*
Friday	*chishanu*	*ngolwesihlanu*
Saturday	*mugovera*	*ngesabatha*
Sunday	*svondo*	*ngesonto*
leopard	*mbada*	*ingwe*
rhinoceros	*chipembere*	*ubhejane*
buffalo	*nyati*	*inyathi*
lion	*shumba*	*isilwane/ngwenyama*
elephant	*nzou*	*indhlovu*
baboon/monkey	*gudo/bveni*	*indwangu/inkawu*
zebra	*mbizi*	*idube*
impala	*mhara*	*impala*
giraffe	*swiza*	*intundla*
hyena	*bere*	*impisi*
warthog	*njiri*	*ingulube yeganga*
hippo	*mvuu*	*imvubu*
man/men	*murume/varume*	*indoda/amadoda*
woman/women	*mukadzi/vakadze*	*umfazi/abafazi*
mr/sir	*changamire*	*umnimzana*
madam	*mudzimai/madzimai*	*inkosikazi/amankazana*
child/children	*mwana/vana*	*umtwana/abantwana*
boy/boys	*mukomana/vakomana*	*umfana/abafana*
girl/girls	*musikana/vasikana*	*inkazana/amankazana*
beer	*doro/whawha*	*utshwala*
bread	*chingwa*	*isinkwa*
eggs	*mazai*	*amaqanda*

fish	*hove*	*inhlanzi*
fruit	*muchero/michero*	*izithelo*
meat	*nyama*	*inyama*
milk	*mukaka*	*ucago*
potatoes	*matapiri*	*amagwili*
rice (cooked)	*mupunga wakabikwa*	*irice ephikiweyo*
salt	*munyu*	*isaudo*
vegetables	*muriwo*	*umbhida/imbhida*
water	*mvura*	*amanzi*
ice/cold	*chando/hunotonhora*	*okuqandayo*
hot	*kupisa*	*kuyatshisha*
small/large	*diki/guru*	*okuncane/ncinyane*
another/more	*rimwe*	*futhi/okunye*
enough	*zvakwana*	*kwenele*
how much	*i marii*	*yimalini*
expensive	*zvinodhura*	*kuyadula*
shop	*chitoro*	*isitolo*
money	*mari*	*imali*
where	*kupi*	*ngaphi*
why	*sei*	*ngani*
when	*rini*	*nini*
how	*sei/nei*	*njani*

GETTING THERE & AROUND

Name Changes

Zimbabwe has been going through a process of Africanising its place and street names. This may be confusing if you're using old editions of maps. The following is a list of changes with the old name in parentheses:

Mberengwa (Belingwe); Chipinge (Chipinga); Dete (Dett); Esigodini (Essexvale); Chivhu (Enkeldoorn); Masvingo (Fort Victoria – also called Nyanda for a while); Kadoma (Gatooma); Gweru (Gwelo); Chegutu (Hartley); Nyazura (Inyazura); Mhangura (Mangula); Marondera (Marandellas); Mashava (Mashaba); Chimanimani (Melsetter); Murewa (Mrewa); Mutoko (Mtoko); Mutorashanga (Mtorashanga); Nkayi (Nkai); Mwenezi (Nuanetsi); Kwe Kwe (Que Que); Harare (Salisbury); Shurugwe (Selukwe); Zvishavana (Shabani); Chinhoyi (Sinoia); Guruwe (Sipolilo); Somabhula (Somabula); Tsholotsho (Tjolotjo); Mutare (Umtali); Mvurwi (Umvukwes); Mvuma (Umvuma); Sango (Vila Salazar) and Hwange (Wankie).

Air

London-Harare Six return flights per week, two by *British Airways* and four by *Air Zimbabwe*. Flights with *KLM* cost £555 return. If you want to save a lot of money by flying direct, however, the London-Lusaka flight by *Aeroflot* works out to be a far better value at £425 return. The ticket is valid for one year.

Paris-Harare *UTA* has one return flight per week via Kinshasa. (You cannot get on this flight in Kinshasa.)

Frankfurt-Harare Two return flights per week by *Air Zimbabwe* via Athens.

Lisbon-Harare One return flight per week by *TAP* via Brazzaville.

Bombay-Harare *Ethiopian Airways* flies Harare-Addis-Bombay. Discounts are available.

Seychelles-Harare *Air France* covers this route via Mauritius and Réunion.

Athens-Harare One flight per week on Friday by *Air Zimbabwe*.

Sydney-Harare One flight per week by *Qantas* via Perth. There is a connection to Johannesburg on this flight.

Zurich-Harare One flight per week by *Swissair* via Geneva and Athens on the way out but direct on the return leg.

Harare-Lilongwe-Blantyre *Air Malawi* are probably the best airline for this flight. You don't have to show currency forms so it works out at around US$60.

Road

Hitching is very easy in Zimbabwe and many travellers prefer it as a way of getting around. You should make an effort to look like a tourist (hang a camera around your neck). All the whites have cars so they tend to be suspicious of others who are apparently so poor they can't afford one; however, they're friendly enough once you tell them you're travelling.

Cycling We've had letters from a few travellers who cycled around the country and recommend it highly. Almost all the roads are surfaced and in excellent repair. In addition, the shoulders of the roads are often surfaced and marked off from the rest of the road by a yellow line to separate them from the vehicular traffic. This was done deliberately so they could be used as cycle lanes. The predictable climate helps considerably, with winter being the most pleasant season. The winds are generally easterly and only rarely strong enough to make cycling difficult. Distances between towns and points of interest are long by European standards, though generally only a day's ride apart. There are plenty of small stores between towns where you can stop and have a drink and a chat. The people you find in these stores are very friendly.

If you're bringing a lightweight bicycle, bear in mind that there is next to nothing available in terms of spares for these in most places, including Harare. You will certainly find no 27-inch tyres for sale anywhere. The local bicycles use either 26-inch or 28-inch wheels, so you can get spares for these. Those who have done it suggest you bring with you all the tools and spare parts you think you may need.

The two best cycle shops in Harare are *Zacks*, Kenneth Kaunda Avenue directly opposite the railway station; and *Manica Cycles*, Second Avenue close to Zacks.

Truck Rental If you're thinking of renting a small truck to visit the game parks, the average price is Z$170 per 400 km for a one-ton utility truck.

Bus There are two types of buses – express and local. The former, operated by *Express Motorways Africa Ltd*, 109 Belvedere Rd, Harare (tel 702121), only operates between the major cities. Their buses are often full so you need to book in advance. The booking office in Harare is at Rezende St (tel 20392). In Bulawayo, book at Musgrove & Watson travel agents; in Mutare book at the Tourist Information Bureau. The following routes apply to buses running in the opposite direction as well:

Harare-Bulawayo The *Express Motorways* bus departs Harare at 7.45 am on Monday, Wednesday, Friday and Saturday. It departs Bulawayo at the same time on Tuesday, Thursday and Saturday and at 1 pm on Sunday. The fare is Z$18.50 one way and the journey takes 6¼ hours. Another company called *Ajayo's* runs buses from Bulawayo to Harare at 7.30 am on Monday, Wednesday and Friday. The buses are of a similar quality but take 6½ hours.

The long-distance 'African' buses depart from Mbare Market bus terminal in Harare Township. To get there from the centre of town, take the local bus with 'Harare' on the signboard (Z$0.13) – local buses labelled 'City' go to the bus terminal near the railway station.

Harare-Mutare Depart Harare at 8 am daily except Sunday; depart Mutare at 2.30 pm daily except Saturday. The fare is Z$7.50 one way and the journey takes 3¾ hours.

Harare-Masvingo Depart Harare at 8 am on Wednesday and Friday; depart Masvingo at 2.25 pm on Friday and Sunday. The journey takes 4½ hours.

Bulawayo-Masvingo Depart Bulawayo at 1.30 pm on Thursday and Saturday; depart Masvingo at 3.30 pm on Wednesday and Friday. The journey takes 21½ hours, but you have to buy a return ticket at Z$117.30.

The white people in Zimbabwe will probably tell you that there are no other buses. This is because they won't go in the other buses with the Africans. The fact is that there are buses to just about everywhere. They're relatively slow and over-crowded, but they are cheap and you're much more likely to meet interesting people on them. They're also quite safe despite what you might hear to the contrary. The only problem about them is that they leave from the bus stations in the African townships and so aren't easy to find. There are also no timetables at these bus stations and people can be infuriatingly vague about departure times. Give these buses a go – you'll undoubtedly raise a few eyebrows, but once the initial shock of seeing a white person using a black people's bus has worn off, you'll find the black people take it in their stride and quickly warm to you. Resident whites will most likely stare at such a spectacle in downright horror or simply not believe their eyes. Two bus companies which have been recommended are the *Zimbabwe Omnibus Co* and the *Shu-Shine Bus Co*. Some examples of these buses are:

Bulawayo-Masvingo This will take you to the Great Zimbabwe ruins. One bus daily departs at about 8.30 am from the corner of Lobengula and Selbourne and arrives at approximately 4.30 pm. The fare is Z$5.40. Get there early. *Zimbabwe Omnibus Company* also cover this route in both directions. Their bus terminus in Bulawayo is at Lobengula St/6th Avenue (tel 74059).

Bulawayo-Victoria Falls The 'Wankie Express' (operated by F Pullen & Co) departs from the bus station at the end of 6th Avenue extension daily at around 9 am and arrives at 3.30 pm. In the opposite direction it departs from the African township in Victoria Falls at 10 am daily and arrives at 4.30 pm. The fare is Z$5.50. You can also pick up this bus opposite Barclays Bank in Victoria Falls. *Zimbabwe Omnibus Co* does this run and costs Z$7. The *Express Motorway* bus costs Z$17.

Mutare-Bulawayo The *Shu-Shine* bus departs about 6.15 am and arrives at about 6 pm.

Mutare-Masvingo The local bus costs Z$5.30.

Rail

Zimbabwe has a good network of railways which connect all the major cities. They're very cheap, especially in 3rd and 4th class. Most trains have four classes, but certain express trains have only 1st and 2nd classes. For internal journeys, bookings open 30 days ahead. For journeys on through trains to Botswana and South Africa, bookings open 90 days ahead. You're advised to book as far ahead as possible. Bedding can be hired for Z$2.35 plus Z$2.35 if you want a mattress. (You have to purchase tickets for bedding at the station and exchange them on the train.)

Bulawayo-Victoria Falls-Bulawayo

Station	Time Daily	Station	Time Daily
Bulawayo	7.00 pm	Victoria Falls	5.30 pm
Hwange	3.39 am	Thomson Junct	8.27 pm

| Thomson Junct | 4.35 am | Hwange | 9.12 pm |
| Victoria Falls | 7.30 am | Bulawayo | 7.15 am |

All classes. There is a buffet car on the train and pasties and tea are brought round at intervals.

Bulawayo-Mafeking-Bulawayo via Botswana

Station	Time		Station	Time	
	Daily	Tues/Thur		Daily	Tues/Thur
Bulawayo	1.30 pm	11.45 am	Mafeking	2.00 pm	9.00 pm
Plumtree	4.20 pm	2.05 pm	Ramatlhabama	4.10 pm	9.30 pm
Francistown	6.26 pm	3.51 pm	Lobatse	5.40 pm	10.40 pm
Palapye	10.15 pm	7.10 pm	Gaborone	7.55 pm	12.27 am
Mahalapye	12.20 am	9.00 pm	Pilane	8.45 pm	1.15 am
Artesia	3.23 am	10.40 pm	Artesia	10.10 pm	2.46 am
Pilane	4.52 am	12.17 am	Mahalapye	1.20 am	5.15 am
Gaborone	6.00 am	1.30 am	Palapye	3.15 am	6.32 am
Lobatse	8.20 am	3.25 am	Francistown	7.23 am	9.56 am
Ramatlhabama	11.04 am	5.00 am	Plumtree	10.05 am	12.09 pm
Mafeking	11.40 am	5.30 am	Bulawayo	12.45 pm	2.10 pm

The daily train has four classes; the Tuesday/Thursday trains have only 1st and 2nd classes. The Tuesday train goes on to Johannesburg and the Thursday train goes on to Cape Town. The daily train has a buffet car between Bulawayo and Ramatlhabama and vice versa. The Tuesday/Thursday trains have a dining car only between Bulawayo and Artesia.

Bulawayo-Harare-Bulawayo

Station	Time		Station	Time	
	Daily	Fri		Daily	Fri
Bulawayo	8.00 pm	7.30 pm	Harare	8.00 pm	7.30 pm
Gweru	1.00 am	12.05 am	Kadoma	11.08 pm	10.25 pm
Kadoma	4.05 am	3.10 am	Gweru	3.05 am	2.05 am
Harare	7.00 am	6.00 am	Bulawayo	7.00 am	6.00 am

The daily train has all classes except on Friday, when it only has 1st and 2nd classes. The 7.30 pm Friday train has only 3rd and 4th classes.

Harare-Mutare-Harare

Station	Time	Station	Time
	Daily		Daily
Harare	9.30 pm	Mutare	9.00 pm
Marondera	11.51 pm	Odzi	9.49 pm
Macheke	12.52 am	Nyazura	11.20 pm
Headlands	2.20 am	Rusapi	12.15 am
Rusapi	3.15 am	Headlands	1.22 am
Nyazura	3.57 am	Macheke	2.50 am
Odzi	5.05 am	Marondera	4.00 am
Mutare	6.00 am	Harare	6.00 am

Note The above schedules are a digest only and do not include many of the smaller stations at which the trains stop.

Direct Connections with South Africa
The following trains have only 1st and 2nd classes available. In South Africa you are not allowed to travel in 3rd class if you're white.

Bulawayo-Johannesburg-Durban

Station	Time Tues	Station	Time Wed
Bulawayo	11.45 am	Durban	6.00 pm
Mafeking arr	5.40 am (Wed)	Johannesburg arr	8.30 am (Thur)
dep	6.10 am	dep	
Johannesburg arr	2.05 pm	Mafeking arr	8.15 pm
dep	6.30 pm	dep	9.00 pm
Durban	9.15 am (Thur)	Bulawayo	2.10 pm (Fri)

Bulawayo-Kimberley-Cape Town

Station	Time Thurs	Station	Time Mon
Bulawayo	11.45 am	Cape Town	2.30 pm
Mafeking arr	5.30 am (Fri)	Kimberley dep	10.15 am (Tues)
dep	6.15 am	Mafeking arr	8.10 pm
Kimberley arr	3.03 pm	dep	9.00 pm
Cape Town	11.00 am	Bulawayo	2.10 pm (Wed)

Bulawayo-Kimberley-Port Elizabeth-East London

Station	Time Thur	Station	Time Mon
Bulawayo	11.45 am	East London	11.15 am
Mafeking arr	5.30 am (Fri)	Port Elizabeth dep	5.00 pm
dep	6.15 am	Kimberley dep	10.15 am (Tue)
Kimberley arr	3.03 pm	Mafeking arr	8.10 pm
Port Elizabeth arr	1.10 pm (Sat)	dep	9.00 pm
East London	12.35 am	Bulawayo	2.10 pm (Wed)

The railway fare structure is based on zones, each costing Z$2.15 (1st class), Z$1.50 (2nd class), Z$0.80 (3rd class) and Z$0.45 (4th class). In Botswana these zone rates change to Z$2.10 (1st class), Z$1.40 (2nd class), Z$0.70 (3rd class). Some examples of zoning are: Bulawayo-Victoria Falls 12 zones; Bulawayo-Harare 12 zones; Bulawayo-Francistown 5 zones; Bulawayo-Mutare 19 zones; Bulawayo-Nyanda 10 zones.

Fares
1st Class

Bulawayo				
Z$9.75	Gweru			
Z$23.40	Z$13.65	Harare		
Z$23.40	Z$33.15	Z$46.80	Victoria Falls	
Z$37.05	Z$27.30	Z$13.65	Z$60.45	Mutare

2nd Class

Bulawayo				
Z$6.75	Gweru			
Z$16.20	Z$9.45	Harare		
Z$16.20	Z$22.95	Z$32.40	Victoria Falls	
Z$25.65	Z$18.90	Z$9.45	Z$41.85	Mutare

4th Class

Bulawayo				
Z$2.00	Gweru			
Z$4.80	Z$2.80	Harare		
			Victoria Falls	
			Z$5.40	Mutare
Z$7.60		Z$5.60		Z$2.80

First class consists of four berths per compartment; 2nd class has six berths per compartment; 3rd class has six berths per compartment, though often more than six people are squeezed in; 4th class is just wooden seats. You can reserve 1st and 2nd class in advance, but not 3rd and 4th class. If you're buying a through-ticket to South Africa, it will have to be either 1st or 2nd class if you're white. The only exception to this is that you can go as far as Mafeking in any class you like so long as you go via Botswana.

Boat

The Lake Kariba ferry sails in either direction between Kariba and Mlibizi (250 km east of Victoria Falls) once per week if there's sufficient passenger demand. The fare is Z$69 including excellent meals and the journey takes 24 hours. As far as seeing animals is concerned, the trip is better from Mlibizi to Kariba, as you are nearer the banks in the daylight hours.

To Zambia

Almost everyone goes via Victoria Falls/ Livingstone for obvious reasons, but if you've already seen the falls there is a bus daily except Sunday direct from Harare to Lusaka. It leaves from the bus station at 7 am, costs Z$6.60 and takes about 11 hours, but it's often fully booked so try and get your ticket in advance. You can, of course, do this journey in stages via the falls either by bus or train. If you arrive by train, the railway station at Victoria Falls is about one km from Zambian customs. Take a taxi from there to the border post (or walk if you have very little baggage) and then have the taxi take you across the bridge and drop you at the Zambian post. If you're walking it's about 1½ km between border posts and about one km from the Zimbabwe post into town. If you arrive after the banks have closed, you can change money at shops but not in the hotels.

There are also border crossing points at Kariba and Chirundu. The road from Chirundu to Lusaka is terrible but this route is the main Harare-Lusaka route. If the border is closed when you get there (after 6 pm on weekdays, after noon on Saturday, all day Sunday) you have a choice of camping or staying at the *Chirundi Valley Motel*, one km from the Zambezi. The motel charges Z$21.80 a single for bed and breakfast (dinner costs Z$5). It is very unpleasant because of the voracious mosquitoes. Money can be changed there. On the Zambian side there is nowhere to stay.

To Botswana

Most travellers take the train from Bulawayo, which goes as far as Mafeking (South Africa) via all the major towns in Botswana – details under 'Rail.' You can go by road but hitching on the Zimbabwean leg of the journey as far as Plumtree is not recommended at present – you may be shot or kidnapped by guerrillas of Nkomo's ZAPU.

To South Africa

The only direct crossing is by road or rail from Bulawayo or Harare to Pretoria and Johannesburg via Beitbridge. Most travellers take the train – details later. It's not advisable to try to hitch-hike through Beitbridge, as South African immigration and customs officials don't like hitch-hikers and will throw every entry requirement in the book at you.

To Mozambique

At present it's possible to go to Malawi via Mozambique along the Nyamapanda-Tete-Zobue road (transit visas for this are easily obtained in Harare). Convoys of trucks leave daily during the week and sometimes on Saturday in either direction, and are escorted by units of the Zimbabwean army. The trip takes all day during daylight hours and is a popular route taken by black Zimbabweans hitching to Malawi. At Tete, the trucks are only allowed across the suspension bridge one at a time, as Soviet tanks weakened the support structure. This route has been opened because Zimbabwean fertilizer is being exchanged for the seasonal corn harvest in Malawi. It may not be repeated, so make enquiries.

BULAWAYO

This is Zimbabwe's second largest city and one of the country's major commercial and industrial centres. It was founded in 1894 on the site of one of Lobengula's kraals (Lobengula was the last of the Matabele kings). Cecil Rhodes used the place as a headquarters on a number of occasions and the rondavel which he constructed still stands in the gardens of Government House. The stone ruins of **Khami**, one of the most important sites of the Rozwi empire, are located 22 km west of the city. The remains date from the 17th century and were occupied until 1820. They consist of a series of terraces and passages supported by huge granite walls, some of which overlook the Khami Gorge. This is one of Zimbabwe's most important archaeological sites and well worth a visit.

Bulawayo is the jumping-off point for a visit to the **Rhodes Matopos National Park**, which begins 32 km south of the city (more later under 'National Parks'). There's also the smaller **Tshabalala Sanctuary** just eight km from the city centre on the Matopos road, which contains a varied selection of wildlife including giraffe, kudu, zebra, impala, wildebeest and water birds. It's open daily from 6 am to 6 pm and you're permitted to walk. The **Chipangali Wildlife Trust**, 23 km from Bulawayo on the main Johannesburg road, operates an orphanage for sick or abandoned young animals, including lions, leopards, cheetahs and many species of antelope and warthog. It's open daily except Monday.

The **National Natural History Museum** in Centenary Park, open daily from 9 am to 5 pm, has excellent tribal cultural displays, a stuffed mammal collection and a room full of Rhodes' memorabilia. The **Railway Museum** is a must for railway buffs. You'll see antique locos, rolling stock and even a 'museum on wheels' – a 1904 passenger coach with original fittings.

Information

The Tourist Office is in City Hall, Fife St between Selbourne Avenue and 8th Avenue (tel 60867).

The Automobile Association is in Fanum House, corner of Selbourne Avenue and Wilson St (tel 70063).

Places to Stay

The *Youth Hostel* (tel 76488), is now on the corner of 3rd St and Townsend Rd, Suburbs, Bulawayo, two km east out of town along 12th Avenue, which becomes 3rd St. Many travellers describe it as dreadful and very unfriendly, and suggest you avoid the place. However, if you want to try it then it costs Z$3 for members and Z$6 for non-members plus 40c for extra blankets. Cooking facilities, cutlery and crockery are provided but the kitchen is

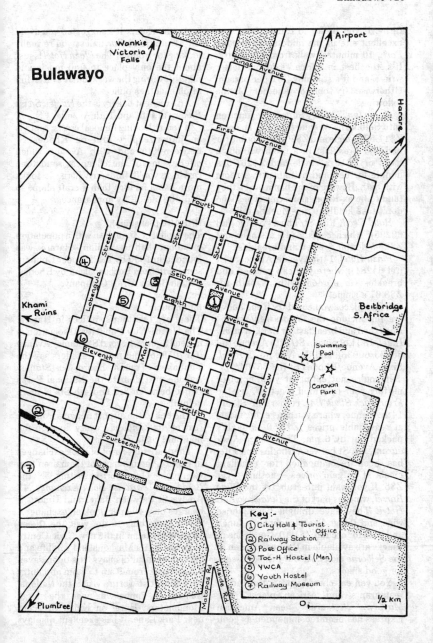

Bulawayo

Key:-
1. City Hall & Tourist Office
2. Railway Station
3. Post Office
4. Toc-H Hostel (Men)
5. YWCA
6. Youth Hostel
7. Railway Museum

filthy. If you prefer to camp, there's an excellent site in the middle of *Caravan Park*, 10 minutes' walk from the centre. It's 'the best in Africa,' said one letter writer, and it's still only Z$1 per person. Otherwise try one or another of the following:

Grey's Inn, 73 Grey St near the junction with Selbourne Avenue (tel 60121), costs Z$11.59 a single and Z$20.09 a double for bed and breakfast in a room without a bath; or Z$16 a single and Z$26.79 a double for bed and breakfast in a room with bath. Beware of the bar crowd – they tend to be ex-Rhodesian army types who don't take kindly to pro-Mugabe talk.

Hotel Cecil, Fife St/Third Avenue (tel 60295), which costs Z$15 a single and Z$25 a double for bed and breakfast.

Plaza Hotel, 14th Avenue/Abercorn St (tel 64281), where you can get bed and breakfast in a room without bath for Z$8.67 a single.

Other places you could try if the above are full include the *Rhodes Matamopos Hotel* (bed and breakfast for Z$8); *Waverly Hotel*, 133 Lobengula St/12th Avenue (tel 60033/60036); and the *New Royal Hotel*, Sixth Avenue/Rhodes St (tel 65764/5).

If you're not eating at your hotel or putting your own food together, try the *Friar Tuck Steak Bar*, corner Fife St and 14th Avenue, where you can get big meals at reasonable prices (Z$3.50-4.50). It's packed out by 6 pm. The *Tavern Restaurant*, 9th St between Rhodes and Fife, has been recommended for excellent meals at bargain prices – nothing over Z$5. If you want pub-grub, try the *Wine Barrel*, which is part of the *Bulawayo Sun Hotel*. They have draught beer, house wine and things like ploughman's lunch and paté for around Z$1.10. Good, cheap snacks are available in the beer garden of the *Selborne Hotel*. Also try the *Grasshut* for good snacks.

You can eat cheaply at a lot of Indian restaurants and African places. The *Mayfayre Restaurant* near American Express has been recommended as good

and quite cheap. It's suggested you avoid the *White Horse Bar* unless you're really looking for trouble. The *Plaza Hotel* is just about the only place to find music and nightlife during the week, but it's often full of plainclothes police.

An excellent bakery is the *Haefeli Swiss Bakery* at Fife and 10th Avenue.

If you're looking for local crafts, there is an import/export firm on Rhodes St between 9th and 10th Avenue which offers some of the cheapest sandstone carvings you'll find anywhere. It looks more like a factory than a craft shop, so don't be put off by appearances.

HARARE (Salisbury)

The capital of Zimbabwe with a population of about half a million, Harare was founded in 1890 by the 'Pioneer Column' sent north from Bechuanaland by Rhodes' British South Africa Company.

Information

There are two tourist offices in Harare. The Harare City Publicity Association is in Cecil Square, Second St/Stanley Avenue (tel 705085), but many travellers say the Zimbabwe Tourist Board on Stanley Avenue next door to the National Parks Office between 3rd and 4th Sts is more helpful.

The bus to the airport departs from the rear of *Air Zimbabwe* every hour on the hour and costs Z$2.60.

There are quite a lot of book exchanges in Harare, though most of them aren't up to much. One worth visiting is the *Booklovers' Paradise Book Exchange*, 48 Angwa St between Baker and Union. It charges only 40c per book on exchange.

For something to do, visit the **Queen Victoria Museum** in the new Civic Centre complex for its Mashonaland wildlife and anthropological displays. It's open seven days a week from 9 am to 5 pm and entry costs 20c. Also worth a visit is the **National Gallery of Zimbabwe** near the large Monomatapa Hotel on Kings Crescent near Park Lane. It has excellent displays of African artifacts, with masks and carvings from all over Africa. The paintings aren't much but show what Zimbabwean modern art is up to. Inexpensive baskets are for sale in the lobby. The gallery is open Tuesday to Sunday from 9 am to 5 pm and entry costs 20c.

Places to Stay

Among the cheapest places to stay are the *Youth Hostel*, 6 Montagu Avenue (tel 26990); *TOC-H*, 163 Union St and 148 Baines Avenue (tel 21566); and *Lady Stanley Hostel*. The Youth Hostel, in an old, attractive house, has separate dormitory accommodation for men and women and costs Z$3 for members and Z$6 for non-members. It offers a quiet, pleasant garden and cooking facilities (cutlery and crockery are provided) and is recommended by many travellers. It's closed between 10 am and 5 pm and the kitchen closes at 10 pm. The mattresses are really dirty but there's hot water and showers and no chores to do. The warden is a fine person, but you should keep a watch on your valuables and any clothes left to dry on the washing lines. Use those lockers! The hostel is a good place to find information on just about any topic of interest to travellers. TOC-H is for men only and costs Z$10 per person if you're only staying one night, Z$8 if you're staying two or more nights. The price includes breakfast. The place is clean but often full. The Lady Stanley Hostel is for women only but is rumoured to be closed. It used to cost Z$2.80 per night including three meals and morning and afternoon tea! If you want to camp, there's a good site at *Coronation Park*, five km southeast of the city on the Mutare Rd. To get there, take a bus marked 'Mabvuku' or 'Tafara' from Manica Rd below Cecil Square (12c).

If you're looking for hotel accommodation, three of the cheapest are the *Elizabeth Hotel*, Nyerere and Manica (tel 708591), which costs Z$8.40-9.52 a single and Z$14-16.24 a double for bed and breakfast (the more expensive rooms have their own bathroom); *Queens' Hotel*, corner Manica and Pioneer Rds (tel 700876), at Z$9.50 a single and Z$15.50 a double (bed and breakfast); and the *Cloisters Hotel*, 121 Baines Avenue (tel 791143/4), which is Z$15.98 for bed, breakfast and dinner (all the rooms have their own bathroom). Other hotels in the same bracket include the *Federal Hotel*, 9 Salisbury St (tel 706118); the *Earlside Hotel*, Fifth St and Selous Avenue (tel 21101); the *Casamia Hotel*, Third St and Central Avenue (tel 790066/7); the *Bronte Hotel*, 132 Baines Avenue (tel 21999/ 21768); and the *Caves Hotel*, 131 Baines Avenue (tel 27641).

If you're not eating at your hotel, try either the *Europa Restaurant*, corner Nyerere and Samora Machel Avenue, a friendly place which offers good, cheap meals; or *Eddie's Takeaways* on Stanley St. Even better is *Natie's Grill*, 1st St between Samora Machel and Union, which offers fantastic thick hamburgers with mushrooms, onions and real Cheddar cheese for Z$3.65, steaks with many exotic sauces, waffles covered with real whipped cream and honey for Z$2 and excellent coffee with real cream for Z$0.50. They also sell beer. The grill is opposite Zambia Airways. Two other places which have been recommended are *Barbours Cafeteria*, Stanley St; and *Homegrown*, corner of Speke Avenue and Moffat St. Meals at the *Earlside Hotel* are cheap and very good value. Breakfast and dinner cost Z$2.30 and lunch Z$3.30.

For moderately priced Greek food try *Demis Taverna*, corner Speke and Moffat. You can make a meal out of just the appetizers (stuffed grape leaves, moussaka) or order the marinated lamb chops – four of them – for around Z$6. It's licenced. *Da Guido's Trattoria* in the shopping complex at Montagu and Salisbury by the Youth Hostel has good pizza and other cheap Italian food. It's very popular.

For somewhere to go in the evening, try *Job's Night Spot*, Nyerere between Forbes

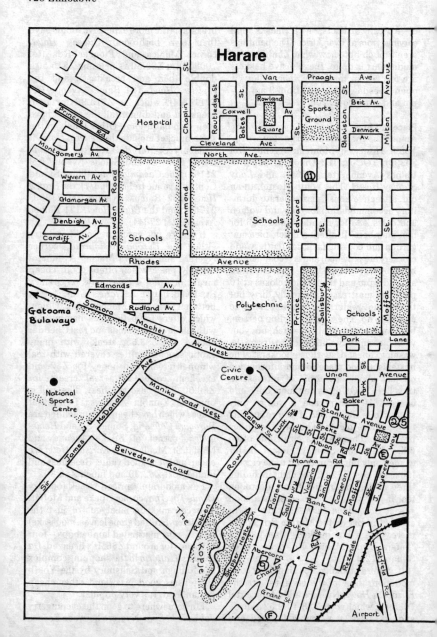

Harare

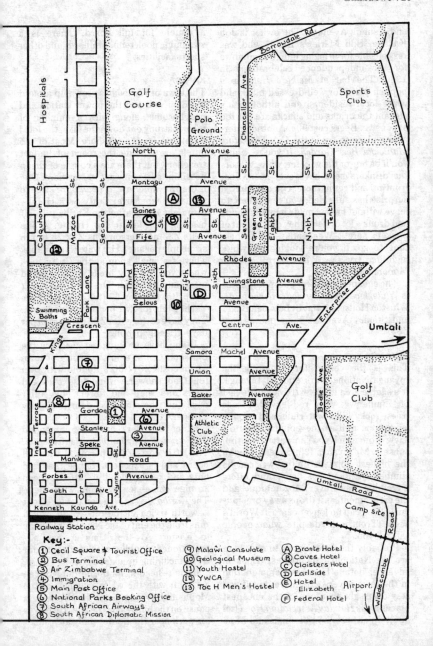

Key:-
(1) Cecil Square & Tourist Office
(2) Bus Terminal
(3) Air Zimbabwe Terminal
(4) Immigration
(5) Main Post Office
(6) National Parks Booking Office
(7) South African Airways
(8) South African Diplomatic Mission

(9) Malawi Consulate
(10) Geological Museum
(11) Youth Hostel
(12) YWCA
(13) Toc H Men's Hostel

(A) Bronte Hotel
(B) Caves Hotel
(C) Cloisters Hotel
(D) Earlside
(E) Hotel Elizabeth
(F) Federal Hotel

and Kaunda Avenues. The owner is Job Kakane, Bob Marley's friend who was responsible for bringing him to Zimbabwe for the independence celebrations in 1980. The bar at *Meikle's Hotel* is a popular place for well-dressed black and white local residents, and although it's elegant the drinks and snacks are not too expensive. Beers cost 90c. Another interesting place to try is the *City Marketing Municipal Beer Garden*. If you're white, you'll be one of the very few white visitors the drinkers here have ever seen. Just front-up and get in there. Once the initial surprise has subsided, you're unlikely to leave without having made a lot of friends and drunk a lot of beer (they drink it out of buckets here!). Weekends are the best time to go. If you're looking for white nightlife, try the *Wine Barrel* at the Monomatapa Hotel.

The cheapest place for passport photos is *Whiteglove Photo Service & Record Bar*, Winston House, Moffat St between Baker and Stanley Avenues. Four photos cost Z$3.

INYANGA

This is the centre for exploring the Inyanga National Park and Mt Inyanga. It's a large area in the extreme north-east of Zimbabwe with red-leaved Msasa trees, rocky hills, waterfalls and prolific wildlife as well as the popular 'World's View' from which you can watch beautiful sunsets. Mt Inyanga (2595 metres high), the highest point in Zimbabwe, can be climbed in about 1½ hours and offers incredible views over Mozambique and the escarpment, as it drops away precipitously. You can no longer camp at World's View (Troutbeck) despite what people will tell you.

Probably the best places to stay here are the National Park lodges. (Book in advance; details later.) Accommodation in the town is very expensive, but if you stay overnight then one of the cheapest places is the *Holiday Association Hotel* (tel 336), which costs Z$14 a single and Z$16 a double for full board. There is a swimming pool, tennis, billiards and other sports facilities.

KARIBA

The town of Kariba has grown up around the dam wall and the power station and has become, along with a number of resorts strung out down the lake, the local substitute for the seashore. Most of the hotels are outside the reach of budget travellers, but there are a couple of cheap possibilities if you want to stay here. One is the *Mophani Bay Caravan Park* close to the (very expensive) Cutty Sark Hotel – turn right 10 km after the Kariba turn-off heading for Makuti and Harare. A site costs Z$3 per person plus Z$2.75 (up to six people per site). Hot water is available. There's a small shop at the Cutty Sark where you can buy bread, milk, canned meat and the like. Or try the *MOTH* campsite, PO Box 67 (tel 409), near the Yacht Club, for Z$2 per person per night. They have cottages for Z$8 per person per day – friendly people.

If you have no camping gear, try the *Christian Centre* near the centre of town which costs Z$11.80 a double with own toilet, hot shower, writing desk, carpeted floors and soap and towel. They offer meals but the club next door is slightly cheaper.

Other travellers have recommended the *Fothergill* and *Spurwing* island resorts. The latter costs Z$25 per night with full board and is excellent. It has thatched huts and really friendly staff. You can arrange game-viewing trips with them. The *Kariba Breeze Hotel* on the lakefront is worth trying in the off-season, which runs from the end of the New Year holiday to Easter. At that time it has air-conditioned doubles with own bath for Z$13 including breakfast.

If you're heading for the border, you can get a lift with the white manager of the Mophani Bay campsite. He lives in a house on the hill beside the site. He leaves for work near the border daily at 7 am.

MASVINGO (Nyanda/Fort Victoria)

Masvingo is the urban centre nearest the **Great Zimbabwe ruins**, one of the most important and impressive archaeological sites in southern Africa. The ruins, 25 km south-east of Masvingo, date back as far as 1200 AD and are estimated to have once housed a population in excess of 10,000. By the time the Portuguese arrived, however, the city was already in decline. Built of stone, the walls range from just over a metre to more than five metres thick and are as high as nine metres. They're certainly worth more than one visit. The site is open daily from 8 am to 5 pm and entry costs Z$1. There's a small museum on the site.

Places to Stay

Despite what you may be told, it's still possible to camp at the Great Zimbabwe ruins. You must buy a ticket (Z$1.50) from the office in the Curio Shop building. The site is next to the parking area and has toilets and cold showers. Watch out for the resident monkeys. Meals are available from the adjacent hotel and are quite cheap. The hotel may also be a good place to find a lift back to Masvingo. If you don't want to camp, try the *Great Zimbabwe Hotel* (tel 2274) at the ruins. A room here costs Z$38 including breakfast. The table d'hote lunch costs Z$8.50. You can get pub-grub at the bar (eg cheeseburgers) for much less. If staying in Masvingo itself, there's a municipal campsite half a km out of town on the Birchenough Bridge/Mutare Rd which costs Z$2 per night.

Hotels in Masvingo itself are generally very expensive – expect to pay Z$25 a single. The *Chevron Hotel* (tel 2054/5) costs Z$27 plus 18% tax plus Z$0.60 'tourist levy' for a double room. The *Flamboyant Hotel* (tel 2005/6) has similar prices.

Near the Great Zimbabwe ruins is Lake Kyle, a popular resort area, though it's quite a distance from the ruins (on the south side) to the recreation area (on the north side). You can stay here at the *Kyle View Chalets & Caravan Park* (tel 223822). The chalets are equipped with shower, toilet and kitchenette and cost Z$7.80; or you can rent an old but adequate on-site van for Z$4. Camping is permitted for Z$4 for two people. There is a food-and-liquor store, and boats can be hired for use on the lake.

You can only walk as far as the entrance – beyond that you must have a vehicle, as this is a game park. If you're lucky, one of the friendly game wardens may give you a lift. It's difficult to hitch out to the Zimbabwe Ruins because there are few cars. There are occasional buses (Z$0.55) and shared taxis (Z$1.50) out to Lake Kyle. Allow several hours either way.

If you're short of money, you might try one of the local missions such as the Canadian one 18 km from town on the way to the ruins.

MUTARE (Umtali)

Mutare is the largest town in eastern Zimbabwe. It sits close to the Mozambique border and is a convenient place from which to visit the nearby Inyanga National Park.

Information

The Tourist Office is in Market Square, Milner Avenue (tel 64711).

Places to Stay

A cheap place to stay is the *Balmoral Hotel*, halfway between the white and black townships. It has a friendly black proprietor and the place is used mostly by black salespeople and commercial travellers. It costs Z$10 a double. If it's full, try the *Christmas Pass Hotel* (tel 63818) five km from Mutare, which costs Z$10 a single and Z$18 a double for bed and breakfast. There's an excellent campsite just below Christmas Pass about two km from Mutare – if you're coming into town by bus, get off before you go all the way into town. It costs Z$3 per night. Ask at the Mutare Tourist Office about *Eventide Cottage* run by Mrs Stubb. It's very romantic, gas-lit and spacious, with four beds for Z$10. Great value.

If you're short of money, ask at the police compound. They may let you sleep there free of charge.

For something to eat, try the takeaway food from *Meikles Department Store*.

If you're looking for good, locally produced handicrafts, try *Jiri Craftshop*. All the items here are produced by local handicapped Zimbabweans.

The *Cecil Kop Game Reserve*, though small, is interesting, with rhinos, elephants, zebras, wildebeest, kudus and monkeys.

VICTORIA FALLS

Among the most spectacular sights in the world, the falls are worth your while and you should spend at least a few days here. They're best seen during the dry season, as that is when you have the advantage of unobscured views, but they're magnificent at any time of year. The Zambezi widens to 1700 metres at the falls and then plunges down a chasm 70 to 110 metres deep across its entire width. The force of the falling water – estimated at 545 million litres per minute during the rainy season – sends clouds of spray high into the sky and sustains a lush rainforest all around. The spray, which often reaches heights of 500 metres, gave rise to the falls' African name – Mosi-O-Tunya or 'smoke that thunders.'

Information

The Tourist Office is on Park Way (tel 202) near the campsite.

Places to Stay

For budget travellers there is a choice of two places to stay. The *National Park lodges*, about six km upriver from the falls, are fine if you have your own transport and are part of a group. Camping costs Z$4 per site; chalets cost a flat Z$20 per night per chalet (six beds, two rooms with bathroom and an open cooking area at the back). The chalets are right out in the bush alongside the Zambezi, where crocodiles crawl up on the banks and hippos can be seen in the river. In addition, there's a wide variety of other animals such as baboons, vervet monkeys, deer, mongeese, wart-hogs and countless species of birds and insects. Bring insect repellent with you.

For those without their own vehicles, the best place to stay is the *Victoria Falls Rest Camp & Caravan Park*, Livingstone Way (PO Box 41, tel 210), 300 metres from the railway station, which has a whole range of accommodation. Camping (with your own tent) costs Z$2.10 per person. If you have your own caravan it's Z$3 per night for up to four people, plus Z$1 for each additional person, plus 10c per person government tax. They also have dormitory-style beds (six beds per room and very comfortable) for Z$4.20 per night per person with bedding, cooking facilities and toilets (but no pots or pans). Chalets cost Z$7.70 per person per night. Both one– and two-bedroom chalets are available, with three beds in each bedroom; there's a minimum charge of Z$10 per day for one bedroom and Z$20 per day for two bedrooms. Pots, pans, bedding, a small refrigerator and firewood are included in the price. Cottages (two bedrooms with a total of six beds and all facilities including pots and pans) are available for Z$8.30 per person per night (minimum charge Z$20). All the above facilities have electricity and are cleaned daily. Meat, eggs, groceries and alcoholic beverages are always available. You can have your laundry done by freelance people who come round every day. A 10% discount is available for groups of 10 or more people or for individuals who stay more than 10 days.

All the tourist hotels in Victoria Falls town itself are expensive – *Victoria Falls Hotel* (tel 344/5) costs Z$75 a single and Z$105 a double, and the *Masaka Sun Hotel* (tel 275) costs about US$67 a double. On the other hand, the Victoria Falls Hotel offers an excellent three-course all-you-can-eat lunch for Z$9 plus tax and a barbeque dinner for Z$9 plus tax. Most travellers find themselves here at least once. You can also get excellent food at the *A'Zambezi River Lodge* (tel 561) upriver from the falls for much the same price as at the Victoria Falls Hotel. You can use the swimming pools at both these places even if you're not staying there. Both the *Rainbow Hotel* and the *Elephant Hills Country Club* are closed.

An excellent African dance show is put on in a simulated African village behind the Victoria Falls Hotel swimming pool every night from 7 to 8 pm. It costs Z\$5.

Other

Bicycles can be rented from *Avis* in Victoria Falls for Z\$6 per day or Z\$1.20 per hour.

If you go into Zambia for the day (no fuss), don't take more than Z\$20; otherwise you'll be contravening currency regulations.

The 'Flight of Angels,' a 20-minute flight over the falls, is worth considering if you have the money – Z\$32. It's been described by many enthusiastic travellers as 'worth every cent.' The 'Booze Cruise' in the early evening on the river above the falls costs Z\$13.80 'but you see more game just walking along the river' according to one traveller, and the price no longer includes the booze.

NATIONAL PARKS

One of the best ways to see Zimbabwe is to use the National Park lodges, caravan sites and camping sites. There are over 250 chalets, cottages and lodges located within the various parks and they're all very reasonably priced. Facilities include basic furniture, refrigerators, bedding and lighting (kerosene pressure lamps, gas or electricity). Campsites in the national parks cost Z\$3 per site (up to six people) and have excellent facilities. Firewood has to be purchased from the park authorities, usually at 50c. Some of the lodges are only open at certain times of the year so you need to make enquiries about this. You don't need to book in

advance at any of the parks as the tourist industry is in the doldrums at present, though you can do so at the Travel Centre, Stanley Avenue, PO Box 8151, Harare (tel 706077). You must report at the park office on arrival at a park even if you have confirmed bookings. Entrance fees to the parks vary.

The only trouble with the national parks is getting there. Local transport is very limited. Local 'African' buses run to or near most parks, but there may be only one every two days or so, which means you really need your own vehicle. Also, you need to take most of your own food and drink. Renting a car isn't cheap (mileage charges are normal in addition to the usual fee), so you have to get a group together to share the cost. *Avis* offers unlimited mileage with a minimum rental period of six days and allows pick-ups and drop-offs without charge at Bulawayo, Harare, Kariba and Victoria Falls. *Hertz* demands a minimum rental period of 10 days if you want unlimited mileage, and they charge you extra if you drop the car off at a place different from the one where you picked it up.

To give you an idea of the costs involved in renting a car and visiting several national parks, here is a breakdown. A VW Golf rented from *Avis* costs about Z\$60 per day (on a six-day minimum hire), a tank of gas costs Z\$40, and accommodation costs around Z\$10 per day (less for couples). If four people share the cost, this is around Z\$30 per day (about US\$10 on the black market).

Recent reports suggest that it's fairly easy to hitch into most parks and that you seldom have to pay for lifts.

Brief details of some of the parks in this country follow:

Chimanimani National Park Private Bag 2063, Chimanimani, tel Chimanimani 03322. Located at the foot of the mountains 21 km from Chimanimani, south of Mutare near the border with Mozambique. Chalets and camping are available. Campsites cost Z$1.50 and include toilets and cold showers. There are good hiking trails over the mountains. An abandoned guesthouse overlooks the hanging valley behind. There are a number of caves where hikers often sleep overnight.

Chinhoyi (Sinoia) Caves Recreational Park

PO Box 193, Chinhoyi, tel 2550. This huge cave, eight km north of Chinhoyi, is one of Zimbabwe's most dramatic attractions. There is a hotel, caravan and campsite. The latter costs Z$3 for two people.

Hwange (Wankie) National Park

Private Bag DT5776, Dete, tel Dett 64. This is Zimbabwe's largest game park, covering over 14,500 square km, and is the place to see animals large and small. Elephants, giraffes, lions, leopards, hippos, crocodiles, buffalo, cheetahs, jackals, zebras, wildebeest and impalas are all here. There are three camps in all – Main Camp, Sinamatella and Robins – as well as a number of bush camps set up in remote areas for the use of those who go on foot safaris. The cost of accommodation in the camps is as follows: Chalets with external cooking facilities Z$4 (maximum three people/one bedroom) and Z$6 (maximum six people/two bedrooms); cottages without cooking facilities Z$5 (maximum three people); family cottages Z$8 (maximum six people); single lodges with kitchen and bathroom Z$10; family lodges with kitchen and bathroom Z$20. The campsites cost Z$3 per site for up to six people. Admission to the park costs Z$3 per person (allows for a stay of one week).

If you have a group and you're thinking of hiring a vehicle to tour the park, Hertz/UTC keep their vehicles near the entrance to the main camp.

You can book a hire vehicle in Victoria Falls, Bulawayo or Harare and arrange to be met on the junction of the main Hwange-Bulawayo road (take the 'Wankie Express' to get there). This will save you a lot of mileage charges.

Kyle Recreational Park

Private Bag 9136, Masvingo, tel 2913. This is a popular resort area 32 km east of Masvingo and across the lake from the Great Zimbabwe ruins (it's 62 km around the lake to the ruins).

You can camp here or rent self-contained thatched cottages which sleep three people for Z$10 per night. There are giraffes, white rhinos, wildebeest, kudus and impalas to be seen in the park. Horse rides are available for Z$4 for two hours together with a guide. Ever gone riding amongst animals like that?

Mana Pools National Park

This park was described by one traveller as being the best game park in Africa after Ngorongoro Crater. Another remarked that people drive all the way from South Africa to see it. One of the reasons is that you are free to walk anywhere your courage will take you, and the opportunities for animal photography are unique. All you have to do is sit under a bush and wait for 40 minutes for the animals to return and then snap away. You can stay in your vehicle if you like, but this would be a wasted opportunity.

The park is only open from 1 May to 31 October. You should book accommodation in advance through the National Parks office in Harare, though this isn't strictly necessary. There is no food for sale in the park or nearby, so you must bring all your own and/or fish (which is permitted). Before entering the park you must check in at the office in Marongora on the main Chirundu-Harare road. Try to avoid the school holiday period which falls in August/September as things can get terribly crowded then.

The accommodation is mostly camping (officially Z£3 per night though you may get it for less). Two lodges are available for Z$20 per day; they sleep up to eight people and have cooking facilities and a refrigerator. You'll come very close to game if camping. Don't be surprised if you bump into elephants or lions when climbing out of your tent!

Ngezi Recreational Park Private Bag 207, Featherstone, tel Mutare 426. Another of the smaller parks in the Mutare area, Ngezi Park is up against the Mozambique border. Lodges and camping are available.

Rhodes Inyanga National Park Private Bag T7901, Mutare, tel Mutare 274. One of the more popular parks in this area. You can get as far as Inyanga village from Mutare by bus. There are beautiful views out over Mozambique. Lodges, chalets and camping are available. Chalets start at Z$7 per night. Campsite fees are Z$3 per night plus Z$1 if you want firewood. If you intend to camp, stock up on food in Mutare, as the local store in Inyanga doesn't have much. You can see most of the attractions on foot, but it's possible to rent horses for Z$4. Have warm clothes handy, as it gets quite cold at night.

There is a daily local bus to this park from Mutare between 6.30 and 7 am; it returns sometime after 9 pm. The fare is Z$2.

Rhodes Matopos National Park Private Bag K5142, Bulawayo, tel Matopos 0-1913. Located 32 km south of Bulawayo, the Matopo Hills are wind-sculpted granite hills and strange balancing rock formations alternating with cool, wooded valleys. They have been a place of retreat for centuries – first for the Bushmen, who left a legacy of painted caves, and then for the Matabele, who fought a fierce rebellion here in the last years of the 19th century. Animals to be seen include the white rhino and the world's largest collection of black eagles.

Also in the park is **Malindidzimu Hill**, otherwise known as **View of the World**, which is associated with local legends about benevolent spirits and is the site of Cecil Rhodes' grave.

There are four sites in all, with lodges, caravan and camping sites. The accommodation at Maleme Dam runs from Z$7 per night for lodges with four beds, kitchen and bathroom, to chalets without kitchen or bathroom for Z$4 per night. Horseback riding through the park is available at Z$4 per hour.

Lake McIlwaine National Park Private Bag 962, Norton, tel Norton 229. Forty km west of Harare on the Bulawayo Rd, this park offers game and boating. A lodge, chalets and camping are available. Cottages are for rent from Z$4.

Vumba Botanical Reserve Private Bag V7472, Mutare, tel Mutare 2127. This park is situated 32 km from Mutare along a steep, winding road in the middle of lush jungle and tea, coffee and banana plantations. There is a *Youth Hostel* at Z$3.50 per night, or you can camp for Z$1.50 – the site is excellent, with hot showers. There's a vague possibility of staying at a *boarding school* at Vumba Heights, but don't count on it – ask for the warden. The *Leopard Rock Hotel* is closed and the *Mountain Lodge Hotel* burned down recently.

Index

738 Index

Thanks to all the following people:

David Abrahamson (USA); Alfred Adam (West Germany); Doug Adamson (Australia); W Aldridge (Australia); Finn Tidemand & Morten Andersen (Denmark); Barbra Andersson; Warren Andrews (UK); Alan Appelbe (Australia); Jane Appleton & Cheryl L Anderson (USA); Alice Armstrong (Swaziland); Alicen Baker (Australia); Phil Baker (Zambia); Yvonne Bardach & David Lloyd (UK); Richard Barker (UK); Peter Barker (Australia); Ray Bates & Inge Bates (Canada); Frank Beier (West Germany); David Bennet (Canada); Julie Bennet (UK); Hans & Manneke van den Berg (Holland); Gunilla Bernang (Sweden); Ian Berrington (S Africa); Mark Berry (USA); Jeb Blakely (USA); Roberto Gonzalez Blanco (Uruguay); Carl Block (Denmark); Steve Boelhouwer (USA); Chris Bollam & Alisen Wheeler (UK); Lindsay Brice (Australia); Peter Brigham & Andy Webley (UK); Simon Caddis & Sara Brimacombe (UK); Mark Bower (UK); Liz Bowles (UK); Valerie & Turbjorn Brodin (Australia & Sweden); Allan Brosnahan (NZ); Cathy Brown (UK); James Brown (UK); Mark Burton (UK); Adam Butler (Italy); Tim Capes (S Africa); Maggs Carlisle & Jo Dodd (UK); Annie Carrington (UK); Frank Carter (Australia); David Ceiriog-Hughes (UK); Brent Chambers (Canada); Andrew Chan; Philip Charpentier (Belgium); Rory Chisholm (UK); Johnny Clarke (UK); J T de Clercq (Holland); Trish Coffey (Liberia); Doug Coggins (USA); Gerry Conway; Gayle Cook & Herb (Australia); Joyce Coope (Ivory Coast); Jim Cowley (Botswana); Helen Crocker (Australia); John Cromber (Australia); David Crotti (Australia); Dr Robert G Cumming (Australia); Torleif Dahlin (Sweden); Steve Dale (UK); Kathleen Darby (UK); Dave Dean (UK); Jay Delehanty (USA); Sean Dennis (Australia); Lynda Desforges & Greg Boyle (UK); Henri Dissenkoen (Holland); Ian Dixon (Australia); Michael Dixon; Paulus Dorlas (Holland); Katherine Dowty (UK); Roger Dunscombe; Naryke van Dyk (Holland); James Earl (Australia); Steve Edelman (USA); Bjorn Edgren (Sweden); Glyn Edwards (Zimbabwe); Hans Eitle (West Germany); Dave Else (UK); Janette Emptage (Australia); Albert van der Ende (Holland); Magnus Engelbrelitsson (Sweden); David Ennis (USA); Don Esty (UK); Michael Evans (UK); Alex Faber (W Germany); Andreas Falk (W Germany); Marc Farrell (Australia); D Faulkner (Zimbabwe); Patricia Fernandes (Canada); Hugh Finlay (Australia); Jonathan Flower (UK); Glen Ford (Canada); Jes Ford & Alison Lescure (UK); Andy Fenton (Kenya); Charles Foster (UK); Rhys Gwilliam & Gael Fox (NZ); Horst Fraunholz (W Germany); G R Fredericks (USA); Jay Friedman (USA); Alasdair Friend (UK); Peter Frumkin (USA); Werner Furrer (Switzerland); Vince Gainey (Kenya); Patricia Gee (Eire); Peter Gillet (UK); Danny Gittings (UK); Dorothy Golden (USA); Ian Graham (Canada); Sarah Graham (NZ); Paul Greenway (Australia); Pierre Gregoire (Canada); Richard Griffin (USA); Michael Hain (W Germany); R Halliwell (UK); Colby Halton-Wingate (USA); Don Hammersely (Australia); Patti Hanagan; Jo Hanson (UK); Jan King & Tom Harriman (USA); Arthur Harris (UK); George Harris (USA); Marc Harrison (UK); Robert Hatwell (UK); Georgina Hayden (Australia); Joh Healy (UK); Thomas Hearron (Swaziland); Roger Hee (USA); Karen Heikhaus (USA); Hans-Peter Heilmair (West Germany); Peter Held (Sweden); Linda Henderson (Australia); Jack Hennesey (Botswana); James Hickman (UK); Eric Hitchings (NZ); Aart Louwrier & Xandra Hilgers (Holland); Dave & Sally Hillebrandt (UK); Christoria Hoffman (W Germany); Charlie Holloway & Diane Bunney; Jamie Hooper; Richard Hosking (UK); Doug Hook (UK); Kevin Hunt (Australia); Mr & Mrs William P Hurst (USA); David Huttner UK); Annie & Stewart Irving (NZ); David Jardine (UK); Keith Jefferis (UK); Tony Jenkins (Canada); Steven E Jeske (USA); Stephen Jobling (Kenya); Helene Johns (Australia); Dave Johnston (UK); Donna Jokinen (Canada); Simon Jolly (Zimbabwe); Fred Jones (USA); Dr David R W Jones (Canada); John Jose (Lesotho); Dr B E Juel-Jenson (UK); Annika Jisvall; Andreas Kalk (West Germany); Paul Kamsteeg (Botswana); Kim Kanger (Sweden); Lars Kasto (Sweden); Harm Hiemstra & Xandra Kause (Holland); Malcolm Keir; Bill Kent (Australia); John Kerr (USA); Eve & Vince Kerrigan (UK); Christine King (NZ); Melvyn R King (UK); K Linda Kivi (Canada); W Klaassen (Tanzania); Claudia Klaus (Switzerland); Andre Kopf (W Germany); Tordis Mastrup Kristensen (Denmark); Nicholas Kristof (UK); Jan Kucera (USA); Jurgen Kuhl (W Germany); Mike Laird (USA); Rick Lamoureux (USA); Charles Landon (S Africa); Walter Lang (W Germany); John Langdon (NZ); Touko Latinew (Ethiopia); Philip Lawler (UK);

Rebecca Lee & Phillipe Dongier (Canada); Renee Leon (Uganda); Dan Lieberfeld (France); Charles Link (Kenya); Margaret Livingston & Todd Miller (USA); Dr Mike Lock (UK); Di Lockwood (UK); Jack Longstaff (Canada); John Lowry (UK); Huber Ludwig (W Germany); Reiner Mai (West Germany); Kim Mack; Janine Madgwick (NZ); Ian McAllister (Botswana); Francis McDonald (Eire); G D MacFarlane (Malawi); Vollene McHarg & Lolita McHarg (Australia); Jack McIlroy (NZ); Ann McVey (Australia); Mette Mark & Claus Juhl (USA); Andrew Mason (Kenya); Helen Malcolm (Australia); Vicki Matchett (NZ); Henk Merkus (Holland); David M'Garry (UK); Paul Mollat (UK); Peter Moor (UK); Jan Myssen (Belgium); Ronald Naar (Holland); Tony Nagypal (Norway); Lynette Newby (NZ); L Newnham (India); Andy Nicholas (UK); T Nicolai (W Germany); Antony Nocera (Australia); Phylis Horst Nofziger (Sudan); Nick Nolan (UK); Ian Norridge (UK); Jeff Norris (USA); John Ovink (Holland); S G Pabalinga (Botswana); Roberto Paloscia (Italy); Piet Pals (Holland); David Paperny (Canada); Morrie Paul (Canada); Peter R Penczer (USA); Simon Penny (Australia); Marie & Kirk Peters (USA); Hans Pfister (Switzerland); Dave Pickhaner & Henry Oak (UK); B Pinar (S Africa); Harald Pitt (W Germany); Mark Pitt (UK); Lesley & Mike Playfair (Australia); Richard Pooley (UK); Krijn J Poppe (Holland); Chas Porter (Zimbabwe); Keith Potter (Swaziland); Allan Poulsen (Denmark); Larry Price; Ian Purcell & Claire (UK); Phyllis A Puffin (USA); Nick Quantock; David W Quinto (USA); Cathy R (USA); Barry Taylor & Tony Rawley (UK); Helen Read (UK); Mark Smalley & Donna Revan (UK); Larry Rice (USA); Keith Richmond (UK); Anton Rijsdijh (Holland); Andy Robertson (Australia); Glen Adam Rogers (Canada); John Ross (UK); Martin Rothman (UK); Trevor Saxty (UK); Jack Sands & Martin Roche (UK); John Rusmore (USA); Candida Saccenti (Italy); Stellan Safvertrom (Sweden); A Sanders (UK); Pete Saunders (NZ); Kevin M Saunders (UK); Cynthia Schember (USA); Jake Schoellkopf (Switzerland); Winfreid Schell (West Germany); Cardine Peter Schimdt (Swaziland); Matthew Schofield (UK); Christina A Scott (S Africa); Mark A Scott (Canada); Rob Seljak (Canada); Lorraine and H Severinsen (UK); Peter Shannon (Australia); Morton Owen Shapiro (USA); Lesley Sharp (USA); Andrew Shisko (Canada); Andy Shoan (UK); David Shoen (USA); Kim Sirenius (Finland); Paul Sitnam (Canada); Werner Simon (West Germany); Rob Smith (UK); Jocelyn Smith (S Africa); Roger Smith (Australia); William Smythe (USA); Adriano Sorgini & Zilda Balero (Brazil); Mike Spence (UK); Maureen Spinks (UK); Mary Stacey (UK); Peter & Wendy Stanczyk (Canada); Stefan & Kristina; Stephen Stocks (Kenya); Alison Stone-Wigg (Kenya); Canon C J Stott (Tanzania); Joachim Strave (Australia); Tim Sturmer (Australia); Paul Suhler (USA); Teresa Sullivan (Zimbabwe); Ray Swanepoel (Transkei); Alan Thatcher (NZ); Fran Thomas & Harry Friedman (USA); Steve Thomas & Annie Thomas (USA); Paula Tavrow (Somalia); Sam Terry (USA); Anders Thoren (Sweden); C Tiems (Holland); Chris Tolley (Swaziland); Gill Tudor (UK); Mark Turner (Australia); Tracey Tyler (USA); Axwel van de Veegaete & Chisi Meyssen (Belgium); Paula & Matt Viney (Australia); Mark Voskamp (Holland); Hans de Vries (Holland); L J Wagenaar (Netherlands); A R Wagener (NZ); Jonnie & Alison Wolf (Sri Lanka); Irmgard & Wolfgang Waldschmidt (W Germany); Adrian Walden (Australia); Gill Walker (UK); Philip Walker (Botswana); B Waloff (Kenya); Simon Warwick (UK); Susan Watts (UK); Niall Watts (Irish Republic); Gerjarn de Weerd (Holland); Jeniffer Westaway (Australia); Bernard Whewell (Australia); J Whitcomb; Anne Whitcombe (USA); Steve Whitt (UK); Rolf Weijburg – Prodotti Rodolpho Productions (Holland); Margaret Williams (USA); Hugh Williamson (UK); Tony Williamson (UK); James Willie (UK); Andrew Wilkinson (UK); Volkmar Wissner (W Germany); Basil Woloff (UK); Brian Wood (UK); Ian Wright (UK); Philip Wullan (UK); Clemens Wurm (West Germany); Chris Yates (UK); Nobunori Yoshida (Japan); Cedric Yoshimoto (Japan); S Zeilikyk; Kate Zeiss (USA); P W Zuidgeest (Holland).